INTERNATIONAL HUMAN RIGHTS IN CONTEXT

LAW, POLITICS, MORALS

INTERNATIONAL HUMAN RIGHTS IN CONTEXT

LAW, POLITICS, MORALS

Text and Materials

Second Edition

HENRY J. STEINER

Jeremiah Smith, Jr. Professor of Law and Director of Law School Human Rights Program, Harvard University

and

PHILIP ALSTON

Professor of International Law, European University Institute, Florence

OXFORD

UNIVERSITY PRESS

OXFORD

UNIVERSITY PRESS

Great Clarendon Street, Oxford OX2 6DP

Oxford University Press is a department of the University of Oxford.
It furthers the Universityís objective of excellence in research, scholarship,
and education by publishing worldwide in

Oxford New York

Auckland Bangkok Buenos Aires Cape Town Chennai
Dar es Salaam Delhi Hong Kong Istanbul Karachi Kolkata
Kuala Lumpur Madrid Melbourne Mexico City Mumbai
Nairobi S„o Paulo Shanghai Taipei Tokyo Toronto

Oxford is a registered trade mark of Oxford University Press
in the UK and in certain other countries

Published in the United States
by Oxford University Press Inc., New York

British Library Cataloguing in Publication Data

(Data available)

Library of Congress Cataloging in Publication Data

(Data available)

ISBN 0-19-829849-8

7 9 10 8

Typeset in Minion by
RefineCatch Limited, Bungay, Suffolk
Printed in Great Britain by
Ashford Colour Press Ltd, Gosport, Hampshire

Preface to the Second Edition

This second edition appears four years after the first. The preface states the premises about the study of human rights that have animated both editions. It also notes the revisions in the second edition that respond to the deep and significant changes of recent years in international human rights.

Basic purposes

The book uses the term 'human rights movement' to include post-1945 governmental, intergovernmental and nongovernmental developments, in both national and international contexts, in the recognition and protection of human rights. A mere half century after this movement was born out of the disasters of the Second World War, human rights ideals inform both the practice and theory of international law and politics. Although the frailties of human rights as an ideal or ideology or state practice are evident, that ideal has become a part of modern consciousness, a lens through which to see the world, a universal discourse, a potent rhetoric and aspiration.

The book critically examines the movement's achievements, which now form an indelible part of our legal, political and moral landscape. The failures, as well as the dilemmas in seeking to realize human rights ideals in the world's diverse cultures, are equally instructive for an understanding of that landscape. Today's university curriculum evidences the significance of international human rights for fields of study as diverse as law, government, international relations and institutions, moral theory, public health, world financial institutions, ecology, economic development, ethnic conflict, religion, education and anthropology.

The book builds on the premise that a basic course in human rights should educate students to see the 'big picture'. Of course it should enable students to master the history, doctrine, and institutional structures of the movement. But it should also persuade students to think critically about the subject as a whole. Thus the text and materials describe, analyse, criticize, propose and provoke, without imposing any single dogma, direction or method for thinking about the history or appropriate path for human rights. The student must reflect on those vexing questions. The knowledge and conceptual framework provided by the book prepares the student seriously engaging with it to work with commitment and critical reflection in a range of roles to advance human rights: advocate, scholar, activist in a governmental or nongovernmental organization, policy analyst.

Principal features of the book

The conceptual framework for the book is set forth in Chapters 1–13 (and readily grasped through the Table of Contents). Chapters 14–16 introduce some additional current topics. The framework consists, in sequence, of the historical development and character of human rights discourse and basic norms; the dilemmas of universalism and cultural relativism; the architecture of international institutions as well as their functions, powers, and interplay with norms; and the relationships between the international and national regimes. Some major themes run through the different parts of the book—for example, changing notions of autonomy and sovereignty, the changing configuration of the public-private divide in human rights ordering, the play of duties and rights in the gradual expansion of the human rights movement, the striking evolution of ideas about the nature and purposes of the movement itself over its half century.

Some understandings informing the entire book follow:

1. Human rights are violated within individual states, not in outer space or on the high seas. One might therefore argue that the study of rights should concentrate on different states—say, human rights *in* Nigeria, *in* Pakistan, Peru, China, the United States, Iran, France. Such a book could offer contextual studies of human rights issues—police brutality, press freedom, religion and the state, discrimination, political pluralism, and so on—that would draw on different national histories and political cultures. It would have the character and high value of studies in comparative law, history and culture.

This book follows a different path. The distinctive aspect of the human rights movement of the last half century has been its invention and creation on the international level. Hence the stress is on the *international* human rights system, as well as on the vital relationships between that system and states' internal orders. Although many illustrations throughout the book draw on human rights violations within one or another state, most of the materials address international norms, processes and institutions, both in their own terms and in terms of their relationships with states' internal orders.

2. What are the sensible boundaries of a book that has an important focus on 'law'? Clearly the coursebook could not achieve its goals if it held to a formal or positivist conception of law that blocked out deeply related fields of inquiry. Thus diverse documents (religious, political, moral, other) and readings from diverse disciplines (anthropology, political and international relations theory, other) interact with formal legal materials (treaties, committee decisions, judicial opinions, other) to form a network of related events and ideas.

This range of readings is readily accessible to university students from academic backgrounds as varied as law, government, political economy, philosophy, theology, business or public health. Human rights courses benefit greatly by including students from such diverse backgrounds, as well as from diverse states and cultures. The first edition, which served as the principal coursebook in human rights courses in a surprising number of countries, was used in both graduate schools and colleges, including faculties and departments of law, government, and international relations.

3. A book based on legal norms and institutions characteristically devotes great attention to the work of courts, the paradigmatic legal institution. Particularly in the Western liberal democracies but also in a growing number of countries in the developing world, courts play a vital role in resolving human rights controversies and developing human rights norms. But where governments are authoritarian and repressive, where violations are serious, systemic and brutal, courts are least relevant. Relative to Western democracies, the judiciary's competence to review executive or legislative action may be sharply reduced or eliminated, its jurisdic-

tion limited, its decrees ignored, its judges subjected to threat or worse. No human rights revolution was ever achieved by court decree. The struggle for rights becomes fully political, even military.

In many states then, courts will at best be marginal actors on human rights issues. With the exception of the European human rights system (and, to a lesser extent, the Inter-American system), the same can be said today about the permanent international tribunals or committees, with respect both to dispute resolution and development of human rights norms. The serious and systemic issues—torture, raw discrimination, corrupt process, ethnic cleansing, genocide, unspeakable poverty, political repression—figure in political processes within states and in international organizations.

For such reasons, and unlike the typical 'casebook', this coursebook devotes less than a fifth of its space to opinions of courts and other tribunals. Many of these opinions are very recent, for it is true that the significance of state constitutional courts has grown over the last decade. South Africa provides one striking example.

4. In vital respects, a book that concentrates on international human rights must assume that students have a rudimentary knowledge of international law. How else can a class discuss matters like treaties and custom, intergovernmental institutions and processes, or internalization of treaty or customary norms within a state? Nonetheless, a substantial percentage of students taking basic courses on human rights lacks that knowledge.

How to handle this situation? In its early chapters, the book provides an introduction to basic conceptions, sources, processes and norms of international law. This introduction hardly achieves the depth and sophistication of a course devoted principally to that rich subject. But it suffices to enable students to grapple with the themes of the coursebook.

5. The study of human rights norms without attention to the international organizations that implement, develop, apply and enforce them would create an air of unreality about the entire enterprise. The architecture, powers, functions and processes of international human rights organizations, intergovernmental and nongovernmental, figure importantly in the book. The student is made aware throughout of the essential and pervasive relationships among norms, institutions, and processes at the international as well as national levels.

6. No one substantive human rights problem and no one region dominates the book. The text and readings draw on many problems to illustrate their themes: free speech and the right to housing, torture and special regimes for ethnic minorities, laws of war and the right to education, Asian and Western views of rights. The chapters illustrate their themes by drawing on many parts of the world, and make particular efforts to present conflicts among regions and cultures in their approaches to and understandings of human rights.

Changes from the first edition

The following summary notes the changes that go beyond the evident updating of text and materials to take account of recent years. About 50 per cent of the text and materials in the book is either new or substantially revised.

There are three organizational changes.

(a)   The old Chapter 13 on gender has been eliminated. In its place, gender issues have been 'mainstreamed' to appear where relevant in different chapters—for example, in Chapter 3's examination of three basic human rights treaties, and in Chapter 5 and 6's discussion of cultural relativism.

(b)   The chapter on economic and social rights now follows the one on civil and political rights, to emphasize their relationships as well as differences, while issues of cultural relativism form a separate Part B of the book.

(c)   The three chapters on intergovernmental organizations now appear in a row, to facilitate comparisons among them before the book turns to nongovernmental organizations.

The remaining changes have to do with the content of the book.

(d)   Chapter 1 complements and updates the 'global snapshots' in the first edition, but adds a section on opinions of national and international tribunals that illustrate the striking expansion of human rights discourse in law, politics and morals.

(e)   To take account of the impressive spread over the last decade of liberal constitutionalism, this edition includes more judicial and committee opinions.

(f)   New topics of growing importance appear, such as the death penalty in Chapter 1, and freedom of religion and children's rights in Chapter 6.

(g)   To take account of a decade of significant changes in the human rights movement—the end of the cold war, globalization and democratization, for example—some topics have been substantially changed. Illustrations include the attention in Chapter 8 to the work of the UN Security Council, in Chapter 10 to democracy's relation to human rights, in Chapter 11 to new understandings of the nongovernmental movement, in Chapter 14 to international criminal tribunals and truth commissions, and in Chapter 16 to effects of globalization on human rights.

Suggestions for use of the coursebook

The text and materials are too extensive to be covered in their entirety in most human rights courses. Choice will surely vary among teachers, depending on the time available for a course and the purposes for which the course is offered. Some suggestions follow.

Although Chapters 1–13 are designed to serve as a whole as a general map and conceptual framework for international human rights, they need not be taught in lock-step. The chapters (with cross references where necessary) can be studied independently outside that framework, and in a different order from that here presented.

Teachers, for example, may prefer more or less stress on the history of the movement, on institutions as opposed to the analysis of norms, or on particular topics like gender, political participation/democracy, or social rights. They may wish to substitute a chapter in Part E for a topic presented in the earlier chapters. If a course means to give more attention than does the book to any particular topic, abundant outside materials to supplement most topics are readily available. The frequent sections on Additional Reading facilitate such a search.

Most of the book could be covered in a single-semester course that met four hours weekly (assuming about 25 pages per course hour). A three-hour course over a semester could then cover about 1,000 pages. A shorter seminar would select chapters as relevant to its purpose.

Practical details and updates on materials

Rather than require students to purchase a separate booklet, basic documents (sharply edited) that are relevant to the materials appear in the book itself, in its Annex on Documents. The book's text refers to frequently cited documents (treaties, declarations, statutes, and so on) only by their titles. An Annex on Citations sets forth official citations and refers to more readily available books or periodicals in which complete (unedited) documents can be found.

Most of the primary and secondary materials are sharply edited in order to make the readings as compact as possible. Omissions (except for footnotes) are indicated by the conventional use of ellipses. Retained footnotes are renumbered within the consecutive footnote numbering of each chapter.

About twice annually, the authors will offer information about post-publication events that bear on topics in the book—treaties and declarations, responses to serious human rights violations, committee decisions, NGO reports, Security Council action, judicial opinions, international conferences, books and articles, and so on. The information will be posted on the following website: www.law.harvard.edu/programs/HRP. Moreover, teachers using the book who wish to call to our attention information that is relevant to the book's topics or who wish to make suggestions for changes in the book may do so through the following e-mail address: ihr@law.harvard.edu. Such information may later appear on the website. Users of this e-mail facility should appreciate that the authors—in view of the great burden that would otherwise be imposed on them—make no commitment whatsoever to respond to any questions, suggestions, or requests for information. The e-mail is intended only to facilitate communication to us about the book in order to assist in its further development and thereby benefit all users.

The authors and their acknowledgements

Henry Steiner, the principal author, was primarily responsible for the book.

Henry Steiner wishes to express his appreciation for the excellent research assistance of several students at Harvard Law School: Ariel Dulitzky (1999), Anthony Lim (2000), Laurie Sickmen (2000), and Lara Stemple (1999). Philip Alston wishes to express his similar appreciation to James Heenan and Mara Bustelo. The authors are grateful to Prof. Craig Scott for helpful suggestions on Chapter 12.

Henry J. Steiner
Philip Alston
April 2000

Summary of Contents

Contents

PART D. STATES AS PROTECTORS AND ENFORCERS OF HUMAN RIGHTS

PART E. CURRENT TOPICS

Acknowledgements

We gratefully acknowledge the permissions extended by the following publishers and authors to reprint excerpts from the indicated publications.

American Anthropological Association. Permission to reprint excerpts from American Anthropological Association's Statement on Human Rights, 49 American Anthropologist 4, 539 (October—December 1947).

American Bar Association. Permission to reprint excerpts from Susan Kilbourne, Placing the Convention of the Rights of the Child in an American Context, Human Rights (Spring 1999).

The American Society of International Law. Excerpts from Donna Sullivan, Advancing the Freedom of Religion or Belief Through the UN Declaration on the Elimination of Religious Tolerance and Discrimination, 82 Am. J. Int. L. 487 (1998). Reproduced with permission from *The American Journal of International Law*, © 1998 The American Society of International Law. Excerpts from Hilary Charleworth, Alienating Oscar? Feminist Analysis of International Law, in Dorinda Dallmeyer (ed.), Reconceiving Reality: Women and International Law (1993); Karen Engle, After the Collapse of the Public/Private Distinction: Strategizing Women's Rights, in Dorinda Dallmeyer (ed.), Reconceiving Reality: Women and International Law (1993). Copyright © 1993 by The American Society of International Law.

Amnesty International Publications, 1 Easton Street, London WC1X 0DJ, www.amnesty.org. Permission to reprint excerpts from Rape and Sexual Abuse: Torture and Ill-Treatment of Women in Detention (1992); Human Rights Principles for Companies (January 1998) from AI Index: ACT 70/01/98 (Amnesty International).

Beacon Press, Boston. Permission to reprint excerpts from Martha Minow, Between Vengeance and Forgiveness. Copyright © 1998 by Martha Minow.

Blackwell Publishers Ltd. Permission to reprint excerpts from Beetham, What Future Economic and Social Rights, Political Studies vol. 43 (1995). Copyright © Political Studies Association; Fabre, Constitutionalising Social Rights, Journal of Poltical Philosophy vol. 6 (1998). Copyright © Blackwell Publishers Ltd; Fortin, Rights Brought Home for Children, Modern Law Review vol. 62 (1999). Copyright © Modern Law Review Ltd; Ewing, The Human Rights Act and Parliamentary Democracy, Modern Law Review vol. 62 (1999). Copyright © Modern Law Review Ltd; Pogany, Constituion making or Constitutional Transformation in Post-Communist Societies, Political Studies Special Issue (1996). Copyright © Political Studies Association.

Boston Review. Yael Tamir, Hands Off Clitoridectomy, 31 Boston Review 21 (1996). Permission granted by Yael Tamir.

The Brookings Institution. Permission to reprint excerpts from Richard Falk, Sovereignty and Human Dignity: The Search for Reconciliation in F. M. Deng and T. Lyons (eds) African Reckoning: A Quest for Good Governance (Brookings Institution 1998).

Cambridge University Press. Permission to reprint excerpts from Daniel Bodansky, Reporting Obligations in Environmental Regimes: Lessons for Human Rights Supervision in P. Alston and J. Crawford (eds) The Future of UN Human Rights Treaty Monitoring (2000); H Steiner, Individual Claims in a World of Massive Violations: What Role for the Human Rights Committee in P. Alston and J. Crawford (eds) The Future of Human Rights Treaty Monitoring (2000).

Carnegie Council on Ethics and International Affairs. Permission to reprint excerpts from Joy Gordon, A Peaceful, Silent, Deadly Remedy: The Ethics of Economic Sanctions, 13 Ethics & Int. Affs. 123 (1999); George A. Lopez, More Ethical Than Not: Sanctions As Surgical Tools, 13 Ethics & Int. Affs. 143 (1999); Larry Cox, Reflections on Human Rights at Century's End, Human Rights Dialogue (Winter 2000); Bahey El Din Hassan, The Credibility Crisis of International Human Rights in the Arab World, Human Rights Dialogue (Winter 2000). © by the Carnegie Council on Ethics and International Affairs.

Carolina Academic Press, Durham, NC. Permission to reprint excerpts from Carol S. Steiker and Jordan M. Steiker, Judicial Developments in Capital Punishment Law, in J. Acker, R. Bohm and C. Lanier, America's Experience with Capital Punishment, pp. 47–76. Copyright 1998 by James R. Axker, Robert M. Bohm and Charles S. Lanier.

The Cato Institute. Permission to reprint excerpts from David Kelley, A Life of One's Own: Individual Rights in the Welfare State (1998).

Columbia University Press. Permission to reprint excerpts from Louis Henkin, The Age of Rights. Copyright © 1990 Columbia University Press.

The Doubleday Broadway Publishing Group, a division of Random House Inc. Permission to reprint excerpts from Desmond Tutu, No Future Without Forgiveness. Copyright © 1999 by Desmond Tutu.

East European Constitutional Review. Cass Sunstein, Against Positive Rights. 2/1 East Eur. Constit'al Rev. 35 (1993).

The Economist. Permission to reprint excerpts from Kalshnikov Kids (10 July 1999); The Non-Governmental Order (18 Dec 1999); How to Make Aid Work (26 June 1999), all copyright © The Economist, London 1999.

NP Engel Verlag. Permission to reprint excerpts from Andrew Drzemczewski and Leyer-Ladewig, Principal Characteristics of the New ECHR Control Mechanism as Established by Protocaol, Human Rights Law Journal 81 (1994); Christian Tomuschat, Quo Vadis Agentoratum?, Human Rights Law Journal 401 (1992); Jorg Polakiewicz, The Application of the European Convention of Human Rights in Domestic Law, Human Rights Law Journal 405 (1996).

Harvard Law Review. Permission to reprint excerpts from Nathaniel Berman, But the Alternative is Despair: European Nationalism and the Modernist Renewal of International Law, 106 Harv. L. Rev. 1792 (1993). Copyright © 1993 by the Harvard Law Review Association.

Harvard University Press. Duncan Kennedy, A Critique of Adjucation. (1997); Adam Kuper, Culture: The Anthropologists Account (1999).

Harvard Women's Law Journal. Permission to reprint excerpts from Tracy Higgins, Anti-Essentialism, Relativism and Human Rights, 19 Harvard Women's L. J. 89 (1996). Copyright © 1996 by the President and Fellows of Harvard College.

Human Rights Watch. Permission to reprint excerpts from Broken People: Caste Violence Against India's 'Untouchables' (1999); Spare the Child; Corporal Punishment in Kenyan Schools (1999); The Scars of Death: Children Abducted by the Lord's Resistance Army in Uganda (1997); Chinese Diplomacy, Western Hypocrisy and the UN Human Rights Commission (1997); Human Rights Watch World Report 2000, The Critique of Military Intervention (1999); Letter to UN Security Council, 1/4/00 (2000); No Guarantees: Sex Discrimination in Mexico's Maquiladora Sector (August, 1996); Business and Human Rights in a Time of Change (1999); Human Rights Watch World Report 2000 (2000). © 1996, 1997, 1999, 2000 by Human Rights Watch.

The Johns Hopkins University Press. Permission to reprint excerpts from Hilary Charlesworth and Christine Chinkin, The Gender of Jus Cogens, 15 Hum. Rts. Q. 63 (1993); James Nickel, How Human Rights Generate Duties to Protect and Provide, 15 Hum. Rts. Q. 77 (1993); Cecilia Medina, The Inter-American Commission on Human Rights and the Inter-American Court of Human Rights: Reflections on a Joint Venture, 12 Hum. Rts. Q. 439 (1990); Stanley Cohen, Government Responses to Human Rights Reports: Claims, Denials, and Counterclaims, 18 Hum. Rts. Q. 517 (1996); Robert Drinan and Teresa Kuo, The Battle for Human Rights in China, 14 Hum. Rts. Q. 21 (1992); Philip Alston and Gerard Quinn, The Nature and Scope of States Parties' Obligations Under the ICESCR, 9 Hum. Rts. Q. 156 (1987). © The Johns Hopkins University Press. Excerpts from A. Clark, E. Friedman, and K. Hochstetler, The Sovereign Limits of Global Civil Society, 51 World Politics (1998). © Center of International Studies, Princeton University. Reprinted by permission of the Johns Hopkins University Press.

International Commission of Jurists. Permission to reprint excerpts from Symposium: The Evolving African Constitultionalism, The Review (1998); excerpts from: Mpazi Sinjela, Constitutionalism in Africa: Emerging Trends, The Review (1998); Bertrand Ramcharan, The Evolving African Constitutionalism, The Review (1998); Amedou Ould-Abdallah, The Rule of Law and Politiocal Liberalisation in Africa (The Review 1998). Permission to reprint excerpts from Ibrahim F. I. Shihata, The World Bank and Human Rights in International Commission of Jurists, Report of a Regional Seminar on Economic, Social and Cultural Rights, Abidjan 1998 (International Commission of Jurists, 1999); Audrey Chapman, A New Approach to Monitoring the International Covenant on Economic, Social and Cultural Rights, The Review No 55 (Dec 1995).

International Monetary Fund. Permission to reprint excerpts from Harold James, From Grandmotherliness to Governance: The Evolution of IMF Conditionality in Finance and Development (December 1998, IMF 1999); Shahid Yusuf, The Changing Development Landscape, 36/4 Finance and Development (1999).

The Hon Justice Michael Kirby AC CMG. Permission to reprint excerpts from Michael Kirby, The Role of International Standards in Australian Courts in P. Alston and M. Chiam (eds), Treaty-Making and Australia: Globalisation Versus Sovereignty (Federation Press 1995).

Michigan Law Review. Permission to reprint excerpts from Martii Koskenniemi, The Pull of the Mainstream, 88 Mich. L. Rev. 1946 (1990).

The New York Review of Books. Permission to reprint excerpts from Amartya

Sen, More Than 100 Million Women Are Missing, 12/20/90; Kenneth Roth, The Court the US Doesn't Want, 11/19/98. Copyright © 1990, 1998, Nyrev., Inc.

The New York Times. Permission to reprint excerpts from Nike Shoe Plant in Vietnam is Called Unsafe for Workers, 11/8/97, p. A1; Bodies Torn From a Grave Leave a Trail of Evidence, 6/29/99, p. A8; Secretive Colombian Courts Survive Protests Over Rights, 6/20/99, p. A21; Amnesty Finds 'Widespread Pattern' of U.S. Rights Violations, 10/5/98, p. A11; Musings on Freedom, by Wearer of Muslim Scarf, 5/12/99, p. A4; Legacy of Rwanda Violence: The Thousands Born of Rape, 9/23/96, p. A1; British Students Facing a New Test: Tuition, 7/24/97, p. A7; Amnesty in Sierre Leone Opposed by Rights Group, 7/26/99, p. A7; In Mexico, Votes Can Be Bought, Study Shows, 7/31/99, p. A4; Held 6 Years Without Trial, Palestinian is Freed by Israel, 7/19/99, p. A6 YNE; Kenyan Tradition Confronted: A Beaten Wife Goes to Court, 10/31/97, p. A5; Globalization Widens Rich-Poor Gap, U.N. Report Says, 7/13/99, p. A8; Russians Lament the Crime of Punishment, 1/8/98, p. A1; 1,500 Executions Cited for Iraq In Past Year, Mostly for Politics, 4/14/98, p. A1; British Report Finds Racism Pervades Police, 2/23/99, p. A5; Massacres of Low-Born Touch Off a Crisis in India, 3/15/99, p. A3; Banned Movement's Head Urges Talks With China, 7/ 24/99, p. A1; Using Gifts as Bait, Peru Sterilizes Poor Women, 2/15/98, p.1; World Bank Emphasizes Role of Free Media in Fighting Graft, 10/11/98, p. 21; A Uganda Tribe Fights Genital Cutting, 7/16/98, p. A8; Letter to the Editor, 11/ 24/93, p. A24; Testing the Limits of Tolerance as Cultures Mix, 3/6/99, p. B9; German Churches, Ever Giving, Ask to Receive, 1/6/98, p. A8; Irking U.S., Yeltsin Signs Law Protecting Orthodox Church, 9/27/97, p. A21; Pope Tells India His Church Has Right to Evangelize, 11/8/99, p. A3; Israeli Learns Some Are More Israeli Than Others, 3/1/98, p. 1; Many in U.S. Back Singapore's Plan to Flog Youth, 4/5/94, p. A6; Checkered Flags; Sovereignty Isn't So Sacred Anymore, 4/18/99, p. 4WK; President Admits 'Don't Ask' Policy Has Been Failure, 12/12/99, p. 1; Turks' High Court Orders Disbanding of Welfare Party, 1/17/98, p. A1; The Precarious Triumph of Human Rights, 8/8/99, p. 8; Virtue by Other Means, 10/26/97, p. WK15; Inquiry Says UN Inertia in '94 Worsened Genocide in Rwanda, 12/17/99, p. A1; Dictators Face the Pinochet Syndrome, 8/22/99, p. WK3; An African Director Faces Trial in His Place of Refuge, 3/1/00, p. A3; Brazil Collides with IMF over a Plan to Aid the Poor, 2/21/00, p. A21. Copyright 1993/94/96/97/98/99/2000 by The New York Times Company.

Notre Dame Law Review. Excerpts from Cass R. Sunstein, Rights and Their Critics, Volume 70, Number 4, the Notre Dame Law Review (1995), 727–757. Reprinted with permission. © by Notre Dame Law Review, University of Notre Dame. The publisher bears responsibility for any errors which have occurred in reprinting or editing.

Oxford University Press. Permission to reprint excerpts from Kenneth Anderson, The Ottowa Convention Banning Landmines, the Role of International Non-Governmental Organisation and the Idea of International Civil Society, in Europeamn Journal of International Law (2000, vol. 11, pp. 144–171); Antonio Cassesse, Ex Iniuria Ius Oritur: Is International Legitimation of Forcible Humanitarian Countermeasures Taking Shape in the World Community? in European Journal of International Law 1999 (1999, vol. 10, pp. 91–120).

The Straits Times. Permission to reprint excerpts from Human Rights: Bridging the Gulf (21 October 1995); SM Lee and his Pragmatic Aproach to Development (28 January 1996); Human Rights: The East Asian Challenge (18 February 1996).

Taylor and Francis Ltd, PO Box 25, Abingdon, Oxfordshire OX14 3UE. Permission to reprint excerpts from K Hayter, Female Circumcision—Is there a Legal Solution?, Journal of Social Welfare and Family Law (1984).

Transaction Publications. Permission to reprint excerpts from Hans Morgenthau, Human Rights and Foreign Policy, in Kenneth Thompson (ed) Moral Dimensions of an American Foreign Policy, Council on Religious and International Affairs (Transation Publications 1984).

Transnational Law and Contemporary Problems. Permission to reprint excerpts from Chidi Anselm Odinaklu, The Individual Complaints Procedures of the African Commission on Human and Peoples' Rights: A Preliminary Assessment, 8 Transnat'l L. & Contemp. Probs. 359 (1998).

The Virginia Journal of International Law. Permission to reprint excerpts from Makau Mutua, The Banjul Charter and the African Cultural Fingerprint: An Evaluation of the Language of Duties, 35 Va. J. Int. L. 339 (1995).

The Yale Journal of International Law. Permission to reprint excerpts from Jose Alvarez, Crimes of State/Crimes of Hate: Lessons from Rwanda, 24 Yale J. Int'l L. 365 (1999); Diane Orentlicher, Separation Anxiety: International Responses to Ethno-Separatist Claims, 23 Yale J. Int. L. (1998).

The Yale Law Journal. Excerpts from Laurence R. Helfer and Anne-Marie Slaughter, Toward a Theory of Effective Supranational Adjudication. Reprinted by permission of The Yale Law Journal Company and Fred B. Rothman & Company from *The Yale Law Journal*, Vol. 107, pages 273–391.

University of California Press. Permission to reprint excerpts from Pnina Lahav, Judgement in Jerusalem: Simon Agranat and the Zionist Century. Copyright © 1997 The Regents of the University of California; Ernst Haas, When Knowledge is Power: Three Models of Change in International Organizations. Copyright © 1989 The Regents of the University of California.

University of Nottingham Centre for Human Rights Law. Permission to reprint excerpts from Vanessa Pupavac, The Infantilisation of the South and the UN Convention of the Rights of the Child' in Human Rights Law Review (March 1998).

University of Pennsylvania Press. Permission to reprint excerpts from Abdullahi Ahmed An-Na'im, State Responsibility under Human Rights Law to Change Religious and Customary Law, in Rebecca Cook (ed) Human Rights of Women; Ann Kent, China, The United Nations and Human Rights (University of Pennsylvania Press 1999).

PART A

CONTEMPORARY HUMAN RIGHTS:
BACKGROUND AND CONTEXT

This coursebook examines the world of contemporary human rights—legal norms, political contexts, moral ideals, human rights discourse, international relations and institutions, governmental and nongovernmental actors, economic development. The list is incomplete, for the boundaries of the subject are steadily expanding. Over a mere half century, the human rights movement that grew out of the Second World War has become an indelible part of our legal, political and moral landscape. The book uses this term 'movement' to include governmental and intergovernmental as well as nongovernmental developments since 1945, unlike some contemporary usage that restricts the term to nongovernmental actors. Given the breadth and complexity of the movement, the coursebook necessarily includes materials from a range of disciplines.

The three principal themes of law, politics and morals are interrelated, indeed inseparable for an understanding of the movement. The political and moral aspects of international human rights are self-evident; it is the international legal aspect that is novel. The rules and standards of contemporary human rights are expressed not only through states' constitutions, laws and practices, but also through treaties and international custom, as well as the work products (decisions about action, forms of adjudication, studies, investigative reports, resolutions, recommendations) of diverse international institutions and organs.

Throughout, the materials underscore the youth of this movement, and the task of students and others committed to its ideals to see themselves not as apprentices learning about an established, even static, framework of ideas and institutions, but rather as shapers and architects of the movement's ongoing development. The book's goal is then not only to train students to work effectively within the present structure and boundaries of the human rights movement, but also to impart a broad as well as critical understanding of it, and to provoke ideas about the directions in which it may be or ought to be heading.

The Preface sets forth the book's pedagogical goals, conceptual structure and formal organization. Students may wish to read it now.

1

Introduction to Human Rights Issues
and Discourse

This introductory chapter assumes no special knowledge about the foundations or content of or argument about rights, human rights, and international human rights. Rather it is meant to spur thoughts about a great range of issues that later chapters examine.

The two parts of the chapter look at these basic questions from complementary perspectives. Part A looks at human rights problems in the large, as they arise and become known. It is not attentive to courts, for in many of the following situations, they will play a marginal role, if a role at all. The medium for looking at these issues is newspaper articles.

Part B moves to an examination of the way that courts, both national courts from many different states and international tribunals, address and argue about the alleged violations of rights that come before them. The topics common to these opinions are the claims of prisoners who have been on death row for many years and allege that their detention constitutes a violation of rights that should lead to relief, and challenges by prisoners sentenced to death to the legality of capital punishment.

A. GLOBAL SNAPSHOTS

The following excerpts from newspaper reports draw you into the diverse human rights problems that plague the world. Many but not all of them refer to rights, or human rights, and thereby indicate the current global currency of that term. After reading these reports, consider the following questions:

> What is the source of the rules or standards under which governmental, intergovernmental, and nongovernmental organizations evaluate and criticize a state?

> What different roles do these types of organizations seem to play?

> How would you identify the alleged human rights violation in each story? Are you clear in each story that (if the reported facts are true) there has been a violation?

Are (international) human rights violations committed only by states, or are nongovernmental forces and individuals also accused of such violations? Do all the stories involve governments as the direct violators of rights?

What steps if any seem to be taken to influence or force a state to end violations?

STORIES ABOUT HUMAN RIGHTS VIOLATIONS

Nike Shoe Plant in Vietnam Is Called Unsafe for Workers
by Steven Greenhouse, *New York Times*, November 8, 1997, p. A1

Undermining Nike's boast that it maintains model working conditions at its factories throughout the world, a prominent accounting firm has found many unsafe conditions at one of the shoe manufacturer's plants in Vietnam.

In an inspection report that was prepared in January for the company's internal use only, Ernst & Young wrote that workers at the factory near Ho Chi Minh City were exposed to carcinogens that exceeded local legal standards by 177 times in parts of the plant and that 77 percent of the employees suffered from respiratory problems.

. . .

The inspection report offers an unusually detailed look into conditions at one of Nike's plants at a time when the world's largest athletic shoe company is facing criticism from human rights and labor groups that it treats workers poorly even as it lavishes millions of dollars on star athletes to endorse its products.

Though other American manufacturers also have problems in overseas plants, Nike has become a lightning rod in the debate because it is seen as able to do more since it earned about $800 million last year on sales of $9.2 billion.

. . .

Like many American apparel makers, Nike uses many subcontractors in Asia, with some 150 factories employing more than 450,000 workers. And like many, that tricky relationship is often offered as a reason for the difficulty in imposing American-style business practices on factories in that part of the world.

. . .

The Ernst & Young report painted a dismal picture of thousands of young women, most under age 25, laboring 10 ½ hours a day, six days a week, in excessive heat and noise and in foul air, for slightly more than $10 a week. The report also found that workers with skin or breathing problems had not been transferred to departments free of chemicals and that more than half the workers who dealt with dangerous chemicals did not wear protective masks or gloves.

. . .

Tien Nguyen, Nike's labor practices manager in Vietnam, said at a news conference yesterday that as soon as Ernst & Young made its confidential report 10 months ago, the company took numerous steps to improve working conditions.

. . .

Bodies Torn From a Grave Leave a Trail of Evidence

by John Kifner, *New York Times*, June 29, 1999, p. A8

. . .

When a French forensic team working for the international war crimes tribunal arrived here at 8 o'clock this morning, they expected to find the bodies of about 150 Kosovo Albanians who other villagers said were killed by Serbian forces on March 28.

There were none. The Serbs seemed to have been here first, dug up the grave and carried the bodies off somewhere, apparently in an effort to destroy evidence before any war crimes trial could take place.

'The bodies are gone now,' said Yves Roy, an investigator on the scene for the tribunal, which is located in The Hague.

But he said there was still plenty of evidence. This site was listed as a count in the war crimes indictment of President Slobodan Milosevic of Yugoslavia and three of his top aides.

. . .

Disappearing bodies, however, are only one problem for the war crimes investigators, who have six teams here now, an official said, with six more soon to be in place. In some areas the bodies are proliferating, with the killing here apparently far greater than anyone had thought, even given the very specific accounts of refugees.

. . .

Striding up a hill, [Mr. Roy] showed where the group of Albanians, almost entirely men, the oldest 96 and the youngest 14, had been separated from the other villagers and marched away to be shot. The shooters, he said, were soldiers of the Yugoslav Army and the special police of the Serbian Interior Ministry.

. . .

Secretive Colombian Courts Survive Protests Over Rights

by Larry Rohter, *New York Times*, June 20, 1999, p. A21

For a decade, terrorism and drug trafficking cases in Colombia have routinely been sent to special tribunals that allow judges, prosecutors and witnesses to remain anonymous.

Now, despite complaints by the United Nations and human rights groups that such practices violate international law and should be abolished, the Colombian Government is moving to extend the life and scope of these so-called 'faceless courts.'

The controversial system had been scheduled to expire on June 30. But new legislation, approved by the Colombian Congress last week and about to be signed by President Andres Pastrana, renews the faceless courts for another eight years and modifies, but does not eliminate, many of the procedures that have been most criticized as denials of fundamental rights.

Beginning July 1, the identities of judges in terrorism and drug cases will no longer be kept secret from lawyers and defendants.

But some prosecutors and witnesses will still be granted anonymity and the law will continue to permit the Government to detain suspects for up to a year while the cases against them are prepared.

Like the old law, the new one infringes on citizens' rights to due process, an effective defense, a fair and speedy public trial and the presumption of innocence, according to an analysis published by the United Nations Commission on Human Rights. "No other place in the world has something quite like this system," said Anders Kompass, director of the United Nations office here. 'It does not correspond to international norms.'

But the Colombian Government maintains that the faceless courts are the only way to deal with the twin plagues of terrorism and drug trafficking that have afflicted this country of 40 million people for decades. Otherwise, officials say, judges, prosecutors and witnesses are likely to be killed by the criminal gangs and guerrilla and paramilitary groups whose offenses are currently prosecuted in the parallel, anonymous system.

. . .

Indeed, the only significant foreign approval has come from the Clinton Administration, whose policy here, other diplomats maintain, is driven primarily by its desire to cut the flow of drugs to the United States.

Amnesty Finds 'Widespread Pattern' of U.S. Rights Violations
by Barbara Crossette, *New York Times*, October 5, 1998, p. A11

Amnesty International, in its first campaign directed at any Western nation, intends to publish a harsh report on the United States on Tuesday, saying American police forces and criminal and legal systems have 'a persistent and widespread pattern of human rights violations'.

. . .

The report is part of a growing effort among human rights organizations to seek 'balance' in reporting by looking at industrialized as well as developing nations. The Clinton Administration has encouraged that trend more than its predecessors, welcoming monitors from the United Nations Human Rights Commission in the face of sharp criticism from some members of Congress.

. . .

. . . Without responses from American officials, [the report] concludes with this statement: 'Across the country thousands of people are subjected to sustained and deliberate brutality at the hands of police officers. Cruel, degrading and sometimes life-threatening methods of constraint continue to be a feature of the U.S. criminal justice system'.

. . .

Pierre Sane, a development expert from Senegal who has been Secretary General of Amnesty International for six years, said in an interview that the United States was chosen as the first Western target because human rights conditions were deteriorating.

. . .

'I think in terms of the severity of what is happening in the U.S., more or less people are aware,' Mr. Sane said. 'They are aware that in the States police can be brutal. They're aware that prisons are not the best place to be in. But what we are concerned with is the lack of action and the complacency. It seems to me that the international community, in terms of standards, is moving really ahead of the standards obtaining in the United States today'.

Musings on Freedom, by Wearer of Muslim Scarf

by Stephen Kinzer, *New York Times*, May 12, 1999, p. A4

Sitting demurely behind her desk dressed in immaculate white, Merve Kavakci does not look like someone who could send a nation of 65 million into turmoil. But because of what she wears, she has done exactly that.

It is not Ms. Kavakci's chic white suit with gold buttons that caused the problem. It is the white scarf that covers her head, coupled with ideas of freedom she developed while living in Texas.

Ms. Kavakci was elected to Parliament last month, but when she entered the parliamentary chamber in Ankara to take her oath of office, pandemonium broke out. More than 100 legislators stood and jeered, failing to break her composure but setting off a political earthquake that is still shaking Turkey.

In the end Ms. Kavakci, 30, left the chamber without taking her oath. It seems like the parliamentary chamber, considered the cathedral of the secular republic, is no place for a woman with a Muslim-style scarf.

. . .

'I was expecting a reaction, but a democratic reaction,' she said of her memorable day in Parliament. 'I believe I had a right to be there. I had been elected like the other 549 members. I am a person like each of them. I campaigned like them, I eat like them, I sleep like them. Because of my personal choice, I don't dress like them. What they said was, "You are not like me so you can't exist." These were the same politicians who campaigned for more democracy, who said they wanted democracy for everyone in this country, freedom of speech, freedom of religion and blah blah blah. If they really wanted democracy they would have supported me in Parliament even if they didn't like the way I dress. But they have a very elastic definition of democracy: democracy for me, but not for you, because you're different'.

. . .

Critics of Ms. Kavakci and her party assert that their long-term goal is to impose a radical form of religious rule that will ultimately destroy freedom in Turkey. They consider her embrace of the language of democracy deeply cynical and mendacious.

. . .

Sitting in front of a Turkish flag in her office, however, Ms. Kavakci said her goal was not to subvert democracy, but to implant it in a country that does not yet fully enjoy it.

. . .

Legacy of Rwanda Violence: The Thousands Born of Rape
by James McKinley, *New York Times*, September 23, 1996, p. A1

Some days, when she looks at her round-faced baby boy, Leonille M. feels that she no longer wants to live.

It is not the child's fault. He peers back at his mother with innocent eyes. But the baby reminds her of all of her family members who died in the massacres that took the lives of at least 500,000 Rwandans, most of them members of the Tutsi ethnic minority, in 1994. He also reminds her of the three soldiers of the majority Hutu group who gang-raped her.

. . .

By conservative estimates, there are 2,000 to 5,000 unwanted children in Rwanda whose mothers were raped during the civil war and mass killings, a new report by Human Rights Watch says. The children, not yet 2, are known in Rwanda as 'enfants mauvais souvenir', children of bad memories.

. . .

The militias were fueled by propaganda that portrayed Tutsi women as high-class seductresses—beautiful women who would corrupt a pure Hutu society. During the widespread violence, women were raped by individuals, gang-raped, raped with sharpened stakes and gun barrels and held in sexual slavery, sometimes alone, sometimes in groups, the report says. In many cases the genitals and breasts of rape victims were mutilated.

. . .

The women who decided to give birth and keep the children have faced a battery of new troubles. Most are in dire financial straits, living on charity and squatting in abandoned houses. Most not only lost their husbands and families in the war, but also their husbands' farms, which were their only means of survival. Some have also taken on dead relatives' children or other orphans, adding to their burdens.

. . .

Others have become outcasts in their own communities. A woman in this position is often accused of being a 'wife of the interhamwe', the Hutu militia that did most of the killing. Many have had to wage battles with their own families to keep the babies, who are seen as 'little interhamwe' by relatives.

. . .

Since widows and rape victims are often stigmatized in Rwandan society, many women have found it impossible to find new husbands or to begin a new life. Many contracted AIDS and other sexually transmitted diseases from the rapists, Mrs. Mukansinga said.

. . .

British Students Facing a New Test: Tuition
by Sarah Lyall, *New York Times*, July 24, 1997, p. A7

The Government announced today that for the first time, Britain plans to impose tuition fees on all college students, effectively abandoning the country's long-held commitment to free higher education for everyone.

For Americans long used to paying fees for even state-run schools or tuition approaching $30,000 a year at Ivy League schools, the proposal—to charge up to $1,600 a year—may seem laughably modest. But the plan also means students would no longer be eligible for Government grants covering room and board, and many graduates will face debts of more than $16,000.

In a nation where free education is considered a basic right, the announcement was taken as a further sign that Prime Minister Tony Blair's new Government is intent on dismantling many most sacred vestiges of Britain's welfare state.

'Free tuition is seen as a right', said Liz Llewellyn, a spokeswoman for the National Union of Students, which says the prospect of leaving school deeply in debt will deter many young people from attending college at all. 'We've always been told that if you choose to go on with your education, the state should pay because you'll give so much back to the state by getting a better job and paying more in taxes'.

The Government's plan was outlined in a speech to the House of Commons this afternoon by David Blunkett, the Secretary for Education and Employment. He said Britain's universities, which face a deficit of up to $3.2 billion in the next decade, had fallen into a financial crisis that could be addressed only by imposing fees.

. . .

Under the Government's plan, all but the poorest students would be expected to pay tuition of up to $1,600 a year, as well as several thousand dollars for room and board. Student loans, to be paid back according to income and over a number of years, would be available for both tuition and living expenses.

. . .

Amnesty in Sierra Leone Opposed by Rights Group
by Paul Lewis, *New York Times*, July 26, 1999, p. A7

Human rights organizations are campaigning against a blanket amnesty granted in Sierra Leone under a peace agreement signed earlier this month to end the brutal eight-year civil war in that tiny, impoverished West African nation.

The tactics of the Revolutionary United Front rebels included deliberately severing arms and legs of civilians, including many children.

The amnesty was extended to the rebels, led by Foday Sanko, who were promised four Government posts as well as 'an absolute and free pardon and reprieve' for their actions since 1991 by the peace deal signed July 7 in Lome, the capital of Togo, Sierra Leone's neighbor.

Human Rights Watch, a New York-based group, and Amnesty International denounced the amnesty provision in letters to the United Nations Secretary General, Kofi Annan, to the members of the Security Council and to Mary Robinson, the United Nations High Commissioner for Human Rights.

'We are now lobbying Security Council members and especially the Netherlands and Canada, which seem the most sympathetic to our views,' Reed Brody, advocacy director at Human Rights Watch, said on Friday.

The Netherlands Representative, Arnold Peter van Walsum, said the amnesty raises an issue of principle 'because we believe peace and accountability are not incompatible, but that does not mean you want people to go on fighting'.

Mr. Annan is due to report to the Council on the Sierra Leone peace agreement on Tuesday. And the Council will then try to adopt a resolution stating its view of the accord.

A British diplomat described the Sierra Leone agreement as 'a very dirty deal but unfortunately the only one available'.

. . .

On the other hand, any perceived weakening of the amnesty granted the rebels in Sierra Leone risks driving them into armed opposition again and restarting one of Africa's longest and cruelest civil wars. Most African governments, diplomats here say, just want to see the fighting ended. Two earlier cease-fire agreements in Sierra Leone broke down.

. . .

In Mexico, Votes Can Be Bought, Study Shows
by Sam Dillon, *New York Times*, July 31, 1999, Saturday, p. A4

One-third of those who voted this month in a crucial Mexican election won by President Ernesto Zedillo's governing party now say they received groceries, scholarships, lottery tickets, crop payments or other government handouts before the vote, according to a new study.

Eighty percent of those who received the gifts voted for the party, the Institutional Revolutionary Party, or PRI, the study found.

The survey, carried out in the state of Mexico, where the party won the Governor's race on July 4, is one of the first measurements of the influence that government aid programs are having in elections in a period when reforms have made outright ballot theft, a common tactic in the past, almost impossible.

. . .

'This is what we call pork in the United States,' Mr. Lund said. But the PRI's power to deliver government aid to constituents is extensive because the party has held presidential power since the 1920s.

. . .

Held 6 Years Without Trial, Palestinian is Freed by Israel
New York Times, July 19, 1999, p. A6 YNE

Israel's longest-held Palestinian detainee returned home today after nearly six years in prison without charge or trial, in a case that brought new scrutiny on Israel's detention practices.

Thirty carloads of family members accompanied the detainee, Osama Barham, after he crossed the checkpoint between Israel and the West Bank, and relatives fired guns in the air as the convoy rolled through his village of Ramin.

Earlier, at the Supreme Court in Jerusalem, Mr. Barham sat smiling, sandwiched between two policemen. Israeli rights activists who had lobbied for his release reached out to shake hands with him.

The court approved a compromise agreement with police officials in which Mr. Barham pledged not to engage in violent activities of any kind in return for his release. 'I want to start anew,' said an elated Mr. Barham, who according to friends wants to begin a career as a human rights activist.

Mr. Barham, 35, was arrested in 1993 for membership in the militant Islamic Holy War group. According to his lawyer, Tamar Peleg-Shavit, the charges and evidence against him have been kept classified for security reasons and there has been no opportunity to publicly counter them. 'It's a human right to have an open and fair hearing, due process,' Ms. Peleg-Shavit said.

In a statement issued after his release, the army said Mr. Barham's detention was extended because he 'did not cease his dangerous activity even when he was in prison'.

Justice Minister Yossi Beilin, a well-known liberal who has come out against administrative detention, welcomed the court's decision. 'I feel relieved knowing that a man who was detained for six years without being told what his crime was, was released from prison', Mr. Beilin said in a statement issued by his office.

Mr. Beilin said he hoped Israel would be able to protect its security interests without violating the basic human rights of prisoners.

. . .

Kenyan Tradition Confronted: A Beaten Wife Goes to Court
New York Times, October 31, 1997, p. A5

Agnes Siyiankoi says her husband used a wooden club the last time he beat her. She had to be carried to the hospital. Ms. Siyiankoi, a 30-year-old Masai, says she suffered 13 years of abuse before deciding to defy tradition and take her husband to court. The case is rare in a country where wife-beating is prevalent and even condoned.

Among the Masai, a southern Kenyan tribe that views women as property, first of their fathers, then of their husbands, the men frequently use force to assert their authority, usually without protest from the women. 'If a man does not beat his wife, he is looked down upon as a weakling,' Ms. Siyiankoi said.

Far from being confined to the Masai, wife-beating is a practice that cuts across the population, with little regard to cultural, economic or educational differences. Although the practice is illegal, women who complain face intense social pressure to conform.

'When I run to my father's house after every severe beating, my mother comforts me and tells me to return to him,' Ms. Siyiankoi said. ' "Look at the scars I've gotten from your father's beatings", she says'.

In a recent survey by the Women Rights Awareness Program, a Kenyan advocacy group, 70 percent of the men and women interviewed said they knew neighbors who beat their wives. Nearly 60 percent said women were to blame for the beatings. Just 51 percent said the men should be punished.

'Even in the few cases taken to court, most victims are pressured by relatives and friends to drop the charges, or settle the case out of court, or change the charge to that of minor assault,' said Millie Odhiambo, of the Kenyan branch of International Federation of Women Lawyers. The group hopes the case will lead to greater awareness that domestic assault is a crime.

Ms. Siyiankoi said she was engaged without her consent to a man her father's age while she was in primary school. She met him the day he came to take her from her father's house. She was 18 and wanted to stay in school. But she said she could not refuse to marry because her father would have cursed her.

After years of abuse, her husband beat her with a club that Masai men use to herd cattle, she says. She was carried to a hospital, which required her to make an official complaint, a regulation that deters many victims of domestic abuse from seeking treatment and speaking out.

. . .

While the case has raised hopes among opponents of wife-beating, it has left Ms. Siyiankoi feeling like an outcast among the Masai. 'Women are very angry with me,' she said. 'It is unheard of in Masailand to put your husband into jail'.

Globalization Widens Rich-Poor Gap, U.N. Report Says
by Judith Miller, *New York Times*, July 13, 1999, p. A8

Globalization is compounding the gap between rich and poor nations and intensifying American dominance of the world's economic and cultural markets, according to the latest human development report published today by the United Nations Development Program.

The 262-page report, the 10th the program has issued, is the first to focus on the spread of the Internet and computer technology as well as the impact of globalization. It concludes that the so-called 'rules of globalization' should be rewritten to save the 60 countries that are worse off they were in 1980 from falling even further behind.

. . .

The report warns that the glaring, growing inequalities in the distribution of wealth pose a 'dangerous polarization' between rich and poor countries.

As in previous reports, it says little about what role the poorest nations themselves play in their predicament. It says little about the corruption and mis-management of resources in many of the poorest countries that have discouraged foreign investment and squandered millions of dollars in foreign aid.

. . .

Russians Lament the Crime of Punishment

by Alessandra Stanley, *New York Times*, January 8, 1998, p. A1

. . .

The Russian penitentiary system competes with that in the United States as one of the largest in the world—each has a population of more than a million inmates. And the Russian system is arguably one of the worst. Prisons are underfinanced, overcrowded and alarmingly unsanitary.

Human rights abuses abound. Tuberculosis is spreading wildly. The Government has no reliable data, but estimates suggest that tuberculosis rates in prisons are anywhere from 20 to 60 times as high as in the rest of the population, which has a TB death rate 24 times that of the United States. As many as 50 percent of Russian prisoners are believed to be infected.

But perhaps the most terrifying aspect of the Russian penal system is pretrial detention. Close to 300,000 people awaiting trial are now in jail. There, a death sentence stalks people who have not yet been convicted of a crime.

Unprotected from the TB epidemic and other infectious diseases, many detainees end up spending two, three and even four years awaiting their day in court in cells as packed as a rush-hour subway car.

. . .

There is no money in the Russian budget to build new prisons or even repair old ones, so efforts to creep closer to Western standards rarely go beyond the paper they are printed on.

. . .

In a report on torture in Russia issued last year, Amnesty International said that 'torture and ill-treatment occur at all stages of detention and imprisonment,' but noted that it was most often reported in pretrial detention.

'Its main purpose appears to be to intimidate detainees and obtain confessions,' the report said. Confessions, more than evidence, are a major part of criminal investigations in Russia.

. . .

'Inmates understand perfectly well that the prison authorities are not responsible for their conditions,' Yuri Aleksandrov, a prisoners' rights activist for the nonprofit agency Novy Dom, said. 'The whole criminal justice system is to blame. It's a mentality that dates back to Stalin'.

. . .

1,500 Executions Cited for Iraq In Past Year, Mostly for Politics

by Barbara Crossette, *New York Times*, April 14, 1998, p. A1

The Government of President Saddam Hussein of Iraq has executed at least 1,500 people in the last year mostly for political reasons, a former Dutch Foreign Minister has concluded in a report to be presented on Tuesday to the United Nations Human Rights Commission.

Most of the deaths occurred during a 'prison-cleansing campaign' in November and December ordered by Mr. Hussein's younger son, Qusay. He directs Iraq's Special Security Organization, one of a number of armed intelligence agencies that sustain an atmosphere of terror in Iraq, diplomats based there say.

The report says that after Qusay Hussein's visit to one prison, Abu Gharib, large numbers of prisoners condemned to death or to sentences of 15 years or more were shot, hanged or electrocuted there and in other prisons. The families of those shot were forced to pay for the bullets used before they could claim the bodies.
. . .

Today in Baghdad, the official Government newspaper Al Qadissiya called Mr. Van der Stoel an agent of American intelligence and Zionism who had been ordered 'to spread lies and put out idiotic reports that no one will take seriously.'
. . .

British Report Finds Racism Pervades Police

by Warren Hoge, *New York Times*, February 23, 1999, p. A5

A long-awaited Government report has found London's police force to be 'riven with pernicious and institutionalized racism' and suggests that chief officers accept that conclusion as a condition of keeping their commands.

The report, which surprised nonwhite leaders with its sweep, makes 70 recommendations for changes in police practices 'designed to usher in a fundamental transformation of Britain's race relations'.

Sir William Macpherson, a retired High Court Justice who was the author of the report and chairman of the eight-month Government inquiry, defined institutional racism as 'the collective failure of an organization to provide an appropriate professional service to people because of their color, culture or ethnic origin'. This is reflected, he said, in 'attitudes and behavior' amounting to discrimination through 'unwitting prejudice, ignorance, thoughtlessness and racist stereotyping'.
. . .

Massacres of Low-Born Touch Off a Crisis in India

by Celia Dugger and Shanker Bigha, *New York Times*, March 15, 1999, p. A3

This hamlet on the edge of a lush, palm-fringed field lay quiet on the moonlit night of Jan. 25. But as the villagers slept, more than 50 upper-caste men, members of an outlawed landowners' army, crept toward them through rustling spears of wheat.

The men fanned out in the dirt lanes, flinging open the doors of mud huts and shouting: 'Kill them! Kill them!' Guns blazing, they massacred 22 people in just a few minutes, among them a 3-year-old boy and his baby sister, who were crying as they huddled in their grandmother's arms.

This massacre of farm workers and their families—untouchables at the bottom of Hinduism's hierarchical social order—was numbingly similar to dozens of others committed during nearly three decades in the eastern state of Bihar.

The state is blessed by mineral wealth and fertile soil but cursed by the nation's highest rates of illiteracy and poverty. Almost 9 out of 10 of the state's 100 million people live in the countryside, and more than half are very poor. The untouchables, who make up 14 percent of the population, are the poorest of the poor.

Bihar is now in the midst of an upheaval that has seen the middle castes depose the upper castes from the seats of political power. The untouchables—now called Dalits, which means ground down in Hindi—have not yet gained an independent political voice, but they have begun grass-roots organizing.

And as they have banded together under various leftist banners to agitate, sometimes violently, for higher wages, a share of land and an end to the sexual exploitation of Dalit women and other humiliations, both middle- and upper-caste landowners have struck back with terror tactics.

'In the American South after the Civil War, the lynchings of blacks were aimed at curbing their uppitiness,' said Ashutosh Varshney, a political scientist at Columbia University. 'India never had slavery, but the Dalits are as close to slavery as you can get. The massacres are aimed at checking their uppitiness'.

Successive governments, dominated by the upper and middle castes, have failed since the 1970s to stop the carnage or to address the harsh social and economic inequalities between the landed and the landless that persist in Bihar and in most of north India.

. . .

Banned Movement's Head Urges Talks With China

by Erik Eckholm, *New York Times*, July 24, 1999, p. A1

. . .

The leader of the fast-spreading spiritual movement banned this week by the Chinese Government asserted yesterday that his group had no political ambitions and called on the Government to engage in dialogue.

'I hope the Chinese Government will try to resolve the matter through dialogue rather than through violence,' Li Hongzhi, leader of the newly outlawed Falun Gong movement, which claims to use exercises to harness cosmic forces, said in an interview yesterday in New York. 'The people's hearts cannot be changed.'

'I don't want to get involved in politics ever,' said Mr. Li, who in 1992 developed a cosmic theory and a movement that says it now has more than 100 million members worldwide. Estimates of the number of followers in China range from two million given by the Government this week to tens of millions claimed by supporters, numbers that cannot be verified.

From his self-imposed exile in New York, Mr. Li is embroiled in one of China's sharpest social rifts in years, as the Government tries to stamp out a movement that has been wildly popular among many retirees, middle-age women and others, mainly in urban areas around the country.

The Government this week described Falun Gong as an illegal political and social force and Mr. Li as an 'evil figure who, by deceiving, has been seriously disrupting social order'.

. . .

Alarmed by the rapid spread of a movement outside the control of the Communist Party, China's leaders detained scores of Falun Gong leaders and mounted a campaign of invective against Mr. Li. Authorities dispersed resulting protests by tens of thousands of followers in at least 30 cities

. . .

Using Gifts as Bait, Peru Sterilizes Poor Women

by Calvin Sims, *New York Times*, February 15, 1998, p. 1

For Magna Morales and Bernadina Alva, peasant Andean women who could barely afford to feed their families, it was a troubling offer but one they found hard to refuse. Shortly before Christmas, Government health workers promised gifts of food and clothing if they underwent a sterilization procedure called tubal ligation.

The operation went well for Mrs. Alva, 26, who received two dresses for her daughter and a T-shirt for her son. But Mrs. Morales, 34, died of complications 10 days after the surgery, leaving three young children and a husband behind. She was never well enough to pick up the promised gifts, and the family was told it could not sue the Government over her death because she had agreed to the procedure.

'When you don't have anything and they offer you clothes and food for your kids, then finally you agree to do it,' said Mrs. Alva, a neighbor of Mrs. Morales in the northern village of Tocache. 'Magna told them that her husband was against the idea, but they told her, "Don't worry, we can do it right now, and tonight you will be back home cooking and your husband will never realize what happened".'

Tales of poor women like Mrs. Morales and Mrs. Alva being pressed and even forced to submit to sterilization operations that have left at least two women dead and hundreds injured have emerged from small towns and villages across Peru in recent weeks in what women's groups, politicians and church leaders here say is an ambitious Government family planning program run amok.

Critics of the program, which was begun in 1995, charge that state health care workers, in a hurry to meet Government-imposed sterilization quotas that offer promotions and cash incentives, are taking advantage of poor rural women, many of whom are illiterate and speak only indigenous Indian languages.

The critics, who include many of the program's early supporters, say the health workers are not telling poor women about alternative methods of contraception or that tubal ligation is nearly always irreversible. They also charge that many state doctors are performing sloppy operations, at times in unsanitary conditions.

'They always look for the poorest women, especially those who don't understand Spanish,' said Gregoria Chuquihuancas, another Tocache resident. 'They
make them put their fingerprint on a sterilization paper they don't understand
because they can't read. If the women refuse, they threaten to cut off the food and
milk programs.'
. . .

World Bank Emphasizes Role of Free Media in Fighting Graft
by Paul Lewis, New York Times, October 11, 1998, p. 21

After surveying the Asian financial crisis, the World Bank has concluded that a
strong and independent news media could be an important protection against
economic mismanagement and government malfeasance in developing nations.

But as the economies of Asian countries and Russia go into free fall, the independent newspapers, magazines, television and radio stations these countries do
have are being dragged down, and many are being forced to scale back their activities.

In an address to the annual meeting of the World Bank and the International
Monetary Fund, James D. Wolfensohn, the bank's president, pointedly included
'the free flow of information' as one of the 'essentials of good governance' on
which, he argued, sustainable economic progress depends.
. . .

World Bank officials, in mulling over the Asian debacle, say they have concluded
that a freer, more aggressive and more critical news media in the region would
have put a brake on the governmental corruption and the so-called crony capitalism that are widely seen as at the heart of today's economic mess.
. . .

QUESTIONS

1. What kinds of human rights violations would you identify, and who would have
committed them, in the articles on the Nike shoe plant, on British students and tuition,
on the massacres in India based on caste, and on globalization and the rich-poor gap?
Are states implicated? Are they the violators? Who is bound by human rights norms?

2. Should rights and related duties be absolute, so that it would be impermissible to
compromise human rights in order to achieve another important goal? How do you
assess the argument of Colombia with respect to the special courts that it now uses, or
the argument about whether it is sensible to grant an amnesty to the insurgents in Sierra
Leone, who committed such terrible atrocities?

3. What categories of human rights violations emerge from these reports? Do any
among them seem amenable to judicial resolution? If not judicial, how might these
violations be ended and disputes be resolved? Are "legal" norms and processes here
relevant?

B. FROM DEATH ROW TO EXECUTION: THE GLOBAL FRAMEWORK FOR CONTEMPORARY HUMAN RIGHTS DISCOURSE

Part A of Chapter 1 drew on newspaper accounts to illustrate the large range of issues that have been brought over the last half century into human rights doctrine and discourse. In seeking to describe the problems, the articles stressed the broad political, social, economic or military context. As in responses to many of today's deepest and gravest human rights problems, they did not draw on the work of courts.

Part B stresses the argument and human rights discourse of courts, those most 'legal' of institutions. It thus takes on a traditional legal character, for the arguments by and decisions of courts stand at the core of legal education and analysis, and of the work of many legal practitioners, including human rights practitioners. It is important to bear in mind that much of the invocation of rights and many of the arguments in these decisions are products of the last half century. The very institutions to which several opinions refer did not previously exist.

It is also important to consider the degree to which these courts and other organs (like the UN Human Rights Committee) form part of some global framework of interaction and discourse, or to the contrary whether the following opinions suggest radically separate worlds of argument and decision in different states and in international as opposed to national courts. Such questions arise as:

> To what extent are the decisions 'connected,' sensitive to other courts' work?

> To what extent is some form of world community developing among the judiciaries of many states with respect to human rights issues?

> Are the new international human rights tribunals part of that community?

The closely related topics here used to examine these issues involve 'death row'—the phenomenon of prisoners sentenced to death who spend many years in prison, often in the parts of prisons reserved for those under death sentence, as they prosecute appeals and seek stays of execution—and the death penalty itself. Prisoners challenge the legality of execution after the 'death row' experience, and challenge the legality of capital punishment itself, under several state constitutional provisions and under the international human rights instruments. The challenges differ among countries and over time, and rest on a few widespread constitutional provisions.

NOTE

Most of the decisions below of national and international tribunals refer to decisions by courts of others states and by international courts and committees created by treaties. The international tribunals here involved are: (1) The European Court of Human Rights, created by the European Convention on Human Rights whose membership is limited to European States. Citizens of European states that submit to the Court's jurisdiction can bring complaints against those states to the Court after exhausting local remedies. See Chapter 10. (2) The Human Rights Committee, created by the International Covenant on Civil and Political Rights. That Committee has the authority to hear complaints brought by a citizen against the state (again after exhausting local remedies) if the state has ratified not only the Covenant but also its Optional Protocol. See Chapter 9.

You should read the provisions (in the Annex on Documents) of the International Covenant and European Convention to which the opinions refer.

CATHOLIC COMMISSION FOR JUSTICE AND PEACE IN ZIMBABWE V. ATTORNEY-GENERAL
Supreme Court of Zimbabwe, 1993
Judgment No. S.C. 73/93, 14 Hum. Rts. L.J. 323 (1993)

[Four men convicted of murder were scheduled to be hanged. The Catholic Commission applied to the Supreme Court for an order prohibiting government authorities from carrying out the sentence. It claimed that the executions were unconstitutional under section 15(1) of the Zimbabwe Constitution, because of the 'dehumanizing factor of prolonged delay', coupled with degrading conditions under which the prisoners were held. The delays in these cases from the time of imposition of the death sentence ranged up to 72 months, considerably in excess of the average period of delay in Zimbabwe for a sentence of death to be carried out. Section 15(1) provides that no person shall be subjected 'to torture or to inhuman or degrading punishment or other such treatment'.

The Court concluded that the appellant had standing to bring the application. It described the harsh prison conditions in which the four defendants were held since the convictions and sentences in 1988, the prisoners' mental anguish during this period, and the torment and taunting inflicted by the guards.

The bulk of the opinion by Gubbay, C.J., concerned the construction of section 15(1) and the attitude of diverse courts toward the factor of delay in executing a sentence of death. The Chief Justice drew on a prior opinion of the Court to say that section 15(1):

> is a provision that embodies broad and idealistic notions of dignity, humanity and decency ... Any punishment or treatment incompatible with the evolving standards of decency that mark the progress of a maturing society ... is repulsive. What might not have been regarded as inhuman decades ago may be revolting to the new sensitivities which emerge as civilisation advances.

In deciding whether a form of treatment is inhuman or degrading, a court makes a value judgment that 'must not only take account of the emerging consensus of values in the civilized international community' as evidenced by decisions of other courts and writings of academics, but also of 'contemporary norms operative in Zimbabwe and the sensitivities of its people'.

The opinion traced 'judicial and academic acceptance of the death row phenomenon'. It quoted from several U.S. Supreme Court decisions describing the mental agony of being on death row and, to the same effect, from a number of opinions of Indian judges. It drew on sociological studies from several countries that 'describe confinement under sentence of death as exquisite psychological torture. . .'.

The opinion dealt in some detail with the 'position' on this issue taken by courts in India and in the United States. Some excerpts follow:]

Although there is no provision in the Indian Constitution, framed in 1948–1950, which expressly proscribes torture or inhuman or degrading punishment or treatment, the Supreme Court of India has filled the void and brought the Bill of Rights in the Constitution into conformity with international norms, as set out in Article 3 of the European Convention for the Protection of Human Rights and Fundamental Freedoms and Article 7 of The International Covenant on Civil and Political Rights. [Zimbabwe was a party to the International Covenant at the time of this decision.] It held in *Francis Coralie Mullin v The Administrator, Union Territory of Delhi* AIR 1983 SC 746 that the right to live with basic human dignity implicit in the right guaranteed under Article 21, included the right not to be subjected to torture or to cruel, inhuman or degrading punishment or treatment. This all-important right was, therefore, read by the Supreme Court into the right to life [Article 21] and made part of domestic jurisprudence.

Taking the right of protection as the base, the Supreme Court has proceeded to consider the question of delay in the carrying out of sentence of death, such delay being a notorious feature of the India legal system.
. . .

On 7 February 1989 the aspect of delay came before five Judges of the Supreme Court in *Triveniben and Others v State of Gujarat and Others* (1989) 1 S.C.J. 383. OZA J, giving the lead judgment, laid down at 393 that the only delay which could be considered in a writ petition was from the date the judgment of the apex court was pronounced (ie) when the judicial process had come to an end. He made it clear that no fixed period could be held to make sentence of death inexecutable and to that extent overruled the decision in *Vatheeswaran's* case, *supra*. SHETTY J in a separate concurring judgment said at 410 paras 74 and 75:

> It has been universally recognised that a condemned person has to suffer a degree of mental torture even though there is no physical mistreatment and no primitive torture . . .
>
> As between funeral fire and mental worry, it is the latter which is more devastating, for, funeral fire burns only the dead body while the mental worry burns the living one. This mental torment may become acute when the judicial verdict is finally set against the accused. Earlier to it, there was every reason for him to hope for acquittal. That hope is extinguished after the final verdict. If, therefore, there is inordinate delay in execution, the condemned prisoner is entitled to

come to the court requesting to examine whether, it is just and fair to allow the sentence of death to be executed.

In *Madhu Mehta v Union of India* [1989] 3 S.C.R. 775, which followed six weeks later, a writ petition brought on behalf on one Gyasi Ram was allowed and the death sentence altered to imprisonment for life. The condemned prisoner had been waiting a decision on his mercy petition by the President of India for over eight years. It was held that he had suffered mental agony of living under the shadow of death for far too long.

(c) The position in the United States of America

The Supreme Court of the United States has never directly addressed the issue of delay in carrying out sentence of death. . . .

. . .

A far more progressive and compassionate approach is evident in *People v Anderson* 493 P. 2d. 8880 (1972). The Supreme Court of California was there concerned with whether the death sentence violated Article 6 of the State's constitutional prohibition against cruel or unusual punishment. In holding that it did, WRIGHT CJ stressed the torturousness of delay involved in the carrying out of the death penalty. He said at 892:.

> It merits emphasis that in assessing the cruelty of capital punishment under article 1, section 6, we are not concerned only with the 'mere extinguishment of life' . . . but with the total impact of capital punishment, from the pronouncement of the judgment of death through the execution itself, both on the individual and on the society which sanctions its use. Our concern is that the execution which ultimately follows pronouncement of the death sentence has in fact become the 'lingering death' which the *Kemmler* court [an earlier-discussed opinion] conceded would be cruel in the constitutional sense.

And continued at 894–895:.

> The cruelty of capital punishment lies not only in the execution itself and the pain incident thereto, but also in the dehumanizing effects of the lengthy imprisonment prior to execution during which the judicial and administrative procedures essential to due process of law are carried out. Penologists and medical experts agree that the process of carrying out a verdict of death is often so degrading and brutalizing to the human spirit as to constitute psychological torture. Respondent concedes the fact of lengthy delays between the pronouncement of the judgment of death and the actual execution, but suggests that these delays are acceptable because they often occur at the instance of the condemned prisoner. We reject this suggestion. An appellant's insistence on receiving the benefits of appellate review of the judgment condemning him to death does not render the lengthy period of impending execution any less torturous or exempt such cruelty from constitutional proscription.

The California State Constitution was later amended in a manner which overruled the decision, by exempting the death penalty from the prohibition against cruel or unusual punishment. Nonetheless, the observations of WRIGHT CJ remain entirely apposite.

The decision of the Supreme Judicial Court of Massachusetts, in *District Attorney for Suffolk District v Watson* Mass. 411 N.E. 2d 1274 (1980) portrays the same advanced perception. It held the death penalty to be violative of the State's Constitution which prohibited cruel punishment. The delay and pain of waiting for execution was an important part of the rationale . . .

. . .

It is, I think, apparent from this survey that both the Supreme Judicial Court of Massachusetts and the Supreme Court of California have indicated an appreciation of the relevance of delay *per se* as a ground of constitutional attack upon the death penalty. The other decisions either failed to view the delay in a constitutional setting, or held that it was not an accountable factor since caused by the condemned prisoner's pursuit, to the full, of his judicial remedies – an approach which 'both ignores the drive for self-preservation and penalises the exercise of a legal right' per the anonymous writer in 1972 Iowa Law Review at 831.

[The court then considered several decisions of the Judicial Committee of the Privy Council in the United Kingdom, on appeals to it from the West Indies. In one of those opinions, *Riley and others v Attorney-General of Jamaica* [1982] 3 All ER 469 (PC), the majority opinion found no breach of the Jamaican constitution in execution of a death sentence. A joint dissenting opinion concluded that there was such a breach. It stated in part:]

> It is no exaggeration, therefore, to say that the jurisprudence of the civilised world, much of which is derived from common law principles and the prohibition against cruel and unusual punishments in the English Bill of Rights, has recognized and acknowledged that prolonged delay in executing a sentence of death can make the punishment when it comes inhuman and degrading. As the Supreme Court of California commented in *People v Anderson* it is cruel and has dehumanizing effects. Sentence of death is one thing: sentence of death followed by lengthy imprisonment prior to execution is another.

. . .

In my respectful view the minority opinion is to be preferred to that of the majority. It applied the liberal interpretation of fundamental rights recommended in *Minister of Home Affairs v Fisher* [an earlier-discussed opinion] and accords with the evolving standards in any civilized country. It was referred to with approval by the Supreme Court of India . . .

. . .

(e) The extradition judgments

In *Soering v United Kingdom* (1989) 11 EHRR 439 the European Court of Human Rights decided for the first time that extradition could amount to a breach of Article 3 (the prohibition against torture or inhuman or degrading treatment or punishment) of the Convention for the Protection of Human Rights and Fundamental Freedoms.

Soering, a German national, was wanted for murder in Bedford County, Virginia, United States of America. He fled to Europe but was arrested in England on a charge of cheque fraud. Six weeks later he was indicted for two brutal murders in Bedford County and, in consequence, the United States requested his extradition under its 1972 Extradition Treaty with Great Britain. . . . Shortly thereafter a hearing was held in England, upon the request of the United States for Soering's extradition, and the court found him extraditable. Appeals against the decision failed and ultimately Soering was ordered to be surrendered to the United States. In the meantime, however, he filed a complaint with the European Commission of Human Rights, which [decided the case against him and then referred the case to the European Court of Human Rights.].

The European Court unanimously found that there was a real risk that a Virginia court would sentence Soering to death and that if he was surrendered for trial, Article 3 would be violated. This determination was based on its assessment of death row conditions at Mecklenburg Correctional Centre. The following passages in the judgment reflect the position of the Court.

. . .

> 106. The period that a condemned prisoner can expect to spend on death row in Virginia before being executed is on average six to eight years. This length of time awaiting death is, as the Commission and the United Kingdom Government noted, in a sense largely of the prisoner's own making in that he takes advantage of all avenues of appeal which are offered to him by Virginia law. The automatic appeal to the Supreme Court of Virginia normally takes no more than six months. The remaining time is accounted for by collateral attacks mounted by the prisoner himself in habeas corpus proceedings before both the State and Federal courts and in applications to the Supreme Court of the United States for certiorari review, the prisoner at each stage being able to seek a stay of execution. The remedies available under Virginia law serve the purpose of ensuring that the ultimate sanction of death is not unlawfully or arbitrarily imposed.
>
> Nevertheless, just as some lapse of time between sentence and execution is inevitable if appeal safeguards are to be provided to the condemned person, so it is equally part of human nature that the person will cling to life by exploiting those safeguards to the full. However well-intentioned and even potentially beneficial is the provision of the complex of post-sentence procedures in Virginia, the consequence is that the condemned prisoner has to endure for many years the conditions on death row and the anguish and mounting tension of living in the ever-present shadow of death.
>
> 111. . . . [H]aving regard to the very long period of time spent on death row in such extreme conditions, with the ever present and mounting anguish of awaiting execution of the death penalty, and to the personal circumstances of the applicant, especially his age and mental state at the time of the offence, the applicant's extradition to the United States would expose him to a real risk of treatment going beyond the threshold set by Article 3. . . . Accordingly, the Secretary of State's decision to extradite the applicant to the United States would, if implemented, give rise to a breach of Article 3.

. . .

In *Re: Kindler and Minister of Justice* (1991) 67 C.C.C. 3d 1 the Supreme Court of Canada, by a majority of four to three, on facts very close to those in the *Soering* case, refused to block the extradition of the fugitive appellant to the United States. It is unnecessary to deal in any detail with the lengthy separate judgments save to indicate, that for the majority, LA FORREST J, at 15 took the view that:

> While the psychological stress inherent in the death-row phenomenon cannot be dismissed lightly, it ultimately pales in comparison to the death penalty. Besides, the fact remains that a defendant is never forced to undergo the full appeal procedure, but the vast majority choose to do so. It would be ironic if delay caused by the appellant's taking advantage of the full and generous avenue of the appeals available to him should be viewed as a violation of fundamental justice.

[The court discussed three cases brought before the UN Human Rights Committee on the question of delay. All three involved Jamaica. The latest of these cases, *Errol Johnson v Jamaica* appears at p. 28, *infra*. The court then considered the period of delay in the four cases before it from the time of imposition of the death sentence, and concluded:]

Making all reasonable allowance for the time necessary for appeal and the consideration of reprieve, these delays are inordinate. As such they create a serious obstacle in the dispensation and administration of justice. They shake the confidence of the people in the very system. It is my earnest belief that the sensitivities of fair-minded Zimbabweans would be much disturbed, if not shocked, by the unduly long lapse of time during which these four condemned prisoners have suffered the agony and torment of the inexorably approaching foreordained death while in demeaning conditions of confinement.

Having regard to the impressive judicial and academic consensus concerning the death row phenomenon, the prolonged delays and the harsh conditions of incarceration, I am convinced that a sufficient degree of seriousness has been attained as to entitle the applicant to invoke on behalf of the condemned prisoners the protection against inhuman treatment afforded them by section 15(1) of the Constitution.

. . .

. . . Humaneness and dignity of the individual are the hallmarks of civilized laws. Justice must be done dispassionately and in accordance with constitutional mandates. . . . For like Article 21 of the Constitution of India, section 15(1) stands as sentinel over human misery, degradation and oppression. Its voice is that of justice and fairness . . .

. . .

THE ORDER

In the result I would order as follows:

1. The application is allowed with costs.
2. The sentences of death passed upon Martin Bechani Bakaka, Luke Kingsize Chiliko, Timothy Mhlanga and John Chakara Zacharia Marichi is, in each case, set aside and substituted with a sentence of imprisonment for life.

. . .

QUESTIONS

1. On what body of law does the court base its decision—Zimbabwe's internal law, a given foreign law, or general principles abstracted from diverse states or an associated group of states (such as Commonwealth states), international law? Some blend thereof?

2. What appears to be the attitude of the court toward decisions by foreign courts or international tribunals? Are they binding? persuasive? simply useful to ventilate an issue and thereby deepen discussion? Does the court pay them any particular deference? Does the fact that Zimbabwe is a state party to the International Covenant on Civil and Political Rights appear to influence the Court's attitude toward the views of the Human Rights Committee created by that Covenant?

3. Would the opinion have gained or lost in persuasiveness if the court had restricted itself to the Zimbabwe constitution and legal developments—case law, statutes, constitution, commentary—internal to Zimbabwe? Or is that no longer plausible with respect to human rights issues?

NOTE

In *Pratt v Attorney General for Jamaica* [1994] 2 AC 1, [1993] 4 All ER 769, a 1993 decision of the Privy Council of the House of Lords in the UK, the two appellants had been convicted in Jamaica in 1979 on a charge of murder in 1977 and were sentenced to death. Since that time, they had been held in death row. On three occasions, before last-minute stays of execution, they had been removed from their cells to an area adjacent to the gallows. In the 13 years before their appeal in 1992 to the Judicial Committee of the Privy Council, the appellants had unsuccessfully sought relief from the death sentence in the Jamaican appellate courts and had also brought the case before two international human rights organs. During the colonial period, cases had routinely been appealed from the highest court of a colony to the Privy Council. As former colonies gained statehood, the practice frequently continued but steadily lost adherents. At the time of this appeal, Jamaica was one of the few states that continued to recognize the appellate jurisdiction of the Privy Council.

Appellants' claim for relief rested on Article 17 of the Jamaican Constitution, which provided in clause (1): 'No person shall be subjected to torture or to inhuman or degrading punishment or other treatment'. The argument was that the long imprisonment on death row constituted inhuman or degrading punishment.

The opinion of the Privy Council was written by Lord Griffiths. It reviewed the complex procedural aspects of the case during the 14-year period when the appellants sought relief. The opinion found considerable responsibility for the delay in the Jamaican judiciary, laws, and government. Lord Griffiths remarked on the circumstances of the appellants.

> The statement of these bare facts is sufficient to bring home to the mind of any person of normal sensitivity and compassion the agony of mind that these men must have suffered as they have alternated between hope and despair . . . facing the gallows . . . [T]here are now 23 prisoners in death row who have been awaiting execution for more than ten years . . . It is against this disturbing background that their Lordships must now determine this constitutional appeal . . .

The opinion stressed that long delays in execution of a death sentence were almost unheard of in the UK, 'If such a situation had been brought to the attention of the court their Lordships do not doubt that the judges would have stayed the execution to enable the prerogative of mercy to be exercized and the sentence to be commuted to one of life imprisonment'.

The opinion discussed a number of cases, including *Catholic Commission for Justice and Peace in Zimbabwe v Attorney-General,* and *Soering v UK* (a decision of the European Court of Human Rights that was discussed in the preceding Zimbabwe decision). It continued:

> In their Lordships' view a state that wishes to retain capital punishment must accept the responsibility of ensuring that execution follows as swiftly as practicable after sentence, allowing a reasonable time for appeal and consideration of reprieve. It is part of the human condition that a condemned man will take every opportunity to save his life through use of the appellate procedure. If the appellate procedure enables the prisoner to prolong the appellate hearings over a period of years, the fault is to be attributed to the appellate system that permits such delay and not to the prisoner who takes advantage of it . . .
>
> The application of the appellants to appeal to the Judicial Committee of the Privy Council and their petitions to the two [international] human rights bodies do not fall within the category of frivolous procedures disentitling them to ask the Board to look at the whole period of delay in this case. The total period of delay is shocking and now amounts to almost 14 years. It is double the time that the European Court of Human Rights considered would be an infringement of art 3 of the European Convention and their Lordships can have no doubt that an execution would now be an infringement of s 17(1) of the Jamaican Constitution. To execute these men now after holding them in custody in an agony of suspense for so many years would be inhuman punishment within the meaning of s 17(1). In the last resort the courts have to accept the responsibility of saying whether the threshold has been passed in any given case and there may be difficult borderline decisions to be made. This, however, is not a borderline case. The delay in this case is wholly unacceptable and this appeal must be allowed.
> . . .
>
> The appropriate order in the present case is that the sentence of death of each appellant should be commuted to life imprisonment.
> . . .
>
> These considerations lead their Lordships to the conclusion that in any case in which execution is to take place more than five years after sentence there will be strong grounds for believing that the delay is such as to constitute 'inhuman or degrading punishment or other treatment'.

NOTE

The United States Supreme Court has not resolved the issue of the constitutionality under the 'cruel and unusual punishments' clause of the Eighth Amendment to the Constitution of executing a sentence of death after a long stay of the prisoner in death row. The Court denied a petition for a writ of certiorari—that is, exercised its discretion to deny review—in a Texas case where the prisoner had spent 17 years on death row: *Lackey v Texas*, 514 U.S. 1045, 115 S. Ct. 1421 (1995). In a separate memorandum, Justice Stevens argued that the case should be reviewed. He suggested that in cases of long delays that were not traceable to the prisoner's abuse of the judicial system by repetitive and frivolous filings, the purpose of retribution may already have been met by the severe punishment inflicted. Moreover, 'the additional deterrent effect from an actual execution now, on the one hand, as compared to 17 years on death row followed by the prisoner's continued incarceration for life, on the other, seems minimal'. Justice Stevens further noted that 'the highest courts in other countries have found arguments such as petitioner's to be persuasive,' citing *Pratt v. Attorney General of Jamaica.*, *supra*. The *Lackey* claim, while 'novel', was 'not without foundation'.

The Court also denied certiorari in *Knight v. Florida* (98-9741) and a related case on November 8, 1999. 120 S. Ct. 459. Justice Thomas, concurring in the denial, stated that he was 'unaware of any support in the American constitutional tradition' for the proposition that a defendant invoking judicial procedures to overturn a death sentence could complain when execution was delayed. It was for this reason, said Thomas, for lack of domestic support, that petitioners had to 'rely' on decisions of the European Court of Human Rights, the Supreme Court of Zimbabwe, the Supreme Court of India, and the Privy Council. 'It is incongruous to arm capital defendants with an arsenal of "constitutional" claims with which they may delay their executions, and simultaneously to complain when executions are inevitably delayed.'

Justice Breyer dissented from the denial of certiorari. He stressed that the long delays in these cases (about 20 years) stemmed in significant part from constitutionally defective death penalty procedures. In these circumstances, 'the claim that time has rendered the execution inhuman is a particularly strong one'. In both cases, sentencing procedures leading to the death penalty had been found unconstitutional in appellate or collateral court proceedings. Thus new sentencing procedures bringing about much delay were required. The new procedures led again to the death penalty.

Justice Breyer referred to the decisions of 'a growing number of courts outside the United States' holding that lengthy delay rendered execution inhuman, degrading, or unusually cruel. He referred to the Pratt opinion, to opinions of the Supreme Courts of India and Zimbabwe, and to decisions of the European Court of Human Rights.

> Obviously this foreign authority does not bind us. After all, we are interpreting a 'Constitution for the United States of America'. . . . [T]his Court has long considered as relevant and informative the way in which foreign courts have applied

standards roughly comparable to our own constitutional standards in roughly comparable circumstances. In doing so, the Court has found particularly instructive opinions of former Commonwealth nations insofar as those opinions reflect a legal tradition that also underlies our own Eighth Amendment. . . . Willingness to consider foreign judicial views in comparable cases is not surprising in a Nation that from its birth has given a 'decent respect to the opinions of mankind'.

In these cases, the foreign courts I have mentioned have considered roughly comparable questions under roughly comparable legal standards. Each court has held or assumed that those standards permit application of the death penalty itself. Consequently, I believe their views are useful even though not binding.

. . .

Finally, the constitutional issue, even if limited to delays of close to 20 years or more, has considerable practical importance. Available statistics indicate that as of two years ago, December 1997, 24 prisoners sentenced to death had been on death row for more than 20 years. At that time 125 prisoners on death row had been sentenced in or before 1980 and therefore may now fall within the relevant category. . . .

In the last decade, the lower federal courts have decided adversely to the prisoner a number of cases posing similar issues.

NOTE

The Human Rights Committee, created by the International Covenant on Civil and Political Rights, has jurisdiction to hear complaints alleging violations of the Covenant that are brought before it by individuals against their own states, provided that those states have ratified the Optional Protocol to the Covenant. Jamaica had ratified the Protocol. The term 'views' is used to describe the Committee's disposition of the complaint, which is known as a 'communication'.

ERROL JOHNSON V. JAMAICA
Communication No. 588/1994, Human Rights Committee
Views of Committee, March 22, 1996
UN Doc. CCPR/C/56/D/588/1994, 5 IHRR 21 (1997)

1. The author of the communication is Errol Johnson, a Jamaican citizen who, at the time of submission of his communication, was awaiting execution at St. Catherine District Prison, Jamaica. He claims to be a victim of violations by Jamaica of articles 6, 7, 10, paragraph 1, and 14, paragraphs 1, 3 (c), (g) and 5, of the International Covenant on Civil and Political Rights. The author is represented by counsel. In early 1995, the offence of which the author was convicted was classified as non-capital murder, and his death sentence was commuted to life imprisonment on 16 March 1995.

2.1 The author was, together with a co-defendant, Irvine Reynolds, convicted

of the murder of one Reginald Campbell and sentenced to death on 15 December 1983 in the Clarendon Circuit Court. . . . [His appeals in Jamaica failed.]
. . .

3.1 It is argued that the author was detained on death row for over 10 years, and that if he were to be executed after such a delay, this would amount to cruel and degrading treatment and/or punishment, in violation of article 7 of the Covenant. In substantiation of his claim, counsel refers to the findings of the Judicial Committee of the Privy Council in *Pratt and Morgan v. Attorney-General of Jamaica* and of the Supreme Court of Zimbabwe in a recent case [set forth at pp. 25 and 19, *supra.*] The fact that the author was held on death row for so long under the appalling conditions of detention at St. Catherine District Prison is said to amount in itself to a violation of article 7.
. . .

8.1 The Committee first has to determine whether the length of the author's detention on death row since December 1983, i.e. over 11 years, amounts to a violation of articles 7 and 10, paragraph 1, of the Covenant. Counsel has alleged a violation of these articles merely by reference to the length of time Mr. Johnson has spent confined to the death row section of St. Catherine District Prison. While a period of detention on death row of well over 11 years is certainly a matter of serious concern, it remains the jurisprudence of this Committee that detention for a specific period of time does not amount to a violation of articles 7 and 10(1) of the Covenant in the absence of some further compelling circumstances. The Committee is aware that its jurisprudence has given rise to controversy and wishes to set out its position in detail.

8.2 . . . [T]he following factors must be considered:

(a) The Covenant does not prohibit the death penalty, though it subjects its use to severe restrictions. As detention on death row is a necessary consequence of imposing the death penalty, no matter how cruel, degrading and inhuman it may appear to be, it cannot, of itself, be regarded as a violation of articles 7 and 10 of the Covenant.

(b) While the Covenant does not prohibit the death penalty, the Committee has taken the view, which has been reflected in the Second Optional Protocol to the Covenant, that article 6 'refers generally to abolition in terms which strongly suggest that abolition is desirable'. . . . Reducing recourse to the death penalty may therefore be seen as one of the objects and purposes of the Covenant.

(c) The provisions of the Covenant must be interpreted in the light of the Covenant's objects and purposes (article 31 of the Vienna Convention on the Law of Treaties). As one of these objects and purposes is to promote reduction in the use of the death penalty, an interpretation of a provision in the Covenant that may encourage a State party that retains the death penalty to make use of that penalty should, where possible, be avoided.

8.3 In light of these factors, we must examine the implications of holding the length of detention on death row, per se, to be in violation of articles 7 and 10. The first, and most serious, implication is that if a State party executes a condemned prisoner after he has spent a certain period of time on death row, it will not be in violation of its obligations under the Covenant, whereas if it refrains from doing so, it will violate the Covenant. An interpretation of the Covenant leading to this result cannot be consistent with the Covenant's object and purpose. The above implication cannot be avoided by refraining from determining a definite period of detention on death row, after which there will be a presumption that detention on death row constitutes cruel and inhuman punishment. . . .

8.4 The second implication of making the time factor per se the determining one, i.e. the factor that turns detention on death row into a violation of the Covenant, is that it conveys a message to States parties retaining the death penalty that they should carry out a capital sentence as expeditiously as possible after it was imposed. This is not a message the Committee would wish to convey to States parties. Life on death row, harsh as it may be, is preferable to death. Furthermore, experience shows that delays in carrying out the death penalty can be the necessary consequence of several factors, many of which may be attributable to the State party. Sometimes a moratorium is placed on executions while the whole question of the death penalty is under review. At other times the executive branch of government delays executions even though it is not feasible politically to abolish the death penalty. The Committee would wish to avoid adopting a line of jurisprudence which weakens the influence of factors that may very well lessen the number of prisoners actually executed. . . .

8.5 Finally, to hold that prolonged detention on death row does not, per se, constitute a violation of articles 7 and 10, does not imply that other circumstances connected with detention on death row may not turn that detention into cruel, inhuman and degrading treatment or punishment. The jurisprudence of the Committee has been that where compelling circumstances of the detention are substantiated, that detention may constitute a violation of the Covenant. This jurisprudence should be maintained in future cases.

8.6 In the present case, neither the author nor his counsel have pointed to any compelling circumstances, over and above the length of the detention on death row, that would turn Mr. Johnson's detention into a violation of articles 7 and 10. The Committee therefore concludes that there has been no violation of these provisions.

. . .

[The Committee did, however, find that Jamaica had violated provisions of Article 14 of the Covenant by its delay in making the trial transcript available to Johnson, for this prevented him from having his appeal determined expeditiously. Hence Johnson was entitled to an effective remedy. Since his death sentence had previously been commuted to life imprisonment, the Committee suggested to Jamaica a further (undesignated) measure of clemency.]

QUESTIONS

1. Do you notice any difference in the structure of argument or style in the opinion of the Human Rights Committee, and in the opinions in the Zimbabwean, American, and

Privy Council decisions? Would you expect international and national tribunals to act differently in these respects?

2. What important differences in the disposition of the prisoners' claims do these opinions reveal? With which decisions, if any, do you agree?

3. All these opinions employ the language of rights; there are several references to international human rights. How then do you explain the differences in outcome, including differences in reasoning and related holdings even when the petitioners are granted relief? Should not rights, like the right to be free of cruel, inhuman or degrading punishment, lead to the same decision everywhere?

NOTE

There follow materials on law-based and other arguments for the retention or abolition of capital punishment: a comment on contemporary aspects of this topic from comparative and international perspectives, and judicial decisions from the United States and South Africa. Again themes of rights and human rights figure importantly in the judicial discussions.

COMMENT ON ASPECTS OF CAPITAL PUNISHMENT

There follow a number of selective observations about capital punishment among states today and about its regulation under international law instruments.[1] Their purpose is to put the descriptions and text of the cases following this Comment into a contemporary perspective that has inevitably been influenced by the human rights movement.

Death Sentences and Executions

As far as known to Amnesty International (AI), the world's largest nongovernmental human rights organization and one committed to the abolition of the death penalty, 1,625 prisoners were executed by 37 states in 1998, while 3,899 people were sentenced to death in 78 states. As AI indicates, 'the true figures are certainly higher'. Of these numbers, 1,067 executions took place in the People's Republic of China, 68 in the United States, and 66 in Iran. There were reports, impossible to confirm, of hundreds of executions in Iraq, and statistics were difficult to obtain from a number of other countries. About 500 prisoners have been executed in the United States since the use of the death penalty was resumed in 1977 (see p. 34, *infra*).

---

[1] Except as otherwise noted, the statistics in this Comment are taken primarily from the Amnesty International website (www.amnesty.org) as of November 1999, which includes current information.

Abolitionist and Retentionist Countries

Over half of the world's countries have abolished the death penalty in law, or in practice, in an ongoing trend over the last decades. After the Second World War, the vast majority of states provided for and used the death penalty. The trend intensified in the 1970s. Since 1990, over 30 countries have abolished capital punishment for ordinary crimes or all crimes. In aggregate figures today, 69 states have abolished the death penalty for all crimes, while 13 states reserved it for designated exceptional crimes, particularly certain wartime crimes. AI argues that 23 states 'can be considered abolitionist *de facto*', since they retain the death penalty but have not carried out executions for at least ten years. Thus in its view, 105 states can today be considered abolitionist, while 90 others retain and use the death penalty.

Abolitionist states in one or another category include the Western European states, and many states from most other parts of the world. Retentionist states include the Muslim states and many states from most other parts of the world. Such significant countries as China, India, Japan, the Russian Federation, and the United States are among the retentionist states. In several countries, including the United States, the number of crimes subject to capital punishment has been on the rise.

Status of Capital Punishment Under International Law

Read Article 6 of the (universal) International Covenant on Civil and Political Rights, and note the limitations, short of abolition, on capital punishment. That Covenant had 144 states parties in March 2000. None of the three major regional treaties—in Africa, Europe, and the Inter-American system—banned capital punishment, though all imposed restrictions on its use. Three more recent treaties now provide for abolition, either totally or with a limited exception for wartime crimes. They are protocols (additions) to the (universal) International Covenant on Civil and Political Rights, and to the regional treaties for Europe and the Inter-American system. The Second Optional Protocol to the International Covenant has 41 states parties, while the 35 parties to Protocol No. 6 to the European Convention on Human Rights constitute a much higher percentage of the total number of parties (41 in March 2000) to that Convention. There are seven parties to the relevant Protocol to the American Convention on Human Rights (25 parties in March 2000). All these documents appear in the Annex on Documents.

Questions about the status of capital punishment under customary international law can be addressed in light of information in Chapter 2.

As Article 6 of the International Covenant indicates, treaties impose a range of restrictions on the use of capital punishment. For the views of the United States about execution of persons who committed the relevant crime when under the age of 18, see p. 1040, *infra.*

The UN Commission on Human Rights, the leading intergovernmental organ concerned primarily with human rights issues, issued Resolution 1999/61 in April

1999 by a vote of 30–11, with 12 abstentions. Such resolutions, while not formally binding on states, can have political and moral significance and influence legal developments. The resolution 'calls upon' states parties to the International Covenant on Civil and Political Rights to join the Second Optional Protocol. It also 'calls upon' states that have retained the death penalty to 'establish a moratorium on executions, with a view to completely abolishing the death penalty'.

The maximum penalty for persons convicted of war crimes, crimes against humanity, or genocide by the International Criminal Tribunals created by the UN Security Council for the Former Yugoslavia and for Rwanda is life imprisonment. The Nuremberg and related trials after the Second World War imposed the death sentence on certain defendants.

Religious views

'Preaching consistency in moral values, Pope John Paul II today urged America's Roman Catholics to extend the crusade to protect human life to include murderers on death row. "The new evangelization calls for followers of Christ who are unconditionally pro-life," the Pope preached to 100,000 people [in St. Louis]. "Modern society has the means of protecting itself, without definitively denying criminals the chance to reform.' He called the death penalty "cruel and unnecessary," and said it was so "even in the case of someone who has done great evil." '. *New York Times*, January 28, 1999, p. A14.

'International law arguments may be less convincing in the Islamic world, where an entrenched and immutable religious doctrine insists upon the death penalty in certain cases. Perhaps there is a role for Islamic legal scholars who can demonstrate an alternative and more progressive view of religious law . . . If there is no universal agreement on the most fundamental of human rights, the right to life, how can anything more be expected in the rest of the catalogue of human rights?' William Schabas, *The Abolition of the Death Penalty in International Law* 307 (2nd edn. 1997).

Arguments about justifications for continuing or abolishing the death penalty

For centuries, law enforcement agencies, defence counsel, criminologists and philosophers, religious figures, and the general public have argued about this issue from many different perspectives. It has become an important issue in political campaigns in democracies. 'Many people still accept the principle of "an eye for an eye, a tooth for a tooth", particularly when atrocious crimes are involved'. Schabas, *supra*, at xii. The debate intensifies as the abolitionist movement has grown over the life of the human rights movement.

The descriptions and text of the judicial decisions following this Comment state many of the leading contemporary arguments, which are cast both in terms of justice and fairness, and in instrumental terms that take into account the effects of capital punishment on the incidence of crime. Frequently such arguments fall within the broad debated categories of retribution, fairness (including the issue of discrimination), and deterrence.

New statistics constantly emerge. For example, in the United States, the state of Illinois reinstated the death penalty in 1977. Since then, it executed 12 men and exonerated 12 after proof of their innocence, some within days of execution. DNA testing has become increasingly significant in proving some convicted killers to be innocent. Since the modern death penalty in the United States began in 1973 (see the following article), about 79 men and women have been released from death row, one for every seven people convicted. *New York Times*, May 23, 1999, p. 16WK.

CAROL STEIKER AND JORDAN STEIKER, JUDICIAL DEVELOPMENTS IN CAPITAL PUNISHMENT LAW

in James Acker, R. Bohm and C. Lanier, America's Experiment with Capital Punishment (1998), at 47

A quarter century ago, the Supreme Court in *Furman v. Georgia* (1972) abolished the death penalty as it was then administered in the United States. Four years later, the Court in *Gregg v. Georgia* (1976) and its quartet of accompanying cases sustained some new death penalty statutes that appeared to address many of the concerns voiced in *Furman*. In doing so, the Court embarked on a course of continuing constitutional regulation of capital punishment in America.

Virtually no one thinks that the constitutional regulation of capital punishment has been a success. But oddly, and we think significantly, critics of the Court's death penalty jurisprudence fall in two diametrically opposed camps. On the one hand, some critics claim that the Court has created an overly complex, absurdly arcane, and minutely detailed body of constitutional law that imposes an unacceptable burden on states' attempts to administer their capital punishment schemes. This set of critics notes the sheer volume of death penalty litigation, the labyrinthine nature of the doctrines that such litigation has spawned, the frequency with which federal courts overturn state-imposed death sentences, and the lengthy delays that occur between the imposition of death sentences and their execution. On the other hand, a different set of critics claims that the Supreme Court has in fact turned its back on regulating the death penalty and no longer even attempts to meet the concerns about the arbitrary and discriminatory imposition of death that animated its 'constitutionalization' of capital punishment in *Furman*. These critics note that the Court's intervention has done little or nothing to remedy the vast over-representation on death row of the young, poor, and mentally retarded or the continuing influence of race on the capital sentencing decision. Under this view, in the anguished words of Justice Harry Blackmun, who twenty years after his dissent in *Furman* radically changed course and argued for the constitutional abolition of the death penalty, the Court has done no more than 'tinker with the machinery of death' (*Callins v. Collins* 1994:1130) .

A sustained examination of the past two decades of constitutional regulation of capital punishment reveals, surprisingly, that both sets of critics are substantially correct. The death penalty is, perversely, both over- and under-regulated. The body of doctrine produced by the Court is enormously complex and its applicability to specific cases difficult to discern; yet, it remains unresponsive to the central animating concerns that inspired the Court to embark on its regulatory regime in the first place. Indeed, most surprisingly, the overall effect of the Supreme Court's quarter century of doctrinal development has been largely to reproduce the pre-*Furman* world of capital sentencing.

. . .

Until the Supreme Court's decision in *Furman v. Georgia* [408 U.S. 238] in 1972, the administration of capital punishment was simply not a subject about which the federal Constitution was thought to have much to say. . . .

[By the 1970's] opponents of capital punishment, buoyed by the 'revolution' in criminal procedure advanced by the Warren Court, had successfully drawn the Court into the constitutional fray. The NAACP Legal Defense Fund led the effort to halt executions through a 'moratorium' strategy by raising a myriad of procedural and substantive challenges to state death penalty schemes in cases in which execution dates were set . . .

. . . *Furman v. Georgia* did not present merely a minor or technical challenge to particular aspects of state death penalty practices, but rather required an encompassing assessment of the moral, political, and practical dimensions of the American system of capital punishment. The immediate effect of *Furman*'s rejection of unguided jury discretion in capital sentencing was to invalidate the death penalty not only in Georgia, but in 38 other states, the District of Columbia, and the federal government. Although *Furman* remains the longest decision ever rendered by the Supreme Court, the majority 'opinion' in the case was a terse one-paragraph invalidating under the Eighth Amendment [The 'cruel and unusual punishments' clause] the death sentences imposed on the three petitioners in the case. . . .

. . .

The extent to which *Furman* was a beginning and not an end to constitutional regulation of the death penalty became clear in 1976, when the Supreme Court considered five new state statutory schemes in light of its decision in *Furman*, upholding three (*Gregg v. Georgia* [428 U.S. 153]; *Jurek v. Texas*; *Proffitt v. Florida*) and striking down two of the schemes (*Woodson v. North Carolina*; *Roberts v. Louisiana*). *Gregg v. Georgia* and its quartet of accompanying cases clarified that the death penalty was not per se invalid under the Eighth Amendment and that the Court would now be involved in the ongoing business of determining which state schemes could pass constitutional muster. . . .

. . .

Desert

At the time of the Court's decision in *Furman*, many jurisdictions in the United States authorized the death penalty not only for murder, but also for crimes such as rape, kidnaping, armed robbery, and even some assaults. Moreover, virtually every death penalty jurisdiction afforded sentencers absolute discretion to impose either death or life imprisonment (or sometimes merely a term of years) in capital cases. The Georgia statute reviewed in *Furman* itself was exemplary: it afforded the jury full discretion to sentence a defendant convicted of forcible rape to death, life imprisonment, or imprisonment for not less than one nor more than 20 years. . . .

One primary problem with such broad and discretionary schemes identified by the *Furman* and *Gregg* Courts was that the state and federal legislatures that drafted such statutes were never required to articulate a theory about the most death-worthy crimes or defendants. The Justices in *Furman* repeatedly noted that the number of those actually sentenced to death represented only a tiny fraction of those eligible to be executed by the broad net cast by the state statutes at issue in the case. The death penalty appeared, in Justice Stewart's evocative image, to strike like 'lightning' (*Furman v. Georgia* 1972:309). . . .

. . . In both *Furman* and *Gregg*, then, the Court's concern about overinclusion— its fear that unbridled sentencing discretion might lead to the execution of those who did not deserve it—was paramount.

Fairness

Distinct from the concern about desert in capital sentencing is the concern about fairness. Even if every defendant sentenced to death under a capital sentencing scheme 'deserved' to die according to the larger community's considered judgment, the scheme could still be subject to challenge on the basis that it treated others, just as 'deserving' as the condemned defendant, more leniently for no reason, or for invidious reasons. In other words, a person sentenced to death could make one of two distinct complaints. He might say simply, 'I don't deserve the death penalty'. But he also might intelligibly say, 'Whether or not I deserve the death penalty, there are other people who also deserve it and who are not getting it'. Thus, a sentencing scheme could avoid the problem of overinclusion (the failure to distinguish the deserving from the undeserving), but still present the problem of underinclusion (the failure to treat equally deserving cases alike).

These two distinct concerns implicate different institutions within the criminal justice system. The task of ascribing desert, and thus avoiding overinclusion, falls largely within the realm of the legislature, which speaks as the voice of the larger community . . . [There] arises the inevitable possibility of arbitrary or even discriminatory enforcement of community norms by the sentencer (usually a jury) in whom resides the ultimate power to pronounce life or death. Unlike its concerns about desert, the *Furman* Court's concerns about fairness were fueled not by the infrequency of the imposition of the death penalty, but rather by the *patterns* of its imposition.

Justice Douglas' concurring opinion in *Furman* presents the clearest expression of the fairness concern—what he himself called the 'equal protection' theme 'implicit' in the Eighth Amendment's proscription of cruel and unusual punishment (at 249). In sounding this theme, Douglas used anecdotal and statistical evidence to demonstrate that the death penalty in the United States was visited disproportionately upon the 'poor, young, and ignorant' and upon 'the Negro, and the members of unpopular groups' (at 250). . . . At no point did Douglas attempt to argue that the defendants before the Court (or the largely poor, young, ignorant, black, or unpopular defendants who had previously been executed) did not 'deserve' the death penalty, by reference either to internal community norms or to some external, Court-imposed notion of proportionality . . .

This focus on fairness, as distinct from desert, was apparent again four years later in *Gregg v. Georgia* (1976): a plurality of the Court upheld Georgia's new capital sentencing scheme partly on the basis that the new statute provided 'clear and objective standards' that would control sentencer discretion 'so as to produce non-discriminatory application' (*Gregg v. Georgia* 1976:198) . . . Indeed, the new Georgia statute most explicitly addressed the *Furman* Court's concerns about discrimination by calling upon the state's highest court to determine in each capital case '[w]hether the sentence of death was imposed under the influence of passion, prejudice, or any other arbitrary factor', based partly on a questionnaire filled out by the trial judge that disclosed whether race played a role in the case (at 211–212, White, J., concurring).

Individualization

One possible response to the *Furman* Court's concerns about desert and fairness was to attempt to control sentencer discretion. This approach, apparent in Georgia's revised statute and also in the new statutes of Florida and Texas, was upheld by the *Gregg* Court in 1976. A second plausible approach, however, was to enact *mandatory* capital sentencing schemes, in which the death penalty was automatically imposed for certain types of crimes. Such schemes would necessarily contain the crucial ingredient of legislative will because they would compel legislatures to agree on circumstances that would require, not merely permit, the imposition of the death penalty. Additionally, such schemes would allow no possibility of discrimination by the sentencer (although the prosecutor, with charging discretion, would clearly have room to maneuver) . . .

In 1976, however, the Supreme Court considered and rejected the mandatory approach, striking down capital statutes from Louisiana and North Carolina, and implicitly dooming all such laws elsewhere. The Court saw mandatory penalties in opposition to rather than in service of the goals of desert and fairness. . . .

. . .

[The] 'respect for humanity' argument built on Justice Brennan's opinion in *Furman* four years earlier, in which he tried to construct an argument against the death penalty based on the idea that '[t]he State, even as it punishes, must treat its members with respect for their intrinsic worth as human beings' (*Furman v. Georgia* 1972:270). Ultimately, Justice Brennan failed to convince his brethren that respect for humanity required the abolition of capital punishment altogether. However, his lengthy *Furman* concurrence did begin to develop a notion of human dignity that formed the basis of the Court's requirement of individualized sentencing.

What no one foresaw at the time, but which by now has become apparent, is the inherent tension between, on the one hand, controlling sentencer discretion so as to promote desert and fairness in the application of the death penalty, and, on the other hand, requiring individualized consideration by the sentencer of all relevant distinguishing traits among defendants. The best means of controlling discretion tend to undermine individualized consideration, and the process of individualized consideration creates opportunities for the free play of the very discretion that needs to be controlled. The 1976 cases, taken together, thus planted the seeds of one of the fundamental instabilities in current death penalty doctrine.

Heightened procedural reliability

Like its commitment to individualized capital sentencing, the Supreme Court's concern for heightened procedural reliability in capital cases built on Justice Brennan's solo concurrence in *Furman*. Just as Justice Brennan elaborated the notion of 'human dignity' implicit in the Court's 'evolving standards of decency' formulation of the Eighth Amendment, he also singlehandedly constructed the now-familiar 'death is different' argument. Arguing that death as a punishment differs in kind, and not merely in degree, from all other punishments, Justice Brennan attempted to demonstrate that its uniqueness as a punishment, both in severity and finality, rendered it cruel and unusual in all circumstances. No other Justices in *Furman* joined in that conclusion (although, arguably, Justice Marshall agreed).

Four years later, however, a plurality of the Court echoed Brennan's *Furman* concurrence by noting, in language that would be repeated many times in future cases:

> Death, in its finality, differs more from life imprisonment than a 100-year prison term differs from one of only a year or two. Because of that qualitative difference, there is a corresponding difference in the need for reliability in the determination that death is the appropriate punishment in a specific case (*Woodson v. North Carolina* 1976:305).

The Court thus concluded that although the practice of individualized sentencing 'generally reflects simply enlightened policy rather than a constitutional imperative', the Eighth Amendment requires individualized sentencing in capital cases (at 304).

The 1976 Court's willingness to require a special decision-making process in capital cases that clearly is not necessary in non-capital proceedings was generated by its concern about the 'reliability' of death verdicts. . . .
. . .

Over the past twenty years, the Court has essentially reaffirmed its basic conclusion of the 1976 cases: that state death penalty practices are subject to constitutional scrutiny but that such scrutiny need not be fatal to the death penalty. Given the number of capital cases litigated in federal court (including the U.S. Supreme Court), the voluminous opinions issued by federal judges, and the scores of death sentences stayed or reversed over that period, one might be tempted to conclude that federal constitutional scrutiny is extraordinarily searching. Close examination of the litigation that has emerged over the past two decades reveals, however, that contemporary death penalty doctrine is in fact remarkably undemanding. It is undeniably true, as many critics have claimed, that the Court's death penalty doctrine is complex, arcane, and minutely detailed. But this complexity does not translate, as the critics seem to assume, into significant impediments to states' efforts to impose the ultimate sanction. Instead, much of the recent capital litigation in the federal courts concerns statutory provisions that state legislatures could readily remedy or that in fact have already been repealed. Indeed, if a state sought to design a capital statute from scratch today, it could easily avoid federal constitutional difficulties and, perhaps more tellingly, could do so without departing significantly from the statutory schemes struck down in *Furman*.

. . .

STATE V. MAKWANYANE

Constitutional Court of the Republic of South Africa, 1995
Case No. CCT/3/94, [1995] 1 LRC 269

[The two appellants were convicted of murder, and sentenced to death by the Witwatersrand Local Division of the Supreme Court. The Appellate Division postponed hearing of the appeals against the death sentence until the new, post-apartheid Constitutional Court decided the question of its constitutionality under the transitional 1993 Constitution. The eleven individual opinions of the Justices of the Constitutional Court were unanimous in holding that the death sentence was unconstitutional. They focused, however, on different constitutional provisions and arguments or elements of the case. There appear below excerpts from the opinion of Justice Chaskalson, President of the Court.]

Relevant provisions of the Constitution

[7] The Constitution

> . . . provides a historic bridge between the past of a deeply divided society charac-
> terised by strife, conflict, untold suffering and injustice, and a future founded on
> the recognition of human rights, democracy and peaceful co-existence and
> development opportunities for all South Africans, irrespective of colour, race,
> class, belief or sex.

It is a transitional constitution but one which itself establishes a new order in South Africa; an order in which human rights and democracy are entrenched and in which the Constitution:

> . . . shall be the supreme law of the Republic and any law or act inconsistent with
> its provisions shall, unless otherwise provided expressly or by necessary implica-
> tion in this Constitution, be of no force and effect to the extent of the
> inconsistency.

[8] Chapter Three of the Constitution sets out the fundamental rights to which every person is entitled under the Constitution and also contains provisions dealing with the way in which the Chapter is to be interpreted by the Courts. It does not deal specifically with the death penalty, but in section 11(2), it prohibits 'cruel, inhuman or degrading treatment or punishment'. There is no definition of what is

to be regarded as 'cruel, inhuman or degrading' and we therefore have to give meaning to these words ourselves.

[9] In *S v Zuma and Two Others* [Constitutional Court Case No. CCT/5/94 (5 April 1995)], this Court dealt with the approach to be adopted in the interpretation of the fundamental rights enshrined in Chapter Three of the Constitution. It gave its approval to an approach which, whilst paying due regard to the language that has been used, is 'generous' and 'purposive' and gives expression to the underlying values of the Constitution. Kentridge AJ, who delivered the judgment of the Court, referred with approval to the following passage in the Canadian case of *R v Big M Drug Mart Ltd*:

> The meaning of a right or freedom guaranteed by the Charter was to be ascertained by an analysis of the purpose of such a guarantee; it was to be understood, in other words, in the light of the interests it was meant to protect.

. . .

[10] . . . [S]*ection* 11(2) of the Constitution must not be construed in isolation, but in its context, which includes the history and background to the adoption of the Constitution, other provisions of the Constitution itself and, in particular, the provisions of Chapter Three of which it is part. It must also be construed in a way which secures for 'individuals the full measure' of its protection. Rights with which *section* 11(2) is associated in Chapter Three of the Constitution, and which are of particular importance to a decision on the constitutionality of the death penalty are included in *section* 9, 'every person shall have the right to life', *section* 10, 'every person shall have the right to respect for and protection of his or her dignity', and *section* 8, 'every person shall have the right to equality before the law and to equal protection of the law'. Punishment must meet the requirements of *sections* 8, 9 and 10; and this is so, whether these sections are treated as giving meaning to *Section* 11(2) or as prescribing separate and independent standards with which all punishments must comply.

[11] Mr. Bizos, who represented the South African government at the hearing of this matter, informed us that the government accepts that the death penalty is a cruel, inhuman and degrading punishment and that it should be declared unconstitutional. The Attorney General of the Witwatersrand, whose office is independent of the government, took a different view, and contended that the death penalty is a necessary and acceptable form of punishment and that it is not cruel, inhuman or degrading within the meaning of section 11(2). He argued that if the framers of the Constitution had wished to make the death penalty unconstitutional they would have said so, and that their failure to do so indicated an intention to leave the issue open to be dealt with by Parliament in the ordinary way. . . .

. . .

[The Court looked to the drafting of the Constitution, to examine why certain provisions were or were not finally included in the Constitution. The failure to deal specifically in the Constitution with capital punishment 'was not accidental'. Different viewpoints were advanced in the early 1990s. Eventually the South

African Law Commission adopted a 'Solomonic solution' that found its way into the Constitution. The death sentence was, in terms, neither sanctioned nor excluded, and it was left to the Constitutional Court to decide whether the pre-constitutional law authorizing capital punishment was consistent with Chapter Three.

The Court then turned to section 11(2) of the Constitution on cruel, inhuman or degrading punishment.]

[27] The principal arguments advanced by counsel for the accused in support of their contention that the imposition of the death penalty for murder is a 'cruel, inhuman or degrading punishment', were that the death sentence is an affront to human dignity, is inconsistent with the unqualified right to life entrenched in the Constitution, cannot be corrected in case of error or enforced in a manner that is not arbitrary, and that it negates the essential content of the right to life and the other rights that flow from it. The Attorney General argued that the death penalty is recognised as a legitimate form of punishment in many parts of the world, it is a deterrent to violent crime, it meets society's need for adequate retribution for heinous offences, and it is regarded by South African society as an acceptable form of punishment. He asserted that it is, therefore, not cruel, inhuman or degrading within the meaning of *section* 11(2) of the Constitution. These arguments for and against the death sentence are well known and have been considered in many of the foreign authorities and cases to which we were referred. We must deal with them now in the light of the provisions of our own Constitution.
. . .

International and foreign comparative law

[33] The death sentence is a form of punishment which has been used throughout history by different societies. It has long been the subject of controversy. As societies became more enlightened, they restricted the offences for which this penalty could be imposed. The movement away from the death penalty gained momentum during the second half of the present century with the growth of the abolitionist movement. In some countries it is now prohibited in all circumstances, in some it is prohibited save in times of war, and in most countries that have retained it as a penalty for crime, its use has been restricted to extreme cases. According to Amnesty International, 1,831 executions were carried out throughout the world in 1993 as a result of sentences of death, of which 1,419 were in China, which means that only 412 executions were carried out in the rest of the world in that year. Today, capital punishment has been abolished as a penalty for murder either specifically or in practice by almost half the countries of the world including the democracies of Europe and our neighbouring countries, Namibia, Mozambique and Angola. . . .

[34] . . . The international and foreign authorities are of value because they analyze arguments for and against the death sentence and show how courts of other jurisdictions have dealt with this vexed issue. For that reason alone they require our attention. They may also have to be considered because of their relevance to section 35(1) of the Constitution, which states:

> In interpreting the provisions of this Chapter a court of law shall promote the values which underlie an open and democratic society based on freedom and equality and shall, where applicable, have regard to public international law applicable to the protection of the rights entrenched in this Chapter, and may have regard to comparable foreign case law.

[35] ... In the context of *section* 35(1), public international law would include non-binding as well as binding law. They may both be used under the section as tools of interpretation. International agreements and customary international law accordingly provide a framework within which Chapter Three can be evaluated and understood, and for that purpose, decisions of tribunals dealing with comparable instruments, such as the United Nations Committee on Human Rights, the Inter-American Commission on Human Rights, the Inter-American Court of Human Rights, the European Commission on Human Rights, and the European Court of Human Rights, and in appropriate cases, reports of specialized agencies such as the International Labour Organization may provide guidance as to the correct interpretation of particular provisions of Chapter Three.

[36] Capital punishment is not prohibited by public international law, and this is a factor that has to be taken into account in deciding whether it is cruel, inhuman or degrading punishment within the meaning of *section* 11(2). International human rights agreements differ, however, from our Constitution in that where the right to life is expressed in unqualified terms they either deal specifically with the death sentence, or authorize exceptions to be made to the right to life by law. ...

...

[40] ... From the beginning, the United States Constitution recognized capital punishment as lawful. The Fifth Amendment (adopted in 1791) refers in specific terms to capital punishment and impliedly recognizes its validity. The Fourteenth Amendment (adopted in 1868) obliges the states, not to 'deprive any person of life, liberty, or property, without due process of law' and it too impliedly recognizes the right of the states to make laws for such purposes. The argument that capital punishment is unconstitutional was based on the Eighth Amendment, which prohibits cruel and unusual punishment. ...

[41] Although challenges under state constitutions to the validity of the death sentence have been successful, the federal constitutionality of the death sentence as a legitimate form of punishment for murder was affirmed by the United States Supreme Court in *Gregg v. Georgia* [428 U.S. 153 (1976)].

...

[42] Statutes providing for mandatory death sentences, or too little discretion in sentencing, have been rejected by the [United States] Supreme Court because they do not allow for consideration of factors peculiar to the convicted person facing sentence, which may distinguish his or her case from other cases. For the same reason, statutes which allow too wide a discretion to judges or juries have also been struck down on the grounds that the exercise of such discretion leads to arbitrary results. In sum, therefore, if there is no discretion, too little discretion, or an unbounded discretion, the provision authorizing the death sentence has been

struck down as being contrary to the Eighth Amendment; where the discretion has been 'suitably directed and limited so as to minimize the risk of wholly arbitrary and capricious action', the challenge to the statute has failed.

[43] Basing his argument on the reasons which found favour with the majority of the United States Supreme Court in *Furman v. Georgia*, [408 U.S. 238 (1972), a decision that struck down the death sentence as there applied and imposed], Mr Trengove contended on behalf of the accused that the imprecise language of section 277, and the unbounded discretion vested by it in the Courts, make its provisions unconstitutional.

[44] Section 277 of the Criminal Procedure Act provides:

(1) The sentence of death may be passed by a superior court only and only in the case of a conviction for—

(a) murder;
(b) treason committed when the Republic is in a state of war;
(c) robbery or attempted robbery, if the court finds aggravating circumstances to have been present;
(d) kidnapping;
(e) child-stealing;
(f) rape.

(2) The sentence of death shall be imposed—

(a) after the presiding judge conjointly with the assessors (if any) . . . has made a finding on the presence or absence of any mitigating or aggravating factors;

and

(b) if the presiding judge or court, as the case may be, with due regard to that finding, is satisfied that the sentence of death is the proper sentence.

. . .

[45] Under our court system questions of guilt and innocence, and the proper sentence to be imposed on those found guilty of crimes, are not decided by juries. In capital cases, where it is likely that the death sentence may be imposed, judges sit with two assessors who have an equal vote with the judge on the issue of guilt and on any mitigating or aggravating factors relevant to sentence; but sentencing is the prerogative of the judge alone. The Criminal Procedure Act allows a full right of appeal to persons sentenced to death, including a right to dispute the sentence without having to establish an irregularity or misdirection on the part of the trial judge. The Appellate Division is empowered to set the sentence aside if it would not have imposed such sentence itself, and it has laid down criteria for the exercise of this power by itself and other courts. . . .

[46] Mitigating and aggravating factors must be identified by the Court, bearing in mind that the onus is on the State to prove beyond reasonable doubt the existence of aggravating factors, and to negative beyond reasonable doubt the presence of any mitigating factors relied on by the accused. Due regard must be paid to the personal circumstances and subjective factors which might have influenced the accused person's conduct, and these factors must then be weighed up

with the main objects of punishment, which have been held to be: deterrence, prevention, reformation, and retribution. In this process '[e]very relevant consideration should receive the most scrupulous care and reasoned attention', and the death sentence should only be imposed in the most exceptional cases, where there is no reasonable prospect of reformation and the objects of punishment would not be properly achieved by any other sentence.

[47] There seems to me to be little difference between the guided discretion required for the death sentence in the United States, and the criteria laid down by the Appellate Division for the imposition of the death sentence. . . .

[48] The argument that the imposition of the death sentence under *section 277* is arbitrary and capricious does not, however, end there. It also focuses on what is alleged to be the arbitrariness inherent in the application of *section 277* in practice. Of the thousands of persons put on trial for murder, only a very small percentage are sentenced to death by a trial court, and of those, a large number escape the ultimate penalty on appeal. At every stage of the process there is an element of chance. The outcome may be dependent upon factors such as the way the case is investigated by the police, the way the case is presented by the prosecutor, how effectively the accused is defended, the personality and particular attitude to capital punishment of the trial judge and, if the matter goes on appeal, the particular judges who are selected to hear the case. Race and poverty are also alleged to be factors.

[49] Most accused facing a possible death sentence are unable to afford legal assistance, and are defended under the *pro deo* system. The defending counsel is more often than not young and inexperienced, frequently of a different race to his or her client, and if this is the case, usually has to consult through an interpreter. *Pro deo* counsel are paid only a nominal fee for the defence, and generally lack the financial resources and the infrastructural support to undertake the necessary investigations and research, to employ expert witnesses to give advice, including advice on matters relevant to sentence, to assemble witnesses, to bargain with the prosecution, and generally to conduct an effective defence. Accused persons who have the money to do so, are able to retain experienced attorneys and counsel, who are paid to undertake the necessary investigations and research, and as a result they are less likely to be sentenced to death than persons similarly placed who are unable to pay for such services.
. . .

[54] The differences that exist between rich and poor, between good and bad prosecutions, between good and bad defence, between severe and lenient judges, between judges who favour capital punishment and those who do not, and the subjective attitudes that might be brought into play by factors such as race and class, may in similar ways affect any case that comes before the courts, and is almost certainly present to some degree in all court systems. . . . Imperfection inherent in criminal trials means that error cannot be excluded; it also means that persons similarly placed may not necessarily receive similar punishment. This needs to be acknowledged. What also needs to be acknowledged is that the possibility of error will be present in any system of justice and that there cannot be perfect equality as between accused persons in the conduct and outcome of criminal trials. We have to accept these differences in the ordinary criminal cases that

come before the courts, even to the extent that some may go to gaol when others similarly placed may be acquitted or receive non-custodial sentences. But death is different, and the question is, whether this is acceptable when the difference is between life and death. Unjust imprisonment is a great wrong, but if it is discovered, the prisoner can be released and compensated; but the killing of an innocent person is irremediable.

. . .

[56] ... The acceptance by a majority of the United States Supreme Court of the proposition that capital punishment is not per se unconstitutional, but that in certain circumstances it may be arbitrary, and thus unconstitutional, has led to endless litigation. Considerable expense and interminable delays result from the exceptionally-high standard of procedural fairness set by the United States courts in attempting to avoid arbitrary decisions. The difficulties that have been experienced in following this path . . . persuade me that we should not follow this route.

The right to dignity

[57] Although the United States Constitution does not contain a specific guarantee of human dignity, it has been accepted by the United States Supreme Court that the concept of human dignity is at the core of the prohibition of 'cruel and unusual punishment' by the Eighth and Fourteenth Amendments. For Brennan J this was decisive of the question in *Gregg v. Georgia.*

> The fatal constitutional infirmity in the punishment of death is that it treats 'members of the human race as nonhumans, as objects to be toyed with and discarded. [It is] thus inconsistent with the fundamental premise of the Clause that even the vilest criminal remains a human being possessed of common human dignity'.

[58] Under our constitutional order the right to human dignity is specifically guaranteed. It can only be limited by legislation which passes the stringent test of being 'necessary'. . . .

[59] In Germany, the Federal Constitutional Court has stressed this aspect of punishment.

> Respect for human dignity especially requires the prohibition of cruel, inhuman, and degrading punishments. [The state] cannot turn the offender into an object of crime prevention to the detriment of his constitutionally protected right to social worth and respect.

[60] That capital punishment constitutes a serious impairment of human dignity has also been recognized by judgments of the Canadian Supreme Court. *Kindler v Canada* [(1992) 6 CRR (2d) SC 4] was concerned with the extradition from Canada to the United States of two fugitives, Kindler, who had been convicted of murder and sentenced to death in the United States, and Ng who was facing a murder charge there and a possible death sentence. Three of the seven judges who heard the cases expressed the opinion that the death penalty was cruel and unusual:

It is the supreme indignity to the individual, the ultimate corporal punishment, the final and complete lobotomy and the absolute and irrevocable castration. [It is] the ultimate desecration of human dignity . . .

[61] Three other judges were of the opinion that:

[t]here is strong ground for believing, having regard to the limited extent to which the death penalty advances any valid penological objectives and the serious invasion of human dignity it engenders, that the death penalty cannot, except in exceptional circumstances, be justified in this country.

In the result, however, the majority of the Court held that the validity of the order for extradition did not depend upon the constitutionality of the death penalty in Canada, or the guarantee in its Charter of Rights against cruel and unusual punishment. The Charter was concerned with legislative and executive acts carried out in Canada, and an order for extradition neither imposed nor authorized any punishment within the borders of Canada.

. . .

The International Covenant on Civil and Political Right

[63] *Ng* [another case, *Ng v. Canada*] and *Kindler* took their cases to the Human Rights Committee of the United Nations, contending that Canada had breached its obligations under the International Covenant on Civil and Political Rights. Once again, there was a division of opinion within the tribunal. In Ng's case [*Ng v. Canada*, Communication No. 469/1991, 5 Nov. 1993] it was said:

The Committee is aware that, by definition, every execution of a sentence of death may be considered to constitute cruel and inhuman treatment within the meaning of article 7 of the covenant.

[64] There was no dissent from that statement. But the International Covenant contains provisions permitting, with some qualifications, the imposition of capital punishment for the most serious crimes. [See Article 6 of the International Covenant, set forth at p. 1383 infra.] In view of these provisions, the majority of the Committee were of the opinion that the extradition of fugitives to a country which enforces the death sentence in accordance with the requirements of the International Covenant, should not be regarded as a breach of the obligations of the extraditing country. In *Ng's* case, the method of execution which he faced if extradited was asphyxiation in a gas chamber. This was found by a majority of the Committee to involve unnecessary physical and mental suffering and, notwithstanding the sanction given to capital punishment, to be cruel punishment within the meaning of article 7 of the International Covenant. In Kindler's case, . . . it was held that the method of execution which was by lethal injection was not a cruel method of execution, and that the extradition did not in the circumstances constitute a breach of Canada's obligations under the International Covenant. [*Kindler v. Canada*, Communication No. 470/1991, 30 July 1993].

. . .

[66] It should be mentioned here that although *articles* 6(2) to (5) of the International Covenant specifically allow the imposition of the death sentence under strict controls 'for the most serious crimes' by those countries which have not abolished it, it provides in *article* 6(6) that '[n]othing in this article shall be invoked to delay or to prevent the abolition of capital punishment by any State Party to the present Covenant'. The fact that the International Covenant sanctions capital punishment must be seen in this context. It tolerates but does not provide justification for the death penalty.

[The opinion then considered the decision by the European Court of Human Rights in *Soering v. United Kingdom* (1989) 11 EHRR 439, involving the question whether the UK would violate the provisions on inhuman and degrading treatment or punishment in Article 3 of the Convention, by extraditing a fugitive to the United States to face murder charges that were subject to capital punishment. In the circumstances, including the experience of 'death row' in the US prisons and possible extradition of the fugitive by the UK for trial in another country that had abolished the death sentence, the European Court concluded that extradition to the United States would violate Article 3.

The opinion next examined a 1980 decision of the Indian Supreme Court holding that capital punishment did not violate the Indian Constitution. It distinguished the Indian decision partly by emphasizing the different wording of relevant provisions in the Constitutions of the two countries].

The right to life

[80] The unqualified right to life vested in every person by *section 9* of our Constitution is another factor crucially relevant to the question whether the death sentence is cruel, inhuman or degrading punishment within the meaning of *section 11(2)* of our Constitution. In this respect our Constitution differs materially from the Constitutions of the United States and India. It also differs materially from the European Convention and the International Covenant. Yet in the cases decided under these constitutions and treaties there were judges who dissented and held that notwithstanding the specific language of the constitution or instrument concerned, capital punishment should not be permitted.

[81] In some instances the dissent focused on the right to life. In *Soering's* case before the European Court of Human Rights, Judge de Meyer, in a concurring opinion, said that capital punishment is 'not consistent with the present state of European civilisation' and for that reason alone, extradition to the United States would violate the fugitive's right to life.

[82] In a dissent in the United Nations Human Rights Committee in *Kindler's* case, Committee member B. Wennergren also stressed the importance of the right to life.

> The value of life is immeasurable for any human being, and the right to life enshrined in article 6 of the Covenant is the supreme human right. It is an obligation of States [P]arties to the Covenant to protect the lives of all human beings on their territory and under their jurisdiction . . .

[83] An individual's right to life has been described as '[t]he most fundamental of all human rights', and was dealt with in that way in the judgments of the Hungarian Constitutional Court declaring capital punishment to be unconstitutional. The challenge to the death sentence in Hungary was based on section 54 of its Constitution which provides:

> (1) In the Republic of Hungary everyone has the inherent right to life and to human dignity, and no one shall be arbitrarily deprived of these rights.

> (2) No one shall be subjected to torture or to cruel or inhuman or degrading punishment.

[84] *Section 8*, the [Hungarian] counterpart of *section 33* of our Constitution, provides that laws

> shall not impose any limitations on the essential content of fundamental rights. According to the finding of the Court, capital punishment imposed a limitation on the essential content of the fundamental rights to life and human dignity, eliminating them irretrievably. As such it was unconstitutional. . . .

. . .

Public opinion

[87] . . . It was disputed whether public opinion, properly informed of the different considerations, would in fact favour the death penalty. I am, however, prepared to assume that it does and that the majority of South Africans agree that the death sentence should be imposed in extreme cases of murder. The question before us, however, is not what the majority of South Africans believe a proper sentence for murder should be. It is whether the Constitution allows the sentence.

[88] Public opinion may have some relevance to the enquiry, but in itself, it is no substitute for the duty vested in the Courts to interpret the Constitution and to uphold its provisions without fear or favour. If public opinion were to be decisive there would be no need for constitutional adjudication. The protection of rights could then be left to Parliament, which has a mandate from the public, and is answerable to the public for the way its mandate is exercised, but this would be a return to parliamentary sovereignty, and a retreat from the new legal order established by the 1993 Constitution. By the same token the issue of the constitutionality of capital punishment cannot be referred to a referendum, in which a majority view would prevail over the wishes of any minority. The very reason for establishing the new legal order, and for vesting the power of judicial review of all legislation in the courts, was to protect the rights of minorities and others who cannot protect their rights adequately through the democratic process. Those who are entitled to claim this protection include the social outcasts and marginalized people of our society. It is only if there is a willingness to protect the worst and the weakest amongst us, that all of us can be secure that our own rights will be protected.

. . .

Cruel, inhuman and degrading punishment

[90] The United Nations Committee on Human Rights has held that the death sentence by definition is cruel and degrading punishment. So has the Hungarian Constitutional Court, and three judges of the Canadian Supreme Court. The death sentence has also been held to be cruel or unusual punishment and thus unconstitutional under the state constitutions of Massachusetts and California.
. . .

[94] Proportionality is an ingredient to be taken into account in deciding whether a penalty is cruel, inhuman or degrading. No Court would today uphold the constitutionality of a statute that makes the death sentence a competent sentence for the cutting down of trees or the killing of deer, which were capital offences in England in the 18th Century. But murder is not to be equated with such 'offences'. The wilful taking of an innocent life calls for a severe penalty, and there are many countries which still retain the death penalty as a sentencing option for such cases. Disparity between the crime and the penalty is not the only ingredient of proportionality; factors such as the enormity and irredeemable character of the death sentence in circumstances where neither error nor arbitrariness can be excluded, the expense and difficulty of addressing the disparities which exist in practice between accused persons facing similar charges, and which are due to factors such as race, poverty, and ignorance, and the other subjective factors which have been mentioned, are also factors that can and should be taken into account in dealing with this issue. It may possibly be that none alone would be sufficient under our Constitution to justify a finding that the death sentence is cruel, inhuman or degrading. But these factors are not to be evaluated in isolation. They must be taken together, and in order to decide whether the threshold set by *section* 11(2) has been crossed they must be evaluated with other relevant factors, including the two fundamental rights on which the accused rely, the right to dignity and the right to life.

[95] The carrying out of the death sentence destroys life, which is protected without reservation under *section* 9 of our Constitution, it annihilates human dignity which is protected under *section* 10, elements of arbitrariness are present in its enforcement and it is irremediable. Taking these factors into account, as well as the assumption that I have made in regard to public opinion in South Africa, and giving the words of *section* 11(2) the broader meaning to which they are entitled at this stage of the enquiry, rather than a narrow meaning, I am satisfied that in the context of our Constitution the death penalty is indeed a cruel, inhuman and degrading punishment.
. . .

Section 33 and limitation of rights

[98] *Section* 33(1) of the Constitution provides, in part, that:

> The rights entrenched in this Chapter may be limited by law of general application, provided that such limitation—
>
>   (a) shall be permissible only to the extent that it is—
>   (i) reasonable; and

> (ii) justifiable in an open and democratic society based on freedom and
>   equality; and
>
> (b) shall not negate the essential content of the right in question.

[99] *Section* 33(1)(b) goes on to provide that the limitation of certain rights, including the rights referred to in *section* 10 and *section* 11 'shall, in addition to being reasonable as required in paragraph (a)(I), also be necessary'.

[100] Our Constitution deals with the limitation of rights through a general limitations clause. As was pointed out by Kentridge AJ in *Zuma's* case, this calls for a 'two-stage' approach, in which a broad rather than a narrow interpretation is given to the fundamental rights enshrined in Chapter Three, and limitations have to be justified through the application of section 33. In this it differs from the Constitution of the United States, which does not contain a limitation clause, as a result of which courts in that country have been obliged to find limits to constitutional rights through a narrow interpretation of the rights themselves. Although the 'two-stage' approach may often produce the same result as the 'one-stage' approach, this will not always be the case.

[101] The practical consequences of this difference in approach are evident in the present case. In *Gregg v. Georgia*, the conclusion reached in the judgment of the plurality was summed up as follows:

> In sum, we cannot say that the judgment of the Georgia legislature that capital punishment may be necessary in some cases is clearly wrong. Considerations of federalism, as well as respect for the ability of a legislature to evaluate, in terms of its particular state, the moral consensus concerning the death penalty and its social utility as a sanction, require us to conclude in the absence of more convincing evidence, that the infliction of death as a punishment for murder is not without justification, and is thus not unconstitutionally severe.

[102] Under our Constitution, the position is different. It is not whether the decision of the State has been shown to be clearly wrong; it is whether the decision of the State is justifiable according to the criteria prescribed by section 33. It is not whether the infliction of death as a punishment for murder 'is not without justification', it is whether the infliction of death as a punishment for murder has been shown to be both reasonable and necessary, and to be consistent with the other requirements of *section* 33. . . .
. . .

[106] Although there is a rational connection between capital punishment and the purpose for which it is prescribed, the elements of arbitrariness, unfairness and irrationality in the imposition of the penalty, are factors that would have to be taken into account in the application of the first component of this test. As far as the second component is concerned, the fact that a severe punishment in the form of life imprisonment is available as an alternative sentence, would be relevant to the question whether the death sentence impairs the right as little as possible.
. . .

[108] The German Constitution does not contain a general limitations clause but permits certain basic rights to be limited by law. According to Professor

Grimm, the Federal Constitutional Court allows such limitation 'only in order to make conflicting rights compatible or to protect the rights of other persons or important community interests . . . any restriction of human rights not only needs constitutionally valid reasons but also has to be proportional to the rank and importance of the right at stake'.

[109] The European Convention also has no general limitations clause, but makes certain rights subject to limitation according to specified criteria. The proportionality test of the European Court of Human Rights calls for a balancing of ends and means. The end must be a 'pressing social need' and the means used must be proportionate to the attainment of such an end. The limitation of certain rights is conditioned upon the limitation being 'necessary in a democratic society' for purposes defined in the relevant provisions of the Convention. . . .

. . .

[112] The Attorney General contended that the imposition of the death penalty for murder in the most serious cases could be justified according to the prescribed criteria. The argument went as follows. The death sentence meets the sentencing requirements for extreme cases of murder more effectively than any other sentence can do. It has a greater deterrent effect than life imprisonment; it ensures that the worst murderers will not endanger the lives of prisoners and warders who would be at risk if the 'worst of the murderers' were to be imprisoned and not executed; and it also meets the need for retribution which is demanded by society as a response to the high level of crime. In the circumstances presently prevailing in the country, it is therefore a necessary component of the criminal justice system. . . .

. . .

Deterrence

[116] The Attorney General attached considerable weight to the need for a deterrent to violent crime. He argued that the countries which had abolished the death penalty were on the whole developed and peaceful countries in which other penalties might be sufficient deterrents. We had not reached that stage of development, he said. If in years to come we did so, we could do away with the death penalty. Parliament could decide when that time has come. At present, however, so the argument went, the death sentence is an indispensable weapon if we are serious about combatting violent crime.

[117] The need for a strong deterrent to violent crime is an end the validity of which is not open to question. The state is clearly entitled, indeed obliged, to take action to protect human life against violation by others. In all societies there are laws which regulate the behaviour of people and which authorise the imposition of civil or criminal sanctions on those who act unlawfully. This is necessary for the preservation and protection of society. Without law, society cannot exist. Without law, individuals in society have no rights. The level of violent crime in our country has reached alarming proportions. It poses a threat to the transition to democracy, and the creation of development opportunities for all, which are primary goals of the Constitution. . . .

. . .

[119] The cause of the high incidence of violent crime cannot simply be

attributed to the failure to carry out the death sentences imposed by the courts. The upsurge in violent crime came at a time of great social change associated with political turmoil and conflict, particularly during the period 1990 to 1994. It is facile to attribute the increase in violent crime during this period to the moratorium on executions. It was a progression that started before the moratorium was announced. There are many factors that have to be taken into account in looking for the cause of this phenomenon. . . .

[120] Homelessness, unemployment, poverty and the frustration consequent upon such conditions are other causes of the crime wave. . . .

[121] We would be deluding ourselves if we were to believe that the execution of the few persons sentenced to death during this period, and of a comparatively few other people each year from now onwards will provide the solution to the unacceptably high rate of crime. There will always be unstable, desperate, and pathological people for whom the risk of arrest and imprisonment provides no deterrent, but there is nothing to show that a decision to carry out the death sentence would have any impact on the behaviour of such people, or that there will be more of them if imprisonment is the only sanction. . . .

[122] The greatest deterrent to crime is the likelihood that offenders will be apprehended, convicted and punished. It is that which is presently lacking in our criminal justice system; and it is at this level and through addressing the causes of crime that the State must seek to combat lawlessness.
. . .

[126] The death sentence has been reserved for the most extreme cases, and the overwhelming majority of convicted murderers are not and, since extenuating circumstances became a relevant factor sixty years ago, have not been sentenced to death in South Africa. I referred earlier to the figures provided by the Attorney General which show that between the amendment of the Criminal Procedure Act in 1990, and January 1995, which is the date of his written argument in the present case, 243 death sentences were imposed, of which 143 were confirmed by the Appellate Division. Yet, according to statistics placed before us by the Commissioner of Police and the Attorney General, there were on average approximately 20,000 murders committed, and 9,000 murder cases brought to trial, each year during this period. Would the carrying out of the death sentence on these 143 persons have deterred the other murderers or saved any lives?

[127] It was accepted by the Attorney General that this is a much disputed issue in the literature on the death sentence. He contended that it is common sense that the most feared penalty will provide the greatest deterrent, but accepted that there is no proof that the death sentence is in fact a greater deterrent than life imprisonment for a long period. . . .
. . .

Retribution

[129] Retribution is one of the objects of punishment, but it carries less weight than deterrence. The righteous anger of family and friends of the murder victim, reinforced by the public abhorrence of vile crimes, is easily translated into a call for vengeance. But capital punishment is not the only way that society has of express-

ing its moral outrage at the crime that has been committed. We have long out-grown the literal application of the biblical injunction of 'an eye for an eye, and a tooth for a tooth'. Punishment must to some extent be commensurate with the offence, but there is no requirement that it be equivalent or identical to it. The state does not put out the eyes of a person who has blinded another in a vicious assault, nor does it punish a rapist, by castrating him and submitting him to the utmost humiliation in gaol. The state does not need to engage in the cold and calculated killing of murderers in order to express moral outrage at their conduct. A very long prison sentence is also a way of expressing outrage and visiting retri-bution upon the criminal.
. . .

[135] In the balancing process, deterrence, prevention and retribution must be weighed against the alternative punishments available to the state, and the factors which taken together make capital punishment cruel, inhuman and degrading: the destruction of life, the annihilation of dignity, the elements of arbitrariness, inequality and the possibility of error in the enforcement of the penalty.
. . .

Conclusion

[144] The rights to life and dignity are the most important of all human rights, and the source of all other personal rights in Chapter Three. By committing ourselves to a society founded on the recognition of human rights we are required to value these two rights above all others. And this must be demonstrated by the State in everything that it does, including the way it punishes criminals. This is not achieved by objectifying murderers and putting them to death to serve as an example to others in the expectation that they might possibly be deterred thereby.
. . .

[146] . . .Taking [all the described] factors into account, as well as the elements of arbitrariness and the possibility of error in enforcing the death penalty, the clear and convincing case that is required to justify the death sentence as a penalty for murder, has not been made out. The requirements of section 33(1) have accord-ingly not been satisfied, and it follows that the provisions of section 277(1)(a) of the Criminal Procedure Act, 1977 must be held to be inconsistent with section 11(2) of the Constitution. In the circumstances, it is not necessary for me to consider whether the section would also be inconsistent with sections 8, 9 or 10 of the Constitution if they had been dealt with separately and not treated together as giving meaning to section 11(2).
. . .

[150] The proper sentence to be imposed on the accused is a matter for the Appellate Division and not for us to decide. . . .
. . .

QUESTIONS

1. Article 6 of the International Covenant on Civil and Political Rights has been much cited and drawn on by both proponents and opponents of capital punishment. In what ways could an abolitionist employ Article 6 to strengthen her position?

2. As an opponent, would you find it advantageous in argument before a court to rely primarily on 'the inherent right to life', as in Article 6(1) of the International Covenant, or on 'cruel, inhuman or degrading treatment or punishment' in Article 7 (compare 'cruel and unusual punishments' in the Eighth Amendment to the U.S. Constitution)? What disadvantages would each have?

3. Would you describe Justice Chaskalson's opinion as ultimately relying on traditional arguments for and against capital punishment that could have been debated by courts anywhere, or relying at least equally on contextual factors that were, if not unique, at least highly specific to South African history and culture? What were the links between these two strands in the opinion?

4. Consider the following comments (reported in Schabas, p. 33, *supra*, at 244) made during a debate in the Parliamentary Assembly of the Council of Europe on the then proposed protocol to the European Convention on Human Rights that would abolish the death penalty. Would you agree or disagree with the speaker, and if the latter, how would you respond to him?

> A Turkish member of the Assembly, Aksoy, said that he supported the report and the recommendation 'in principle', but that it did not take sufficient account of the particular situation of certain member States. He suggested that because of differing economic, social and political structures it was not possible to apply identical sentences in all countries. Were he Swedish, Swiss, Norwegian, Austrian or German, he would most certainly support total abolition of the death penalty, said Aksoy. Yet it would be a grave error to recommend abolition in countries where political assassination and terrorism are organized on a systematic scale.

5. With reference to the preceding opinions on death row and capital punishment, consider (a) the comparative, or horizontal, dimension to the human rights movement—that is, the spread among states of abolition of capital punishment and the cross-referencing by states to each other's legislation or constitutional decisions on this issue. Consider also (b) the vertical dimension—that is, the relation between treaties and decisions or resolutions of international organs on this issue and what states decide to do. Are this (a) horizontal movement among states and (b) vertical movement to create international law and institutions that then influence states, discrete or interrelated phenomena? If the latter, in what ways are the horizontal and vertical movements related to each other? Do they appear to constitute equal parts of an international 'human rights movement'?

6. Identify the range of actors of all descriptions in the worldwide debates over death row and the death penalty, and the ways in which they appear to interact with others, whether cooperatively or in a hostile way.

ADDITIONAL READING

On the death penalty see: Amnesty International, *When the State Kills . . .*, *The Death Penalty: A Human Rights Issue* (1989); R. Hood, *The Death Penalty: A World-Wide Perspective* (2nd edn 1998); N. Rodley, *The Treatment of Prisoners under International Law* (2nd edn 1999); W. Schabas, *The Death Penalty as Cruel Treatment and Torture: Capital Punishment Challenged in the World's Courts* (1996); and W. Schabas, *The Abolition of the Death Penalty in International Law* (2nd edn 1997).

2

Up to Nuremberg: Background to the Human Rights Movement

In its discussion of the death row phenomenon and the legality of the death penalty, Chapter 1(B) concentrated on the law—often the constitutional law—of different states. The courts of these states referred with some frequency to international organizations and to treaties, but they devoted most of their analysis to their own and to foreign legal systems. Except for the opinion of an international body (the Human Rights Committee) on a death row case, that chapter did not place international law at centre stage.

Chapters 2–4, on the other hand, concentrate on the international-law aspects of the human rights movement. Why has this path been followed? After all, it is possible to study human rights issues not at the international level but in the detailed contexts of different states' histories, socio-economic and political structures, legal systems, religions, cultures and so on. With respect to its legal dimension, a human rights course that was so organized would stress the internal law of states as well as foreign and comparative law. It would engage in a contextual and comparative analysis of bodies of internal law. It could devote its full attention to states like China, Saudi Arabia, Italy, the United States, or Guatemala. It could stress the recent trend in many states toward (at least as a formal matter) liberal constitutionalism. For such a study of human rights, international law could play a peripheral role, relevant only when it exerted some clear influence on the national scene or had a place in the basic logic of a judicial decision.

The attractiveness of such an approach becomes more apparent when one contrasts with international human rights many other international subjects where international law occupies, indeed *must* occupy, a central position. Imagine, for example, that this coursebook's interest were not human rights but the humanitarian law of war (rules for the conduct of war), or the regulation of fisheries, or immunities of diplomats from arrest, or the regulation of trade barriers like tariffs. Each of those fields is inherently, intrinsically, *international* in character. Each involves relations *between* states or between citizens of one state and other states. We could not profitably examine any one of them without examining international custom and treaties, international institutions and processes.

In a basic respect, violations of human rights are different. Not only are they generally rooted within states rather than in interstate engagements, but they need not on their surface involve any international consequences whatsoever. (Of course systemic and severe human rights violations that start as 'internal' matters—for example, recurrent violence against an ethnic minority—could well have international consequences, perhaps by leading to refugee flows abroad or by angering other states whose populations are related by ethnicity to the oppressed minority.) In typical instances of violations, the police of state X torture defendants to extract confessions; the attorney general of X shuts the opposition press as elections approach; prisoners are raped by their guards; courts decide cases according to executive command; women or a minority group are barred from education or certain work. Each of these events could profitably be studied entirely within a state's (or region's, culture's) internal framework, just as law students in many countries traditionally concentrate on their country's internal legal-political system, including that system's provision for civil liberties and human rights.

Nonetheless, since the Second World War it would be inadequate or even misleading to develop a framework for the study of human rights in many countries without including as a major ingredient the international legal and political aspects of the field: laws, processes and institutions. In today's world, human rights is characteristically imagined as a movement involving international law and institutions, as well as a movement involving the spread of liberal constitutions among states. Internal developments in many states have been much influenced by international law and institutions, as well as by pressures from other states trying to enforce international law.

Internal or comparative approaches to human rights law and the truly international aspects of human rights are now rarely 'split'. Rather they are complexly intertwined and reciprocally influential with respect to the growth of human rights norms, the causes and effects of their violations, the reactions and sanctions of intergovernmental bodies or other states, the transformations of internal orders, and so on.

From another perspective as well it would be impossible to grasp the character of the human rights movement without a basic knowledge about international law and its contributions to it. The movement's aspirations to universal validity are necessarily rooted in that body of law. Many of the distinctive organizations intended to help to realize those aspirations are creations of international law.

For such reasons, this coursebook frequently examines but does not concentrate on the internal law and politics of one or a few states. It relates throughout this 'horizontal' strand of the human rights movement, as constitutionalism spreads among states, to the 'vertical' strand of the new international law that is meant to bind states and that is implemented by the new international institutions. Both the horizontal and vertical dimensions of the human rights movement are vital. But the truly novel developments of the last half century have involved primarily this second dimension. This chapter begins the book's inquiry into it.

Chapter 2 has a dual function. It sketches the doctrines and principles in an older international law that served as background to and precedents for the human rights movement that took root and developed after the Second World War. Moreover, it uses the cases expressing those doctrines and principles to examine basic sources of and understandings about international law, particularly custom and treaty. The two tasks are intertwined. The opinions, while developing substantive knowledge about the international law preceding the Second World War, address questions such as: By what means or methods have the international rules and standards of the human rights movement been developed? By what processes are international legal rules made, elaborated, applied, and changed?

To aid the reader in thinking about these questions, scholars' articles accompany the different decisions. The excerpts below are compact and abstract, and sparse in their illustrations. But the opinions of tribunals to which they are linked offer those illustrations.

Several of the opinions and scholarly writings in the chapter draw on Article 38 of the Statute of the International Court of Justice, the judicial organ of the United Nations that was created by the UN Charter of 1945. That article has long served as a traditional point of departure for examining questions about the sources of international law.[1] It repeats in relevant respects the provisions of the 1921 Statute of its predecessor court, the Permanent Court of International Justice that was linked to the League of Nations and effectively died during the Second World War. It reads:

> 1. The Court, whose function is to decide in accordance with international law such disputes as are submitted to it, shall apply:
>
>   a. international conventions, whether general or particular, establishing rules expressly recognized by the contesting states;
>   b. international custom, as evidence of a general practice accepted as law;
>   c. the general principles of law recognized by civilized nations;
>   d. subject to the provisions of Article 59 [stating that decisions of the Court have no binding force except between the parties to the case], judicial decisions and the teachings of the most highly qualified publicists of the various nations, as subsidiary means for the determination of rules of law.

Although Article 38 instructs this particular Court about the method of applying international law to resolve disputes, its influence has extended to other international tribunals, to national courts, and indeed generally to argument based on international law that is made in settings other than courts.

The Article takes a positivist perspective. It defines the task of the Court in terms of its *application* of an identifiable body of international law. Its skeletal list, one that omits important contemporary processes of international law-making that are examined in Chapter 3, expresses a formal conception of the judicial function that is radically different from that of, say, a legal realist.

---

[1] The Court can only hear cases to which states are parties: Article 34 of the Statute. A state's consent is necessary for the Court to exercise jurisdiction over it. That consent generally refers to the Court's adjudicating all 'legal disputes' concerning the 'interpretation of a treaty', a 'question of international law', the exist ence of a fact which, if established 'would constitute a breach of an international obligation', and the reparation to be made for breach of an international obligation: Article 36. Statute of the International Court of Justice, T.S. No. 993 (at p, 25) (U.S.).

NOTE

The chapter has the following organization: Section A examines customary law, and illustrates its theme through a national court decision in a field now known as the humanitarian laws of war. Section B examines aspects of general principles of law and natural law, in the context of an arbitral decision on the law of state responsibility for injury to aliens. Section C examines treaty law by drawing on a decision of the Permanent Court of International Justice on the minorities regime in Europe between the two World Wars. Section D looks at the judgment at Nuremberg after the Second World War, at the very threshold of the human rights movement. Section E offers some scholar's views about the background to the human rights movement and the character of international law.

A. LAWS OF WAR AND CUSTOMARY INTERNATIONAL LAW

NOTE

The following decision in *The Paquete Habana* deals with an earlier period in the development of the laws of war, here naval warfare, and with a theme that became central in the later treaty development of this field—the protection of noncombatant civilians and their property (here, civilian fishing vessels) against the ravages of war. Within the framework of the laws of war, this case involves *jus in bello*, the ways in which war ought to be waged, rather than the related but distinct *jus ad bellum*, the determination of those conditions (if any) in which a *just* or justified war can be waged, in which war is legal.

In its analysis of the question before it, the US Supreme Court here illustrates a classical understanding of customary international law.

THE PAQUETE HABANA
Supreme Court of the United States, 1900
175 U.S. 677, 20 S.Ct. 290

MR. JUSTICE GRAY DELIVERED THE OPINION OF THE COURT

These are two appeals from decrees of the district court of the United States for the southern district of Florida condemning two fishing vessels and their cargoes as prize of war.

Each vessel was a fishing smack, running in and out of Havana, and regularly engaged in fishing on the coast of Cuba; sailed under the Spanish flag; was owned by a Spanish subject of Cuban birth, living in the city of Havana; was commanded by a subject of Spain also residing in Havana; and her master and crew had no interest in the vessel, but were entitled to shares, amounting in all to two thirds, of her catch, the other third belonging to her owner. Her cargo consisted of fresh fish, caught by her crew from the sea, put on board as they were caught, and kept and sold alive. Until stopped by the blockading squadron she had no knowledge of the existence of the war or of any blockade. She had no arms or ammunition on board, and made no attempt to run the blockade after she knew of its existence, nor any resistance at the time of the capture.

. . .

Both the fishing vessels were brought by their captors into Key West. A libel for the condemnation of each vessel and her cargo as prize of war was there filed on April 27, 1898; a claim was interposed by her master on behalf of himself and the other members of the crew, and of her owner; evidence was taken, showing the facts above stated; and on May 30, 1898, a final decree of condemnation and sale was entered, 'the court not being satisfied that as a matter of law, without any ordinance, treaty, or proclamation, fishing vessels of this class are exempt from seizure'.

Each vessel was thereupon sold by auction; the Paquete Habana for the sum of $490; and the Lola for the sum of $800. There was no other evidence in the record of the value of either vessel or of her cargo. . . .

. . .

We are then brought to the consideration of the question whether, upon the facts appearing in these records, the fishing smacks were subject to capture by the armed vessels of the United States during the recent war with Spain.

By an ancient usage among civilized nations, beginning centuries ago, and gradually ripening into a rule of international law, coast fishing vessels, pursuing their vocation of catching and bringing in fresh fish, have been recognized as exempt, with their cargoes and crews, from capture as prize of war.

This doctrine, however, has been earnestly contested at the bar; and no complete collection of the instances illustrating it is to be found, so far as we are aware, in a single published work, although many are referred to and discussed by the writers on international law, notable in 2 Ortolan, *Règles Internationales et Diplomatie de la Mer* (4th ed.) lib. 3, chap. 2, pp. 51–56; in 4 Calvo, *Droit International* (5th ed.) 2367–2373; in De Boeck, *Propriété Privé Ennemie sous Pavillon Ennemie*, §§191–196; and in Hall, *International Law* (4th ed.) 148. It is therefore worth the while to trace the history of the rule, from the earliest accessible sources, through the increasing recognition of it with occasional setbacks, to what we may now justly consider as its final establishment in our own country and generally throughout the civilized world.

The earliest acts of any government on the subject, mentioned in the books, either emanated from, or were approved by, a King of England.

In 1403 and 1406 Henry IV. issued orders to his admirals and other officers, entitled 'Concerning Safety for Fishermen—*De Securitate pro Piscatoribus*'. By an order of October 26, 1403, reciting that it was made pursuant to a treaty between himself and the King of France; and for the greater safety of the fishermen of either country, and so that they could be, and carry on their industry, the more safely on the sea, and deal with each other in peace; and that the French King had consented that English fishermen should be treated likewise,—it was ordained that French fishermen might, during the then pending season for the herring fishery, safely fish for herrings and all other fish, from the harbor of Gravelines and the island of Thanet to the mouth of the Seine and the harbor of Hautoune. ...

The same custom would seem to have prevailed in France until towards the end of the seventeenth century. For example, in 1675, Louis XIV. and the States General of Holland by mutual agreement granted to Dutch and French fishermen the liberty, undisturbed by their vessels of war, of fishing along the coasts of France, Holland, and England. ...

The doctrine which exempts coast fishermen, with their vessels and cargoes, from capture as prize of war, has been familiar to the United States from the time of the War of Independence.
...

In the treaty of 1785 between the United States and Prussia, article 23 ... provided that, if war should arise between the contracting parties, 'all women and children, scholars of every faculty, cultivators of the earth, artisans, manufacturers, and fishermen, unarmed and inhabiting unfortified towns, villages, or places, and in general all others whose occupations are for the common subsistence and benefit of mankind, shall be allowed to continue their respective employments, and shall not be molested in their persons, nor shall their houses or goods be burnt or otherwise destroyed, nor their fields wasted by the armed force of the enemy, into whose power, by the events of war, they may happen to fall; but if anything is necessary to be taken from them for the use of such armed force, the same shall be paid for at a reasonable price'. ...

Since the United States became a nation, the only serious interruptions, so far as we are informed, of the general recognition of the exemption of coast fishing vessels from hostile capture, arose out of the mutual suspicions and recriminations of England and France during the wars of the French Revolution.
...

On January 24, 1798, the English government by express order instructed the commanders of its ships to seize French and Dutch fishermen with their boats. ... After the promulgation of that order, Lord Stowell (then Sir William Scott) in the High Court of Admiralty of England condemned small Dutch fishing vessels as prize of war. In one case the capture was in April, 1798, and the decree was made November 13, 1798. *The Young Jacob and Johanna*, 1 C.Rob. 20. ...

On March 16, 1801, the Addington Ministry, having come into power in England, revoked the orders of its predecessors against the French fishermen; maintaining, however, that 'the freedom of fishing was nowise founded upon an agreement, but upon a simple concession', that 'this concession would be always subordinate to the convenience of the moment', and that 'it was never extended to the great fishery, or to commerce in oysters or in fish'. And the freedom of the coast fisheries was again allowed on both sides. ...

Lord Stowell's judgment in *The Young Jacob and Johanna*, 1 C.Rob. 20, above cited, was much relied on by the counsel for the United States, and deserves careful consideration.

The vessel there condemned is described in the report as 'a small Dutch fishing vessel taken April, 1798, on her return from the Dogger bank to Holland'; and Lord Stowell, in delivering judgment, said: 'In former wars it has not been usual to make captures of these small fishing vessels; but this rule was a rule of comity only, and not of legal decision; it has prevailed from views of mutual accommodation between neighbouring countries, and from tenderness to a poor and industrious order of people. In the present war there has, I presume, been sufficient reason for changing this mode of treatment; and as they are brought before me for my judgment they must be referred to the general principles of this court; they fall under the character and description of the last class of cases; that is, of ships constantly and exclusively employed in the enemy's trade'. And he added: 'it is a further satisfaction to me, in giving this judgment, to observe that the facts also bear strong marks of a false and fraudulent transaction'.

Both the capture and the condemnation were within a year after the order of the English government of January 24, 1798, instructing the commanders of its ships to seize French and Dutch fishing vessels, and before any revocation of that order. Lord Stowell's judgment shows that his decision was based upon the order of 1798, as well as upon strong evidence of fraud. Nothing more was adjudged in the case.

But some expressions in his opinion have been given so much weight by English writers that it may be well to examine them particularly. The opinion begins by admitting the known custom in former wars not to capture such vessels; adding, however, 'but this was a rule of comity only, and not of legal decision'. Assuming the phrase 'legal decision' to have been there used, in the sense in which courts are accustomed to use it, as equivalent to 'judicial decision', it is true that so far as appears, there had been no such decision on the point in England. The word 'comity' was apparently used by Lord Stowell as synonymous with courtesy or goodwill. But the period of a hundred years which has since elapsed is amply sufficient to have enabled what originally may have rested in custom or comity, courtesy or concession, to grow, by the general assent of civilized nations, into a settled rule of international law. . . .

The French prize tribunals, both before and after Lord Stowell's decision, took a wholly different view of the general question. . . .

The English government [by orders in council of 1806 and 1810] unqualifiedly prohibited the molestation of fishing vessels employed in catching and bringing to market fresh fish. . . .

Wheaton, in his Digest of the Law of Maritime Captures and Prizes, published in 1815, wrote: 'It has been usual in maritime wars to exempt from capture fishing boats and their cargoes, both from views of mutual accommodation between neighboring countries, and from tenderness to a poor and industrious order of people. This custom, so honorable to the humanity of civilized nations, has fallen into disuse; and it is remarkable that both France and England mutually reproach each other with that breach of good faith which has finally abolished it'. Wheaton, Captures, chap. 2, 18.

This statement clearly exhibits Wheaton's opinion that the custom had been a general one, as well as that it ought to remain so. His assumption that it had been abolished by the differences between France and England at the close of the last century was hardly justified by the state of things when he wrote, and has not since been borne out.

. . .

In the war with Mexico, in 1846, the United States recognized the exemption of coast fishing boats from capture. . . .

In the treaty of peace between the United States and Mexico, in 1848, were inserted the very words of the earlier treaties with Prussia, already quoted, forbidding the hostile molestation or seizure in time of war of the persons, occupations, houses, or goods of fishermen. 9 Stat. at L. 939, 940.

. . .

France in the Crimean war in 1854, and in her wars with Italy in 1859 and with Germany in 1870, by general orders, forbade her cruisers to trouble the coast fisheries, or to seize any vessel or boat engaged therein, unless naval or military operations should make it necessary.

. . .

Since the English orders in council of 1806 and 1810 . . . in favor of fishing vessels employed in catching and bringing to market fresh fish, no instance has been found in which the exemption from capture of private coast fishing vessels honestly pursuing their peaceful industry has been denied by England or by any other nation. And the Empire of Japan (the last state admitted into the rank of civilized nations), by an ordinance promulgated at the beginning of its war with China in August, 1894, established prize courts, and ordained that 'the following enemy's vessels are exempt from detention', including in the exemption 'boats engaged in coast fisheries', as well as 'ships engaged exclusively on a voyage of scientific discovery, philanthrophy, or religious mission'. Takahashi, International Law, 11, 178.

International law is part of our law, and must be ascertained and administered by the courts of justice of appropriate jurisdiction as often as questions of right depending upon it are duly presented for their determination. For this purpose, where there is no treaty and no controlling executive or legislative act or judicial decision, resort must be had to the customs and usages of civilized nations, and, as evidence of these, to the works of jurists and commentators who by years of labor, research, and experience have made themselves peculiarly well acquainted with the subjects of which they treat. Such works are resorted to by judicial tribunals, not for the speculations of their authors concerning what the law ought to be, but for trustworthy evidence of what the law really is. Hilton v. Guyot, 159 U.S. 113, 163, 164, 214, 215, 40 L.Ed. 95, 108, 125, 126, 16 Sup.Ct.Rep. 139.

. . .

Chancellor Kent says: 'In the absence of higher and more authoritative sanctions, the ordinances of foreign states, the opinions of eminent statesmen, and the writings of distinguished jurists, are regarded as of great consideration on questions not settled by conventional law. In cases where the principal jurists agree, the presumption will be very great in favor of the solidity of their maxims; and no civilized nation that does not arrogantly set all ordinary law and justice at defiance will venture to disregard the uniform sense of the established writers on international law'. 1 Kent, Com. 18.

It will be convenient, in the first place, to refer to some leading French treatises on international law, which deal with the question now before us, not as one of the law of France only, but as one determined by the general consent of civilized nations. . . . [Discussion of French treatises omitted.]
. . .

No international jurist of the present day has a wider or more deserved reputation than Calvo, who, though writing in French, is a citizen of the Argentine Republic, employed in its diplomatic service abroad. In the fifth edition of his great work on international law, published in 1896, he observes, in 2366, that the international authority of decisions in particular cases by the prize courts of France, of England, and of the United States is lessened by the fact that the principles on which they are based are largely derived from the internal legislation of each country; and yet the peculiar character of maritime wars, with other considerations, gives to prize jurisprudence a force and importance reaching beyond the limits of the country in which it has prevailed. He therefore proposes here to group together a number of particular cases proper to serve as precedents for the solution of grave questions of maritime law in regard to the capture of private property as prize of war. Immediately, in 2367, he goes on to say: 'Notwithstanding the hardships to which maritime wars subject private property, notwithstanding the extent of the recognized rights of belligerents, there are generally exempted, from seizure and capture, fishing vessels'. . . .

The modern German books on international law, cited by the counsel for the appellants, treat the custom by which the vessels and implements of coast fishermen are exempt from seizure and capture as well established by the practice of nations. Heffter, 137; 2 Kalterborn, 237, p. 480; Bluntschli, 667; Perels, 37, p. 217.
. . .

Two recent English text-writers cited at the bar (influenced by what Lord Stowell said a century since) hesitate to recognize that the exemption of coast fishing vessels from capture has now become a settled rule of international law. Yet they both admit that there is little real difference in the views, or in the practice, of England and of other maritime nations; and that no civilized nation at the present day would molest coast fishing vessels so long as they were peaceably pursuing their calling and there was no danger that they or their crews might be of military use to the enemy. . . .

But there are writers of various maritime countries, not yet cited, too important to be passed by without notice. . . .

[The opinion quotes from writing from the Netherlands, Spain, Austria, Portugal and Italy.]

This review of the precedents and authorities on the subject appears to us abundantly to demonstrate that at the present day, by the general consent of the civilized nations of the world, and independently of any express treaty or other public act, it is an established rule of international law, founded on considerations of humanity to a poor and industrious order of men, and of the mutual convenience of belligerent states, that coast fishing vessels, with their implements and supplies, cargoes and crews, unarmed and honestly pursuing their peaceful calling of catching and bringing in fresh fish, are exempt from capture as prize of war. . . .

. . .

This rule of international law is one which prize courts administering the law of nations are bound to take judicial notice of, and to give effect to, in the absence of any treaty or other public act of their own government in relation to the matter.

. . .

To this subject in more than one aspect are singularly applicable the words uttered by Mr. Justice Strong, speaking for this court: 'Undoubtedly no single nation can change the law of the sea. The law is of universal obligation and no statute of one or two nations can create obligations for the world. Like all the laws of nations, it rests upon the common consent of civilized communities. It is of force, not because it was prescribed by any superior power, but because it has been generally accepted as a rule of conduct. Whatever may have been its origin, whether in the usages of navigation, or in the ordinances of maritime states, or in both, it has become the law of the sea only by the concurrent sanction of those nations who may be said to constitute the commercial world. . . . [Of these facts] we may take judicial notice. Foreign municipal laws must indeed be proved as facts, but it is not so with the law of nations'. The Scotia, 14 Wall. 170, 187, 188, sub nom. Sears v. The Scotia, 20 L.Ed. 822, 825, 826.

The position taken by the United States during the recent war with Spain was quite in accord with the rule of international law, now generally recognized by civilized nations, in regard to coast fishing vessels.

On April 21, 1898, the Secretary of the Navy gave instructions to Admiral Sampson, commanding the North Atlantic Squadron, to 'immediately institute a blockade of the north coast of Cuba, extending from Cardenas on the east to Bahia Honda on the west'. Bureau of Navigation Report of 1898, appx. 175. The blockade was immediately instituted accordingly. On April 22 the President issued a proclamation declaring that the United States had instituted and would maintain that blockade, 'in pursuance of the laws of the United States, and the law of nations applicable to such cases'. 30 Stat. at L. 1769. And by the act of Congress of April 25, 1898, chap. 189, it was declared that the war between the United States and Spain existed on that day, and had existed since and including April 21. 30 Stat. at L. 364.

On April 26, 1898, the President issued another proclamation which, after reciting the existence of the war as declared by Congress, contained this further recital: 'It being desirable that such war should be conducted upon principles in harmony with the present views of nations and sanctioned by their recent practice'. This recital was followed by specific declarations of certain rules for the conduct of the war by sea, making no mention of fishing vessels. 30 Stat. at L. 1770. But the proclamation clearly manifests the general policy of the government to conduct the war in accordance with the principles of international law sanctioned by the recent practice of nations. . . .

Upon the facts proved in either case, it is the duty of this court, sitting as the highest prize court of the United States, and administering the law of nations, to declare and adjudge that the capture was unlawful and without probable cause; and it is therefore, in each case,—

Ordered, that the decree of the District Court be reversed, and the proceeds of the sale of the vessel, together with the proceeds of any sale of her cargo, be restored to the claimant, with damages and costs.

MR. CHIEF JUSTICE FULLER, WITH WHOM CONCURRED MR. JUSTICE HARLAN AND MR. JUSTICE MEKENNA, DISSENTING

The district court held these vessels and their cargoes liable because not 'satisfied that as a matter of law, without any ordinance, treaty, or proclamation, fishing vessels of this class are exempt from seizure'.

This court holds otherwise, not because such exemption is to be found in any treaty, legislation, proclamation, or instruction granting it, but on the ground that the vessels were exempt by reason of an established rule of international law applicable to them, which it is the duty of the court to enforce.

I am unable to conclude that there is any such established international rule, or that this court can properly revise action which must be treated as having been taken in the ordinary exercise of discretion in the conduct of war.

. . . .

This case involves the capture of enemy's property on the sea, and executive action, and if the position that the alleged rule *proprio vigore* limits the sovereign power in war be rejected, then I understand the contention to be that, by reason of the existence of the rule, the proclamation of April 26 must be read as if it contained the exemption in terms, or the exemption must be allowed because the capture of fishing vessels of this class was not specifically authorized.

The preamble to the proclamation stated, it is true, that it was desirable that the war 'should be conducted upon principles in harmony with the present views of nations and sanctioned by their recent practice', but the reference was to the intention of the government 'not to resort to privateering, but to adhere to the rules of the Declaration of Paris'; and the proclamation spoke for itself. The language of the preamble did not carry the exemption in terms, and the real question is whether it must be allowed because not affirmatively withheld, or, in other words, because such captures were not in terms directed.

. . .

It is impossible to concede that the Admiral ratified these captures in disregard of established international law and the proclamation, or that the President, if he had been of opinion that there was any infraction of law or proclamation, would not have intervened prior to condemnation.

In truth, the exemption of fishing craft is essentially an act of grace, and not a matter of right, and it is extended or denied as the exigency is believed to demand.

It is, said Sir William Scott, 'a rule of comity only, and not of legal decision'.

. . .

It is difficult to conceive of a law of the sea of universal obligation to which Great Britain has not acceded. And I am not aware of adequate foundation for imputing to this country the adoption of any other than the English rule.

. . .

It is needless to review the speculations and repetitions of the writers on international law. Ortolan, De Boeck, and others admit that the custom relied on as consecrating the immunity is not so general as to create an absolute international rule; Heffter, Calvo, and others are to the contrary. Their lucubrations may be persuasive, but not authoritative.

In my judgment, the rule is that exemption from the rigors of war is in the control of the Executive. He is bound by no immutable rule on the subject. It is for him to apply, or to modify, or to deny altogether such immunity as may have been usually extended.

. . .

COMMENT ON THE HUMANITARIAN LAW OF WAR

The opinion in *The Paquete Habana* has the aura of a humane world in which, if war occurs, the fighting should be as compassionate in spirit as possible. It rests the rule of exemption of coastal fishing vessels 'on considerations of humanity to a poor and industrious order of men, and [on] the mutual convenience of fishing vessels'. The opinion seems more than a mere 14 years distant from the savagery of the First World War I, let alone that war's successors during this century with their massive atrocities and civilian casualties in engagements of close to total war by one or both sides.

The intricate body of international humanitarian law considered by the Supreme Court grew out of centuries of primarily customary law, although custom was supplemented and informed centuries ago by selective bilateral treaties. Custom remains essential to argument about the laws of war to this day, indeed to the subject matter jurisdiction of the International Criminal Tribunal for the Former Yugoslavia discussed in Chapter 14. But this field is increasingly dominated by multilateral treaties that have both codified customary standards and rules and developed new ones in numerous international conferences. Multilateral declarations and treaties started to achieve prominence in the second half of the nineteenth century. The treaties now include the Hague Conventions concluded around the turn of the century, the four Geneva Conventions of 1949 (as well as two significant protocols of 1977 to those conventions), and several discrete treaties since the Second World War on matters like bans on particular weapons and cultural property.

The basic Geneva Conventions (188 states parties as of March 2000) and the two Protocols (Protocol No. 1, 156 parties; Protocol No. 2, 149 parties) cover a vast range of problems stemming from land, air or naval warfare, including the protection of wounded combatants and prisoners of war, of civilian populations and civilian objects affected by military operations or present in occupied territories, and of medical and religious personnel and buildings. As suggested by this list, the provisions of the four Conventions and the two Protocols constitute the principal contemporary regulation of *jus in bello*.

This entire corpus of custom and treaties has come to be know as the 'international humanitarian law of war', the broad purpose being—in the words of the landmark St. Petersburg Declaration of 1868—'alleviating as much as possible the calamities of war'. Here lies the tension, even contradiction, within this body of law. Putting aside the question of a war's legality (an issue central to the Judgment of the International Military Tribunal at Nuremberg, p. 115, *infra*, and today governed by the UN Charter), a war fought in compliance with the standards and rules of the laws of war permits massive intentional killing or wounding and massive other destruction that, absent a war, would violate the most fundamental human rights norms.

Hence all these standards and rules stand at some perilous and problematic divide between brutality and destruction (i) that is permitted or privileged and (ii) that is illegal and subject to sanction. Standards like 'proportionality' in choosing military means or like the avoidance of 'unnecessary suffering' to the civilian population are employed to help to draw the line. The powerful ideal of reducing human suffering that animates this humanitarian law of war thus is countered by the goal of state parties to a war—indeed, in the eyes of states, the paramount goal—of gaining military objectives and victory while reducing as much as possible the losses to one's own armed forces.

The generous mood of *The Paquete Habana* toward the civilian population and its food-gathering needs was reflected in the various Hague Conventions regulating land and naval warfare that were adopted during the ensuing decade. Note Article 3 of the Hague Convention of 1907 on Certain Restrictions with Regard to the Exercise of the Right to Capture in Naval War, 36 Stat. 2396, T.S. No. 544, which proclaimed in 1910: 'Vessels used exclusively for fishing along the coast . . . are exempt from capture . . .'.

The efforts to protect civilian populations and their property took on renewed vigor after the Second World War through the Geneva Conventions of 1949. Consider Article 48 of Protocol No. 1 to the Geneva Conventions, adopted in 1977. Article 48 enjoins the parties to a conflict to 'distinguish between the civilian population and combatants and between civilian objects and military objectives'. Their operations are to be directed 'only against military objectives'. Article 52 defines military objectives to be 'objects which, by their nature, location, purposes or use make an effective contribution to military action and whose total or partial destruction, capture or neutralization, in the circumstances ruling at the time, offers a definite military advantage'. Article 54 is entitled, 'Protection of Objects Indispensable to the Survival of the Civilian Population'. It states that '[s]tarvation of civilians as a method of warfare is prohibited'. Specifically, parties are prohibited from attacking or removing 'objects indispensable to the survival of the civilian population, such as foodstuffs . . . , for the specific purpose of denying them for their sustenance value to the civilian population or to the adverse Party. . . .'. An exception is made for objects used by an adverse party as sustenance 'solely' for its armed forces or 'in direct support of military action'.

Consider some special characteristics of *The Paquete Habana*.

(1) Note the emphasis on the fact that the Supreme Court here sat as a *prize court* administering the law of nations, and note its references to the international character of the law maritime. Indeed, the Court almost assumed the role of an international tribunal, a consideration stressed in the excerpts from the scholar Calvo. Nonetheless, the Court's statement that 'international law is part of our law' and must be 'ascertained and administered by courts of justice' as often as 'questions of right' depending on it are presented for determination, has been drawn on

in many later judicial decisions in the United States involving unrelated international law issues.

(2) An antiquarian aspect of the decision and period is that the naval personnel who captured the fishing vessels participated in the judicial proceedings, for at the time of the war captors were entitled to share in the proceeds of the sale of lawful prizes. That practice has ended and proceeds are now paid into the Treasury. 70A Stat. 475 (1956), 10 U.S.C.A. 7651–81.

(3) The Court looked to a relatively small number of countries for evidence of state practice, dominantly in Western Europe. It referred to Japan as 'the last state admitted into the rank of civilized nations'. Even at the start of the twentieth century, the world community creating international law was a small and relatively cohesive one. Contrast the multinational and multicultural character of an assembly of states today drafting a convention on the laws of war or a human rights convention, and imagine the range of states to which references might be made in a contemporary judicial opinion considering the customary law of international human rights.

COMMENT ON THE ROLE OF CUSTOM

The Supreme Court decision in *The Paquete Habana* raises basic questions about custom, which has been referred to as oldest and original source of international law. Customary law remains indispensable to an adequate understanding of human rights law. It figures in many fora, from the broad debates about human rights within the United Nations to the arguments of counsel before an international or national tribunal.

Customary law refers to conduct, or the conscious abstention from certain conduct, of states that becomes in some measure a part of international legal order. By virtue of a developing custom, particular conduct may be considered to be permitted or obligatory in legal terms, or abstention from particular conduct may come to be considered a legal duty.

Consider the 1950 statement of a noted scholar describing the character of the state practice that can build a customary rule of international law: (1) 'concordant practice' by a number of states relating to a particular situation; (2) continuation of that practice 'over a considerable period of time'; (3) a conception that the practice is required by or consistent with international law; and (4) general acquiescence in that practice by other states.[2] Other scholars have contested some of these observations, and today many authorities would contend that custom has long been a less rigid, more flexible and dynamic force in law-making.

Clause (b) of Article 38(1) states that the ICJ shall apply 'international custom, as evidence of a general practice accepted as law'. The phrase is as confusing as it is terse. Contemporary formulations of custom have overcome some difficulties in

---

[2] M. Hudson, Working Paper on Article 24 of the Statute of the International Law Commission, UN Doc. A/CN.4/16, March 3, 1950, p. 5.

understanding it, but three of the terms there used remain contested and vexing: 'general', 'practice', and 'accepted as law'.

Section 102 of the *Restatement (Third), Foreign Relations Law of the United States*, presents a contemporary and clearer formulation of customary law that draws broadly on scholarly, judicial and diplomatic sources. Many authorities on international law, certainly in the developed world and to varying degrees in the states of the Third World, could accept that formulation as an accurate description and guide. After including custom as one of the sources of international law, the *Restatement* provides in clause (2): 'Customary international law results from a general and consistent practice of states followed by them from a sense of legal obligation'.

Each of these terms—'general', 'consistent', 'practice', 'followed', and 'sense of legal obligation'—is defined in a particular way. For example, the *Restatement*'s comments on Section 102 say:

> state practice includes diplomatic acts and instructions, public measures, and official statements, whether unilateral or in combination with other states in international organizations;
> inaction may constitute state practice as when a state acquiesces in another state's conduct that affects its legal rights;
> the state practice necessary may be of 'comparatively short duration';
> a practice can be general even if not universally followed;
> there is no 'precise formula to indicate how widespread a practice must be, but it should reflect wide acceptance among the states particularly involved in the relevant activity'.

The *Restatement* also addresses the question of the sense of legal obligation, or *opinio juris* in the conventional Latin phrase. For example; to form a customary rule, 'it must appear that the states follow the practice from a sense of legal obligation' (*opinio juris sive necessitatis*); hence a practice generally followed 'but which states feel legally free to disregard' cannot form such a rule; *opinio juris* need not be verbal or in some other way explicit, but may be inferred from acts or omissions. The comments also note that a state that is created after a practice has ripened into a rule of international law 'is bound by that rule'.

The *Restatement* (in the Reporter's Notes to Section 102) notes some of the perplexities in the concept of customary law:

> Each element in attempted definitions has raised difficulties. There have been philosophical debates about the very basis of the definition: how can practice build law? Most troublesome conceptually has been the circularity in the suggestion that law is built by practice based on a sense of legal obligation: how, it is asked, can there be a sense of legal obligation before the law from which the legal obligation derives has matured? Such conceptual difficulties, however, have not prevented acceptance of customary law essentially as here defined.

Consider the need to evaluate state practice with respect to (1) *opinio juris* and (2) the reaction of other states to a given state's conduct. Suppose that what is at issue in a case is a state's 'abstention'—for example, state X neither arrests nor asserts judicial jurisdiction over a foreign ambassador, which is one aspect of the law of diplomatic immunities that developed as customary law long before it was subjected to treaty regulation. During the period when this customary law was being developed, it would have been relevant to inquire why states generally did not arrest or prosecute foreign ambassadors. For example, assume that X asserted that it was not legally barred from such conduct but merely exercised its discretion, as a matter of expediency or courtesy, not to arrest or prosecute. Abstention by X coupled with such an explanation would not as readily have contributed to the formation of a customary legal rule. On the other hand, assume that a decision by the executive or courts of X not to arrest or assert judicial jurisdiction over the ambassador rested explicitly on the belief that international law required such abstention. Such practice of X would then constitute classic evidence of *opinio juris*.

Consider a polar illustration, where X acts in a way that immediately and adversely affects the interests of other states rather than abstains from conduct. Suppose that X imprisons without trial the ambassador from state Y, or imprisons many local residents who are citizens of Y. Surely it has not acted out of a sense of an international law *duty*. If it considered international law to be relevant at all, it may have concluded that its conduct was not prohibited by customary law, that customary law was here permissive. Or it may have decided that even if imprisonment was prohibited, it would nonetheless violate international law.

In this type of situation, the conception of *opinio juris* is less relevant, indeed irrelevant to the state's conduct. The state did not act out of duty. What does appear central to a determination of the legality of X's conduct is the *reaction* of other states—in this instance, particularly Y. That reaction of Y might be one of tacit acquiescence, thus tending to support the legality of X's conduct, or, more likely on the facts here given, Y might make a diplomatic protest or criticize X's action in other ways as a violation of international law. Action and reaction, acts by a state perhaps accompanied by claims of the act's legality, followed by reaction-responses by other states adversely affected by those acts, here constitute the critical components of the growth of a customary rule

These simplified illustrations suggest some of the typical dynamics of traditional customary international law. What is common to both illustrations—abstention from arrest, and arrest—is that the interests of at least two states were directly involved: at least the acting state X, and state Y. Of course states other than Y may well have taken an interest in X's action; after all, those states also have ambassadors and citizens in foreign countries. All of these possibilities are relevant to understanding *The Paquete Habana*.

Relationships between Treaties and Custom

Thus far we have considered custom independently of treaties (whose elements are described at p. 103, *infra*). But these two 'sources' or law-making processes of international law are complexly interrelated. For example, the question often arises of the extent to which a treaty should be read in the light of preexisting custom. A treaty norm of great generality may naturally be interpreted against the back-ground of relevant state practice or policies. In such contexts, the question whether the treaty is intended to be 'declaratory' of preexisting customary law or to change that law may become relevant.

Moreover, treaties may give birth to rules of customary law. Assume a succession of bilateral treaties among many states, each containing a provision giving indigent aliens who are citizens of the other state party, the right to counsel at the government's expense in a criminal prosecution. The question may arise whether these bilateral treaties create a custom that would bind a state not party to any of them. Polar arguments will likely be developed by parties to such a dispute, for example: (1) The non-party state cannot be bound by those treaties since it has not con-sented. The series of bilateral treaties simply constitutes special exceptions to the traditional customary law that leaves the state's discretion unimpaired on this matter. Indeed, the necessity that many states saw for treaties underscores that no obligation existed under customary law. (2) A solution worked out among many states should be considered relevant or persuasive for the development of a cus-tomary law setting standards for all countries. Similarly, the network of treaties may have become dense enough, and state practice consistent with the treaty may have become general enough, to build a customary norm binding all states. Article 38 of the Vienna Convention signals rather than resolves this issue by stating that nothing in its prior articles providing generally that a treaty does not create obliga-tions for a third state precludes a rule set forth in a treaty from becoming binding on a third State 'as a customary rule of international law, recognized as such'.

In contemporary international law, broadly ratified multilateral treaties are more likely than a series of bilateral treaties to generate the argument that treaty rules have become customary law binding non-parties. Some of the principal human rights treaties, for example, have about 140 state parties from all parts of the world. Of course, one must distinguish between substantive norms in multi-lateral treaties that are alleged to constitute custom binding non-parties, and insti-tutional arrangements created by the treaties in which parties have agreed, for example, to submit reports or disputes to a treaty organ.

AKEHURST'S MODERN INTRODUCTION TO INTERNATIONAL LAW

Peter Malanczuk (7th revised edn 1997), at 39

[The following excerpts develop some themes about custom in the preceding Comment.]

. . .

Where to Look for Evidence of Customary Law

The main evidence of customary law is to be found in the actual practice of states, and a rough idea of a state's practice can be gathered from published material—

from newspaper reports of actions taken by states, and from statements made by government spokesmen to Parliament, to the press, at international conferences and at meetings of international organizations; and also from a state's laws and judicial decisions, because the legislature and the judiciary form part of a state just as much as the executive does. At times the Foreign Ministry of a state may publish extracts from its archives; for instance, when a state goes to war or becomes involved in a particular bitter dispute, it may publish documents to justify itself in the eyes of the world. But the vast majority of the material which would tend to throw light on a state's practice concerning questions of international law— correspondence with other states, and the advice which each state receives from its own legal advisers—is normally not published; or, to be more precise, it is only recently that efforts have been made to publish digests of the practice followed by different states. . . .

Evidence of customary law may sometimes also be found in the writings of international lawyers, and in judgments of national and international tribunals, which are mentioned as subsidiary means for the determination of rules of law in Article 38(1)(d) of the Statute of the International Court of Justice.

Similarly, treaties can be evidence of customary law; but great care must be taken when inferring rules of customary law from treaties, especially bilateral ones. For instance, treaties dealing with a particular subject matter may habitually contain a certain provision; thus, extradition treaties almost always provide that political offenders shall not be extradited. It has sometimes been argued that a standard provision of this type has become so habitual that it should be regarded as a rule of customary law, to be inferred even when a treaty is silent on that particular point. On the other hand, why would states bother to insert such standard provisions in their treaties, if the rule existed already as a rule of customary law? . . . [T]he mere existence of identical bilateral treaties does not generally support a corresponding norm of customary law. At least the network of bilateral treaties must be widespread before it can amount to state practice resulting in customary law.

The case of multilateral treaties is different and may definitely constitute evidence of customary law. If the treaty claims to be declaratory of customary law, or is intended to codify customary law, it can be quoted as evidence of customary law even against a state which is not a party to the treaty . . .
. . .

The Problem of Repetition

It has sometimes been suggested that a single precedent is not enough to establish a customary rule, and that there must be a degree of repetition over a period of time. . . .

In the *Nicaragua* case [*Nicaragua v. US (Merits)*, ICJ Rep. 1986, para. 186] the ICJ held:

> It is not to be expected that in the practice of States the application of the rules in question should have been perfect, in the sense that States should have refrained, with complete consistency, from the use of force or from intervention in each other's internal affairs. The Court does not consider that, for a rule to be estab-

lished as customary, the corresponding practice must be in absolutely rigorous conformity with the rule. In order to deduce the existence of customary rules, the Court deems it sufficient that the conduct of States should, in general, be consistent with such rules, and that instances of State conduct inconsistent with a given rule should generally have been treated as breaches of that rule, not as indications of the recognition of a new rule.

In sum, *major* inconsistencies in the practice (that is, a large amount of practice which goes against the 'rule' in question) prevent the creation of a customary rule.
. . .

There remains the question of what constitutes 'general' practice. This much depends on the circumstances of the case and on the rule at issue. 'General' practice is a relative concept and cannot be determined in the abstract. It should include the conduct of all states, which can participate in the formulation of the rule or the interests of which are specially affected. 'A practice can be general even if it is not universally accepted; there is no precise formula to indicate how widespread a practice must be, but it should reflect wide acceptance among the states particularly involved in the relevant activity'. Therefore, in the law of the sea, the practice of sea powers and maritime nations will have greater significance than the practice of land-locked states, while in the law governing outer space activities, the practice of the United States and Russia will exert a more dominant influence than that of Burundi or Chile. . . .

What is certain is that general practice does not require the unanimous practice of all states or other international subjects. This means that a state can be bound by the general practice of other states even against its wishes if it does not protest against the emergence of the rule and continues persistently to do so (persistent objector). Such instances are not frequent and the rule also requires that states are sufficiently aware of the emergence of the new practice and law. . . .
. . .

What States Say and What States Do

It is sometimes suggested that state practice consists only of what states do, not of what they say. For instance, in his dissenting opinion in the *Fisheries* case, Judge Read argued that claims made to areas of the sea by a state could not create a customary rule unless such claims were enforced against foreign ships. [ICJ Rep. 1951, 116, 191] But in the later *Fisheries Jurisdiction* cases ten of the fourteen judges inferred the existence of customary rules from such claims, without considering whether they had been enforced [*UK v. Iceland (Merits)*, ICJ Rep. 1974, 3, at 47, 56–8, 81–8, 119–20, 135, 161] . . . Similarly, the Nuremberg Tribunal cited resolutions passed by the League of Nations Assembly and a Pan-American Conference as authority for its finding that aggressive war was criminal according to the 'customs and practices of states'. [Excerpts from this opinion appear at p. 115, *infra.*] The better view therefore appears to be that state practice consists not only of what states do, but also of what they say.

This becomes even clearer if one takes the fact into account that in the modern world states have found new means of communication. . . .
. . .

The Psychological Element in the Formation of Customary Law (opinio iuris)

. . .

The technical name given to this psychological element is *opinio iuris sive neces-sitatis* (*opinio iuris* for short). It is usually defined as a conviction felt by states that a certain form of conduct is required by international law. This definition presupposes that all rules of international law are framed in terms of duties. But that is not so; in addition to rules laying down duties, there are also permissive rules, which permit states to act in a particular way (for example, to prosecute foreigners for crimes committed within the prosecuting state's territory) without making such actions obligatory. In the case of a rule imposing a duty, the traditional definition of *opinio iuris* is correct; in the case of a permissive rule, *opinio iuris* means a conviction felt by states that a certain form of conduct is *permitted* by international law.

There is clearly something artificial about trying to analyse the psychology of collective entities such as states. Indeed, the modern tendency is not to look for direct evidence of a state's psychological convictions, but to infer *opinio iuris* indirectly from the actual behaviour of states. Thus, official statements are not required; *opinio iuris* may be gathered from acts or omissions. . . .

. . .

Moreover, if states are clearly divided on whether a certain conduct (such as non-recourse to nuclear weapons over the past fifty years) constitutes the expression of an *opinio iuris* (in this case that the use of nuclear weapons is illegal), it is impossible to find that there is such *opinion iuris*.

. . .

Customary law has a built-in mechanism of change. If states are agreed that a rule should be changed, a new rule of customary international law based on the new practice of states can emerge very quickly; thus the law on outer space developed very quickly after the first artificial satellite was launched. If the number of states supporting a change, or the number of states resisting a change, is small, they will probably soon fall into line with the practice of the majority. The real difficulty comes when the states supporting the change and the states resisting the change are fairly evenly balanced. In this case change is difficult and slow, and disagreement and uncertainty about the law may persist for a long time until a new consensus emerges, as, for example, in the dispute about the width of the territorial sea . . .

'Instant' Customary Law

A special problem is the existence or non-existence of the category of '*diritto spontaneo*' or 'instant customary international law' which has been brought to the forefront by some authors, such as Roberto Ago and Bin Cheng. The result is to deny the significance of state practice and the relevance of the time factor in the formation of customary international law and to rely solely on *opinion iuris*, as expressed in non-binding resolutions and declarations, as the constitutive element of custom.

. . . [C]hanges in the international law-making process have modified the concept of modern customary law in several respects, including the tendency that it is made with relative speed, written in textual form, and is more elaborate than traditional custom. The possibility of 'instant' customary international law, or '*droit spontane*', based upon *opinio iuris* only and without the requirement of any practice, however, has remained a matter of dispute. In view of the nature of the decentralized international legal system and the elementary role of state practice as the objective element in the formation of customary law, enabling one to distinguish it from non-binding commitments, *opinio iuris* on its own, even if clearly established for some states as the subjective element, does not suffice to establish general custom in controversial areas. In addition, the very notion of 'custom' implies some time element and 'instant custom' is a contradiction in terms, although it appears that this is more a matter of appropriate terminology than of substance.

. . .

Universality and the Consensual Theory of International Law

It has already been suggested that the practice followed by a small number of states is sufficient to create a customary rule, if there is no practice which conflicts with that rule. But what if some states oppose the alleged rule? Can the opposition of a single state prevent the creation of a customary rule? If so, there would be very few rules, because state practice differs from state to state on many topics. On the other hand, to allow the majority to create a rule against the wishes of the minority would lead to insuperable difficulties. How large must the majority be? In counting the majority, must equal weight be given to the practice of Guatemala and that of the United States? If, on the other hand, some states are to be regarded as more important than others, on what criteria is importance to be based? Population? Area? Wealth? Military power? . . .

. . .

. . . The International Court of Justice has emphasized that a claimant state which seeks to rely on a customary rule must prove that the rule has become binding on the defendant state. The obvious way of doing this is to show that the defendant state has recognized the rule in its own state practice (although recognition for this purpose may amount to no more than failure to protest when other states have applied the rule in cases affecting the defendant's interests). But it may not be possible to find any evidence of the defendant's attitude towards the rule, and so there is a second—and more frequently used—way of proving that the rule is binding on the defendant: by showing that the rule is accepted by other states. In these circumstances the rule in question is binding on the defendant state, unless the defendant state can show that it has expressly and consistently rejected the rule since the earliest days of the rule's existence; dissent expressed after the rule has become well established is too late to prevent the rule binding the dissenting state. Thus, in the *Fisheries* case, the International Court of Justice held that a particular rule was not generally recognized, but added: 'In any event, the . . . rule would appear to be inapplicable as against Norway, inasmuch as she has always opposed any attempt to apply it to the Norwegian coast'.

The problem of the 'persistent objector', however, has recently attracted more attention in the literature. Can a disagreeing state ultimately and indefinitely remain outside of new law accepted by the large majority of states? Do emerging rules of *ius cogens* require criteria different to norms of lesser significance? Such questions are far from settled at this point in time. . . .

. . .

Ius cogens

Some of the early writers on international law said that a treaty would be void if it was contrary to morality or to certain (unspecified) basic principles of international law. The logical basis for this rule was that a treaty could not override natural law. With the decline of the theory of natural law, the rule was largely forgotten, although some writers continued to pay lip-service to it.

Recently there has been a tendency to revive the rule, although it is no longer based on natural law. . . . The technical name now given to the basic principles of international law, which states are not allowed to contract out of, is 'peremptory norms of general international law', otherwise known as *ius cogens*.

Article 53 of the Convention on the Law of Treaties [see Annex on Documents] provides as follows:

> A treaty is void if, at the time of its conclusion, it conflicts with a peremptory norm of general international law. For the purposes of the present Convention, a peremptory norm of general international law is a norm accepted and recognized by the international community of States as a whole as a norm from which no derogation is permitted and which can be modified only by a subsequent norm of general international law having the same character.

What is said about treaties being void would also probably apply equally to local custom. . . .

Although cautiously expressed to apply only 'for the purposes of the present Convention', the definition of a 'peremptory norm' is probably valid for all purposes. The definition is more skilful than appears at first sight. A rule cannot become a peremptory norm unless it is 'accepted and recognized [as such] by the international community of states *as a whole*'. . . . It must find acceptance and recognition by the international community at large and cannot be imposed upon a significant minority of states. Thus, an overwhelming majority of states is required, cutting across cultural and ideological differences.

At present very few rules pass this test. Many rules have been suggested as candidates. Some writers suggest that there is considerable agreement on the prohibition of the use of force, of genocide, slavery, of gross violations of the right of people to self-determination, and of racial discrimination. Others would include the prohibition on torture. In an obscure *obiter dictum* in the *Barcelona Traction* case in 1970, the ICJ referred to 'basic rights of the human person', including the prohibition of slavery and racial discrimination and the prohibition of aggression and genocide, which it considered to be 'the concern of all states', without, however, expressly recognizing the concept of *ius cogens*. [ICJ Rep. 1970 3, paras. 33 and 34]. But, apart from the 'basic rights of the human person' mentioned in the

Barcelona Traction case, the only one which at present receives anything approaching general acceptance is the rule against aggression.
. . .

MARTTI KOSKENNIEMI, THE PULL OF THE MAINSTREAM
88 Mich. L. Rev. 1946 (1990)

. . . [I]nternational lawyers have had difficulty accounting for rules of international law that do not emanate from the consent of the states against which they are applied. In fact, most modern lawyers have assumed that international law is not really binding unless it can be traced to an agreement or some other meeting of wills between two or more sovereign states. Once the idea of a natural law is discarded, it seems difficult to justify an obligation that is not voluntarily assumed.
. . .

   The matter is particularly important in regard to norms intended to safeguard basic human rights and fundamental freedoms. If the only states bound to respect such rights and freedoms are the states that have formally become parties to the relevant instruments—and even then only within the scope of their often compromised wordings and multiple reservations—then many important political values would seem to lack adequate protection. It is inherently difficult to accept the notion that states are legally bound not to engage in genocide, for example, only if they have ratified and not formally denounced the 1948 Genocide Convention. Some norms seem so basic, so important, that it is more than slightly artificial to argue that states are legally bound to comply with them simply because there exists an agreement between them to that effect, rather than because, in the words of the International Court of Justice (ICJ), noncompliance would 'shock[] the conscience of mankind' and be contrary to 'elementary considerations of humanity'.
. . .

   . . . To what extent are states bound by humanitarian or human rights norms regardless of treaties, by way of customary law? The subject, an important one, is situated in a theoretical mine field. Although it seems clear that not all international law can be based upon agreement, it seems much less clear what else, then, it may be founded upon. . . . A Grotian lawyer would not, of course, perceive a great difficulty. He would simply say that some norms exist by force of natural reason or social necessity. Such an argument, however, is not open to a modern lawyer or court, much less an international court, established for the settlement of disputes between varying cultures, varying traditions, and varying conceptions of reason and justice. Such conceptions seem to be historically and contextually conditioned, so that imposing them on a nonconsenting state seems both political and unjustifiable as such.
   It is, I believe, for this reason—the difficulty of justifying conceptions of natural justice in modern society—that lawyers have tended to relegate into 'custom' all those important norms that cannot be supported by treaties. In this way, they

might avoid arguing from an essentially naturalistic—and thus suspect—position. 'Custom' may seem both less difficult to verify and more justifiable to apply than abstract maxims of international justice.

...

Professor Meron [an authority on humanitarian law whose book is here under review] follows this strategy. Although he accepts the category of 'general principles' as a valid way to argue about human rights and humanitarian norms, he does not use this argumentative tack. Nor does he examine whether, or to what extent, such norms might be valid as natural law. His reason for so doing is clearly stated: he wishes to 'utilize irreproachable legal methods' to enhance 'the credibility of the norms' for which he argues. The assumption here is that to argue in terms of general principles or natural justice is to engage in a political debate and to fall victim to bias and subjectivism. Following his rationalistic credo, Meron hopes to base human rights and humanitarian norms on something more tangible, something that jurists can look at through a distinct (objective, scientific) method and thus ground their conclusions in a more acceptable way—a way that would also better justify their application against nonconsenting states.

The starting point—hoping to argue nontreaty-based human rights and humanitarian norms as custom—however, does not fare too well in Professor Meron's careful analysis of pertinent case law and juristic opinion. He accepts the orthodox 'two-element theory' of custom (*i.e.*, for custom to exist, there must be both material practice to that effect and the practice must have been motivated by a belief that it is required by law (p. 3)), yet case law contains little to actually support such a theory, although passages paying lip service to it are abundant....

...

... [The rest of material practice and the *opinio juris*] is useless, first, because the interpretation of 'state behavior' or 'state will' is not an automatic operation but involves the choice and use of conceptual matrices that are controversial and that usually allow one to argue either way. But it is also, and more fundamentally, useless because we do not wish to condone anything that states may do or say, and because it is really our certainty that genocide or torture is illegal that allows us to understand state behavior and to accept or reject its legal message, not state behavior itself that allows us to understand that these practices are prohibited by law. It seems to me that if we are uncertain of the latter fact, then there is really little in this world we can feel confident about.

In other words, finding juristic evidence (a precedent, a habitual behaviour, a legal doctrine) to support such a conclusion adds little or nothing to our reasons for adopting it. To the contrary, it contains the harmful implication that it is *only* because this evidence is available that we can justifiably reach our conclusion. It opens the door for disputing the conclusion by disputing the presence of the evidence, or for requiring the same evidence in support of some other equally compelling conclusion, when that evidence might not be so readily available.

It is, of course, true that people are uncertain about right and wrong. The past two hundred years since the Enlightenment and the victory of the principle of arbitrary value have done nothing to teach us about how to know these things or how to cope with our strong moral intuitions. But one should not pretend that this uncertainty will vanish if only one is methodologically 'rigorous'. If the development of the human sciences has taught us anything during its short history, it is that the effort to replace our loss of faith in theories about the right and the good with an absolute faith in our ability to understand human life as a matter of social 'facts' has been a failure. We remain just as unable to derive norms from the facts of state behavior as Hume was. And we are just as compelled to admit that everything we know about norms which are embedded in such behavior is conditioned by an anterior—though at least in some respects largely shared—criterion of what is right and good for human life.

. . .

QUESTIONS

1. Suppose that an international tribunal rather than US courts had heard this controversy, and had sought to decide it within the framework of Article 38 of the Statute of the International Court of Justice. Assuming that this tribunal came to the same conclusion, would any observations in the Supreme Court's opinion likely have been omitted or changed by such an international tribunal? Which observations? Suppose, for example, that the historical record was identical with that reported by the Supreme Court except for the fact that the United States had consistently objected to this rule of exemption and had often refused to follow it.

2. Does the method of the Court in 'ascertaining' the customary rule appear consistent with some of the observations about the nature of custom and the processes for its development in the preceding readings? Consider, for example, how the Supreme Court deals with:

   (i) the issue of *opinio juris*, and its relation to comity, grace, concession, or discretion;
   (ii) the relevance of treaties, as expressing a customary norm or as special rules (*lex specialis*) negating the existence of a custom; and
   (iii) the departure from the rule of exemption during the Napoleonic wars, as a temporary interruption of or as aborting an emerging custom.

About which of these three aspects of the opinion does the dissenting opinion differ? How would you have argued against the Court's resolution of these three aspects?

3. How do you assess Koskenniemi's argument about customary law? How would you make the argument that the decision in *The Paquete Habana* in fact supports Koskenniemi's view of what underlies argument about customary law?

QUESTION

The Comment on Aspects of Capital Punishment, together with the article following it by Carol Steiker and Jordan Steiker and the Makwanyane case, at pp. 31–53, *supra*, convey some sense of the ideas and data that characterize contemporary discussion about the legality of the death penalty under national laws (primarily constitutional law) and under the international law of human rights. Advocates acting on behalf of prisoners in death row or acting generally in the public interest have argued in countries like the United States that the death penalty is now barred by customary international law. Of course their elaborated arguments involve more extensive research, broader and more detailed information, and more developed moral and legal perspectives on the death penalty than appear in Chapter 1(B).

Assume that execution in the United States of a prisoner pursuant to a court judgment imposing capital punishment would be upheld, in the circumstances of the particular case, as constitutional under federal law. Assume further that an argument that such execution violates customary international law would, if agreed with by the US Supreme Court, have internal effects in the United States (a question raised in Chapter 12).

Based on the materials in Chapter 1(B), and in light of the preceding discussions of custom, make the argument that customary international law bars the death penalty. In making that argument, consider also the possible relevance of the excerpts from Oscar Schachter's book at p. 90, *infra*. Based on the same sources, make the opposing argument as well.

Take account of the evidence of state practice and of *opinio juris*, and of the major difference between ascertaining customary law through state interaction in a case like *The Paquete Habana* and ascertaining customary law in a death penalty case.

ADDITIONAL READING

On the laws of war see: T. Meron, *Human Rights and Humanitarian Norms as Customary Law* (1989); D. Fleck (ed.), *The Handbook of Humanitarian Law in Armed Conflicts* (1995); and G. Best, *War and Law Since 1945* (1994). On custom see: M. Byers, *Custom, Power and the Power of Rules* (1999); and H. Charlesworth, 'Customary International Law and the Nicaragua Case', 11 Aust. Y. B. Int. L. 1 (1988).

B. STATE RESPONSIBILITY, GENERAL PRINCIPLES, AND NATURAL LAW

COMMENT ON THE LAW OF STATE RESPONSIBILITY

The *Chattin* case described *infra* was decided under a 1923 General Claims Convention between the United States and Mexico, 43 Stat. 1730, T.S. No. 678. That treaty provided that designated claims against Mexico of US citizens (and vice versa) for losses or damages suffered by persons or by their properties that (in the case of the US citizens) had been presented to the US government for interposition with Mexico and that had remained unsettled 'shall be submitted to a Commission consisting of three members for decision in accordance with the principles of international law, justice and equity'. Each state was to appoint one member, and the presiding third commissioner was to be selected by mutual agreement (and by stipulated procedures failing agreement).

These arbitrations grew out of and further developed the law of state responsibility for injuries to aliens, a branch of international law that was among the important predecessors to contemporary human rights law. That body of law addressed only certain kinds of conflicts—not including, for example, conflicts originating in the first instance in a dispute between a claimant state (X) and a respondent state (Y). Thus it did not cover a dispute, say, based on a claim by X that Y had violated international law by its invasion of X's territory or by its imprisonment of X's ambassador.

Rather, the claims between states that were addressed by the law of state responsibility for injuries to aliens grew out of disputes arising in the first instance between a citizen-national of X and the government of Y. For example, respondent state Y allegedly imprisoned a citizen of claimant state X without hearing or trial, or seized property belonging to citizens of X—allegations which, if true, could show violations of international law. Note that these illustrations involve action leading to injury of X's citizens by governmental officials or organs (executive, legislative, judicial) of Y. The law of state responsibility required that the conduct complained of be that of the state or, in less clear and more complex situations, be ultimately attributable to the state.

In the normal case, the citizen of X would seek a remedy within Y, probably through its judiciary—release from jail, return of the seized property or compensation for it. Indeed, before invoking the aid of his own government, the citizen of X would generally be required under the relevant treaty to pursue such a path, to 'exhaust local remedies'. But that path could prove to be fruitless, because of lack of recourse to Y's judiciary, because that judiciary was corrupt, or because of Y's law adverse to the citizen of X that would certainly be applied by its judiciary. In such circumstances, the injured person may turn to his own government X for diplomatic protection.

The 1924 decision of the Permanent Court of International Justice in the *Mavrommatis Palestine Concessions (Jurisdiction)* case, P.C.I.J., Ser. A, No. 2, gave classic expression to such diplomatic protection. It pointed out that when a state took up the cause of one of its subjects (citizens-nationals) in a dispute originating between that subject and respondent state, the dispute:

> entered upon a new phase; it entered the domain of international law, and became a dispute between two States. . . . It is an elementary principle of international law that a State is entitled to protect its subjects, when injured by acts contrary to international law committed by another State, from whom they have been unable to obtain satisfaction through the ordinary channels. By taking up the case of one of its subjects and by resorting to diplomatic action or international judicial proceedings on his behalf, a State is in reality asserting its own rights—its right to ensure, in the person of its subjects, respect for the rules of international law.

Precisely what action to take, what form of diplomatic protection to extend, lay within the discretion of the claimant state. If it decided to intervene and thereby make the claim its own, it might espouse the claim through informal conversations with the respondent state, or make a formal diplomatic protest, or exert various economic and political pressures to encourage a settlement (extending at times to military intervention), or, if these strategies failed, have recourse to international tribunals. Such recourse was infrequent. International tribunals to whose jurisdiction states had consented for the resolution of disputes between them were rare. Moreover, states were reluctant to raise controversies between their citizens and foreign states to the level of interstate conflict before an international tribunal except where a clear national interest gave reason to do so.

An arbitral tribunal to which the claimant state turned may have been created by agreement between the disputing states to submit to it designated types of disputes. That agreement may have been part of a general arbitration treaty (which after the Second World War found scant use) covering a broad range of potential disputes between the two parties. Or it may have been a so-called compromissory clause (*compromis*) in a treaty dealing with a specific subject that bound the parties to submit to arbitration disputes that might arise under that treaty. Of course, two states could always agree to submit specified disputes to arbitration, as in the 1923 General Claims Convention between the United States and Mexico under which *Chattin* was decided.

In 1921, *ad hoc* arbitral tribunals were first supplemented by an international court, the Permanent Court of International Justice provided for in the Covenant of the League of Nations. Again, problems of states' consent to jurisdiction and states' reluctance to start interstate litigation limited the role of that court (and indeed the role of its successor, the International Court of Justice created under the Charter of the United Nations) in developing the law of state responsibility (or, today, in developing the international law of human rights).

The growth in the nineteenth and twentieth centuries of the law of state responsibility for injury to aliens was the product of and evidenced by a range of state interactions—diplomatic protests and responses, negotiated settlements, arbitral decisions—and the writings of scholars. Before the Second World War, there was little attempt at formal codification or creative development of this body of law through treaties—that is, treaties spelling out the content of what international law required of a state in its treatment of aliens.

As it developed, the international law of state responsibility reflected the more intense identification of the individual with his state (or later, the identification of the corporation with the state of its incorporation, or of most of its shareholders) that accompanied the nationalistic trends of that era. This body of law would not have developed so vigorously but for Western colonialism and economic imperialism that reached their zenith during this period. Transnational business operations centered in Europe, and later in the United States as well, penetrated those regions now known as the Third World or developing countries. The protection afforded aliens under international law had obvious importance for the foreign operations of transnational corporations that were often directed by foreign nationals.

In such circumstances, given the links between the success and wealth of corporations in their foreign ventures and national wealth and power, the security of the person and property of a national or corporation operating in a foreign part of the world became a concern of his or its government. That concern manifested itself in the vigorous assertion of diplomatic protection and in the enhanced activity of arbitral tribunals. In the late nineteenth and early twentieth centuries, some such arbitrations occurred under the pressure of actual or threatened military force by the claimant states, particularly against Latin American governments.

A statement in an arbitral proceeding in 1924 by Max Huber, a Judge of the Permanent Court of International Justice, cogently expressed some basic principles of that era's consensus (among states of the developed world) about the law of state responsibility:[3]

> . . . It is true that the large majority of writers have a marked tendency to limit the responsibility of the State. But their theories often have political inspiration and represent a natural reaction against unjustified interventions in the affairs of certain nations. . . .
> . . . The conflicting interest with respect to the problem of compensation of aliens are, on the one hand, the interest of a State in exercising its public power in its own territory without interference or control of any nature by foreign States and, on the other hand, the interest of the State in seeing the rights of its nationals established in foreign countries respected and well protected.
> Three principles are hardly debatable:
>
> . . .
>
> (2) In general, a person established in a foreign country is subject to the territorial legislation for the protection of his person and his property, under the same conditions as nationals of that country.
> (3) A State whose national established in another State is deprived of his rights has a right to intervene *if the injury constitutes a violation of international law.* . . .
> . . . The territorial character of sovereignty is so essential a trait of contemporary public law that foreign intervention in relationships between a territorial State and individuals subject to its sovereignty can be allowed only in extraordinary cases. . . .
> . . . This right of intervention has been claimed by all States; only its limits are under discussion. By denying this right, one would arrive at intolerable results: international law would become helpless in the face of injustices tantamount to the negation of human personality, for that is the subject which every denial of justice touches.
> . . . No police or other administration of justice is perfect, and it is doubtless necessary to accept, even in the best administered countries, a considerable margin of tolerance. However, the restrictions thus placed on the right of a State to intervene to protect its nationals assume that the general security in the country of residence does not fall below a certain standard. . . .

How was it determined whether, in Huber's words, an 'injury' to an alien 'con-

---

[3] Judge Huber delivered these remarks in his role as a Reporter (in effect, arbitrator) in a dispute between Great Britain and Spain. British Claims in the Spanish Zone of Morocco, 2 U.N.R.I.A.A. 615, 639 (1924).

stitutes a violation of international law', or whether the administration of justice in a given country fell below 'a certain standard'? To what materials would, for example, an arbitral tribunal turn for help in defining the content of that standard? What types of argument and justifications would inform the development of this body of international law? Decisions in the many arbitrations, including the *Chattin* case below, shed light on these questions.

COMMENT ON THE *CHATTIN* CASE

The *Chattin* case[4] is among the more interesting of the arbitral decisions. Chattin, a US citizen, was a conductor on a railroad in Mexico from 1908 to 1910, when he was arrested for embezzlement of fares. His trial was consolidated with those of several other Americans and Mexicans who had been arrested on similar charges. In February 1911 he was convicted and sentenced to two years' imprisonment. His appeal was rejected in July 1911. In the meantime the inhabitants of Mazatlán, during a political uprising, threw open the doors of the jail and Chattin escaped to the United States. In asserting Chattin's claims, the United States argued that the arrest was illegal, that Chattin was mistreated while in prison, that his trial was unreasonably delayed, and that there were irregularities in the trial. It claimed that Chattin suffered injuries worth $50,000 in compensation.

Of the three members of the Claims Commission, one came from the United States (Nielsen) and another from Mexico (MacGregor). Each wrote an opinion. Excerpts from the opinion of the third Commissioner follow:

COMMISSIONER VAN VOLLENHOVEN

[This opinion examined a range of complaints about the conduct of the trial. The Commissioner gave particular attention to three such complaints.

(1) Chattin claimed that he had not been duly informed of the charges. The opinion concluded that this claim was 'proven by the record, and to a painful extent'. The principal complainant, an American manager of the railroad company, made full statements to the Court 'without ever being confronted with the accused and his colleagues', and indeed was 'allowed to submit to the Court a series of anonymous written accusations. . . . It is not shown that the confrontation between Chattin and his accusers amounted to anything like an effort on the Judge's part to find out the truth'. Nonetheless Chattin was generally aware of the details of the investigation.

(2) Van Vollenhoven dismissed Chattin's charge that witnesses were not sworn as irrelevant, 'as Mexican law does not require an 'oath' (it is satisfied with a solemn promise, *protesta*, to tell the truth), nor do international standards of civilization'.

(3) Van Vollenhoven found the charge that the hearings in open court lasted

---

[4] *United States of America (B.E. Chattin) v. United Mexican States*, United States-Mexican Claims Commission, 1927. Opinions of Commissioners under the 1923 Convention between the United States and Mexico, 1927–27, at 422, 4 U.N.R.I.A.A. 282.

only five minutes was proven by the record. That hearing was 'a pure formality', in which written documents were confirmed and defence counsel said only a word or two. The opinion concludes that 'the whole of the proceedings discloses a most astonishing lack of seriousness on the part of the Court', and cites instances where the judge failed to follow leads or examine certain people.]

Neither during the investigations nor during the hearings in open court was any such thing as an oral examination or cross-examination of any importance attempted. It seems highly improbable that the accused have been given a real opportunity during the hearings in open court, freely to speak for themselves. It is not for the Commission to endeavor to reach from the record any conviction as to the innocence or guilt of Chattin and his colleagues; but even in case they were guilty, the Commission would render a bad service to the Government of Mexico if it failed to place the stamp of its disapproval and even indignation on a criminal procedure so far below international standards of civilization as the present one. If the wholesome rule of international law as to respect for the judiciary of another country ... shall stand, it would seem of the utmost necessity that appellate tribunals when, in exceptional cases, discovering proceedings of this type should take against them the strongest measures possible under constitution and laws, in order to safeguard their country's reputation.

[Nonetheless, the opinion found the record sufficient to warrant a conviction of Chattin and rejected a charge that the court was biased against American citizens, since four Mexicans were also convicted.]

Bringing the proceedings of Mexican authorities against Chattin to the test of international standards ... there can be no doubt of their being highly insufficient. Inquiring whether there is convincing evidence of these unjust proceedings ... the answer must be in the affirmative. Since this is a case of alleged responsibility of Mexico for injustice committed by its judiciary, it is necessary to inquire whether the treatment of Chattin amounts even to an outrage, to bad faith, to wilful neglect of duty, or to an insufficiency of governmental action recognizable by every unbiased man ... and the answer here again can only be in the affirmative.

   [Taking all these factors into account, the opinion concluded that] it would seem proper to allow in behalf of this claimant damages in the sum of $5,000.00.

COMMISSIONER NIELSEN (CONCURRING)
[In his concurring opinion, Commissioner Nielsen took a comparative approach with respect to criminal procedure.]

Comparisons pertinent and useful in the instant case must be made with the systems obtaining in countries which like Mexico are governed by the principles of the civil law, since the administration of criminal jurisprudence in those countries differs so very radically from the procedure in criminal cases in countries in which the principles of Anglo-Saxon law obtain. This point is important in considering the arguments of counsel for the United States regarding irrelevant evidence and hearsay evidence appearing in the record of proceedings against the accused. From the standpoint of the rules governing Mexican criminal procedure conclusions respecting objections relative to these matters must be grounded not on the fact that a judge received evidence of this kind but on the use he made of it.

[Nielsen observed that counsel for Mexico had stressed that during the period of investigation a Mexican judge was at liberty to receive anything placed before him, including anonymous accusations. Although European procedure allowed 'a similar measure of latitude' for judges, there was one essential difference: after proceedings before a judge of investigation, the case is taken over by another judge who conducts the actual trial. Thus, said Nielsen, under the French law of the period]

the preliminary examination does not serve as a foundation for the verdict of the judge who decided as to the guilt of the accused. The examination allows the examining judge to determine whether there is ground for formal charge, and in case there is, to decide upon the jurisdiction. The accused is not immediately brought before the court which is to pass upon his guilt or innocence. His appearance in court is deferred until the accusation rests upon substantial grounds. This trial is before a judge whose functions are of a more judicial character than those of a judge of investigation employing inquisitorial methods in the nature of those used by a prosecutor. When the period of investigation was completed in the cases of Chattin and the others with whom his case was consolidated, the entire proceedings so far as the Government was concerned were substantially finished, and after a hearing lasting perhaps five minutes, the same judge who collected evidence against the accused sentenced them. . . . International law requires that in the administration of penal laws an alien must be accorded certain rights. There must be some grounds for his arrest; he is entitled to be informed of the charge against him; and he must be given opportunity to defend himself.

[Nielsen, 'having further in mind the peculiarly delicate character of an examination of judicial proceedings by an international tribunal, as well as the practical difficulties inherent in such examination', concluded that the Commission should render a small award based on the mistreatment of Chattin during the period of investigation.]

COMMISSIONER MACGREGOR (DISSENTING)

[In his dissent, Commissioner MacGregor referred to the charge that the trial proper lasted only five minutes, 'implying thereby that there was really no trial and that Chattin was convicted without being heard'. This was an 'erroneous criticism which arises from the difference between Anglo-Saxon procedure and that of other countries'. Mexican criminal procedure consisted of two parts: preliminary proceedings (sumario) and plenary proceedings (plenario). In the sumario, evidence is gathered, investigations occur, the judge or defendant can cross examine. When the judge concludes that there are sufficient facts to establish a case, the sumario ends as the record is given to all parties to be certain that they do not request more testimony and so that they can make final pleas. Then a public hearing (plenario) is held 'in which the parties very often do not have anything further to allege'. That hearing is formal, and serves little new function. Such occurred in the *Chattin* case.]

In view of the foregoing explanation, I believe that it becomes evident that the charge, that there was no trial proper, can not subsist, for, in Mexican procedure, it is not a question of a trial in the sense of Anglo-Saxon law, which requires that the case be always heard in plenary proceedings, before a jury, adducing all the circumstances and evidence of the cause, examining and cross-examining all the witnesses, and allowing the prosecuting attorney and counsel for the defense to make their respective allegations. International law insures that a defendant be judged openly and that he be permitted to defend himself, but in no manner does it oblige these things to be done in any fixed way, as they are matters of internal regulation and belong to the sovereignty of States. . . . . I admit that [other deficiencies] exist and that they show that the Judge could have carried out the investigation in a more efficient manner, but the fact that it was not done does not mean any violation of international law.

. . .

I consider that this is one of the most delicate cases that has come before the Commission and that its nature is such that it puts to a test the application of principles of international law. It is hardly of any use to proclaim in theory respect for the judiciary of a nation, if, in practice, it is attempted to call the judiciary to account for its minor acts. It is true that sometimes it is difficult to determine when a judicial act is internationally improper and when it is so from a domestic standpoint only. In my opinion the test which consists in ascertaining if the act implies damage, wilful neglect, or palpable deviation from the established customs becomes clearer by having in mind the damage which the claimant could have suffered. There are certain defects in procedure that can never cause damage which may be estimated separately, and that are blotted out or disappear, to put it thus, if the final decision is just. There are other defects which make it impossible for such decision to be just. The former, as a rule, do not engender international liability; the latter do so, since such liability arises from the decision which is iniquitous because of such defects. To prevent an accused from defending himself, either by refusing to inform him as to the facts imputed to him or by denying him a hearing and the use of remedies; to sentence him without evidence, or to impose on him disproportionate or unusual penalties, to treat him with cruelty and discrimination; are all acts which per se cause damage due to their rendering a just decision impossible. But to delay the proceedings somewhat, to lay aside some evidence, there existing other clear proofs, to fail to comply with the adjective law in its secondary provisions and other deficiencies of this kind, do not cause damage nor violate international law. Counsel for Mexico justly stated that to submit the decisions of a nation to revision in this respect was tantamount to submitting her to a régime of capitulations. All the criticism which has been made of these proceedings, I regret to say, appears to arise from lack of knowledge of the judicial system and practice of Mexico, and, what is more dangerous, from the application thereto of tests belonging to foreign systems of law. For example, in some of the latter the investigation of a crime is made only by the police magistrates and the trial proper is conducted by the Judge. Hence the reluctance in accepting that one same judge may have the two functions and that, therefore, he may have to receive in the preliminary investigation (instrucción) of the case all kinds of data, with the obligation, of course, of not taking them into account at the time of judgment, if they have no probative weight. . . . [The foreign-law procedure is used to understand what is a trial or open trial imagining at the same time that it must have the sacred forms of common-law and without remembering that the same goal is reached by many roads. And the same can be said when speaking of the manner of taking testimony of witnesses, of cross-examination, of holding confrontations, etc. . . . In view of the above considerations, I am of the opinion that this claim should be disallowed.

NOTE

These three opinions of the Commissioners underscore the methodological problems in developing a minimum international standard of criminal procedure out of such diverse materials—a diversity that was restricted in *Chattin* to Europe and Latin America, hence far less perplexing than today's worldwide diversity of legal cultures and criminal processes. A treaty was relevant to *Chattin*, but as indicated above, it addressed the scope and structure of the arbitration between the United States and Mexico rather than the international norms of criminal procedure to be applied. The only reference of the General Claims Convention to applicable norms was the terse provision in Article 1 that claims should be submitted to the tripartite Commission 'for decision in accordance with the principles of international law, justice and equity'.

Today a dispute like that in *Chattin* could draw on a human rights treaty, the International Covenant on Civil and Political Rights to be discussed in Chapter 3 that (as of March 2000) had 144 state parties. Article 14 of that Covenant dealing with criminal trials provides in relevant part:

> 1. All persons shall be equal before the courts. . . . [E]veryone shall be entitled to a fair and public hearing by [an] impartial tribunal. . . .
> 2. Everyone . . . shall have the right to be presumed innocent until proved guilty according to law.
> 3. . . . [E]veryone shall be entitled to the following minimum guarantees. . . .
>
> (d) To be tried in his presence and to defend himself in person or through legal assistance of his own choosing . . . ;
> (e) To examine, or have examined, the witnesses against him and to obtain the attendance and examination of witnesses on his behalf. . . .

QUESTIONS

1. Why is international law relevant to this decision? Were there any international factors in the trial and conviction and, if so, how do they compare with the international factors in *The Paquete Habana*?

2. How would you identify the most serious problem in the judicial process leading to Chattin's conviction—say, on the basis of a comparison with judicial processes in other legal systems? Does the van Vollenhoven opinion implicate the Mexican system of criminal justice structurally, so that any convictions within it would fall short of an international standard? Or is its criticism limited to the facts of this particular case?

3. How do the Commissioners approach the task of identifying an 'international standard of civilization' (or, within the terms of the 1923 Convention, the relevant 'international law, justice and equity') against which they are to test the legality of the conviction? Do they resort to customary international law? Do the excerpts from Oscar Schachter's *International Law in Theory and Practice* that follow these questions offer any guidance?

4. Would the tribunal's task have been much simpler if there had been a treaty between the United States and Mexico regulating treatment of aliens that included Article 14 of the ICCPR? Would Article 14 have resolved the basic issues on its face?

OSCAR SCHACHTER, INTERNATIONAL LAW IN THEORY AND PRACTICE
(1991), at 50

Ch. IV. General Principles and Equity

. . .

The Broad Expanse of General Principles of Law

We can distinguish five categories of general principles that have been invoked and applied in international law discourse and cases. Each has a different basis for its authority and validity as law. They are:

(1) The principles of municipal law 'recognized by civilized nations'.

(2) General principles of law 'derived from the specific nature of the international community'.

(3) Principles 'intrinsic to the idea of law and basic to all legal systems'.

(4) Principles 'valid through all kinds of societies in relationships of hierarchy and co-ordination'.

(5) Principles of justice founded on 'the very nature of man as a rational and social being'.

Although these five categories are analytically distinct, it is not unusual for a particular general principle to fall into more than one of the categories. For example, the principle that no one shall be a judge in his own cause or that a victim of a legal wrong is entitled to reparation are considered part of most if not all, systems of municipal law and as intrinsic to the basic idea of law.

Our first category, general principles of municipal law, has given rise to a considerable body of writing and much controversy. Article 38(1)(c) of the Statute of Court does not expressly refer to principles of national law but rather general principles 'recognized by civilized nations'. . . . Elihu Root, the American member of the drafting committee, prepared the text finally adopted and it seemed clear that his amendment was intended to refer to principles 'actually recognized and applied in national legal systems'. The fact that the subparagraph was distinct from those on treaty and custom indicated an intent to treat general principles as an independent source of law, and not as a subsidiary source. As an independent source, it did not appear to require any separate proof that such principles of national law had been 'received' into international law.

However, a significant minority of jurists holds that national law principles, even if generally found in most legal systems, cannot *ipso facto* be international law. One view is that they must receive the *imprimatur* of State consent through custom or treaty in order to become international law. The strict positivist school adheres to that view. A somewhat modified version is adopted by others to the effect that rules of municipal law cannot be considered as recognized by civilized nations unless there is evidence of the concurrence of States on their status as international law. Such concurrence may occur through treaty, custom or other evidence of recognition. This would allow for some principles, such as *res judicata*, which are not customary law but are generally accepted in international law. . . .

. . .

. . . The most important limitation on the use of municipal law principles arises from the requirement that the principle be appropriate for application on the international level. Thus, the universally accepted common crimes—murder, theft, assault, incest—that apply to individuals are not crimes under international law by virtue of their ubiquity. . . .

At the same time, I would suggest a somewhat more positive approach for the emergent international law concerned with the individual, business companies, environmental dangers and shared resources. Inasmuch as these areas have become the concern of international law, national law principles will often be suitable for international application. This does not mean importing municipal rules 'lock, stock and barrel', but it suggests that domestic law rules applicable to such matters as individual rights, contractual remedies, liability for extra-hazardous activities, or restraints on use of common property, have now become pertinent for recruitment into international law. In these areas, we may look to representative legal systems not only for the highly abstract principles of the kind referred to earlier but to more specific rules that are sufficiently widespread as to be considered 'recognized by civilized nations'. . . .

The second category of general principles included in our list comprises principles derived from the specific character of the international community. The most obvious candidates for this category of principles are . . . the necessary principles of co-existence. They include the principles of *pacta sunt servanda*, non-intervention, territorial integrity, self-defence and the legal equality of States. Some of these principles are in the United Nations Charter and therefore part of treaty law, but others might appropriately be treated as principles required by the specific character of a society of sovereign independent members.

. . .

The foregoing comments are also pertinent to the next two categories of general principles. The idea of principles '*jus rationale*' 'valid through all kinds of human societies' . . . is associated with traditional natural law doctrine. At the present time its theological links are mainly historical as far as international law is concerned, but its principal justification does not depart too far from the classic natural law emphasis on the nature of 'man', that is, on the human person as a rational and social creature.

The universalist implication of this theory—the idea of the unity of the human species—has had a powerful impetus in the present era. This is evidenced in at least three significant political and legal developments. The first is the global movements against discrimination on grounds of race, colour and sex. The second is the move toward general acceptance of human rights. The third is the increased fear of nuclear annihilation. These three developments strongly reinforce the universalistic values inherent in natural law doctrine. They have found expression in numerous international and constitutional law instruments as well as in popular movements throughout the world directed to humanitarian ends. Clearly, they are a 'material source' of much of the new international law manifested in treaties and customary rules.

In so far as they are recognized as general principles of law, many tend to fall within our fifth category—the principles of natural justice. This concept is well known in many municipal law systems (although identified in diverse ways). 'Natural justice' in its international legal manifestation has two aspects. One refers to the minimal standards of decency and respect for the individual human being that are largely spelled out in the human rights instruments. We can say that in this aspect, 'natural justice' has been largely subsumed as a source of general principles by the human rights instruments . . .

ADDITIONAL READING

On state responsbility see: 'Symposium: State Responsibility', 10 Eur. J. Int. L. 339 (1999); A. Randelzhofer and C. Tomuschat (eds.), *State Responsibility and the Individual: Reparation in Instances of Grave Violations of Human Rights* (1999); J. Weiler, A. Cassese and M. Spinedi (eds.), *International Crimes of State: A Critical Analysis of the ILC's Draft Article 19 on State Responsibility*; and R. Lillich, 'The Current Status of the Law of State Responsibility', in Lillich (ed.) *International Law of State Responsibility for Injuries to Aliens* (1983).

C. INTERWAR MINORITIES REGIME AND THE ROLE OF TREATIES

COMMENT ON THE MINORITIES REGIME AFTER THE FIRST WORLD WAR

The *Minority Schools in Albania* opinion that follows illustrates treaties as a source and major expression of international law, and introduces another field of international law that influenced the growth of the human rights movement. This Comment provides some background to the opinion.

Treaties and other special regimes to protect minorities have a long history in international law dating from the emergence in the seventeenth century of the modern form of the political state, sovereign within its territorial boundaries. Within Europe religious issues became a strong concern since states often included more than one religious denomination, and abuse by a state of a religious minority could lead to intervention by other states where that religion was dominant. Hence peace treaties sometimes included provisions on religious minorities. In the eighteenth and nineteenth centuries, the precarious situation of Christian minorities within the Ottoman Empire and of religious minorities in newly independent East European or Balkan states led to outbreaks of violence and to sporadic treaty regulation.

The First World War ushered in an era of heightened attention to problems of racial, religious or linguistic minorities. The collapse of the great Austro-Hungarian and Ottoman multinational empires, and the chaos as the Russian empire of the Romanoffs was succeeded by the Soviet Union, led to much redrawing of maps and the creation of new states. President Wilson's Fourteen Points, however compromised they became in the Versailles Treaty and later arrangements, nonetheless exerted influence on the postwar settlements. In it and other messages, Wilson stressed the ideals of the freeing of minorities and the related 'self-determination' of peoples or nationalities. That concept of self-determination, so politically powerful and open to such diverse interpretations, continues to this day to be much disputed and to have profound consequences. It not only appears in the UN Charter but is given a position of high prominence in the two principal human rights covenants.

From concepts like self-determination and out of the legacy of nineteenth-century liberal nationalism that saw the development of nation-states like Germany and Italy, the principle of nationalities took on a new force. Here was another ambiguous and disputed concept—the 'nation' or 'nationality' as distinct from the political state, the nation (often identified with a 'people') defined in cultural or historical terms, often defined more concretely in racial, linguistic and religious terms. One goal in displacing the old empires with new or redrawn states was to identify the nation with the state—ideally, to give each 'nation' its own state. Membership in a 'nation' would ideally be equivalent to membership in a 'state' consisting only or principally of that nation.

Within the pure realization of this ideal, all 'Poles', for example, would be situated in Poland; there would be no 'Polish' national minority in other states, and other 'nationalities' would not be resident in Poland. Indeed, the detaching of Poland after the First World War from the empires and states that had absorbed different parts of it represented one of the few instances of relatively strict congruence between the 'nation' and 'state'. There were polar moves, for example the creation of Yugoslavia as a multiethnic state that after 70 years has had such tragic consequences.

Of course the goal of total identification of state with nation—a goal itself disputed and in contradiction with other conceptions of the political state that did not emphasize cultural homogeneity or ethnic purity—could not be realized. Life and history were and remain too various and complex for such precise correlation. The nineteenth century examples of Germany and Italy, for example, were far from unitary; each had its national, ethnic, linguistic, and religious minorities. National or ethnic homogeneity could be achieved in the vast majority of the world's states only by the compulsory and massive migrations of minority groups, migrations far more systematic and coercive than were some of the population movements and exchanges after the First World War. A 'nation' defined, say, in linguistic-religious terms would generally transcend national boundaries and be located in the territories of two or several sovereign states in the new world created by the postwar settlements. A Greek-speaking Christian minority would, for example, be present in the reconfigured Muslim Albania.

Bear in mind another confusing linguistic usage. The term 'national' is generally used in international law to signify the subjects or citizens of a state. Hence members of the 'German' nation (in the sense of a 'people' and 'culture') living in Poland could be Polish 'nationals' in the sense of being citizens of Poland. Or they could possess only German citizenship and be alien residents in Poland. In the *Minority Schools in Albania* case that follows, members of the Greek-speaking Christian minority (part of a 'nation' in the cultural or ethnic sense) in Muslim Albania were 'nationals' (citizens) of Albania. One can imagine the ambiguity attending the frequent usage of the term 'national minorities', which could mean at least (1) a group in a state belonging in the cultural or ethnic sense to a 'nation' that constituted a minority in that state, or (2) all minorities in a state who were 'nationals' (citizens) of that state.

After the First World War, the victorious powers and the new League of Nations sought to address this situation. They confronted the impossibility, even if it were desirable, of creating ethnically homogeneous states. Hence they had to deal with the continuing presence in states of minorities which had frequently been abused in ways ranging from economic discrimination to pogroms and other violence that could implicate other states, spill across international boundaries and lead to war. The immediate trigger for the outbreak of the First World War in the tormented Balkans was fresh in memory.

President Wilson had proposed that the Covenant of the League of Nations include norms governing the protection of minorities that would have embraced all members of the League. The other major powers rejected this approach, preferring discrete international arrangements to handle discrete problems of minorities in particular states of Central-East Europe and the Balkans rather than a universal treaty system. This compromise led to the regime of the so-called Minorities Treaties that were imposed on the new or reconfigured states of Central-East Europe and the Balkans.

For some states like Austria and Hungary, provisions for minority protection were included in the peace treaties. Other states like Poland or Greece signed minority protection treaties with the allied and associated powers. Some states like Albania and Lithuania made minority protection declarations as a condition for their membership in the League of Nations. There were also bilateral treaties protecting minorities such as one between Germany and Poland. Note that one of the features of this new regime was to insulate the victorious powers from international regulation of their treatment of their own citizens belonging to minorities.

Although there were significant variations among these treaties and declarations, many provisions were common. The 1919 Minorities Treaty between the Principal Allied and Associated Powers and Poland served as a model for later treaties and declarations. It provided for protection of life and liberty and religious freedom for all 'inhabitants of Poland'. All Polish nationals (citizens) were guaranteed equality before the law and the right to use their own language in private life and judicial proceedings. Members of racial, religious or linguistic minorities were guaranteed 'the same treatment and security in law and in fact' as other Polish nationals, and the right to establish and control at their expense their own religious, social and educational institutions. In areas of Poland where a 'considerable proportion' of Polish nationals belonged to minorities, an 'equitable share' of public funds would go to such minority groups for educational or religious purposes. In view of the particular history of oppression and violence, there were specific guarantees for Jews.

Jan Herman Burgers[5] has described the special regimes formed by the minority provisions as follows:

> . . .[T]he regime consisted of three categories of obligations. Firstly, it guaranteed full and complete protection of life and liberty to all *inhabitants* of the country or region concerned, without distinction of birth , nationality, language, race or religion. Secondly, it guaranteed that all nationals would be equal before the law and would enjoy the same civil and political rights, without distinction as to race, language or religion. Thirdly, it provided for a series of special guarantees for nationals belonging to minorities, for instance concerned the use of their language and the right to establish social and religious institutions.

Like other minority treaties and declarations, the Polish treaty's provisions were placed under the guarantee of the League of Nations to the extent that 'they affect persons belonging to' minority groups. The League developed procedures to implement its duties, including a right of petition to it by beleaguered minorities claiming that a treaty regime or declaration had been violated, and including a minorities committee given the task of seeking negotiated solutions to such dis-

---

[5] 'The Road to San Francisco: The Revival of the Human Rights Idea in the Twentieth Century', 14 Hum. Rts. Q. 447 (1992), at 450.

putes. As shown by the *Minority Schools in Albania* case, the Council of the League could invoke in accordance with its usual procedures the advisory opinion jurisdiction of the Permanent Court of International Justice (PCIJ), the first international court (supplementing *ad hoc* arbitral tribunals as in the *Chattin* case). The Court was created by the League in 1921, became dormant in the Second World War, and was then succeeded by the International Court of Justice created under the UN Charter.

MINORITY SCHOOLS IN ALBANIA
Advisory Opinion, Permanent Court of International Justice, 1935
Series A/B-No. 64

[In 1920, the Assembly of the League of Nations adopted a recommendation requesting that if Albania were admitted into the League, it 'should take the necessary measures to enforce the principles of the Minorities Treaties' and to arrange the 'details required to carry this object into effect' with the Council of the League. Albania was admitted to membership a few days later. In 1921 the Council included on its agenda the question of protection of minorities in Albania.

The Greek government, in view of the presence of a substantial Christian minority of Greek origin in (dominantly Muslim) Albania, communicated to the League proposals for provisions going beyond the Minorities Treaties that were related to Christian worship and to education in the Greek language. The Council commissioned a report, and the reporter submitted to it a draft Declaration to be signed by Albania and formally communicated to the Council. The Declaration was signed by Albania and submitted to the Council in 1921, with basic similarities to but some differences from the typical clauses of the Minorities Treaties. The Council decided that the stipulations in the Declaration about minorities should be placed under the guarantee of the League from the date of the Declaration's ratification by Albania, which took place in 1922.

The first paragraph of Article 5 of the Declaration, at the core of the dispute that later developed, provided as follows:

> Albanian nationals who belong to racial, linguistic or religious minorities, will enjoy the same treatment and security in law and in fact as other Albanian nationals. In particular, they shall have an equal right to maintain, manage and control at their own expense or to establish in the future, charitable, religious and social institutions, schools and other educational establishments, with the right to use their own language and to exercise their religion freely therein.

Over the years, numerous changes in the laws and practices of the Albanian government led to questions about compliance with the Declaration. In 1933, the Albanian National Assembly modified Articles 206 and 207 of the Constitution, which had provided that 'Albanian subjects may found private schools' subject to government regulation, to state:

> The instruction and education of Albanian subjects are reserved to the State and

will be given in State schools. Primary education is compulsory for all Albanian nationals and will be given free of charge. Private schools of all categories at present in operation will be closed.

The new provisions affecting Greek-language and other private schools led to petitions and complaints to the League from groups including the Greek minority in Albania. Acting within its regular powers, the Council requested the Permanent Court of International Justice in 1935 to give an advisory opinion whether, in light of the 1921 Declaration as a whole, Albania was justified in its position that it had acted in conformity with 'the letter and the spirit' of Article 5 because (as Albania argued) its abolition of private schools was a general measure applicable to the majority as well as minority of Albanian nationals.

There follow excerpts from the opinion for the PCIJ and from a dissenting opinion. For present purposes, the Albanian Declaration can be understood as tantamount to a treaty. The opinions draw no relevant distinction between the two, and refer frequently to the Minorities Treaties to inform their interpretation of the Declaration.]

The contention of the Albanian Government is that the above-mentioned clause imposed no other obligation upon it, in educational matters, than to grant to its nationals belonging to racial, religious, or linguistic minorities a right equal to that possessed by other Albanian nationals. Once the latter have ceased to be entitled to have private schools, the former cannot claim to have them either. This conclusion, which is alleged to follow quite naturally from the wording of paragraph I of Article 5, would, it is contended, be in complete conformity with the meaning and spirit of the treaties for the protection of minorities, an essential characteristic of which is the full and complete equality of all nationals of the State, whether belonging to the majority or to the minority. On the other hand, it is argued, any interpretation which would compel Albania to respect the private minority schools would create a privilege in favour of the minority and run counter to the essential idea of the law governing minorities. Moreover, as the minority régime is an extraordinary régime constituting a derogation from the ordinary law, the text in question should, in case of doubt, be construed in the manner most favourable to the sovereignty of the Albanian State.

According to the explanations furnished to the Court by the Greek Government, the fundamental idea of Article 5 of the Declaration was on the contrary to guarantee freedom of education to the minorities by granting them the right to retain their existing schools and to establish others, if they desired; equality of treatment is, in the Greek Government's opinion, merely an adjunct to that right, and cannot impede the purpose in view, which is to ensure full and effectual liberty in matters of education. Moreover, the application of the same régime to a majority as to a minority, whose needs are quite different, would only create an apparent equality, whereas the Albanian Declaration, consistently with ordinary minority law, was designed to ensure a genuine and effective equality, not merely a formal equality.

. . .

As the Declaration of October 2nd, 1921, was designed to apply to Albania the general principles of the treaties for the protection of minorities, this is the point of view which, in the Court's opinion, must be adopted in construing paragraph 1 of Article 5 of the said Declaration.

The idea underlying the treaties for the protection of minorities is to secure for certain elements incorporated in a State, the population of which differs from them in race, language or religion, the possibility of living peaceably alongside that population and co-operating amicably with it, while at the same time preserving the characteristics which distinguish them from the majority, and satisfying the ensuing special needs.

In order to attain this object, two things were regarded as particularly necessary, and have formed the subject of provisions in these treaties.

The first is to ensure that nationals belonging to racial, religious or linguistic minorities shall be placed in every respect on a footing of perfect equality with the other nationals of the State.

The second is to ensure for the minority elements suitable means for the preservation of their racial peculiarities, their traditions and their national characteristics.

These two requirements are indeed closely interlocked, for there would be no true equality between a majority and a minority if the latter were deprived of its own institutions, and were consequently compelled to renounce that which constitutes the very essence of its being as a minority.

In common with the other treaties for the protection of minorities, and in particular with the Polish Treaty of June 28th, 1919, the text of which it follows, so far as concerns the question before the Court, very closely and almost literally, the Declaration of October 2nd, 1921, begins by laying down that no person shall be placed, in his relations with the Albanian authorities, in a position of inferiority by reason of his language, race or religion. . . .

. . .

In all these cases, the Declaration provides for a régime of legal equality for all persons mentioned in the clause; in fact no standard of comparison was indicated, and none was necessary, for at the same time that it provides for equality of treatment the Declaration specifies the rights which are to be enjoyed equally by all.

. . .

It has already been remarked that paragraph 1 of Article 5 consists of two sentences, the second of which is linked to the first by the words *in particular:* for a right apprehension of the second part, it is therefore first necessary to determine the meaning and the scope of the first sentence.

This sentence is worded as follows:

> Albanian nationals who belong to racial, linguistic or religious minorities, will enjoy the same treatment and security in law and in fact as other Albanian nationals.

The question that arises is what is meant by the *same treatment and security in law and in fact.*

It must be noted to begin with that the equality of all Albanian nationals before the law has already been stipulated in the widest terms in Article 4. As it is difficult to admit that Article 5 set out to repeat in different words what had already been said in Article 4, one is led to the conclusion that 'the same treatment and security in law and in fact' which is provided for in Article 5 is not the same notion as the equality before the law which is provided for in Article 4.
...

This special conception finds expression in the idea of an equality in fact which in Article 5 supplements equality in law. All Albanian nationals enjoy the equality in law stipulated in Article 4; on the other hand, the equality between members of the majority and of the minority must, according to the terms of Article 5, be an equality in law and in fact.

It is perhaps not easy to define the distinction between the notions of equality in fact and equality in law; nevertheless, it may be said that the former notion excludes the idea of a merely formal equality; that is indeed what the Court laid down in its Advisory Opinion of September 10th, 1923, concerning the case of the German settlers in Poland (Opinion No. 6), in which it said that:

> There must be equality in fact as well as ostensible legal equality in the sense of the absence of discrimination in the words of the law.

Equality in law precludes discrimination of any kind; whereas equality in fact may involve the necessity of different treatment in order to attain a result which establishes an equilibrium between different situations.

It is easy to imagine cases in which equality of treatment of the majority and of the minority, whose situation and requirements are different, would result in inequality in fact; treatment of this description would run counter to the first sentence of paragraph 1 of Article 5. The equality between members of the majority and of the minority must be an effective, genuine equality; that is the meaning of this provision.

The second sentence of this paragraph provides as follows:

> In particular they shall have an equal right to maintain, manage and control at their own expense or to establish in the future, charitable, religious and social institutions, schools and other educational establishments, with the right to use their own language and to exercise their religion freely therein.

This sentence of the paragraph being linked to the first by the words 'in particular', it is natural to conclude that it envisages a particularly important illustration of the application of the principle of identical treatment in law and in fact that is stipulated in the first sentence of the paragraph. For the institutions mentioned in the second sentence are indispensable to enable the minority to enjoy the same treatment as the majority, not only in law but also in fact. The abolition of these institutions, which alone can satisfy the special requirements of the minority groups, and their replacement by government institutions, would destroy this equality of treatment, for its effect would be to deprive the minority of the institutions appropriate to its needs, whereas the majority would continue to have them supplied in the institutions created by the State.

Far from creating a privilege in favour of the minority, as the Albanian Government avers, this stipulation ensures that the majority shall not be given a privileged situation as compared with the minority.

It may further be observed that, even disregarding the link between the two parts of paragraph 1 of Article 5, it seems difficult to maintain that the adjective 'equal', which qualifies the word 'right', has the effect of empowering the State to abolish the right, and thus to render the clause in question illusory; for, if so, the stipulation which confers so important a right on the members of the minority would not only add nothing to what has already been provided in Article 4, but it would become a weapon by which the State could deprive the minority régime of a great part of its practical value. It should be observed that in its Advisory Opinion of September 15th, 1923, concerning the question of the acquisition of Polish nationality (Opinion No. 7), the Court referred to the opinion which it had already expressed in Advisory Opinion No. 6 to the effect that 'an interpretation which would deprive the Minorities Treaty of a great part of its value is inadmissible'.

. . .

The idea embodied in the expression 'equal right' is that the right thus conferred on the members of the minority cannot in any case be inferior to the corresponding right of other Albanian nationals. In other words, the members of the minority must always enjoy the right stipulated in the Declaration, and, in addition, any more extensive rights which the State may accord to other nationals.

. . .

The construction which the Court places on paragraph 1 of Article 5 is confirmed by the history of this provision.

[Analysis of the proposals of the Greek Government and replies of the Albanian Government during the period of drafting of the Declaration omitted.]

The Court, having thus established that paragraph 1 of Article 5 of the Declaration, both according to its letter and its spirit, confers on Albanian nationals of racial, religious or linguistic minorities the right that is stipulated in the second sentence of that paragraph, finds it unnecessary to examine the subsidiary argument adduced by the Albanian Government to the effect that the text in question should in case of doubt be interpreted in the sense that is most favourable to the sovereignty of the State.

. . .

For these reasons,

The Court is of opinion,

by eight votes to three,

that the plea of the Albanian Government that, as the abolition of private schools in Albania constitutes a general measure applicable to the majority as well as to the minority, it is in conformity with the letter and spirit of the stipulations laid down in Article 5, first paragraph, of the Declaration of October 2nd, 1921, is not well founded.

. . .

DISSENTING OPINION BY SIR CECIL HURST, COUNT ROSTWOROWSKI, AND MR.
NEGULESCO

The undermentioned are unable to concur in the opinion rendered by the Court.
They can see no adequate reason for holding that the suppression of the private
schools effected in Albania in virtue of Articles 206 and 207 of the Constitution of
1933 is not in conformity with the Albanian Declaration of October 2nd, 1921.

. . .

The construction of the paragraph is clear and simple. The first sentence stipulates for the treatment and the security being the same for the members of the
minority as for the other Albanian nationals. The second provides that as regards
certain specified matters the members of the minority shall have an equal right.
The two sentences are linked together by the words 'In particular' (*notamment*).
These words show that the second sentence is a particular application of the
principle enunciated in the first. If the rights of the two categories under the first
sentence are to be the same, the equal right provided for in the second sentence
must indicate equality between the same two categories, viz. the members of the
minority and the other Albanian nationals. The second sentence is added because
the general principle laid down in the first sentence mentions only 'treatment and
security in law and in fact'—a phrase so indefinite that without further words of
precision it would be doubtful whether it covered the right to establish and maintain charitable, religious and social institutions and schools and other educational
establishments, but the particular application of the general principle of identity
of treatment and security remains governed by the dominating element of equality
as between the two categories.

The word 'equal' implies that the right so enjoyed must be equal in measure to
the right enjoyed by somebody else. '*They shall have an equal right*' means that the
right to be enjoyed by the people in question is to be equal in measure to that
enjoyed by some other group. A right which is unconditional and independent of
that enjoyed by other people cannot with accuracy be described as an 'equal right'.
'Equality' necessarily implies the existence of some extraneous criterion by reference to which the content is to be determined.

If the text of the first paragraph of Article 5 is considered alone, it does not
seem that there could be any doubt as to its interpretation. It is, however, laid
down in the Opinion from which the undersigned dissent that if the general
purpose of the minority treaties is borne in mind and also the contents of the
Albanian Declaration taken as a whole, it will be found that the 'equal right'
provided for in the first paragraph of Article 5 cannot mean a right of which the
extent is measured by that enjoyed by other Albanian nationals, and that it must
imply an unconditional right, a right of which the members of the minority
cannot be deprived.

. . .

As the opinion of the Court is based on the general purpose which the minorities treaties are presumed to have had in view and not on the text of Article 5,
paragraph 1, of the Albanian Declaration, it involves to some extent a departure

from the principles hitherto adopted by this Court in the interpretation of international instruments, that in presence of a clause which is reasonably clear the Court is bound to apply it as it stands without considering whether other provisions might with advantage have been added to it or substituted for it, and this even if the results following from it may in some particular hypothesis seem unsatisfactory.

. . .

Furthermore, the suppression of the private schools—even if it may prejudice to some appreciable extent the interests of a minority—does not oblige them to abandon an essential part of the characteristic life of a minority. In interpreting Article 5, the question whether the possession of particular institutions may or may not be *important* to the minority cannot constitute the decisive consideration. There is another consideration entitled to equal weight. That is the extent to which the monopoly of education may be of importance to the State. The two considerations cannot be weighed one against the other: Neither of them—in the absence of a clear stipulation to that effect—can provide an objective standard for determining which of them is to prevail.

International justice must proceed upon the footing of applying treaty stipulations impartially to the rights of the State and to the rights of the minority, and the method of doing so is to adhere to the terms of the treaty—as representing the common will of the parties—as closely as possible.

. . .

If the intention of the second sentence: 'In particular they [the minority] shall have an equal right . . .', had been that the right so given should be universal and unconditional, there is no reason why the draftsman should not have dealt with the right to establish institutions and schools in the earlier articles [of the Declaration that set up fixed and universal standards for all Albanians on matters like protection of life and free exercise of religion]. The draftsman should have dealt with the liberty to maintain schools and other institutions on lines similar to those governing the right to the free exercise of religion, which undoubtedly is conferred as a universal and unconditional right. Instead of doing so the right conferred upon the minority is an 'equal' right . . .

. . .

COMMENT ON FURTHER ASPECTS OF THE MINORITY TREATIES

The *Minority Schools in Albania* opinions address many current issues that remain vexing. The discussions about the nature of 'equality' and assurances thereof, in particular about equality 'in law' and 'in fact', inform contemporary human rights law as well as constitutional and legislative debates in many states with respect to issues like equal protection and affirmative action. The question whether the Declaration and the Court's opinion recognized only the rights of individual members of a minority, or also the right of the minority itself as a collective or group, remains one that vexes the discussion of minority rights. Protection aiming at the cultural survival of minorities continues to raise the troubling issue of which types of minorities merit such protection, and whether assurance of equal protection (with the majority) is sufficient for the purpose.

But if the issues debated within the minorities regime remain, the regime itself has disappeared. Over the next two decades, its norms were roundly violated. Its international machinery within the League of Nations proved to be ineffectual, partly for the same lack of political will that led to other disastrous events in the interwar period. The failure of the regime was tragic in its consequences. Its noble purposes were distorted or blunted or ignored as Europe of the 1930s moved toward the horrors of the Second World War, the Holocaust and the brutalization and slaughter of so many other minorities. The settlements, norms and institutions after the Second World War designed to prevent further savagery against minorities stressed different principles and created radically different institutions, principally within the universal human rights system built in and around the United Nations.

Nonetheless, it is important to recognize the distinctive dilemmas and advances as well as the shortcomings of this minorities regime. Sovereignty in the sense of a state's (absolute) internal control over its own citizens was to some extent eroded. Treaties-declarations subjected aspects of the state's treatment of its own citizens to international law and international processes—that is, citizens who were members of a racial, religious or linguistic minority. Although the norms were expressed in bilateral treaties or declarations, the regime took on a multilateral aspect through its incorporation into the League as well as through the large number of nearly simultaneous treaties and declarations. The whole scheme was informed by multilateral planning, in contrast with the centuries-old examples of sporadic bilateral treaties protecting (usually religious) minorities. Minorities became a matter of formal international concern, the treaties-declarations fragmented the state into different sections of its citizens, and international law reached beyond the law of state responsibility to protect some of a state's own citizens.

The precise issue of the *Minority Schools in Albania* case is now addressed in the 1960 UNESCO Convention against Discrimination in Education. Article 5(1)(c) recognizes the 'right of members of national minorities to carry on their own educational activities, including the maintenance of schools and, depending on the educational policy of each State, the use or the teaching of their own language... '. The article subjects this right to several provisos. For example, its exercise should not prevent minorities from understanding the culture and language of the larger community as well, or prejudice national sovereignty.

COMMENT ON TREATIES

Treaties have inevitably figured in this chapter's prior discussions—for example, the bilateral treaties whose relevance to custom was debated in *The Paquete Habana,* or the convention underlying the *Chattin* litigation. As noted above, the Albanian Declaration can be understood for present purposes as tantamount to a treaty, for the opinions do not distinguish between the two and refer to the

Minorities Treaties to advance their interpretation of the Declaration. Hence this Comment, and particularly its sections on issues like interpretation, is here relevant.

In Article 38(1) of the Statute of the International Court of Justice, the Court is instructed in clause (a) to apply 'international conventions, whether general or particular, establishing rules expressly recognized by the contesting states'. Treaties thus head the list. They have become the primary expression of international law and, particularly when multilateral, the most effective if not the only path toward international regulation of many contemporary problems. Multilateral treaties have been the principal means for development of the human rights movement. One striking advantage of treaties over custom should be noted. Only treaties can create, and define the powers or jurisdiction of, international institutions in which state parties participate and to which they may owe duties.

The terminology for this voluminous and diverse body of international law varies. International agreements are referred to as pacts, protocols (generally supplemental to another agreement), covenants, conventions, charters, exchanges of notes and concordats (agreements between a nation and the Holy See), as well as treaties—terms that are more or less interchangeable in legal significance. Within the internal law of some countries such as the United States, the term 'treaty' (as contrasted, say, with international executive agreement) has a particular constitutional significance.

Consider the different purposes which treaties serve. Some reaching critical national interests have a basic political character: alliances, peace settlements, control of atomic weapons. Others, while less politically charged, also involve relationships between governments and affect private parties only indirectly: agreements on foreign aid, cooperation in the provision of governmental services such as the mails. But treaties often have a direct and specific impact upon private parties. For many decades, tariff accords, income tax conventions, and treaties of friendship, commerce and navigation have determined the conditions under which the nationals or residents of one signatory can export to, or engage in business activities within, the other signatory's territory. Most significant for this book's purposes, human rights treaties have sought to extend protection to all persons against governmental abuse.

Domestic analogies to the treaty help to portray its distinctive character: contract and legislation. Some treaties settling particular disputes resemble an accord and satisfaction under contract law: an agreement over boundaries, an agreement to pay a stated sum as compensation for injury to the receiving nation or its nationals. Others are closer in character to private contracts of continuing significance or to domestic legislation for they regulate recurrent problems by defining rights and obligations of the parties and their nationals: agreements over rules of navigation, income taxation, or the enforcement of foreign-country judgments. The term 'international legislation' to describe treaties has therefor gained some currency, particularly with respect to multilateral treaties such as those on human rights that impose rules on states intended to regulate their conduct. The Albanian Declaration and the many bilateral treaties that formed part of the minorities regime of the period come within this description.

Nonetheless, domestic legislation differs in several critical respects from the characteristic treaty. A statute is generally enacted by the majority of a legislature and binds all members of the relevant society. Even changes in a constitution, which usually require approval by the legislature and other institutions or groups, can be accomplished over substantial dissent. The ordinary treaty, on the other hand, is a consensual arrangement. With few exceptions, such as Article 2(6) of the UN Charter, it purports to bind or benefit only parties. Alteration of its terms by one state party generally requires the consent of all.

Consider the institution of contract. Like the treaty, a contract can be said to make or create law between the parties—for within the facilitative framework of governing law but subject to that law's mandatory norms and constraints, courts recognize and enforce contract-created duties. The treaty shares a contract's consensual basis, but treaty law lacks the breadth and relative inclusiveness of a national body of contract law. It has preserved a certain Roman law flavor ('*pacta sunt servanda*', '*rebus sic stantibus*') acquired during the long period from the Renaissance to the nineteenth century, when continental European scholars dominated the field. But treaty law often reflects the diversity of approaches to domestic contract law that lawyers bring to the topic, a diversity that is particularly striking on issues of treaty interpretation.

Duties Imposed by Treaty Law

Whatever its purpose or character, the international agreement is generally recognized from the perspective of international law as an authoritative starting point for legal reasoning about any dispute to which it is relevant. The maxim *pacta sunt servanda* is at the core of treaty law. It embodies a widespread recognition that commitments publicly, formally and (more or less) voluntarily made by a nation should be honoured. As stated in Article 26 of the Vienna Convention on the Law of Treaties (see below): 'Every treaty in force is binding upon the parties to it and must be performed by them in good faith'.

Whatever the jurisprudential or philosophical bases for this norm, one can readily perceive the practical reasons for and the national interests served by adherence to the principle that *pacta sunt servanda*. The treaty represents one of the most effective means for bringing some order to relationships among states or their nationals, and for the systematic development of new principles responsive to the changing needs of the international community. It is the prime legal form through which that community can realize some degree of stability and predictability, and seek to institutionalize ideals like peaceful settlement of disputes and protection of human rights.

Acceptance of the primary role of the treaty does not, however, mean that a problem between two countries is adequately solved from the perspective of legal ordering simply by execution of a treaty with satisfactory provisions. A body of law has necessarily developed to deal with questions analogous to those addressed by domestic contract law—for example, formation of a treaty, its interpretation and performance, remedies for breach, and amendment or termination. But that body of law is often fragmentary and vague, reflecting the scarcity of decisions of international tribunals and the political tensions which some aspects of treaty law reflect.

There have been recurrent efforts to remedy this situation through more or less creative codification of the law of treaties. The contemporary authoritative text grows out of a United Nations Conference on the Law of Treaties that adopted in 1969 the Vienna Convention on the Law of Treaties, UN Doc, A/CONF, 39/27, 63 A.J.I.L. 875 (1969). That Convention became effective in 1980 and (as of March 2000) had been ratified by 90 states from all regions of the world. Excerpts from it appear in the Annex on Documents. For reasons stemming largely from tensions between the Executive and the Congress over authority over different types of international agreements, the United States has not ratified the Vienna Convention. Nonetheless, in its provisions on international agreements the *Restatement (Third), Foreign Relations Law of the United States* (1987) 'accepts the Vienna Convention as, in general, constituting a codification of the customary international law governing international agreements, and therefore as foreign relations law of the United States. . . .' Vol. I, p. 145.

Treaty Formation

A treaty is formed by the express consent of its parties. Although there are no precise requirements for execution or form, certain procedures have become standard. By choice of the parties, or in order to comply with the internal rules of a signatory country that are considered at pp. 999–1029 *infra*, it may be necessary to postpone the effectiveness of the agreement until a national legislative body has approved it and national executive authorities have ratified it. Instruments of ratification for bilateral agreements are then exchanged. In the case of multilateral treaties, such instruments are deposited with the national government or international organization that has been designated as the custodian of the authentic text and of all other instruments relating to the treaty, including subsequent adhesions by nations that were not among the original signatories. Thereafter a treaty will generally be proclaimed or promulgated by the executive in each country.

Consent

Given the established principle that treaties are consensual, what rules prevail as to the character of that consent? Do domestic law contract principles about the effect of duress carry over to the international field?

In a domestic legal system, a party cannot enforce a contract which was signed by a defendant at gunpoint. One could argue that victorious nations cannot assert rights under a peace treaty obtained by a whole army. It is not surprising that the large powers are reluctant to recognize that such forms of duress can invalidate a treaty. If duress were a defence, it would be critical to define its contours, for many treaties result from various forms of military, political or economic pressure. The paucity of and doubts about international institutions with authority to develop answers to such questions underscore the reluctance to open treaties to challenge on these grounds.

The different approaches of the victorious Western powers towards the defeated nations in the First World War and the Second World War reflect the growing awareness that treaties, whatever their 'legal' character, will survive only insofar as they bring satisfactory solutions to developing political, economic and social problems. Even from a legal perspective, the advent of the UN Charter after the Second World War, with its explicit rejection of war as a permitted instrument of national policy, may herald some evolution of legal doctrine in this field. Article 52 of the Vienna Convention states: 'A treaty is void if its conclusion has been procured by the threat or use of force in violation of the principles of international law embodied in the Charter of the United Nations'. Attempts at Vienna to broaden the scope of coercion to include economic duress failed, although they resulted in a declaration condemning the use of such practices.

Reservations

Problems of consent that have no precise parallel in national contract law arise in connection with reservations to treaties, i.e., unilateral statements made by a state accepting a treaty 'whereby it purports to exclude, or vary the legal effect of certain provisions of the treaty in their application to a state' (Article 2(1)(d) of the Vienna Convention). With bilateral treaties, no conceptual difficulties arise: ratification with reservations amounts to a counteroffer; the other state may accept (or reject) explicitly or may be held to have tacitly accepted it by proceeding with its ratification process or with compliance with the treaty. With multilateral treaties the problems may be quite complex. The traditional rule said that acceptance by all parties was required. The expanding number of states has required more flexibility.

Given the increased number of reservations, some of great significance, that many states are attaching to their ratifications of basic human rights treaties, questions about those reservations' validity under general treaty law or under the terms of a specific treaty have become matters of high concern within the human rights movement. See pp. 439–441 and 1043–1044, *infra*.

Violations of and Changes in Treaties

Violation of a treaty may lead to diplomatic protests and a claim before an international tribunal. But primarily because of the limited and qualified consents of nations to the jurisdiction of international tribunals, the offended party will usually resort to other measures. In a national system of contract law, well developed rules govern such measures. They may distinguish between a minor breach not authorizing the injured party to terminate its own performance, and a material breach providing justification for such a move. Article 60 of the Vienna Convention provides that a material breach (as defined) of a bilateral treaty entitles the other party to terminate the treaty or suspend its performance thereunder. These rules necessarily grow more complex for multilateral treaties. For reasons that Chapters 2 and 3 describe, they may have little relevance for the ways that states respond to violations of human rights treaty norms by other states.

Amendments raise additional problems. The treaty's contractual aspect suggests that the consent of all parties is necessary. Parties may however agree in advance (see Article 108 of the UN Charter) to be bound with respect to certain matters by the vote of a specified number. Such provisions in a multilateral treaty bring it closer in character to national legislation. They may be limited to changes which do not impose new obligations upon a dissenting party, although a state antagonistic to an amendment could generally withdraw. Absent some such provisions, a treaty may aggravate rather than resolve a fundamental problem of international law, how to achieve in a peaceful manner the changes in existing arrangements that are needed to adapt them to developing political, social or economic conditions.

One of the most contentious issues in treaty law is whether the emergence of conditions that were unforeseeable or unforeseen at the time of the treaty's conclusion terminates or modifies a party's obligation to perform. This problem borders the subject of treaty interpretation, considered *infra*, since it is often described as a question whether an implied condition or an escape clause, called the *clausula rebus sic stantibus*, should be read into a treaty. Mature municipal legal systems have developed rules for handling situations where the performance of one party is rendered impossible or useless by intervening conditions. 'Impossibility', 'frustration', 'force majeure', and 'implied conditions' are the concepts used in Anglo-American law.

At the international level, possibilities of changes in conditions that upset assumptions underlying an agreement are enhanced by the long duration of many treaties, the difficulty in amending them and the rapid political, economic and social vicissitudes in modern times. Thus nations, including the United States, have occasionally used *rebus sic stantibus* as the basis for declaring treaties no longer effective. Article 62 of the Vienna Convention states that a 'fundamental change of circumstances' which was not foreseen by the parties may not be invoked as a ground for terminating a treaty unless '(a) the existence of those circumstances constituted an essential basis of the consent of the parties to transform the extent of obligations still to be performed under the treaty'.

Treaty Interpretation

There is no shortcut to a reliable sense of how a given treaty will be construed. Even immersion in a mass of diplomatic correspondence and cases would not develop such a skill. In view of the variety of treaties and of approaches to their interpretation, such learning would more likely shed light on the possibilities than provide a certain answer to any given question.

One obstacle to helpful generalization about treaty interpretation is the variety of purposes which treaties serve. Different approaches are advisable for treaties that lay down rules for a long or indefinite period, in contrast with those settling past disputes. The long-term treaty must benefit from a certain flexibility and room for development if it is to survive changes in circumstances and relations between the parties. Changes in conditions like those that make *rebus sic stantibus* an attractive doctrine may lead a court or executive official to interpret a treaty flexibly so as to give it a sensible application to new circumstances.

The very style of a treaty will influence the approach of an official charged with interpreting it. Certain categories, such as income tax conventions, lend themselves to a detailed draftsmanship that will often be impractical and undesirable in a constitutional document such as the UN Charter. Conventions such as those relating to human rights necessarily use broad and abstract terms and standards like fairness or *ordre public.*

In a national legal system, lawyers and courts can seek to give specific content to general statutory standards by resort to a common law background or to a constitutional tradition, indeed by reference to the entire legal culture and society within which these standards become operative. Interpretation can reach towards generally understood practices, customs or purposes—even if the lawyer or judge may encounter choice and contradiction in practices and purposes rather than consensus. It may be far more difficult to interpret treaty standards of comparable generality that embrace an international community with diverse national traditions. The problem becomes acute in multilateral treaties among nations from different regions and cultures, for one method of securing agreement to a treaty in the first instance may be to conceal rather than resolve differences through resort to general standards. In addition, the difficulty in achieving agreement over amendments to long-continuing multilateral treaties may encourage their draftsmen to express a 'consensus' through norms of a general character, which have a better chance of surviving and carrying their broad purposes through changed conditions among the signatories.

Maxims similar to those found in domestic fields exist for treaties as well. The Vienna Convention contains several. Article 31 provides that a 'treaty shall be interpreted in good faith in accordance with the ordinary meaning to be given to the terms of the treaty in their context and in the light of its object and purpose'. Article 32 goes on to add that recourse may be had to supplementary means if Article 31 interpretation produces a meaning that is 'ambiguous or obscure' or an outcome 'manifestly absurd or unreasonable'.

One way to build a framework for construing treaties is to consider the continuum which lies between 'strict' interpretation according to the 'plain meaning' of the treaty, and interpretation according to the interpreter's view of the best means of implementing the purposes or realizing the principles expressed by the treaty. Of course both extremes of the spectrum are untenanted. One cannot wholly ignore the treaty's words, nor can one always find an unambiguous and relevant text that resolves the immediate issue.

Part of the difficulty is that treaties may be drafted in several languages. If domestic courts deem it unwise to 'make a fortress out of the dictionary', it would seem particularly unwise when dictionaries in several languages (and in different legal systems according different meanings to linguistically similar terms) must be resorted to. Sometimes corresponding words in the different versions may shed more light on the intended meaning; at other times, they are plainly inconsistent.

Reliance upon literal construction or 'strict' interpretation may however be an attractive method or technique to an international tribunal that is sensitive to its weak political foundation. It may be tempted to take refuge in the position that its decision is the ineluctable outcome of the drafter's intention expressed in clear text, and not a choice arrived at on the basis of the tribunal's understanding of policy considerations or relevant principles that may resolve a dispute over interpretation. Reliance on legislative history or *travaux préparatoires* can achieve the same result of placing responsibility on the drafters. The charge of 'judicial legislation' evokes strong reactions in the United States; it inevitably influences judges of international tribunals and heightens the temptation to take refuge in the dictionary.

Treaties and International Organizations

In addition to setting forth specific rules which are to govern the conduct of the parties, a treaty may establish machinery for the development of further norms. This applies particularly to multilateral agreements, which may be specialized or general in subject matter, regional or worldwide in scope. At its simplest, such a treaty may provide for periodic meetings at which the signatories' representatives will exchange views. From such discussions the representatives may go on to negotiate new agreements, for the presence of delegates from several countries makes possible the adjustment at one time of interlocking problems that affect each of them. At the next level, the treaty may authorize the parties' delegates to pass advisory or recommendatory resolutions. Such meetings can produce draft conventions which will be submitted to the members for consideration and possible ratification.

In more advanced arrangements the structure created by treaty will include organs or agencies exercising stated powers. Sometimes they are authorized to mediate or put pressure on disputants to arbitrate. Sometimes their authority extends to issuing non-binding declarations on relevant issues and recommendatory resolutions. Such powers can go further and include competence to issue binding interpretations of the treaty as well as regulations, directives or resolutions binding upon the parties (a limited legislative function), or to apply the treaty to specific situations in an authoritative way (a limited judicial function). Finally, the treaty may give a stated majority of the members the power to amend the agreement with respect to some or all provisions so as to bind all parties.

At some point in this progression we find that the treaty has created an international 'organization'. The growth of a permanent staff maintaining a continuous interim activity and the acquisition of a budget and buildings signal the emergence of a distinct entity with some life of its own. The members may endow this entity with a juridical personality and empower it to make contracts or treaties with private parties or governments and be a party to lawsuits. They may also confer upon the organization and its officials various immunities.

Such international organizations' concerns and functions now include diverse fields like peacekeeping, trade and monetary matters, fisheries and other regimes of the high seas, environmental protection, the regulation of basic commodities, and protection of human rights. In all such cases, the issues to be addressed do not lend themselves to adequate resolution through the development of customary rules, through a network of bilateral treaties, or through multilateral treaties that contain only substantive rules without institutional mechanisms for their promotion, implementation or enforcement. Such organizations may be universal or regional. Issues of human rights, for example, figure pervasively in the work of the United Nations and fully occupy some organs within the UN such as the Commission on Human Rights (Chapter 8). There are also regional human rights organizations in Europe, the Americas and Africa (Chapter 10).

QUESTIONS

1. The types of protections or assurances given by treaty to a distinctive group within a larger polity can be categorized in various ways, including the following. The assurance can be *absolute* (fixed, unconditional) or *contingent* (dependent on some reference group). For example, treaties of commerce between two states may reciprocally grant to citizens of each state the right to reside (for business purposes) and do business (as aliens) in the other state. Some assurances in such treaties will be absolute—for example, citizens of each state are given the right to buy or lease real property for residential purposes in the other state. Other assurances will be contingent—for example, citizens of each state are given the right to organize a corporation and qualify to do business in the other state on the same terms as citizens of that other state (so called 'national treatment'). Within this framework, how would you characterize the rights given to members of a designated minority by the Albanian Declaration? Do the majority and dissenting opinions differ about how to characterize them?

2. If you were a member of the Greek-speaking Christian minority, would you have been content with a Declaration that contained no more than a general equal protection clause? If not, why not? How would you justify your argument for more protection?

3. Would Albania have been justified in imposing some control on the Greek schools, such as defining subjects to be taught and censoring teaching materials that, say, urged independence from Albania?

4. Why do the opinions refer to this minorities regime as 'extraordinary'? In what respects does it depart from classical conceptions of international law, or differ from the law of state responsibility?

5. Does a treaty necessarily solve the problems of the method to be employed in 'identifying' and 'applying' international law that were present in *The Paquete Habana* and *Chattin*? How would you characterize the methodologies or conceptions of interpretation that the majority and dissenting opinions reveal? How do those approaches to interpretation differ with respect to their basic assumptions about the relation between the minorities regime and general international law?

6. Consider how close to or distant from the minorities regime Article 27 of the International Covenant on Civil and Political Rights appears on its face to be. It provides:

> In those States in which ethnic, religious or linguistic minorities exist, persons belonging to such minorities shall not be denied the right, in community with the other members of their group, to enjoy their own culture, to profess and practise their own religion, or to use their own language.

ADDITIONAL READING

On the minorities regime see N. Berman, ' "But the Alternative is Despair": European Nationalism and the Modernist Renewal of International Law', 106 Harv. L. Rev. 1792 (1993); P. Thornberry, *International Law and the Rights of Minorities*; and P. de Azcarate, *The League of Nations and National Minorities* (1945). On treaty law see: B. Simma, 'Human Rights and General International Law: A Comparative Analysis', in 4 Collected Courses of the Academy of European Law 1 (1995); and P. Reuter, *Introduction to the Law of Treaties* (3rd edn 1995).

D. JUDGMENT AT NUREMBERG

COMMENT ON THE NUREMBERG TRIAL

The trial at Nuremberg in 1945–1946 of major war criminals among the Axis powers, dominantly Nazi party leaders and military officials, gave the nascent human rights movement a powerful impulse. The UN Charter that became effective in 1945 included a few broad human rights provisions. But they were more programmatic than operational, more a programme to be realized by states over time than a system in place for application to states. Nuremberg, on the other hand, was concrete and applied: prosecutions, convictions, punishment. The prosecution and the Judgment of the International Military Tribunal in this initial, weighty trial for massive crimes committed during the war years were based on concepts and norms, some of which had deep roots in international law and some of which represented a significant development of that law that opened the path toward the later formulation of fundamental human rights norms.

The striking aspect of Nuremberg was that the trial and Judgment applied international law doctrines and concepts to impose criminal punishment on individuals for their commission of any of the three types of crimes under international law that are described below. The notion of crimes against the law of nations for which violators bore an individual criminal responsibility was itself an older one, but it had operated in a restricted field. As customary international law developed from the time of Grotius, certain conduct came to be considered a violation of the law of nations—in effect, a universal crime. Piracy on the high seas was long the classic example of this limited category of crimes. Given the common interest of all nations in protecting navigation against interference on the high seas outside the territory of any state, it was considered appropriate for the state apprehending a pirate to prosecute in its own courts. Since there was no international criminal tribunal, prosecution in a state court was the only means of judicial enforcement. To the extent that the state courts sought to apply the customary international law defining the crime of piracy, either directly or as it had become absorbed into national legislation, the choice of forum became less significant, for state courts everywhere were in theory applying the same law.

One specialized field, the humanitarian laws of war, had long included rules regulating the conduct of war, the so-called *jus in bello*. This body of law imposed sanctions against combatants who committed serious violations of the restrictive rules. Such application of the laws of war, and its foundation in customary norms and in treaties, figure in the Judgment, *infra*. But the concept of individual criminal responsibility was not systematically developed. It achieved a new prominence and a clearer definition after the Nuremberg Judgment, primarily through the Geneva Conventions of 1949 and their 1977 Protocols (noted at p. 67, *supra*). Gradually other types of conduct have been added to this small list of individual crimes under international law—for example, slave trading long prior to Nuremberg and genocide thereafter. The 1990s saw two large advances in such respects on the Geneva Conventions: the provisions for the International Criminal Tribunals for the former Yugoslavia and for Rwanda, and the completion of a draft treaty for a permanent International Criminal Court, all discussed in Chapter 14.

As the Second World War came to an end, the Allied powers held several conferences to determine what policies they should follow towards the Germans responsible for the war and for the systematic barbarity and annihilation of the period. The wartime destruction and civilian losses were known. The nature and extent of the Holocaust were first becoming widely known. These conferences culminated in the (United States, USSR, Britain, France) London Agreement of August 8, 1945, 59 Stat. 1544, E.A.S. No. 472, in which the parties determined to constitute 'an International Military Tribunal for the trial of war criminals'. The Charter annexed to the Agreement provided for the composition and basic procedures of the Tribunal and stated the criminal provisions for the trials in its three critical articles:

Article 6.
The Tribunal established by the Agreement referred to in Article 1 hereof for the trial and punishment of the major war criminals of the European Axis countries shall have the power to try and punish persons who, acting in the interests of the European Axis countries, whether as individuals or as members of organizations, committed any of the following crimes.

The following acts, or any of them, are crimes coming within the jurisdiction of the Tribunal for which there shall be individual responsibility:

(a) *Crimes Against Peace*: namely, planning, preparation, initiation or waging of a war of aggression, or a war in violation of international treaties, agreements or assurances, or participation in a common plan or conspiracy for the accomplishment of any of the foregoing;

(b) *War Crimes*: namely, violations of the laws or customs of war. Such violations shall include, but not be limited to, murder, ill-treatment or deportation to slave labor or for any other purpose of civilian population of or in occupied territory, murder or ill-treatment of prisoners of war or persons on the seas, killing of hostages, plunder of public or private property, wanton destruction of cities, towns or villages, or devastation not justified by military necessity;

(c) *Crimes Against Humanity*: namely, murder, extermination, enslavement, deportation, and other inhumane acts committed against any civilian population, before or during the war, or persecutions on political, racial or religious grounds in execution of or in connection with any crime within the jurisdiction of the Tribunal, whether or not in violation of the domestic law of the country where perpetrated.

Leaders, organizers, instigators and accomplices participating in the formulation or execution of a common plan or conspiracy to commit any of the foregoing crimes are responsible for all acts performed by any persons in execution of such plan.

Article 7.

The official position of defendants, whether as Heads of State or responsible officials in Government Departments, shall not be considered as freeing them from responsibility or mitigating punishment.

Article 8.

The fact that the Defendant acted pursuant to order of his Government or of a superior shall not free him from responsibility, but may be considered in mitigation of punishment if the Tribunal determines that justice so requires.

Note the innovative character of these provisions. Although the Tribunal of four judges (one from each of the major Allied Powers) was restricted to the four victorious powers creating it, nonetheless the Tribunal had this international character in its formation and composition, and to that extent was radically different from the national military courts before which the laws of war had to that time generally been enforced. At the core of the Charter lay the concept of international crimes for which there would be 'individual responsibility', a sharp departure from the then-existing customary law or conventions which stressed the duties of (and sometimes sanctions against) states. Moreover, in defining crimes within the Tribunal's jurisdiction, the Charter went beyond the traditional 'war crimes' (paragraph (b) of Article 6) in two ways.

First, the Charter included the war-related 'crimes against peace'—so-called *jus ad bellum*, in contrast with the category of war crimes or *jus in bello*. International law had for a long time been innocent of such a concept. After a slow departure during the post-Reformation period from earlier distinctions of philosophers, theologians, and writers on international law between 'just' and 'unjust' wars, the European nations moved towards a conception of war as an instrument of national policy, much like any other, to be legally regulated only with respect to *jus in bello*, the manner of its conduct. The Covenant of the League of Nations did not frontally challenge this principle, although it attempted to control aggression through collective decisions of the League. The interwar period witnessed some fortification of the principles later articulated in the Nuremberg Charter, primarily through the Kellogg-Briand pact of 1927 that is referred to in the Judgment. Today the UN Charter requires members (Article 2(4)) to 'refrain in their international relations from the threat or use of force' against other states, while providing (Article 51) that nothing shall impair 'the inherent right of individual or collective self-defense if an armed attack occurs against a Member . . . '. When viewed in conjunction with the Nuremberg Charter, those provisions suggest the contemporary effort to distinguish not between 'just' and 'unjust' wars but between the permitted 'self-defence' and the forbidden 'aggression'—the word used in defining 'crimes against peace' in Article 6(a) of that Charter.

Second, Article 6(c) represented an important innovation. There were few precedents for use of the phrase 'crimes against humanity' as part of a description of international law, and its content was correspondingly indeterminate. On its face, paragraph (c) might have been read to include the entire programme of the Nazi government to exterminate Jews and other civilian groups, in and outside Germany, whether 'before or during the war', and thus to include not only the Holocaust but also the planning for and early persecution of Jews and other groups preceding the Holocaust. Moreover, that paragraph appeared to bring within its scope the persecution or annihilation by Germany of Jews who were German nationals as well as those who were aliens. This would represent a great advance on the international law of state responsibility to aliens as described at pp. 81–92, *supra*. Note, however, how the Judgment of the Tribunal interpreted Article 6(c) with respect to these observations.

In other respects as well, the concept of 'crimes against humanity', even in this early formulation, developed the earlier international law. War crimes were committed by combatants; crimes against humanity could be committed by civilians as well. War crimes could cover discrete as well as systematic action by a combatant— an isolated murder of a civilian by a combatant as well a systematic policy of wanton destruction of towns. Crimes against humanity were directed primarily to planned conduct, to systematic conduct.

In defining the charges against the major Nazi leaders tried at Nuremberg and its successor tribunals, the Allied powers took care to exclude those types of conduct which had not been understood to violate existing custom or conventions and in which they themselves had engaged—for example, the massive bombing of cities with necessarily high tolls of civilians that were indeed aimed at demoralization of the enemy.

JUDGMENT OF NUREMBERG TRIBUNAL
International Military Tribunal, Nuremberg (1946)
41 Am.J.Int.L. 172 (1947)

. . .

[*The Law of the Charter*]

The jurisdiction of the Tribunal is defined in the [London] Agreement and Charter, and the crimes coming within the jurisdiction of the Tribunal, for which there shall be individual responsibility, are set out in Article 6. The law of the Charter is decisive, and binding upon the Tribunal.

The making of the Charter was the exercise of the sovereign legislative power by the countries to which the German Reich unconditionally surrendered; and the undoubted right of these countries to legislate for the occupied territories has been recognized by the civilized world. The Charter is not an arbitrary exercise of power on the part of the victorious Nations, but in the view of the Tribunal, as will be shown, it is the expression of international law existing at the time of its creation; and to that extent is itself a contribution to international law.

... With regard to the constitution of the Court, all that the defendants are entitled to ask is to receive a fair trial on the facts and law.

The Charter makes the planning or waging of a war of aggression or a war in violation of international treaties a crime; and it is therefore not strictly necessary to consider whether and to what extent aggressive war was a crime before the execution of the London Agreement. But in view of the great importance of the questions of law involved, the Tribunal has heard full argument from the Prosecution and the Defence, and will express its view on the matter.

It was urged on behalf of the defendants that a fundamental principle of all law—international and domestic—is that there can be no punishment of crime without a pre-existing law. '*Nullum crimen sine lege, nulla poena sine lege.*' It was submitted that *ex post facto* punishment is abhorrent to the law of all civilized nations, that no sovereign power had made aggressive war a crime at the time that the alleged criminal acts were committed, that no statute had defined aggressive war, that no penalty had been fixed for its commission, and no court had been created to try and punish offenders.

In the first place, it is to be observed that the maxim *nullum crimen sine lege* is not a limitation of sovereignty, but is in general a principle of justice. To assert that it is unjust to punish those who in defiance of treaties and assurances have attacked neighboring states without warning is obviously untrue, for in such circumstances the attacker must know that he is doing wrong, and so far from it being unjust to punish him, it would be unjust if his wrong were allowed to go unpunished. . . .

This view is strongly reinforced by a consideration of the state of international law in 1939, so far as aggressive war is concerned. The General Treaty for the Renunciation of War of 27 August 1928, more generally known as the Pact of Paris or the Kellogg-Briand Pact, was binding on 63 nations, including Germany, Italy and Japan at the outbreak of war in 1939. . . .

... The nations who signed the Pact or adhered to it unconditionally condemned recourse to war for the future as an instrument of policy, and expressly renounced it. After the signing of the Pact, any nation resorting to war as an instrument of national policy breaks the Pact. In the opinion of the Tribunal, the solemn renunciation of war as an instrument of national policy necessarily involves the proposition that such a war is illegal in international law; and that those who plan and wage such a war, with its inevitable and terrible consequences, are committing a crime in so doing. War for the solution of international controversies undertaken as an instrument of national policy certainly includes a war of aggression, and such a war is therefore outlawed by the Pact. . . .

... The Hague Convention of 1907 prohibited resort to certain methods of waging war. These included the inhumane treatment of prisoners, the employment of poisoned weapons, the improper use of flags of true, and similar matters. Many of these prohibitions had been enforced long before the date of the Convention; but since 1907 they have certainly been crimes, punishable as offenses against the law of war; yet the Hague Convention nowhere designates such practices as criminal, nor is any sentence prescribed, nor any mention made of a court to try and punish offenders. For many years past, however, military tribunals have tried and punished individuals guilty of violating the rules of land warfare laid down by this Convention. In the opinion of the Tribunal, those who wage aggressive war are doing that which is equally illegal, and of much greater moment than a breach of one of the rules of the Hague Convention. . . . The law of war is to be found not only in treaties, but in the customs and practices of states which gradually obtained universal recognition, and from the general principles of justice applied by jurists and practised by military courts. This law is not static, but by continual adaptation follows the needs of a changing world. Indeed, in many cases treaties do no more than express and define for more accurate reference the principles of law already existing.

. . .

All these expressions of opinion, and others that could be cited, so solemnly made, reinforce the construction which the Tribunal placed upon the Pact of Paris, that resort to a war of aggression is not merely illegal, but is criminal. The prohibition of aggressive war demanded by the conscience of the world, finds its expression in the series of pacts and treaties to which the Tribunal has just referred.

. . .

. . . That international law imposes duties and liabilities upon individuals as well as upon States has long been recognized. . . . Crimes against international law are committed by men, not by abstract entities, and only by punishing individuals who commit such crimes can the provisions of international law be enforced.

. . .

The authors of these acts cannot shelter themselves behind their official position in order to be freed from punishment in appropriate proceedings. Article 7 of the Charter expressly declares:

> The official position of Defendants, whether as heads of State, or responsible officials in Government departments, shall not be considered as freeing them from responsibility, or mitigating punishment.

On the other hand the very essence of the Charter is that individuals have international duties which transcend the national obligations of obedience imposed by the individual state. He who violates the laws of war cannot obtain immunity while acting in pursuance of the authority of the state if the state in authorizing action moves outside its competence under international law.

It was also submitted on behalf of most of these defendants that in doing what they did they were acting under the orders of Hitler, and therefore cannot be held responsible for the acts committed by them in carrying out these orders. The Charter specifically provides in Article 8:

> The fact that the Defendant acted pursuant to order of his Government or of a superior shall not free him from responsibility, but may be considered in mitigation of punishment.

The provisions of this article are in conformity with the law of all nations. That a soldier was ordered to kill or torture in violation of the international law of war has never been recognized as a defense to such acts of brutality, though, as the Charter here provides, the order may be urged in mitigation of the punishment. The true test, which is found in varying degrees in the criminal law of most nations, is not the existence of the order, but whether moral choice was in fact possible.

. . .

War Crimes and Crimes against Humanity

. . . War Crimes were committed on a vast scale, never before seen in the history of war. They were perpetrated in all the countries occupied by Germany, and on the High Seas, and were attended by every conceivable circumstance of cruelty and horror. There can be no doubt that the majority of them arose from the Nazi conception of 'total war', with which the aggressive wars were waged. For in this conception of 'total war,' the moral ideas underlying the conventions which seek to make war more humane are no longer regarded as having force or validity. Everything is made subordinate to the overmastering dictates of war. Rules, regulations, assurances, and treaties all alike are of no moment; and so, freed from the restraining influence of international law, the aggressive war is conducted by the Nazi leaders in the most barbaric way. Accordingly, War Crimes were committed when and wherever the Führer and his close associates thought them to be advantageous. They were for the most part the result of cold and criminal calculation.

. . .

. . . Prisoners of war were ill-treated and tortured and murdered, not only in defiance of the well-established rules of international law, but in complete disregard of the elementary dictates of humanity. Civilian populations in occupied territories suffered the same fate. Whole populations were deported to Germany for the purposes of slave labor upon defense works, armament production, and similar tasks connected with the war effort. Hostages were taken in very large numbers from the civilian populations in all the occupied countries, and were shot as suited the German purposes. Public and private property was systematically plundered and pillaged in order to enlarge the resources of Germany at the expense of the rest of Europe. Cities and towns and villages were wantonly destroyed without military justification or necessity.

. . .

Murder and Ill-treatment of Civilian Population

Article 6(b) of the Charter provides that 'ill-treatment . . . of civilian population of or in occupied territory . . . killing of hostages . . . wanton destruction of cities, towns, or villages' shall be a war crime. In the main, these provisions are merely declaratory of the existing laws of war as expressed by the Hague Convention, Article 46. . . .

. . .

One of the most notorious means of terrorizing the people in occupied territories was the use of concentration camps . . . [which] became places of organized and systematic murder, where millions of people were destroyed.

In the administration of the occupied territories the concentration camps were used to destroy all opposition groups. . . .

A certain number of the concentration camps were equipped with gas chambers for the wholesale destruction of the inmates, and with furnaces for the burning of the bodies. Some of them were in fact used for the extermination of Jews as part of the 'final solution' of the Jewish problem. . . .

. . .

Slave Labor Policy

Article 6(b) of the Charter provides that the 'ill-treatment or deportation to slave labor or for any other purpose, of civilian population of or in occupied territory' shall be a War Crime. The laws relating to forced labor by the inhabitants of occupied territories are found in Article 52 of the Hague Convention. . . . The policy of the German occupation authorities was in flagrant violation of the terms of this convention. . . . [T]he German occupation authorities did succeed in forcing many of the inhabitants of the occupied territories to work for the German war effort, and in deporting at least 5,000,000 persons to Germany to serve German industry and agriculture.

. . .

Persecution of the Jews

The persecution of the Jews at the hands of the Nazi Government has been proved in the greatest detail before the Tribunal. It is a record of consistent and systematic inhumanity on the greatest scale. Ohlendorf, Chief of Amt III in the RSHA from 1939 to 1943, and who was in command of one of the Einsatz groups in the campaign against the Soviet Union testified as to the methods employed in the extermination of the Jews. . . .

When the witness Bach Zelewski was asked how Ohlendorf could admit the murder of 90,000 people, he replied: 'I am of the opinion that when, for years, for decades, the doctrine is preached that the Slav race is an inferior race, and Jews not even human, then such an outcome is inevitable'.

. . .

. . . The Nazi Party preached these doctrines throughout its history, *Der Stürmer* and other publications were allowed to disseminate hatred of the Jews, and in the speeches and public declarations of the Nazi leaders, the Jews were held up to public ridicule and contempt.

. . . By the autumn of 1938, the Nazi policy towards the Jews had reached the stage where it was directed towards the complete exclusion of Jews from German life. Pogroms were organized, which included the burning and demolishing of synagogues, the looting of Jewish businesses, and the arrest of prominent Jewish business men. . . .

It was contended for the Prosecution that certain aspects of this anti-Semitic policy were connected with the plans for aggressive war. The violent measures taken against the Jews in November 1938 were nominally in retaliation for the killing of an official of the German Embassy in Paris. But the decision to seize Austria and Czechoslovakia had been made a year before. The imposition of a fine of one billion marks was made, and the confiscation of the financial holdings of the Jews was decreed, at a time when German armament expenditure had put the German treasury in difficulties, and when the reduction of expenditure on armaments was being considered. . . .

It was further said that the connection of the anti-Semitic policy with aggressive war was not limited to economic matters. . . .

The Nazi persecution of Jews in Germany before the war, severe and repressive as it was, cannot compare, however, with the policy pursued during the war in the occupied territories. . . . In the summer of 1941, however, plans were made for the 'final solution' of the Jewish question in Europe. This 'final solution' meant the extermination of the Jews. . . .

The plan for exterminating the Jews was developed shortly after the attack on the Soviet Union. . . .

. . .

. . . Adolf Eichmann, who had been put in charge of this program by Hitler, has estimated that the policy pursued resulted in the killing of 6 million Jews, of which 4 million were killed in the extermination institutions.

The Law Relating to War Crimes and Crimes against Humanity

. . .

The Tribunal is of course bound by the Charter, in the definition which it gives both of War Crimes and Crimes against Humanity. With respect to War Crimes, however, as has already been pointed out, the crimes defined by Article 6, Section (b), of the Charter were already recognized as War Crimes under international law. They were covered by Articles 46, 50, 52, and 56 of the Hague Convention of 1907, and Articles 2, 3, 4, 46, and 51 of the Geneva Convention of 1929. That violation of these provisions constituted crimes for which the guilty individuals were punishable is too well settled to admit of argument.

But it is argued that the Hague Convention does not apply in this case, because of the 'general participation' clause in Article 2 of the Hague Convention of 1907. That clause provided:

> The provisions contained in the regulations (Rules of Land Warfare) referred to in Article 1 as well as in the present Convention do not apply except between contracting powers, and then only if all the belligerents are parties to the Convention.

Several of the belligerents in the recent war were not parties to this Convention.

In the opinion of the Tribunal it is not necessary to decide this question. The rules of land warfare expressed in the Convention undoubtedly represented an advance over existing international law at the time of their adoption. But the convention expressly stated that it was an attempt 'to revise the general laws and customs of war', which it thus recognized to be then existing, but by 1939 these rules laid down in the Convention were recognized by all civilized nations, and were regarded as being declaratory of the laws and customs of war which are referred to in Article 6(b) of the Charter.

. . .

With regard to Crimes against Humanity there is no doubt whatever that polit-ical opponents were murdered in Germany before the war, and that many of them were kept in concentration camps in circumstances of great horror and cruelty. The policy of terror was certainly carried out on a vast scale, and in many cases was organized and systematic. The policy of persecution, repression, and murder of civilians in Germany before the war of 1939, who were likely to be hostile to the Government, was most ruthlessly carried out. The persecution of Jews during the same period is established beyond all doubt. To constitute Crimes against Human-ity, the acts relied on before the outbreak of war must have been in execution of, or in connection with, any crime within the jurisdiction of the Tribunal. The Tri-bunal is of the opinion that revolting and horrible as many of these crimes were, it has not been satisfactorily proved that they were done in execution of, or in connection with, any such crime. The Tribunal therefore cannot make a general declaration that the acts before 1939 were Crimes against Humanity within the meaning of the Charter, but from the beginning of the war in 1939 War Crimes were committed on a vast scale, which were also Crimes against Humanity; and insofar as the inhumane acts charged in the Indictment, and committed after the beginning of the war, did not constitute War Crimes, they were all committed in execution of, or in connection with, the aggressive war, and therefore constituted Crimes against Humanity.

[The opinion considered individually each of the 22 defendants at this first trial of alleged war criminals. It found 19 of the defendants guilty of one or more counts of the indictment. It imposed 12 death sentences. Most convictions were for War Crimes and Crimes against Humanity, the majority of those convicted being found guilty of both crimes.]

NOTE

Note the following statement in Ian Brownlie, *Principles of Public International Law* (4th edn 1990), at 562:

> But whatever the state of the law in 1945, Article 6 of the Nuremberg Charter has since come to represent general international law. The Agreement to which the Charter was annexed was signed by the United States, United Kingdom, France, and USSR, and nineteen other state subsequently adhered to it. In a resolution adopted unanimously on 11 December 1946, the General Assembly affirmed 'the principles of international law recognized by the Charter of the Nuremberg Tribunal and the judgment of the Tribunal'.

There has been considerable expansion in the definitions of two of the crimes defined in Article 6. The field of individual criminal responsibility for war crimes has been both expanded and clarified, through provisions of the Geneva Conven-tions of 1949 and later instruments. Particularly relevant are the provisions for 'grave breaches' in these conventions, described at p. 1135, *infra*. The concept of crimes against humanity has expanded greatly in coverage and shed some limitations placed on it by the Judgment of the Tribunal. Such developments are described in the materials dealing with the current International Criminal Tribunals for the Former Yugoslavia and for Rwanda and with the proposed International Criminal Court in Chapter 14. The notion of 'crimes against peace', however, has fallen into relative disuse.

The problem of *ex post facto* trials has received much commentary, some of which appears *infra*. See in this connection Article 15 of the International Covenant on Civil and Political Rights (in Annex on Documents).

Compare with the Nuremberg Judgment the following provisions of the Convention on the Prevention and Punishment of the Crime of Genocide (130 parties as of March 2000) bearing on personal responsibility. The treaty parties 'confirm' in Article I that genocide 'is a crime under international law which they undertake to prevent and to punish'. Article 2 defines genocide:

> In the present Convention, genocide means any of the following acts committed with intent to destroy, in whole or in part, a national, ethnical, racial or religious group, as such:
>
> (a) Killing members of the group;
> (b) Causing serious bodily or mental harm to members of the group;
> (c) Deliberately inflicting on the group conditions of life calculated to bring about its physical destruction in whole or in part;
> (d) Imposing measures intended to prevent births within the group;
> (e) Forcibly transferring children of the group to another group.

Persons committing acts of genocide 'shall be punished, whether they are constitutionally responsible rulers, public officials or private individuals'. (Art. IV). The parties agree (Art. V) to enact the necessary legislation to give effect to the Convention and 'to provide effective penalties for persons guilty of genocide'. Under Art. VI, persons charged with genocide are to be tried by a tribunal 'of the State in the territory of which the act was committed, or by such international penal tribunal as may have jurisdiction with respect to those Contracting Parties which shall have accepted its jurisdiction'. No international penal tribunal of general jurisdiction has been created.

VIEWS OF COMMENTATORS

There follow a number of authors' observations about the charges, the Judgment and the principles in the Nuremberg trials.

(1) In a review of a book by Sheldon Glueck entitled *The Nuremberg Trial and Aggressive War* (1946), the reviewer George Finch, 47 Am.J.Int.L. 334 (1947), makes the following arguments:

> As the title indicates, this book deals with the charges at Nuremberg based upon the planning and waging of aggressive war. The author has written it because in his previous volume he expressed the view that he did not think such acts could

be regarded as 'international crimes'. He has now changed his mind and believes 'that for the purpose of conceiving aggressive war to be an international crime, the Pact of Paris may, together with other treaties and resolutions, be regarded as evidence of a sufficiently developed *custom* to be accepted as international law' (pp. 4–5). . . .

The reviewer fully agrees with the author in regard to the place of custom in the development of international law. He regards as untenable, however, the argument not only of the author but of the prosecutors and judges at Nuremberg that custom can be judicially established by placing interpretations upon the words of treaties which are refuted by the acts of the signatories in practice, by citing unratified protocols or public and private resolutions of no legal effect, and by ignoring flagrant and repeated violations of non-aggression pacts by one of the prosecuting governments which, if properly weighed in the evidence, would nullify any judicial holding that a custom outlawing aggressive war had been accepted in international law. . . .

(2) In his article, 'The Nurnberg Trial', 33 Va. L. Rev. 679 (1947), at 694, Francis Biddle, the American judge on the Tribunal, commented on the definition of 'crimes against humanity' in Article 6(c) of the Charter:

. . . The authors of the Charter evidently realized that the crimes enumerated were essentially domestic and hardly subject to the incidence of international law, unless partaking of the nature of war crimes. Their purpose was evidently to reach the terrible persecution of the Jews and liberals within Germany before the war. But the Tribunal held that 'revolting and horrible as many of these crimes were', it had not been established that they were done 'in execution of, or in connection with' any crime within its jurisdiction. After the beginning of the war, however, these inhumane acts were held to have been committed in execution of the war, and were therefore crimes against humanity.

. . .

Crimes against humanity constitute a somewhat nebulous conception, although the expression is not unknown to the language of international law. . . . With one possible exception . . . crimes against humanity were held [in the Judgment of the Tribunal] to have been committed only where the proof also fully established the commission of war crimes. Mr. Stimson suggested [that the Tribunal eliminate from its jurisdiction matters related to pre-war persecution in Germany], which involved 'a reduction of the meaning of crimes against humanity to a point where they became practically synonymous with war crimes'. I agree. And I believe that this inelastic construction is justified by the language of the Charter and by the consideration that such a rigid interpretation is highly desirable in this stage of the development of international law.

(3) Professor Hans Kelsen, in 'Will the Judgment in the Nuremberg Trial Constitute a Precedent in International Law?', 1 Int. L. Q. 153 (1947) at 164, was critical of several aspects of the London Agreement and the Judgment. But with respect to the question of retroactivity of criminal punishment, he wrote:

The objection most frequently put forward—although not the weightiest one—
is that the law applied by the judgment of Nuremberg is an ex post facto law.
There can be little doubt that the London Agreement provides individual punishment for acts which, at the time they were performed were not punishable,
either under international law or under any national law. . . . However, this rule
[against retroactive legislation] is not valid at all within international law, and is
valid within national law only with important exceptions. [Kelsen notes several
exceptions, including the rule's irrelevance to 'customary law and to law created
by a precedent, for such law is necessarily retroactive in respect to the first case to
which it is applied. . . .']

A retroactive law providing individual punishment for acts which were illegal
though not criminal at the time they were committed, seems also to be an
exception to the rule against ex post facto laws. The London Agreement is such
a law. It is retroactive only in so far as it established individual criminal
responsibility for acts which at the time they were committed constituted violations of existing international law, but for which this law has provided only
collective responsibility. . . . Since the internationally illegal acts for which the
London Agreement established individual criminal responsibility were certainly
also morally most objectionable, and the persons who committed these acts
were certainly aware of their immoral character, the retroactivity of the law
applied to them can hardly be considered as absolutely incompatible with
justice.

(4) In his biography entitled *Harlan Fiske Stone: Pillar of the Law* (1956),
Alpheus Thomas Mason discussed Chief Justice Stone's views about the involvement of Justices of the US Supreme Court in extrajudicial assignments and, in
particular, Stone's views about President Truman's appointment of Justice Robert
Jackson to be American Prosecutor at the trials. The following excerpts (at 715) are
all incorporations by Mason in his book of quotations of Chief Justice Stone's
remarks.

So far as the Nuremberg trial is an attempt to justify the application of the power
of the victor to the vanquished because the vanquished made aggressive war, . . . I
dislike extremely to see it dressed up with a false facade of legality. The best that
can be said for it is that it is a political act of the victorious States which may be
morally right. . . . It would not disturb me greatly . . . if that power were openly
and frankly used to punish the German leaders for being a bad lot, but it disturbs
me some to have it dressed up in the habiliments of the common law and the
Constitutional safeguards to those charged with crime.

Jackson is away conducting his high-grade lynching party in Nuremberg. . . . I
don't mind what he does to the Nazis, but I hate to see the pretense that he is
running a court and proceeding according to common law. This is a little too
sanctimonious a fraud to meet my old-fashioned ideas.

(5) Professor Herbert Wechsler, in '*The Issues of the Nuremberg Trial*', 62 Pol.
Sci. Q. 11 (1947), at 23 observed:

. . . [M]ost of those who mount the attack [on the Judgment on contentions
including ex post facto law] hasten to assure us that their plea is not one of

immunity for the defendants; they argue only that they should have been disposed of politically, that is, dispatched out of hand. This is a curious position indeed. A punitive enterprise launched on the basis of general rules, administered in an adversary proceeding under a separation of prosecutive and adjudicative powers is, in the name of law and justice, asserted to be less desirable than an ex parte execution list or a drumhead court-martial constituted in the immediate aftermath of the war. . . . Those who choose to do so may view the Nuremberg proceeding as 'political' rather than 'legal'—a program calling for the judicial application of principles of liability politically defined. They cannot view it as less civilized an institution than a program of organized violence against prisoners, whether directed from the respective capitals or by military commanders in the field.

(6) Mark Osiel, in *Mass Atrocity, Collective Memory, and the Law* (1997), comments on charges against the defeated states (at 122):

For the Nuremberg and Tokyo courts, it mattered little to the validity of criminal proceedings against Axis leadership that Allied victors had committed vast war crimes of their own. Unlike the law of tort, criminal law has virtually no place for 'comparative fault', no doctrinal device for mitigating the wrongdoing or culpability of the accused in light of the accusers'. . . . For the public, however, . . . it mattered *greatly* in gauging the legitimacy of the trials that they seemed tendentiously selective, aimed at focusing memory in partisan ways. It mattered for such listeners that the defendants . . . had constituted only a single side to a two- or multi-sided conflict, one in which other parties had similarly committed unlawful acts on a large scale. This unsavory feature of the Nuremberg judgment has undermined its authority in the minds of many, weakening its normative weight.

(7) David Luban, in *Legal Modernism* (1994), describes what he sees as a confusion in the Nuremberg charges (at 336):

This idea that Nuremberg was to be the Trial to End All Wars seems fantastic and naïve forty years (and 150 wars) later. It has also done much to vitiate the real achievements of the trial, in particular the condemnation of crimes against humanity. To end all war, the authors of the Nuremberg Charter were led to incorporate an intellectual confusion into it. The Charter criminalized aggression; and by criminalizing aggression, the Charter erected a wall around state sovereignty and committed itself to an old-European model of unbreachable nation-states.

But crimes against humanity are often, even characteristically, carried out by states against their own subjects. The effect, and great moral and legal achievement, or criminalizing such acts and assigning personal liability to those who order them and carry them out is to pierce the veil of sovereignty. As a result, Article 6(a) pulls in the opposite direction from Articles 6(c), 7 and 8, leaving us . . . with a legacy that is at best equivocal and at worst immoral.

QUESTIONS

1. Recall clause (c) of Article 38(1) of the Statute of the ICJ, and the comments thereon of Oscar Schachter, at p. 91, *supra*. Should the Tribunal have relied on that clause to respond to charges of *ex post facto* application of Article 6(c) to individuals who were responsible for the murder of groups of Germans or aliens?

2. Do you agree with the Tribunal's restrictive interpretation of Article 6(c)? Consider the commentary above of Francis Biddle.

3. How do you evaluate the criticism by Finch of the Tribunal's use of treaties in deciding whether customary international law included a given norm? Recall the comments about the growth of customary law by Schachter.

4. How do you evaluate the criticism of the Nuremberg trial by Chief Justice Stone? by Osiel? by Luban?

5. Why do you suppose that Article 6(a) on crimes against peace (wars of aggression) has fallen into disuse with respect to individual criminal liability and was omitted from the criminal provisions in the Statute for the International Criminal Tribunal for the Former Yugoslavia?

6. How do you now assess the significance and consequences of Nuremberg? Even if you agree with some or several of the criticisms above, do you nonetheless conclude that the trial and judgment were justified in their actual historical forms?

ADDITIONAL READING

On Nuremberg see three books by Telford Taylor: *Nuremberg Trials: War Crimes and International Law* (1949); *Nuremberg and Vietnam: An American Tragedy* (1978); and *The Anatomy of the Nuremberg Trials: A Personal Memoir* (1992). See also Memorandum Submitted by the Secretary-General, *The Charter and Judgment of the Nürnberg Tribunal: History and Analysis*, U.N. Doc. A/CN.4/5 (1949); and Egon Schwelb, 'Crimes against Humanity', 23 Brit. Ybk. Int. L. 178 (1946). More generally see: T. Meron, *War Crimes Law Comes of Age: Essays* (1998).

E. PERSPECTIVES ON INTERNATIONAL LAW

This section concludes the chapter with two readings of scholars in the field. The following observations of Louis Henkin review some themes developed in the prior sections and describe other antecedents in international law to contemporary human rights. The excerpts from Oscar Schachter's book offer jurisprudential and political views about the nature of international law.

LOUIS HENKIN, INTERNATIONAL LAW: POLITICS, VALUES AND FUNCTIONS
216 Collected Courses of Hague Academy of International Law 13 (Vol. IV, 1989), at 208

Chapter X
STATE VALUES AND OTHER VALUES: HUMAN RIGHTS

. . .

That until recently international law took no note of individual human beings may be surprising. Both international law and domestic legal norms in the Christian world had roots in an accepted morality and in natural law, and had common intellectual progenitors (including Grotius, Locke, Vattel). But for hundreds of years international law and the law governing individual life did not come together. International law, true to its name, was law only between States, governing only relations between States on the State level. What a State did inside its borders in relation to its own nationals remained its own affair, an element of its autonomy, a matter of its 'domestic jurisdiction'.

Antecedents of the International Law of Human Rights

In fact, neither the international political system nor international law ever closed out totally what went on inside a State and what happened to individuals within a State. Early, international law began to attend to internal matters that held special interest for other States, and those sometimes included concern for individual human beings, or at least redounded to the benefit of individual human beings. But what was in fact of interest to other States, and what was accepted as being of legitimate interest to other States (and therefore to the system and to law), were limited *a priori* by the character of the State system and its values. Of course, every State was legitimately concerned with what happened to its diplomats, to its diplomatic mission and to its property in the territory of another State. States were concerned, and the system developed norms to assure, that their nationals (and the property of their nationals) in the territory of another State be treated reasonably, 'fairly', and the system and the law early identified an international standard of justice by which a State must abide in its treatment of foreign nationals. States also entered into agreements, usually on a reciprocal basis, promising protection or privilege—freedom to reside, to conduct business, to worship—to persons with whom the other State party to the treaty identified because of common religion or ethnicity.

Concern for individual human welfare seeped into the international system in the eighteenth and nineteenth centuries in other discrete, specific respects. In the nineteenth century, European (and American) States abolished slavery and slave trade. Later, States began to pursue agreements to make war less inhumane, to outlaw some cruel weapons to safeguard prisoners of war, the wounded, civilian populations. It is noteworthy that, in these instances, even less-than-democratic States began to attend to human values, though humanitarian limitations on the conduct of war may have brought significant cost to the State's military interests.

Following the First World War, concern for individual human beings was reflected in several League of Nations programmes. Building on earlier precedents in the nineteenth century, the dominant States pressed selected other States to adhere to 'minorities treaties' guaranteed by the League, in which States Parties assumed obligations to respect rights of identified ethnic, national or religious minorities among their inhabitants. . . . The years following the First World War also saw a major development in international concern for individual welfare, a development that is often overlooked and commonly underestimated: the International Labour Office (now the International Labour Organisation (ILO)) was established and it launched a variety of programmes including a series of conventions setting minimum standards for working conditions and related matters.

In general, the principles of customary international law that developed, and the special agreements that were concluded, addressed only what happened to *some* people inside a State, only in respects with which other States were in fact concerned, and only where such concern was considered their proper business in a system of autonomous States. One can only speculate as to why States accepted these norms and agreements, but it may be reasonable to doubt whether those developments authentically reflected sensitivity to human rights generally. States attended to what occurred inside another State when such happenings impinged on their political-economic interests. States were concerned, and were deemed legitimately concerned, for the freedoms, privileges, and immunities of their diplomats because an affront to the diplomat affronted his prince (or his State), and because interference with a diplomat interfered with his functions and disturbed orderly, friendly relations. Injury to a foreign national or to his or her property was also an affront to the State of his or her nationality, and powerful States exporting people, goods, and capital to other countries in the age of growing mercantilism insisted on law that would protect the State interests that these represented.

. . .

Humanitarian developments in the law of war reflected some concern by States to reduce the horrors of war for their own people and a willingness in exchange to reduce them for others. Powerful States promoted minorities treaties because mistreatment of minorities with which other States identified threatened international peace. Those treaties were imposed selectively, principally on nations defeated in war and on newly created or enlarged States; they did not establish general norms requiring respect for minorities by the big and the powerful as well; they did not require respect for individuals who were not members of identified minorities, or for members of the majority. . . .

Even the ILO conventions, perhaps, served some less-than-altruistic purposes. Improvement in the conditions of labour was capitalism's defence against the spectre of spreading socialism which had just established itself in the largest country in Europe. States, moreover, had a direct interest in the conditions of labour in countries with which they competed in a common international market: a State impelled to improve labour and social conditions at home could not readily do so unless other States did so, lest the increase in its costs of production render its products non-competitive.

I have stressed the possibly political-economic (rather than humanitarian) motivations for early norms and agreements, identifying a State's concern for the welfare of some of its nationals as an extension of its Statehood and perhaps reflecting principally concern for State interests and values. If some norms and agreements in fact were motivated by concern for a State's own people generally, they did not reflect interest in the welfare of those in other countries, or of human beings generally. State interests rather than individual human interests, or at best the interests of a State's own people rather than general human concerns, also inspired voluntary inter-State co-operation to promote reciprocal economic interests. Occasional assistance to other States, even if for the benefit of the people of that State (as in flood or earthquake relief), was voluntary, out of friendship and generosity (rather than legal obligation), and was provided to the receiving State and penetrated its society only lightly and only with its consent.

I would not underestimate the influence of ideas of rights and constitutionalism in the seventeenth and eighteenth centuries, and of a growing and spreading enlightenment generally: Locke, Montesquieu, other Encyclopedists, Rousseau; the example of the Glorious Revolution in England and the establishment of constitutionalism in the United States; the influence of the French Declaration of the Rights of Man and of the Citizen. Such ideas and examples have influenced developments inside countries, but they did not easily enter the international political and legal system. Concern by one country for the welfare of individual human beings inside another country met many obstacles, not least the conception and implications of Statehood in a State system. The human condition in other countries and the treatment of individuals by other Governments were not commonly known abroad since they were not included in the information sources of the time. Information (and concern) were filtered through the State system and through diplomatic sources, and human values as such were not the business of diplomacy. For those reasons, and for other reasons flowing from the State system, other States took little note and expressed little concern for what a Government did to its own citizens. In general, the veil of Statehood was impermeable. If occasionally something particularly horrendous happened—a massacre, pogrom—and was communicated and made known by the available media of communication, it evoked from other States more-or-less polite diplomatic expressions of regret, not on grounds of law but of *noblesse oblige* or of common princely morality wrapped in Christian charity (whose violation gave princes and Christianity a bad name).

Even if the implications of Statehood had not been an obstacle, as regards any but the grossest violations of what we now call human rights, few if any States had moral sensitivity and moral standing to intercede. When a State invoked an international standard of justice on behalf of one of its nationals abroad, it may have been invoking a standard unknown and unheeded at home. Few States had constitutional protections and not many had effective legislative or common-law protections for individual rights. Torture and police brutality, denials of due process, arbitrary detention, perversions of law, were not wildly abnormal. Surely, few States recognized political freedom—freedom of speech, association and assembly, universal suffrage. Many States denied religious freedom to some, and few States granted complete religious toleration; full equality to members of other than the dominant religion was slow in coming anywhere. Women were subject to rampant and deep-rooted inequalities and domination, often to abuse and oppression. Even today such violations are not the stuff of dramatic television programmes and do not arouse international revulsion and reaction; in earlier times, surely, violations of what are today recognized as civil and political rights caused little stir outside the country. A State's failure to provide for the economic and social welfare of its inhabitants was wholly beyond the ken of other States. There were no alert media of information and few civil rights or other non-governmental organizations to sensitize and activate people and Governments.

. . .

OSCAR SCHACHTER, INTERNATIONAL LAW
IN THEORY AND PRACTICE
(1991) at 5

Ch. I. The Nature and Reality of International Law

. . .

The uses of law and the role of power

In discussing the complexity of international law and its relative autonomy, we have more or less assumed its 'reality'. We did so while recognizing that it is a product of political and social forces, that it is dependent on behaviour and that it is an instrument to meet changing ends and values. All these aspects give rise to questions as to the reality of international law. These questions are epitomized in the not uncommon view that we cannot have genuine and effective law in a society of sovereign States dominated by power and self-interest. . . .

One way of approaching the issues is to consider the views of the sceptics of international law—those who doubt, for one reason or another, that international law can contribute significantly to international order. Four kinds of sceptical positions merit our attention. The first emphasizes the dominance of power over law. The second asserts the dependence of international law on the will of national States. A third position points to the deep divisions of belief, aims and culture in international society and questions whether a common authoritative legal system is realizable. The fourth sceptical position lays stress on the fragility of a legal system that lacks centralized institutions to determine authoritatively what the law is and to enforce it. I will discuss the reasoning behind these positions and comment on their validity.

The thesis that law is subordinate to power is commonly referred to as a 'realist' (or 'realpolitik') point of view. Power, in this context, refers to the ability of a State to impose its will on others or, more broadly, to control outcomes contested by others. The components of power are military, economic, political and psychological; international society exhibits, in striking degree, an unequal distribution of these components of power. The unequal distribution of power is a pervasive and dominating element in the relations of States. States strive to augment their power, perceiving power sometimes as an end in itself and more commonly as a means to attain more freedom of action and other objectives. For the realist, the crucial importance of power and the pursuit of self-interest by States make it virtually inevitable that the law—both in its creation and application—should yield to those determinants. Law may play a subordinate role as an aid to stability, a 'gentle civilizer of events' but it cannot be relied on 'to suppress the chaotic and dangerous aspirations of governments'. Political theorists reach similar conclusions in their analysis of the State system. From a 'structural' standpoint (as they sometimes put it), a system based on the sovereignty of States is a system of 'co-ordinate relations', in which formal authority is decentralized. While this fundamental condition does not rule out the use of a legal system to provide a required degree of order and predictability, the individual States in the last analysis are not subordinated to any superior authority. Hence the effective limits on their action derive from their own perception of national interest and the countervailing power of others. In consequence, as Raymond Aron has put it, international society is 'an anarchical order of power in which might makes right'.

These general theoretical conclusions accord with the widespread popular belief that in international relations power rather than law governs. . . . The fact that legal arguments are almost always made by the alleged violators only tends to add to the cynicism about law since such self-serving legal arguments are not submitted to adjudication or other third-party determinations. The absence of compulsory or generally accepted judicial settlement of international disputes is taken as compelling evidence that the law is not taken seriously and hence that 'power politics' prevails.

Since we cannot deny the crucial role of power in the relations of States, we should seek to understand its specific impact on the international legal system. Plainly, international law is not an ideal construct, created and given effect solely in terms of its internal logic. Nor can it be understood only as an instrument to serve human needs and aims (though it is that too). International law must also be seen as the product of historical experience in which power and the 'relation of forces' are determinants. Those States with power (i.e., the ability to control the outcomes contested by others) will have a disproportionate and often decisive influence in determining the content of rules and their application in practice. Because this is the case, international law, in a broad sense, both reflects and sustains the existing political order and distribution of power.

. . . A popular view, probably prevalent all over the world, is that powerful States, like powerful individuals in many countries, can often flout the law and get away with it. . . .

We need to consider not only that States break the rules but also that they generally conform to them even against their immediate interest. Nobody denies that States, powerful and not so powerful, observe international law most of the time. There are various reasons why they do so. Much compliance can be attributed to institutionalized habit; officials follow the rules as a matter of practice, and in countless decisions they look to treaty obligations, to precedents that evidence custom and to general principles of law expounded in treatises and manuals. Many of the decisions involve no apparent clash of law and self-interest but numerous cases arise in which a government refrains from action (or non-action) that it would otherwise take if there were no legal grounds limiting its discretion. This is most evident when specific treaties apply—say, of commerce, navigation, reciprocal exchanges—but it is also true of the many cases covered by the unwritten customary rules applicable to many areas of inter-State relations. We must remember that the law is not applied as if it were governed by a computer programmed to respond to every contingency. In actuality, a good part of law observance takes place because the officials concerned do not even consider the option of violation; they have, so to speak, 'internalized' the rules so that possibilities of action contrary to the law do not even rise to conscious decision-making. It would, for example, be virtually certain today that a State would not consider sending its troops in to another country to collect revenues to pay a debt (as the United States once did in Haiti). Nor would it consider asserting jurisdiction over foreign flag vessels on the high seas. We often tend to forget how much of the basic law of nations is so thoroughly embedded in the minds and habits of officials that it is given effect without conscious decision making.

It is of course also true that cases arise in which officials do have to consider whether the law should be applied when it appears to be in the immediate interest of the government not to do so. The responses to such situations depend on a variety of considerations. Most obviously, governments will weigh a possible breach by them against their interest in reciprocal observance by the other party. They will also consider the likelihood of retaliation and other self-help measures by that party. Nor would they ignore the negative consequences of a reputation for repudiating their obligations. In many countries, officials would be sensitive to anticipated criticism by influential domestic leaders or groups who place high value on the country's reputation for legality generally or on observance of the particular obligations involved. The possibility of judicial enforcement in domestic tribunals may in some cases serve as a deterrent to non-compliance. Remedies by the aggrieved State may also be available under some circumstances in international mechanisms, perhaps through arbitral or judicial means or through loss of benefits under treaty régimes. . . . Violations, in short, are rarely cost-free even to powerful States.

. . .

The dependency of international law on the will of states

. . . If States have no superior authority and their relations are 'co-ordinate', rather than hierarchical, does it not follow that a State is bound only by the legal rules to which it agrees to submit? . . .

These questions are as old as international law itself and have given rise to considerable theoretical writing. The idea that the will of States is the basis of international law and hence that the law is dependent on the consent of States is referred to in international law theory as 'voluntarism' or 'consensualism'. Voluntarism is not only a theory held by academic scholars. It is also an expression of the strongly held conception of State sovereignty dominant in most governments. . . .

The general idea that international law rests on the will of the States has been applied in various ways, with quite different significance. It has been applied to international law as a whole (particularly customary law) and to particular rules of international law. In regard to the latter, the requirement of consent has been directed both to the creation of new rules of law and to their use in particular cases. We will sort out the questions raised in each category by considering the following five propositions:

(1) international law as a general system is accepted by all States and hence is an expression of their will:

. . .

(3) the creation of a new rule or repeal of an old rule of customary law requires the consent of States;

(4) a State which has not consented to a customary law rule is free at any time to reject its application to the State;

(5) any State is free to exercise its sovereign right to reject the application of a customary law rule on the ground that it is not in accordance with that State's will.

(I should note that the term customary law rule as used above is intended to refer not only to rules in the narrow sense of that term but also to principles, standards, practices, concepts and procedures that are considered as legal grounds for asserting rights and obligations.)

(1) The first proposition asserts an empirical fact amply supported by practice. A possible objection is that the acceptance of international law cannot be attributed to the 'will' of the States since they have no choice in the matter. The very claim to be a State with authority over a given territory and population involves recognition of the basic international law rules. We shall consider this further in regard to the second proposition. However, even if it is true that 'membership' in any society presupposes adherence to its basic rules (*ubi societas, ibi ius*), it is not inconsistent with the fact that States accept the particular system of international law now in force. At least in that sense, the system rests on their consent just as a domestic law system may be said to rest basically on the consent of the people. Without their general consent, there could be no durable operative system of law. Although voluntarism in this form may seem to be a 'weak' version, it is important to recognize that the system of law has in general been accepted by the community of States. Acceptance of the system is in itself a plausible basis for the obligation to abide by the particular rules valid in that system.

. . .

(3) The third proposition is that the creation of a new rule or repeal of an existing rule requires the consent of States. Inasmuch as customary law arises through uniformities of State conduct accompanied by the belief of States that they are conforming to what amounts to a legal obligation, the States that participated in such conduct and recognize the obligation created by it can reasonably be considered to have consented to the rule thus established. . . .

How many States are required to establish 'general' practice and how frequent, numerous and consistent the practice must be are questions which cannot be answered in categorical propositions. Generality, frequency, density, consistency, duration are in principle required but whether they are met in regard to a specific rule depends on the circumstances of the case. This seems to leave the emergence of customary law rather mysterious. It is not easy to generalize about the factors that should help in deciding how many States are enough, how 'dense' the practice need be, how long in time and so on. . . . For our present purpose, it is enough to note the broad agreement among authorities that general custom does not require universal consent of all States. . . .

(4) The most significant test of voluntarist-consensualist theory is raised by the fourth proposition—namely that a State is not bound by a rule to which it has not consented. The proposition requires critical analysis. Non-consenting States divide into two categories: (1) States that have manifested neither acceptance nor objection: (2) States which have openly objected to the rule in general or to its specific application to the objecting State. If we accept the principle that general custom does not require universal consent it follows that the assent of a particular State is not necessary for a general rule to come into being and to bind all States. . . .

A special problem is presented by the second category of non-consenting States—those that have openly manifested their dissent to a customary rule. One might ask why a dissenting State should be able to avoid a general customary rule if universal consent is not considered necessary and nonassenting States are considered bound. . . . Even if this is accepted as law, it is subject to some limitations.
. . .

. . . It may be questioned whether the exception for a dissenting State would apply to a new principle of customary law regarded as fundamental or of major importance. If . . . principles are regarded as fundamental and of major import-ance to the generality of States with respect to an area beyond any State's jurisdiction, a good case can be made for denying the dissenting State the right to avoid the obligations that all other States incur as a consequence of the acceptance of the new principles. The issue cannot reasonably be decided solely by reference to voluntarist theory. It would be germane to consider a variety of factors including the circumstances of adoption of the new principle, the reasons for its importance to the generality of States, the grounds of dissent, and the relevant position of the dissenting States. . . .

(5) The fifth proposition constitutes the 'strongest' use of voluntarist theory. It would allow a State to reject the application of a customary rule to it simply on the ground that it was contrary to the State's present will. No State, to my knowledge, has openly espoused that position. It would amount to a denial of customary law and it is most unlikely that any State would be prepared to take that position. However, a State may seek to avoid submitting to a rule by adopting a more moderate form of consensualism. . . . A strong preference in favour of State sovereignty and voluntarism on the part of members of a tribunal (or other decision-makers) will tend to raise the threshold of practice and *opinio juris* considered necessary to establish a universal rule.

Voluntarism in a somewhat different guise can also be found when a State objects to a rule on the ground that it is incompatible with a vital interest of the State. In such case, the recalcitrant State rests not simply on its will per se but on a superior norm of self-interest that is said to prevail over law. . . .

Significantly, no State appears to claim a right of this kind although some have interpreted self-defence broadly (as we shall see) or have turned to general notions of sovereignty and independence to justify departing from rules that are deemed against their vital interest.
. . .

NOTE

Compare with Schachter's views about the relationship between law and force the following observations of Stanley Hoffmann, in 'The Study of International Law and the Theory of International Relations', 1963 Proc. Am. Soc. Int. L. 26:

> It is however essential for the social scientist to understand that law is not merely a policy among others in the hands of statesmen, but that it is a tool with very special characteristics and roles. . . . Most important is the fact that law has a distinct solemnity of effects: it is a normative instrument that creates rights and duties. Consequently it has a function that is both symbolic and conservative; it enshrines, elevates, consecrates the interests or ideas it embodies. We understand, thus, why law is an important stake in the contests of nations. What makes international law so special a tool for states is this solemnity of effects, rather than the fact that its norms express common interests; for this is far too simple: some legal instruments such as peace treaties reflect merely the temporary, forced convergence of deeply antagonistic policies. A situation of dependence or of superiority that is just a fact of life can be reversed through political action, but once it is solemnly cast in legal form, the risks of action designed to change the situation are much higher: law is a form of policy that changes the stakes, and often 'escalates' the intensity, of political contests; it is a constraint comparable to force in its effects.

ADDITIONAL READING

M. Byers (ed.), *The Role of Law in International Politics: Essays in International Relations and International Law* (2000); S. Ratner and A.-M. Slaughter (eds), Symposium on Method in International Law, 93 Am. J. Int'l L. 291 (1999); I. Brownlie, *Principles of Public International Law* (5th edn 1998); M. Koskenniemi, *Apology and Utopia* (1989); I. Shearer, *Starke's International Law* (11th edn 1994); R. Jennings and A. Watts. *Oppenheim's International Law* (9th edn 1992); B. Simma et al. (eds), *The Charter of the United Nations: A Commentary* (1994).

3

Civil and Political Rights

Chapter 3 introduces basic instruments of the human rights movement that concern civil and political rights; Chapter 4 addresses economic and social rights. As the two chapters indicate, these are not airtight categories. Many treaties declare rights that straddle the two basic covenants in these fields, or that fall clearly within the domains of both of them. Many rights are hard to categorize. Nonetheless, at their core, the conventional distinctions are clear, whatever the relationships and interdependency between the two categories. Freedom from torture, equal protection, and the right to form political associations fall within this chapter; the right to health care or food comes within the next.

Both chapters explore instruments that are at the core of the *universal* human rights system—universal in that it is based on treaties that aim at worldwide membership. Chapter 11 explores three *regional* human rights systems, based on treaties whose membership is restricted to states in a particular region: the European Convention for the Protection of Human Rights and Fundamental Freedoms (known as the European Convention on Human Rights) (40 states parties as of March 2000), the American Convention on Human Rights (25 parties), and the African Charter on Human and Peoples' Rights (53 parties).

The core of the universal system consists of the United Nations Charter and related instruments. Three such instruments, composing the so-called International Bill of Rights, stand out in significance: the Universal Declaration of Human Rights of 1948, and two principal covenants that became effective in 1976: the International Covenant on Civil and Political Rights (ICCPR), discussed herein, and the International Covenant on Economic, Social and Cultural Rights (ICESCR), discussed in Chapter 4. As of March 2000, the ICCPR had 144 states parties, the ICESCR 142 parties.

Chapter 3 also examines the Convention on the Elimination of All Forms of Discrimination against Women (CEDAW), a major treaty (165 states parties) that took form decades after the ICCPR and that reveals different concerns, goals and strategies of the human rights movement. Comparison of the ICCPR and CEDAW offers useful insights into the evolution of civil and political rights. The chapter concludes with a shorter section on the effect of the human rights movement, as part of broader international law developments of the last half century including the growth of intergovernmental organizations, on conceptions of customary international law and related modes of argument about custom.

A. FROM THE UNITED NATIONS CHARTER TO THE INTERNATIONAL COVENANT ON CIVIL AND POLITICAL RIGHTS

COMMENT ON THE CHARTER AND THE ORIGINS OF THE HUMAN RIGHTS MOVEMENT

The human rights movement is not simply a matter of fundamental postulates, ideologies, and norms—rules, standards, principles. To the contrary, these basic elements are imbedded in institutions, some of them state and some international, and in related international processes. In particular, it is impossible to grasp this movement adequately without an appreciation of its close relation to and reliance on international organizations. Both the universal and regional human rights systems have vital links to such intergovernmental organizations. For example, the basic instruments of the universal system were drafted within the different organs of the United Nations and adopted by its General Assembly, before (in the case of the treaties) being submitted to states for ratification. (As Chapter 11 makes clear, nongovernmental organizations also play a vital role.)

Moreover, the United Nations Charter itself first gave formal and authoritative expression to the human rights movement that began at the end of the Second World War. Since its birth in 1945, the UN has served as a vital institutional spur to the development of the movement, as well as serving as a major forum for many-sided debates about it. The purpose of the present comments is to call attention to aspects of the UN and its Charter that bear on the examination of basic rights instruments. Readers should now become familiar with the provisions (in the Documents Annex) of the Charter that are referred to below. Other Charter provisions figure in later chapters.

Charter Provisions

Consider first the Charter's radical transformation of the branch of the laws of war concerning *jus ad bellum* (p. 114, *supra*). Recall that for several centuries that body of law had addressed almost exclusively *jus in bello*, the rules regulating the conduct of warfare rather than the justice or legality of the waging of war. The International Military Tribunal at Nuremberg was empowered to adjudicate 'crimes against peace,' part of *jus ad bellum* and the most disputed element of that Tribunal's mandate.

The Charter builds on the precedents to which the Nuremberg Judgment (p. 115, *supra*) refers and states the UN's basic purpose of securing and maintaining peace. It does so by providing in Article 2(4) that UN members 'shall refrain in their international relations from the threat or use of force against the territorial integrity or political independence of any state', a rule qualified by Article 51's provision that nothing in the Charter 'shall impair the inherent right of individual or collective self-defence if an armed attack occurs' against a member.

The Charter's references to human rights are scattered, terse, even cryptic. The term 'human rights' appears infrequently, although in vital contexts. Note its occurrence in the following provisions: second paragraph of the Preamble, Article 1(3), Article 13(1)(b), Articles 55 and 56, Article 62(2) and Article 68.

Several striking characteristics of these provisions emerge. Many have a promotional or programmatic character, for they refer principally to the purposes or goals of the UN or to the competences of different UN organs: 'encouraging respect for human rights,' 'assisting in the realization of human rights', 'promote . . . universal respect for, and observance of, human rights'. Not even a provision such as Article 56, which refers to obligations of the Member States rather than of the UN, contains the language of obligation. It notes only that states 'pledge themselves' to action 'for the achievement' of purposes including the promotion of observance of human rights. Note that only one substantive human right receives direct mention in the Charter: equal protection.

The UN and the Universal Declaration

Despite proposals to the contrary, the Charter stopped shy of incorporating a bill of rights. Instead, there were proposals for developing one through the work of a special commission that would give separate attention to the issue. That commission was contemplated by Charter Article 68, which provides that one of the UN organs, the Economic and Social Council (ECOSOC), 'shall set up commissions in economic and social fields and for the promotion of human rights'. In 1946, ECOSOC established the Commission on Human Rights (referred to in this book as the UN Commission), which has evolved over the decades to become the world's single most important human rights organ. Chapter 8 examines its work. At this earlier time, the new Commission was charged primarily with submitting reports and proposals on an international bill of rights.

The UN Commission first met in its present form early in 1947, its members (representatives of the state members of the Commission) including such distinguished founders of the human rights movement as René Cassin of France, Charles Malik of the Lebanon, and Eleanor Roosevelt of the United States. Some representatives urged that the draft bill of rights under preparation should take the form of a declaration—that is, a recommendation by the General Assembly to Member States (see Charter Article 13) that would exert a moral and political influence on states rather than constitute a legally binding instrument. Other representatives urged the Commission to prepare a draft convention containing a bill of rights that would, after adoption by the General Assembly, be submitted to states for their ratification.

The first path was followed. In 1948, the UN Commission adopted a draft Declaration, which in turn was adopted by the General Assembly that year as the Universal Declaration of Human Rights (UDHR), with 48 states voting in favour and eight abstaining—Saudi Arabia, South Africa, and the Soviet Union together with four East European states and a Soviet republic whose votes it controlled. (It is something of a jolt to realize today, in a decolonized and fragmented world of over 190 states, that UN membership in 1948 stood at 56 states.)

The Universal Declaration was meant to precede more detailed and comprehensive provisions in a single convention that would be approved by the General Assembly and submitted to states for ratification. After all, within the prevailing concepts of human rights at that time, the UDHR seemed to cover most of the field, including economic and social rights (see Articles 22–26) as well as civil and political rights. But during the years of drafting—years in which the Cold War took harsher and more rigid form, and in which the United States strongly qualified the nature of its commitment to the universal human rights movement— these matters became more contentious. The human rights movement was buffeted by ideological conflict and the formal differences of approach in a polarized world. One consequence was the decision in 1952 to build on the UDHR by dividing its provisions between two treaties, one on civil and political rights, the other on economic, social and cultural rights. This history is set forth in more detail at pp. 244–245, *infra*.

The plan to use the Universal Declaration as a springboard to treaties triumphed, but not as quickly as anticipated. The two principal treaties—the International Covenant on Civil and Political Rights (ICCPR) and the International Covenant on Economic, Social and Cultural Rights (ICESCR)—made their ways through the drafting and amendment processes in the Commission, the Third Committee and the General Assembly, where they were approved only in 1966. Another decade passed before the two Covenants achieved the number of ratifications necessary to enter into force.

During the 28 years between 1948 and 1976, specialized human rights treaties such as the Genocide Convention entered into force. But not until the two principal Covenants became effective did a treaty achieve as broad coverage of human rights topics as the Universal Declaration. It was partly for this reason that the UDHR became so broadly known and frequently invoked. During these intervening years, it was the only broad-based human rights instrument available. To this day, it:

> has retained its place of honor in the human rights movement. No other document has so caught the historical moment, achieved the same moral and rhetorical force, or exerted as much influence on the movement as a whole. . . . [T]he Declaration expressed in lean, eloquent language the hopes and idealism of a world released from the grip of World War II. However self-evident it may appear today, the Declaration bore a more radical message than many of its framers perhaps recognized. It proceeded to work its subversive path though many rooted doctrines of international law, forever changing the discourse of international relations on issues vital to human decency and peace.[1]

In some sense the constitution of the entire movement, it has remained the single most cited human rights instrument.

---

[1] Henry Steiner, 'Securing Human Rights: The First Half-Century of the Universal Declaration, and Beyond', *Harvard Magazine*, September–October 1998, p. 45.

Other UN Organs Related to Human Rights

Together with the UN Commission, other UN organs have played major roles in developing universal human rights. Their full significance with respect to drafting and approving treaties or declarations, monitoring, censuring, and authorizing or ordering state action becomes apparent through readings in Chapters 3, 4, 8 and 14. A brief description follows.

Chapter IV of the Charter sets forth the composition and powers of the General Assembly. Those powers are described in Articles 10–14 in terms such as 'initiate studies', 'recommend', 'promote', 'encourage' and 'discuss'. Particularly relevant are Articles 10 and 13. Article 10 authorizes the General Assembly to 'discuss any questions or any matters within the scope of the present Charter [and] . . . make recommendations to the Members of the United Nations . . . on any such questions or matters'. Article 13 authorizes the General Assembly to 'make recommendations' for the purpose of, *inter alia,* 'assisting in the realization of human rights'.

Contrast the stronger and more closely defined powers of the Security Council under Chapter VII. Those powers range from making recommendations to states parties about ending a dispute, to the power to authorize and take military action 'to maintain or restore international peace and security' (Article 42) after the Council 'determine[s] the existence of any threat to the peace, breach of the peace, or act of aggression' (Article 39). Under Article 25, member states 'agree to accept and carry out' the Security Council's decisions on these and other matters. No such formal obligation of states attaches to recommendations or resolutions of the General Assembly.

Two of the seven Main Committees of the General Assembly—committees of the whole, for all UN members are entitled to be represented on them—have also participated in the drafting or other processes affecting human rights. The Social, Humanitarian and Cultural Committee (Third Committee) and the Legal Committee (Sixth Committee) have reviewed drafts of proposed declarations or conventions and often added their comments to the document submitted to the plenary General Assembly for its ultimate approval.

Historical Sequence and Typology of Instruments

That part of the universal human rights movement consisting of intergovernmental instruments—that is, excluding for present purposes both national laws and nongovernmental institutions forming part of the movement—can be imagined as a four-tiered normative edifice, the tiers described generally in the order of their chronological appearance.

(1) The UN Charter, at the pinnacle of the human rights system, has relatively little to say about the subject. But what it does say has been accorded great significance. Through interpretation and extrapolation, as well as frequent invocation, the sparse text has constituted a point of departure for inventive development of the entire movement.

(2) The Universal Declaration of Human Rights, viewed by some as a further

elaboration of the brief references to human rights in the Charter, occupies in important ways the primary position of constitution of the entire movement.

(3) The two principal covenants, which alone among the universal treaties have broad coverage of human rights topics, develop in more detail the basic categories of rights that figure in the Universal Declaration, and include additional rights as well. These covenants together with the UDHR form what is generally referred to as the International Bill of Rights.

(4) A host of multilateral human rights treaties (usually termed 'conventions', for there are only the two basic 'covenants'), as well as resolutions or declarations with a more limited or focused subject than the comprehensive International Bill of Rights, have grown out of the United Nations (drafting by UN organs, approval by the General Assembly) and (in the case of treaties) have been ratified by large numbers of states. They develop further the content of rights that are more tersely described in the two covenants or, in some cases, that escape mention in them. This fourth tier consists of a network of treaties, most but not all of which became effective after the two Covenants, including: the Convention on the Prevention and Punishment of the Crime of Genocide, effective 1951 (130 states parties as of March 2000), the International Convention on the Elimination of all Forms of Racial Discrimination, 1969 (155 parties), the Convention on the Elimination of all Forms of Discrimination against Women, 1981 (165 parties), the Convention against Torture and other Cruel, Inhuman or Degrading Treatment or Punishment, 1987 (118 parties), and the Convention on the Rights of the Child, 1990 (191 parties). This book discusses to one or another degree all these instruments.

NOTE

Consider the following observations in Louis Henkin, *International Law: Politics, Values and Functions*, 216 Collected Courses of The Hague Law Academy of International Droit (Vol. IV, 1989), at 215.

> The United Nations Charter, a vehicle of radical political-legal change in several respects, did not claim authority for the new human rights commitment it projected other than in the present consent of States. Unlike the international standard of justice for foreign nationals, which derived from the age of natural law and clearly reflected common acceptance of some natural rights[2], the Charter is a 'positivist' instrument. It does not invoke natural rights or any other philosophical basis for human rights. (The principal Powers could not have agreed on any such basis.) The Charter Preamble links human rights with human dignity but treats that value as self-evident, without need for justification. Nor does the Charter define either term or give other guidance as to the human rights that human dignity requires. In fact, to help justify the radical penetration of the State monolith, the Charter in effect justifies human rights as a State value by linking it to peace and security.
>
> Perhaps because we now wish to, we tend to exaggerate what the Charter did

---

[2] [Eds] See, e.g., the discussion of the law of state responsibility and the *Chattin* case, pp. 81–92, *supra*.

for human rights. The Charter made the promotion of human rights a purpose of the United Nations; perhaps without full appreciation of the extent of the penetration of Statehood that was involved, it thereby recognized and established that relations between a State and its own inhabitants were a matter of international concern. But the Charter did not erode State autonomy and the requirement of State consent to new human rights law. . . .

. . . Surely, the Charter did not provide, clearly and explicitly, that every State party to the Charter assumes legal obligations not to violate the human rights, or some human rights, of persons subject to its jurisdiction.

In 1945, the principal Powers were not prepared to derogate from the established character of the international system by establishing law and legal obligation that would penetrate Statehood in that radical way; clearly, they themselves were not ready to submit to such law. Small Powers and non-governmental organizations indeed proposed the addition to the Charter of an international bill of rights, but it was not done. . . .

COMMENT ON RELATIONSHIPS BETWEEN THE UNIVERSAL DECLARATION AND THE ICCPR

Readers should now become familiar with the Universal Declaration and the substantive part (Articles 1–27) of the International Covenant on Civil and Political Rights. The comparisons below between the UDHR and the ICCPR assume that familiarity.

(1) Under international law, approval by the General Assembly of a declaration like the UDHR has a different consequence from a treaty that has become effective through the required number of ratifications. Of course the declaration will have solemn effects as the formal act of a deliberative body of global importance. Its subject matter, like that of the UDHR, may be of the greatest significance. But when approved or adopted, it is hortatory and aspirational, recommendatory rather than, in a formal sense, binding.

The Covenant, on the other hand, binds the states parties in accordance with its terms, subject to such formal matters as reservations (see p. 439, *infra*). Of course this statement of international law doctrine and its basic postulate, *pacta sunt servanda*, does not end discussion. The content of important provisions of a treaty may long remain in dispute among the states parties. Differences over interpretation will likely arise; some states will disagree with others as to what even basic provisions of the Covenant (such as, in the case of the ICCPR, the 'right to life') mean and require. What indeed is the 'commitment'? In absence of a consensus, which state party or which international institution can provide an answer, decision, interpretation that most parties will view as authoritative? Even if there is a widespread consensus about meaning, one must confront the question of whether states will honour this 'binding' commitment and, if not, whether the UN or some Member States will apply pressure against violators sufficient to persuade them to comply. Does or should the probability of enforcement against violators have any bearing on the legally binding character of an international agreement? Such questions underlie much of the discussion in Part C of this book.

One must take account of these and other qualifications to the apparently clear contrast between 'binding' and 'hortatory' instruments. In the case of the UDHR, the years have further blurred that contrast. The constant invocation of the Declaration as the fountainhead or constitution or grand statement of the human rights movement has its effect on how it is viewed. Arguments have developed for viewing all or part of the Declaration as legally binding, either as a matter of customary international law or as an authoritative interpretation of the UN Charter.

(2) A resolution of the General Assembly with the formal status of a recommendation can hardly create an international institution with defined membership, structure and powers. Neither can customary international law. A treaty can. The Charter creates numerous organs distinct from but related to the UN itself. The ICCPR creates an ongoing institution, a treaty organ: the Human Rights Committee. That organ gives institutional support to the Covenant's norms, for the Covenant imposes on states parties formal obligations (such as the submission of periodic reports) to the Committee. This Committee (referred to in this book as the ICCPR Committee and examined in Chapter 9) is charged with the performance of the tasks defined both in the Covenant and in its Optional Protocol effective in 1976 (95 states parties as of March 2000).

(3) Both the UDHR and ICCPR are terse about their derivations or foundations in moral and political thought. Such statements as are made that have the character of justifications or explanations appear in the preambles (with a few exceptions such as Article 21 of the UDHR and Article 25 of the ICCPR). But clearly these instruments differ radically from, say, a tax treaty that expresses a compromise and temporary convergence of interests among its states parties. They speak to matters deep, lasting, purportedly universal. What then are the intuitions that shape them, their sources in intellectual history, important guides to their interpretation and evolution?

(4) Many rights declared in the Covenant closely resemble the provisions of the Universal Declaration, although they are stated in considerably greater detail. Compare, for example, the requirements for criminal trials in Articles 10 and 11 of the Universal Declaration with the analogous provisions in Articles 14 and 15 of the Covenant.

(5) *Individual* rights characterize these instruments. Group or collective rights—that is, rights that pertain to and are exercised by the collectivity as such—are rare. In a few cases, they are either asserted or hinted at in the Covenant, most directly in Articles 1 (on self-determination of peoples) and 27 (on survival of cultures). These provisions are absent from the Universal Declaration. Both the UDHR and the ICCPR refer to the family as the 'natural and fundamental group unit of society'. On the other hand, it should be kept in mind that rights cast in terms of the individual, such as the right to equal protection or the right to practice one's religion, have an inherent group character, either in the sense that the identity at issue in denials of equal protection is a group identity (race, ethnicity, gender, religion) or in the sense that the right is generally practised in community with others (as suggested by ICCPR Article 27).

(6) In both instruments the idea of *rights* dominates with respect to indi-

viduals. Duties characteristically attach to the state. Article 29(1) of the Declaration does provide that everyone 'has duties to the community in which alone the free and full development of his personality is possible'. The Covenant has no article referring to individuals' *duties*, though its Preamble has such a clause.

(7) Article 17 of the Declaration on the 'right to own property' and protection against arbitrary deprivation thereof does not figure among the rights declared in the Covenant.

(8) The UDHR goes beyond the bare declaration of rights to provide (Article 8) that everyone has the 'right to an effective remedy by the competent national tribunals' for violations of fundamental rights. The remedial structure of the ICCPR goes much further. In Article 2, states parties agree to 'ensure' to all persons within their territory the rights recognized by the Covenant, and to adopt such legislative or other measures as may be necessary to achieve that goal. Moreover, the parties undertake to 'ensure' that any person whose rights are violated 'shall have an effective remedy', and that 'the competent authorities shall enforce such remedies when granted'. They undertake in particular 'to develop the possibilities of judicial remedy'.

(9) Two types of provisions in the ICCPR limit states' obligations thereunder:

(a) Article 4 dealing with a public emergency ('which threatens the life of the nation and the existence of which is officiallly proclaimed') permits under closely stated conditions a temporary *derogation*—that is, deviation in the way of detracting—from many of the rights declared by the Covenant. Thus states may consciously, purposively depart from such rights as those in Article 9 relating to arrest and detention. Note that under paragraph (2) certain rights are non-derogable.

(b) A number of articles include *limitation clauses*—that is, provisions indicating that a given right cannot be absolute but must be adapted to meet a state's interest in protecting public safety, order, health or morals, or national security. See, for example, Articles 18 and 19. In Articles 21 and 22, the limitation clause is phrased in terms of permitting those restrictions on a right 'which are necessary in a democratic society'. Compare the broad provision of Article 29(2) of the UDHR, which is not linked to a specific right. Note that the limitation clauses may overlap with but are not identical with the common problem of resolving conflicts between rights (such as rights to speech and to privacy) that also may lead to a 'limitation' of one or the other right.

(10) Article 5 of the UDHR bans 'cruel, inhuman or degrading' punishment, but that instrument does not refer to capital punishment as such. See Article 6, para. 2 of the ICCPR. The Second Optional Protocol to the ICCPR, Aiming at the Abolition of the Death Penalty, became effective in 1991 (41 states parties as of March 2000). Article 1 provides that 'No one within the jurisdiction of a State Party to the present Protocol shall be executed. . . . Each State Party shall take all necessary measures to abolish the death penalty within its jurisdiction'. Recall the discussion about measures affecting capital punishment at pp. 31–34, *supra*.

One can organize or classify the rights declared in the Declaration and Covenant in various ways, depending on the purpose of the typology. Consider the adequacy of the following scheme that embraces most of the Covenant's rights, although it excludes such distinctive provisions as ICCPR Article 1 on the self-determination of peoples and Article 27 on the enjoyment by minorities of their own cultures:

(a) Protection of the individual's physical integrity, as in provisions on torture, arbitrary arrest, and arbitrary deprivation of life;

(b) procedural fairness when government deprives an individual of liberty, as in provisions on arrest, trial procedure and conditions of imprisonment;

(c) equal protection norms defined in racial, religious, gender and other terms;

(d) freedoms of belief, speech and association, such as provisions on political advocacy, the practice of religion, press freedom, and the right to hold an assembly and form associations; and

(e) the right to political participation.

These five categories of rights can be imagined as on a spectrum. At one extreme lie killing or torture over which there exists a broad formal-verbal consensus among states (whatever the degree of ongoing violation of the relevant rights by many states). At the other extreme lie rights whose purposes, basic meanings and even validity are formally disputed. For example, few if any states (even those that practise it) formally justify torture. A good number of states, however, may justify some form of religious or gender discrimination stemming from religious belief or customary practices, and argue that such practices should be viewed as consistent with the goals of the human rights movement. Or states that reject the core practices of political democracy may justify different forms of political organization ranging from hereditary leadership to a theocracy.

Among the intergovernmental organs or institutions referred to in this Comment, some such as the UN Commission are mandated by the UN Charter, others such as the ICCPR Committee by distinct treaties. As a matter of convenience, the first set is often referred to as 'Charter-based' organs/institutions and the second set as 'treaty-based' organs/institutions.

Despite this distinction, bear in mind that the entire universal human rights regime is related to the United Nations. The human rights treaties are distinct from the Charter only up to a point. Thus the ICCPR and the other treaties noted in category (4) above all grew within the UN, from the time that they were first drafted in an organ like the UN Commission to their final approval by the General Assembly and submission to states for ratification. Typically for such other treaties, the ICCPR provides for a number of ongoing links to the UN. Article 45 indicates that the Annual Report of the ICCPR Committee should be submitted by that Committee to the General Assembly. Note also the provisions for amendment of the ICCPR in Article 51. Moreover, each of these separate treaty regimes like the ICCPR depends for funding on the regular biennial budget adopted by the General Assembly.

QUESTIONS

1. Relying only on the preambles and texts of the UDHR and the ICCPR, how would you identify the reasons for those instruments, their justifications in moral and political thought, the moral and political traditions from which they derive? Why do you suppose there was such a sparse statement of reasons or justifications in these instruments?

2. Do you see in either of these instruments any departure from 'universal' premises, rights, and related obligations of states? That is, are there concessions in any provisions to different cultures or regions that would allow those cultures or regions to privilege their own traditions rather than follow these instruments' rules—for example, by inflicting certain severe modes of criminal punishment, or governing by theocracy or inherited rule, or imposing restrictions on minority religions or on activities of women?

3. Article 2 of the ICCPR includes states' undertakings 'to respect and to ensure to all individuals' the recognized rights. States parties must 'ensure' that persons whose rights are violated have an 'effective remedy'. Competent authorities 'shall enforce such remedies when granted'.

   a. Is it accurate to say that rights are borne by individuals, and duties are borne only by states since the ICCPR is concerned only with state violations? Who may violate, say, your right to bodily security? Who may violate your right to political participation under Article 25, or your right to procedural due process under Article 14?
   b. Is it accurate to say that the duties of the state are entirely 'negative', in the sense of requiring no more than that the state generally keep its 'hands off' individuals, and refrain from certain conduct such as discrimination? Is it accurate to say that fulfilment by the state of its duties would then be cost-free?

NOTE

Understandings of the Universal Declaration have inevitably changed over time. Appreciation of that change, as well as of the continuities in understanding, illuminate the general evolution of the human rights movement as well as changing perceptions of international law. There follow some excerpts from an influential book by a preeminent scholar of international law of his generation, Hersch Lauterpacht. At the time of the book's publication, the Declaration was novel and untested as to its character and significance.

H. LAUTERPACHT, INTERNATIONAL LAW AND HUMAN RIGHTS
(1950), at 61

Chapter 4: The Subjects of the Law of Nations, the Function of International Law, and the Rights of Man

. . .

What have been the reasons which have prompted the changes in the matter of subjects of international law, with regard both to international rights and to international duties? These causes have been numerous and manifold. They have included, with reference to the recognition of the individual as a subject of international rights, the acknowledgment of the worth of human personality as the ultimate unit of all law; the realisation of the dangers besetting international peace as the result of the denial of fundamental human rights; and the increased attention paid to those already substantial developments in international law in which, notwithstanding the traditional dogma, the individual is in fact treated as a subject of international rights. Similarly, in the sphere of international duties there has been an enhanced realisation of the fact that the direct subjection of the individual to the rule of international law is an essential condition of the strengthening of the ethical basis of international law and of its effectiveness in a period of history in which the destructive potentialities of science and the power of the machinery of the State threaten the very existence of civilised life.

Above all, with regard to both international rights and international duties the decisive factor has been the change in the character and the function of modern international law. The international law of the past was to a large extent of a formal character. It was concerned mainly with the delimitation of the jurisdiction of States. Substantial portions of it were devoted to immunities of States, their diplomatic representatives, and their property. In so far as it was concerned with substantive law, it was mainly concerned with the law of war. There is not much difference in this respect between the treatises of the early publicists and those of modern writers. In traditional international law the individual played an inconspicuous part because the international interests of the individual and his contacts across the frontier were rudimentary. This is no longer the case. . . .

. . .

For it is in relation to State sovereignty that the question of subjects of international law has assumed a special significance. Critics of the traditional theory have treated it as an emanation of the doctrine of sovereignty. in their view it is State sovereignty—absolute, petty, and overbearing—which rejects, as incompatible with the dignity of States, the idea of individuals as units of that international order which they have monopolised and thwarted in its growth. It is the sovereign State, with its claim to exclusive allegiance and its pretensions to exclusive usefulness that interposes itself as an impenetrable barrier between the individual and the greater society of all humanity. . . .

. . .

While statements such as that individuals are only objects and not subjects of international law have been shown here to be devoid of substance, they reveal clearly the intimate connexion between the question of the subjects of international law and the notion of 'human rights and fundamental freedoms'. . . . The claim of the State to unqualified exclusiveness in the field of international relations was tolerable at a time when the actuality and the interdependence of the interests of the individual cutting across national frontiers were less obvious than they are today. It is this latter fact which explains why the constant expansion of the periphery of individual rights—an enduring feature of legal development—cannot stop short of the limits of the State. What is much more important, the recognition of the individual, by dint of the acknowledgment of his fundamental rights and freedoms, as the ultimate subject of international law, is a challenge to the doctrine which in reserving that quality exclusively to the State tends to a personification of the State as a being distinct from the individuals who compose it, with all that such personification implies. That recognition brings to mind the fact that, in the international as in the municipal sphere, the collective good is conditioned by the good of the individual human beings who comprise the collectivity. It denies, by cogent implication, that the corporate entity of the State is of a higher order than its component parts. . . .

. . . An international legal system which aims at effectively safeguarding human freedom in all its aspects is no longer an abstraction. It is as real as man's interest in the guarantee and the preservation of his inalienable rights as a rational and moral being. International law, which has excelled in punctilious insistence on the respect owed by one sovereign State to another, henceforth acknowledges the sovereignty of man. For fundamental human rights are rights superior to the law of the sovereign State. The hope, expressed by Emerson, that 'man shall treat with man as a sovereign state with a sovereign state' may be brought nearer to fruition by sovereign States recognising the duty to treat man with the respect which traditional law exacted from them in relation to other States. To that vital extent the recognition of inalienable human rights and the recognition of the individual as a subject of international law are synonymous. To that vital extent they both signify the recognition of a higher, fundamental law not only on the part of States but also, through international law, on the part of the organized international community itself. That fundamental law, as expressed in the acknowledgment of the ultimate reality and the independent status of the individual, constitutes both the moral limit and the justification of the international legal order. . . .

Chapter 5: The Idea of Natural Rights in Legal and Political Thought

The object of the present Section of this book . . . is to enquire into the relation between, on the one hand, the conceptions of the law of nature and the natural rights of man, and, on the other hand, the effective acknowledgment of these rights by international law in general and an International Bill of Human Rights in particular. . . .

. . . The law of nature and natural rights can never be a true substitute for the positive enactments of the law of the society of States. When so treated they are inefficacious, deceptive and, in the long run, a brake upon progress. However, while they are bound to be mischievous when conceived as an alternative to changes in the law, they are of abiding potency and beneficence as the foundation of its ultimate validity and as a standard of its approximation to justice. Inasmuch as, upon final analysis, they are an expression of moral claims, they are a powerful level of legal reform. The moral claims of today are often the legal rights of tomorrow. The law of nature, even when conceived as an expression of mere ethical postulates, is an inarticulate but powerful element in the interpretation of existing law. Even after human rights and freedoms have become part of the positive fundamental law of mankind, the ideas of natural law and natural rights which underlie them will constitute that higher law which must forever remain the ultimate standard of fitness of all positive law, whether national or international. . . .

. . .

. . . [T]he question of the relation of the individual to the State—and his protection against the State—has been a perennial problem of law and politics. That problem has consisted in the reconciliation of two apparently conflicting factors. The first is that the State, however widely its object may be construed, has no justification and no valid claim to obedience except as an instrument for securing the welfare of the individual human being. The second is that the State—though not necessarily the existing sovereign State—has come to be recognized as the absolute condition of the civilized existence of man and of his progression towards the full realisation of his faculties. It is a matter of absorbing interest to note how, in the history of political and legal thought and action, the conflict between these two factors has been bridged by the notion, variously disguised, of the fundamental, natural, inherent or inalienable rights of man. These are the bounds which, it has been asserted, the Leviathan of the State must not transgress. . . .

[Lauterpacht then turns to historical antecedents of 'the notion and the doctrine of natural, inalienable rights of man pre-existent to and higher than the positive law of the State'. He observes that 'ideas of the law of nature date back to antiquity', and briefly describes such ideas and notions of natural right in Greek philosophy and the Greek state, in Roman thought, in the Middle Ages, and in the Reformation and the period of Social Contract. Lauterpacht then addresses 'fundamental rights in modern constitutions'.]

In the nineteenth and twentieth centuries the recognition of the fundamental rights of man in the constitutions of States became, in a paraphrase of Article 38 of the Statute of the Permanent Court of International Justice, a general principle of the constitutional law of civilised States. It became part of the law of nearly all European States. . . . After the First World War it was adopted by Germany and most of the new European States. The All-Russia Congress proclaimed in January, 1918, a 'declaration of the rights of the toiling and the exploited peoples' which was incorporated as Part I of the Constitution of 5 July, 1918. That declaration was considerably extended in the Constitution of 1936. Other States which subsequently succumbed to the wave of totalitarianism did not dispense in their revised constitutions—like those of Poland of 1935 and Roumania of 1938—with a list of fundamental rights. The Latin-American States followed in the nineteenth

and twentieth centuries the general trend practically without exception. . . . States
on the Asiatic continent followed suit. . . . The Turkish Constitution of 1928 did
not refrain from similar terminology vividly reminiscent of the Declaration of
1789: 'Every Turk is born and lives free. . . . The limits, for every one, of freedom,
which is a natural right, are the limits of the freedom of others'. . . . The Constitution of Japan of 3 November, 1946, laid down, in Article 11, 'that the people shall
not be prevented from enjoying any of the fundamental rights' and that 'these
fundamental rights guaranteed to the people by the constitution shall be conferred upon the people of this and future generations as eternal and inviolate
rights'. . . .

    . . . [T]here is one objection to the notion of natural rights which, far from
invalidating the essential idea of natural rights, is nevertheless in a sense
unanswerable. It is a criticism which reveals a close and, indeed, inescapable connexion between the idea of fundamental rights on the one hand and the law of
nature and the law of nations on the other. That criticism is to the effect that, in
the last resort, such rights are subject to the will of the State: that they may—and
must—be regulated, modified, and if need be taken away by legislation and, possibly, by judicial interpretation; that, therefore, these rights are in essence a revocable part of the positive law of a sanctity and permanence no higher than the
constitution of the State either as enacted or as interpreted by courts and by
subsequent legislation. . . .

. . .

Chapter 17: The Universal Declaration of Human Rights

The Universal Declaration of Human Rights . . . has been hailed as an historic
event of profound significance and as one of the greatest achievements of the
United Nations. . . . Mrs. Roosevelt, Chairman of the Commission on Human
Rights and the principal representative of the United States on the Third Committee, said: 'It [the Declaration] might well become the international Magna Carta of
all mankind . . . Its proclamation by the General Assembly would be of importance
comparable to the 1789 proclamation of the Declaration of the Rights of Man, the
proclamation of the rights of man in the Declaration of Independence of the
United States of America, and similar declarations made in other countries'. . . .

. . .

    The practical unanimity of the Members of the United Nations in stressing the
importance of the Declaration was accompanied by an equally general repudiation
of the idea that the Declaration imposed upon them a legal obligation to respect
the human rights and fundamental freedoms which it proclaimed. The debates in
the General Assembly and in the Third Committee did not reveal any sense of
uneasiness on account of the incongruity between the proclamation of the universal character of the human rights forming the subject matter of the Declaration
and the rejection of the legal duty to give effect to them. The delegates gloried in
the profound significance of the achievement whereby the nations of the world
agree as to what are the obvious and inalienable rights of man—so obvious and
fundamental that they considered the suggestion of describing them as grounded
in nature to impart to the Declaration an undesirable element of controversy and

confusion—but they declined to acknowledge them as part of the law binding upon their States and Governments. . . .

. . . [T]he representative of the United States, in the same statement before the General Assembly in which she extolled the virtues of the Declaration, said: 'In giving our approval to the declaration today, it is of primary importance that we keep clearly in mind the basic character of the document. It is not a treaty; it is not an international agreement. It is not and does not purport to be a statement of law or of legal obligation. . . .'

. . .

. . . It is now necessary to consider the view, expressed in various forms, that, somehow, the Declaration may have an indirect legal effect.

In the first instance, it may be said—and has been said—that although the Declaration in itself may not be a legal document involving legal obligations, it is of legal value inasmuch as it contains an authoritative interpretation of the 'human rights and fundamental freedoms' which do constitute an obligation, however imperfect, binding upon the Members of the United Nations. It is unlikely that any tribunal or other authority administering international law would accept a suggestion of that kind. To maintain that a document contains an authoritative interpretation of a legally binding instrument is to assert that that former document itself is as legally binding and as important as the instrument which it is supposed to interpret. . . .

. . . [T]here would seem to be no substance in the view that the provisions of the Declaration may somehow be of importance for the interpretation of the Charter as a formulation, in this field, of the 'general principles of law recognized by civilised nations'. The Declaration does not purport to embody what civilized nations generally recognize as law. . . . The Declaration gives expression to what, in the fullness of time, ought to become principles of law generally recognized and acted upon by States Members of the United Nations. . . .

. . .

Undoubtedly the Declaration will occasionally be invoked by private and official bodies, including the organs of the United Nations. But it will not—and cannot—properly be invoked as a source of legal obligation. . . .

Not being a legal instrument, the Declaration would appear to be outside international law. Its provisions cannot form the subject matter of legal interpretation. There is little meaning in attempting to elucidate, by reference to accepted canons of construction and to preparatory work, the extent of an obligation which is binding only in the sphere of conscience. . . .

The fact that the Universal Declaration of Human Rights is not a legal instrument expressive of legally binding obligations is not in itself a measure of its importance. It is possible that, if divested of any pretence to legal authority, it may yet prove, by dint of a clear realisation of that very fact, a significant landmark in the evolution of a vital part of international law. . . .

. . .

The moral authority and influence of an international pronouncement of this nature must be in direct proportion to the degree of the sacrifice of the sovereignty of States which it involves. Thus conceived, the fundamental issue in relation to the moral authority of the Declaration can be simply stated: That authority is a function of the degree to which States commit themselves to an effective recognition of these rights guaranteed by a will and an agency other than and superior to their own. . . .

Its moral force cannot rest on the fact of its universality—or practical universality—as soon as it is realised that it has proved acceptable to all for the reason that it imposes obligations upon none. . . .

Undoubtedly, no Bill of Rights, however rigid may be its legal obligations and however drastic its instrumentalities of enforcement, can prove effective unless, by education and enlightenment, it secures the support of the public opinion of the world. But public opinion in support of such aims cannot be created by pronouncements expressing 'a common standard of achievement'. It is accurate, in this respect, to compare the Declaration of 1948 with that of [the French Declaration of] 1789 and similar constitutional pronouncements. These may not have been endowed, from the very inception, with all the remedies of judicial review and the formal apparatus of enforcement. But they became, from the outset, part of national law and an instrument of national action. They were not a mere philosophical pronouncement. . . . One of the governing principles of the Declaration—a principle which was repeatedly affirmed and which is a juridical heresy—is that it should proclaim rights of individuals while scrupulously refraining from laying down the duties of States. To do otherwise, it was asserted, would constitute the Declaration a legal instrument. But there are, in these matters, no rights of the individual except as a counterpart and a product of the duties of the State. There are no rights unless accompanied by remedies. That correlation is not only an inescapable principle of juridical logic. Its absence connotes a fundamental and decisive ethical flaw in the structure and conception of the Declaration. . . .

NOTE

Preceding observations about the Universal Declaration have stressed the priority that it gives to rights (over duties) and the dominance of *individual* (as opposed to group or collective) rights. Consider the following argument about the character of the Declaration, based on an analysis of its drafters and drafting, by Mary Ann Glendon, in *Rights from Wrongs* (manuscript ch. 9, Random House, forthcoming):

> Revisiting the Declaration as it looked to the men and women who participated in its creation discloses three nearly forgotten features that bear importantly on contemporary problems of interpretation and implementation: . . . (3) Its parts were meant to be understood in relation to each other and the whole . . . [T]he currently prevalent 'pick and choose' approach is not a legitimate method of dealing with its interlocking rights.
> . . .
> Those closely involved in the drafting process seem to have taken for granted that human dignity was the Declaration's touchstone. . . . The framers fleshed

out the concept of human dignity by connecting it to a particular conception of personhood. The Declaration's 'everyone' is not an isolated individual, but a person who is constituted, in important ways, by and through relationships with others. 'Everyone' is envisioned as uniquely valuable in himself . . . but 'Everyone' is expected to act towards others 'in a spirit of brotherhood'. 'Everyone' is depicted as situated in a variety of specifically named, real-life relationships of mutual dependence: marriage, families, communities, religious groups, workplaces, associations, societies, cultures, nations and an emerging international order. Though its main body is devoted to basic freedoms, the Declaration begins and ends with exhortations to solidarity (Articles 1 and 29). Whatever else may be said of him or her, the Declaration's 'everyone' is not a lone bearer of rights.
. . .

The Declaration's membership in what may be called the 'dignitarian' family of post-World-War II constitutions differentiates it in subtle, but significant, ways from the older, more individualistic and 'libertarian' rights tradition of the Anglo-American nations. . . . In dignitarian traditions . . . rights tend to be formulated so as to make clear their limits, and their relation to one another, as well as to the responsibilities that belong to citizens and the state. Charters in this tradition . . . accord an equally high priority to freedom, but it is a freedom grounded in dignity and linked with solidarity. . . . [T]he interpreter must respect the priorities established in the text and strive to optimize the scope of each principle involved.

QUESTION

As a principle of interpretation, in what direction (if any) would this understanding of the UDHR point with respect to, say, (1) a question of freedom of speech as applied to hate speech, (2) a question of individual liberty in relation to the right of others to an adequate standard of living, (3) a question of equal protection in relation to a claim for gay marriage? What is the relation between this understanding and a declaration expressed in terms of individual duties?

NOTE

Note the following observations about the progressive or immediate character of the state's obligations under the ICCPR, in Dominic McGoldrick, *The Human Rights Committee* (1991), at 12:

There were marked differences of opinion during the drafting on the matter of the obligations that would be incurred by a State party to the ICCPR. Some representatives argued that the obligations under the ICCPR were absolute and immediate and that, therefore, a State could only become a party to the ICCPR after, or simultaneously with, its taking the necessary measures to secure those rights. If there were disparities between the Covenant and national law they could best be met by reservations. . . .

Against this view it was argued that the prior adoption of the necessary measures in domestic law was not required by international law. . . .
. . .

Proposals to provide that the necessary measures be taken within a specified
time limit or within a reasonable time were rejected as was a suggestion that each
State fix its own time limit in its instrument of ratification. The only clear
intentions of the [UN Commission on Human Rights] that emerged were those
of avoiding excessive delays in the full implementation of the Covenant and of
not introducing the general notion of progressiveness that was a feature of the
obligations under the then draft [International Covenant on Economic, Social
and Cultural Rights].

The objections to the draft article 2(2) were again voiced in the Third Committee but the provision remained unchanged. The Committee's report stated
that:

> It represented the minimum compromise formula, the need for which,
> particularly in new States building up their body of legislation, was
> manifest. The notion of implementation at the earliest possible
> moment was implicit in article 2 as a whole. Moreover, the reporting
> requirement in article 49 (later article 40) would indeed serve as an
> effective curb on undue delay.

NOTE

It is frequently stated that all rights declared in the ICCPR are 'equal and interdependent'. Within that formulation, the right of an indigent person to be
assigned legal assistance in a criminal case in Article 14(3) (c) is of the same rank
as, interdependent with, the right not to be tortured in Article 7. The following
readings explore this issue of equality or hierarchy. Note how the question may
change with the purpose for which the question is asked. These readings are
concerned primarily with derogation during emergencies.

THEO VAN BOVEN, DISTINGUISHING CRITERIA OF HUMAN RIGHTS

in Karel Vasak and Alston (eds.), The International Dimensions of Human Rights, Vol. 1 (1982), at 43

There is another argument against making a distinction between fundamental
human rights and other human rights. Such a distinction might imply that there is
a hierarchy between various human rights according to their fundamental character. However, in modern human rights thinking the indivisibility of human
rights and fundamental freedoms is prevalent. This idea of indivisibility presupposes that human rights form, so to speak, a single package and that they cannot
rank one above the other on a hierarchical scale.

This may all be true, but there still remain weighty arguments which militate in
favour of distinguishing fundamental human rights from other human rights.

Such fundamental rights can also be called elementary rights or supra-positive rights. i.e. rights whose validity is not dependent on their acceptance by the subjects of law but which are at the foundation of the international community. . . .

. . .

. . . The intensity of the prevailing sentiments against racism and racial discrimination, the awareness of urgency and the political climate have made the principle of racial non-discrimination one of the foundations of the international community as represented in the UN. Members of this community are bound by this principle on the basis of the UN Charter, even if they do not adhere to the various international instruments specifically aimed at the elimination of racial discrimination and apartheid. . . .

There is also a great deal of law in humanitarian conventions and in international human rights instruments supporting the existence of very fundamental human rights. This is that part of human rights law which does not permit any derogation even in time of armed conflict or in other public emergency situations threatening the life of the nation. The common article 3 of the four Geneva Conventions of 1949, setting out a number of minimum humanitarian standards which are to be respected in cases of conflict which are not of an international character, enumerates certain acts which 'are and shall remain prohibited at any time and in any place whatsoever'. The following acts are mentioned: '(a) violence to life and person, in particular murder of all kinds, mutilation, cruel treatment and torture; (b) taking of hostages; (c) outrages upon personal dignity, in particular, humiliating and degrading treatment; (d) the passing of sentences and the carrying out of executions without previous judgment pronounced by a regularly constituted court, affording all the judicial guarantees which are recognized as indispensable by civilized nations'. The universal validity of these fundamental prescriptions is underlined by the words 'at any time and in any place whatsoever' in this common article 3 of the four 1949 Geneva Conventions.

The International Covenant on Civil and Political Rights enumerates in article 4, para. 2, the rights from which no derogation is allowed in time of public emergency. . . . Regional human rights conventions contain a similar clause enumerating provisions from which no derogation may be made.

The fact that in a number of comprehensive human rights instruments at the worldwide and the regional level, certain rights are specifically safeguarded and are intended to retain their full strength and validity notably in serious emergency situations, is a strong argument in favour of the contention that there is at least a minimum catalogue of fundamental or elementary human rights.

. . .

NOTE

Compare with van Boven's observations those in Theodor Meron, *On a Hierarchy of International Human Rights*, 80 Am. J. Int. L. 1 (1986), at 21:

> . . . Hierarchical terms constitute a warning sign that the international community will not accept any breach of those rights. Historically, the notions of

'basic rights of the human person' and 'fundamental rights' have helped establish the erga omnes principle, which is so crucial to ensuring respect for human rights. Eventually, they may contribute to the crystallization of some rights, through custom or treaties, into hierarchically superior norms, as in the more developed national legal systems.

Yet the balance of pros and cons does not necessarily weigh clearly on the side of the pros. Resort to hierarchical terms has not been matched by careful consideration of their legal significance. Few criteria for distinguishing between ordinary rights and higher rights have been agreed upon. There is no accepted system by which higher rights can be identified and their content determined. Nor are the consequences of the distinction between higher and ordinary rights clear. Rights not accorded quality labels, i.e., the majority of human rights, are relegated to inferior, second-class, status. Moreover, rather than grapple with the harder questions of rationalizing human rights lawmaking and distinguishing between rights and claims, some commentators are resorting increasingly to superior rights in the hope that no state will dare—politically, morally and perhaps even legally—to ignore them. In these ways, hierarchical terms contribute to the unnecessary mystification of human rights, rather than to their greater clarity.

Caution should therefore be exercised in resorting to a hierarchical terminology. Too liberal an invocation of superior rights such as 'fundamental rights' and 'basic rights,' as well as *jus cogens*, may adversely affect the credibility of human rights as a legal discipline.

In a report on its Fiftieth Session in 1994, the Human Rights Committee created by the ICCPR noted a proposal submitted to it for a possible draft optional protocol to that instrument that would add Article 9 paras. 3 and 4 (arrest and detention) and Article 14 (criminal procedure) to the list of non-derogable provisions under Article 4(2). The Committee's reaction was negative. It 'was satisfied that States parties generally understood that the right to habeas corpus and *amparo* should not be limited in situations of emergency', and that the remedies provided in the relevant parts of Article 9, 'read in conjunction with article 2 were inherent in the Covenant as a whole'. There was a 'considerable risk' that such an optional protocol 'might implicitly invite States parties to feel free to derogate from the provisions of article 9 of the Covenant during states of emergency if they do not ratify the proposed optional protocol'. UN Doc. A/49/40, paras. 22–25.

QUESTIONS

1. How does the doctrine of *jus cogens* differ from the effort urged by Van Boven to work out some hierarchy of rights, whether for the purposes indicated by Common Article 3 of the Geneva Conventions or for purposes of stating non-derogable rights in situations of emergency?

2. Does the list of non-derogable rights in Article 4 of the ICCPR necessarily express some abstract, general hierarchy of rights in terms of their 'fundamental' importance or some similar criterion? How do you compare the rights there listed with others that are derogable? Can you suggest another purpose and criterion for deciding on a list of non-derogable rights in Article 4?

3. Suppose that you are a director of an international nongovernmental human rights organization, like Human Rights Watch or the International Commission of Jurists. You must vote on next year's agenda for that organization indicating what types of violations it should investigate, taking account of budget constraints and other limited resources. In general, are there issues or regions to which you would give priority with respect to monitoring and reporting and attempting to achieve change? From this perspective, how do you react to the views of van Boven and Meron about equality or hierarchy among human rights norms?

4. Suppose that you are part of a new, reforming and popularly elected government of State X that has just displaced a decade-long repressive, brutal regime that was forced from power by popular uprisings. Suspected enemies of the regime were arrested, tortured, killed. Discrimination among ethnic groups was rampant. Courts were tools of the government. Political participation and speech were repressed. Of course your political and material resources are now limited. How would you start to think about agendas and priorities for the new X with respect to realization of human rights norms?

NOTE

The issue arose in the 1990s of a state party's right to withdraw from the ICCPR, which unlike many treaties has no provision about termination of obligations. The Human Rights Committee created by the ICCPR issued in 1997, at its 61st session, its General Comment 26 on this question. (The authority of the Committee to issue such comments, as well as their significance, are examined at pp. 731–738, *infra*.) Excerpts follow:

> 1. The International Covenant on Civil and Political Rights does not contain any provision regarding its termination and does not provide for denunciation or withdrawal. Consequently, the possibility of termination, denunciation or withdrawal must be considered in the light of applicable rules of customary international law which are reflected in the Vienna Convention on the Law of Treaties. On this basis, the Covenant is not subject to denunciation or withdrawal unless it is established that the parties intended to admit the possibility of denunciation or withdrawal or a right to do so is implied from the nature of the treaty.
>
> 2. [The Committee noted that some separate state agreements related to the ICCPR were subject to denunciation or withdrawal by the parties, as were other human rights treaties.] It can. . .be concluded that the drafters of the Covenant deliberately intended to exclude the possibility of denunciation. . . .
>
> 3. Furthermore, it is clear that the Covenant is not the type of treaty which, by

its nature, implies a right of denunciation. Together with the simultaneously prepared and adopted International Covenant on Economic, Social and Cultural Rights, the Covenant codifies in treaty form the universal human rights enshrined in the Universal Declaration of Human Rights, the three instruments together often being referred to as the 'International Bill of Human Rights'. As such, the Covenant does not have a temporary character typical of treaties where a right of denunciation is deemed to be admitted, notwithstanding the absence of a specific provision to that effect.

4. The rights enshrined in the Covenant belong to the people living in the territory of the State party. The Human Rights Committee has consistently taken the view . . .that once the people are accorded the protection of the rights under the Covenant, such protection devolves with territory and continues to belong to them, notwithstanding change in government of the State party, including dismemberment in more than one State or State succession. . . .

5. The Committee is therefore firmly of the view that international law does not permit a State which has ratified or acceded or succeeded to the Covenant to denounce it or withdraw from it.

ADDITIONAL READING

L. Henkin (ed.), *The International Bill of Rights: Th Covenant on Civil and Political Rights* (1981); P. Lauren, *The Evolution of International Human Rights* (1999); J. Morsink, *The Universal Declaration of Human Rights: Origins, Drafting, and Intent* (1999); G. Alfredsson and A. Eide, *The Universal Declaration of Human Rights: A Common Standard of Achievement* (1999); B. van der Heijden and B. Tahzib-Lie (eds.), *Reflections on the Universal Declaration of Human Rights: A Fiftieth Anniversary Anthology* (1998); W. Korey, *NGOs and the Universal Declaration of Human Rights* (1998); Y. Danieli *et al.* (eds.), *Universal Declaration of Human Rights: 50 Years and Beyond* (1999); and P. Baehr, C. Flinterman and M. Senders (eds.), *Innovation and Inspiration: Fifty Years of the Universal Declaration of Human Rights* (1999).

B. WOMEN'S RIGHTS AND CEDAW

The study of women's rights illustrates the increasing ambition, breadth and complexity of the human rights movement. We see a proliferation of instruments and institutions, world conferences and NGO initiatives, active proposals in many directions, and growing conflicts about premises and goals within the women's movement itself. Goals and strategies different from the ICCPR become prominent. Such complexity is captured in an innovative and ambitious treaty, the Convention on the Elimination of All Forms of Discrimination against Women (CEDAW, effective 1981, 165 states parties in March 2000).

Of the several blind spots in the early development of the human rights movement, none is as striking as that movement's failure to give to violations of women's (human) rights the attention, and in some respects the priority, that they require. It is not only that these problems adversely affect half of the world's population. They affect everyone, for a deep change in women's circumstances and possibilities produces change throughout social, economic and political life.

Even in fields where the human rights movement acted with vigour in setting standards, passing resolutions and at times imposing sanctions—for example, racial discrimination—it is often the case that progress has been measured or slight, and that problems of the most serious character remain entrenched. Nonetheless, it is instructive to contrast the vigor of the movement in trying to 'eliminate' racial discrimination with its relative apathy until the last decade in responding to gender discrimination—and to explore why this is so.

The materials in this Section B suggest the complexly interwoven socio-economic, legal, political and cultural strands to the problem of women's sub-ordination and to the content of women's rights. Although a systematic study of economic and social rights must await Chapter 4, Section B demonstrates in many ways the interrelationships and functional interdependence of civil-political and economic-social rights. The title to CEDAW incorporates a classic civil-political issue, discrimination, but the content of this convention's rights and the work of its Committee range more broadly. Moreover, when one focuses specifically on what appear to be women's issues, links between them and other aspects of social order (disorder) appear pervasive. All is interrelated. The problem is truly systemic.

One important aspect of women's rights, although inevitably figuring in some of the discussions in this section, receives closer attention in Chapters 5 and 6. Those chapters use gender issues to illustrate the conflict between universalism and cultural relativism.

1. BACKGROUND TO CEDAW: SOCIO-ECONOMIC CONTEXT, DISCRIMINATION, AND ABUSE

These introductory materials present reports about women's circumstances in different parts of the world. They suggest the complex relationships among diverse phenomena that bear on women's rights. Several themes recur in the readings.

(1) Legal norms capture and reinforce deep cultural norms and community practices. They entrench ideas and help give them the sense of being natural, part of the inevitable order of things.

(2) Reformers and advocates of deep legal and cultural transformation insist that change is possible, so that what was seen as natural or inevitable comes to be understood as socially constructed and thus contingent, open to change.

(3) Property rights and economic dependence interact with patterns of authority within family and workplace, and with vital issues like education, health, and political participation.

(4) Major economic and political programmes, like a development or privatization scheme or structural adjustment requirements or a stress on deregulated

markets and trade, may impose particular and severe costs on women that are not apparent on the face of the programmes.

(5) The statistics created by bureaucracies or scholars structure and confine the imagination. They are often viewed as objective data, without awareness of the disputable methods and categories that determine their formulation. What they record as well as what they do not record influence policies as well as perceptions. New methods and categories in the statistical tables prepared by such institutions as the United Nations Development Program introduce new criteria to judge women's (and other groups') circumstances and progress.

INITIAL REPORT OF GUATEMALA SUBMITTED TO THE CEDAW COMMITTEE
CEDAW/C/Gua/1–2, 2 April 1991

[CEDAW requires in Article 18 that states parties submit periodic reports on 'measures which they have adopted to give effect' to CEDAW's provisions. Those reports 'may indicate factors and difficulties affecting the degree of fulfillment of obligations' under CEDAW. The reports are to be submitted to the Committee created by Article 17 of CEDAW. In its introduction to this report, Guatemala noted the difficulty of assembling it, stressing that 'studies of this type are only a recent innovation'. The task of preparation 'has also been a positive exercise in thought, analysis and self-appraisal with respect to the position of women in Guatemala in 1983, and the changes made to date'. That work stimulated action to design 'strategies and targets . . . to improve the situation encountered in the short and medium term'. The following excerpts from the report address Articles 5 and 16 of the Convention.]

Article 5

46. Guatemala is a multi-ethnic, multi-cultural and multilingual country with traditional, cultural patterns that reinforce the subordination of women on the social, cultural, economic and political planes. Extended Guatemalan families in the country and nuclear families in the city are governed by a patriarchal system in which decisions are taken by men (husband, father or eldest son), who are considered the heads of the household, a role assumed by women only in their absence.

47. In Guatemalan society the man is expected to be the breadwinner, the legal representative, the repository of authority; the one who must 'correct' the children, while the mother is relegated to their care and upbringing, to household tasks, and to 'waiting on' or looking after her husband or partner. These roles often have to be performed in addition to engaging in some profitable activity which generates earnings that are always regarded as 'complementary'.

48. For their childhood, little boys and girls are guided towards work considered 'masculine' or 'feminine'; for example, boys play at working outside the home as carpenters, mechanics, farmers or pilots, and in all those jobs that are

considered 'tough' or that require physical strength. Girls, on the other hand, are taught to interest themselves in cooking, weaving, sewing, washing, ironing, or cleaning the house and, especially, caring for the children and helping the mother, as a responsibility and duty more than just a game.

49. Care of the children is strictly considered the responsibility of the mother, grandmother, and/or sister; and in the event of divorce, separation or dissolution of the marriage, custody of the children is generally awarded to the mother.

50. The aforementioned patterns vary slightly with the socio-economic stratum, which generally also determines the social class to which the women belong and which in addition is related to their level of education and knowledge.

51. Notwithstanding what has been said, the woman is the chief social agent in the majority of spheres of action. An empirical profile of a Guatemalan woman may cover the following characteristics.

52. She is responsible for family health and hygiene and for the supervision of the formal and informal upbringing of the children in the home; she organizes and maintains living and sanitary conditions and a supply of water for domestic use. She produces nutritional supplements for the family, including animal proteins (cattle, sheep and goats) and sources of vitamins (fruit and vegetables); she is the one in charge of the purchase, preparation, stocking and distribution of food within the home. In addition, she manages the family income, ensuring that payment in kind and in cash is used in such a way as to maximize the material well-being of the family.

53. She takes responsibility for generating additional income or for producing consumer goods when her partner's income does not cover the minimum family requirements.

54. In the case of an irresponsible father, the entire responsibility for the support of the children devolves upon her, reflected in particular by a considerable increase in her hours of work.

55. Her work is poorly paid or not paid at all and is generally of low productivity owing to lack of access to capital.

56. It is falsely assumed that the man is the one who makes the principal economic contributions to the family, for which reason he is the owner and beneficiary of all payments and services.

57. The educational level of the woman is low, which reflects on the effectiveness of her efforts to maintain and improve the health, feeding, housing and other living conditions of her family.

58. In the paid work that she does, her salary is inferior to a man's and her instability in the sense of a job is greater.

59. The man has traditionally been considered the 'head of the household'.

Article 16

184. Family relations in Guatemala, as regards the guardianship, wardship, trusteeship and adoption of children, the ownership of property, its disposition and enjoyment, etc. are governed by the Guatemalan Civil Code (Decree-Law No. 106).
. . .

190. The woman's rights and responsibilities in marriage are as follows:

. . .

(2) The husband owes his wife protection and assistance, and must provide her with all the means necessary to maintain the household, in accordance with his financial resources. The woman has a special right and duty to nurture and care for her children during their minority, and to take charge of domestic affairs.

. . .

(5) The woman may be employed or ply a trade, occupation, public office or business, where she is able to do so without endangering the interests and the care of her children, or other needs of her household.

. . .

197. Married women are restricted in representing the marriage and in administration of marital assets, roles which are assigned by law to the husband, and this constitutes a relative incapacity.

198. Parental authority is a right which is virtually forbidden to women, since it is assigned to the father. Women only come to exercise this right when the father is imprisoned or legally barred from such.

. . .

201. The legal context allows the husband to object to the wife engaging in activities outside the home, thus barring her from the right and freedom to work. The legal context restricts her right to personal fulfilment in areas outside her function as mother and housewife and restricts her personal liberty.

. . .

203. A judicial declaration of paternity in cases of rape, rape of juveniles and abduction is dependent on the conduct of the mother, based on what the law terms 'notoriously disorderly conduct', an express form of discrimination against women and the product of conception resulting from forced intercourse.

. . .

209. Adultery defined as an 'offence against honour' protects the legal right of filiation and 'the interests of the family', but makes a clear distinction concerning the gravity of the act, depending on whether it involves the man or the woman, providing a tougher sentence for the woman; the proof and the procedure are different in the two cases, so that in practice it is only applied to women.

210. Offences 'against life' in which women are most affected are defined as abortion, which is defined as criminal conduct by which the death of the foetus is caused deliberately, within the mother's womb or by its premature expulsion. Medical abortion to avoid danger to the health or death of the mother, or due to deformities of the foetus, is not punishable. This is not envisaged when it is the result of rape.

211. With regard to the offence of rape, the punishment is graded according to the age of the victim and the relationship of authority which may exist between the victim and the offender. Reference is made to the 'honourable woman', requiring that the offender has used seduction, promise of marriage or deceit and the woman is a virgin; this emphasizes the value of 'honour', defining it as an offence against honour rather than against personal integrity, as would be correct.

212. Maltreatment of women and children and domestic violence are not

defined as offences against the person and in practice are lumped together with injuries, coercion and threats, causing serious difficulties with regard to proof and other procedural problems.
. . .

COMMENT ON WOMEN'S SOCIAL AND ECONOMIC CONDITIONS

The status of women within the international human rights regime and the task of ensuring human rights for women are incomprehensible without taking into account the social and economic conditions that characterize women's lives around the world. Much information appears in later materials in this section addressing issues such as violence against women. This Comment sets forth some basic statisics.

Later readings underscore the degree to which rights abuses are strongly correlated to victims' slight social and economic power, hence political power. Those who are most vulnerable to human rights abuses often lack the favour or protection of the state, as well as the power within their communities to protect and further their basic needs and interests.

According to virtually every indicator of social well-being and status—political participation, legal capacity, access to economic resources and employment, wage differentials, levels of educations and health care—women fare significantly and sometimes dramatically worse than men. The following information from the *Human Development Report* for 1993 of the United Nations Development Programme suggests the dimensions of the problem (at p. 25):

> *Literacy*—Women are much less likely than men to be literate. In South Asia, female literacy rates are only around 50% those of males. . . . in Nepal 35% . . . Sudan 27%. Women make up two-thirds of the world's illiterates.
>
> *Higher education*—Women in developing countries lag far behind men. In Sub-Saharan Africa, their enrolment rates for tertiary education are only a third of those of men. Even in industrial countries, women are very poorly represented in scientific and technical study. . . .
>
> *Employment*—In developing countries women have many fewer job opportunities; the employment participation rates of women are on average only 50% those of men (in South Asia 29% and in the Arab States only 16%) . . . . Wage discrimination is also a feature of industrial countries; in Japan, women receive only 51% of male wages. Women who are not in paid employment are, of course, far from idle. Indeed, they tend to work much longer hours than men. . . .
>
> *Health*—Women tend on average to live longer than men. But in some Asian and North African countries, the discrimination against women—through neglect of their health or nutrition—is such that they have a shorter life expectancy. . . .
>
> *National statistics*—Women are often invisible in statistics. If women's unpaid housework were counted as productive output in national income accounts, global output would increase by 20–30%.

Although employment outside the home provides women with increased income and often social status, employment remains a major source of discrimination. Women are doubly disadvantaged, occupying lower status and lower wage jobs in virtually every society while retaining the overwhelming burden of child care and household responsibilities. Alternatively, the labour women do outside caring for the family may remain unvalued and uncompensated (to a large extent, unvalued because uncompensated) where it does not form part of the cash economy. Consider the following (*Human Development Report* for 1993, at p. 45):

> By 1990, women's share of the total economically active population in the industrial countries increased dramatically to 42%. In East Asia, it had risen to 43%, in Latin America and the Caribbean to 32%, and in North Africa and the Arab States to 13%.
>
> But women are generally employed in a restricted range of jobs—in low-paid, low-productivity work. . . . In Africa, about 78% of economically active women work in agriculture (compared with 64% for men) . . .
>
> Low status is reflected in low productivity and low pay, with women's earnings frequently only 50–80% those of men. . . .

Contrary to the expectations that many hold, economic development is not an automatic route to the relative advancement of women within society. As stated in the same *Report* at p. 26:

> Japan, despite some of the world's highest levels of human development, still has marked inequalities in achievement between men and women. . . . In education, the tertiary enrolment ratio for females is only two-thirds that of males.
>
> Similarly [in Japan] in employment, women are considerably worse off. Women's average earnings are only 51% those of men, and women are largely excluded from decision-making positions: they hold only 7% of administrative and managerial jobs.
>
> Their representation is even lower in the political sphere. . . . [O]nly 2% of parliamentary seats are held by women, and at the ministerial level there are no women at all. . . .

In fact, there is considerable evidence that the well-being of women can be at risk rather than advanced through development including economic globalization and restructuring, in view of the types of jobs and wages that will be available for them, and the effects on welfare services of a stress on deregulated markets and free trade. Women's tasks in the process of development tend to remain those involving long hours at basic labour like water collection, while men receive the necessary technical assistance.

The structural adjustment programmes that were intended to manage the debt crises endured by many developing countries during the 1980s further exacerbated the precarious situation of women. The orthodox formula for economic reform that was promoted by institutions such as the World Bank and the International Monetary Fund involved some or all of the following elements: privatization of government services and corporations, economic deregulation and liberalization of trade, and reduction in the civil service and social services spending. As a consequence, these programmes have led to sharp cutbacks in 'social safety net' spending in health, education and social services. The burden often fell disproportionately on women and children.[3] The materials in Chapter 16 discuss some contemporary changes in the policies of intergovernmental financial organizations and greater attention to the situation of women and other groups particularly at risk.

In East and Central European states and the former Soviet Union, the burden of transition to market economies has similarly been borne disproportionately by women, despite their education levels that frequently exceed men's. In the new privatized economies, job retraining programmes have been targeted principally toward men, and vital supports for working women like free or subsidized child care facilities are disappearing or have been privatized.[4]

Statistics covering all or some of the years 1991–1996 are available at a website dated 1 December 1997, www.un.org/Depts/unsd/gender/.htm. They are drawn largely from *The World's Women 1995: Trends and Statistics*, published as an official document for the Fourth World Conference on Women in Beijing in 1995 and as a UN sales publication.

AMARTYA SEN, MORE THAN 100 MILLION WOMEN ARE MISSING
New York Review of Books, December 20, 1990, at 61

It is often said that women make up a majority of the world's population. They do not. This mistaken belief is based on generalizing from the contemporary situation in Europe and North America, where the ratio of women to men is typically around 1.05 or 1.06, or higher. In South Asia, West Asia, and China, the ratio of women to men can be as low as 0.94, or even lower, and it varies widely elsewhere in Asia, in Africa, and in Latin America. How can we understand and explain these differences, and react to them?

At birth, boys outnumber girls everywhere in the world, by much the same proportion—there are around 105 or 106 male children for every 100 female children. Just why the biology of reproduction leads to this result remains a subject of debate. But after conception, biology seems on the whole to favor women. . . . When given the same care as males, females tend to have better survival rates than males.

Women outnumber men substantially in Europe, the US, and Japan, where, despite the persistence of various types of bias against women (men having distinct advantages in higher education, job specialization, and promotion to senior

[3] Third Periodic Report of Ecuador to CEDAW Committee, CEDAW/C/ECU/3, 10 January 1992; Lourdes, Beneria and Feldman (eds.), *Unequal Burden: Economic Crises, Persistent Poverty, and Women's Work* (1992); Akua Kuenyehia, 'The Impact of Structural Adjustment Programs on Women's International Human Rights: The Example of Ghana', in Rebecca Cook (ed.), *Human Rights of Women:* *National and International Perspectives* (1994), at 422.

[4] Barbara Einhorn, *Cinderella Goes to Market: Citizenship, Gender and Women's Movements in East Central Europe* (1993); UN Centre for Social Development and Humanitarian Affairs, *The Impact of Economic and Political Reform on the Status of Women in Eastern Europe* (1992).

executive positions, for example), women suffer little discrimination in basic nutrition and health care. . . .

The fate of women is quite different in most of Asia and North Africa. In these places the failure to give women medical care similar to what men get and to provide them with comparable food and social services results in fewer women surviving than would be the case if they had equal care. In India, for example, except in the period immediately following birth, the death rate is higher for women than for men fairly consistently in all age groups until the late thirties. This relates to higher rates of disease from which women suffer, and ultimately to the relative neglect of females, especially in health care and medical attention. Similar neglect of women vis-à-vis men can be seen also in many other parts of the world. The result is a lower proportion of women than would be the case if they had equal care—in most of Asia and North Africa, and to a lesser extent Latin America.

This pattern is not uniform in all parts of the third world, however. Sub-Saharan Africa, for example, ravaged as it is by extreme poverty, hunger, and famine, has a substantial excess rather than deficit of women, the ratio of women to men being around 1.02. The 'third world' in this matter is not a useful category, because it is so diverse.

. . .

To get an idea of the numbers of people involved in the different ratios of women to men, we can estimate the number of 'missing women' in a country, say, China or India, by calculating the number of extra women who would have been in China or India if these countries had the same ratio of women to men as obtain in areas of the world in which they receive similar care. If we could expect equal populations of the two sexes, the low ratio of 0.94 women, to men in South Asia, West Asia, and China would indicate a 6 percent deficit of women; but since, in countries where men and women receive similar care, the ratio is about 1.05, the real shortfall is about 11 percent. In China alone this amounts to 50 million 'missing women', taking 1.05 as the benchmark ratio. When that number is added to those in South Asia, West Asia, and North Africa, a great many more than 100 million women are 'missing'. These numbers tell us, quietly, a terrible story of inequality and neglect leading to the excess mortality of women.

To account for the neglect of women, two simplistic explanations have often been presented or, more often, implicitly assumed. One view emphasizes the cultural contrasts between East and West (or between the Occident and the Orient), claiming that Western civilization is less sexist than Eastern. That women outnumber men in Western countries may appear to lend support to this Kipling-like generalization. . . . The other simple argument looks instead at stages of economic development, seeing the unequal nutrition and health care provided for women as a feature of underdevelopment, a characteristic of poor economies awaiting economic advancement.

. . .

Despite their superficial plausibility, neither the alleged contrast between 'East' and 'West', nor the simple hypothesis of female deprivation as a characteristic of economic 'underdevelopment' gives us anything like an adequate understanding of the geography of female deprivation in social wellbeing and survival. We have to examine the complex ways in which economic, social, and cultural factors can influence the regional differences.

It is certainly true that, for example, the status and power of women in the family differ greatly from one region to another, and there are good reasons to expect that these social features would be related to the economic role and independence of women. For example, employment outside the home and owning assets can both be important for women's economic independence and power; and these factors may have far-reaching effects on the divisions of benefits and chores within the family and can greatly influence what are implicitly accepted as women's 'entitlements'.

[Sen discusses decision-making within the family as the pursuit of cooperation 'in which solutions for the conflicting aspects of family life are implicitly agreed on'. Analysis of these 'cooperative conflicts' in different regions and cultures can 'provide a useful way of understanding the influences that affect the "deal" that women get in the division of benefits within the family'. Perceptions of who is doing 'productive' work or contributing to the family's welfare can be very influential, and such social perceptions are 'of pervasive importance in gender inequality', particularly 'in sustaining female deprivation in many of the poorer countries'.

Division of a family's joint benefits are apt to be more favourable to women if (1) they earn outside income, (2) their work is recognized as productive, (3) they own some economic resources or hold economic rights, and (4) there is an understanding of ways in which women are deprived. 'Considerable empirical evidence' suggests that gainful employment such as working outside the home for a wage as opposed to unpaid housework 'can substantially enhance the deal that women get'. Not only access to funds but also women's status and standing in the family improve. Moreover, women bring home experience of the outside world, a form of education. Such factors can 'counter the relative neglect of girls as they grow up', as women are seen as economic producers.

Sen discusses the different situation in China, where other explanatory factors may be important, such as the strong measures to control the size of families in the framework of a strong cultural preference for boys.]

In comparing different regions of Asia and Africa, if we try to relate the relative survival prospects of women to the 'gainful employment' of both sexes—i.e., work outside the home, possibly for a wage—we do find a strong association. . . .
. . .

Analyses based on simple conflicts between East and West or on 'underdevelopment' clearly do not take us very far. The variables that appear important—for example, female employment or female literacy—combine both economic and cultural effects. To ascribe importance to the influence of gainful employment on women's prospects for survival may superficially look like another attempt at a simple economic explanation, but it would be a mistake to see it this way. The deeper question is why such outside employment is more prevalent in, say, sub-Saharan Africa than in North Africa, or in Southeast and Eastern Asia than in Western and Southern Asia. Here the cultural, including religious, backgrounds of the respective regions are surely important. Economic causes for women's deprivation have to be integrated with other—social and cultural—factors to give depth to the explanation.

Of course, gainful employment is not the only factor affecting women's chances of survival. Women's education and their economic rights—including property rights—may be crucial variables as well. Consider the state of Kerala in India. . . . It does not have a deficit of women—its ratio of women to men of more than 1.03 is closer to that of Europe (1.05) than those of China, West Asia, and India as a whole (0.94). The life expectancy of women at birth in Kerala, which had already reached sixty-eight years by the time of the last census in 1981 (and is estimated to be seventy-two years now), is considerably higher than men's sixty-four years at that time (and sixty-seven now). While women are generally able to find 'gainful employment' in Kerala—certainly much more so than in Punjab—the state is not exceptional in this regard. What is exceptional is Kerala's remarkably high literacy rate: not only is it much higher than elsewhere in India, it is also substantially higher than in China, especially for women.

NOTE

It was the rare report of a human rights NGO before the 1990s that gave specific attention to human rights violations against women, although women often figured with men as victims in reports dealing with themes like arbitrary detention, disappearances, or torture. Numbers of NGOs have been organized during the past decade that were devoted to women's human rights issues, and leading NGOs of general scope now frequently address women's problems.

There follow two NGO reports exclusively on violence against women, in one case violence perpetrated directly by the state and in the other violence occurring in the home and followed by state inaction.

AMNESTY INTERNATIONAL, RAPE AND SEXUAL ABUSE: TORTURE AND ILL TREATMENT OF WOMEN IN DETENTION
(1992), at 1

. . .

. . . In countries around the world, government agents use rape and sexual abuse to coerce, humiliate, punish and intimidate women. When a policeman or a soldier rapes a woman in his custody, that rape is no longer an act of private violence, but an act of torture or ill-treatment for which the state bears responsibility. . . .

Yet many governments persistently refuse to recognize that rape and sexual abuse by government agents are serious human rights violations. In country after country effective investigations into cases of rape do not take place nor are the perpetrators brought to justice. From the emergency zones of Peru, for instance,

AI has received dozens of reports of members of the security forces raping women and girls. AI [Amnesty International] knows of no official investigations into such incidents since the state of emergency was first declared in October 1981 and the current government has not demonstrated the political will to institute such investigations. In 1986 a Peruvian prosecutor told an AI delegation in Ayacucho that rape was to be expected when troops were conducting counter-insurgency operations, and that prosecutions for such assaults were unlikely.

Even when public outrage forces officials into conducting investigations and prosecutions, the punishments imposed by the courts on government agents found guilty of rape are seldom commensurate with the enormity of the crime. . . .

Although men are sometimes raped in custody by government agents, it is a form of torture primarily directed against women, and to which women are uniquely vulnerable. Women are also more likely to suffer sexual abuse and harassment short of rape, including fondling, verbal humiliation, excessive body searches, and other intentionally degrading treatment. . . .

When governments use military force to suppress armed insurgency movements, troops are often given extensive powers and are not held accountable to civilian legal authorities for their actions. In the course of counter-insurgency operations, government soldiers sometimes use rape and sexual abuse to try and extract information from women suspected of involvement with the armed opposition or even to punish women who simply live in areas known to be sympathetic to the insurgents. The indiscriminate use of torture and ill-treatment also helps create a permanent sense of fear and insecurity, against which the capacity for independent political action can be dulled or thwarted. The official failure to condemn or punish rape gives it an overt political sanction, which allows rape and other forms of torture and ill-treatment to become tools of military strategy.

. . .

Maria Nicolaidou was among 33 young men and women detained in Athens, Greece on 2 November 1991 after policemen found them sticking up political posters. The detainees were taken to a police station, where all 12 of the women were ordered to strip naked and were kept in an open room in full view of a number of policemen, who made obscene gestures and comments. Several of the women said they were beaten by police officers. . . .

In many countries policemen use sexual harassment and threats of rape as an interrogation tactic. The interrogators may be after something specific, like information or a signature on a confession, or they may simply want to frighten the victim and other local women. Rose Ann Maguire was arrested in July 1991 in Northern Ireland and held for five days in Castlereagh interrogation centre. During questioning sessions, she was reportedly sexually harassed, physically abused and threatened with death. . . .

Dozens of Palestinian women and children detained in the Israeli-Occupied Territories have reportedly been sexually abused or threatened in sexually explicit language during interrogation. Fatimah Salameh was arrested near Nablus in July. Her interrogators allegedly threatened to rape her with a chair leg and told her they would photograph her naked and show the pictures to her family. 'They called me a whore and said that a million men had slept with me,' she said. Fatimah Salameh agreed to confess to membership in an illegal organization and was sentenced to 14 months' imprisonment. . . .

In Turkey rape and sexual abuse are frequently used in attempts to extract confessions from both men and women during interrogation. . . .

Some women are raped or sexually abused because they happen to be the wives, mothers, daughters or sisters of men the authorities cannot capture. These women become substitutes for the men in their families and government agents torture and abuse them to punish and shame their male relatives or to coerce these men into surrendering.

. . .

Pregnant women who are tortured or hurt in inhumane conditions face the additional threat of suffering miscarriage or permanent injury. The special needs of pregnant women are recognized in international instruments such as the United Nations Standard Minimum Rules for the Treatment of Prisoners. Some governments not only ignore these needs, but take advantage of the vulnerability of pregnant women to inflict severe physical and emotional pain.

Wafa' Murtada was a 27-year-old civil engineer and nearly nine months pregnant when the Syrian authorities arrested her in September 1987. The authorities apparently suspected her husband, Yahya Murtada, of belonging to a banned opposition group and tried to extract the names of his associates from her through torture. Wafa' Murtada gave birth in prison and lost her child, apparently because of the torture. She was held without charge or trial until her recent release from Fara' Falastin detention centre in Damascus.

. . .

Some governments pursue policies that result in persistent human rights violations against people of particular ethnic or national origin. Indigenous peoples, who are often denied civil and political rights, have little recourse against the governments that allow these violations to occur. Those who work on their behalf have also been attacked. . . .

All government agents who encourage, condone or participate in the rape of women in their custody should be brought to justice. Yet many of the perpetrators go free because their victims are too terrified or ashamed to file a complaint. Some women try to obliterate the memory of the assault; others feel degraded and fear that they would be shunned or abandoned if they reveal what has been done to them. In some traditional societies raped women are thought to be tainted or defiled, and the economic and social pressures to conceal a rape can be considerable: if a married woman is raped, her husband may exercise his right to desert her; a single woman who has been raped may no longer be seen as fit for marriage. . . .

Many rape victims are threatened with additional violence if they complain to anyone about the attack. . . .

And some governments maintain legislation making it possible for the victims of rape to be charged with criminal offences. Under Pakistan's Hudood Ordinance, women convicted of extra-marital sexual relations—including rape and adultery—can be sentenced to be publicly whipped, imprisoned or stoned to death. In August 1989 two nurses were raped at gunpoint by three interns in a

Karachi hospital. One of the victims tried to file a complaint and was herself charged with admitting to sexual intercourse. As a result of the charges she has lost her job and her marital engagement has been broken off. 'No one else can ever know how I feel inside,' she said. 'I may seem all right on the outside but inside I feel as if I no longer exist.'

. . .

AMERICAS WATCH, CRIMINAL INJUSTICE: VIOLENCE AGAINST WOMEN IN BRAZIL
(1992), at 12

. . .

I. Introduction

In April of this year, Americas Watch, together with the Women's Rights Project of Human Rights Watch, travelled to Brazil to assess the response of the Brazilian government to the problem of domestic violence. This report contains the findings of that mission. It focuses on wife-murder, domestic battery and rape. It constitutes the first report of the newly formed Women's Rights Project of Human Rights Watch which monitors violence against women and discrimination on the basis of sex throughout the world.

The crime of domestic violence is not unique to Brazil. According to recent United Nations reports, it exists in all regions, classes and cultures. Women all over the world and from all walks of life are at risk from violence in the home, usually at the hands of their husband or lover. Although the exact number of abused women will probably never be known, available information indicates unequivocally that domestic violence is a common and serious problem in developed and developing countries alike.

Although domestic violence is common and widespread, it has traditionally been perceived as a private, family problem, beyond the scope of state responsibility. Indeed, in the past husbands have had the legal right to punish or even kill their wives with impunity. Only gradually changing social attitudes and increased reporting have propelled the problem into the public eye. And as the nature and severity of violence in the home has become evident, so has the responsibility of governments to prosecute such abuse as they would any other violent crime.

. . .

Moreover, female victims still have little reason to expect that their abusers— once denounced—will ever be punished. A police chief in Rio de Janeiro told Americas Watch that to her knowledge, of more than 2,000 battery and sexual assault cases registered at her station in 1990, not a single one had ended in punishment of the accused. The São Luis women's police station in the northeastern state of Maranhão reported that of over 4,000 cases of physical and sexual assault registered with the station, only 300 were ever forwarded for processing and only two yielded punishment for the accused.

Brazil's criminal law is part of the problem. In the Brazilian Penal Code, rape is defined as a crime against custom rather than a crime against an individual person—society rather than the female victim is the offended party. Most other sex crimes are deemed crimes only if the victim is a 'virgin' or 'honest' woman. If a woman does not fit this 'customary' stereotype, she is likely to be accused of having consented to the crime and it is unlikely to be investigated. Moreover, pursuit of these cases by law depends on the initiative of the victim, not the state; if at anytime she desists from prosecution the case will be dropped. Of over 800 cases of rape reported to the São Paulo women's police stations from 1985 to 1989, less than 1/4 were ever investigated.

Marital rape, in particular, is severely under-reported and least likely to be prosecuted. While marital rape theoretically is included within the general prohibition against rape, in practice it is not commonly viewed by the courts as a crime. Under the Brazilian Civil Code, the refusal of sexual relations is cause for legal separation. According to several attorneys with whom Americas Watch spoke, when a husband uses violence to compel his wife to have sexual relations, it is viewed by the courts as enforcing the wife's conjugal obligations, not as rape. As a result, rape in the home, with the exception of incest, is almost never punished.
. . .

II. BACKGROUND
A. The role of the Women's Movement
. . .

Women's increased economic and political power coupled with the development of autonomous and state-affiliated women's institutions, enabled the women's movement to press for fundamental changes in the state's response to gender-specific violence. In 1985, women's groups, together with the state council on women, persuaded São Paulo's opposition party mayor to establish a woman's police station, staffed entirely by women and dedicated solely to crimes of violence against women, excluding homicide, which was not viewed as a gender-specific crime. By late 1985, eight women's police stations (Delegacias De Defesa Da Mulher, hereafter delegacias) had opened in the state of São Paulo, and by 1990 there were 74 throughout the country.

The women's *delegacias* represented an integrated approach to the problem of domestic violence. They were designed to investigate gender-specific crimes, and to provide psychological and legal counseling.The female police officers (*delegadas*) were to receive training in all aspects of domestic violence, from its psychological impact to the legal remedies available to the victim. . . .
. . .

In 1984, women's rights advocates secured Brazil's adoption of the Convention on the Elimination of All Forms of Discrimination Against Women (CEDAW), although with several reservations.[5] In 1986, the women's movement held a

---

[5] Brazil entered reservations regarding the sections of the Convention that guarantee the equal rights of men and women to choose their residence and domicile, to have equal rights to enter into marriage, during marriage and at its dissolution, and to have the same personal rights, including the right to choose a family name. Brazil also entered reservations to the Convention article according the same rights 'for both spouses in respect of ownership, acquisition, management, administration, enjoyment and disposition of property

national constitutional forum to draft a list of recommendations for consideration by the Constituent Assembly, which was elected in the 1986 congressional elections to take up the task of writing a new Brazilian Constitution. . . .

The new Constitution, enacted in 1988, reflects many of the national women's movement's demands. In particular, Article 226, Paragraph 8 provides that 'the state should assist the family, in the person of each of its members, and should create mechanisms so as to impede violence in the sphere of its relationships'. Similar provisions have been adopted in state constitutions throughout Brazil.

. . .

Yet, there is still a long way to go. Changes in political and economic power since the onset of the new republic have diminished the scope and effectiveness of initiatives launched in the euphoria of the early years. . . .

. . .

B. Domestic violence: statistical evidence

. . . A marked difference emerged in the nature of violence suffered by women as opposed to men. For Brazilian men, murder and physical abuse primarily involve acquaintances or strangers and occur outside the home. For Brazilian women, the opposite is true. The 1988 census showed that men were abused by relatives (including spouses) only ten percent of the time, while women are related to their abuser in over half of the cases of reported physical violence.

. . .

. . . Examples of physical abuse cited in a 1989 study of violence against women in the state of Pernambuco included beating tying up and spanking, burning the genitals and breasts with cigarettes, strangulation, inserting objects in the victim's vagina (such as bottles and pieces of wood) and throwing alcohol and fire on the victim. The study also noted repeated physical abuse of pregnant women in which the aggressors 'aimed for the womb, breasts and vagina'.

. . .

HILARY CHARLESWORTH AND CHRISTINE CHINKIN, THE GENDER OF *JUS COGENS*
15 Hum. Rts Q. 63 (1993)

[The authors, drawing on Article 53 of the Vienna Convention on the Law of Treaties and scholarly writing, stress the principal characteristics of the concept of *jus cogens* as normative superiority and universality, the first inevitably associated with the second. Proponents of the concept emphasize its contribution to the collective international order by playing a role similar to that of constitutionally protected rights in domestic order. The authors argue that, despite the provision in Article 53 that inconsistent treaties are void, the doctrine has had little formal or practical consequence. Its significance is primarily symbolic and hortatory in purporting to express the deeper conscience of mankind. But, the authors contend, the concept of *jus cogens* should not be viewed as universal, for its present content—particularly the category of human rights often designated as norms of *jus cogens*—privileges the experiences of men over women by giving differential protection. The following excerpts advance that claim.]

Although human rights law is often regarded as a radical development in international law because of its challenge to that discipline's traditional public/private dichotomy between states and individuals, it has retained the deeper, gendered, public/private distinction. In the major human rights treaties, rights are defined according to what men fear will happen to them, those harms against which they seek guarantees. The primacy traditionally given to civil and political rights by Western international lawyers and philosophers is directed towards protection for men within their public life—their relationship with government. The same importance has not been generally accorded to economic and social rights which affect life in the private sphere, the world of women, although these rights are addressed to states. This is not to assert that when women are victims of violations of the civil and political rights they are not accorded the same protection, but that these are not the harms from which women most need protection.

All the violations of human rights typically included in catalogues of *jus cogens* norms are of undoubted seriousness; genocide, slavery, murder, disappearances, torture, prolonged arbitrary detention, and systematic racial discrimination. The silences of the list, however, indicate that women's experiences have not directly contributed to it. For example, although race discrimination consistently appears in *jus cogens* inventories, discrimination on the basis of sex does not. And yet sex discrimination is an even more widespread injustice, affecting the lives of more than half the world's population. While a prohibition on sex discrimination, as racial discrimination, is included in every general human rights convention and is the subject of a specialized binding instrument, sexual equality has not been allocated the status of a fundamental and basic tenet of a communal world order.

Of course women as well as men suffer from the violation of the traditional canon of *jus cogens* norms. However the manner in which the norms have been constructed obscures the most pervasive harms done to women. One example of this is the 'most important of all human rights', the right to life set out in Article 6 of the Civil and Political Convenant which forms part of customary international law. The right is concerned with the arbitrary deprivation of life through public action. Important as it is, the protection from arbitrary deprivation of life or liberty through public actions does not address the ways in which being a women is in itself life-threatening and the special ways in which women need legal protection to be able to enjoy their right to life. . . .

A number of recent studies show that being a women may be hazardous even from before birth due to the practice in some areas of aborting female fetuses because of the strong social and economic pressure to have sons. Immediately after birth womanhood is also dangerous in some societies because of the higher incidence of female infanticide. During childhood in many communities girls are breast-fed for shorter periods and later fed less so that girls suffer the physical and mental effects of malnutrition at higher rates than boys. Indeed in most of Asia and North Africa, women suffer great discrimination in basic nutrition and health care leading to a disproportionate number of female deaths. The well-documented phenomenon of the 'feminization' of poverty in both the developing and developed world causes women to have a much lower quality of life than men.

Violence against women is endemic in all states; indeed international lawyers could observe that this is one of those rare areas where there is genuinely consistent and uniform state practice. . . .

The United Nations system has not ignored the issue of violence against women. . . . A United Nations report on violence against women observes that '[v]iolence against women in the family has . . . been recognized as a priority area of international and national action. . . . All the research evidence that is available suggests that violence against women in the home is a universal problem, occurring across all cultures and in all countries'. . . .

The great level of documented violence against women around the world is unaddressed by the international legal notion of the right to life because that legal system is focussed on 'public' actions by the state. A similar myopia can be detected also in the international prohibition on torture. A central feature of the international legal definition of torture is that it takes place in the public realm: it must be 'inflicted by or at the instigation of or with the consent or acquiescence of a public official or other person acting in an official capacity'. Although many women are victims of torture in this 'public' sense, by far the greatest violence against women occurs in the 'private' nongovernmental sphere.

. . .

The problematic structure of traditionally asserted *jus cogens* norms is also shown in the more controversial 'collective' right to self-determination. The right allows 'all peoples' to 'freely determine their political status and freely pursue their economic, social and cultural development'. Yet the oppression of women within groups claiming the right of self-determination has never been considered relevant to the validity of their claim or to the form self-determination should take. An example of this is the firm United States support for the Afghani resistance movement after the 1979 Soviet invasion without any apparent concern for the very low status of women within traditional Afghani society. Another is the immediate and powerful United Nations response after Iraq's 1990 invasion of Kuwait. None of the plans for the liberation or reconstruction of Kuwait were concerned with that state's denial of political rights to women. Although some international pressure was brought to bear on the Kuwaiti government during and after the invasion to institute a more democratic system, the concern did not focus on the political repression of women and was quickly dropped.

. . .

Feminist rethinking of *jus cogens* would also give prominence to a range of other human rights; the right to sexual equality, to food, to reproductive freedom, to be free from fear of violence and oppression, and to peace. . . . In the particular context of the concept of *jus cogens*, which has an explicitly promotional and aspirational character, it should be possible for even traditional international legal theory to accommodate rights that are fundamental to the existence and dignity of half the world's population. . . .

. . .

2. CEDAW: PROVISIONS AND COMMITTEE

COMMENT ON PROTECTION OF WOMEN UNDER CONVENTIONS PRIOR TO CEDAW

Of course women benefit, and are meant to benefit, from provisions of the basic human rights instruments on state-inflicted torture or killing, denials of due process, freedom of speech and so on. The emphasis of this Comment is on issues of distinctive concern to women, on issues related to gender whether or not they so appear on the surface.

One fundamental protection of women stems from the assurance of equal protection. Such protection has been a dominant theme in the human rights movement, and prohibition of discrimination because of sex has been an essential ingredient of that theme. It is true that application of the equal protection principle in the field of women's rights raises particularly subtle and difficult problems, but the thrust of that principle is also direct and clear on basic issues like voting or admission to higher study.

Recall the stress on the equal protection norm in the following provisions in the UN Charter and the International Bill of Rights.

1. The Charter's preamble states the determination of the peoples of the United Nations to reaffirm faith 'in the equal rights of men and women'. Article 1(3) sets forth the organization's purpose of promoting respect for human rights 'for all without distinction as to race, sex, language, or religion'. Article 55(c) is to similar effect.

2. Article 2 of the Universal Declaration states that 'everyone' is entitled to the rights declared 'without distinction of any kind, such as race, colour, sex, language, religion, political or other opinion, national or social origin, property, birth or other status'. Under Article 16, men and women are 'entitled to equal rights as to marriage, during marriage and at its dissolution'.

3. Under Article 2 of the ICCPR, states undertake to ensure to all within their territory the rights recognized in the Covenant 'without distinction of any kind'. The list of prohibited distinctions is identical with that above in the UDHR. States further undertake in Article 3 to 'ensure the equal right of men and women' to enjoyment of all rights set forth in the Covenant. Under Article 23(4), states are to take 'appropriate steps to ensure equality of rights and responsibilities of spouses as to marriage, during marriage and at its dissolution'. Article 26 contains undertakings by states to prohibit discrimination on the same grounds as those identified in the UDHR.

4. Similar anti-discrimination provisions appear in the International Covenant on Economic, Social and Cultural Rights.

These instruments have been sharply criticized, in terms of both their substantive provisions bearing explicitly or implicitly on women and the means by which those provisions have been implemented. Some of the most trenchant analyses have been made by scholars and advocates writing from a feminist perspective—for present purposes, a perspective that examines instruments so as to identify their overt or covert bearing on women, particularly with respect to gender bias.

Consider, for example, the following analysis of Article 16 of the UDHR by Helen Holmes.[6] The article states that '[t]he family is the natural and fundamental group unit of society and is entitled to protection by society and the State'. Holmes notes the widely divergent definitions of the family in different cultures—nuclear, extended, matrilineal, patrilineal, and so on—and asserts that 'those with the power to implement Article 16 will implement it to conform to their own concepts of "family"'. She notes the ongoing conflicts over the advantages and disadvantages of different types of families, including the prototypical ideal in the developed West of the nuclear family. She questions the wisdom or fairness, in the midst of such conflicts and changing perceptions, of institutionalizing a vision of the family as (quoting from the Article 16) the 'natural and fundamental group unit'.

What, moreover, is meant by (again quoting) 'protection by society and the State' of the family? What are such protection's implications, say, for divorce or for the desire of a child to leave a family because of abuse or other reasons? How will such protection be reconciled with the provisions about children in Article 25(2)? Holmes asks whether protection of the family would in fact amount to the defence of patriarchy and hierarchy.

Another critic, Laura Reanda, develops related perspectives on the older human rights corpus.[7] Writing in 1981, she observes that the main international human rights organs like the UN Commission on Human Rights or the ICCPR Human Rights Committee 'do not appear to deal specifically with violations of the human rights of women, except in a marginal way or within the framework of other human rights issues'. Through the UN Commission on the Status of Women and the CEDAW Committee, p. 188, *infra*, there has been a 'ghettoization' of questions relating to women and their relegation to structures endowed with less power and resources than the general human rights structures.

Reanda notes that the periodic reports submitted by states to the Human Rights Committee under Article 40 of the ICCPR rarely deal with the situation of women and, when they do so, generally stress laws on the books rather than custom or practice. Thus 'forms of oppression not specifically defined in the Covenant tend to be neglected'. She continues (at p. 15):

> It is well known, for instance, that in many states parties to the Covenant, discriminatory practices against women persist, whether in law or in fact, such as segregation from public life, polygamy, the dowry system, bride-price, and genital mutilation. Another example is forced prostitution, which is considered a form of slavery by other United Nations organs but has never been raised in connection with the antislavery provision of the Covenant.

---

[6] 'A Feminist Analysis of the Universal Declaration of Human Rights', in Carol Gould (ed.), *Beyond Domination: New Perspectives on Women and Philosophy* (1983), at 250.

[7] 'Human Rights and Women's Rights: The United Nations Approach', 3 Hum. Rts. Q. 11 (No. 2 1981).

While none of these institutions and practices are specifically mentioned by the Covenant, it is hard to see how women can be guaranteed the full enjoyment of the human rights and fundamental freedoms to which they are entitled under the Covenant so long as these and other forms of oppression continue. To bring these practices under the purview of the Covenant, however, would require a concerted effort in terms of fact-gathering and interpretation, and there is no evidence that this is among the goals of the Committee. In fact, none of these practices has been mentioned in state reports or in the debates of the Committee. It would appear that the interpretation given to the Covenant so far is that the Covenant does not apply to these obvious violations of the human rights of women.

NOTE

Section 702 of the *Restatement (Third), Foreign Relations Law of the United States*, p. 233, *infra*, sets forth categories of the contemporary *customary* international law of human rights. It provides that a state violates international law if, 'as a matter of state policy, it practices, encourages, or condones' conduct that includes genocide, torture, systematic racial discrimination, or 'a consistent pattern of gross violations of internationally recognized human rights.' The section does not include gender discrimination among the seven identified categories. Note the *Restatement*'s comments following the text of Section 702.

    a. *Scope of customary law of human rights.* This section includes as customary law only those human rights whose status as customary law is generally accepted (as of 1987) and whose scope and content are generally agreed. The list is not necessarily complete, and is not closed: human rights not listed in this section may have achieved the status of customary law, and some rights might achieve that status in the future.

. . .

    b. *Gender discrimination.* The United Nations Charter (Article 1(3)) and the Universal Declaration of Human Rights (Article 2) prohibit discrimination in respect of human rights on various grounds, including sex. Discrimination on the basis of sex in respect of recognized rights is prohibited by a number of international agreements, including the Covenant on Civil and Political Rights, the Covenant on Economic, Social and Cultural Rights, and more generally by the Convention on the Elimination of All Forms of Discrimination Against Women, which, as of 1987, had been ratified by 91 states and signed by a number of others. The United States had signed the Convention but had not yet ratified it. The domestic laws of a number of states, including those of the United States, mandate equality for, or prohibit discrimination against, women generally or in various respects. Gender-based discrimination is still practiced in many states in varying degrees, but freedom from gender discrimination as state policy, in many matters, may already be a principle of customary international law. . . .

COMMENT ON CEDAW'S SUBSTANTIVE PROVISIONS

The Convention is among the many that elaborate in one particular field the norms and ideals that are generally and tersely stated in the Universal Declaration, and stated somewhat more amply in the ICCPR. Its preamble suggests how deeply the issues run and that the norms of this Convention must be placed in a broader transformative context. It recognizes 'that a change in the traditional role of men as well as the role of women in society and in the family is needed to achieve full equality between men and women'.

The reader should be familiar with the provisions of the Convention.

Article 1: Note three vital characteristics of the definition of 'discrimination against women'. (a) The article refers to *effect* as well as *purpose*, thus directing attention to the consequences of governmental measures as well as the intentions underlying them. (b) The definition is not limited to discrimination through 'state action' or action by persons acting under colour of law, as are the definitions of many rights such as the definition of torture under the Convention against Torture. (c) The definition's range is further expanded by the concluding phrase, 'or any other field'.

Article 2: The goals stated in this article are to be pursued 'without delay'. Consider the possible meanings of the terms 'equality' in clause (a) and 'any act of discrimination' in clause (c). Note the breadth of clauses (e) and (f) with respect to the private, non-governmental sectors of society, particularly in relation to the definition in Article 1. Note throughout the Convention the blurred lines between the private and public spheres of life, and the range of obligations on states to intervene in the private sector, to go beyond 'respect' in order to 'protect', 'ensure', and 'promote'.

Article 3: Note the grand goal set forth for states, to 'ensure the full development and advancement of women', and consider whether the other human rights instruments examined contain a similar conception for any group, or for people in general.

Article 4: This 'affirmative action' clause, however qualified, appears as well in the Convention on the Elimination of all Forms of Racial Discrimination, but not in the ICCPR. Consider this Article 4 in relation to Article 2(e) and (f), and Article 11.

Article 5: The breadth and aspiration of this article are surely striking. Provisions such as Article 10(c) impose a similar obligation on states in defined contexts. Other human rights treaties lack a similar provision, although Article 2 of the Racial Discrimination Convention comes close. Consider how a state in good faith might decide on 'appropriate measures' under this article, bearing in mind the injunction in Article 2 to proceed 'without delay' as well as the claims of the Convention's other provisions.

Articles 6–16: These articles evidence how a treaty devoted to one set of problems—here, ending discrimination against women and achieving equality—makes possible discrete, disaggregated treatment of the different issues relevant to these problems. Clearly the variety and detail in these articles would have been out of place, indeed impossible, in a treaty of general scope like the ICCPR. Note the great range of verbs that are used throughout these articles to define states parties' duties, including: eliminate, provide, encourage, protect, introduce, accord, ensure.

Article 6 is typical of many provisions in requiring a state party to regulate specific non-governmental activity.

Articles 7–9, to the contrary, deal with the traditional notion of state action, here barring discrimination by the state.

Article 10 concerns a particular field, education, and lists specific goals which, in their totality, take on a programmatic character. Note paragraph (h) on family planning and its relationship to three other provisions: Articles 12(1), 14(2)(b) and 16(e). The Convention does not address as such the question of abortion.

Article 12 together with a number of other provisions indicate the degree to which CEDAW involves and interrelates the classical categories of civil-political rights and economic-social rights. It imposes a limited duty to provide free health care.

Article 14 disaggregates women's problems in regional and functional terms. It underscores strategies for realizing goals that permeate the entire Convention, such as mobilization through functional grass roots groups and participation in local decision making. CEDAW is not a convention in which solutions are to be provided only by the central authority of the state.

Article 16 orders the states to sweep away a large number of fundamental, traditional discriminations against and forms of subordination of women. Like several other articles, it could be understood as a complement to, one specification of, the broad goals stated in Article 5. Compare its provisions with the Report of Guatemala, p. 160, *supra*.

NOTE

More states have entered reservations to their ratification of CEDAW than of any other human rights treaties. Some reservations seriously qualify a state's commitment, particularly those that base the reservation on conflicting principles or rules in a religion or culture The Comment at p. 439, *infra*, gives examples of reservations and examines them in the context of a discussion about universalism and cultural relativism.

COMMENT ON TYPES OF STATE DUTIES IMPOSED BY HUMAN RIGHTS TREATIES

To understand the significance and implications of the rights stated in the ICCPR, CEDAW and other human rights treaties, it is helpful to examine the related duties/obligations of states—even though human rights conventions rarely talk of duties. Attention to such duties both clarifies the significance of the related rights and thus helps to sort out ideas, and points to strategies of change. The effort, then, is to decompose a right into its related state duties, and thereby gain a clearer notion of the content or proposed content of the right itself.

Some of these duties can fairly be called correlative (corresponding) to the right—for example, implying from my right not to be tortured the state's correlative duty not to torture me. As a practical matter and from a functional perspective, other duties may be necessary implications from the nature of a given right even if they are not spelled out in treaty text—for example, a state's duty to create and operate electoral institutions and processes if the citizen's right to vote is to be realized.

Different rights may point to different types of state's duties. All depends on the nature of the right, on the problems that it was meant to overcome or to prevent. Some types of state duties described below are more prominent in the ICCPR, some in CEDAW, some in the International Covenant on Economic, Social and Cultural Rights discussed in Chapter 4, or in other human rights treaties. Identifying the multiple duties that may be relevant to any one right sharpens an understanding of what is distinctive to and necessary to realize that right.

Two points should be kept in mind as we examine different kinds of rights from the perspective of related variable state duties.

(1) At the start of the human rights movement, much weight was given to a distinction between so-called 'negative' and 'positive' rights. The negative rights basically imposed a duty of 'hands-off', a duty of a state's non-interference with, say, an individual's physical security. Thus, the right not to be tortured was imagined to impose only such a negative duty—the state's correlative duty not to torture. Positive rights, on the other hand, imposed affirmative (positive) duties on the state—in the classic case, a duty to provide food (food stamps/subsidies and so on) if such provision was essential to satisfy the right to food. Thus economic and social rights such as the right to food were considered positive rights, which frequently required financial expenditures by the state, unlike the classic negative rights that were thought to require merely abstention from unjustified interference with another person. It will be important to consider how much of this negative-positive distinction remains valid in the light of the illustrations and analysis below.

(2) Rights are not static. They evolve. They broaden or contract over time. One way of understanding an expansion of the content of a given right (to speech, to food) is to examine the duties related to that right, and to inquire whether and how they have expanded. The argument for a broader construction of a given right often amounts to the claim that further duties ought to be imposed on the state in order to satisfy the right. Consider some examples. The right to speech implies at a minimum the government's correlative duty not to interfere with it. A modest expansion of the right imposes the further duty on government to protect a speaker against deliberate interference by nonstate actors. An argument for further expansion can be based on the claim that government must facilitate speech by assuring access of political groups to the media (that is, to newspapers or electronic media whether or not owned or controlled by the state). Such arguments for expansion of duties can constitute a strategy of change. So attention to duties,

how they differ among rights within a treaty and among treaties, and how they change over time is one vital way of examining and fostering change in the human rights movement as a whole.

The following scheme of five types of state duties derives from but modifies earlier writings, particularly Henry Shue, *Basic Rights* (2nd edn 1996), and G. J. H. van Hoof, 'The Legal Nature of Economic, Social and Cultural Rights', in Philip Alston and K. Tomasevski (eds), *The Right to Food* (1984), at 97.

(1) **Respect** Rights of Others

This duty requires the state to treat persons equally, to respect their individual dignity and worth, and hence not to interfere with or impair their declared rights, whether physical security rights or rights to fair process, equal protection, speech or political participation. This duty of respect has often been described as 'negative' in the sense of being a 'hands-off' duty. The broad idea is not to worsen an individual's situation by depriving that person of the enjoyment of a declared right.

Of course the observance by states of this duty of respect would itself, without any further duties of states, lead to a vast improvement in the human condition. In this sense, the duty of respect can be seen to lie at the core of the human rights movement. Observance would avoid most of the worst calamities: the genocides, massacres, and tortures. The duty of respect is in this sense allied to the 'anti-disaster' element of the human rights movement. But observance would achieve far more, such as realizing basic conditions for a democratic society.

For many but not all rights declared in the treaties, the duty of respect reaches beyond states to individuals and nonstate entities. A person's right to bodily security or to vote imposes a correlative duty on all other person to refrain from interfering with it (a classic 'hands-off' right). On the other hand, the other duties identified in categories (2)–(5) below are in most cases associated only with the state. Under the human rights treaties, individuals or nonstate entities do not, for example, bear direct duties to protect other individuals against physical attack or to provide housing for them. Such issues about the character and range of individual duties are considered elsewhere at pp. 324 and 1132, *infra*. This Comment covers only state duties.

(2) **Create Institutional Machinery** Essential to Realization of Rights

Some rights may be impaired or effectively annulled not only by government's direct interference with them (torture, preventing a citizen from expressing ideas or voting), but also by its failure to put in place the institutional machinery essential for the realization or practice of the right. Political participation offers a simple illustration. A citizen's right to vote means little unless a government maintains fair electoral machinery that makes possible the act of voting, counting of ballots and so on. Voting rights are, then, hardly cost-free for government. It is not simply a matter of 'hands off'. Public funds must be expended to create the infrastructure on which the practical realization of the right depends. The negative-positive distinction, while having some utility, is inadequate to describe this duty, as well as the state obligation to institutionalize rights that is described in category (3) below.

(3) **Protect** Rights/**Prevent** Violations

Several human rights treaties make explicit the state's duty to protect against and to prevent violations of rights—for example, Article 2 of the ICCPR that gives victims of violations the right to a remedy. Again institutional machinery is required, in this instance to comply with a specific command of the treaties. In the case of the ICCPR, that command is expressed through the state's duty in Article 2 to 'ensure to all individuals' the recognized rights. States must then do the necessary to ensure. Surely they must provide a police force to protect people against violations of their rights (to physical security, or free speech, or property) either by state or nonstate ('private') actors. They must create normative systems like tort or criminal law, as well as institutions like courts or jails, processes like civil suits or criminal prosecutions, in order to maintain a system of justice that provides remedies for violations and imposes sanctions on violators. This duty to protect has been vital to the development of CEDAW and women's rights. As in category (2) above, the state's duty to protect/prevent involves state expenditures.

The negative-positive rights distinction is not helpful. The classic 'negative' rights here demand the classic 'positive' protection. It is difficult to imagine a right for which this is not true. As Henry Shue, in *Basic Rights* (2nd edn 1996) puts it:

> All these activities and institutions [of government, like police, courts, jails] are attempts at providing social guarantees for individuals' security so that they are not left to face alone forces that they cannot handle on their own. How much more than these expenditures one thinks would be necessary in order for people actually to be reasonably secure . . . depends on one's theory of violent crime, but it is not unreasonable to believe that it would involve extremely expensive, 'positive' programs . . . A demand for physical security is not normally a demand simply to be left alone, but demand to be protected against harm. It is a demand for positive action. . . .

Note that the concepts of protect and prevent, though linked in this category (3), can take on quite different meanings, depending on context. For example, promotion of cultural change (category (5) below) about, say, violence against women may help to prevent such violence. Prevention may then be realized in the long run well outside such everyday forces for protection as police.

(4) **Provide** Goods and Services to Satisfy Rights

The state's duty here is primarily to provide material resources to the rights-bearer, like housing or food or health care, matters associated with the International Covenant on Economic, Social and Cultural Rights that Chapter 4 examines. (Resources provided by the state may go directly from it to the individual rights bearer, as by providing food stamps or subsidized public housing, *or* it may go indirectly to the ultimate beneficiary through, say, subsidies to construction firms that will then offer low-rent housing.) Unlike the duty of respect (do not worsen the situation of the rights-bearer), this duty to provide generally is meant to improve the situation of the rights-bearer.

It is most evident and explicit in this category (4) that the state must expend public funds to meet its duties. It is for this reason that state duties related to welfare rights have most frequently been described as affirmative (positive). Unlike categories (2) and (3) above, both of which also involve state expenditures, these expenditures are at the core of, are the very essence of, the individual right. They are not merely incidental to it, essential means to realize some other right, as for example state expenditures for police are essential to fulfil a duty to protect.

On the other hand, the realization of economic and social rights need not depend on 'direct' or 'indirect' provision by the state in the sense described above. Other, radically different policies may achieve the goal of satisfying a right to, say, food. For example, one way of overcoming poverty and malnutrition in rural areas might be to undertake a programme of expropriation and land reform that would increase employment and yield and thereby make more people self-sufficient with respect to food. Again, monetary or fiscal policy designed to lower unemployment and hence malnutrition and homelessness could reduce the need for direct provision of funds or goods. Such characteristic policies of the modern welfare state may then make the direct or indirect provision of funds or goods measures of last rather than first resort.

(5) **Promote** Rights

This state duty refers to bringing about changes in public consciousness or perception or understanding about a given problem or issue, with the purpose of alleviating the problem. In certain contexts, such promotion of rights may be a useful or indeed essential path toward their better recognition by nonstate actors. Like the duty of protection, it generally requires the state to expend funds and create the institutions that are necessary to promoting acceptance of the right. Thus a state's duty to promote often involves public education— for example, school education or public campaigns meant to change attitudes about violence toward women or children. Promotion plays a vital role in CEDAW.

Promotion underscores the point that these categories of duties are not discrete. They are often complexly interrelated, and indeed overlap. For example, fulfilment of a duty to promote may bear on the duty not only to provide but also to protect, as when the state promotes and disseminates knowledge about the evil consequences of discrimination that may reduce the incidence of, say, racism or homophobic violence.

NOTE

The distinction between negative and positive rights was developed by a number of theorists to demonstrate the superiority of civil and political over economic and social rights, discussed in Chapter 4. Within this distinction, it was often asserted that the first category of rights was exclusively negative, while the second was positive, and moreover that only negative rights could qualify as genuine rights. Consider the following observations in Maurice Cranston, 'Are There Any Human Rights?', in 112/4 Daedalus 12 (1983):

> The traditional political and civil rights are not difficult to institute. For the most part, they require governments, and other people generally, to leave a man alone.... Do not injure, arrest, or imprison him. To respect a man's right to life, liberty , and property is not a very costly exercise. As Locke and others have explained, it requires a system of law that recognizes those rights to protect those rights. But rulers are not called up to do anything that it is unreasonable to expect of them.... Political ... rights can be secured by fairly simple legislation. Since those rights are largely rights against government interference, the greatest effort will be directed toward restraining the government's own executive arm. But this is no longer the case where economic and social rights are concerned. ...

JAMES NICKEL, HOW HUMAN RIGHTS GENERATE DUTIES TO PROTECT AND PROVIDE
15 Hum. Rts. Q. 77 (1993), at 80

[The following excerpts, which use different terms from those appearing in the preceding Comment, bear out and expand some ideas in that Comment.]

The feasibility of a general right is typically concerned with the duties or burdens of several parties. For example, an adequate response to the claim-to freedom from torture will involve a high-priority duty to refrain from torturing. This duty not to torture can feasibly be borne and fulfilled by all, so this duty can be addressed to everyone. But an adequate response to the claim-to freedom from torture also requires finding individuals or institutions that can protect people against torture. As noted earlier, this positive duty, although connected with a universal right, need not be addressed to everyone, or even to some worldwide agency. The claim-to freedom from torture may be universal without all of the corresponding duties being universal in the sense of being against everyone, or against some worldwide agency. All that is required is that for every rightholder, there is at least one agent or agency with duties to protect that person from torture.

To illustrate how this might work, consider the addressees of the right to freedom from torture. First, all persons and all institutions have duties to refrain from torturing, from using torture to achieve their ends. This part of the claim-against *is* universal in the sense of being against everyone. Second, each government has the duty or responsibility to protect people within its territory from torture, to take steps to prevent, deter, and stop torture. Negative duties to refrain fall on everyone; positive duties to protect fall on governments. In addition to these primary addressees of the right against torture, one can also identify secondary addressees who bear secondary or back-up responsibilities connected with the right against torture. The people of a country are secondary addressees with respect to fundamental rights. They bear the responsibility of creating and maintaining a political system that respects and protects the right to freedom from torture. International institutions such as the United Nations and the World Bank are also secondary addressees. They bear the responsibility of assisting, encouraging, and—if necessary—pressuring governments to refrain from torture and to provide protections against torture. One should keep in mind here that if adequate national or international institutions are unavailable, there is the option of reforming existing institutions or creating new ones. Successful action to change the institutions available to uphold rights can make a difference in which rights are justifiable.

Once plausible addressees for the right are identified, one must next show that these addressees can successfully bear the burdens that the right would impose on them, or in other words, one must examine the issue of 'feasibility'. . . .
. . .

One advantage of the emphasis on duties connected with rights is that it moves the debate in the direction of implementation, towards the question of who has to do what if these rights are to be realized. In the case of the right to education in Brazil, an emphasis on the duties connected with this right would lead one to ask, who bears primary responsibility for educating the millions of youngsters in Brazil whose parents are too poor to pay for their education. Many of these children are not in school, and many others are in schools of extremely low quality. Under this analysis, the Brazilian government bears this primary responsibility, and accordingly it ought to be sternly criticized for its historic failure to invest much in educational opportunities to the children of the poor. The citizens of Brazil are the secondary addressees of this right, and they bear the responsibility to act politically to bring about changes in government agencies to effectively implement the right to education. . . .

A second practical advantage of emphasizing the duties connected with rights is that questions of priority among rights, and among rights and other important social goals necessarily move to center stage. Political discussions of these matters have often been very shallow and have tended to use overly broad categories, such as the contrast between 'civil and political rights' and 'economic and social rights', that obscure more than they illuminate.

A third practical advantage of emphasizing the duties connected with rights is that this emphasis will inevitably lead to discussions of the inadequacies of the contemporary international political and economic order. National governments are primary addressees of human rights, yet they frequently have problems of inadequate resources, corruption, fragile legal structures and processes, and weak commitments to democracy. Seeking both general and specific ways to address these sorts of problems is a natural extension of a concern for human rights that takes seriously the duties associated with rights.
. . .

QUESTIONS

1. Consider CEDAW's stress (as in its title) on eliminating discrimination to achieve equality between men and women, as well as its means for realizing that equality. The phrase 'on the basis of equality of men and women' recurs in many of its articles. Compare the notion of equality in the ICCPR—say, in ICCPR Article 3 ('to ensure the equal rights of men and women to the enjoyment of all civil and political rights' in that covenant), or ICCPR Article 26 ('All persons are equal before the law and are entitled without any discrimination to the equal protection of the law'). Are the two treaties' conceptions of equality identical, similar, very different?

2. Note that CEDAW has no provision specifically addressing bodily security in the manner that other human rights instruments do by, for example, prohibiting arbitrary deprivation of life, torture, or arbitrary detention. What provisions of CEDAW would you rely on to assert a woman's right to bodily security?

3. Do the provisions of CEDAW on their face make any concession to cultural relativism, to cultural diversity in regional, ethnic, religious or other terms? Or do they insist throughout on universal application of its norms without variation?

4. Under Article 2, states parties agree to pursue the required policies, 'by all appropriate means and without delay'. Contrast the description of state obligations in Article 2 of the Covenant on Economic, Social and Cultural Rights: 'achieving progressively the full realization' of the recognized rights. Is this textual contrast accurate with respect to CEDAW? How do you understand the question of CEDAW's 'time frame' in comparison, say, with the ICCPR?

5. Which provisions of CEDAW fall into which of the categories of state duties that are described in the preceding Comment and article? Does any one category appear to dominate? Which category represents the most significant change from the ICCPR?

6. Anti-discrimination measures followed a certain chronology both in the United States and in the international human rights movement: prohibition first of racial discrimination and then of types of sex discrimination, while today the debate rages about what measures to take, indeed whether to take measures, against discrimination on the basis of sexual orientation

As far as the international movement is concerned, racism was considered an evil from the start. Because of its connections with the issues of apartheid and colonialism it fuelled the entire movement. Sex discrimination was also barred in the Universal Declaration of Human Rights, but had to wait decades longer to become a focus of attention and to be incorporated into the mainstream discussion of human rights. The normative consensus regarding gender discrimination started to develop much later. Today that consensus obtains on certain core issues, while on many others dispute continues at the practical, doctrinal and ideological level in political fora and within the women's movement. As yet we see no consensus at the universal level regarding the rights of sexual minorities or the right to sexual orientation.

Why this sequence? Is it significant, or merely an accident of history? Do the feared consequences of ending discrimination differ radically among these three fields? Is there an implicit hierarchy, some forms of discrimination being considered worse than others? What explanations can you offer?

NOTE

Two institutions within the universal human rights system are concerned exclusively with women's rights. The older of the two, the UN Commission on the Status of Women, is formally the body with primary responsibility for monitoring and encouraging implementation of international law on women's rights.[8] It was established by the General Assembly at the same time as the Human Rights Commission, but it has been a less effective and influential body.

The more significant and influential organ has been the Committee formed under CEDAW. Hence the following materials examine only the CEDAW Committee, a 'treaty organ' rather than a 'Charter organ' within the distinction made at p. 145, *supra*. Chapter 9 will examine the ICCPR Committee and other treaty organs. It will also discuss a proposed Optional Protocol and communications procedure for the CEDAW Committee that the present materials omit. You should now read Articles 17–21 of the Convention.

ANDREW BYRNES, THE COMMITTEE ON THE ELIMINATION OF DISCRIMINATION AGAINST WOMEN
in Philip Alston (ed.), The United Nations and Human Rights: A Critical Appraisal (2nd edn forthcoming)

[Byrnes notes that the UN General Assembly, in deciding on the appropriate type of supervisory body for CEDAW, drew on the model of the ICCPR Committee. Thus the CEDAW Committee was constituted as a body of independent experts given the task of monitoring states' efforts to meet their obligations through review of periodic reports submitted by the states parties. The Committee's importance has steadily increased over its life, partly as a consequence of the greater attention given women's rights on the world scene, from world conferences to new international instruments.

Committee members have had diverse backgrounds, from fields like sociolgoy, medicine, international relations, education, political science, law, and government. Lawyers, once dominant, now constitute less than a third of the membership. With one exception from Sweden in 1982–1984, all Committee members have been women. Byrnes continues:]

---

[8] See Sandra Coliver, 'United Nations Commission on the Status of Women: Suggestions for Enhancing its Effectiveness', 9 Whittier L. Rev. 435 (1987).

This is perhaps no surprise, since the membership of treaty bodies reflects one national selection process multiplied many times, and in most countries there is likely to be a higher percentage of women than men working on issues relating to women's equality, thus making it more likely that a woman will be nominated. Nevertheless, perhaps the time has come for the Committee and States Parties to consider once again whether some members of CEDAW should be men. Given that they should be experts in the fields covered by the Convention, one beneficial effect of a better gender balance would be to avoid the impression that all-female membership may create, namely that discrimination against women is a concern only of women, and not something that men should be concerned with.

At the same time, the all-female membership of CEDAW must be seen in the context of the overall gender imbalance in the treaty bodies. The overwhelming majority of treaty body members are still male, though the number of women has increased slightly in recent years. When the question of CEDAW's women-only membership was raised in the late 1980s, part of CEDAW's riposte was that it was premature to seek to achieve gender balance in CEDAW's membership while the gender imbalances on the other committees had not been addressed.

[Byrnes notes that the Committee's primary function is to consider the periodic reports of states, but it has given increasing time to drafting its general recommendations and providing input to the world conferences on women's issues. Reports are reviewed at a public meeting to which representatives of the reporting state are invited. The conventional description of the process is that of a 'constructive dialogue'.]

Nonetheless, this does not mean that the Committee's consideration of a State report involves an uncritical and mutually congratulatory discussion of the State report. Individual committee members, and indeed the Committee as a whole, are regularly critical of either the technical limitations of a State report (for example, failure to comply with the Committee's guidelines, or the substantive position in the country as revealed in the report (and also frequently more clearly in non-governmental reports). Both in individual comments and in the Committee's collective concluding comments on a report, extremely critical assessments have been made, although the Committee seeks to express a balanced view.

. . .

Following the meetings with the State Party, the country rapporteur will draft concluding comments, for adoption by the Committee. These are made available to the State Party and the public at the end of the session. . . . This standard format consists of an introduction, a section on positive aspects. . . ., a section 'on factors and difficulties affecting the implementation of the Convention', a section identifying principal areas of concern, and a final section containing concrete suggestions and recommendations in response to the problems identified by the Committee.

[Byrnes then addresses the theme of 'developing a jurisprudence of the Convention', and considers general recommendations.]

The challenge facing CEDAW has been to ensure that the Convention continues to address contemporary violations of women's human rights. The Committee is able to interpret the Convention in a dynamic fashion through its questioning of States Parties during the examination of reports, and the adoption of *General recommendations*. The Committee has not adopted a narrow approach to interpreting the treaty, but has used its limited interpretative powers to ensure that the provisions of the Convention are applied to serious violations, both old and new. Its use of *General recommendations* is becoming an increasingly important part of that process.

[Byrnes concludes that CEDAW, whatever its difficulties of resources and marginalization in its early years, 'now operates in a reasonably favorable environment'.]

The Committee now has both the substantive and other support that it did not previously have, it has been accepted as one of the treaty body family and is now more open to the experience and innovations adopted by other committees, while the climate for advancing women's human rights within the framework of the United Nations remains positive. Knowledge of the Committee is more widespread, and there is a broad constituency at the national and international level with a commitment to supporting the work of the Committee.

The critical question is whether the activities of CEDAW under the Convention have made a meaningful contribution to the pursuit of equality for women at the national, regional and local level. The impact of an international instrument and reviews carried out in New York may seem a long way from women's everyday lives and it will be rare that the work of CEDAW has an immediate and direct effect of this sort. Rather, it is through influencing law-making, policy-making, judicial decisions and providing support for women claiming the rights guaranteed by the Convention to them that the Committee can help to make a difference. There is a growing body of evidence that the reporting procedure has helped to bring [change in] reporting countries. The Committee's jurisprudence in the form of its *General recommendations* is beginning to provide a useful resource for policymakers, judges and lawyers and women's rights advocates in their efforts to translate national constitutional and other guarantees into practice. Finally, the Committee has influenced international policymaking on a number of issues through its contributions to the series of world conferences held throughout the 1990s, and has begun to influence the activities of international agencies in a number of ways.

Notwithstanding these contributions, CEDAW faces many challenges in the future. The Committee's supporters and critics are becoming increasingly demanding in their scrutiny of the efficiency of its work, and many international and national NGOs have high expectations of the difference that CEDAW can make to the realisation of women's equality at the national level. The strain under which the treaty system as a whole is operating, the need for CEDAW to expand its efforts to collaborate with and influence other bodies to incorporate gender in their human rights and other work, and the additional workload and challenges that will come with the adoption of an optional protocol will continue to extend CEDAW as an institution, its members individually, and those who support its work.

[The proposed optional protocol to which Byrnes refers is discussed at p. 777, *infra*.]

CONCLUDING OBSERVATIONS OF CEDAW COMMITTEE ON THIRD AND FOURTH PERIODIC REPORTS OF CHINA
CEDAW/C/1999/1/L.1/Add.7, 1999
www.un.org/womenwatch/daw/cedaw

[At its 20th session in 1999, the Committee considered China's combined third and fourth periodic reports under Article 18 of CEDAW that were submitted in 1997. It summarized the presentation of the report to the Committee by the representative of China, who asserted that China had made substantial progress toward meeting the goals of CEDAW. The Committee stated:

> 7. In conclusion, the representative noted that despite the tremendous amount of work done to promote women's full participation in development, quite a number of women in rural areas lived in poverty, more than 100 million women were still illiterate, and in the transition from a planned economy to a market economy and the reform process, large numbers of women workers had been laid off and were experiencing difficulties finding new employment. The participation of women in political life was still low, incidents of violations of women's rights continued to occur and certain social evils persisted. He emphasized, however, that his Government was determined to continue its efforts, and welcomed the support of the international community in that regard.

The document then set forth the Committee's concluding observations.]

17. The Committee expresses its appreciation to the Government of China for submitting its combined third and fourth periodic reports. However . . . the report does not incorporate sufficient statistical data disaggregated by sex, comparing the current situation to that at the time of the previous report.
. . .

21. The Committee acknowledges with appreciation the comprehensive efforts undertaken by the Government of China to implement the Convention since the consideration of its second periodic report in 1992. These efforts are indicative of the political will of the Government to eliminate discrimination and to advance equality between women and men. The Committee reaffirms that the Convention recognizes that women's rights include civil, political, economic, social and cultural rights and that they are an inalienable, integral and indivisible part of universal human rights.
. . .

23. The Committee commends the Government for the elaboration of programmes to ensure implementation of those laws, and especially the Programme for the Development of Chinese Women (1995–2000). It notes the achievements of the Government in ensuring social and economic rights for hundreds of millions of people. It also notes that economic reforms in recent years have brought about strong and steady economic growth. The Committee commends the efforts of the Government to combine economic restructuring with concern for the social well-being of China's citizens. It commends, in particular, the Government's efforts to alleviate poverty, to address the unemployment of women, to modify gender stereotypes, including in the mass media, to initiate legal awareness campaigns and to reduce illiteracy of women in rural areas. . . .

24. The Committee welcomes the overall increase of facilities and personnel for maternal health care, the greater access to family planning services and to primary health care. It commends the Government for its collaboration with UNFPA to initiate a pilot family planning programme, based on voluntary participation, information and freedom of choice. The Committee welcomes in particular the Government's strong and unequivocal objection to the use of coercive measures in implementation of its population policy.
. . .

26. The Committee notes that the great size and diversity of China pose special challenges to the realization of equality between women and men.

27. The Committee notes that the persistence of prejudice and stereotypical attitudes concerning the role of women and men in the family and in society, based on views of male superiority and the subordination of women, constitutes a serious impediment to the full implementation of the Convention.

28. The Committee considers that the gap between the situation of women in urban areas and those in rural and remote areas constitutes a major obstacle to the full implementation of the Convention.

29. The Committee notes with concern the adverse impact of economic restructuring on women in the transition from a planned economy to a market economy, and in particular the gender-specific consequences for women's employment and re-employment.

30. The Committee is concerned that the Government's approach to the implementation of the Convention has an apparent focus on the protection of women rather than on their empowerment Thus, the central machinery responsible for government policy is the National Working Committee on Women and Children, perpetuating the identification of women with children. Similarly, in the area of women's health, there is a focus on mother-child health, limited to women's reproductive function. Likewise, labour laws and regulations overemphasize the protection of women.

31. The Committee recommends that the Government re-examine its approach to realizing gender equality, with an emphasis on the human rights framework of the Convention and the empowerment of women. The Government should encourage a country-wide social dialogue that advocates equality between women and men, and a comprehensive public campaign aimed at changing traditional attitudes.

. . .

33. Although the Convention is an integral part of Chinese law, the Committee is concerned that the Women's Law does not contain a definition of discrimination against women. It is also concerned that the Women's Law does not provide for effective remedies in cases of violation of the law. It is unclear whether the Convention can be, or ever has been, invoked in a court of law, and what the outcome of such cases might have been.

34. The Committee recommends that the Government adopt legislation that expressly prohibits gender discrimination, including unintentional and indirect discrimination, in accordance with the definition in article 1 of the Convention. It also recommends that the Government improve the availability of means of redress, including legal remedies, under the Women's Law. The Government should provide legal aid to women who suffer discrimination in its various forms, to assist them in the realization of their rights. It should also widely publicize all these measures so that adequate enforcement of the law can be ensured. . . .

35. The Committee is concerned about the diverse forms of violence against women in China, including custodial violence, sexual abuse, domestic violence, sexual violence and sexual harassment in the workplace. The Committee is also concerned that economic conditions may contribute to an increase in violence against women.

36. The Committee recommends that the Government examine and revise its laws and policies on violence against women in the light of the Committee's general recommendation 19. . . .

37. The Committee recommends that the Government consider the possibility of extending an invitation to the Special Rapporteur on Violence against Women, including its causes and consequences, to visit China and all its provinces.

38. The Committee is concerned that prostitution, which is often a result of poverty and economic deprivation, is illegal in China.

39. The Committee recommends decriminalization of prostitution. Given the HIV/AIDS pandemic, the Committee also recommends that due attention be paid to health services for women in prostitution. The Government is also urged to take measures for the rehabilitation and reintegration of prostitutes into society.
. . .

42. The Committee is concerned that the proportional representation of women in all spheres of public life, and especially at the higher decision-making levels, has increased only minimally since the consideration of China's second report.

43. The Committee urges the Government to adopt temporary special measures within the meaning of article 4, paragraph 1 of the Convention to increase the number of women at the higher echelons of Government. . . .
. . .

46. The Committee is concerned about the economic situation of women in the transition from a centrally planned to a market economy. The rising unemployment of women, difficulties in finding new employment, the lack of enforcement of labour laws for women workers and the continuing categorization of certain jobs as unsuitable for women are of particular concern. The Committee is

concerned that retraining of unemployed women for jobs in the service sector may lead to further gender segregation of the labour market, with women being trapped in low-wage sectors. . . .

. . .

49. The Committee recognizes that population growth is a genuine and severe problem and that considerable progress has been made in providing family planning services, but expresses concern about various aspects of the implementation of China's population policy, including the following:

(a) The Committee notes with concern that only 14 per cent of men use contraceptives, thus making contraception and family planning overwhelmingly a woman's responsibility. In the light of the fact that vasectomy is far less intrusive and costly than tubal ligation, targeting mainly women for sterilization may amount to discrimination;

(b) Notwithstanding the Government's clear rejection of coercive measures, there are consistent reports of abuse and violence by local family planning officials. These include forced sterilizations and abortions, arbitrary detention and house demolitions, particularly in rural areas and among ethnic minorities;

(c) The Committee is concerned about the growing disparity in the male/female sex ratio at birth as an unintended consequence of the population policy, owing to the discriminatory tradition of son preference. The shortage of females may also have long-term implications regarding trafficking in women;

(d) The Committee is concerned about illegal practices of sex-selective abortion, female infanticide and the non-registration and abandonment of female children. The Committee expresses particular concern about the status of 'out-of-plan' and unregistered children, many of them girls, who may be officially non-existent and thus not entitled to education, health care or other social benefits.

. . .

51. Recognizing that male children, especially in rural and remote areas, remain responsible for supporting people in old age, the Government should explicitly address the linkages between economic security in old age and its family planning policies. It should take all appropriate measures to modify and eliminate son preference, inter alia, by expanding educational and employment opportunities for women in rural areas. The Government should enforce laws against sex-selective abortion, female infanticide and abandonment of children and remove all legal disabilities from 'out-of-plan' and unregistered children.

. . .

53. The Committee recommends that all government policy and planning for rural areas, including micro-credit, small enterprise development and other income-generating projects, be developed with the full and active participation of rural women. Urgent attention should be given to addressing women's suicide rates through measures such as the provision of mental health services and a better understanding of the causes of these suicides. Women's studies centres could be encouraged to undertake the necessary research. The Government is urged to ensure that women have equal enjoyment of land rights independent of their marital status.

. . .

56. In the light of the diversity of the country and its population, the Committee repeats the request it made in its concluding comments on China's second periodic report, that the Government provide in its reports a breakdown of information by provinces and autonomous regions and also include information on ethnic minorities particularly the Uyghur and Tibetan peoples.

57. The Committee urges the Government to translate the Convention on the Elimination of All Forms of Discrimination against Women into local languages. It recommends a comprehensive public campaign to improve legal literacy of the Convention and to raise awareness of gender equality as a societal goal and of women's rights as human rights. . . .

. . .

QUESTIONS

1. Do these excerpts from the concluding observations suggest that the Committee is urging compliance with the full range of duties described in the typology of duties at p. 182, *supra*, or that it is giving priority to one strategy and related duty? What strategy would you employ if you were a member of the Committee?

2. What relationships do the concluding observations suggest between civil-political and economic-social rights?

3. In what ways and to what extent do the concluding observations bear on the conduct of nonstate/private actors?

4. In what ways, if any, could these concluding observations serve to put pressure on the Chinese government to act in accordance with the recommendations?

5. Based on these excerpts, how do you assess the utility or significance for realizing the goals of CEDAW of these periodic reports and reactions by the Committee? Can you think of ways in which the reports and reactions could be improved?

GENERAL RECOMMENDATION NO. 23 OF CEDAW COMMITTEE, 16th Sess., 1997

www.un.org/womenwatch/daw/cedaw/recomm.htm

[This General Recommendation is entitled Political and Public Life and is based on Article 7 of CEDAW.]

. . .

5. Article 7 obliges States parties to take all appropriate measures to eliminate discrimination against women in political and public life and to ensure that they enjoy equality with men in political and public life. The obligation specified in

article 7 extends to all areas of public and political life and is not limited to those areas specified in subparagraphs (a), (b) and (c). The political and public life of a country is a broad concept. It refers to the exercise of political power, in particular the exercise of legislative, judicial, executive and administrative powers. The term covers all aspects of public administration and the formulation and implementation of policy at the international, national, regional and local levels. The concept also includes many aspects of civil society, including public boards and local councils and the activities of organizations such as political parties, trade unions, professional or industry associations, women's organizations, community-based organizations and other organizations concerned with public and political life.
. . .

8. Public and private spheres of human activity have always been considered distinct, and have been regulated accordingly. Invariably, women have been assigned to the private or domestic sphere, associated with reproduction and the raising of children, and in all societies these activities have been treated as inferior. By contrast, public life, which is respected and honoured, extends to a broad range of activity outside the private and domestic sphere. Men historically have both dominated public life and exercised the power to confine and subordinate women within the private sphere.
. . .

10. In all nations, the most significant factors inhibiting women's ability to participate in public life have been the cultural framework of values and religious beliefs, the lack of services and men's failure to share the tasks associated with the organization of the household and with the care and raising of children. In all nations, cultural traditions and religious beliefs have played a part in confining women to the private spheres of activity and excluding them from active participation in public life.

11. Relieving women of some of the burdens of domestic work would allow them to engage more fully in the life of their communities. . . .

12. Stereotyping, including that perpetrated by the media, confines women in political life to issues such as the environment, children and health, and excludes them from responsibility for finance, budgetary control and conflict resolution. The low involvement of women in the professions from which politicians are recruited can create another obstacle. In countries where women leaders do assume power this can be the result of the influence of their fathers, husbands or male relatives rather than electoral success in their own right.
. . .

14. No political system has conferred on women both the right to and the benefit of full and equal participation. While democratic systems have improved women's opportunities for involvement in political life, the many economic, social and cultural barriers they continue to face have seriously limited their participation. Even historically stable democracies have failed to integrate fully and equally the opinions and interests of the female half of the population. Societies in which women are excluded from public life and decision-making cannot be described as democratic. . . . The examination of States parties' reports shows that where there is full and equal participation of women in public life and

decision-making, the implementation of their rights and compliance with the Convention improves.

15. . . . Under article 4, the Convention encourages the use of temporary special measures in order to give full effect to articles 7 and 8. Where countries have developed effective temporary strategies in an attempt to achieve equality of participation, a wide range of measures has been implemented, including recruiting, financially assisting and training women candidates, amending electoral procedures, developing campaigns directed at equal participation, setting numerical goals and quotas and targeting women for appointment to public positions such as the judiciary or other professional groups that play an essential part in the everyday life of all societies. The formal removal of barriers and the introduction of temporary special measures to encourage the equal participation of both men and women in the public life of their societies are essential prerequisites to true equality in political life. In order, however, to overcome centuries of male domination of the public sphere, women also require the encouragement and support of all sectors of society to achieve full and effective participation, encouragement which must be led by States parties to the Convention, as well as by political parties and public officials. . . .

16. The critical issue, emphasized in the Beijing Platform for Action is the gap between the de jure and de facto, or the right as against the reality of women's participation in politics and public life generally. Research demonstrates that if women's participation reaches 30 to 35 per cent (generally termed a 'critical mass'), there is a real impact on political style and the content of decisions, and political life is revitalized.

. . .

22. The system of balloting, the distribution of seats in Parliament, the choice of district, all have a significant impact on the proportion of women elected to Parliament. Political parties must embrace the principles of equal opportunity and democracy and endeavour to balance the number of male and female candidates.

. . .

25. Article 7 (b) . . . requires States parties to ensure that women have the right to participate fully in and be represented in public policy formulation in all sectors and at all levels. This would facilitate the mainstreaming of gender issues and contribute a gender perspective to public policy-making.

26. States parties have a responsibility, where it is within their control, both to appoint women to senior decision-making roles and, as a matter of course, to consult and incorporate the advice of groups which are broadly representative of women's views and interests.

27. States parties have a further obligation to ensure that barriers to women's full participation in the formulation of government policy are identified and overcome. These barriers include complacency when token women are appointed, and traditional and customary attitudes that discourage women's participation.

When women are not broadly represented in the senior levels of government or are inadequately or not consulted at all, government policy will not be comprehensive and effective.

28. While States parties generally hold the power to appoint women to senior

cabinet and administrative positions, political parties also have a responsibility to ensure that women are included in party lists and nominated for election in areas where they have a likelihood of electoral success. States parties should also endeavour to ensure that women are appointed to government advisory bodies on an equal basis with men and that these bodies take into account, as appropriate, the views of representative women's groups. It is the Government's fundamental responsibility to encourage these initiatives to lead and guide public opinion and change attitudes that discriminate against women or discourage women's involvement in political and public life.

29. Measures that have been adopted by a number of States parties in order to ensure equal participation by women in senior cabinet and administrative positions and as members of government advisory bodies include: adoption of a rule whereby, when potential appointees are equally qualified, preference will be given to a woman nominee; the adoption of a rule that neither sex should constitute less than 40 per cent of the members of a public body; a quota for women members of cabinet and for appointment to public office; and consultation with women's organizations to ensure that qualified women are nominated for membership in public bodies and offices and the development and maintenance of registers of such women in order to facilitate the nomination of women for appointment to public bodies and posts. Where members are appointed to advisory bodies upon the nomination of private organizations, States parties should encourage these organizations to nominate qualified and suitable women for membership in these bodies.

. . .

31. Examination of the reports of States parties also demonstrates that in certain cases the law excludes women from exercising royal powers, from serving as judges in religious or traditional tribunals vested with jurisdiction on behalf of the State or from full participation in the military. These provisions discriminate against women, deny to society the advantages of their involvement and skills in these areas of the life of their communities and contravene the principles of the Convention.

32. . . . Political parties should be encouraged to adopt effective measures to . . .ensure that women have an equal opportunity in practice to serve as party officials and to be nominated as candidates for election.

33. Measures that have been adopted by some political parties include setting aside for women a certain minimum number or percentage of positions on their executive bodies, ensuring that there is a balance between the number of male and female candidates nominated for election, and ensuring that women are not consistently assigned to less favourable constituencies or to the least advantageous positions on a party list. States parties should ensure that such temporary special measures are specifically permitted under anti-discrimination legislation or other constitutional guarantees of equality.

34. Other organizations such as trade unions and political parties have an obligation to demonstrate their commitment to the principle of gender equality in their constitutions, in the application of those rules and in the composition of their memberships with gender-balanced representation on their executive boards

so that these bodies may benefit from the full and equal participation of all sectors of society and from contributions made by both sexes. These organizations also provide a valuable training ground for women in political skills, participation and leadership, as do non-governmental organizations (NGOs).

. . .

35. Under article 8, Governments are obliged to ensure the presence of women at all levels and in all areas of international affairs. This requires that they be included in economic and military matters, in both multilateral and bilateral diplomacy, and in official delegations to international and regional conferences.

36. From an examination of the reports of States parties, it is evident that women are grossly under-represented in the diplomatic and foreign services of most Governments, and particularly at the highest ranks. Women tend to be assigned to embassies of lesser importance to the country's foreign relations and in some cases women are discriminated against in terms of their appointments by restrictions pertaining to their marital status. . . .

. . .

39. The globalization of the contemporary world makes the inclusion of women and their participation in international organizations, on equal terms with men, increasingly important. The integration of a gender perspective and women's human rights into the agenda of all international bodies is a government imperative. Many crucial decisions on global issues, such as peacemaking and conflict resolution, military expenditure and nuclear disarmament, development and the environment, foreign aid and economic restructuring, are taken with limited participation of women. This is in stark contrast to their participation in these areas at the non-governmental level.

40. The inclusion of a critical mass of women in international negotiations, peacekeeping activities, all levels of preventive diplomacy, mediation, humanitarian assistance, social reconciliation, peace negotiations and the international criminal justice system will make a difference. In addressing armed or other conflicts, a gender perspective and analysis is necessary to understand their differing effects on women and men.

Recommendations

[This section identifies concrete measures to be implemented and specifies the details and statistical data on these issues to be provided in the periodic state reports.]

GENERAL RECOMMENDATION NO. 19 OF CEDAW COMMITTEE, 11th Sess., 1992

UN Doc. A/47/38, 1 Int. Hum. Rt. Rep. 25 (1994)
www.un.org/womenwatch/daw/cedaw/recomm.htm

[This General Recommendation is entitled Violence against Women.]

. . .

[Background]

1. Gender-based violence is a form of discrimination that seriously inhibits women's ability to enjoy rights and freedoms on a basis of equality with men.
. . .

4. The Committee concluded that not all the reports of States parties adequately reflected the close connection between discrimination against women, gender-based violence, and violations of human rights and fundamental freedoms. The full implementation of the Convention required States to take positive measures to eliminate all forms of violence against women.

5. The Committee suggested to States parties that in reviewing their laws and policies, and in reporting under the Convention, they should have regard to the following comments of the Committee concerning gender-based violence.

[General Comments]

6. The Convention in article 1 defines discrimination against women. The definition of discrimination includes gender-based violence, that is, violence that is directed against a woman because she is a woman or that affects women disproportionately. It includes acts that inflict physical, mental or sexual harm or suffering, threats of such acts, coercion and other deprivations of liberty. Gender-based violence may breach specific provisions of the Convention, regardless of whether those provisions expressly mention violence.

7. Gender-based violence, which impairs or nullifies the enjoyment by women of human rights and fundamental freedoms under general international law or under human rights conventions, is discrimination within the meaning of article 1 of the Convention. These rights and freedoms include:

    (a) The right to life;
    (b) The right not to be subject to torture or to cruel, inhuman or degrading treatment or punishment;
    (c) The right to equal protection according to humanitarian norms in time of international or internal armed conflict;
    (d) The right to liberty and security of person;
    (e) The right to equal protection under the law;
    (f) The right to equality in the family;
    (g) The right to the highest standard attainable of physical and mental health;
    (h) The right to just and favourable conditions of work.

8. The Convention applies to violence perpetrated by public authorities. Such acts of violence may breach that State's obligations under general international human rights law and under other conventions, in addition to breaching this Convention.

9. It is emphasized, however, that discrimination under the Convention is not restricted to action by or on behalf of Governments (see articles 2(e), 2(f) and 5). For example, under article 2 (e) the Convention calls on States parties to take all

appropriate measures to eliminate discrimination against women by any person, organization or enterprise. Under general international law and specific human rights covenants, States may also be responsible for private acts if they fail to act with due diligence to prevent violations of rights or to investigate and punish acts of violence, and for providing compensation.

[Comments on Specific Articles of the Convention]

. . .

Articles 2(f), 5 and 10(c)

11. Traditional attitudes by which women are regarded as subordinate to men or as having stereotyped roles perpetuate widespread practices involving violence or coercion, such as family violence and abuse, forced marriage, dowry deaths, acid attacks and female circumcision. Such prejudices and practices may justify gender-based violence as a form of protection or control of women. The effect of such violence on the physical and mental integrity of women is to deprive them of the equal enjoyment, exercise and knowledge of human rights and fundamental freedoms. While this comment addresses mainly actual or threatened violence, the underlying consequences of these forms of gender-based violence help to maintain women in subordinate roles and contribute to their low level of political participation and to their lower level of education, skills and work opportunities.

12. These attitudes also contribute to the propagation of pornography and the depiction and other commercial exploitation of women as sexual objects, rather than as individuals. This in turn contributes to gender-based violence.

. . .

Article 11

17. Equality in employment can be seriously impaired when women are subjected to gender-specific violence, such as sexual harassment in the workplace.

18. Sexual harassment includes such unwelcome sexually determined behaviour as physical contact and advances, sexually coloured remarks, showing pornography and sexual demands, whether by words or actions. Such conduct can be humiliating and may constitute a health and safety problem; it is discriminatory when the woman has reasonable grounds to believe that her objection would disadvantage her in connection with her employment, including recruitment or promotion, or when it creates a hostile working environment.

Article 12

19. States parties are required by article 12 to take measures to ensure equal access to health care. Violence against women puts their health and lives at risk.

20. In some States there are traditional practices perpetuated by culture and tradition that are harmful to the health of women and children. These practices include dietary restrictions for pregnant women, preference for male children and female circumcision or genital mutilation.

. . .

Article 16 (and Article 5)

22. Compulsory sterilization or abortion adversely affects women's physical and mental health, and infringes the right of women to decide on the number and spacing of their children.

23. Family violence is one of the most insidious forms of violence against women. It is prevalent in all societies. . . .

[Specific Recommendations]

24. In light of these comments, the Committee on the Elimination of Discrimination against Women recommends:

(a) States parties should take appropriate and effective measures to overcome all forms of gender-based violence, whether by public or private act;

(b) States parties should ensure that laws against family violence and abuse, rape, sexual assault and other gender-based violence give adequate protection to all women, and respect their integrity and dignity. Appropriate protective and support services should be provided for victims. Gender-sensitive training of judicial and law enforcement officers and other public officials is essential for the effective implementation of the Convention;

(c) States parties should encourage the compilation of statistics and research on the extent, causes and effects of violence, and on the effectiveness of measures to prevent and deal with violence;

(d) Effective measures should be taken to ensure that the media respect and promote respect for women;

(e) States parties in their report should identify the nature and extent of attitudes, customs and practices that perpetuate violence against women, and the kinds of violence that result. They should report the measures that they have undertaken to overcome violence, and the effect of those measures;

(f) Effective measures should be taken to overcome these attitudes and practices. States should introduce education and public information programmes to help eliminate prejudices which hinder women's equality;

. . .

(k) States parties should establish or support services for victims of family violence, rape, sex assault and other forms of gender-based violence, including refuges, specially trained health workers, rehabilitation and counselling;

. . .

(m) States parties should ensure that measures are taken to prevent coercion in regard to fertility and reproduction, and to ensure that women are not forced to seek unsafe medical procedures such as illegal abortion because of lack of appropriate services in regard to fertility control;

. . .

COMMENT ON INTERNATIONAL INSTRUMENTS ON VIOLENCE AGAINST WOMEN

In 1993, the General Assembly adopted a Declaration on the Elimination of Violence against Women.[9] The Preamble asserted that the Declaration would 'strengthen and complement' the process of effective implementation of CEDAW, and recognized that violence against women 'is a manifestation of historically unequal power relations between men and women, which have led to domination over and discrimination against women'. Violence is 'one of the crucial social mechanisms by which women are forced into a subordinate position'.

Article 1 provides that 'violence against women' means gender-based violence, including threats thereof or coercion, 'whether occurring in public or in private life'.

Article 2 states that such violence encompasses family violence including battering, sexual abuse of children, marital rape, female genital mutilation and 'other traditional practices harmful to women', It also covers violence within the general community such as sexual abuse, sexual harassment or intimidation at work or in educational institutions or elsewhere, trafficking in women and forced prostitution. All violence 'perpetrated or condoned' by the state is also covered.

Article 4 provides that 'States should condemn violence against women and should not invoke any custom, tradition or religious consideration to avoid their obligations with respect to its elimination'. States should therefor 'pursue by all appropriate means and without delay a policy of eliminating violence' and to this end should take stated measures. Those measures include the exercise of 'due diligence to prevent, investigate and, in accordance with national legislation, punish acts of violence against women, whether those acts are perpetrated by the State or by private persons'. The state is to adopt measures, 'especially in the field of education, to modify the social and cultural patterns of conduct of men and women and to eliminate prejudices, customary practices and all other practices based on the idea of the inferiority or superiority of either of the sexes and on stereotyped roles for men and women'.

To date only one treaty directly addresses this issue. In June 1994, the Organization of American States adopted the Inter-American Convention on the Prevention, Punishment and Eradication of Violence Against Women[10] (effective March 1995, with 29 states parties in March 2000). Like the UN Declaration, its preambular paragraphs recognize that violence against women is 'a manifestation of the historically unequal power relations between women and men'. The substantive provisions and the definition of the Convention's reach echo provisions in the Declaration.

This Convention is, however, more explicit in recognizing the broad scope and nature of violence, encompassing (Art. 2) 'physical, sexual and psychological violence'. Article 3 makes explicit a woman's rights 'to be free from violence in both the public and private sphere'.

[9] U.N. Doc. A/48/629, reprinted in 33 Int. Leg. Mat. 1050 (1994).
[10] 33 Int. Leg. Mat. 1534 (1994).

States agree (Art. 7) 'to pursue, by all appropriate means and without delay, policies to prevent, punish and eradicate such violence'. These duties include due diligence in investigating and imposing penalties for violence, and the establishment of effective legal procedures including protective measures for women.

NOTE

In 1994, the UN Economic and Social Council (Decision 1994/254) endorsed the resolution of the UN Human Rights Commission (Resolution 1994/45) to appoint for a three-year term a special rapporteur on violence against women, its causes and consequences. The special rapporteur is empowered to engage in field missions either independently or jointly with other rapporteurs and working groups; to seek and receive information from governments, other treaty bodies, specialized agencies of the UN and NGOs; and to consult with the CEDAW Committee in the course of her investigations. Radhika Coomarasawamy from Sri Lanka was appointed to this post, which she continues to hold in 1999. She has submitted annual reports to the Commission on her work.

SPECIAL RAPPORTEUR ON VIOLENCE AGAINST WOMEN, PRELIMINARY REPORT
Commission on Human Rights, E/CN.4/1995,42, 22 November 1994

[The following excerpts from the Preliminary Report of Radhika Coomaraswamy are taken from sections entitled 'Historically unequal power relations', and 'Cultural ideology'.]

49. ... [V]iolence against women is a manifestation of historically unequal power relations between men and women. Violence is part of a historical process and is not natural or born of biological determinism. The system of male dominance has historical roots and its functions and manifestations change over time. The oppression of women is therefore a question of politics, requiring an analysis of the institutions of the State and society, the conditioning and socialization of individuals, and the nature of economic and social exploitation. The use of force against women is only one aspect of this phenomenon, which relies on intimidation and fear to subordinate women.

50. Women are subject to certain universal forms of abuse .... It is argued that any attempt to universalize women's experience is to conceal other forms of oppression such as those based on race, class or nationality. This reservation must be noted and acknowledged. And yet it must be accepted that there are patterns of patriarchal domination which are universal, though this domination takes a number of different forms as a result of particular and different historical experiences. ...

54. The institution of the family is also an arena where historical power relations are often played out. On the one hand, the family can be the source of

positive nurturing and caring values where individuals bond through mutual respect and love. On the other hand, it can be a social institution where labour is exploited, where male sexual power is violently expressed and where a certain type of socialization disempowers women. Female sexual identity is often created by the family environment. The negative images of the self which often inhibit women from realizing their full potential may be linked to familial expectation. The family is, therefore, the source of positive humane values, yet in some instances it is the site for violence against women and a socialization process which may result in justifying violence against women.

. . .

57. In the context of the historical power relations between men and women, women must also confront the problem that men control the knowledge systems of the world. Whether it be in the field of science, culture, religion or language, men control the accompanying discourse. Women have been excluded from the enterprise of creating symbolic systems or interpreting historical experience. It is this lack of control over knowledge systems which allows them not only to be victims of violence, but to be part of a discourse which often legitimizes or trivializes violence against women. . . .

. . .

64. The ideologies which justify the use of violence against women base their discussion on a particular construction of sexual identity. The construction of masculinity often requires that manhood be equated with the ability to exert power over others, especially through the use of force. Masculinity gives man power to control the lives of those around him, especially women. The construction of femininity in these ideologies often requires women to be passive and submissive, to accept violence as part of a woman's estate. Such ideologies also link a woman's identity and self-esteem to her relationship to her father, husband or son. An independent woman is often denied expression in feminine terms. In addition, standards of beauty, defined by women, often require women to mutilate themselves or damage their health, whether with regard to foot binding, anorexia nervosa and bulimia. It is important to reinvent creatively these categories of masculinity and femininity, devoid of the use of force and ensuring the full development of human potential.

. . .

67. Certain customary practices and some aspects of tradition are often the cause of violence against women. Besides female genital mutilation, a whole host of practices violate female dignity. Foot binding, male preference, early marriage, virginity tests, dowry deaths, sati, female infanticide and malnutrition are among the many practices which violate a woman's human rights. Blind adherence to these practices and State inaction with regard to these customs and traditions have made possible large-scale violence against women. States are enacting new laws and regulations with regard to the development of a modern economy and modern technology and to developing practices which suit a modern democracy, yet it seems that in the area of women's rights change is slow to be accepted.

QUESTIONS

1. With reference to the typology of state duties at p. 180, *supra*, categorize the different duties which states are to bear under the two general recommendations. Does any one category appear to represent a priority for the Committee? Would you, as a Committee member, have established a clear priority for one or both recommendations?

2. In what ways do these general recommendations reach beyond state conduct to regulate the conduct of nonstate/private parties, whether health providers or others? Is any of this regulation direct, in the sense that the Committee imposes duties on such nonstate parties? Do the recommendations point toward criminal sanctions imposed by the state against private parties not complying with the stated policies?

3. How do you react to the provisions in the General Recommendation on Political and Public Life on affirmative action, either by the state or by political parties? As a member of the Committee, which if any of these provisions would you oppose?

4. How would you describe the relative weight of civil-political rights and economic-social rights in the two recommendations? Are the two categories of rights kept discrete or intricately integrated?

5. In what respects, if any, do you believe that these general recommendations broaden the duties of states that CEDAW imposes?

6. What influence do you believe that these general recommendations will have on the conduct of states? What measures are at the Committee's disposal to put pressure on states to comply?

7. In what ways is the state involved in the acts and practices described in paras. 11, 12 and 20 of the General Recommendation on Violence against Women? Is it suggested that those perpetrating the described acts are themselves violating the Convention? In this respect, does the UN Declaration on Violence go further than the General Recommendation in that it addresses primarily the offensive conduct of nonstate actors? Why does the state figure at all in this Declaration?

8. The Preliminary Report of the Special Rapporteur states in para. 64 (on ideologies justifying violence against women) that it is 'important to reinvent creatively these categories of masculinity and femininity'. (a) Do you agree with this proposal? (b) From the proposal's perspective, how would you draft a governmental programme for sharply reducing violence against women? What function would the criminal law serve? Other types of law?

COMMENT ON EFFORTS TOWARDS US RATIFICATION OF CEDAW

Ratification has been considered by the United States on several occasions and, in October 1994, almost occurred. The President had submitted the Convention to the Senate, and the Senate Committee on Foreign Relations recommended the Senate's consent to ratification.[11] It observed among other things that failure to ratify had limited US leadership in the promotion of equality for women.

The Committee recommended ratification subject to a number of reservations, understandings and declarations, including the following:

> [T]he Constitution and laws of the United States establish extensive protections against discrimination, reaching all forms of governmental activity as well as significant areas of non-governmental activity. However, individual privacy and freedom from governmental interference in private conduct are also recognized as among the fundamental values of our free and democratic society. The United States understands that by its terms the Convention requires broad regulation of private conduct, in particular under Articles 2, 3 and 5. The United States does not accept any obligation under the Convention to enact legislation or to take any other action with respect to private conduct except as mandated by the Constitution and laws of the United States.

The Committee also proposed reservations to the right to equal pay understood as comparable worth, the right to paid maternity leave, and any obligation under Articles 5, 7, 8 and 13 of the Convention that might restrict constitutional rights to speech, expression and association.

Five senators (a Republican minority) on the Committee objected to ratification. Their statement of Minority Views recognized the 'unfortunate prevalence of violence and human rights abuses against women around the world' and shared the 'majority's strong support for eliminating discrimination against women'. Nonetheless, they were not 'persuaded' that CEDAW was 'a proper or effective means of pursuing that objective'. The Minority Views made the following points:

> (1) CEDAW may enable ratifying states to generate 'political capital', but is 'unlikely to convince governments to make policy changes they would otherwise avoid'.
>
> (2) Countries like the United States 'must guard against treaties that overreach', and must not promise 'more than we can deliver or we risk diluting the moral suasion that undergirds existing covenants'. Indeed, the fear exists that 'creating another set of unenforceable international standards will further dilute respect for international human rights'.
>
> (3) More than 30 states ratifying CEDAW have made significant reservations, sometimes 'so broad as to appear to be at variance with the object and purpose of the treaty itself'. The Minority Views drew illustrations from Islamic states.

---

[11] See S384–10, Exec. Rep. Sen. Comm. on For. Rel., October 3, 1994. Various related documents and the text of all reservations are set forth in 89 Am. J. Int. L. 102 (1995).

The statement questioned 'whether such behavior does not, in fact, "cheapen the coin" of human rights treaties generally'. These reservations suggest that CEDAW 'may reach beyond the necessarily restrictive scope of an effective human rights treaty'.

(4) 'Improvement in the status of women in countries such as India, China, and Sudan will ultimately be made in those countries, not in the United States Senate'.

(5) Evolution of 'internationally accepted norms' on human rights 'is important and must be carefully encouraged. It must, however, take place within an international system of sovereign nations with differing cultural, religious and political systems. Pushing a normative agenda beyond that system's ability to incorporate it leads, we believe, to what is represented by this convention. . . . '

In the end, as the session of Congress came to an end, the Convention never reached the Senate floor.

There has been little subsequent action. President Clinton sent a letter to Congressional leaders on March 11, 1998, seeking their support for gaining Senate consent to ratification.[12] There the matter rests.

QUESTIONS

1. Which objections to ratification of CEDAW that were set forth in the Minority Views seem particular to CEDAW, and which could refer generally to many human rights treaties?

2. The Minority Views state that CEDAW 'may reach beyond the necessarily restrictive scope of an effective human rights treaty'. The Views refer to the differing cultural, religious and political systems among states, and assert that '[p]ushing a normative agenda beyond [the international system's] ability to incorporate it leads . . . to what is represented by this convention. . . . ' Does CEDAW raise special and more difficult problems for US ratification than did the ICCPR? If so, why?

NOTE

Another mechanism within the international system has been increasingly used to advance human rights as well as other objectives: large inter-governmental conferences organized around specific themes. These conferences provide an occasion for governments to discuss and perhaps ultimately agree on common strategies of action to resolve issues of global concern. Recent conferences have included the 1990 World Summit for Children, the 1992 Rio de Janeiro Conference on Environment and Development, the 1993 Second World Conference on Human Rights at Vienna, the 1994 Cairo Conference on Population and Development, the

---

[12] Weekly Compilation of Presidential Documents, March 16, 1998.

1995 Copenhagen World Summit for Social Development, and the Fourth World Conference on Women in Beijing in 1995.

These conferences are by no means identical in structure or flavour; the character of each is influenced by the particular purpose or issue at hand. Nonetheless, recent conferences have tended to follow a similar format. Apart from publicizing the Member States' recognition of the importance of the subject under consideration, the main object of the Conference is often to obtain agreement on a draft document, such as a declaration or charter, and on a related programme of action.

Much of the difficult work in identifying the nature of the issue and proposing solutions to particular problems, is accomplished prior to the opening of the conference. An initial draft may be drawn up by a branch of the UN Secretariat. Expert group meetings are often convened around specific issues or areas of concern. Through a series of regional and global preparatory meetings attended by delegations of the Member States, the draft document may be refined or significantly altered. By the time the conference opens, normally a significant portion of the text or programme has been agreed upon. At this point, it becomes a 'battle of the brackets'—the term arises from the practice of bracketing clauses in the text that are not yet agreed on—that is to say, an exercise in resolving the parts of the programme that have remained contentious.

Throughout this process, sometimes at parallel meetings designed to facilitate it, NGOs engage in an attempt to influence the substance of the document, by providing relevant information to the Secretariat, lobbying Member States or publicizing issues of concern in the press. Reflecting NGOs' increasing influence and activity, it is becoming more common for Member States to consult with them—at least ones from their own countries—prior to establishing their positions, and even to include NGO representation in their official delegations to the preparatory and world conferences.

There follow excerpts from one of the major world meetings involving women and gender as a major theme, the UN World Conference on Human Rights in Vienna, in 1993.

VIENNA DECLARATION AND PROGRAMME OF ACTION
UN World Conference on Human Rights, Vienna, 1993 14 Hum. Rts. L. J. 352 (1993)

The World Conference on Human Rights . . .
  Solemnly adopts the Vienna Declaration and Programme of Action.
. . .

18. The human rights of women and of the girl-child are an inalienable, integral and indivisible part of universal human rights. The full and equal participation of women in political, civil, economic, social and cultural life, at the national, regional and international levels, and the eradication of all forms of discrimination on grounds of sex are priority objectives of the international community. . . .

. . .

37. The equal status of women and the human rights of women should be integrated into the mainstream of United Nations system-wide activity. These issues should be regularly and systematically addressed throughout relevant United Nations bodies and mechanisms. In particular, steps should be taken to increase cooperation and promote further integration of objectives and goals between the Commission on the Status of Women, the Commission on Human Rights, the Committee for the Elimination of Discrimination against Women, the United Nations Development Fund for Women, the United Nations Development Programme and other United Nations agencies. In this context, cooperation and coordination should be strengthened between the Centre for Human Rights and the Division for the Advancement of Women.

38. In particular, the World Conference on Human Rights stresses, the importance of working towards the elimination of violence against women in public and private life, the elimination of all forms of sexual harassment, exploitation and trafficking in women, the elimination of gender bias in the administration of justice and the eradication of any conflicts which may arise between the rights of women and the harmful effects of certain traditional or customary practices, cultural prejudices and religious extremism. . . .

39. . . . States are urged to withdraw reservations that are contrary to the object and purpose of the Convention or which are otherwise incompatible with international treaty law.

40. . . . The Commission on the Status of Women and the Committee on the Elimination of Discrimination against Women should quickly examine the possibility of introducing the right of petition through the preparation of an optional protocol to the Convention on the Elimination of All Forms of Discrimination against Women. The World Conference on Human Rights welcomes the decision of the Commission on Human Rights to consider the appointment of a special rapporteur on violence against women at its fiftieth session.

41. . . . [T]he World Conference on Human Rights reaffirms, on the basis of equality between women and men, a woman's right to accessible and adequate health care and the widest range of family planning services, as well as equal access to education at all levels.

42. Treaty monitoring bodies should include the status of women and the human rights of women in their deliberations and findings, making use of gender-specific data. States should be encouraged to supply information on the situation of women *de jure* and *de facto* in their reports to treaty monitoring bodies. The World Conference on Human Rights notes with satisfaction that the Commission on Human Rights adopted at its forty-ninth session resolution 1993/46 of 8 March 1993 stating that rapporteurs and working groups in the field of human rights should also be encouraged to do so. Steps should also be taken by the Division for the Advancement of Women in cooperation with other United Nations bodies, specifically the Centre for Human Rights, to ensure that the human rights activities of the United Nations regularly address violations of women's human rights, including gender-specific abuses. Training for United Nations human rights and humanitarian relief personnel to assist them to recognize and deal with human

rights abuses particular to women and to carry out their work without gender bias should be encouraged.

43. The World Conference on Human Rights urges Governments and regional and international organizations to facilitate the access of women to decision-making posts and their greater participation in the decision-making process. It encourages further steps within the United Nations Secretariat to appoint and promote women staff members in accordance with the Charter of the United Nations, and encourages other principal and subsidiary organs of the United Nations to guarantee the participation of women under conditions of equality.

3. THE PUBLIC/PRIVATE DIVIDE: DISCRIMINATION AND VIOLENCE BY NONGOVERNMENTAL ACTORS

Earlier materials in this chapter sometimes described abuse of women not by state ('public') but by nongovernmental ('private') actors and action. This theme—the relevance of the public-private divide—inevitably surfaces with respect to women's rights, as much as, if not more than, with respect to other human rights fields.

The distinction between these two terms or concepts is stated in different ways. In the preceding paragraph, it had to do with the nature or character of the actor (governmental or nongovernmental). From other perspectives, the distinction concerns different spheres of life and action. The 'private' is frequently associated with the home, family, domestic life. The 'public' is identified with the interactions of a working life: salaried employment, business, professions, the give and take of the market, being 'out in the world'.

The following readings examine some of the issues presented by opposition of private and public:

> the practical, political and ideological significance of the divide;
> the shifting boundary line between the two as conceptions of their significance and content change;
> the degree to which human rights instruments should require states parties to regulate non-governmental (private)conduct; and
> the degree to which non-governmental actors should themselves become directly subject to duties under international human rights law and liable for their violation.

The readings start with what has become a classic judicial opinion in international human rights because of its clarification of a state's duty with respect to violence committed by non-governmental actors, and with questions by Theodor Meron about the effects of CEDAW on the realm of the private. The further readings by contemporary feminists suggest the importance of keeping clear the different meanings of private and public, as well as the need to distinguish between the conception of 'privacy' and the various definitions of the private-public divide.

VELÁSQUEZ RODRIGUEZ CASE
Inter-American Court of Human Rights, 1988
Ser. C, No. 4, 9 Hum. Rts L. J. 212 (1988)

[A petition against Honduras was received by the Inter-American Commission of Human Rights, alleging that one Velásquez was arrested without warranty by national security units of Honduras. Knowledge of his whereabouts was consistently denied by police and security forces. Velásquez had disappeared. Petitioners argued that through this conduct, Honduras had violated several articles of the American Convention on Human Rights. After hearings and conclusions, the Commission referred the matter to the Inter-American Court of Human Rights, whose contentious jurisdiction had been recognized by Honduras. The Court concluded that Honduras had violated the Convention.

In the excerpts below, the Court addresses the issue of just what the obligations of Honduras were under the Convention? Was Honduras obligated only to 'respect' individual rights and not directly violate them, as by torture or illegal arrest? Or was Honduras obligated to take steps, within reasonable limits, to protect people like Velásquez from seizure even by nongovernmental, private persons? In an earlier portion of the opinion, the Court had found that the Honduran state was implicated in the arrest and disappearance, and that the acts of those arresting Velásquez could be imputed to the state. In the present excerpts, the Court reviews that information, and considers what might be the responsibility of Honduras even if the seizure and disappearance of Velásquez were caused by private persons unconnected with the government.]

161. Article 1(1) of the Convention provides:

> 1. The States Parties to this Convention undertake to respect the rights and freedoms recognized herein and to ensure to all persons subject to their jurisdiction the free and full exercise of those rights and freedoms. . . .

. . .

164. Article 1(1) is essential in determining whether a violation of the human rights recognized by the Convention can be imputed to a State Party. In effect, that article charges the States Parties with the fundamental duty to respect and guarantee the rights recognized in the Convention. Any impairment of those rights which can be attributed under the rules of international law to the action or omission of any public authority constitutes an act imputable to the State, which assumes responsibility in the terms provided by the Convention itself.

165. The first obligation assumed by the States Parties under Article 1(1) is 'to respect the rights and freedoms' recognized by the Convention. . . .

166. The second obligation of the States Parties is to ['ensure'] the free and full exercise of the rights recognized by the Convention to every person subject to its jurisdiction. This obligation implies the duty of the States Parties to organize the governmental apparatus and, in general, all the structures through which public power is exercised, so that they are capable of juridically ensuring the free and full

enjoyment of human rights. As a consequence of this obligation, the States must prevent, investigate and punish any violation of the rights recognized by the Convention and, moreover, if possible attempt to restore the rights violated and provide compensation as warranted for damages resulting from the violation.
. . .

169. According to Article 1(1), any exercise of public power that violates the rights recognized by the Convention is illegal. . . .

170. This conclusion is independent of whether the organ or official has contravened provisions of internal law or overstepped the limits of his authority. Under international law a State is responsible for the acts of its agents undertaken in their official capacity and for their omissions, even when those agents act outside the sphere of their authority or violate internal law.
. . .

172. Thus, in principle, any violation of rights recognized by the Convention carried out by an act of public authority or by persons who use their position of authority is imputable to the State. However, this does not define all the circumstances in which a State is obligated to prevent, investigate and punish human rights violations, nor all the cases in which the State might be found responsible for an infringement of those rights. An illegal act which violates human rights and which is initially not directly imputable to a State (for example, because it is the act of a private person or because the person responsible has not been identified) can lead to international responsibility of the State, not because of the act itself, but because of the lack of due diligence to prevent the violation or to respond to it as required by the Convention.
. . .

174. The State has a legal duty to take reasonable steps to prevent human rights violations and to use the means at its disposal to carry out a serious investigation of violations committed within its jurisdiction, to identify those responsible, impose the appropriate punishment and ensure the victim adequate compensation.

175. This duty to prevent includes all those means of a legal, political, administrative and cultural nature that promote the safeguard of human rights and ensure that any violations are considered and treated as illegal acts, which, as such, may lead to the punishment of those responsible and the obligation to indemnify the victims for damages. It is not possible to make a detailed list of all such measures, as they vary with the law and the conditions of each State Party. Of course, while the State is obligated to prevent human rights abuses, the existence of a particular violation does not, in itself, prove the failure to take preventive measures. . . .
. . .

177. In certain circumstances, it may be difficult to investigate acts that violate an individual's rights. The duty to investigate, like the duty to prevent, is not breached merely because the investigation does not produce a satisfactory result. Nevertheless, it must be undertaken in a serious manner. . . . Where the acts of private parties that violate the Convention are not seriously investigated, those parties are aided in a sense by the government, thereby making the State responsible on the international plane.

178. In the instant case, the evidence shows a complete inability of the procedures of the State of Honduras, which were theoretically adequate, to ensure the investigation of the disappearance of Manfredo Velásquez and the fulfillment of its duties to pay compensation and punish those responsible, as set out in Article 1(1) of the Convention.

179. As the Court has verified above, the failure of the judicial system to act upon the writs brought before various tribunals in the instant case has been proven. Not one writ of habeas corpus was processed. No judge had access to the places where Manfredo Velásquez might have been detained. The criminal complaint was dismissed.

180. Nor did the organs of the Executive Branch carry out a serious investigation to establish the fate of Manfredo Velásquez. There was no investigation of public allegations of a practice of disappearances nor a determination of whether Manfredo Velásquez had been a victim of that practice. The Commission's requests for information were ignored to the point that the Commission had to presume, under Article 42 of its Regulations, that the allegations were true. . . .

. . .

182. The Court is convinced, and has so found, that the disappearance of Manfredo Velásquez was carried out by agents who acted under cover of public authority. However, even had that fact not been proven, the failure of the State apparatus to act, which is clearly proven, is a failure on the part of Honduras to fulfill the duties it assumed under Article 1(1) of the Convention, which obligated it to guarantee Manfredo Velásquez the free and full exercise of his human rights.

. . .

THEODOR MERON, HUMAN RIGHTS LAW-MAKING IN THE UNITED NATIONS
(1986), at 60

. . .

. . . [Article 1 of the] Convention on the Elimination of All Forms of Discrimination Against Women clearly extends the prohibition of discrimination to private life. . . .

The provisions of the Convention on the Elimination of All Forms of Discrimination Against Women apply to a broad range of activities: unintentional as well as international discrimination is prohibited (as indicated by the 'effect' clause); private as well as public actions are regulated (as indicated by the phrase 'and other field'). By proscribing practices which have the effect of discriminating against women, the Convention guards against the use of facially neutral criteria as a pretext for discrimination, for instance the use of height and weight requirements which are not related to the requirements of the job and which tend to exclude women as a group. The 'effects' standard avoids the difficulties inherent in proving specific discriminatory motive. The prohibition of unintentional discrimination is necessary to achieve systemic change, because policies undertaken without discriminatory motive may perpetuate inequalities established by prior acts of purposeful discrimination. . . .

The definition of discrimination against women does not prohibit certain distinctions *per se*, but only when they have the purpose or the effect of denying women the enjoyment of human rights and fundamental freedoms on a basis of equality with men. . . . [T]he Committee on the Elimination of Racial Discrimination has tended to regard all ethnic distinctions as suspect, unless made in the context of affirmative action, without engaging in a substantive inquiry as to whether they have in fact had an adverse effect on the enjoyment of 'rights'. If the parties to the Convention on the Elimination of All Forms of Discrimination Against Women and the Committee established under Art. 17 follow a similar approach, a further expansion in the reach of the Convention would result. . . .

It is not clear whether it was appropriate to extend the field of application of the Convention to encompass even private, interpersonal relations (except, of course, when the conduct which is challenged takes forms customarily regulated pursuant to the police power). It is certainly true that discrimination against women in personal and family life is rampant and may obviate equal opportunities which may be available in public life. There is danger, however, that state regulation of interpersonal conduct may violate the privacy and associational rights of the individual and conflict with the principles of freedom of opinion, expression, and belief. Such regulation may require invasive state action to determine compliance, including inquiry into political and religious beliefs. Attempts to regulate discrimination in interpersonal conduct may invite abuse of the discretion vested in the State by the broad language of Art. 1.

. . .

[Article 5 of the Convention] mandates regulation of social and cultural patterns of conduct regardless of whether the conduct is public or private. Coupled with the broad and vague language of the preambular sentence discussed above ('all appropriate measures'), para. (a) might permit States to curtail to an undefined extent privacy and associational interests and the freedom of opinion and expression. Moreover, since social and cultural behaviour may be patterned according to factors such as ethnicity or religion, state action authorized by para. (a) which is directed towards modifying the way in which a particular ethnic or religious group treats women may conflict with the principles forbidding discrimination on the basis of race or religion.

The danger of intrusive state action and possible violation of the rights of ethnic or religious groups might have been mitigated by limiting state action to educational measures. Social and cultural patterns of conduct could be regulated by the substantive provisions which govern actual practices in a particular field, for example employment practices, without loss of substantive rights under the Convention.

. . .

HILARY CHARLESWORTH, ALIENATING OSCAR? FEMINIST ANALYSIS OF INTERNATIONAL LAW

in Dorinda Dallmeyer (ed.), Reconceiving Reality: Women and International Law (1993), at 1

...

Feminist analysis has only just begun in international law. . . . One reason is that there are very few women scholars and practitioners of international law and the discipline operates as a men's club. Another is the abstract nature of the concepts and subjects of international law which do not seem to impinge directly on women's lives. Another, perhaps, is the emphasis placed in modern international law discourse on the significance of differences of race, culture, and nationality and the consequent lack of interest in another significant variable such as gender. Yet another is the generally positivist or realist cast of international legal theory which is inhospitable to feminist inquiry. Finally, the fact that international law deals in matters of life and death, of war and peace, of 'real decision-making power' has kept it a male preserve.

...

From charting the failure of the international legal system to take women seriously, feminist analysis must proceed to explore the unspoken commitments of apparently neutral principles of international law and the ways that male perspectives are institutionalized in it. . . . For example, the operation of the much-invoked principle of self-determination has often exacerbated the oppression of women: Afghanistan, Kuwait, and the former Yugoslavia are recent examples of this. The right operates with respect to 'peoples'—groups defined ethnically— even if half the persons comprising the people have no power within it. What does the much-heralded human right to democracy promise to women? Most formulations of international human rights are quite irrelevant to women's lives, being based on what men most fear will happen to them.

The most explicit commitment of the current international legal order, of course, is to the concept of the state and any feminist analysis must investigate this dedication. For a time feminists accepted the state as a neutral institution which could be persuaded to accommodate women's interests. The failure of this project has led to new understandings of the state, primarily in a national context. . . .

...

Historically, the formation of the state depended on a sexual division of labor and the relegation of women to a private, domestic, devalued sphere. Men dominated in the public sphere of citizenship and political and economic life. The state institutionalized the patriarchal family both as the qualification for citizenship and public life and also as the basic socio-economic unit. The functions of the state were identified with men. Rebecca Grant notes, 'Women experienced the effects of wars and other manifestations of state conduct. But it was left to men—citizens of the state—to formulate policy for dealing with other states'.

The distinction between public and private spheres which is at the heart of the traditional notion of the state has had a defining influence on international law and tenacity in international legal doctrine. Thus the United Nations Charter makes the (public) province of international law distinct from the (private) sphere of domestic jurisdiction; . . . Even international human rights law, which is regarded as radically challenging the traditional distinction between international and domestic concerns, targets 'public', state-sanctioned violations rather than those that have no apparent direct connection to the state. . . .

Accepting statehood and sovereignty as givens in the international legal order narrows our imaginative universe and the possibilities of reconstruction. What direction does feminist analysis suggest for reconceiving the state? A. S. Runyan and V. S. Peterson point out the unique character of feminist critiques of the state in that 'they have never been mounted in the name of women taking over state power'. They deal instead with new conceptions of power. . . . At the very least a feminist state would need to have as its goal the eradication of the cultural distinction which underpins women's exclusion from power: the gendered public/private dichotomy. It is sometimes assumed that the feminists aim at the eradication of the state. But in fact it is worth noting that even when contemporary state structures have broken down, patriarchy flourishes. Indeed women are usually in a significantly worse position in times of state crisis. The fate of women in Bosnia-Herzegovina at the current time underlines this.

If the state as a patriarchal, hierarchical, militarized entity is transformed, many principles of international law will need to be revised. The major sources of international law set out in Article 38 of the Statute of the International Court of Justice, conventions and custom, are the product of state action. If a feminist account of the state gives priority to participatory democracy, non-state actors will be able to contribute to the creation of international law. Moreover, international law may become more flexible. . . .

. . .

. . . At this stage in feminist analysis of international law, then, deconstruction and reconstruction are difficult to separate. Deconstruction has transformative potential because it reduces the imaginative grip of the traditional theories. As Elizabeth Gross observes, all feminist theories are subversive strategies. They are 'forms of guerrilla warfare, striking out at points of patriarchy's greatest weakness, its blindspots'. They reveal the 'partial and partisan instead of the universal or representative position' of patriarchal discourse.

. . .

NOTE

In her article 'Accountability in International Law for Violations of Women's Rights by Non-State Actors', appearing in Dorinda Dallmeyer (ed.), *Reconceiving Reality: Women and International Law* (1993), at 93, Rebecca Cook inquires why it is necessary or useful to inquire into a state's accountability in international law for violations of women's rights by nonstate actors including private persons. She suggests:

> Women's experiences confirm the endemic character of denials of rights committed by public agencies, for instance regarding access to government, to polit-

ical power, and to legal status based on nationality. Women's initial experiences of discrimination arise more intimately, however, through their inferior status as daughters and impaired access to education, employment, wage equity, and equitable distribution of family assets. Vulnerability to domestic violence may be encountered as daughters, sisters, brides, and wives. Accordingly, women's exposure to discrimination and other denials of human rights will originate through acts of private persons and institutions, and will continue at this level as women mature to recognize parallel denials of rights directly attributable to state action that they encounter in the political, economic and other spheres of national life. The denials of rights that states permit women to suffer in their private relationships are an important part of the total subjugation of women.

Women's human rights warrant defense when their violation originates in state action and also in private action. It is not a reason to disregard privately originating violations because violations also occur in the public sector of national life, or because they remain unremedied when they are directly attributable to organs of the state, or because they are more difficult to tackle when they arise through non-state actors. . . . The identification of violations of women's rights both by organs of state and by conduct of non-state actors for which the state can be shown accountable are complementary goals, and not alternatives to or in competition with each other.

Menno Kamminga in his Book *Inter-State Accountability for Violations of Human Rights* distinguishes the terms 'accountability' and 'responsibility'. Accountability is claimed to involve a duty to provide an explanation or account for an act apparently contrary to an international obligation. Responsibility involves a duty to provide appropriate reparation for an internationally wrongful act. Responsibility can be a means of discharging accountability, but accountability is a wider concept because a state may be able to explain an act of apparent violation of international law in a way that does not involve its responsibility can be understood as a limited sub-category of accountability.

More mechanisms exist through international institutions and under terms of human rights treaties to allow states to meet accountability for their practices and responses to private conduct than exists to compel the narrower obligation to meet state responsibility. . . .

KAREN ENGLE, AFTER THE COLLAPSE OF THE PUBLIC/ PRIVATE DISTINCTION: STRATEGIZING WOMEN'S RIGHTS
in Dorinda Dollmeyer (ed.), Reconceiving Reality: Women and International Law (1993), at 143

. . .

Central to the critiques of international law have been analyses of the public/ private distinction. They generally take one of two forms. Either women's rights advocates argue that public international law, and particularly human rights theory, is flawed because it is not really universal. That is, because international law excludes from its scope the private, or domestic sphere—presumably the space in which women operate—it cannot include them. Or advocates argue that international law does not really exclude the private, but rather uses the public/private divide as a convenient screen to avoid addressing women's issues.

Those who take the first approach, then, take for granted that public international law in its present form cannot enter what they see as the private sphere. For women to be included, they maintain, international law must be reconceptualized to include the private.

Those who take the second approach, on the other hand, assume that doctrinal tools are present in international law—particularly in human rights law—to accommodate women. The public/private dichotomy, they assert, is both irrational and inconsistently applied. According to this second approach, the human rights regime and states are disingenuous in their claim that they do not enter the private sphere. The private sphere is entered all the time, for example, through regulation of the family, or the ability to impute to states the acts of non-state actors in disappearance cases. Moreover, these critics argue, a state's failure to protect rights in the private sphere is not distinguishable from direct state action. Finally, they point out that the human rights regime applies a double standard when talking about women. The international legal regime would never argue, for example, that it could not intervene to ensure that states end certain forms of 'private' violence, such as cannibalism or slavery.

. . .

Concentrating too much on the public/private distinction excludes important parts of women's experiences. Not only does such a focus often omit those parts of women's lives that figure into the 'public', however that gets defined, it also assumes that 'private' is bad for women. It fails to recognize that the 'private' is a place where many have tried to be (such as those involved in the market), and that it might ultimately afford protection to (at least some) women.

. . .

[. . . The critiques of the private-public distinction] make us think of the unregulated private as something that is necessarily bad for women. We rarely look at the ways in which privacy (even if only because it seems the best available paradigm) is seen by at least some women to offer them protection. A number of examples immediately come to mind, each of which centers on women's bodies and, not surprisingly, on women's sexuality. The language of privacy, and sketching out zones of privacy, many would argue, is our best shot at legally theorizing women's sexuality. In United States legal jurisprudence, the First Amendment has been used to a similar end as often seen in the debates about pornography.

Examples of where 'the private' is sometimes seen to have liberating potential for women are abortion (which is most obvious to us in the United States); battering; the protection of 'alternative' sexual lifestyles; prostitution; right to wear the veil as protection from sexual harassment; right to participate in *or be free of* clitoridectomies, sati, breast implants, the wearing of spike-heeled shoes. Failure to focus on these issues affecting women's relationships to our bodies obscures the ways that many women see their lives.

. . . [T]he critiques often prevent us from taking seriously women who claim not to want the regulation or protection of international law. Arguments about 'culture', particularly those that attempt to use claims of cultural integrity or community to maintain practices that some women might find abhorrent, get transformed into arguments about the private. That is, women's rights advocates often treat these arguments as though they are yet another manifestation of the mainstream legal regime's exclusion of the private or women (or both) at all costs. As a result, advocates either ignore those women who defend practices they see as an important part of their culture, or assume that such women are replete with false consciousness.

. . .

. . . [T]he critiques often lead us to conspiracy theories. Our exclusion indicates that they're all out to get us. We point out that *they* don't include *us* in the mainstream, that *they* give *us* our own marginal institutions and then ensure that the institutions lack enforcement mechanisms, that *they* don't really care about *us* or take us seriously. We rarely ask, though, who *they* are, who *we* are, and why they're out to get us. We also fail to notice that others are singing a similar tune to our own. Those who argue for economic and social rights, for example, seem to feel just as isolated and outside as women's advocates do. In fact, sometimes it seems that international law, particularly human rights law, has been built by its own criticism. That is every time some group or cause feels outside the law, it pushes for inclusion, generally through a new official document. The vast proliferation of human rights documents, then, is as much a testament to exclusion as it is to inclusion.

. . .

COMMENT ON THE PUBLIC/PRIVATE DIVIDE AND EXPANSION OF THE HUMAN RIGHTS MOVEMENT

Chapter 3 has examined several ideas about the significance of the public-private divide for human rights law and policy. This Comment summarizes different ways in which the human rights movement has weakened the distinction, or the significance of the distinction, between public and private and thereby opened paths toward expansion in coverage and application of international human rights norms.

In the context of human rights as elsewhere, the terms 'public' and 'private' have a protean character. Their meanings depend on the purpose for which they are employed, on their context, and indeed on the historical period in which they are used. Even when intended to serve merely as descriptive terms of classification, the terms carry much historical and ideological baggage that bears on human rights concerns.

Consider some of the explicit and implicit uses of distinctions between the public and private in Chapters 2 and 3. From the start, individuals were the beneficiaries of the human rights movement. In the UHDR and human rights treaties, they were declared to be the bearers of rights (with a few exceptions for group rights such as peoples seeking self-determination). States were the primary bearers of the range of duties identified in the Comment at p. 180, *supra*. Protection of individuals against states was surely the primary original purpose of these instruments.

One continuing use of 'public' and 'private' has indeed been to identify the state and government with the public, and individuals with the private. Within this distinction individuals are then private, 'nonstate' actors, as indeed are other nonstate (nongovernmental) actors such as business entities and public interest groups like human rights nongovernmental organizations. To some extent, the human rights norms benefiting individuals also benefit these nonstate entities—for example, the right to advocacy of public interest organizations, or the right of business corporations to a fair trial.

The materials in this section of Chapter 3 on 'The Public-Private Divide' have also drawn on other conceptions of this divide. The feminist and other scholarship on women's issues and human rights has stressed the ideological connotations in the use of these terms: the 'public' domain of business and the market (a man's world) is set against the 'private' domain of home and family (a woman's world). The categories do not fit comfortably with the division sketched in the preceding paragraph. Thus the 'private' (in the sense of 'nonstate') man who works in the larger economy and polity forms part of the 'public' domain and takes part in 'public' life, while women confined to family work are both as 'private' as nonstate actors and as participants in the 'private' domain and 'private' life.

The challenge to this distinction and its many implications for the lives and capacities of men and women has been central to the women's movement. CEDAW expresses throughout its rejection of most of these implications and its intention of making the worlds of public and private equally accessible to men and women. The readings in this section also demonstrate the significance to women's issues of the related but distinct concept of 'privacy' that figures in the human rights instruments (for example, Article 17 of the ICCPR).

* * * * *

The balance of this Comment addresses the question of regulation by international human rights instruments of the state ('public') and of nonstate parties ('private'). Over the half century of the human rights movement, both treaty and customary law have expanded the degree to which duties and responsibilities are directly imposed on individual actors as well as states. If violated, those duties may lead to individual criminal liability under international law. In its discussion of the Nuremberg Judgment, Chapter 2 introduced this topic. In that context, and in the broad context of war crimes as they have subsequently developed, the individuals convicted of crimes were generally identified with and in some way part of the state and its activities: leaders, bureaucrats, members of armed forces, and so on.

But other categories of individual crimes have developed greatly since Nuremberg: the crime of genocide, crimes against humanity. This expansion of individual criminal liability is made evident in the Statutes of the International Criminal Tribunals for the Former Yugoslavia and Rwanda, and of the proposed International Criminal Court, all described in Chapter 14. Individuals charged with genocide or crimes against humanity are not necessarily state-related, and indeed may be acting in violation of state law. Moreover, other types of international criminal liability based on treaties, such as the crime of hijacking aircraft, also reach 'nonstate' (and in this sense 'private') individuals. In all such instances, criminal liability stems directly from international law, although the formal basis of prosecution may be a state law based on an international criminal provision. An analogy with respect to individual civil liability is provided by the United States Alien Tort Statute, examined at p. 1049, *infra*.

* * * * *

In two significant respects that Chapter 3 underscores, the human rights movement has reached beyond state conduct in very different ways from individual criminal liability to bring within its regulatory scope much conduct by individuals and nonstate entities.

(1) A state's duty to protect individuals against interference with their rights by nonstate actors. A prime illustration is the state's duty under the ICCPR (Article 2) and CEDAW (Article 2) to protect individuals against types of interference by nonstate actors that violate their rights. The Comment on types of state duties at p. 180, *supra*, as well as the Velásquez Rodriguez case illustrate this duty. But unlike the preceding category of international criminal liability for, say, crimes against humanity, international law does not here *directly* regulate the interfering nonstate actors. Those actors are not subjected to criminal or other liability under international law. Rather it is the state that the human rights treaty obligates to offer reasonable protection to individuals against such interference. Such protection will often include not only police protection but also a system of state criminal law under which offenders may be prosecuted.

For the most part, this indirect regulation of nonstate actors flows from a state's general duty to protect against interferences that is derived, for example, from a state's commitment in a treaty to 'ensure' recognized rights (Article 2 of the ICCPR, Article 1 of the American Convention at issue in Velásquez Rodriguez). Some treaties go beyond so general a state duty and impose on the state the duty to protect against a specific type of interference by nonstate actors like business firms. For example, Articles 2(e) and 11 of CEDAW require states parties to eliminate discrimination in employment. It remains for the state to decide what regulation it will impose on business employers, including what type of remedial or enforcement measures it will enact to meet its obligation.

(2) Other state duties that blur or eliminate the public-private distinction. The Comment on types of state duties, drawing particularly on CEDAW, includes the duty to 'promote'. Promotion of changes of attitude in a population will involve a range of public policies, education, and other means of achieving the goals of cultural transformation that, for example, are stated in Article 5 of CEDAW. The traditional realms of public and private are deeply interrelated and implicated. Distinctions between state and nonstate actors blur. All actors, all sectors of economic and political life and of family life, participate in the formation and transformation of culture that are here at issue.

The human rights movement offers other diverse illustrations of the breakdown of traditional public-private categories. Nonstate actors have achieved importance in the human rights movement in ways other than becoming bearers of duties or targets of state regulation. Chapter 11, for example, explores the growing role of human rights nongovernmental organizations, including their formal participation in the processes of intergovernmental organizations and their influence on the development of human rights norms. Chapter 16 examines the powerful role of multinational enterprises. Again the traditional distinctions between public and private actors and processes lose some of their force and significance.

QUESTIONS

1. How do you assess the 'danger of intrusive state action' to which Meron refers? Do such dangers as may appear to you stem from the degree to which (a) CEDAW regulates private or nongovernmental actors and acts, (b) requires changes in cultural attitudes and customary practices, or both?

2. 'Two radically different conceptions are presented in the readings of how violence against women by non-state actors leads to the conclusion that the relevant state has violated international human rights. (1) The state fails to act reasonably through the processes of the criminal law to protect against violence, to punish the violators, and to deter further violence. (2) There is no division of state and society or culture, no satisfactory way of distinguishing between the public and private with respect to the exercise of power against women. In this context, private power is public power. The state is deeply implicated in cultural attitudes that foster violence, and can meet its human rights duties only by changing those attitudes. It is not a matter of patching up criminal laws or enforcement here or there, but of transforming deep structures of beliefs and behavior'.

a. Is this an accurate description of the readings? If not, how would you formulate the different conceptions at work?

b. Are both conceptions, one or the other, or neither one, appropriate for a human rights treaty on women's rights?

3. 'CEDAW is more of a long-run political platform or program than a human rights treaty concerned with equal protection.' Do you agree? If so, what follows from it?

ADDITIONAL READING

On women's rights generally see: K. Askin and D. Koenig (eds.), *Women and International Human Rights Law* (Vols. 1–2, 1999); R. Cook (ed.), *Human Rights of Women* (1994); D. Dallmeyer (ed.), *Reconceiving Reality: Women and International Law* (1993); M. Nussbaum, *Sex and Social Justice* (1999); W. Renteln et al. (eds.), *Human Rights of Women—International and African Perspectives* (1998); S. Fredman, 'Less Equal Than Others—Equality and Women's Rights', in C. Gearty and A. Tompkins (eds.), Understanding Human Rights (1996); articles in 12 Aust. Y.B. Int. L. 177–293 (1992). On CEDAW see M. Bustelo, 'CEDAW at the Crossroads', in P. Alston and J. Crawford (eds.), *The Future of UN Human Rights Treaty Monitoring* 79 (2000). On the public-private divide see A. Clapham, *Human Rights in the Private Sphere* (1993).

On issues of public and private, see: A. Clapham, *Human Rights in the Private Sphere* (1993); M. Forde, 'Non-Governmental Interferences with Human Rights', 54 Brit. Ybk. Int. L. 253 (1985); C. MacKinnon, 'On Torture: A Feminist Perspective on Human Rights', in K. Mahoney and P. Mahoney (eds.), *Human Rights in the Twenty-First Century* 21 (1993); F. Olsen, 'Feminist Critiques of the Public/Private Distinction', in D. Dallmeyer (ed.), *Reconceiving Reality: Women and International Law* (1993), at 157; C. Pateman,

'Feminist Critiques of the Public/Private Distinction', in S.J. Benn and Gaus (eds.), *Public and Private in Social Life* (1983), at 281.

C. THE CONTINUING ROLE OF CUSTOM AND THE SIGNIFICANCE OF UN RESOLUTIONS

Given the multitude of human rights treaties, one might conclude that resort to customary international law and to general principles as components of argument about international law is no longer necessary. Since treaties occupy the field, recourse thereto should be sufficient.

That conclusion would be wrong. As components of argument about international human rights, custom and general principles retain great importance, although less in their classical methods and forms as sketched in Chapter 2, than in their contemporary transformed character. Custom occupies a central role in legal argument about matters as diverse as litigation under the Alien Tort Statute in the United States in Chapter 12 and interpretation of the subject matter jurisdiction of the International Criminal Tribunals for the Former Yugoslavia and for Rwanda in Chapter 14.

This Section C suggests the influence on the development of the human rights movement over the last half century of older and contemporary notions of international customary law. It thus explores the significance of new ingredients of argument about international human rights such as resolutions and declarations voted by the UN General Assembly, or recommendations of treaty bodies. Chapter 3 is rich in illustrations of these contemporary ingredients of international law, from the Universal Declaration itself to the documents issued by the ICCPR Committee and the CEDAW Committee.

OPPENHEIM'S INTERNATIONAL LAW (ROBERT JENNINGS AND ARTHUR WATTS, EDS.)
Vol. 1 (9th edn 1992), at 4

That part of international law that is binding on all states, as is far the greater part of customary law, may be called *universal* international law, in contradistinction to *particular* international law which is binding on two or a few states only. *General* international law is that which is binding upon a great many states. General international law, such as provisions of certain treaties which are widely, but not universally, binding and which establish rules appropriate for universal application, has a tendency to become universal international law.

One can also distinguish between those rules of international law which, even though they may be of universal application, do not in any particular situation give rise to rights and obligations *erga omnes*, and those which do. Thus, although all states are under certain obligations as regards the treatment of aliens, those obligations (generally speaking) can only be invoked by the state whose nationality

the alien possesses: on the other hand, obligations deriving from the outlawing of acts of aggression, and of genocide, and from the principles and rules concerning the basic rights of the human person, including protection from slavery and racial discrimination, are such that all states have an interest in the protection of the rights involved.[13] Rights and obligations *erga omnes* may even be created by the actions of a limited number of states. There is, however, no agreed enumeration of rights and obligations *erga omnes*, and the law in this area is still developing, as it is in the connected matter of a state's ability, by analogy with the *actio popularis* (or *actio communis*) known to some national legal systems, to institute proceedings to vindicate an interest as a member of the international community as distinct from an interest vested more particularly in itself. . . .
. . .

States may, by and within the limits of agreement between themselves, vary or even dispense altogether with most rules of international law. There are, however, a few rules from which no derogation is permissible. The latter—rules of *ius cogens*, or peremptory norms of general international law—have been defined in Article 53 of the Vienna Convention on the Law of Treaties 1969 (and for the purpose of that Convention) as norms 'accepted and recognised by the international community of states as a whole as a norm from which no derogation is permitted and which can be modified only by a subsequent norm of general international law having the same character'; and Article 64 contemplates the emergence of new rules of *ius cogens* in the future.

Such a category of rules of *ius cogens* is a comparatively recent development and there is no general agreement as to which rules have this character. The International Law Commission regarded the law of the Charter concerning the prohibition of the use of force as a conspicuous example of such a rule. Although the Commission refrained from giving in its draft Articles on the Law of Treaties any examples of rules of *ius cogens*, it did record that in this context mention had additionally been made of the prohibition of criminal acts under international law, and of acts such as trade in slaves, piracy or genocide, in the suppression of which every state is called upon to cooperate; the observance of human rights, the equality of states and the principle of self-determination. The full content of the category of *ius cogens* remains to be worked out in the practice of states and in the jurisprudence of international tribunals. . . .

The operation and effect of rules of *ius cogens* in areas other than that of treaties are similarly unclear. Presumably no act done contrary to such a rule can be legitimated by means of consent. . . .

---

[13] [Eds.] The authors here refer in a footnote to the *Case Concerning The Barcelona Traction, Light and Power Company, Limited (New Application 1962) (Belgium v. Spain)* [1970] ICJ Rep. 4. The relevant portion of that opinion of the International Court of Justice reads, at paras 33–34: '[A]n essential distinction should be drawn between the obligations of a State towards the international community as a whole, and those arising vis-à-vis another State in the field of diplomatic protection. By their very nature, the former are the concern of all States. In view of the importance of the rights involved, all States can be held to have a legal interest in their protection; they are obligations *erga omnes*. Such obligations derive, for example, in contemporary international law, from the outlawing of acts of aggression, and of genocide, as also from the principles and rules concerning the basic rights of the human person, including protection from slavery and racial discrimination . . .'

OSCAR SCHACHTER, INTERNATIONAL LAW IN THEORY AND PRACTICE

(1991), at 85

Ch. VI. Resolutions and Political Texts

. . .

Few issues of international law theory have aroused as much controversy as that engendered by resolutions and declarations of the General Assembly which appear to express principles and rules of law. Their adoption by large majorities through voting or consensus procedures has been seen by many as attempts to impose obligatory norms on dissenting minorities and to change radically the way in which international law is made.

It is, of course, true that such resolutions are not a formal source of law within the explicit categories of Article 38 (1) of the Statute of the International Court of Justice. . . .

. . . As the central global forum for the international community, with the competence to discuss all questions of international concern, with institutional continuity and a constitutional framework of agreed purposes and principles, the Assembly has become a major instrument of States for articulating their national interests, and seeking general support for them. The conception of Assembly resolutions as expressions of common interests and the 'general will' of the international community has been a natural consequence. It also has naturally followed that in many cases the effort is made to transform the 'general will' thus expressed into law. One obvious way of accomplishing that transformation is to use a resolution as a basis for the preparation of a treaty by the Assembly itself or by a diplomatic conference convened by it. The treaties are then open for adherence by member States and other States. . . .

Legal uncertainty has, however, been created when the Assembly adopted resolutions which purported to assert legal norms without recourse to the treaty process. Such resolutions 'declared the law' either in general terms or as applied to a particular case. Neither in form nor in intent were they recommendatory. Surprising as it may seem, the authority of the General Assembly to adopt such declaratory resolutions was accepted from the very beginning. At its first session, in 1946, the Assembly considered the Nuremberg Principles and they 'affirmed' them in a unanimous resolution. In another resolution adopted at the same session, genocide was declared a crime under international law. This, too, was unanimous. No one questioned the Assembly's competence to adopt such resolutions despite the absence of explicit Charter authority to do so. The Assembly also interpreted and applied the Charter in particular cases, characterizing certain conduct as illegal. The resolutions condemning South Africa for apartheid and for its administration of South West Africa fall into this category. The competence of the Assembly to do this—that is, to designate conduct as illegal under the Charter and to assert obligations and rights applicable in particular cases—was not questioned.

What was, however, in question was the legal force of the declarations of law, whether general or particular. Could they be considered 'binding' when the Assembly lacked constitutional authority to adopt mandatory decisions concerning the subjects dealt with? If not binding, were they authoritative in some other sense? Was unanimity or near-unanimity a requirement for their authority? If nearly all States agreed on what is the law, was there a sufficient reason to deny effect to that determination? These and related questions gave rise to official perplexity and a considerable body of legal analysis. . . .

Lawyers are accustomed to pouring new wine into old bottles and keeping the old labels. Thus, the law-declaring resolutions that construed and 'concretized' the principles of the Charter—whether as general rules or in regard to particular cases—may be regarded as authentic interpretation by the parties of their existing treaty obligations. To the extent that they were interpretation, and agreed by all the member States, they fitted comfortably into an established source of law. . . .

But as we know the line between interpretation and new law is often blurred. Whenever a general rule is construed to apply to a new set of facts, an element of novelty is introduced; in effect, new content is added to the existing rule. This is even clearer when an authoritative body re-defines and makes more precise an existing rule or principle. In any such case, the question of degree can be raised: how far does the 'new' rule go beyond the agreed meaning of the old rule? Is the Charter being amended or simply interpreted? The answer is provided, not by logical analysis, but by the responses of those deemed competent to decide— namely, the States parties to the treaty. If they all agree in a formal resolution that the Charter means what the resolution says it does, that will be regarded as 'authentic' (that is, authoritative) interpretation. . . .

We come now to the declaratory resolution that purports to state the law independently of any Charter rule. . . . When all the States in the United Nations declare that a . . . norm is legally binding, it is difficult to dismiss that determination as ultra vires—or reduce it to a recommendation—because it was made in the General Assembly. The fact is that the declaration purports to express the *opinio juris communis*, not a recommendation. . . .

The . . . question is whether the assertion in good faith by all States that a norm is legally binding is sufficient to validate the norm as law even though State practice is negligible or inconclusive. International lawyers differ on the answer. . . .

. . .

. . . Much of the debate has focused on the choice between two polar categories: 'binding' and 'hortatory' (i.e., without legal force *et al*). That categorization— however clear it may appear—seems much less appropriate than treating the law-declaring resolutions as evidence for the asserted proposition of law.

. . .

Ch. XV. International Human Rights

. . .

Human Rights as Customary International Law

. . .

. . . [A] juristic debate has taken place for some years on whether human rights in whole or in part has become part of general customary international law. . . . If we have so extensive a network of treaty obligations, as suggested earlier, how important is it to determine the extent of customary law? Two answers may be given. First despite the many treaties and the considerable numbers of States parties to most of them, a significant number of States have not adhered to many of the treaties. They are therefore neither bound by the treaty obligations nor entitled to invoke those obligations against the parties. It is therefore of some consequence to determine their obligations and rights under customary law. A second reason is that the recognition of human rights in customary law allows not only the treaty non-parties, but also the parties to have recourse to international law remedies not provided for in the treaties. . . .

Whether human rights obligations have become customary law cannot readily be answered on the basis of the usual process of customary law formation. States do not usually make claims on other States or protest violations that do not affect their nationals. In that sense, one can find scant State practice accompanied by *opinio juris*. Arbitral awards and international judicial decisions are also rare except in tribunals based on treaties such as the European and Inter-American courts of human rights. The arguments advanced in support of a finding that rights are a part of customary law rely on different kinds of evidence. They include the following:

— the incorporation of human rights provisions in many national constitutions and laws;
— frequent references in United Nations resolutions and declarations to
  the 'duty' of all States to observe faithfully the Universal Declaration of
  Human Rights;
— resolutions of the United Nations and other international bodies condemning specific human rights violations as violative of international
  law;
— statements by national officials criticizing other States for serious
  human rights violations;
— a dictum of the International Court of Justice that obligations erga
  omnes in international law include those derived 'from the principles
  and rules concerning the basic rights of the human person' (*Barcelona
  Traction* Judgment, 1970);
— some decisions in various national courts that refer to the Universal
  Declaration as a source of standards for judicial decision.

None of the foregoing items of 'evidence' of custom conform to the traditional criteria. General statements by international bodies (such as the United Nations General Assembly or the Tehran Conference on Human Rights) that the 'Universal Declaration constitutes an obligation for the members of the international community' are not without significance, but their weight as evidence of custom cannot be assessed without considering actual practice. National constitutions and legislation similarly require a measure of confirmation in actual behaviour. One can readily think of numerous constitutions that have incorporated many of the provisions of the Universal Declaration or other versions of human rights norms, but these provisions are far from realization in practice. Constitutions with human rights provisions that are little more than window-dressing can hardly be cited as significant evidence of practice or 'general principles' of law.

Should we then reject all of the affirmations of human rights principles as obligatory on the ground that infringements are widespread, often gross and generally tolerated by the international community? Or should we minimize the negative practice and treat the verbal affirmations as persuasive evidence that the Universal Declaration has now become customary law? Some international lawyers answering this second question in the affirmative have asserted that the Declaration 'is now part of the customary law of nations and therefore binding on all States'.

Although only a few legal scholars have taken this position, they are often cited by human rights advocates in national tribunals and in publications. The argument for treating the Declaration as law is also bolstered by noting that its principles have been included in many national constitutions and laws and consequently may be reasonably regarded as 'general principles of law accepted by civilized nations', a source of general international law under Article 38 of the Statute of the International Court of Justice. . . . . A third theory for attributing legal force to the Declaration is premised on the provision of the United Nations Charter (Article 56) that pledges members to take action to achieve certain ends of the Charter, including human rights. It is suggested that the Declaration by authoritatively spelling out the recognized human rights gives specific content to the obligation.

These three lines of legal argument are generally linked by their proponents in human rights advocacy. It is not inconceivable that in time they will carry the day for the Declaration to be treated as obligatory. However, for the present, their reach exceeds their grasp. Neither governments nor courts have accepted the Universal Declaration as an instrument with obligatory force. Many have, of course, lauded its principles as standards to be achieved and in specific instances have rhetorically relied on the Declaration as a touchstone of legality. . . . But these particular references fall short of recognizing the Declaration as obligatory in law. It remains difficult to do so in the face of the clear intention of the governments to consider it as non-binding. . . .

This conclusion, however, does not dispose of claims that some important human rights included in the Declaration have become customary law (and/or general principles of law) and therefore binding on all States. The evidence for this must, of course, focus on the specific rights in question. As noted earlier, such evidence is rarely to be found in the traditional patterns of State practice involving claims and counter-claims between two States. Instead, one must look for 'practice' and *opinio juris* mainly in the international forums where human rights issues are actually discussed, debated and sometimes resolved by general consensus. These are principally organs of the United Nations and of regional bodies. In those settings, governments take positions on a general and specific level: they censure, condemn, or condone particular conduct. An evaluation of those actions and their effects on State conduct provides a basis for judgments on whether a particular right or principle has become customary international law. Such inquiries may have to be broadened to include pronouncements by national leaders, legislative enactments, judicial opinions, and scholarly studies. No single event will provide the answer. One essential test is whether there is a general conviction that particular conduct is internationally unlawful. Occasional violations do not nullify a rule that is widely observed. The depth and intensity of condemnation are significant indicators of State practice in this context. The extent of agreement across geographical and political divisions is also pertinent. Applying these indicators on a global scale is obviously not an easy task, nor is it a one-time effort. Attitudes, practices and expectations are in flux and judgments may often change. Nonetheless there is little doubt that some human rights are recognized as mandatory for all countries, irrespective of treaty. The most obvious are the prohibitions against slavery, genocide, torture and other cruel, inhuman and degrading treatment. No government would contend that these prohibitions apply only to parties to the treaties that outlaw them. The list does not stop there. The ALI Restatement (Third) of 1987[14] adds the following actions as unlawful 'for a state to practice, encourage or condone:

—   The murder or causing the disappearance of individuals;
—   Prolonged arbitrary detention;
—   Systematic racial discrimination.'

The Restatement's list also includes a more general category as violative of customary law, to wit: 'consistent patterns of gross violations of internationally recognized human rights'. . . .

The Restatement's enumeration of customary law human rights is well-founded as far as it goes, but developments affecting human rights in the past decade indicate that the list of customary law rights may have significantly increased. Studies carried out for the United Nations Commission on Human Rights which have examined national laws on a global scale as well as governmental and scholarly statements reveal that several rights have been widely invoked as principles of general international law. The examples include:

—   The right to self-determination of peoples;
—   The individual right to leave and return to one's country;
—   The principle of non-refoulement for refugees threatened by persecution.

There is a well-intentioned tendency among human rights lawyers to add to the list of customary law rights, especially 'due process' rights. Theodor Meron, for example, has suggested that a number of basic rights of the accused stipulated in the Covenant on Political and Civil Rights (Article 14) are also customary law. His indicators are the inclusion of these rights in national law generally and references to them in treaties and other international instruments. However, evidence that these rights are secured in most countries is lacking. . . . Even where they are on the books, they are often honored in the breach, not the observance. . . .

---

[14]   [Eds.] *Restatement (Third), Foreign Relations Law of the United States* (1987). Section 702, to which the text refers, appears at p. 233, *infra*.

However, recent developments in various parts of the world indicate that certain human rights have penetrated deeply into the consciousness of peoples in many countries. Violations are more and more resented in places where previously they had been ignored or seen as unavoidable. Most striking in this respect are the changes in Eastern Europe and in the Soviet Union in recent years (especially 1987–1990). Individual human rights were emphasized in the popular demands and given effect in the new political arrangements. The rights were asserted as fundamental entitlements recognized by the international community. Protection against arbitrary arrest, against political trials and against lack of procedural rights were emphasized. Freedom of speech and of peaceful assembly were demanded as basic rights. Political participation through genuine elections, ensured by secret ballot, was another salient demand. It is true that these rights are in the International Covenant on Civil and Political Rights to which the USSR and other States in Eastern Europe have long been parties though not in substantial compliance. But the treaty compliance issue was subsidiary; the main point was that the rights were now demanded as basic and essential whether or not in treaties. The dramatic reversal of the long prevalent political statist ideology had worldwide repercussions, foremost of which was an intensified awareness of the importance of basic rights.

. . .

Present tendencies also suggest that other human rights may be on their way to acceptance as general international law, especially in virtue of their widespread inclusion in national law plus general recognition of their international significance. Several economic and social rights may well meet that dual test—in particular, the right to basic sustenance, and to public assistance in matters of health, welfare and basic education. ILO practice indicates that trade union rights, including freedom of association, are widely accepted as 'international common law'. Also significant is the widespread recognition of the rights of women to full equality and to protection against discrimination. These rights have been affirmed and emphasized in numerous declarations as well as in some international conventions, though in many respects the gap between the proclaimed rights and actual conditions remains great. A positive trend is that many countries have enacted legislation that prohibits gender discrimination by State action. The prevalence of these laws in conjunction with the United Nations Charter's prohibition of discrimination based on sex provides a strong argument for holding that such discrimination is an international delict.

. . .

Whatever the doctrinal theory, the political dynamics that mark the demands for human rights make it almost certain that the international law of human rights will continue to have a deeper and broader basis than the treaties alone. The powers that govern States are not immune from pressures based on a social consciousness of the limits of State authority. . . .

. . .

ROSALYN HIGGINS, PROBLEMS AND PROCESS: INTERNATIONAL LAW AND HOW WE USE IT
(1994), at 19

One of the special characteristics of international law is that violations of law can lead to the formation of new law. Of course, this characteristic is more troublesome for those who regard law as rules, and less troublesome for those who regard law as process. But whether one believes that international law consists of rules that have been derived from consent or natural law; or whether one believes international law is a process of decision-making, with appropriate reliance on past trends of decision-making in the light of current context and desired outcomes, there still remains the question of how the 'rules' or the 'trend of decision' change through time. And, in so far as these rules or trends of decisions are based on custom, then there is the related question of what legal significance is to be given to practice that is inconsistent with the perceived rules or trends of decision.
. . .

If a customary rule loses its normative quality when it is widely ignored, over a significant period of time, does this not lead to a relativist view of the substantive content of international law, with disturbing implications? . . .

A second example: all states agree that international law prohibits genocide (and that this total prohibition is today rooted in customary international law and not just in treaty obligations). So what if some states from time to time engage in genocide? Here we may safely answer that genocide, while it sometimes occurs and while its very nature makes *all* norm compliance shocking, is certainly not the majority practice. The customary law that prohibits genocide remains intact, notwithstanding appalling examples of non-compliance. Let us look at a third, more difficult example. No one doubts that there exists a norm prohibiting torture. No state denies the existence of such a norm; and, indeed, it is widely recognized as a customary rule of international law by national courts. But it is equally clear from, for example, the reports of Amnesty International, that *the great majority* of states systematically engage in torture. If one takes the view that non-compliance is relevant to the retention of normative quality, are we to conclude that there is not really any prohibition of torture under customary international law? . . .
. . .

New norms require both practice and *opinio juris* before they can be said to represent customary international law. And so it is with the gradual death of existing norms and their replacement by others. The reason that the prohibition on torture continues to be a requirement of customary international law, even though widely abused, is not because it has a higher normative status that allows us to ignore the abuse, but because *opinio juris* as to its normative status continues to exist. No state, not even a state that tortures, believes that the international law prohibition is undesirable and that it is not bound by the prohibition. A new norm cannot emerge without both practice and *opinio juris*; and an existing norm does not die without the great majority of states engaging in both a contrary practice and withdrawing their *opinio juris.*

RESTATEMENT (THIRD) THE FOREIGN RELATIONS LAW OF THE UNITED STATES
American Law Institute (1987), Vol. 2, 161

§702. Customary International Law of Human Rights

A state violates international law if, as a matter of state policy, it practices, encourages, or condones

(a) genocide,
(b) slavery or slave trade,
(c) the murder or causing the disappearance of individuals,
(d) torture or other cruel, inhuman, or degrading treatment or punishment,
(e) prolonged arbitrary detention,
(f) systematic racial discrimination, or
(g) a consistent pattern of gross violations of internationally recognized human rights.

Comment:

a. Scope of customary law of human rights. This section includes as customary law only those human rights whose status as customary law is generally accepted (as of 1987) and whose scope and content are generally agreed. The list is not necessarily complete, and is not closed: human rights not listed in this section may have achieved the status of customary law, and some rights might achieve that status in the future.

b. State policy as violation of customary law. In general, a state is responsible for acts of officials or official bodies, national or local, even if the acts were not authorized by or known to the responsible national authorities, indeed even if expressly forbidden by law, decree or instruction. The violations of human rights cited in this section, however, are violations of customary international law only if practiced, encouraged, or condoned by the government of a state as official policy.
. . .

A government may be presumed to have encouraged or condoned acts prohibited by this section if such acts, especially by its officials, have been repeated or notorious and no steps have been taken to prevent them or to punish the perpetrators. . . .

Even when a state is not responsible under this section because a violation is not state policy, the state may be responsible under some international agreement that requires the state to prevent the violation. . . .
. . .

l. Gender discrimination. The United Nations Charter (Article 1(3)) and the Universal Declaration of Human Rights (Article 2) prohibit discrimination in respect of human rights on various grounds, including sex. Discrimination on the basis of sex in respect of recognized rights is prohibited by a number of international agreements, including the Covenant on Civil and Political Rights, the Covenant on Economic, Social and Cultural Rights, and more generally by the Convention on the Elimination of All Forms of Discrimination Against Women,

which, as of 1987, had been ratified by 91 states and signed by a number of others. The United States had signed the Convention but had not yet ratified it. The domestic laws of a number of states, including those of the United States, mandate equality for, or prohibit discrimination against, women generally or in various respects. Gender-based discrimination is still practiced in many states in varying degrees, but freedom from gender discrimination as state policy, in many matters, may already be a principle of customary international law. . . .
. . .

   m. Consistent pattern of gross violations of human rights. The acts enumerated in clauses (a) to (f) are violations of customary law even if the practice is not consistent, or not part of a 'pattern', and those acts are inherently 'gross' violations of human rights. Clause (g) includes other infringements of recognized human rights that are not violations of customary law when committed singly or sporadically (although they may be forbidden to states parties to the International Covenants or other particular agreements); they become violations of customary law if the state is guilty of a 'consistent pattern of gross violations' as state policy. A violation is gross if it is particularly shocking because of the importance of the right or the gravity of the violation. All the rights proclaimed in the Universal Declaration and protected by the principal International Covenants are internationally recognized human rights, but some rights are fundamental and intrinsic to human dignity. Consistent patterns of violation of such rights as state policy may be deemed 'gross' *ipso facto.* These include, for example, systematic harassment, invasions of the privacy of the home, arbitrary arrest and detention (even if not prolonged); denial of fair trial in criminal cases; grossly disproportionate punishment; denial of freedom to leave a country; denial of the right to return to one's country; mass uprooting of a country's population; denial of freedom of conscience and religion; denial of personality before the law; denial of basic privacy such as the right to marry and raise a family; and invidious racial or religious discrimination. A state party to the Covenant on Civil and Political Rights is responsible even for a single, isolated violation of any of these rights; any state is liable under customary law for a consistent pattern of violations of any such right as state policy.

   n. Customary law of human rights and jus cogens. Not all human rights norms are peremptory norms (*jus cogens*), but those in clauses (a) to (f) of this section are, and an international agreement that violates them is void.

   o. Responsibility to all states (erga omnes*).* Violations of the rules stated in this section are violations of obligations to all other states and any state may invoke the ordinary remedies available to a state when its rights under customary law are violated.

NOTE

In the United States, the *Restatements of Law* represent an important reference for many legal issues, although they have no official, legal status. These *Restatements* are adopted and promulgated by the American Law Institute, a private organization not affiliated with the United States Government, whose membership consists of judges, legal academicians, and lawyers involved in private practice and in government. The drafts presented to the Institute for its approval and adoption are generally prepared by leading academicians, who may consult advisory committees with a broader membership.

Such was the case with the *Restatement (Third) of the Foreign Relations Law of the United States*, other portions of which appear in later chapters. The introduction to that *Restatement* states (at p. ix) that it is 'in no sense an official document of the United States'. It notes that in some particulars its rules 'are at variance' with positions taken by the United States Government. Nonetheless, despite this independence and non-official status, it is inevitable that a *Restatement* dealing with international law will in general reflect the broad positions taken by the United States rather than, say, inconsistent or polar positions taken by other, perhaps hostile states.

NOTE

Professor Louis Henkin was the chief reporter for *Restatement (Third) of the Foreign Relations Law of the United States*. Consider his comments in 'Human Rights and State "Sovereignty"' Ga. J. Int'l & Comp. L. 31 (1995/96), at 37:

> ... [T]here is now a significant, and increasing, amount of such non-conventional law of human rights. But though that law is not made by treaty, it ... differs from traditional customary law in fundamental respects. Traditional customary law was not made; it resulted. . . . Now, in our time, non-conventional law is being *made*, purposefully, knowingly, wilfully, and concern for human rights has provided a principal impetus to its growth. . . .
>
> [Henkin refers to the *Restatement*'s list of violations in Section 702.] Where does this law come from? The Restatement . . . supports the non-conventional human rights law it restates by invoking the traditional indicia of traditional customary law—state practice with a sense of legal obligation. But the Reporters of the Restatement admitted that the state practice supporting non-conventional human rights law looks different, is different. . . .
>
> . . . I suggest that such law is 'constitutional' in a new sense. The international system, having identified contemporary human values, has adopted and declared them to be fundamental law, international law. But, in a radical derogation from the axiom of 'sovereignty', that law is not based on consent: at least, it does not honor or accept dissent, and it binds particular states regardless of their objection.
>
> How did this happen? Conceptually, it may have sneaked into the law on the back of another idea, *ius cogens*. . . . *ius cogens* . . . does not reflect ancient custom or traditional natural law; it has not been built by state practice. Also, it does not require consent of every state: it reflects 'general' consensus . . .
>
> And so, international non-conventional human rights law is ... like ius cogens. . . . [I]t is not the result of practice but the product of common consensus from which few dare dissent . . .

QUESTIONS

1. How would you identify the basic differences between contemporary changes in the notion of customary international law and the traditional notions described at pp. 69–78, *supra*?

2. What would you identify as the likely causes of such changes?

3. How do the readings in this section bear on the criticism by Koskenniemi, at p. 78, *supra*, of the classical mode of argument about customary international law?

4. More than a decade after *Restatement (Third)* was approved, would you change in any respect the position taken with respect to gender discrimination? If so, why? (The information at pp. 442–444, *infra*, on reservations to CEDAW may influence your answer.)

5. Suppose that a group of persons hostile to a given minority and unconnected to the state or government attack members of that minority. The state security apparatus (police, prosecutors) gives less attention to such attacks and the related harm than it does to crimes against other members of society.

a. What provision(s) of the ICCPR would be relevant to the claim that (i) members of the group have violated that treaty, or (ii) the state itself has violated it? What bearing does *Restatement* §702 have on these questions?

b. Does either the ICCPR or §702 require or support (a) a civil action for monetary compensation based on international law and brought by a victim against members of the group, or (b) a criminal action based on international law brought by the state against the group members who attacked the victim?

NOTE

The analyses in Chapter 3 of the UDHR, ICCPR and CEDAW raise basic questions about the effect of the human rights movement, as well as of other trends in international relations and law over these decades, on traditional notions of state sovereignty. Those questions become particularly salient with respect to issues of implementation of the basic treaties, ranging from UN debates or monitoring by intergovernmental or nongovernmental organizations to bilateral or collective economic pressures on violator states and enforcement that may include military intervention. For such reasons, these questions are examined in Chapter 8.

ADDITIONAL READING

On custom see M. Byers, *Custom, Power and the Power of Rules* (1999); B. Simma and P. Alston, 'The Sources of Human Rights Law: Custom, Jus Cogens, General Principles', 12 Aust. Y. B. Int. L. 82 (1992); and M. Ragazzi, *The Concept of International Obligations* Erga Omnes (1997)

4

Economic and Social Rights

A. SOCIO-ECONOMIC CONTEXT AND HISTORICAL BACKGROUND

The Universal Declaration of Human Rights recognizes two sets of human rights: the 'traditional' civil and political rights, as well as economic, social and cultural rights. In transforming the Declaration's provisions into legally binding obligations, the United Nations adopted two separate International Covenants which, taken together, constitute the bedrock of the international normative regime for human rights. Chapter 3 concentrated on the ICCPR. This chapter explores the companion International Covenant on Economic, Social and Cultural Rights (ICESCR).

The 'official' position, dating back to the Universal Declaration and reaffirmed in innumerable resolutions since that time, is that the two covenants and sets of rights are, in the words adopted by the second World Conference on Human Rights in Vienna, 'universal, indivisible and interdependent and interrelated. The international community must treat human rights globally in a fair and equal manner, on the same footing, and with the same emphasis.' (Vienna Declaration, para. 5). But this formal consensus masks a deep and enduring disagreement over the proper status of economic, social and cultural rights. At one extreme lies the view that these rights are superior to civil and political rights in terms of an appropriate value hierarchy and in chronological terms. Of what use is the right to free speech to those who are starving and illiterate? At the other extreme we find the view that economic and social rights do not constitute rights (as properly understood) at all. Treating them as rights undermines the enjoyment of individual freedom, distorts the functioning of free markets by justifying large-scale state intervention in the economy, and provides an excuse to downgrade the importance of civil and political rights.

Although variations on these extremes have dominated both diplomatic and academic discourse, the great majority of governments have taken some sort of intermediate position. For the most part that position has involved (a) support for the equal status and importance of economic and social rights (as of March 2000, 142 states were parties to the ICESCR, compared with 144 parties to the ICCPR), together with (b) failure to take steps to entrench those rights constitutionally, to adopt legislative or administrative provisions based explicitly on the recognition of specific economic and social rights as international human rights, or to provide effective means of redress to individuals or groups alleging violations of those rights. Indeed, one of the puzzles in the field lies in the rare invocation of the ICESCR in the play of internal politics or in the judiciaries in most states, compared with the frequent invocation of civil and political rights provisions of the UDHR, the ICCPR, and regional instruments such as the European Convention on Human Rights.

Even before the final adoption of the UDHR, the debate over the relationship between the two sets of rights had become a casualty of the Cold War: the Communist countries abstained from voting on its adoption by the General Assembly on the grounds that the economic and social rights provisions were inadequate. Moreover, at least since the 1970s, it has taken on an important North-South dimension. As a result, the debate carries a lot of ideological baggage. It is diffuse, often not well thought through and inextricably linked to some of the most basic political choices confronting any society. With the rejection of communism and the widespread embrace of free-market economic solutions within the ongoing process of globalization, economic and social rights are certain to remain among the most controversial issues in the years ahead. Those issues will have important implications for other aspects of human rights law.

In a statement to the Vienna World Conference in 1993, the UN Committee on Economic, Social and Cultural Rights (hereafter the ESCR Committee) drew attention to:

> [t]he shocking reality . . . that States and the international community as a whole continue to tolerate all too often breaches of economic, social and cultural rights which, if they occurred in relation to civil and political rights, would provoke expressions of horror and outrage and would lead to concerted calls for immediate remedial action. In effect, despite the rhetoric, violations of civil and political rights continue to be treated as though they were far more serious, and more patently intolerable, than massive and direct denials of economic, social and cultural rights . . . . Statistical indicators of the extent of deprivation, or breaches, of economic, social and cultural rights have been cited so often that they have tended to lose their impact. The magnitude, severity and constancy of that deprivation have provoked attitudes of resignation, feelings of helplessness and compassion fatigue. Such muted responses are facilitated by a reluctance to characterize the problems that exist as gross and massive denials of economic, social and cultural rights. Yet it is difficult to understand how the situation can realistically be portrayed in any other way.[1]

SOCIAL AND ECONOMIC STATISTICS

In a 1999 report on progress since the Vienna Conference, the UN High Commissioner for Human Rights was highly critical of the limited achievements. Other recent assessments of world trends attach particular importance to the growing

---

[1] UN Doc. E/1993/22, Annex III, paras 5 and 7.

gap between rich and poor. The following excerpts convey a sense of the current socio-economic context for debate about economic and social rights.

Report of the United Nations High Commissioner for Human Rights to the Economic and Social Council
UN Doc. E/1999/96.

4. . . . [D]espite examples of progress, it remains painfully clear that the fundamental rights to decent living conditions, food, basic health care and education . . . are widely being denied . . . The 1999 *State of the World's Children Report* . . . warns that nearly a billion people, a sixth of humanity, are functionally illiterate and will enter the twenty-first century unable to read a book or sign their names. Two-thirds of them are women . . . And the 1998 *Human Development Report* . . . points out the bleak reality that, of the 4.4 billion people in developing countries, nearly three-fifths lack basic sanitation, almost a third have no access to clean water, a quarter do not have adequate housing, a fifth have no access to modern health services, a fifth of children do not attend school and approximately a fifth do not have enough dietary energy and protein.

5. One area of particular urgency is the eradication of extreme poverty. The latest report of the World Bank indicates that the recent financial and economic crisis has driven large parts of populations into poverty—measured by the World Bank as income of less than US$ 1 per day. The victims of poverty are in fact denied almost all rights—not only to adequate food, health care and housing, but also to participation in political processes; access to information and education; fair legal treatment and the normal benefits of citizenship. These conditions are compounded for the most vulnerable, in particular children and women, who in some parts of the world are being increasingly exploited through trafficking, forced labour and prostitution. The Bank's report speaks about the failure of existing economic strategies to combat poverty and calls for new, socially oriented approaches.

6. The globalization of markets, capital, communication and technology changes the face of the world, opening new opportunities and creating new challenges. While the benefits of these transformations are undeniable for millions of people in all regions, it is also undeniable that still larger numbers of the world's population are being pushed to the margins of society, economically and socially, in part because of this complex process. In developing and developed countries alike, a clear trend towards a smaller percentage of the population receiving a greater share of wealth, while the poorest simultaneously lose ground, must be addressed.

. . .

Latest World Bank Poverty Update Shows Urgent Need to Better Shield Poor in Crises
World Bank News Release No.99/2214/S, June 2, 1999.

In sum, the global picture that emerges at the end of the 1990s is one of stalled progress, with the major exception of China, owing to the East Asian crisis, rising numbers of poor people in India, continued rises in Sub-Saharan Africa, and a sharp worsening in ECA [Eastern Europe and Central Asia] ... [I]f there is no change in the proportion of people in poverty over the course of the decade—at 30 percent living below a $1 a day—that would imply an increase from 1.3 billion living under $1 a day in 1993 to around 1.5 billion in 1999.

Efforts to Improve Human Welfare Stall on the Threshold of the New Millenium
World Bank News Release No. 99/2152/S, April 26, 1999.

According to *World Development Indicators 1999* ... [in] Eastern Europe and the countries of the former Soviet Union (FSU), millions of people have seen their living standards deteriorate sharply during their difficult move towards establishing modern market economies. In 1989, about 14 million people in the transition economies of the FSU were living under a poverty line of four dollars a day. By the mid-1990s, that number was about 147 million, or about one-person-in- three.

In parts of Sub-Saharan Africa, hard-won increases in life expectancy have been wiped out by HIV/AIDS, and from 1980–1996, growth in the school-age population has consistently outpaced the numbers of primary school enrollments. Furthermore, foreign aid levels are at their lowest levels in almost 50 years.
...

Inequality has increased most rapidly in Eastern Europe and the countries of the former Soviet Union since the collapse of Communism. In Russia, the number of people living in poverty (less then $4 per day) soared from about 2 million in 1987 to 66 million—four out of ten Russians—by 1995.

During the past decade, inequality has also increased in countries as diverse as Brazil, Bangladesh, China, Malaysia and Thailand. In 34 developing countries—including Jordan, Malaysia, Russia, Peru, South Africa, Ukraine, Venezuela, and Zambia—the richest 20 percent of the population receives more than half the country's income, while the poorest 20 percent gets less than 5 percent.

Number of Hungry in Developing World Down by 40 Million in Five Years But Increasing in Many Poor Countries
UN Food and Agriculture Organization Press Release 99/61, 14 October 1999.

Every night, almost 800 million people in the developing world go to sleep hungry, [according to] *The State of Food Insecurity in the World* [1999, issued by FAO].

That is more than the combined population of Europe and North America—a 'hungry continent' of women, men and children who may never reach their physical and mental potential because they do not have enough to eat.

The number of undernourished people in the developing world has fallen by 40 million, from 830 million to 790 million between 1990/1992 and 1995/1997. This decline, however, represents the extraordinary achievement of just 37 countries, which realized reductions totaling 100 million. Across the rest of the developing world, the number of people who are chronically undernourished actually increased by almost 60 million.

... At the 1996 World Food Summit, 186 countries committed themselves to halve the number of undernourished to 400 million in the developing world by 2015. To achieve the Summit goal, the rate of progress needs to be stepped up by 150 per cent to [achieve] 20 million fewer hungry people each year.

... Around...26 million [people] in Eastern Europe and the former USSR and 8 million in the industrialized countries are estimated to be undernourished.

One in Five People Had Difficulty Satisfying Basic Needs in 1995, Census Bureau Reports
U.S. Department of Commerce News, July 9, 1999.

In 1995, about 49 million people [in the United States]—about 1 in 5—lived in a household whose members had difficulty satisfying basic needs, according to a report released today by the Commerce Department's Census Bureau.

The report...takes a look at households who didn't make mortgage or rent payments, failed to pay utility bills and/or had service shut off, didn't get enough to eat, needed to see a doctor or dentist but didn't or otherwise could not meet essential expenses.

...

Other key findings:

— more than one-third (18.1 million) of all people living in households with unmet basic needs were children (under 18 years old)
   ...
— About 1 in 20 people (5 percent) lived in a household whose members sometimes did not get enough to eat.
— Lack of health insurance strongly increased the probability that a person in the household who needs to see a doctor did not. ....

QUESTION

How are these statistics relevant to international human rights? Are they the equivalent of, for example, Amnesty International reports listing the number of reported incidents of torture or extrajudicial executions worldwide, all clearly human rights violations? Is the ESCR Committee over-reacting when it claims that we tolerate 'breaches of economic, social and cultural rights which, if they occurred in relation to civil and political rights, would provoke expressions of horror and outrage'?

COMMENT ON HISTORICAL ORIGINS OF ECONOMIC AND SOCIAL RIGHTS

The historical origins of the recognition of economic and social rights are diffuse. Those rights have drawn strength from the injunctions expressed in different religious traditions to care for those in need and those who cannot look after themselves. In Catholicism, papal encyclicals have long promoted the importance of the right to subsistence with dignity, while 'liberation theology' has sought to build upon this 'preferential option for the poor'. Virtually all of the major religions manifest comparable concern for the poor and oppressed.[2] Other sources include philosophical analyses and political theory from authors as diverse as Thomas Paine, Karl Marx, Immanuel Kant and John Rawls; the political programmes of the nineteenth century Fabian socialists in Britain, Chancellor Bismarck in Germany (who introduced social insurance schemes in the 1880s), and the New Dealers in the United States; and constitutional precedents such as the Mexican Constitution of 1917, the first and subsequent Soviet Constitutions, and the 1919 Constitution of the Weimar Republic (embodying the *Wohlfahrtsstaat* concept).

This comment concentrates on the evolution of these ideas in international human rights law. The most appropriate starting point is the International Labour Organisation (ILO). Established by the Treaty of Versailles in 1919 to abolish the 'injustice, hardship and privation' which workers suffered and to guarantee 'fair and humane conditions of labour', it was conceived as the response of Western countries to the ideologies of Bolshevism and Socialism arising out of the Russian Revolution.[3]

In the inter-war years, the ILO adopted international minimum standards in relation to a wide range of matters which now fall under the rubric of economic and social rights. They included, *inter alia*, conventions dealing with freedom of association and the right to organize trade unions, forced labour, minimum working age, hours of work, weekly rest, sickness protection, accident insurance, invalidity and old-age insurance, and freedom from discrimination in employment. The Great Depression of the early 1930s emphasized the need for social protection of those who were unemployed and gave a strong impetus to full employment policies such as those advocated by Keynes in his *General Theory of Employment, Interest and Money* (1936).

Partly as a result of these developments, various proposals were made during the

---

[2] See Martin Shupack, 'The Churches and Human Rights: Catholic and Protestant Human Rights Views as Reflected in Church Statements', 6 Harv. Hum. Rts. J. 127 (1993).

[3] Virginia Leary, 'Lessons from the Experience of the International Labour Organisation', in Philip Alston (ed.), *The United Nations and Human Rights: A Critical Appraisal* (1992), at 582.

drafting of the UN Charter for the inclusion of provisions enshrining the maintenance of 'full employment' as a commitment to be undertaken by Member States. The strongest version, known after its principal proponents as the 'Australian Pledge', committed UN members to take action to secure 'improved labour standards, economic advancement, social security, and employment for all who seek it'.[4]

Despite significant support, the United States opposed the proposal on the grounds that any such undertaking would involve interference in the domestic, economic and political affairs of states. Ultimately agreement was reached on Article 55(a) of the Charter, which simply states that the United Nations shall promote 'higher standards of living, full employment, and conditions of economic and social progress and development' but does not call for specific follow-up at the international level.

US opposition in this context did not signify the rejection of economic and social rights per se.[5] Indeed, in 1941 President Roosevelt had nominated 'freedom from want' as one of the four freedoms that should characterize the future world order. He spelled out this vision in his 1944 State of the Union address.[6]

> We have come to a clear realization of the fact that true individual freedom cannot exist without economic security and independence. 'Necessitous men are not free men.' People who are out of a job are the stuff of which dictatorships are made.
>
> In our day these economic truths have become accepted as self-evident. We have accepted, so to speak, a second bill of rights, under which a new basis of security and prosperity can be established for all—regardless of station, race, or creed.
>
> Among these are:
>
> The right to a useful and remunerative job in the industries, or shops, or farms, or mines of the Nation;
> The right to earn enough to provide adequate food and clothing and recreation;
> The right of every farmer to raise and sell his products at a return which will give him and his family a decent living;
> The right of every businessman, large and small, to trade in an atmosphere of freedom from unfair competition and domination by monopolies at home or abroad;
> The right of every family to a decent home;
> The right to adequate medical care and the opportunity to achieve and enjoy good health;
> The right to adequate protection from the economic fears of old age, sickness, accident, and unemployment;
> The right to a good education.

---

[4] See generally Ruth Russell and Jean Muther, *A History of the United Nations Charter: The Role of the United States 1940–1945* (1958), at 786.

[5] See generally Louis Sohn, *The Human Rights Movement: From Roosevelt's Four Freedoms to the Interdependence of Peace, Development, and Human Rights* (1995).

[6] Eleventh Annual Message to Congress (January 11, 1944), in J. Israel (ed.), *The State of the Union Messages of the Presidents* (1966), Vol. 3, at 2881.

All of these rights spell security. And after this war is won we must be prepared
to move forward, in the implementation of these rights, to new goals of human
happiness and well-being.

This approach was subsequently reflected in a draft international Bill of Rights,
completed in 1944, by a Committee appointed by the American Law Institute. In
addition to listing the rights contained in the US Bill of Rights (the first ten
amendments to the Constitution), the Institute's proposal advocated international
recognition of a range of rights and acceptance of the correlative duties in relation
to education, work, reasonable conditions of work, adequate food and housing,
and social security. (See Statement of Essential Human Rights, UN Doc. A/148
(1947), Arts 11–15.) In relation to each of the proposed rights, a Comment by the
Committee drew attention to the fact that it had already been recognized in the
'current or recent constitutions' of many countries; e.g. 40 countries in the case of
the right to education; 9 for the right to work; 11 for the right to adequate housing;
27 for the right to social security.

Although these proposals of the Committee were never formally endorsed by
the American Law Institute, they were submitted to the United Nations and were
to prove highly influential in the preparation of the first draft of the Universal
Declaration in 1947. In the drafting of Articles 22–28 of the UDHR, strong support for the inclusion of economic and social rights came from the United States
(a delegation led by Eleanor Roosevelt), Egypt, several Latin American countries
(particularly Chile) and from the (Communist) countries of Eastern Europe. Australia and the United Kingdom opposed their inclusion,[7] as did South Africa which
objected first that 'a condition of existence does not constitute a fundamental
human right merely because it is eminently desirable for the fullest realisation of
all human potentialities' and secondly that if the proposed economic rights were
to be taken seriously it would be 'necessary to resort to more or less totalitarian
control of the economic life of the country'.[8]

After the adoption of the Universal Declaration in 1948, the next step was to
translate the rights it recognized in Articles 22–28 into binding treaty obligations.
This process took from 1949 to 1966. The delay was due to reasons including the
Cold War, developing US opposition to the principle of international human
rights treaties, and the scope and complexity of the proposed obligations. By 1955,
the main lines of what was to become the ICESCR were agreed.

The following analysis of the drafting process, prepared by the United Nations,
captures the main dilemmas and controversies relating to the inclusion of economic, social and cultural rights.[9]

> . . . [Between 1949 and 1951 the Commission on Human Rights worked on a
> single draft covenant dealing with both of the categories of rights. But in 1951
> the General Assembly, under pressure from the Western-dominated Commis-

---

[7] See B. Andreassen, 'Article 22', A. and W. B. Eide,
'Article 25', in G. Alfredsson and A. Eide (eds.), *The
Universal Declaration of Human Rights* (1999).

[8] UN Doc. E/CN.4/82/Add.4 (1948) 11, 13.

[9] Annotations on the Text of the Draft International Covenants on Human Rights, UN Doc. A/
2929 (1955), at 7.

sion, agreed to draft two separate covenants] . . . to contain 'as many similar provisions as possible' and to be approved and opened for signature simultaneously, in order to emphasize the unity of purpose.

. . .

8. Those who were in favour of drafting a single covenant maintained that human rights could not be clearly divided into different categories, nor could they be so classified as to represent a hierarchy of values. All rights should be promoted and protected at the same time. Without economic, social and cultural rights, civil and political rights might be purely nominal in character; without civil and political rights, economic, social and cultural rights could not be long ensured . . .

9. Those in favour of drafting two separate covenants argued that civil and political rights were enforceable, or justiciable, or of an 'absolute' character, while economic, social and cultural rights were not or might not be; that the former were immediately applicable, while the latter were to be progressively implemented; and that, generally speaking, the former were rights of the individual 'against' the State, that is, against unlawful and unjust action of the State, while the latter were rights which the State would have to take positive action to promote. Since the nature of civil and political rights and that of economic, social and cultural rights, and the obligations of the State in respect thereof, were different, it was desirable that two separate instruments should be prepared.

10. The question of drafting one or two covenants was intimately related to the question of implementation. If no measures of implementation were to be formulated, it would make little difference whether one or two covenants were to be drafted. Generally speaking, civil and political rights were thought to be 'legal' rights and could best be implemented by the creation of a good offices committee, while economic, social and cultural rights were thought to be 'programme' rights and could best be implemented by the establishment of a system of periodic reports. Since the rights could be divided into two broad categories, which should be subject to different procedures of implementation, it would be both logical and convenient to formulate two separate covenants.

11. However, it was argued that not in all countries and territories were all civil and political rights 'legal' rights, nor all economic, social and cultural rights 'programme' rights. A civil or political right might well be a 'programme' right under one régime, an economic, social or cultural right a 'legal' right under another. A covenant could be drafted in such a manner as would enable States, upon ratification or accession, to announce, each in so far as it was concerned, which civil, political, economic, social and cultural rights were 'legal' rights, and which 'programme' rights, and by which procedures the rights would be implemented.

. . .

COMMENT ON THE ICESCR AND THE CHARACTER OF THE RIGHTS

This Covenant was adopted by the General Assembly in Res. 2200A (XXI) of 16 December 1966 and entered into force on 3 January 1976. It is divided into five 'Parts'. Part I (like Part I of the ICCPR) recognizes the right of peoples to self-determination; Part II defines the general nature of states parties obligations; Part

III enumerates the specific substantive rights; Part IV deals with international implementation; and Part V contains typical final provisions of a human rights treaty. The enumeration in Part III recognizes the rights to work and to just and favourable conditions of work; to rest and leisure; to form and join trade unions and to strike; to social security; to special protection for the family, mothers and children; to an adequate standard of living, including food, clothing and housing; to physical and mental health; to education; and to scientific and cultural life. The right to property, although recognized in the Universal Declaration, was not included, primarily because of the inability of governments to agree on a formulation governing public takings and the compensation therefor.

Economic and social rights are not in any sense restricted to the ICESCR, a world apart from all other human rights treaties. To the contrary, they figure in other major treaties. For example, both the Convention on the Elimination of All Forms of Discrimination against Women discussed in Chapter 3 and the Convention on the Rights of the Child examined in Chapter 6 contain extensive obligations on states of an economic and social character.

To grasp the following materials, it is important to become familiar now with Parts II and III of the Covenant (see the Annex on Documents).

Differences between the ICESCR and the ICCPR

There are many differences between the two major Covenants, including terminology. For example, the ICCPR contains terms such as 'everyone has the right to. . .', or 'no one shall be. . .', whereas the ICESCR usually employs the formula 'States Parties recognize the right of everyone to. . .'. Two major differences should be noted, both appearing in the key provision of Article 2(1). First, the obligation of states parties stated in that provision is recognized to be subject to the availability of resources ('to the maximum of its available resources'). And second, the obligation is one of progressive realization ('with a view to achieving progressively').

This language has been subject to conflicting critiques. On the one hand, it is often suggested that the nature of the obligation under the ICESCR is so onerous that virtually no government will be able to comply. Developing countries, in particular, are seen to be confronting an impossible challenge. On the other hand, it is argued that the relative open-endedness of the concept of progressive realization, particularly in light of the qualification about availability of resources, renders the obligation devoid of meaningful content. Governments can present themselves as defenders of economic and social rights without international imposition of any precise constraints on their policies and behaviour. A related criticism is that the Covenant imposes only 'programmatic' obligations upon governments—that is, obligations to be fulfilled incrementally through the ongoing execution of a programme. It therefore becomes difficult if not impossible to determine when those obligations ought to be met or indeed have been met.

Interdependence of the two Covenants

The interdependence of the two categories of rights has always been part of UN doctrine. The UDHR, at the very start of the human rights movement, included both categories without any sense or separateness or priority. The Preamble to the ICESCR, in terms mirroring those used in the ICCPR, states that 'in accordance with the Universal Declaration . . . , the ideal of free human beings enjoying freedom from fear and want can only be achieved if conditions are created whereby everyone may enjoy his economic, social and cultural rights, as well as his civil and political rights'.

The interdependence principle, apart from its use as a political compromise between advocates of one or two covenants, reflects the fact that the two sets of rights can neither logically nor practically be separated in watertight compartments. Civil and political rights may constitute the condition for and thus be implicit in economic and social rights. Or a given right might fit equally well within either covenant, depending on the purpose for which it is declared. Some illustrations follow:

(1) The right to form trade unions is contained in the ICESCR, while the right to freedom of association is recognized in the ICCPR.
(2) The ICESCR recognizes various 'liberties' and 'freedoms' in relation to scientific research and creative activity.
(3) While the right to education and the parental liberty to choose a child's school are dealt with in the ICESCR (Art. 13), the liberty of parents to choose their child's religious and moral education is recognized in the ICCPR (Art. 18).
(4) The prohibition of discrimination in relation to the provision of, and access to, educational facilities and opportunities can be derived from both Art. 2 of the ICESCR and Art. 26 of the ICCPR.
(5) Even the European Convention on Human Rights, which is generally considered to cover only civil and political rights issues, states (in Art. 2 of Protocol 1) that 'no person shall be denied the right to education'.

Economic rights, social rights, cultural rights

The ICESCR does not make explicit any distinction between economic and social rights. Commentators differ as to their characterization of one or the other of the declared rights, or ignore the distinction. Consider the following comment:

> No clear divisions can be made among the different rights declared in the Covenant. Most rights evidence both economic and social concerns. In some, the economic and workplace character is dominant—for example, rights to work and to favorable conditions of work such as wages necessary for a 'decent living', or rights to form and advocate through trade unions (Articles 6–8). Articles 11–14 of the Covenant have a different character. They range from rights to 'the highest attainable standard of physical and mental health,' to rights to education

and 'an adequate standard of living'. Article 11 defines such a standard of living to include 'adequate food, clothing and housing'.

... I shall call these rights in Articles 11–14 'social rights', even though they have important economic consequences ... Some, such as those in Article 11 on adequate housing and food, are often referred to as social welfare rights. They address and primarily affect those parts of a population on the bottom rungs of the socio-economic ladder. By concentrating on the least well off, the most deprived population, they speak more directly than other parts of the Covenant to the purpose of reducing poverty. On the other hand, other social rights like those to health care, education and social security, address needs not only of the economically marginal population but of all citizens.[10]

Although the title of the ICESCR expressly refers to 'cultural rights' and Art. 15(1) recognizes 'the right of everyone ... to take part in cultural life', such rights have attracted relatively little attention in this context. Rather, they have tended to be dealt with in relation to the ICCPR, whether under its non-discrimination clause (Art. 2(1)), the minorities provision (Art. 27), or specific rights such as freedoms of expression, religion, and association and the right to 'take part in the conduct of public affairs'. The consequence has been a clear neglect of the specifically economic and social rights dimensions of cultural rights.

General observations

The greatest challenge is to identify effective approaches to implementation—i.e. to the means by which economic, social and cultural rights can be given effect and governments can be held accountable to fulfil their obligations. The Covenant says only that governments must use 'all appropriate means' to work towards the stated ends. Such means may be universally valid or relevant or may be quite specific to a particular culture or legal system. The Covenant gives no further pointers, beyond noting that 'appropriate means' includes 'particularly the adoption of legislative measures'. It is clear, however, that neither legislation nor effective remedies of a judicial nature, which are both central to the domestic implementation framework contained in the ICCPR (Art. 2), will play the same roles or *per se* be sufficient in relation to the ICESCR.

The principal UN body concerned with economic, social and cultural rights is the Committee on Economic, Social and Cultural Rights[11], established in 1987 to monitor the compliance of states parties with their obligations under the Covenant (sometimes referred to as the ICESCR Committee). An initial report by each state party is due within two years, and subsequent reports are required at five-yearly intervals. The Committee consists of eighteen independent experts, elected by the Economic and Social Council for four-year terms and reflecting an equitable geographic distribution. Its principal activities are the examination of states parties' reports culminating in the adoption of 'concluding observations' thereon, and the adoption of 'general comments'.

---

[10] Henry Steiner, 'Social Rights and Economic Development: Converging Discourses?', 4 Buffalo Hum. Rts. L. Rev. 25 (1998), at 27.

[11] Philip Alston was Chairperson of the Committee from 1991–1999.

QUESTIONS

1. Does the notion of 'progressive realization' appear distinctive to the ICESCR, or does it appear to be applicable to the ICCPR and to CEDAW? Consider, for example, the application of Article 25 of the ICCPR (right to political participation and to elections) to a state party to that Covenant that has been under authoritarian rule for 50 years. Consider the application of Articles 3 and 26 of the ICCPR to a state imposing severe gender discrimination on its population. Is the notion that, like torture, the state is under an obligation immediately to achieve what these articles require? What is the relevance of Article 40(1) of the ICCPR to this question? What of the duties of promotion of states under Article 5 of CEDAW?

2. Is the idea of resource constraints distinctive to the ICESCR? Like 'progressive realization', the term does not appear in the ICCPR or CEDAW. Can you imagine rights in those instruments whose full realization would be affected by resource constraints that other states would be likely to take into account?

B. CHALLENGES TO ECONOMIC AND SOCIAL RIGHTS

COMMENT ON GOVERNMENTAL AMBIVALENCE

Economic and social rights have been challenged on many grounds. Governments have been especially ambivalent in relation to them, both at the national level and in international fora. Consider the following examples:

- Applicants for membership of the Council of Europe must undertake to ratify the European Convention on Human Rights, but are not required to give assurances of any type as to the European Social Charter (which is the European Convention's counterpart in the field of economic and social rights). As of May 1, 2000, 17 of the Council's 41 members had not ratified either the 1961 Charter or the 1996 revision; and
- The Organization of American States adopted an Additional Protocol to the American Convention on Human Rights in the Area of Economic, Social and Cultural Rights (the 'Protocol of San Salvador') in 1988. Not until November 1999 had 11 countries, compared with 25 parties to the Convention itself, become parties to it, so that the Protocol could enter into force.

The only open hostility to this group of rights has come from the United States, whose attitude has varied considerably from one administration to another. Under President Johnson the United States voted in the General Assembly in 1966 in favour of adopting the Covenant. Although neither the Nixon nor Ford Administrations were opposed to these rights, neither actively promoted them. The Carter

Administration adopted a different approach epitomized by Secretary of State Vance's 'Law Day Speech' at the University of Georgia, in which he defined human rights as including:

> First, . . . the right to be free from governmental violation of the integrity of the person . . . . Second, . . . the right to the fulfilment of such vital needs as food, shelter, health care and education . . . . Third, . . . the right to enjoy civil and political liberties . . . . .[12]

In 1978, President Carter signed the Covenant and sent it to the Senate for its advice and consent to ratification. No action was taken on the Covenant by the Senate, even in Committee. This approach was reversed by the Reagan and Bush Administrations which opposed the concept of economic and social rights on the grounds that while:

> the urgency and moral seriousness of the need to eliminate starvation and poverty from the world are unquestionable . . . the idea of economic and social rights is easily abused by repressive governments which claim that they promote human rights even though they deny their citizens the basic . . . civil and political rights.[13]

Subsequently, in international fora, the United States opposed measures designed to promote economic and social rights. In 1993, Secretary of State Christopher indicated that the Clinton Administration would press for ratification of the Covenant, although no timetable was set and no action has since been taken. In contrast, the United States strongly opposed all references to the right to adequate housing and the right to adequate food, respectively, during negotiations at successive UN-sponsored world conferences in 1996 on human settlements (Istanbul) and food (Rome). But the United States was almost alone and both conferences voted overwhelming to adopt the terminology of economic and social rights. The State Department's *Country Report on Human Rights Practices for 1999* continued the practice first introduced in 1982 of not addressing economic, social and cultural rights, although a limited range of labour rights issues is addressed.

The United States is not alone in its ambivalence, however. Although formal support for economic, social and cultural rights has been near universal, in practice no group of states has consistently followed up its rhetorical support at the international level with practical and sustained programmes of implementation. The most vocal proponents of these rights have made few concrete proposals. Thus a group of 14 developing countries which in 1999 urged the UN Commission on Human Rights to give higher priority to economic, social and cultural rights could only suggest that equal budgetary and human resources be devoted to each of the two sets of rights.[14] One of the countries, however, submitted the

---

[12] 76 Dept. of State Bulletin 505 (1977).
[13] Introduction, U.S. Dept of State, *Country Reports on Human Rights Practices for 1992*, 5.
[14] UN Doc. E/CN.4/1999/120, para. 103(b).

following comment on a proposal to appoint a special rapporteur to investigate situations with respect to economic, social and cultural rights:

> The Government of Cuba is of the opinion that it is not appropriate . . . Such a step would be contrary to United Nations efforts to simplify the Organization's structures and make them more efficient and effective . . . [Such a rapporteur] could only give an inventory of rights that are not being realized and of daily calamities in all parts of the world, with which we are all familiar. What is needed . . . [is] to take more decisive steps towards the inalienable right to development, understood not only as economic growth but also as eradication of poverty . . . '.

For that purpose, Cuba indicated that the onus is on the developed countries, for whom the provision of assistance to developing countries is 'a moral and historical obligation'.[15]

Against this background of political ambivalence, the readings now examine some of the ideological, theoretical and legal problems that frequently arise in debates at both the national and international levels. The materials tend to emphasize the United States debate, partly because the United States has been the key dissenter on these issues in international fora and partly because US-style economic liberalism is increasingly being followed elsewhere.

Consider the following remarks of Louis Henkin, writing before the fundamental US domestic welfare reforms of the mid-1990s, and the DeShaney case that follows:

> Let there be no doubt. The United States is now a welfare state. But the United States is not a welfare state by constitutional compulsion. Indeed, it became a welfare state in the face of powerful constitutional resistance: federalism and, ironically, notions of individual rights—economic liberty and freedom of contract—held the welfare state back for half a century; and a constitutional amendment was required to permit the progressive income tax which was essential to make the welfare state possible. Jurisprudentially, the United States is a welfare state by grace of Congress and of the states . . .
>
> . . . Surely the United States has moved far from 'negative' government, from thinking that the poor are a special and natural category of people and are not the responsibility of society and government but only of church and charity. In theory, Congress could probably abolish the welfare system at will, and the states could probably end public education. But that is a theoretical theory. The welfare system and other rights granted by legislation (for example, laws against private racial discrimination) are so deeply imbedded as to have near-constitutional sturdiness . . . And Americans have begun to think and speak of social security and other benefits as matters of entitlement and right.[16]

---

[15] UN Doc. E/CN.4/1998/25, para. 16.

[16] Henkin, 'International Human Rights and Rights in the United States', in Theodor Meron (ed.), *Human Rights in International Law* (1984), at 43.

COMMENT ON THE DESHANEY CASE

No one judicial decision can capture the complexity of issues about state duties that are based in a state's constitution. This Comment describes a suggestive decision of the US Supreme Court: *DeShaney v. Winnebago County Department of Social Services*, 489 U.S. 189, 109 S. Ct. 998 (1989). (Bear in mind that the United States was not party to the ICESCR, and that the US Constitution does not declare rights or duties of an economic-social nature that are close in character to the provisions of the ICESCR.)

The petitioner, Joshua DeShaney, was a very young boy who was repeatedly and seriously beaten by his father. He and his mother sued for damages from the respondent, the Department of Social Services (DSS) of the state of Wisconsin, under a federal statute, 42 U.S.C. §1983 bearing on the denial of constitutional rights. He claimed that, by failing to protect him, the DSS had denied him the liberty guaranteed by the Due Process Clause of the Fourteenth Amendment to the Constitution ('No State shall . . . deprive any person of life, liberty, or property, without due process of law').

Joshua lived with his twice-divorced father, to whom an earlier court decision had awarded custody. From 1982 to 1984, DSS was advised on several occasions that Joshua might be a victim of child abuse. On several occasions, local hospitals to which Joshua had been admitted with multiple bruises and abrasions had informed DSS of its suspicions. A former wife of the father had termed the father 'a prime case for child abuse.' An ad hoc 'team' of experts formed by Winnebago County had concluded there was insufficient evidence of child abuse to remove Joshua from his home, but recommended measures to which the father had agreed. A DSS caseworker then made monthly visits to the DeShaney home, observed suspicious injuries, noted that the father had broken his agreement, and 'dutifully recorded' such information in her files, together with her 'continuing suspicion' that Joshua was being physically abused, 'but she did nothing more.' In 1984, the father beat four-year-old Joshua into a life-threatening coma. Joshua suffered severe brain damage and was expected to spend his life confined to an institution for the profoundly retarded.

This action in a federal district court claimed that DSS violated Joshua's rights under the Due Process Clause by failing to intervene to protect him against a risk of violence which it knew of or ought to have known. Joshua was thereby deprived of his liberty interest in freedom from unjustified intrusions on his personal security. In a 6–3 decision, the Supreme Court affirmed the decision of the Court of Appeal denying the claim. Chief Justice Rehnquist's opinion for the Court said in part:

> But nothing in the language of the Due Process Clause itself requires the State to protect the life, liberty, and property of its citizens against invasion by private actors. The Clause is phrased as a limitation of the State's power to act, not as a guarantee of certain minimal levels of safety and security . . . [I]ts language cannot fairly be extended to impose an affirmative obligation on the State to ensure that those interests do not come to harm through other means. Nor does history support such an expansive reading of the constitutional text. Like its

counterpart in the Fifth Amendment, the Due Process Clause of the Fourteenth Amendment was intended to prevent government [quoting from a prior decision] 'from abusing [its] power, or employing it as an instrument of oppression.' . . . Its purpose was to protect the people from the State, not to ensure that the State protected them from each other. The Framers [of the Constitution] were content to leave the extent of governmental obligation in the latter area to the democratic political processes.

Consistent with these principles, our cases have recognized that the Due Process Clauses generally confer no affirmative right to governmental aid, even where such aid may be necessary to secure life, liberty, or property interests of which the government itself may not deprive the individual. . . . As a general matter, then, we conclude that a State's failure to protect an individual against private violence simply does not constitute a violation of the Due Process Clause.

The opinion further rejected petitioners' contention that, 'even if the Due Process Clause imposes no affirmative obligation on the State to provide the general public with adequate protective services, such a duty may arise out of certain "protective relationships" created or assumed by the State with respect to particular individuals.' It distinguished prior cases imposing such a duty when the state took individuals into its custody, as in prisons or mental health institutions.

A dissenting opinion of Justice Brennan stated in part:

It may well be, as the Court decides, that the Due Process Clause as construed by our prior cases creates no general right to basic governmental services. That, however, is not the question presented here. . . . No one, in short, has asked the Court to proclaim that, as a general matter, the Constitution safeguards positive as well as negative liberties.

Criticizing the majority opinion's emphasis on state *inaction* as the asserted basis for the state's liability, Justice Brennan stressed the degree to which the state in this case had indeed *acted* (1) by encouraging citizens and other state agencies to rely on the DSS to handle instances of child abuse, and (2) by actively intervening through DSS in several ways in this case. He drew an analogy between the facts in *DeShaney* and the custody cases that Justice Rehnquist had concluded were not in point. 'My disagreement with the Court arises from its failure to see that inaction can be every bit as abusive of power as action, that oppression can result when a State undertakes a vital duty and then ignores it.'

In his dissenting opinion, Justice Blackmun termed the facts and decision 'a sad commentary upon American life.'

NOTE

In *Rights Talk* (1991), at 96, Mary Ann Glendon criticized the Court's opinion in *DeShaney*. Noting that the majority opinion had 'correctly' pointed out that the Constitution 'does not establish affirmative government obligations to come to the aid of citizens,' she stressed that it 'could have emphasized the extent to which our political regime, by statute, has long been one in which state and federal governments alike have committed themselves in principles and in practice to a vast array of affirmative governmental obligations.'

> By giving the impression that the United States Constitution somehow embodies a no-duty-to-rescue rule writ large, the opinion . . . miseducates the public about the American version of the welfare state, and about the role of citizens in shaping and reshaping it. . . . A characterization of American constitutional law by the nation's highest court that *appears* to put these statutory welfare commitments in tension with our basic constitutional values becomes part of the dynamics that will affect the future course of those commitments.

Rather, the Court should have emphasized that the Constitution 'permits— although it does not require—a responsive, affirmatively acting state.' Such emphasis would have helped 'to bring together the two halves of the divided American political soul—our insistence on limiting government, and our commitment to protecting the weak and the helpless.'

QUESTION

Compare the typical wording of provisions of the international human rights instruments on 'rights' ('everyone' or 'every person' shall have a specified right) and on state duties (see Article 2 of the ICCPR), with the wording of the United States Constitution in the Bill of Rights (the first eight amendments to the Constitution) and the Fourteenth Amendment. Do the international instruments more readily permit the imposition on the state of 'affirmative' duties of protection? What provisions of the ICCPR point toward such duties, particularly (as in *DeShaney*) a duty to protect against acts of private (nonstate) actors? Do such provisions have counterparts in the U.S. Constitution? (Of course, as Justice Rehnquist notes but only summarily discusses, a country's legal and political history and ideology are also here at issue.)

NOTE

In the following readings, David Beetham gives a broad overview of the principal critiques of economic and social rights, while David Kelley presents the case in favour of an 'individualist political philosophy that prizes freedom' and is not compatible with such rights.

DAVID BEETHAM, WHAT FUTURE FOR ECONOMIC AND SOCIAL RIGHTS?
43 Political Studies 41 (1995).

. . .

. . . It is argued, typically, that the list of so-called 'rights' in the [UDHR and the ICESCR] can at most be a statement of aspirations or goals rather than properly of *rights*. For an entitlement to be a human right it must satisfy a number of conditions: it must be fundamental and universal; it must in principle be definable in justiciable form; it should be clear who has the duty to uphold or implement the right; and the responsible agency should possess the capacity to fulfil its obligation. The rights specified in the Covenant do not satisfy these conditions, it is argued.

Indeed, they would seem to fail on every count. They confuse the fundamental with the merely desirable, or that which is specific to the advanced economies (holidays with pay, free higher education, the right of everyone to the continuous improvement of living conditions). Even those that are fundamental cannot in principle be definable in justiciable form. At what level can the deprivation of nutrition, sanitation or health care be sufficient to trigger legal redress? And whose duty is it to see that these 'rights' are met—national governments, international institutions, the UN itself? If it is governments, can they be required to provide what they do not have the means or capacity to deliver? . . . While we may reasonably require them to *refrain* from torturing their citizens, it is not obvious that we can equally require them to guarantee them all a livelihood, adequate accommodation and a healthy environment. Moreover for them to do so, it is contended, would require a huge paternalist and bureaucratic apparatus and a corresponding extension of compulsory taxation, both of which would interfere with another basic right, the right to freedom.

. . .

[The author recounts the 'depressing litany' of recent developments in relation to economic and social rights and suggests that] two alternative responses are possible. One is to conclude that the incorporation of economic and social rights in the human rights canon is simply spitting in the wind, when hundreds of millions suffer from malnutrition and vulnerability to disease and starvation. Worse, it is an insult to them to insist on their 'human rights' when there is no realistic prospect of these being upheld. . . .

The opposite response is to insist that human rights most urgently need asserting and defending, both theoretically and practically, where they are most denied. Indeed the language of rights only makes sense at all in a context where basic requirements are vulnerable to standard threats (could we imagine a 'right' to clean air in a pre-industrial society?). The human rights agenda has therefore necessarily an aspirational or promotional dimension; but it is not mere rhetoric. The purpose of the two covenants and their monitoring apparatus is to cajole state signatories into undertaking the necessary domestic policy and legislation to ensure their citizens the protection of their rights in practice. This promotional aspect of the human rights agenda is not only addressed to those whose responsibility it is to secure the rights in question. It also serves as a legitimation for the deprived in their struggles to realize their rights on their own behalf, by providing a set of internationally validated standards to which they can appeal.

. . .

So I start with the definition of social and economic rights. Can they be defined in such a way that they meet the criteria for a human right of being fundamental, universal and clearly specifiable?

. . .

. . . [In terms of the first two criteria] a minimum agenda of economic and social rights will aim to secure those basic material conditions for human agency that modern experience has shown to be both necessary and effective. These are not that remarkable actually. Both the defenders of a 'basic needs' approach within development economics and human rights theorists would converge on a minimum core of rights such as the following: the right to food of an adequate nutritional value, to clothing, to shelter, to basic (or primary) health care, clean water and sanitation, and to education to at least primary level. Although there may be other things to be added to this list (see below), it provides the foundation, together with the crucial principle of non-discriminatory access.

. . .

If the rights in the above list can meet the criteria of being both fundamental and universally applicable, can they also meet the test of specificity, such that it is possible to specify a level below which a given right can be said to be denied? Even the level of necessary nutrition, which seems to be the most objectively definable, will vary according to person and circumstance. The level of clothing or shelter needed will vary according to the climate. And the need for health care and education, as is well known, is almost infinitely expandable as knowledge increases. Here there will inevitably be a *certain* arbitrariness about defining the required standard for a human right as that of primary health care and education, although that standard is based upon a general agreement that these constitute significant thresholds. That some minimum standards need to be established, however, is necessary to the idea of a 'core' of rights, and to the assumption of the UN Committee on ESCR that such rights can increasingly be justiciable, and amenable to individual petition and complaint. In any case, the methods needed are perhaps not that complex for determining when girls are discriminated against in access to education, when children die through lack of food or clean water, or when people sleep rough because they have no access to housing; nor for deciding on the kind of comparative statistics—on infant mortality rates, life expectancy rates, literacy rates, school attendance rates, etc.,—which can serve as evidence of rights denials.

. . .

DAVID KELLEY, A LIFE OF ONE'S OWN: INDIVIDUAL RIGHTS AND THE WELFARE STATE
(1998), at 1

In our personal lives, most of us realize that the world doesn't owe us a living. . . .

Yet in our public lives we have accepted an obligation to provide food, shelter, jobs, education, pensions, medical care, child support, and other goods to every member of society. The premise of the welfare state—the sprawling network of programs for transferring wealth from taxpayers to recipients—is that the world *does* owe us a living. If someone is unable or unwilling to support himself, the government will provide food stamps, housing subsidies, and possibly cash assistance as well. . . .

. . .

. . . [T]he welfare state is a specific historical phenomenon. In its modern form it is just over 100 years old. During the 1880s, Germany under Otto von Bismarck created social insurance programs for old age, job-related accidents, and other medical costs. Great Britain began building its welfare state, partly on Bismarck's model, in the early years of this century. In the United States, . . . the major welfare programs were created during the 1930s and 1960s . . .

. . . The welfare state . . . rests on an idea. The thinkers and activists who built it insisted that the social provision of goods be treated as a right possessed by all people as citizens, rather than as an act of charity or noblesse oblige, a gift from some to others. . . .

. . .

[Ch.] 2. What is a Welfare Right?

. . . America remains unique in the role that rights play in the national culture. [The Declaration of Independence reflects the principles of Enlightenment individualism, including] the idea that the individual's primary need is for liberty: the freedom to act without interference, to be secure against assault on his person or property, to think and speak his mind freely, to keep the fruits of his labor. And while government is necessary to secure that freedom, it is also the greatest danger to it. Thus, the concept of rights served two functions in the political theory of the Enlightenment: to legitimate government and to control it. . . .

It is against that background that we must understand the concept of welfare rights, a concept that reflects a more expansive view of the role of government than anything envisioned by the classical liberals of the Enlightenment. 'For Jefferson, . . . the poor had no right to be free from want', observes legal scholar Louis Henkin. 'The framers saw the purposes of government as being to police and safeguard, not to feed and clothe and house' . . .

. . .

Welfare rights differ from the classical rights to life, liberty, and property in the nature of the claim that they embody. . . .

The primary difference is one of content, a difference in what it is that people are said to have a right *to*. The classical rights are rights to freedom of action, whereas welfare rights are rights to goods. That distinction has often been described as the difference between 'freedom from' and 'freedom to'. The classical rights guarantee freedom from interference by others—and may thus be referred to as liberty rights—whereas welfare rights guarantee freedom to have various things that are regarded as necessities. What that means, in essence, is that the classical liberty rights are concerned with processes, whereas welfare rights are concerned with outcomes.

Liberty rights set conditions on the way in which individuals interact. Those rights say that we cannot harm, coerce, or steal from each other as we go about our business in life, but they do not guarantee that we will succeed in our business. . . .

Welfare rights, by contrast, are intended to guarantee success, at least at a minimum level. They are conceived as entitlements to have certain goods, not merely to pursue them. They are rights to have the goods provided by others if one cannot (or will not) earn them oneself. . . .

. . .

On whom does the obligation fall [to provide what welfare rights require]? Here is another point of difference between liberty and welfare rights. One person's liberty rights impose on every other human being the obligation to respect them. I am obliged not to murder or steal from other individuals, even those I have never encountered and with whom I have no relationship. But am I obliged to respect their welfare rights? No advocate of welfare rights would say that a poor person has a right to appear at my door and demand food, or a place to sleep, or any of the other goods to which he is said to have a right. The obligation to supply those goods does not fall upon me as a particular individual; it falls upon all of us indifferently, as members of society. . . . Insofar as welfare rights are implemented through government programs, for example, the obligation is distributed among all taxpayers.

. . .

To implement the liberty rights of individuals, government must protect them against incursions by other individuals. . . . The laws involved are relatively simple; they essentially prohibit specific types of actions. The government apparatus required is relatively small, the 'night-watchman state' of classical liberalism. The only significant expense involved is that of the military, to protect against foreign aggression.

The implementation of welfare rights requires a much more activist form of government. The welfare state typically involves large-scale transfer programs . . . through which wealth is transferred from taxpayers to those on whom the state confers entitlements to various goods.

. . .

. . . [T]he administration of the transfer programs is enormously complex by contrast with the relatively simple prohibitions involved in protecting the rights to life, liberty, and property. The welfare state involves government in running large-scale business enterprises: pension plans, health insurance, and so on. A complex set of regulations is required to define the entitlements of people, depending on the diverse circumstances of their lives, and a large bureaucracy is required to enforce those regulations. [Kelley also refers to the high amount of total spending on social welfare by government at all levels in the United States.]

Liberty and welfare rights differ, finally, in the level at which it is possible to implement them. The economic and technological development of a society affects the degree to which it can provide welfare rights to its members. A preindustrial society obviously cannot guarantee access to modern medical equipment and procedures. Even in a wealthy society, the potential demand for goods like health care or insurance against economic risks is open-ended. If individuals have rights to at least minimum levels of such goods, then the political process must decide what constitutes the minimum, the level that represents need rather than luxury. There is no universal and nonarbitrary standard for distinguishing need from luxury and thus for defining the content of welfare rights. It depends on the level of wealth in a given society.

The implementation of liberty rights, however, is not historically relative in the same way. The protection of an individual's liberty rights requires that other individuals, and the government itself, refrain from forcibly harming or constraining him or appropriating his property. The ability to forbear such actions is not a function of wealth. . . .

. . .

In short, liberty rights reflect an individualist political philosophy that prizes freedom, welfare rights a communitarian or collectivist one that is willing to sacrifice freedom. . . .

QUESTIONS

1. Beetham and Kelley both stress the redistributive character of social welfare programmes and their high expense. Need welfare programmes necessarily rest on, say, progressive taxation at higher rates for the rich to finance distributions in cash or kind to the needy? Does Article 2 of the ICESCR itself suggest how high social welfare expenses must be, whether in total or per capita terms or in terms of percentages of the national budget?

2. According to Kelley, liberty rights 'say that we cannot harm, coerce or steal from each other'. In this sense, the category of 'liberty rights' seems to fit well with most rights declared in the ICCPR. With respect to the ICCPR, in what ways does Kelley understate the complexity and expense of 'liberty rights', and thus overstate the distinctions with 'welfare rights'?

NOTE

Recall the discussion of negative and positive rights at pp. 181–184 in Chapter 3. That discussion involved comparisons between civil-political and economic-social rights that are relevant to Kelley's argument and to the following readings.

STEPHEN HOLMES AND CASS R. SUNSTEIN, THE COST OF RIGHTS: WHY LIBERTY DEPENDS ON TAXES
(1999), at 1

The opposition between two fundamentally different sorts of claim—between 'negative rights' . . . and 'positive rights' . . .—is quite familiar. But it is anything but self-evident. It does not appear anywhere in the [US] Constitution, for one thing. It was wholly unknown to the American framers. So how does it arise? . . .
. . .

This dichotomy has taken deep root in common thought and expression. Those Americans who wish to be left alone prize their immunities from public interference, it is said, while those who wish to be taken care of seek entitlements to public aid. Negative rights ban and exclude government; positive ones invite and demand government. The former require the hobbling of public officials, while the latter require their affirmative intervention. Negative rights typically protect liberty; positive rights typically promote equality. The former shield a private realm, whereas the latter reallocate tax dollars . . . The former rights include the rights of property and contract and, of course, freedom from being tortured by the police; the latter encompass rights to food stamps, subsidized housing, and minimal welfare payments.
. . .

The attraction of this categorization stems partly from the moral warning or moral promise it is believed to convey. Conservative devotees of the positive/negative rights distinction routinely urge, for instance, that welfare rights are potentially infantilizing and exercised on the basis of resources forked out free of charge by the government. Classical liberal rights, they add by way of contrast, are exercised autonomously, American-style, by hardy and self-sufficient individuals who spurn paternalism and government handouts.

. . . Instead of protecting us from government, this conservative story continues, welfare rights make people dependent on government, thus eroding 'real freedom' in two different ways: by unfairly confiscating the private assets of the wealthy and imprudently weakening the self-sufficiency of the poor. . . .

. . .[In contrast] progressives applaud the rise of positive guarantees—interpreting this as a sign of political learning and an improved understanding of the requirements of justice. . . . The eventual rise of positive rights registered a novel appreciation of the need to supplement non-interference with public provision.

One and the same distinction, in effect, obligingly serves two contrary outlooks.
. . .

The Cost of Remedies

'Where there is a right, there is a remedy' is a classical legal maxim. Individuals enjoy rights, in a legal as opposed to a moral sense, only if the wrongs they suffer are fairly and predictably redressed by their government. This simple point goes a long way toward disclosing the inadequacy of the negative rights/positive rights distinction. What it shows is that all legally enforced rights are necessarily positive rights.

Rights are costly because remedies are costly. Enforcement is expensive, especially uniform and fair enforcement; and legal rights are hollow to the extent that they remain unenforced. Formulated differently, almost every right implies a correlative duty, and duties are taken seriously only when dereliction is punished by the public power drawing on the public purse. . . .

. . .

The financing of basic rights through tax revenues helps us see clearly that rights are public goods: taxpayer-funded and government-managed social services designed to improve collective and individual well-being. All rights are positive rights.

QUESTIONS

1. Based on the preceding readings, how would you identify the salient distinctions between civil-political and economic-social rights? (Of course, they need not be the same as the distinctions drawn in these readings.)

2. To what degree do you find valid the contrasting characterizations of these two categories in some of the readings: rights versus needs or claims, negative versus positive, individual versus collective, determinate versus open textured, law versus policy?

C. THE BEARER AND NATURE OF DUTIES UNDER THE ICESCR

Recall that under the ICCPR, many rights could be violated by individuals as well as by the state—for example, the right to bodily security, or to free speech and assembly. Is this true as well of the core rights under the ICESCR, like the right to an adequate standard of living, including housing and food? Who bears duties that are correlative to or implied by such rights, only states, or individuals as well? And how can those duties be best described?

IMMANUEL KANT, THE DOCTRINE OF VIRTUE,
in The Metaphysics of Morals (1797, M. J. Gregor, trans. 1964), at 116

[24.] When we are speaking of laws of duty (not laws of nature) and, among these, of laws governing men's external relations with one another, we are considering a moral (intelligible) world where, by analogy with the physical world, attraction and repulsion bind together rational beings (on earth). The principle of mutual love admonishes men constantly to come nearer to each other; that of the respect which they owe each other, to keep themselves at a distance from one another. And should one of these great moral forces fail, 'then nothingness (immorality), with gaping throat, would drink the whole kingdom of (moral) beings like a drop of water'. . . .

[25.] In this context, however, love is not to be taken as a feeling (aesthetic love), i.e. a pleasure in the perfection of other men; it does not mean emotional love (for others cannot oblige us to have feelings). It must rather be taken as a maxim of benevolence (practical love), which has beneficence as its consequence.

The same holds true of the respect to be shown to others: it is not to be taken merely as the feeling that comes from comparing one's own worth with another's (such as mere habit causes a child to feel toward his parents, a pupil toward his teacher, a subordinate in general toward his superior). Respect is rather to be taken in a practical sense (*observantia aliis praestanda*), as a maxim of limiting our self-esteem by the dignity of humanity in another person.

Moreover, the duty of free respect to others is really only a negative one (of not exalting oneself above others) and is thus analogous to the juridical duty of not encroaching on another's possessions. Hence, although respect is a mere duty of virtue, it is considered narrow in comparison with a duty of love, and it is the duty of love that is considered wide.

The duty of love for one's neighbour can also be expressed as the duty of making others' ends my own (in so far as these ends are only not immoral), The duty of respect for my neighbour is contained in the maxim of not abasing any other man to a mere means to my end (not demanding that the other degrade himself in order to slave for my end).

By the fact that I fulfill a duty of love to someone I obligate the other as well: I make him indebted to me. But in fulfilling a duty of respect I obligate only myself, contain myself within certain limits in order to detract nothing from the worth that the other, as a man, is entitled to posit in himself.

. . .

[30.] It is every man's duty to be beneficent—that is, to promote, according to his means, the happiness of others who are in need, and this without hope of gaining anything by it.

For every man who finds himself in need wishes to be helped by other men. But if he lets his maxim of not willing to help others in turn when they are in need become public, i.e. makes this a universal permissive law, then everyone would likewise deny him assistance when he needs it, or at least would be entitled to. Hence the maxim of self-interest contradicts itself when it is made universal law— that is, it is contrary to duty. Consequently the maxim of common interest—of beneficence toward the needy—is a universal duty of men, and indeed for this reason: that men are to be considered fellow-men—that is, rational beings with needs, united by nature in one dwelling place for the purpose of helping one another.

. . .

[Casuistical Questions]

. . .

The ability to practice beneficence, which depends on property, follows largely from the injustice of the government, which favours certain men and so introduces an inequality of wealth that makes others need help. This being the case, does the rich man's help to the needy, on which he so readily prides himself as something meritorious, really deserve to be called beneficence at all?

. . .

[38.] Every man has a rightful claim to respect from his fellow-men and is reciprocally obligated to show respect for every other man.

Humanity itself is a dignity; for man cannot be used merely as a means by any man (either by others or even by himself) but must always be treated at the same time as an end. . . .

PROVISIONS IN RELIGIOUS TEXTS ON CHARITABLE GIVING

Isaiah, Ch. 58 (Holy Scriptures, Masoretic Text, 1917)

[The reference is to a fast of repentance.]

Behold, in the day of your fast ye pursue your business, and exact all your labours.

Behold, ye fast for strife and contention, and to smite with the fist of wickedness;

Ye fast not this day so as to make your voice to be heard on high.

Is such the fast that I have chosen? The day for a man to afflict his soul?

Is it to bow down his head as a bulrush, and to spread sackcloth and ashes under him?

Wilt thou call this a fast, and an acceptable day to the Lord?

Is not this the fast that I have chosen? To loose the fetters of wickedness, to undue the bands of the yoke,

And to let the oppressed go free, and that ye break every yoke?

Is it not to deal thy bread to the hungry, and that thou bring the poor that are cast out to thy house?

When thou seest the naked, that thou cover him, and that thou hide not thyself from thine own flesh?

. . .

And if thou draw out thy soul to the hungry, and satisfy the afflicted soul;

Then shall thy light rise in darkness, and thy gloom be as the noonday;

And the Lord will guide thee continually, and satisfy thy soul in drought, and make strong thy bones;

And thou shalt be like a watered garden, and like a spring of water, whose waters fail not.

Matthew, Ch. 26 (Holy Bible, King James Version)

When the Son of man shall come in his glory, and all the holy angels with him, then shall he sit upon the throne of his glory;

. . .

Then shall the King say unto them on his right hand. Come, ye blessed of my Father, inherit the kingdom prepared for you from the foundation of the world.

For I was an hungered, and ye gave me meat; I was thirsty, and ye gave me drink; I was a stranger, and ye took me in;

Naked, and ye clothed me. I was sick, and ye visited me; I was in prison, and ye came unto me.

Then shall the righteous answer him, saying, Lord, when saw we thee an hungred, and fed thee, or thirsty, and gave thee drink?

. . .

And the King shall answer and say unto them. Verily I say unto you, Inasmuch as you have done it unto any of the least of these my brethren, ye have done it unto me.

Surah 63: Al Munafiqun, 9 and 10 (Holy Qur'an, Abdullah Yusuf 'Ali trans. 1989)

O ye who believe!
Let not your riches
Or your children divert you
From the remembrance of Allah.
If any act thus,
The loss is their own.
And spend something (in charity)
Out of the substance
Which We have bestowed
On you

QUESTIONS

1. 'If we were to make a rough analogy, Kant's duty of respect recalls the ICCPR, while the duty of beneficence recalls the ICESCR.' Do you agree or disagree, and why?

2. Compare as a group the verses from the Hebrew Bible, the Christian Bible, and the Qur'an *with* Article 11 of the ICESCR. Based on these religious texts and on the prior readings in this chapter, what similarities and what differences do you find with respect to the invocation of rights and duties, and with respect to who bears what rights or duties?

3. A critic of economic-social rights might respond to these readings by saying that they well illustrate the distinction which must be drawn between ethical or moral duties on the one hand, and legal obligations which are correlative to human rights on the other. Would you agree?

NOTE

This section concludes with the views of the ICESCR Committee on the issue of obligations. Although the Covenant contains no provision authorizing the Committee to make a binding interpretation of the nature and scope of the states' obligations in question, the Committee is in a position to adopt more or less authoritative statements of interpretation in the form of 'general comments' such as these.

COMMITTEE ON ECONOMIC, SOCIAL AND CULTURAL RIGHTS, GENERAL COMMENT NO. 3 (1990)
UN Doc. E/1991/23, Annex III

The nature of States parties obligations (article 2, paragraph 1)

1. Article 2 . . . describes the nature of the general legal obligations undertaken by States parties to the Covenant. Those obligations include both what may be termed (following the work of the International Law Commission) obligations of conduct and obligations of result . . . [W]hile the Covenant provides for progressive realization and acknowledges the constraints due to the limits of available resources, it also imposes various obligations which are of immediate effect. Of these, two are of particular importance in understanding the precise nature of States parties obligations. One of these, . . . is the 'undertaking to guarantee' that relevant rights 'will be exercised without discrimination . . . '.

2. The other is the undertaking in article 2(1) 'to take steps', which in itself, is not qualified or limited by other considerations . . . . [W]hile the full realization of the relevant rights may be achieved progressively, steps towards that goal must be taken within a reasonably short time after the Covenant's entry into force for the States concerned. Such steps should be deliberate, concrete and targeted as clearly as possible towards meeting the obligations recognized in the Covenant.

3. The means which should be used in order to satisfy the obligation to take steps are stated in article 2(1) to be 'all appropriate means, including particularly the adoption of legislative measures'. The Committee recognizes that in many instances legislation is highly desirable and in some cases may even be indispensable. For example, it may be difficult to combat discrimination effectively in the absence of a sound legislative foundation for the necessary measures. In fields such as health, the protection of children and mothers, and education, as well as in respect of the matters dealt with in articles 6 to 9, legislation may also be an indispensable element for many purposes.

4. . . . [H]owever, the adoption of legislative measures, as specifically foreseen by the Covenant, is by no means exhaustive of the obligations of States parties. Rather, the phrase 'by all appropriate means' must be given its full and natural meaning . . . . [T]he ultimate determination as to whether all appropriate measures have been taken remains for the Committee to make.

. . .

7. Other measures which may also be considered 'appropriate' for the purposes of article 2(1) include, but are not limited to, administrative, financial, educational and social measures.

. . .

9. . . . The concept of progressive realization constitutes a recognition of the fact that full realization of all economic, social and cultural rights will generally not be able to be achieved in a short period of time. In this sense the obligation differs significantly from that contained in article 2 of the Covenant on Civil and Political Rights which embodies an immediate obligation to respect and ensure all of the relevant rights. Nevertheless, the fact that realization over time, or in other words progressively, is foreseen under the Covenant should not be misinterpreted as depriving the obligation of all meaningful content. It is on the one hand a necessary flexibility device, reflecting the realities of the real world and the difficulties involved for any country in ensuring full realization of economic, social and cultural rights. On the other hand, the phrase must be read in the light of the overall objective, indeed the *raison d'être* of the Covenant which is to establish clear obligations for States parties in respect of the full realization of the rights in question. It thus imposes an obligation to move as expeditiously and effectively as possible towards that goal. Moreover, any deliberately retrogressive measures in that regard would require the most careful consideration and would need to be fully justified. . . .

10. . . . [T]he Committee is of the view that a minimum core obligation to ensure the satisfaction of, at the very least, minimum essential levels of each of the rights is incumbent upon every State party. Thus, for example, a State party in which any significant number of individuals is deprived of essential foodstuffs, of essential primary health care, of basic shelter and housing, or of the most basic forms of education is, prima facie, failing to discharge its obligations under the Covenant. If the Covenant were to be read in such a way as not to establish such a minimum core obligation, it would be largely deprived of its *raison d'être*. By the same token, it must be noted that any assessment as to whether a State has discharged its minimum core obligation must also take account of resource constraints applying within the country concerned. Article 2(1) obligates each State party to take the necessary steps 'to the maximum of its available resources'. In order for a State party to be able to attribute its failure to meet at least its minimum core obligations to a lack of available resources it must demonstrate that every effort has been made to use all resources that are at its disposition in an effort to satisfy, as a matter of priority, those minimum obligations.

11. . . . [T]he obligations to monitor the extent of the realization, or more especially of the non-realization, of economic, social and cultural rights, and to devise strategies and programmes for their promotion, are not in any way eliminated as a result of resource constraints. . . .

12. Similarly, the Committee underlines the fact that even in times of severe resource constraints whether caused by a process of adjustment, of economic recession, or by other factors, the vulnerable members of society can and indeed must be protected by the adoption of relatively low-cost targeted programmes.

. . .

COMMITTEE ON ECONOMIC, SOCIAL AND CULTURAL RIGHTS, GENERAL COMMENT NO. 12 (1999)
UN Doc. E/C.12/1999/5

The right to adequate food (article 11)

. . .

15. The right to adequate food, like any other human right, imposes three types or levels of obligations on States parties: the obligations to *respect*, to *protect* and to *fulfil*. In turn, the obligation to *fulfil* incorporates both an obligation to *facilitate* and an obligation to *provide*. The obligation to *respect* existing access to adequate food requires States parties not to take any measures that result in preventing such access. The obligation to *protect* requires measures by the State to ensure that enterprises or individuals do not deprive individuals of their access to adequate food. The obligation to *fulfil* (*facilitate*) means the State must pro-actively engage in activities intended to strengthen people's access to and utilization of resources and means to ensure their livelihood, including food security. Finally, whenever an individual or group is unable, for reasons beyond their control, to enjoy the right to adequate food by the means at their disposal, States have the obligation to *fulfil* (*provide*) that right directly. This obligation also applies for persons who are victims of natural or other disasters.

. . .

QUESTIONS

1. A "right to" some economic-social good like housing or food tells us little until we know what kinds of duties the state has to enable people to realize that right. All lies in the definition of those duties.' Comment, and illustrate this assertion with a description of the kinds of state duties that might be relevant to coming closer to achieving the 'right to adequate food'.

2. Consider the analysis of economic and social rights in terms of the levels of obligation specified by the Committee in its General Comment No. 12 (1999):

   a. Whatever its conceptual interest, how useful do you find this analysis in terms of identifying the precise legal obligations that flow from the provisions of the Covenant?
   b. Does the framework also have utility for understanding the implications of civil and political rights? Can you apply the scheme to, say, the right to freedom from torture or the right to political participation through voting?
   c. In general, how do you view the distinction between the ICCPR and ICESCR that is so often signalled by commentators—namely, that economic-social rights are to be realized progressively? Does the different wording of the ICCPR indicate that all the civil-political rights declared therein must be realized immediately? Or are some such rights also, indeed inevitably, subject to progressive rather than immediate realization? If so, which ones?

3. The Committee's statement in para. 10 concerning minimum core obligations constitutes a major 'clarification' of the obligations of states parties. How would you critique this interpretation if you were the representative of a government which is unsympathetic to these rights?

ADDITIONAL READING

On the issue of obligations see: Philip Alston and Gerard Quinn, 'The Nature and Scope of States Parties' Obligations Under the International Covenant on Economic, Social and Cultural Rights', 9 Hum. Rts Q. 156 (1987); and G. J. H. van Hoof, 'The Legal Nature of Economic, Social and Cultural Rights: A Rebuttal of Some Traditional Views', in Philip Alston and Katarina Tomasevski (eds.), *The Right To Food* 97 (1984). For philosophical discussions of the nature of economic and social rights see: Alan Gewirth, *The Community of Rights* (1997); Ellen Frankel Paul et al. (eds.), *Economic Rights* (1992); Partha Dasgupta, *An Inquiry into Well-Being and Destitution* (1993); Martha Nussbaum and A. Sen (eds.), *The Quality of Life* (1993); Amartya Sen, *Inequality Reexamined* (1992); and Raymond Plant, *Modern Political Thought* (1991).

D. THE RELATIONSHIP BETWEEN THE TWO SETS OF RIGHTS

The phrase first coined in 1950 and then adapted at the 1993 Vienna World Conference—that all rights are 'indivisible and interdependent and interrelated'—expresses the international community's attempt to resolve in the context of its discussions of human rights the longstanding debate over the relationship between freedom and equality. But the constant reaffirmation of the slogan of indivisibility has not prevented regular claims that one set of rights or the other must in fact be accorded priority. Throughout the 1980s the United States claimed that because 'the idea of economic and social rights is easily abused by repressive governments', it would omit all discussion of those rights from its focus. China has constantly sought to downgrade civil and political rights on the grounds that 'when poverty and lack of adequate food are commonplace and people's basic needs are not guaranteed, priority should be given to economic development'.[17] The Right to Development has also often been used as a surrogate for this claim (see p. 1420, *infra*).

International human rights NGOs have tended to be pre-occupied with civil and political rights despite occasional affirmations of intent to adopt a broader focus.

In the materials that follow we consider different perspectives on the relationship between the two sets of rights before turning to a case study of the Dalits ('untouchables') of India. This is a classic example of the ways in which the

---

[17] Statement by the Chinese Representative to the Vienna World Conference, 1993, p. 3.

situation of both sets of rights often appears to be inextricably linked. For the most part it has been the economic and social rights dimension which has been neglected or deferred. The question that arises is whether the downgrading of these rights is a defensible strategy, even if it may be problematic in terms of principle.

AMARTYA SEN, FREEDOMS AND NEEDS
The New Republic (January 10 and 17, 1994) 31 at 32

. . .

. . . Do needs and rights represent a basic contradiction? Do the former really undermine the latter? I would argue that this is altogether the wrong way to understand, first, the force of economic needs and, second, the salience of political rights. The real issues that have to be addressed lie elsewhere, and they involve taking note of extensive interconnections between the enjoyment of political rights and the appreciation of economic needs. Political rights can have a major role in providing incentives and information toward the solution of economic privation. But the connections between rights and needs are not merely instrumental, they are also constitutive. For our conceptualization of economic needs depends on open public debates and discussions, and the guaranteeing of those debates and those discussions requires an insistence on political rights.

. . .

Those who are skeptical of the relevance of political rights to poor countries would not necessarily deny the basic importance of political rights. Some of them would not even deny my contention that the nastiness of the violation of liberty can go well beyond other forms of disadvantage. Instead their arguments turn on the impact of political rights on the fulfillment of economic needs, and they take this impact to be firmly negative and overwhelmingly important.

The belief abounds that political rights correlate negatively with economic growth. Indeed, something of a 'general theory' of this relationship between political liberty and economic prosperity has been articulated recently by that unlikely theorist Lee Kuan Yew, the former prime minister of Singapore; and the praise of the supposed advantages of 'the hard state' in promoting economic development goes back a long way in the development literature . . . now reasonably well understood; a variety of factors played a part, including the use of international markets, an openness to competition, a high level of literacy, successful land reforms and the provision of selective incentives to encourage growth and exports. There is *nothing* to indicate that these economic and social policies were inconsistent with greater democracy, that they had to be sustained by the elements of authoritarianism actually present in South Korea. The danger of taking *post hoc* to be *propter hoc* is as real in the making of such political and strategic judgments as it is in any empirical reasoning.

Thus the fundamental importance of political rights is not refuted by some allegedly negative effect of these rights on economic performance. In fact, the instrumental connections may even give a very positive role to political rights in the context of deprivations of a drastic and elementary kind: whether, and how, a government responds to intense needs and sufferings may well depend on how much pressure is put on it, and whether or not pressure is put on it will depend on the exercise of political rights (such as voting, criticizing, protesting and so on).

Consider the matter of famine. I have tried to argue elsewhere that the avoidance of such economic disasters as famines is made much easier by the existence, and the exercise, of various liberties and political rights, including the liberty of free expression . . . . But famines have never afflicted any country that is independent, that goes to elections regularly, that has opposition parties to voice criticisms, that permits newspapers to report freely and to question the wisdom of government policies without extensive censorship.

. . .

Why might we expect a general connection between democracy and the nonoccurrence of famines? The answer is not hard to seek. Famines kill millions of people in different countries in the world, but they do not kill the rulers. The kings and the presidents, the bureaucrats and the bosses, the military leaders and the commanders never starve. And if there are no elections, no opposition parties, no forums for uncensored public criticism, then those in authority do not have to suffer the political consequences of their failure to prevent famine. Democracy, by contrast, would spread the penalty of famine to the ruling groups and the political leadership.

There is, moreover, the issue of information. A free press, and more generally the practice of democracy, contributes greatly to bringing out the information that can have an enormous impact on policies for famine prevention, such as facts about the early effects of droughts and floods, and about the nature and the results of unemployment . . . . Indeed, I would argue that a free press and an active political opposition constitute the best 'early warning system' that a country threatened by famine can possess.

. . .

In making such arguments, of course, there is the danger of exaggerating the effectiveness of democracy. Political rights and liberties are permissive advantages, and their effectiveness depends on how they are exercised. Democracies have been particularly successful in preventing disasters that are easy to understand, in which sympathy can take an especially immediate form. Many other problems are not quite so accessible. Thus India's success in eradicating famine is not matched by a similar success in eliminating non-extreme hunger, or in curing persistent illiteracy or in relieving inequalities in gender relations. While the plight of famine victims is easy to politicize, these other deprivations call for deeper analysis, and for greater and more effective use of mass communication and political participation—in sum, for a fuller practice of democracy.

. . .

Human lives suffer from miseries and deprivations of various kinds, some more amenable to alleviation than others. The totality of the human predicament would be an undiscriminating basis for the social analysis of needs. There are many things that we might have good reason to value if they were feasible, maybe even immortality; yet we do not see them as needs. Our conception of needs relates to our analysis of the nature of deprivations, and also to our understanding of what can be done about them. Political rights, including freedom of expression and discussion, are not only pivotal in inducing political responses to economic needs, they are also central to the conceptualization of economic needs themselves.

QUESTIONS

1. Is Sen's analysis consistent with the indivisibility thesis or does it give a clear priority to civil and political rights?

2. How would you make the counter argument, that economic and social rights should enjoy a clear priority over civil and political rights?

3. Can you think of contradictions between the two sets of rights, i.e. situations where attention to the requirements of one set (say, civil-political rights) limits the possibilities of realizing the other?

4. In 1992 the ESCR Committee asserted that 'there is no basis whatsoever to assume that the realization of economic, social and cultural rights will necessarily result from the achievement of civil and political rights', or that democracy can be a sufficient condition for their realization unless it is accompanied by targeted policies. Is this consistent with Sen's analysis? Does it seem to you to be empirically verifiable?

5. Lee Kuan Yew, who is quoted by Sen, has long sought to defend the approach that he instituted during his many years as Prime Minister of Singapore. Consider the following description of Singaporean social policies:

> [It is government policy] not to provide direct funds to individuals in its 'welfare' programs. Instead, much is spent on education, public housing, health care and infrastructure build-up as human capital investments to enable the individual and the nation as a whole to become economically competitive in a capitalist world. . . .For those who fall through the economic net. . .public assistance is marginal and difficult to obtain. . . .The government's position is that 'helping the needy' is a moral responsibility of the community itself and not just of the state. So construed, the recipients of the moral largesse of the community are to consider themselves privileged and bear the appropriate sense of gratitude.[18]

Does such an approach give priority to economic and social rights or does it instead put economic growth ahead of both sets of rights? If Singapore were to decide to become a party to the ICESCR, would it need to change such policies?

6. Comment on the following view of the ESCR Committee:

> [The ICESCR] neither requires nor precludes any particular form of govern-

---

[18] Beng-Huat Chua, 'Australian and Asian Perceptions of Human Rights', in I. Russell, P. van Ness and Beng-Huat Chua (eds.), *Australia's Human Rights Diplomacy* (1992), at 95.

ment or economic system . . ., provided only that it is democratic and that all human rights are thereby respected. Thus, in terms of political and economic systems the Covenant is neutral and its principles cannot accurately be described as being predicated exclusively upon the need for, or the desirability of, a socialist or capitalist system, or a mixed, centrally planned, or laisser-faire economy, or upon any other particular approach . . . (General Comment No. 3 (1990), para. 8).

HUMAN RIGHTS WATCH, BROKEN PEOPLE: CASTE VIOLENCE AGAINST INDIA'S 'UNTOUCHABLES'
(1999), at 1

More than one-sixth of India's population, some 160 million people, live a precarious existence, shunned by much of society because of their rank as 'untouchables' or Dalits—literally meaning 'broken' people—at the bottom of India's caste system. Dalits are discriminated against, denied access to land, forced to work in degrading conditions, and routinely abused at the hands of the police and of higher-caste groups that enjoy the state's protection. In what has been called India's 'hidden apartheid', entire villages in many Indian states remain completely segregated by caste. National legislation and constitutional protections serve only to mask the social realities of discrimination and violence faced by those living below the 'pollution line'.

Despite the fact that 'untouchability' was abolished under India's constitution in 1950, the practice of 'untouchability'—the imposition of social disabilities on persons by reason of their birth in certain castes—remains very much a part of rural India. 'Untouchables' may not cross the line dividing their part of the village from that occupied by higher castes. They may not use the same wells, visit the same temples, drink from the same cups in tea stalls, or lay claim to land that is legally theirs. Dalit children are frequently made to sit in the back of classrooms, and communities as a whole are made to perform degrading rituals in the name of caste.

Most Dalits continue to live in extreme poverty, without land or opportunities for better employment or education. With the exception of a minority who have benefited from India's policy of quotas in education and government jobs, Dalits are relegated to the most menial of tasks, as manual scavengers, removers of human waste and dead animals, leather workers, street sweepers, and cobblers. Dalit children make up the majority of those sold into bondage to pay off debts to upper-caste creditors. Dalit men, women, and children numbering in the tens of millions work as agricultural laborers for a few kilograms of rice or Rs. 15 to Rs. 35 (US$0.38 to $0.88) a day. Their upper-caste employers frequently use caste as a cover for exploitative economic arrangements: social sanction of their status as lesser beings allows their impoverishment to continue.

Dalit women face the triple burden of caste, class, and gender. Dalit girls have been forced to become prostitutes for upper-caste patrons and village priests.

Sexual abuse and other forms of violence against women are used by landlords and the police to inflict political 'lessons' and crush dissent within the community. . . .

The plight of India's 'untouchables' elicits only sporadic attention within the country. Public outrage over large-scale incidents of violence or particularly egregious examples of discrimination fades quickly, and the state is under little pressure to undertake more meaningful reforms. Laws granting Dalits special consideration for government jobs and education reach only a small percentage of those they are meant to benefit. Laws designed to ensure that Dalits enjoy equal rights and protection have seldom been enforced. Instead, police refuse to register complaints about violations of the law and rarely prosecute those responsible for abuses that range from murder and rape to exploitative labor practices and forced displacement from Dalit lands and homes.

Political mobilization that has resulted in the emergence of powerful interest groups and political parties among middle- and low-caste groups throughout India since the mid-1980s has largely bypassed Dalits. . . .

Lacking access to mainstream political organizations and increasingly frustrated with the pace of reforms, Dalits have begun to resist subjugation and discrimination in two ways: peaceful protest and armed struggle. Particularly since the early 1990s, Dalit organizations have sought to mobilize Dalits to protest peacefully against the human rights violations suffered by their community. These movements have quickly grown in membership and visibility and have provoked a backlash from the higher-caste groups most threatened—both economically and politically—by Dalit assertiveness. Police, many of whom belong to these higher-caste groups or who enjoy their patronage, have arrested Dalit activists, including social workers and lawyers, for activity that is legal and on charges that show the police's political motivation. Dalit activists are jailed under preventive detention statutes to prevent them from holding meetings and protest rallies, or charged as 'terrorists' and 'threats to national security'. Court cases drag on for years, costing impoverished people precious money and time.

Dalits who dare to challenge the social order have been subject to abuses by their higher-caste neighbors. Dalit villages are collectively penalized for individual 'transgressions' through social boycotts, including loss of employment and access to water, grazing lands, and ration shops. For most Dalits in rural India who earn less than a subsistence living as agricultural laborers, a social boycott may mean destitution and starvation.

In some states, notably Bihar, guerrilla organizations advocating the use of violence to achieve land redistribution have attracted Dalit support.
. . .

This report is about caste, but it is also about class, gender, poverty, labor, and land. For those at the bottom of its hierarchy, caste is a determinative factor for the attainment of social, political, civil, and economic rights.
. . .

J. DRÈZE AND A. SEN, HUNGER AND PUBLIC ACTION
(1989), at 257

. . .

When it comes to enhancing basic human capabilities and, in particular, beating persistent hunger and deprivation, the role played by public support—including public delivery of health care and basic education—is hard to replace.

. . .

. . . [T]he crucial role of public support in removing endemic deprivation is visible not only in the achievements and failures of developing countries today, but also in the historical experiences of the rich and industrialized countries. This is well illustrated by the sharp increases in longevity in Britain during the decades of the world wars, which were periods of rapid expansion of public support in the form of public food distribution, employment generation and health care provisioning (not unconnected with the war efforts). There is nothing particularly ad hoc in the findings regarding the contribution of public support to human lives in the developing countries today.

Public action is not, of course, just a question of public delivery and state initiative. It is also, in a very big way, a matter of participation by the public in the process of social change. . . . [P]ublic participation can have powerful positive roles in both 'collaborative' and 'adversarial' ways vis-à-vis governmental policy. The collaboration of the public is an indispensable ingredient of public health campaigns, literacy drives, land reforms, famine relief operations, and other endeavours that call for cooperative efforts for their successful completion. On the other hand, for the initiation of these endeavours and for the government to act appropriately, adversarial pressures from the public demanding such action can be quite crucial. For this adversarial function, major contributions can be made by political activism, journalistic pressures and informed public criticism. Both types of public participation—collaborative and adversarial—are important for the conquest of famines and endemic deprivation.

To emphasize the vital role of public action in eliminating hunger in the modern world must not be taken as a general denial of the importance of incentives, nor indeed of the particular role played by the specific incentives provided by the market mechanism. Incentives are, in fact, central to the logic of public action. But the incentives that must be considered are not only those that offer profits in the market, but also those that motivate governments to implement well-planned public policies, induce families to reject intrahousehold discrimination, encourage political parties and the news media to make reasoned demands, and inspire the public at large to cooperate, criticize and coordinate. This complex set of social incentives can hardly be reduced to the narrow—though often important—role of markets and profits.

. . .

QUESTIONS

1. As the adviser to a local human rights NGO, what general governmental strategy would you suggest to respond to the problems of Dalits? Would government programmes to provide economic and social rights figure at the outset of that strategy, or at a later stage in your recommendations, or at all? Would it make sense to focus solely on civil and political rights, on the theory that such rights, when genuinely assured and exercised, will themselves open the paths toward economic and social progress?

2. 'The proposals in Drèze and Sen blur the line between provision of economic and social rights (in the classical sense of distributing food) and a range of other government policies to the point of near disappearance. It would appear that a government can satisfy the "right of everyone to. . .adequate food" stated in Article 11 of the ICESCR by long-run programs radically different from traditional notions of provision to the needy out of tax revenues gathered by the welfare state. Perhaps paragraph (2) of Article 11 says as much. Much more than redistribution through the tax system is involved. In such provisions the ICESCR reveals its potentially radical character by proposing deep structural change in economic and social institutions.' Comment.

E. JUSTICIABILITY AND THE ROLE OF COURTS IN DEVELOPING ECONOMIC AND SOCIAL RIGHTS

The accountability of governments and other entities, as well as the availability of a remedy in cases of a violation, are indispensable elements of international human rights law. Yet economic, social and cultural rights are often characterized as 'mere' programmatic rights, in the sense that they require only a general programme of measures designed to promote realization of rights. Relative to Article 2 of the ICCPR, Article 2 of the ICESCR is weak with respect to implementation. For many governments, it seems to follow that traditional legal remedies such as court actions are either inappropriate or at best impracticable. This section examines that assumption.

In the view of many observers, justiciability (i.e. whether the courts can, and at least sometimes will, provide a remedy for aggrieved individuals claiming a violation of those rights) need not be seen as an indispensable characteristic of a human right, whatever its relevance to the understanding and analysis of 'legal rights' within, say, a liberal democracy. In the clear case, the right to political participation declared in Article 25 of the ICCPR will hardly be vindicated by a court within an authoritarian regime that has long violated many provisions of that Covenant. It remains nonetheless a human right, to be vindicated in most cases through paths and strategies distinct from the formal legal system.

Despite such illustrations, programmatic approaches that depend solely upon legislatures and/or administrative agencies for the implementation of economic and social rights have left many observers, lawyers in particular, uneasy. After all, within some basic understandings and analyses of legal rights, such rights demand remedies, individual remedies.[19] The ICESCR Committee has sought to respond to this issue in two of its General Comments,[20] an excerpt from one of which follows.

COMMITTEE ON ECONOMIC, SOCIAL AND CULTURAL RIGHTS, GENERAL COMMENT NO. 9 (1998)
UN Doc. E/1999/22, Annex IV

Domestic Application of the Covenant
A. The duty to give effect to the Covenant in the domestic legal order

1. ... The central obligation in relation to the Covenant is for States parties to give effect to the rights recognized therein. By requiring governments to do so 'by all appropriate means', the Covenant adopts a broad and flexible approach which enables the particularities of the legal and administrative systems of each State, as well as other relevant considerations, to be taken into account.

2. But this flexibility co-exists with the obligation upon each State Party to use *all* the means at its disposal to give effect to the rights recognised in the Covenant. In this respect, the fundamental requirements of international human rights law must be borne in mind. Thus the norms themselves must be recognised in appropriate ways within the domestic legal order, appropriate means of redress, or remedies, must be available to any aggrieved individual or group, and appropriate means of ensuring governmental accountability must be put in place.
. . .

C. The role of legal remedies

Legal or judicial remedies?

9. The right to an effective remedy need not be interpreted as always requiring a judicial remedy. Administrative remedies will, in many cases, be adequate . . . . Any such administrative remedies should be accessible, affordable, timely, and effective. . . . [But] whenever a Covenant right cannot be made fully effective without some role for the judiciary, judicial remedies are necessary.

Justiciability

10. In relation to civil and political rights, it is generally taken for granted that judicial remedies for violations are essential. Regrettably, the contrary presumption is too often made in relation to economic, social and cultural rights. This discrepancy is not warranted either by the nature of the rights or by the relevant Covenant provisions. The Committee has already made clear that it considers many of the provisions in the Covenant to be capable of immediate implementation. Thus in General Comment No. 3 it cited, by way of example: articles 3,

---

[19] See the discussion of rights and adjudication thereof at pp. 286–299, *infra*.
[20] See also General Comment No. 3 (1990), UN Doc. E/1991/23, Annex III, paras. 5–6.

7(a)(i), 8, 10(3), 13(2)(a), 13(3), 13(4) and 15(3). It is important in this regard to distinguish between justiciability (which refers to those matters which are appropriately resolved by the courts) and norms which are self-executing (capable of being applied by courts without further elaboration). While the general approach of each legal system needs to be taken into account, there is no Covenant right which could not, in the great majority of systems, be considered to possess at least some significant justiciable dimensions. It is sometimes suggested that matters involving the allocation of resources should be left to the political authorities rather than the courts. While the respective competences of the different branches of government must be respected, it is appropriate to acknowledge that courts are generally already involved in a considerable range of matters which have important resource implications. The adoption of a rigid classification of economic, social and cultural rights which puts them, by definition, beyond the reach of the courts would thus be arbitrary and incompatible with the principle that the two sets of human rights are indivisible and interdependent. It would also drastically curtail the capacity of the courts to protect the rights of the most vulnerable and disadvantaged groups in society.

NOTE

The rights referred to by the Committee in the preceding General Comment No. 9 are equal rights of men and women (Art. 3), equal pay for equal work (Art. 7(a)(i)), the right to form and join trade unions and the right to strike (Art. 8), the right of children to special protection (Art. 10(3)), the right to free, compulsory, primary education (Art. 13(2)(a)), the liberty to choose a non-public school (Art. 13(3)), the liberty to establish schools (Art. 13(4)), and the freedom for scientific research and creative activity (Art. 15(3)). The extent to which these rights are actually justiciable varies considerably from one country to another.

In relation to the remaining rights in the ICESCR, such as the rights to work (Art. 6), health (Art. 12), food, clothing, housing (Art. 11) and education (Art. 13), Vierdag concludes a lengthy critique of the Covenant in the following terms:[21]

> What are laid down in provisions such as Articles 6, 11 and 13 of the ICESCR are consequently not rights of individuals, but broadly formulated programmes for governmental policies in the economic, social and cultural fields.
>
> It is suggested that it is misleading to adopt an instrument that by its very title and by the wording of its relevant provisions purports to grant 'rights' to individuals but in fact appears not to do so, or to do so only marginally. It is also regrettable that, in this way, a notion of 'right' is introduced into international law that is utterly different from the concept of 'right of an individual' as it is traditionally understood in international law and employed in practice . . . .

[21] E. Vierdag, 'The Legal Nature of the Rights Granted by the International Covenant on Economic, Social and Cultural Rights', 9 Neths. Ybk. Int. L. 69 (1978), at 103.

QUESTIONS

1. The first two paragraphs of the preceding Note each list a group of rights declared in the ICESCR. Should the two lists necessarily be treated similarly with respect to the issue of justiciability, i.e. either all amenable to adjudication or none amenable? Or should one draw a basic distinction between the kinds of rights in the two lists? What distinction, and what consequences might it suggest?

2. Article 8 of the Universal Declaration of Human Rights states that 'Everyone has the right to an effective remedy by the competent national tribunals for acts violating the fundamental rights granted him by the constitution or by law.' There is nothing to indicate that this was intended to apply only to civil and political rights, for of course the UDHR declares economic and social rights as well. The ICCPR (Art. 2(3)(b)) requires States parties to 'develop the possibilities of judicial remedy', but there is no equivalent provision in the ICESCR. Can Art. 2(1) of the ICESCR reasonably be interpreted as requiring the provision of judicial remedies? Or does this distinction between the two covenants speak to the issue that Vierdag raises?

NOTE

The following readings look at these questions of the constitutionalization of economic-social rights from different perspectives and take radically different approaches to the related issue of justiciability.

CÉCILE FABRE, CONSTITUTIONALISING SOCIAL RIGHTS
6 J. Polit. Phil. 263 (1998), at 280–83

... Now, the institutional logic of social rights is said to preclude their constitutionalisation because judges lack the *legitimacy* and/or the *competence* to deal with such issues. That is, it is claimed that they ought not to be allowed to adjudicate constitutional social rights because it is the democratic majority's moral right to allocate resources as they see fit, and/or they should not be allowed to adjudicate these rights because they are not equipped to do so. I shall examine these two claims in turn.

There are two reasons why one might think that the judiciary does not have the legitimacy to adjudicate constitutional social rights. First, were it to do so, it would have to interfere with the drawing of the budget, thereby encroaching upon one of the main prerogatives of the legislature.

... It may be that there are no welfare policies which give effect to constitutional social rights; or it may be that there are such policies but that they do not, or so it is claimed, give people what the constitution entitles them to get. The judiciary has two courses of actions. It can either ask the government to implement welfare policies or to allocate resources in such a way as to respect people's social rights, or it can draft policies itself and decide in great detail how resources should be allocated. I believe it should do the first; that is, it should remind the government that it is under a duty to do x: it should not tell the government *how* to fulfil this duty, precisely so as to allow for greater scope in democratic decision-making.

The second reason why it is thought that the judiciary does not have the legitimacy to adjudicate constitutional social rights is the following. . . . [R]esources are scarce and the interests protected by social rights are therefore likely to conflict. As a result, adjudicating between them requires that very difficult choices be made (who will get resources? homeless people or the sick?) which will shape what society looks like. Only the elected representatives of the people, it is argued, ought to be allowed to make those difficult choices. Now, admittedly, these may be difficult matters to deal with; however, adjudicating conflicts between interests protected by negative rights may be as difficult (how, for instance, is one to decide that someone's interest in privacy has been violated by someone else's exercise of their freedom of speech?), and if one thinks that the judiciary can adjudicate the latter conflicts on the grounds that the value of autonomy must be protected from attacks by the democratic majority then one must argue that the judiciary has legitimacy to adjudicate conflicts between the interests protected by social rights, precisely because these interests must be safeguarded for people to be autonomous.

Whether judges are competent to deal with constitutional social rights raises different issues. Judges, it is said, are not competent to ask the government to allocate resources in certain ways: they do not have the training and the information-gathering tools that are required to decide whether funds have been spent the way they should have and whether a particular individual got the resources the constitution entitles him to have. In fact, or so it is argued, faced with such difficulties, judges would be unwilling to adjudicate social rights, which would give their constitutionalisation no more than symbolic value. . . . [Judges] now increasingly assess whether resources have been allocated according to the law, most notably, in the UK, with respect to education, housing and health care, which suggests that they would not be reluctant to adjudicate constitutional social rights. These judgements are usually taken into account by governments, and have led some governments to adjust their welfare policies. This tells us two things. First, courts have not always been reluctant to adjudicate allocations of resources. Second, when they have done so, they have done so with some degree of success.

Now, it is likely that they are not always as successful as they should be. However, to bemoan this fact and reject constitutional social rights on that ground is misguided. Clearly, poring over budget reports and assessing welfare policies require some specific skills; but there is no reason why specialised judges could not be trained to acquire those skills, or could not seek advice from independent experts, as they actually already do.

[The author then asks whether judges are well placed to adjudicate individual cases and tentatively concludes that it might sometimes] be virtually impossible for them to assess whether a social right of a given *individual* has been violated. However, that is no reason to reject the constitutionalisation of social rights altogether. The government could be put under weaker constitutional constraints, which could be formulated as follows: 'the government of the day must take all steps to ensure that it satisfies social rights to minimum income, housing, education and health care, as far as it can, within the constraints of resources reasonably available to pursue them'. The judiciary would be able, I think, to make sure that the government does indeed take those steps. Furthermore, there are other ways of protecting constitutional social rights than constitutional judicial review of individual cases, which admittedly would not offer as good a protection, but would offer some protection nonetheless. For example, one might provide for group action, whereby associations of, say, homeless people, would be able to challenge government housing policies on grounds of unconstitutionality. Or one might provide for constitutional judicial *preview* of the law, as is the case in France and in the Republic of Ireland. . . .

CASS SUNSTEIN, AGAINST POSITIVE RIGHTS
2/1 East Eur. Constit'al Rev. 35 (1993)

. . .

If we look at the actual and proposed constitutions for Eastern Europe, we will find a truly dazzling array of social and economic rights. . . .

I think that this is a large mistake, possibly a disaster. It seems clear that Eastern European countries should use their constitutions to produce two things: (a) firm liberal rights—free speech, voting rights, protection against abuse of the criminal justice system, religious liberty, barriers to invidious discrimination, property and contract rights; and (b) the preconditions for some kind of market economy. The endless catalogue of what I will be calling 'positive rights', many of them absurd, threatens to undermine both of these important tasks.

Three qualifications are necessary at the outset. First, the argument against these rights applies with distinctive force to countries in the unique position of transition from Communism to a market economy. Other countries, especially in the West, are in a much different situation, and here it is by no means clear that social and economic rights would be harmful. . . .

Second, there is a big difference between what a decent society should provide and what a good constitution should guarantee. A decent society ensures that its citizens have food and shelter; it tries to guarantee medical care; it is concerned to offer good education, good jobs, and a clean environment. . . . If the Constitution tries to specify everything to which a decent society commits itself, it threatens to become a mere piece of paper, worth nothing in the real world. . . . Opposition to social and economic rights in the Constitution does not entail a belief that nations in Eastern Europe should eliminate social and economic programs that provide crucial protection against the vicissitudes of the free market.

Third, not all positive rights are the same. The right to education, for example, is more readily subject to judicial enforcement than the right to a clean environment. Some of the relevant rights pose especially severe risks; others are relatively harmless. But I believe that few of them belong in Eastern European constitutions. Here's why:

Governments should not be compelled to interfere with free markets. Some positive rights establish government interference with free markets as a constitutional obligation. For countries that are trying to create market economies, this is perverse. A constitution that prevents the operation of free labor markets may defeat current aspirations in Eastern Europe. Recall that the Hungarian Constitution protects not merely the right to equal pay for equal work, but also the right to an income conforming with the quantity and quality of work performed. This provision will have one of two consequences. (a) If the provision is to mean something, courts will have to oversee labor markets very closely, [in which case] it will be impossible to have a labor market. (b) The relevant provisions will be ignored—treated as goals or aspirations not subject to legal enforcement. . . .

The Hungarian provision is an extreme example, but similar problems are raised by provisions calling for specified maximum hours, for paid parental leave, for paid holidays, and much else. Many of these provisions may make sense if they are placed in ordinary legislation. But this is where they belong—not in the constitution. The constitution should not undertake close control of the private sphere, of civil society and economic markets. . . . Perhaps some small companies in the East should be allowed to get ahead by paying their workers a great deal in return for long hours, or for less in the way of leave; perhaps not. Perhaps medical care should not be free—especially for people who have the money to pay for it. These issues should be subject to democratic debate, not constitutional foreclosure.

Many positive rights are unenforceable by courts. Courts lack the tools of a bureaucracy. They cannot create government programs. They do not have a systematic overview of government policy. In these circumstances, it is unrealistic to expect courts to enforce many positive rights. . . . One of the enduring legacies of Communism is a large degree of cynicism about constitutions—a belief that constitutions may be pretty, but that they do not have meaning in the real world. If the right to 'the highest possible level of physical health' is not subject to judicial enforcement, perhaps the same will become true of the right to free speech and to due process of law.

The inclusion of many positive rights could work against general current effort to diminish sense of entitlement to state protection and to encourage individual initiative. . . . [I]f positive dispensations from the state are seen as a matter of individual entitlement, there can be corrosive effects on individual enterprise and initiative. This effect can be seen in both the West and the East. The risk of corrosion is no reason to eliminate programs that provide for subsistence. But in today's Eastern Europe, it is important to undertake a cultural shift through which people will look less to the state for their support, and more to their own efforts and enterprise. . . . A constitution that indiscriminately merges guarantees of 'just pay' and 'recreation' with traditional liberal rights is likely to send just the wrong signals.
. . .

In these circumstances, what ought to be done? I suggest three routes for the future. First, people now drafting constitutions for Eastern Europe should delete or minimize provisions that call for positive rights. . . .

Second, [they] might put the positive rights in a separate section, . . . making clear that such rights are not for judicial enforcement, that they occupy a separate status, and that they are intended to set out general aspirations for public officials and for the citizenry at large.

Third, judges and lawyers in Eastern Europe . . . might adopt the notion that rights are 'nonjusticiable'—not subject to judicial enforcement—when they call for large-scale interference with the operation of free markets, or when they call for managerial tasks not within judicial competence. Any such notion must, however, make it clear that courts will vigorously enforce the basic political and civil rights whose violation was a daily affair under Communist rule—rights such as free speech, religious liberty, freedom from police abuse, due process, and nondiscrimination on grounds of ethnicity, race, religion, and sex.

QUESTIONS

1. What desirable goals might human rights proponents expect the constitutional recognition of economic and social rights to achieve? Are there ways of mitigating the negative consequences that Sunstein describes?

2. Sunstein refers to some positive rights as absurd. Which rights might they be? The right to periodic holidays with pay has often been cited as evidence of the utopian and counter-productive concepts enshrined in the ICESCR. Why is it included in the Covenant, and is it in your view symptomatic of what might be wrong with the Covenant?

3. Fabre's proposed formulation looks rather like the obligation expressed in Article 2(1) of the ICESCR. Take some current examples of welfare policy in your country and reflect on whether they could be impugned on the basis of such a formulation.

4. Since at least 1992 the Israeli Knesset (parliament) has been considering various proposals for a Basic Law dealing with social rights. In 1997, the Ministry of Justice proposed the inclusion of the following formulation in such a law:

> The State of Israel will pursue the promotion and development of the conditions required for the guarantee of an existence worthy of human dignity to all residents, including, in this respect, matters of employment, education, health, housing, social welfare and environment, as determined by law or in accordance [with] the law or governmental decisions.

How would you evaluate this proposal, taking account of the fact that Israel is a party to the ICESCR?

. . .

NOTE

Although there is no formal requirement in the ICESCR that economic and social rights be constitutionally enshrined by states, there are many examples of such provisions. While the façade constitutions of the Soviet Union and other Communist states of the pre-1989 period are often cited in order to discredit such an approach, the practice is far more widespread than this reference point might suggest. Even in the United States, for example, the right to education is recognized in the constitutions of many of the 50 component states.[22]

The following materials emphasize the experience of courts in India and South Africa in deciding cases involving claims based on rights to housing and health. Note that the issues arise in these cases under state constitutions rather than under the ICESCR. Nonetheless, the decisions have an obvious bearing on international human rights, for the issues raised are close to those that would be encountered by courts in most countries seeking to give effect within domestic law to, say, Article 11 of the Covenant.

When reading these decisions, bear in mind several aspects of the question of justiciability that underlie some of the courts' discussion.

(1) Are the rights as recognized in the ICESCR formulated in a manner that is sufficiently precise to enable judges to apply them in concrete cases?

(2) To the extent that such cases will involve decisions about public spending priorities, should such decisions remain the exclusive domain of the executive and legislature?

(3) Are judges well suited in terms of their expertise, social and political background and the facilities available to them to make such decisions?

(4) Does the justiciability test need to be applied to issues of economic and social rights in a narrow, traditional manner, or are there more creative approaches, still involving the courts in some way, which would satisfy those demanding formal, institutionalized measures of implementation for economic and social rights?

COMMENT ON INDIA AND 'DIRECTIVE PRINCIPLES'

In India the concept of 'directive principles of state policy' was originally developed in contra-distinction to that of 'fundamental rights'. Such principles are considered to be distinct from, and usually inferior in status to, rights that appear in the constitution without the qualification 'directive'. They appear in different forms in diverse constitutions including those of Ireland, Papua New Guinea and Nigeria. The Indian experience holds the greatest interest for our purposes. The Indian Constitution of 1950 contains one chapter dealing with 'fundamental rights' which consists largely of civil and political rights which figure in litigation as do a great range of legal claims, and another chapter dealing with 'directive principles of state policy'. Some illustrations from the Constitution follow.

---

[22] Allen Hubsch, 'Note: The Emerging Right to Education under State Constitutional Law', 65 Temple L. Rev. 1325 (1992).

Part III. Fundamental Rights

. . .

Article 21. No person shall be deprived of his life or personal liberty except according to procedure established by law.

. . .

Part IV. Directive Principles of State Policy

. . .

Article 37. The provisions contained in this Part shall not be enforced by any court, but the principles therein laid down are nevertheless fundamental in the governance of the country and it shall be the duty of the State to apply these principles in making laws.

Article 39. The State shall, in particular, direct its policy towards securing—

   (a) that the citizens, men and women equally, have the right to an adequate means of livelihood;

   (b) that the ownership and control of the material resources of the community are so distributed as best to subserve the common good;

   (c) that the operation of the economic system does not result in the concentration of wealth and means of production to the common detriment;

   (d) that there is equal pay for equal work for both men and women;

   (e) that the health and strength of workers, men and women, and the tender age of children are not abused and that citizens are not forced by economic necessity to enter avocations unsuited to their age or strength;

   (f) that children are given opportunities and facilities to develop in a healthy manner and in conditions of freedom and dignity and that childhood and youth are protected against exploitation and against moral and material abandonment.

. . .

Article 41. The State shall, within the limits of its economic capacity and development, make effective provision for securing the right to work, to education and to public assistance in cases of unemployment, old age, sickness and disablement, and in other cases of undeserved want.

. . .

Article 47. The State shall regard the raising of the level of nutrition and the standard of living of its people and the improvement of public health as among its primary duties . . .

Over the years the Indian courts as well as the legislature have redefined the relationship between fundamental rights and directive principles. The important element in the present context is the extent to which the directive principles have gone from being clearly non-justiciable to their providing the basis of a right of action at first instance before the Indian Supreme Court. The relationship between the two has been summarized as follows:

The Supreme Court has gone through various phases in interpreting the relationship between fundamental rights and directive principles. Initially there was a firm adherence to the supremacy of fundamental rights. After several constitutional amendments, public debate and disputes over court decisions, the

Supreme Court has adopted a more balanced and integrated approach in order to interpret harmoniously the two chapters.[23]

UPENDRA BAXI, JUDICIAL DISCOURSE: THE DIALECTICS OF THE FACE AND THE MASK
35 J. of the Indian Law Institute 1 (1993), at 7

[In this reading Baxi describes the way in which the directive principles have been used in the context of what is sometimes called 'public interest litigation', or what he prefers to term 'social action litigation' (SAL).]

... The procedure is that of epistolary jurisdiction, where letters written by ordinary citizens to courts get converted into writ petitions. And these letters do not allege violation of fundamental rights of their authors; the authors allege such violation of the rights of the impoverished groups of Indian society—be they people in custody, victims of police violence, forced, bonded, migrant, contract labour, child workers, rickshaw pullers, hawkers, self-employed people, pensioners, pavement dwellers, slum dwellers, fishermen or Sri Lankan Tamils used as bonded labourers. The law of standing, that is persons who can bring complaints of rights-violation, has been thus revolutionised; and access to constitutional justice has been fully democratised.

The second major procedural innovation brought in by SAL is the collection of social data and legal evidence concerning the plight of these impoverished groups. Courts now appoint socio-legal commissions of public citizens, social scientists and others to examine the conditions alleged to be violative of people's rights; and the reports of the commission, constituted at state expense, provide the material for doing justice. Increasingly, universities and research institutes are directed by the court to function as commissions.
...

The third major aspect of the SAL is in the area of relief. Compensation and rehabilitation for victims deprived of their fundamental rights now constitute a constitutional right; the Supreme Court undertook a detailed monitoring of the rehabilitation of the blinded of Bhagalpur and since then has fashioned many a measure of compensation and rehabilitation; it has ordered the administration of theosuplhate injections to the Bhopal victims and upheld the constitutional validity of the Bhopal Act by reading into it the obligation to provide monthly interim relief ... ; it has provided elaborate directives for treatment of prisoners and undertrials in jails; it has given specific directives for humane and just conditions of work for migrant workers and forced labourers.

The fourth salient aspect of the SAL is the development of constitutional jurisprudence itself. The right to compensation for violation of fundamental rights is now fully emergent. Indians have now a right to speedy trial though nowhere

---

[23] De Villiers, 'The Socio-Economic Consequences of Directive Principles of State Policy: Limitations on Fundamental Rights', 8 S. Af. J. Hum. Rts. 188 (1992), at 198.

explicitly formulated by the Constitution. The custodial inmates have a right to dignity and immunity from cruel, unusual or degrading treatment . . . . Above all, the jurisprudence of SAL insists on a simple postulate of civilized jurisprudence: administration shall act in accordance with the law and the Constitution. This is a monumental achievement of SAL jurisprudence . . .

Fifth, without being exhaustive, the SAL processes have at times resulted in a mini-takeover of the administrative regime of certain institutions of administration, which have displayed a congenital inability to work in accordance with the law and the Constitution. The most conspicuous illustration of this, perhaps, is the Agra Protective Home for Women, virtually run by the judiciary for well over ten years. The Supreme Court is doing its best to enable, by constant invigilation, the State of Bihar to ensure proper prison administration, to the point of maintenance of the record of undertrial and convict populations in the various jails of Bihar. In environmental cases, the Supreme Court has ordered the closure or monitored the pollution potential of private industries. The State High Courts have not lagged behind in these and related areas.

. . .

But when, at the end of the day, judicial orders arrive, the executive is left with a series of rather painful choices. To implement them is to engage in tasks of renovation of power which the executive loathes in the first place: e.g., appointment of vigilance committees under the bonded labour law, prosecution of officers allegedly guilty of blindings, torture and tyrannies, expansion of the minimum wage of factories inspectorate, avoidance of sex-based discrimination in public works, including famine relief, running of remand homes for women and juvenile institutions in accordance with its own declared laws and policies, and reformation of jails. The SAL outcomes are not perceived as opportunities to reshape power but rather as obstacles in the exercise of real power.

. . .

. . . Constitutional adjudication in SAL becomes, then, a dialogue between judiciary and executive on the nature of public power and its public purposes. The executive has yet to accept the role of the pupil, although the courts have all too eagerly donned the didactic robes of pedagogues for democracy and constitutionalism.

OLGA TELLIS v. BOMBAY MUNICIPAL CORPORATION
Supreme Court of India, 1985
AIR 1986 Supreme Court 18

CHANDRACHUD, C.

1. These Writ Petitions portray the plight of lakhs [hundreds of thousands] of persons who live on pavements and in slums in the city of Bombay. They constitute nearly half the population of the city. The first group of petitions relates to pavement dwellers while the second group relates to both pavement and Basti or slum dwellers. Those who have made pavements their homes exist in the midst of

filth and squalor, which has to be seen to be believed. Rabid dogs in search of stinking meat and cats in search of hungry rats keep them company. They cook and sleep where they ease, for no conveniences are available to them. Their daughters come of age, bathe under the nosy gaze of passers by, unmindful of the feminine sense of bashfulness. The cooking and washing over, women pick lice from each other's hair. The boys beg. Menfolk without occupation snatch chains with the connivance of the defenders of law and order; when caught, if at all, they say: 'Who doesn't commit crimes in this city?'

It is these men and women who have come to this Court to ask for a judgment that they cannot be evicted from their squalid shelters without being offered alternative accommodation. They rely for their rights on Art. 21 of the Constitution which guarantees that no person shall be deprived of his life except according to procedure established by law. They do not contend that they have a right to live on the pavements. Their contention is that they have a right to live, a right which cannot be exercised without the means of livelihood. They have no option but to flock to big cities like Bombay, which provide the means of bare subsistence. They only choose a pavement or a slum which is nearest to their place of work. In a word, their plea is that the right to life is illusory without a right to the protection of the means by which alone life can be lived. And, the right of life can only be taken away or abridged by a procedure established by law, which has to be fair and reasonable, not fanciful or arbitrary such as is prescribed by the Bombay Municipal Corporation Act or the Bombay Police Act. . . .

[The petitioners in the two batches of Writ Petitions included pavement dwellers and slum residents, as well as a journalist and civil liberties organizations. The typical petitioner was a landless labourer in rural areas unable to find a job and moving to Bombay to find work even at extremely low wages. In one instance described by the Court, the Chief Minister of Maharashtra (the state including Bombay) announced that all pavement dwellers would be evicted and deported to their places of origin, and directed respondent Bombay Municipal Corporation to demolish pavement dwellings and evict the dwellers. He explained: 'It is a very inhuman existence. These structures are flimsy and open to the elements. During the monsoon there is no way these people can live comfortably'. When one petitioner's shelter was demolished, he like many others returned and rebuilt it. The Court observed: 'It is like a game of hide and seek. . . . Their main attachment to those places is the nearness thereof to their place of work'.

Petitioners claimed that the decision to demolish violated, among other provisions, Article 21 of the Constitution. They sought a declaration that relevant provisions of the Bombay Municipal Corporation Act also violated Article 21 and sought appropriate relief, including restoration of the sites to their former occupants.

The counter-affidavits of the Government of Maharashtra, the Bombay Municipal Corporation and other respondents raised numerous issues, including: No person has a legal right to encroach on a public right of way; numerous hazards of health and safety thereby arise, from human filth to anti-social acts like theft and prostitution and generally increased criminal tendencies. The Government asserted that it provided housing assistance to weaker elements of society, but 'any allocation for housing has to be made after balancing the conflicting demands from various priority sectors. The paucity of resources is a restraining factor on the ability of the State to deal effectively' with housing issues. The Government's broad policy was to reverse the rate of growth of large cities and disperse people to small and medium towns. The Government described its various welfare pro-grammes and expenses for housing, and observed:

> The phenomenon of poverty has to be tackled on an All-India basis by making the gains of development available to all sections of the society through a policy of equitable distribution of income and wealth. Urbanisation is a major problem facing the entire country, the migration of people from the rural to the urban areas being a reflection of the colossal poverty existing in the rural areas. The rural poverty cannot, however, be eliminated by increasing the pressure of popu-lation on metropolitan cities like Bombay.

Other Maharashtra officials stated in their affidavits that the state had put certain vacant lands aside near Bombay for re-settlement of the slum dwellers, and that it was the state's policy 'to provide alternative accommodation' to certain slum dwellers who had been 'censused' and who possessed identity cards.

After a detailed account of the arguments and statistical information set forth in the pleadings, the Court stated its views.]

. . .

32. . . . For purposes of argument, we will assume the factual correctness of the premise that if the petitioners are evicted from their dwellings, they will be deprived of their livelihood. Upon that assumption, the question which we have to consider is whether the right to life includes the right to livelihood. We see only one answer to that question, namely, that it does. The sweep of the right to life conferred by Art. 21 is wide and far-reaching. It does not mean merely that life cannot be extinguished or taken away as, for example, by the imposition and execution of the death sentence, except according to procedure established by law. That is but one aspect of the right to life. An equally important facet of that right is the right to livelihood because, no person can live without the means of living, that is, the means of livelihood. If the right to livelihood is not treated as a part of the constitutional right to life, the easiest way of depriving a person of his right to life would be to deprive him of his means of livelihood to the point of abrogation. . . . That, which alone makes it possible to live, leave aside what makes life livable, must be deemed to be an integral component of the right to life. Deprive a person of his right to livelihood and you shall have deprived him of his life. Indeed, that explains the massive migration of the rural population to big cities. . . .

33. Article 39(a) of the Constitution, which is a Directive Principle of State Policy, provides that the State shall, in particular, direct its policy towards securing that the citizens, men and women equally, have the right to an adequate means of livelihood. Art. 41, which is another Directive Principle, provides, inter alia, that the State shall, within the limits of its economic capacity and development, make

effective provision for securing the right to work in cases of unemployment and of undeserved want. Article 37 provides that the Directive Principles, though not enforceable by any Court, are nevertheless fundamental in the governance of the country. The Principles contained in Arts. 39(a) and 41 must be regarded as equally fundamental in the understanding and interpretation of the meaning and content of fundamental rights. If there is an obligation upon the State to secure to the citizens an adequate means of livelihood and the right to work, it would be sheer pedantry to exclude the right to livelihood from the content of the right to life. The State may not, by affirmative action, be compellable to provide adequate means of livelihood or work to the citizens. But, any person, who is deprived of his right to livelihood except according to just and fair procedure established by law, can challenge the deprivation as offending the right to life conferred by Art. 21.
. . .

35. . . . It would be unrealistic on our part to reject the petitions on the ground that the petitioners have not adduced evidence to show that they will be rendered jobless if they are evicted from the slums and pavements. Commonsense, which is a cluster of life's experiences, is often more dependable than the rival facts presented by warring litigants.
. . .

37. Two conclusions emerge from this discussion: one, that the right to life which is conferred by Art. 21 includes the right to livelihood and two, that it is established that if the petitioners are evicted from their dwellings, they will be deprived of their livelihood. But the Constitution does not put an absolute embargo on the deprivation of life or personal liberty. By Art. 21, such deprivation has to be according to procedure established by law. In the instant case, the law which allows the deprivation of the right conferred by Art. 21 is the Bombay Municipal Corporation Act. . . .

[The opinion referred to sections of that Act prohibiting structures causing obstruction in streets, and (Section 314) authorizing removal of such structures by the Commissioner 'without notice'. Petitioners claimed that authority to cause demolition 'without notice' (no notice was given or hearing was held in this case) made the procedure 'arbitrary and unreasonable'.

The Court stated that it was 'essential that the procedure prescribed by law for depriving a person of his fundamental right [under Article 21], in this case the right to life, must conform to the norms of justice and fairplay'. It had no doubt that the general procedure for removal spelled out in Article 314 'cannot be regarded as unreasonable, unfair or unjust'. Public properties intended for the convenience of the general public had to be protected against interfering private use. Putting up a dwelling on the pavement amounted to a trespass.

But the provision about notice was troubling. Article 314 did not forbid notice; it gave the Commissioner discretion to proceed without notice. It had to be construed to authorize action without notice only sparingly and in the exceptional case (such as need for speed), for failure to give notice excluded 'principles of natural justice'. Respondents had argued that no hearing was necessary to trespassers on public property, who indeed committed a crime in so doing. But, said the Court, petitioners had used public properties for an unauthorized purpose not to commit an offence or annoy anyone but

> to find a habitat in places which are mostly filthy or marshy, out of sheer help-lessness. It is not as if they have a free choice to exercise. . . . The encroachments . . . are involuntary acts in that sense that those acts are compelled by inevitable circumstances and are not guided by choice.

Notice would give opportunity for response and argument, for dialogue preceding the eviction action which might thereby be judged to be arbitrary. It heightened the chance of law observance and accuracy of judgment of the state authority. Hence the procedure followed in this case was defective.

The Court stated that it normally would have directed the Municipal Corporation to afford petitioners a hearing to show why their encroachments on pavements should not be removed. 'But the opportunity which was denied by the Commissioner was granted by us in an ample measure, both sides having made their contentions elaborately. . . .' In the light of those contentions, the Court concluded that the Commissioner 'was justified in directing the removal of the encroachments'. Judicial relief was however necessary in view of the failure of notice and the related hearing at which petitioners could have presented arguments and statistics such as those presented before the Court. Hence the Court proposed 'to pass an order which, we believe, [the Commissioner] would or should have passed, had he granted a hearing to them and heard what we did'. The opinion continued:]

> 55. . . . [W]hat is of crucial importance to the question of thinning out the squatters' colonies in metropolitan cities is to create new opportunities for employment in the rural sector and to spread the existing job opportunities evenly in urban areas. Apart from the further misery and degradation which it involves, eviction of slum and pavement dwellers is an ineffective remedy for decongesting the cities. In a highly readable and moving account of the problems which the poor have to face, Susan George says (*How the other Half Dies—The Real Reasons for World Hunger* (Pelican Books)):

> > So long as thorough-going land reform, re-grouping and distribution of resources to the poorest, bottom half of the population does not take place, Third World countries can go on increasing their production until hell freezes and hunger will remain, for the production will go to those who already have plenty—to the developed world or to the wealthy in the Third World itself. Poverty and hunger walk hand in hand. (Page 18).

> 56. We will close with a quotation from the same book which has a message:

> > Malnourished babies, wasted mothers, emaciated corpses in the streets of Asia have definite and definable reasons for existing. Hunger may have been the human race's constant companion and 'the poor may always be with us', but in the twentieth century, one cannot take this fatalistic view of the destiny of

millions of fellow creatures. Their condition is not inevitable but is caused by identifiable forces within the province of rational human control. (p. 15)

57. To summarise, . . . pavement dwellers who were censused or who happened to be censused in 1976 should be given, though not as a condition precedent to their removal, alternate pitches at Malavani or at such other convenient place as the Government considers reasonable but not farther away in terms of distance; slum dwellers who were given identity cards and whose dwellings were numbered in the 1976 census must be given alternate sites for the resettlement: slums which have been in existence for a long time, say for twenty years or more, and which have been improved and developed will not be removed unless the land on which they stand or the appurtenant land, is required for a public purpose, in which case, alternate sites or accommodation will be provided to them: the 'Low Income Scheme Shelter Programme' which is proposed to be undertaken with the aid of the World Bank will be pursued earnestly: and, the 'Slum Upgradation Programme (SUP)' under which basic amenities are to be given to slum dwellers will be implemented without delay. In order to minimise the hardship involved in any eviction, we direct that the slums, wherever situated, will not be removed until one month after the end of the current monsoon season, that is, until October 31, 1985 and, thereafter, only in accordance with this judgment. . . .

QUESTIONS

1. 'Courts overstep their proper roles by making radical interpretations of constitutional terms that expand both state duties and courts' power. The *Olga Tellis* decision reads a right to livelihood or work at a living wage (an economic-social right) into the right to life (a classic civil-political right), and moreover ties housing to the right to a livelihood. It thereby converts a "directive principle" into a "fundamental right". In light of this decision, every economic-social right that contributes importantly to an adequate life becomes part of the right to life. What economic and social planning now stands outside a court's jurisdiction? The court has become the legislature of the welfare state.' Comment, as applied to the *Olga Tellis* decision.

2. Does the Court interpret the right to life to give all persons a right to employment, to a living wage, to a home? If so, are these rights absolute, or are they subject to limitations? What kinds of limitations? Which state institutions decide on the content of the right and the limitations? What seems to be the role of courts?

3. The opinion, including its quotations from other sources, suggests a range of ways in which a state might satisfy the relevant constitutional provisions. What might they be? Do they involve measures other than direct state provision of, say, employment or housing?

4. Compare Articles 39(a) and 41 of the Indian Constitution with Articles 2, 6 and 7 of the ICESCR. Are they equivalent with respect to the obligations put on the state, or are there significant differences between them?

5. Suppose that the petitioners had relied on the ICESCR as well as the Indian Constitution, and that the Court decided the case by applying both the Constitution (which it did) and Articles 2, 6, 7 and 11 of the ICESCR. Should the decision and the orders set forth at the end of the opinion have remained the same with respect to application of the ICESCR?

6. As a human rights advocate, would you welcome this opinion or view it as a defeat for your cause? What parts of it might be helpful to support your position in future advocacy?

7. In light of the Indian SAL experience as described by Baxi, is it desirable for 'constitutional adjudication' to have become 'a dialogue between judiciary and executive on the nature of public power and its public purposes'? From the perspective of promoting human rights, is it desirable for the judiciary to have 'donned the didactic roles of pedagogues for democracy and constitutionalism'? What do you think would be the symptoms of the Indian Supreme Court's failure 'to evolve PIL [Public Interest Litigation] on a sound jurisprudential footing'?

NOTE

When South Africa's post-apartheid constitution was being debated, consideration was given to following the directive principles approach in relation to social rights. This was rejected, however, and full constitutional recognition was accorded to them. In its judgment in the *Soobramoney* case below, the South African Constitutional Court explored the limits of the right not to be refused medical treatment. It referred in particular to an Indian case, *Samity*, which dealt with a similar issue. Key provisions of the Constitution (1996) are provided below, followed by excerpts from the two cases.

Chapter 1 Founding Provisions
Section 1.
The Republic of South Africa is one sovereign democratic state founded on the following values:

(a) Human dignity, the achievement of equality and the advancement of human rights and freedoms.

. . .

Chapter 2 Bill of Rights
Section 7. Rights
(1) This Bill of Rights is a cornerstone of democracy in South Africa. It enshrines the rights of all people in our country and affirms the democratic values of human dignity, equality and freedom.
(2) The state must respect, protect, promote and fulfil the rights in the Bill of Rights.
(3) The rights in the Bill of Rights are subject to the limitations contained or referred to in section 36, or elsewhere in the Bill.

. . .

Section 10. Human dignity.

Everyone has inherent dignity and the right to have their dignity respected and protected.

Section 11. Life

Everyone has the right to life.

. . .

Section 27. Health care, food, water and social security

(1) Everyone has the right to have access to—

(a) health care services, including reproductive health care;
(b) sufficient food and water; and
(c) social security, including, if they are unable to support themselves and their dependants, appropriate social assistance.

(2) The state must take reasonable legislative and other measures, within its available resources, to achieve the progressive realisation of each of these rights.

(3) No one may be refused emergency medical treatment.

. . .

Section 39. Interpretation of Bill of Rights

(1) When interpreting the Bill of Rights, a court, tribunal or forum—

(a) must promote the values that underlie an open and democratic society based on human dignity, equality and freedom;
(b) must consider international law; and
(c) may consider foreign law.

(2) When interpreting any legislation, and when developing the common law or customary law, every court, tribunal or forum must promote the spirit, purport, and objects of the Bill of Rights.

SOOBRAMONEY v. MINISTER OF HEALTH (KWAZULU-NATAL)

Constitutional Court of South Africa, Case CCT 32/97, 27 November 1997

www.law.wits.ac.za/judgements/soobram.html

CHASKALSON P:

[1] The appellant, a 41 year old unemployed man, is a diabetic who suffers from ischaemic heart disease and cerebro-vascular disease which caused him to have a stroke during 1996. In 1996 his kidneys also failed. Sadly his condition is irreversible and he is now in the final stages of chronic renal failure. His life could be prolonged by means of regular renal dialysis. He has sought such treatment from the renal unit of the Addington state hospital in Durban. The hospital can, however, only provide dialysis treatment to a limited number of patients. The renal unit has 20 dialysis machines available to it, and some of these machines are in poor condition. Each treatment takes four hours and a further two hours have to be allowed for the cleaning of a machine, before it can be used again for other treatment. Because of the limited facilities that are available for kidney dialysis the

hospital has been unable to provide the appellant with the treatment he has requested.

[2] ... Additional dialysis machines and more trained nursing staff are required to enable it to do this, but the hospital budget does not make provision for such expenditure. The hospital would like to have its budget increased but it has been told by the provincial health department that funds are not available for this purpose.

[3] Because of the shortage of resources the hospital follows a set policy in regard to the use of the dialysis resources. Only patients who suffer from acute renal failure, which can be treated and remedied by renal dialysis are given automatic access to renal dialysis at the hospital. Those patients who, like the appellant, suffer from chronic renal failure which is irreversible are not admitted automatically to the renal programme. A set of guidelines has been drawn up and adopted to determine which applicants who have chronic renal failure will be given dialysis treatment. ...

[The opinion noted that under these guidelines that stress the long-run prospects of those seeking dialysis, appellant did not qualify for such treatment. He alleged that he could not afford treatment at private hospitals, and he sought a judicial order directing Addington Hospital to provide the necessary treatment. His application was dismissed, and he then applied for leave to appeal to the Constitutional Court. His claim was based on sections 27(3) and 11 of the 1996 Constitution, *supra.*

The Court stressed the great disparities in wealth in South Africa, and the deplorable conditions and poverty in which millions of people lived, including lack of access to adequate health facilities. It referred to the commitment in the preamble of the Constitution to address these issues 'and to transform our society into one in which there will be human dignity, freedom and equality. . .', and to Sections 26 and 27, *supra.*]

. . .

[11] What is apparent from these provisions is that the obligations imposed on the state by sections 26 and 27 in regard to access to housing, health care, food, water and social security are dependent upon the resources available for such purposes, and that the corresponding rights themselves are limited by reason of the lack of resources. Given this lack of resources and the significant demands on them that have already been referred to, an unqualified obligation to meet these needs would not presently be capable of being fulfilled. This is the context within which section 27(3) must be construed.

[14] Counsel for the appellant argued that section 27(3) should be construed consistently with the right to life entrenched in section 11 of the Constitution and that everyone requiring life-saving treatment who is unable to pay for such treatment herself or himself is entitled to have the treatment provided at a state hospital without charge.

[15] This Court has dealt with the right to life in the context of capital punishment but it has not yet been called upon to decide upon the parameters of the

right to life or its relevance to the positive obligations imposed on the state under various provisions of the bill of rights. In India the Supreme Court has developed a jurisprudence around the right to life so as to impose positive obligations on the state in respect of the basic needs of its inhabitants. Whilst the Indian jurisprudence on this subject contains valuable insights it is important to bear in mind that our Constitution is structured differently to the Indian Constitution. Unlike the Indian Constitution ours deals specifically in the bill of rights with certain positive obligations imposed on the state, and where it does so, it is our duty to apply the obligations as formulated in the Constitution and not to draw inferences that would be inconsistent therewith.

[16] This should be done in accordance with the purposive approach to the interpretation of the Constitution which has been adopted by this Court. . . .

[17] The purposive approach will often be one which calls for a generous interpretation to be given to a right to ensure that individuals secure the full protection of the bill of rights, but this is not always the case, and the context may indicate that in order to give effect to the purpose of a particular provision 'a narrower or specific meaning' should be given to it.

[18] In developing his argument on the right to life counsel for the appellant relied upon a decision of a two-judge bench of the Supreme Court of India in *Paschim Banga Khet Mazdoor Samity and others v. State of West Bengal and another*, where it was said:

> The Constitution envisages the establishment of a welfare State at the federal level as well as at the State level. In a welfare State the primary duty of the Government is to secure the welfare of the people. Providing adequate medical facilities for the people is an essential part of the obligations undertaken by the Government in a welfare State. The Government discharges this obligation by running hospitals and health centres which provide medical care to the person seeking to avail those facilities. Article 21 imposes an obligation on the State to safeguard the right to life of every person. Preservation of human life is thus of paramount importance. The Government hospitals run by the State and the medical officers employed therein are duty bound to extend medical assistance for preserving human life. Failure on the part of a Government hospital to provide timely medical treatment to a person in need of such treatment results in violation of his right to life guaranteed under Article 21.

These comments must be seen in the context of the facts of that case which are materially different to those of the present case. It was a case in which constitutional damages were claimed. The claimant had suffered serious head injuries and brain haemorrhage as a result of having fallen off a train. He was taken to various hospitals and turned away, either because the hospital did not have the necessary facilities for treatment, or on the grounds that it did not have room to accommodate him. As a result he had been obliged to secure the necessary treatment at a private hospital. It appeared from the judgment that the claimant could in fact have been accommodated in more than one of the hospitals which turned him away and that the persons responsible for that decision had been guilty of misconduct. This is precisely the sort of case which would fall within section 27(3).

It is one in which emergency treatment was clearly necessary. The occurrence was sudden, the patient had no opportunity of making arrangements in advance for the treatment that was required, and there was urgency in securing the treatment in order to stabilize his condition. The treatment was available but denied.

[19] In our Constitution the right to medical treatment does not have to be inferred from the nature of the state established by the Constitution or from the right to life which it guarantees. It is dealt with directly in section 27. If section 27(3) were to be construed in accordance with the appellant's contention it would make it substantially more difficult for the state to fulfill its primary obligations under sections 27(1) and (2) to provide health care services to 'everyone' within its available resources. It would also have the consequence of prioritising the treatment of terminal illnesses over other forms of medical care and would reduce the resources available to the state for purposes such as preventative health care and medical treatment for persons suffering from illnesses or bodily infirmities which are not life threatening. In my view much clearer language than that used in section 27(3) would be required to justify such a conclusion.

[20] Section 27(3) itself is couched in negative terms—it is a right not to be refused emergency treatment. The purpose of the right seems to be to ensure that treatment be given in an emergency, and is not frustrated by reason of bureaucratic requirements or other formalities. A person who suffers a sudden catastrophe which calls for immediate medical attention, such as the injured person in *Paschim Banga Khet Mazdoor Samity v. State of West Bengal,* should not be refused ambulance or other emergency services which are available and should not be turned away from a hospital which is able to provide the necessary treatment. What the section requires is that remedial treatment that is necessary and available be given immediately to avert that harm.

[21] The applicant suffers from chronic renal failure. To be kept alive by dialysis he would require such treatment two to three times a week. This is not an emergency which calls for immediate remedial treatment. It is an ongoing state of affairs resulting from a deterioration of the applicant's renal function which is incurable. In my view section 27(3) does not apply to these facts.

[22] The appellant's demand to receive dialysis treatment at a state hospital must be determined in accordance with the provisions of sections 27(1) and (2) and not section 27(3). These sections entitle everyone to have access to health care services provided by the state 'within its available resources'.

. . .

[24] At present the Department of Health in KwaZulu-Natal does not have sufficient funds to cover the cost of the services which are being provided to the public. In 1996–1997 it overspent its budget by R152 million, and in the current year it is anticipated that the overspending will be R700 million rand unless a serious cutback is made in the services which it provides. The renal unit at the Addington Hospital has to serve the whole of KwaZulu-Natal and also takes patients from parts of the Eastern Cape. There are many more patients suffering from chronic renal failure than there are dialysis machines to treat such patients. This is a nation-wide problem and resources are stretched in all renal clinics throughout the land. Guidelines have therefore been established to assist the per-

sons working in these clinics to make the agonizing choices which have to be made in deciding who should receive treatment, and who not. These guidelines were applied in the present case.

[25] By using the available dialysis machines in accordance with the guidelines more patients are benefited than would be the case if they were used to keep alive persons with chronic renal failure, and the outcome of the treatment is also likely to be more beneficial because it is directed to curing patients, and not simply to maintaining them in a chronically ill condition. It has not been suggested that these guidelines are unreasonable or that they were not applied fairly and rationally when the decision was taken by the Addington Hospital that the appellant did not qualify for dialysis.

. . .

[28] . . . It is estimated that the cost to the state of treating one chronically ill patient by means of renal dialysis provided twice a week at a state hospital is approximately R60,000 per annum. If all the persons in South Africa who suffer from chronic renal failure were to be provided with dialysis treatment—and many of them, as the appellant does, would require treatment three times a week—the cost of doing so would make substantial inroads into the health budget. And if this principle were to be applied to all patients claiming access to expensive medical treatment or expensive drugs, the health budget would have to be dramatically increased to the prejudice of other needs which the state has to meet.

[29] The provincial administration which is responsible for health services in KwaZulu-Natal has to make decisions about the funding that should be made available for health care and how such funds should be spent. These choices involve difficult decisions to be taken at the political level in fixing the health budget, and at the functional level in deciding upon the priorities to be met. A court will be slow to interfere with rational decisions taken in good faith by the political organs and medical authorities whose responsibility it is to deal with such matters.

[30] . . . The dilemma confronting health authorities faced with such cases was described by Sir Thomas Bingham MR in in *R v. Cambridge Health Authority, ex parte B*:[24]

> . . . health authorities of all kinds are constantly pressed to make ends meet. . . .
> Difficult and agonising judgments have to be made as to how a limited budget is
> best allocated to the maximum advantage of the maximum number of patients.
> That is not a judgment which the court can make.

[31] One cannot but have sympathy for the appellant and his family, who face the cruel dilemma of having to impoverish themselves in order to secure the treatment that the appellant seeks in order to prolong his life. The hard and unpalatable fact is that if the appellant were a wealthy man he would be able to procure such treatment from private sources; he is not and has to look to the state to provide him with the treatment. But the state's resources are limited and the appellant does not meet the criteria for admission to the renal dialysis programme.

---

[24] [1995] 2 All ER 129 (CA) at 137d–f.

Unfortunately, this is true not only of the appellant but of many others who need access to renal dialysis units or to other health services. There are also those who need access to housing, food and water, employment opportunities, and social security. . . .

The state has to manage its limited resources in order to address all these claims. There will be times when this requires it to adopt a holistic approach to the larger needs of society rather than to focus on the specific needs of particular individuals within society.

[37] . . . The appeal . . . is dismissed.

NOTE

The facts of *Paschim Banga Khet Mazdoor Samity v. State of West Bengal* are summarized above in para. 18 of the *Soobramoney* case. The Indian Court held that the denial of treatment to Samity at various government hospitals when he was in a serious condition violated his right to life under Article 21 of the Indian Constitution, *supra*. In addition to awarding compensation and taking favourable note of a range of procedural reforms introduced by the State Government in West Bengal in relation to hospital admissions, the Court went on to spell out a broader range of policies for the government to institute to meet its constitutional obligations. Some illustrations of what was required in order that 'proper medical facilities are available for dealing with emergency cases' follow:

> 1. Adequate facilities are available at the Primary Health Centres where the patient can be given immediate primary treatment so as to stabilize his condition;
>
> . . .
>
> 3. Facilities for giving Specialist treatment are increased and are available at the hospitals at District level and Sub-Division level having regard to the growing needs:
>
> . . .
>
> 5. Proper arrangement of ambulance is made for transport of a patient from the Primary Health Centre to the District hospital or Sub-Division hospital and from the District hospital or Sub-Division hospital to the State hospital:
>
> 6. The ambulance is adequately provided with necessary equipment and medical personnel:
>
> . . .
>
> 16. It is no doubt true that financial resources are needed for providing these facilities. But at the same time it cannot be ignored that it is the constitutional obligation of the State to provide adequate medical services to the people. Whatever is necessary for this purpose has to be done. In the context of the constitutional obligation to provide free legal aid to a poor accused this Court has held that the State cannot avoid its constitutional obligation in that regard on account of financial constraints. The said observations would apply with equal, if not greater, force in the matter of discharge of constitutional obligation of the State to provide medical aid to preserve human life. In the matter of allocation of funds for medical services the said constitutional obligation of the State has to be

kept in view. It is necessary that a time-bound plan for providing these services should be chalked out . . . and steps should be taken to implement the same. . . .

17. The Union of India is a party to these proceedings. Since it is the joint obligation of the Centre as well as the States to provide medical services it is expected that the Union of India would render the necessary assistance in the improvement of the medical services in the country on these lines.

. . .

QUESTIONS

1. Precisely how does the Court resolve the issue in *Soobramoney* through its interpretation of Article 27(3)? Why are paragraphs (1) and (2) of Article 27 relevant?

2. 'In *Soobramoney*, the Court plays the role of super legislature, determining how to allocate funds between social welfare and other purposes and indeed among welfare categories such as health or housing.' Do you agree? If not, how would you describe the role that the Court here plays in applying social rights stated in the Constitution? On what text in the opinion would you base your view of the matter?

3. Compare the rights at issue in this case with 'directive principles' in the Indian Constitution. Are these rights in the South African Constitution viewed in effect by the Court as directive principles?

4. '[The opinion by President Chaskalson and a concurring opinion by Justice Sachs] barely distinguish between the languages of rights and cost-benefit. They underscore both the goal of social justice and the necessity of management to achieve the effective use of resources. These are understood, naturally presented, as complementary and interdependent rather than antagonistic or even alternative discourses. Deciding on the full operational definition of the right requires that "agonizing choices" be made, choices about cost efficiency and vexing trade-offs. These intertwined decisions are vital to the very content and significance of the right: the type of health care system, the funding, the priorities and coverage in terms of both persons and problems.'[25] Do you agree with this analysis of the Chaskalson opinion; if so, what text in the opinion supports it? Do you agree that the interpretation of a constitutional 'right', a 'human right', will often and indeed necessarily involve cost-benefit, consequentialist reasoning and argument in order to determine the content of the right? Would this be true also of a civil or political right—for example, determining the legality under Article 25 of the ICCPR (the right to political participation and elections) of a state's ban of political parties explicitly based on a given religion or ethnic group?

5. How do you assess the micro-management of hospitals in the orders of the Court in *Samity* that were designed to implement a constitutional right? Is Question (4) relevant as well here?

6. In *Soobramoney* the court refers to *Samity* in support of its proposition that only 'remedial treatment that is necessary *and available*' (emphasis added) need be given. Is this consistent with the overall approach of the Indian Court?

[25] Henry Steiner, 'Social Rights and Economic Development', *supra* n. 10, at 33.

ADDITIONAL READING

Craig Scott and P. Macklem, 'Constitutional Ropes of Sand or Justiciable Guarantees: Social Rights in a New South African Constitution?', 141 U. Penn. L. Rev. 1 (1992); Sheetal Shah, 'Illuminating the Possible in the Developing World: Guaranteeing the Human Right to Health in the Developing World', 32 Vanderbilt J. Transnat'l L. 435 (1999); Erika de Wet, *The Constitutional Enforceability of Economic and Social Rights* (1996); J. Bakan and D. Schneiderman (eds.), *Social Justice and the Constitution: Perspectives on a Social Union for Canada* (1992); M. Cappelletti, *The Judicial Process in Comparative Perspective* (1989); and O. Mendelsohn and M. Vicziany, *The Untouchables: Subordination, Poverty and the State in Modern India* (1998).

F. RESOURCE CONSTRAINTS OR POLITICAL WILL?

Much of the criticism of the concept of economic and social rights is premised on the assumption that wealthy industrialized countries may be able to afford policies designed to protect such rights, but developing countries, countries 'in transition to democracy', and others needing to practice fiscal austerity (a group of countries that covers all but a small elite among states) do not enjoy the luxury of being able to pursue such policies. In particular, the great majority of developing countries has no chance of meeting any 'minimum core obligation' in respect of these rights. For example, Maurice Cranston has written that: '[f]or a government to provide social security . . . it has to have access to great capital wealth. . . . The government of India, for example, simply cannot command the resources that would guarantee' each Indian an adequate standard of living.[26] For many critics it follows that, in the absence of large-scale international aid or of rapid domestic economic growth (or both), the government's hands are tied and little can be expected of it in response to its obligations under the Covenant. (Note that the issue of international aid is considered in Chapter 16, *infra*.) Pressures to reduce the size of the public sector, to privatize various functions previously performed by governments, and to stimulate growth by reducing taxes, all render governments less able to accept responsibility for economic and social rights.

The following readings examine such views.

---

[26] 'Human Rights: Real and Supposed', in D.D.Raphael (ed.), *Political Theory and the Rights of Man* 43 (1967), at 51.

MYRON WEINER, CHILD LABOUR IN DEVELOPING COUNTRIES: THE INDIAN CASE
2 Int. J. Children's Rts. 121 (1994)

Governments do not advocate child labour or oppose compulsory education. . . . Why, then, is child labour so widespread in developing countries? Why are so many children not in school?

The answers are well known and widely accepted. Governments in developing countries, it is said, lack the financial resources for universal compulsory primary school education; governments lack the administrative resources to enforce child labour laws; poor families need the labour and the income of their children; and children and their parents often find the schools in developing countries irrelevant to meet their needs.

By drawing upon examples from India, I will argue that these explanations are unsatisfactory. India is the world's largest producer of non-school going child workers; a review of the Indian experience will therefore help in understanding the reasons for the persistence of child labour not only in India but perhaps also in other developing states. I propose to develop three alternative explanations, firstly, that child labour is not simply an unfortunate feature of low income developing countries that cannot be eliminated until national incomes grow but is in fact sustained by government policies on primary education; secondly, that in India the establishment of compulsory primary education has not been in the interests of the middle classes who are concerned with the expansion of government expenditures on higher education; and finally, that child labour has become part of the government's industrial strategy to promote the small scale sector and to expand exports.

. . .

. . . [One] conclusion is that the establishment of compulsory education is a necessary condition for the reduction and abolition of child labour. Without compulsory education governments are unable to enforce child labour laws. In one country after another the phased extension of the age of compulsory education went hand in hand with a phased extension of restrictions on the employment of children. If the school-leaving age is lower than the age of admission to employment, children are likely to illegally seek employment, and the enforcement of child labour laws is rendered more difficult. It is administratively easier to monitor school attendance than to monitor children in the work place, and easier to force parents to send their children to school than to force employers not to hire children. No country has successfully ended child labour without first making education compulsory. So long as children are free not to attend school, they will enter the labour force.

India need not wait until incomes rise to make primary education universal and compulsory. The sooner India acts, the quicker will be the fall in the illiteracy rate, the more likely it is that child labour will be reduced, and the greater are the prospects for a reduction in fertility rates as children are no longer seen as financial assets to the family. But Indian policy makers continue to be mired in a set of views that preclude their taking the necessary steps to get children into school and out of the labour force and a set of industrial policies that promote the employment of children in the small scale sector. Moreover, these views are so widely shared in India that no political parties of the left or right, none of the trade unions, no religious organizations, and not even the educational establishment is pressing for policy changes. There is little indication of fundamental rethinking within the state or central governments. Even officials who recognize that regular school attendance is a solution to the problem of child labour continue to believe that the responsibility of sending children to school should be with parents, not with the state. Policy makers continue to believe that parents should be permitted to send their children into the labour force, and that child labour cannot be eliminated while there is poverty. Government policy is to work around the fringes of the problem: promote adult literacy campaigns, provide non-formal education to working children, and provide free school lunches to encourage children to remain in school. But neither the central nor the state governments have been willing to do what has been done historically by every developed and now by many developing countries: declare that all children ages six to twelve or fourteen *must* attend school, that parents, no matter how needy, will *not be* permitted to remove their children from school, that school attendance *will* be enforced by local authorities, and that the government *will* be obligated to locate a primary school within reasonable distance of all school age children. Only through such a policy will it be possible to end child labour in India, and within a generation raise India's literacy rate to that of other large developing countries.

UNITED NATIONS DEVELOPMENT PROGRAMME, HUMAN DEVELOPMENT REPORT
(1990), at 4

. . .

7. Developing countries are not too poor to pay for human development and take care of economic growth.

The view that human development can be promoted only at the expense of economic growth poses a false tradeoff. It misstates the purpose of development and underestimates the returns on investment in health and eduction. These returns can be high, indeed. Private returns to primary education are as high as 43% in Africa, 31% in Asia and 32% in Latin America. Social returns from female literacy are even higher—in terms of reduced fertility, reduced infant mortality, lower school dropout rates, improved family nutrition and lower population growth.

Most budgets can, moreover, accommodate additional spending on human development by reorienting national priorities. In many instances, more than half the spending is swallowed by the military, debt repayments, inefficient parastatals, unnecessary government controls and mistargetted social subsidies. Since other resource possibilities remain limited, restructuring budget priorities to balance economic and social spending should move to the top of the policy agenda for development in the 1990s.

Special attention should go to reducing military spending in the Third World— it has risen three times as fast as that in the industrial nations in the last 30 years, and is now approaching $200 billion a year. Developing countries as a group spend more on the military (5.5% of their combined GNP) than on education and health (5.3%). In many developing countries, current military spending is sometimes two or three times greater than spending on education and health. There are eight times more soldiers than physicians in the Third World.

Governments can also do much to improve the efficiency of social spending by creating a policy and budgetary framework that would achieve a more desirable mix between various social expenditures, particularly by reallocating resources:

— from curative medical facilities to primary health care programmes,
— from highly trained doctors to paramedical personnel,
— from urban to rural services,
— from general to vocational education,
— from subsidising tertiary education to subsidising primary and secondary education,
— from expensive housing for the privileged groups to sites and services projects for the poor,
— from subsidies for vocal and powerful groups to subsidies for inarticulate and weaker groups and
— from the formal sector to the informal sector and the programmes for the unemployed and the underemployed.

Such a restructuring of budget priorities will require tremendous political courage. But the alternatives are limited, and the payoffs can be enormous.
. . .

COMMITTEE ON ECONOMIC, SOCIAL AND CULTURAL RIGHTS, GENERAL COMMENT NO. 11 (1999)
UN Doc. E/C.12/1999/4

Plans of action for primary education

1. Article 14 of the [ICESCR] requires each State party which has not been able to secure compulsory primary education, free of charge, to undertake within two years, to work out and adopt a detailed plan of action for the progressive implementation, within a reasonable number of years, to be fixed in the plan, of the principle of compulsory primary education free of charge for all. . . .
. . .

5. Article 14 contains a number of elements which warrant some elaboration in the light of the Committee's extensive experience in examining State party reports.

6. *Compulsory.* The element of compulsion serves to highlight the fact that

neither parents, nor guardians, nor the State is entitled to treat as optional the decision as to whether the child should have access to primary education. . . .

7. *Free of charge.* The nature of this requirement is unequivocal. The right is expressly formulated so as to ensure the availability of primary education without charge to the child, parents or guardians. Fees imposed by the Government, local authorities or the school, and other direct costs, constitute disincentives to the enjoyment of the right and may jeopardize its realization. They are also often highly regressive in effect. Their elimination is a matter which must be addressed by the required plan of action. Indirect costs, such as compulsory levies on parents (sometimes portrayed as being voluntary, when in fact they are not), or the obligation to wear a relatively expensive school uniform, can also fall into the same category. Other indirect costs may be permissible, subject to the Committee's examination on a case-by-base basis. . . .

8. *Adoption of a detailed plan.* The State party is required to adopt a plan of action within two years. This must be interpreted as meaning within two years of the Covenant's entry into force for the State concerned, or within two years of a subsequent change in circumstances which has led to the non-observance of the relevant obligation. This obligation is a continuing one . . . . The plan must cover all of the actions which are necessary in order to secure each of the requisite component parts of the right and must be sufficiently detailed so as to ensure the comprehensive realization of the right. Participation of all sections of civil society in the drawing up of the plan is vital and some means of periodically reviewing progress and ensuring accountability are essential. Without those elements, the significance of the article would be undermined.

9. *Obligations.* A State party cannot escape the unequivocal obligation to adopt a plan of action on the grounds that the necessary resources are not available. If the obligation could be avoided in this way, there would be no justification for the unique requirement contained in article 14 which applies, almost by definition, to situations characterized by inadequate financial resources. By the same token, and for the same reason, the references to 'international assistance and cooperation' in articles 2.1 and 23 of the Covenant are of particular relevance in this situation. Where a State party is clearly lacking in the financial resources and/or expertise required to 'work out and adopt' a detailed plan, the international community has a clear obligation to assist.

10. *Progressive implementation.* . . . Unlike the provision in article 2.1, however, article 14 specifies that the target date must be 'within a reasonable number of years' and moreover, that the time-frame must 'be fixed in the plan'. In other words, the plan must specifically set out a series of targeted implementation dates for each stage of the progressive implementation of the plan. . . .

QUESTIONS

1. Weiner's analysis rejects resource constraints as a significant impediment to the realization of the right to universal primary education. If you accept his analysis, is there any reason not to find the Government of India in violation of its obligations under the

ICESCR (which it ratified in 1979)? Is this a case in which cultural factors (religious, caste-based, and gender-based) could be appropriately drawn on to justify governmental inaction in response to claims of economic and social rights? Or is it one that highlights the need to insist upon respect for those human rights?

2. Is the *Human Development Report*'s prescription convincing? Is it only the poor developing countries which should be adopting such priorities?

G. TOWARDS MORE EFFECTIVE MONITORING

The monitoring of economic, social and cultural rights is made especially challenging by the scope of the rights, the diversity of the means by which they might be made operational, and the inevitably complex relationship between rights and resources. In legal terms, the challenge is how to take account in a monitoring system of the provisions in the ICESCR calling for 'progressive realization' to the 'maximum of available resources', while acknowledging that financial and administrative capacities vary dramatically from one state to another. The ESCR Committee has sought to combine a 'minimum core content' approach which yields a universal minimum standard with an emphasis upon the need for each state to establish 'benchmarks' against which its performance can be measured both internally and by external monitoring bodies.

This section examines a case study of the Committee in action, and then considers other approaches that have been suggested.

1. SUPERVISION BY THE ESCR COMMITTEE: A CASE STUDY OF HOUSING

Neither the UN Commission on Human Rights nor its Sub-Commission has been very active in relation to the implementation of economic, social and cultural rights, although several important studies have been undertaken by the latter. The principal responsibility has thus fallen to the ESCR Committee, established in 1987 to supervise compliance by states parties with their obligations under the ICESCR.

In many respects, the Committee functions in the same way as the ICCPR Human Rights Committee, examined in Chapter 10, infra. On the basis of regular reports submitted by states parties in accordance with the Committee's 'reporting guidelines', and of its own deliberations as in the drafting of 'general comments', the ESCR Committee seeks to achieve three principal objectives: (1) developing the normative content of the rights recognized in the Covenant; (2) acting as a catalyst to state action in developing national 'benchmarks' and devising appropriate mechanisms for establishing accountability, and providing means of vindication to aggrieved individuals and groups at the national level; and (3) holding states accountable at the international level through the examination of reports.

The following case study, focused on the right to adequate housing, considers the type of reports that the Committee has sought to elicit through its guidelines, the use it has made of 'general comments' to develop the content of the right, and the outcome of the examination of a report by Nigeria. The process, a reasonably typical one, consisted of the following steps:

29 October 1993: ICESCR enters into force for Nigeria, three months after ratification.

29 October 1995: Initial (comprehensive) report due within two years of entry into force. Nigeria is requested to follow the Committee's reporting guidelines and provide detailed descriptive and statistical information.[27]

23 February 1996: The report is submitted, translated into the different UN languages and published as an official UN document.

10 December 1996: The Chairperson of the ESCR Committee sends a letter to the Nigerian Government indicating that 'the Committee has received information from a variety of sources, alleging that large-scale forced evictions are being undertaken in Lagos and that many more are planned in the months ahead. One estimate submitted to the Committee suggests that as many as 1.2 million people in 15 slum areas might be affected by the proposed measures'. The letter states that the government's report is lacking in factual detail and that additional information on housing matters is essential if the Committee is to be able to evaluate the evidence effectively.

23 May 1997: The Committee's five-person Working Group sends a list of specific questions to the Government to form the principal focus of the dialogue. The list takes into account information from 'all available sources', including information from NGOs which is thought to be reliable. A written response prior to the Committee session is requested.

January 1998: The Government submits additional information but does not answer the questions.

27 April 1998: The Committee holds a three-hour public session during which NGOs present information on Nigeria and other reports currently before the Committee.

29–30 April 1998: The Committee devotes nine hours to a 'dialogue' with the Government in which precise answers are sought to specific questions posed by any member of the Committee. The expert member from Nigeria recuses himself from participation.

13 May 1998: The Committee drafts its 'concluding observations' in closed session and they are made public. NGOs circulate them within Nigeria and the UN issues a press release with details, puts them on its website, and includes them in the Committee's Annual Report.

---

[27] The guidelines and most of the other documents referred to in this case study are available on the website of the UN High Commissioner for Human Rights at: <www.unhchr.ch/tbs>.

COMMITTEE ON ECONOMIC, SOCIAL AND CULTURAL RIGHTS, REPORTING GUIDELINES
UN Doc. E/1991/23, Annex IV

[These guidelines, adopted by the Committee in 1991 and subject to revision over time, regulate the form and contents of the reports that states parties to the ICESCR are required to submit. An initial report is required within two years of ratification and periodic reports are due every five years thereafter.]

The right to adequate housing

(a) Please furnish detailed statistical information about the housing situation in your country.

(b) Please provide detailed information about those groups within your society that are vulnerable and disadvantaged with regard to housing. Indicate, in particular:

(i) The number of homeless individuals and families;

(ii) The number of individuals and families currently inadequately housed and without ready access to basic amenities . . . ;

(iii) The number of persons currently classified as living in 'illegal' settlements or housing;

(iv) The number of persons evicted within the last five years . . . .

. . .

(c) Please provide information on the existence of any laws affecting the realization of the right to housing.

(d) Please provide information on all other measures taken to fulfil the right to housing, . . .

. . .

4. Please give details on any difficulties or shortcomings encountered . . . and on the measures taken to remedy . . . them.

COMMITTEE ON ECONOMIC, SOCIAL AND CULTURAL RIGHTS, GENERAL COMMENT No. 4 (1991)
UN Doc. E/1992/23, Annex III

The right to adequate housing (art. 11(1) of the Covenant)

. . .

7. In the Committee's view, the right to housing should not be interpreted in a narrow or restrictive sense which equates it with, for example, the shelter provided by merely having a roof over one's head or views shelter exclusively as a commodity. Rather it should be seen as the right to live somewhere in security, peace and dignity . . . .

8 . . . . While adequacy is determined in part by social, economic, cultural, climatic, ecological and other factors, the Committee believes that it is nevertheless

possible to identify certain aspects of the right that must be taken into account for this purpose in any particular context. They include the following:

(a) Legal security of tenure. . . . Notwithstanding the type of tenure, all persons should possess a degree of security of tenure which guarantees legal protection against forced eviction, harassment and other threats . . . .

(b) Availability of services, materials, facilities and infrastructure. An adequate house must contain certain facilities essential for health, security, comfort and nutrition [including] . . . sustainable access to . . . safe drinking water, energy for cooking, heating and lighting, sanitation and washing facilities, means of food storage, refuse disposal, site drainage and emergency services;

(c) Affordability. . . . [C]osts associated with housing should be at such a level that the attainment and satisfaction of other basic needs are not threatened or compromised;

(d) Habitability. . . . [I]n terms of providing the inhabitants with adequate space and protecting them from cold, damp, heat, rain, wind or other threats to health, structural hazards, and disease vectors . . . .

(e) Accessibility. . . .

(f) Location. Adequate housing must be in a location which allows access to employment options, health-care services, schools, child-care centres and other social facilities. This is true both in large cities and in rural areas where the temporal and financial costs of getting to and from the place of work can place excessive demands upon the budgets of poor households. Similarly, housing should not be built on polluted sites nor in immediate proximity to pollution sources that threaten the right to health of the inhabitants;

(g) Cultural adequacy. . . .

. . .

10. Regardless of the state of development of any country, there are certain steps which must be taken immediately. . . . [M]any of the measures required to promote the right to housing would only require the abstention by the Government from certain practices and a commitment to facilitating 'self-help' by affected groups. To the extent that any such steps are considered to be beyond the maximum resources available to a State party, it is appropriate that a request be made as soon as possible for international cooperation in accordance with articles 11(1), 22 and 23 of the Covenant, and that the Committee be informed thereof.

. . .

12. While the most appropriate means of achieving the full realization of the right to adequate housing will inevitably vary significantly from one State party to another, the Covenant clearly requires that each State party take whatever steps are necessary for that purpose. This will almost invariably require the adoption of a national housing strategy. . . .

13. Effective monitoring of the situation with respect to housing is another obligation of immediate effect. . . .

COMMITTEE ON ECONOMIC, SOCIAL AND CULTURAL RIGHTS, SUMMARY RECORDS

UN Doc. E/C.12/1998/SR. 6, 3 May 1998

Held at the Palais des Nations, Geneva, on Wednesday, 28 April 1998, at 3 p.m.

Initial report of Nigeria (E/1990/5/Add.31, E/C.12/Q/NIGERIA/1)

. . .

11. Mr. PILLAY [Committee member] said that he wished to ask two questions. First, was it not true to say that, since Nigeria was plagued by political instability, poor management, galloping inflation and rampant corruption, the majority of Nigerians did not enjoy their economic, social and cultural rights? Second, did the rule of law apply in Nigeria? The report stated that the country's Constitution was modelled on the United States, yet it appeared that the military Federal Government's decrees superseded the powers of all courts and even prevailed over the application of the Covenant. The representative of Nigeria had mentioned human rights seminars being organized for magistrates and judges, yet material available to the Committee indicated the existence of a financial crisis in the judiciary. The salaries of judges, magistrates and court officers were said to be extremely low, the number of court rooms insufficient and their condition poor. It was therefore no wonder that bribery was reported to be common among the judiciary. The delegation's comments on those points would be appreciated.

. . .

UN Doc. E/C.12/1998/SR. 8, 4 May 1998.

Held at the Palais des Nations, Geneva, on Thursday, 29 April 1998, at 3 p.m.

. . .

6. Mr. PILLAY pointed out that questions 32–35 of the list of issues . . . had not been answered. Specifically . . . he wondered whether the delegation agreed with the estimate that there were 7 million people homeless in Nigeria. Was it true that 35 per cent of the income of the lower-paid workers went on housing, and that 80 per cent of the population lived in uninhabitable houses, unable to afford decent housing because of their low incomes, high rents and galloping inflation?

7. It had been estimated that over one million people had been affected by forced evictions. What measures was the Government taking to remedy the situation of those persons? Had the Government taken into account the provisions of General Comments 4 and 7 of the Committee, which required prior consultation, compensation and resettlement of the victims of evictions, and would it take them into account in the event of future evictions?

8. . . . [I]t appeared that in May 1996 the Nigerian Government had flouted a Federal High Court order and forcibly evicted people from Harvey Road in Lagos.

. . .

17. Mrs. BONOAN-DANDAN, . . . observed that all reports on forced eviction in Nigeria had stated that women were frequently verbally abused, beaten and raped, and left homeless and poverty-stricken after eviction. What . . . support had the Government extended to [such] women . . .?

18. Mr. TEXIER said that a report to the Committee in May 1997 had referred to the eviction by the Ministry of Labour and Housing of some 250,000 street traders from streets and areas beneath bridges in Lagos after only 7 days' notice. In the process of eviction, their merchandise and shelters had been destroyed but no compensation had ever been paid. . . .

. . .

21. Mr. OSAH ([Representative of the Government of] Nigeria), replying to questions raised, said that although he had no figures on the homeless, the figure of 7 million seemed most improbable; it might include the many who slept in the streets but who were not necessarily homeless, and the large numbers moving to the cities in search of work, who were usually homeless only temporarily, until they found alternative accommodation.

22. The questions concerning inadequate housing appeared to be based on the view that the whole of Nigeria was a shanty town where no decent accommodation or drinking water was available. That was not true, certainly of Lagos and other urban areas. Suitable and adequate accommodation with all the basic facilities was provided for workers: a 3 or 4-bedroomed flat or bungalow in the case of senior Government officials and 1 or 2-bedroomed flats for the lower brackets, according to their status in the service. Workers in the private sector were provided with very good home and office accommodation.

23. In the case of the apparent disregard of an order of the Federal High Court in Lagos, to which Mr. Pillay had referred, the Government's decision to proceed with the Harvey Road project had been prompted by environmental considerations. . . . He assured the Committee that the Military Governor in Lagos, who had jurisdiction over the Harvey Road estate, was a fine officer, very popular with the people, who would never have evicted anyone without adequate preparation and compensation. As far as the rule of law was concerned, therefore, he believed that the High Court's decision had been respected.

. . .

28. The CHAIRPERSON pointed out that the delegation's responses to the questions were not answering the Committee's needs. Certain events had been alleged, and, unless the Committee could find a reason to doubt that they had occurred, it must conclude that they had in fact done so. In the absence of any effective rebuttal, it had to draw its own conclusions.

. . .

33. The CHAIRPERSON felt that he should again remind the delegation that the provisions of the law were one thing and their application another. . . . If the Committee could be given statistics for the number of evictions, in Lagos alone, over the last two or three years, the number of successful cases brought against such evictions, and the amount of compensation that had allegedly been paid to those evicted, it would have a factual basis on which to make its assessment. Unfortunately, the responses it was receiving did not go in that direction.

34. Mr. OSAH (Nigeria) said that the obligations of States parties were clearly stipulated in the Covenant. In the case of article 11, the State had fulfilled its obligations by making adequate provision in the law. . . .

. . .

38. In response to the question about the effect of evictions on women and the elderly, he said that the individuals affected had the right to compensation. Notice was usually given and adequate arrangements made to move them out so that the Government could complete its project. There was no discrimination in such entitlement.

. . .

80. The CHAIRPERSON thanked the Nigerian delegation for its presence and for the answers it had provided. The Committee would, after due deliberation, formulate its concluding observations

COMMITTEE ON ECONOMIC, SOCIAL AND CULTURAL RIGHTS, CONCLUDING OBSERVATIONS ON THE REPORT OF NIGERIA
UN Doc. E/C.12/1/Add.23, 13 May 1998

. . .

23. The Committee expresses its deep concern about the rising number of home-less women and young girls, who are forced to sleep in the streets where they are vulnerable to rape and other forms of violence.

24. Children are not much better off. Many resort to prostitution to feed themselves. The rate of school drop-outs at the primary school age is over 20 percent. Twelve million children are estimated to hold one job or another. For those who go to school, up to 80 or more are crammed in dilapidated classrooms meant originally to take only a maximum of 40. . . . Nigerian law does not provide equal treatment to children born in wedlock and those born out of wedlock. . . . Almost thirty percent of Nigerian children suffer malnutrition and its damaging consequences. . . .

25. The Committee is greatly disturbed that 21 percent of the population of Nigeria live below the poverty line in spite of the country's rich natural resources. . . .

. . .

27. The Committee is appalled at the great number of homeless people and notes with concern the acute housing problem in Nigeria where decent housing is scarce and relatively expensive. The urban poor, especially women and children, are forced to live in make-shift cheap dumps or shelters in appalling and degrading conditions representing both physical and mental illnesses hazards. Safe treated pipe-borne water is available to about fifty percent of urban dwellers but only to 30 percent of rural inhabitants. By and large only 39 percent of Nigeria's population has adequate access to clean drinking water.

28. The Committee notes with concern that gross under-funding and inadequate management of health services led during the last decade to rapid

deterioration of health infrastructures in hospitals. The 1996 budget capital allocation to health and social services was N. 1.7 billion, only 3.5 percent of total capital
allocations to federal ministries. Frequently, hospital patients not only have had to
buy drugs but have also had to supply needles, syringes and suture threads, in
addition to paying for bed space. . . .

. . .

E. Suggestions and Recommendations

. . .

34. The restoration of democracy and the rule of law are prerequisites for the
implementation of the [ICESCR] in Nigeria. Elimination of the practice of governing by military decree, the strengthening of the authority of the Nigerian judiciary
and the Human Rights Commission are necessary first steps to restore confidence
in the regime's intentions to reinstitute democratic civilian rule.

. . .

42. The Committee urges the Government of Nigeria to cease forthwith the
massive and arbitrary evictions of people from their homes and take such
measures as are necessary in order to alleviate the plight of those who are
subject to arbitrary evictions or are too poor to afford a decent accommodation.
In view of the acute shortage of housing, the Government of Nigeria should
allocate adequate resources and make sustained efforts to combat this serious
situation.

43–44. [The Committee called for a new report—in effect a special report not
normally required—to be submitted within two years and urged the Government
to disseminate the Committee's Concluding Observations].

QUESTIONS

1. Based on this example, how would you evaluate the monitoring process? What
criteria of effectiveness would you apply? In what circumstances could the outcome in
this case be considered to be effective?

2. Are the demands upon states parties as reflected in the reporting guidelines and
the General Comment unrealistically high? Can you think of any accompanying measures that might make states more likely to meet the reporting requirements?

2. A 'VIOLATIONS APPROACH'

AUDREY CHAPMAN, A NEW APPROACH TO MONITORING THE INTERNATIONAL COVENANT ON ECONOMIC, SOCIAL AND CULTURAL RIGHTS

International Commission of Jurists, The Review, No. 55, December 1995, at 23

The thesis of this paper is that effective monitoring of the International Covenant on Economic, Social and Cultural Rights is not currently taking place and that rectifying this situation requires a change in the paradigm for evaluating compliance with its provisions. Monitoring is central to the realization of the rights enumerated in the Covenant. Without systematic and ongoing collection and analysis of relevant data, countries which ratify or accede to the Covenant cannot be held accountable for implementation. 'Progressive realization', the current standard used to assess the performance of State parties, renders economic, social, and cultural rights very difficult to monitor. A 'violations approach' constitutes a more feasible alternative. . . .

. . .

. . . Systematic monitoring of the degree to which countries have implemented these rights has five methodological preconditions:

1. conceptualisation of the specific components of each enumerated right and the concomitant obligations of State parties;
2. delineation of performance standards related to each of these components, including relevant indicators;
3. collection of relevant data, appropriately disaggregated by sex and a variety of other variables;
4. development of a computerised information management system for processing these data; and
5. analysis of these data so as to be able to ascertain the performance of a particular country. For reasons which will be discussed below, none of these five preconditions are currently being met.

. . . Evaluating progressive realization within the context of 'the maximum of its available resources' considerably complicates the methodological requirements outlined above: this standard assumes that valid expectations and concomitant obligations of State parties under each enumerated right are not uniform or universal but instead relative to levels of development and available resources. This necessitates the development of a multiplicity of performance standards to fit the many social, developmental, and resource contexts appropriate to specific countries.

. . .

Evaluating the progressive realization of economic, social, and cultural rights requires the availability of comparable statistical data from several periods in time in order to assess trends. Measuring progressive realization requires an assessment

not only of current performance, but also of whether a State is moving expeditiously and effectively towards the goal of full implementation. Consistent with
the Committee's reporting guidelines, much of these data would be disaggregated
in relevant categories, including gender, ethnicity, race, region, socio-economic
groups, urban/rural divisions, and linguistic groups. . . .

A thorough evaluation would therefore require complicated analyses of an
enormous quantity of data. Many governments do not have appropriate data of
good quality for this type of analysis. . . . Moreover, analysis of these data to
evaluate performance, were such data to be available, requires statistical expertise
that members of the United Nations Committee on Economic, Social and Cultural
Rights, staff of the UN Centre for Human Rights, and nongovernmental organizations do not generally possess.

. . .

. . . What is being advocated here is the open and explicit adoption of a violations oriented review process for evaluating compliance with the Covenant. . . .

. . .

To facilitate monitoring the Covenant, this article proposes a tripartite categor-
isation of violations. The three categories are:

1. violations resulting from actions, policies, and legislation on the part of
   the government;
2. violations related to patterns of discrimination; and
3. violations related to the State's failure to fulfil minimum core obligations
   of enumerated rights.

Violations resulting from State actions, policies, and legislation are the type of
violation most comparable to infractions of civil and political rights. These are
predominantly acts of commission, activities of States or governments which contravene standards set in the Covenant. Others are policies or laws which create
conditions inimical to the realization of recognized rights. . . .

The following list provides some examples of the types of State initiatives that
would qualify for the first category of violations:

- interference with the rights of association, to form labour unions, and to
  strike (Article 8(1));
- forced evictions and removals of persons from their homes by State agencies (Article 11(1));
- coercive birth control practices, including abortions and large-scale steril-
  isation, such as those being carried out in several Asian countries, most
  notably China, as a matter of State policy to accomplish fertility control
  (Article 12);
- legalisation or policy support for medical or cultural practices which
  endanger girls' or women's health, such as female circumcision (Article
  12);

. . .

Violations related to patterns of discrimination also represent a fundamental breach of the Covenant. Under the Covenant, State parties have the immediate obligation to ensure non-discrimination. . . .

. . .

Examples abound of violations reflecting discriminatory policies and actions by State parties, both in the failure to ensure non-discrimination and in initiatives and policies which perpetuate or worsen forms of discrimination. These include the following:

. . .

- Women's health needs are rarely given equal resources. Many countries do not incorporate reproductive health services in primary care, health problems predominantly or solely affecting women tend to not receive sufficient attention, and women are rarely included in research trials (Article 12).
- In countries where single-sex schooling is common, there is frequently a serious imbalance in the number of school places available and the quality of schools designated for boys and girls, resulting in a lack of equality of educational opportunity (Article 13).
- In some countries, ethnic and linguistic minorities are denied the right to use their native language for schooling or broadcasting (Article 15(1a)).

The third category of violations consists of those resulting from the failure to fulfil minimum core obligations. In its third General Comment, the Committee 'is of the view that a minimum core obligation to ensure the satisfaction of, at the very least, minimum essential levels of each of the rights is incumbent upon every State party'. Similarly, the Committee underscores that even in times of severe resources constraints the vulnerable members of society 'can and indeed must' be protected by the adoption of relatively low-cost targeted programs. Women constitute one such vulnerable and neglected community. The Committee has yet to define the minimum obligations related to specific rights. Although there is an urgent need for the Committee or other experts to proceed to define this core, some of these violations of omission are so obvious and blatant that they can already be identified. They include the following:

. . .

- Countries often fail to implement laws and regulations related to obligations outlined in the Covenant. For example, child labour continues in many countries despite laws prohibiting employment of children under the age of 14.
- Although Article 13 requires the introduction of free and compulsory primary education, and Article 14 mandates that countries which lack free and compulsory primary education develop a detailed plan of action within two years of becoming a State party, many countries fail to do so.

. . . By anticipating the kinds of violations that monitors are likely to encounter, an inventory can provide the foundation for formulating instructions and guides on what monitors should consider and check in relationship to specific rights. Through a better understanding of the most significant violations, it will also be possible to develop standards and indicators to evaluate compliance with the Covenant. . . .

QUESTIONS

1. What distinguishes the 'violations approach' advocated by Chapman from that reflected in the Committee's approach in the case of Nigeria?

2. Does the following statement by the Committee in its General Comment No. 12 (1999) on the right to adequate food (UN Doc. E/C.12/1999/5) satisfy the criticism directed at the Committee by Chapman?

> 17. Violations of the Covenant occur when a state fails to ensure the satisfaction of, at the very least, the minimum essential level required to be free from hunger. In determining which actions or omissions amount to a violation of the right to food, it is important to distinguish the inability from the unwillingness of a State party to comply. . . .
>
> 18. Furthermore, any discrimination in access to food, as well as to means and entitlements for its procurement, on the grounds [stated in article 2(2)] . . . constitutes a violation of the Covenant.
>
> 19. Violations of the right to food can occur through the direct action of States or other entities insufficiently regulated by States. These include: the formal repeal or suspension of legislation necessary for the continued enjoyment of the right to food; denial of access to food to particular individuals or groups, whether the discrimination is based on legislation or is pro-active; the prevention of access to humanitarian food aid in internal conflicts or other emergency situations; adoption of legislation or policies which are manifestly incompatible with pre-existing legal obligations relating to the right to food; and failure to regulate activities of individuals or groups so as to prevent them from violating the right to food of others, or the failure of a State to take into account its international legal obligations regarding the right to food when entering into agreements with other States or with international organizations.

3. INDICATORS AND BENCHMARKS

Various commentators, including Chapman, have emphasized the importance of developing comprehensive statistical indicators as a means by which to monitor compliance with the ICESCR. But apart from the many technical challenges mounted against most formal indicators, the Committee's experience to date shows that the great majority of states—both developed and developing—are extremely reluctant, or genuinely unable, to gather and publish such comprehensive statistical indicators in relation to the rights recognized in the ICESCR.

The Committee has so far preferred a strategy which focuses on 'benchmarks'.

The analysis by Alston seeks to distinguish benchmarks from indicators. The review by UNDP that concludes this section outlines the role that might be played by poverty strategies.

PHILIP ALSTON, INTERNATIONAL GOVERNANCE IN THE NORMATIVE AREAS

in UNDP, Background Papers: Human Development Report 1999, at 15–18

The most useful approach to overcoming the lack of national-level action in relation to these rights is that of benchmarking. Extensive work has been done in recent years on the elaboration of a wide range of economic and social 'indicators' of development. . . . But indicators differ in very significant ways from . . . benchmarks . . . . [I]t is useful to highlight some of the characteristics of indicators. For the most part, they are essentially statistical in nature [and the] need for objectivity, quantifiability and accuracy point in turn to the technical expertise required in order to compile [them]. The same applies to their subsequent interpretation, which should take account of the known weaknesses of the process, and compensate for any likely biases or other suspected shortcomings. Accordingly, a significant number of caveats or qualifications will usually be attached to the use of any given indicator. Finally, the capacity to gather, analyze and make use of the data required for indicators is heavily dependent upon the availability of the appropriate technical expertise and resources.

In contrast, benchmarks are . . . targets established by governments, on the basis of appropriately consultative processes, in relation to each of the economic, social and cultural rights obligations that apply in the state concerned. Those targets will be partly quantitative (and thus more closely assimilated to indicators) and partly qualitative. They will be linked to specific time frames. And they will provide a basis upon which the reality of 'progressive realization', contained in [the ICESCR] can be measured. Benchmarks will initially differ significantly from one country to another, reflecting both the 'available resources' and the priority concerns in each country. Over time, however, one would expect a gradual coming together of the approaches without necessarily ever leading to a formal systematization or uniformity.

Thus, the setting of a benchmark, and the identification of the criteria by which it is to be measured, are not dependent upon, or limited by, the availability of a technically accepted indicator or of detailed statistical data linked to that indicator. Benchmarks can be more subjective and more tailored to a specific context than indicators because they are firmly rooted in the human rights framework. The manner in which they are set should be consultative rather than technocratic, and opportunities should be available for the social partners and civil society in general to make inputs into their design and evaluation.

Also unlike indicators, benchmarks should be linked to mechanisms of accountability in the sense that failure to reach a given benchmark should trigger an appropriate remedial response. Both the nature of the trigger and of the relevant remedies are matters to be determined in lights of domestic considerations . . . .

. . .

. . . Individuals must be empowered to participate in decisions relating to the steps to be taken towards meeting those rights and be given the opportunity to contribute to monitoring and evaluation processes. In this sense, civil and political rights can be seen not only as ends in themselves, but also as a vital means by which to facilitate the realization of economic, social and cultural rights.

. . .

UNITED NATIONS DEVELOPMENT PROGRAMME, UNDP POVERTY REPORT 1998
(1998), at 15

A series of goals and targets for poverty reduction have been established at recent UN Conferences—as well as in the 1996 OECD-DAC strategy, *Shaping the 21st Century*. In order to achieve consistency between these, the OECD-DAC, the UN system and the World Bank have joined forces to agree on the indicators that will be used in monitoring progress toward these targets.

  • *Income poverty*—The global target here is that between 1993 and 2015 the proportion of people living in extreme poverty will be halved. The indicator for this will be the poverty headcount ratio—the proportion of the population whose income or consumption falls below $1 per day. On this basis, the required reduction is from 30 per cent to 15 per cent. However, built into this target is another requirement that the depth of poverty (the average income of those below the poverty line) should not get worse. It was also agreed that individual countries could, for their own purposes, replace the $1-per-day threshold with a nationally chosen poverty line.

  • *Relative poverty*—The target is to increase the national consumption of the poorest fifth of the population.

  • *Malnutrition*—The global target is that between 1995 and 2005 the proportion of malnourished children should halve, and halve again between 2005 and 2015. The indicator for this will be the proportion of children under five who are underweight. This is a good indicator since it combines the effects of both current and past malnourishment.

  • *Literacy*—The general target for adult illiteracy (age 15–24) is that between 1990 and 2015 it be reduced globally by three quarters, and that it be the same for men and women. This means reducing global male and female illiteracy rates to 8 per cent by 2015.

. . .

Setting targets Governments have made a commitment to poverty reduction that requires setting national time-bound goals and targets—and establishing monitoring systems that are reliable and transparent. Many have set such targets, but not nearly enough. Out of 130 countries surveyed by UNDP, only 38 countries so far have specific targets for the reduction or eradication of extreme poverty, and only 39 have done so for the reduction of overall poverty.

. . .

If the poorest countries are to achieve major reductions in poverty, they will need substantial external funding. The prospects are not promising. During the 1970s and 1980s, official development assistance (ODA) from the members of the DAC of the OECD remained stable at around 0.35 per cent of donors' combined GDP. But since the early 1990s, the volume of aid has declined steadily—and is now at an all-time low of 0.22 per cent. . . .

. . .

What is critically important is that only 38 countries have targets for extreme poverty and 39 for overall poverty. This underlines the need for many to make concrete, time-bound commitments to poverty eradication. China proposes, for example, to eliminate extreme poverty by the turn of the century. Among other countries that have set targets are:

. . .

- *Tanzania*: with extreme poverty around 36 per cent, it plans to reduce this by half by 2010 and eradicate it by 2020.
- *India*: with overall poverty at 36 per cent, it plans to reduce this to 18 per cent by 2002 and to below five per cent by 2012.

. . .

. . . One problem in the past has been that poverty strategies have often set ambitious targets but backed them up with few resources. Governments need to set realistic targets. . . .

. . .

QUESTION

Could or should the approach to poverty strategies promoted by UNDP be made an integral part of the monitoring strategy for the ICESCR?

ADDITIONAL READING

For specialized bibliographies see: Philip Alston, *Economic and Social Rights: A Bibliography* (2000); Amnesty International, 'Publications on Health and Human Rights Themes: 1992– 1998', 4 Health and Human Rights 215 (1999). On the ICESCR in general see: 'The Limburg Principles on the Implementation of the International Covenant on Economic, Social and Cultural Rights', 9 Hum. Rts Q 122 (1987); 'The Maastricht Guidelines on Violations of Economic, Social and Cultural Rights', 20 Hum. Rts Q 691 (1998); Matthew Craven, *The International Covenant on Economic, Social and Cultural Rights: A Perspective on its Development* (1995); Paul Hunt, *Reclaiming Social Rights: International and Comparative Perspectives* (1996); Asbjørn Eide, C. Krause and A. Rosas (eds.), *Economic, Social and Cultural Rights: A Textbook* (1994); Danilo Türk, 'The Realization of Economic, Social and

Cultural Rights: Final Report Submitted by the Special Rapporteur', UN Doc. E/CN.4/Sub.2/1992/16; Franz Matscher (ed.), *The Implementation of Economic and Social Rights* (1991); Ralph Beddard and D. Hill (eds.), *Economic, Social and Cultural Rights: Progress and Achievement* (1992); Fons Coomans and Fried van Hoof, *The Right to Complain about Economic, Social and Cultural Rights* (1995); Scott Leckie, 'Another Step towards Indivisibility: Identifying the Key Features of Violations of Economic, Social and Cultural Rights', 20 Hum. Rts Q 81 (1998).

On some specific rights see: Asbjørn Eide, 'The Right to Adequate Food and to be Free from Hunger: Updated Study', UN Doc. E/CN.4/Sub.2/1999/12; Centre on Housing Rights and Evictions, *Forced Evictions and Human Rights: A Manual for Action* (1999); Brigit Toebes, *The Right to Health as a Human Right in International Law* (1999); Human Rights Program, Harvard Law School and the François-Xavier Bagnoud Center for Health and Human Rights, *Economic and Social Rights and the Right to Health* (1995); Audrey R. Chapman (ed.), *Health Care Reform: A Human Rights Approach* (1994); Clair Apodaca, 'Measuring Women's Economic and Social Rights Achievement', 20 Hum. Rts Q 139 (1998).

In relation to the work of the ICESCR Committee see: Philip Alston, 'The Committee on Economic, Social and Cultural Rights', in P. Alston (ed.), *The United Nations and Human Rights: A Critical Appraisal* (2nd edn 2000); Craig Scott, 'Reaching Beyond (Without Abandoning) the Category of "Economic, Social and Cultural Rights"', 21 Hum. Rts Q. 633 (1999); Kitty Arambulo, *Strengthening the Supervision of the International Covenant on Economic, Social and Cultural Rights: Theoretical and Procedural Aspects* (1999).

PART B

WHAT ARE RIGHTS, ARE THEY EVERYWHERE, AND EVERYWHERE THE SAME? CHALLENGES TO UNIVERSALISM AND CONFLICTS AMONG RIGHTS

The preceding chapters surely conveyed no sense of a uniform, coherent, uncontested human rights movement. From the controversies over death row and capital punishment in Chapter 1 to the disputes over the substance and implications of economic and social rights in Chapter 4, we have seen major differences among states' legal orders as well as ongoing struggles over the meaning of treaty provisions and the content of customary law. Such contests and struggles within and about the human rights movement can be contrasted with conduct (torture, summary executions, racial discrimination, sham trials, and so on) that the vast majority of states throughout the world view as violations of universally accepted human rights norms.

Part B concentrates on such contests and disputes, exploring them more systematically than did the prior materials. It raises questions that were earlier bypassed, such as the nature of rights and rights discourse, and the opposition between universalism and cultural relativism in one's understanding of the character of the human rights movement. Conceptual and theoretical writings introduce these notions. They are either accompanied by graphic illustrations and case studies in Chapter 5, or followed by them in Chapter 6, which examines concrete instances of conflicts among rights and of claims that an asserted right lacks universal validity.

5

Rights, Duties, and Cultural Relativism

Thus far the materials have described but barely commented on the fundamental characteristic of the UDHR and ICCPR, their foundation in the rhetoric and concept of *rights*. Many view that rhetoric as unproblematic, as the central and inevitable component of a universal discourse about human dignity and humane treatment of individuals by governments. Others, to the contrary, view a discourse about rights as alien and harmful to their states or cultures, disruptive of traditional social structures, subversive of authority. Consider the following queries:

(1) Why does the language of rights dominate the texts of the declarations and treaties as well as, in many states, the new constitutions and even the slogans and polemics of political debate?

(2) Is that language intrinsically superior to other possible ones—for example, the language of duties that might lead to a Universal Declaration of Human Duties? Is rights language essential to the values and goals of the human rights movement? Or is the currency of that language a matter of historical contingency, in that the postwar movement to protect human dignity found its roots in liberal political cultures in which rights had long ago taken root.

(3) Does a particular substantive content necessarily attach to the language of rights? For example, do 'rights' necessarily express the principles of the liberal political tradition, as with respect to nondiscrimination, or fair procedures, or freedom of religion or speech? Or are rights empty receptacles that are open to many different types of values and ideas, some of which might be antagonistic to the liberal tradition?

(4) Universality informs the discourse and content of rights in the UDHR and the basic treaties. But why should we accept that the stated norms are universal? Are arguments about their universal character accepted worldwide? Or do some parts of the world view many important provisions in the basic human rights instruments as particular to the Western liberal tradition?

These are the questions that we encounter in Chapter 5. The first three sets of questions are addressed in Section A, while Section B explores the last set under the broad rubric of cultural relativism. Chapter 6 builds on these discussions by illustrating the broad ideas developed in them through examination of several concrete issues.

A. THE NOTION OF 'RIGHTS': ORIGINS AND RELATION TO 'DUTIES'

We here consider different understandings, historical and contemporary, of the notion of 'rights' and inquire whether rights have inherent implications for a society's moral, political and socio-economic order. For example, does rights rhetoric in a constitution and statutes, or in a dominant moral and political theory, point to an individualistic, communitarian, or other type of society? Does it necessarily assume certain institutional arrangements for government, such as a constitutional separation of powers and an independent judiciary?

The readings begin with brief descriptions of the evolution from earlier concepts of natural law and natural rights to contemporary notions of rights in domestic and international contexts.

BURNS WESTON, HUMAN RIGHTS
20 New Encyclopedia Britannica (15th ed 1992)

. . .

The expression 'human rights' is relatively new, having come into everyday parlance only since World War II and the founding of the United Nations in 1945. It replaces the phrase 'natural rights', which fell into disfavour in part because the concept of natural law (to which it was intimately linked) had become a matter of great controversy, and the later phrase 'the rights of Man' . . .

. . .

It was primarily for the 17th and 18th centuries, however, to elaborate upon this modernist conception of natural law as meaning or implying natural rights. The scientific and intellectual achievements of the 17th century . . . encouraged a belief in natural law and universal order; and during the 18th century, the so-called Age of Enlightenment, a growing confidence in human reason and in the perfectability of human affairs led to its more comprehensive expression. Particularly to be noted are the writings of the 17th-century English philosopher John Locke— arguably the most important natural law theorist of modern times—and the works of the 18th-century Philosophes centred mainly in Paris, including Montesquieu, Voltaire, and Jean-Jacques Rousseau. Locke argued in detail, mainly in writings associated with the Revolution of 1688 (the Glorious Revolution), that certain rights self-evidently pertain to individuals as human beings (because they existed in 'the state of nature' before humankind entered civil society); that chief among them are the rights to life, liberty (freedom from arbitrary rule), and property; that, upon entering civil society (pursuant to a 'social contract'), humankind surrendered to the state only the right to enforce these natural rights, not the rights themselves; and that the state's failure to secure these reserved natural rights (the state itself being under contract to safeguard the interests of its members) gives rise to a right to responsible, popular revolution. The Philosophes, building on Locke and others and embracing many and varied currents of thought with a common supreme faith in reason, vigorously attacked religious and scientific dogmatism, intolerance, censorship, and social-economic restraints. They sought to discover and act upon universally valid principles harmoniously governing nature, humanity, and society, including the theory of the inalienable 'rights of Man' that became their fundamental ethical and social gospel.

All this liberal intellectual ferment had, not surprisingly, great influence on the Western world of the late 18th and early 19th centuries. Together with the practical example of England's Revolution of 1688 and the resulting Bill of Rights, it provided the rationale for the wave of revolutionary agitation that then swept the West, most notably in North America and France. Thomas Jefferson, who had studied Locke and Montesquieu and who asserted that his countrymen were a 'free people claiming their rights as derived from the laws of nature and not as the gift of their Chief Magistrate', gave poetic eloquence to the plain prose of the 17th century in the Declaration of Independence proclaimed by the 13 American Colonies on July 4, 1776: 'We hold these truths to be self-evident, that all men are created equal, that they are endowed by their Creator with certain unalienable Rights, that among these are Life, Liberty and the Pursuit of Happiness'. Similarly, the Marquis de Lafayette . . . imitated the pronouncements of the English and American revolutions in the [French] Declaration of the Rights of Man and of the Citizen of August 26, 1789. Insisting that 'men are born and remain free and equal in rights', the declaration proclaims that 'the aim of every political association is the preservation of the natural and imprescriptible rights of man', identifies these rights as 'Liberty, Property, Safety and Resistance to Oppression', and defines 'liberty' so as to include the right to free speech, freedom of association, religious freedom, and freedom from arbitrary arrest and confinement (as if anticipating the Bill of Rights added in 1791 to the Constitution of the United States of 1787).

In sum, the idea of human rights, called by another name, played a key role in the late 18th- and early 19th-century struggles against political absolutism. It was, indeed, the failure of rulers to respect the principles of freedom and equality, which had been central to natural law philosophy almost from the beginning, that was responsible for this development . . .

. . . [B]ecause they were conceived in essentially absolutist—'inalienable', 'unalterable', 'eternal'—terms, natural rights were found increasingly to come into conflict with one another. Most importantly, the doctrine of natural rights came under powerful philosophical and political attack from both the right and the left.

In England, for example, conservatives Edmund Burke and David Hume united with liberal Jeremy Bentham in condemning the doctrine, the former out of fear that public affirmation of natural rights would lead to social upheaval, the latter out of concern lest declarations and proclamations of natural rights substitute for effective legislation. In his *Reflections on the Revolution in France* (1790), Burke, a believer in natural law who nonetheless denied that the 'rights of Man' could be derived from it, criticized the drafters of the Declaration of the Rights of Man and of the Citizen for proclaiming the 'monstrous fiction' of human equality, which, he argued, serves but to inspire 'false ideas and vain expectations in men destined to travel in the obscure walk of laborious life'. Bentham, one of the founders of Utilitarianism and a nonbeliever, was no less scornful. 'Rights', he wrote, 'is the child of law; from real law come real rights; but from imaginary laws, from "law of nature", come imaginary rights. . . . Natural rights is simple nonsense; natural and imprescriptible rights (an American phrase), rhetorical nonsense, nonsense upon stilts'. Hume agreed with Bentham: natural law and natural rights, he insisted, are unreal metaphysical phenomena.

This assault upon natural law and natural rights, thus begun during the late 18th century, both intensified and broadened during the 19th and early 20th centuries. John Stuart Mill, despite his vigorous defense of liberty, proclaimed that rights ultimately are founded on utility. The German jurist Friedrich Karl von Savigny, England's Sir Henry Maine, and other historicalists emphasized that rights are a function of cultural and environmental variables unique to particular communities. And the jurist John Austin and the philosopher Ludwig Wittgenstein insisted, respectively, that the only law is 'the command of the sovereign' (a phrase of Thomas Hobbes) and that the only truth is that which can be established by verifiable experience. By World War I, there were scarcely any theorists who would or could defend the 'rights of Man' along the lines of natural law. . . .

Yet, though the heyday of natural rights proved short, the idea of human rights nonetheless endured in one form or another. The abolition of slavery, factory legislation, popular education, trade unionism, the universal suffrage movement—these and other examples of 19th-century reformist impulse afford ample evidence that the idea was not to be extinguished even if its transempirical derivation had become a matter of general skepticism. But it was not until the rise and fall of Nazi Germany that the idea of rights—human rights—came truly into its own. . . .

. . .

To say that there is widespread acceptance of the principle of human rights on the domestic and international planes is not to say that there is complete agreement about the nature of such rights or their substantive scope—which is to say, their definition. Some of the most basic questions have yet to receive conclusive answers. Whether human rights are to be viewed as divine, moral, or legal entitlements; whether they are to be validated by intuition, custom, social contract theory, principles of distributive justice, or as prerequisites for happiness; whether they are to be understood as irrevocable or partially revocable; whether they are to be broad or limited in number and content—these and kindred issues are matters of ongoing debate and likely will remain so as long as there exist contending approaches to public order and scarcities among resources.

. . .

DAVID SIDORSKY, CONTEMPORARY REINTERPRETATIONS OF THE CONCEPT OF HUMAN RIGHTS
in Sidorsky (ed.), Essays on Human Rights (1979), at 89

. . .

In a context in which escalating rhetorical support for human rights as a cause célèbre coexists with systematic abuse of many of these rights, it is not surprising that the very meaning of human rights has become contested. Radically different definitions and interpretations of human rights have been proposed, each of which claims the banner of human rights. . . .

. . .

In turning to the contemporary interpretations and the current uses of the concept of human rights, even before examining the ways in which the idea is contested, an appropriate starting point is the recognition that the term seems to be fulfilling two different, although consistent, functions. On the one hand, the phrase *universal human rights* is used to assert that universal norms or standards are applicable to all human societies. This assertion has its roots in ancient ideas of universal justice and in medieval notions of natural law. . . .

On the other hand, the idea of human rights is used to affirm that all individuals, solely by virtue of being human, have moral rights which no society or state should deny. This idea has its classic source in seventeenth- and eighteenth-century theories of natural rights. . . .

. . .

The Theory of Natural Rights

The theory of natural rights had a major influence in the development of the political self-consciousness of modern Western society. The idea of natural rights as the sole justification for any political society was a challenge to all established political authority. From the perspective of the theory of natural rights, all the recognized theories of legitimacy—the divine rights of kings, the pragmatic necessity of stable political rule, conformity to divine or natural law or rootedness in historical and institutional traditions—were inadequate. A political regime was justified only if it satisfied the natural rights of its citizens.

The current function of the theory of human rights, unlike the doctrine of natural rights, is not primarily that of serving as a principle of legitimacy within a particular national state. It has become part of an effort to develop standards of achievement with respect to citizens' rights within an international community. Yet it is significant in this context to recognize the continuity between the traditional theory of natural rights and recent formulations of human rights. Six elements of that continuity merit special examination.

First, it was characteristic of theorists of natural rights to develop a list of specific rights. Although these rights allegedly derived from the universal and evident desires of all men, the content of various bills or declarations of rights differed. The appearance or omission of a specified right, like the right to property, was an index of the importance given in social policy to the defense or realization of that right. This tradition has been adopted in the theory of human rights and has resulted, for example, in the articulation of the more extended list of thirty rights that mark the Universal Declaration of Human Rights.

Second, in all traditional theories of natural rights, such rights were ascribed only to human beings . . .

The further implication is that any human being, solely by virtue of his potential ability to exercise rational choice, had rights. It was in this sense that the theory of natural rights proposed the equality of all men. Since having natural rights was intrinsically connected to being a human being, there was a basis for the later transition from the phraseology of *natural rights* to that of *human rights*.

Third, a major characterization of natural rights derived from this belief that rights are the properties of persons capable of exercising rational choice. For, when men asserted their natural rights they were expressing their autonomy as individuals. Hence, the model or pattern for the exercise of natural rights became the protection of the sphere of the autonomous individual from arbitrary incursion by the state or other coercive association. The listing of the right to life, for example, did not involve a commitment to the extension or universalization of health care or to actions for shaping a safer environment but to a rule of law that would restrain arbitrary acts of violence, especially those of governmental authorities, against individuals. Similarly, the natural right to liberty did not refer to support of policies that would enhance self-realization through the universalization of education, but it did require the legal protection of individuals against arbitrary imprisonment.

Since the natural rights of men were bound intrinsically to their capacity to exercise rational choice as autonomous beings, the list of natural rights comprised what have been termed negative freedoms, rather than positive liberty, that is, the freedoms that protect the individual *from* the invasion of his domain of selfhood or privacy rather than the freedom of the individual or group *to* achieve its purposes or ideals. This stress is evident in the many detailed lists of the declarations or bills or rights that proliferated in the late eighteenth and early nineteenth centuries. The inclusion of a number of human rights that relate to social and economic development is a point of difference between the classic theory of natural rights and the theory that led to the Universal Declaration of Human Rights. That inclusion, and the priority to be assigned to social and economic rights, has become the single most contested item in discussions of contemporary theory of human rights.
. . .

Fifth, natural rights, as the adjective shows, derive from the order of *nature* or from the nature of 'natural man' but not from society or history. Indeed, as truths of nature they were held to be rationally self-evident: that is, if the meaning of the term is understood, then all rational beings could intuitively know that men had natural rights. In this view, the recognition that the theory of natural rights had its genesis in the rise to power of the middle class no more shows the relativity of natural rights than the fact that the calculus was discovered in seventeenth-century Germany or England makes its truth relative to that place and time. While rational intuition is no longer relevant for the contemporary views of human rights, the belief that rights are universal, and not relative, to particular social or historical culture has become, if anything, even more important in their use as international norms.

. . .

NOTE

The following readings describe their authors' understandings of basic character-istics of rights in contemporary legal and political discourse and argument. The brief excerpt from Eugene Kamenka distinguishes claims of rights from other types of claims. Duncan Kennedy analyzes rights discourse as it has evolved in a liberal political culture such as the United States. He is thus more attentive to the role of rights in adjudication than are most of the materials in this coursebook, which examine rights discourse in the framework not of judicial opinions but of broader political processes—advocacy and speeches, UN resolutions, committee reports, investigative missions, scholarly writings and so on. Nonetheless, the analysis and critique of rights in Kennedy's book inform rights discourse through-out the international human rights movement as well. In the two readings that follow, Cass Sunstein and Karl Klare respond in different ways to aspects of the broad 'critique of rights' that schools of thought and groups throughout the world have developed over recent decades.

Ideas in these readings are central to grasping the special characteristics, strengths and weaknesses of a movement based on rights, whether rights language figures in broad political debates or in the opinions of courts.

EUGENE KAMENKA, HUMAN RIGHTS, PEOPLES' RIGHTS
in James Crawford (ed.), The Rights of Peoples (1988), at 127

Rights are claims that have achieved a special kind of endorsement or success: legal rights by a legal system; human rights by widespread sentiment or an international order. All rights arise in specific historical circumstances. They are claims made, conceded or granted by people who are themselves historically and socially shaped. They are asserted by people on their own behalf or as perceived and endorsed implications of specific historical traditions, institutions and arrange-ments or of a historically conditioned theory of human needs and human aspir-ations, or of a human conception of a Divine plan and purpose. In objective fact as opposed to (some) subjective feeling, they are neither eternal nor inalienable, neither prior to society or societies nor independent of them. Some such rights can be singled out, and they often are singled out, as social ideals, as goals to strive toward. But even as such, they cannot be divorced from social content and context.

Claims presented as rights are claims that are often, perhaps usually, presented as having a special kind of importance, urgency, universality, or endorsement that makes them more than disparate or simply subjective demands. Their success is dependent on such endorsement—by a government or a legal system that has power to grant and protect such rights, by a tradition or institution whose authority is accepted in those circles that recognize these claims as rights, by wide-spread social sentiment, regionally, nationally, or internationally.

Claims, whether presented as rights or not, conflict. So do the traditions, institutions and authorities that endorse the claim as a right. They conflict both with each other and, often, in their internal structure, implications and working out. . . .

The concept of human rights is no longer tied to belief in God or natural law in its classical sense. But it still seeks or claims a form of endorsement that transcends or pretends to transcend specific historical institutions and traditions, legal systems, governments, or national and even regional communities. Like moral claims more generally, it asserts in its own behalf moral and sometimes even logical priority—connection with the very concept (treated as morally loaded) of what it means to be a human being or a person, or of what it means to behave morally. These are questions on which moral philosophers do have a certain expertise, at least in seeing where the difficulties lie, and on which they, like ordinary people throughout the world, have long disagreed and continue to disagree.

DUNCAN KENNEDY, A CRITIQUE OF ADJUDICATION
(1997), at 305

[Kennedy, a leading scholar in the critical legal studies movement that started in the United States and spread to other countries, devotes part of his book to the examination and critique of rights. He is not directly concerned with the substance of rights—for example, whether a right to free speech should have broader or narrower boundaries—but rather with the discourse of rights itself, with the way in which advocates and courts argue and reason about rights. Thus Kennedy examines matters such as the assumptions made by courts and advocates about rights, the distinctive characteristics of rights rhetoric, and the types of reasoning (legal and other) that are explicitly or implicitly involved in the interpretation, elaboration and application of rights to given cases or contexts.

These ideas, although rooted in this book in the American experience, bear directly on rights discourse in the international human rights movement. The ideas below figure in the responses by Karl Klare and Cass Sunstein to criticism of rights and rights rhetoric that appear in the next following materials.

Kennedy notes that rights 'play a central role in the American mode of political discourse'. He describes rights as 'mediators' between two elements or domains in that discourse: *value judgments*, which he describes as matters of preference, related to subjectivity of views and to 'philosophical' premises; and *factual judgments* (also referred to as *factoid*) that represent the domain of the scientific, the empirical, objective judgments.

A few excerpts from the chapters on rights follow.]

[I]t seems to me that in American political discourse [the ways of under-standing the nature of rights] all presuppose a basic distinction between rights argument and other kinds of normative argument. The point of an appeal to a right, the reason for making it, is that it *can't be reduced* to a mere 'value judgment' that one outcome is better than another. Yet it is possible to make rights arguments about matters that fall outside the domain commonly understood as factual, that is, about political or policy questions of how the government ought to act. In other words, rights are mediators between the domain of pure value judgments and the domain of factual judgments.

The word 'mediation' here means that reasoning from the right is understood to have properties from both sides of the divide: 'value' as in value judgment, but 'reasoning' as in 'logic', with the possibility of correctness. Rights reasoning, in short, allows you to be right about your value judgments, rather than just stating 'preferences', as in 'I prefer chocolate to vanilla ice cream'. The mediation is possible because rights are understood to have two crucial properties.

First, they are 'universal' in the sense that they derive from needs or values or preferences that every person shares or ought to share. For this reason, everyone does or ought to agree that they are desirable. This is the first aspect of rights as mediators: they follow from values but are neither arbitrary nor subjective because they are universal.

Second, they are 'factoid', in the sense that 'once you acknowledge the existence of the right, then you have to agree that its observance *requires x, y*, and *z*'. For example, everyone recognizes that the statement 'be good' is too vague to help resolve concrete conflicts, even though it is universal. But once we have derived a *right* from universal needs or values, it is understood to be possible to have a relatively objective, rational, determinate discussion of how it ought to be instantiated in social or legal rules.

. . .

I pointed out [earlier] that rights occupy an ambiguous status with respect to the distinction between rules and reasons for rules. 'Congress shall make no law abridging the freedom of speech' is an enacted rule of the legal system, but 'protecting freedom of speech' is a reason for adopting a rule, or for choosing one interpretation of a rule over another. In this second usage, the right is understood to be something that is outside and preexists legal reasoning.

The outside right is something that a person has even if the legal order doesn't recognize it and even if 'exercising' it is illegal. 'I have the right to engage in homosexual intercourse, even if it is forbidden by the sodomy statutes of every government in the universe'. Or 'slavery denies the right to personal freedom, which exists in spite of and above the law of slave states'.

The Constitution, and state and federal statutes, legalize some highly abstract outside rights, such as the right of free speech in the First Amendment or of property in the Fourteenth. Positive law also legalizes less abstract rights that are understood to derive from more abstract, but not enacted, outside rights. . . .

. . .

[Kennedy observes that these 'outside' rights, which preexist any incorporation of them into law (for example, the right not to be tortured by state officials exists whether or not the formal legal system incorporates it and thus makes it a 'legal' right), can be analogized to 'natural rights' in classical liberal political theory.

When a party to litigation makes a legal claim of right, other factors come into play, such as the 'duty of interpretive fidelity' of judges who are bound by the legal formulation of the right and have a duty to be faithful to it in their interpretation and application. The adjudication of constitutional rights brings all these problems together. When incorporated in a constitution, such as the First Amendment to the United States Constitution, constitutional rights 'are both legal rights embedded in and formed by legal argumentative practice (legal rules) and entities that "exist" prior to and outside the constitution'. Thus argument based on constitutional rights involves both 'legal argument (under a duty of interpretive fidelity) and legislative argument (appealing to the political values of the community)'. By 'legislative argument', Kennedy refers to the broad range of arguments based on preferences, values, and policies that are characteristically advanced by opposing parties and interests within the legislative political process.

Kennedy then discusses legal rights in legal reasoning. He notes that rights arguments 'are open to the same analysis of open texture of indeterminacy as legal argument in general'. He describes one of the ways in which the critique of legal rights collapses the distinction between rights-based argument and policy argument in general. For example, suppose that a claimant appeals to the right to free speech to urge a court to interpret some rule in a way that protects free speech. The court will frequently 'balance' the conflicting claims, perhaps the right to free speech and (with respect to sexually abusive speech in the workplace) the other party's right to a nonabusive workplace. What determines the balance struck by the court is not any logical chain of reasoning from the asserted right, or from two asserted conflicting rights, but the court's 'considering obviously open-textured arguments from morality, social welfare, expectations, and institutional competence and administrability'.]

The upshot, when both sides are well represented, is that the advocates confront the judge with two plausible but contradictory chains of rights reasoning, one proceeding from the plaintiff's rights and the other from the defendant's. Yes, the employer has property rights, but the picketers have free-speech rights. Yes, the harasser has free-speech rights, but the harassed has a right to be free of sex discrimination in the workplace. Yes, the landowner has the right to do whatever he wants on his land, but his neighbor has a right to be free from unreasonable interference. And each chain is open to an internal critique.

Sometimes the judge more or less arbitrarily endorses one side over the other; sometimes she throws in the towel and balances. The lesson of practice for the doubter is that the question involved cannot be resolved without resort to policy, which in turn makes the resolution open to ideological influence. The critique of legal rights reasoning becomes just a special case of the general critique of policy argument: once it is shown that the case requires a balancing of conflicting rights claims, it is implausible that it is the rights themselves, rather than the 'subjective' or 'political' commitments of the judges, that are deciding the outcome.

. . .

People sometimes say, 'A critique of rights? But if you got rid of rights, then the state could do anything it wanted to you! What about the right of privacy? We wouldn't have any way to object to state intrusion!' They are just missing the point!

In the Western democracies, rights 'exist' in the sense that there are legal rules limiting what people can do to one another and limiting the executive and the legislature. The critique of rights recognizes the reality of rule-making, rule-following, and rule-enforcing behavior. It is about faith in the rational procedures through which legislators, adjudicators, or enforcers elaborate gaps, conflicts, and ambiguities in the 'text' of inside or outside rights.

There is nothing in the critique that might suggest a reduction in the rights of citizens vis-à-vis their governments. Having lost one's faith in rights discourse is perfectly consistent with, indeed often associated with, a passionate belief in radical expansion of citizen rights against the state. Moreover, loss of faith is consistent with advocacy of greatly increased tenant rights in dealings with landlords, as well as with the reverse, just as it is consistent with favoring more or less government control over abortion decisions. It is not about the question of how we ought to define rights but rather about how we should *feel about the discourse in which we claim them.*

. . .

CASS SUNSTEIN, RIGHTS AND THEIR CRITICS
70 Notre Dame L. Rev. 727 (1995), at 730

[This article, though written with respect to ongoing debate about rights in the United States, bears also on the international discourse of rights. The author begins with six different categories of charges against rights (categories A–F), drawn from judicial opinions and from such critics (none of whom would individually employ the same six categories) as Professors Mary Ann Glendon and Duncan Kennedy. Category A refers to the social foundations of rights, and to the view of critics that the rhetoric of rights, typically cast in individualistic terms, obscures the point that rights are essentially social and collective in character. Indeed, they depend on collective institutions and communal support. This confusion, critics say, makes it difficult to draw lines between 'rights that are desirable from the social point of view and rights that are not'. The article turns to the second category:]

B. *The Rigidity of Rights*

Other critics charge that rights have a strident and absolutist character, and that for this reason they impoverish political discourse. Rights do not admit of compromise. They do not allow room for competing considerations. For this reason, they impair and even foreclose deliberation over complex issues not realistically soluble by simple formulas.

Rooted in nineteenth-century ideas of absolute sovereignty over property, rights are said to be ill-adapted to what we usually need, that is, a careful discussion of trade-offs and competing concerns. If rights are (in Ronald Dworkin's suggestive and influential phrase, criticized below) 'trumps', they are for that very reason harmful to the difficult process of accommodating different goals and considerations in resolving such thorny problems as abortion, the environment, and plant closings.

C. Indeterminacy

In one of his greatest aphorisms, Justice Holmes wrote that '[g]eneral propositions do not decide concrete cases'. Rights, of course, take the form of general propositions. For this reason they are said to be indeterminate and thus unhelpful.

If we know that there is a right to private property, we do not know whether an occupational safety and health law or a law requiring beach access is permissible. In fact, we know relatively little. Standing by itself, the constitutional protection against government 'takings' tells us very little about how to handle particular problems. This is true of rights generally. To say that there is a right to equal protection of the law is not to say, for example, that affirmative action programs are acceptable, mandatory, or prohibited. In fact, the right to equal protection of the law requires a great deal of supplemental work to decide cases. The right must be specified in order to have concrete meaning. The specification will depend on premises not contained within the announcement of the right itself. Rights purport to solve problems, but when stated abstractly—it is claimed—they are at most the beginning of a discussion.

Perhaps the area of free speech is the most vivid illustration. Everyone agrees that such a right exists; but without supplemental work, we cannot know how to handle the hard questions raised by commercial speech, libel, obscenity, or campaign finance restrictions. A serious problem with modern free speech discussions is that the term 'free speech' tends to be used as if it handled the hard questions by itself.

D. Excessive Individualism

A different objection is that rights are unduly individualistic and associated with highly undesirable characteristics, including selfishness and indifference to others. Rights miss the 'dimension of sociality'; they posit selfish, isolated individuals who assert what is theirs, rather than participating in communal life. Rights, it is said, neglect the moral and social dimensions of important problems.

The important and contested right of privacy, for example, is said to have emerged as an unduly individual right, rooted in the 'property paradigm' and loosened from connections to others. Critics urge that this conception of the issues involved in the so-called privacy cases misses crucial aspects of the relevant problems—abortion, family living arrangements, and the asserted right to die. Such issues do not involve simple privacy; they call up a range of issues about networks of relationships, between individuals and the state, between individuals and families, between individuals and localities. Perhaps the abortion issue is especially problematic when conceived in terms of a 'right to privacy'. Many people, on both sides of the abortion controversy, are uncomfortable with the 'privacy' rhetoric. Inattentive to the unborn or to the situation of mothers, American law has been said to have, perversely, left the pregnant woman genuinely alone, without people 'willing to help her either to have the abortion she desired, or to keep and raise the child who was eventually born'.

. . .

E. Protection of Existing Distributions and Practices

To some critics, a key problem with rights is that they tend to be used for what the critics see as pernicious ends. Partly because rights are indeterminate in the abstract, they can be used as an excessively conservative and antidemocratic force, protecting existing distributions from scrutiny and change. Some people think that the historical function of rights has been to insulate current practice from legitimate democratic oversight . . .

. . .

F. Rights Versus Responsibilities

A final and especially prominent objection is that the emphasis on rights tends to crowd out the issue of responsibility. In American law and in American public discourse, some critics complain, it is too rare to find the idea that people owe duties to each other, or that civic virtue is to be cultivated, prized, and lived. Rights, and especially new protections of rights since the 1960s, are said to be a major problem here.

In a simple formulation: People who insist on their rights too infrequently explore what it is right to do. Or they become dependent on the official institutions charged with safeguarding rights, rather than doing things for themselves. The controversy over whether rights turn women or blacks into a 'dependent class' is in part about this issue. People who insist that their status as victims entitles them to enforce their legal rights may not conceive of themselves in ways that engender equality and equal citizenship.

. . .

[The author then turns to clarification of some conceptual issues raised by the criticism, and concludes that the critique, while embodying some limited and important truths, 'does not by any means support a general challenge to rights.' Sunstein starts by noting the position advanced by many rights advocates that rights refer to important human interests 'that operate as "trumps", in the sense that they cannot be compromised by reference to collective policies or goals.' He doubts that this conception is helpful.]

. . .The first problem is that almost every right is defeasible at some point, and defeasible just because the collective interest is very strong. In American law, no right is absolute. If, for example, the rest of the human race will be eliminated because of the protection of a right, the right will certainly be redefined or legitimately infringed, probably under some version of the 'compelling interest' test. The real question then becomes when rights are defeasible because of collective justifications—under what conditions and for what reasons. The formula of 'trumps' is misleading for this reason. We need to know what sorts of reasons are admissible and how weighty they must be; these are the key questions in the exploration of rights.

Rights characteristically limit the kinds of arguments that can be used by way of justification, and they characteristically require justification of special weight. Above all, rights exclude certain otherwise admissible reasons for action. But ideas of this kind do not support the 'trumps' metaphor and indeed lead in quite different directions.

The second problem is that many conceptual puzzles are raised by the understanding of right as interests operating 'against' the collectivity. Often rights are something that the collectivity recognizes and protects in order to protect its interests. If this is so, there is no easy opposition between rights and the collectivity. . . . Rights are collectively conferred and designed to promote collective interests. They are protected by social institutions for social reasons. If such cases, rights may in a sense operate against the collectivity once they are conferred; governments may not take property just because it wants to do so. But even in such cases, rights are guaranteed in the first instance both by and for the collectivity (which of course has no existence apart from the individuals who compose it).
. . .

[Sunstein turns his attention to what he describes as 'truths and partial truths' in the 'highly eclectic' views of the critics of rights. He observes:]

It is also important to point out that references to rights can make for unduly rigid understandings of complex problems and can sometimes stop discussion in its tracks before analysis has even started. Claims of right often have the vices of rules. Even worse, rights can be conclusions masquerading as reasons. In thinking about claims of right, it is often necessary to be detailed and concrete about the social consequences of competing courses of action. The invocation of 'rights' can be a serious obstacle to this process. Consider, for example, the current debates over regulation of the electronic media, violent pornography, hate speech at universities, or advertising for cigarettes. To say that any restriction on these forms of expression violates the 'right to free speech' may in the end be correct; but this requires a long and complex argument, not a shorthand phrase. The claim of a 'right to free speech' is far too general and abstract to support the argument. Here it does seem important and true to say that rights, stated abstractedly, do not solve concrete cases. They are indeterminate until they are specified.

As they operate in law, rights generally *are* specified. Hence the rights protected by the Constitution and the common law are far from indeterminate, however hard it is to know what they are when stated abstractly. The claim of indeterminacy is for this reason far too broad. The problem, to which the critics have correctly drawn attention, lies in the use of general claims of right to resolve cases in which the specification has not yet occurred.

It is also true that efforts to think about many social and economic problems in terms or rights can obscure those problems. A claimed right to clean air and water or to safe products and workplaces makes little sense in light of the need for close assessment, in particular cases, of the advantages of greater environmental protection or more safety, as compared with the possible accompanying disadvantages—higher prices, lower wages, less employment, and more poverty. Perhaps the legal system will create rights of a kind after it has undertaken this assessment. But to the extent that the regulatory programs of the 1970s were billed as simple vindications of 'rights', they severely impaired political deliberation about their content and about the necessity for trade-offs.

. . .

D. Confusions and Misconceptions

Despite the various partial truths in the attack on rights, there is a pervasive problem in that attack: Rights need not have the functions or consequences that they are alleged to have. The challenge to rights is properly directed against certain kinds of rights, not against rights in general. At most, the challenge to rights creates a contingent, partial warning about the appropriate content of rights and about the possibly harmful role of certain social institutions safeguarding rights. It is not what it purports to be, that is, a general claim about rights as a social institution. More specifically, the current devaluation of rights suffers from two serious problems. Both of these problems are products of some pervasive confusions.

Many critics of rights complain about what they see as a cultural shift from the 1960s, in which rights have crowded out responsibilities. Simply as a matter of cultural description, the claim is far too crude. In some areas, including for example sexuality, it is plausible to say that a belief in private autonomy has prevailed at the expense of a commitment to responsible behavior. But in other areas, the last few decades have witnessed an increase in social and legal responsibilities and a decreased commitment to rights. Consider, for example, cigarette smoking; corporate misconduct; air and water pollution; sexual harassment; and racist and sexist speech. In all of these areas, people who were formerly autonomous, and free to act in accordance with their own claims of right, are now subject to socially and sometimes legally enforced responsibilities. We have seen, in the last few decades, a redefinition of areas of right and a redefinition of areas of responsibility. I do not intend to celebrate these redefinitions, but only to suggest that purely as a matter of description, there has been no general shift from responsibility to rights.

. . .

The second problem is that the critics seem to think that the explosion of 'rights talk' accounts for certain social failures, including failures of social responsibility. This is far too simple a claim. In fact, the opposite is as likely true—failures of social responsibility give rise to assertions of rights. In any case, the claimed association depends on empirical claims that are highly speculative and that lack clear support.

The two problems can be brought together if we attend to a familiar conceptual confusion. Often critics write as if rights and responsibilities are opposed, or as if those who favor the former are completely different from these who favor the latter. As they see it, rights are individual, atomistic, selfish, crude, licentious, antisocial, and associated with the Warren Court. Responsibilities, on the other hand, are seen as collective, social, altruistic, nuanced, and associated with appropriate or traditional values. But this understanding is quite inadequate, for some rights lack the characteristics claimed for them, and other rights have the features associated with responsibilities.

For example, the right to freedom of speech may be owned by individuals, but it is a precondition for a highly social process, that of democratic deliberation. That right keeps open the channels of communication; it is emphatically communal in character. It ensures a sine qua non of sociality, an opportunity for people to speak with one other. Indeed, everyone who owns a speech right does so partly so as to contribute to the collectivity; it is this fact that explains the government's inability to 'buy' speech rights even when a speaker would like to sell. So too, the right to associational freedom is hardly individualistic. It is meant precisely to protect collective action and sociality.

. . .

The claimed opposition between rights and responsibilities faces some additional difficulties as well. Rights of the most traditional sort, including property, may be the necessary conditions for enabling a sense of collective responsibility to flourish. People without rights to their property may be so dependent on official will that they cannot exercise their responsibilities as citizens. Moreover, a principal characteristic of totalitarian states is the endless cataloguing of responsibilities owed by citizens to the state. The Soviet Constitution was an ignoble example. For example, that Constitution created a duty 'to make thrifty use of the people's wealth', 'to preserve and protect socialist property', to 'work conscientiously', and 'to concern themselves with the upbringing of children'. The Soviet Constitution offers a cautionary note against enthusiasm for responsibilities, at least if these are to be treated as an explicit, legally codified concern of the state (putting the Hohfeldian point to one side).

. . .

KARL KLARE, LEGAL THEORY AND DEMOCRATIC RECONSTRUCTION
25 U. of Brit. Colum. L. Rev. 69 (1991), at 97

[The author here discusses the appropriate place of 'rights' in the formal legal structures and guarantees and in the legal-political discourse of the postcommunist states of Central-East Europe. He concludes that 'it seems obvious that postcommunist law should be founded upon an explicit charter of human rights guarantees. How could there be any doubt of the central place of rights in democratic legal reconstruction?' Nonetheless, Klare notes, recent debates among Western legal scholars have developed a serious 'critique of rights', and he undertakes to summarize 'some of the major lines of criticism advanced by the rights skeptics'. The following excerpts deal with two aspects of this critique and Klare's responses thereto.]

A second branch of rights skepticism concerns the efficacy and limitations of the rights tradition in relationship to social change. [T]he skeptics call attention to certain self-imposed limitations internal to rights discourse stemming from its embrace of the public/private distinction. Rights thinking has predominantly concerned the relationship between the individual and the state. As traditionally understood, the human rights project is to erect barriers between the individual and the state, so as to protect human autonomy and self-determination from being violated or crushed by governmental power.

Unquestionably, a just society requires such protections, but human freedom can also be invaded or denied by nongovernmental forms of power, by domination in the so-called 'private sphere'. Human dignity is denied by *de jure* racial segregation, but it is also denied by employers who discriminate on the basis of race. Laws barring adult homosexuals from privately and consensually expressing their sexuality deny freedom and autonomy, but so, too, do homophobic social practices such as housing discrimination and gay bashing. The expression of dissent can be inhibited by the cost of media access as well as by abuses of state power. Rights charters almost invariably concern restrictions on state power and therefore leave intact many forms of 'private' domination, including hierarchies of class, race, gender and sexual preference. The skeptics argue that the vision of freedom embodied in the rights tradition is for this reason partial and incomplete.

Given the injustices committed by the Stalinist regimes, it is understandable that the first priority of postcommunist lawyers is to guard against the abuse of state power . . . . Granting this, the argument goes, to realize freedom in all aspects of life, to establish arrangements in all social contexts that will be committed to human dignity, self-realization and equality, requires a deep transformation, in both East and West, not only of governmental but also of non-state institutions and practices that are left untouched by conventional human rights doctrine. A strong version of rights skepticism suggests that the fixation on the individual/state relationship in the rights tradition actually diverts intellectual and political resources from other, needed approaches to social justice.

Here again, it is conceivable that rights discourse can be transformed to accommodate these criticisms; that we can articulate a panoply of self-determination rights in social and economic life. . . .

This brings us to a third aspect of contemporary rights skepticism, the so-called 'indeterminacy critique'. In its strongest versions, rights discourse purports to supply a political criteria for evaluating institutions and practices and for resolving social conflict. The very power of a claim of right is that it is founded upon universal values, that it transcends all particular understandings of appropriate social organization. A successful rights claimant trumps majoritarian sentiment regarding the good life. . . .

. . .

. . . The initial problem is that many of the most important rights concepts are formulated at an exceedingly high level of abstraction. Because human rights concepts tend to be very elastic and open-ended, they are capable of being given a wide range of meanings, including inconsistent meanings. Take freedom of speech, for example. One meaning is the right to dissent and to criticize the powers that be. Yet the right to free speech can also be given quite a different meaning, as, e.g., in the American cases barring government from trying to prevent the distortion of the electoral process by corporate campaign contributions. In the former interpretation, free speech permits individuals to unfreeze hierarchy and open up political debate, whereas in the latter case, the right to free speech is mobilized to reinforce domination by entrenched power. Or, take the right to privacy, the right to be left alone by government with regard to certain intimate matters. For most feminists, this connotes a right to choice about reproduction and abortion. But the right to privacy regarding intimate personal matters has long had a less savory invocation as a justification for why courts should not intervene to prevent or punish domestic violence. An interesting aspect of rights-fixated political cultures, such as we have in the United States, is that anybody and everybody can and does formulate their political claims in rights terms.

Thus, rights concepts are sufficiently elastic so that they can mean different things to different people. People who seek to reinforce hierarchy and perpetuate domination can speak the language of rights, often with sincerity. But there is an even deeper problem. Even those who would consistently invoke rights in the service of self-determination, autonomy and equality find that rights concepts are internally contradictory. That is because, like all of legal discourse, rights theory is an arena of conflicting conceptions of justice and human freedom. For example, democratic thinking, particularly within the liberal tradition, contains conceptions of rights as freedom of action and also of rights as guarantors of security. It contains conceptions of rights as protection from state power and also of rights to invoke state power to protect the individual from powerful private groups. Proponents of democracy have advanced conceptions of rights to freedom of association and also conceptions of rights of excluded minorities to insist on membership in important groups. Rights theories contain conceptions of equality as identical treatment of those similarly situated and also theories of equality as protection for those not similarly situated. Human rights discourse holds that its claims are universal yet also embodies a belief in the right of all peoples to cultural autonomy and self-determination.

Thus, choices must be made in elaborating any structure of human rights guarantees, just as in the course of specifying market structures, and the choices bear socially and politically significant consequences.

The problem is that rights discourse itself does not provide neutral decision procedures with which to make such choices.

. . .

. . . My point here is that, by itself, rights discourse does not and probably cannot provide us with the criteria for deciding between conflicting claims of right. In order to resolve rights conflicts, it is necessary to step outside the discourse. One must appeal to more concrete and therefore more controversial analyses of the relevant social and institutional contexts than rights discourse offers; and one must develop and elaborate conceptions of and intuitions about human freedom and self-determination by reference to which one seeks to assess rights claims and resolve rights conflicts.

If the processes of concretizing rights concepts and of resolving rights conflicts extend beyond the traditional discourse of rights onto the terrain of social theory and political philosophy, it follows that rights rhetoric must be politicized in order to serve as a foundation for legal reconstruction. . . . Surely it is insufficient to think of human rights practice in terms of obtaining the correct list of rights and then enacting them into a code. Rather, postcommunist lawyers must think of rights discourse and rights charters as relatively open media in which to advance visions of socially desirable institutions and practices. That is, the rights founda-tion of legal reconstruction is an invitation to make political philosophy, not only in promulgating the initial charters, but at every step along the way of articulating and interpreting rights concepts and filling them with concrete legal and insti-tutional meaning. But this revised, 'politicized' conception of human rights dis-course and practice in postcommunist legal reconstruction sits uneasily with the idea of an autonomous rule of law that is ostensibly the basis of the whole enterprise.

. . .

NOTE

A number of different understandings about rights—their nature, content and consequences—appear in the readings in Chapters 3 and 4. Consider the following lists, setting forth in the left column assertions or understandings about rights that typify much (not all) rights discourse within liberal societies, in opposition to a list in the right column of very different understandings, some of which inform the discussion about cultural relativism in Section B of this chapter, and some of which are related to utilitarian or policy-oriented argument.

inalienable	as opposed to	socially constructed, given and taken
absolute		contingent
universal		particular, culturally specific
eternal, ahistorical		time bound, historicist
rights based on equal human dignity		rights based on utility, power

QUESTIONS

1. How damaging to a rights-oriented international movement are the criticisms about rights discourse and argument that are developed (and in some cases, responded to) in the preceding articles? To which of them is the UDHR or the covenants and treaties examined in Chapters 3 and 4 most vulnerable?

2. Kennedy and Klare both stress that, at a given point, rights-based assertions give out, and a claimant or judge or other decision-maker must resort to (Kennedy) 'open-textured arguments from morality, social welfare, expectations, and institutional com-petence and administrability'. Klare stresses that 'choices must be made in elaborating

any structure of human rights guarantees . . . and the choices bear socially and politically significant consequences. The problem is that rights discourse itself does not provide neutral decision procedures with which to make such choices. . . . In order to
resolve rights conflicts, it is necessary to step outside the discourse'.

Apply these observations to a conception as basic as the 'right to life'. What 'choices'
about the meaning of this conception are before treaty-makers, legislatures, courts or
advocates elaborating this right, and through what methods or processes can those
choices be resolved? What different issues are posed by, say, a 'right to health care'?

3. Kennedy, Klare and Sunstein all stress the significance of the indeterminacy of
rights-based argument, including the problem of conflicting rights. Kennedy notes that
these features of 'open texture or indeterminacy' are open to the same analysis 'as legal
argument in general'. That is, they are not particular to rights. Give some examples,
other than those stated in the preceding writings, of pressing and difficult issues raised
by the ICCPR, CEDAW or the ICESCR that stem from the indeterminacy of the texts or
contradictions among rights? How would you start to go about resolving a concrete
issue about the content and reach of a right that involves indeterminacy or contradiction (say, right to speech and right to privacy)? Bear in mind that for many international
human rights issues, it will be impractical or impossible to invoke the jurisdiction of a
court that could issue a 'binding' precedent.

COMMENT ON DUTIES

The following readings describe and analyze duty-oriented rather than rights-
oriented social ordering through law and cultural tradition. Robert Cover comments on the legal culture of Judaism with its stress on obligations imposed by
God rather than on rights. He suggests historical reasons why Western states and
Judaism developed in these different ways. Jomo Kenyatta describes aspects of the
education of the young in the Gikuyu people in Kenya, particularly the inculcation
of elements of social obligations and duty. Although the cultural and religious
contexts and the content of the duties referred to are radically different in these
readings, they both suggest important consequences of an orientation towards
duty/obligation and the gap between such an orientation and the liberal political
culture that influenced the human rights movement.

Note that the duties/obligations referred to in these readings are *not* the same as
duties within a *scheme of rights* that are correlative to the described rights. For
example, the individual's basic right to be free from torture imposes a correlative
(corresponding) duty on the state not to torture. The following readings talk of
duties imposed on *individuals* rather than on the state or some other collective
entity. Article 29(1) of the UDHR offers an analogy to such use of duties, as does
the preamble to the ICCPR. But explicit language of individual duty to other
individuals (other than the implied, traditional correlative duties), to society, or
to the state in the universal human rights system is rare. A closer analogy to
the present readings, particularly the excerpts from Kenyatta, is provided by the
African Charter on Human and Peoples' Rights, examined at p. 354, *infra*.

ROBERT COVER, OBLIGATION: A JEWISH JURISPRUDENCE OF THE SOCIAL ORDER
5 J. of Law and Relig. 65 (1987)

I. Fundamental Words

Every legal culture has its fundamental words. When we define our subject this weekend as human rights, we also locate ourselves in a normative universe at a particular place. The word 'rights' is a highly evocative one for those of us who have grown up in the post-enlightenment secular society of the West. . . .

Judaism is, itself, a legal culture of great antiquity. It has hardly led a wholly autonomous existence these past three millennia. Yet, I suppose it can lay as much claim as any of the other great legal cultures to have an integrity to its basic categories. When I am asked to reflect upon Judaism and human rights, therefore, the first thought that comes to mind is that the categories are wrong. I do not mean, of course, that basic ideas of human dignity and worth are not powerfully expressed in the Jewish legal and literary traditions. Rather, I mean that because it is a legal tradition Judaism has its own categories for expressing through law the worth and dignity of each human being. And the categories are not closely analogous to 'human rights'. The principal word in Jewish law, which occupies a place equivalent in evocative force to the American legal system's 'rights', is the word 'mitzvah' which literally means commandment but has a general meaning closer to 'incumbent obligation'.

Before I begin an analysis of the differing implications of these two rather different key words, I should like to put the two words in a context—the contexts of their respective myths. For both of us these words are connected to fundamental stories and receive their force from those stories as much as from the denotative meaning of the words themselves. The story behind the term 'rights' is the story of social contract. The myth postulates free and independent if highly vulnerable beings who voluntarily trade a portion of their autonomy for a measure of collective security. The myth makes the collective arrangement the product of individual choice and thus secondary to the individual. 'Rights' are the fundamental category because it is the normative category which most nearly approximates that which is the source of the legitimacy of everything else. Rights are traded for collective security. But some rights are retained and, in some theories, some rights are inalienable. In any event the first and fundamental unit is the individual and 'rights' locate him as an individual separate and apart from every other individual.

I must stress that I do not mean to suggest that all or even most theories that are founded upon rights are 'individualistic' or 'atomistic'. Nor would I suggest for a moment that with a starting point of 'rights' and social contract one must get to a certain end. Hobbes as well as Locke is part of this tradition. And, of course, so is Rousseau. Collective solutions as well as individualistic ones are possible but, it is the case that even the collective solutions are solutions which arrive at their destination by way of a theory which derives the authority of the collective from the individual. . . .

The basic word of Judaism is obligation or mitzvah. It, too, is intrinsically bound up in a myth—the myth of Sinai. Just as the myth of social contract is essentially a myth of autonomy, so the myth of Sinai is essentially a myth of heteronomy. Sinai is a collective—indeed, a corporate—experience. The experience at Sinai is not chosen. The event gives forth the words which are commandments. In all Rabbinic and post Rabbinic embellishment upon the Biblical account of Sinai this event is the Code for all Law. All law was given at Sinai and therefore all law is related back to the ultimate heteronomous event in which we were chosen-passive voice.

. . .

What have these stories to do with the ways in which the law languages of these respective legal cultures are spoken? Social movements in the United States organize around rights. When there is some urgently felt need to change the law or keep it in one way or another a 'Rights' movement is started. Civil rights, the right to life, welfare rights, etc. The premium that is to be put upon an entitlement is so coded. When we 'take rights seriously' we understand them to be trumps in the legal game. In Jewish law, an entitlement without an obligation is a sad, almost pathetic thing. . . .

Indeed, to be one who acts out of obligation is the closest thing there is to a Jewish definition of completion as a person within the community. A child does not become emancipated or 'free' when he or she reaches maturity. Nor does she/he become *sui juris*. No, the child becomes bar or bat mitzvah, literally one who is of the obligations. Traditionally, the parent at that time says a blessing. Blessed is He that has exonerated me from the punishment of this child. The primary legal distinction between Jew and non-Jew is that the non-Jew is only obligated to the 7 Noachide commandments. . . .

The Uses of Rights and Obligations

The Jewish legal system has evolved for the past 1900 years without a state and largely without much in the way of coercive powers to be exercised upon the adherents of the faith. I do not mean to idealize the situation. The Jewish communities over the millennia have wielded power. Communal sanctions of banning and shunning have been regularly and occasionally cruelly imposed on individuals or groups. Less frequently, but frequently enough, Jewish communities granted quasi-autonomy by gentile rulers, have used the power of the gentile state to discipline dissidents and deviants. Nonetheless, there remains a difference between wielding a power which draws on but also depends on pre-existing social solidarity, and, wielding one which depends on violence. . . .

In a situation in which there is no centralized power and little in the way of coercive violence, it is critical that the mythic center of the Law reinforce the bonds of solidarity. Common, mutual, reciprocal obligation is necessary. The myth of divine commandment creates that web . . . . It was a myth that created legitimacy for a radically diffuse and coordinate system of authority. But while it created room for the diffusion of authority it did not have a place for individualism. One might have independent and divergent understandings of the obligations imposed by God through his chosen people, but one could not have a world view which denied the obligations.

The jurisprudence of rights, on the other hand, has gained ascendance in the Western world together with the rise of the national state with its almost unique mastery of violence over extensive territories. Certainly, it may be argued, it has been essential to counterbalance the development of the state with a myth which a) establishes the State as legitimate only in so far as it can be derived from the autonomous creatures who trade in their rights for security—i.e., one must tell a story about the State's utility or service to us, and b) potentially justifies individual and communal resistance to the Behemoth. It may be true as Bentham so aptly pointed out that natural rights may be used either apologetically or in revolutionary fashion, and there is nothing in the concept powerful enough analytically to constrain which use it shall be put to. Nevertheless, it is the case that natural right apologies are of a sort that in their articulation they limit the most far-reaching claims of the State, and the revolutionary ideology that can be generated is also of a sort which is particularly effective in countering organic statist claims.

Thus, there is a sense in which the ideology of rights has been a useful counter to the centrifugal forces of the western nation state while the ideology of mitzvoth or obligation has been equally useful as a counter to the centripetal forces that have beset Judaism over the centuries.

. . .

. . . [T]he Maimonides system contrasts the normative world of mitzvoth with the world of vanity—hebel. It seems that Maimonides, in this respect, as in so many others has hit the mark. A world centered upon obligation is not, really cannot be, an empty or vain world. Rights, as an organizing principle, are indifferent to the vanity of varying ends. But mitzvoths because they so strongly bind and locate the individual must make a strong claim for the substantive content of that which they dictate. The system, if it's content be vain, can hardly claim to be a system. The rights system is indifferent to ends and in its indifference can claim systemic coherence without making any strong claims about the fullness or vanity of the ends it permits.

. . .

JOMO KENYATTA, FACING MOUNT KENYA: THE TRIBAL LIFE OF THE GIKUYU
(1965), at 109

[These excerpts are taken from a description by Kenyatta, who later became the first post-colonial president of Kenya, of the Gikuyu people (often rendered in English as 'Kikuyu') in that country. The excerpts stress elements of duty inculcated in Gikuyu children, and appear in Ch. 5, 'System of Education.']

[The children] are also taught definitely at circumcision the theory, as it were, of respect to their parents and kinsfolk. Under all circumstances they must stay with them and share in their joys and sorrows. It will never do to leave them and go off to see the world whenever they take the notion, especially when their parents are in their old age. They must give them clothes, look after their garden, herd their cattle, sheep and goats, build their grain stores and houses. It thus becomes a part of their outlook on life that their parents shall not suffer want nor continue to labour strenuously in their old age while their children can lend a hand and do things to give them comfort.

This respect and duty to parents is further emphasised by the fact that the youth or girl cannot advance from one stage to another without the parent's will and active assistance. The satisfaction of all a boy's longings and ambitions depends on the father's and family's consent. . . .

. . .

The teaching of social obligations is again emphasised by the classification of age-groups to which we have already referred. This binds together those of the same status in ties of closest loyalty and devotion. Men circumcised at the same time stand in the very closest relationship to each other. When a man of the same age-group injures another it is a serious magico-religious offence. They are like blood brothers; they must not do any wrong to each other. It ranks with an injury done to a member of one's own family. The age-group (*riika*) is thus a powerful instrument for securing conformity with tribal usage. The selfish or reckless youth is taught by the opinion of his gang that it does not pay to incur displeasure. He will not be called to eat with the others when food is going. He may be put out of their dances, fined, or even ostracised for a time. If he does not change his ways he will find his old companions have deserted him.

. . . The age-groups do more than bind men of equal standing together. They further emphasise the social grades of junior and senior, inferior and superior. We see the same principle in evidence all through the various grades . . .

Owing to the strength and numbers of the social ties existing between members of the same family, clan and age-group, and between different families and clans through which the tribe is unified and solidified as one organic whole, the community can be mobilised very easily for corporate activity. House-building, cultivation, harvesting, digging trap-pits, putting up fences around cultivated fields, and building bridges, are usually done by the group; hence the Gikuyu saying: '*Kamoinge koyaga ndere*', which means collective activities make heavy tasks easier. In the old days sacrifices were offered and wars were waged by the tribe as a whole or by the clan. Marriage contracts and ceremonies are the affairs of families and not of individuals. Sometimes even cattle are bought by joint effort. Thus the individual boy or girl soon learns to work with and for other people. An old man who has no children of his own is helped by his neighbour's children in almost everything. His hut is built, his garden dug, firewood is cut and water is fetched for him. If his cattle, sheep or goats are lost or in difficulties the children of his neighbour will help to bring them back, at great pains and often at considerable risk. The old man reciprocates by treating the children as though they were his own. Children learn this habit of communal work like others, not by verbal exhortations so much as by joining with older people in such social services . . . All help given in this way is voluntary, and kinsfolk are proud to help one another. There is no payment or expectation of payment. They are well feasted, of course. This is not regarded as payment, but as hospitality. The whole thing rests on the principle of reciprocal obligations. It is taken for granted that the neighbour whom you assist in difficulty or whose house you help to build will do the same for you when in similar need. Those who do not reciprocate these sentiments of neighbourliness are not in favour . . . .

. . .

The selfish or self-regarding man has no name or reputation in the Gikuyu community. An individualist is looked upon with suspicion and is given a nickname of *mwebongia*, one who works only for himself and is likely to end up as a wizard. He may lack assistance when he needs it. . . .

In the Gikuyu community there is no really individual affair, for every thing has a moral and social reference. The habit of corporate effort is but the other side of corporate ownership; and corporate responsibility is illustrated in corporate work no less than in corporate sacrifice and prayer.

In spite of the foreign elements which work against many of the Gikuyu institutions and the desire to implant the system of wholesale Westernisation, this system of mutual help and the tribal solidarity in social services, political and economic activities are still maintained by the large majority of the Gikuyu people. It is less practised among those Gikuyu who have been Europeanised or detribalised. The rest of the community look upon these people as mischief-makers and breakers of the tribal traditions, and the general disgusted cry is heard: '*Mothongo ne athogonjire borori*', i.e. the white man had spoiled and disgraced our country.

. . .

The striking thing in the Gikuyu system of education, and the feature which most sharply distinguishes it from the European system of education, is the primary place given to personal relations. Each official statement of educational policy repeats this well-worn declaration that the aim of education must be the building of character and not the mere acquisition of knowledge. . . .

. . .

QUESTIONS

1. 'A duty-based social order seems inherently less subject to universalization (with respect to the duties imposed on individuals) than a rights-based social order (with respect to the rights attributed to individuals). That is, the content of duties (obligations toward elders, toward the community, toward God) seems to be very particular and bound to a given context, a product of a given religion or political or social culture, whereas individuals' rights seem to be more divorced from a particular context and can therefore be stated more abstractly.' Do you agree? Any examples?

2. '"Individual rights" necessarily imply equality among all rights holders, which is to say among all members of society. This in fact is what the contemporary human rights instruments declare. To the contrary, duties can be (and frequently are) defined so as to impose hierarchy, status, and discrimination in a given social order'. Do you agree? Any examples?

3. 'Different from a regime of rights, a regime of duties intrinsically exerts an inward, centripetal force. It draws individual duty-bearers into the society, connects them

intricately with other individuals and the community in a variety of ways, blurs the separate identity of the individual from society, and leads to a more communal and collective structure of life.' Do you agree?

4. Note that Article 2(3) of the ICCPR requires states to provide all persons whose rights have been violated with 'an effective remedy', and to develop particularly the possibilities of 'judicial remedy'. Do rights imply a preference for or even require individual (judicial or other) remedies against the state, whereas a regime of individual duties is less likely to provide such remedies?

COMMENT ON DUTY PROVISIONS OF NATIONAL CONSTITUTIONS

In modern constitutions, as in human rights treaties, provisions conferring rights on individuals far outnumber those imposing duties. There appear below English translations of articles in a number of state constitutions that, as of recent dates, expressed such duties. Presented here in isolation from the context of the constitutions and political societies in which they take meaning, these articles serve merely to illustrate the range of such duties. Within their national contexts, they may be understood or interpreted to impose slight or significant duties, which moreover may be viewed merely as hortatory or may be subject to enforcement by civil or criminal actions brought by the state or by nonstate parties.

Belarus

Article 53: Everyone shall respect the dignity, rights, liberties, and legitimate interests of others.

Article 55: It shall be the duty of everyone to protect the environment.

Cambodia

Article 47: Parents shall have the duty to take care of and educate their children to become good citizens. Children shall have the duty to take good care of their elderly mother and father according to Khmer traditions.

China

Article 42: (3) Work is the glorious duty of every able-bodied citizen. All working people in state enterprises and in urban and rural economic collectives should perform their tasks with an attitude consonant with their status as masters of the country. . . .

Article 49: (2) Both husband and wife have the duty to practice family planning. (3) Parents have the duty to rear and educate their minor children, and children who have come of age have the duty to support and assist their parents.

Article 54: It is the duty of citizens of the People's Republic of China to safeguard the security, honour, and interests of the motherland; they must not commit acts detrimental to the security, honour and interests of the motherland.

India

Article 51A: It shall be the duty of every citizen of India . . . (b) to cherish and follow the noble ideals which inspired our national struggle for freedom; . . . (e) to promote harmony and the spirit of common brotherhood amongst all the people of India transcending religious, linguistic and regional or sectional diversities; to renounce practices derogatory to the dignity of women; . . . (g) to protect and improve the natural environment . . . and to have compassion for living creatures. . . .

Iraq

Article 10: Social solidarity is the first foundation for the Society. Its essence is that every citizen accomplishes his duty in full, and that the Society guarantees the citizen's rights and liberties in full.

Article 32: (2) Work is an honor and a sacred duty for every able citizen, and is indispensable by the necessity to participate in building the society, protecting it, and realizing its evolution and prosperity.

Italy

Article 4: The Republic recognizes the right of all citizens to work and promotes such conditions as will make this right effective. (2) Every citizen shall undertake, according to his possibilities and his own choice, an activity or a function contributing to the material and moral progress of society.

Poland

Article 86: Everyone shall care for the quality of the environment and shall be held responsible for causing its degradation. The principles of such responsibility shall be specified by statute.

Portugal

Article 49: (1) All citizens who are over 18 years old have the right to vote. . . . (2) The exercise of the right to vote is personal and constitutes a civic duty.

Article 58: (1) Everyone has the right to work. (2) The duty to work is inseparable from the right to work. . . . (3) It is the duty of the State, by implementing plans for economic and social policy, to safeguard the right to work. . . .

Article 78: (1) Everyone has the right to cultural enjoyment and creation, and the duty to preserve, defend, and increase the cultural heritage. [Subsequent provisions in Article 78 spell out the state's duties.]

Saudi Arabia

Article 12: The consolidation of national unity is a duty, and the state will prevent anything that may lead to disunity, sedition and separation.

Spain

Article 45: (1) Everyone has the right to enjoy an environment suitable for the development of the person as well as the duty to preserve it.

Thailand

Article 68: Every person shall have a duty to exercise his or her right to vote at an election. The person who fails to attend an election for voting without notifying the appropriate cause of such failure shall lose his or her right to vote as provided by law.

Uganda

Article 39: The exercise and enjoyment of rights and freedoms is inseparable from the performance of duties and obligations, and accordingly, it shall be the duty of every citizen . . . (c) to foster national unity and live in harmony with others; (d) to engage in gainful employment for the good of himself, the family, the common good and to contribute to the national development; . . . (f) to contribute to the well-being of the community where the citizen lives; (g) to protect and safeguard the environment; and (h) to promote democracy and the rule of law.

QUESTIONS

1. Which if any of the preceding provisions are inconsistent with, or indeed threaten, the basic human rights declared by the leading international instruments? Which if any do you view as implicitly incorporated in those instruments?

2. How do you understand, and would you support for your own country's constitution, the provisions relating to work, to environment, and to voting?

A UNIVERSAL DECLARATION OF HUMAN RESPONSIBLITIES
Proposed by InterAction Council, 1997
in Hans Küng and Schmidt (eds.), A Global Ethic and Global Responsibilities
(1998), at 6

[The InterAction Council consists of about 25 former heads of state and government who have been addressing long-term global issues. The members (who endorsed the proposed Declaration) included Helmut Schmidt (Germany), Lord Callaghan of Cardiff (UK), Jimmy Carter (United States), and other former heads of state from such countries as Australia, Brazil, Costa Rica, Cyprus, Israel, Japan, Lebanon, Singapore, Thailand, and Zambia. The Council submitted the proposed Declaration to the UN Secretary General for consideration for its proclamation by the UN General Assembly as a 'common standard for all peoples and all nations'.

The introductory text to the Declaration notes that 'traditionally we have spoken of human rights, and indeed the world has gone a long way in their international recognition and protection since the Universal Declaration of Human Rights . . . [I]t is time now to initiate an equally important quest for the acceptance of human duties or obligations'. The concept of human obligations 'serves to balance the notions of freedom and responsibility; while rights relate more to freedom, obligations are associated with responsibility'. The two are 'interdependent'. Since the enlightenment, the West has been associated with rights and individualism. In the East, 'the notions of responsibility and community have prevailed'.

> Without a proper balance, unrestricted freedom is as dangerous as imposed social responsibility. Great social injustices have resulted from extreme economic freedom and capitalist greed, while at the same time cruel oppression of people's basic liberties has been justified in the name of society's interests or communist ideals.

Excerpts from the Declaration follow.]
. . .

Article 1

Every person, regardless of gender, ethnic origin, social status, political opinion, language, age, nationality, or religion, has a responsibility to treat all people in a humane way.
. . .

Article 3

No person, no group or organization, no state, no army or police stands above good and evil; all are subject to ethical standards. Everyone has a responsibility to promote good and to avoid evil in all things.

Article 4

All people, endowed with reason and conscience, must accept a responsibility to each and all, to families and communities, to races, nations, and religions in a spirit of solidarity: What you do not wish to be done to yourself, do not do to others.

Article 5

Every person has a responsibility to **respect life**. No one has the right to injure, to torture or to kill another human person. This does not exclude the right of justified self-defense of individuals or communities.

. . .

Article 7

Every person is infinitely precious and must be protected unconditionally. The animals and the natural environment also demand protection. All people have a responsibility to protect the air, water and soil of the earth for the sake of present inhabitants and future generations.

Article 8

Every person has a responsibility to behave with integrity, honesty and fairness. No person or group should rob or arbitrarily deprive any other person or group of their property.

Article 9

All people, given the necessary tools, have a responsibility to make serious efforts to overcome poverty, malnutrition, ignorance, and inequality. They should promote sustainable development all over the world in order to assure dignity, freedom, security and justice for all people.

Article 10

All people have a responsibility to develop their talents through diligent endeavor; they should have equal access to education and to meaningful work. Everyone should lend support to the needy, the disadvantaged, the disabled and to the victims of discrimination.

Article 11

All property and wealth must be used responsibly in accordance with justice and for the advancement of the human race. Economic and political power must not be handled as an instrument of domination, but in the service of economic justice and of the social order.

. . .

Article 14

The freedom of the media to inform the public and to criticize institutions of society and governmental actions, which is essential for a just society, must be used with responsibility and discretion. Freedom of the media carries a special responsibility for accurate and truthful reporting. Sensational reporting that degrades the human person or dignity must at all times be avoided.

Article 15

While religious freedom must be guaranteed, the representatives of religions have a special responsibility to avoid expressions of prejudice and acts of discrimination toward those of different beliefs. They should not incite or legitimize hatred, fanaticism and religious wars, but should foster tolerance and mutual respect between all people.

Article 16

All men and all women have a responsibility to show respect to one another **and understanding** in their partnership. No one should subject another person to sexual exploitation or dependence. Rather, sexual partners should accept the responsibility of caring for each other's well-being.

Article 17

In all its cultural and religious varieties, marriage requires love, loyalty and forgiveness and should aim at guaranteeing security and mutual support.

Article 18

Sensible family planning is the responsibility of every couple. The relationship between parents and children should reflect mutual love, respect, appreciation and concern. No parents or other adults should exploit, abuse or maltreat children.

Article 19

Nothing in this Declaration may be interpreted as implying for any state, group or person any right to engage in any activity or to perform any act aimed at the destruction of any of the responsibilities, rights and freedom set forth in this Declaration and in the Universal Declaration of Human Rights of 1948.

QUESTIONS

1. Which if any of the duties in the proposed Declaration cause you concern from the perspective of weakening or even contradicting basic human rights norms? Could the UDHR and the proposed Declaration comfortably co-exist?

2. Implicit in the Declaration are objections to a universal declaration cast dominantly in the language of rights. Could those objections be met by reformulation of some of the rights? Or do the objections challenge the very language, the intrinsic properties, of rights?

COMMENT ON COMPARISONS BETWEEN RIGHTS AND DUTIES IN THE AFRICAN CHARTER AND IN OTHER HUMAN RIGHTS INSTRUMENTS

The newest, the least developed or effective (in relation to the European and Inter-American regimes), the most distinctive and the most controversial of the three established regional human rights regimes involves African states. In 1981 the Assembly of Heads of States and Government of the Organization of African Unity adopted the African Charter on Human and Peoples' Rights. It entered into force in 1986. As of March 2000, 53 African states were parties.

The present discussion of the Charter emphasizes the distinctive attention that the African system gives to duties as well as rights. (The American Declaration on the Rights and Duties of Man, p. 869, *infra*, includes ten articles on individual duties. The American Convention on Human Rights does not give special attention to duties.) This distinctive emphasis is obvious on the face of the African Charter, even before one considers any elaboration or application of the provisions on duties by the African Commission. You should now become familiar with the provisions of the Charter set forth in the Annex on Documents. Other aspects of the Charter, and of the role of the Commission created by it, are discussed at pp. 920–937 *infra*.

The Charter's Preamble itself suggests some of the striking differences from other human rights instruments, universal and regional. Its key theme is regional cultural distinctiveness, as when it refers to '[t]aking into consideration the virtues of [African states'] historical tradition and the values of African civilization'.

Rights

Consider first Chapter 1 of Part I, dealing with 'human and peoples' rights'.

1. Compare the important opening provisions (Articles 1 and 2) of the Charter on the obligations of states with the analogous provisions in Article 2 of the ICCPR.

2. Several of the rights are expressed in ways that differ in wording from equivalent provisions in other instruments but that amount in the large to a similar conception. See, for example, Article 4.

3. Many rights are expressed in significantly different ways from the equivalent provisions in, say, the ICCPR. Compare, for example, Article 7 of the Charter on criminal procedure with Articles 14 and 15 of the ICCPR; and Article 13 of the Charter on political participation with Article 25 of the ICCPR. Note the respects in which Article 25 is more specific.

4. The protection of the property right in Article 14 recalls Article 17 of the UDHR but finds no equivalent in the ICCPR. The European Convention as first drafted included no such provision, but its First Protocol extends protection to the property right.

5. Some provisions state familiar norms, but illustrate them or make them specific in ways that recall Africa's experience with the Western slave trade and

with colonization. They bear out the phrase in the Preamble quoted above. See, for example, Articles 5, 19 and 20. Other provisions refer to abuses in Africa's own post-colonial history, such as Article 12(5) that recalls Uganda's expulsion of its citizens of Asian descent.

6. A number of provisions draw attention to the attempts of the states to reconcile humane treatment of individuals with their interests in territorial integrity and security. See for example, Article 23(2).

7. Compare the characteristic limitations on rights in the Charter with those in the ICCPR. See, for example, Articles 18(3) and 22(2) of the ICCPR. Compare with them Article 6 of the Charter, assuring the right to liberty 'except for reasons and conditions previously laid down by law'; Article 8 providing that freedom of conscience and religion are 'subject to law and order'; and Article 10 declaring the right to free association 'provided that [the individual] abides by the law'. See also Articles 11 and 12(2).

8. Note that the Charter has no provision for derogation of rights in situations of national emergency, equivalent to Article 4 of the ICCPR.

9. The Charter includes economic-social rights as in Articles 15 and 16, but does not qualify these rights with respect to their progressive realization and with respect to resource constraints to which the rights are subject, as does Article 1 of the International Covenant on Economic, Social and Cultural Rights.

10. The Charter includes several collective or peoples' rights, sometimes referred to as 'third-generation' human rights, in provisions like those in Articles 23 and 24 dealing with peoples' rights 'to national and international peace and security' and 'to a generally satisfactory environment favourable to their development.' The Charter's title itself signals the importance of this feature.

Duties

Consider now the distinctive Chapter 2 of Part I, on 'duties'. As prior materials in this chapter stress, references to 'duties' are not alien to human rights instruments: Article 29 of the UDHR, the preamble to the ICCPR, indeed the preamble to the UN Charter itself.

Nonetheless, the Charter is the first human rights treaty to include an enumeration of, to give forceful attention to, individuals' duties. In this respect, it goes well beyond the conventional notion that duties may be correlative to rights, such as the obvious duties of states that are correlative (corresponding) to individual rights—for example, states' duties not to torture or to provide a structure for voting in political elections. The Charter also goes beyond correlative duties of individuals that many human rights instruments explicitly or implicitly impose— for example, an individual's right to bodily security imposes a duty an other individuals not to invade that right. The Charter differs by defining duties that are not simply the 'other side' of individual rights, and that run from individuals to the state as well as to other groups and individuals. Hence the Charter directly raises the issues of universalism and cultural relativism that are addressed in Part B of this chapter and in Chapter 6.

Depending on their interpretation and their possible application within the

African human rights regime, the duties declared in the Charter could constitute part of the deep structure of the society contemplated by that instrument. For example, they could determine in basic ways the relationships between the individual on the one hand, and society and state on the other. They could resolve in specific ways the tension between the individual and the collective. They could contradict some provisions in the Charter's preceding elaboration of rights.

Note some of the vital phrases in Articles 27–29. Article 27 refers to duties towards one's 'family and society, the State and other legally recognized communities and the international community'. Rights are to be exercised with 'due regard to the rights of others, collective security, morality and common interest'.

The language of Article 29 is striking. Note such phrases as the 'harmonious development of the family', 'cohesion and respect', 'serve the national community', 'not to compromise the security of the state', 'strengthen social and national solidarity', 'strengthen positive African cultural values in [one's] relations with other members of the society', and 'contribute to the best of [one's] abilities . . . to the promotion and achievement of African unity'.

This theme of solidarity appears also in the African Charter's definitions of rights. Article 10(2) protects individuals against being compelled 'to join an association', but '[s]ubject to the obligation of solidarity provided for in Article 29'. Article 25 provides that states must 'promote and ensure through teaching, education and publication' respect for the rights declared and to assure that such rights 'as well as corresponding obligations and duties are understood'.

That is, depending on their interpretation and application, duties and ideals of solidarity may impinge in clear and serious ways on the Charter's definitions of rights themselves. Moreover, the Charter imposes individual duties not only on the state but also on different groups or communities within (or perhaps transcending) that state.

Consider some of the problems raised by these provisions about individual duties:

1. Sometimes what appear to be conventional terms of reference may bear plural meanings that affect the nature of the duty. For example, what definition applies to the word 'family' in Article 27—the nuclear or extended family? In the African context, one might think of the extended family. Nonetheless, the only specific reference to family relationships in the three articles on duties deals with parents and children (Article 29(1)).

Or how are we to understand 'society' in Article 27—as referring to the nation state, or to prevailing social and cultural structures within the state? It is striking that the article does not mention or seem to include ethnic groups, for they are frequently not 'legally' recognized.

2. As in the other two articles on duties, the requirements put on the individual by Article 28 raise the question of whether, and by whom, these duties are to be enforced. Who or what institution is to give meaning and application to them, or even provide general guidance for their performance? To the present, the African Commission has taken no steps toward interpretation or general elaboration of the provisions on duties. The question remains open whether the three articles are to constitute in some sense 'binding' and enforceable obligations.

3. The duties are of such breadth and so ambiguous in their connotations that a regime of serious enforcement without some degree of prior elaboration is difficult to imagine. Consider, for example, Article 28's provision that non-discrimination is not simply a duty of the state, but individuals also must not discriminate against other individuals. The article does not list any forbidden grounds for discrimination. Nor does it on its face distinguish between discrimination in the so-called private and public spheres—that is, discrimination in personal social relationships, and in employment or housing.

4. Article 29 raises a host of such issues, none more salient than the question whether it imposes on individuals a duty to uphold extant, traditional structures ranging from the family to the government. The critical terms seem to be 'harmonious', 'cohesion', 'community', 'security', 'social and national solidarity', 'territorial integrity', 'positive African cultural values', 'moral well-being of society', and last but not least, 'African unity'. How are these injunctions to be reconciled with the rights earlier declared?

Consider the following analysis of duties and their relationships both to rights and to African tradition and culture.

MAKAU MUTUA, THE BANJUL CHARTER AND THE AFRICAN CULTURAL FINGERPRINT: AN EVALUATION OF THE LANGUAGE OF DUTIES
35 Va. J. Int. L. 339 (1995), at 344

. . .

. . .In the West, the language of rights primarily developed along the trajectory of claims against the state; entitlements which imply the right to seek an individual remedy for a wrong. The African language of duty, however, offers a different meaning for individual/state-society relations: while people had rights, they also bore duties. The resolution of a claim was not necessarily directed at satisfying or remedying an individual wrong. It was an opportunity for society to contemplate the complex web of individual and community duties and rights to seek a balance between the competing claims of the individual and society.

The principles and ideals common to all these conceptions are, according to the author's own observations of various African societies, respect for, and protection of, the individual and individuality within the family and the greater socio-political unit; deference to age because a long life is generally wise and knowledgeable; commitment and responsibility to other individuals, family, and community; solidarity with fellow human beings, especially in times of need; tolerance for difference in political views and personal ability; reciprocity in labor issues and for generosity; and consultation in matters of governance. As aptly put by Cohen, many African cultures value the group—one should never die alone, live alone, remain outside social networks unless one is a pariah, insane, or the carrier of a feared contagious disease. Corporate kinship in which individuals are responsible for the behavior of their group members is a widespread tradition. But in addition, the individual person and his or her dignity and autonomy are carefully protected in African traditions, as are individual rights to land, individual competition for public office, and personal success.

. . .

This conception, that of the individual as a moral being endowed with rights but also bounded by duties, proactively uniting his needs with the needs of others, was the quintessence of the formulation of rights in pre-colonial societies. It radically differs from the liberal conception of the individual as the state's primary antagonist. Moreover, it provides those concerned with the universal conception of human rights with a basis for imagining another dialectic: the harmonization of duties and rights . . .

While it is true that no culture is static, and that normative cultural values are forever evolving, it is naive to think that a worldview can be eroded in a matter of decades, even centuries. Why should the concession be made that the individualist rights perspective is 'superior' to more community-oriented notions? As Cobbah has noted, 'in the same way that people in other cultures are brought up to assert their independence from their community, the average African's worldview is one that places the individual within his community'.

. . .

. . .While acknowledging that it is impossible to recapture and re-institute pre-colonial forms of social and political organization, this Article nonetheless asserts that Africa must partially look inward, to its pre-colonial past, for possible solutions. Certain ideals in pre-colonial African philosophy, particularly the conception of humanity, and the interface of rights and duties in a communal context as provided for in the African Charter, should form part of that process of reconstruction. The European domination of Africa has wrought social changes which have disabled old institutions by complicating social and political processes. Pre-colonial and post-colonial societies now differ fundamentally. In particular, there are differences of scale; states now have large and varied populations. Moreover, states possess enormous instruments of control and coercion, and their tasks are now without number. While this is true, Africa cannot move forward by completely abandoning its past.

. . .

The series of explicit duties spelled out in articles 27 through 29 of the African Charter could be read as intended to recreate the bonds of the pre-colonial era among individuals and between individuals and the state. They represent a rejection of the individual 'who is utterly free and utterly irresponsible and opposed to society'. In a proper refection of the nuanced nature of societal obligations in the pre-colonial era, the African Charter explicitly provides for two types of duties: direct and indirect. A direct duty is contained, for example, in article 29(4) of the Charter which requires the individual to 'preserve and strengthen social and national solidarity, particularly when the latter is threatened'. There is nothing inherently sinister about this provision; it merely repeats a duty formerly imposed on members of pre-colonial communities. If anything, there exists a heightened need today, more than at any other time in recent history, to fortify communal relations and defend national solidarity. The threat of the collapse of the post-colonial state, as has been the case in Liberia, Somalia, and Rwanda, is only too real. Political elites as well as the common citizenry, each in equal measure, bear the primary responsibility for avoiding societal collapse and its devastating consequences.

The African Charter provides an example of an indirect duty in article 27(2), which states that 'the rights and freedoms of each individual shall be exercised with due regard to the rights of others, collective security, morality and common interest'. . . .

Duties are also grouped according to whether they are owed to individuals or to larger units such as the family, society, or the state. Parents, for example, are owed a duty of respect and maintenance by their children. Crippling economic problems do not allow African states to contemplate some of the programs of the welfare state. The care of the aged and needy falls squarely on family and community members. This requirement—a necessity today—has its roots in the past: it was unthinkable to abandon a parent or relative in need. The family guilty of such an omission would be held in disgrace and contempt pending the intervention of lineage or clan members. Such problems explain why the family is considered sacred and why it would be simply impracticable and suicidal for Africans to adopt wholesale the individualist conception of rights. . . .

. . .

The duties that require the individual to strengthen and defend national independence, security, and the territorial integrity of the state are inspired by the continent's history of domination and occupation by outside powers over the centuries. The duties represent an extension of the principle of self-determination, used in the external sense, as a shield against foreign occupation. Even in countries where this history is lacking, the right of the state to be defended by its citizens can trump certain individual rights, such as the draft of younger people for a war effort. Likewise, the duty to place one's intellectual abilities at the service of the state is a legitimate state interest, for the 'brain drain' has robbed Africa of massive intellect. In recognition of the need for the strength of diversity, rather than its power to divide, the Charter asks individuals to promote African unity, an especially critical role given arbitrary balkanization by the colonial powers and the ethnic animosities fostered within and between the imposed states.

. . . It is now generally accepted that one of the strikes against the pre-colonial regime was its strict separation of gender roles and, in many cases, the limitation on, or exclusion of, women from political participation. The discriminatory treatment of women on the basis of gender in marriage, property ownership, and inheritance, and the disproportionately heavy labor and reproduction burdens were violations of their rights.

However, these are not the practices that the Charter condones when it requires states to assist families as the 'custodians of morals and traditional values'. Such an interpretation would be a cynical misreading of the Charter. The reference is to those traditional values which enhanced the dignity of the individual and emphasized the dignity of motherhood and the importance of the female as the central link in the reproductive chain; women were highly valued as equals in the process of the regeneration of life. The Charter guarantees, unambiguously and without equivocation, the equal rights of women in its gender equality provision by requiring states to 'eliminate every discrimination against women' and to protect women's rights in international human rights instruments. Read in conjunction with other provisions, the Charter leaves no room for discriminatory treatment against women.

. . .

. . . [C]ritics who question the value of including duties in the Charter point only to the theoretical danger that states might capitalize on the duty concept to violate other guaranteed rights. The fear is frequently expressed that emphasis on duties may lead to the 'trumping' of individual rights if the two are in opposition. . . .

. . .

This Article is not intended to dismiss concerns about the potential for the misuse of the duty/rights conception by political elites to achieve narrow, personal ends. However, any notions are subject to abuse by power-hungry elites. There is no basis for concluding that the duty/rights conception is unique in this respect. While it is true that the pre-colonial context in which the conception originally worked was small in scale and relatively uncomplicated, the argument made here is not about magnitudes. Instead, the ideals that can be distilled from the past are the central thrust of this argument. Is it possible to introduce in the modern African state grassroots democracy, deepening it in neighborhood communities and villages in the tradition of the pre-colonial council of elders? Can the family reclaim its status as the basic organizational political unit in this re-democratization process? Is it possible to create a state of laws—where elected officials are bound by checks and balances—as in the days of the old where chiefs were held accountable, at times through destooling? Can the state and the family devise a 'social security' system in which the burden of caring for the aged and the needy can be shared? Is it possible to require individuals to take responsibility for their actions in matters relating to sexuality, community security, and self-help projects in the construction of community schools and health centers, utilizing concepts such as harambee, the Kenyan slogan for pulling together?. . . These are the typical questions that the new formulation of human rights must ask in the context of recreating the African state to legitimize human rights on the continent.

. . . Part of the reason for the failure of the post-colonial state to respect human rights lies in the seemingly alien character of that corpus. The African Charter's duty/rights conception is an excellent point of departure in the reconstruction of a new ethos and the restoration of confidence in the continent's cultural identity. It reintroduces values that Africa needs most at this time: commitment, solidarity, respect, and responsibility. Moreover, it also represents a recognition of another reality. Individual rights are collective in their dimension. 'Their recognition, their mode of exercise and their means of protection' is a collective process requiring the intervention of other individuals, groups, and communities. The past, as the Africans of the old used to say, is part of the living. It ought to be used to construct a better tomorrow.

QUESTIONS

1. Does Mutua's article (a) explain and seek to justify in terms of African history and culture the relevant provisions of the Charter, or (b) seek to reconcile those provisions with the human rights movement, or (c) both? Do you believe that he succeeds in the second task? Does he suggest that the West and Africa should in some respects go their separate ways, or that Africa has indeed much to teach the West about the directions of its own rights-oriented thought?

2. Does the Charter protect an advocate of radical reform who seeks significant changes in her state with respect to gender relationships or the character of the family? How, for example, would you reconcile the provisions of Article 29 with Article 18, to the effect that the state should 'ensure the elimination of every discrimination against women'? How would you state your argument for the supremacy of Article 18? Are you persuaded by Mutua's argument?

3. What effect might Articles 27–29 have on the Charter's provisions for speech and association, which are the very conditions of effective political participation? Are Mutua's views here helpful?

4. 'Whatever the African Charter says, African states like all states are subject to the universal human rights system of the UDHR and the two basic Covenants. If there is a conflict, if this regional regime requires or permits state conduct that universal norms prohibit, those norms must prevail. Else the "universal" human rights movement collapses into regional anarchy'. Comment.

NOTE

As prior readings underscore, rights as a fundamental language of law, politics and morals grew within and are associated with the Western liberal tradition. This is not, however, to say that the claims, interests, values and ideals expressed through rights language in the basic human rights instruments are exclusive to the Western liberal tradition. Many of them, as we have seen, may be expressed through other languages as well—for example, the language of duty and responsibility.

To place the basic instruments in historical context, and as background for the discussion of cultural relativism in Section B, it will be helpful to have in mind some notions about liberal political thought and the liberal state. The following Comment sketches basic characteristics.

COMMENT ON SOME CHARACTERISTICS OF THE LIBERAL POLITICAL TRADITION

Observers from different regions and cultures can agree that the human rights movement, with respect to its language of rights and the civil and political rights that it declares, stems principally from the liberal tradition of Western thought.

That observation lies at the core of argument by states from non-Western parts of the world that some basic provisions in instruments like the UDHR or ICCPR are inappropriate and inapplicable to their circumstances. Those instruments, the argument goes, purport to give a genuinely universal expression to certain tenets of liberal political culture. But those tenets fit poorly with states outside that culture. Thus liberal thought and practices inform much contemporary debate about the meaning and relevance of cultural relativism.

For the purpose of facilitating some comparisons between liberalism and the human rights movement, this Comment sketches characteristics that observers would associate with the different expressions of the liberal tradition during this century. The Comment has a limited historical scope. It does not reach back to the origins of liberal thought in the seventeenth century and Age of Enlightenment, or to changes in that body of thought in the nineteenth century.

The liberal political tradition has never been and surely is not today a monolithic body of thought requiring one and only one form of government. The very term 'liberal' has assumed different meanings, from the liberal economics associated with the *laissez faire* school of the nineteenth century to contemporary associations of liberalism in a country like the United States with a more active and engaged state concerned with the general welfare of the population and with regulation of the market and nongovernmental actors—the modern regulatory and welfare state so familiar to Western states.

The contemporary expressions of liberal thought by theorists like Dworkin or Rawls depart significantly from the writings of the classical theorists influencing its development, like Bentham, Kant, Locke, Mill, Rousseau and Tocqueville. The differences among such classical writers are reflected in the distinct versions of liberal ideology and the varied structures and practices of self-styled liberal democracies. This variety and ongoing transformation suggest caution in making inclusive and dogmatic comparisons between, say, liberalism and the human rights movement, which has during this last half century generated its own internal conflicts and has itself undergone significant change.

No characteristic of the liberal tradition is more striking than its emphasis on the individual. Liberal political theory and the constitutive instruments of many liberal states frequently employ basic concepts or premises like the dignity and autonomy of the individual, and the respect that is due the individual. The vital concept of equality informs these terms: the equal dignity of all human beings, the equal respect to which individuals are entitled, the equal right for self-realization. It is not then surprising that equal protection and equal opportunities without repressive discrimination constitute so cardinal a value of contemporary liberalism. In general, the protection of members of minorities against invidious discrimination continues to be a central concern for the liberal state.

Such stress on the individual informs basic justifications for the state. The liberal state rests on, its very legitimacy stems from, the consent of the people within it. Within liberal theory, that consent is both hypothetical, as in the notion of a social contract among the inhabitants of a state of nature to create the political state, and institutionalized through typical practices such as periodic elections. Such ideas are explicit in the basic human rights instruments. Note Article 21 of the UDHR ('The will of the people shall be the basis of the authority of government') and Article 25 of the ICCPR (the importance of elections 'guaranteeing the free expression of the will of the electors').

From the start, liberal theory has been attentive to the risk of abuse of the individual by the state. The rights language that is found in constitutional bills of rights, statutory provisions for basic rights, political traditions not expressed in positive law, and writings of theorists and advocates respond to this need for protection against the state. The rights with which the individual is endowed limit governmental power—the right not to be tortured, not to be discriminated against on stated grounds.

Historically the protection of the property right against interference by the state and others played a major role in liberal theory. Indeed, questions of the relationships between liberalism and free enterprise or capitalism have long been debated. They take on a particular pungency in the post Cold-War world of spreading markets, spreading democracy, and globalization.

Sometimes the types of rights just referred to are described as 'negative': the hands-off or non-interference rights (don't touch), or the right to be interfered with (as by arrest, imprisonment) only pursuant to stated processes. It is partly the prominence of the rights related to notions of individual liberty, autonomy and choice and the right related to property protection that produces the sharp division in much liberal thought between the state and individual, between government and nongovernmental sectors, between what are often referred to as the public and private realms or spheres of action.

This conception of negative rights, and of negative freedom as the absence of external constraints, together with the historical alliance of political liberalism with conceptions of a free market and *laissez faire*, led to liberalism's early emphasis on sharply limited government. The tension between that early ideology and background, and the growing emphasis over more than a century on the welfare and regulatory functions of the modern liberal state, remain central to much political and moral debate today.

That debate is related to an opposition that has developed in liberal thought between *negative* rights or negative liberty (freedom), and *positive* or *affirmative* rights or liberty (freedom). Those terms have acquired different meanings, to be explored in this and later chapters. For example, 'positive rights' have been described as entitlements of individuals that the state not simply respect the 'private' sphere of inviolability of the individual (the negative rights), but also 'act' in particular ways to benefit the individual, perhaps by providing education or health care. In this sense, the 'positive rights' of individuals such as the right to education or health care impose duties on the state to provide the necessary institutions or resources. Compare the Comment on state duties at p. 180, *supra*.

In a different and more ample sense, *positive liberty* has been described as 'liberty to' as opposed to 'liberty from'—for example, the liberty to realize oneself, to satisfy one's real interests, to achieve individual self-determination. One form of such positive liberty facilitated by the state would be governmental policies and institutions fostering the active political participation of citizens in electoral and other processes that help to determine the exercise of public power. Through such positive liberty, the individual can participate in the creation and recreation of self and state. The state readily and naturally becomes involved in this search of individuals for positive liberty, characteristically by creating the conditions that make the individual quest more likely to succeed, but at the dangerous authoritarian extreme by attempting to define the content of genuine self-realization and by coercing individuals to achieve it.

What an individual should seek in life, what idea of the good in life that individual holds, how the individual seeks self-realization, remain in the liberal state matters of individual choice to which both negative and positive conceptions of rights and freedom are relevant. That state must be open to a variety of ends, a variety of conceptions of the good, that individuals will express. The liberal state must then be a pluralist state. Its structure of rights, going beyond the rights to personal security and equal protection to include rights of conscience and speech and association, facilitates and protects the many types of diversity within pluralism, as well as ongoing argument in the public arena about the forms and goals of social and political life.

Precisely what governmental structures best realize such liberal principles is among the disputed features of the liberal tradition. The liberal state is closely associated with the ideal of the rule of law, hence with some minimum of separation of government powers such as an independent judiciary that can protect individual rights against executive abuse. The fear of tyranny of the majority lies at the foundation of the argument for restrictions on governmental power through a constitutional bill of rights limiting or putting conditions on what government can do. How to enforce that bill of rights against the executive and legislature has never achieved a consensus among liberal states. They vary in the degree to which they subject legislative action to judicial review, hence in the degree to which governmental power, even if supported by a freely voting majority of the population, can abridge or transform or abolish rights. The trend among democracies over the last few decades has been toward judicial review of legislative as well as executive action.

The liberal tradition continues to be subjected to deep challenges from within and without, and thus continues its process of evolutionary change. During and particularly after the Cold War, its interaction with states of the developing world posed complex issues in relation to efforts of some of those states to develop new forms of government and economy. For example, the relationships in the former Communist states of Central and East Europe between liberalism, privatization and property rights, markets and regulation thereof, and the provision of welfare remain ambiguous and in flux. More generally, questions of the relationship between liberalism and a market economy, or liberalism and ethnic nationalism, have assumed heightened prominence. In a Western country such as the United States, liberalism responds to challenges from diverse perspectives such as communitarian ideas, civic republicanism, and multiculturalism (cultural particularism).

Some of these contemporary challenges underscore a continuing debate within liberalism, the two sides to which can lead to significantly different political and social orders: *individual* or *group* identity as primary. The group may be—to use the conventional porous and overlapping terms—national, linguistic, religious, cultural, ethnic. At the extreme, it is not compatible with the liberal creed for a governing order to subordinate individuals fully to the demands of such kinds of groups. With respect to the core values of liberalism, individual rights remain lexically prior to the demands of a culture or group, to the claims of any collective identity or group solidarity.

Nonetheless, the liberal state is hardly hostile to groups as such. It is not blind to the influence of groups (religious, cultural, ethnic) or of group and cultural identity in shaping the individual. Indeed, the political life of modern liberal democracies is largely constituted by the interaction, lobbying and other political participation of groups, some of which are natural in their defining characteristic (race, sex, elderly citizens), some formed out of shared interests (labour unions, business associations, environmental groups). The liberal state, by definition committed to pluralism, must accommodate different types of groups, and maintain the framework of rights in which they can struggle for recognition, power and survival.

Such issues indicate how much is open and debated within liberalism about the significance of the priority of the individual in the contemporary liberal state—or different types of liberal states. Should we, for example, understand the 'individual' *abstractly*, as similar in vital respects everywhere, both within the same state and universally? Or do we understand the individual *contextually*, as influenced or even determined by ethnic, cultural, national, religious and other traditions and communities? Should we even phrase the question in such dramatic contrasts, or should we rather assume that the answers are too complex for any clear choice between them?

Since the birth of the human rights movement, and particularly since the collapse of the Soviet Union, such issues about the individual and the collective have taken on great pungency in the contradictions bred, on the one hand, by the spread of both liberal ideology with its emphasis on the individual and of market ideology with its stress on private initiative, and on the other hand, by the often savage bursts of ethnic nationalism in many parts of the world with their stress on collective rather than individual identity.

The emphasis in both liberalism and the human rights movement on individual 'rights' leads to one final observation related to several of this chapter's readings. Rights are no more determinate in meaning, no less susceptible to varying interpretations and disputes among states, than any other moral, political or legal conception—for example, 'property', or 'sovereignty', or 'consent', or 'national security'. Within liberal states, different institutional solutions have been brought to the question of who should determine and develop the content of rights, who should resolve the many and puzzling conflicts among rights. In the international arena, this problem becomes all the more complex. What mechanisms, what institutional framework, what allocation or separation of powers, what blend of overtly political and judicial resolution of these issues, will we find in the international human rights movement? Such issues are examined in Part C of this coursebook.

ADDITIONAL READING

On theories of rights see the following collections: M. Ishay (ed.), *The Human Rights Reader: Major Political Essays, Speeches, and Documents from the Bible to the Present* (1997); J. Waldron (ed.), *Theories of Rights* (1984); C. Nino (ed.), *Rights* (1992); D. Boaz (ed.), *The Libertarian Reader* (1997). In relation to duties see: D. Selbourne, *The Principle of Duty* (1994); and F. Van Hoof, 'A Universal Declaration of Human Responsibilities: Far-Sighted or Flawed', in M. Bulterman, A. Hendriks, and J. Smith (eds.), *To Baehr in Our Minds* (1998), at 55.

  On liberalism see: H. Laski, *The Rise of Liberalism* (1936); G. De Ruggiero, *The History of European Liberalism* (1927); N. Rosenblum (ed.), *Liberalism and the Moral Life* (1989); M. Sandel (ed.), *Liberalism and its Critics* (1984); C. Taylor, 'What's Wrong with Negative Liberty', in A. Ryan (ed.), *The Idea of Freedom* (1979), at 175. More generally see R. Rorty, *Contingency, Irony, and Solidarity* (1989); R. Unger, *Democracy Realized* (1998); A. Gewirth, *The Community of Rights* (1998); and C. Nino, *The Ethics of Human Rights* (1991).

B. UNIVERSALISM AND CULTURAL RELATIVISM

COMMENT ON THE UNIVERSALIST-RELATIVIST DEBATE

The question of the 'universal' or 'relative' character of the rights declared in the major instruments of the human rights movement has been a source of debate and contention from the movement's start. These alternative understandings of the character of human rights have been cast in different but related ways—for example, 'absolute' rights (compare 'universal') as opposed to 'contingent' rights (compare 'relative'), or imperialism in imposing rights (compare 'universal') as opposed to self-determination of peoples (compare 'relative'). The contest between these positions took on renewed vigor as the human rights movement slowly developed, and in important respects weakened, earlier understandings of the scope of national sovereignty and of domestic jurisdiction that had enjoyed greater strength. Indeed, significant links have developed over the decades between some of the claims associated with cultural relativism and claims of sovereign autonomy for a state to follow its own path.

  Put simply, the partisans of universality claim that international human rights like rights to equal protection, physical security, free speech, freedom of religion and free association are and must be the same everywhere. This claim applies at least as to the rights' general content, for advocates of the position that rights are universal must concede that many basic rights (such as the right to a fair criminal trial) allow for culturally influenced forms of implementation or realization (i.e., states are not required to use the Anglo-American jury to assure a fair trial; states need not follow any one particular voting system to meet the requirement of a government that represents the will of the people).

  Advocates of cultural relativism claim that (most, some) rights and rules about morality are encoded in and thus depend on cultural context, the term 'culture' often being used in a broad and diffuse way that reaches beyond indigenous traditions and customary practices to include political and religious ideologies and institutional structures. Hence notions of right (and wrong) and moral rules based on them necessarily differ throughout the world because the cultures in which they take root and inhere themselves differ. This relativist position can then be understood simply to assert as an empirical matter that the world contains an impressive diversity in views about right and wrong that is linked to the diverse underlying cultures.

But the strong relativist position goes beyond arguing that there is—as a matter of fact, empirically—an impressive diversity. It attaches an important consequence to this diversity: that no transcendent or transcultural ideas of right can be found or agreed on, and hence that no culture or state (whether or not in the guise of enforcing international human rights) is justified in attempting to impose on other cultures or states what must be understood to be ideas associated particularly with it. In this strong form, cultural relativism necessarily contradicts a basic premise of the human rights movement.

On their face, human rights instruments (which in their treaty form mean to impose legal obligations, to convert moral rules into legal rules) are surely on the 'universalist' side of this debate. The landmark instrument is the *Universal* Declaration of Human Rights, parts of which have clearly become customary international law. The two Covenants, with numerous states parties from all the world's regions, also speak in universal terms: 'everyone' has the right to liberty, 'all persons' are entitled to equal protection, 'no one' shall be subjected to torture, 'everyone' has the right to an adequate standard of living. Neither in the definitions of rights nor in the limitation clauses (such as limitations of rights because of public order or policy or public health) does the text of these basic instruments make any explicit concession to cultural variation. (The regional instruments examined in Chapter 10, and particularly the aspects of the African Charter on Human and Peoples' Rights examined at p. 354, *supra*, do express an important degree of cultural variation.)

To the relativist, these instruments and their pretension to universality may suggest primarily the arrogance or 'cultural imperialism' of the West, given the West's traditional urge—expressed for example in political ideology (liberalism) and in religious faith (Christianity)—to view its own forms and beliefs as universal, and to attempt to universalize them. Moreover, the push to universalization of norms is said by some relativists to destroy diversity of cultures and hence to amount to another path toward cultural homogenization in the modern world. But the debate between these two positions follows no simple route. It is open to a range of views and strategies that the materials in this Section B explore at a general and theoretical level—and that the case studies in Chapter 6 further probe.

During the Cold War, such debates (sometimes no more than highly politicized accusations, routine polemics) were dominantly between the Communist world (and its sympathizers) and the Western democracies. The Western democracies charged the Communist world with violating many basic rights, particularly those of a civil and political character. That world replied both by charging the West with violations of the more important economic and social rights, and by asserting that the political and ideological structures of Communist states pointed toward a different understanding of rights.

That debate died more-or-less together with the Soviet Union, though some of its themes survive in different form. Today the universal-relative debate takes place primarily in a North-South (or West-East) framework between developed and less developed countries, or in a religious (West-Islam) framework. It also includes nonstate actors such as indigenous peoples.

NOTE

The three introductory readings come out of the rich anthropological literature on culture and cultural relativism. Anthropologists have long had to wrestle with these issues, in the context of their ethnographic writings about diverse cultures whose practices and values depart radically from the West. Often those practices would be subject to serious moral criticism from the perspectives of Western thought. The anthropological writings have sought primarily to describe, explain, and understand the alien culture, within the framework of one or another theoretical perspective or methodology. They have not historically sought to pass judgement on the practices involved, to condemn or praise even as they describe.

Thus the role of the anthropologist has traditionally been very different from that of the human rights investigator who monitors and reports and the human rights advocate who works to arrest the described violations. To be sure, investigators and advocates may also seek to understand and to describe the cultural contexts in which they are working. But those working with the large international human rights organizations characteristically combine their description with moral and legal assessment of a given state's conduct against international human rights standards. They will in appropriate cases condemn the state's conduct and urge the state or others to take corrective or coercive measures. Their work is inherently judgmental, normatively based. They seek to vindicate and advance the human rights movement.

As noted in the readings, the traditional anthropologists' approach to these questions has come under recurrent challenge. Questions have been raised about the appropriate stance of the anthropologist toward practices and values that are offensive from a Western viewpoint. Ought she to be critical of them, or on the contrary be tolerant and accepting, or simply be distant and neutral while in the role of observer and explainer. If critical, under what standards would she criticize?

Most of the anthropological debate on such issues developed before the international human rights movement became prominent in the 1970s, and makes no reference to that movement. The Statement on Human Rights, p. 372, *infra*, is an exception to this observation. Moreover, bear in mind in the following readings that the human rights movement addresses primarily states—and primarily individuals' rights against the state—whereas ethnographic writings involve primarily peoples or tribes or societies, which may be nonstate (often sub-state) entities or which in any event are objects of study distinct from the political organization and political acts of the state itself.

ELVIN HATCH, CULTURE AND MORALITY: THE RELATIVITY OF VALUES IN ANTHROPOLOGY
(1983), at 8

... Herskovits wrote that cultural relativism developed because of

> the problem of finding valid cross-cultural norms. In every case where criteria to evaluate the ways of different peoples have been proposed, in no matter what aspect of culture, the question has at once posed itself: 'Whose standards?' ... [T]he need for a cultural relativistic point of view has become apparent because of the realization that there is no way to play this game of making judgments across cultures except with loaded dice.

Ethical relativism is generally conceived as standing at the opposite pole from absolutism, which is the position that there is a set of moral principles that are universally valid as standards of judgment. One absolutist ethical theory is the traditional Christian view that right and wrong are God-given, and that all people may be judged according to Christian values. A wide range of purely secular ethical theories have also developed . . . .

It is the *content* of moral principles, not their existence, that is variable among human beings. It seems that all societies have some form of moral system, for people everywhere evaluate the actions of kinsmen, neighbors, and acquaintances as virtuous, estimable, praiseworthy, and honorable, or as unworthy, shameful, and despicable. These evaluations take objective form as sanctions, such as open praise or rebuke; and in extreme cases, violence and execution. The ubiquity of the moral evaluation of behavior apparently is a feature which sets humanity apart from other organisms. . . .
. . .

Chapter 4. The Call for Tolerance

... By and large ethical relativists have been anthropologists and not philosophers, and it is chiefiy in the anthropological literature that we find arguments in its favor. Two people in particular have stood out as its proponents in the United States, Melville Herskovits and Ruth Benedict, both of whom were students of Boas. Almost without exception, the philosophers are disapproving, for usually they mention ethical relativism only to criticize it while in the course of arguing some other ethical theory.

At least two very different versions of ethical relativism have been advanced by anthropologists, and these need to be distinguished since they have their own faults and virtues. The first is sometimes classified (erroneously, as we shall see) as a form of skepticism, and I will call it the Boasian version of ethical relativism. . . . Skepticism in ethics is the view that nothing is really either right or wrong, or that there are no moral principles with a reasonable claim to legitimacy. It has been suggested that the Boasian position differs from this on one main point: Boasian relativism implies that principles of right and wrong do have some validity, but a very limited one, for they are legitimate only for the members of the society in which they are found. The values of the American middle class are valid for middle-class Americans, but not for the Trobriand Islanders, and vice versa.

Philosophers have presented a wide range of arguments against Boasian ethical relativism . . . According to this argument, Boasian relativism is in essence a moral theory that gives a central place to one particular value. . . . It contains a more or less implicit value judgment in its call for tolerance: it asserts that we *ought* to respect other ways of life . . . Herskovits wrote: 'The very core of cultural relativism is the social discipline that comes of respect for differences—of mutual respect. Emphasis on the worth of many ways of life, not one, is an affirmation of the values in each culture.
. . .

. . . The call for tolerance was an appeal to the liberal philosophy regarding human rights and self-determinism. It expressed the principle that others ought to be able to conduct their affairs as they see fit, which includes living their lives according to the cultural values and beliefs of their society. Put simply, what was at issue was human freedom.

The call for tolerance (or for the freedom of foreign peoples to live as they choose) was a matter of immediate, practical importance in light of the pattern of Western expansion. As Western Europeans established colonies and assumed power over more and more of the globe, they typically wanted both to Christianize and civilize the indigenous peoples. Christian rituals were fostered or imposed, and 'pagan' practices were prohibited, sometimes with force. The practice of plural marriage was condemned as a barbaric custom, and Western standards of modesty were enforced in an attempt to improve morals by covering the body. In the Southwest of North America, Indians who traditionally had lived in scattered encampments were made to settle in proper villages like 'civilized' people. The treatment of non-Western societies by the expanding nations of the West is a very large blot on our history, and had the Boasian call for tolerance—and for the freedom of others to define 'civilization' for themselves—been heard two or three centuries earlier, this blot might not loom so large today.
. . .

To develop a moral theory around the principle of tolerance raises the need to justify that principle: what reasons or grounds can be given to make the case that cultural differences ought to be respected? . . . The relativists make the error of deriving an 'ought' statement from an 'is' statement. To say that values vary from culture to culture is to describe (accurately or not) an empirical state of affairs in the real world, whereas the call for tolerance is a value judgment of what ought to be, and it is logically impossible to derive the one from the other. The fact of moral diversity no more compels our approval of other ways of life than the existence of cancer compels us to value ill-health.

Let us assume that we do find a set of values shared by all cultures. Would the relativist want to claim that these moral principles are legitimate ones for the world to embrace? What if the universal standard we discover is that all people are intolerant of other cultures—which is not very far-fetched? Clearly the ethical relativists would not throw aside their value of tolerance, but they would be forced to recognize that it is an error to think that the presence or absence of universal values among human cultures is a suitable base on which to build a moral philosophy.

. . .

Chapter 5. The Limits of Tolerance

The Boasian version of ethical relativism is subject to even harsher criticism . . . in its commitment to the status quo. The approval it enjoins seems to be absolute, leaving no room for judgment . . .

. . .

The moral principle of tolerance that is proposed by Boasian relativism carries the obligation that one cannot be indifferent toward other ways of life—it obligates us to approve what others do. So if missionaries or government officials were to interfere in Yanomamo affairs for the purpose of reducing violence, the relativist would be obligated to oppose these moves in word if not action. Similarly, by the strict logic of relativism, Chagnon was wrong to insist that the mother feed her emaciated child. The Boasian relativist is placed in the morally awkward position of endorsing the infant's starvation, the rape of abducted women, the massacre of whole villages . . .

Chapter 6. A Growing Disaffection

. . . .

We can now understand why ethical relativism has fallen on such hard times in spite of the resurgence of pessimism during the 1960s and later. First, it has been the experience of most anthropologists that non-Western peoples (and especially Third World nations) want change, at least to some extent: second, it is clear that they are often disadvantaged if it does not come; third, anthropologists by and large have altered their thinking about the relativity of material interests and improvement: most today consider these to be general values that can be applied throughout the world.

Not only has relativism fallen on hard times, it has become the subject of angry criticism, much of it from the Third World, which tends to conceive anthropologists as conservative in their attitudes toward change and therefore as promoting the subservience of the underdeveloped nations. . . .

. . .

Whatever the cause, according to the radical critique, relativism has played directly into the hands of the oppressors throughout the world by its tacit support of the status quo. The relativists have not recognized that the exotic cultures to which they grant equal validity are poverty-stricken, powerless, and oppressed. William Willis comments that the relativist 'avoids the distress and misery' of foreign peoples who are 'cringing and cursing at the aggressive cruelty' of the Western nations (p. 126). This avoidance of the matter of oppression 'helps explain the lack of outrage that has prevailed in anthropology until recent years'. Willis writes: 'Since relativism is applied only to 'aboriginal' customs, it advises colored peoples to preserve those customs that contributed to initial defeat and subsequent exploitation . . . . Hence, relativism defines the good life for colored peoples differently than for white people, and the good colored man is the man of the bush' (p. 144). Instead of leaving cultures as they are, as museum pieces, we should help to bring about change—or, better, we should help the oppressed to bring about change.

. . .

AMERICAN ANTHROPOLOGICAL ASSOCIATION, STATEMENT ON HUMAN RIGHTS
49 Amer. Anthropologist No. 4, 539 (1947)

[In 1947, the Commission on Human Rights created under the UN Charter was considering proposals for a declaration on basic human rights. Ultimately the instrument took the form of the Universal Declaration of Human Rights voted by the UN General Assembly in 1948. The Statement from which the following excerpts are taken was submitted to the Commission in 1947 by the Executive Board of the American Anthropological Association. It uses several terms or designations to refer to the pending document that became the UDHR.]

The problem faced by the Commission on Human Rights of the United Nations in preparing its Declaration on the Rights of Man must be approached from two points of view. The first, in terms of which the Declaration is ordinarily conceived, concerns the respect for the personality of the individual as such and his right to its fullest development as a member of his society. In a world order, however, respect for the cultures of differing human groups is equally important.

These are two facets of the same problem, since it is a truism that groups are composed of individuals, and human beings do not function outside the societies of which they form a part. The problem is thus to formulate a statement of human rights that will do more than just phrase respect for the individual as an individual. It must also take into full account the individual as a member of the social group of which he is a part, whose sanctioned modes of life shape his behavior, and with whose fate his own is thus inextricably bound.

. . . How can the proposed Declaration be applicable to all human beings and not be a statement of rights conceived only in terms of the values prevalent in the countries of Western Europe and America?

. . .

If we begin, as we must, with the individual, we find that from the moment of his birth not only his behavior, but his very thought, his hopes, aspirations, the moral values which direct his action and justify and give meaning to his life in his own eyes and those of his fellows, are shaped by the body of custom of the group of which he becomes a member. The process by means of which this is accomplished is so subtle, and its effects are so far-reaching, that only after considerable training are we conscious of it. Yet if the essence of the Declaration is to be, as it must, a statement in which the right of the individual to develop his personality to the fullest is to be stressed, then this must be based on a recognition of the fact that the personality of the individual can develop only in terms of the culture of his society.

. . .

... Doctrines of the 'white man's burden' have been employed to implement economic exploitation and to deny the right to control their own affairs to millions of peoples over the world, where the expansion of Europe and America has not meant the literal extermination of whole populations. Rationalized in terms of ascribing cultural inferiority to these peoples, or in conceptions of their backwardness in development of their 'primitive mentality', that justified their being held in the tutelage of their superiors, the history of the expansion of the western world has been marked by demoralization of human personality and the disintegration of human rights among the peoples over whom hegemony has been established.

The values of the ways of life of these peoples have been consistently misunderstood and decried. Religious beliefs that for untold ages have carried conviction and permitted adjustment to the Universe have been attacked as superstitious, immoral, untrue. And, since power carries its own conviction, this has furthered the process of demoralization begun by economic exploitation and the loss of political autonomy....

We thus come to the first proposition that the study of human psychology and culture dictates as essential in drawing up a Bill of Human Rights in terms of existing knowledge:

1. *The individual realizes his personality through his culture, hence respect for individual differences entails a respect for cultural differences.*

There can be no individual freedom, that is, when the group with which the individual identifies himself is not free. There can be no full development of the individual personality as long as the individual is told, by men who have the power to enforce their commands, that the way of life of his group is inferior to that of those who wield the power.
. . .

2. *Respect for differences between cultures is validated by the scientific fact that no technique of qualitatively evaluating cultures has been discovered.*

This principle leads us to a further one, namely that the aims that guide the life of every people are self-evident in their significance to that people....

3. *Standards and values are relative to the culture from which they derive so that any attempt to formulate postulates that grow out of the beliefs or moral codes of one culture must to that extent detract from the applicability of any Declaration of Human Rights to mankind as a whole.*

Ideas of right and wrong, good and evil, are found in all societies, though they differ in their expression among different peoples. What is held to be a human right in one society may be regarded as anti-social by another people, or by the same people in a different period of their history. The saint of one epoch would at a later time be confined as a man not fitted to cope with reality. Even the nature of the physical world, the colors we see, the sounds we hear, are conditioned by the language we speak, which is part of the culture into which we are born.

The problem of drawing up a Declaration of Human Rights was relatively simple in the eighteenth century, because it was not a matter of *human* rights, but of the rights of men within the framework of the sanctions laid by a single society. . . .

Today the problem is complicated by the fact that the Declaration must be of worldwide applicability. It must embrace and recognize the validity of many different ways of life. It will not be convincing to the Indonesian, the African, the Indian, the Chinese, if it lies on the same plane as like documents of an earlier period. . . .

. . .

NOTE

In 1983, the creation of a new national park in Sri Lanka displaced the last remnant of the Wanniya-laeto people from the last portion of forests where they had long been hunters and gatherers. Since then, the people have struggled to preserve their culture. In 1996 the American Anthropological Association acted to aid this group by sending a letter to the Prime Minister of Sri Lanka protesting the treatment of the Wanniya-laeto and asking that they again be given access to the lands on the park. As reported in Daniel Goleman, Anthropology Group Takes Activist Stand to Protect Cultures, *New York Times*, March 19, 1996, p. C11, the action was taken by a Committee for Human Rights recently established by the Association

> in a step designed to move anthropology as a profession to an activist stance taken only erratically in the past, and usually by individual anthropologists. The letter marked the first time the anthropological association itself has actively intervened in a dispute, although it has taken political positions in the past.

The Committee's chair described its mandate as broad, and stated that 'our concern is with any group of persons where assaults on their cultural ways have put them in danger'. The Committee has taken up other causes involving mistreatment and displacement of indigenous groups by action of the World Bank or national governments.

The move within the Association toward activism ignited a debate in the field between those protesting that such advocacy and intervention blurs professional objectivity, and others who argued that anthropologists 'have both a moral and professional obligation to protect the people who make the discipline possible by opening their way of life to study'. The debate was described by some as a 'generational schism' within the profession. Those trained in recent decades were more likely to be taught that 'their profession demanded an activist stand'. As one anthropologist put it, 'I teach . . . that people have a right to their culture and that human rights concerns are inextricably bound up with being an anthropologist'. The Association's letter protesting Sri Lanka's conduct toward the Wanniya-laeto contended that its action violated international law.

QUESTION

Does the intervention by the American Anthropological Association described in the preceding Note deviate from or support the 1947 Statement of the Association? Does it bring the Association closer to the work of human rights NGOs?

NOTE

The preceding readings did not examine the notion of culture itself as they explored issues of universalism and respect for different cultures. Yet the human rights discourse of the last half century directly raises the question of what the different proponents in the ongoing debate mean by culture, or cultural tradition or identity. What is being asserted by the claim that a given state or region must be free to follow its own 'cultural tradition', even if thereby violating norms in universal treaties? Many meanings of the term appear and disappear in this debate; often 'culture' as a justification for difference is not referred to as such but is implicit in a state's argument. Or that broad term is disaggregated into some of its complex components, such as language or religion.

Meanings of culture may also differ across the divides of different languages. Consider some definitions for 'culture' in the American Heritage Dictionary of the English Language (1969).

> . . . 4. Intellectual and social formation. 5. The totality of socially transmitted behavior patterns, arts, beliefs, characteristic of a community or population. 6. A style of social and artistic expression peculiar to a society or class. 7. Intellectual and artistic activity.

In his 1999 book, *Culture: The Anthropologists' Account*, Adam Kuper explores this concept over two centuries of Western intellectual history and anthropology. He raises questions pertinent to human rights inquiry about the premises, methods, and validity of cultural analysis. He also suggests ways in which contemporary concepts like multiculturalism and globalism tap into the debate on universalism and relativism. The following excerpts suggest the variety of premises and theories that have informed anthropological and political use of this ever-changing concept, and the importance of bringing awareness of the term's complexity to current human rights controversies that take legal as well as political form.

ADAM KUPER, CULTURE: THE ANTHROPOLOGISTS' ACCOUNT
(1999), at 2

Introduction: Culture Wars

. . .

Everyone is into culture now. For anthropologists, culture was once a term of art. Now the natives talk culture back at them. '"Culture"—the word itself, or some local equivalent, is on everyone's lips', Marshall Sahlins has observed. 'Tibetans and Hawaiians, Ojibway, Kwakiutl, and Eskimo, Kazakhs and Mongols, native Australians, Balinese, Kashmiris, and New Zealand Maori: all discover they have a "culture"'. The monolingual speakers of Kayapo in the South American tropical forest use the Portuguese term *cultura* to describe their traditional ceremonies. Maurice Godelier describes a migrant laborer returning to his New Guinea people, the Baruya, and proclaiming: 'We must find strength in our customs, we must base ourselves on what the Whites call culture'. Another New Guinean tells an anthropologist, 'If we didn't have *kastom*, we would be just like white men.' Sahlins cites all these instances to illustrate a general proposition: 'The cultural self-consciousness developing among imperialism's erstwhile victims is one of the more remarkable phenomena of world history in the later twentieth century'.

These erstwhile victims may even develop critical discourses on culture. Gerd Baumann has shown that in Southall, a multi-ethnic suburb in West London, people 'question what the terms "*culture*" and "*community*" may signify in the first place. The terms themselves become pivotal points in the making of a Southall culture'. However, even anti-Western nationalists may simply appropriate the dominant international rhetoric of culture to affirm the unique identity of their own people, with no fear of self-contradiction. 'We consider the main threat to our society at the present time', says a fundamentalist Iranian politician, 'to be a cultural one'. . . .

. . .

It goes without saying that culture means something rather different to market researchers in London, a Japanese mogul, New Guinean villagers, and a radical clergyman in Teheran, not to mention Samuel Huntington. There is nevertheless a family resemblance between the concepts they have in mind. In its most general sense, culture is simply a way of talking about collective identities. Status is also in play, however. Many people believe that cultures can be measured against each other, and they are inclined to esteem their own culture more highly than that of others. They may even believe that there is only one true civilization, and that the future not only of the nation but of the world depends on the survival of their culture. . . .

Whereas the patriots of Western Civ claim the high ground of the great tradition, the multiculturalists celebrate the diversity of America and champion the cultures of the marginal, the minorities, the dissidents, the colonized. The culture of the establishment is denounced as oppressive. Minority cultures empower the weak: they are authentic; they speak to real people; they sustain variety and choice;

they feed dissent. All cultures are equal, or should be treated as equal. 'So culture as a theme or topic of study has replaced society as the general object of inquiry among progressives', Fred Inglis writes, with only a touch of irony. But while conservatives reject these arguments, they agree that culture establishes public standards and determines national destiny. And when people of different nations and ethnic groups meet, whole cultures confront each other. Something must give in this confrontation.

Culture is also often used in a different sense, to refer to the high art that is enjoyed by the happy few. But it is not simply a private accomplishment. The well-being of the whole nation is at stake if art and scholarship are threatened. . . .
. . .

A French, a German, and an English theory of culture are often loosely identified. Alternatively, and equally loosely, Enlightenment, Romantic, and Classical discourses are distinguished. These are rough-and-ready labels for complex constructs that have regularly been taken to pieces and reassembled in new patterns, adapted, pronounced dead, revived, renamed, revamped, and generally subjected to a variety of structural transformations. Yet however crude, this classification does provide an initial orientation. Even the most imaginative and original thinkers can generally be placed in one or another of these central traditions, each of which specifies a conception of culture and puts it to work within a particular theory of history.

In the French tradition, civilization is represented as a progressive, cumulative, distinctively human achievement. Human beings are alike, at least in potential. All are capable of civilization, which depends on the unique human gift for reason. No doubt civilization has progressed furthest in France, but in principle it may be enjoyed, if perhaps not quite to the same degree, by savages, barbarians, and other Europeans. . . .

[The author then describes the 'ideological opposition' to this secular creed, asserting 'national tradition against cosmopolitan civilization'.]

Unlike scientific knowledge, the wisdom of culture is subjective. Its most profound insights are relative, not universal laws. What is true on one side of the Pyrenees may be error on the other side. But if the cultural faith is eroded, life loses all meaning. While material civilization was tightening its iron grip on every European society, individual nations therefore struggled to sustain a spiritual culture, expressed above all in language and the arts. The authentic *Kultur* of the German people was surely to be preferred to the artificial *Civilization* of a cosmopolitan, materialistic French-speaking elite. In any case, cultural difference was natural. There is no common human nature. 'I have seen Frenchmen, Italians, Russians', wrote the French counter-revolutionary de Maistre. 'But as for man, I declare that I have never in my life met him; if he exists, he is unknown to me.' (Henry James may have had this aphorism in mind when he wrote, 'Man isn't at all one, after all—it takes so much of him to be American, to be French, etc.')

These two traditions of thinking about culture developed in dialectical opposition to each other. A central theme of Enlightenment thinkers was human progress, whereas their opponents were interested in the particular destiny of a nation. In the Enlightenment view, civilization was engaged in a great struggle to overcome the resistance of traditional cultures, with their superstitions, irrational prejudices, and fearful loyalties to cynical rulers. (Voltaire said he would rest in peace only when the last king was strangled in the entrails of the last priest.) For the party of the Counter-Enlightenment, the defining enemy was rational, scientific, universal civilization: the Enlightenment itself. Associated with material values, with capitalism, and often with foreign political and economic influence, this civilization menaced authentic culture and condemned age-old crafts to obsolescence. Cosmopolitanism corrupted language. Rationalism disturbed religious faith. Together they eroded the spiritual values on which the organic community depended.

. . .

As the human sciences crystallized, competing schools of thought drew on these classic perspectives. Central themes of the Enlightenment view of the world, or of the French ideology, reemerged in nineteenth-century positivism, socialism, and utilitarianism. In the twentieth century, the idea of a progressive, scientific world civilization was translated into the theory of modernization, and then the theory of globalization. In the short run, culture was a barrier to modernization (or industrialization, or globalization), but modern civilization would in the end trample over local, less efficient traditions. Culture was invoked when it became necessary to explain why people were clinging to irrational goals and self-destructive strategies. Development projects were defeated by cultural resistance. Democracy crumbled because it was alien to the traditions of a nation. Rational choice theories could not account for what economists despairingly call 'stickiness,' entrenched ways of thinking and doing that persist in the face of the most compelling arguments. Culture was the fallback, to explain apparently irrational behavior. Culture also accounted for the disappointing outcome of many political reforms. Tradition was the refuge of the ignorant and fearful, or the recourse of the rich and powerful, jealous of any challenge to their established privileges.

From another point of view, the resistance of local cultures to globalization might be respected, even celebrated. This was the perspective of the heirs to the Counter-Enlightenment. The romantic, or German, tradition was also not static. It underwent its own transformations, though always exhibiting an elective affinity with idealism, relativism, historicism, a hermeneutic style of analysis, and what we now call identity politics. . . .

But even if they decked themselves out in the latest fashions, the classical ideas about culture did not have the field to themselves. They confronted new rivals, the greatest of which made its appearance with the publication of Darwin's *The Origin of Species* in 1859. Even the least scientific thinker could not ignore the challenge after Darwin extended his argument to human beings in *The Descent of Man* in 1871. The possibility now had to be faced that human universals and human differences could be explained in biological terms. Culture might follow natural laws. . . .

The challenge of a biological theory of human progress and human difference provoked the development of what was in some ways a new conception of culture.

Culture was now conceived of in opposition to biology. It was culture that marked human beings off from other animals, and nations from other nations. And it was not inherited biologically, but learned, acquired, even borrowed. . . .
. . .

Virchow's associate, Adolf Bastian (who became the first director of the great Berlin museum of ethnology in 1886), attempted to demonstrate that, like races, cultures are hybrids. There are no pure cultures, distinctive and enduring. Every culture draws on diverse sources, depends on borrowings, and is in flux. Human beings are very much alike, and every culture is rooted in a universal human mentality. Cultural differences were caused by the challenges presented by the local natural environment, and by the contacts between human populations. Borrowing was the primary mechanism for cultural change. And since cultural changes were the consequence of chance local processes—environmental pressures, migrations, trade—it followed that history has no fixed pattern of development.

This liberal Berlin anthropology has been characterized as a blend of Enlightenment and Romantic ideas, but it is actually based on a double rejection. If cultures are open, syncretic, and unstable, then obviously they cannot express unchanging, essential identities, or an underlying racial character. And if cultural changes are the consequence of chance local factors, then it must follow that there are no general laws of history. Above all, however, the Berlin school insisted that culture works in a very different way from biological forces—and might even override them.

Franz Boas, a student of Virchow and Bastian, introduced this approach into American anthropology. . . . The Boasians were skeptical about universal laws of evolution. They also repudiated racial explanations of difference, a matter of enduring political importance in the United States. The fundamental Boasian thesis was that culture makes us, not biology. We become what we are by growing up in a particular cultural setting; we are not born that way. Race, and also sex and age, are cultural constructs, not immutable natural conditions. The implication is that we can be made over into something better, perhaps learning from the tolerant people of Samoa, or the perfectly balanced Balinese.

This was a powerfully attractive idea in twentieth-century America, but the alternative, racial understanding of cultural difference remained a potent challenge. The idea of culture could actually reinforce a racial theory of difference. Culture could be a euphemism for race, fostering a discourse on racial identities while apparently abjuring racism. Anthropologists might fastidiously distinguish between race and culture, but in popular usage 'culture' referred to an innate quality. The nature of a group was evident to the naked eye, expressed to equal effect in skin color, facial characteristics, religion, morals, aptitudes, accent, gestures, and dietary preferences. This stubborn confusion persists. . . .

Culture is always defined in opposition to something else. It is the authentic, local way of being different that resists its implacable enemy, a globalizing, material civilization. Or it is the realm of the spirit, embattled against materialism. Or it is the human capacity for spiritual growth that overcomes our animal nature. Within the social sciences, culture appeared in yet another set of contrasts: it was the collective consciousness, as opposed to the individual psyche. At the same time, it stood for the ideological dimension of social life as against the mundane organization of government, factory, or family. . . .

. . .

[In his concluding chapter on Culture, Difference, Identity, the author observes:]

Modern theories about culture recycle earlier ones, and lend themselves to similar political purposes. Each also confronts well-worn objections that are posed by its rivals. Formulated in ambiguous and weak terms, the theories all say something that is now rather obvious, hardly remarkable, even if the diffuse light they shed may sometimes be helpful. They retain the power to shock, even to interest, only if they are stated in very strong terms—but then their claims seem to be over the top, not to be reconciled with what we know from our own experience. At full strength, moreover, we may suspect that they are not good for the health.

These theories also have fundamental weaknesses in common. Complex notions like culture, or discourse, inhibit an analysis of the relationships among the variables they pack together. Even in sophisticated modern formulations, culture—or discourse—tends to be represented as a single system, though one shot through with arguments and inconsistencies. However, to understand culture, we must first deconstruct it. Religious beliefs, rituals, knowledge, moral values, the arts, rhetorical genres, and so on should be separated out from each other rather than bound together into a single bundle labeled culture, or collective consciousness, or superstructure, or discourse. Separating out these elements, one is led on to explore the changing configurations in which language, knowledge, techniques, political ideologies, rituals, commodities, and so on are related to each other.

. . .

. . . [I]f the elements of a culture are disaggregated, it is usually not difficult to show that the parts are separately tied to specific administrative arrangements, economic pressures, biological constraints, and so forth. 'A "culture,"' Eric Wolf concluded, 'is thus better seen as a series of processes that construct, reconstruct, and dismantle cultural materials, in response to identifiable determinants.'

For Roy D'Andrade, a central feature of modern cognitive anthropology has been precisely

> the breaking up of culture into parts . . . cognitively formed units—features, prototypes, schemas, propositions, theories, etc. This makes possible a *particulate* theory of culture; that is, a theory about the 'pieces' of culture, their composition and relations to other things.

D'Andrade's conception of culture is psychological—it is 'in the mind'—but a similar point could be made if culture is conceived of rather as a public discourse, comparable to a language. It would still make sense to break it up into parts, and then to see whether elements in the complex mix of culture may have their own specific (though not fixed) 'relations to other things'. Perhaps kinship and the division of labor by sex have something to do after all with the biology of reproduction; or, as Foucault insisted, knowledge is to be understood in relation to power; or, as Bourdieu writes, the arts should be analyzed with reference to funding, and to the prestige they lend to the connoisseur; and cultural identity may make sense only when it is placed in the context of a particular electoral system.

In short, it is a poor strategy to separate out a cultural sphere, and to treat it in its own terms. . . . For the same sort of reason, cultural identity can never provide an adequate guide for living. We all have multiple identities, and even if I accept that I have a primary cultural identity, I may not want to conform to it. Besides, it would not be very practical. I operate in the market, live through my body, struggle in the grip of others. If I am to regard myself only as a cultural being, I allow myself little room to maneuver, or to question the world in which I find myself. Finally, there is a moral objection to culture theory. It tends to draw attention away from what we have in common instead of encouraging us to communicate across national, ethnic, and religious boundaries, and to venture between them.

NOTE

Kuper's suggestion for unpacking the notion of culture and cultural identity to divide them into their many, and often closely interrelated, aspects makes obvious historical sense with respect to language. Vital to theorists of ethnicity and nationalism and to the forces behind the formation of nation states in nineteenth century Europe, language continues to play a major role in the building of states (the revival of Hebrew as an official language in Israel). It also has figured importantly in internal ethnic conflicts in which groups identified (among other ways) by a different language demand some form of autonomy within the state (the Basque community in Spain), or sovereign independence (the Tamil Tigers in the Sri Lankan conflict). The human rights movement itself has been sensitive to language issues, particularly within the Council of Europe but also in the universal movement—for example, Article 27 of the ICCPR (members of ethnic, religious and linguistic minorities have the right, in community with other group members, 'to enjoy their own culture, to profess and practice their own religion, or to use their own language').

The resurgence of movements for ethnic group identity through the revival of languages has become a feature of a world simultaneously marked by trends toward globalization and hence toward homogenization, as well as by the growth of regional organizations as in Europe that limit state sovereignty. A newspaper report (Marlise Simons, 'In New Europe, a Lingual Hodgepodge', *New York Times*, October 17, 1999, p. 4NE) summarizes trends in West Europe. It refers to a radio station in Brittany, France, that broadcasts only in Breton, 'a Celtic language spoken for more than 2,000 years that until recently seemed doomed to disappear'. The station manager states: 'Saving the culture of Brittany is very much on people's minds. This generation is no longer embarrassed about speaking or being Breton'. Activists in the pro-Breton movement employ the modern technology of software to spread the language and send their children to bilingual schools. A Breton novelist observed: 'We now accept that our identity can have several layers.

We can feel European and French and Breton all at once. But the answer is to remain open. If not, you become a bastion, a Serbia'.

The article reports that in recent years 'greater tolerance has allowed for more teaching of Occitan, Basque, Corsican and Alsation in France's schools'. The trend, reflecting a larger one in Europe as a whole, has its sharp critics. The head of the French Academy observed that teaching regional languages is 'an enterprise that can destroy the unity of the nation . . . Why sacrifice a glorious language to local dialects'. Other national examples include the return of Gaelic to schools in Scotland and Wales, school courses in Northern Italy in Friulian, Dutch radio broadcasts in Frisian, and Finnish broadcasts in Saami. A German author on regional identity observes:

> Brussels bureaucrats may try to steamroller us into oneness, but people are stubborn. The more global and uniform our civilization, the more people want to anchor themselves in their own culture. The fact is, Europe has a few thousand years of settled cultures. It can't simply turn into an American-type melting pot.

Such ideas figure importantly in the ongoing debates about cultural relativism and cultural integrity in relation to universal human rights that are described in Chapter 6.

NOTE

Consider:

BRITANNUS   (*shocked*):
               Caesar, this is not proper.
THEODOTUS   (*outraged*):
               How?
CAESAR   (*recovering his self-possession*):
               Pardon him Theodotus: he is a barbarian, and thinks that the customs of his tribe and island are the laws of nature.
               George Bernard Shaw, *Caesar and Cleopatra*, Act II

The following articles examine cultural relativism from the perspective of two major religions and related national cultures: Hinduism and Islam. They express two different but related approaches to this issue.

Pannikar inquires into equivalents of international human rights in a non-Western culture. He concentrates on India, and on the 'traditional Hindu, Jain and Buddhist conceptions of reality'. He takes the broad position that '[t]there are no trans-cultural values, for the simple reason that a value exists as such only in a given cultural context. But there may be cross-cultural values, and a cross-cultural critique is indeed possible'. Noting that human rights are 'trampled upon in the East as well as the West', he asks whether human rights perhaps are not observed today 'because in their present form they do not represent a universal symbol powerful enough to elicit understanding and agreement'.

An-Na'im examines the 'Muslim world'. Committed to international human rights and of the Islamic faith, he argues that 'human rights advocates in the Muslim world must work within the framework of Islam to be effective . . . [and] should struggle to have their interpretations of the relevant [Islamic] texts adopted as the new Islamic scriptural imperatives for the contemporary world'. Those interpretations would be broadly consistent with the norms of international human rights. An-Na'im is then attentive to the relation between the international system and a given religious tradition, and to the possibility of reconciliation through reinterpretation of the tradition, rather than through identification of cross-cultural values among different systems.

PANNIKAR, IS THE NOTION OF HUMAN RIGHTS A WESTERN CONCEPT?
120 Diogenes 75 (1982)

. . .

I. The Method of Inquiry

It is claimed that Human Rights are universal. This alone entails a major philosophical query. Does it make sense to ask about conditions of universality when the very question about conditions of universality is far from universal? Philosophy can no longer ignore this inter-cultural problematic. Can we extrapolate the concept of Human Rights, from the context of the culture and history in which it was conceived, into a globally valid notion? Could it at least *become* a universal symbol? Or is it only one particular way of expressing—and saving—the *humanum*?

Although the question posed in the title is a legitimate one, there is something disturbing in this formulation as it was given to me. At least at first glance, it would seem to offer only one alternative: either the notion of Universal Human Rights is a Western notion, or it is not. If it is, besides being a tacit indictment against those who do not possess such a valuable concept, its introduction into other cultures, even if necessary, would appear as a plain imposition from outside. It would appear, once again, as a continuation of the colonial syndrome, namely the belief that the constructs of one particular culture (God, Church, Empire, Western civilization, science, modern technology, etc.) have, if not the monopoly, at least the privilege of possessing a universal value which entitles them to be spread over all the Earth. If not, that is, if the concept of Universal Human Rights is not exclusively a Western concept, it would be difficult to deny that many a culture has let it slumber, thus again giving rise to an impression of the indisputable superiority of Western culture. . . .

. . . [T]he problem is how, from the [locus or context] of one culture, to understand the constructs of another. It is wrong-headed methodology to begin by asking. Does another culture also have the notion of Human Rights?—assuming that such a notion is absolutely indispensable to guarantee human dignity. No question is neutral, for every question conditions its possible answers.

... Meanings are not transferable here. Translations are more delicate than heart transplants. So what must we do? We must dig down to where a homogeneous soil or a similar problematic appears: we must search out the *homeomorphic equivalent*—to the concept of Human Rights in this case. ...[1]

... If, for instance, Human Rights are considered to be the basis for the exercise of and respect for human dignity, we should investigate how another culture satisfies the equivalent need—and this can be done only once a common ground (a mutually understandable language) has been worked out between the two cultures. Or perhaps we should ask how the idea of a just social and political order could be formulated within a certain culture, and investigate whether the concept of Human Rights is a particularly appropriate way of expressing this order. A traditional Confucian might see this problem of order and rights as a question of 'good manners' or in terms of his profoundly ceremonial or ritual conception of human intercourse, in terms of *li*. A Hindu might see it another way, and so on.
...

... Human Rights are one window through which one particular culture envisages a just human order for its individuals. But those who live in that culture do not see the window. For this they need the help of another culture which sees through another window.

II. Assumptions and Implications of the Western Concept

...

1. At the basis of the discourse on Human Rights there is the assumption of a *universal human nature* common to all peoples. Otherwise, a Universal Declaration could not logically have been proclaimed. This idea in its turn is connected with the old notion of a Natural Law.

But the contemporary Declaration of Human Rights further *implies*:

a) that this human nature must be *knowable*. ...

b) that this human nature is known by means of an equally universal organ of knowledge, generally called *reason*. Otherwise, if its knowledge should depend on a special intuition, revelation, faith, decree of a prophet or the like, Human Rights could not be taken as *natural* rights—inherent in Man. ...

c) ... Man is the master of himself and the universe. He is the supreme legislator on Earth—the question of whether a Supreme Being exists or not remains open, but ineffective.

2. The second assumption is that of the *dignity of the individual*. Each individual is, in a certain sense, absolute, irreducible to another. This is probably the major thrust of the Modern question of Human Rights. Human Rights defend

---

[1] The two words Brahman and God, for instance, are neither analogous nor merely equivocal (nor univocal, of course). They are not exactly equivalent either. They are homeomorphic. They perform a certain type of respectively corresponding function in the two different traditions where these words are alive.

the dignity of the individual *vis-à-vis* Society at large, and the State in particular.

But this in turn implies:

a) not only the distinction but also the *separation* between individual and society. In this view the human being is fundamentally the individual. Society is a kind of superstructure, which can easily become a menace and also an alienating factor for the individual. Human Rights are there primarily to protect the individual;

b) the *autonomy* of humankind *vis-à-vis* and often versus the Cosmos . . . The individual stands in between Society and World Human Rights defend the autonomy of the human individual;

c) . . . The individual has an inalienable dignity because he is an end in himself and a kind of absolute. You can cut off a finger for the sake of the entire body, but can you kill one person to save another?

3. The third assumption is that of a *democratic social order.* Society is assumed to be not a hierarchical order founded on a divine will or law or mythical origin, but a sum of 'free' individuals organized to achieve otherwise unreachable goals. Human Rights, once again, serve mainly to protect the individual. Society here is not seen as a family or a protection, but as something unavoidable which can easily abuse the power conferred on it (precisely by the assent of the sum of its individuals). This Society crystallizes in the State, which theoretically expresses the will of the people, or at least of the majority. . . .

This implies:

a) that each individual is seen as equally important and thus equally responsible for the welfare of society. . . .

b) that Society is nothing but the sum total of the individuals whose wills are sovereign and ultimately decisive. . . .

c) that the rights and freedoms of the individual can be limited only when they impinge upon the rights and freedoms of other individuals, and in this way majority rule is rationally justified. . . .

. . . [The Universal] Declaration clearly was articulated along the lines of the historical trends of the Western world during the last three centuries, and in tune with a certain philosophical anthropology or individualistic humanism which helped justify them.

III. Cross-Cultural Reflections

1. Is the Concept of Human Rights a Universal Concept?

The answer is a plain *no.* . . .

No concept as such is universal. Each concept is valid primarily where it was conceived. If we want to extend its validity beyond its own context we shall have to justify the extrapolation. . . . To accept the fact that the concept of Human Rights *is* not universal does not yet mean that it *should* not *become* so. Now in order for a concept to become universally valid it should fulfill at least two conditions. . . . [I]t should be the universal point of reference for any problematic regarding human dignity. In other words, it should displace all other homeomorphic equivalents and be the pivotal center of a just social order. To put it another way, the culture which has given birth to the concept of Human Rights should also be called upon to become a universal culture. This may well be one of the causes of a certain uneasiness one senses in non-Western thinkers who study the question of Human Rights. They fear for the identity of their own cultures.

. . .

The following parallelism may be instructive. To assume that without the explicit recognition of Human Rights life would be chaotic and have no meaning belongs to the same order of ideas as to think that without the belief in one God as understood in the Abrahamic tradition human life would dissolve itself in total anarchy. This line of thinking leads to the belief that Atheists, Buddhists and Animists, for instance, should be considered as human aberrations. In the same vein: either Human Rights, or chaos. This attitude does not belong exclusively to Western culture. To call the stranger a barbarian is all too common an attitude among the peoples of the world. . . .

There are no trans-cultural values, for the simple reason that a value exists as such only in a given cultural context. But there may be cross-cultural values, and a cross-cultural critique is indeed possible. The latter does not consist in evaluating one cultural construct with the categories of another, but in trying to understand and criticize one particular human problem with the tools of understanding of the different cultures concerned, at the same time taking thematically into consideration that the very awareness and, much more, the formulation of the problem is already culturally bound. Our question is then to examine the possible cross-cultural value of the issue of Human Rights, an effort which begins by delimiting the cultural boundaries of the concept. The dangers of cultural westocentrism are only too patent today.

a) We have already mentioned the particular historical origins of the Declaration of Human Rights. To claim universal validity for Human Rights in the formulated sense implies the belief that most of the peoples of the world today are engaged in much the same way as the Western nations in a process of transition from more or less mythical *Gemeinschaften* (feudal principalities, self-governing cities, guilds, local communities, tribal institutions . . .) to a 'rationally' and 'contractually' organized 'modernity' as known to the Western industrialized world. This is a questionable assumption. No one can predict the evolution (or eventual disintegration) of those traditional societies which have started from different material and cultural bases and whose reaction to modern Western civilization may therefore follow hitherto unknown lines.

. . .

b) We may now briefly reconsider the three assumptions mentioned above. . . . We shall limit ourselves here to [examining the assumptions of the Universal Declaration with respect to] the very broad umbrella of a pre-Modern, non-Western state of mind.

i) There is certainly a *universal human nature* but, first of all, this nature does not need to be segregated and fundamentally distinct from the nature of all living beings and/or the entire reality. Thus exclusively *Human* Rights would be seen as a violation of 'Cosmic Rights' and an example of self-defeating anthropocentrism, a novel kind of apartheid. To retort that 'Cosmic Rights' is a meaningless expression

would only betray the underlying cosmology of the objection, for which the phrase makes no sense. But the existence of a different cosmology is precisely what is at stake here. We speak of the laws of nature; why not also of her rights?[2]
. . .

Thirdly, to proclaim the undoubtedly positive concept of Human Rights may turn out to be a Trojan horse, surreptitiously introduced into other civilizations which will then all but be obliged to accept those ways of living, thinking and feeling for which Human Rights is the proper solution in cases of conflict. . . .

ii) Nothing could be more important than to underscore and defend the *dignity of the human person*. But the person should be distinguished from the individual. The individual is just an abstraction, i.e. a selection of a few aspects of the person for practical purposes. My *person*, on the other hand, is also in 'my' parents, children, friends, foes, ancestors and successors. 'My' person is also in 'my' ideas and feelings and in 'my' belongings. If you hurt 'me', you are equally damaging my whole clan, and possibly yourself as well. Rights cannot be individualized in this way. Is it the right of the mother, or of the child?—in the case of abortion. Or perhaps of the father and relatives as well? Rights cannot be abstracted from duties; the two are correlated. The dignity of the human person may equally be violated by your language, or by your desecrating a place I consider holy, even though it does not 'belong' to me in the sense of individualized private property. You may have 'bought' it for a sum of money, while it belongs to me by virtue of another order altogether. An individual is an isolated knot; a person is the entire fabric around that knot, woven from the total fabric of the real. The limits to a person are not fixed, they depend utterly on his or her personality. Certainly without the knots the net would collapse; but without the net, the knots would not even exist.

To aggressively defend my individual rights, for instance, may have negative, i.e. unjust, repercussions on others and perhaps even on myself. The need for consensus in many traditions—instead of majority opinion—is based precisely on the corporate nature of human rights.
. . .

iii) *Democracy* is also a great value and infinitely better than any dictatorship. But it amounts to tyranny to put the peoples of the world under the alternative of choosing either democracy or dictatorship. Human Rights are tied to democracy. Individuals need to be protected when the structure which is above them (Society, the State or the Dictator—by whatever name) is not qualitatively superior to them, i.e. when it does not belong to a higher order. Human rights is a legal device for the protection of smaller numbers of people (the minority or the individual) faced with the power of greater numbers . . . In a hierarchical conception of reality, the particular human being cannot defend his or her rights by demanding or exacting

---

[2] [Eds.] The author here uses a number of related concepts. *Cosmos* refers broadly to a universe regarded as an orderly and harmonious whole. *Cosmology* refers generally to a branch of philosophy concerned with the origin and structure of the universe. An *anthropocentric* view refers to one in which man is viewed as a central fact of the universe, and reality is interpreted in terms of human values and experiences. *Anthropomorphism* refers to the attribution of human characteristics to inanimate or natural phenomena.

them independently of the whole. The wounded order has to be set straight again, or it has to change altogether. Other traditional societies have different means to more or less successfully restore the order. . . .

. . .

IV. An Indian Reflection

. . .

The starting point here is not the individual, but the whole complex concatenation of the Real. In order to protect the world, for the sake of the protection of this universe, says Manu, He, Svayambhu, the Self-existent, arranged the castes and their duties. Dharma is the order of the entire reality, that which keeps the world together. The individual's duty is to maintain his 'rights'; it is to find one's place in relation to Society, to the Cosmos, and to the transcendent world.

. . .

3. Human Rights are not Rights only. They are also duties and both are interdependent. Humankind has the 'right' to survive only insofar as it performs the duty of maintaining the world (*lokasamgraha*). We have the 'right' to eat only inasmuch as we fulfill the duty of allowing ourselves to be eaten by a hierarchically higher agency. Our right is only a participation in the entire metabolic function of the universe.

We should have, if anything, a Declaration of Universal Rights and Duties in which the whole of Reality would be encompassed. Obviously, this demands not only a different anthropology but also a different cosmology and an altogether different theology—beginning with its name. . . .

. . .

6. Both systems (the Western and the Hindu) make sense from and within a given and accepted myth. Both systems imply a certain kind of consensus. When that consensus is challenged, a new myth must be found. The broken myth is the situation in India today, as it is in the world at large. That the rights of individuals be conditioned only by their position in the net of Reality can no longer be admitted by the contemporary mentality. Nor does it seem to be admissible that the rights of individuals be so absolute as not to depend at all on the particular situation of the individual.

In short, there is at present no endogenous theory capable of unifying contemporary societies and no imposed or imported ideology can be simply substituted for it. A mutual fecundation of cultures is a human imperative of our times.

. . .

V. By Way of Conclusion

Is the concept of Human Rights a Western conception?
 Yes.
 Should the world then renounce declaring or enforcing Human Rights?
. . .

 No.
 Three qualifications, however, are necessary:
 1. For an authentic human life to be possible within the *megamachine* of the

modern technological world, Human Rights are imperative. This is because the development of the notion of Human Rights is bound up with and given its meaning by the slow development of that megamachine. How far individuals or groups or nations should collaborate with this present-day system is another question altogether. But in the contemporary political arena as defined by current socio-economic and ideological trends, the defense of Human Rights is a sacred duty. Yet it should be remembered that to introduce Human Rights (in the definite Western sense, of course) into other cultures before the introduction of *technicul-ture* would amount not only to putting the cart before the horse, but also to preparing the way for the technological invasion—as if by a Trojan horse, as we have already said. And yet a technological civilization without Human Rights amounts to the most inhuman situation imaginable. The dilemma is excruciating. This makes the two following points all the more important and urgent.

2. Room should be made for other traditions to develop and formulate their own homeomorphic views corresponding to or opposing Western 'rights'. Or rather, these other world traditions should make room for themselves, since no one else is likely to make it for them. This is an urgent task; otherwise it will be impossible for non-Western cultures to survive, let alone to offer viable alternatives or even a sensible complement. Here the role of a cross-cultural philosophical approach is paramount. The need for human pluralism is often recognized in principle, but not often practiced, not only because of the dynamism which drives the paneconomic ideology, linked with the megamachine, to expand all over the world, but also because viable alternatives are not yet theoretically worked out.

. . .

ABDULLAH AHMED AN-NA'IM, HUMAN RIGHTS IN THE MUSLIM WORLD
3 Harv. Hum. Rts. J. 13 (1990)

Introduction

Historical formulations of Islamic religious law, commonly known as Shari'a, include a universal system of law and ethics and purport to regulate every aspect of public and private life. The power of Shari'a to regulate the behavior of Muslims derives from its moral and religious authority as well as the formal enforcement of its legal norms. As such, Shari'a influences individual and collective behavior in Muslim countries through its role in the socialization processes of such nations regardless of its status in their formal legal systems. For example, the status and rights of women in the Muslim world have always been significantly influenced by Shari'a, regardless of the degree of Islamization in public life. Of course, Shari'a is not the sole determinant of human behavior nor the only formative force behind social and political institutions in Muslim countries.

. . .

I conclude that human rights advocates in the Muslim world must work within the framework of Islam to be effective. They need not be confined, however, to the particular historical interpretations of Islam known as Shari'a. Muslims are obliged, as a matter of faith, to conduct their private and public affairs in accordance with the dictates of Islam, but there is room for legitimate disagreement over the precise nature of these dictates in the modern context. Religious texts, like all other texts, are open to a variety of interpretations. Human rights advocates in the Muslim world should struggle to have their interpretations of the relevant texts adopted as the new Islamic scriptural imperatives for the contemporary world.

A. Cultural Legitimacy for Human Rights

The basic premise of my approach is that human rights violations reflect the lack or weakness of cultural legitimacy of international standards in a society. Insofar as these standards are perceived to be alien to or at variance with the values and institutions of a people, they are unlikely to elicit commitment or compliance. While cultural legitimacy may not be the sole or even primary determinant of compliance with human rights standards, it is, in my view, an extremely significant one. Thus, the underlying causes of any lack or weakness of legitimacy of human rights standards must be addressed in order to enhance the promotion and protection of human rights in that society.

. . . This cultural illegitimacy, it is argued, derives from the historical conditions surrounding the creation of the particular human rights instruments. Most African and Asian countries did not participate in the formulation of the Universal Declaration of Human Rights because, as victims of colonization, they were not members of the United Nations. When they did participate in the formulation of subsequent instruments, they did so on the basis of an established framework and philosophical assumptions adopted in their absence. For example, the pre-existing framework and assumptions favored individual civil and political rights over collective solidarity rights, such as a right to development, an outcome which remains problematic today. Some authors have gone so far as to argue that inherent differences exist between the Western notion of human rights as reflected in the international instruments and non-Western notions of human dignity. In the Muslim world, for instance, there are obvious conflicts between Shari'a and certain human rights, especially of women and non-Muslims.

. . . In this discussion, I focus on the principles of legal equality and nondiscrimination contained in many human rights instruments. These principles relating to gender and religion are particularly problematic in the Muslim world.

. . .

II. Islam, Shari'a and Human Rights

. . .

A. The Development and Current Application of Shari'a

To the over nine hundred million Muslims of the world, the Qur'an is the literal and final word of God and Muhammad is the final Prophet. During his mission, from 610 A.D. to his death in 632 A.D., the Prophet elaborated on the meaning of the Qur'an and supplemented its rulings through his statements and actions. This body of information came to be known as Sunna. He also established the first Islamic state in Medina around 622 A.D. which emerged later as the ideal model of an Islamic state. . . .

While the Qur'an was collected and recorded soon after the Prophet Muhammad's death, it took almost two centuries to collect, verify, and record the Sunna. Because it remained an oral tradition for a long time during a period of exceptional turmoil in Muslim history, some Sunna reports are still controversial in terms of both their authenticity and relationship to the Qur'an.

Because Shari'a is derived from Sunna as well as the Qur'an, its development as a comprehensive legal and ethical system had to await the collection and authentication of Sunna. Shari'a was not developed until the second and third centuries of Islam. . . .

. . .

Shari'a is not a formally enacted legal code. It consists of a vast body of jurisprudence in which individual jurists express their views on the meaning of the Qur'an and Sunna and the legal implications of those views. Although most Muslims believe Shari'a to be a single logical whole, there is significant diversity of opinion not only among the various schools of thought, but also among the different jurists of a particular school. . . .

Furthermore, Muslim jurists were primarily concerned with the formulation of principles of Shari'a in terms of moral duties sanctioned by religious consequences rather than with legal obligations and rights and specific temporal remedies. They categorized all fields of human activity as permissible or impermissible and recommended or reprehensible. In other words, Shari'a addresses the conscience of the individual Muslim, whether in a private, or public and official, capacity, and not the institutions and corporate entities of society and the state.

. . .

Whatever may have been the historical status of Shari'a as the legal system of Muslim countries, the scope of its application in the public domain has diminished significantly since the middle of the nineteenth century. Due to both internal factors and external influence, Shari'a principles had been replaced by European law governing commercial, criminal, and constitutional matters in almost all Muslim countries. Only family law and inheritance continued to be governed by Shari'a. . . .

Recently, many Muslims have challenged the gradual weakening of Shari'a as the basis for their formal legal systems. Most Muslim countries have experienced mounting demands for the immediate application of Shari'a as the sole, or at least primary, legal system of the land. These movements have either succeeded in gaining complete control, as in Iran, or achieved significant success in having aspects of Shari'a introduced into the legal system, as in Pakistan and the Sudan. Governments of Muslim countries generally find it difficult to resist these demands out of fear of being condemned by their own populations as anti-Islamic. Therefore, it is likely that this so-called Islamic fundamentalism will achieve further successes in other Muslim countries.

The possibility of further Islamization may convince more people of the urgency of understanding and discussing the relationship between Shari'a and human rights, because Shari'a would have a direct impact on a wider range of human rights issues if it became the formal legal system of any country. . . .

I believe that a modern version of Islamic law can and should be developed. Such a modern 'Shari'a' could be, in my view, entirely consistent with current standards of human rights. These views, however, are appreciated by only a tiny minority of contemporary Muslims. To the overwhelming majority of Muslims today, Shari'a is the sole valid interpretation of Islam, and as such *ought* to prevail over any human law or policy.

B. Shari'a and Human Rights

In this part, I illustrate with specific examples how Shari'a conflicts with international human rights standards. . . .

. . .

The second example is the Shari'a law of apostasy. According to Shari'a, a Muslim who repudiates his faith in Islam, whether directly or indirectly, is guilty of a capital offense punishable by death. This aspect of Shari'a is in complete conflict with the fundamental human right of freedom of religion and conscience. The apostasy of a Muslim may be inferred by the court from the person's views or actions deemed by the court to contravene the basic tenets of Islam and therefore be tantamount to apostasy, regardless of the accused's personal belief that he or she is a Muslim.

The Shari'a law of apostasy can be used to restrict other human rights such as freedom of expression. A person may be liable to the death penalty for expressing views held by the authorities to contravene the official view of the tenets of Islam. Far from being an historical practice or a purely theoretical danger, this interpretation of the law of apostasy was applied in the Sudan as recently as 1985, when a Sudanese Muslim reformer was executed because the authorities deemed his views to be contrary to Islam.[3]

A third and final example of conflict between Shari'a and human rights relates to the status and rights of non-Muslims. Shari'a classifies the subjects of an Islamic state in terms of their religious beliefs: Muslims, *ahl al-Kitab* or believers in a divinely revealed scripture (mainly Christian and Jews), and unbelievers. In modern terms, Muslims are the only full citizens of an Islamic state, enjoying all the rights and freedoms granted by Shari'a and subject only to the limitations and restrictions imposed on women. *Ahl al-Kitab* are entitled to the status of *dhimma*, a special compact with the Muslim state which guarantees them security of persons and property and a degree of communal autonomy to practice their own religion and conduct their private affairs in accordance with their customs and laws. In exchange for these limited rights, *dhimmis* undertake to pay *jizya* or poll tax and submit to Muslim sovereignty and authority in all public affairs. . . .

---

[3] . . . The Salman Rushdie affair illustrates the serious negative implications of the law of apostasy to literary and artistic expression. Mr Rushdie, a British national of Muslim background, published a novel entitled, The Satanic Verses, in which irreverent reference is made to the Prophet of Islam, his wives, and leading companions. Many Muslim governments banned the book because their populations found the author's style and connotations extremely offensive. The late Imam Khomeini of Iran sentenced Rushdie to death *in absentia* without charge or trial. . . .

According to this scheme, non-Muslim subjects of an Islamic state can aspire only to the status of *dhimma*, under which they would suffer serious violations of their human rights. *Dhimmis* are not entitled to equality with Muslims. [Economic and family law illustrations omitted.]

. . .

IV. A Case Study: The Islamic Dimension of The Status of Women

. . .

The present focus on Muslim violations of the human rights of women does not mean that these are peculiar to the Muslim world.[4] As a Muslim, however, I am particularly concerned with the situation in the Muslim world and wish to contribute to its improvement.

The following discussion is organized in terms of the status and rights of Muslim women in the private sphere, particularly within the family, and in public fora, in relation to access to work and participation in public affairs. This classification is recommended for the Muslim context because the personal law aspects of Shari'a, family law and inheritance, have been applied much more consistently than the public law doctrines.[5] The status and rights of women in private life have always been significantly influenced by Shari'a regardless of the extent of Islamization of the public debate.

A. Shari'a and the Human Rights of Women

. . . The most important general principle of Shari'a influencing the status and rights of women is the notion of *qawama*. *Qawama* has its origin in verse 4:34 of the Qur'an: 'Men have *qawama* [guardianship and authority] over women because of the advantage they [men] have over them [women] and because they [men] spend their property in supporting them [women]'. According to Shari'a interpretations of this verse, men as a group are the guardians of and superior to women as a group, and the men of a particular family are the guardians of and superior to the women of that family.

. . . For example, Shari'a provides that women are disqualified from holding general public office, which involves the exercise of authority over men, because, in keeping with the verse 4:34 of the Qur'an, men are entitled to exercise authority over women and not the reverse.

Another general principle of Shari'a that has broad implications for the status

---

[4] It is difficult to distinguish between Islamic, or rather Shari'a, factors and extra-Shari'a actors affecting the status and rights of women. The fact that women's human rights are violated in all parts of the world suggests that there are universal social, economic, and political factors contributing to the persistence of this state of affairs. Nevertheless, the articulation and operation of these factors varies from one culture or context to the next. In particular, the rationalization of discrimination against the denial of equality for women is based on the values and customs of the particular society. In the Muslim world, these values and customs are supposed to be Islamic or at least consistent with the dictates of Islam. It is therefore useful to discuss the Islamic dimension of the status and rights of women.

[5] The private/public dichotomy, however, is an artificial distinction. The two spheres of life overlap and interact. The socialization and treatment of both men and women at home affect their role in public life and vice versa. While this classification can be used for analysis in the Muslim context, its limitations should be noted. It is advisable to look for both the private and public dimensions of a given Shari'a principle or rule rather than assume that it has only private or public implications.

and rights of Muslim women is the notion of *al-hijab*, the veil. This means more than requiring women to cover their bodies and faces in public. According to Shari'a interpretations of verses 24:31, 33:33,[6] 33:53, and 33:59[7] of the Qur'an, women are supposed to stay at home and not leave it except when required to by urgent necessity. When they are permitted to venture beyond the home, they must do so with their bodies and faces covered. *Al-hijab* tends to reinforce women's inability to hold public office and restricts their access to public life. They are not supposed to participate in public life, because they must not mix with men even in public places.

... In family law for example, men have the right to marry up to four wives and the power to exercise complete control over them during marriage, to the extent of punishing them for disobedience if the men deem that to be necessary.[8] In contrast, the co-wives are supposed to submit to their husband's will and endure his punishments. While a husband is entitled to divorce any of his wives at will, a wife is not entitled to a divorce, except by judicial order on very specific and limited grounds. Another private law feature of discrimination is found in the law of inheritance, where the general rule is that women are entitled to half the share of men.

In addition to their general inferiority under the principle of *qawama* and lack of access to public life as a consequence of the notion of *al-hijab*, women are subjected to further specific limitations in the public domain. For instance, in the administration of justice, Shari'a holds women to be incompetent witnesses in serious criminal cases, regardless of their individual character and knowledge of the facts. In civil cases where a woman's testimony is accepted, it takes two women to make a single witness. *Diya*, monetary compensation to be paid to victims of violent crimes or to their surviving kin, is less for female victims than it is for male victims.

... These overlapping and interacting principles and rules play an extremely significant role in the socialization of both women and men. Notions of women's inferiority are deeply embedded in the character and attitudes of both women and men from early childhood.

...

C. Muslim Women in Public Life

A similar and perhaps more drastic conflict exists between reformist and conservative trends in relation to the status and rights of women in the public domain. Unlike personal law matters, where Shari'a was never displaced by secular law, in most Muslim countries, constitutional, criminal, and other public law matters have come to be based on secular, mainly Western, legal concepts and institutions.

---

[6] [O Consorts of the Prophet . . .] And stay quietly in your houses, and make not a dazzling display, like that of the former Times of Ignorance; and establish regular prayer, and give regular charity; and obey God and His Apostle. And God only wishes to remove all abomination from you, ye Members of the Family, and to make you pure and spotless.

[6] O Prophet! Tell thy wives and daughters, and the believing women, that they should cast their outer garments over their persons (when abroad): that is most convenient, that they should be known (as such) and not molested. And God is Oft-Forgiving, Most Merciful.

[8] Polygamy is based on verse 4:3 of the Qur'an. The husband's power to chastise his wife to the extent of beating her is based on verse 4:34 of the Qur'an.

Consequently, the struggle over Islamization of public law has been concerned with the re-establishment of Shari'a where it has been absent for decades, or at least since the creation of the modern Muslim nation states in the first half of the twentieth century. In terms of women's rights, the struggle shall determine whether women can keep the degree of equality and rights in public life they have achieved under secular constitutions and laws.

. . .

. . . Educated women and other modernist segments of society may not be able to articulate their vision of an Islamic state in terms of Shari'a, because aspects of Shari'a are incompatible with certain concepts and institutions which these groups take for granted, including the protection of all human rights. To the extent that efforts for the protection and promotion of human rights in the Muslim world must take into account the Islamic dimension of the political and sociological situation in Muslim countries, a modernist conception of Islam is needed.

V. *Islamic Reform and Human Rights*

. . .

Islamic reform needs must be based on the Qur'an and Sunna, the primary sources of Islam. Although Muslims believe that the Qur'an is the literal and final word of God, and Sunna are the traditions of his final Prophet, they also appreciate that these sources have to be understood and applied through human interpretation and action. . . .

A. *An Adequate Reform Methodology*

. . . The basic premise of my position, based on the work of the late Sudanese Muslim reformer *Ustadh* Mahmoud Mohamed Taha, is that the Shari'a reflects a historically-conditioned interpretation of Islamic scriptures in the sense that the founding jurists had to understand those sources in accordance with their own social, economic, and political circumstances. In relation to the status and rights of women, for example, equality between men and women in the eight and ninth centuries in the Middle East, or anywhere else at the time, would have been inconceivable and impracticable. It was therefore natural and indeed inevitable that Muslim jurists would understand the relevant texts of the Qur'an and Sunna as confirming rather than repudiating the realities of the day.

In interpreting the primary sources of Islam in their historical context, the founding jurists of Shari'a tended not only to understand the Qur'an and Sunna as confirming existing social attitudes and institutions, but also to emphasize certain texts and 'enact' them into Shari'a while de-emphasizing other texts or interpreting them in ways consistent with what they believed to be the intent and purpose of the sources. Working with the same primary sources, modern Muslim jurists might shift emphasis from one class of texts to the other, and interpret the previously enacted texts in ways consistent with a new understanding of what is believed to be the intent and purpose of the sources. This new understanding would be informed by contemporary social, economic, and political circumstances in the same way that the 'old' understanding on which Shari'a jurists acted was informed by the then prevailing circumstances. The new understanding would

qualify for Islamic legitimacy, in my view, if it is based on specific texts in opposing
the application of other texts, and can be shown to be in accordance with the
Qur'an and Sunna as a whole.

For example, the general principle of *qawama*, the guardianship and authority
of men over women under Shari'a, is based on verse 4:34 of the Qur'an.

... This verse presents *qawama* as a consequence of two conditions: men's
advantage over and financial support of women. The fact that men are generally
physically stronger than most women is not relevant in modern times where the
rule of law prevails over physical might. Moreover, modern circumstances are
making the economic independence of women from men more readily realized
and appreciated. In other words, neither of the conditions—advantages of physical
might or earning power—set by verse 4:34 as the justification for the *qawama* of
men over women is tenable today.

The fundamental position of the modern human rights movement is that all
human beings are equal in worth and dignity, regardless of gender, religion, or
race. This position can be substantiated by the Qur'an and other Islamic sources as
understood under the radically transformed circumstances of today. For example,
in numerous verses the Qur'an speaks of honor and dignity for 'humankind' and
'children of Adam', without distinction as to race, color, gender, or religion. By
drawing on those sources and being willing to set aside archaic and dated interpretations of other sources, such as the one previously given to verse 4:34 of the
Qur'an, we can provide Islamic legitimacy for the full range of human rights for
women.

Similarly, numerous verses of the Qur'an provide for freedom of choice and
non-compulsion in religious belief and conscience.[9] These verses have been either
de-emphasized as having been 'overruled' by other verses which were understood
to legitimize coercion, or 'interpreted' in ways which permitted such coercion. For
example, verse 9:29 of the Qur'an was taken as the foundation of the whole system
of *dhimma*, and its consequent discrimination against non-Muslims. Relying on
those verses which extoll freedom of religion rather than those that legitimize
religious coercion, one can argue now that the *dhimma* system should no longer be
part of Islamic law and that complete equality should be assured regardless of
religion or belief. The same argument can be used to abolish all negative legal
consequences of apostasy as inconsistent with the Islamic principle of freedom of
religion. [Discussion omitted of mechanisms and methods within Islam for development and reform.]

... The ultimate test of legitimacy and efficacy is, of course, acceptance and
implementation by Muslims throughout the world.

B. Prospects for Acceptance and Likely Impact of the Proposed Reform

...

... Governments of Muslim countries, like many other governments, formally
subscribe to international human rights instruments because, in my view, they

---

[9] See, for example, verse 2:256 of the Qur'an which provides: 'Let there be no compulsion in religion: Truth stands out clear from error . . . ' In verse 18:29 God instructs the Prophet: 'Say, the Truth is from your Lord. Let him who will, believe, and let him who will, reject [it]'.

find the human rights idea an important legitimizing force both at home and abroad . . .

Nevertheless, the proposed reform will probably be resisted because it challenges the vested interests of powerful forces in the Muslim world and may upset male-dominated traditional political and social institutions. These forces probably will try to restrict opportunities for a genuine consideration of this reform methodology. . . .

Consequently, the acceptance and implementation of this reform methodology will involve a political struggle within Muslim nations as part of a larger general struggle for human rights. I would recommend this proposal to participants in that struggle who champion the cause of justice and equality for women and non-Muslims, and freedom of belief and expression in the Muslim world. Given the extreme importance of Islamic legitimacy in Muslim societies, I urge human rights advocates to claim the Islamic platform and not concede it to the traditionalist and fundamentalist forces in their societies. I would also invite outside supporters of Muslim human rights advocates to express their support with due sensitivity and genuine concern for Islamic legitimacy in the Muslim world.
. . .

QUESTIONS

1. Pannikar and An-Na'im suggest two very different approaches to the questions of how to understand divergences among cultures with respect to human rights issues and how to go about finding common ground. How would you describe them? Does either or do both appear helpful in resolving contemporary disputes over, say, gender discrimination or capital punishment?

2. Pannikar appears to follow his challenge to the notion of universal human rights with the observation that human rights are imperative 'within the megamachine of the modern technological world'. Compare Cover's references (p. 343, *supra*) to the 'almost unique mastery of violence' of the modern state and of 'communal resistance to the Behemoth'. What do you understand these observations to mean? Do they amount to a distinctive modern justification for a human rights system that would displace religious or regional norms?

NOTE

Consider the following observation in Rosalyn Higgins, *Problems and Process: International Law and How We Use It* (1994), at 96:

It is sometimes suggested that there can be no fully universal concept of human rights, for it is necessary to take into account the diverse cultures and political systems of the world. In my view this is a point advanced mostly by states, and by liberal scholars anxious not to impose the Western view of things on others. It is rarely advanced by the oppressed, who are only too anxious to benefit from perceived universal standards. The non-universal, relativist view of human rights is in fact a very state-centred view and loses sight of the fact that human rights are human rights and not dependent on the fact that states, or groupings of states, may behave differently from each other so far as their politics, economic policy, and culture are concerned. I believe, profoundly, in the universality of the human spirit. Individuals everywhere want the same essential things: to have sufficient food and shelter; to be able to speak freely; to practise their own religion or to abstain from religious belief; to feel that their person is not threatened by the state; to know that they will not be tortured, or detained without charge, and that, if charged, they will have a fair trial. I believe there is nothing in these aspirations that is dependent upon culture, or religion, or stage of development. They are as keenly felt by the African tribesman as by the European city-dweller, by the inhabitant of a Latin American shanty-town as by the resident of a Manhattan apartment.

Compare the following writings of Howard and Schachter with respect to their conceptions of human dignity, and the relationship of those conceptions to human rights. Consider how these conceptions differ, and what the consequences of that difference might be for the content or style of expression of a human rights regime.

RHODA HOWARD, DIGNITY, COMMUNITY, AND HUMAN RIGHTS

In Abdullahi An-Na'im (ed.), Human Rights in Cross-Cultural Perspective (1991), at 81

. . .

. . . [Most] known human societies did not and do not have conceptions of human rights. Human rights are a moral good that one can accept—on an ethical basis—and that everyone ought to have in the modern state-centric world. To seek an anthropologically based consensus on rights by surveying all known human cultures, however, is to confuse the concepts of rights, dignity, and justice. One can find affinities, analogues, and precedents for the actual content of internationally accepted human rights in many religious and cultural (geographic and national) traditions; but the actual concept of *human* rights, as will be seen, is particular and modern, representing a radical rupture from the many status-based, nonegalitarian, and hierarchical societies of the past and present . . .

Human rights are a modern concept now universally applicable in principle because of the social evolution of the entire world toward state societies. The concept of human rights springs from modern human thought about the nature of justice; it does not spring from an anthropologically based consensus about the values, needs, or desires of human beings. As Jack Donnelly puts it, the concept of human rights is best interpreted by constructivist theory:

Human rights aim to establish and guarantee the conditions necessary for the development of the human person envisioned in . . . [one particular] underlying moral theory of human nature, thereby bringing into being that type of person. . . . The evolution of particular conceptions or lists of human rights is seen in the constructivist theory as the result of the *reciprocal interactions of moral conceptions and material conditions of life*, mediated through social institutions such as rights.

Human rights tend to be particularly characteristic of liberal and/or social democratic societies. . . .

Human rights adhere to the human being *by virtue of being human, and for no other reason.* . . .

This means that the human being who holds rights holds them not only against the state, but also against 'society', that is, against his or her community or even family. This orientation is a radical departure from the way most human societies in the past—and many in the present—have been or are organized. For most human societies, insofar as 'rights' might be considered to be applicable at all, collective or communal rights would be preferred to individual human rights . . . . Collective or community rights imply permissible inegalitarian ranking of members in the interests of preservation of 'tradition'.

I define human dignity as *the particular cultural understandings of the inner moral worth of the human person and his or her proper political relations with society*. Dignity is not a claim that an individual asserts against a society; it is not, for example, the claim that one is worthy of respect merely because one is a human being. Rather, dignity is something that is granted at birth or on incorporation into the community as a concomitant of one's particular ascribed status, or that accumulates and is earned during the life of an adult who adheres to his or her society's values, customs, and norms: the adult, that is, who accepts normative cultural constraints on his or her particular behavior. . . .

Many indigenous groups (that is, the remnants of precapitalist societies destroyed—physically, culturally, or both—during the process of European conquest and/or settlement) now make claims for the recognition of their collective or communal rights. When they do so they are not primarily interested in the human rights of the individual members of their collectivities. Rather, they are interested in the recognition of their *collective dignity*, in the acknowledgment of the value of their collective way of life as opposed to the way of life of the dominant society into which they are unequally 'integrated' . . . .
. . .

Thus in most known past or present societies, human dignity is not private, individual, or autonomous. It is public, collective, and prescribed by social norms. The idea that an individual can enhance his or her 'dignity' by asserting his or her human rights violates many societies' most fundamental beliefs about the way social life should be ordered. Part of the dignity of a human being consists of the quiet endurance and acceptance of what a human rights approach to the world would consider injustice or inequality . . . .
. . .

What then is a human being? For many societies, the human being is the person who has learned and obeys the community's rules. A nonsocial atomized individual is not human; he or she is a species of 'other'—perhaps equivalent to a (presocialized) child, a stranger, a slave, or even an animal. There is very little room in most societies for Mead's 'I'—the individual, self-reflective being—to emerge over the 'me', that part of a being that absorbs his or her community's culture and faithfully follows the rules and customs expected of a person of his or her station. The human group takes precedence over the human person.

. . .

This does not mean that human rights are not relevant, in the late twentieth century, to those societies in the world that retain precapitalist, nonindividualist notions of human dignity, honor, and the social order. The rise of the centralized state makes human rights relevant the world over. It does mean that to look for universalistic 'roots' of human rights in different social areas of the world . . . or in different religious traditions, is to abstract those societies and religions from culture and history. One can find, in Judaism and Christianity for example, strong moral analogues to the content—although not the concept—of contemporary human rights. But one can also find moral precepts justifying inequality and denial of what are now considered fundamental human rights. . . .

. . .

. . . All societies do have underlying conceptions of human dignity and social justice. These conceptions can be identified; and certain commonalities of belief, for example, in the social value of work, can also be located on a transcultural basis. But in most known human societies, dignity and justice are not based on any idea of the *inalienable right* of the *physical*, socially *equal* human being against the claims of family, community, or the state. They are based on just the opposite, that is, the *alienable privileges* of *socially unequal* beings, considered to embody gradations of humanness according to socially defined status categories entitled to different degrees of respect.

While all societies have underlying concepts of dignity and justice, few have concepts of rights. Human rights, then, are a particular expression of human dignity. In most societies, dignity does not imply human rights. There is very little cultural—let alone universal—foundation for the concept, as opposed to the content, of human rights. The society that actively protects rights both in law and in practice is a radical departure for most known human societies. . . .

. . .

OSCAR SCHACHTER, HUMAN DIGNITY AS A NORMATIVE CONCEPT
77 Am. J. Int. L. 848 (1983)

The 'dignity of the human person' and 'human dignity' are phrases that have come to be used as an expression of a basic value accepted in a broad sense by all peoples.

Human dignity appears in the Preamble of the Charter of the United

Nations as an ideal that 'we the peoples of the United Nations' are 'determined' to achieve . . . .

The term dignity is also included in Article 1 of the Universal Declaration of Human Rights. . . .

. . .

The Helsinki Accords in Principle VII affirm that the participating states will promote the effective exercise of human rights and freedoms, 'all of which derive from the inherent dignity of the human person'.

References to human dignity are to be found in various resolutions and declarations of international bodies. National constitutions and proclamations, especially those recently adopted, include the ideal or goal of human dignity in their references to human rights. Political leaders, jurists and philosophers have increasingly alluded to the dignity of the human person . . . . No other ideal seems so clearly accepted as a universal social good.

We do not find an explicit definition of the expression 'dignity of the human person' in international instruments or (as far as I know) in national law. Its intrinsic meaning has been left to intuitive understanding, conditioned in large measure by cultural factors. . . .

. . .

An analysis of dignity may begin with its etymological root, the Latin 'dignitas' translated as worth (in French, 'valeur'). One lexical meaning of dignity is 'intrinsic worth'. Thus, when the UN Charter refers to the 'dignity and worth' of the human person, it uses two synonyms for the same concept. The other instruments speak of 'inherent dignity', an expression that is close to 'intrinsic worth'.

What is meant by 'respect' for 'intrinsic worth' or 'inherent dignity' of a person? 'Respect' has several nuanced meanings: 'esteem', 'deference', 'a proper regard for', 'recognition of'. These terms have both a subjective aspect (how one feels or thinks about another) and an objective aspect (how one treats another). Both are relevant to our question, but it seems more useful to focus on the latter aspect for purposes of practical measures.

One general answer to our question is suggested by the Kantian injunction to treat every human being as an end, not as a means. Respect for the intrinsic worth of every person should mean that individuals are not to be perceived or treated merely as instruments or objects of the will of others. This proposition will probably be generally acceptable as an ideal. There may be more question about its implications. I shall suggest such implications as corollaries of the general proposition.

The first is that a high priority should be accorded in political, social and legal arrangements to individual choices in such matters as beliefs, way of life, attitudes and the conduct of public affairs. Note that this is stated as a 'high priority', not an absolute rule. We may give it more specific content by applying it to political and psychological situations. In the political context, respect for the dignity and worth of all persons, and for their individual choices, leads, broadly speaking, to a strong emphasis on the will and consent of the governed. . . .

. . .

... [W]e believe that the idea of human dignity involves a complex notion of the individual. It includes recognition of a distinct personal identity, reflecting individual autonomy and responsibility. It also embraces a recognition that the individual self is a part of larger collectivities and that they, too, must be considered in the meaning of the inherent dignity of the person ...

We are led more deeply into the analysis of human dignity when we consider its relation to the material needs of human beings and to the ideal of distributive justice. Few will dispute that a person in abject condition, deprived of adequate means of subsistence, or denied the opportunity to work, suffers a profound affront to his sense of dignity and intrinsic worth. Economic and social arrangements cannot therefore be excluded from a consideration of the demands of dignity. At the least, it requires recognition of a minimal concept of distributive justice that would require satisfaction of the essential needs of everyone.
...

... The general idea that human rights are derived from the dignity of the person is neither truistic nor neutral. It has two corollaries that challenge conceptions prevalent in some societies and ideologies. The first corollary is the idea that basic rights are not given by authority and therefore may not be taken away; the second is that they are rights of the person, every person. It is not unrealistic to assume that ideas of this kind will have a role in challenging existing attitudes. When they are found in official declarations, they become part of the instruments of change, sometimes loudly proclaimed, at other times almost imperceptibly affecting ideas of legitimacy.
...

... Respect for human dignity may be realized in other ways than by asserting claims of right. In many cases, the application of a 'rights approach' to affronts to dignity would raise questions involving existing basic rights such as free speech. In other cases, respect for dignity may be more appropriately and effectively attained through social processes such as education, material benefits, political leadership and the like ...

These observations indicate that the central idea of human dignity has a wide range of applications outside of the sphere of human rights. It is therefore of some importance to treat it as a distinct subject and to consider ways that respect for dignity can be fostered through public and private agencies.

ADDITIONAL READING

On cultural relativism see: K. Dalacoura, *Islam, Liberalism and Human Rights* (1998); E. Cotran and A. Sherif (eds.), *Democracy, The Rule of Law and Islam* (1999); A. Pollis and P. Schwab (eds.), *Human Rights: Cultural and Ideological Perspectives* (1979); and T. Dunne and N. Wheeler (eds.), *Human Rights in Global Politics* (1999).

6

Conflicting Traditions and Rights: Illustrations

Against the background of Chapter 5, with its examination of rights discourse and its presentation of different perspectives on universalism and cultural relativism, this chapter explores four topics that are among the human rights issues now in debate among and within countries.

These materials do more than illustrate conflicts stemming from a state's violation of widely recognized human rights norms. In such instances—for example, torture, racial discrimination, denial of fair judicial process, repression of political advocacy—there may be no dispute over the validity of the norm. There are simply alleged violations, perhaps denied by the accused state, perhaps justified by that state on one or another ground, perhaps drawing no response.

In the illustrations below, two different phenomena become central to the debate. (1) The asserted universal norm itself may be challenged, perhaps on the ground that it lacks universal validity, or that it conflicts with ultimate religious commands, or that it violates long-standing tradition that assures cultural integrity and survival. That is, the legitimacy or validity of the human rights norm is itself challenged. In such respects, this chapter's illustrations further develop the theme of cultural relativism. (2) Sometimes related to cultural relativism and sometimes distinct, the second phenomenon involves a conflict among rights that are all recognized to some extent in the leading human rights instruments. The dispute is formally internal to the human rights corpus. What, for example, are the respective boundaries of rights that in given contexts squarely conflict with each other? Freedom of religious belief and practice may conflict with nondiscrimination norms; freedom of speech may conflict with the protection of minority groups. As materials in Chapter 5(A) made clear, such types of conflict are endemic to rights discourse, as they are to law in general.

The illustrations in this chapter of both these phenomena cut deeply and sometimes painfully into the human rights movement. Materials elsewhere in the coursebook offer further illustrations of both categories of illustrations. See, for example, the discussions of death row and capital punishment at pp. 18–55, *supra*; of free speech and hate speech at pp. 749–761, *infra*; and of homosexuality and human rights at pp. 818–836, *infra*.

In several of the following studies, the issues have to do with family, gender, and religion—interrelated topics that have characterized much discussion of the last decade about cultural relativism and that often involve conflicting rights. Thus the studies examine gender and family in relation to a state's or ethnic group's internal custom, or in relation to religion. They also examine the rights of children. Other illustrations in this chapter range more broadly, to include group rights and group autonomy with respect to religious law, and differing regional perspectives (particularly certain East Asian perspectives) on culture and universalism of human rights norms.

The problems discussed in this chapter have become acute within many developing countries. In recent decades, such countries experienced strong external and internal pressures to rethink and revise, sometimes radically, their traditional beliefs and practices. The relentless assault of the developed world on other cultures, the penetration of those cultures by trade, investment, high-tech media, and tourism, as well as the universalization of ideas and values like human rights, have launched transformative processes that are often referred to under the broad rubric of globalization. The challenge to a state or region's traditional ways and to other state practices that depart from the universal human rights instruments increasingly comes from internal groups as well as from international advocates and organizations. The battle is joined.

A. GENDER

1. CUSTOM AND CULTURE

The potential for conflict in a large number of states between the objectives of several human rights treaties, on the one hand, and customary laws and practices as well as religious beliefs, on the other, has become a salient contemporary concern. Gender-related issues are here prominent. To some extent, traditional norms and local custom that retain power and influence impose different roles and duties on men and women. To some extent, such problems stem from the increasing power and prominence in recent years of fundamentalist religious groups, many of which actively oppose the transformative impetus of the human rights movement with respect to traditional gender roles. Such conflicts assume a large significance, since the control and influence over women of customary law and religious belief may far exceed that of modern state-secular law.

Customary laws and practices may conflict with prohibitions in the text of ICCPR and CEDAW or in the action taken by the bodies created by these two treaties. Recall Articles 2(f) and 5(a) of CEDAW that require states to take all appropriate measures to modify or abolish customs, practices, and social and cultural patterns of conduct that constitute discrimination or that are based on the idea of inferiority or on stereotyped roles for women.

This section begins with a reading that explores some problems in developing a feminist perspective on human rights related to gender, problems that bear on the following case studies. It then explores a practice that is variously referred to, with strikingly different political and moral innuendo and sometimes agendas, as female circumcision *or* female genital mutilation. The materials continue with other themes relating gender to custom and culture: problems of land ownership under internal customary law, and problems posed by immigrants to Western states who carry with them native practices that they wish to continue.

TRACY HIGGINS, ANTI-ESSENTIALISM, RELATIVISM, AND HUMAN RIGHTS
19 Harvard Women's L. J. 89 (1996)

During the Fourth United Nations World Conference on Women [in 1995], cultural differences among women presented a series of practical and theoretical problems. The practical problems arose out of the enormous task of negotiating among a large group of people a single, albeit complex, document that would set an agenda for addressing the problems of women globally. Differences in culture, language, religion, and education presented complications at every stage of the process. As a theoretical matter, such differences presented a less immediate but in some ways more difficult and persistent problem: In the face of profound cultural differences among women, how can feminists maintain a global political movement yet avoid charges of cultural imperialism?

This theoretical dilemma has become a serious political hurdle for global feminism as the challenge of cultural relativism permeates the politics of any discussion of women's rights on the international stage. For example, at the 1994 United Nations Population Conference in Cairo, the Vatican joined with several Muslim governments to condemn what they viewed as the imposition of Western norms of sexual license and individual autonomy on the rest of the world . . . .

Feminist responses to this charge are complicated and sometimes conflicting. On the one hand, feminists note that culture and religion are often cited as justifications for denying women a range of basic rights, including the right to travel, rights in marriage and divorce, the right to own property, even the right to be protected by the criminal law on an equal basis with men. Women have much to lose, therefore, in any movement away from a universal standard of human rights in favor of deference to culture. On the other hand, feminists acknowledge that feminism itself is grounded in the importance of participation, of listening to and accounting for the particular experiences of women, especially those on the margins of power. Indeed, much feminist criticism of traditional human rights approaches has focused on the tendency of international policymakers to exclude women's experiences and women's voices. Thus, the claim that Western concepts of women's equality are exclusionary or imperialist strikes at the heart of one of feminism's central commitments—respect for difference.

In short, both the move to expand universal human rights to include those rights central to women's condition and the move toward a relativist view of human rights are consistent with and informed by feminist theory. Indeed, the tension between them reflects a tension within feminism itself, between describing women's experience collectively as a basis for political action and respecting

differences among women. Addressing this tension, this Article endeavors to sort out the degree to which feminism, by virtue of its own commitments, must take cultural defenses seriously, particularly when articulated by women themselves.
. . .

Despite the general consensus [over the universality of human rights that was reflected in the Universal Declaration], differences have persisted over the scope and priorities of the international human rights agenda, differences that are translated with surprising frequency into the rhetoric of universality versus cultural relativism, imperialism versus self-determination. Notwithstanding the language of universality, the question remains: To what extent may a state depart from international norms in the name of culture? . . .
. . .

The influence of the universalist/relativist divide on the politics of human rights is perhaps nowhere more evident than in debates over women's rights as human rights. Cultural relativists have targeted feminism itself as a product of Western ideology and global feminism as a form of Western imperialism. Ironically, cultural relativists have accused feminist human rights activists of imposing Western standards on non-Western cultures in much the same way that feminists have criticized states for imposing male-defined norms on women. The complexity of this debate has sown confusion among feminist human rights activists, undermining the effectiveness of the global feminist movement . . .

[Higgins considers the criticism of some feminists that the movement in general has been characterized by 'essentialism'—that is, the belief that many categories (like gender) or groups (like women) have a real, true essence, and thus fixed properties that define what they are. Essentialism in this sense is likely to be linked to a universalist position.]

Much incisive and insightful criticism, particularly by feminists of color, has revealed that treating gender difference as the primary concern of feminism has had the effect of reinforcing gendered categories and collapsing differences among women. These critics have argued convincingly that early feminist descriptions of women's experience focused on white, middle-class, educated, heterosexual women. Consequently, the political priorities of the women's movement in the West (e.g., equal access to education and employment, abortion rights) have reflected the most urgent concerns of a relatively more powerful group of women . . . Accused of essentialism, feminists who theorized a commonality among women were criticized for committing the dual sin of reinforcing patriarchal assumptions about women as a group and marginalizing some women along the lines of race, class, and sexual orientation.

Despite its theoretical and political vulnerabilities, the practical appeal of essentialism, like the appeal of universalism, persists. Essentialist assumptions offer the promise of uniting women in a way that transcends or precedes politics . . .

Much feminist activism on the international level has been premised on two assumptions, both of which may be characterized as essentialist: first, that women share types of experiences and are oppressed in particular ways as women; and second, that these experiences are often different than those of men . . . [F]eminist progress in reshaping the scope of the international human rights agenda stands as an important example of the power of organizing around assumptions of commonality.

. . .

[Higgins explores two views about culture and coercion that are relevant to a response by feminists who are committed to universalism to the criticisms and challenge of cultural relativists and anti-essentialists. The first view has to do with the tendency in some strands of cultural relativism to 'essentialize' the local culture itself and in the process to obscure coercion.]

Feminists have questioned arguments based on a simple assertion of cultural integrity for several reasons. First, cultural relativists may inadequately attend to the degree to which power relationships within the culture itself constrain the ability of individuals to renegotiate cultural norms. Yet, this inattention is inconsistent with a concern about coercion. The relativist cannot criticize Western imperialism and at the same time ignore non-Western states' selective use of the defense of culture in the service of state power. The risk of such intra-cultural coercion seems especially great when that selective invocation of culture has differential effects on groups within the state such as minority ethnic or racial groups or women.

Second, cultural relativist arguments may oversimplify the complexity and fluidity of culture by treating culture as monolithic and moral norms within a particular culture as readily ascertainable. Yet, a single, inward glance at Western culture reveals the absurdity of this assumption. The multiplicity of beliefs in the United States (or even within a single community or family) about the legitimacy of abortion or the role of women in the family illustrates the complexity of translating imperfectly shared assumptions into evaluative standards. Such oversimplification seems inconsistent with the very premises of cultural relativism. Indeed, cultural relativists' tendency to describe differences in terms of simple opposition—Western versus non-Western—without exploring how specific cultural practices are constituted and justified 'essentializes' culture itself.

Treating culture as monolithic fails to respect relevant intra-cultural differences just as the assumption of the universality of human rights standards fails to respect cross-cultural differences. Cultural differences that may be relevant to assessing human rights claims are neither uniform nor static. Rather, they are constantly created, challenged, and renegotiated by individuals living within inevitably overlapping cultural communities.

This oversimplification of culture may lead relativists to accept too readily a cultural defense articulated by state actors or other elites on the international level, actors that tend not to be women. Yet, it seems unlikely that a cultural defense offered by the state will adequately reflect the dynamic, evolving, and possibly conflicting cultural concerns of its citizens.

Given the complexity and multiplicity of culture, the ability or inclination of heads of state to identify and translate cultural practices into specific defenses against the imposition of Western human rights norms is questionable. Feminists

in particular have cited example after example in which culture has been selectively and perhaps cynically invoked to justify oppressive practices.

. . .

[The second view about culture and coercion raises the question of the role of
private ordering in coercion.]

In contrast to cultural relativists and liberal pluralists, feminist anti-essentialists
are centrally concerned with the interplay between culture and self, exploring ways
in which culture constructs gendered individuals. . . . [F]eminism emphasizes the
role of private power. The most important premise of this feminist view is that the
sex/gender system is substantially a product of culture rather than divine will,
human biology or natural selection. Implicit in this assumption is the claim that
cultural norms—language, law, myth, custom—are not merely products of human
will and action but also define and limit the possibilities for human identity.

Connected with this view of cultural limitations on human subjectivity is the
notion that cultural norms function as a source of power and control within
modern society. Consistent with this recognition, many feminists have rejected a
theory of power that posits monolithic control held by a coherent or unified
sovereign. Yet, it is precisely this model of power that traditional human rights
standards are designed to regulate and to which cultural relativists often defer
when exercised within cultural boundaries. In contrast, feminists . . . have
emphasized the degree to which power is exercised both from above, by sovereigns,
and within concrete social interactions and relationships—in short, through culture. For feminists, culture itself becomes a source of control and a site of resistance, a form of power that feminist human rights activists must engage directly
along with more traditional public and private forms.

. . .

Conclusion

Confronted with the challenge of cultural relativism, feminism faces divergent
paths, neither of which seems to lead out of the woods of patriarchy. The first path,
leading to simple tolerance of cultural difference, is too broad. To follow it would
require feminists to ignore pervasive limits on women's freedom in the name of an
autonomy that exists for women in theory only.

The other path, leading to objective condemnation of cultural practices, is too
narrow. To follow it would require feminists to dismiss the culturally distinct
experiences of women as false consciousness. Yet to forge an alternative path is
difficult, requiring feminists to confront the risks inherent in global strategies for
change.

Building upon women's shared experiences inevitably entails a risk of mis-
description, or worse, cooptation but contains the promise of transforming and
radicalizing women's understanding of their own condition. Emphasizing difference threatens to splinter women politically, undermining hard-won progress, but
may simultaneously uncover new possibilities for re-creating gender relations.
Forging a combined strategy that respects both commonality and difference
requires feminists to acknowledge that we cannot eliminate the risk of coercion
altogether, but the risk of inaction is also ever present.

VIEWS OF COMMENTATORS ABOUT FEMALE CIRCUMCISION/GENITAL MUTILATION

A Traditional Practice that Threatens Health—Female Circumcision

40 World Health Organization Chronicle 31 (1986)

. . .

The traditional practices of a society are closely linked with the living conditions of the people and with their beliefs and priorities. In societies where women's needs have been subordinated to those of men, traditional practices often serve to reinforce their disadvantage, with direct and indirect effects on their health.

Traditionally, the reproductive role of women is surrounded by myths and taboos that underpin practices pertaining to menstruation, pregnancy and child-birth. Some of these practices are health-promoting but many are dangerous, even life-threatening. . . .

. . .

One traditional practice that has attracted much attention in the last decade is female circumcision. Although not the most lethal of the practices affecting women's health, its adverse effects are undeniable. Seventy million women are estimated to be circumcised, with several thousand new operations performed each day. It is a custom that is still widespread only in Africa north of the equator, though mild forms of female circumcision are reported from some countries in Asia too. However, history reveals that female circumcision of some kind has been practised at one time or another on every continent. . . .

. . .

There are three main types of female circumcision.

1. *Circumcision proper*, known in Muslim countries as *sunna* (which means 'traditional'), is the mildest but also the rarest form. It involves the removal only of the clitoral prepuce.
2. *Excision* involves the amputation of the whole of the clitoris and all or part of the labia minora.
3. *Infibulation*, also known as *Pharaonic circumcision*, involves the amputation of the clitoris, the whole of the labia minora, and at least the anterior two-thirds and often the whole of the medial part of the labia majora. The two sides of the vulva are then stitched together with silk, catgut or thorns, and a tiny silver of wood or a reed is inserted to preserve an opening for urine and menstrual blood. The girl's legs are usually bound together from ankle to knee until the wound has healed, which may take anything up to 40 days.

Initial circumcision is carried out before a girl reaches puberty, the age range being anywhere from one week to 14 years. The operation is generally the responsibility of the traditional midwife, who rarely uses even a local anaesthetic. She is assisted by a number of women to hold the child down, and these frequently include the child's own relatives. . . .

. . .

Most of the adverse health consequences are associated with Pharaonic circumcision. Haemorrhage and shock from the acute pain are immediate dangers of the
operation, and, because it is usually performed in unhygienic circumstances, the
risks of infection and tetanus are considerable. . . .

Implantation dermoid cysts are a very common complication; these often grow
to the size of a grapefruit. . . .

Infections of the vagina, urinary tract and pelvis occur frequently. Pelvic infection can result in sterility. Between 20% and 25% of infertility in Sudan has been
attributed to Pharaonic circumcision.

Not surprisingly, a woman who has been infibulated suffers great difficulty and
pain during sexual intercourse, which can be excruciating if a neuroma has formed
at the point of section of the dorsal nerve of the clitoris. Consummation of
marriage often necessitates the opening up of the scar by the husband using his
fingers, a razor or a knife. Very little research has been done on the sexual experience of circumcised women, a subject surrounded by taboos and personal inhib-
ition in most societies. However, the operation is known to destroy much or all of
the vulval nerve and pressure endings, and seems likely to delay arousal and impair
orgasm. One study among infibulated women found that few even knew of the
existence of orgasm.

During childbirth infibulation causes a variety of serious problems including
prolonged labour and obstructed delivery, with increased risk of fetal brain damage and fetal loss. . . .

Though some observers believe female circumcision was originally a means of
suppressing female sexuality and attempting to ensure chaste or monogamous
behaviour, others believe that it was started long ago among herders as a protection against rape for the young girls who took the animals out to pasture. In fact its
origins have proved impossible to trace. Not surprisingly, a variety of reasons are
advanced by its adherents for continuing to support the practice today. As the
word 'sunna' suggests, some Muslim people believe it is religiously ordained.
However, there is no support for female circumcision in the Koran, nor is it
practised in Saudi Arabia, the cradle of Islam. Other adherents believe that intact
female genitalia are 'unclean'; that an uncircumcised woman is likely to be pro-
miscuous; even that the operation improves the life chances of a woman's off-
spring. Some say it is a ritual initiation into womanhood.

None of the reasons given bears close scrutiny. They are, in fact, rationalizations
for a practice that has woven itself into the fabric of some societies so completely
that 'reasons' are no longer particularly relevant, since invalidating them does not
stop the practice.

Significantly, female circumcision is usually associated with poverty, illiteracy
and low status of women—with communities in which people face hunger, ill-
health, overwork, lack of clean water. In such settings an uncircumcised woman is
stigmatized and not sought in marriage, which helps explain the paradox that the
victims of the practice are also its strongest proponents. They can scarcely afford
not to be. In the best of circumstances, people are reluctant to question tradition
or take an independent line lest they lose social approval. In poverty-stricken

communities struggling to survive, social acceptance and support may mean the difference between life and death.

However, the signs are that education and a widening range of choices for women are slowly but surely undermining the practice. And men, too, from societies that customarily circumcise their women are beginning to express their own ambivalence or outright dislike of the custom. . . .

. . .

Wherever a colonial administration of the past or a government of today has tried to ban it outright, it has simply been practised with greater secrecy, and those suffering health complications have been inhibited from seeking professional help. Such an approach ignores the fact that those practising female circumcision believe in it, and that deeply entrenched attitudes of and towards circumcised women cannot be changed overnight. It ignores the need to *replace* the practice and not merely repress it: girls and women need to find other forms and types of social status, approval, and respectability. It ignores, too, the fact that the operation is a principal source of income to traditional birth attendants and even midwives, who cannot afford to relinquish it unless an alternative living is available.

Roman Catholic missionaries in Ethiopia in the sixteenth century tried to stop the practice among their converts, but when men refused to marry the girls a reversal of the policy had to be demanded urgently from Rome. Today abolitionists who attempt to move fast similarly come up against the brick wall of a conservative society feeling itself threatened, or, if the campaigners are outsiders, against suspicion that they are meddling in cultural affairs that are none of their business. Many of these lessons have been learned, and the present approach is through national or local organizations, using as far as possible the skills and experience of those whose work is among villagers normally, such as teachers, social workers and health personnel.

. . .

In August 1982 WHO made a formal statement of its position to the United Nations Commission on Human Rights. This statement endorsed the recommendations of the Khartoum seminar, namely:

— that governments should adopt clear national policies to abolish the practice, and to inform and educate the public about its harmfulness;
— that programmes to combat it should recognize its association with extremely adverse social and economic conditions, and should respond sensitively to women's needs and problems;
— that the involvement of women's organizations at the local level should be encouraged, since it is with them that awareness and commitment to change must begin.

In the same statement the Organization expressed its unequivocal opposition to any medicalization of the operation, advising that under no circumstances should it ever be performed by health professionals or in health establishments.

. . .

Female Genital Mutiliation: Proposals for Change

Minority Rights Group International, Report 92/3 (1992), at 11.

. . .

Female genital mutilation is a complex issue, for it involves deep-seated cultural practices which affect millions of people. However, it can be divided into (at least) four distinct issues.

1 *Rights of women.* Female genital mutilation is an extreme example of the general subjugation of women, sufficiently extreme and horrifying to make women and men question the basis of what is done to women, what women have accepted and why, in the name of society and tradition.

The burning of Indian widows and the binding of the feet of Chinese girl children are other striking examples, sharp enough and strange enough to throw a spotlight on other less obvious ways in which women the world over submit to oppression. . . .

. . .

2 *Rights of children.* An adult is quite free to submit her or himself to a ritual or tradition, but a child, having no formed judgement, does not consent but simply undergoes the operation (which in this case is irrevocable) while she is totally vulnerable. The descriptions available of the reactions of children—panic and shock from extreme pain, biting through the tongue, convulsions, necessity for six adults to hold down an eight-year-old, and death—indicate a practice comparable to torture.

Many countries signatory to Article 5 of the Universal Declaration of Human Rights (which provides that no one shall be subjected to torture, or to cruel, inhuman or degrading treatment) violate that clause. Those violations are discussed and sometimes condemned by various UN commissions. . . .

. . .

In September 1990, the United Nations Convention on the Rights of the Child went into force. It became part of International Human Rights Law. Under Article 24(3) it states that:

> States Parties shall take all effective and appropriate measures with a view to abolishing traditional practices prejudicial to the health of children.

. . .

3 *The right to good health.* There is no medical reputable practitioner who insists that mutilation is good for the physical or mental health of girls and women. . . .

. . .

Legislation

In Africa

Formal legislation forbidding genital mutilation, or more precisely infibulation, exists in the Sudan. A law first enacted in 1946 allows for a term of imprisonment up to five years and/or a fine. However, it is not an offence (under Article 284 of the Sudan Penal Code for 1974) 'merely to remove the free and projecting part of the clitoris'.

. . .

In September 1982, President Arap Moi took steps to ban the practices in Kenya, following reports of the deaths of 14 children after excision. A traditional practitioner found to be carrying out this operation can be arrested by the Chiefs Act and brought before the law.

. . .

In Western countries

A law prohibiting female excision, whether consent has been given or not, came into force in Sweden in July 1982, carrying a two-year sentence. In Norway, in 1985, all hospitals were alerted to the practice. Belgium has incorporated a ban on the practice. Several states in the USA have incorporated female genital mutilation into their criminal code.

In the UK, specific legislation prohibiting female circumcision came into force at the end of 1985. A person found guilty of an offence is liable to up to five years' imprisonment or to a fine. . . .

. . .

Kay Boulware-Miller, Female Circumcision: Challenges to the Practice as a Human Rights Violation

8 Harv. Womens L. J. 155 (1985), at 165.

. . .

A. *The Rights of the Child*

The Declaration of the Rights of the Child, adopted by the UN General Assembly in 1959, asserts that children must be guaranteed the opportunity to develop physically in a healthy and normal way.

. . .

First, to challenge female circumcision as a violation of the rights of the child suggests that women who permit the operation are incompetent and abusive mothers who, in some ways, do not love their children. The success of this approach therefore depends in part on how it is implemented; if African women are offended by the implication that they are poor mothers, they will likely reject the children's rights argument altogether.

The second problem with the rights of the child approach is that it conflicts with parents' desires to rear children independently and their notions of what is in their children's best interests. While women may not wish to see their daughters harmed, they may also feel strongly that they should be able to rear their children according to their own cultural norms and traditions. Besides, if mothers value the economic, social, and cultural benefits of the operation, they are unlikely to be persuaded that it should not be performed on their daughters. Moreover, the strong social and cultural pressures to continue the practice work against parents who would prefer not to submit their daughters to the operation. . . .

The third problem with this approach is that it almost exclusively focuses on the physical harm done to a child when she is circumcised and does not address the positive feelings she may have as a circumcised woman. In African communities with strong cultural and traditional ties, the perceived need to be circumcised mitigates the hellish remembrances of the event. Little girls who are initially hurt, betrayed, and degraded by the operation later come to feel socially and morally acceptable because they have been circumcised. As the girls grow into women they may forget the pain and argue that the practice need not be banned. Furthermore, it is difficult to attack a practice as harmful to children when it later gives them both social and economic benefits.

A final problem with approaching this issue from the rights of the child perspective is that many young girls believe that they want to be circumcised. The stigma associated with not being circumcised attaches early, virtually compelling a choice to undergo the operation. . . .

To argue that the girls themselves are opposed to the operation is therefore difficult; indeed, recent studies indicate that adolescent girls 'voluntarily' undergo the operation.

In some cases, however, African girls recognize how horrifying the practice can be. One reason given for the large number of Ethiopian girls in the Eritrean People's Liberation Front Army is that they were running away from forced marriages and the 'knife.' Others who have been circumcised feel outraged and betrayed by the *excieuse* (the man or woman who circumcised them), their fathers, their aunts, but most of all by their mothers.

. . .

C. The Right to Health

The right to health argument, which attacks female circumcision for producing menacing health problems, is likely to be successful. Women and governments in Africa accept this approach because it can be integrated into pre-existing values and social and economic priorities, and does not require a reformulation of rights and policies. Combatting female circumcision as a violation of the right to health may therefore help unify the campaign to eradicate it.

African women accept the right to health argument for a number of reasons. First, as sexuality is not an openly discussed topic among most African women, they can more easily discuss the operation in terms of health effects. Further, since African countries face numerous health problems that demand immediate attention, framing the issue in terms of a right to health is seen as more legitimate than arguing for sexual or corporal integrity.

. . .

Isabelle Gunning, Arrogant Perception, World Travelling and Multicultural Feminism: The Case of Female Genital Surgeries

23 Colum. Hum. Rts. L. Rev. 189 (1991–92), at 238.

. . .

Arguably, most of the activity reviewed and criticized by the human rights system is not culturally based. In cases of torture or forced disappearances, accused governments generally deny the fact or any knowledge thereof. With a cultural practice, the condemned act is acknowledged and defended: the practice is viewed 'as conduct which has evolved for a specific purpose within a culture and is endorsed as a legitimate expression of that purpose'. However governments may not be actually involved in the practice, because private citizens willingly nurture their cultural norms.

One problem therefore is whether human rights which, like the rest of international law, is aimed at public or government actions can be used to alter the behavior of private parties. Feminists have argued persuasively that the public-private distinction is a false one and that the real question is not whether law, in this case human rights law, should apply to the private as well as the public, but rather 'what types of private acts are and are not protected'. If one can decide that a particular act is a violation, even if performed by private citizens, one can hold governments responsible. For example, when one reviews the international definition of torture one sees that it is not only active or direct government participation which is prohibited, but also government 'consent or acquiescence'.

It may be argued that that language is designed to hold accountable governments that are believed to be responsible for torturous acts but who have created sufficient 'plausible deniability' to make it difficult to prove complicity. Still, it reflects a willingness to pressure governments to do something about 'private' acts. The practical problem is that if governments really do not have control over private actions, then the primary tool of human rights enforcement, governmental embarrassment, will not be nearly as effective. This is particularly true with a practice like female genital surgeries, where the governments involved may either refuse to be embarrassed or become angry at the attack on the culture; thus they reject the interference. Moreover, even if a government is embarrassed, the cost of implementing an eradication law, as has been explained, could be enormously socially disruptive and ineffective.

. . .

. . . One is not stuck between choosing 'universal standards' and 'everything is relative'. It is not that there are 'universals' out there waiting to be discovered. But through dialogue, shared values can become universal and be safeguarded. The process by which these universal standards are created is important. A dialogue, with a tone that respects cultural diversity, is essential. From that dialogue a consensus may be reached, understanding that as people and cultures interact they do change and learn from each other.

CEDAW, Female Circumcision

General Recommendation. No. 14, 9th Sess., 1990.
Un Doc. A/45/38/1 Int. Hum. Rts. Re. 21 (No. 1, 1994).

[The Committee on the Elimination of Discrimination against Women (see p. 188, *supra*), created by the Convention on the Elimination of all Forms of Discrimination against Women, is authorized to make general recommendations based on reports that it receives from the states parties.]

Recommends that States parties:

(a)   Take appropriate and effective measures with a view to eradicating the practice of female circumcision. Such measures could include:

   (i)   The collection and dissemination by universities, medical or nursing associations, national women's organizations or other bodies of basic data about such traditional practices;
   (ii)   The support of women's organizations at the national and local levels working for the elimination of female circumcision and other practices harmful to women;
   (iii) The encouragement of politicians, professionals, religious and community leaders at all levels, including the media and the arts, to co-operate in influencing attitudes towards the eradication of female circumcision;
   (iv) The introduction of appropriate educational and training programmes and seminars based on research findings about the problems arising from female circumcision;

(b)   Include in their national health policies appropriate strategies aimed at eradicating female circumcision in public health care. Such strategies could include the special responsibility of health personnel, including traditional birth attendants, to explain the harmful effects of female circumcision;

(c)   Invite assistance, information and advice from the appropriate organizations of the United Nations system to support and assist efforts being deployed to eliminate harmful traditional practices;

(d)   Include in their reports to the Committee under articles 10 and 12 of the Convention on the Elimination of All Forms of Discrimination against Women information about measures taken to eliminate female circumcision.

K. Hayter, Female Circumcision—Is There a Legal Solution?

J. of Soc. Welf. L. (U.K.) 323 (Nov. 1984), at 355.

[These remarks concerned a pending bill in Parliament to prohibit female circumcision in the U.K.]

Clearly the effects of female circumcision and the enforced suppression of female sexuality is to be abhorred. The overall response of members of the House of Lords reflects this view, as summarised in the speech of Baroness Gaitskell's where she states, 'The primitive attitude to female circumcision rests not only on tradition, but on the male desire for the female to be pure for him . . . That is not only the most cruel, but also . . . the most primitive, and the most important aspect of the matter which we should reject'. But is this moral indignation sufficient to justify legal intervention to prohibit consensual acts performed on women over 16 in accordance with the cultural requirements of a minority group? Support for the view that it is can be seen in the statement of Lord Devlin, in his Maccabean Lecture in 1959 entitled *The Enforcement of Morals*. Here it is argued that legal intervention is justified where in the collective moral judgment of a society a practice cannot be tolerated. But unless moral repugnance can be founded on the broader principle that all acts amounting to sexual oppression of women are not to be tolerated, legislation on this issue could be interpreted as purely discriminatory against the minority groups concerned. It is interesting to note here that clitoradectomies were openly performed on children and women in England and the United States as late as 1945 as a 'cure' for masturbation and 'promiscuity'. The demise of this practice in recent years may indicate a general change in attitudes towards female sexuality. If this is correct then, it is suggested, the legality of certain western practices will also require review. Purely elective cosmetic surgery is an obvious case where the right of the individual to consent to treatment is not seriously questioned. Breast reduction, for example, is an unnecessary and mutilating operation involving considerable pain and scarring to the patient. If justification for its performance were called for, medical evidence of anxiety and depression brought on by the woman's dissatisfaction with her body would undoubtedly be sufficient to outweigh the injury inherent in the treatment. Indeed, the Government's proposed amendment to the Bill which would safeguard the right of western women to undergo surgery on mental health grounds reinforces this view. Precisely the same justification would be pleaded in support of the legality of female circumcision and should, by analogy, in the absence of further justification for its prohibition, be sufficient. In both cases the women's perception of themselves reflects the demands of the social group to which they belong. This justification is the greater in the case of female circumcision where its necessity extends beyond mere aesthetic appeal, being crucial to the women's status within the group.

Additionally, the imposition of the moral values of the majority onto minority groups would seem inappropriate in a multiracial society in which the current trend is towards tolerance of others' cultural practices. An analogy can be drawn here between female circumcision and the circumcision of Jewish males, which does receive social and legal tolerance. Clearly nice distinctions can be drawn between a mere custom in the case of female circumcision and a strict religious requirement in the latter case. But is this really the criteria to be used to limit the bounds of toleration? The essential element in both appears to be the unquestioned and entrenched nature of the practices which are part of the social fabric of the groups concerned. Arguably both should, prima facie, be tolerated on this basis alone. A valid distinction between the two practices, however, is the degree of injury involved in female circumcision which is not associated with male circumcision.

. . . . Legal intervention is, however, justified to protect persons from what is offensive or injurious, particularly where the individual is young, weak in body or mind or in a state of particular physical or economic dependence. Arguably the practice of female circumcision bears characteristics which bring it within these exceptions thus justifying legal intervention, which are not present in other forms of elective surgery. Clearly it is applicable to the circumcision of female children and this approach has been taken to prohibit indigenous practices, notably the tattooing of minors. To subject women over 16 to the same degree of legal paternalism appears, prima facie, to be a denial of their right to self-determination and a slight on the intellectual capacity of the women members of these groups. This issue underlies objections to legal limitations on a woman's right to elect for abortion. It is possible, however, that the cloistered lifestyle and acute state of economic dependence in which the women practising female circumcision find themselves may provide some justification for a paternalistic approach here. Access to research findings and wider views which refute the necessity for female circumcision are denied to them and the traditional view of the practice is enforced within the closed environment. They are not, therefore, in a position to form a balanced judgment in their own best interests. By criminalising female circumcision the law may assist in freeing women who are powerless to help themselves by reducing the social pressure to conform.

AAWORD, A Statement on Genital Mutilation

Miranda Davies (ed.), *Third World-Second Sex: Women's Struggles and National Liberation* (1983), at 217.

[The Association of African Women for Research and Development (AAWORD) is a group of African women researchers dedicated to doing women's research from an African perspective. They are based in Dakar, Senegal where their first official meeting was held in December 1977.]

. . .

This new crusade of the West has been led out of the moral and cultural prejudices of Judaeo-Christian Western society: aggressiveness, ignorance or even contempt, paternalism and activism are the elements which have infuriated and then shocked many people of good will. In trying to reach their own public, the new crusaders have fallen back on sensationalism, and have become insensitive to the dignity of the very women they want to 'save'. They are totally unconscious of the latent racism which such a campaign evokes in countries where ethnocentric prejudice is so deep-rooted. And in their conviction that this is a 'just cause', they have forgotten that these women from a different race and a different culture are also *human beings*, and that solidarity can only exist alongside self-affirmation and mutual respect.

. . .

AAWORD, whose aim is to carry out research which leads to the liberation of African people and women in particular, *firmly condemns* genital mutilation and all other practices—traditional or modern—which oppress women and justify exploiting them economically or socially, as a serious violation of the fundamental rights of women.

. . .

However, as far as AAWORD is concerned, the fight against genital mutilation, although necessary, should not take on such proportions that the wood cannot be seen for the trees. . . .

. . . [T]o fight against genital mutilation without placing it in the context of ignorance, obscurantism, exploitation, poverty, etc., without questioning the structures and social relations which perpetuate this situation, is like 'refusing to see the sun in the middle of the day'. This, however, is precisely the approach taken by many Westerners, and is highly suspect, especially since Westerners necessarily profit from the exploitation of the peoples and women of Africa, whether directly or indirectly.

Feminists from developed countries—at least those who are sincerely concerned about this situation rather than those who use it only for their personal prestige—should understand this other aspect of the problem. They must accept that it is a problem for *African women*, and that no change is possible without the conscious participation of African women. . . .

. . .

Hope Lewis, Between 'Irua' and 'Female Genital Mutilation'

8 Harv. Hum. Rts. J. 1 (1995), at 31

A primary concern expressed in African feminist texts is the tendency among Western human rights activists to essentialize the motivations for practicing FGS [Female Genital Surgery] as rooted either in superstition or in the passive acceptance of patriarchal domination. In rejecting these characterizations, African feminists seek to recapture and control the representation of their own cultural heritage.

. . .

The African feminist literature on FGS emphasizes the importance of the cultural context in which FGS occurs and the complexity of the justifications for its continued practice. It contends that western feminist discourse fails to ask the questions that would help place its patriarchal aspects in a broader context: Are boys initiated at the same time as girls? Are the risk and consequences of initiation rituals for boys as life-threatening and long-lasting as they are for girls? What socioeconomic purposes does FGS serve for a particular group? Are there alternative ways of fulfilling those purposes or challenging their necessity? If so, how should domestic and international actors identify and support those alternatives? Finally, do domestic and international actors contribute to the continuation of harmful traditional practices?

Barbara Crossette, A Uganda Tribe Fights Genital Cutting

New York Times, July 16, 1998, p. A8

For the Sabiny people of eastern Uganda, 1998 is a circumcision year—as are all even years—when girls as well as boys would normally be expected to endure a painful rite of passage to young adulthood. But not this time, said G. W. Cheborian, chairman of the Sabiny Elders Association, a council of clan leaders. While young men of 14 to about 22 will still take part in elaborate circumcision ceremonies in December to mark their entry into manhood, for many if not most girls and young women, there will be no genital cutting.

In the last few years the Sabiny people have waged a campaign to abolish female genital mutilation and replace it with a symbolic ritual declaring the girl a woman without maiming her for life, Mr. Cherborian said in an interview. Last week Mr. Cheborian received the 1998 United Nations Population Award for the work that the Sabiny elders have done in their remote, mountainous Kapchorwa region of Uganda.

The Sabiny Elders—after first converting themselves from proponents to opponents of female genital cutting—attracted the attention of health and population experts by finding their own way to deal with a practice that is widely condemned by women's groups and passionately defended by traditionalists in Africa, where it is most prevalent. The elders' campaign is being studied by other Africans as an example of how to deal with a culturally sensitive taboo within a traditional society.

Mr. Cheborian, who describes himself as 'about 71,' said that even among the Sabiny—130,000 people, according to Uganda's last census in 1991—there were still those who clung to the tradition. 'But most of our children are educated now,' he said. 'The girls say, "Father, this time I am not going to go along with your idea"'.

A decade ago the Sabiny, a collection of rural clans engaged in small-scale farming, were committed enough to the practice of genital cutting that they made it a requirement. That put them into conflict with the Ugandan Government, which discourages the practice. The tension only increased Sabiny tenacity on the subject, Ugandans say.

Then in 1992, Sabiny chiefs formed the Elders Association and began a systematic review of their traditions. 'The main reason was to identify those which are values for retaining, improve those which required improvement, so that they are consistent with modern life,' Mr. Cheborian said, speaking in English. He said that those values that were no longer acceptable were singled out to be 'discarded or abandoned.'

From the beginning, he said, the focus was on the genital cutting of girls. But the elders met resistance and did not have the necessary resources to wage an effective grass-roots campaign. A few years ago the United Nations Population Fund stepped in with some support.

'We started in 1996, and we have been very active on the ground for about two years now,' Mr. Cheborian said. By the end of that year, 'it appeared that we had reduced the circumcision of girls by 36 percent,' he added.

. . .

'What we have done is to tell parents about the harmful parts of circumcising females,' Mr. Cheborian said. 'This included the pain, the very serious bleeding and fainting because of the bleeding. Because of the open cuts, there is a risk of H.I.V.-AIDS affecting the person. 'We told them that when that part which is cut forms a scar, that reduces the opening of the passage, so later when a mother wants to deliver, she finds a lot of labor problems' . . . Fathers and mothers alike 'have come to understand that it is harmful,' he said. 'Fathers are now on our side.'

. . .

Merwine, Letter to Editor

New York Times, November 24, 1993, at A24.

To the Editor:
A. M. Rosenthal condemns female circumcision, a traditional practice common to many African and Arabic peoples, as 'female mutilation' . . . From the Western liberal tradition, and certainly from a feminist perspective, Mr. Rosenthal is correct.

However, from the African viewpoint the practice can serve as an affirmation of the value of woman in traditional society.

This tradition has long been a source of conflict between Western and African values.

. . .

The operation completed, a fee was provided by the young women, usually in the form of a cooked meal, to their moruithia. At this point, they became full members of the Kikuyu and were no longer considered girls.

The importance of the ceremony among traditional Kikuyu cannot be understated, for each girl showed by her act of courage that she was ready to be married. Of equal importance, she now became a member of an age-set. An age-set is a group of people of similar age who tend to act together in their society for the rest of their lives. To the Kikuyu, female circumcision is much more than a mere physical act.

. . .

The sentiments expressed long ago in Kenya are almost certainly shared by the peoples who practice the custom today. To demand, as Mr. Rosenthal does, that economic aid be used to force a change in a tradition central to many Africans and Arabs is the height of ethnocentrism.

A better approach would be for Western peoples to try to understand the importance of these traditions to those who practice them. The West could encourage Africans to have the surgical part of the ceremony performed by competent medical practitioners. That would eliminate potential infection and restrict the extent of excision. This is being done in many African states. Such a policy would allow the West to uphold its values while avoiding the appearance of arrogance.

Yael Tamir, Hands Off Clitoridectomy

31 Boston Review 21 (Summer 1996) ; www.polisci.mit.edu/BR21.3/Tamir.html

. . .

Clitoridectomy is obviously a deplorable practice. It is, among other things, an extremely painful, traumatizing mutilation of young girls that leaves them permanently disfigured and deprived of sexual enjoyment. We should express no sympathy toward those who practice it, and support those who struggle to end it.

But we also should be suspicious about the role of clitoridectomy in current political debate. Despite their liberal appearance, references to clitoridectomy commonly reveal a patronizing attitude toward women, suggesting that they are primarily sexual beings. Moreover, those references involve a certain degree of dishonesty. They intentionally widen the gap between our culture and those in which clitoridectomy is practiced, thus presenting those other cultures as incommensurable with ours. The effect of this distancing is to disconnect criticism of their practices from criticism of our own, and turn reflection on other cultures into yet another occasion for celebrating our special virtues. We should resist such self-congratulation. And if we do, the debate about clitoridectomy takes on an entirely different cast.

. . .

Moreover, we are all aware of painful practices of body piercing, tattooing, and abnormal elongation of lips, ear lobes, and necks. National Geographic runs cover photos of women and men who have undergone such severe malformations, not in protest but as a neutral representation of other ways of life with their different conceptions of beauty. So hostility to clitoridectomy is not driven principally by concerns about physical suffering. Those who object to it would be no less hostile if it were performed in hygienic conditions under anesthesia.

It might be said that these examples are all irrelevant as they do not include the mutilation of the body. But when is the body improved and when is it mutilated? Are parents who force their children to wear braces mutilating their children's teeth or improving them? In most cases, the answer depends on one's conception of beauty. . . . To be sure, parents say (sincerely) that these treatments will improve their children's life chances, self-image, and social standing. But parents who perform clitoridectomy on their daughters invoke precisely the same arguments.

Furthermore, it seems clear that Western conceptions of female beauty encourage women to undergo a wide range of painful, medically unnecessary, and potentially damaging processes—extreme diets, depilation, face lifts, fat pumping, silicone implants. Of course, adult women do these things to their own bodies, and, it is said, their decisions are freely made. But would our gut reaction to female circumcision be very different if it were performed on consenting adults? It is not unlikely that girls at the age of 13 or 14, who are considered in traditional societies as adults mature enough to wed and bear children, would 'consent' to the mutilation of their bodies if they were convinced that marriage and children were contingent on so doing. Many women who followed the tradition of Sati seemed to do it as a matter of choice. Did their 'consent' make this tradition defensible? Women 'consent' to such practices because the alternative is even more painful—a life of solitude, humiliation, and deprivation.

. . .

Perhaps, then, we object to clitoridectomy because it is performed on minors. But think of the parents in our culture who foster in their daughters bad eating habits that might destroy their teeth or their vital organs, or, in more tragic cases, lead to life-threatening eating disorders. Are we ready to judge these parents as harshly as we judge parents who require clitoridectomies?

In both cases, parents sincerely believe that they are serving the interests of their children and allowing them to live what is, according to their conception of the good, a meaningful life. Both cases may thus be taken to demonstrate that parents are not the most trustworthy guardians of their children, but why should one case be more harshly judged than the other?

. . .

The common answer is that clitoridectomy damages women's sexual organs, thus depriving them of sexual enjoyment—a basic need, perhaps even a right. One may wonder, however, when precisely our society became so deeply committed to women's sexual enjoyment.

. . .

Sexual enjoyment has acquired a mythical status in our society, advocated both as the most sublime and most corruptive pleasure. Advocates of clitoridectomy see the corruption: Performing clitoridectomy will restrict the sexual desires of women, thereby turning them into more chaste and righteous wives and mothers. They believe that the pursuit of sexual pleasures may lead a person astray, and that women are more likely to be influenced by such desires and act unscrupulously.

Both assumptions are also well grounded in the Western tradition. The failure to control the pursuit of sexual pleasures was seen by religious thinkers, as well as by many secular liberals, as undermining virtue, fostering bad habits and pernicious behavior, and hindering the possibility of true love (either of God or of other human beings). In the Christian tradition celibacy was affirmed as the highest ideal, and 'sex within marriage was regarded as an evil necessary for the continuation of the species'.

. . .

. . . Societies discriminate, dominate, and abuse their members in various ways, but there is something common to all expressions of oppression. We should place this core aspect, repeated in all traditions in different forms, at the center of our criticism. In the cases discussed here, it is not a particular practice but a set of ill-motivated efforts to control the sexuality of women and to restrict their ability to compete for social and political resources that we should find reprehensible.

Does the overwhelming disgust at clitoridectomy signal an emerging social commitment to structural change—to ensuring equal social, economic, and political status for women? I'm afraid not. Of course, the absence of such commitment is no justification for clitoridectomy. My purpose, however, is not to justify clitoridectomy, but to expose the roots of the deep hostility to it—to reveal the smug, unjustified self-satisfaction lurking behind the current condemnation of clitoridectomy. Referring to clitoridectomy, and emphasizing the distance of the practice from our own conventions, allows us to condemn them for what they do to their women, support the struggle of their women against their primitive, inhuman culture, and remain silent on the status of women in our society.

. . .

Multicultural exchanges raise acute concerns not because they point to the incommensurability of cultures, or the impossibility of cross-cultural conversation, but because they confront us with our own deficiencies. . . .

[This article of Yael Tamir was followed by several commentators on the article. One such commentator, Martha Nussbaum, wrote:]

> I am prepared to agree with Tamir to this extent. The attention give FGM seems to me somewhat disproportionate, among the many gross abuses the world practices against women—lack of equality under the law, lack of equal access to education, sex-selective infanticide and feticide, domestic violence, marital rape, rape in police custody, and many more. . . . [T]he reason for this focus is not a fascination with sex but the relative tractability of FGM as a practical problem, given the fact that it is already widely resisted and indeed illegal; how much harder to grapple with women's legal inequality before Islamic courts, their pervasive danger, their illiteracy. . . . Surely Tamir is right that we should not focus on this one abuse while relaxing our determination to make structural changes that would bring women closer to full equality worldwide.

NOTE

As comments in the preceding readings make clear, the practice of female genital mutilation raises the distinctive question of who (if anyone), which party or actor, is violating international human rights. Apparently no state enforces the practice, or instructs or advocates through its affiliated religious or educational institutions that the practice be continued.

The practice then raises the question addressed in the discussions of the ICCPR and CEDAW in Chapter 3: the degree to which the human rights movement regulates directly or indirectly the conduct of non-state—and in this sense, private—actors. Again we consider the reach of the human rights movement to 'private' actors and to actions that cannot readily be attributed directly to the 'public' state, another instance of the public-private question that recurs throughout the coursebook.

Note that this question also points towards the serious obstacles to practical implementation of human rights norms, even by states that are hostile to and seek to curb the challenged practice. A government may find it difficult to disregard the sentiments of politically powerful groups or segments of society that wish to maintain religious or customary law. Moreover, a state's motivation to bring about change will depend on that change's relation to other state objectives and on the depth of the socio-cultural roots of the practices. Indeed, the state might not possess the necessary influence or power to proceed. Authority may be divided among the central government and regional or ethnic leaders. The supervision and enforcement of some customary laws may rest not with the state but with another body, such as a religious court or officials. And as the preceding materials have indicated, secular remedies, even if available, may have limited utility or not even be the best route to follow for critics of the practice.

QUESTIONS

1. African state X is a party to the ICCPR and CEDAW. Its government takes no formal, legal position on female genital mutilation, which is undergone by a substantial number of girls in X in the different ways described in the readings. No law, no subsidy, no official policy, requires or facilitates or prohibits the practice. Suppose that you are a member of a nongovernmental human rights organization in X criticizing this widespread practice before an international human rights body such as the committees created by the ICCPR (see Chapter 9) and CEDAW, on the ground that it violates those treaties.

    a. Precisely what is the violation, and whom would you charge with committing it? The state? Why? If not the state, are any nonstate actors subject to duties under these instruments?

    b. On what provisions of these treaties would you rely for your claim of a human rights violation. What arguments would you make based on them?

2. 'It's no wonder that challenges to female circumcision have generated so much controversy in states where it is practiced. Could the line-up be worse from the perspective of getting things done? It's West vs. the rest, the uneducated and backward rest. It's whites vs. non-whites. It's science vs. culture.' Comment. If you agree, how would you attempt to change this line-up?

NOTE

The following materials extend the discussion of tradition and customary law to other practices, particularly restrictions related to gender on land inheritance and ownership.

ABDULLAHI AHMED AN-NA'IM, STATE RESPONSIBILITY UNDER INTERNATIONAL HUMAN RIGHTS LAW TO CHANGE RELIGIOUS AND CUSTOMARY LAW

in Rebecca Cook (ed.), Human Rights of Women (1994), at 167

[The author argues that a state's responsibility for conforming its domestic laws and practices to its international law obligations to protect and promote human rights 'applies not only to laws enacted by formal legislative organs of the state but also to those attributed to religious and customary sources or sanctions', no matter how enacted or implemented. He notes that Articles 2(f) and 5(a) of CEDAW cover customary practices within that convention's states parties. The article stresses the importance of assuring that the human rights standards are seen as legitimate within the culture where they are to be implemented, and notes that decisions about what is legitimate may well be contested within the culture and influenced by power relationships.

An-Na'im talks of the need for a moral and political 'overlapping consensus' among major cultural traditions of the world to support 'universal' norms, and for internal validation within a cultural tradition when a perhaps uncongenial universal norm is to be implemented with it. Thus

> norms of the international system should be validated in terms of the values and institutions of each culture, and also in terms of shared or similar values and institutions of all cultures. This can be achieved . . . through what I call 'internal discourse' within the framework of each culture, and 'cross-cultural dialogue' among the various cultural traditions of the world.

The excerpts below set forth the author's suggestions of how to change religious and customary norms.]

The authority of religious and customary laws is commonly perceived to derive from either the people's religious beliefs or their communal practice from time immemorial. That is to say, the common perception is that the validity of religious laws is ensured by divine sanction, while the utility of customary laws is assumed to have been proven through long experience. Since the two sources of authority overlap, they can be invoked interchangeably or in combination. . . .

This common perception of the authority of religious and customary laws is founded on a complex web of economic, social and political factors, and tends to reflect existing power relations within the community. The perception is also maintained and promoted through processes of individual socialization and communal identification. While it is useful to understand its basis and dynamics, it may not be necessary or desirable to challenge or repudiate the perception itself in order to change the religious and customary laws it legitimizes. It is important to remember that the objective is to bring religious and customary laws into conformity with international human rights law, not to extinguish religious and customary laws themselves or transform their jurisprudential character. In any case, whether, to what extent, and how indigenous perceptions about religious and customary laws should and can be challenged, changed, or modified should be left to the process of internal discourse . . . An external effort to impose change would probably be perceived as an exercise in cultural imperialism, and rejected as such.

It should also be emphasized that religious and customary laws can, and usually are, implemented independently of the structures and mechanisms of the state. The state might try to regulate the operation of these laws, for example, by providing for procedural safeguards to be enforced by administrative organs or tribunals. But it can neither immediately eradicate the practice of these laws altogether, nor transform their nature and content, at least not without engaging in massive oppression and intimidation of the particular population over a long period of time. Even if the state were able and willing to maintain such a program as a high priority in its domestic policies, such policy or practice would be totally unacceptable from a human rights point of view.

An effort to change religious and customary laws in accordance with international human rights law should seek to persuade people of the validity and utility of the change. Such persuasion must, of course, be grounded in a complete and realistic understanding of the rationale or authority of these laws, and of the way they operate in practice. For example, customary land tenure practices that assign ownership or possession of land to men rather than women might be apparently justified or rationalized on the ground that only men can cultivate or otherwise use the land in order to support their families. Beyond that apparent rationale, however, such practices will probably also rely on assumptions about the competence and 'proper' roles of men and women in society. This type of underlying rationale can be strong enough to override or negate efforts by the state to change or regulate customary land tenure practices.

For instance, the state may introduce a different land distribution scheme in order to give women their share, and seek to enforce this through an official land registration system. Nevertheless, previous customary land tenure practices may persist 'off the record', with the apparent acquiescence of the women who are supposed to benefit from the enforcement of the new system. An effort to change this aspect of customary law must take into account and address not only apparent economic and sociological factors or justifications, but also the circumstances and underlying rationales that might cause the practice to continue despite attempts at legal regulation or change by the state.

Similarly, one or more justifications may be given for the practice of female genital mutilation. A more sophisticated inquiry, however, may reveal other rationales or underlying assumptions, for example, about male/female sexuality and roles, power relations, and economic and political interests . . .

In view of these factors, it is clear that the only viable and acceptable way of changing religious and customary laws is by transforming popular beliefs and attitudes, and thereby changing common practice. This can be done through a comprehensive and intensive program of formal and informal education, supported by social services and other administrative measures, in order to change people's attitudes about the necessity or desirability of continuing a particular religious or customary practice. To achieve its objective, the program must not only discredit the religious or customary law or practice in question, but also provide a viable and legitimate alternative view of the matter. Such an alternative view of an existing practice can be either the simple discontinuation of the practice in question or the substitution of another.

Since the original practice derives its authority from religious or customary sanction, an effort to discredit it (and to substitute another where appropriate) must draw its authority from the same source on which the original practice was founded. This effort must also be presented through a reasoning or rationale intelligible to the affected population. For example, efforts to change customary land tenure practices must seek to challenge and discredit whatever economical, sociological, or other rationale is perceived by the population at large to support or justify those practices. Such efforts must also seek to challenge and discredit the original practice in ways that are relevant to, and understood and accepted by, the population in question.

. . .

. . . A highly motivated and capable constituency, for instance, can cultivate popular political support for change, and pressure the state into ratifying the relevant treaty or into increasing or effectuating its commitment to implement change in accordance with international human rights law. Conversely, the existence of an official commitment can encourage the growth of an active local constituency, or facilitate the development of broadly based political support for change. This dynamic is part of the process of internal discourse whereby the proponents of an internationally recognized human right seek to justify and legitimize that right in terms of their own culture, as explained above.

In addition to these internal aspects, there is also the external dimension of the process of changing religious or customary laws. External actors can support and influence the process of internal discourse through cross-cultural dialogue. . . . However, it is crucial that external support and influence be provided in ways that enhance, rather than undermine, the integrity and efficacy of the internal discourse. The process of cultural legitimation will be undermined, if not totally repudiated, by even the appearance of imposition of extra-cultural values and norms. External actors should support and encourage indigenous actors who are engaging in internal discourse to legitimize and effectuate a particular human right. . . .

The need for cultural sensitivity and discretion in providing external support is underscored by the fact that those acting as internal agents of change are liable to be regarded by local religious or political forces as subversive elements acting on behalf of the imperial interests of alien powers and cultures. This may appear obvious and elementary in such a political struggle, where the internal 'guardians' of tradition and the status quo would want to seize on every opportunity and pretext in their efforts to undermine the credibility of the proponents of changing religious or customary laws. . . .

. . .

EPHRAHIM V. PASTORY

Tanzania High Court, 1990
87 Int. L. Rep. 106 (1992)

[Pastory inherited some clan land from her father by a valid will. She sold it to a stranger who was not a clan member. Ephrahim, Pastory's nephew and a clan member, filed a suit requesting the Primary Court to declare that the land was void since females had no power under Haya customary law to sell clan land. The Primary Court declared the sale void and ordered Pastory to restore the funds to the purchaser. The District Court, on appeal, overturned that decision, holding that the sale was valid but, since it was made without the clan's consent (see *infra*), the nephew was at liberty to redeem the land by paying back the purchase price. The nephew appealed to the High Court.

The Court observed at the outset that '[w]omen's liberation is high on the agenda in this appeal'. It stated that Haya customary law was 'clear on the point', for para. 20 of the Declaration of Customary Law provided that '[w]omen can inherit, except for clan land, which they may receive in usufruct [for their lifetime] but may not sell. However, if there is [no] male of that clan, women may inherit such land in full ownership'. A book on *Customary Law of Haya Tribe* indicated that a male member of the clan could sell clan land with the consent of clan members, but if the sale were made without such consent, other clan members could *redeem* the land by repaying the purchase price to the purchaser.

The opinion referred to a prior decision holding that courts were bound by the applicable customary law. Any changes in customary law had to be 'initiated by altering the customs of the community where they originate'. Thus (said the prior decision) it did not 'fall to this Court to decide that such law is inappropriate to modern development and conditions'. But, the present Court noted, there had been a recent change in judicial attitudes. The opinion by Justice Mwalusanya continued:]

. . . In his booklet *Socialism and Rural Development* Mwalimu J. K. Nyerere states:

> Although every individual was joined to his fellow by human respect, there was in most parts of Tanzania, an acceptance of one human inequality. Although we try to hide the fact and despite the exaggeration which our critics have frequently indulged in, it is true that the women in traditional society were regarded as having a place in the community which was not only different, but was also to some extent inferior . . . This is certainly inconsistent with our socialist conception of the equality of all human beings and the right of all to live in such security and freedom as is consistent with equal security and freedom from all other. If we want our country to make full and quick progress now, it is essential that our women live in terms of full equality with their fellow citizens who are men.

And as long ago as 1968 Mr Justice Saidi (as he then was) pointed out the inherent wrong in this discriminatory customary law. It was in the case of

Ndewawiosia d/o HDcamtzo v. Imanuel s/o Malasi: (1968) HCD No 127. He *inter alia* said:

> Now it is abundantly clear that this custom, which bars daughters from inherit-
> ing clan land and sometimes their own father's estate, has left a loophole for
> undeserving clansmen to flourish within the tribe. Lazy clan members anxiously
> await the death of their prosperous clansmen who happens to have no male issue
> and as soon as death occurs they immediately grab the estate and mercilessly
> mess up things in the dead man's household, putting the widow and daughters
> into terrible confusion, fear, and misery.
> . . .

But the customary law in question has not been changed up to this day. The
women are still suffering at the hands of selfish clan members.

What is more is that since the *Bill of Rights* was incorporated in our 1977
Constitution *vide* Act No 15/1984 by Article 13(4) discrimination against women
has been prohibited. But some people say that, that is a dead letter. And the
Universal Declaration of Human Rights (1948) which is part of our Constitution by
virtue of Article 9(1)(f) prohibits discrimination based on sex as per Article 7.
Moreover Tanzania has ratified the *Convention on the Elimination of all Forms of
Discrimination against Women*. That is not all. Tanzania has also ratified the *African Charter on Human and Peoples Rights* which in Article 18(3) prohibits discrimination on account of sex. And finally Tanzania has ratified the *International
Covenant on Civil and Political Rights* which in Article 26 prohibits discrimination
based on sex. The principles enunciated in the above named documents are a
standard below which any civilized nation will be ashamed to fall. It is clear from
what I have discussed that the customary law under discussion flies in the face of
our Bill of Rights as well as the international conventions to which we are
signatories.
. . .

It has been provided by Section 5(1) of the Constitution (Consequential, Transitional and Temporary Provisions) Act No 16 of 1984 that with effect from March
1988 *the courts* will construe the existing law, including customary law:

> with such modifications, adoptions, qualifications and exceptions as may be
> necessary to bring it into conformity with the provisions of the Fifth Consti-
> tutional Amendment Act No 15/1984 i.e. Bill of Rights.
> . . .

Now what was the intention of Parliament of Tanzania to pass Section 5(1) of
Act 16/1984 and what was the mischief that it intended to remedy?

There can be no doubt that Parliament wanted to do away with all oppressive
and unjust laws of the past. It wanted all existing laws (as they existed in 1984)
which were inconsistent with the Bill of Rights to be inapplicable in the new era or
be treated as modified so that they are in line with the Bill of Rights. It wanted the
courts to modify by construction those existing laws which were inconsistent with
the Bill of Rights such that they were in line with the new era. . . .

If Parliament meant otherwise it could have said so in clear words. Many
countries in the Commonwealth which had to incorporate Bill of Rights in their

constitutions have expressly indicated what they wanted to be the position of the existing law after the introduction of the Bill of Rights in the constitutions. For example in Sri Lanka Article 18(3) of their 1972 Constitution clearly states that: 'all existing law shall operate notwithstanding any inconsistency with the provisions of the Bill of Rights'. . . .

But we in Tanzania did not want to adopt the above provisions which 'saved' the existing law operating prior to the introduction of the Bill of Rights. We wanted to start with a clean slate, a new *grundnorm*. . . .
. . .

I have found as a fact that Section 20 of the *Rules of Inheritance* GN No 436/1963 of the Declaration of Customary Law, is discriminatory of females in that unlike their male counterparts, they are barred from selling clan land. That is inconsistent with Article 13(4) of the Bill of Rights of our Constitution which bars discrimination on account of sex. Therefore under Section 5(1) of Act 16/1984 I take Section 20 of the *Rules of Inheritance* GN No 436/1963 to be *now modified and qualified* such that males and females have now equal rights to inherit and sell clan land. . . . The disposal of the clan land to strangers without the consent of the clansmen is subject to the fiat that any other clan member can *redeem* that clan land on payment of the purchase price to the purchaser. That now applies to both males and females. . . .

From now on, females all over Tanzania can at least hold their heads high and claim to be equal to men as far as inheritance of clan land and self-acquired land of their father's is concerned. It is part of the long road to women's liberation. But there is no cause for euphoria as there is much more to do in other spheres. One thing which surprises me is that it has taken a simple, old rural woman to champion the cause of women in this field but not the elite women in town who chant jejune slogans years on end on women's lib but without delivering the goods. To the male chauvinists they should remember what that English novelist John Gay (1685–1732) had said in *The Beggar's Opera*:

> Fill every glass, for wine inspires us,
> And fires us, with courage, love and joy,
> Women and wine should life employ.
> Is there aught else on earth desirous?
> If the heart of a man is depressed with cares,
> The mist is dispelled when a woman appears.

It is hoped that, from the time the woman has been elevated to the same place as the man, at least in respect of inheritance of clan land, then the mist will be dispelled.
. . .

Like the District Court I hold that the sale was valid. The appellant can redeem that clan land on payment of Shs. 300,000. I give the appellant six months from today to redeem the clan land, otherwise if he fails, the land becomes the property of the purchaser . . . .

MAGAYA v. MAGAYA
Supreme Court of Zimbabwe, 1999
Judgment No. S.C. 210/98, [1999] 3 LRC 35

[Shonhiwa Lennon Magaya, the deceased, died intestate. His eldest child, Venia Magaya, was by his first wife. His three sons were by his second wife. His estate included a house where he was living at the time of his death. Venia Magaya went to community court to claim ownership of the estate. A son of the second wife opposed her claim to ownership, and ultimately the court ruled in his favour, the presiding magistrate stating that 'Venia is a lady [and] therefore cannot be appointed to [her] father's estate when there is a man.' Venia Magaya appealed to the Supreme Court, which dismissed the appeal and thus upheld the decision awarding the estate to the son.

Judge Muchechetere, the presiding judge on that court, stated that he would dismiss the appeal because the matter 'relates to customary law being applied to an estate of an African who married according to African law and custom'. Article 68(1) of the Administration of Estates Act provides that when 'any African who has contracted a marriage according to African law and custom . . . dies intestate his estate shall be administered and distributed according to the customs and usages of the tribe or people to which he belonged'. The deceased belonged to the Shona tribal grouping in Zimbabwe It was conceded that the two basic tribal groupings in Zimbabwe, the Shona and Ndebele, 'have broadly similar customs and usages on succession and inheritance', which were similar to many tribal groupings in South Africa. As the opinion stated, 'What is common and clear . . . is that under the customary law of succession of the above tribes males are preferred to females as heirs'.

That rule, the court observed, 'constitutes a *prima facie* discrimination against females and could therefore be a *prima facie* breach' of the Zimbabwe Constitution. Section 23(1) and (2) of the Constitution state that 'no law shall make any provision that is discriminatory either of itself or in its effect'. A law is regarded as discriminatory if 'persons of a particular description by race, tribe, place or origin, political opinions, colour or creed are . . . subjected to a . . . disability to which other persons of another such description are not made subject'. The court, noting that the provisions of Section 23 did not prohibit discrimination based on sex, said that 'even if they did on account of Zimbabwe's adherence to gender equality enshrined in international human rights instruments', Section 23(3) states a relevant exception to the rule of non-discrimination. That exception covers 'devolution of property on death or other matters of personal law [as well as] the application of African customary law in any case involving Africans'.

Judge Muchechetere then considered the relevance of a 1982 Act (the Majority Act) that granted full legal capacity to everybody over the age of 18, including the capacity to acquire and own interests in property independently, and including matters of customary law.]

The question to consider is whether the 'disabilities' and 'discrimination' suffered by women under customary law were based on 'their perpetual minority'. In [the earlier cited] *Mwazozo's* case I came to the conclusion that they were not based on their perpetual minority but on the nature of African society, especially the patri-lineal, matrilineal or bilateral nature of some of them. I reasoned that the concepts of 'minority' and 'majority' status were not known to African customary law but that they were common law concepts which, in my view, should only be used in customary law situations with great care. And I attempted to explain why allowing female children to inherit in a broadly patrilineal society such as in the present case, would disrupt the African customary laws of that society. Although my explanations may have been too general, I still consider them broadly correct. . . .

I agree with what [a cited author] Bennett says about the nature of African society. The learned author states that at the heart of the African socio-political order lay the family, a unit that was extended both vertically and horizontally to encompass a wide range of people who could be called 'kin'. The family was therefore the focus of social concern. In the circumstances, individual interests were submerged in the common weal and the system stressed individual duties instead of his or her rights. And the legal relationships of most consequence in customary law were those of a family's dealings with other families, not those flowing from one person's relations with another.

At the head of the family there was a patriarch, or a senior man, who exercised control of the property and lives of women and juniors. It is from this that the status of women is derived. The woman's status is therefore basically the same as that of any junior male in the family. Mr. Neube [*amicus curiae*] conceded that males in a family are as subordinate to the partriarch as females until they are 'liberated' [which] generally comes with the death of the patriarch and the male 'taking over' or with the male moving away from the family and founding his own family. . . .

In my understanding of African society, especially that of a patrilineal nature, the 'perpetual discrimination' against women stems mainly from the fact that women were always regarded as persons who would eventually leave their original family on marriage . . . to join the family of their husbands. It was reasoned that in their new situation . . . they could not be heads of their original families as they were more likely to subject the interests of the original family to those of their new family. . . . It was also reasoned that the appointment of female heirs would be tantamount to diverting the property of the original family to that of her new family. . . . [H]er property would be inherited by her children who would be members of the new family. This, in my view, would be a distortion of the prin-ciples underlying customary law of succession and inheritance.
. . .

. . . [T]he accepted position is, on all the authorities, that the heir inherits the property and responsibilities of the deceased. [Under the direction or with the approval of the heir, that property could be] distributed to or divided amongst various relatives and acquaintances. This may be done because of the wishes of the deceased, expressed before his death, or because of the heir's desire to discharge his responsibilities of looking after the family. . . .

[The court then described its understanding of the role of the heir in assuming the status of the deceased, in guiding the family and caring for the needs of minor children as well as seeing to the widow's needs. These responsibilities of the heir under customary law had indeed been enforced by courts. For all such reasons, the Majority Act should not be interpreted 'so widely that it would give women additional rights which interfered with and distorted some aspects of customary law', particularly in view of the Constitution's explicit exemption for such law.]

[Counsel] urged this court to, in any event, exercise its discretional law-making role to ensure that women are not excluded from being appointed heiresses at customary law. . . . They argued that this was necessary because the system of appointing single male heirs had caused untold hardship to the deceased's widows and dependants in that the heirs have too often not lived up to their responsibilities and used all the deceased's property for their own personal benefit. They also argued that the change would be proper because culture and custom are dynamic and change with changes in society and in particular the fact that urbanisation has made African society less and less patriarchal. It was further argued that the change would be in keeping with the principle of advancing gender equality enshrined in the international human rights instruments to which Zimbabwe is a party. [Eds. Zimbabwe is a party to CEDAW. Treaties do not have domestic legal effect in Zimbabwe until Parliament enacts implementing legislation that incorporates them into domestic law.]

While I am in total agreement with the submission that there is a need to advance gender equality in all spheres of society, I am of the view that great care must be taken when African customary law is under consideration. In the first place, it must be recognized that customary law has long directed the way African people conducted their lives and the majority of Africans in Zimbabwe still live in rural areas and still conduct their lives in terms of customary law. In the circumstances, it will not readily be abandoned, especially by those such as senior males who stand to lose their positions of privilege. . . .

Secondly, the application of customary law generally is sanctioned by the Constitution and some would elevate this to a right having been conferred by the Constitution.

Thirdly, the application of customary law, especially in inheritance and succession, is in a way voluntary, that is to Africans married under customary law or those who choose to be bound by it. It could therefore be argued that there should be no or little interference with a person's choice. . . .

In view of the above, I consider it prudent to pursue a pragmatic and gradual change which would win long term acceptance rather than legal revolution initiated by the courts. [The opinion then quotes from the author Bennet.]

> The obligation to care for family members, which lies at the heart of the African social system, is a vital and fundamental value, which Africa's Charter on Human and People's Rights is careful to stress. Paragraph 4 of the Preamble to the Charter urges parties to pay heed to 'the virtues of [the African] historical tradition and the values of African civilisation,'. . . . Article 29(1), in particular, states that each person is obliged to preserve the harmonious development of the

family and to work for the cohesion and respect of the family. . . . [These provisions of the Charter are examined at p. 354, *supra*.]

[The court expressed doubt about the judicial capacity to reform customary law, given the complexity of such law. Reform would necessarily go beyond holding a customary norm void; it would have to provide new rules. But those rules would be imposed without the full investigation of social context and consultation with interested parties that a legislature could offer.

Moreover, the court noted, the legislature had recently reformed the succession of estates of persons subject to customary law. If the deceased in this case had died after October 1997 his estate would have been administered under the amended Act, which repealed Section 68(1), *supra*. 'So as far as succession under customary law is concerned the law has now been reformed'.]

QUESTIONS

1. As counsel for appellant in the *Magaya* case, how would you respond to the court's observation that the decision to marry under customary law was a voluntary choice by the parties to the marriage, and hence there was little or no basis for a court to interfere with the consequences of that choice?

2. "It is not simply a matter of inheritance. This typical disability of women under the customary law of many African states has a pervasive effect on women's lives. Surely it impairs their ability to exercise reproductive rights, to get an education, and equally serious matters." If you made this argument to a court or legislature, how would you bear it out?

3. The court in *Ephrahim v. Pastory* points to the 'inherent wrong' in the discriminatory customary law, for 'lazy clan members' profit when there is no male issue and 'grab the estate and mercilessly mess up things' to the detriment of the widow and daughters. On the other hand, the court in the *Magaya* case stresses that the Shona customary law imposes serious responsibilities on the male heirs, such as duties of support out of the inherited property to family members of the deceased. The assumption is that these duties are honoured. That is, the customary law consists of a complex, interrelated network of rules.

Taking the more charitable view of the customary practice, how would you take account of these relationships between inheritance and responsibilities in proposing a reform that eliminates gender discrimination, particularly in view of the court's description of how women, when they marry, join another and primary family?

BARBARA CROSSETTE, TESTING THE LIMITS OF
TOLERANCE AS CULTURES MIX
New York Times, March 6, 1999, p. B9

In Maine, a refugee from Afghanistan was seen kissing the penis of his baby boy, a
traditional expression of love by this father. To his neighbors and the police, it was
child abuse, and his son was taken away. In Seattle, a hospital tried to invent a
harmless female circumcision procedure to satisfy conservative Somali parents
wanting to keep an African practice alive in their community. The idea got buried
in criticism from an outraged public.

How do democratic, pluralistic societies like the United States, based on
religious and cultural tolerance, respond to customs and rituals that may be repel-
lent to the majority? As new groups of immigrants from Asia and Africa are added
to the demographic mix in the United States, Canada and Europe, balancing
cultural variety with mainstream values is becoming more and more tricky.

Many Americans confront the issue of whether any branch of government
should have the power to intervene in the most intimate details of family life.

'I think we are torn,' said Richard A. Shweder, an anthropologist at the University of Chicago and a leading advocate of the broadest tolerance for cultural
differences. 'It's a great dilemma right now that's coming up again about how
we're going to deal with diversity in the United States and what it means to be an
American.'

Anthropologists have waded deeply into this debate, which is increasingly
engaging scholars across academia, as well as social workers, lawyers and judges
who deal with new cultural dimensions in immigration and asylum. Some, like
Mr. Shweder, argue for fundamental changes in American laws, if necessary, to
accommodate almost any practice accepted as valid in a radically different society
if it can be demonstrated to have some social or cultural good.

For example, although Mr. Shweder and others would strongly oppose importing such practices as India's immolation of widows, they defend other controversial practices, including the common African ritual that opponents call female
genital mutilation, which usually involves removing the clitoris at a minimum.
They say that it is no more harmful than male circumcision and should be
accommodated, not deemed criminal, as it now is in the United States and several
European countries. At the Harvard Law School, Martha Minow, a professor who
specializes in family and school issues, said that intolerance often arises when the
behavior of immigrants seems to be 'nonmodern, nonscientific and nonrational'.
She cites as an example the practice of 'coining' among Cambodians, where hot
objects may be pressed on a child's forehead or back as cures for various maladies,
leaving alarming welts that for teachers and social workers set off warnings of child
abuse.

Americans are more than happy to accept new immigrants when their traditions seem to reinforce mainstream ideals. There are few cultural critics of the
family values, work ethic or dedication to education found among many East
Asians, for example.

But going more than halfway to tolerate what look like disturbing cultural practices unsettles some historians, aid experts, economists and others with experience in developing societies. Such relativism, they say, undermines the very notion of progress. What's more, it raises the question of how far acceptance can go before there is no core American culture, no shared values, left.

Many years of living in a variety of cultures, said Urban Jonsson, a Swede who directs the United Nations Children's Fund, Unicef, in sub-Saharan Africa, has led him to conclude that there is 'a global moral minimum', which he has heard articulated by Asian Buddhists and African thinkers as well as by Western human rights advocates.

'There is a nonethnocentric global morality,' he said, and scholars would be better occupied looking for it rather than denying it. 'I am upset by the anthropological interest in mystifying what we have already demystified. All cultures have their bad and good things.'

. . .

Scholars like Mr. Shweder are wary of attempts to catalogue 'good' and 'bad' societies or practices . . . [H]e helped form a group of about 15 legal and cultural experts to investigate how American law affects ethnic customs among African, Asian, Caribbean and Latin American immigrants.

. . .

'Despite our pluralistic ideals, something very much like a cultural un-American activities list seems to have begun circulating among powerful representatives and enforcers of mainstream culture', the group says in its statement. 'Among the ethnic minority activities at risk of being dubbed "un-American" are the use of disciplinary techniques such as shaming and physical punishment, parent/child co-sleeping arrangements, rituals of group identity and ceremonies of initiation involving scarification, piercing and genital alterations, arranged marriage, polygamy, the segregation of gender roles, bilingualism and foreign language use and many more'.

Some sociologists and anthropologists on this behavioral frontier argue that American laws and welfare services have often left immigrants terrified of the intrusive power of government. The Afghan father in Maine who lost his son to the social services, backed by a lower court, did not prevail until the matter reached the state Supreme Court, which researched the family's cultural heritage and decided in its favor—while making clear that this was an exceptional case, not a precedent.

Spanking, puberty rites, animal sacrifices, enforced dress codes, leaving children unattended at home and sometimes the use of narcotics have all been portrayed as acceptable cultural practices. But who can claim to be culturally beyond the prevailing laws and why?

. . .

Paradoxically, while some Americans want judgment-free considerations of immigrants' practices and traditional rituals in the countries they come from, asylum seekers from those same countries are turning up at American airports begging to escape from tribal rites in the name of human rights. Immigration lawyers and judges are thus drawn into a debate that is less and less theoretical.

Mr. Jonsson of Unicef . . . labels those who would condemn many in the third world to practices they may desperately want to avoid as 'immoral and unscientific.' In their academic towers, Mr. Jonsson said, cultural relativists become 'partners of the tormentors'.

Jessica Neuwirth, an international lawyer who is director of Equality Now, a New York-based organization aiding women's groups in the developing world and immigrant women in this country, asks why the practices that cultural relativists want to condone so often involve women: how they dress, what they own, where they go, how their bodies can be used.

'Culture is male-patrolled in the way that it is created and transmitted,' she said. 'People who control culture tend to be the people in power, and who constitutes that group is important. Until we can break through that, we can't take the measure of what is really representative'.

. . .

NOTE

A federal criminal statute in the United States, entitled Female Genital Mutilation, was enacted in 1996, 18 U.S.C.A. §116 (West Supp. 1998). Section 116 provides:

(a) Except as provided in subsection (b), whoever knowingly circumcises, excises, or infibulates the whole or any part of the labia majora or labia minora or clitoris of another person who has not attained the age of 18 years shall be fined under this title or imprisoned not more than 5 years, or both.

(b) A surgical operation is not a violation of this section if the operation is— [Clauses (1) and (2) refer to the operation's being necessary to health/medical purposes and being performed by a licensed medical practitioner.]

(c) In applying subsection (b)(1) , no account shall be taken of the effect on the person on whom the operation is to be performed of any belief on the part of that person, or any other person, that the operation is required as a matter of custom or ritual.

In arguing for this legislation while the bill was pending, Senator Reid urged the United States to be more attentive to this practice, and said (142 Cong. Rec. S8972, July 26, 1996):

As African immigrants move throughout the world, taking this barbaric practice with them, many women are working to halt the practice in their new communities. Few are willing to speak up in their traditional communities. But this is occurring in countries where they immigrate. . . . The United States, I believe, is a world leader and needs to realize its influence in the world. I do not believe it is our place to go into other countries and dictate their traditions. But, at the same time, we need to show African governments that we take this issue seriously. We need help from others in the international community.

QUESTION

Serious issues involving cultural practices of immigrants have arisen in numerous Western states. For example, France witnessed a long-lasting dispute involving judicial decisions and passionate public debate over the question whether Muslim girls from North Africa or Turkey who were attending the state secular schools should be allowed to wear scarves, often associated with a sense of their practice and obligations as Muslim girls or women. What kinds of considerations would you think pertinent to a decision by a state whether to permit or ban a particular practice that deviated from community practice and norms—for example, the scarf at school that is generally denied to schoolgirls, or the instances reported in the article by Crossette involving conduct between spouses or between parent and child within the family? Should the immigrant, at least with respect to the applicability of the civil and criminal law, be fully assimilated to the long-present citizen?

2. RESERVATIONS to CEDAW

The Women's Convention (pp. 176–211, *supra*) remains the leader among human rights treaties with respect to the number of reservations that its states parties have entered. Some of these reservations deal with issues similar to those discussed in Section 1, namely conflicts between custom or religion and human rights norms. Others bring in different types of concerns about CEDAW.

This section starts with a description of the international law criteria for assessing the validity of reservations.

COMMENT ON TREATY RESERVATIONS

Article 2(1)(d) of the Vienna Convention on the Law of Treaties defines a reservation to mean 'a unilateral statement' made by a state when ratifying a treaty 'whereby it purports to exclude or to modify the legal effect of certain provisions of the treaty in their application to that State'. Article 19 provides that a state ratifying a treaty may make a reservation unless it is 'prohibited by the treaty' or 'is incompatible with the object and purpose of the treaty'. Section 313 of the *Restatement (Third), Foreign Relations Law of the United States* (1987), is to the same effect. Comment (g) to Section 313 refers to the terms *declaration* and *understanding*.

> When signing or adhering to an international agreement, a state may make a unilateral declaration that does not purport to be a reservation. Whatever it is called, it constitutes a reservation in fact if it purports to exclude, limit, or modify the state's legal obligation. Sometimes, however, a declaration purports to be an 'understanding', an interpretation of the agreement in a particular respect. Such an interpretive declaration is not a reservation if it reflects the

accepted view of the agreement. But another contracting party may challenge the expressed understanding, treating it as a reservation which it is not prepared to accept.

The International Court of Justice addressed the question of the effect of reservations to a multilateral human rights treaty in its 1951 advisory opinion on *Reservations to the Genocide Convention*,[1] which influenced the Vienna Convention's provisions above. The principal questions put to the I.C.J. by the UN General Assembly was whether a reserving state could be regarded as a party to the Genocide Convention if its reservation was objected to by one or more existing parties but not by others, and, if so, what effect the reservation then had between the reserving state and the accepting or rejecting parties.

In responding to that question,[2] the Court addressed the 'traditional concept . . . that no reservation was valid unless it was accepted by all the contracting parties without exception. . . . ' In the context of the Genocide Convention, the Court found it 'proper' to take into account circumstances leading to 'a more flexible application of this principle'. It emphasized the universal character and aspiration of multilateral human rights treaties. Widespread ratifications had 'already given rise to greater flexibility in the international practice' concerning them.

After concluding that the Genocide Convention (whose provisions were silent on the issue of reservations) permitted a state to enter a reservation, the Court considered 'what kind of reservations may be made and what kind of objections may be taken to them'. It underscored the special character of the Convention, which was 'manifestly adopted for a purely humanitarian and civilizing purpose.' In such a convention the contracting States do not have any interests of their own; they merely have, one and all, a common interest in the achievement of 'accomplishment of those high purposes which are the *raison d'être* of the convention'. In such circumstances, one cannot 'speak of individual advantages or disadvantages to States, or of the maintenance of a perfect contractual balance between rights and duties'. Permitting any one state party that objected to another state's reservation of any type to block adherence to the convention by that other state would frustrate the convention's goal of universal membership.

On the other hand, the Court could not accept the argument that 'any State entitled to become a party to the Genocide Convention may do so while making any reservation it chooses by virtue of its sovereignty'. It followed that 'it is the compatibility of a reservation with the object and purpose of the Convention that must furnish the criterion for the attitude of a State in making the reservation on accession as well as for the appraisal by a State in objecting to the reservation'.

The high number of reservations that have accompanied ratification of CEDAW have become a regrettably notorious feature of the Convention, which is in this respect first among the human rights treaties. By way of contrast, few states have

---

[1] Advisory Opinion, 1951 I.C. J. 15.

[2] The Court concluded (1) that a state whose reservation has been objected to by one or more parties but not by others can be regarded as a party to the Convention 'if the reservation is compatible with the object and purposes of the Convention', and (2) that a state party objecting to a reservation that it views as incompatible with the Convention can consider the reserving state not to be a party.

entered reservations to the Convention on Racial Discrimination. Moreover, many of the CEDAW reservations are directed to fundamental provisions.

Unlike the ICCPR, which is silent on the issue, CEDAW addresses reservations in Article 28(2), which prohibits those incompatible with the 'object and purpose' of the Convention. Tolerance of reservations has been urged on various grounds— for example, the desirability of securing widespread participation in treaties serving a 'purely humanitarian and civilizing purpose' (in the words of the *Genocide Convention* case above), and hence the reluctance to view a ratification as invalid because of its reservations. A commentator emphasizes another ground:[3]

> Most states are apprehensive about the possible consequences of accepting a human rights treaty, not least because such treaties may have a dynamic force and interpretation of their scope and impact is less certain that that of commercial treaties. . . . Reservations are seen to offer an assurance that the state can protect its interest to the fullest extent possible.

Other commentators have considered reservations to Article 2 to be 'manifestly incompatible' with the object and purpose of the Convention.[4] As noted below, several states parties have objected to these reservations on grounds that they threaten the integrity of the Convention and the human rights regime in general. Reservations that purport to be applying and thus to be consistent with Article 28(2) of CEDAW raise issues of religious intolerance and of cultural relativism. The net result, claims one commentator, has been the diffuse and widespread view that international obligations assumed through the ratification of CEDAW are somehow 'separate and distinct' from and less binding than those of other human rights treaties.[5]

Consider the following suggestions of Rebecca Cook about criteria for distinguishing between reservations that are compatible and incompatible with the Convention:[6]

> The thesis of this article is that the object and purpose of the Women's Convention are that states parties shall move progressively towards elimination of all forms of discrimination against women and ensure equality between men and women. Further, states parties have an obligation to provide the means to move progressively toward this result. Although the Women's Convention envisions that states parties shall move progressively towards elimination of all forms of discrimination against women and ensure equality between men and women, reservations to the Convention's substantive provisions pose a threat to the achievement of this goal . . . Accordingly, reservations that contemplate the provision of means towards the pursuit of this goal will be regarded as compatible with 'the object and purpose of the treaty' as provided by article 28(2) of the Women's Convention and article 19(c) of the Vienna Convention. Similarly, any

[3] Rebecca Cook, Reservations to the Convention on the Elimination of All Forms of Discrimination against Women, 30 Va. J. Int. L. 643, 650 (1990).
[3] Belinda Clark, The Vienna Convention Reserva-

tions Regime and the Convention on Discrimination against Women, 85 Am J. Int. L. 281 (1991).
[5] *Ibid.*
[6] Rebecca Cook, n. 3, *supra*, at 648.

reservation that contemplates enduring inconsistency between state law or practice and the obligations of the Women's Convention is incompatible with the
treaty's object and purpose.

As of January 2000, 67 states parties to CEDAW had entered reservations or
declarations, either addressed to a specific provision or of a general character that
embraced the convention as a whole. Ten had registered objections to some of
those reservations. Selected illustrations from several states, as well as a characteristic objection to a reservation by another state party to CEDAW, appear below.[7]

Austria

Austria reserves its right to apply the provision of article 7(b) as far as service in
the armed forces is concerned, and the provision of article 11 as far as night work
of women and special protection of working women is concerned, within the
limits established by national legislation.

Bangladesh

The Government of the People's Republic of Bangladesh does not consider as
binding upon itself the provisions of articles 2, 13(a) and 16(1)(c) and (f) as they
conflict with Shariah law based on Holy Koran and Sunna.

Belgium

The application of article 7 shall not affect the validity of the provisions of the
Constitution . . . which reserves for men the exercise of royal powers . . .

Brazil

The Government of the Federative Republic of Brazil hereby expresses its reservations to article 15, paragraph 4, and to article 16, paragraph 1(a),(c),(g) and
(f). . . .

Egypt

Reservation to the text of article 9, paragraph 2, concerning the granting to women
of equal rights with men with respect to the nationality of their children, without
prejudice to the acquisition by a child born of a marriage of the nationality of his
father. . . . It is clear that the child's acquisition of his father's nationality is the
procedure most suitable for the child and that this does not infringe upon the
principle of equality between men and women, since it is customary for a women

---

[7] The full text of all reservations etc. is available on the UN website at www.un.org/Depts/Treaty/final/ts2/newfiles/part_boo/iv_boo/iv_8.html. Note that the reservations listed above made by Bangladesh in relation to Arts. 13(a) and 16(1)(f), and those made by Belgium and Brazil, have all subsequently been withdrawn.

to agree, upon marrying an alien, that her children shall be of the father's nationality.

Reservation to the text of article 16 concerning the equality of men and women in all matters relating to marriage and family relations during the marriage and upon its dissolution, without prejudice to the Islamic Shariah provisions where by women are accorded rights equivalent to those of their spouses so as to ensure a just balance between them. This is out of respect for the sacrosanct nature of the firm religious beliefs which govern marital relations in Egypt and which may not be called in question and in view of the fact that one of the most important bases of these relations is an equivalency of rights and duties so as to ensure complementarity which guarantees true equality between the spouses, not a quasi-equality that renders the marriage a burden on the wife. . . . The provisions of the Shariah lay down that the husband shall pay bridal money to the wife and maintain her fully and shall also make a payment to her upon divorce, whereas the wife retains full rights over her property and is not obliged to spend anything on her keep. The Shariah therefore restricts the wife's rights to divorce by making it contingent on a judge's ruling, whereas no such restriction is laid down in the case of the husband.

The Arab Republic of Egypt is willing to comply with the content of [article 2], provided that such compliance does not run counter to the Islamic Shariah.

France

The Government of the French Republic declares that no provision of the Convention must be interpreted as prevailing over provisions of French legislation which are more favourable to women than to men.

Ireland

[Re Article 16(1)(d,f)] Ireland is of the view that the attainment in Ireland of the objectives of the Convention does not necessitate the extension to men of rights identical to those accorded to women in respect of the guardianship, adoption and custody of children born out of wedlock and reserves the right to implement the Convention subject to that understanding.

Malta

The Government of Malta does not consider itself bound by subparagraph (e) of Article 16, in so far as the same may be interpreted as imposing an obligation on Malta to legalize abortion.

Singapore

In the context of Singapore's multi-racial and multi-religious society and the need to respect the freedom of minorities to practise their religious and personal laws, the Republic of Singapore reserves the right not to apply the provisions of articles

2 and 16 where compliance with these provisions would be contrary to their religious or personal laws.

Singapore interprets article 11, paragraph 1, in the light of the provisions of article 4, paragraph 2 as not precluding prohibitions, restrictions or conditions on the employment of women in certain areas, or on work done by them where this is considered necessary or desirable to protect the health and safety of women or the human foetus. ....

Turkey

The Government of the Republic of Turkey [makes reservations] with regard to the articles of the Convention dealing with family relations which are not completely compatible with the provisions of the Turkish Civil Code. ....

Objections

Germany

The Federal Republic of Germany considers that the reservations made by Egypt regarding article 2, article 9, paragraph 2, and article 16, by Bangladesh regarding article 2, article 13 (*a*) and article 16, paragraph 1 (*c*) and (*f*), by Brazil regarding article 15, paragraph 4, and article 16, paragraph 1 (*a*), (*c*), (*g*) and (*h*), by Jamaica regarding article 9, paragraph 2, by the Republic of Korea regarding article 9 and article 16, paragraph 1 (*c*), (*d*), (*f*) and *g*), and by Mauritius regarding article 11, paragraph 1 (*b*) and (*d*), and article 16, paragraph 1 (*g*), are incompatible with the object and purpose of the Convention (article 28, paragraph 2) and therefore objects to them. In relation to the Federal Republic of Germany, they may not be invoked in support of a legal practice which does not pay due regard to the legal status afforded to women and children in the Federal Republic of Germany in conformity with the above-mentioned articles of the Convention.

This objection shall not preclude the entry into force of the Convention as between Egypt, Bangladesh, Brazil, Jamaica, the Republic of Korea, Mauritius and the Federal Republic of Germany.

QUESTIONS

1. Which of the preceding reservations do you view as objectionable? Which of them raise issues of cultural relativism? Only those based on a state's local custom or religion?

2. Consider the reservations of Bangladesh and Egypt. What arguments would you make for the validity of those reservations under the criteria stated in the Vienna Convention and CEDAW?

3. How do you assess the criteria suggested by Cook? Would any of the reservations above be treated differently by you under her criteria?

ADDITIONAL READING

On treaty reservations see: A. Pellet, *Fourth Report on Reservations to Treaties*, UN Doc A/CN.4/1999 (1999); B. Simma, 'Reservations to Human Rights Treaties: Some Recent Developments', in G. Hafner *et al* (eds.), *Liber Amicorum Professor Seidl-Hohenveldern (1998) 30*; C. Redgwell, 'Reservations to Treaties and Human Rights Committee General Comment No. 24 (52), 46 Int. & Comp. L. Q. 390 (1997)'.

B. RELIGION

No topic generates more controversy—or indeed more complex ideas—than relationships between (1) institutionalization of religion in the state or religious belief or practice and (2) human rights norms. From one perspective, religious beliefs and human rights are complementary expressions of similar ideas, even though religious texts invoke the language of duties rather than rights. Important aspects of the major religious traditions—canonical text, scholarly exegesis, ministries—provide the foundation for, or reinforce, many basic human rights. Evident examples include rights to bodily security, or to economic and social provision for the needy. From another perspective, religious traditions may impinge on human rights, and religious leaders may assert the primacy of those traditions over rights. The banner of cultural relativism may here be held high. If notions of state sovereignty represent one powerful concept and a force that challenges and seeks to limit the reach of the international human rights movement, religion can then represent another.

The topics in Section B explore selected issues within this large theme. They involve the distinction sketched by some scholars between freedom *of* religion, and freedom *from* religion. The first freedom is threatened primarily by state conduct that prohibits public expression of religious belief and sharply restricts religious practice or ritual. Such conduct may stem from an ideologically secular state (such as the Peoples' Republic of China) that seeks to limit the role of organized religions, or at the other extreme from fundamentalist states that will not tolerate other forms of religious expression. The second freedom *from* again is threatened primarily by the state, which may impose the beliefs or practices of an official or dominant religion on all citizens, whatever their religious community (if any, for some citizens will be secular or atheist). In such circumstances, human rights other than the right to freedom of religion may be implicated. Forms of gender discrimination enforced by the state may find roots in sacred religious text. The state may repress certain speech that is widely viewed as offensive to the dominant religion. And so on.

These issues do not involve a simple dichotomy of the 'state' and 'citizens'. As the materials in Chapters 5 and 6 have illustrated, religion-based restraints or obligations may be rooted in a broad religious culture that is both closely related to and distinct from the state, and that may be insisted on or enforced by a range of nonstate actors. Religion and society will often be as apt a framework for discussion as religion and state. The state itself may adopt many attitudes and pursue many policies, from support of the religious culture, to a pose of neutrality, to active opposition to its teachings and demands.

The following materials start with a comparative survey of questions of religion and state and freedom of religion. These comparisons among states highlight a vital issues that permeates this Section B: what are the links between religious communities, or one religious community, and the state? The spectrum is large, from notions of separation that are so strong in the United States (the 'establishment' clause of the First Amendment to the Constitution, the metaphor used by courts of the 'wall of separation'), to the pervasive interrelationships in several countries between Islam and the state.

Section B continues with analyses of ways in which the international human rights instruments address the broad array of issues sketched in the preceding paragraphs. It next examines a pressing current issue, that of proselytism. The final part of this section concentrates on one form of link between religion and the state, namely bodies of religion-based personal law and sometimes special religious courts that are distinctive to and govern separate religious communities.

1. INTRODUCTION: COMPARATIVE PERSPECTIVES

COLE DURHAM, PERSPECTIVES ON RELIGIOUS LIBERTY: A COMPARATIVE FRAMEWORK

in Johan van der Vyver and Witte (eds.), Religious Human Rights in Global Perspective (1996), at 12

. . .

A Comparative Model for Analyzing Religious Liberty

Up to this point, we have identified various cultural tensions that make religion potentially divisive and the countervailing considerations that have helped moderns since Locke to understand how respect for religion and its potential divisiveness can result in stabilization rather than disintegration of a society and its political institutions. We turn now to an effort to provide a comparative framework for possible configurations of religious and state institutions and resulting patterns of religious freedom.

Threshold Conditions for Religious Liberty

An initial consideration in any generalized reflection on religious liberty is the recognition that there are certain threshold conditions that must be met before religious liberty can emerge. Briefly stated, there must be some measure of (1) pluralism, (2) economic stability, and (3) political legitimacy within the society in question. In addition, (4) there must be some willingness on the part of differing religious groups and their adherents to live with each other. Each of these threshold conditions deserves fuller analysis, but only a few comments are possible here.

Minimal Pluralism. Until some measure of divergence in fundamental belief systems emerges in a society, the question of religious liberty does not even arise. One can imagine a primitive society, for example, in which all the members of the community share assumptions about the nature of the physical and moral cosmos and in which agreement is so pervasive that questions of religious liberty and dissent would not arise.

Given human propensities to disagree and struggle with each other concerning fundamental issues, it seems difficult to imagine such pristine social homogeneity enduring for long. This difficulty is evident even within nuclear families, and is all the more likely to emerge in societies of any complexity. On the other hand, one can imagine societies enduring for substantial periods in which dominant religious views achieve effective consensus. Some medieval Christian communities no doubt functioned in this manner.

Similarly, one can imagine a society maintaining a sense of its own homogeneity by conceptualizing dissenters as strangers or foreigners. That is, group differentiation may obscure the emergence of incipient pluralism. Each group is committed to its own understanding of the world. Struggles between rival groups are understood as battles for the dominance of one outlook over another. Particularly if exit (or expulsion) from one group is easy, the home group remains homogeneous and the need for religious liberty is not perceived. Dissent appears as treason, betrayal, or at a minimum, as the mark of an outsider. Issues of religious liberty only begin to arise when differences between outlooks must be taken seriously as an unavoidable part of the relevant community.

. . .

Political Legitimacy. Since religion can be a powerful legitimizing (or delegitimizing) force in a society, the likelihood of achieving religious liberty is reduced to the extent that a regime's political legitimacy is weak. Such a regime is likely either to exploit the legitimizing power of a dominant religion (with concomitant risks of oppression for dissenting groups) or to view religion in general as a threat. In either case, religious liberty suffers.

. . .

Religious Respect for Rights of Those with Differing Beliefs. Religious liberty for all is not possible in a context in which one religious group not only rejects the beliefs of another group but is unwilling to live with that group. If the intolerant group is dominant, it will persecute adherents of other groups. If not, it is likely to attract persecution itself because of efforts to actualize its religious views. In either event, religious liberty will not be fully actualized in the community because there will be at least one group that feels inhibited in actualizing its religious beliefs.

This problem can only be solved if there are grounds within a religious tradition calling for toleration of or respect for the rights of others to have divergent beliefs. Fortunately, there are resources within most religious traditions that support according others such respect. . . .

. . .

The Relationship Between Religious Freedom Rights and Church-State Separation

With the foregoing analysis of threshold conditions for religious freedom in mind, we can turn to a comparative analysis of different types of church-state systems. The degree of religious liberty in a particular society can be assessed along two dimensions—one involving the degree to which state action burdens religious belief and conduct and another involving the degree of identification between government and religious institutions. In the United States, because of the wording of the religion clause of the First Amendment of the U.S. Constitution, these two dimensions are thought of respectively as the 'free exercise' and 'establishment' aspects of religious liberty. But for comparative purposes, it is useful to think more broadly in terms of varying degrees of religious freedom and church-state identification.

At least in lay thought, there is a tendency to assume that there is a straight-forward linear correlation between these two values that could be represented as shown in Figure 1.

This picture considerably oversimplifies matters. The primary difficulties arise in connection with the church-state identification gradient and its correlation to the religious freedom continuum. Few religious establishments have ever been so totalistic as to achieve complete identification of church and state. To the extent that extreme situation is reached or approached, there is clearly an absence of religious freedom. This is obviously true for adherents of minority religions, and even the majority religion is likely to suffer because of extensive state involvement in or regulation of its affairs or due to the enervation that results from excessive dependence of religious institutions on the state.

At the other end of the church-state identification continuum, things seem more confused. The mere fact that a state does not have a formally established church does not necessarily mean that it has a separationist regime characterized by rigorous non-identification with religion. Moreover, there is considerable dis-agreement about the exact configuration of relationships between church and state that maximizes religious liberty, and it may well be that the optimal configuration for one culture may be different than that for another. Further, it is not clear whether 'non-identification' accurately marks the end of this particular continuum. Non-establishment and separation may mark intermediate points along a longer continuum that actually ends with 'negative' identification: i.e., overt hostility or persecution. But if persecution lies at both ends of the church-state

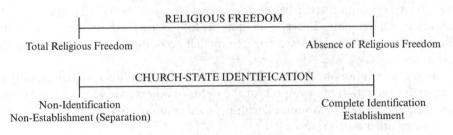

Figure 1

identification continuum, it is not at all clear how this continuum correlates with the religious liberty continuum.

[The author draws on an article by George Ryskamp, The Spanish Experience in Church-State Relations: A Comparative Study of the Interrelationship between Church-State Identification and Religious Liberty, 1980 Brigham Young Univ. L. Rev. 616, including that article's diagram using the same two continua as in Figure 1 above. But countries in Ryskamp's diagram appear at different points of the two continua; there is no precise correlation. The author challenges Ryskamp's location of several countries on these continua, but asks generally 'why states located at opposite ends of the identification gradient should be located so close to each other on the religious freedom gradient'.]

The answer to this seeming puzzle lies in reconceptualizing the church-state identification continuum as a loop that correlates with the religious freedom continuum as shown in Figure 3.

This model accurately reflects the fact that both strong positive and strong negative identification of church and state correlate with low levels of religious freedom. In both situations, the state adopts a sharply defined attitude toward one or more religions, leaving little room for dissenting views.
. . .

Another significant aspect of religious liberty clarified by the model is that one cannot simply assume that the more rigidly one separates church and state, the more religious liberty will be enhanced. At some point, aggressive separationism becomes hostility toward religion. Mechanical insistence on separation at all costs may accordingly push a system toward inadvertent insensitivity and ultimately intentional persecution. Stalinist constitutions generally had very strong church-state separation provisions, but these can hardly be said to have maximized religious liberty. Rather, they were construed as a demand that religion should be excluded from any domain where the state was present. But in a totalitarian state, this became a demand in practice that religion be marginalized to the vanishing point. . . .

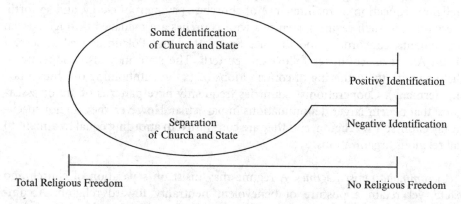

Figure 3

. . .

Turning first to the identification continuum, one can conceive it as a representation of a series of types of church-state regimes. Beginning at the positive identification end of the continuum, one first encounters *absolute theocracies* of the type one associates with stereotypical views of Islamic fundamentalism. In fact, a range of regimes is possible in Muslim theory, depending on the scope given to internal Muslim beliefs about toleration and also depending on the extent to which flexible interpretation of Shari'a law creates normative space for modernization.

Established Churches. The notion of an 'established church' is vague, and can in fact cover a range of possible church-state configurations with very different implications for the religious freedom of minority groups. At one extreme, a regime with an established church that is granted a strictly enforced monopoly in religious affairs is closely related to one with theocratic rule. Spain or Italy at some periods are classical exemplars. The next position is held by countries that have established religion that tolerates a restricted set of divergent beliefs. An Islamic country that tolerates 'people of the Book' (but not others) would be one example; a country with an established Christian church that tolerates a number of major faiths, but disparages others would be another. The next position is a country that maintains an established church, but guarantees equal treatment for all other religious beliefs. Great Britain would be a fitting example.

Endorsed Churches. The next category consists of regimes that fall just short of formally affirming that one particular church is the official church of a nation, but acknowledge that one particular church has a special place in the country's traditions. This is quite typical in countries where Roman Catholicism is predominant and a new constitution has been adopted relatively recently (at least since Vatican II). The endorsed church is specially acknowledged, but the country's constitution asserts that other groups are entitled to equal protection. . . .

Cooperationist Regimes. The next category of regime grants no special status to dominant churches, but the state continues to cooperate closely with churches in a variety of ways. Germany provides the prototypical example of this type of regime, though it is certainly not alone in this regard. Most notably, the cooperationist state may provide significant funding to various church-related activities, such as religious education or maintenance of churches, payment of clergy, and so forth. Very often in such regimes, relations with churches are managed through special agreements, concordats, and the like. Spain, Italy and Poland as well as several Latin American countries follow this pattern. The state may also cooperate in helping with the gathering of contributions (e.g., the withholding of 'church tax' in Germany). Cooperationist countries frequently have patterns of aid or assistance that benefit larger denominations in particular. However, they do not specifically endorse any religion, and they are committed to affording equal treatment to all religious organizations. . . .

. . .

Accommodationist Regimes. A regime may insist on separation of church and state, yet retain a posture of benevolent neutrality toward religion. Accommodationism might be thought of as cooperationism without the provision of any direct financial subsidies to religion or religious education. An accommodationist regime would have not qualms about recognizing the importance of religion as part of national or local culture, accommodating religious symbols in public settings, allowing tax, dietary, holiday, Sabbath, and other kinds of exemptions, and so forth. Many scholars in the United States argue that the United States religion clause should be construed to allow a more accommodationist approach to religious liberty. Note that the growth of the state intensifies the need for accommodation. As state influence becomes more pervasive and regulatory burdens expand, refusal to exempt or accommodate shades into hostility.

Separationist Regimes. As suggested by the earlier comments on Stalinist church-state separation, the slogan 'separation of church and state' can be used to cover a fairly broad and diverse range of regimes. At the benign end, separationism differs relatively little from accommodationism. The major difference is that separationism, as it names suggests, insists on more rigid separation of church and state. Any suggestion of public support for religion is deemed inappropriate. Religious symbols in public displays such as Christmas creches are not allowed. Even indirect subsidies to religion through tax deductions or tax exemptions are either suspect or proscribed. Granting religiously-based exemptions from general public laws is viewed as impermissible favoritism for religion. No religious teaching or indoctrination of any kind is permitted in public schools (although some teaching about religions from an objective standpoint may be permitted). The mere reliance on religious premises in public argument is deemed to run afoul of the church-state separation principle. Members of the clergy are not permitted to hold public office.

More extreme forms of separationism make stronger attempts to cordon off religion from public life. One form this can take is through tightening the state monopoly on certain forms of educational or social services. In the educational realm, the state can ban home schooling altogether, can proscribe private schools, or can submit either of the foregoing to such extensive accreditation requirements that it is virtually impossible for independent religious education to function. Different regimes make differing judgments about the extent to which religious marriages will be recognized. A range of social or charitable services (including health care) may be regulated in ways that make it difficult for religious organizations to carry out their perceived ministries in this area. 'Separation' in its most objectionable guise demands that religion retreat from any domain that the state desires to occupy, but is untroubled by intrusive state regulation and intervention in religious affairs.

. . .

Hostility and Overt Persecution. The test in this area is how smaller religious groups are treated. Government officials seldom persecute larger religious groups (though this was certainly not unheard of in communist lands). Persecution can take the form of imprisonment of those who insist on acting in accordance with divergent religious beliefs. In its most egregious forms, it involves 'ethnic cleansing' or most extreme, genocide. More typical problems involve less dramatic forms of bureaucratic roadblocks which cumulatively have the effect of significantly impairing religious liberty. These can take the form of denying or delaying registration (granting entity status) and obstructing land use approvals.

With the foregoing categories in mind, the relationship between the more refined identification gradient and the religious freedom gradient can be modeled as shown in Figure 4.

There is some room for argument about which type of regime should be displayed as the type most likely to maximize religious liberty. My contention is that accommodationist regimes have the best claim to this position. Historical experience suggests that maximal religious liberty tends to be achieved when church-state identification is in the accommodation or non-hostile separation mode. Of course, substantial religious liberty can also exist in cooperationist or endorsed church regimes, at least where genuine religious equality is present. However, there is always a sense in such regimes that smaller religious communities have a kind of second-class status, and to the extent that public funds are directly supporting programs of major churches, there is a sense that members of religious minorities are being coerced to support religious programs with which they do not agree. As between separationist and accommodationist regimes, accommodationism has the edge in contemporary settings where the modern secular 'performance state' has emerged with its welfare and regulatory dimensions. As state action or influence pervades more and more of social life, wooden insistence on separation too easily slips into marginalization of religion. Moreover, as regulations proliferate, there is increased demand for exceptions that can sensitively accommodate religious needs. In the last analysis, if accommodation can be achieved without undue difficulty, a regime which fails to accommodate manifests a lesser degree of religious liberty.

Advocates of stricter separation tend to invoke notions of equality to argue

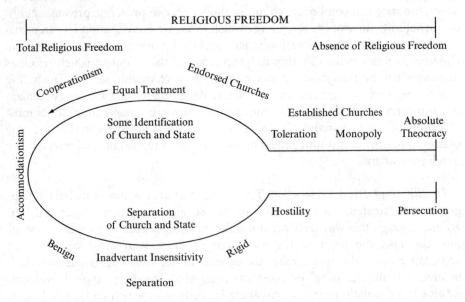

Figure 4

against accommodation. Accommodating a religious need or practice, the argument goes, inevitably involves giving religious individuals or groups special treatment, and this violates requirements of state neutrality and equal protection. This overlooks the fact that differential treatment does not necessarily violate equality norms if there is a rational basis for the differentiation. Protecting religious freedom rights provides not merely a rational basis but a compelling justification for reasonable accommodations. In the last analysis, making such accommodations (or alternatively, using the least burdensome means—from the standpoint of the religious practice affected—in pursuing state ends) is the best way to assure that the dignity of religiously different persons is afforded equal respect. Treating others with understanding of their differences shows far deeper respect than allocating everyone to equally Procrustean beds.

Differences in cultural or historical background may also affect the particular approach that best maximizes religious liberty in a particular country. For example, accommodating religious instruction in schools may be more important in a country such as Germany, where school secularization is associated historically with the religious persecutions of Bismarck's *Kulturkampf* and the Nazi *Kirchenkampf.* In the United States, in contrast, introduction of indoctrination-style instruction in the public schools appears violative of long-entrenched church-state traditions. More generally, it is often the case that essentially similar conduct will have different cultural meaning in different national settings. Religious liberty must be sensitive to these shifting social realities.

The church-state identification loop is useful not only in comparing types of institutional configurations, but also in keeping institutional issues in perspective. It is useful to note, for example, that the often highly polarized constitutional debates in the United States are in fact debates about which of a fairly narrow range of institutional options is optimal. . . .
. . .

DINAH SHELTON AND ALEXANDRE KISS, A DRAFT MODEL LAW ON FREEDOM OF RELIGION

in Johan van der Vyver and J. Witte, Jr. (eds.), Religious Human Rights in
Global Perspective (1996), at 572

. . .

The freedom to have a religion means that the government does not prescribe orthodoxy or prohibit particular religions or beliefs. In practice, this is not always the case. Among the examples that may be cited, Indonesia bans the Jehovah's Witness religion because of 'its aggressive manner in propagating its teachings, trying to convert other adherents to this faith'. According to the government, 'misleading cults' are banned in order to maintain peace and harmony between and among adherents of the various religions. 'Without the Government's handling in the matter, the activities of "cults" (including Jehovah's Witnesses and Baha'is) may create disturbances and disrupt the existing religious tolerance'.

Similar justifications are put forward by other states that ban specific religions. In some countries, coercion is employed to force renunciation of banned religions.

Short of banning, laws may severely interfere with minority religions. In Pakistan, the Ahmadis are prevented by law from calling themselves Muslims and using Muslim practices in worship or in the public manifestations of their faith.

Both bans and restrictions may be imposed when the state is viewed as the beneficiary or object of religious liberty. The Saudi Arabian government states '[o]ur view is that freedom of religion (which is a basic issue in the Universal Declaration of Human Rights) has double edges: (a) The freedom *of any country* to adhere to, protect and preserve its religion. (b) The respect and tolerance towards religious minorities of the country's citizens as long as they respect the constitutional tenets of their country'.

. . .

The constitutions of some states establish the primacy of a religion over the state, granting privileges that are incompatible with religious liberty and non-discrimination. Even in states with excellent human rights records, links between religion and state pose problems. In Norway, the king and a majority of the cabinet are required to be members of the state church. Christianity is still a mandatory subject in the Norwegian public schools. Nonconformists have been permitted to teach it since 1969 as long as they do so in accordance with evangelical Lutheran doctrine. Only in 1964 was the constitution amended to guarantee all inhabitants the free exercise of religion. A 1969 Law Concerning Religious Denominations extends the right to form denominations and stipulates that groups registered with the Department of Justice may receive financial aid from both the national and municipal governments on the same basis as parishes of the state church in proportion to their membership statistics. The majority remains opposed to disestablishment of the state church. It is seen as 'a public institution in which membership does not require a commitment of faith and which presently has approximately equal numbers of atheists and "personal Christians" on its rolls'.

In England, the Anglican Church remains at the center of public policy and has substantial support from the state. Prime ministers appoint bishops and the House of Lords contains 26 Anglican bishops who are the lords spiritual. The Parliament can rule on doctrinal and liturgical matters—most recently on the issue of ordination of women. Although there may be little real intervention in the internal affairs of the church, its strongly privileged position can be seen to discriminate against minority religions.

State budgets provide for some religious denominations in Spain, Italy, Greece, Belgium, and Luxembourg. Religious taxes exist in Austria, Switzerland, Denmark, Germany, Norway, and Finland. Indirect support is provided in France, Great Britain, the Netherlands, and Sweden.

Established religions exist in all parts of the world. In Africa, the constitutions of the Comores, Mauritania, Libya, and Somalia proclaim Islam as the religion of the state. Libya also declares that 'the Holy Koran is the constitution of the Socialist People's Libyan Arab Jamahiriya'. In the Sudan, all legislation must conform to Islamic prescriptions. The head of state must be a Muslim, and non-Muslims are incompetent to testify against Muslims. Propagation of heretical beliefs is a crime.

In contrast, the constitution of Botswana specifically recognizes the individual's right to propagate his religion. Proselytizing or converting others is permissible.

Subordination of religion to the state can have pernicious effects on religious liberty equal to those in states where the government is subordinate to religion. Revolutionary governments sometimes repress religious activities, providing that no one may invoke religious liberty 'to hinder the state in its work of establishing the socialist order'.

Some states limit the political activities of clergy or religious officials, on the pretext of maintaining the separation of religion and state. Such exclusionary laws have sometimes placed legislatures or courts in the position of deciding who constitutes 'clergy' or officials of religion.

Mexico's constitution contains some of the more restrictive provisions. Its articles provide that no minister of any faith may be a candidate for elected office. Article 130 provides that ministers cannot form associations for political purposes or rally in favor of or against any candidate, political party or association. Neither can they oppose the laws of the country or its institutions, or attack in any way the patriotic symbols in their public meetings, religious ceremonies, religious propaganda or publications. It is strictly forbidden to establish any kind of political associations. It is also forbidden to hold political meetings in the churches. . . .
. . .

NOTE

The two preceding articles provide rich illustrations of different types of relationships between religion and state throughout the world. The First Amendment to the United States Constitution, prohibiting Congress from making laws 'respecting an establishment of religion, or prohibiting the free exercise thereof', would appear to stand at the end of a spectrum with respect to establishment, although as Durham demonstrates, it is problematic to place the United States at the extreme, for all depends on how the spectrum is defined. For example, the United States and Iran (excerpts from the Iranian Constitution appear below) do represent extremes with respect to involvement of religion in state, and state in religion. But the United States would be located on a different point in a spectrum if states like Iran were at one end, and states hostile to and suppressing all religious belief and practice (which of course would be non-establishment states) were at the other.

Although there continues to be extensive constitutional litigation in the United States with respect to both the 'establishment' and 'free exercise' clauses, it is important to bear in mind that, relative to most of the countries discussed below, 'the often highly polarized constitutional debates in the United States are in fact debates about which of a fairly narrow range of institutional options is optimal'. Durham, *supra*. Hence the following discussion concentrates on societies and states that depart substantially or radically from the ideology, constitutional doctrine, and practice in the United States.

The following newspaper articles on issues of religion and state in Germany and Russia, and the excerpts from the Iranian Constitution, provide greater detail about some aspects of relationships between state and religion and of freedom of religion in these few states. Sections 3 and 4 below provide further illustrations from Greece, Israel and India.

EDMUND ANDREWS, GERMAN CHURCHES, EVER GIVING, ASK TO RECEIVE
New York Times, Jan. 6, 1998, p. A8

. . .

Under an unusual century-old system, religious institutions in Germany get almost all their revenue from a 9 percent church surtax imposed on the income tax of every registered Catholic, Protestant and Jew. Taxpayers are asked to declare their religion on their income tax returns, and churchgoers are pressed to register their religion with the Government. Those who are not members of the religions covered by the tax do not pay it, nor do those who have taken the bureaucratic step of revoking their registration.

Church taxes totaled about $11 billion in 1996, almost as much as the sin tax on cigarettes. In striking contrast to the United States, with its separation of church and state, Germany uses its religion taxes for the salaries of priests and rabbis, the construction of churches and a sprawling array of church-run social programs, from Christian day-care centers and kindergartens to drug-counseling clinics and hospitals.

But now the church-state partnership is cracking. With 4.3 million Germans, or more than 11 percent of the work force, unemployed, and thus paying no taxes, church revenue fell about 4 percent in 1996. It could have plunged as much as 10 percent in 1997. That would represent a combined drop in revenues for all religions of more than $1 billion.

. . .

Germany's church tax supports three main religious groups: the Evangelical Churches, an umbrella organization of Protestants that oversees the Lutheran, Reform and United Protestant branches; Roman Catholicism, and Judaism. Protestants, most of them Lutherans, account for 45 percent of the German population, with Roman Catholics at 37 percent. Jews represent only a small percentage. Muslims and others are not part of the tax structure.

Much like German industry, German religion is now preaching the need to cut costs, become more efficient and refocus priorities. In Munich, Protestant leaders even got a free strategic analysis from the management consultants McKinsey & Company. And they are talking about trying to wean themselves, at least partly, from the tax system.

In early November, Protestant leaders in Hesse announced plans to cut 25 percent of spending on 19 programs, like psychological counseling and adult education. Pastors will also be sent into retirement as soon as they turn 60, while new seminarians will be kept out. In addition, the church will sharply reduce its extensive support for kindergartens and cut the number of religion teachers it sends to public schools.

. . .

The financial crunch is causing religious people at all levels to rethink their partnership with the Government. It began when the state took it upon itself to tax people who went to church and to funnel that money back to the denominations. In exchange, the churches assumed a range of nonreligious responsibilities in areas like adult education and social work as well as providing religious instruction in public schools.

. . .

As Mr. Holle and fellow seminarians wrote in a dissident newspaper they recently started, 'The greatest danger for the churches is not primarily financial, but rather the anonymity and unapproachability of its functionaries'. Mr. Holle argues that if churches relied on direct contributions from parishioners, as they do in the United States, people would identify more closely with their churches and dig more deeply into their pockets. But many Germans view the idea of passing a collection plate as tasteless.

. . .

But the churches cannot wean themselves so easily from the system. Officials of the Roman Catholic Bishops' Conference in Bonn noted, for instance, that while the church now pays the state more than $100 million a year for its tax collection service, that cost could triple if the job was privately undertaken.

Meanwhile, churches have begun to pull away from responsibilities not directly related to church life. In the case of kindergartens, Protestant officials want to force either the state or parents to pay more. Under the budget plan here in Hesse, the church's contribution to kindergarten costs would drop to 15 percent, from 40 percent in some schools. And children who do not belong to the church will have to pay extra.

. . .

Mr. Holle and his classmates, in an unusually scathing and public criticism, have accused the church leadership of succumbing to the 'dictatorship of finance'. 'Our church leadership is built on sand,' the group of seminarians wrote in their newspaper. 'No ideas, no heart, its eye on commerce.'

. . .

MICHAEL GORDON, IRKING U.S., YELTSIN SIGNS LAW PROTECTING ORTHODOX CHURCH
New York Times, September 27, 1997, p. A1

Spurning appeals from the United States, President Boris N. Yeltsin signed a new law today that protects the Russian Orthodox Church from competition with other Christian faiths. Western church leaders deplored the law, saying it threatens religious freedom in Russia.

. . .

The law creates a hierarchy of religious groups, with the Russian Orthodox Church firmly ensconced in the first and most privileged category while rival Christian groups are afforded a secondary status.

. . .

The Senate has passed a spending bill that would cut $200 million in aid to Russia in six months if the law proves to discriminate against minority religions . . .

. . .

Critics acknowledge that some Western European nations have state religions. But Russia's Constitution prohibits a state religion. The Vatican warned today that the legislation could lead to discrimination against minority religions. So did the Archbishop of Canterbury, the Most Rev. George Carey, who is the leader of the Anglican Church.

'It is the most sweeping legislative rollback of human rights since the birth of post-Soviet Russia,' said Lawrence Uzzell, representative here of the Keston Institute, which monitors religious freedom in the former Communist countries of Europe.

The dispute has its roots in the upsurge of religious activity following the breakup of the Soviet Union. Catholics, Mormons, mainline and evangelical Protestants and non-Christian religious sects sought to minister to Russians' spiritual needs.

That distressed the Russian Orthodox Church, which was determined to maintain its dominance and to squash challenges from dissidents in its own ranks. The church's tacit support of President Yeltsin during the 1996 election campaign also enhanced its political influence, and it began to militate for a new law.

. . .

. . . [T]he Russian Orthodox Church continued its campaign, appealing to a nationalist and sympathetic Parliament. Some Western officials believe that the [Clinton]Administration . . . underestimated the political strength of the Orthodox Church and failed to use the summer months to influence the terms of the new legislation that was bound to follow.

. . .

Under the new law, religious organizations, like the Russian Orthodox Church, that the authorities certify as having been active 15 or more years ago qualify for full rights and privileges. Jewish and Islamic organizations are also included. Those organizations would have the right to own property, control radio and television stations and distribute religious literature. They would be entitled to tax exemptions and could conduct services in hospitals and cemeteries.

But religions organizations that do not satisfy the 15-year rule would see their activities restricted. They would be able to carry out financial transactions and conduct charity work, but they would not have the right to operate schools, distribute religious literature or invite foreigners to work as clergy or preachers.

A third category of religious groups—those that choose not to register and whose registration is not accepted—would be subject to more stringent restrictions.

Russian officials insist that the new law is needed to safeguard Russians against fanatical groups and dangerous sects. Foreign Minister Yevgeny M. Primakov even told American diplomats that the law would discourage 'mass suicides,' like those of the Heaven's Gate cult in California. Patriarch Aleksy, II, the leader of the Orthodox Church, praised the new law. 'Today's law is another step toward perfecting the legislation that secures and defends the rights of Russia's believers,' he said.

But critics say it will hamper the activities of mainstream religious groups. Methodists, for instance, would not satisfy the 15–year rule and therefore would not be able to sell or give away religious literature or run schools.

CONSTITUTION OF IRAN
1979 (as amended)

[Events of the last few years underscore the severe tensions and at times outright conflict between the forces for religious or secular rule in Iran. In the process, the implications and very meaning of the 1979 revolution against the Shah led by Ayatollah Khomeini (Khumayni), and the Constitution that it spawned, are brought into public debate. The paradoxes and indeed contradictions of Iran's complex governmental structure (religious leader, institutionalization of Islamic principles, elected president and assembly) are reflected in the excerpts below from the Constitution.]

Article 1 [Form of Government]

The form of government of Iran is that of an Islamic Republic, endorsed by the people of Iran on the basis of their longstanding belief in the sovereignty of truth and Koranic justice, in the referendum of 29 and 30 March 1979, through the affirmative vote of a majority of 98.2% of eligible voters, held after the victorious Islamic Revolution led by Imam Khumayni.

Article 2 [Foundational Principles]

The Islamic Republic is a system based on belief in:

(1) the One God (as stated in the phrase 'There is no god except Allah'), His exclusive sovereignty and right to legislate, and the necessity of submission to His commands;

(2) Divine revelation and its fundamental role in setting forth the laws;

. . .

(6) the exalted dignity and value of man, and his freedom coupled with responsibility before God; in which equity, justice, political, economic, social, and cultural independence, and national solidarity are secured by recourse to: (a) continuous leadership of the holy persons, possessing necessary qualifications, exercised on the basis of the Koran and the Sunnah, upon all of whom be peace; . . .

Article 3 [State Goals]

In order to attain the objectives specified in Article 2, the government of the Islamic Republic of Iran has the duty of directing all its resources to the following goals:

(1) the creation of a favorable environment for the growth of moral virtues based on faith and piety and the struggle against all forms of vice and corruption;

(2) raising the level of public awareness in all areas, through the proper use of the press, mass media, and other means;

. . .

(7) ensuring political and social freedoms within the framework of the law;

(8) the participation of the entire people in determining their political, economic, social, and cultural destiny;

. . .

Article 4 [Islamic Principle]

All civil, penal financial, economic, administrative, cultural, military, political, and other laws and regulations must be based on Islamic criteria. This principle applies absolutely and generally to all articles of the Constitution as well as to all other laws and regulations, and the wise persons of the Guardian Council are judges in this matter.

. . .

Article 6 [Administration of Affairs]

In the Islamic Republic of Iran, the affairs of the country must be administered on the basis of public opinion expressed by the means of elections, including the election of the President, the representatives of the Islamic Consultative Assembly, and the members of councils, or by means of referenda in matters specified in other articles of this Constitution.

. . .

Article 8 [Community Principle]

In the Islamic Republic of Iran, 'al-'amr bilma'ruf wa al-nahy 'an al-munkar' is a universal and reciprocal duty that must be fulfilled by the people with respect to one another, by the government with respect to the people, and by the people with respect to the government. The conditions, limits, and nature of this duty will be specified by law. (This is in accordance with the Koranic verse 'The believers, men and women, are guardians of one another; they enjoin the good and forbid the evil'. [9:71])

. . .

Article 12 [Official Religion]

The official religion of Iran is Islam and the Twelver Ja'fari school, and this principle will remain eternally immutable. Other Islamic schools are to be accorded full respect, and their followers are free to act in accordance with their own jurisprudence in performing their religious rites. These schools enjoy official status in matters pertaining to religious education, affairs of personal status (marriage, divorce, inheritance, and wills) and related litigation in courts of law. In regions of the country where Muslims following any one of these schools constitute the majority, local regulations, within the bounds of the jurisdiction of local councils, are to be in accordance with the respective school, without infringing upon the rights of the followers of other schools.

Article 13 [Recognized Religious Minorities]

Zoroastrian, Jewish, and Christian Iranians are the only recognized religious minorities, who, within the limits of the law, are free to perform their religious rites and ceremonies, and to act according to their own canon in matters of personal affairs and religious education.

Article 14 [Non-Muslims' Rights]

In accordance with the sacred verse 'God does not forbid you to deal kindly and justly with those who have not fought against you because of your religion and who have not expelled you from your homes' [60:8], the government of the Islamic Republic of Iran and all Muslims are duty-bound to treat non-Muslims in conformity with ethical norms and the principles of Islamic justice and equity, and to respect their human rights. This principle applies to all who refrain from engaging in conspiracy or activity against Islam and the Islamic Republic of Iran.
. . .

Article 19 [No Discrimination, No Privileges]

All people of Iran, whatever the ethnic group or tribe to which they belong, enjoy equal rights; color, race, language, and the like, do not bestow any privilege.

Article 20 [Equality Before Law]

All citizens of the country, both men and women, equally enjoy the protection of the law and enjoy all human, political, economic, social, and cultural rights, in conformity with Islamic criteria.

Article 21 [Women's Rights]

The government must ensure the rights of women in all respects, in conformity with Islamic criteria, and accomplish the following goals:

(1) create a favorable environment for the growth of woman's personality and the restoration of her rights, both the material and intellectual;
. . .

(3) establishing competent courts to protect and preserve the family;
. . .

(5) the awarding of guardianship of children to worthy mothers, in order to protect the interests of the children, in the absence of a legal guardian.
. . .

Article 23 [Freedom of Belief]

The investigation of individuals' beliefs is forbidden, and no one may be molested or taken to task simply for holding a certain belief.

Article 24 [Freedom of the Press]

Publications and the press have freedom of expression except when it is detrimental to the fundamental principles of Islam or the rights of the public. The details of this exception will be specified by law.
. . .

Article 27 [Freedom of Assembly]

Public gatherings and marches may be freely held, provided arms are not carried and that they are not detrimental to the fundamental principles of Islam.

. . .

Article 57 [Separation of Powers]

The powers of government in the Islamic Republic are vested in the legislature, the judiciary, and the executive powers, functioning under the supervision of the absolute religious Leader and the Leadership of the Ummah, in accordance with the forthcoming articles of this Constitution. These powers are independent of each other.

Article 58 [Legislature]

The functions of the legislature are to be exercised through the Islamic Consultative Assembly, consisting of the elected representatives of the people. Legislation approved by this body, after going through the stages specified in the articles below, is communicated to the executive.

. . .

Article 60 [Executive]

The functions of the executive, except in the matters that are directly placed under the jurisdiction of the Leadership by the Constitution, are to be exercised by the President and the Ministers.

Article 61 [Judiciary]

The functions of the judiciary are to be performed by courts of justice, which are to be formed in accordance with the criteria of Islam, and are vested with the authority to examine and settle lawsuits, protect the rights of the public, dispense and enact justice, and implement the Divine limits.

Article 62 [Election]

(1) The Islamic Consultative Assembly is constituted by the representatives of the people elected directly and by secret ballot.

(2) The qualifications of voters and candidates, as well as the nature of election, will be specified by law.

. . .

Article 64 [270 Members, Religious Representatives]

(1) There are to be two hundred seventy members of the Islamic Consultative Assembly. . . .

(2) The Zoroastrians and Jews will each elect one representative; Assyrian and Chaldean Christians will jointly elect one representative; and Armenian Christians in the north and those in the south of the country will each elect one representative.

(3) The delimitation of the election constituencies and the number of representatives will be determined by law.

. . .

Article 107 [Religious Leader]

(1) After the demise of Imam Khumayni, the task of appointing the Leader shall be vested with the experts elected by the people. The experts will review and consult among themselves concerning all the religious men possessing the qualifications specified in Articles 5 and 109. . . .

. . .

Article 109 [Leadership Qualifications]

(1) Following are the essential qualifications and conditions for the Leader:

a. Scholarship, as required for performing the functions of religious leader in different fields.
b. Justice and piety, as required for the leadership of the Islamic Ummah.
c. Right political and social perspicacity, prudence, courage, administrative facilities, and adequate capability for leadership.

. . .

Article 110 [Leadership Duties and Powers]

(1) Following are the duties and powers of the Leadership:

1. Delineation of the general policies of the Islamic Republic of Iran after consultation with the Nation's Exigency Council.
2. Supervision over the proper execution of the general policies of the system.
3. Issuing decrees for national referenda.
4. Assuming supreme command of the Armed Forces.
5. Declaration of war and peace and the mobilization of the Armed Forces.
6. Appointment, dismissal, and resignation of:

    a. the religious men on the Guardian Council,
    b. the supreme judicial authority of the country,
    c. the head of the radio and television network of the Islamic Republic of Iran,
    d. the chief of the joint staff,
    e. the chief commander of the Isalmic Revolution Guards Corps, and
    f. the supreme commanders of the Armed Forces.

7. Resolving differences between the three wings of the Armed Forces and regulation of their relations.
8. Resolving the problems which cannot be solved by conventional methods, through the Nation's Exigency Council.
9. Signing the decree formalizing the election of the President of the Republic by the people. The suitability of candidates for the Presidency of the Republic, with respect to the qualifications specified in the Constitution, must be confirmed before elections take place by the Guardian Council, and, in the case of the first term of a President, by the Leadership.
10. Dismissal of the President of the Republic, with due regard for the inter-

ests of the country, after the Supreme Court holds him guilty of the violation of his constitutional duties, or after a vote of the Islamic Consultative Assembly testifying to his incompetence on the basis of Article 89.

...

Article 144 [Islamic Army]

The Army of the Islamic Republic of Iran must be an Islamic Army, i.e., committed to Islamic ideology and the people, and must recruit into its service individuals who have faith in the objectives of the Islamic Revolution and are devoted to the cause of realizing its goals.

...

Article 167 [Rule of Law for Judiciary]

The judge is bound to endeavor to judge each case on the basis of the codified law. In case of the absence of any such law, he has to deliver his judgment on the basis of authoritative Islamic sources and authentic fatawa. ....

QUESTIONS

1. What similarities and what differences would you stress in comparing the Western states noted above with respect to relationships between religion and state?

2. What similarities and what differences would you stress in comparing the Western states noted above as a whole with the Muslim states of the Middle East?

3. What do you believe to be the likely implications of a close (or closer than the United States) relationship between religion and state for nondiscrimination among religions or their adherents? Indeed, is equal protection of religions by the state a necessary condition to freedom of religion?

2. INTERNATIONAL LAW PERSPECTIVES

Here we turn to the universal human rights instruments. Note the limited degree to which those instruments have developed ideas about religion and state or religion and human rights, at least in relation to their far greater development of human rights ideas in fields like race, gender, or democratic participation. A major issue in this Part B is why this should be the case.

GENERAL COMMENT NO. 22 (ON ARTICLE 18) OF THE HUMAN RIGHTS COMMITTEE
Adopted 1993, UN Doc. HRI/GEN/1/Rev.1 (1994), at 35

[The Human Rights Committee created by the International Covenant on Civil and Political Rights has authority to issue 'general comments,' effectively used by the Committee to issue interpretive comments on the Covenant's provisions. This General Comment addresses Article 18 of the ICCPR, which states rights related to religious belief and freedom. See pp. 731–738, *infra*, for a discussion of General Comments and their effects.]

Article 18, ICCPR

1. Everyone shall have the right to freedom of thought, conscience and religion. This right shall include freedom to have or to adopt a religion or belief of his choice, and freedom, either individually or in community with others and in public or private, to manifest his religion or belief in worship, observance, practice and teaching.

2. No one shall be subject to coercion which would impair his freedom to have or to adopt a religion or belief of his choice.

3. Freedom to manifest one's religion or beliefs may be subject only to such limitations as are prescribed by law and are necessary to protect public safety, order, health, or morals or the fundamental rights and freedoms of others.

4. The States Parties to the present Covenant undertake to have respect for the liberty of parents and, when applicable, legal guardians to ensure the religious and moral education of their children in conformity with their own convictions.

General Comment No. 22

. . .

2. Article 18 protects theistic, non-theistic and atheistic beliefs, as well as the right not to profess any religion or belief. The terms 'belief' and 'religion' are to be broadly construed. Article 18 is not limited in its application to traditional religions or to religions and beliefs with institutional characteristics or practices analogous to those of traditional religions. . . .

3. Article 18 distinguishes the freedom of thought, conscience, religion or belief from the freedom to manifest religion or belief. It does not permit any limitations whatsoever on the freedom of thought and conscience or on the freedom to have or adopt a religion or belief of one's choice. These freedoms are protected unconditionally. . . .

4. The freedom to manifest religion or belief may be exercised 'either individually or in community with others and in public or private'. The freedom to manifest religion or belief in worship, observance, practice and teaching encompasses a broad range of acts. The concept of worship extends to ritual and ceremonial acts giving direct expression to belief, as well as various practices integral to such acts, including the building of places of worship, the use of ritual formulae and objects, the display of symbols, and the observance of holidays and days of rest. The

observance and practice of religion or belief may include not only ceremonial acts but also such customs as the observance of dietary regulations, the wearing of distinctive clothing or headcoverings, participation in rituals associated with certain stages of life, and the use of a particular language customarily spoken by a group. In addition, the practice and teaching of religion or belief includes acts integral to the conduct by religious groups of their basic affairs, such as the freedom to choose their religious leaders, priests and teachers, the freedom to establish seminaries or religious schools and the freedom to prepare and distribute religious texts or publications.

5. The Committee observes that the freedom to 'have or to adopt' a religion or belief necessarily entails the freedom to choose a religion or belief, including the right to replace one's current religion or belief with another or to adopt atheistic views, as well as the right to retain one's religion or belief. Article 18.2 bars coercion that would impair the right to have or adopt a religion or belief, including the use of threat of physical force or penal sanctions to compel believers or non-believers to adhere to their religious beliefs and congregations, to recant their religion or belief or to convert. . . .

6. The Committee is of the view that article 18.4 permits public school instruction in subjects such as the general history of religions and ethics if it is given in a neutral and objective way. . . . The Committee notes that public education that includes instruction in a particular religion or belief is inconsistent with article 18.4 unless provision is made for non-discriminatory exemptions or alternatives that would accommodate the wishes of parents and guardians.

7. In accordance with article 20, no manifestation of religion or belief may amount to propaganda for war or advocacy of national, racial or religious hatred that constitutes incitement to discrimination, hostility or violence. . . .

8. Article 18.3 permits restrictions on the freedom to manifest religion or belief only if limitations are prescribed by law and are necessary to protect public safety, order, health or morals, or the fundamental rights and freedoms of others. The freedom from coercion to have or to adopt a religion or belief and the liberty of parents and guardians to ensure religious and moral education cannot be restricted. In interpreting the scope of permissible limitation clauses . . . limitations may be applied only for those purposes for which they were prescribed and must be directly related and proportionate to the specific need on which they are predicated. . . .

9. The fact that a religion is recognized as a state religion or that it is established as official or traditional or that its followers comprise the majority of the population, shall not result in any impairment of the enjoyment of any of the rights under the Covenant, including articles 18 and 27, nor in any discrimination against adherents to other religions or non-believers. In particular, certain measures discriminating against the latter, such as measures restricting eligibility for government service to members of the predominant religion or giving economic privileges to them or imposing special restrictions on the practice of other faiths, are not in accordance with the prohibition of discrimination based on religion or belief and the guarantee of equal protection under article 26. . . .

10. If a set of beliefs is treated as official ideology in constitutions, statutes, proclamations of ruling parties, etc., or in actual practice, this shall not result in any impairment of the freedoms under article 18 or any other rights recognized under the Covenant nor in any discrimination against persons who do not accept the official ideology or who oppose it.

. . .

DECLARATION ON THE ELIMINATION OF ALL FORMS OF INTOLERANCE AND OF DISCRIMINATION BASED ON RELIGION OR BELIEF
G.A. Res. 36/55, 1981

The General Assembly

. . .

Considering that the disregard and infringement of human rights and fundamental freedoms, in particular of the right to freedom of thought, conscience, religion or whatever belief, have brought, directly or indirectly, wars and great suffering to mankind, especially where they serve as a means of foreign interference in the internal affairs of other States and amount to kindling hatred between peoples and nations,

Considering that religion or belief, for anyone who professes either, is one of the fundamental elements in his conception of life and that freedom of religion or belief should be fully respected and guaranteed,

Considering that it is essential to promote understanding, tolerance and respect in matters relating to freedom of religion and belief . . .,

. . .

Proclaims this Declaration on the Elimination of All Forms of Intolerance and of Discrimination Based on Religion or Belief:

Article 1

1. Everyone shall have the right to freedom of thought, conscience and religion. This right shall include freedom to have a religion or whatever belief of his choice, and freedom, either individually or in community with others and in public or private, to manifest his religion or belief in worship, observance, practice and teaching.

2. No one shall be subject to coercion which would impair his freedom to have a religion or belief of his choice.

3. Freedom to manifest one's religion or belief may be subject only to such limitations as are prescribed by law and are necessary to protect public safety, order, health or morals or the fundamental rights and freedoms of others.

Article 2

1. No one shall be subject to discrimination by any State, institution, group of persons, or person on the grounds of religion or other belief.

2. For the purposes of the present Declaration, the expression 'intolerance and discrimination based on religion or belief' means any distinction, exclusion, restriction or preference based on religion or belief and having as its purpose or as its effect nullification or impairment of the recognition, enjoyment or exercise of human rights and fundamental freedoms on an equal basis.

Article 3

Discrimination between human being on the grounds of religion or belief constitutes an affront to human dignity and a disavowal of the principles of the Charter of the United Nations, and shall be condemned as a violation of the human rights and fundamental freedoms proclaimed in the Universal Declaration of Human Rights and enunciated in detail in the International Covenants on Human Rights, and as an obstacle to friendly and peaceful relations between nations.

Article 4

1. All States shall take effective measures to prevent and eliminate discrimination on the grounds of religion or belief in the recognition, exercise and enjoyment of human rights and fundamental freedoms in all fields of civil, economic, political, social and cultural life.

2. All States shall make all efforts to enact or rescind legislation where necessary to prohibit any such discrimination, and to take all appropriate measures to combat intolerance on the grounds of religion or other beliefs in this matter.

Article 5

1. The parents or, as the case may be, the legal guardians of the child have the right to organize the life within the family in accordance with their religion or belief and bearing in mind the moral education in which they believe the child should be brought up.

2. Every child shall enjoy the right to have access to education in the matter of religion or belief in accordance with the wishes of his parents or, as the case may be, legal guardians, and shall not be compelled to receive teaching on religion or belief against the wishes of his parents or legal guardians, the best interests of the child being the guiding principle.

. . .

Article 6

In accordance with article I of the present Declaration, and subject to the provisions of article 1, paragraph 3, the right to freedom of thought, conscience, religion or belief shall include, inter alia, the following freedoms:

. . .

- (d) To write, issue and disseminate relevant publications in these areas;
- (e) To teach a religion or belief in places suitable for these purposes;
- (f) To solicit and receive voluntary financial and other contributions from individuals and institutions;
- (g) To train, appoint, elect or designate by succession appropriate leaders called for by the requirements and standards of any religion or belief;

(h) To observe days of rest and to celebrate holidays and ceremonies in accordance with the precepts of one's religion or belief;

(i) To establish and maintain communications with individuals and communities in matters of religion and belief at the national and international levels.

Article 7

The rights and freedoms set forth in the present Declaration shall be accorded in national legislation in such a manner that everyone shall be able to avail himself of such rights and freedoms in practice.

. . .

Article 8

Nothing in the present Declaration shall be construed as restricting or derogating from any right defined in the Universal Declaration of Human Rights and the International Covenants on Human Rights.

DONNA SULLIVAN, ADVANCING THE FREEDOM OF RELIGION OR BELIEF THROUGH THE UN DECLARATION ON THE ELIMINATION OF RELIGIOUS TOLERANCE AND DISCRIMINATION
82 Am. J. Int. L. 487 (1988), at 488

[The General Assembly adopted this Declaration in 1981 by consensus, 19 years after efforts began in the UN system to develop protections for religious freedom that went beyond Article 18 of the ICCPR. As the author notes, this long delay in producing a Declaration—not a Convention—may be attributed partly 'to the potential for controversy inherent in the subject matter itself'. The excerpts below discuss a few of the Declaration's provisions.]

Although it lacks, of course, the nature of an international agreement, the Declaration is 'regarded throughout the world as articulating the fundamental rights of freedom of religion and belief'. The Declaration gives specific content to the general statements of the rights to freedom of religion or belief and freedom from discrimination based on religion or belief contained in the major human rights instruments. . . . That the United Nations General Assembly intended that it be normative and not merely hortatory is apparent from its Articles 4 and 7. . . . There is no consensus on whether the prohibition of discrimination on grounds of religion or belief already constitutes a norm of customary law. As the Declaration acquires concrete material content through its implementation, it will contribute to the acceptance of the customary law status of this important principle.

. . .

I. *Preliminary Observations*

The norms stated in the Declaration hold a striking potential for conflict with other rights; consequently, the task of applying the Declaration to concrete situations will challenge human rights advocates to devise interpretive approaches that will maximize the protection afforded to all the rights implicated. Two general features of the Declaration are likely to affect the resolution of such conflicts. First, it is directed primarily toward actions taken by governments, or by individuals who do not subscribe to a given religion or belief, against individuals who do hold and practice that belief. Interactions among members of the same religious groups are therefore not easily analyzed under the Declaration. Second, application of the Declaration is most straightforward when the belief or practice under consideration corresponds to a typically Western model of religion, in which religious institutions and authority are structurally separable from political and other social institutions. The greater degree to which religious power may be structurally distinct from political power under this model than it is under other systems does not necessarily imply a formal separation of church and state. Indeed, the protections offered in the Declaration are not premised upon the separation of church and state and are clearly distinguished in this regard from First Amendment rights under the United States Constitution.

. . .

II. The Scope of Article 1

. . .

[Coercion]

Coercive forms of persuasion, which attack the intellectual and psychological aspects of belief, should be encompassed by the prohibited forms of coercion. In two common situations, such 'moral' coercion generates conflict between principles stated in the Declaration itself. Proselytizing activities, the first of these, by their very nature attempt moral compulsion to some degree. [Such activities are examined in Section 3, *infra.*]

A desire to avoid the implicit approval of proselytizing was one of the considerations underlying the omission from the Declaration of an explicit reference to the freedom to change one's religion or belief. . . .

The right of individuals to maintain their own beliefs is central to the concerns that motivated the drafting of the Declaration itself. This principle necessarily entails not only the right to retain a belief, but also the freedom to choose a belief without coercion, including the right to reject one's current belief and accept another. Although explicit reference to the right to change beliefs was dropped from the Declaration, that right remains implicit in the right to have a religion or belief. Moreover, Article 8, the savings clause of the Declaration, preserves the standards set forth in the Universal Declaration of Human Rights and the International Covenants on Human Rights. . . . The Universal Declaration affirms the freedom to change beliefs and the Political Covenant refers to the freedom to adopt a religion or belief.

Nonetheless, the parameters of the right to change one's religion or belief remain uncertain, as illustrated by the difficulty of evaluating the treatment to be accorded apostates and heretics under the Declaration, a second area implicated by the prohibition of coercion. Apostasy and heresy present potential conflicts between the right of individuals to believe what they choose and the right of religious groups to promulgate doctrine as a part of religious practice. Such conflict illustrates the difficulty encountered in attempting to reconcile competing religious interests. History is replete with examples of religious persecution perpetrated in the guise of punishment for heresy. . . .

. . .

[Boundary Between Religion and Politics]

Arguments that the conduct restricted by the state is not religious in nature or that the individuals and groups affected are not engaged in religious activities are often advanced as a means of circumventing the broadly framed requirements of paragraph 3 [of Article 1]. All too frequently, a state seeking to suppress religious freedoms characterizes the activities of religious groups and leaders as impermissible political action or subversion. The absence of a definition of religion or belief may facilitate such denials of the true basis for restrictions or oppression by the state, but probably has little substantive effect upon whether states will commit such abuses.

Governments do have a legitimate interest in controlling violence against the state or disruptions of public order, and may do so by using methods consistent with other human rights obligations. Nonetheless, governmental violations of religious freedoms and persecution of religious leaders and groups under the pretense of restraining impermissible political activity are far more prevalent than is the use of a religious identity to camouflage actions motivated by purely partisan political concerns. . . .

. . . Many religious doctrines or beliefs dictate standards of social conduct and responsibility, and require believers to act accordingly. For those adherents who follow such precepts of social responsibility, the distinction between religious and political activities may be artificial. For example, pacifist religious convictions may prompt an individual to participate in public protest, to refuse to pay taxes used for military expenses and to attempt to influence decisions made by political leaders. Religious beliefs inevitably assume political significance in such circumstances.

Indeed, the intensity with which believers commonly assert their faith, the highly organized character of many religious groups and the magnitude of their followings lend those groups formidable political power. Moreover, the structural separation of secular and religious authority is obviously not a universal feature of societies, as demonstrated by Iran. Finally, political beliefs are presumably subsumed within the general category of 'beliefs' to which the Declaration extends and are protected under that rubric. . . .

. . .

III. The Scope of the Prohibition of Discrimination and Intolerance

. . . [B]y prohibiting acts that have a discriminatory effect as well as purpose, the Declaration reaches not only the discriminatory imposition of civil, political, economic, legal or social disabilities, but also the extension of benefits to some religious groups and not others. For example, if governments grant tax-exempt status to certain religious groups only, other groups will be required to devote financial resources to tax payments that otherwise would have been available to fund their religious activities. Such schemes thus have a discriminatory effect upon the groups not allotted benefits.

. . .

[Intolerance]

. . . Two general views have been taken of the meaning of 'intolerance' and its significance in the Declaration. The first, that the term lacks juridical meaning and refers to prejudice or a state of mind, was advanced during the drafting process, and has been emphasized subsequently in discussions of educational measures to promote the Declaration. The second view, that intolerance refers to conduct manifesting hatred or prejudice based on religion or belief as well as to a state of mind, underlies descriptions of various human rights violations, such as attacks upon the physical integrity of the person, as intolerance.

. . . The view that intolerance describes the emotional, psychological, philosophical and religious attitudes that may prompt acts of discrimination or violations of religious freedoms is persuasive. Where intolerance fuels such conduct as killing or the destruction of property, these acts constitute violations of substantive international human rights, such as the right to life, and, in most cases, violations of national law. If intolerance motivates deprivations of the freedom to manifest religion or belief, these acts again constitute violations of substantive rights protected by the Declaration itself.

The distinction between intolerance and discrimination may be usefully analogized to the distinction between racial prejudice and racism. Attitudes of hatred and fear toward religious groups may be rooted in phenomena such as histories of conflict between religious communities and the competing interests underlying those conflicts, religious doctrines that condemn nonbelievers and condone their oppression or eradication, state propaganda against religious belief, and racial or ethnic conflict. So understood, intolerance is not a particular type of violation of religious freedom or of discrimination, but the attitudes that may motivate such violations.

From this interpretation it follows that educational measures to eradicate intolerance are of vital significance. Educational activities obviously lie within the scope of the 'appropriate' measures contemplated by Article 4(2), although no express reference to such activities appears in the Declaration. Efforts to promote and implement the Declaration should compensate for the omission of a provision explicitly calling for educational measures by emphasizing the importance of such activities.

A second approach to combating intolerance, which was proposed during drafting but rejected, is to prohibit the expression of ideas based on religious hatred and the incitement of hatred and discrimination based on religion or belief. [See the discussion of hate speech at pp. 749–761, *infra.*]

. . .

[Religious Law and Human Rights Law]

Although the rights to establish religious courts and administer religious law are not stated in the Declaration, religious tribunals and the implementation of religious law are manifestations of religious belief to which the protections of Article 1 should apply. Nevertheless, the extent to which religious law may be administered without restrictions by the state or without limitations derived from other human rights obligations may vary with the substantive content of the law itself, and with the scope of the subject matter and personal jurisdiction vested in the religious courts.

Religious law may incorporate elements hostile to various human rights, infringing upon those rights to differing degrees. At one end of the spectrum, for example, may be dress codes for women that have the effect of reinforcing societal beliefs that relegate women to inferior status in public life. At the other end of the continuum are the extreme violations of such rights as the freedom from torture and the right to life by practices such as mutilation and suttee. Other conflicts between religious tenets and human rights fall at different points along this spectrum. For example, rules of procedure, such as evidentiary laws that assign lesser weight to testimony by women, may infringe substantive rights by impairing the ability to obtain legal protection for those rights. Attempts to resolve conflicts between religious law and human rights norms may be fruitless where religious doctrine insists upon the immutability of the sacred law or its supremacy over human rights norms.

A major area of conflict between religious law and human rights law is that of women's rights ... [C]ertain broad principles relevant to the principal types of conflicts can usefully be delineated. Religious tenets governing rights associated with the life of the family, particularly those pertaining to marriage and divorce, inheritance and personal status, frequently set religious law in opposition to the prohibition of discrimination against women. Compare, for example, Articles 5 and 10(c) of the Discrimination Against Women Convention with Article 5(2) of the Declaration ...

Article 15 of the Discrimination Against Women Convention guarantees women equality with men before the law and legal capacity identical to that of men in civil matters, but the status of women before religious tribunals or secular courts applying religious law is not clarified by this guarantee. Religious laws governing personal status obviously determine not only the religious rights of women, but also important legal rights, including those regulating economic resources ... [Illustrations from Islamic and Jewish law are omitted. Religious law in relation to gender and religious belief of minorities is discussed at pp. 491–511, *infra.*]

. . .

QUESTIONS

1. In what respects does the General Comment of the Human Rights Committee appear to go beyond Article 18 itself with respect to notions of religious freedom, and beyond the 1981 Declaration? What implications have Article 18 and the 1981 Declaration for the issue of 'establishment'?

2. Does the Declaration reach beyond action by the state to cover conduct (that is, to require or prohibit certain conduct) by private (nonstate) actors? If so, under what provisions and with respect to what kinds of conduct?

3. How would you resolve apparent conflicts between the Declaration and other human rights instruments—for example, requirements of nondiscrimination in employment under CEDAW and a religiously based belief that women should not be given certain kinds of employment? Do the savings clauses—Article 8 of the Declaration and Article 23 of CEDAW—provide an answer?

4. Under the Declaration, what are the state's duties with respect to religious intolerance that expresses itself in interactions among individuals and nonstate entities but that state organs or officials do not themselves urge or actively reinforce? The same as a state's duties under CEDAW?

5. Assess the consistency of the provisions of the Iranian Constitution with (a) Article 18 of the ICCPR, and (b) the 1981 Declaration, assuming (contrary in some instances to fact) that all religious faiths including Sunni Moslems, Christians of all sects, Jews, Baha'is, and others are allowed freely to hold and observe their religious beliefs and to practice their religious commandments in groups and in houses of worship. How likely is it that a state committed to a constitution similar to Iran's will afford freedom of religion to all faiths?

NOTE

Consider the following comments in Malcolm Evans, *Religious Liberty and International Law in Europe* (1997), at 257. The author speculates about prospects for a convention on religious freedom and discrimination, and notes that the complexity and variety of views on religious issues suggests how arduous the legal and political paths would be toward agreement on its provisions. He notes that there have been suggestions for such a treaty in the UN Commission on Human Rights and the Sub-Commission, and that reports examining this possibility have been prepared. Evans states that these reports highlight one factor among the many that need to be addressed in preparing such a treaty—namely, 'the intolerant attitude of believers themselves. This is seen as a handicap which can be overcome with copious doses of education concerning human rights'. He quotes from one such report, which observed that:

the reservations concerning religious freedom that have been expressed . . .

should be dealt with patiently and deliberately, through further dialogue. Such dialogue should take into account the factors, be based on internationally established principles . . . and set a long-term course without any concessions. . . . The only way to make progress in promoting religious freedom is to avoid categorical, inflexible attitudes. . . .

Reacting to these observations and to similar ones in other reports, Evans states:

If this means anything, it means that the freedom of religion does not include the right to adhere to a religion which is intolerant of the beliefs of others. On this view, 'Human Rights' has itself become a 'religion or belief' which is itself as intolerant of other forms of value systems which may stand in opposition to its own central tenets as any of those it seeks to address.

Evans also refers to a recommendation of the Parliamentary Assembly of the Council of Europe that described the current 'crisis of values' in society, and the inadequacy of a market society to meet needs for (quoting from the recommendation) 'individual well-being and social responsibility. The recourse to religion as an alternative has, however, to be reconciled with the principles of democracy and human rights'. Evans expresses his opinion about these assertions:

In seeking to assert itself in this fashion, the international community risks becoming the oppressor of the believer, rather than the protector of the persecuted. Clearly the time is not yet ripe for a convention: not because of the unwillingness of States to adopt such an instrument, but because of the reluctance of the international community to accept that in the religious beliefs of others the dogmas of human rights are met with an equally powerful force which must be respected, not overcome.

QUESTIONS

1. Do you agree with the views of Evans about resolution of the tension between 'religious beliefs of others and the dogmas of human rights'? In what directions would his views point, for example, with respect to dealing with gender discrimination based on religion?

2. Do you agree that the time is not ripe for a convention? Given all the problems, what kind of changes from the terms of the 1981 Declaration would you advocate in such a convention, and what strategies would you follow in working toward agreement among diverse states and religions on the proposed terms?

3. PROSELYTISM

KOKKINAKIS v. GREECE
European Court of Human Rights, 1993
Ser. A, No. 260-A, 17 EHRR 397

[Minos Kokkinakis, a Greek national, was born in 1919 into an Orthodox Christian family. In 1936, he became a Jehovah's Witnesses, a Christian sect originating in the nineteenth century, and known for intense door-to-door canvassing by its members. He was arrested more than 60 times for proselytism, and on several occasions imprisoned for a period of months. In 1986, he and his wife called at the home of a Mrs. Kyriakaki to engage her in discussion about religion. Her husband, cantor at a local Orthodox church, informed the police who arrested him. Kokkinakis was convicted under Law No. 1363/1938 of the crime of engaging in proselytism and was sentenced to four months' imprisonment. The Court of Appeal upheld the conviction. The Court of Cassation dismissed an appeal, rejecting the plea that the Law violated Article 13 of the Greek Constitution and hence could not be applied.

Kokkinakis then brought a case against Greece before the European Commission of Human Rights, claiming that his conviction violated provisions of the European Convention on Human Rights. Greece, a party to that Convention, had accepted the jurisdiction of the Commission to hear individual complaints. The Commission found that Greece had violated Article 9 of the Convention. It then referred the case to the European Court of Human Rights, whose jurisdiction Greece had also accepted. (The jurisdiction and work of this Court are examined at pp. 808–867, *infra*.)

Section 4 of Law No. 1363/1938, as later amended, made 'engaging in proselytism' a crime, and further provided:

> 2. By 'proselytism' is meant, in particular, any direct or indirect attempt to intrude on the religious beliefs of a person of a different religious persuasion, with the aim of undermining those beliefs, either by any kind of inducement or promise of an inducement or moral support or material assistance, or by fraudulent means or by taking advantage of his inexperience, trust, need, low intellect or naïvety.

The Greek Constitution of 1975 stated in Article 3 that the 'dominant religion in Greece is that of the Christian Eastern Orthodox Church'. The opinion of the European Court of Human Rights noted:

> Greece's successive Constitutions have referred to the Church as being 'dominant'. The overwhelming majority of the population are members of it, and, according to Greek conceptions, it represents de jure and de facto the religion of the State itself, a good number of whose administrative and educational functions (marriage and family law, compulsory religious instruction, oaths sworn by members of the Government, etc.) it moreover carries out. Its role in public life

is reflected by, among other things, the presence of the Minister of Education and Religious Affairs at the sessions of the Church hierarchy at which the Archbishop of Athens is elected and by the participation of the Church authorities in all official State events; the President of the Republic takes his oath of office according to Orthodox ritual (Article 33 para. 2 of the Constitution); and the official calendar follows that of the Christian Eastern Orthodox Church.

Article 13 of the Constitution provided:

> 1. Freedom of conscience in religious matters is inviolable. The enjoyment of personal and political rights shall not depend on an individual's religious beliefs.
> 2. There shall be freedom to practise any known religion; individuals shall be free to perform their rites of worship without hindrance and under the protection of the law. The performance of rites of worship must not prejudice public order or public morals. Proselytism is prohibited.

Several accounts appeared in the opinions of the Greek courts of the interaction between Kokkinakis and Kryiakaki. The trial court stated that the defendant:

> attempted to proselytise and, directly or indirectly, to intrude on the religious beliefs of Orthodox Christians, with the intention of undermining those beliefs, by taking advantage of their inexperience, their low intellect and their naïvety. In particular, they went to the home of [Mrs Kyriakaki] . . . and told her that they brought good news; by insisting in a pressing manner, they gained admittance to the house and began to read from a book on the Scriptures which they interpreted with reference to a king of heaven, to events which had not yet occurred but would occur, etc., encouraging her by means of their judicious, skilful explanations . . . to change her Orthodox Christian beliefs.

The Court of Appeal repeated this account, and added that Kokkinakis began to read out passages from Holy Scripture, which he:

> skillfully analysed in a manner that the Christian woman, for want of adequate grounding in doctrine, could not challenge, and at the same time offered her various similar books and importunately tried, directly and indirectly, to undermine her religious beliefs. He must consequently be declared guilty of the above-mentioned offence.

One appeal judge dissented, asserting that no evidence showed that Kyriakaki was particularly inexperienced in Orthodox Christian belief or was of particularly low intellect or naïve.

There follow excerpts from the opinion of the European Court:]

[A 1953 judgment of the Greek Supreme Administrative Court had stated with respect to the meaning of the prohibition of proselytism that the Constitutional ban]

> means that purely spiritual teaching does not amount to proselytism, even if it demonstrates the errors of other religions and entices possible disciples away

from them, who abandon their original religions of their own free will; this is because spiritual teaching is in the nature of a rite of worship performed freely and without hindrance. Outside such spiritual teaching, which may be freely given, any determined, importunate attempt to entice disciples away from the dominant religion by means that are unlawful or morally reprehensible constitutes proselytism as prohibited by the aforementioned provision of the Constitution.

18. The Greek courts have held that persons were guilty of proselytism who . . . offered a scholarship for study abroad; . . . distributed 'so-called religious' books and booklets free to 'illiterate peasants' or to 'young schoolchildren'; or promised a young seamstress an improvement in her position if she left the Orthodox Church, whose priests were alleged to be 'exploiters of society'.

[The opinion noted that the Jehovah's Witnesses movement had been present in Greece for about a century, and that its membership in Greece was estimated to be between 25,000 and 70,000. Between 1975 and 1992, 4,400 members had been arrested, 1,233 committed to trial, and 208 convcited, some for other offences than proselytism. It then turned to Kokkinakis's claim that Article 9 of the European Convention had been violated.]

28. The applicant's complaints mainly concerned a restriction on the exercise of his freedom of religion. The Court will accordingly begin by looking at the issues relating to Article 9 (art. 9), which provides:

> 1. Everyone has the right to freedom of thought, conscience and religion; this right includes freedom to change his religion or belief and freedom, either alone or in community with others and in public or private, to manifest his religion or belief, in worship, teaching, practice and observance.
> 2. Freedom to manifest one's religion or beliefs shall be subject only to such limitations as are prescribed by law and are necessary in a democratic society in the interests of public safety, for the protection of public order, health or morals, or for the protection of the rights and freedoms of others.

29. The applicant did not only challenge what he claimed to be the wrongful application to him of section 4 of Law no. 1363/1938. His submission concentrated on the broader problem of whether that enactment was compatible with the right enshrined in Article 9 (art. 9) of the Convention . . . He pointed to the logical and legal difficulty of drawing any even remotely clear dividing-line between proselytism and freedom to change one's religion or belief and, either alone or in community with others, in public and in private, to manifest it, which encompassed all forms of teaching, publication and preaching between people.

The ban on proselytism, which was made a criminal offence during the Metaxas dictatorship, was not only unconstitutional, Mr Kokkinakis submitted, but it also formed, together with the other clauses of Law no. 1363/1938, 'an arsenal of prohibitions and threats of punishment' hanging over the adherents of all beliefs and all creeds.

Mr Kokkinakis complained, lastly, of the selective application of this Law by the administrative and judicial authorities; it would surpass 'even the wildest academic hypothesis' to imagine, for example, the possibility . . . that an Orthodox Christian would be prosecuted for proselytising on behalf of the 'dominant religion'.

. . .

31. . . . According to Article 9, freedom to manifest one's religion is not only exercisable in community with others, 'in public' and within the circle of those whose faith one shares, but can also be asserted 'alone' and 'in private'; furthermore, it includes in principle the right to try to convince one's neighbour, for example through 'teaching', failing which, moreover, 'freedom to change [one's] religion or belief', enshrined in Article 9, would be likely to remain a dead letter.

. . .

33. . . . [The limitations clause in Article 9(2)] refers only to 'freedom to manifest one's religion or belief'. In so doing, it recognises that in democratic societies, in which several religions coexist within one and the same population, it may be necessary to place restrictions on this freedom in order to reconcile the interests of the various groups and ensure that everyone's beliefs are respected.

. . .

36. The sentence passed by the Lasithi Criminal Court and subsequently reduced by the Crete Court of Appeal (see paragraphs 9–10 above) amounts to an interference with the exercise of Mr Kokkinakis's right to 'freedom to manifest [his] religion or belief'. Such an interference is contrary to Article 9 unless it is 'prescribed by law', directed at one or more of the legitimate aims in paragraph 2 and 'necessary in a democratic society' for achieving them.

. . .

[Kokkinakis claimed that the requirement that a prohibition be 'prescribed by law' had not been met by Section 4 of the Greek Law. The definition of proselytism had no 'objective' base, perhaps a deliberate decision 'to make it possible for any kind of religious conversation or communication to be caught by the provision'. The Law was vague throughout, using phrases like an 'indirect attempt' to intrude on religious beliefs.

> Punishing a non-Orthodox Christian even when he was offering 'moral support or material assistance' was tantamount to punishing an act that any religion would prescribe and that the Criminal Code required in certain emergencies. . . . Consequently, no citizen could regulate his conduct on the basis of this enactment. . . .

The Court noted that it was indeed essential to avoid 'excessive rigidity' in legislation in order to keep pace with changing circumstances. Many criminal statutes 'to a greater or lesser extent are vague'. Practice under the proselytism statute and a "body of settled national case-law interpreting the Law were such as to 'enable Mr. Kokkinakis to regulate his conduct in the matter'. Hence the Law was 'prescribed by law' within the meaning of Article 9(2).

The Court next inquired into whether there had been a 'legitimate aim' for the Law within the meaning of Article 9(2).]

43. In the applicant's submission, religion was part of the 'constantly renewable flow of human thought' and it was impossible to conceive of its being excluded from public debate. A fair balance of personal rights made it necessary to accept that others' thought should be subject to a minimum of influence, otherwise the result would be a 'strange society of silent animals that [would] think but . . . not express themselves, that [would] talk but . . . not communicate, and that [would] exist but . . . not coexist'.

44. Having regard to the circumstances of the case and the actual terms of the relevant courts' decisions, the Court considers that the impugned measure was in pursuit of a legitimate aim under Article 9 para. 2, namely the protection of the rights and freedoms of others, relied on by the Government.

[The Court turned to the requirement that a restrictive measure be 'necessary in a democratic society.']

45. Mr Kokkinakis did not consider it necessary in a democratic society to prohibit a fellow citizen's right to speak when he came to discuss religion with his neighbour. He was curious to know how a discourse delivered with conviction and based on holy books common to all Christians could infringe the rights of others. Mrs Kyriakaki was an experienced adult woman with intellectual abilities; it was not possible, without flouting fundamental human rights, to make it a criminal offence for a Jehovah's Witness to have a conversation with a cantor's wife. Moreover, the Crete Court of Appeal, although the facts before it were precise and absolutely clear, had not managed to determine the direct or indirect nature of the applicant's attempt to intrude on the complainant's religious beliefs; its reasoning showed that it had convicted the applicant 'not for something he had done but for what he was'.
. . .

46. The Government . . . pointed out that if the State remained indifferent to attacks on freedom of religious belief, major unrest would be caused that would probably disturb the social peace.

47. The Court has consistently held that a certain margin of appreciation is to be left to the Contracting States in assessing the existence and extent of the necessity of an interference, but this margin is subject to European supervision, embracing both the legislation and the decisions applying it, even those given by an independent court. The Court's task is to determine whether the measures taken at national level were justified in principle and proportionate.
. . .

48. First of all, a distinction has to be made between bearing Christian witness and improper proselytism. The former corresponds to true evangelism, which a report drawn up in 1956 under the auspices of the World Council of Churches describes as an essential mission and a responsibility of every Christian and every Church. The latter represents a corruption or deformation of it. It may, according to the same report, take the form of activities offering material or social advantages with a view to gaining new members for a Church or exerting improper pressure on people in distress or in need; it may even entail the use of

violence or brainwashing; more generally, it is not compatible with respect for the freedom of thought, conscience and religion of others.

Scrutiny of section 4 of Law no. 1363/1938 shows that the relevant criteria adopted by the Greek legislature are reconcilable with the foregoing if and in so far as they are designed only to punish improper proselytism, which the Court does not have to define in the abstract in the present case.

49. The Court notes, however, that in their reasoning the Greek courts established the applicant's liability by merely reproducing the wording of section 4 and did not sufficiently specify in what way the accused had attempted to convince his neighbour by improper means. None of the facts they set out warrants that finding.

That being so, it has not been shown that the applicant's conviction was justified in the circumstances of the case by a pressing social need. The contested measure therefore does not appear to have been proportionate to the legitimate aim pursued or, consequently, 'necessary in a democratic society . . . for the protection of the rights and freedoms of others'.

50. In conclusion, there has been a breach of Article 9 (art. 9) of the Convention.

. . .

[Since a breach of the Convention had been found, the Court found it unnecessary to consider an additional charge of Kokkinakis, namely that his conviction also violated Article 10, protecting freedom of expression. It held that Greece was to pay Kokkinakis 400,000 drachmas for non-pecuniary damage and 2,789,500 drachmas for costs and expenses. There follow some excerpts from the separate concurring and dissenting opinions.]

PARTLY CONCURRING OPINION OF JUDGE PETTITI

I was in the majority which voted that there had been a breach of Article 9 but I considered that the reasoning given in the judgment could usefully have been expanded.

Furthermore, I parted company with the majority in that I also took the view that the current criminal legislation in Greece on proselytism was in itself contrary to Article 9.

. . .

In the first place, I take the view that what contravenes Article 9 (art. 9) is the Law. . . . [T]he definition is such as to make it possible at any moment to punish the slightest attempt by anyone to convince a person he is addressing.

. . . [T]the mere threat of applying a provision, even one that has fallen into disuse, is sufficient to constitute a breach.

The expression "proselytism that is not respectable", which is a criterion used by the Greek courts when applying the Law, is sufficient for the enactment and the case-law applying it to be regarded as contrary to Article 9.

. . .

. . . [T]he haziness of the definition leaves too wide a margin of interpretation for determining criminal penalties.

. . .

Proselytism is linked to freedom of religion; a believer must be able to communicate his faith and his beliefs in the religious sphere as in the philosophical sphere. Freedom of religion and conscience is a fundamental right and this freedom must be able to be exercised for the benefit of all religions and not for the benefit of a single Church, even if this has traditionally been the established Church or 'dominant religion'.

Freedom of religion and conscience certainly entails accepting proselytism, even where it is 'not respectable'. Believers and agnostic philosophers have a right to expound their beliefs, to try to get other people to share them and even to try to convert those whom they are addressing.

The only limits on the exercise of this right are those dictated by respect for the rights of others where there is an attempt to coerce the person into consenting or to use manipulative techniques.

The other types of unacceptable behaviour—such as brainwashing, breaches of labour law, endangering of public health and incitement to immorality, which are found in the practices of certain pseudo-religious groups—must be punished in positive law as ordinary criminal offences. Proselytism cannot be forbidden under cover of punishing such activities.

. . .

. . . Non-criminal proselytism remains the main expression of freedom of religion. Attempting to make converts is not in itself an attack on the freedom and beliefs of others or an infringement of their rights.

. . .

Spiritual, religious and philosophical convictions belong to the private sphere of beliefs and call into play the right to express and manifest them. Setting up a system of criminal prosecution and punishment without safeguards is a perilous undertaking, and the authoritarian regimes which, while proclaiming freedom of religion in their Constitutions, have restricted it by means of criminal offences of parasitism, subversion or proselytism have given rise to abuses . . . .

The wording adopted by the majority of the Court in finding a breach, namely that the applicant's conviction was not justified in the circumstances of the case, leaves too much room for a repressive interpretation by the Greek courts in the future, whereas public prosecution must likewise be monitored. In my view, it would have been possible to define impropriety, coercion and duress more clearly and to describe more satisfactorily, in the abstract, the full scope of religious freedom and bearing witness.

. . .

DISSENTING OPINION OF JUDGE VALTICOS

. . .

Let us look now at the facts of the case. On the one hand, we have a militant Jehovah's Witness, a hardbitten adept of proselytism, a specialist in conversion, a martyr of the criminal courts whose earlier convictions have served only to harden him in his militancy, and, on the other hand, the ideal victim, a naïve woman, the wife of a cantor in the Orthodox Church (if he manages to convert her, what a triumph!). He swoops on her, trumpets that he has good news for her (the play on words is obvious, but no doubt not to her), manages to get himself let in and, as an experienced commercial traveller and cunning purveyor of a faith he wants to spread, expounds to her his intellectual wares cunningly wrapped up in a mantle of universal peace and radiant happiness. Who, indeed, would not like peace and happiness? But is this the mere exposition of Mr Kokkinakis's beliefs or is it not rather an attempt to beguile the simple soul of the cantor's wife? Does the Convention afford its protection to such undertakings? Certainly not.

. . .

I should certainly be inclined to recommend the Government to give instructions that prosecutions should be avoided where harmless conversations are involved, but not in the case of systematic, persistent campaigns entailing actions bordering on unlawful entry.

That having been said, I do not consider in any way that there has been a breach of the Convention.

. . .

MAKAU MUTUA, LIMITATIONS ON RELIGIOUS RIGHTS: PROBLEMATIZING RELIGIOUS FREEDOM IN THE AFRICAN CONTEXT
in Johan D. van der Vyver and J. Witte, Jr. (eds.), Religious Human Rights in Global Perspective (1996), at 417

. . . With the African theater as the basic laboratory, I intend to unpack the meaning of religious freedom at the point of contact between the messianic faiths and African religions and illustrate how that meeting resulted in a phenomenon akin to cultural genocide.

The main purpose here is not merely to defend forms of religion or belief but rather to problematize the concept of the right to the free exercise of messianic faiths, which include the right to proselytize in the marketplace of religions. In societies, such as the African ones where religion is woven into virtually every aspect of life, its delegitimization can easily lead to the collapse of social norms and cultural identities. The result, as has been the case in most of Black Africa, is a culturally disconnected people, neither African nor European nor Arab. In other words, I shall argue that imperial religions have necessarily violated the individual conscience and the communal expressions of Africans and their communities by subverting African religions.

In so doing, they have robbed Africans of essential elements of their humanity.

. . .

Since the right to religious freedom includes the right to be left alone—to choose freely whether and what to believe—the rights regime by requiring that African religions compete in the marketplace of ideas incorrectly assumes a level playing field. The rights corpus not only forcibly imposes on African religions the obligation to compete—a task for which as non-proselytizing, non-competitive, creeds they are not historically fashioned—but also protects evangelizing religions in their march towards universalization. In the context of religious freedom, the privileging by the rights regime of the competition of ideas over the right against cultural invasion, in a skewed contest, amounts to condoning the dismantling of African religions. I also argue that the playing field, the one crucial and necessary ingredient in a fair fight, is heavily weighted against Africans. Messianic religions have either been forcibly imposed or their introduction was accomplished as part of the cultural package borne by colonialism. Missionaries did not simply offer Jesus Christ as the savior of benighted souls; his salvation was frequently a pre-condition for services in education and health, which were quite often the exclusive domain of the church and the colonial state. It makes little sense to argue that Africans could avoid acculturation by opting out of the colonial order; in most cases the embrace of indigenous societies by the European imperial powers was so violent and total that conformity was the only immediate option. In making this argument I shall also rely on notions of human rights law which, as I shall seek to show, suggest that indigenous beliefs have a right to be respected and left alone by more dominant external traditions.

This reasoning poses serious questions that go to the root of the rights regime. Some difficulties are obvious. A key ideal of the human rights movement, and indeed of liberalism, is the unwavering commitment to the open society in which the freedom to advance, receive, and disseminate ideas is assumed necessary for the greater social good. Though not absolute—permissible limitations can be placed on what ideas and under what circumstances advocacy is allowed by the law—this commitment creates a rights regime conundrum in conversations about the universality of human rights norms. Questions arise about the validity of the advocacy of certain norms beyond the borders of their origin. The right of advocacy itself and its centrality in the human rights corpus becomes an issue. . . . Could theocratic states, for example, seek protection for their political orders and social systems under the rights corpus? Other examples come to mind: should human rights law invade cultures that subordinate women and seek to eradicate gender bias through advocacy? Are these acceptable forms of advocacy which the human rights movement should protect? Ultimately, one must ask, who decides what is good for the universe and what should be advocated transnationally?
. . .

A discussion about limitations on religious rights at first blush appears to frustrate some of the major ideals of the human rights movement. It raises the question about the tension between the restriction of the right to evangelize or advocate a point of view and one of the central ideals of the human rights movement, the promotion of diversity and the right to advocate ideas or creeds. An exploration of the manner in which the human rights corpus ought to view religious rights—whether further to limit or to expand the protections they currently enjoy—raises this fundamental tension: how does a body of principles that promotes diversity and difference protect the establishment and manifestation of religious ordering that seeks to destroy difference and forcibly impose an orthodoxy in Africa—as both Christianity and Islam, the two major proselytizing religions, attempted, and in many cases successfully did? Precisely because of the ethos of universalization common to both, the messianic faiths sought to eradicate, with the help of the state, all other forms of religious expression and belief and close off any avenues through which other competing faiths could be introduced or sustained. This coerced imposition of a religious orthodoxy implies a desire and a social philosophy to seek the forcible destruction of that which is different. Yet, it seems inconceivable that the human rights movement would have intended to protect the 'right' of certain religions to 'destroy' others. . . .

. . .

. . . Although Article 18 of the ICCPR guarantees the 'right to freedom of thought, conscience and religion', and provides for certain limitations, it does not spell out the duties that must be borne by proselytizing religions. I attempt in this chapter to balance the interests of these religions with those of African societies, both individual and collective, and to explore ways, if possible, in which the respectful co-existence between these radically different spiritualities could be imagined and worked out.

. . .

The two basic human rights documents—the Universal Declaration of Human Rights and the International Covenant on Civil and Political Rights—seek to entrench and encourage the free exchange of ideas and the respect for difference and diversity. The emphasis placed on the importance of creating and maintaining a diverse society is one of the most striking characteristics of human rights law. Diversity is encouraged, though not required, by the rights corpus in cultural, religious, political, and other endeavors and pursuits. Through this emphasis, human rights law 'evidences throughout its hostility to imposed uniformity' . . .

. . .

Taken together, the provisions advocating difference and diversity and those providing explicitly for religious rights, would seem to allow proselytization by the messianic religions, although they also provide for certain limitations which might be read as possibly excluding certain modes of evangelization. For example, proselytization through force, coercion, or in the context of colonization would appear to be excluded.

Although human rights law amply protects the right to proselytize through the principles of free speech, assembly, and association, the 'pecking' order of rights problematizes the right to evangelize where the result is the destruction of other cultures or the closure of avenues for other religions. It is my argument that the most fundamental of all human rights is that of self-determination and that no other right overrides it. Without this fundamental group or individual right, no other human right could be secured, since the group would be unable to determine for its individual members under what political, social, cultural, economic, and legal order they would live. Any right which directly conflicts with this right ought to be void to the extent of that conflict. Traditionally, the self-determination principle has been employed to advance the cause of decolonization or to overcome other forms of external occupation. The principle was indispensable to the decolonization process. This usage of the principle—as a tool for advancing demands for external self-determination—could be expanded to disallow cultural and religious imperialism or imposition by external agencies through acculturation, especially where the express intent of the 'invading' culture or religion, as was the case in Africa, is to destroy its indigenous counterparts and seal off the entry or growth of other traditions. Furthermore, the principle could also be read to empower internal self-determination, that is, the right of a people to 'cultural survival'. This usage of self-determination is advanced by the Draft Declaration on the Rights of Indigenous Peoples. It is also an argument against cultural genocide. It is one of the ideas advanced by advocates of autonomy regimes for minorities: unless groups are given protection against invasion and control by others, their cultural and ethnic identities could be quashed by more powerful cultures and political systems. The violent advocacy of the messianic religions in Africa could be seen as a negation of this right particularly because religion is often the first point of attack in the process of acculturation.

Christianity and Islam forcibly entered Africa not as guests but as masters. The two traditions came either as conquerors or on the backs of conquerors. As they had done elsewhere, they were driven by the belief and conviction of their own innate superiority—and conversely what they saw as barbaric African religions and cultures. This belief was not a function of an objective assessment and reflection about African religions and cultures. It was born of the contempt and ignorance of that which was different and the exaggerated importance of the messianic faiths. . . . The West was able through coercion, intimidation, trickery, and force to impose a new political, social, cultural, and thanks to the missionaries, religious order in Africa. African political, social, and religious traditions were delegitimized virtually overnight.

. . .

HAROLD BERMAN, RELIGIOUS RIGHTS IN RUSSIA AT A TIME OF TUMULTUOUS TRANSITION: A HISTORICAL THEORY

in Johan van der Vyver and J. Witte (eds.), Religious Human Rights in Global Perspective (1996), at 301

. . .

'Are you a believer?' I once asked a Muscovite. He replied, 'I'm Russian, I'm Orthodox'.

During a visit to Moscow in September, 1994, I had the opportunity to ask questions about this ethnic dimension of Russian Christianity in a two-hour interview with a representative of the Moscow Patriarchate. In defending the aborted 1993 legislation, he said that the Lutherans should be free to give religious leadership to the German population of Russia, the Roman Catholics to the Polish population of Russia, the Jews to the Jews, the Muslims to the Turks in Russia, and so forth—but the Russians . . ., the ethnic Russians, the *russkie*, he said, belong chiefly to Russian Orthodoxy.

It is difficult for Western Christians to accept, or even to understand, the belief in ethnic Christian churches. In the Western Christian tradition, now embodied in secular constitutional law in most countries and adopted by the human rights covenants, religious freedom is conceived primarily in terms of the religious faith of the individual believer, including his right to manifest that faith in collective bodies which are conceived to be voluntary associations. . . .

It is, above all, this conception of the common Christian faith of the people, the *narod,* of Russian nationality that is the principal source of opposition to the influx of foreign evangelical missionaries. It is not the purpose of the vast majority of these missionaries to draw Russians away from Russian Orthodoxy, and for the most part they have attracted Russians who formerly were atheist or agnostic. When I made this point to the representative of the Moscow Patriarchate with whom I spoke in 1994, he replied: 'It is true that after more than 75 years of Marxist-Leninist education and Communist Party pressure, a great many Russians are ignorant of Russian Orthodoxy or indifferent to it. But their roots are Orthodox. It is our task to return them to Orthodoxy'.
...

But the objection to foreign missionaries goes deeper. The historical argument of the Patriarchate is directed not only to the past but also to the present and future. Russia is now experiencing a severe spiritual crisis, which, in the view not only of the Moscow Patriarchate but of many Russian people, whether or not they are believers, is being aggravated by the foreign evangelical missionaries. My informant in the Moscow Patriarchate expressed this point in the following way:

'The changes now taking place in Russia', he said, 'including especially the economic reforms, require a new post-Soviet psychology among the people. For three generations the people has been brought up on a simple monolithic ideology that is now repudiated. The belief in Soviet superiority is gone. The belief in progress toward a bright future is gone. The people feels lost'.

'The foreign evangelical missionaries,' he continued, 'know that there is a spiritual crisis but they do not understand it. In fact, they are offering to the people another simple solution. Like the Communists, they offer salvation in return for a commitment which requires little effort. "Just believe, and you will be saved." This reinforces the old psychology, in which simple slogans were offered in return for immediate minimum rewards but great rewards in the future. Russian Orthodoxy is more complex and more difficult. It teaches not rewards but sacrifice. It teaches the positive value of suffering. Its spiritual demands are great'.

My interlocutor went on to a different aspect of the same theme of spiritual crisis. 'In the past,' he said, 'whenever there has been a spiritual crisis of this intensity, the people has turned to the Russian Church. That was true at the time of the Napoleonic Wars. It was true in the First World War. It was true even under Stalin in the Second World War. Now we are in a comparable crisis. Moreover, both the extreme nationalist on the right and the radical democrats on the left can be reconciled on this point, namely, that to meet our spiritual crisis it is important that a strong role be played not only by the Russian Orthodox Church but also by other traditional Russian confessions, confessions that have been tested by repression for seventy-five years and that have forged a fraternal relationship with each other'.

I responded that many think the Russian Orthodox Church is simply afraid of competition. 'Not at all,' he replied, 'But Russia needs time to recover her health before they descend on us. The Russian Orthodox Church is like a very sick person that is only beginning to recover her health'.

'Moreover,' he added, 'we lack both the material and the human resources needed to compete on an equal basis. The foreign missionaries are pouring huge sums of money into evangelization, paying for billboard advertisements and for television programs featuring American preachers and hiring huge stadiums for spreading their message'. Also in human resources, the Russian Church, he said, is lacking in people who are trained to attract outsiders. 'For 75 years we were permitted to talk only to the faithful in our congregations. We are only beginning now to educate clergy in how to speak to non-believers'.

. . .

'The August law,' my informant said, 'was a reaction against the premature invasion of Western missionaries. Of course we do not want to violate international law or our own constitution or principles of human rights. But we hope that those legal and moral norms can be adapted to enable us to meet the acute spiritual crisis that now confronts us'.

. . .

ALESSANDRA STANLEY, POPE TELLS INDIA HIS CHURCH HAS RIGHT TO EVANGELIZE
New York Times, November 8, 1999, p. A3

Summoning all his moral authority, Pope John Paul II tried today to persuade leaders of other religions here that interfaith understanding should lead them to recognize the Roman Catholic Church's right to evangelize. 'Religious freedom constitutes the very heart of human rights', the pope, on a three-day visit to India, said at a interreligious gathering that included Hindus, Muslims, Sikhs, Jews and representatives of several other faiths. 'Its inviolability is such that individuals must be recognized as having the right even to change their religion, if their conscience so demands.'

But that is an argument that many religious leaders in India accept only with difficulty. Christian conversions are at the heart of a political and religious dispute that has made the 79-year-old pope's visit a tense one. Christian proselytizing is fuel for Muslim fundamentalists, but it is also a source of uneasiness between the pope and some of his more moderate and like-minded religious peers.

'Conversions are a fundamental right,' Samdhong Rinpoche, a Buddhist monk who is the speaker of the Tibetan Parliament in exile, said after leaving the podium he shared with the pope. 'But what we fear is that between indoctrination and anybody's inner-consciousness to choose his religion, there is a clean line.' 'Any kind of action to encourage, or to persuade or to motivate in favor of any particular religion, that is a form of conversion that we as Buddhists cannot recommend,' the monk said.

. . .

. . . Shankaracharya Madhavananda Saraswati, a moderate Hindu leader who has criticized fundamentalist protests against the visit . . . also expressed private misgivings about Christian evangelization. He said later that Hindus could not really ever be diverted from their original faith: 'Religion comes from the heart.

Something may change outwardly, but what is inside remains with the human being forever. That does not change'.

The pope, who came to India to close a synod of Asian bishops, has declared the evangelization of Asia, where Catholics remain a tiny minority, to be one of the church's top priorities for the next millennium. He said it was a 'mystery' why Christ is largely unknown on the continent and added, 'The peoples of Asia need Jesus Christ and his Gospel'.

In India, however, Hindu fundamentalists accuse Christian missionaries, who are most active in poor rural and tribal areas, of preying on the most susceptible in society—buying their souls with education, medical aid and economic assistance.

Anti-Christian attacks by Hindu fundamentalists, often encouraged by political extremists, have increased dramatically in the last two years, with more than 150 recorded incidents of church lootings, beatings, rapes and killings. In Orissa, the state that was recently devastated by a cyclone, a missionary and his two young children were killed in January.

The pope came to India with two agendas: He preached ardently for religious tolerance for all faiths, but also instructed his own to convert new followers. To even the mildest leaders of other religions, the two messages do not easily blend.

'Religious people are more busy with increasing the number of their followers rather than paying attention to the challenges that beset religion,' Acharya Mahapragya, head of the Jain faith, said at the podium. Speaking through a lavender-colored surgical mask—Jains are Hindus who revere all forms of life and veil their speech to prevent their breath from destroying living micro-organisms—he was the only leader, besides the pope, to address the issue of conversions publicly.

In the current climate, some Indian Catholics say, their simplest acts of charity are misunderstood. 'We help people with scholarships and medical aid,' said Bartholomew Abraham, 40, a businessman who traveled almost 1,500 miles by train to see the pope. 'If we were really bribing converts, after 2,000 years we wouldn't still only be 2 percent of the population'.

The pope wants church leaders to adapt their pastoral style to suit the culture and customs of their native lands, and he showed the way today by presiding over a colorful sitar Mass for 40,000 worshipers in Nehru Stadium. The Mass coincided with the most important Hindu celebration of the year, Diwali, the festival of light, which was noisily celebrated all over New Delhi with fireworks. At the Mass, under a huge abstract poster of Mother Teresa of Calcutta, women in brown and gold saris danced before the altar while a choir of sitar-players performed Indian-style hymns.

. . .

NOTE

Consider the following observations of Claude Lévi-Strauss in *Race and History* (1958), at 12. Rather than view the diversity of cultures as a 'natural phenomenon', people 'have tended rather to regard diversity as something abnormal or outrageous', to the point of rejecting 'out of hand the cultural institutions . . . which are furthest removed from those with which we identify ourselves'. One sees 'crude reactions', 'instinctive antipathy', 'repugnance' toward ways of life or beliefs to which we are unaccustomed and which we term 'barbarous'.

Nonetheless, collaboration between cultures has been the key to achievement. The greater achievements stem not from 'isolated' cultures but from those which have 'combined their play' through such means as migration, borrowing, trade or warfare. 'For, if a culture were left to its own resources, it could never hope to be "superior"'. Indeed, the greater the diversity between the cultures concerned, the 'more fruitful' such a 'coalition of cultures' will be.

Lévi-Strauss turns to a problem stemming from his preceding observations, that of cultural uniformity. He proposes some solutions to it, but emphasizes that he is describing a process that is inherently 'contradictory'. That is, progress requires collaboration among cultures, but 'in the course of their collaboration, the differences in their contributions will gradually be evened out, although collaboration was originally necessary and advantageous simply because of these differences.' To this contradiction he finds no clear solution. He stresses that

> man must, no doubt, guard against the blind particularism which would restrict the dignity of humankind to a single race, culture or society; but he must never forget, on the other hand, that no section of humanity has succeeded in finding universally applicable formulas; and that it is impossible to imagine mankind pursuing a single way of life for, in such a case, mankind would be ossified.

The currents toward both unification and diversity are essential. One must preserve diversity as such, diversity itself, the idea and substance of it, rather than any one historically realized form. One must look for 'stirrings of new life, foster latent potentialities', and see each form of diversity as 'contributions to the fullness of all the others'.

QUESTIONS

1. How do you assess the Kokkinakis opinion? Do you find justification for any restriction on proselytizing other than those related to coercion, undue imposition on the listener, and similar matters?

2. How do you assess Mutua's views? Can they be limited to matters or religion, or would his arguments carry with the same effect to other attributes of a culture, such as discrimination, or extreme forms of punishment, or authoritarian rule by priests or by elders of a community? How would you seek to resolve the tensions that Mutua underscores, such as arguments in favor of cultural variety and survival as opposed to arguments for universal norms?

3. How do you compare the arguments advanced in the article by Berman by a representative of the Moscow Patriarchate with respect to proselytizing in Russia with Mutua's arguments about Africa? What similarities and differences? How do both compare with the apparent position of the Greek government in Kokkinakis? Should these

different arguments carry different weight with respect to assessing the legality of restrictions on proselytizing under the ICCPR or the European Convention?

4. 'The human rights instruments are very attentive to the rights of parents to persuade their children to particular beliefs, including religious beliefs and related practices. For example, Article 18(4) of the ICCPR commits the states parties "to have respect for the liberty of parents . . . to ensure the religious and moral education of their children in conformity with their own convictions". Religious belief is of fundamental importance to a human being. Why should parents be given this authority, and states then be permitted to prohibit efforts of others to persuade adults to a different belief?' Respond.

5. 'If cultural survival and maintenance of old traditions, religious and other, is to prevail, it must do so by the inner strength of these traditions, by their ability to resist, not through the state's protection in the form of banning foreign ideas and influence of a religious or other character. Here as elsewhere, consumer choice in the larger marketplace of ideas should prevail. Cultures grow through interaction, not through artificial isolation.' Comment.

4. AUTONOMY REGIMES: RELIGION-BASED PERSONAL LAW

COMMENT ON AUTONOMY REGIMES

Autonomy regimes refer to governmental systems or sub-systems within a state that are directed or administered by a minority or its members. They take many forms. Three general types figure in this discussion, each subject to variations that range from strong to weak regimes. In each case, a distinguishing mark of the regime is that it depends on legal authorization—customary, statutory, or constitutional law. In most instances, the state's formal legal system defines the powers and scope of the regime. That is, autonomy regimes are instituted in law, and those governing or administering them exercise a form of governmental power.

This section examines the first type, personal law regimes. They provide that members of a defined ethnic group will be governed with respect to matters of personal law—marriage, divorce, perhaps adoption, succession, and so on—by a body of law distinctive to it, usually religious in character. Thus all members of a religious community—Jews, Muslims and members of different Christian communities in the illustration below of Israel; Hindus and Muslims in the illustration below from India—may be subject to a religion-based personal law system, that could be applied by religious courts or by the normal secular courts. Depending on the state, members of such groups may or may not be able to 'opt out' from the religious law by selecting a nationwide secular law.

A second type of regime has a territorial organization, and hence is plausible only when the ethnic minority at issue is regionally concentrated—as is true, for example, of the Tamil minority in Sri Lanka or the Kurdish minority in several states. This organization may take the form of a component part of a federalism, or of a regional government to which powers have been devolved within a unitary state. The ethnic minority exercises one or another degree of political control over the territory and to that degree governs its own affairs. Contemporary illustrations include Catalonia in Spain, or ethnically-based states in India.

The third type, power-sharing regimes, assures that one or several ethnic groups will benefit from a particular form of participation in governance, in economic activity, or in other fields. Like personal law regimes, it does not demand that the ethnic minority be regionally concentrated. Power-sharing can assume many forms. It may affect the composition of the national legislature—for example, through provision that members of an ethnic minorities are entitled to elect a stated percentage of legislators through the use of separate voting rolls specific to the minority. It may require approval by a majority of the legislative representatives of a minority group before certain changes—say, a change to constitutional provisions giving the minority group stated protections—can be made. Belgium and Lebanon illustrate relatively successful and failed power-sharing arrangements.

The universal human rights corpus is silent with respect to such kinds of autonomy regimes, although different provisions of the leading instruments provide a foundation for arguments that such regimes are consistent or inconsistent with human rights. Consider Article 27 of the ICCPR, which has become the preeminent human rights norm for discussion of rights and protections of minorities and their members. It provides:

> In those States in which ethnic, religious or linguistic minorities exist, persons belonging to such minorities shall not be denied the right, in community with the other members of their group, to enjoy their own culture, to profess and practise their own religion, or to use their own language.

Note several aspects of this provision: (1) It refers to 'minorities' rather than to 'peoples', as in the provision in ICCPR Article 1 for self-determination of 'peoples'. (2) It protects 'persons belonging to' minorities rather than the minorities themselves. (3) Nonetheless, the right is to be exercised 'in community with the other members' of a minority.

Individual or Collective Rights

Most rights declared in the human rights instruments have an individual character. Many of them are at the same time germane, indeed essential, to the formation of groups. Thus the rights to advocacy and association are vital to the organization of interest groups. Moreover, certain rights such as those identified in Article 27 are inherently collective, such as the right of members of minorities to use their own language or practice their own religion. Indeed, Article 27 states that such rights may be exercised 'in community with the other members' of a linguistic, religious or other ethnic group.

Other types of rights that are characteristically expressed in individual terms, such as the right to equal protection in ICCPR Articles 2(1) and 26, also have a group aspect. The prohibited governmental conduct amounts to the disadvantaging of an individual because of that individual's group characteristic or identity. It is the individual's link to the group that provides the very occasion for discrimination. Moreover, the entire group benefits from the protection against discrimination accorded to any one of its members.

What then would be the nature of a 'right' to an autonomy regime? If we assume that such a right exists—say, to a distinctive personal law, or to a form of power-sharing—it would have a markedly different character even from the individual rights noted above that have some collective or group association. Autonomy rights are unmistakably collective, in the sense that they can be exercised *only* by the group—by its spokespersons or representatives, however they are selected—and cannot be reduced to or expressed through individual rights of its members. The group itself would have bargained for the autonomy arrangements that are confirmed in law, statutory or constitutional. Officials or official institutions of the group—its clergy, a regional government, an ethnic political party—implement and administer autonomy schemes.

COMMENT ON STATE, RELIGION, AND PERSONAL LAW IN ISRAEL

[Alexandra Lahav and Ofrit Liviatan provided invaluable assistance in the research for and writing of this Comment.]

Background

Established in 1948 in the aftermath of the Holocaust and after a half century of a Zionist movement working toward a national homeland for Jews, Israel has a population that is about 80 per cent Jewish and 15 per cent Muslim. (This comment concerns only the Jewish and Muslim populations.) Muslims form the principal part of the Arab minority in Israel.

The state's Declaration of Independence provides that Israel will be a 'Jewish state.' It also promises that the state will provide for equality of rights for all its citizens, and will guarantee freedom of religion and conscience. Israel has no constitution. The protection of civil liberties and basic rights was achieved through judicial decisions and through the Basic Laws of 1992—laws enjoying a superior normative status, requiring in some instances super-majorities for their enactment and amendment (itself possible only by a later Basic Law), viewed by some commentators as an incipient constitution, One such law declares that '[h]uman rights in Israel ... will be safeguarded in the spirit of the principles contained in the Declaration of Independence'.

A Basic Law provides that 'the values of the State of Israel as a Jewish and Democratic State' are the basis of human rights in Israel. The official ideology of the state asserts that its Jewish and democratic characters are compatible, and that the state is equally committed to both. Israel (that is, the internationally recognized state, excluding those parts of the West Bank and Gaza that Israel continues to occupy and that are now subject to final status negotiations with the Palestinian Authority) constitutes a political democracy: free and open elections, peaceful transfers of governments within its parliamentary system, independent judiciary, free association and press, civilian control of the military, and broad support for democratic institutions. Arab political parties compete in elections and hold seats in the Knesset (Parliament). Certain legislation, such as restrictions on participation in elections of political parties advocating change in the character of Israel as the state of the Jewish people or parties inciting to racism, limited popular participation through the vote. But recent Supreme Court decisions have narrowed this restriction, leaving room for more political parties to advocate policies making Israeli fully a state of "all its citizens."In addition, the serious threats over the decades to national security have led to restraints on a number of human rights.

In 1992, the Knesset brought about a 'constitutional revolution' by codifying through Basic Laws fundamental freedoms such as liberty , dignity, privacy, and freedom of occupation. This legislation strengthened the normative value of such rights by putting special burdens on future legislation limiting them. Rights to equality and religious freedom were omitted from these laws because of strong opposition by the orthodox religious parties, which feared that 'constitutionalization' of religious rights would limit the Knesset's ability to enact legislation urged by religious interests that would institute religious norms or further support religious institutions.

Despite the Declaration of Independence and Basic Laws, serious issues remain with respect to the state's treatment of the Arab minority in terms of equality of state benefits and services including education. Moreover, army veterans (with few exceptions such as Druze and recent immigrants such as Russian Christians, only Jews serve in the army) benefit in a variety of ways from those services, such as subsidized housing. Land ownership and development has proved to be a particularly difficult issue. The policies developed prior to the establishment of Israel by groups facilitating settlement by Jews—like the Jewish Agency and the Jewish National Fund, institutions that have a quasi-governmental character—long continued in effect. For example, only Jews were eligible for leasing or purchasing those lands that were under the control of the Jewish National Fund (about 13 per cent of state-owned land). Those policies are now judicially limited.

The most prominent illustration of the Jewish character of the state is the 1950 Law of Return, conferring on Jews in all countries the right to settle in Israel and receive automatically Israeli citizenship. Except for certain family members of Jews, non-Jews seeking to immigrate must receive permission to do so. (There is no necessary connection between the definition of a Jew for purposes of the Law of Return and the *Halachic* (Jewish law) definition.) But Jewish identity is expressed in many day-by-day ways, including religious and historical/ethnic state symbols such as the flag, the national emblem and anthem. The Hebrew language, revived as a modern tongue under the impetus of the Zionist movement, dominates, although Arabic also constitutes an official language. Other illustrations of the religious and cultural aspects of the state's Jewish identity include: official observance of the Sabbath and of religious and national holidays (including, for example, the suspension of state transportation systems) as days of rest (though non-Jews may observe their days of rest); maintenance by the state of *kashrut* (Jewish dietary laws) in public institutions; and significant state support of Jewish educational institutions. Nonetheless, Judaism is not an 'official state religion' in the sense of legal provision for its preferred treatment as such over other religious faiths or for pervasive absorption of traditional Jewish law into the Israeli legal system.

Personal-religious bodies of law and communities

The Israeli legal and political systems reveal extraordinary complexity in the relationships between a national, territorial, and secular legal order including all residents of Israel within its scope, and a personal, religious law and religious courts. This comment bypasses the detail and complexity of the resulting mixed system—for example, the ever-shifting boundaries between secular/civil and religious law and courts. It stresses the relevance of religious law and courts to personal law.

The religious court system in Israel is based on the *Millet* system, a legacy of the Ottoman Empire that collapsed in the First World War. Ottoman law granted an important degree of autonomy to the Christian and Jewish communities living under its control, particularly with respect to personal law. This heritage of religious pluralism was continued under British Mandatory Rule that succeeded Ottoman rule and continued almost until the founding of the State of Israel.

The jurisdiction of religious courts derives from legislative grant. The Palestine Order of Council, 1922, Section 47, issued by the Mandatory Government established (in effect, continued with some changes) the jurisdiction of religious tribunals over matters of personal status. This Order of Council recognized ten religious communities, including Jewish, Muslim, and a number of Christian sects, each with its own court system and judges and religiously based personal law. The Israeli Government added two more communities (the Druz and the Baha'i).

Extensive Israeli legislation over the half century has regulated in changing ways all or particular religious communities

The jurisdiction of religious courts is limited to matters of personal status. The Palestine Order of Council defined 'matters of personal status' to include such matters as marriage, divorce, alimony, maintenance, guardianship, successions, wills. The Israeli Government deleted from this list adoption, inheritance, wills and legacies. These matters are now handled in civil courts, unless both parties to a dispute consent to the jurisdiction of the relevant religious court.

All the religious courts exercise an exclusive jurisdiction over members of the respective communities, no matter what the personal religious convictions (believer, agnostic, atheist) or ritual or other observance may be. Thus two Jews or two Muslims who view themselves as secular and non-believers and who wish to marry in Israel must do so within the relevant religious court system—that is, respectively the Rabbinical and Shari'a courts—that will apply, respectively, orthodox Jewish law and Islamic law. Indeed, it is the decisions of the religious courts that form the basis of religious law in the relevant community. If a matter of 'personal status' committed to religious law appropriately arises before a civil court that has jurisdiction to pass on it, that court will itself apply the relevant religious law.

Jurisdiction is exclusive for all religious courts with respect to marriage and divorce. On other matters like inheritance or adoption, jurisdiction is concurrent with civil courts. In such situations, both parties' consent is required to permit adjudication by a religious court. Islamic courts have the broadest subject-matter jurisdiction, as was true under the Ottoman system. When a dispute arises about whether a question falls into the category of 'personal status,' the matter is decided by a judicial panel.

The religious courts derive their authority from legislation and are effectively state organs. State finances support the courts, including in most cases payment of the judges' salaries. Judges for both court systems are appointed by the President of Israel on the recommendation of a nominating committee headed by the Minister of Religious Affairs and including members of the concerned religious community. In some respects, the provisions regulating appointment, salary and related matters are more favourable to the Rabbinical courts and judges than to the Islamic (Shari'a) courts and judges.

There is no civil mechanism for deciding religious affiliation, even in the event that two religions claim the same individual. Generally the issue is decided by the application of religious law. For example, under religious law as applied by the Rabbinical courts, a person's status as a 'Jew' generally depends on the mother's religious status or would follow from orthodox conversion to Judaism in Israel or non-orthodox (that is, conservative or reform) conversion abroad.

A growing number of statutes enacted by the Knesset apply to and govern organization of and adjudication in religious courts, including the appointment and salaries of judges, women's equal rights in matters like family or common property, and laws affecting adoption and guardianship. Such regulation rarely interferes with matters of exclusive jurisdiction of the religious courts such as marriage and divorce.

Religious courts are also required to abide by the Basic Laws enacted by the Knesset (such as the Basic Law: Human Dignity and Freedom) and by fundamental constitutional principles insofar as the application of these laws and principles does not contravene the basic tenets of the religious law—and unless legislation explicitly exempts the religious courts from such laws (as generally is the case for marriage and divorce).

Rabbinical Courts

The Rabbinical courts apply orthodox (Halachic) Jewish law, as opposed to strains of non-orthodox belief such as the different understandings of Judaism and Jewish ritual in the Conservative and Reform movements that are dominant among Jews in many countries including the United States. About 20 per cent of the population is now Orthodox.

This hegemonic status of Orthodox Judaism stems from an agreement in 1947, just before the founding of Israel, between the Executive of the Jewish Agency represented by David Ben-Gurion, later the first prime minister, and the ultra Orthodox World Agudah Movement. The agreement provided for (1) the establishment of the Sabbath (Saturday) as the legal day of rest for Jews and all state institutions, (2) the observance of Jewish dietary laws in all state institutions, (3) the establishment of a religious school network supported by the state, and (4) the continuation of rabbinical control over the personal status laws applied to Jews. Israel's multi-party parliamentary democracy based on proportional representation and government coalitions has so functioned as to enable the relatively small Orthodox parties to exert considerable political influence on the Knesset and Prime Minister in enactment of such legislation as strong Sabbath laws prohibiting industrial and commercial activities and most public transportation, or state support for orthodox institutes of learning with exemption of students in such institutions from military service that is mandatory for others. In the last decade, non-orthodox Jewish movements have succeeded in winning a series of court cases that upset some traditional practices excluding women and non-orthodox Jews from, say, religious councils.

In order to marry, a Jewish citizen of Israel must meet the Orthodox Halachic requirements that are applied in the Rabbinical courts. For example, a Jew may marry only another Jew, and even within the Jewish community, certain types of marriages are forbidden. For other situations—for example, Jews who wish to marry non-Jews or to marry persons converted to Judaism under the supervision of a conservative or reform rather than orthodox rabbi—the traditional option is to marry abroad. Civil marriages from foreign jurisdictions (such as nearby Cyprus that is popular for such purposes) are recognized in Israel by the Ministry of the Interior and by the civil courts system. Such marriages are not recognized by the rabbinical court system.

Under religious law, divorce requires prior authorization by the Rabinnical courts, even if it is based on mutual consent of the parties. After such authorization, a husband must deliver to his wife a consent (called a *Get*) to dissolution of the marriage. A woman whose husband refuses to grant her a *Get* in accordance with the Rabbinical court's judgment of divorce may, after stautory reforms, request the Attorney General to intervene. In that case, the Attorney General may bring the matter into civil court, which may imprison the husband until he implements the Rabinnical court's judgment. Until the *Get* is granted by the man, the woman remains under serious, personal restriction.

As a reaction to this situation, a significant 'alternative marriage' industry has developed that alleviates the situation for people who do not follow the prescribed route through Rabbinical courts. In fact, if not by law, a number of paths have developed toward being considered married, through the conservative or reform movements in Judaism. Israeli legislation and judicial decisions have also created an extensive jurisprudence, to the point where a cohabiting couple have almost the same rights as married couples with respect to such matters as succession, legitimacy of children, and social security. Moreover, recent years have seen the growth of 'family courts' that have assumed much of the same jurisdiction as religious court with respect to issues like custody, alimony, maintenance, or division of property, thus holding the religious courts to exclusive formal control of marriage and divorce.

NOTE

On ratification of the ICCPR, Israel included the following reservation:

> With reference to Article 23 of the Covenant, and any other provision to which
> the present reservation may be relevant, matters of personal status are governed
> in Israel by the religious laws of the parties concerned. To the extent that such law
> is inconsistent with its obligations under the Covenant, Israel reserves the right
> to apply that law.

On ratification of CEDAW, Israel included the following reservation:

> The State of Israel hereby expresses its reservation with regard to Article 16 of the
> Convention, to the extent that laws on personal status which are binding on the
> various religious communities in Israel do not conform with the provisions of
> that article.

NOTE

As indicated in the preceding Comment, different aspects of the Israeli legal and
political system that are unrelated to religious law or belief discriminate between
Jews and Arabs. They bear on the larger issue of treatment of the Jewish and Arab
communities that inhabits personal law as well. Consider the following newspaper
article.

SERGE SCHMEMANN, ISRAELI LEARNS SOME ARE MORE ISRAELI THAN OTHERS
New York Times, March 1, 1998, p. 1

Three years ago, Adel Kaadan saw an ad in the paper for lots on this hilltop near his
village. The view was spectacular, the infrastructure modern, the school good and
the price right. So he came and asked for an application to join the cooperative.
The clerk hemmed and hawed, and finally said no. No Arabs.

'It was a slap in the face,' said Mr. Kaadan, one of about a million Arabs who live
in Israel proper and hold Israeli citizenship, out of a total population of 5.8
million. 'It was an earthquake for me. I work in a military hospital. They let me
save their lives, but to live next to them, no'.

So Mr. Kaadan sued. . . . On the surface, the case does not seem so wrenching.
The community of Katsir is neither particularly religious nor nationalistic. Mr.
Kaadan is hardly a radical or a revolutionary; he speaks fluent Hebrew, and many
of the residents here know him from the hospital.

His quest, however, touches the very heart of the unresolved conflict in Israel's
founding principles, which define the country both as a Jewish state and a democratic state granting equal rights to all citizens. The inherent contradiction . . . has
never been fully tested on the fundamental question of a citizen's right to land. . . .

'This is one of the most difficult and complex judicial decisions that I have ever come across', the president of the Supreme Court, Aharon Barak, declared at a hearing on Feb. 10, pleading with both sides to find a compromise before March 10. 'We are not ready yet for this sort of judicial decision, which has unforseen consequences', he said. 'I suggest that you reach a compromise and avoid a judicial decision, since it is hard to know which way it will go.'

. . .

The case also comes as many Jews in Israel and abroad fervently defend the right of Jews to settle in Arab neighborhoods in East Jerusalem and in the West Bank, though the legal issues are different. These instances have provoked much denunciation of Palestinian laws against selling land to Jews. They have been described as akin to Nazi Germany's 'Nuremberg laws', which restricted the Jews' rights to property, among other things.

Dressed in his hospital whites, Mr. Kaadan chatted cheerily in Hebrew. . . . He said that he had worked side by side with Jews for 23 years as a medical assistant at an Israeli hospital, where he had many Israeli friends, and that he had no problem with the idea of his daughters attending Jewish schools. He insisted that he was simply in search of a better quality of life. . . .

. . .

Technically, Mr. Kaadan sued not to buy property but to lease it. In Israel, 93 percent of the land is owned by the state or by one of two agencies, the Development Authority and the Jewish National Fund. They in turn lease it to other agencies or developers.

In many towns, like Katsir, land is leased to the Jewish Agency, an international, nongovernmental body set up in the 1920s to settle Jews from around the world in Israel. The Jewish Agency then sublets the land to various Jewish cooperatives, which offer long-term leases to residents. Katsir, founded in 1982, is one of 600 to 700 such towns across Israel.

The lawyer handling Mr. Kaadan's suit, Dan Yakir [of the Association for Civil Rights in Israel], said the heart of the case was the fact that the Jewish Agency, under its own bylaws, is required to lease land only to Jews. The civil rights association has asked the Supreme Court to rule that it is illegal for the state to lease lands to an agency that discriminates in its use of the lands. . . . Among the reasons cited is the Israeli Declaration of Independence, which says the state must 'insure complete equality of social and political rights to all inhabitants irrespective of nationality, race or sex'.

. . .

NOTE

On March 8, 2000, the Israeli High Court of Justice decided the case of *Kaaden v. Israel Land Authority* (H.C. 6698/95), growing out of the preceding *New York Times* account. Petitioners were an Arab couple living in an Arab settlement who wished to build a home in Katzir, a communal settlement established in 1982 by the Jewish Agency (via the Israel Land Authority) for such a purpose. The Society accepted only Jewish members and hence refused to accept petitioners, who claimed that the policy constituted discrimination on the basis of religion or nationality that was prohibited by law with respect to state land.

The Court's opinion by President (of the Court) Barak concluded that the principle of equality prohibited the state from distinguishing among citizens on such bases; that principle applied also to allocation of state land. Jews and non-Jews were citizens with equal rights. Nor could the state allocate land to the Jewish Agency knowing that the Agency would permit only Jews to use the land. Even if the Jewish Agency could distinguish between Jews and non-Jews, it could not do so in allocating state land.

The Court's opinion was carefully limited to facts of the immediate case. It did not cover past allocations of state land, and it spoke only to the particular circumstances of the communal settlement of Katzir—that is, not deciding about other types of settlements such as *kibbutzim* and *moshavim* that gave rise to different problems. The state was ordered to consider petitioner's request 'based on the principle of equality', while also 'considering various relevant factors—including those factors affecting the Jewish Agency and the current residents of Katzir,' as well as 'numerous legal issues.' The state was to reach its decision 'with deliberate speed.'

QUESTIONS

1. Clearly religious arrangements of the type imbedded in the Israeli legal system, if instituted with respect to any religion or religions in the United States, would violate the establishment clause of the First Amendment to the Constitution. Does such 'establishment' in Israel, including the prominence of Jewish religion and tradition in basic state symbols, itself indicate that freedom of religion has also been violated? Or do freedom of religion and establishment co-exist in Israel?

2. (a) Suppose that two non-believing Israeli citizens who (by the rules regulating their personal status) are Jews or Muslims wish to marry in a ceremony consistent with their moral beliefs and conscience. Does either couple have a substantial claim that the Israeli legal system denies the couple a human right? What right? Does the ICCPR help? Does CEDAW help? (b) Is the situation the same if, say, an Israeli Jew and Israeli Muslim wish to marry but neither wishes to convert to the other's religion? (c) Suppose that two Israeli Jews who adhere to the beliefs and ritual of Conservative or Reform Judaism wish to be married in Israel by a Conservative or Reform rabbi. What result, and what human rights claim?

3. 'Whatever questions about religion may arise in Israel, equal protection is not among them. With minor exceptions that do not rise to the level of human rights concerns, each religious community is treated equally by provision for its own courts applying its own religious law to personal law matters.' Comment.

4. Does the Israeli system suggest a general, structural conflict between autonomy regimes for religious, linguistic, cultural or other communities, and the rights declared in the ICCPR? If so, how would you describe that conflict? In the light of ICCPR Art. 27 and the general value attached by the human rights movement to protecting diversity and allowing communities to maintain their own distinctive traditions, what suggestions do you have for resolving any such conflict—for example, recommended changes in Israeli legislation?

ADDITIONAL READING

Relevant sources in English include A. Dowty, *The Jewish State a Century Later* (1998); D. Kretzmer, *The Legal Status of the Arabs in Israel* (1990); A. Barak, 'The Constitutionalization of the Israeli Legal System as a Results of the Basic Laws and its Effect on Procedural and Substantive Criminal Law', 31 Israel L. Rev. 3 (1997); A. Maoz, 'Religious Human Rights in the State of Israel', in J. van der Vyver and J. Witte (eds.), *Religious Human Rights in Global Perspective* (1996), at 349; A. Rosen-Zvi, 'Family and Inheritance Law', in A. Shapira and K.C. DeWitt-Arar (eds.), *Introduction to the Law of Israel* (1995), at 75.

COMMENT ON PERSONAL-RELIGIOUS LAW IN INDIA

[Balakrishnan Rajagopal provided invaluable assistance in the research for and writing of this comment and the later comment in this section.]

The problematic relationship between secular law and personal or religious law runs deep in Indian history. The Hindu population forms a vast majority, while the principal minority population of Muslims measure about 10 per cent of the population, or close to 100 million people. Rulers including the colonial British had long recognized that attempts to displace the traditional laws of religious communities with secular law, regional or national, could have explosive consequences. They had generally respected such religiously based laws, at least with respect to the traditional scope of personal law on matters like family (marriage, divorce, and so on) and inheritance. Hence Muslims were governed on such matters by the Shari'a, while Hindus and other communities were governed by their own personal laws.

During the British colonial rule, a secular legal order embracing all of India slowly developed through public laws relating to such typical matters as crimes, property, evidence, and negotiable instruments. At the same time, legislation interfered with religious beliefs on selected practices such as Sati (the self-immolation of a widow on her husband's funeral pyre) and enabled a widow's remarriage. Since there were no separate religious courts, the upshot was that the secular courts applied a substantial body of religious law to people belonging to the different religious communities on a range of matters of personal law. That law remained largely uncodified, in its customary forms. The resulting confusion and contradiction were to some extent resolved for Muslims by the Shariat Act of 1937 under which Muslims were to be governed by religious law on matters related to the family.

The Constitution framed in 1949 soon after India's independence recognized a number of basic human rights, (some of them subject to such traditional limitations as public order and morality). Provisions among the Constitution's 'Fundamental Rights' that are germane to this comment include:

> Art. 14: 'The State Shall not deny to any person equality before the law or the equal protection of the laws'.
> Art. 15: Subject to exceptions permitting the State to make special provision for women and children and to advance backward classes of citizens, the State 'shall not discriminate against any citizen on grounds only of religion, race, caste, sex, place of birth or any of them'.
> Art. 25: All persons 'are equally entitled to freedom of conscience and the right freely to profess, practise and propagate religion'.
> Art. 29: Any section of citizens 'having a distinct language, script or culture of its own shall have the right to conserve the same'.

The Constitution also took a step toward building a more inclusive national, secular legal order by declaring in non-binding language in Article 44 that the state should 'endeavor to secure for the citizens a uniform civil code throughout the territory of India'. The debates in the Constituent Assembly on the draft of (what became) Article 44 anticipated the difficulties to follow, as some members of the Assembly argued for a qualification to the effect that no community of people would be required to surrender its personal law, a part of its religion and culture. The argument was that the new secular state should not interfere with the way of life and religion of the people. The rhetoric of 'freedom' to practice one's own religion figures in the debates, and there were warnings of serious unrest if such an attempt were made.

In general, these debates underscored the tension between the universalizing rhetoric of the Hindu members and the relativistic rhetoric of the Muslim members. But some speeches observed that many in the Hindu majority would oppose a mandatory and inclusive uniform civil code displacing (Hindu) personal law on matters like inheritance, a personal law which gave women a subordinate status. There were strong challenges to all such 'isolationist' positions and pleas for restricting religion to its 'legitimate' sphere that didn't interfere with the evolution of a strong, consolidated Indian nation.

The dual secular-religious structure of Indian law was reinforced in the post-independence period. Hindu customary law was codified in the 1950s, while secular marriage laws were enacted which permitted (but did not require) 'civil' marriages for interreligious couples. The Special Marriages Act of 1954 permitted application to interreligious marriage of the secular Indian Succession Act of 1925, provided that parties performed their marriages under the Act.

In general, persons within the same religious community who married became inescapably subject to their religion's personal law. But exceptions developed, and the situation today is complex. To simplify: (1) Any two persons, irrespective of religion, can marry under the Special Marriage Act of 1954. This is a civil secular marriage by registration before a state official. Secular law governs family matters like divorce. (2) But the legal effects of such a marriage on matters like succession differ for individuals depending on whether one party or both of the married couple are Hindus. For example, if both are Hindus, they are governed by the Hindu Succession Act, 1955, whereas if one or both are non-Hindus, they are governed by the Indian Succession Act, 1955. But relatively few marriages are performed under the Special Marriages Act of 1954.

The consequence of these original provisions for the new state and a half century of changes is that the legal system has remained bifurcated, with the secular order including (as relevant to family matters) the criminal law, criminal procedure law, transfer of property law, and special laws regulating matters like inter-religious marriages, as well as marriages between couples belonging to the same religion who wish to be significantly exempted from their religious laws. Tensions over this situation grew with the resurgent Hindu nationalism of the 1980s and the political strategies of the Muslim leadership.

It was in this climate that the Supreme Court of India decided in 1985 the following case.

MOHAMMED AHMED KHAN V. SHAH BANO BEGUM
Supreme Court of India (1985), 2 Sup. Ct. Cases 556

[In this opinion, the Supreme Court affirmed a judgment of the High Court awarding Shah Bano, the former wife of Mohammed Ahmed Khan, a monthly maintenance from him of Rs. 179.20 (the equivalent at the time of about $14). The application was brought under Section 125 of the 1973 Code of Criminal Procedure, a national law. That section covers former wives like Shah Bano who had not remarried and were unable to maintain themselves. It authorizes the court to issue an order, backed by civil and criminal sanctions, for a monthly allowance. Such criminal procedure was faster and more efficient than the alternative civil-process route. Unlike a number of civil laws like the Hindu Adoptions and Maintenance Act, Section 125 was open to women of all religions. Since the adoption in 1872 of the Criminal Procedure Code from which the 1973 Code was drawn, divorced women of all faiths had regularly applied for maintenance under Section 125.

The panel of five judges (all of whom were Hindu) of the Supreme Court of India decided unanimously. The excerpts from the opinion of Chief Justice Chandrachud, and the Comment following the opinion, use two terms that require definition. *Iddat* refers to a period of three months following a divorce, while *Mahr* refers to a dower or marriage settlement.]

1. This appeal does not involve any question of constitutional importance but, that is not to say that it does not involve any question of importance. Some questions which arise under the ordinary civil and criminal law are of a far-reaching significance to large segments of society which have been traditionally subjected to unjust treatment. Women are one such segment. '*Na stree swatantra-*

marhati' said Manu, the Law giver: The woman does not deserve independence. And, it is alleged that the 'fatal point in Islam is the degradation of woman'. To the Prophet is ascribed the statement, hopefully wrongly, that 'Woman was made from a crooked rib, and if you try to bend it straight, it will break; therefore treat your wives kindly'.

2. This appeal, arising out of an application filed by a divorced Muslim woman for maintenance under Section 125 of the Code of Criminal Procedure, raises a straightforward issue which is of common interest not only to Muslim women, not only to women generally but, to all those who, aspiring to create an equal society of men and women, lure themselves into the belief that mankind has achieved a remarkable degree of progress in that direction. . . .

3. Does the Muslim Personal Law impose no obligation upon the husband to provide for the maintenance of his divorced wife? Undoubtedly, the Muslim husband enjoys the privilege of being able to discard his wife whenever he chooses to do so, for reasons good, bad or indifferent. Indeed, for no reason at all. But, is the only price of that privilege the dole of pittance during the period of iddat? And, is the law so ruthless in its inequality that, no matter how much the husband pays for the maintenance of his divorced wife during the period of iddat, the mere fact that he has paid something, no matter how little, absolves him for ever from the duty of paying adequately so as to enable her to keep her body and soul together? Then again, is there any provision in the Muslim Personal Law under which a sum is payable to the wife 'on divorce'? These are some of the important, though agonising, questions which arise for our decision.

. . .

7. Under Section 125(1)(a), a person who, having sufficient means, neglects or refuses to maintain his wife who is unable to maintain herself, can be asked by the court to pay a monthly maintenance to her at a rate not exceeding five hundred rupees. By clause (b) of the Explanation to Section 125(1), 'wife' includes a divorced woman who has not remarried. These provisions are too clear and precise to admit of any doubt or refinement. The religion professed by a spouse or by the spouses has no place in the scheme of these provisions. Whether the spouses are Hindus or Muslims, Christians or Parsis, pagans or heathens, is wholly irrelevant in the application of these provisions. The reason for this is axiomatic, in the sense that Section 125 is a part of the Code of Criminal Procedure, not of the civil laws which define and govern the rights and obligations of the parties belonging to particular religions, like the Hindu Adoptions and Maintenance Act, the Shariat, or the Parsi Matrimonial Act. Section 125 was enacted in order to provide a quick and summary remedy to a class of persons who are unable to maintain themselves. What difference would it then make as to what is the religion professed by the neglected wife, child or parent? Neglect by a person of sufficient means to maintain these and the inability of those persons to maintain themselves are the objective criteria which determine the applicability of Section 125. Such provisions, which are essentially of a prophylactic nature, cut across the barriers of religion. True, that they do not supplant the personal law of the parties but, equally, the religion professed by the parties or the state of the personal law by which they are governed, cannot have any repercussion on the applicability of such laws unless,

within the framework of the Constitution, their application is restricted to a defined category of religious groups or classes. The liability imposed by Section 125 to maintain close relatives who are indigent is founded upon the individual's obligation to the society to prevent vagrancy and destitution. That is the moral edict of the law and morality cannot be clubbed with religion. . . .
. . .

9. Under Section 488 of the Code of 1898, the wife's right to maintenance depended upon the continuance of her married status. Therefore, that right could be defeated by the husband by divorcing her unilaterally as under the Muslim Personal Law, or by obtaining a decree of divorce against her under the other systems of law. It was in order to remove this hardship that the Joint Committee recommended that the benefit of the provisions regarding maintenance should be extended to a divorced woman, so long as she has not remarried after the divorce.
. . .

10. The conclusion that the right conferred by Section 125 can be exercised irrespective of the personal law of the parties, is fortified, especially in regard to Muslims, by the provision contained in the Explanation to the second proviso to Section 125(3) of the Code. That proviso says that if the husband offers to maintain his wife on condition that she should live with him, and she refuses to live with him, the Magistrate may consider any grounds of refusal stated by her, and may make an order of maintenance notwithstanding the offer of the husband, if he is satisfied that there is a just ground for passing such an order. According to the Explanation to the proviso:

> If a husband has contracted marriage with another woman or keeps a mistress, it shall be considered to be just ground for his wife's refusal to live with him.

It is too well-known that 'A Mahomadan may have as many as four wives at the same time but not more. If he marries a fifth wife when he has already four, the marriage is not void, but merely irregular'. (See *Mulla's Mahomedan Law*, Eighteenth Edition, paragraph 255, page 285, quoting *Baillie's Digest of Moohummudan Laws*; and *Ameer Ali's Mahomedan Law*, Fifth Edition, Vol. II, page 280.) The explanation confers upon the wife the right to refuse to live with her husband if he contracts another marriage, leave alone 3 or 4 other marriages. It shows, unmistakably, that Section 125 overrides the personal law, if there is any conflict between the two.
. . .

12. The next logical step to take is to examine the question, on which considerable argument has been advanced before us, whether there is any conflict between the provisions of Section 125 and those of the Muslim Personal Law on the liability of the Muslim husband to provide for the maintenance of his divorced wife.

13. The contention of the husband and of the interveners who support him is that, under the Muslim Personal Law, the liability of the husband to maintain a divorced wife is limited to the period of iddat. In support of this proposition, they rely upon the statement of law on the point contained in certain text books. In *Mulla's Mahomedan Law* (Eighteenth Edition, para 279, page 301), there is a

statement to the effect that, 'After divorce, the wife is entitled to maintenance during the period of iddat'.

. . .

Tyabji's Muslim Law (Fourth Edition, para 304, pages 268–269), contains the statement that:

> On the expiration of the iddat after talaq, the wife's right to maintenance ceases, whether based on the Muslim Law, or on an order under the Criminal Procedure Code.

. . .

14. These statements in the text books are inadequate to establish the proposition that the Muslim husband is not under an obligation to provide for the maintenance of his divorced wife, *who is unable to maintain herself*. One must have regard to the entire conspectus of the Muslim Personal Law in order to determine the extent, both in quantum and in duration, of the husband's liability to provide for the maintenance of an indigent wife who has been divorced by him. . . .

15. There can be no greater authority on this question than the Holy Quran, 'the Quran, the Sacred Book of Islam, comprises in its 114 Suras or chapters, the total of revelations believed to have been communicated to Prophet Muhammed, as a final expression of God's will'. (*The Quran*—Interpreted by Arthur J. Arberry.) Verses (Aiyats) 241 and 242 of the Quran show that there is an obligation on Muslim husbands to provide for their divorced wives. The Arabic version of those Aiyats and their English translation are reproduced below:

. . .

18. In *The Running Commentary of the Holy Quran* (1964 Edition) by Dr Allamah Khadim Rahmani Nuri, Aiyat 241 is translated thus:

> 241: And for the divorced woman (also) a provision (should be made) with fairness (in addition to her dower); (This is) a duty (incumbent) on the reverent.

19. In *The Meaning of the Glorious Quran, Text and Explanatory Translation,* by Marmaduke Pickthall, (Taj Company Ltd., Karachi), Aiyat 241 is translated thus:

> 241: For divorced women a provision in kindness: A duty for those who ward off (evil).

20. Finally, in *The Quran Interpreted* by Arthur J. Arberry, Aiyat 241 is translated thus:

> 241: There shall be for divorced women provision honourable—an obligation on the godfearing.
> So God makes clear His signs for you: Happily you will understand.

. . .

22. These Aiyats leave no doubt that the Quran imposes an obligation on the Muslim husband to make provision for or to provide maintenance to the divorced wife. The contrary argument does less than justice to the teachings of the Quran. As observed by Mr M. Hidayatullah in his introduction to *Mulla's Mahomedan*

Law, the Quran is Al-furqan, that is, one showing truth from falsehood and right from wrong.

. . .

27. It is contended on behalf of the appellant that the proceedings of the Rajya Sabha dated December 18, 1973 (volume 86, column 186), when the bill which led to the Code of 1973 was on the anvil, would show that the intention of the Parliament was to leave the provision of the Muslim Personal Law untouched. In this behalf, reliance is placed on the following statement made by Shri Ram Niwas Mirdha, the then Minister of State, Home Affairs:

> Dr Vyas very learnedly made certain observations that a divorced wife under the Muslim law deserves to be treated justly and she should get what is her equitable or legal due. Well, I will not go into this, but say that we would not like to interfere with the customary law of the Muslims through the Criminal Procedure Code. If there is a demand for change in the Muslim Personal Law, it should actually come from the Muslim Community itself and we should wait for the Muslim public opinion on these matters to crystalize before we try to change this customary right or make changes in their personal law. Above all, this is hardly, the place where we could do so. But as I tried to explain, the provision in the Bill is an advance over the previous situation. Divorced women have been included and brought within the ambit of Clause 125, but a limitation is being imposed by this amendment to Clause 127, namely, that the maintenance orders would cease to operate after the amounts due to her under the personal law are paid to her. This is a healthy compromise between what has been termed a conservative interpretation of law or a concession to conservative public opinion and liberal approach to the problem. We have made an advance and not tried to transgress what are the personal rights of Muslim women. So this, I think, should satisfy hon. Members that whatever advance we have made is in the right direction and it should be welcomed.

28. It does appear from this speech that the Government did not desire to interfere with the personal law of the Muslims through the Criminal Procedure Code. It wanted the Muslim community to take the lead and the Muslim public opinion to crystalise on the reforms in their personal law. However, we are not concerned with the question whether the Government did or did not desire to bring about changes in the Muslim Personal Law by enacting Sections 125 and 127 of the Code. As we have said earlier and, as admitted by the Minister, the Government did introduce such a change by defining the expression 'wife' to include a divorced wife. . . .

29. It must follow from this discussion, unavoidably a little too long, that the judgments of this Court in *Bai Tahira* (Krishna Iyer, J., Tulzapurkar, J. and Pathak, J.) and *Fuzlunbi* (Krishna Iyer, J., one of us, Chinnappa Reddy, J. and A. P. Sen, J.) are correct. Justice Krishna Iyer who spoke for the Court in both these cases, relied greatly on the teleological and schematic method of interpretation so as to advance the purpose of the law. These constructional techniques have their own importance in the interpretation of statutes meant to ameliorate the conditions of suffering sections of the society. We have attempted to show that taking the language of the statute as one finds it, there is no escape from the conclusion that a

divorced Muslim wife is entitled to apply for maintenance under Section 125 and that, Mahr is not a sum which, under the Muslim Personal Law, is payable on divorce.

. . .

31. It is a matter of deep regret that some of the interveners who supported the appellant, took up an extreme position by displaying an unwarranted zeal to defeat the right to maintenance of women who are unable to maintain themselves. The written submissions of the All India Muslim Personal Law Board have gone to the length of asserting that it is irrelevant to inquire as to how a Muslim divorcee should maintain herself. The facile answer of the Board is that the Personal Law has devised the system of Mahr to meet the requirements of women and if a woman is indigent, she must look to her relations, including nephews and cousins, to support her. This is a most unreasonable view of law as well as life. . . .

32. It is also a matter of regret that Article 44 of our Constitution has remained a dead letter. It provides that 'The State shall endeavour to secure for the citizens a uniform civil code throughout the territory of India'. There is no evidence of any official activity for framing a common civil code for the country. A belief seems to have gained ground that it is for the Muslim community to take a lead in the matter of reforms of their personal law. A common Civil Code will help the cause of national integration by removing disparate loyalties to laws which have conflicting ideologies. No community is likely to bell the cat by making gratuitous concessions on this issue. It is the State which is charged with the duty of securing a uniform civil code for the citizens of the country and, unquestionably, it has the legislative competence to do so. A counsel in the case whispered, somewhat audibly, that legislative competence is one thing, the political courage to use that competence is quite another. We understand the difficulties involved in bringing persons of different faiths and persuasions on a common platform. But, a beginning has to be made if the Constitution is to have any meaning. Inevitably, the role of the reformer has to be assumed by the courts because, it is beyond the endurance of sensitive minds to allow injustice to be suffered when it is so palpable. But piecemeal attempts of courts to bridge the gap between personal laws cannot take the place of a common Civil Code. Justice to all is a far more satisfactory way of dispensing justice than justice from case to case.

33. Dr Tahir Mahmood in his book *Muslim Personal Law* (1977 Edition, pages 200–202), has made a powerful plea for framing a uniform Civil Code for all citizens of India. He says: 'In pursuance of the goal of secularism, the State must stop administering religion-based personal laws'. He wants the lead to come from the majority community but, we should have thought that, lead or no lead, the State must act. It would be useful to quote the appeal made by the author to the Muslim community:

Instead of wasting their energies in exerting theological and political pressure in order to secure an 'immunity' for their traditional personal law from the state's legislative jurisdiction, the Muslims will do well to begin exploring and demonstrating how the true Islamic laws, purged of their time-worn and anachronistic interpretations, can enrich the common civil code of India.

. . .

34. Before we conclude, we would like to draw attention to the Report of the Commission on Marriage and Family Laws, which was appointed by the Government of Pakistan by a Resolution dated August 4, 1955. The answer of the Commission to Question 5 (page 1215 of the Report) is that

> a large number of middle-aged women who are being divorced without rhyme or reason should not be thrown on the streets without a roof over their heads and without any means of sustaining themselves and their children.

The Report concludes thus:

> In the words of Allama Iqbal, 'the question which is likely to confront Muslim countries in the near future, is whether the law of Islam is capable of evolution— a question which will require great intellectual effort, and is sure to be answered in the affirmative'.

35. For these reasons, we dismiss the appeal and confirm the judgment of the High Court. The appellant will pay the costs of the appeal to respondent 1, which we quantify at rupees ten thousand. It is needless to add that it would be open to the respondent to make an application under Section 127(1) of the Code for increasing the allowance of maintenance granted to her on proof of a change in the circumstances as envisaged by that section.

COMMENT ON AFTERMATH OF SHAH BANO

Within the divided Muslim community, the 'progressives' supported the judgment while the 'fundamentalists' opposed it. A statutory body, the Muslim Personal Law Board, started a campaign for legislation to reverse the ruling. It should be noted that, under great pressure from her community, Shah Bano retracted her involvement in the case and made a public statement rejecting the judgment of the Court and disassociating herself from it.

The ruling Congress Party, concluding that the judgment was a political liability for it, introduced a 1986 bill, the Muslim Women (Protection of Rights in Divorce) Act, that effectively reversed the judgment. That Act required a divorced Muslim woman's former husband only to return the Mahr and pay maintenance during the period of iddat. Thereafter, the maintenance ordered by a court would become the responsibility of the woman's children, parents, or certain relatives, or ultimately of the administrators of Muslim trust funds.

This Act, which has been challenged on constitutional grounds, in fact intensified rather than resolved the problems created by the Shah Bano judgment. The Indian government continues the process of drafting a uniform civil code covering these matters to satisfy feminists and progressives, while the Hindu political right has also pressed on the issue of a uniform civil code for its own political reasons. Leaders of the Hindu right talked of the offensive stand of the Muslim community which opposed the Shah Bano judgment, and argued that the uniform civil code was a vital means of protecting the national sovereignty.

Several cases in the Indian judiciary subsequent to *Shah Bano* have raised issues of equality versus culture. In *Sarla Mugdal v. Union of India and Ors.*, (1995) 3 Sup. Ct. Cases 635, the Court held invalid the second marriage of a Muslim when the first marriage had not been dissolved, although pursuant to Islamic law the second marriage was valid. The Court stated:

> Those who preferred to remain in India after the partition, fully knew that the Indian leaders did not believe in two-nation or three-nation theory and that in the Indian Republic, there was to be only one Nation—the Indian Nation—and no community could claim to remain a separate entity on the basis of religion. In this view of the matters, no community can oppose the introduction of a uniform civil code for all the citizens in the territory of India. *(at 650).*

The Court also directed the Government to take steps to implement Article 44 by preparing a uniform civil code.

In *Ahmedabad Women Action Group and Ors. v. Union of India*, (1997) Sup. Ct. Cases 573, the Court backed off from the strong language of the preceding case and dismissed constitutional challenges to the Muslim practices of polygamy and triple talaq (a form of divorce under the Shariat that allows the husband to annul a marriage upon proclaiming talaq three times). The Court stated that the case presented only 'issues of State policies with which the Court will not not ordinarily have any concern'.

NOTE

India ratified CEDAW subject to the following reservation:

> With regard to articles 5(a) and 16(1) of [CEDAW]. the Government of the Republic of India declares that it shall abide by and ensure these provisions in conformity with its policy of non-interference in the personal affairs of any Community without its initiative and consent.

QUESTIONS

1. From the perspective of human rights concerns, identify the significant distinctions between Israel and India with respect to their systems of personal-religious law and the relationships in each state between that law and national civil law and national courts. Is the 'national' always identified with the secular, or with the 'universal' perspective on human rights, while the separate bodies of personal law are identified with the religious and cultural relativism?

2. Broadly speaking what are the similarities and differences between the arguments advanced by members of the Hindu and Muslim communities in the legislative and public debates over the issues presented? What differences of viewpoint appear within each community? What conceptions of the nation, and of the secular as opposed to the religious, emerge?

3. Do the cited provisions of the Indian Constitution seem to provide a clear direction for the Court to follow, or do they further complicate the issues?

4. Since the Court in *Shah Bano* decides in favour of the application of the national law, why does it examine the case under the Muslim Personal Law as well? How do you assess that discussion?

5. Theories of right, or human rights in general, do not figure in the opinion. What international human rights not discussed by the Court might have been advanced by Shah Bano in support of her claim for maintenance under the national law? What provisions of what human rights treaties could have been relied on?

6. The Act succeeding and displacing the Shao Bano opinion provides an option for parties, by mutual consent, to be governed by Section 125 of the Criminal Procedure Code. Does this option resolve any problems that you may have with the Act? How realistic do you think it will be in practice?

ADDITIONAL READING

On Indian personal-religious law, see: *Mayne's Hindu Law and Usage* (13th edn 1991); Mulla *Principles of Hindu Law* (16th edn 1990); N. Purohit, *Principles of Mohammedan Law* (1995). On family law generally, see F.C.V. Subba Rao, *Family Law in India: Hindu Law and Mohammedan Law* (7th edn 1995).

On religion and human rights generally, see: K. Boyle and J. Sheen (eds.), *Freedom of Religion and Belief: A World Report* (1997); M. Evans, *Religious Liberty and International Law in Europe* (1997); C. Gustafson and P. Juviler (eds.), *Religion and Human Rights: Competing Claims?* (1999); I. Bloom, J.P. Martin and W. Proudfoot (eds.), *Religious Diversity and Human Rights* (1996); G. Robbers (ed.), *State and Church in the European Union* (1996); M. Marty and R. Scott Appelby (eds.), *Accounting for Fundamentalisms* (1994); A.E. Mayer, *Islam and Human Rights: Tradition and Politics* (3rd edn 1999); M. McConnell, 'Religious Freedom at a Crossroads', 59 U. Cal. L. Rev. 115 (1992).

C. CHILDREN

The UN Convention on the Rights of the Child (CRC) was adopted by the UN General Assembly on November 20, 1989 and entered into force in record time on September 2, 1990. As of January 1, 2000 it had been ratified by 191 States. Only Somalia and the United States remain outside the treaty regime. This development is all the more remarkable in view of the relative novelty of the concept of children's rights, and the fact that the CRC is the most comprehensive single treaty in the human rights field. Moreover, it was ratified by a significant number of states that had previously failed to ratify the two major Covenants. The Convention's coverage is considerable: it applies to 'every human being below the age of 18 years unless, under the law applicable to the child, majority is attained earlier' (Art. 1), thus putting the burden on the state to justify instances in which a lower age limit is prescribed.

The following readings trace the process through which the treaty was drafted, and then consider some objections that have been raised by conservative groups in the United States and their counterparts elsewhere, as well as by commentators speaking from a Third World perspective. The readings then examine two major issues in relation to which children's rights have played an especially important role in recent years: corporal punishment and the use of children as soldiers.

You should now read the excerpts from the CRC in the Annex on Documents.

NIGEL CANTWELL, THE ORIGINS, DEVELOPMENT AND SIGNIFICANCE OF THE UNITED NATIONS CONVENTION ON THE RIGHTS OF THE CHILD

in S. Detrick (ed.), The United Nations Convention on the Rights of the Child: A Guide to the 'Travaux Préparatoires' (1992), at 19

The first mention of the 'rights of the child' as such in an internationally recognised text dates back to 1924, when the Assembly of the League of Nations passed a resolution endorsing the Declaration of the Rights of the Child promulgated the previous year by the Council of the non-governmental 'Save the Children International Union'. The League's members were invited 'to be guided by the principles' of this five-point document, which became known as the Declaration of Geneva and retained currency for a quarter of a century. In 1948, it served as the basis for a slightly expanded, seven-point Declaration adopted by the General Assembly of the newly-constituted United Nations. Then came the Declaration of the Rights of the Child promulgated by the U.N. General Assembly on November 20, 1959, and which is still valid today. It was this text that was the springboard for the initiative to draft a convention.

The essential theme underlying all of these non-binding declarations was that children need special protection and priority care. This reflected the overwhelming concerns of the first half of the twentieth century as regards children, particularly because of the realities and ramifications of the two World Wars . . .

In the 'North', the late Sixties and the Seventies witnessed progressive but rapid change in these attitudes. There was also a great deal of confusion as to what 'the rights of the child' really implied, despite the tentative definition given in the 1959 Declaration. . . . Were 'children's rights' to be seen in opposition to those of adults? Did they involve 'pupil power' and/or autonomy from parents? In the Seventies, such were the questions being asked about the rights of the child, which was at that time aptly termed 'a concept in search of a definition'.

. . .

[In 1978, Poland tabled a proposed convention, modelled closely on the 1959 Declaration so as to build on the existing consensus. It failed to gain support. Instead, an open-ended Working Group of the UN Commission on Human Rights was established, and met from 1979 until 1988 when the draft of the present Convention was completed and sent to the General Assembly for adoption. Since it was 'open-ended', any of the 43 states then represented on the Commission could participate, and other states could send observers who could make statements, as could intergovernmental organizations and nongovernmental organizations in consultative status with ECOSOC.

The Working Group acted on the basis of consensus; no proposal was taken to a vote. This led to a very lengthy process, and the consensus system 'resulted in the abandonment of certain proposals, notwithstanding the support of a clear majority'. One casualty was a proposal to limit medical experimentation on children, for no formulation could be found to satisfy all delegations.]

Another major factor which affected the functioning of the Working Group, more especially in its early years, was the political climate. The change in the atmosphere of the meetings as of 1985, when East-West relations began to thaw in earnest, was remarkable. It contributed greatly to the Working Group being able gradually to move into top gear from then on, since it reduced to a minimum the purely political statements and negotiation that had previously been a hallmark of the discussions.

. . .

Participants in the Drafting Process

The hesitation that characterised governments' reactions to the proposal for a convention on the rights of the child was reflected in the level of their participation. During the early years, never more than thirty countries took part in meetings of the Working Group, rising to forty as of the mid-Eighties. The industrialised countries were significantly over-represented in all stages. Fears that the outcome would be a heavily Northern-oriented text were widespread and justified. They were attenuated only by particularly active participation on the part of certain developing countries (Algeria, Argentina, Senegal and Venezuela were remarkable in this respect) as well as, in 1988, a sudden last-minute surge of delegates from the South, many from States with Islamic law.

A key feature in the successful functioning of the Working Group—for it was indeed successful, and increasingly so as time went on—was continuity in the composition of government delegations.

. . .

If the active participation of most individual governments generally left much to be desired, the presence and impact of intergovernmental organisations can only be qualified as scandalously weak. To be sure, the International Labour Organisation made certain it was represented in particular during discussions on the child labour article (see Article 32), and UNICEF finally realised the importance of the future Convention for its work, sending strong delegations as of 1986. But the United Nations Development Programme (UNDP), United Nations

Educational, Scientific and Cultural Organisation (UNESCO), the United Nations High Commissioner for Refugees (UNHCR) and, most notably, the World Health Organisation (WHO) (whose definition of 'health' means that a wide range of the Convention's provisions are directly germane to its mandate) were rarely to be found. Their potential technical contribution would no doubt have helped to resolve, more efficiently at the very least, many of the substantive problems that came up during the debates. Their studied absence, on the other hand, remains one of the great mysteries of the drafting process.

The NGO Contribution

As noted previously, the third category of participants, in addition to governments and intergovernmental organisations, was composed of recognized non-governmental organisations (NGOs). It is generally acknowledged in the international community that the NGOs had a direct and indirect impact on this Convention that is without parallel in the history of drafting international instruments.

. . .

[In 1983 an NGO Ad Hoc Group was created in order to develop joint proposals and ensure greater coherence among the NGOs.]

. . .

Throughout the remainder of the drafting process, the NGO Ad Hoc Group submitted annual reports to the Working Group, setting out and explaining their proposals and concerns. In addition, they began holding briefing sessions for government representatives as well as, at a more general level, producing materials and organising meetings to arouse awareness about the future Convention and foster understanding of its importance.

The extent of the overall NGO contribution is, understandably, by no means always clear from the travaux préparatoires. The success of the NGOs' activities to promote support for the Convention was, for example, undoubtedly instrumental in getting many governments to take the drafting process more seriously, and in giving the Working Group a renewed sense of purpose. This was all the more so when, in 1987, the NGO Group joined with UNICEF in publicly promoting the objective of having the Convention ready for adoption by the U.N. General Assembly in 1989. Furthermore, the Group's proposals were increasingly being presented by government delegates during the Working Group meetings, rather than directly by the NGOs themselves. None of these instances of NGO impact could be reflected in the reports of the Working Group. However, reviewing the final text of the Convention, the Ad Hoc Group was able to identify at least thirteen substantive articles or paragraphs for whose inclusion in the text the NGOs had been primarily responsible.

. . .

Issues of Controversy

Whilst every paragraph of every article was the subject of debate—sometimes protracted—a number of substantive issues broached in the draft Convention caused major controversy.

The first of these in fact aroused disagreement because it was not broached: the issue in question was the definition of the minimum age of the child. There were of course two groups of countries with irreconcilably opposed standpoints as to the moment when childhood begins—at conception or at birth. Substantive discussion was pointless. Neither side could ever agree to what would have been a definition of the child in Article 1 essentially either permitting or outlawing abortion. Nor could any formulation be found for that article which would allow each society to adopt its own standard in this regard. Yet there was just one relevant point on which all could agree: that, as stated in the Preamble of the 1959 Declaration on the Rights of the Child, the child 'needs special safeguards and care, including appropriate legal protection, both before as well as after birth'. Such legal protection could include, but would not require, the prohibition of abortion. Not without difficulty, the Working Group finally came to a consensus that explicit reference to the formulation in the Declaration would be made in the Preamble to the Convention, and that there would be no mention of minimum age in Article 1.

The second major problem area concerned freedom of religion. The initial formulation of Article 14, modelled on the text of Article 18 of the International Covenant on Civil and Political Rights, included reference to 'the freedom to have or to adopt a religion . . . of his choice'. It was subsequently pointed out in the strongest terms that, under Islam, a child does not have the right to choose another religion, and that the right contained in the Covenant could only be held to apply to adults. This put the drafters in a delicate situation. What attitude was to be taken towards the elimination of a right of the child in the future Convention which was already conferred by a well-established international human rights instrument without restriction as to the age of the beneficiary? Reluctantly, in the end, the proponents of retaining the full right agreed to drop all reference to choice, 'in the spirit of compromise'.

The third issue that provoked considerable problems was adoption. . . .

The final example of controversial issues concerns the age at which children should be permitted to take part in armed conflict (see Article 38). There is little doubt that this was, and remains, the most hotly-debated question of the drafting process. The NGOs and many governments fought tirelessly for years to ensure that, even if it had to be conceded that children could be recruited into the armed forces as of age fifteen, at least they be prohibited from taking a direct part in hostilities until they had reached eighteen years. The final consensus was uncomfortable to say the least. At the last meeting of the Working Group, the United States delegate—ostensibly alone but clearly benefiting from the silent support of several other delegations—categorically refused to give such protection to the fifteen to seventeen age-group. . . .

. . .

At last a Convention on the Rights of the Child

By its genesis, scope, content and very existence, this Convention ranks as a landmark . . . .

. . .

The Convention is extraordinarily comprehensive in scope. It covers all the traditionally-defined areas of human rights—civil, political, economic, social and cultural. In doing so, however, it has shied away from distinguishing between these areas and, on the contrary, has happily tended to underscore the indivisibility, mutual reinforcement and equal importance of all rights. (The only exception to this is the explicit mention of 'economic, social and cultural rights' in Article 4). In order precisely to avoid that traditional categorization, with its negative historical connotations, many commentators have preferred to describe and analyse the scope of the Convention in terms of rights relating to 'protection', 'provision' (of services and material benefits) and 'participation' (in society and in decisions affecting the child him- or herself)—the three Ps.

. . .

[T]he Convention constitutes a major leap forward in standard-setting on children's issues. On a general level, we can note the introduction of 'participation' rights which had never before been incorporated in a child-focused international instrument. More specifically, the following are among the most notable improvements and innovations which the Convention sets out:

> Best interests of the child; primary consideration (see Article 3): This article is fundamental to the whole Convention in that it stipulates that the child's best interests must be a 'primary consideration' in all actions concerning children . . .
>
> Preservation of identity (see Article 8): . . . The Working Group included this provision at the suggestion of Argentina in the light of mass 'disappearances' of children whose identity papers had been deliberately falsified and family ties arbitrarily severed.
>
> Child's right to express opinions (see Article 12): The right of the child not only to express an opinion but also to have that opinion taken into account in matters that affect him or her is a highly significant recognition of the need to give children a greater say in their own lives.
>
> Prevention of abuse by those having care (see Article 19): The feature of special interest in this article is the emphasis placed on the prevention of intra-familial abuse and neglect, which has never previously figured in a binding instrument.
>
> Adoption (see Article 21): this article is of special importance because of the emphasis it places on the need for strong safeguards surrounding the adoption process—especially as regards inter-country adoption. . . .
> . . .
> Health and access to care (see Article 24): . . . [T]his article stands out because it mentions—for the first time in a binding international instrument—a state obligation to work towards the abolition of traditional practices, such as female circumcision and preferential treatment of male children. . . .
> . . .
> Torture/Capital punishment (see Article 37): The aspect of special note in

this article is the inclusion of the principle that deprivation of liberty must be looked upon as a last resort and, if it is nonetheless ordered, must be limited to the shortest possible period of time.

. . .

Treatment in penal matters (see Article 40): . . . [I]nternational norms in this sphere have been significantly upgraded.

. . .

Dissemination of the principles and provision of the Convention (see Article 42): . . . it is the first time that specific and explicit recognition has been given to the need for children themselves to receive information on their rights.

VANESSA PUPAVAC, THE INFANTILIZATION OF THE SOUTH AND THE UN CONVENTION ON THE RIGHTS OF THE CHILD

Universty of Nottingham Centre for Human Rights Law, Human Rights Law Review, March 1998, at 3

To question children's rights has been described as a modern-day heresy. Few writers have critically examined the implications of the UN Convention on the Rights of the Child . . . The common assumption is that the institutionalization of children's rights at the international level can only result in the improvement of the lives of children around the world. The provisions of the Convention are not felt to be problematic. . . .

The universalization of Western childhood

. . . [To] what extent is its approach appropriate to ameliorating the plight of children? Whilst there is an international consensus of concern for children, that does not mean that there is a consensus about the policies needed to bring about an improvement in child welfare. The experience and perceptions of childhood vary fundamentally in different countries, but the Convention assumes a model of childhood that is universally applicable 'based on the notion that children everywhere have the same basic needs and that these can be met with a standard set of responses'. . . .

An examination of the provisions of the Convention reveals that the universal standards of the Convention are based on a Western concept of childhood and Western social policies which emphasize the role of individual causations and professional interventions and de-emphasize the influence of the wider social, economic, political and cultural circumstances.

. . .

The Western model of childhood is based on the idea that children should be protected from the adult world. The Western conception of childhood as a time of play and training for adulthood has become the universal standard to be enforced under the Convention to the age of eighteen. The Western 'protective view of childhood', as Aron Bar-On explains, 'has resulted from a combination of circumstances that are not part of the experience of most countries in the South'. This construction of childhood arose in the particular circumstances of the Northern developed countries late in their industrialization which consequently led to the removal of children from the labour market into education. However, the rationale of the Convention is that, irrespective of the level of development of a country, children can have a childhood by empowering children with rights and re-orientating social policy to ensure that the best interests of the child are of primary consideration. In other words, the Convention requires the universal attainment of a modern Western childhood without the industrialization and development that was considered a prerequisite to this modern construction of childhood as a period of dependency and protection.

Childhood remains a luxury that is unrealisable for the majority of the population in developing countries. Children in developing countries usually have to take on adult roles at a much earlier age than in industrial countries. . . .

. . .

Infantilization of the South

. . .

The institutionalizing and globalizing of Western models of childhood under the Convention means that the experience of childhood in developing countries is outlawed. For example, children in many parts of the world have to act as adults, commonly as child soldiers or child labourers, which is condemned by proponents of children's rights. As Allison James points out, the consequence of the setting of specific age limits for children, prescribing their participation in some spheres whilst proscribing others 'means that those children whose actions take place outside the limits set for "childhood" become pathologized' and that 'the Western ideology of childhood as a period of happiness and innocence works to exclude those for whom it is not'. Southern societies are judged as having violated their children because the lives of the children do not conform to the image of child-hood held in the West.

. . . The singling out of the plight of children implicitly blames the adult population for their suffering. Their plight becomes a sign of the moral failings of their society. The imperative of the best interests of the child gives outside agencies the legitimacy and powers to intervene. Thus Southern societies through the failure to comply with Western childhoods become permanent objects of outside intervention. In other words, the discourse on children's rights infantilizes the South.

. . .

. . . The problems of children cannot be put down to a lack of awareness of the interests of the child in individual states nor can their plight be alleviated without taking into account the wider political, economic and international context. With the best will or parenting classes in the world, many parents and their societies are unable to ensure their children are properly fed and clothed, receive education and do not have to work. . . . Whilst there has not been a general improvement in the welfare of children in the last decade, the discourse of children's rights suggests that the plight of children in the Third World is due to the moral failings of their societies.

SUSAN KILBOURNE, PLACING THE CONVENTION ON THE RIGHTS OF THE CHILD IN AN AMERICAN CONTEXT
Human Rights, Spring 1999, at 27

Opposition to U.S. Ratification: Facts and Fictions

The United States participated in the lengthy drafting process of the CRC and became a signatory to the treaty in 1995. However, the CRC has not yet been transmitted by the White House to the Senate for the advice and consent needed for ratification. The primary reason for this delay is that the political climate in the Senate and the country is remarkably hostile to ratification.

Even though the CRC has not been generally publicized within the United States, there are vocal opponents, mostly conservative religious organizations. . . . They have been quite successful at motivating members to contact their senators to express opposition to ratification. In fact, Senate staffers report that they have received 100 opposition letters for every letter in support of the CRC.

The fact sheets, magazine articles, fund-raising appeals, Websites, and video-tapes published by opposition organizations paint a picture of the CRC as a radical and dangerous document that will guarantee unlimited government interference in family life. The CRC has been variously described as 'the most dangerous attack on parents' rights in the history of the United States', 'the ultimate program to annihilate parental authority', and a 'tool for perverts'.

Two types of arguments can be discerned in opposition materials. First, a great deal of general criticism of the United Nations and human rights treaties is proffered. Opponents making this argument are concerned that U.S. ratification of the CRC would cause the United States to give up some of its sovereignty and would result in violations of states' rights and damage to our system of federalism.

. . .

Second, and more politically inflammatory, opponents argue that the CRC 'strips parents of rights' . . . Although the CRC's provisions 'are worthy principles, deserving of support, especially in repressive regimes such as Iraq, Libya and Albania', critics fear that there is great potential for abusing parental rights.

. . . These interpretations seem to be based on misunderstandings about the implementation process or distortions of the CRC's text. For example, according to opposition publications:

• Under Article 13, 'parents would be subject to prosecution for any attempt to prevent their children from interaction (sic) with pornography, rock music, or television'.

• Article 14 gives children 'a legal right to object to all religious training. Alternatively, children may assert their right against parental objection to participate in occult, Muslim or Buddhist worship services'.

• Article 15 could prevent parents 'from forbidding their child to associate with people deemed to be objectionable companions . . . [C]hildren could claim a "fundamental" right to join gangs, cults, and racist organizations over parental objection.'

• Article 16 'gives the child a virtually absolute "right of privacy" to be enforced at law against all others, including parents. Presumably, this privacy right includes the right to have an abortion without parental consent, the right to fornication and homosexual conduct within the home, the right to view obscenity within the home, and the right to obtain and use birth control'.

• Article 43 'calls for a Committee' of 10 experts of high moral stature 'to investigate and prosecute parents who violate their children's rights'.

. . .

Even though most of the critical arguments are based on distorted or erroneous readings of the CRC, a few opposition points are valid and are likely to pose political problems in the United States. First, the Committee on the Rights of the Child has interpreted the CRC to require the prohibition of corporal punishment, even within the family. Whether corporal punishment is acceptable and effective in American society is debatable. Nevertheless, if the United States was to implement this requirement, many parents would object on privacy or religious grounds. Second, Article 29 seems to require the federal government to impose 'values curricula' on primary educational institutions, including private schools. This would probably violate the First Amendment and would certainly be controversial. Third, critics claim that the guarantee of privacy in Article 16, when read in combination with the Article 24(f) provision that state parties 'develop . . . family planning education and services', establishes abortion rights for children. However, a close reading of the text and the drafting history demonstrates that the CRC is neutral on abortion. Other areas of the CRC that may pose legal problems in the United States include the incarceration and capital punishment of juvenile offenders. These issues do not involve parental rights and are therefore less politically volatile.

Most, if not all, of these valid concerns can be addressed through the process of developing Reservations, Understandings, and Declarations (RUDs).

. . .

Would the Convention on the Rights of the Child fix [problems in the United States of murders of and crimes by children, of poverty and lack of health insurance?] Of course not. But the CRC *would* provide a tool for advocates to help bring about changes in legislation and in the implementation of programs for children. It would provide a framework against which we can measure our governmental policies for children—policies that are currently scattered among many agencies and levels of government, with no coordination or oversight. . . .

QUESTION

If you were trying to persuade groups hostile to the CRC of the advantages of ratification by the United States, what arguments would you make?

COMMENT ON RESERVATIONS TO CRC

As with the other principal UN human rights treaties (see Chapter 10), the CRC establishes a supervisory body to monitor implementation of the Convention. The

Committee on the Rights of the Child was set up in 1991. It consists of ten members (of 'recognised competence in the field' and serving 'in their personal capacity'—Art. 43(2)), elected for four-year terms. The Committee meets three times a year for sessions of three weeks' duration, with an additional week devoted to Working Group meetings at the end of each session. As of May 1, 2000 the Committee had received 182 reports, including 36 periodic (i.e. as opposed to initial) reports. Of those, it had reviewed only 109 initial reports and 9 periodic reports.

The Committee is by far the best provided for of the six UN human rights treaty bodies, and has benefited from a special Action Plan supported by voluntary contributions as well as extensive support from UNICEF. It has also been systematically supported by an NGO Group which facilitates the submission of alternative reports from NGO sources within each of the countries whose official report is being examined by the Committee. The Group has a full-time Liaison Officer in Geneva for this purpose.

The Committee's output consists primarily of the 'concluding observations' adopted at the end of its examination of each report. It also holds regular 'days of general discussion' which enable the Committee to receive expert, including NGO, inputs on specific themes such as children and the media, children in armed conflict, economic exploitation of children, the girl child, juvenile justice, children with disabilities, and children living with HIV/AIDS.

As with CEDAW (see pp. 439–444, *supra*), the CRC has been ratified with an extensive number of declarations and reservations. Consider the following official statements:[8]

Germany

The Federal Republic of Germany . . . declares that the provisions of the Convention are also without prejudice to the provisions of national law concerning

a) legal representation of minors in the exercise of their rights;
b) rights of custody and access in respect of children born in wedlock;
c) circumstances under family and inheritance law of children born out of wedlock.

The Government . . . regrets the fact that under article 38 (2) of the Convention even fifteen-year-olds may take a part in hostilities as soldiers, because this age limit is incompatible with the consideration of a child's best interest (article 3(1) of the Convention). It declares that it will not make any use of the possibility afforded by the Convention of fixing this age limit at fifteen years.

Guatemala

With reference to article 1 of the Convention, . . . Guatemala declares that article 3 of its Political Constitution establishes that: 'The State guarantees and protects human life from the time of its conception, as well as the integrity and security of the individual'.

---

[8] Taken from: www.un.org/Depts/Treaty/final/ts2/newfiles/part_boo/iv_boo/iv_11.html.

Malaysia

The Government of Malaysia accepts the provisions of the Convention on the Rights of the Child but expresses reservations with respect to articles 1, 2, 7, 13, 14, 15, [. . .], 28, [paragraph 1 (a)], 37, [. . .] of the Convention and declares that the said provisions shall be applicable only if they are in conformity with the Constitution, national laws and national policies of the Government of Malaysia.

United Kingdom

Where at any time there is a lack of suitable accommodation or adequate facilities for a particular individual in any institution in which young offenders are detained, or where the mixing of adults and children is deemed to be mutually beneficial, the United Kingdom reserves the right not to apply article 37(c) in so far as those provisions require children who are detained to be accommodated separately from adults.

Syria

The Syrian Arab Republic has reservations on the Convention's provisions which are not in conformity with the Syrian Arab legislations and with the Islamic Shari-ah's principles, in particular the content of article (14) related to the Right of the Child to the freedom of religion, and articles 2 and 21 concerning the adoption.

Singapore

The Republic of Singapore considers that a child's rights as defined in the Convention, in particular the rights defined in articles 12 to 17, shall in accordance with articles 3 and 5 be exercised with respect for the authority of parents, schools and other persons who are entrusted with the care of the child and in the best interests of the child and in accordance with the customs, values and religions of Singapore's multi-racial and multi-religious society regarding the place of the child within and outside the family.

(2) The Republic of Singapore considers that articles 19 and 37 of the Convention do not prohibit—

(a) the application of any prevailing measures prescribed by law for maintaining law and order in the Republic of Singapore;
(b) measures and restrictions which are prescribed by law and which are necessary in the interests of national security, public safety, public order, the protection of public health or the protection of the rights and freedoms of others; or
(c) the judicious application of corporal punishment in the best interest of the child.

(3) The Constitution and the laws of the Republic of Singapore provide adequate protection and fundamental rights and liberties in the best interests of the child. The accession to the Convention by the Republic of Singapore does not imply the acceptance of obligations going beyond the limits prescribed by the Constitution of the Republic of Singapore nor the acceptance of any obligation to introduce any right beyond those prescribed under the Constitution.

. . .

Norway (Objection)

The Government of Norway considers that reservation (3) made by the Republic of Singapore, due to its unlimited scope and undefined character, is contrary to the object and purpose of the Convention, and thus impermissible under article 51, paragraph 2, of the Convention.

Furthermore, the Government of Norway considers that declaration (2) made by the Republic of Singapore, in so far as it purports to exclude or to modify the legal effect of articles 19 and 37 of the Convention, also constitutes a reservation impermissible under the Convention, due to the fundamental nature of the rights concerned and the unspecified reference to domestic law.

For these reasons, the Government of Norway objects to the said reservations made by the Government of Singapore.

NOTE

Partly as a result of the CRC, an increasing number of states have included children's rights provisions in their constitutions. The extent of the provisions varies greatly, as does the degree to which the provisions of the CRC are reflected. One of the strongest examples of a new constitution which has drawn obvious inspiration from the CRC is that of South Africa, adopted in 1996. Section 28 provides that:

(1) Every child has the right—

(a) to a name and a nationality from birth;

(b) to family care or parental care, or to appropriate alternative care when removed from the family environment;

(c) to basic nutrition, shelter, basic health care services and social services;

(d) to be protected from maltreatment, neglect, abuse or degradation;

(e) to be protected from exploitative labour practices;

(f) not to be required or permitted to perform work or provide services that—

(i) are inappropriate for a person of that child's age; or

(ii) place at risk the child's well-being, education, physical or mental health or spiritual, moral or social development;

(g) not to be detained except as a measure of last resort, in which case, in addition to the rights a child enjoys under sections 12 and 35, the child may be detained only for the shortest appropriate period of time, and has the right to be—

(i) kept separately from detained persons over the age of 18 years; and

(ii) treated in a manner, and kept in conditions, that take account of the child's age;

(h) to have a legal practitioner assigned to the child by the state, and at state expense, in civil proceedings affecting the child, if substantial injustice would otherwise result; and

(i) not to be used directly in armed conflict, and to be protected in times of armed conflict.

(2) A child's best interests are of paramount importance in every matter concerning the child.

(3) In this section 'child' means a person under the age of 18 years.

The balance of this Section C on children's rights is divided into two case studies. The following materials address the first study, on corporal punishment.

HUMAN RIGHTS WATCH, SPARE THE CHILD: CORPORAL PUNISHMENT IN KENYAN SCHOOLS
(1999), at 3

. . .

For most Kenyan children, violence is a regular part of the school experience. Teachers use caning, slapping, and whipping to maintain classroom discipline and to punish children for poor academic performance. The infliction of corporal punishment is routine, arbitrary, and often brutal. Bruises and cuts are regular by-products of school punishments, and more severe injuries (broken bones, knocked-out teeth, internal bleeding) are not infrequent. At times, beatings by teachers leave children permanently disfigured, disabled or dead.
. . .

Kenyan law restricts the use of school-based corporal punishment. According to the Education (School Discipline) Regulations, corporal punishment may only be administered for certain behavior, after a full inquiry, and in the presence of a witness, but not in the presence of other pupils. Only the headteacher is permitted to administer corporal punishment, and he or she must use a cane or strap of regulation size, hitting boys on the buttocks and girls on the palm of the hand. The headteacher may give no more than six strokes as punishment, and must keep a written record of all the proceedings. In 1996 the Director of Education reportedly issued a statement banning the imposition of corporal punishment, although no ban has ever been enforced, and the Education (School Discipline) Regulations continue to authorize the punishment.

Illegal and severe forms of corporal punishment remain widespread, according to over two hundred Kenyan children interviewed by Human Rights Watch. . . . In the twenty schools we visited, we found the use and abuse of corporal punishment were uniform: corporal punishment appeared to be equally widespread at urban schools and rural schools, at schools catering to the middle and upper middle classes and schools catering to the poor, and at schools in different regions, or with different ethnic and religious populations.

In Kenya, the most common method of corporal punishment involves teachers striking students with a 'cane': generally an uneven wooden stick of two to three feet in length, with a diameter of approximately three-fourths of an inch. Some teachers also punish students by flogging them with whips made of rubber (from strips of old car tires), with heavier canes, or simply by slapping, kicking, or pinching. For the most part, boys are hit on the backside, while girls are hit on the palm of the hand. At times, however, children are beaten on other parts of the body. . . .

. . .

Group punishments were widely reported: if a school did not perform well on national exams, for instance, an entire class might be caned regardless of the individual performance of each student. Similarly, if graffiti was found in a classroom, the whole class might be caned if the culprit could not be identified. . . .

. . .

The Ministry of Education appears to have done little to enforce the provisions of the Education (School Discipline) Regulations, which limit how corporal punishment may be imposed. . . .

Awareness-raising campaigns and training for practicing teachers on discipline and alternatives to corporal punishment in schools are virtually nonexistent. Instructors are rarely disciplined by headteachers or by the Ministry of Education, even for inflicting serious injuries on the children under their care. . . .

. . .

The judicial system is generally not a practical alternative for redress for school corporal punishment. Since most families cannot afford attorneys, they have little access to the courts, or prospects of prevailing in legal action if they do. Furthermore, the judicial system is not strong, with judicial processes slow, and judgments difficult to enforce.

Perhaps most disturbing, Human Rights Watch received numerous reports, from children and parents, of serious retaliation against people who challenged severe corporal punishment. . . .

. . .

Various forms of corporal punishment (and other punishments like manual labor) have a long pedigree in Kenya. Many Kenyans told Human Rights Watch that physical chastisement has long been accepted in Kenyan homes. The Kenyan government school system arose in the days of British colonial government, and adopted nineteenth-century British traditions of school discipline, including the widespread use of the cane.

. . .

Although most Kenyans we met told Human Rights Watch that corporal punishment should never be so severe as to cause lasting injury to a child, few of those interviewed perceived corporal punishment as a human rights issue, or even as a major cause for concern. . . .

. . .

School corporal punishment in Kenya has a high degree of cultural acceptance, even approval. Although some teachers inflict severe forms of corporal punishment on students out of deliberate cruelty, probably the great majority of teachers genuinely intend to 'educate' children by caning or whipping them. To the extent that children are seriously injured, many Kenyans are willing to write such incidents off as tragic exceptions in a generally acceptable system, the result of the occasional sadistic teacher or of unfortunate but unavoidable accidents. . . .

. . .

Recommendations:

To the Government of Kenya, generally:

- Amend the Education Act of 1968 and the Education (School Discipline) Regulations to abolish the use of corporal punishment in all Kenyan schools, public and private.
- The Attorney General should introduce the long-awaited redrafted Children's Bill to parliament for debate and ratification. The bill should abolish corporal punishment of children in all institutions, including regular schools and correctional schools.

. . .

- Support programs that educate parents, teachers, and society at large about the harm of corporal punishment and the existence of effective alternatives.

. . .

MANY IN U.S. BACK SINGAPORE'S PLAN TO FLOG YOUTH
New York Times, April 5, 1994, p. A6

Spare the rod and spoil the child may no longer be an axiom of American parenting, but many Americans are surprisingly unsympathetic to the plight of an Ohio youth who was convicted of vandalizing cars in Singapore and now faces a flogging in that country.

Michael P. Fay, 18 years old, was sentenced to four months in prison, a $2,215 fine and six lashes on his bare buttocks with a rattan cane by a martial arts expert after pleading guilty last October to vandalizing cars with spray paint and eggs and tearing down traffic signs in Singapore, where he lived with his mother and stepfather.

. . .

President Clinton and Representative Tony P. Hall, an Ohio Democrat, have appealed to the Singapore Government, arguing that the flogging, which may cause permanent scars, is excessive punishment for the youth.

. . .

Chin Hock Seng, first secretary at the Singapore Embassy, told The Associated Press that more than 100 letters and 200 phone calls had been received from Americans in recent weeks. 'The vast majority express very strong support for Singapore,' Mr. Chin said.

A spokesman for The Dayton Daily News, Mr. Fay's hometown newspaper, also said its mail was running against the youth.

And on the streets of Washington, there was little compassion for the young man. Women were slightly more sympathetic, worrying about the physical damage done by caning.

'If you've ever had your antenna ripped off your car, you can sympathize with the Government of Singapore,' said Ben Johnson, 26, a media relations director of Ein Communications Inc., a public relations firm. 'Lash him. Vandalism is a cowardly and insubordinate act.'

. . .

The enthusiasm for such measures reflects American frustration with crime and young miscreants, some experts say.
. . .

[An Amnesty International official, Estrellita Jones] said that the law, which her organization has protested for years, violates international laws and is 'unusually cruel and degrading' punishment.

'This is not the paddle or the whip that some of us got in public school,' she said. 'They tie you down like an animal. This is a very traumatic experience both mentally and physically.'

Ms. Jones said for 1,218 floggings in Singapore reported to Amnesty International in 1987 and 1988, Singaporeans accounted for 984 and foreigners for 234.

NOTE

In *Tryer v. United Kingdom*, 25 April 1978, (No. 26) 2 EHRR 1, the European Court of Human Rights held that three strokes of the birch administered by the local police against the bare bottom of a fifteen-year-old (carrying out a juvenile court sentence) was degrading treatment in violation of the ECHR. A separate opinion of Judge Fitzmaurice said in part:

> 12. I have to admit that my own view may be coloured by the fact that I was brought up and educated under a system according to which corporal punishment of schoolboys . . . was regarded as the normal sanction for serious misbehaviour, and even sometimes for what was much less serious. . . . [T]hese beatings were carried out without any of the safeguards attendant on Mr Tyrer's: no parents, nurses or doctors were ever present. They also not infrequently took place under conditions of far greater intrinsic humiliation than in his case. Yet I cannot remember that any boy felt degraded or debased. Such an idea would have been thought rather ridiculous. . . . [I]ndeed, such is the natural perversity of the young of the human species that these occasions were often seen as matters of pride and congratulation . . .

JANE FORTIN, RIGHTS BROUGHT HOME FOR CHILDREN
62 Modern L. Rev. 359 (1999)

. . .

Children's Family Life and the Use of Corporal Punishment

. . . [N]either Article 8 [on private and family life] nor indeed any of the other Articles in the [European Convention of Human Rights, pp. 1423–27, *infra*] cope very adequately with attempts to ensure that children are protected from over-authoritarian parents within the privacy of the home. This weakness has undermined attempts to outlaw the use of corporal punishment in British homes. As is well known, the continued lawfulness of corporal punishment in private homes and independent schools was strongly criticised by the Committee on the Rights of the Child. Challenges employing the [U.K.] Human Rights Act 1998 may eventually achieve its complete abolition in private homes. The use of the European Convention certainly had a dramatic success in gradually curtailing corporal punishment in schools. Rulings by the European Court against the United Kingdom for allowing this form of punishment, thereby infringing the rights of parents and children, prompted legislation in 1986 outlawing its use in all state schools. A later decision of the European Court led to further legislation in 1993 warning independent schools that they could not lawfully administer corporal punishment which could be described as being 'inhuman or degrading'. In other words, they were directed to heed the terms of Article 3 regarding the punishment of their pupils. The School Standards and Framework Act 1998 finally outlawed the use of corporal punishment in all schools, state and independent alike. Indeed, it goes much further than previous legislation in so far as it makes the use of corporal punishment in schools unlawful not only for civil purposes but also for criminal purposes.

Despite the Convention being utilised to attack the legality of corporal punishment in schools, it had not hitherto been used by children as a means of challenging their *parents'* use of corporal punishment in the home. It was recently established, however, that Article 3 [prohibiting 'inhuman or degrading treatment or punishment'] can protect children against such parental behaviour. A young British boy successfully argued that his step-father's ability to beat him with a garden cane at intervals over a period of a week, as a form of punishment, without any criminal sanction, infringed his rights under Article 3. The European Court confirmed the European Commission's unanimous decision in the boy's favour. [*A. v. United Kingdom*, 23 September 1998, HUDOC REF 00000999] Like the Commission, it considered that the United Kingdom government must take responsibility for providing children with practical and effective state protection against treatment or punishment contrary to Article 3. This it had manifestly failed to do since a jury had been able to acquit the step-father of behaviour of a severity clearly prohibited by Article 3. Both Commission and Court emphasised their view that the English common law defence to a charge of assault against a child, namely that the parent's behaviour amounted to 'reasonable chastisement', undermined the law's ability to protect children's rights. As in other recent case law, both bodies attached importance to the way in which the UN Convention on the Rights of the Child protects children's rights in this context. Indeed, the Commission discussed at some length the criticisms levelled by the Committee on the Rights of the Child at British law on this topic.

The impact of the recent decision was restricted by the European Court's failure to suggest that corporal punishment *per se* amounts to a violation of a child's rights under Article 3. Indeed, it reasserted its earlier view that it depends on the circumstances of each case whether ill-treatment reaches the level of severity required to infringe Article 3. Unfortunately this allows the decision to be downplayed by arguing that it merely precludes parents from treating their children in a particularly brutal way. Thus the Health Minister rapidly responded to it by claiming that the 'overwhelming majority of parents know the difference between smacking and beating'. Nevertheless, the government has accepted that the law requires clarifying to 'reflect the view that violence against children is unacceptable and promote better protection for children without getting in the way of normal family life'.

It seems clear that, at the very least, the parental right to administer lawful chastisement must be revoked and that parents must be warned that discipline amounting to 'inhuman or degrading treatment' is legally prohibited. The legislative attempt at providing comprehensible guidance to schools on the type of punishment falling into such a category suggests that parents will be left in an extremely confused state. Certainly such a change would not bring about the complete abolition of corporal punishment that many consider is required. Experience elsewhere shows that laws of such kind can be extremely effective. Research in Sweden suggests a strong decrease in the use of physical punishment since 1979 when the law there was changed prohibiting any form of smacking children. Nevertheless, to introduce such a change here would be highly controversial and not one that any government would contemplate making with equanimity. . . .

. . .

NOTE

When the CRC was being drafted, several proposals were made to outlaw corporal punishment. They were not taken up in relation to Art. 37, and a more general formulation was adopted in Art. 28(2). A detailed comparative study of national approaches undertaken for the UN in 1983 concluded that 'reasonable and moderate physical punishment is now lawful in most jurisdictions as part of the parents' right of correction'.[9] The Committee on the Rights of the Child, however, has attached considerable importance to the issue and has taken a strong line in its concluding observations on states' reports. The following is a sampling of its statements:

United Kingdom (UN Doc. CRC/C/15/Add.34):
[T]he Committee is worried about the national legal provisions dealing with reasonable chastisement within the family. The imprecise nature of the expression of reasonable chastisement as contained in these legal provisions may pave the way for it to be interpreted in a subjective and arbitrary manner. Thus, the Committee is concerned that legislative and other measures relating to the physical integrity of children do not appear to be compatible with the provisions and principles of the Convention, including those of its articles 3, 19 and 37.

Bangladesh (CRC/C/15/Add.74):
The persistence of corporal punishment and its acceptance by the society and instances of violence by law-enforcement officials against abandoned or 'vagrant' children [are matters] of serious concern.

---

[9] A. Pappas, *Law and the Status of the Child* xlv (1983).

Republic of Korea (UN Doc. CRC/C/15/Add.51):
[T]he Committee is concerned at . . . the persistence of corporal punishment, widely envisaged by parents and teachers as an educational measure. . . .

Poland (UN Doc. CRC/C/15/Add.31):
The Committee is also preoccupied by the existence on a large scale of child abuse and violence within the family and the insufficient protection afforded by the existing legislation in that regard . . . [It] further suggests that the clear prohibition of torture or other cruel, inhuman or degrading treatment or punishment, as well as the ban on corporal punishment in the family, be reflected in the national legislation. In this field, the Committee also suggests the development of procedures and mechanisms to monitor complaints of maltreatment and cruelty within or outside the family.

The Committee is following in the footsteps of a long line of statements adopted under UN auspices, but none of which is formally binding in character. For example, the 1985 'Beijing Rules', the UN's Standard Minimum Rules for the Administration of Juvenile Justice, provide that: 'Juveniles shall not be subject to corporate punishment' (rule 17(3)) and the 1990 United Nations Rules for the Protection of Juveniles Deprived of their Liberty state that 'All disciplinary measures constituting cruel inhuman or degrading treatment shall be strictly prohibited, including corporal punishment' (rule 67). In its General Comment 20 (1992) the Human Rights Committee indicated that the prohibition [in article 7] of the ICCPR must extend to corporal punishment, including excessive chastisement ordered as punishment for a crime or as an educative or disciplinary measure.

QUESTIONS

1. Singapore did not ratify the CRC until 1995 and, as of January 1, 2000, it had not become a party to the ICCPR or the Torture Convention. What would the legal arguments be on either side if a Committee member wanted to challenge the legality of the use of the rattan on a 17 year old?

2. Comment on the following statement: 'All the available evidence indicates that the great majority of cultures either tolerate or actively condone at least some mild forms of corporal punishment. Given that the CRC is silent on the issue, it is highly inappropriate for the ten members of the Committee to take it upon themselves to seek to change both the culture and the laws in countries around the world'.

3. Does the Committee's approach to this issue leave any room for a public-private divide—that is, perhaps regulating only corporal punishment by public institutions/employees such as public school teachers? Should it do so?

4. How would you go about trying to bring schools and other institutions in Kenya

into compliance with the CRC? What strategies, what alliances, what sanctions? Compare the earlier materials on female genital mutilation.

5. How would you respond to the critique by Pupavac?

6. It was reported in September 1999 that some 300 towns across the United States have introduced curfew laws that, for example, require all children under 17 to be home by 11 p.m. on weekdays and midnight on the weekends, with exceptions for work or church activities. In 1996 police arrested 140,000 juveniles for curfew violations, which was more than the total arrests for all juvenile violent crimes put together.[10] Are such laws likely to be consistent with the provisions of the CRC?

7. Are issues of corporal punishment as much matters of 'culture', and cultural relativism, as say gender roles or the degree of tolerance of minority religions? Would you expect as much resistance to changes bringing states into compliance with the CRC as with CEDAW?

NOTE

The balance of materials in the chapter involves the second case study, child soldiers.

HUMAN RIGHTS WATCH CHILDREN'S RIGHTS PROJECT, THE SCARS OF DEATH: CHILDREN ABDUCTED BY THE LORD's RESISTANCE ARMY IN UGANDA
(1997), at 1

I. Summary and Recommendations
. . .

In northern Uganda, thousands of children are victims of a vicious cycle of violence, caught between a brutal rebel group and the army of the Ugandan government. The rebel Lord's Resistance Army (LRA) is ostensibly dedicated to overthrowing the government of Uganda, but in practice the rebels appear to devote most of their time to attacks on the civilian population: they raid villages, loot stores and homes, burn houses and schools, and rape, mutilate and slaughter civilians unlucky enough to be in their path.

[A]fter each raid, the rebels take . . . young children. . . .

[They] prefer children of fourteen to sixteen, but at times they abduct children as young as eight or nine, boys and girls alike. They tie the children to one another, and force them to carry heavy loads of looted goods as they march them off into the bush. Children who protest or resist are killed. Children who cannot keep up or become tired or ill are killed. Children who attempt to escape are killed.

---

[10] 'Lights Out', *The Economist*, September 18, 1999, p.30.

Their deaths are not quick—a child killed by a single rebel bullet is a rarity. If one child attempts to escape, the rebels force the other abducted children to kill the wouldbe escapee, usually with clubs or machetes. Any child who refuses to participate in the killing may also be beaten or killed.

The rebels generally bring their captives across the border to a Lord's Resistance Army camp in Sudan. In the bush in Sudan, a shortage of food and water reduces many children to eating leaves for survival; deaths from dysentery, hunger and thirst are frequent. Living conditions in the Lord's Resistance Army camp are slightly better, because the Sudanese government supplies the Lord's Resistance Army with both food and arms in exchange for assistance in fighting the rebel Sudanese People's Liberation Army (SPLA).

Those children who reach the Lord's Resistance Army camp are forced to serve the rebels. Smaller children may be made to run errands, fetch water or cultivate the land; girls as young as twelve are given to rebel commanders as 'wives'. All of the children are trained as soldiers, taught to use guns and to march.

The Lord's Resistance Army enforces discipline through a combination of violence and threats. Children who do not perform their assigned tasks to the rebels' satisfaction are beaten. Children who flout rebel orders are beaten or killed, often by other abducted children. Failed escape attempts continue to be punished by death, and successful escape attempts lead to retaliation: if one sibling escapes, the rebels often kill the other sibling, or return to the child's home village and slaughter any surviving relatives.

In effect, children abducted by the Lord's Resistance Army become slaves: their labor, their bodies and their lives are all at the disposal of their rebel captors.

Once they have been trained (and sometimes before being trained), the children are forced to fight, both in Uganda and in Sudan. In Sudan, the children are forced to help raid villages for food, and fight against the Sudan People's Liberation Army. In Uganda, the children are also made to loot villages, fight against Ugandan government soldiers, and help abduct other children. When the rebels fight against the Ugandan government army, they force the captive children to the front; children who hang back or refuse to fire are beaten or killed by the rebels, while those who run forward may be mown down by government bullets.

The Lord's Resistance Army's use of children as combatants is an extreme example of a troubling worldwide trend toward increased reliance on child soldiers in conflicts of all sorts. Graca Machel, who headed the United Nations Study on the Impact of Armed Conflict on Children, has pointed out that the proliferation of inexpensive light weapons has contributed to the increased use of children as soldiers:

> [T]he reality is that children have increasingly become targets, and not incidental victims [of war], as a result of conscious and deliberate decisions made by adults. . . . War violates every right of the child. . . . The injury to children—the physical wounds, the psychosocial distress, the sexual violence—are affronts to each and every humanitarian impulse that inspired the Convention on the Rights of the Child.

. . .

Recommendations To the United Nations

. . .

[T]he U.N. Working Group on a Draft Optional Protocol to the Convention on the Rights of the Child on Involvement of Children in Armed Conflicts should uncompromisingly seek to raise to eighteen the minimum age at which people may be recruited into armed forces and participate in hostilities (whether that recruitment is voluntary or compulsory, and whether it is into governmental or nongovernmental armed forces). African states should be encouraged to participate actively in the working group.

KALASHNIKOV KIDS
The Economist, July 10, 1999, at 26

. . . [I]n Sierra Leone . . . 6,000 children were recently combatants. . . .

The United Nations reckons that children, defined as those under 18 years old, are active participants in conflicts stretching from west and central Africa to the Balkans, Latin America, Sri Lanka and Afghanistan. In Uganda, for example, the UN Children's Fund, Unicef, estimates that as many as 8,000 have been abducted by rebels since 1995. Another 15,000 are said by Amnesty International, a non-governmental organisation based in Britain, to be in the ranks of Colombia's security forces and many more are in paramilitary groups there. According to the Coalition to Stop the Use of Child Soldiers, a group of religious and peace groups headquartered in Switzerland, 300,000 children in over 60 countries are soldiers.

. . .

[T]here are problems of definition. What is a child? Is it the same in all cultures? A Tamil might well be married at 14 and expect to fulfil other manly duties, but it is against the law in Britain to take a wife at that age. A 12-year-old gun-toter seems clearly unacceptable; a 17-year-old, less so. And what is a soldier? Not all of them fight, or even risk their lives. Many ordinary children suffer horribly during the kind of vicious civil war that throws up lots of child soldiers. At least the soldiers are likely to get a handful of food for their pains.

Despite these ambiguities, two trends are worth thinking about. Children tend to be used heavily as soldiers during prolonged civil wars; and such civil wars abound at present. And although children were once recruited only when the supply of adult fighters ran short, the youngest are now often recruited first.

There are logical reasons for this. First, there are more children around, proportionally, in most of the relevant places. Thanks to demography, poverty and persistent fighting, in much of Africa south of the Sahara, for example, half the people are now under 18 years old. Then too children are often easier to attract than adults. . . .

When they cannot be tempted into the ranks, children can be forced more easily than adults. Once secured, they are more readily moulded into unquestioning fighters. . . . The youngest will often develop the sort of loyalty that stems from knowing no other way of life.

Despite—sometimes because of—their size, children can do valuable work as
scouts, spies, messengers and decoys. Even ten-year-olds can learn to carry and use
lightweight but lethal weapons, such as M16 semi-automatic rifles or the omni-
present aluminium Kalashnikov AK-47s. They may be more willing than older
companions to do the most dangerous jobs, such as laying and clearing mines,
serving as suicide bombers or infiltrating villages. . . .

Finally, children are an economical addition to the force. They need less food
than adult soldiers, take up less space and can do without a wage. . . .

. . . Olara Otunnu, the UN Special Representative for Children and Armed
Conflict . . ., says that 2m children have been killed in situations of armed conflict
since 1987, and three times that number have been seriously injured or permanently disabled. As civilians' share of casualties in war has rocketed this century (up
from 5% in the first world war to 48% in the second and around 90% today), the
involvement of children has also grown.

But for child soldiers in particular there are more risks. On top of the obvious
dangers of injury or death during combat, they tend to live harsh lives. Some are
punished, or killed, for making mistakes. . . .

Day-to-day injuries from carrying heavy loads, as well as damage to ears and
eyes from gunfire, are well documented. Drug addiction, malnutrition and sexually transmitted diseases are common among bands of child soldiers in different
continents.

Then there are the emotional effects. Large numbers of children have seen
atrocities. . . . Sometimes, in order to humiliate a village under attack and destroy
its social order, the youngest boy in the ranks of the attackers is ordered to execute
the village chief. . . .

The impact of all this not only on the child but on society as a whole is
dreadful. . . .

This week about 100 government representatives, UN staff and aid workers
gathered in Montevideo, the capital of Uruguay, for the second of four international conferences on child soldiers. They discussed how to stop the recruitment
of children by armies, paramilitary groups and civil-defence bodies.

That is a difficult (and some would say impossible) task. The differences among
the three categories are immense. Some child soldiers are recruited, openly and
legally, into national armies where care is taken over their training and welfare. A
second lot, such as those with self-defence committees in Mozambique or the 'village
guards' in Algeria, fight to protect their families and villages. A third type are those
who are taken away from their communities, often forcibly, by groups that may have
started life with a political agenda but frequently end up as common criminals.

The first sort are the easiest to do something about but the least in need of
rescue. It is not illegal under international law to recruit a 15-year-old as a soldier.
The UN Convention on the Rights of the Child . . . establishes the age of 18 as the
end of childhood. It forbids, for example, the death penalty for children and sets
other standards for their protection. An exception has been made for soldiering,
allowing recruitment at 15.

The British navy, for example, recruits 16-year-old school-leavers. The British
army starts hiring them at 17 and now has 4,991 under-18-year-olds (1,000 more

than two years ago) in its employ . . . The American army, too, recruits and deploys 17-year-olds. . . . [I]n 1997 the American army had 2,880 17-year-olds on active duty.

The minority of countries that recruit at this age argue that, if they left it any later, the young people would turn to other employment: more than half of military personnel in Britain joined before their 18th birthdays. Some make a different point, that society benefits if lads without job prospects are taken off the streets and into useful training before unappealing habits form.

Their opponents say that only the most careful systems—for example, that in Australia, where young recruits are monitored by a host of psychologists, chaplains and other folk as well as given training suitable to their age—can protect children from what they see as the unhealthy rigours of military life. It is inconsistent, they say, for governments that do not allow young people to vote, buy alcohol, drive, marry without their parents' consent or accept certain kinds of civilian employment to send them into mortal danger instead.

Their campaign to raise the minimum age for soldiering from 15 to 18 in the children's-rights convention is gradually gaining momentum, though perhaps not for the reasons put forward. Many western countries want to reduce their armed forces anyway. . . .

. . . On June 17th [1999] members of the International Labour Organization voted unanimously to ban the employment of those younger than 18 in hazardous work, including prostitution, drug-smuggling and soldiering. (Only young conscripts are prohibited; young volunteers will still be allowed—though definitions of 'voluntary' among the very poor could prove a touch theoretical.)

Is 18 a reasonable cut-off? It smacks of an attempt by developed countries to force their values on the rest of the world, where children get down to things earlier. But at least, . . . if 18 becomes the legal minimum, then—even allowing for the difficulty of telling a child's age in places where malnutrition may make him look younger than he is or hard labour make him older—13- and 14-year-olds are less likely to end up clutching Kalashnikovs.

If the minimum recruiting age is raised by amending international agreements (and America and Britain are notable stand-outs against it), it will affect only national armies. A far bigger worry is unofficial armed groups, the civil-defence or rebel-cum-criminal gangs that draw boys and girls into their maw during prolonged civil wars. They are not confined to poor countries: a few children fight for the KLA (Kosovo Liberation Army) in Yugoslavia and rather more for the PKK (Kurdistan Workers' Party) in Turkey.

. . . Stopping such groups from using children as soldiers is much harder than stopping governments, as they are unlikely to be much affected by the opinions of either international do-gooders or voters (who might anyway—who knows?—consider enlisting child soldiers preferable to communal destruction). But because these groups usually defend villages, and thus move around less than rebel bands, their activities can be monitored more easily. Some outside carrots and sticks—money to demobilise, the threat of harsh penalties if recruiting child soldiers comes to be classified as a war crime—could have some effect. It is, frankly, a long shot.

Even longer are the odds against winning hearts and minds among the third group. Yet the sort of child soldier for whom life is worst, and from whom the greatest threat to stability and peace is later likely to come, is an abducted child who becomes a fighter. . . .

. . .

[F]oreign countries and institutions, [Otunnu] argues, should make it clear to any rebel group aspiring to govern that recognition and aid will be harder to win if the group has used child soldiers. This may sound like pie in the sky, but such arguments are making a little progress. The Sudan People's Liberation Army has pledged not to use child soldiers. So have both the Tamil Tigers and the Sri Lankan government.

Until 1998, the UN Security Council had not even discussed the issue of child soldiers. Since then, however, the subject has been raised several times, and expert witnesses have been questioned. The fate of children under arms is now recognized as an important part of peace negotiations in many parts of the world, with implications not only for successful demobilization but also for policies on health, education and nurturing democracy. As with the campaign to ban landmines, it is the gradual realisation of the dimensions of the problem, rather than any multilateral posturing, that has the best chance of solving it in time.

NOTE

In April 2000, the UN Commission on Human Rights (Res. 2000/59) approved two draft optional protocols to the CRC dealing respectively with the involvement of children in armed conflict, and the sale of children, child prostitution and child pornography. The General Assembly is expected to adopt both. The first requires States Parties to 'take all feasible measures to ensure that members of their armed forces who have not attained the age of 18 years do not take a direct part in hostilities' and to ensure that such persons 'are not compulsorily recruited into their armed forces'.

The Security Council, however, after many years of resisting the inclusion of human rights issues on its agenda (see pp. 649–53 *infra*), was put under considerable public pressure to react to the challenges described above. On August 25, 1999 it adopted the following resolution.

Security Council Resolution 1261 (1999)

The Security Council,
Noting recent efforts to bring to an end the use of children as soldiers in violation of international law, in [ILO Convention No. 182 of 1999] . . . and in the Rome Statute of the International Criminal Court in which conscripting or enlisting children under the age of fifteen into national armed forces or using them to participate actively in hostilities is characterized as a war crime,

1. Expresses its grave concern at the harmful and widespread impact of armed conflict on children . . .;

2. Strongly condemns the targeting of children in situations of armed conflict, . . .;

. . .

5. Welcomes and encourages efforts by all relevant actors at the national and international level to develop more coherent and effective approaches to the issue of children and armed conflict;

6. Supports the work of the open-ended inter-sessional working group of the Commission on Human Rights on a draft optional protocol to the Convention on the Rights of the Child on the involvement of children in armed conflict, and expresses the hope that it will make further progress with a view to finalizing its work;

. . .

13. Urges States and all relevant parts of the United Nations system to intensify their efforts to ensure an end to the recruitment and use of children in armed conflict in violation of international law through political and other efforts, including promotion of the availability of alternatives for children to their participation in armed conflict;

. . .

15. Urges States and the United Nations system to facilitate the disarmament, demobilization, rehabilitation and reintegration of children used as soldiers in violation of international law . . .;

. . .

19. Requests the Secretary-General to ensure that personnel involved in United Nations peacemaking, peacekeeping and peace-building activities have appropriate training on the protection, rights and welfare of children, and urges States and relevant international and regional organizations to ensure that appropriate training is included in their programmes for personnel involved in similar activities;

. . .

21. Decides to remain actively seized of the matter.

QUESTIONS

1. How do you evaluate the response of the Security Council, keeping in mind that the United Kingdom and the United States are permanent members of the Council? Is it problematic that the reliance upon existing international law means that no change in policy or practice is required of developed countries, whereas developing countries are clearly targeted in view of practices within their territories?

2. Or do the proposals to ban under 18 recruitment, as *The Economist* suggests, smack 'of an attempt by developed countries to force their values on the rest of the world, where children get down to things earlier'?

3. Can matters of 'principle' in such debates reasonably be expected to transcend more mundane but nonetheless defensible practical considerations? Is a utopian element inevitable and desirable in drawing up the agendas of human rights groups?

ADDITIONAL READING

P. Alston, S. Parker and J. Seymour (eds.), *Children, Rights, and the Law* (1992); G. Van Bueren, *The International Law on the Rights of the Child* (1995); M. Freeman and P. Veerman (eds.), *The Ideologies of Children's Rights* (1992); Gerison Lansdown, 'The Reporting Process under the Convention on the Rights of the Child', in Philip Alston and James Crawford (eds.), *The Future of UN Human Rights Treaty Monitoring* 113 (2000); Mac Darrow, 'The Committee on the Rights of the Child', in P. Alston (ed.), *The United Nations and Human Rights: A Critical Appraisal* (2nd edn 2000); Susan Bitensky, 'Spare the Rod, Embrace our Humanity: Toward a New Legal Regime Prohibiting Corporal Punishment of Children', 31 University of Michigan Journal of Law Reform 353–474 (1998); David Orentlicher, 'Spanking and Other Corporal Punishment of Children by Parents: Overvaluing Pain, Undervaluing Children', 35 Houston Law Review 147–85 (1998); 'Corporal Punishment: Special Issue', 17 Children's Legal Rights Journal 2–46 (1997); I. Hyman, F. Cavallo and J. Stafford, 'Corporal punishment in America: Cultural Wars in Politics, Religion and Science', 17 Children's Legal Rights J. 36 (1997); J. Kuper, *International Law Concerning Child Civilians in Armed Conflict* (1997); and G. Goodwin-Gill and I. Cohn, *Child Soldiers* (1994).

D. EAST ASIAN PERSPECTIVES

During the Cold War, the primary context for argument over universalism and relativism was the conflict between the West and Communist states, particularly between the United States and the Soviet Union. Today the debate has shifted to address fundamental differences between Western states' views of basic human rights and universalism, on the one hand, and Islamic states or a number of East Asian states intent on economic development, on the other. We concentrate here on such Asian states, where the primary parties to the debate have been the United States and China. The Government of Singapore, particularly in view of the position of its former and powerful prime minister, Lee Kuan Yew, has made a sustained and serious contribution to the debate.

These brief glimpses into the argument are sufficient to suggest some of the difficulties in characterizing it. What here is at issue? Are the positions taken in the following readings another illustration of cultural relativism, based on different East Asian traditions and religions from the West, similar in such respects to the prior studies in this chapter? What notions of culture and religion are stressed? What relevance have the other issues raised by authors like Kausikan, such as the need for economic development and the asserted condition to such development, namely social stability? Are these matters also issues of cultural variation and relativism?

BILHARI KAUSIKAN, ASIA'S DIFFERENT STANDARD
92 Foreign Policy 24 (1993)

East and Southeast Asia must respond to a new phenomenon: Human rights have become a legitimate issue in interstate relations. How a country treats its citizens is no longer a matter for its own exclusive determination. Others can and do legitimately claim a concern. There is an emerging global culture of human rights. . . .

In response, East and Southeast Asia are reexamining their own human rights standards.

. . . But there is a more general acceptance of many international human rights norms, even among states that have not acceded to the two covenants or are accused by the West of human rights abuses.

The human rights situation in the region, whether measured by the standard of civil and political rights or by social, cultural, and economic rights, has improved greatly over the last 20 years. As countries in the region become more prosperous, secure, and self-confident, they are moving beyond a purely defensive attitude to a more active approach to human rights. All the countries of the region are party to the U.N. Charter. None has rejected the Universal Declaration. There are references to human rights in the constitutions of many of the countries in the region. Countries like China, Indonesia, and even Burma have not just brushed aside Western criticism of their human rights records but have tried to respond seriously, asserting or trying to demonstrate that they too adhere to international human rights norms. They tend to interpret rather than reject such norms when there are disagreements. They discuss human rights with Western delegations. They have released political prisoners; and Indonesia, for instance, has even held commissions of inquiry on alleged abuses and punished some officials found guilty.

Abuses and inconsistencies continue. But it is too simplistic to dismiss what has been achieved as mere gestures intended to appease Western critics. Such inclinations may well be an element in the overall calculation of interests. And Western pressure undeniably plays a role. But in themselves, self-interest and pressure are insufficient and condescendingly ethnocentric Western explanations. They do less than justice to the states concerned, most of which have their own traditions in which the rulers have a duty to govern in a way consonant with the human dignity of their subjects, even if there is no clear concept of 'rights' as has evolved in the West. China today, for all its imperfections, is a vast improvement over the China of the Cultural Revolution. So too has the situation in Taiwan, South Korea, and the Association of Southeast Asian Nations (ASEAN) improved. Western critics who deny the improvements lose credibility.
. . .

The diversity of cultural traditions, political structures, and levels of development will make it difficult, if not impossible, to define a single distinctive and coherent human rights regime that can encompass the vast region from Japan to Burma, with its Confucianist, Buddhist, Islamic, and Hindu traditions. Nonetheless, the movement toward such a goal is likely to continue. What is clear is that

there is a general discontent throughout the region with a purely Western interpretation of human rights. The further development of human rights there will be
shaped primarily by internal developments, but pressure will continue to come
from the United States and Europe.

Human rights did not evolve in a vacuum. During the Cold War, the Western
promotion of human rights was shaped by and deployed as an ideological instrument of the East-West struggle. The post-Cold War human rights dialogue
between the West and Asia will be influenced by the power structure and dynamics
of a more regionalized world, built around the United States, Europe, and Asia,
which is replacing Cold War alliances and superpower competition. Trade and
security will, as always, be foremost on the international agenda, and human rights
will not be an issue of the first order. But human rights touch upon extraordinarily
delicate matters of culture and values. And human rights issues are likely to
become more prominent.

. . .

Meanwhile, relations among the United States, Europe, and Asia may lead the
West to use human rights as an instrument of economic competition. . . .

The lengthening catalogue of rights and freedoms in international human rights
law now encompasses such matters as pay, work conditions, trade unions, standard
of living, rest and leisure, welfare and social security, women's and children's
rights, and the environment. The pressures and temptation to link economic concerns with human rights will certainly rise if economic strains increase. That is not
to say that the West is insincere in its commitment to human rights. But policy
motivations are rarely simple; and it is difficult to believe that economic considerations do not to some degree influence Western attitudes toward such issues as,
say, the prison labor component of Chinese exports, child labor in Thailand, or
some of the AFL-CIO complaints against Malaysian labor practices. President Bill
Clinton's declared intention to press for human rights in China in return for
continuing to grant most-favored-nation trading status to Beijing makes the linkage explicit.

But efforts to promote human rights in Asia must also reckon with the altered
distribution of power in the post-Cold War world. Power, especially economic
power, has been diffused. For the last two decades, most of East and Southeast Asia
has experienced strong economic growth and will probably keep growing faster
than other regions well into the next century. . . .

Of course, the economic growth has not been even. The United States and
Europe are still major markets for almost all East and Southeast Asian countries,
many of whom remain aid recipients. But Western leverage over East and Southeast Asia has been greatly reduced. The countries in the region are reacting
accordingly. . . .

East and Southeast Asia are now significant actors in the world economy. There
is far less scope for conditionality and sanctions to force compliance with human
rights. The region is an expanding market for the West. . . .

. . .

. . . [T]he trend, already evident under Reagan and Bush in the attendant
strains between the United States and many Asian countries, is away from rights as

relatively precisely defined in international law, toward the promotion of hazier notions of 'freedom' and 'democracy'. The human rights apparatus is now even more open to manipulation by competing legislative, executive, judicial, media, and special interests devoted to such transcendent American values.

. . .

. . . Distance makes it easier to be virtuous; proximity makes for prudence. If, for instance, tough sanctions break the grip of the State Law and Order Restoration Council in Burma or the Communist party in China, the results could be violent. If disorder breaks out in Burma or China, it is not the United States or Europe that will pay the immediate price. Is the West prepared to intervene and remain engaged, perhaps for decades, to restore order? China will be a formidable political and economic force by the turn of the century. That does not mean human rights abuses in China must be overlooked. But if the promotion of human rights ignores Chinese realities and interests, expect China to find ways to exert counter-vailing pressures. And it will have the wherewithal to try to reshape any international order it sees as threatening.

For the first time since the Universal Declaration was adopted in 1948, countries not thoroughly steeped in the Judeo-Christian and natural law traditions are in the first rank: That unprecedented situation will define the new international politics of human rights. It will also multiply the occasions for conflict. In the process, will the human rights dialogue between the West and East and Southeast Asia become a dialogue of the deaf, with each side proclaiming its superior virtue without advancing the common interests of humanity? Or can it be a genuine and fruitful dialogue, expanding and deepening consensus? The latter outcome will require finding a balance between a pretentious and unrealistic universalism and a paralyzing cultural relativism. The myth of the universality of all human rights is harmful if it masks the real gap that exists between Asian and Western perceptions of human rights. The gap will not be bridged if it is denied.

The June 1993 Vienna U.N. conference on human rights did not even attempt to do so. The West went to Vienna accusing Asia of trying to undermine the ideal of universality, and determined to blame Asia if the conference failed. Inevitably, Asia resisted. The result after weeks of wrangling was a predictable diplomatic compromise ambiguous enough so all could live with it, but that settled very few things. There was no real dialogue between Asia and the West, no genuine attempt to address the issues or forge a meeting of the minds. If anything, the Vienna conference may only have hardened attitudes on both sides and increased the deep skepticism with which many Asian countries regard Western posturing on human rights.

. . .

For many in the West, the end of the Cold War was not just the defeat or collapse of communist regimes, but the supreme triumph and vindication of Western systems and values. It has become the lens through which they view developments in other regions. There has been a tendency since 1989 to draw parallels between developments in the Third World and those in Eastern Europe and the former USSR, measuring all states by the advance of what the West regards as 'democracy'. That is a value-laden term, itself susceptible to multiple interpretations, but usually understood by Western human rights activists and the media as the establishment of political institutions and practices akin to those existing in the United States and Europe.

There is good reason to doubt whether the countries of the former USSR and Eastern Europe will really evolve into 'democracies' anytime soon, however this term is defined, or even whether such a transformation would necessarily always be for the better, given the ethnic hatreds in the region. But the Western approach is ideological, not empirical. The West needs its myths; missionary zeal to whip the heathen along the path of righteousness and remake the world in its own image is deeply ingrained in Western (especially American) political culture. It is entirely understandable that Western human rights advocates choose to interpret reality in the way they believe helps their cause most.

. . .

The hard core of rights that are truly universal is smaller than many in the West are wont to pretend. Forty-five years after the Universal Declaration was adopted, many of its 30 articles are still subject to debate over interpretation and application—not just between Asia and the West, but within the West itself. Not every one of the 50 states of the United States would apply the provisions of the Universal Declaration in the same way. It is not only pretentious but wrong to insist that everything has been settled once and forever. The Universal Declaration is not a tablet Moses brought down from the mountain. It was drafted by mortals. All international norms must evolve through continuing debate among different points of view if consensus is to be maintained.

Most East and Southeast Asian governments are uneasy with the propensity of many American and some European human rights activists to place more emphasis on civil and political rights than on economic, social, and cultural rights. They would probably not be convinced, for instance, by a September 1992 report issued by Human Rights Watch entitled *Indivisible Human Rights: The Relationship of Political and Civil Rights to Survival, Subsistence and Poverty*. They would find the report's argument that 'political and civil rights, especially those related to democratic accountability', are basic to survival and 'not luxuries to be enjoyed only after a certain level of economic development has been reached' to be grossly overstated. Such an argument does not accord with their own historical experience. That experience sees order and stability as preconditions for economic growth, and growth as the necessary foundation of any political order that claims to advance human dignity.

The Asian record of economic success is a powerful claim that cannot be easily dismissed. Both the West and Asia can agree that values and institutions are important determinants of development. But what institutions and which values? The individualistic ethos of the West or the communitarian traditions of Asia? The consensus-seeking approach of East and South-east Asia or the adversarial institutions of the West? . . .

. . .

One explanation of the contradictions in Asian attitudes is that popular pressures against East and Southeast Asian governments may not be so much for 'human rights' or 'democracy' but for good government: effective, efficient, and honest administrations able to provide security and basic needs with good opportunities for an improved standard of living. To be sure, good government, human rights, and democracy are overlapping concepts. Good government requires the protection of human dignity and accountability through periodic fair and free elections. But they are not always the same thing; it cannot be blithely assumed, as many in the West have, that more democracy and human rights will inevitably lead to good government, as the many lost opportunities of the Aquino government demonstrated. The apparent contradictions mirror a complex reality: Good government may well require, among other things, detention without trial to deal with military rebels or religious and other extremists; curbs on press freedoms to avoid fanning racial tensions or exacerbating social divisions; and draconian laws to break the power of entrenched interests in order to, for instance, establish land reforms.

Those are the realities of exercising authority in heterogeneous, unevenly modernized, and imperfectly integrated societies with large rural populations and shallow Western-style civic traditions. . . .

. . .

Future Western approaches on human rights will have to be formulated with greater nuance and precision. It makes a great deal of difference if the West insists on humane standards of behavior by vigorously protesting genocide, murder, torture, or slavery. Here there is a clear consensus on a core of international law that does not admit of derogation on any grounds. The West has a legitimate right and moral duty to promote those core human rights, even if it is tempered by limited influence. But if the West objects to, say, capital punishment, detention without trial, or curbs on press freedoms, it should recognize that it does so in a context where the international law is less definitive and more open to interpretation and where there is room for further elaboration through debate. The West will have to accept that no universal consensus may be possible and that states can legitimately agree to disagree without being guilty of sinister designs or bad faith. Trying to impose pet Western definitions of 'freedom' and 'democracy' is an incitement to destructive conflict, best foregone in the interest of promoting real human rights.

The international law on human rights provides a useful, relatively precise, and common framework for the human rights dialogue between West and East. It helps prevent 'human rights' from becoming a mere catchphrase for whatever actions the West finds contrary to its preferences or too alien to comprehend. But the implementation, interpretation, and elaboration of the international law on human rights is unavoidably political. It must reflect changing global power structures and political circumstances. It will require the West to make complex political distinctions, perhaps refraining from taking a position on some human rights issues, irrespective of their merits, in order to press others where the prospects for consensus are better.

. . .

Yet it is only through such thickets of compromise, contradiction, and ambiguity that further progress on human rights can be made. Those in the West concerned about human rights in East and Southeast Asia, therefore, must be asked a simple question: Do you ultimately want to do good, or merely posture to make yourselves feel good?

NOTE

Consider the relevance to Kausikan's remarks of the following information:

(1) In 1987 the Singapore Government detained various social workers and activists. Several U.S. Congressmen wrote to complain about the detentions. A statement (in reply) of the Minister for Home Affairs stressed the fragility and heterogeneity of Singapore.

> We are vulnerable to powerful centrifugal forces and volatile emotional tides. Like many other developing countries, Singapore's major problem of nationhood is simply to stay united as one viable nation. . . . Singapore has repeatedly encountered subversive threats from within and without. . . . The very secrecy of covert operations precludes garnering evidence to meet the standards of the criminal law for conviction. In many cases of racial agitation, the process of trial itself will provide further opportunity for inflammatory rabble rousing. . . . Preventive detention is not a blemish marring our record; it is a necessary power underpinning our freedom.[11]

(2) The *New York Times*, January 18, 1995, p. A6, reported that a Singapore court found a US scholar and US-owned newspaper (the *International Herald Tribune*) guilty of contempt of court over a published opinion article that was critical of what it called 'intolerant regimes' in Asia that use 'a compliant' judiciary to drive opposition politicians into bankruptcy through defamation and other suits. Heavy fines were imposed. The Justice noted that the article's clear reference was to Singapore, and that the description of compliant courts had 'scandalized the Singapore judiciary'. The US State Department had protested this contempt proceeding, noting that 'people have a right to freedom of expression'.

Responding to similar critical allegations in the past about suits brought by members of the governing party, the Singapore government had insisted that the cases were decided on the merits without pressure on the judiciary. A few months earlier, a judicial decision found that the same newspaper had defamed the former Prime Minister (Lee Kuan Yew) through its reference to 'dynastic politics' in Singapore and other Asian states. It was public knowledge that Lee desired to see his son eventually become Prime Minister, but Lee claimed that the article amounted to an accusation of nepotism.

(3) A speech by Prime Minister Goh in which he 'delivered a wide-ranging denunciation of liberal ideas' was reported in *The Australian*, August 23, 1994, p. 10. Stating that Singapore could not accept unmarried single-parent families, Goh noted that 'unmarried mothers would no longer be allowed to buy government-subsidised flats direct from the Housing Development Board'. Goh also reaffirmed the Government's refusal to allow female civil servants the same medical benefits

---

[11] Quoted in Yash Ghai, 'Human Rights and Governance: The Asia Debate', 15 Aust. Y.B. Int. L. I (1994), at 9.

as their male counterparts, explaining that 'changing the rule would alter the balance of responsibility between men and women'. He further said that the government policy of stopping aid to families when they broke up was harsh but right. It was the Government's underlying philosophy to 'channel rights, benefits and privileges through the head of the family so that he can enforce the obligations and responsibilities of family members'. To promote family togetherness, Mr. Goh announced a government grant of \$30,000 (\$27,000) for people who want to buy a flat near their parents. The Prime Minister acknowledged some problems, noting that Singaporeans were 'more preoccupied with materialism and individual rewards', and that divorce rates were rising.

ARTICLES ON EAST ASIA/SINGAPORE AND HUMAN RIGHTS, THE STRAITS TIMES (SINGAPORE)

Human Rights: Bridging the Gulf

by Susan Sim, *The Straits Times* (Singapore), October 21, 1995, p. 32.

. . .

It is perhaps not so much for specific human rights abuses that Singapore has attracted considerable attention from human rights activists as for the government's clear articulation of a viable alternative position.

What some have called the 'Singapore School' of critics, led by Mr Lee himself, is challenging the Western idea that the individual is inviolable and must be placed above societal order.

Singapore diplomats like Mr Kishore Mahbubani and Bilahari Kausikan, who both spent several months in the United States researching human rights issues, have written articles, published in American journals, which call for a reassertion of indigenous Asian values and traditions that have contributed to the prosperity and stability of many Southeast and East Asian countries.

Their articles have also suggested that the absence of such values might explain the social decay in the West, especially the United States.

In a sense the Singapore Government's differences with the international human rights groups—which tend not to like being tagged as 'western groups' even though their members and financial sources are primarily from the West—are a reflection of an East-West gulf.

Many Western commentators dismiss this notion as simplistic and intellectually dishonest, pointing to the many commonalities in Asian and Western intellectual traditions. Asians, they argue, do not have a stranglehold on communitarianism or strong work ethics. Confucianism as perpetuated by present-day Asian governments is remarkably similar to the Protestant work ethic.

Yet a survey conducted by American political analyst David Hitchcock last year shows that Asian academics, think tank experts, officials, businessmen, journalists, religious and cultural leaders do tend to have different moral perspectives from their American counterparts.

Asian respondents in his study picked as their top three choices of societal values, in descending order: orderly society, harmony and accountability of public officials.

Americans, on the other hand, chose freedom of expression, personal freedom and rights of the individual.

They also did not think that an orderly society, harmony, rights of society, respect for authority and consensus were of critical importance to fellow Americans.

SM Lee and his Pragmatic Approach to Development

by Susan Sim, *The Straits Times* (Singapore), January 28, 1996, p. 4.

. . .

[Lee Kuan Yew's] position, reflected in interviews with various Western and Asian magazines and in his speeches over the last few years, has been unyielding.

Among the core tenets:

— Values are learnt differently in West and East, with one's mother's milk, and Western-style democracy requires certain cultural impulses absent in many Asian societies.

— The exuberance of democracy leads to undisciplined and disorderly conditions inimical to development.

— Asian leaders are right to put the material needs of their people first, even if they have to be brutal to attain that goal, although brutality for its own sake is undesirable.

— Participatory politics will come to Asian societies as they develop, but the process is slow and to hasten it according to the dictates of the West is to court disaster.

. . .

Human Rights: The East Asian Challenge

by Susan Sim, *The Straits Times* (Singapore), February 18, 1996, p. 1, SR4.

. . .

Often overlooked in the polemics are more nuanced viewpoints articulated by critical Asian intellectuals. They do not believe that 3.4 billion Asians of diverse ethnic, linguistic and religious hues subscribe to a single set of beliefs completely different from those held by nearly a billion people in Europe and America.

At the same time, they find it difficult to accept that a common standard of moral conduct can be adhered to by all mankind, transcending all national and cultural differences.

Yet, as Singapore's then Foreign Minister Wong Kan Seng said at the Vienna conference: 'Diversity cannot justify gross violations of human rights. Murder is murder whether perpetrated in America, Asia or Africa. No one claims torture as part of his cultural heritage'.

There is a large core of rights which all states agree to protect, regardless of whether they have signed any of the UN human rights covenants.

The debate is thus really about what other rights are worthy of state protection.

And this is where historical, cultural and religious factors may have a bearing on whether an Asian alternative to traditional Western conceptions of human rights does exist.

. . .

More intractable a problem is what one workshop participant, law lecturer Kevin Tan from the National University of Singapore, calls the 'priority issue'.

Does development come before human rights? Should certain civil and political liberties be put on hold while collective economic and social interests are advanced? Put more simplistically, do you give a starving man a loaf of bread or a milkcrate to vent his spleen on the passing world?

Mr Tan does not think many developing countries have a choice.

'What many East Asian states are fighting for is not really the right to forge their own version of human rights, but for the right to be modern. Asian modernity rather than Asian democracy or Asian human rights,' he argues.

History, he says, is replete with examples of how strong leaders transformed their societies without an overly stringent adherence to the rule of law, or an extravagant regard for human rights.

And East Asian governments, having recognized this fact, have framed their debates along these lines.

HUMAN RIGHTS IN CHINA
Information Office of the State Council, Beijing, 1991

[This White Paper represents the most important official statement made by the government of the Peoples' Republic of China on human rights issues. The excerpts are taken from Section X, 'Active Participation in International Human Rights Activities'.]

China pays close attention to the issue of the right to development. China believes that as history develops, the concept and connotation of human rights also develop constantly. . . . To the people in the developing countries, the most urgent human rights are still the right to subsistence and the right to economic, social and cultural development. Therefore, attention should first be given to the right to development. . . .

Over a long period in the UN activities in that human rights field, China has firmly opposed to any country making use of the issue of human rights to sell its own values, ideology, political standards and mode of development, and to any country interfering in the internal affairs of other countries on the pretext of human rights, the internal affairs of developing countries in particular, and so hurting the sovereignty and dignity of many developing countries. Together with other developing countries, China has waged a resolute struggle against all such acts of interference, and upheld justice by speaking out from a sense of fairness. China has always maintained that human rights are essentially matters within the domestic jurisdiction of a country. Respect for each country's sovereignty and non-interference in internal affairs are universally recognized principles of international law, which are applicable to all fields of international relations, and of course applicable to the field of human rights as well. Section 7 of Article 2 of the Charter of the United Nations stipulates that 'Nothing contained in the present Charter shall authorize the United Nations to intervene in matters which are essentially within the domestic jurisdiction of any state' . . . . These provisions of international instruments reflect the will of the overwhelming majority of countries to safeguard the fundamental principles of international law and maintain a normal relationship between states. They are basic principles that must be followed in international human rights activities. The argument that the principle of non-interference in internal affairs does not apply to the issue of human rights is, in essence, a demand that sovereign states give up their state sovereignty in the field of human rights, a demand that is contrary to international law. Using the human rights issue for the political purpose of imposing the ideology of one country on another is no longer a question of human rights, but a manifestation of power politics in the form of interference in the internal affairs of other countries. Such abnormal practice in international human rights activities must be eliminated.

China is in favor of strengthening international cooperation in the realm of human rights on the basis of mutual understanding and seeking a common ground while reserving differences. However, no country in its effort to realize and protect human rights can take a route that is divorced from its history and its economic, political and cultural realities. . . . It is neither proper nor feasible for any country to judge other countries by the yardstick of its own mode or to impose its own mode on others. Therefore, the purpose of international protection of human rights and related activities should be to promote normal cooperation in the international field of human rights and international harmony, mutual understanding and mutual respect. Consideration should be given to the differing views on human rights held by countries with different political, economic and social systems, as well as different historical, religious and cultural backgrounds. International human rights activities should be carried on in the spirit of seeking common ground while reserving differences, mutual respect, and the promotion of understanding and cooperation.

China has always held that to effect international protection of human rights, the international community should interfere with and stop acts that endanger world peace and security, such as gross human rights violations caused by colonialism, racism, foreign aggression and occupation, as well as apartheid, racial discrimination, genocide, slave trade and serious violation of human rights by international terrorist organizations. . . .

. . . Interference in other countries' internal affairs and the pushing of power politics on the pretext of human rights are obstructing the realization of human rights and fundamental freedoms.

NOTE

The Second World Conference on Human Rights, held in Vienna in June 1993, was preceded by regional preparatory meetings in four parts of the world. A group of Asian countries held such a regional meeting in Bangkok earlier that year. It culminated in the Bangkok Governmental Declaration.[13]

In that Declaration, the participating states emphasized (para. 5) 'principles of respect for national sovereignty and territorial integrity as well as non-interference in the internal affairs of States, and the non-use of human rights as an instrument of political pressure'. Although para. 7 stressed the universality of human rights and that no violation could be justified, para. 8 asserted that human rights 'must be considered in the context of a dynamic and evolving process of international norm-setting, bearing in mind the significance of national and regional particularities and various historical, cultural and religious backgrounds'.

Human rights nongovernmental organizations (NGOs) from the Asia-Pacific region also gathered at Bangkok to transact their business immediately before the intergovernmental meeting began: The Bangkok NGO Declaration on Human Rights provided in para. 1:

> *Universality.* We can learn from different cultures in a pluralistic perspective. . . . Universal human rights are rooted in many cultures. We affirm the basis of universality of human rights which afford protection to all of humanity. . . . While advocating cultural pluralism, those cultural practices which derogate from universally accepted human rights, including women's right, must not be tolerated. *As human rights are of universal concern and are universal in value, the advocacy of human rights cannot be considered to be an encroachment upon national sovereignty.*

The Vienna Declaration[14] adopted by states at the Second World Conference on Human Rights, provides in Sec. I, para. 5 that:

> [a]ll human rights are universal, indivisible, and interdependent and inter-related. . . . While the significance of national and regional particularities and various historical, cultural and religious backgrounds must be borne in mind, it is the duty of States, regardless of their political, economic and cultural systems, to promote and protect all human rights and fundamental freedoms.

QUESTIONS

1. 'It is sheer evasion of the real issue for a state labeled a violator of human rights to contend (as does Kausikan, a government official in Singapore) that Western advocacy of human rights is to an important degree a way of supporting the material interests of Western states in opening foreign markets to Western investment and trade, and generally in spreading market economies.' Comment.

2. Is Kausikan's argument one of cultural relativism, the defence of a traditional or religious culture against invasion and annihilation by the West? What international human rights norms that purport to be universal does he challenge, and why? How does his argument compare with those based on customary norms (gender, for example) or on religious dogma?

3. If one can read Kausikan's observations and the excerpts from the PRC White Paper to say that states making economic progress find that human rights endanger that progress, how would you reply to these arguments? Would you agree or disagree, and why?

4. In its White Paper, the PRC invokes the traditional rhetoric of domestic jurisdiction. Does that rhetoric appear to rest on cultural relativism? Or on other grounds?

5. The illustrations at the end of the White Paper indicate where the PRC would support international enforcement of human rights, even if involving substantial interference with a state. Do these illustrations have any common theme or characteristic? Do any of them, from a Western perspective, implicate the PRC?

NOTE

The two following writings by Ghai and Donnelly consider cultural relativism in general, but bear on the preceding questions.

YASH GHAI, HUMAN RIGHTS AND GOVERNANCE: THE ASIA DEBATE
15 Austral. Y. Bk. Int. L. 1 (1994), at 5

... It is easy to believe that there is a distinct Asian approach to human rights because some government leaders speak as if they represent the whole continent when they make their pronouncements on human rights. This view is reinforced because they claim that their views are based on perspectives which emerge from the Asian culture or religion or Asian realities. The gist of their position is that human rights as propounded in the West are founded on individualism and therefore have no relevance to Asia which is based on the primacy of the community. It is also sometimes argued that economic underdevelopment renders most of the political and civil rights (emphasised in the West) irrelevant in Asia. Indeed, it is sometimes alleged that such rights are dangerous in view of fragmented nationalism and fragile Statehood.

It would be surprising if there were indeed one Asian perspective, since neither Asian culture nor Asian realities are homogenous throughout the continent. All the world's major religions are represented in Asia, and are in one place or another State religions (or enjoy a comparable status: Christianity in the Philippines, Islam in Malaysia, Hinduism in Nepal and Buddhism in Sri Lanka and Thailand). To this list we may add political ideologies like socialism, democracy or feudalism which animate peoples and governments of the region. Even apart from religious differences, there are other factors which have produced a rich diversity of cultures. A culture, moreover, is not static and many accounts given of Asian culture are probably true of an age long ago. Nor are the economic circumstances of all the Asian countries similar. Japan, Singapore and Hong Kong are among the world's most prosperous countries, while there is grinding poverty in Bangladesh, India and the Philippines. The economic and political systems in Asia likewise show a remarkable diversity, ranging from semi-feudal kingdoms in Kuwait and Saudi Arabia, through military dictatorships in Burma and formerly Cambodia, effectively one party regimes in Singapore and Indonesia, communist regimes in China and Vietnam, ambiguous democracies in Malaysia and Sri Lanka, to well established democracies like India. There are similarly differences in their economic systems, ranging from tribal subsistence economies in parts of Indonesia through highly developed market economies of Singapore, Hong Kong and Taiwan and the mixed economy model of India to the planned economies of China and Vietnam. Perceptions of human rights are undoubtedly reflective of these conditions, and suggest that they would vary from country to country.

Perceptions of human rights are reflective of social and class positions in society. What conveys an apparent picture of a uniform Asian perspective on human rights is that it is the perspective of a particular group, that of the ruling elites, which gets international attention. What unites these elites is their notion of governance and the expediency of their rule. For the most part, the political systems they represent are not open or democratic, and their publicly expressed views on human rights are an emanation of these systems, of the need to justify authoritarianism and occasional repression. It is their views which are given wide publicity domestically and internationally.
. . .

. . . [S]ome Asian governments claim that their societies place a higher value on the community than in the West, that individuals find fulfilment in their participation in communal life and community tasks, and that this factor constitutes a primary distinction in the approach to human rights. . . . This argument is advanced as an instance of the general proposition that rights are culture specific.

The 'communitarian' argument is Janus-faced. It is used against the claim of universal human rights to distinguish the allegedly Western, individual-oriented approaches to rights from the community centred values of the East. Yet it is also used to deny the claims and assertions of communities in the name of 'national unity and stability'. It suffers from at least two further weaknesses. First, it overstates the 'individualism' of Western society and traditions of thought. . . .

Secondly, Asian governments (notwithstanding the attempt in the Singapore Paper to distinguish the 'nation' and the community) fall into the easy but wrong assumption that they or the State are the 'community'. . . . Nothing can be more destructive of the community than this confiliation. The community and State are different institutions and to some extent in a contrary juxtaposition. The community, for the most part, depends on popular norms developed through forms of consensus and enforced through mediation and persuasion. The State is an imposition on society, and unless humanised and democratised (as it has not been in most of Asia), it relies on edicts, the military, coercion and sanctions. It is the tension between them which has elsewhere underpinned human rights. In the name of the community, most Asian governments have stifled social and political initiatives of private groups. . . . Governments have destroyed many communities in the name of development or State stability. . . .

Another attack on the community comes from the economic, market oriented policies of the governments. Although Asian capitalism appears to rely on the family and clan associations, there is little doubt that it weakens the community and its cohesion. The organising matrix of the market is not the same as that of the community. Nor are its values or methods particularly 'communitarian'. The moving frontier of the market, seeking new resources, has been particularly disruptive of communities which have managed to preserve intact a great deal of their culture and organisation during the colonial and post-colonial periods. The emphasis on the market, and with it individual rights of property are also at odds with communal organisation and enjoyment of property. . . .

A final point is the contradiction between claims of a consensus and harmonious society, and the extensive arming of the state apparatus. The pervasive use of draconian legislation like administrative detention, disestablishment of societies, press censorship, and sedition, belies claims to respect alternative views, promote a dialogue, and seek consensus. The contemporary State intolerance of opposition is inconsistent with traditional communal values and processes. . . .

JACK DONNELLY, UNIVERSAL HUMAN RIGHTS IN THEORY AND PRACTICE
(1989), at 118

. . .

4. *Culture and relativism*

The cultural basis of cultural relativism must be considered too, especially because numerous contemporary arguments against universal human rights standards strive for the cachet of cultural relativism but actually are entirely without cultural basis.

Standard arguments for cultural relativism rely on such examples as the precolonial African village, Native American tribes, and traditional Islamic social systems, but we have seen that human rights are foreign to such communities, which employed other mechanisms to protect and realize human dignity . . . [W]here there is a thriving indigenous cultural tradition and community, arguments of cultural relativism offer a strong defense against outside interference—including disruptions that might be caused by introducing 'universal' human rights.

Such communities, however, are increasingly the exception rather than the rule. They are not, for example, the communities of the teeming slums that hold an ever-growing proportion of the population of most Third World states. Even most rural areas of the Third World have been substantially penetrated, and the local culture 'corrupted', by foreign practices and institutions, including the modern state, the money economy, and 'Western' values, products, and practices. In the Third World today we see most often not the persistence of traditional culture in the face of modern intrusions, or even the development of syncretic cultures and values, but rather a disruptive 'Westernization', cultural confusion, or the enthusiastic embrace of 'modern' practices and values. In other words, the traditional culture advanced to justify cultural relativism far too often no longer exists. But communitarian defenses of traditional practices usually cannot be extended to modern nation-states and contemporary nationalist regimes.

Therefore, while recognizing the legitimate claims of self-determination and cultural relativism, we must be alert to cynical manipulations of a dying, lost, or even mythical cultural past. We must not be misled by complaints of the inappropriateness of 'Western' human rights made by repressive regimes whose practices have at best only the most tenuous connection to the indigenous culture; communitarian rhetoric too often cloaks the depredations of corrupt and often Westernized or deracinated elites.

Arguments of cultural relativism are far too often made by economic and political elites that have long since left traditional culture behind. While this may represent a fundamentally admirable effort to retain or recapture cherished traditional values, it is at least ironic to see largely Westernized elites warning against the values and practices they have adopted.

. . .

. . . Leaders sing the praises of traditional communities—while they wield arbitrary power antithetical to traditional values, pursue development policies that systematically undermine traditional communities, and replace traditional leaders with corrupt cronies and party hacks. Such cynical manipulation of tradition occurs everywhere.

. . .

The cynicism of many claims of cultural relativism can also be seen in the fact that far too often they are for foreign consumption only. The same elites that raise culture as a defense against external criticisms based on universal human rights often ruthlessly suppress inconvenient local customs, whether of the majority or of a minority. National unification certainly will require substantial sacrifices of local customs, but the lack of *local* cultural sensitivity shown by many national elites that strongly advocate an international cultural relativism suggests a very high degree of self-interest.

. . .

ADDITIONAL READING

On Asian perspectives see: J. Bauer and D. Bell (eds.), *The East Asian Challenge for Human Rights* (1999); D. Kelly and A. Reid, *Asian Freedoms: The Idea of Freedom in East and Southeast Asia* (1998); W. de Bary, *Asian Values and Human Rights: A Confucian Communitarian Perspective* (1998); and W. de Bary and Tu Weiming (eds.), *Confucianism and Human Rights* (1998).

PART C

INTERNATIONAL HUMAN RIGHTS ORGANIZATIONS

Part C turns to an examination of the international organizations embodying, developing, monitoring and enforcing the rules and standards of the human rights movement whose character and evolution were explored in Part A. The invention of organizations by the movement has been among its most striking and important features. None of the institutions[1] discussed in Part C existed before the end of the Second World War.

Neither Part A nor Part C can fully exclude the other and become an airtight compartment. Norms and institutions are too intricately and fundamentally connected. For example, several UN organs necessarily figured in Chapter 3's discussion of the development of the UDHR, ICCPR and CEDAW, as well as in Chapter 4's discussion of the ICESCR. They did so because standard-setting, the grandest achievement of the human rights movement's first half century, began within these new international institutions—drafting by the UN Commission on Human Rights, for example. Similarly, the materials in Part C, though stressing institutions' role in implementation of treaties, necessarily involve their law-making powers as well through their interpretive comments on treaty texts and the dispute-resolving decisions by international committees or courts that rest on such texts.

Nonetheless our concerns here sharply change. These new chapters look at institutions as such: constitutional structures, processes, functions, powers. Above all, the chapters are concerned with institutions' role in elaboration, implementation and enforcement rather than standard-setting.

Part C examines intergovernmental and nongovernmental organizations, both universal and regional in scope, whose work involves primarily international human rights. Inevitably its materials pose broader issues about international organizations or institutions in general, whatever their fields of specialization. An analogy to Part A is pertinent. There we gave some attention to characteristics of international law as such, as essential background to the study of international human rights norms. Here too we give brief attention to characteristics of international organizations as such.

Chapter 7 brings into discussion some broader characteristics of international institutions. The remaining Chapters 8–11 in Part C start with the UN Charter human rights organs (or bodies), continue with treaty organs, move to regional human rights organizations in Europe, the Americas and Africa, and conclude with nongovernmental human rights organizations.

---

[1] A word about terminology. The authors' text in this book uses the terms '*organization*' and '*institution*' more or less interchangeably. Excerpts from writings by other authors included in this book may, however, attach particular meanings to one or the other term. For example, some scholars of international 'organizations' view that designation as indicating possession of specific legal attributes, such as juridical personality and capacity to sue. From this perspective, the United Nations is the paradigmatic 'organization'. On the other hand the Human Rights Committee created under the ICCPR, a treaty *organ* or *body* (interchangeable terms), would not readily fit within such a meaning of the term. Some scholars view the term 'institution' as suggesting a richer and more complex and autonomous entity that goes beyond the form of a rudimentary organization that merely organizes states within a loose cooperative framework. There is indeed little agreement.

7

The Need for International Institutions and their Challenge to Notions of Sovereignty

A. SOME BASIC NOTIONS

Except for nongovernmental organizations, the international institutions and organs examined in Part C were created by multilateral treaties or derive their authority and legitimacy from decisions taken within the framework of those treaties. Customary international law does not, cannot create institutions. These materials explore the more developed and complex institutional arrangements, going well beyond the kind of rudimentary organization created by a multilateral treaty that, say, provides only for periodic meetings of states parties to exchange views on certain matters or to draft conventions to be submitted to states for ratification.

The principal treaties relevant to Part C—the UN Charter, the ICCPR and its Optional Protocol, and the treaties creating the three regional human rights systems—each creates a distinctive human rights regime involving both norms and one or more treaty organs intended to perform stated functions by exercising stated powers. To one or another extent, that regime (or organization) takes on a life of its own. It will have one or many of such attributes as its own officials, staff and budget. Despite its pervasive links with the states parties creating it (parties that are directly represented in the membership of many Charter organs such as the UN General Assembly or the UN Commission on Human Rights), the regime or organization can be meaningfully considered separately from those parties (unlike, say, the 'rudimentary' form of organization described above). If in some major respects it depends entirely on the states parties' 'will' as expressed in voting or other forms of decision-making, in other major respects the regime/organization possesses autonomy. Thus a regime organ like the UN Commission on Human Rights or the European Court of Human Rights becomes a significant participant in international relations, expanding on the traditional international system of sovereign states and qualitatively changing the nature of international law and life.

There follow excerpts from the Table of Contents of a leading treatise on the subject that suggest one framework, a formal typology, for thinking about the constitution and operations of international institutions. It indicates how much choice states have, how many possibilities are before them, when they negotiate about the original form or the reform of multilateral institutions. The excerpts include the entire section of the Table of Contents on voting since a reading below draws on voting arrangements to illustrate its argument.

HENRY SCHERMERS, INTERNATIONAL INSTITUTIONAL LAW
(1980), at ix

Table of Contents

NOTE

Schermers has set forth formal distinctions between two categories of international organizations that figure in the following chapters.[2]

> *Non-Governmental Organizations*: By far the largest number of international organizations is established and governed by individual people. . . . In order to obtain legal personality such organizations must be established under the law of a State. . . . Legally, their position is not different from other organizations under that law. . . . Under international law all organizations established by individual citizens are classified as non-governmental, even if they perform important governmental tasks. [Schermers cites the International Committee of the Red Cross as an example of performing governmental tasks.] There is no generally recognized definition of non-governmental organizations. In a sense, international companies . . . are international organizations.
>
> *Governmental Organizations*: An international organization is characterized as a governmental organization, or as a public international organization, when it is established by an interstate agreement. With very few exceptions. . . . the required interstate agreement is expressed in a treaty. This treaty is usually called the constitution of the organization. . . . We noted above that some non-governmental organizations perform governmental tasks. It is equally possible that a governmental organization is established for a commercial purposes, *e.g.* the launching and exploitation of a satellite. . . .
>
> Most international organizations are no more than fora where States cooperate. . . . [But] factually many international organizations have some governmental power of their own. . . . Though [such organizations'] autonomous tasks are still limited in number, they have led to a general recognition that international organizations have their own legal personality under international law. Together with the States they form the subjects which create the international legal order.

COMMENT ON RELATIONS BETWEEN NORMS AND INSTITUTIONS

Imagine a human rights system consisting solely of the rules or principles growing out of declarations, treaties and customary law. That is, we 'assume away' the UN organs dealing with human rights issues, the organs under treaties like the ICCPR, and regional human rights organs. We do away entirely with the 'institutionalization' of norms in these different entities.

Simply imagining a human rights system shorn of its intergovernmental institutions and processes makes clear how profoundly different the human rights movement would be. Only state governments and state institutions would be available to meet the need for standard-setting; for the development, monitoring, implementation and enforcement of norms; and for dispute resolution. Of course one hopes that most states would take their obligations seriously, acting consist-

---

[2] 'The International Organizations', in Mohammed Bedjaoui (ed.), *International Law: Achievements and Prospects* (1991) at 67.

ently with their treaty obligations through their own equivalent constitutional norms or through specific internalization of treaty norms (see Chapter 12). One also knows, however, that no state will so act all the time, that many states will be persistent and serious violators, and that a number among them will engage in brutal and systematic abuses. From the international perspective, human rights norms would be freely floating rather than anchored in any international regime, dependent for their effectiveness on the willingness of one or many treaty parties to apply pressures to delinquent states. Whatever the inadequacies of existing international human rights institutions, in such imagined circumstances a state party to the basic treaties that commits serious violations would have much less to fear.

The problem is compounded in the light of a distinctive feature of the enforcement of international human rights norms. States parties to a human rights treaty lack the usual material incentives (as exist in, say, a trade or establishment treaty) to act against violator state Y. The violation consists in Y's abuse of *its own* citizens. Why should state X invest its energies in trying to persuade state Y to stop such conduct? It would generally be foolish to assume that sustained inquiry into Y's abuses, let alone serious pressures and sanctions against Y, would originate in X or other states parties, which at most might suspend economic or military aid to the delinquent state (see Chapter 13). The inquiries, debates, threats and pressures of international organizations may persuade Y to more serious thought.

It should then be no surprise that the traditional defences by states of sovereignty and domestic jurisdiction are asserted today more strongly against the powers or actions of international institutions that involve implementation, enforcement, or dispute resolution—that may indeed involve physical intervention—than against standard-setting as such. Through its collective acts and decisions—ranging from the holding of a debate, investigative missions and resolutions, or the imposition of sanctions to physical intervention—the institution can inflict serious costs on the delinquent state. It becomes the bridge between states (the very creators of international norms) and the norms themselves. It can make those norms 'real'.

All the intergovernmental institutions and organs examined in Part C reflect this tension or contradiction. States create institutions that, to one or another degree, are meant to influence their behaviour or discipline them. Much depends on the institution's architecture—its constitution and processes, its modes of decision-making such as majority vote or consensus, its powers. In states' decisions about architecture lie some of the most acerbic fights and deepest divisions in the human rights movement.

The following readings raise basic questions about international institutions that recur in specific institutional contexts in the later specialized chapters.

INIS CLAUDE, SWORDS INTO PLOWSHARES
(4th edn., 1984), at 6

... To understand that international agencies are products not of the aspirations of idealists standing outside of and above international politics, but of the necessities felt by statesmen operating within the arena of international politics, is to sense the fact that international organization is a functional response to the complexities of the modern state system, an organic development rooted in the realities of the system rather than an optional experiment fastened upon it. For one who grasps this fact, the issue of whether we should have international organization is no more meaningful than the issue of whether urbanization should result in the provision of more extensive public services and the imposition of more elaborate governmental regulations. One recognizes international organization as a distinctive modern aspect of world politics, a relatively recent growth, but an established trend. Particular organizations may come and go, but international organization as a generic phenomenon is here to stay. The collapse of the League of Nations led almost automatically to consideration of the nature of its replacement, and similar failure by the United Nations might be expected to produce the same reaction. A sense of history provides the basis for the understanding that international organization has become a necessary part of the system for dealing with international problems, and that 'to organize or not to organize' is no longer an open question for statesmen or a useful one for students of international relations.

...

... The problems confronted by international organizations may be divided into two categories: constitutional problems—the problems *of* international organizations, and substantive problems—the problems *with which* the organizations are designed to grapple. The first group consists of internal matters, related to the management and functioning of the organizations, while the second includes external issues requiring solution. Constitutional problems are occasioned *by* the establishment of international organizations; substantive problems are the occasions *for* the establishment of such agencies.

However definite the dividing line between these two classes of problems may be in logic, it is not so in practice. The nature and intensity of world problems determine the nature and scope of organizational efforts, and thereby define the constitutional problems which emerge. Decisions concerning the internal development of international agencies are inevitably influenced by external political considerations, and, conversely, the solution of substantive political problems is affected by the degree of constitutional development achieved by international organizations. The two problem areas cannot be divorced.

One of the major tasks of twentieth-century statesmanship is to strike a balance between obsessive concern with institutional problems—which makes international organization an end in itself, and exclusive concentration upon substantive issues of current world politics—which neglects the building of an adequate institutional apparatus for international relations....

... It is useful for statemen to be reminded that they cannot expect international organizations to serve them well, now or in the future, if their urge to exploit these institutions for immediate political advantage overrides all consideration of the requirements of sound constitutional development. International organizations cannot become effective means to the ends that states envisage unless they are treated, to some degree, as ends in themselves.

. . .

NOTE

The excerpts from Ernst Haas stress the issue of control by one or a few states of the processes and powers of an international organization. That issue permeates Chapter 8's materials on the UN General Assembly and Commission on Human Rights.

ERNST HAAS, WHEN KNOWLEDGE IS POWER
(1990), at 57

All international organizations have a heterogeneous membership. Their members differ in size, military power, population, resource endowment, and degree of industrialization. The members also differ greatly from one another in the extent to which they are permeable—that is, subject to being 'penetrated' economically, culturally, and politically by their stronger neighbors.

Most organizations have their own 'superpower' capable of playing a hegemonic role if it chose to do so. All organizations (except those of Eastern and Western Europe) count democratic, totalitarian, and authoritarian governments among their members. Even organizations that consist almost entirely of economically less developed countries display significant differences in the degree of development among their members. All universal organizations include members with capitalist, socialist, and mixed economies.

All organizations are characterized by major inequalities in power, however defined, among their members. Consequently, they are subject to rule by hegemonic states or hegemonic coalitions of states. The hegemony need not be expressed in the direct imposition of the preferences of the stronger on the weaker. It usually takes the form of higher financial contributions and disproportionate roles for the nationals of the stronger members in organizational secretariats. At the extreme, this kind of hegemony is illustrated by the role of the United States in U.N. agencies. On the one hand, a decision to reduce American financial contributions from 25 percent of the budget to 20 percent threatened to ruin organizational programs. On the other hand, the United States had been signally unsuccessful in translating its superpower status into consistent influence over the content of programs, having lost many programmatic battles for almost two decades except in organizations in which greater power is recognized in the form of weighted voting.

In addition to disproportionate influence due to financial prowess or voting privilege, the principle of sovereign equality is also contradicted in practice by the tendency of the more powerful states to constitute themselves into an inner elite that is consulted far more consistently by the formal heads of secretariats, commissions, and councils than are representatives of less important states. Membership in this elite differs with topic and issue. It almost always includes the delegates of the superpowers and of Japan, Britain, France, West Germany, India, and, increasingly, Brazil in organizations to which these states belong. But it may also include the delegates of smaller states if the country in question happens to be salient to the issue at stake. Sweden, Singapore, and Tanzania have played inner-elite roles on some occasions in the United Nations.

. . .

International organizations share a certain marginality with respect to the core activities in international politics. Few foreign policy initiatives depend on international organizations for their success. States risk little by investing symbolically in the programs of such organizations; the core of one's foreign policy remains intact even if little concrete help is provided by the organizations. In most instances, any result from a symbolic investment in organizational action will not be experienced until much later. Foreign policy relies on nonorganizational means to a far greater extent than on institutionalized multi-lateral efforts. There are, of course, exceptions for large and small states. Immediate benefits can accrue from a successful peacekeeping operation for the losing side in a war; ambitious economic development and technical assistance projects are sources of prestige and employment for one's nationals; a country beset with refugees benefits immediately from multilateral aid; even the superpowers may benefit from a successful mediation to prevent crisis escalation. The great lines of foreign policy, however, are only marginally and gradually influenced by what goes on in international organizations.

NOTE

The following article by David Kennedy talks of the 'move' toward institutions as key to the understanding of modern international law. These excerpts stress the complex, dual, even contradictory positions of states with respect to institutions. States parties make the treaty that creates the institution in which they become members. They lead lives 'within and without the institution'. They form part of its internal processes, participating in decisions about its external action. At the same time they remain sovereign, autonomous states that can become the objects of such action. Through his discussion of different voting arrangements, Kennedy illustrates some of these dilemmas.

DAVID KENNEDY, A NEW STREAM OF INTERNATIONAL LAW SCHOLARSHIP
7 Wisc. Int. L. J. 1 (1988), at 39

. . .

. . . [F]ew areas of public international law doctrine today remain free of the network of institutions understood to have been set in motion in 1918. The corpus of modern doctrine . . . is relentlessly procedural, harnessing each substantive aspiration into the policy objective of some institutional regime. Seen either from history or doctrine, then, the move to institutions is the key to modern international law.

From this perspective, institutions—and the discipline of international institutions—are different from doctrines. . . . Public international law turns to institutions, turns into institutions, as a turn to practice, to engagement with sovereign society, as a move to realism and the politics of regime management. We see then, in the relationship between our two disciplines—public international law and international institutions—a familiar division of labor. The one handles issues of independent legal judgment, the other problems of sovereign engagement. Of course this image is an oversimplification—we saw the repetition throughout public international law of a shrewd equivocation about the independence and normative nature of international law doctrine, and we are likely to find the discipline of international institutions riddled with doctrinal independence, procedural channels, consensual covenants, and the like.

But still, between them they handle international law's more general aspiration to both remain independent and connect with sovereign power. Perhaps this can be done ever so much better the more the division is blurred, or the division of labor proliferated throughout both disciplines. At least we never need face either sovereign autonomy or legal dominion in their pure form. They exist only as rather unstable and hesitant invocations and reference points. . . .

. . .

Questions of constitutional structure are normally considered in relationship to a constituting text—be it the League Covenant, the U.N. Charter or the U.N. Convention of the Law of the Sea. The texts establishing international institutions are remarkably similar in basic structure. In broad outline, all set out the membership, decisionmaking procedures, and respective competences of legislative and administrative organs. Sometimes provision for reference to an independently established or integrated dispute settlement procedure is added. . . .

Leaving dispute resolution aside for a moment, no document seems complete, seems fully to have established a plenary [legislative plenary organ] if it does not indicate who will participate, how they will decide and how their collective being will be known. This pattern repeats the temporal logic of establishment: signatories are transformed into members, the interactions of members are structured, and the organ which they constitute is named. Membership marks a break between life within and without the institution. The organ is the name given the object established. Voting inserts a text between these two moments—both reminiscent of the particularity of members and generative of the constituted organ. The basic historical narrative could hardly be more familiar—a move from politics through text to institutional action.

. . .

. . . Focus for a moment on voting. People writing about institutional design in our discipline have devoted a great deal of energy to voting structure—the allocation of votes among members or the voting configurations required for action. On the one hand, the voting mechanism seems completely internal to the organization, a mere procedure for translating membership into organ activity. Such a sense focuses reformist energy on a technical procedure which might easily be changed, even if it seems too removed from context to provide a fully convincing account of the institution's practices. On the other hand, the voting mechanism draws a connection between the original members and the activities of their institution—connecting the preinstitutional context to the actions of the organization. The result is a double position—within and without the institution.

As such, voting exists uneasily between membership—itself the break between the institution and its creators—and organs—themselves the link between the institution and its context and object. Voting reaches back to members, defining them, and forward to organs, reminding them of their past. The problem of voting is to translate membership into action, orchestrating a smooth movement from constitution as members (frozen in the intentions of the establishing document) to institutional action within the competences of the organ in question. Voting thus both marks the inside of the plenary and asserts a relationship with both a preinstitutional constituency and an implementing organization, thereby linking two constituted beings—states as members with institutions as actors. . . .

. . .

This central relationship demands much of voting. It must accommodate both the authority of sovereign members and the cooperative activity of the institution. . . . Voting must move from sovereign autonomy to cooperation. . . .

. . .

. . . [Voting] must both ratify and express a particular distribution of power merely promised states by membership and be the mechanism by which the community makes up its collective mind and expresses itself vis-a-vis specific state powers—a relationship posited by the instrumental posture of organs. If the institution must be open and closed, voting must be deferential to and expressive of state power and yet also control, channel and ultimately reapportion that power as the voice and mind of the international institution. . . .

. . .

. . . Over the past sixty-five years, scholars considering voting in international institutions have advocated plenary decisionmaking by unanimity, majority vote and consensus. They have expressed their enthusiasm for and disillusionment with each scheme in remarkably similar terms. Each, in turn, has been credited with an ability simultaneously to defer to sovereign authority and express sovereign cooperation. As each decisionmaking scheme fell out of favor, it was criticized for permitting or encouraging either the anarchy of organizational collapse or the tyranny of institutional capture.

During the Hague period, and into the first days of the League [of Nations], scholars defended unanimity voting as a move from sovereign decentralization, in which international law could grow only through the relatively cumbersome mechanism of treaty drafting or the quite lengthy process of customary accretion, to institutionalization. At the turn of the century, unanimity symbolized the achievement of an institutional life among states, for it permitted autonomous sovereigns to sit in standing plenaries without forswearing their sovereign prerogative.

By the mid-1930s, unanimity no longer seemed so attractive. Scholars began to suggest that the League either need not, as a matter of law, or did not, as a matter of practice, continue to abide by a rigid unanimity rule. These texts advanced arguments against unanimity and in favor of some alternative voting scheme (usually majority voting) to those which had been advanced in support of unanimity during the preceding period.

Unanimity, as a matter of theory and practice, could neither respect sovereign autonomy nor generate sovereign cooperation. It permits states to be held hostage by one bad actor, both preventing international action and centralizing international authority so as to override sovereign authority. By reducing international cooperation to the lowest common denominator of sovereign accord, unanimity emasculates the institution and sabatoges cooperation. In short, unanimity slows the momentum of institutional life and permits backsliding to anarchy.

Majority voting seemed much better. It would decentralize international authority, allowing states to defend their interests without waiting for the go ahead from one recalcitrant sovereign. At the same time, majority voting allows for more powerful and decisive institutional action, rendering the international institution persuasive by keeping it in touch with the greater part of the community. A strong international institution, in turn, fosters community. These arguments prevailed in 1945, and the post-war institutions exhibit a veritable cornucopia of majoritarian and weighted voting formulas.

By the mid-1960s, however, the luster was off majoritarianism. Weighted and majority voting—and particularly the veto—seemed a step backward, away from organization toward anarchy or irrelevance. On the one hand, majority voting produces a tyranny of the majority, allowing international organizations to be far too assertive, thereby threatening the sovereign authority of the minority. On the other hand, majority voting is the enemy of international cooperation. By encouraging rash decisions which reflect passing fads, majority voting leaves the institution powerless in the face of sovereign autonomy. By ignoring the interests of the minority, it debases the currency of international institutional outputs and causes the institution to lose respect. Majority voting fails the cooperative sovereign as much as the autonomous one.

By 1975, the fashionable international institution made up its mind by consensus. By exactly translating political reality into institutional action, consensus keeps the institution in step with all states. The minority feels attended to, included, respected: neither the big powers nor the blocs are able to control the majority any more. Consensus is the perfect form of institutional deference. Moreover, consensus permits the institution to make powerful decisions and ensures compliance with such decisions as are taken. The very experience of coming to consensus builds community. Finally, as we might expect, by 1980, the bloom was beginning to be off consensus—and the reasons were familiar. The institution was hostage to one hold out autonomous state—and the individual sovereign felt bullied into agreement by a powerful consensus building plenary practice.

This rather fickle rotation among voting procedures repeats the same arguments in each generation. Good procedures instantiate both autonomy and cooperation among sovereigns. Bad procedures fail to banish the threats of anarchy and tyranny. The move from one to another—from unanimity to majoritarianism to consensus—also marks a certain maturity. Although the arguments for and against consensus sound similar to those advanced for and against unanimity, these procedures are quite dissimilar. In many ways, consensus is the very opposite of a voting mechanism, producing no actual record of inter-sovereign accord, it seems to presume the accord behind the institutional output.

We might say that unanimity positions voting close to membership, consensus close to organs. Seen this way, the move among voting mechanisms is simply a repetition of the more general institutionalizing move from membership through voting to organs. Unanimity suggests an immature plenary, constantly recapitulating the moment of establishment. Consensus suggests a mature organizational voice finally released from its members. Majority voting seems a middle ground, a half-way house of trust, in which formalization of minority rights is still necessary to shackle the organ to members.

. . .

NOTE

The attraction of international organizations as a means of solving international problems was perhaps at its height after the Second World War, an attraction and enthusiasm captured in the creation of the United Nations. Over the decades, enthusiasm waned as it became clear that institutions could simply incorporate the polarities and conflicts of the 'outside' world, become lethargic administrators through inertia and stale bureaucracy, and experience manipulation and corruption. They could share many vices of states themselves.

With the end of the Cold War, fresh hopes looked less to the creation of new institutions than to the revivification of existing ones, particularly the UN. Those hopes too have faded. Much current discussion looks toward reforms of major institutions like the UN to permit them to play a more significant and effective role.

Human rights institutions are fully part of this cycle of enthusiasm and despair. Each of the later chapters involves evaluation of existing institutions and inquires into the kinds of changes that are necessary, desirable, feasible. Some of the current proposals for reform are modest. Others are basic and structural, such as proposals for change in the membership and veto power within the UN Security Council, or for participation of nongovernmental organizations in the work of the General Assembly.

Part of the assessment of the structure, efficiency and achievements of existing human rights institutions may usefully involve comparisons with other types of international regimes—perhaps the very different types of institutions in such diverse fields as the law of the sea, or trade, or environment. The following article suggests some basic differences between human rights and environmental regimes.

DANIEL BODANSKY, REPORTING OBLIGATIONS IN ENVIRONMENTAL REGIMES: LESSONS FOR HUMAN RIGHTS SUPERVISION

in Philip Alston and J. Crawford (eds.), The Future of UN Human Rights Treaty Monitoring 361 (2000), at 363

. . .

B. Some differences between international environmental and human rights law

. . .

First, international law is grounded in the need for mutual action. Most international environmental problems—certainly all global ones—cannot be addressed by individual states acting alone; they require collective effort. In contrast, human rights obligations do not depend on reciprocity in the same way. States owe obligations not to one another, but to individuals; moreover, one state's respect for human rights does not depend on, and may not be conditioned on, compliance by other states. This has an important implication for reporting: in international environmental law, unlike human rights law, one of the principal functions of reporting is to provide assurances to states that their own efforts to protect the environment are being reciprocated. Otherwise, those efforts may count for nothing; indeed they may give non-complying states a competitive advantage.

Second, international environmental law is typically directed at the control of private rather than governmental conduct. To be sure, environmental duties fall in the first instance on governments, and some are aimed at governmental behaviour (for example, environmental impact assessments are usually required only for governmental actions). But most environmental harm results from the behaviour of private actors and will be solved only through changes in private behaviour. In contrast, human rights have traditionally been conceived as rights *vis-à-vis* governments which can be violated only, or at least primarily, by governmental conduct. In the parlance sometimes used in connection with economic, social and cultural rights, international environmental law consists primarily of duties to 'protect', while human rights law has tended to focus on duties to 'respect'. Again, this difference has an important implication for reporting: in international environmental regimes, reports must often address not only governmental actions, but individual and business behaviour.

Thirdly, human rights treaty regimes tend to be more legalistic in nature than international environmental regimes. Once an issue is conceived in terms of rights, it is removed from the political arena of competing interests and policies. Perhaps for this reason, the paradigmatic institution established by human rights treaties is the expert committee, composed largely of lawyers. In contrast, the central institution established by international environmental agreements is the conference of the parties, whose primary task is political, namely to direct the implementation and evolution of the regime. Even the more specialized implementation committees established by some international environmental agreements are generally composed of government rather than independent experts, and take a political rather than a strictly legal approach to compliance questions.

The more obviously 'political' character of international environmental regimes is reflected not only in institutional and procedural arrangements, but also in substantive obligations, which often reflect political compromises struck in order to achieve agreement. Of course, human rights agreements also are the product of negotiation, but with an important difference. In human rights agreements, the end point of the negotiations is a common core of human rights to be respected. In contrast, international environmental negotiations often involve a process of outright horse-trading that, on the one hand, results in different requirements for different countries, but, by virtue of that fact, allows more stringent and specific requirements to be adopted than would otherwise be possible.

. . .

C. An overview of international environmental reporting

. . .

. . .[E]nvironmental reporting has an additional function, apart from individual compliance: reporting contributes to the factual basis for decisions about whether to develop new or amended norms, and thus subserves a legislative function. A notable feature of environmental regimes is their dynamic quality. In contrast to human rights agreements, which tend to be relatively stable, environmental regimes need to evolve, often quite rapidly, in response to changes in the nature of environmental problems and our understanding of them. Environmental reporting contributes to this essentially legislative process in two ways, first, by contributing to scientific understanding of a problem (for example, national inventories of greenhouse gas emissions give a better picture of what is actually taking place in the atmosphere), and second, by allowing an assessment of the overall progress of states towards achieving the objectives of an agreement. . . .

. . .

QUESTIONS

Do you agree with Bodansky's assessment of the human rights regime as relatively 'legal' compared with the more 'political' environmental regime? As relatively state-oriented in its attentions rather than attentive to nongovernmental actors? Do you have the sense that institutions must be tailored to fit the needs of radically different international fields, and hence naturally, inevitably, will differ significantly in their basic characteristics?

HENRY STEINER, INDIVIDUAL CLAIMS IN A WORLD OF MASSIVE VIOLATIONS: WHAT ROLE FOR THE HUMAN RIGHTS COMMITTEE?

in Philip Alston and J. Crawford (eds.), The Future of UN Human Rights Treaty Monitoring 15 (2000), at 19

[This article examines the significance of individual complaints before the Human Rights Committee under the Optional Protocol to the ICCPR, examined in Chapter 9. The following excerpts address international human rights institutions generally.]

[The structure of the Human Rights Committee], like that of many of the new human rights institutions, was problematic from the start. The burst of energies, the idealism and imagination that generated treaties and created their implementing organs necessarily pushed the architecture of international institutions in novel directions. The architects could have found no adequate and convincing models to realize the novel goals of the young human rights regimes. The institutions had no *necessary* character, no *traditional* form or functions. Their structure could not be derived from some self-evident or reigning theory of international law or institutions—in the way, for example, that the institutions of a state newly become democratic might naturally reflect tried and valued notions such as the separation of powers.

The architecture was rather invented to fit the moment, to express the compromises between divergent viewpoints and draw into the treaties as many states as possible. Hence the different treaty institutions, as well as the UN organs provided for in the UN Charter, had a contingent character that distinguished them from most norms of the treaties. As times changed and new situations developed, there was little reason to reconsider the rules against torture, discrimination, or censorship, but much reason to reconsider the adequacy of institutions.

The structure and powers of these institutions were serious matters, for the treaty organs could readily be understood to threaten states more than the norms themselves. Ratification of a treaty that declared human rights norms could be advantageous to a state unlikely to honour its commitments. That state now formally participated on the side of the angels in a developing international discourse, and in a relatively costless way. A profound cynicism, a contempt directed not only to the content of the norms but also to their inefficacy, informed many such ratifications. Anchoring norms in institutions, however, raises the cost of joining. Institutions make rights more effective by threatening or taking actions that may lead a state to comply. Institutions with real power cut to the bone of sovereignty. No wonder that intense fights over the provisions creating the new institutions became the rule.

. . .

. . . International law has long stated many norms that grow out of state conduct and correspond closely with most states' interests and behaviour (diplomatic immunities, exclusive territorial control, rules of navigation). But human rights instruments, together with related international law developments such as peacekeeping norms and the contemporary humanitarian law of armed conflict, shatter that correspondence. For most states, these treaties represent more aspiration than achievement. Their ideals are not embedded in but, to the contrary, tower above state behaviour. Their stance is deeply critical, their aim transformative.

International [human rights organs] are inevitably sensitive to this gap, and to the tensions that it generates. Relative to, say, [government institutions] in states within the liberal and democratic traditions, they often enjoy only precarious political support. Their room for bold decision-making is correspondingly limited, at least for decision-making that criticizes and regulates state conduct. Moreover, to a far greater degree than in national contexts, international human rights organs confront formidable differences in culture and tradition that have given rise to arguments between the proponents of universalism and of cultural relativism. . . .

B. SOVEREIGNTY AND DOMESTIC JURISDICTION

At its very threshold and to this day, the human rights movement has inevitably confronted antagonistic claims based on conceptions of sovereignty. How could its premises coexist with the then-reigning conceptions of state sovereignty? Or have the nature of the state, and the content of that protean concept as well as of allied concepts like domestic jurisdiction and autonomy, themselves undergone substantial change over the half century of this movement?

For reasons suggested in Part A of this Chapter, international organizations with powers of elaboration, implementation, application and enforcement pose issues of state sovereignty in the most acute form. They can indeed 'cut to the bone', whether their ultimate power be to order military intervention or to impose conditions on needed loans that restructure parts of a local economy. Hence Part B offers an appropriate context in which to consider the issues more broadly.

Nonetheless, the basic ideas in Part B will be familiar from earlier chapters examining the normative content (and disputes thereover) of the human rights movement. Indeed, those chapters could not have avoided them. In one or another of its meanings or incarnations, the notion of sovereignty inserts itself into many of the diverse topics in this coursebook. The introduction in Chapter 2 to international law inevitably considered the clash between international regulation and state governments' internal control of their polity—cases like *Chattin* or *Minority Schools in Albania*, for example. States' arguments based on sovereignty provided counterpoint in Chapter 3 to the description of the growth of the human rights movement. States' claims based on notions of cultural relativism in Chapters 5 and 6 often spoke the language of autonomy and sovereign independence. The broad theme of sovereignty in its modern dress(es) continues to inform discussion in the following chapters: topics including actions of the UN Security Council under Chapter VII of the Charter (Chapter 8); supranational regional organizations as in Europe that appropriate former economic, political and human rights prerogatives of the state (Chapter 10); claims of internal ethnic autonomy and self-determination (Chapter 15); and changing notions of internal sovereignty and independence or interdependence in an era of globalization, free trade and deregulated markets (Chapter 16).

Consider at the outset brief comments of several scholars about the meaning of this notion in contemporary international law and argument.

Malanczuk[3] notes that the origin of the modern theory lies in internal analyses of state structure, analyses that reach to writings of theorists like Machiavelli, Bodin and Hobbes. Originally used to describe the commands of a sovereign within a state (internal sovereignty), sovereignty later came to be used to describe as well the relationship of the ruler towards other rulers or states (external sovereignty, a continuing deep concern of international law). He suggests that the word 'sovereignty' should be replaced by 'independence'. 'In so far as 'sovereignty' means anything in addition to 'independence', it is not a legal term with any fixed meaning but a wholly emotive term. Everyone knows that states are powerful, but the emphasis on sovereignty exaggerates their power and encourages them to abuse it . . .'.

Brownlie[4] states that:

> sovereignty and equality of states represent the basic constitutional doctrine of the law of nations, which governs a community consisting primarily of states having a uniform legal personality. If international law exists, then the dynamics of state sovereignty can be expressed in terms of law, and, as states are equal and have legal personality, sovereignty is in a major aspect a relation to other states (and to organizations of states) defined by law.

He describes the principal corollaries of states' sovereignty and equality as

> (1) a jurisdiction, prima facie exclusive, over a territory and the permanent population living there; (2) a duty of non-intervention in the area of exclusive jurisdiction of other states; and (3) the dependence of obligations arising from customary law and treaties on the consent of the obligor.

Koskenniemi[5] observes that it is 'notoriously difficult to pin down the meaning of sovereignty', but that nonetheless the literature characteristically starts with a definition. Usually the concept is connected with ideas of independence (external sovereignty) and self-determination (internal sovereignty). He quotes a classic definition in an arbitral decision to the effect that sovereignty 'in the relations between States signifies independence: independence in regard to a portion of the globe is the right to exercise therein, to the exclusion of any other States, the functions of a State'. Sovereignty thus implies freedom of action by a state.

If, argues Koskenniemi, this or any agreed-on definition of sovereignty had a clear, ascertainable meaning, then 'whether an act falls within the State's legitimate

---

[3] Peter Malanczuk, *Akehurst's Modern Introduction to International Law* (7th edn., 1997), 17–18.
[4] Ian Brownlie, *Principles of Public International Law* (4th edn. 1990), Ch. XIII, 287.
[5] Martti Koskenniemi, *From Apology to Utopia: The Structure of International Legal Argument* (1989), Ch. 4.

sphere of action could always be solved by simply applying [that definition] to the case'. But '[t]here simply is no fixed meaning, no natural extent to sovereignty at all'. Thus in disputes between two states, each may base its argument on its own sovereignty. Assuming that 'sovereignty had a fixed content would entail accepting that there is an antecedent material rule which determines the boundaries of State liberty regardless of the subjective will or interest of any particular State'. Such material boundaries not stemming from the free choice of the state 'will appear as unjustified coercion'. It is indeed 'impossible to define "sovereignty" in such a manner as to contain our present perception of the State's full subjective freedom and that of its objective submission to restraints to such freedom'.

STEPHEN KRASNER, SOVEREIGNTY: ORGANIZED HYPOCRISY
(1999), at 9

[Krasner identifies four different ways in which the term sovereignty is commonly used: domestic, interdependence, international legal, and Westphalian sovereignty.]

Domestic sovereignty

The intellectual history of the term sovereignty is most closely associated with domestic sovereignty.

. . . Domestic sovereignty, the organization and effectiveness of political author-ity, is the single most important question for political analysis, but the organiza-tion of authority within a state and the level of control enjoyed by the state are not necessarily related to international legal or Westphalian sovereignty.

. . .

Interdependence sovereignty

In contemporary discourse it has become commonplace for observers to note that state sovereignty is being eroded by globalization. Such analysts are concerned fundamentally with questions of control, not authority. The inability to regulate the flow of goods, persons, pollutants, diseases, and ideas across territorial bound-aries has been described as a loss of sovereignty.

. . .

Interdependence sovereignty, or the lack thereof, is not practically or logically related to international legal or Westphalian sovereignty. A state can be recognized as a juridical equal by other states and still be unable to control movements across its own borders. Unregulated transborder movements do not imply that a state is subject to external structures of authority, which would be a violation of Westphal-ian sovereignty. Rulers can lose control of transborder flows and still be recognized and be able to exclude external actors.

. . .

International legal sovereignty

The third meaning of sovereignty, international legal sovereignty, has been concerned with establishing the status of a political entity in the international system. Is a state recognized by other states? Is it accepted as a juridical equal? Are its representatives entitled to diplomatic immunity? Can it be a member of international organizations? Can its representatives enter into agreements with other entities?

. . .

The classic model of international law is a replication of the liberal theory of the state. The state is treated at the international level as analogous to the individual at the national level. Sovereignty, independence, and consent are comparable with the position that the individual has in the liberal theory of the state.

International legal sovereignty . . . does not guarantee that legitimate domestic authorities will be able to monitor and regulate developments within the territory of their state or flows across their borders; that is, it does not guarantee either domestic sovereignty or interdependence sovereignty.

. . .

Westphalian sovereignty

Finally, sovereignty has been understood as the Westphalian model, an institutional arrangement for organizing political life that is based on two principles: territoriality and the exclusion of external actors from domestic authority structures. Rulers may be constrained, sometimes severely, by the external environment, but they are still free to choose the institutions and policies they regard as optimal. Westphalian sovereignty is violated when external actors influence or determine domestic authority structures.

Domestic authority structures can be infiltrated through both coercive and voluntary actions, through intervention and invitation. Foreign actors, usually the rulers of other states, can use their material capabilities to dictate or coerce changes in the authority structures of a target; they can violate the rule of non-intervention in the internal affairs of other states.

. . .

While Westphalian sovereignty can be compromised through invitation as well as intervention, invitation has received less notice in the literature because observers have confounded international legal and Westphalian sovereignty. Intervention violates both. Invitation violates only Westphalian sovereignty. Invitation occurs when a ruler voluntarily compromises the domestic autonomy of his or her own polity. Free choices are never inconsistent with international legal sovereignty.

Invitations can, however, infringe domestic autonomy. Rulers may issue invitations for a variety of reasons, including tying the hands of their successors, securing external financial resources, and strengthening domestic support for values that they, themselves, embrace. Invitations may sometimes be inadvertent; rulers might not realize that entering into an agreement may alter their own domestic institutional arrangements. Regardless of the motivation or the perspicacity of rulers, invitations violate Westphalian sovereignty by subjecting internal authority structures to external constraints. The rulings of the European Court of Justice, for instance, have legitimacy in the judicial systems of the member states of the European Union. IMF conditionality agreements, which may include stipulations requiring changes in domestic structures, carry weight not only because they are attached to the provision of funding but also because the IMF has legitimacy for some actors in borrowing countries derived from its claims to technical expertise. Human rights conventions can provide focal points that alter conceptions of legitimacy among groups in civil society and precipitate possibly unanticipated changes in the institutional arrangements of signatory states.

... [T]he most important empirical conclusion of the present study is that the principles associated with both Westphalian and international legal sovereignty have always been violated. Neither Westphalian nor international legal sovereignty has ever been a stable equilibrium from which rulers had no incentives to deviate. . . .

. . .

GEORGES ABI-SAAB, THE CHANGING WORLD ORDER AND THE INTERNATIONAL LEGAL ORDER: THE STRUCTURAL EVOLUTION OF INTERNATIONAL LAW BEYOND THE STATE-CENTRIC MODEL

in Y. Sakamoto (ed.), Global Transformation: Challenges to the State System (1994), at 439

The origins of the present international legal order go back to the disintegration of what Vinogradoff has called 'the World State of Medieval Christendom', as a result of the Reformation and the Wars of Religion in Europe. Its traits were fixed in the Peace of Westphalia, which definitively broke away from the formally theocratic character and hierarchic structure of the existing system, invalidating once and for all the assumption—already negated in practice—of the double allegiance of princes to Pope and Emperor, and replacing it by a new egalitarian set-up epitomized in the dictum '*cujus regio, ejus religio*' (each region follows its prince's religion).

This formula provided the basis for the coexistence of princes adhering to different versions of 'truth' (i.e. with different ideologies), the Wars of Religion having shown that neither camp was in a position to impose its truth on the other. It thus recognized, in terms of the ideological conflict of the moment (to which it was supposed to provide a final and stable solution), the paramountcy of every prince in his territory and over his subjects; whence the twin legal principles, governing the new international distribution of power, of sovereignty and equality (or of the 'sovereign equality' of Article 2(1) of the UN Charter).

In other words, as the legal system was meant to govern relations between antagonistic units, it had to gloss over the sources of their antagonism. It thus postulated a horizontal international structure where no hierarchy prevailed; where princes were 'sovereign', both in the sense of exercising exclusive power over their territory and their subjects (internal sovereignty), and in the sense of depending on no higher authority in the international sphere (external sovereignty or independence). But in order to maintain this situation, princes had to recognize each other (i.e. to be considered) as legally equal on the international level, regardless of size, wealth, strength, form of government, religion, or ideology.

Given the main purpose of the system of making it possible for antagonistic units to coexist, it aimed—to borrow the words of David Mitrany—at keeping them 'peacefully apart' rather than at bringing them 'actively together'. In the logic of this system, there was only one general obligation, the obligation to respect the sovereignty of others. It was an essentially passive obligation of abstention, of not trespassing on the spatial and functional confines of their sovereignty.

But if the sovereigns decided to establish or entertain relations, the system provided them with the 'legal recipes' or the 'how to do' formulae. In other words, to the extent that relations did take place, international law provided them with a convenient frame of reference. Indeed, the most developed chapters of classical international law fall in this category, such as the law of diplomatic and consular relations, and the law of treaties and of state responsibility.

Two important consequences flowed from this scheme of things, one relating to the representation of the new system of its rising subjects, the states, the other to the consistency and structure of the system itself. And both reflected its patently 'state-centric', indeed its 'state-deist', character.

In the first place, the internal logical construct of the system sketched above inexorably gave rise to the image of a 'hermetic state', a black box, or a 'billiard-ball' (to use Arnold Wolfers' term). Thus, in the perspective or contemplation of classical international law, states are opaque balls, whose inside we cannot see (or should feign not seeing), which are all formally equal, and which can come into contact only on the periphery or from the outside.

Obviously, this was a representation that did not completely correspond to reality even then (i.e. in the middle of the seventeenth century); much less since the industrial revolution; and even less so in our time, as we can witness in our daily lives. But it is on its basis that much of the principles and rules of international law that are still with us today have been moulded and developed.

As far as the consistency (or density) and structure of the system are concerned, states did not want to give with the left hand what they had just acquired with the right, namely their affranchisement from any and all dependence on, or submission to, a higher authority. They particularly did not want to see (re)established above them any new superior instance, whatever it might be. The new structure of international law thus had a precise and well-delimited (as well as limited) task: formally to sanction the new distribution of power in international society, i.e. to legitimize and sanction sovereignty in its newly acquired sense, without encroaching or trespassing on it.

. . .

In conclusion, two remarks are in order concerning the real social hold of this initial design, and the place of the ensuing system in the world then and now.

First, what is described above is the inner logic of the system or the manner in which it was initially articulated, in the light and as a function of the new constellation of power in the civil society it purported to regulate. But its 'fit' to external social reality comprised a good part of artifice and reification. For when we speak of the centrality and all-inclusiveness or all-mightiness of the state, we are speaking of the abstract model, on the basis of abstract equality. In reality, this model eliminates from its field of vision sources of inequality and conflict of interests, and the attendant vulnerability of weak states to diktats and interventions by stronger powers, usually on the pretext of alleged violations of international law by the former, put forward and unilaterally acted upon by the latter, in the absence of autonomous organs capable of objectively verifying their veracity at the request of either party.

In the second place, it should be recalled that, at its inception, this system was not the only one contending for the status of international legal order. It had to coexist, even in Europe, with the system of Islam as well as with other existing regional systems with similar universalist pretentions. However, with time, it progressively managed to dispose of these contending systems, either by direct control, via its subjects, of large parts of the non-Western world through colonialism; or, for those communities that managed to remain formally independent (e.g. because they served as a buffer between two European empires or to avoid upsetting the European balance of power), through forced assimilation, in order to qualify as 'civilized nations'.

Thus, what started objectively as a regional system in the seventeenth century, ended up becoming the universal system by the end of the nineteenth century.

. . .

NOTE

The following readings underscore the significance of international human rights for the internal distribution of power within a state, suggest new understandings of sovereignty that might impose internal human rights observance upon the legitimacy of a state's defensive invocation of the concept, and challenge and defend the notion of the sovereign state itself.

HENRY STEINER, THE YOUTH OF RIGHTS
104 Harv. L. Rev. 917 (1991), at 929

. . . Unlike many components of classical international law, the human rights movement was not meant to work out matters of reciprocal convenience among states—for example, sovereign or diplomatic immunities—or to aim only at regulating areas of historical conflict among states—for example, uses of the sea or airspace, or treatment by a state of its alien population. Rather it reached broad areas of everyday life within states that are vital to the internal rather than international distribution of political power. As international law's aspirations grew, as that law became more critical of and hence more distanced from states' behavior, the potential for conflict between human rights advocates within a state and that state's controlling elites escalated.

Even the most consensual of rights, the right not to be tortured, has a subversive potential. If, as [an] Amnesty International report suggests, torture amounts to the price of dissent because it is 'most often used as an integral part of a government's security strategy', abolishing torture lowers that price. Oppressive regimes prefer to keep the price high.

Other rights included in the *Universal Declaration* and the *Civil–Political Rights Covenant* influence the structure of government more directly. Abolishing discrimination on grounds of race, ethnicity, religion, or gender can radically alter economic and social arrangements and redirect political power. Protecting rights of speech, expression, and association will give citizens not only security against arbitrary state action, but also the chance to develop a diverse and vibrant civil society that can influence the directions of the state as effectively as governmental policies influence it. Entrenched structures of domination—landholding patterns, power over rural labor, virtual enslavement of children or women or given minorities—may become open to effective challenge.

The stakes for power rise as we move further along the spectrum of human rights. The major human rights instruments empower citizens to 'take part' in government and to vote in secrecy in genuine, periodic, and nondiscriminatory elections. In given circumstances, an authoritarian government can stop torturing and arresting without surrendering its monopoly of power. As events in Eastern Europe illustrate, however, such a government cannot grant the right to political participation without signing its death warrant. 'Throw out the rascals' speaks the more dramatically after decades of unchosen and oppressive regimes.

. . .

Particular clusters of civil-political rights thus challenge many of the world's governments in unavoidable, implacable ways. To some extent the range of human rights that I have mentioned respond to a 'disaster' dimension of the human rights movement. From that perspective, the movement seeks primarily to avert or terminate catastrophes stemming from gross abuses of power—at the extreme another genocide, at less draconian levels the systematic violations of rights to physical integrity in many repressive states. The premise to its goal of protection is captured in the familiar maxim, 'Power tends to corrupt and absolute power corrupts absolutely'. Its modern roots lie in the rule of law tradition, in the notion of law as fences protecting us from each other and, most important, from the state.

But the aspirations of the human rights movement reach beyond the goal of preventing disasters. The movement also has a 'utopian' dimension that envisions a vibrant and broadly based political community. Such a vision underscores the potential of the human rights movement for conflict with regimes all over the world. A society honoring the full range of contemporary human rights would be hospitable to many types of pluralism [and unwilling to embrace or impose] one final truth, at least to the point of allowing and protecting difference. It would not stop at the protection of negative rights but would encourage citizens to exercise their right to political participation, one path toward enabling peoples to realize the right to self-determination. It would ensure room for dissent and alternative visions of social and political life by keeping open and protecting access to the roads toward change.

Violations of human rights, particularly those of a systematic character, are then never gratuitous. Correctly or incorrectly, those holding power understand abuse and terror as instrumental to their keeping it. Sadism and cruelty will be all too evident, but they are harnessed to a politically purposeful scheme rather than fostered or permitted by states for their own sake. [The sorry condition of human rights] in many states should generally be traced to a recurrent structural phenomenon related to power and ideology rather than to individual pathologies.

The fight over rights therefore becomes the right over the redistribution of power—sometimes direct and unadorned, sometimes imbedded in ideological struggles or in complex ethnic conflicts. How else could South African elites view the insistence of political opponents on one-person-one-vote? How else could the former communist leaders of Eastern Europe have viewed demands for political pluralism? Moreover, some leaders succeeding to power in societies undergoing transformation will surely experience the desire to retain it, denouncing the rights that they now proclaim. The struggle is ongoing, relentless.

. . .

QUESTION

Richard Falk (*On Human Governance: Towards a New Global Politics* (1995), at 251), observes that 'sovereignty and democracy are profoundly affected by the realization of human rights. . . . In particular, the citizenry is morally and legally empowered to the extent it appreciates that its leaders can be challenged when they transgress the restraints on power as contained in the international law of human rights. In these regards, the protection of human rights represents a radical tendency in our historical period . . .'.

Given the observations of Steiner and Falk with respect to the human rights movement's radical effects on internal power and external sovereignty, why would any state sign up to a human rights treaty in other than bad faith?

RICHARD FALK, SOVEREIGNTY AND HUMAN DIGNITY: THE SEARCH FOR RECONCILIATION
in Francis Deng and Lyons (eds.), African Reckoning: A Quest for Good Governance (1998), at 12

If the doctrine of sovereignty could be erased from the minds of political leaders, would it reduce those forms of human suffering associated with extreme governmental failure? Would such an erasure strengthen sentiments of human solidarity on which an ethos of collective responsibility and individual accountability depends?

This still dominant image of sovereignty is essentially negative, a prerogative to resist claims and encroachments coming from outside national boundaries—the right to say no. Such a view of sovereignty is especially prevalent among sub-Saharan countries, which look back on their pre-independence past in sorrow and anger because of the harms generally perceived to have resulted from the predatory interventions that lay at the core of the colonial experience. With this image still uppermost in political consciousness, the acquisition of independence and with it sovereign rights was most often and influentially understood as an inversion of colonialism. Instead of complete domination from *outside* the country, there was now to be unencumbered freedom to act *inside* borders.

But the predicaments of postcolonial Africa are very different from those of colonial Africa. If one follows the lines of reasoning that flow from the American and French Revolutions, sovereignty inheres ultimately not in the state but in the citizenry and is associated with the rights of people, although it may be exercised by the people's representatives. Such international moral, legal, and political ideas as the right of self-determination and the right of development are direct expressions of this understanding of sovereignty, but such an understanding has not yet formally conditioned the interplay between state, society, and the organized international community.

Under present circumstances sovereignty calls for a more balanced, complex view of this foundational idea of the contemporary state that continues to provide the ideological underpinning of world order. The spread of support for human rights and the emergence of a norm of democratic entitlement [lend] credence to the view that the state is itself the subject of obligations as well as entitled to rights, and that these obligations may be implemented both by a politics of resistance on the part of citizens and by a process of humanitarian intervention by the international community. This conditioning of sovereignty is further evolved in relation to the capacity of a state to carry out governmental functions. When the state fails to provide governance, other political actors are needed to protect a vulnerable citizenry from the perils of chaos and civil strife as well as from unleashed forces of ethnic and religious extremism. This is particularly true in much of Africa where the intermediate structures of civil society are very weak, offering little protection in the event that government institutions at the center collapse or even seriously erode.

. . .

Aside from doctrinal confusion, manipulation, and uncertainty, there is a clear trend away from the idea of unconditional sovereignty and toward a concept of responsible sovereignty. Governmental legitimacy that validates the exercise of sovereignty involves adherence to minimum humanitarian norms and a capacity to act effectively to protect citizens from acute threats to their security and well-being that derive from adverse conditions within a country. As with other fundamental norms and principles, sovereignty evolves in relation to practice and to changes in community expectations. . . .

NOTE

Compare the following comment of Margaret Keck and Kathryn Sikkink:[6]

... Northerners within networks usually see third world leaders' claims about sovereignty as the self-serving positions of authoritarian or, in any case, elite actors. They consider that a weaker sovereignty might actually improve the political clout of the most marginalized people in developing countries.

In the south, however, many activists take quite a different view. Rather than seeing sovereignty as a stone wall blocking the spread of desired principles and norms, they recognize its fragility and worry about weakening it further. The doctrines of sovereignty and nonintervention remain the main line of defense against foreign efforts to limit domestic and international choices that third world states (and their citizens) can make. Self-determination, because it has so rarely been practiced in a satisfactory manner, remains a desired, if fading, utopia. Sovereignty over resources, a fundamental part of the discussions about a new international economic order, appears particularly to be threatened by international action on the environment. Even where third world activists may oppose the policies of their own governments, they have no reason to believe that international actors would do better, and considerable reason to suspect the contrary. In developing countries it is as much the idea of the state, as it is the state itself, that warrants loyalty.

...

... The issue of sovereignty, for third world activists, is deeply embedded in the issue of structural inequality.

QUESTIONS

1. If you were to flesh out Falk's notion of 'responsible sovereignty', what ingredients might it contain? The entire human rights corpus? What consequences might flow from a failure to exercise such 'responsible sovereignty' because of, say, gross and massive human rights violations like massacres of political opponents? What entities—states, IGOs, NGOS, others—might impose those consequences?

2. How do you assess the comment of Keck and Sikkink? Do you understand it to be consistent with Falk's proposal?

3. Compare with the preceding readings the following observation of Martii Koskenniemi:

Statehood survives and should continue to survive for the foreseeable future because its formal-bureaucratic rationality provides a safeguard against the totalitarianism inherent in a commitment to substantive values, which forces those values on people not sharing them.

...

---

[6] *Activists beyond Borders: Advocacy Networks in International Politics* (1998), at 215.

These reflections . . . do not require an unreserved commitment to statehood . . . [It] remains a second best—defensible but only to the extent that there can be no general agreement about the authentic purpose of social life. . . .[7]

Is the human rights movement one which has a 'commitment to substantive values' involving an inherent 'totalitarianism'? Has the movement moved toward 'general agreement about the authentic purposes of social life', thereby legitimating its erosion of state sovereignty?

NOTE

The following readings highlight key elements in ongoing political debate about state sovereignty within the United Nations in connection with UN peacekeeping and other activities, and in connection with the NATO military intervention in Yugoslavia (examined at pp. 653–62, *infra*).

VIEWS OF GOVERNMENT LEADERS

Each year the UN General Assembly holds a 'general debate', in the course of which world leaders reflect on the major issues of current concern. During the 1999 debate questions of sovereignty, intervention and interference in domestic affairs were extremely prominent. The following excerpts, descriptions (rather than direct quotations) of the comments at the debate, are taken from UN press releases.[8]

Kofi Annan, United Nations Secretary-General:

State sovereignty was being redefined by the forces of globalization and internal cooperation . . . The State was now widely understood to be the servant of the people and not vice versa. At the same time, individual sovereignty had been enhanced by a renewed consciousness of the right of every individual to control his or her own destiny. Those parallel developments did not lend themselves to simple conclusions. They did, however, 'demand of us a willingness to think anew' about how the United Nations responded to the political, human rights and humanitarian crises affecting so much of the world . . .

Abdelaziz Bouteflika, President of Algeria:

He did not deny the right of the public opinion of the northern hemisphere to denounce the breaches of human rights where they existed, and the United

---

[7] 'The Future of Statehood', 32 Harvard Int'l L. J. 397, 404 (1991).

[8] Taken from UN Press Releases GA/9595 (20 September 1999), GA/9606 (24 September 1999), and GA/9608 (25 September 1999).

Nations had the right and the duty to help suffering humanity. However, the countries of the OAU remained extremely sensitive to any undermining of their sovereignty—not only because it was their final defence against the rules of an unequal world, but also because they were not taking part either in the decision-making process by the Security Council, or in the monitoring of their implementation.

He said that the debate on the concept of interference in internal matters seemed far from finished, as several questions required exact answers. Among those were the questions of where aid stopped and interference began; what lines were to be drawn between the humanitarian, the political and the economic; and if interference was valid only for weak or weakened States. In any case, interference in internal affairs could only take place with the consent of the State in question.

S. Jayakumar, Foreign Minister of Singapore:

[T]he United Nations must work within the framework of the state system. . . . It could do nothing its Members did not expressly allow. Its basis was the principle of sovereign equality of all its Members. It also stressed the concomitant principle of non-interference in internal affairs.

However, those premises were now under assault, he continued. Two forces—the pressures of a truly integrated world economy and the end of the Cold War—were impelling change. Neither force was adequately understood. Globalization affected the very notion of statehood and government as they had so far been perceived. The essential function of any government was to govern and provide public goods and services to its citizens within its borders. But in a globalized economy, national borders no longer encompassed sufficient territory to function as self-contained economic units. Financial geography and economic geography no longer coincided with political geography. The challenge facing sovereign states was no longer one of interaction with other states. The real challenge was now within each state, forcing a reconceptualization of the very idea of government and statehood, and requiring a change of mindset that would be difficult and painful to achieve. What was required was an unprecedented and qualitatively new kind of international cooperation calling for redefinition of what constituted 'states' and 'national interests'. For that kind of international cooperation to take root, it must be shown to be superior to any other political alternative.

It was here . . . that the interplay of globalization and the post-Cold War international order complicated matters. The Cold War had imposed identities that transcended nationalism. Its end provided an opportunity to seek reassurance and a new identity in real or imagined ethnic nationalisms. The resulting proliferation of states and the lack of a clear organizing principle had made international cooperation problematic. Unfortunately, the reaction to this mismatch between economic and political geography had been a new protectionism and xenophobic nationalisms—or, where a country felt strong and confident enough, a new kind of extraterroriality in which strong states tried to project their national laws and standards beyond their boundaries. There had, of course, been regional responses to this need for a new kind of cooperation. But relying on regionalism as more than a stopgap in a globalized world created latent instability.

Surin Pitsuwan, Minister for Foreign Affairs for Thailand:

[T]raditional concepts of security were woefully inadequate to meet the new challenges faced by humankind. 'More and more, we in the international community are being faced with the conflicts within States', he said 'not between or among States as in the past'. Rather than State rights, State interests, State sovereignty, the international community now had to grapple with the defence of the 'common good', the protection of 'rights beyond borders' and intervention to promote and safeguard humanitarian ideals and objectives. To that end he proposed a transfer of the traditional preoccupation with the security and sovereignty of the State to serious consideration on the emerging concept of 'human security'.

QUESTION

The UN Secretary-General calls for a willingness to think anew, while the Singaporean Foreign Minister proposes a redefinition of the terms 'state' and 'national interests'. What type of alternative approaches might enable the international system to respond more effectively to the challenges identified by various commentators? Is this in fact a debate which can only move forward incrementally on the basis of successive *ad hoc* innovations?

JUDITH MILLER, CHECKERED FLAGS: SOVEREIGNTY ISN'T SO SACRED ANYMORE
New York Times, April 18, 1999, p. 4WK

At the century's last session of the Commission on Human Rights, Secretary General Kofi Annan of the United Nations unveiled a doctrine with profound implications for international relations in the new millennium. The air strikes against Yugoslavia, he said on April 7, showed that the world would no longer permit nations intent on committing genocide to 'hide' behind the United Nations charter, which has traditionally safeguarded national sovereignty.

The protection of human rights, he said, must 'take precedence over concerns of state sovereignty'. 'As long as I am Secretary General', said Mr. Annan, the United Nations 'will always place human beings at the center of everything we do'. This was not the Secretary General acting alone. He was, he acknowledged, only embracing an 'evolving' international norm. He also acknowledged that using force to protect human rights poses 'fundamental challenges' to the United Nations.

In fact, an erosion of sovereignty when it conflicts with human rights standards is reflected in many events of the last decade. . . . [References to such events included the International Criminal Tribunals for Yugoslavia and Rwanda and the U.K. litigation concerning the extradition of Pinochet].

To a certain extent, analysts agree, Mr. Annan's own stance is a reaction to his own searing experience as the head of peacekeeping in Rwanda, when more than half a million people were slaughtered as the Security Council withdrew United Nations forces.

Some argue that Mr. Annan has merely blessed a 'given' of the political climate today: the growing importance of human rights to the United Nations and many of its 185 members. This was most evident in the Security Council's overwhelming rejection two weeks ago of a resolution condemning NATO's air strikes as illegal on grounds that the Security Council had not authorized them. Only Namibia joined Russia and China, the co-sponsors of the motion, in arguing that Serbia's treatment of its Albanian minority was essentially an internal matter.

Mr. Annan's doctrine, predictably, has won praise from the burgeoning human rights community. But others argue that though well-intentioned, it is naive, dangerous and likely to increase tensions and paralysis within the Security Council.

And at least one close adviser to Mr. Annan worries that intervening to save white Europeans (albeit Muslims) in Kosovo, after having ignored even worse massacres in Rwanda and elsewhere, leaves the United Nations open to charges of selective morality and double standards. Others argue that in a world with some 40 million refugees and displaced people, Mr. Annan's stance risks stretching United Nations resources to unbearable limits.

. . .

In speeches and articles last year, Mr. Annan . . . signaled his growing anxiety about the violations of rights occurring in Kosovo. Nation-states are not going to disappear, he wrote in the journal 'Humanitarian Intervention'. Respect for the 'fundamental sovereignty, territorial integrity, and political independence of states' will remain a 'cornerstone of the international system'. Nevertheless, he said last summer in Rome, the principle of sovereignty cannot provide 'excuses for the inexcusable'. The United Nations charter, he reminded people in England last June, 'was issued in the name of "the peoples", not the governments, of the United Nations'.

. . .

And for Europe, the question of appearing indifferent to repression and brutality was especially evocative. Even Germany, which since World War II has resisted the use of force to solve political problems, did not want to end the century by appearing cold toward an echo of the atrocities it caused 60 years ago. Paraphrasing Foreign Minister Joschka Fischer of Germany, the diplomat said the decision for Germany was between 'no more wars' and 'no more Auschwitzes'. It, like the rest of NATO, chose to go to war this time.

NOTE

Consider the following comparison between Kosovo and Chechnya:[9]

. . .

So the question arises: What is the world to make of the new doctrine it thought was emerging—a doctrine that seemed, after Bosnia and Kosovo and East Timor, to be empowering the bulk of the world to intervene in countries that abused their own citizens. Large parts of the world, it seemed, were embracing the idea that universal standards of human rights were putting at least some limits on sovereignty.

But now comes the harshest test of that doctrine: Russia, a humbled super-power desperate to hold together its very territory, not to mention its national pride, in the face of international condemnation of its methods. 'Human rights are no reason to interfere in the internal affairs of a state', Russia's Foreign Minister, Igor Ivanov, protested last week, offering the same argument that Russia and President Slobodan Milosevic of Yugoslavia made during last spring's NATO air war against the Serbian attempt at 'ethnic cleansing' in Kosovo. The difference, of course, is that some countries are more sovereign than others. Sheer power still counts.

. . .

With Russia (and China) having a veto in the Security Council, consensus on outside intervention to protect civilians in Chechnya is as unlikely as it would be in Tibet, but that does not mean Western nations are hypocritical in refraining from an intervention that could prove suicidal, so long as they urge Russia to stop and think again.

. . .

COMMENT ON DOMESTIC JURISDICTION

In the human rights context, especially within the United Nations, the many perspectives on sovereignty have been brought into debate primarily in the context of two issues: (1) the interplay between Article 2(7), on the one hand, and Articles 55–56 of the Charter and provisions of human rights treaties, on the other; and (2) proposed action by the Security Council in response to a threat to international peace and security or in cases of humanitarian intervention, such as in Kosovo in 1999. Article 2(7) reads:

Nothing contained in the present Charter shall authorize the United Nations to intervene in matters which are essentially within the domestic jurisdiction of any State . . ., but this principle shall not prejudice the application of enforcement measures under Chapter VII.

Although this provision does not sit easily with the undertakings in Articles 55–56 to cooperate with the UN in promoting respect for human rights, nor with the explicit duties of states set forth in the human rights treaties, the tensions were left

[9] Craig Whitney, 'Hands Off, The No Man's Land in the Fight for Human Rights', *New York Times*, December 12, 1999, p. WK1.

to be dealt with over time through the developing practice of UN organs. Apart from mandating the creation of a Commission on Human Rights, the Charter did not spell out the measures that it envisaged might be taken to give effect to one of the UN's principal purposes, listed in Article 1(3), of promoting and encouraging respect for human rights. The General Assembly was empowered to 'discuss any questions or any matters within the scope of the . . . Charter' (Article 10) and to 'initiate studies and make recommendations for the purpose of . . . [*inter alia*] assisting in the realization of human rights' (Article 13). Neither the type of studies nor the ways in which they might be prepared were spelled out. Nor was it clear what, if any, limits applied to the type of recommendations that might be made. So the task remained of working out the relationship between the traditional themes of state sovereignty in paragraphs (1) and (7) of Article 2 with the internationalist spirit of Article 1 and the later human rights provisions.

Some critics have stressed that the Charter did not give the Assembly or other UN organs the power to make authoritative interpretations of these or any other provisions. In Watson's view, 'as a result, the power of autointerpretation still remains with individual states'.[10] Each state, when addressed by a UN organ (other than the Security Council acting under explicit powers), would then decide for itself whether or not the matter raised was part of its *domaine reservé* (domestic jurisdiction) and thus off limits to the UN under Article 2(7). The overwhelming majority of commentators have rejected this analysis, and have instead argued that (1) the General Assembly must have the power to interpret its own mandate, including the implications of Article 2(7); (2) a teleological approach should be applied in interpreting Article 2(7) in the light of the (developing) purposes of the Organization (Article 1); (3) the resolutions of the UN and other bodies have made clear that a narrow interpretation is to be given to Article 2(7); and (4) as legitimate matters of international concern, human rights cannot reasonably be characterized as being exclusively an internal matter.

Over the course of more than half a century, UN organs have systematically reduced the scope claimed for the domestic jurisdiction 'defence'. The early case of South Africa was critical. Although Article 2(7) was invoked in many diplomatic exchanges and public statements by a variety of states in the late 1940s and early 1950s, apartheid led to a major breakthrough. A special Commission on the Racial Situation in the Union of South Africa appointed by the General Assembly in 1952 concluded that Article 2(7) prohibited only 'dictatorial interference', a phrase interpreted as implying 'a peremptory demand for positive conduct or abstention—a demand which, if not complied with, involves a threat of or recourse to compulsion . . .'. Article 2(7) referred 'only to direct intervention in the domestic economy, social structure, or cultural arrangements of the State concerned but does not in any way preclude recommendations, or even inquiries conducted outside the territory of such State'.[11] The Commission's report gave rise to extensive debate, in which South Africa took the position that the General Assembly could not even discuss the subject of race relations in that country. Only

---

[10] James Shand Watson, *Theory and Reality in the International Protection of Human Rights* (1999), at 205.
[11] UN Doc. A/2505 (1953), 16–22.

rarely today does one hear even distant echoes of that extreme position. (Later developments with respect to South Africa are described at p. 649, *infra*.)

Although regularly invoked, the domestic jurisdiction defence proved equally unsuccessful in relation to debate and recommendations about other cases such as those of Vietnam in the early 1960s, Israel since the late 1960s, Chile in the 1970s and countries such as Iran and Afghanistan in the 1980s.[12] It has been difficult to assemble a wide range of governments to advance a strong defensive interpretation (that is, a broad interpretation) of Article 2(7) that is consistent, because states arguing for such an interpretation in their own defence have nonetheless occasionally or frequently insisted that measures be taken against other violator states.

The only significant exception in this regard has been the People's Republic of China, which has abstained in the UN from condemning human rights violations in other states of which it clearly did not approve. But even China supported resolutions condemning human rights violations in Afghanistan, southern Africa and the Israeli Occupied Territories, and has expressed its concern about human rights violations in countries such as Indonesia in the late 1990s. Recall China's contemporary views about human rights, domestic jurisdiction and intervention that appear in the excerpts from the 1991 White Paper on Human Rights in China, at p. 547, *supra*.

The end of the Cold War brought a dramatic change of policy by many states and within the UN with respect to domestic jurisdiction. For example, Poland had insisted in 1983, when its own declaration of martial law was under scrutiny, that UN organs could even consider human rights questions in a particular state only 'if the following criteria were met: firstly, that a particular situation represented a gross, massive and flagrant violation of human rights and fundamental freedoms; secondly, that the situation represented a consistent pattern of such violations; thirdly, that the situation endangered international peace and security; and lastly, that consideration of the situation was without prejudice to the functions and powers of organs already in existence'.[13] But by October 1991 Poland endorsed the following conclusion of the Moscow Meeting of the Conference on the Human Dimension of the Conference on Security and Co-operation in Europe (the CSCE, or Helsinki process, described at p. 791, *infra*):

> The participating States emphasize that issues relating to human rights, funda-
> mental freedoms, democracy and the rule of law are of international concern, as
> respect for these rights and freedoms constitutes one of the foundations of the
> international order. They categorically and irrevocably declare that the commit-
> ments undertaken in the field of the human dimension of the CSCE are matters
> of direct and legitimate concern to all participating States and do not belong
> exclusively to the internal affairs of the State concerned.[14]

Today the issue of domestic jurisdiction is rarely raised in other than a perfunc-

---

[12] Menno Kamminga, *Inter-State Accountability for Violations of Human Rights* (1992).
[13] UN Doc. E/CN.4/1983/SR.40/Add.1.
[14] 30 Int. Leg. Mat. 1670, 1672 (1991).

tory manner in UN fora. Even when raised by a state like China whose human rights record is under criticism, a substantive debate about a resolution or other aspects of the criticism usually takes place and the outcome (a resolution, say, passed or defeated) reflects a variety of legal and political considerations among which Article 2(7) as such is not a substantial factor.

ADDITIONAL READING

Classic works on sovereignty include: Bertrand de Jouvenel, *Sovereignty: An Inquiry into the Political Good* (1957); F.H. Hinsley, *Sovereignty* (2nd edn., 1986); A. Milward, *The European Rescue of the Nation-State* (1992); and L. Gross, 'The Peace of Westphalia 1648–1948', 42 Am. J. Int. L. 20 (1948). More recent collections focusing on globalization, etc., and its implications are: T.J. Biersteker and C. Weber (eds.), *State Sovereignty as a Social Construct* (1996); G. Lyons and M. Mastanduno (eds.), *Beyond Westphalia: State Sovereignty and International Intervention* (1995); R. Jackson and A. James (eds.), *States in a Changing World* (1993); Gunther Teubner (ed.), *Global Law without a State* (1997). See also: Oscar Schachter, 'The Decline of the Nation State and its Implications for International Law', 36 Colum. J. Trans. L. 7 (1997); J. Klabbers, 'Clinching the Concept of Sovereignty: Wimbledon Redux', 3 Austrian Rev. Int. & Eur. L. 345 (1998); Hendrik Spruyt, *The Sovereign State and its Competitors* (1994); Jens Bartelson, *A Genealogy of Sovereignty* (1995). Sovereignty is also dealt with in much of the recent literature on civil society, NGOs, and humanitarian intervention. On domestic jurisdiction, see H. Lauterpacht, *International Law and Human Rights* (1950); R. Higgins, *The Development of International Law through the Political Organs of the United Nations* (1963); L. Sohn, 'The New International Law: Protection of the Rights of Individuals Rather than States', 32 Am. U. L. Rev. 1 (1982).

Intergovernmental Enforcement of Human Right Norms: The United Nations System

This chapter takes a systematic look at the United Nations human rights system insofar as it bears on enforcement. It thereby complements earlier chapters, which looked at that system with respect to the generation of norms. The stress here is on the UN as an organization, and on the roles and effectiveness of its different organs or bodies concerned with human rights. The materials trace the evolution of these organs over several decades, examine the UN's significant procedures or processes in this field, suggest criteria for evaluation of the UN's record, and explore possible reforms.

A. CONCEPTIONS OF ENFORCEMENT

For individuals whose human rights are being violated, and for the groups that seek to defend them, the effectiveness of the UN's human rights system depends to an important degree upon its ability to 'enforce' respect for the legal norms that originated within it. But the very concept of such international 'enforcement' is controversial and resisted by a significant number of governments (a few of which do so overtly, while many others use more subtle methods). As suggested by Chapter 7, it is therefore not surprising that the UN's often hotly contested efforts to establish institutions and procedures capable of securing enforcement have been less successful than its work in setting human rights standards, often consensually.

An evaluation of the UN's performance will be strongly influenced by the observer's starting point or perspective on world order.

1. Do we assume that the 'globalization' of issues such as human rights is desirable, even unavoidable, so that a nation's treatment of its own nationals is a legitimate concern of all others (an *erga omnes* approach, p. 234, *supra*)? Or do we hold to a more traditional image of the sovereign state that emphasizes the inviolability of national boundaries for human rights as well as other purposes?

2. Even if the former, do we envisage a world in which an effective multilateral organization (which might or might not be the UN) should be able to act against the will of the government(s) concerned to enforce universal norms? Or do we believe that although some degree of globalization is inevitable, say with respect to standard-setting, the actual implementation by individual governments of those standards, each in its own way, remains the most effective, desirable or realistic approach?

3. Are we prepared to accept that the measures that we would happily support against another country might, in a different context, be applied against our own? Do we assume that international enforcement actions must be applied equally to powerful nations and to smaller states, so that we should only adopt policies that can be applied across the board, consistently?

The answers to such questions depend partly on the definition of enforcement. Do we refer only to the relatively rare peacekeeping and so-called 'police' actions that involve the presence in a state of UN or other foreign forces? The only use of the term 'enforcement' in the UN Charter occurs in relation to the enforcement under Chapter VII of decisions of the Security Council (Article 45). This has led some international lawyers to equate enforcement with the use of, or threat to use, economic or other sanctions or armed force. Although most dictionary definitions of enforcement include an element of compulsion, it is nonetheless true that compulsion may be moral as well as physical. It is also true that the use of force for human rights purposes has won increasing support in recent years, especially in light of developments in relation to Kosovo and East Timor, but this is surely not what is meant by calls for the UN to 'enforce', routinely, universal human rights norms.

At the other extreme from the use of sanctions or armed force, enforcement has been defined as 'comprising all measures intended and proper to induce respect for human rights'.[1] That definition could extend to the other extreme of UN action, the frequent debates or recommendatory resolutions of the General Assembly. But such a definition is so open-ended that it provides no criteria against which to evaluate the UN's performance. It puts the emphasis on intentions rather than on results achieved, and suggests that 'enforcement' measures might be confined to the adoption of resolutions and other such hortatory activities of the UN.

In the following reading, Louis Henkin discusses notions of compliance and enforcement and suggests differences in this regard between international law in general and international human rights law in particular.

---

[1] Rudolf Bernhardt, 'General Report', in Bernhardt and Jolowicz (eds.), *International Enforcement of Human Rights* (1985), at 5.

LOUIS HENKIN, INTERNATIONAL LAW: POLITICS, VALUES AND FUNCTIONS
in 216 Collected Courses of the Hague Academy of International Law 13 (Vol. IV, 1989), at 251

Compliance with international law as to civil and political rights ... takes place within a State and depends on its legal system, on its courts and other official bodies. But, as with other international obligations, the international system can exert influence on the State to comply. ... States observe international law from developed habit and from commitment to order generally; because States have an interest in maintaining norms which they themselves made or to which they consented and in which all have a common interest (or which represent agreed compromises and accommodations); because the system has developed a (less-than-perfect) culture of compliance; because of the availability of 'horizontal enforcement' so that a would-be violator is deterred by the anticipated response of the victim State or of others which would visit undesirable consequences upon a violator. These inducements do not work in the same way for human rights law, precisely because that law promotes human values rather than State values. Because a State's commitments under human rights law are directed towards its own people and may require major internal readjustments, the habit of compliance with international standards may not have developed; indeed, ingrained attitudes and habits inconsistent with those standards may have to be broken, and established practices abandoned. Even after 40 years under the Universal Declaration, even years after States were persuaded to make legal commitments to human rights, many States have not yet 'internalized' their international human rights undertakings, have not developed strong commitment to constitutionalism, rights and the rule of law, have not established institutions to nurture that commitment.

The general culture of compliance with international law also is less effective for human rights law. The international human rights system is still 'settling in'. States have not yet wholly shed the idea that conditions inside a State, including how a State treats its own inhabitants, are no one else's business. ... States have not yet wholly assimilated the fact that they have an *international obligation* to respect the rights of their citizens, that an act of torture or other inhuman treatment, for example, is a violation of an international law.

Compliance with international human rights obligations—i.e., respect for human rights at home—is more responsive to domestic forces, to the domestic constitutional culture, than to any international culture pressing for compliance with international human rights norms. The causes of human rights violations are cultural, political, internal, close to home—an underdeveloped commitment to constitutionalism, to the rule of law, to the idea of individual rights, to limitations on government; political-social-economic underdevelopment and instability; evil or stupid State leaders, fostering a culture that tolerates brutality and repression; inefficient administration. In such circumstances, external inducements to comply with international human rights law are remote and not readily felt.

Horizontal enforcement, the principal inducement for international compliance generally, also works differently and less effectively for human rights. Like other

international obligations, human rights undertakings run to other States, to the other parties to a covenant or convention, or to all States when the obligation is under customary law and *erga omnes*. . . . In principle, human rights obligations, like other international obligations, create rights in the promisees and afford them remedies. But while State promisees are entitled to pursue such remedies, they have not been sufficiently motivated to do so and do not in fact do so. For the real beneficiaries are not the State promisees but the inhabitants of the promisor State, and, in general, States—even if they have adhered to international agreements—do not have a strong interest in human rights generally, and are not yet politically acclimated and habituated to responding to violations of rights of persons abroad other than their own nationals. Many States, themselves still lacking an entrenched human rights culture, themselves vulnerable to charges of violation, are reluctant to respond (surely to respond unilaterally) to a violation by another friendly State of the human rights of the State's own inhabitants. What is more, the principal element of horizontal deterrence is missing. A State promisee cannot respond to a violation by retaliation or the threat of retaliation; such retaliation would itself violate human rights. And the threat that 'if you violate the human rights of your inhabitants, we will violate the human rights of our inhabitants' hardly serves as a deterrent. The result is that the temptation to violate human rights law is stronger than for other international law while fear of reaction by other States or of other adverse consequences is weaker.
. . .

. . .[F]or these (and other) reasons, the International Human Rights Movement has developed special 'enforcement machinery'.

Special enforcement machinery has followed two principal tracks. Some has been established by particular human rights agreements, such as the Human Rights Committee under the Covenant on Civil and Political Rights and the commissions and courts under the European and American conventions. A second track of enforcement consists of United Nations bodies—the General Assembly, the Economic and Social Council (ECOSOC), and especially the Human Rights Commission and its subsidiary units. Their activities are sometimes seen as politics, not law, but these bodies invoke norms and are properly seen as part of the enforcement system.

It is difficult to assess which of these 'tracks' has been more successful; surely they have both contributed to compliance. But they work differently. A monitoring body created by a human rights covenant or convention addresses only compliance by States parties to that agreement and only with the norms established by the agreement. The mandate, authority and procedures of the monitoring body are defined by the agreement. United Nations bodies, on the other hand, often address human rights issues as part of their general mandate as defined by the United Nations Charter and by General Assembly resolutions. They are not themselves monitoring bodies, but have sometimes created *ad hoc* monitors and have sometimes condemned violations. In principle, they might address human rights violations by virtually any State, since nearly all States are parties to the United Nations Charter; in fact, political bodies are likely to address only selected, dramatic human rights violations by selected countries.
. . .

Surely, horizontal enforcement is available to enforce the customary law of human rights. Obligations of customary law in respect of human rights are *erga omnes* [see p. 234, *supra*] and all States can act (peacefully) to induce compliance. They can protest, make claims, and even bring suit if the parties had consented to the compulsory jurisdiction of the International Court of Justice or to some relevant system of arbitration.

. . .

International human rights law benefits significantly from enforcement also by political bodies [that are within the UN system, as well as by bodies created by the human rights treaties]: In general, international political bodies have attended only to the enforcement of norms of extraordinary political significance such as the law of the Charter on the use of force, but political bodies have devoted extraordinary efforts to promoting law on human rights and for that and other reasons they have not avoided the demands of enforcement of—inducing compliance with—that law.

If law is politics, enforcement of law in the inter-State system is also heavily political. Political influence brought to bear in the organs and suborgans of the United Nations determined the enforcement machinery that found its way into covenants and conventions. (Political forces, I have suggested, have influenced also how that machinery has worked.) But United Nations bodies themselves have also been an arena for charges of human rights violations, sometimes evoking resolutions of condemnation.

One cannot appraise these activities with precision or with confidence, but clearly they have served as some inducement to terminate or mitigate violations, perhaps even as some deterrent. Political bodies, however, are subject to their own political laws. The larger bodies—notably the United Nations General Assembly—are more visible, more newsworthy, therefore more 'politicized', therefore less likely to apply human rights norms judicially, impartially. In such bodies, human rights are more susceptible to being subordinated to non-human rights consider-ations. There, voting, including 'bloc-voting', has led to 'selective targeting' of some States, sometimes exaggerating their violations, and overlooking those of other States, including some that are guilty of gross violations. Smaller political bodies, such as the Human Rights Commission, are also inhabited by government representatives concerned for State values and friendly relations, but increasingly they are able to be somewhat less 'political', more evenhanded, as well as more activist in the cause of human rights.

. . .

QUESTIONS

1. Is the term 'enforcement' the right term to use to describe what you would like the UN to be able to do in response to its findings that gross violations of human rights are taking place or are likely to take place? Are there other powers, stopping short of this sense of 'enforcement', that you would wish to vest in the UN or any other international organization to respond to gross violations?

2. Allegations of politicization, the use of double standards, or special treatment are recurring themes in discussions of international human rights decision-making processes. Is 'politicization' in this sense synonymous with taking 'political' considerations into account in arriving at a decision? Would you prefer a process of decision-making in intergovernmental organs that excluded 'all' political considerations from certain aspects of the process of decision-making, or from the entire process? Consider, for example, fact-finding in a given situation involving allegations of gross violations, or the decision of what action if any to take if gross violations are found.

B. THE UN SYSTEM: CHARTER-BASED INSTITUTIONS

The UN's human rights machinery consists of a 'two-track' approach:

(1) *Charter-based organs* (a) whose creation is directly mandated by the UN Charter, such as the General Assembly, the Economic and Social Council and the Commission on Human Rights, or (b) which have been authorized by one of those bodies, such as the Sub-Commission on the Promotion and Protection of Human Rights, and the Commission on the Status of Women; and

(2) *Treaty-based organs* such as the Human Rights Committee formed under the ICCPR, referred to in this book as the 'ICCPR Committee' in order to reduce confusion with the UN Commission on Human Rights that is identified as the 'UN Commission', that have been created by six other human rights treaties originating in UN processes. These organs are intended to monitor compliance by states with their obligations under those treaties.

The focus of this Chapter is on Charter-based organs. Treaty-based organs are dealt with especially in Chapters 3 (CEDAW), 4 (ESCR Committee) and 10 (ICCPR Committee). While the work of the UN Commission is of particular importance, other UN organs are also significant. The organizational structure is reflected in the chart below.

COMMENT ON CHARTER ORGANS

Note the following elements of the chart. First, the highly successful post-War decolonization processes overseen by the UN rendered the *Trusteeship Council* superfluous. It suspended operation in 1994. Second, although the number of cases taken before the *International Court of Justice* has grown substantially over the past decade or so, and has included cases with a major human rights component in relation to self-determination and genocide, the jurisprudence that the ICJ has generated has had only a limited impact on the normative underpinnings of

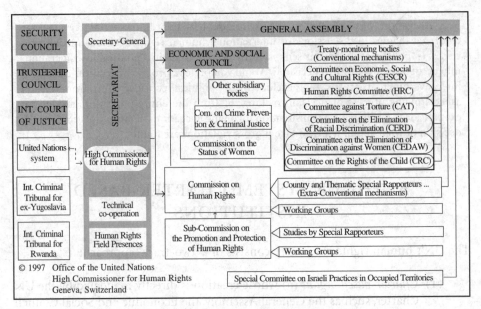

Figure 8.1 UN Human Rights Organizational Structure
Source: www.unhchr.ch/hrostr.htm

the international human rights regime. Third, although the *Economic and Social Council* (ECOSOC) once played a major role as an intermediary between the Assembly and the Commission, and still has a theoretically important role of coordination within an increasingly disparate UN system, its contributions to the human rights debate since the 1970s have been minimal and its coordination efforts have had little practical impact. In formal terms, the Commission reports to ECOSOC and any Commission resolution or decision with financial consequences requires the latter's approval, unless an earlier authorization can be invoked. It is extremely rare for ECOSOC to refuse to endorse what the Commission has decided. There is, however, one area in which the role of the Council remains significant—in relation to the granting of 'consultative status' with the UN to nongovernmental organizations. See p. 979, *infra*.

Finally, mention should be made of the *Commission on the Status of Women*. It was established in 1946 and reports to the Council in relation to policies to promote women's rights in the political, economic, civil, social and educational fields. It consists of 45 governmental representatives, who normally meet for only eight days each year, and its mandate now includes follow-up to the Platform of Action adopted by the Fourth World Conference on Women, held in Beijing in 1995. In 1999 it completed the task of drafting an optional protocol permitting individual complaints to be lodged under the CEDAW Convention, p. 777, *infra*.

Consider now the organs whose work is examined in this Chapter. Until the mid-1990s, the *Security Council* was extremely reluctant to become involved in human rights matters. Since that time, its role in the field has become significant.

The *Secretariat* is led by the *Secretary-General*, who is appointed for five years by the General Assembly on the recommendation of the Security Council. A nominee may thus be vetoed by any of the five permanent members of the Council. The Secretary-General is the chief administrative officer of the UN and also exerts important moral authority within the wider international system. Successive Secretaries-General have been very reluctant to embrace human rights concerns actively for fear of offending governments and jeopardizing their wider role in the promotion of international peace and security. For example, just a few months before the General Assembly created the post of High Commissioner for Human Rights in December 1993, Secretary-General Boutros-Ghali strongly opposed the initiative. Kofi Annan, of Ghana, the Secretary-General since 1 January 1997, has taken a more active human rights stance than any of his predecessors and has overseen a process of 'mainstreaming' human rights throughout the organization. As a result, bodies dealing with issues from economic development to peacekeeping and beyond have been encouraged to address systematically the human rights dimensions of their mandates.

Under the Secretary-General, the *High Commissioner for Human Rights* (HCHR) is the UN official with principal responsibility for human rights. In formal terms she is subject to the direction and authority of the Secretary-General and acts within the mandate given her by the policy organs (the General Assembly, ECOSOC and the UN Commission). The High Commissioner is appointed by the Secretary-General with the approval of the General Assembly, due regard being paid to geographical rotation, for a four-year term with the possibility of one renewal. The first High Commissioner was José Ayala-Lasso, of Ecuador, who served from 1994–97 and was succeeded by Mary Robinson, the former President of Ireland. In 2000 the Office employed 160 'professional' and 66 'general service' staff. From the regular UN budget it receives around $22–24 million and in extra-budgetary resources it receives something over $40 million.

The HCHR's mandate was originally spelled out in GA Res. 48/141 (1993), which established the Office as one of the outcomes of the Vienna World Conference on Human Rights. The tasks include, *inter alia*, to promote and protect the effective enjoyment of civil, cultural, economic, political and social rights, including the right to development; to provide advisory services and technical and financial assistance in the field of human rights to states that request them; to coordinate UN education and public information programmes in the field of human rights; to play an active role in removing the obstacles to the full realization of human rights; to engage governments in a dialogue to secure respect for human rights; and to enhance international cooperation for the promotion and protection of human rights. A major development in recent years has been the establishment of field operations in some 20 countries, including (i) monitoring cum technical cooperation presences in Burundi, Cambodia, Colombia, Bosnia and Herzegovina, Croatia, the Democratic Republic of the Congo and Yugoslavia; (ii) cooperative presences with the UN Departments of Peace-Keeping and Political Affairs in Angola, the Central African Republic, Liberia, Sierra Leone and Abkhazia, Georgia; and (iii) technical cooperation presences in Malawi, South Africa, southern Africa, Togo, Gaza, Mongolia, Guatemala and El Salvador.

The main part of this Chapter concentrates on the work of the UN Commission on Human Rights. Since the debates, declarations, resolutions and recommendations of the General Assembly, the vital plenary organ, play an important role, various readings draw also on its work. A brief description of each of these organs follows.

The *General Assembly.* As noted above (p. 589), the Charter empowers the Assembly to 'discuss any questions or any matters within the scope of the ... Charter' (Article 10) and to 'initiate studies and make recommendations for the purpose of ... [*inter alia*] assisting in the realization of human rights' (Article 13). The Assembly's principal significance derives from the fact that it is composed of all UN Member States, each of which has one vote regardless of population, wealth or other factors. While most issues are decided by a simple majority vote, decisions on important questions, such as those on peace and security, admission of new Members, and budgetary matters, require a two-thirds majority. Nevertheless, much of its work is carried out on a consensus basis, thus avoiding the need for a vote. The Assembly meets from September to December each year and at other times as required. Its resolutions are not *per se* legally binding but they are an important reflection of the will of the world community. Much of the debate and drafting occurs in six Main Committees, three of which are of particular relevance to human rights: the Third (Social, Humanitarian and Cultural issues); the Fifth (Administrative and Budgetary issues); and the Sixth (Legal issues).

The *Commission on Human Rights.* Established in 1946, it currently consists of 53 member governments elected for three-year terms by the ECOSOC. It meets annually for six weeks in Geneva from mid-March to late April. Since 1992 there has also been provision for emergency sessions. Four have been held as of April 2000 (two relating to the former Yugoslavia, one each to Rwanda and East Timor). The tendency of the UN generally to promote geographical and political balance through a system of regional groupings influences much of the work of the Commission. The five groups are Asia, Africa, Eastern Europe, Latin America, and Western Europe and Others—the last category including Canada, Australia and New Zealand, and, in practice, the United States. Thus, for example, the position of Chairperson rotates annually among the groups and the regional groups caucus regularly during the Commission's annual session. Working groups of five member governments are commonly established to ensure that one member from each group can be included.[2] While the Commission occupies a lower place in the organizational hierarchy than either the Assembly or the ECOSOC, in the human rights area it is actually more significant in many respects than those other bodies.

A sense of the scale of the Commission's activities can be derived from the statistics for 1999, when a total of 3,240 persons participated in its six-week session. They included 587 persons representing the 53 Member States, 568 representing 91 other states, 217 representing 29 UN and other international organizations, and 1,824 representing 212 NGOs which were observing the proceedings or participating in them in a specific defined way (UN Doc. E/CN.4/2000/8, Annex). These figures included 37 'dignitaries' (such as heads of state or government, foreign ministers, or heads of international organizations) who addressed

---

[2] This arrangement has so operated as to exclude Israel, from any group and hence to deny it the possibility of being elected to the Commission. It was never admitted to the Asian region, within which it falls geographically, but the Western Europe group is currently negotiating its admission.

the Commission. In all, 485 documents, representing 6,278 pages in the English version alone, were issued for the session. A total of 82 resolutions were adopted, only 24 of which required a vote. A further 13 decisions dealing with procedural matters were also adopted.

The final UN body to which reference should be made is the *Sub-Commission on the Promotion and Protection of Human Rights* (known from 1947 to 1999 as the Sub-Commission on Prevention of Discrimination and Protection of Minorities). In contrast to the Commission, which is composed entirely of governmental representatives, the Sub-Commission consists of 26 independent experts, elected by the Commission upon the nomination of governments. It meets for four weeks annually in Geneva in August, although its session is generally preceded by various Working Groups dealing with communications (complaints under the 1503 procedure, see below p. 612), the rights of indigenous populations, contemporary forms of slavery, and minorities.

The degree of independence of its members varies radically. It has long stood out because of its relative independence, its flexible agenda and working methods, its preparedness to act as a pressure group *vis-à-vis* its parent body (the Commission), and its ambiguous and often antagonistic relationship with that parent. It has come under increasing attack in the late 1990s and agreed in 1999 not to adopt resolutions on country situations which are already under consideration by the Commission. It previously played an important role by adopting resolutions which put pressure on the Commission to go further than it previously had. The Sub-Commission continues to generate a range of detailed studies on subjects such as human rights and income distribution, systematic rape during armed conflict, or the right to adequate food.

In contrast with the treaty-based bodies earlier discussed, the Charter-based bodies are political organs which have a much broader mandate to promote awareness, to foster respect, and to respond to violations of human rights standards. They derive their legitimacy and their mandate, in the broadest sense, from the human rights provisions of the Charter. Consider the following contrasts between the two types of organs.

> Treaty-based organs are distinguished by: a limited clientele consisting only of states parties to the treaty in question; concerns stemming from the terms of the treaty; a particular concern with developing the normative understanding of the relevant rights; a limited range of procedural options for dealing with matters of violation; consensus-based decision-making to the greatest extent possible; and often a non-adversarial relationship with states parties (particularly with respect to state reports) based on the concept of a 'constructive dialogue'.

> By contrast, the political organs generally: focus on a diverse range of issues; insist that every state is an actual or potential client (or respondent), regardless of its specific treaty obligations; work on the basis of a constantly expanding mandate, which should be capable of responding to crises as they emerge; engage, as a last resort, in adversarial actions *vis-à-vis* states; rely more heavily upon NGO inputs and public opinion generally to ensure the effectiveness of their work; take decisions by often strongly contested majority voting; pay

comparatively little attention to normative issues; and are very wary about establishing specific procedural frameworks within which to work, preferring a more *ad hoc* approach in most situations.

The materials that follow emphasize three features of these institutions. First, the concern of most UN organs—surely of the Commission—is overwhelmingly with civil and political rights rather than with the economic and social rights examined in Chapter 4. Second, the emphasis is on responding to relatively discrete but gross and noticeable violations—large numbers of disappearances or killings of political opponents, violent ethnic conflict, a declaration of martial law. The principal emphasis is not on what might be termed persistent, endemic, and commonplace violations that are often ignored by other states—including such serious violations as systematically entrenched discrimination against women or particular minority groups, or control of the press. Third, these organs give little attention to consciousness-raising through education or promotional activities that many observers would identify as indispensable components of an effective UN programme.

Perhaps the principal criterion used by the vast majority of governments and commentators in assessing the UN's performance is the extent to which it reacts effectively to gross violations. But this criterion should not be accepted uncritically. A significant amount of the UN's important work concentrates on longer term, structural dimensions of human rights issues: standard-setting, the promotion of greater awareness of those standards both within (e.g. in peacekeeping, or in the work of the World Bank and UN Development Programme) and outside the UN system, and the provision of advice and assistance (formerly known in the UN human rights context as 'advisory services' but now referred to as 'technical co-operation'). The organization of world conferences has also been important, particularly for present purposes those relating to human rights (Vienna 1993), women (Beijing 1995) and racism (South Africa 2001).

C. FACT-FINDING

Fact-finding is a term which has long been used to describe the function of international human rights monitors whose task is to ascertain what is going on in a given situation and to report thereon in relation to international human rights standards. The notion that the international community would seek to 'find facts' that may not accord with, or even flatly contradict, those provided officially by a sovereign government would have been virtually unthinkable not many years ago. For example, when the 1907 Hague Convention relating to international commissions of inquiry was adopted, its scope was carefully limited so as to cover only 'disputes involving neither honour nor essential interests'. Today, international fact-finding is an accepted and relatively common activity. It is carried out not only by a large number of international organizations but also by individual states and above all NGOs.

Fact-finding depends for its credibility and potential impact upon the extent to which it is perceived to have been thorough, politically objective and procedurally fair. For that reason attempts have been made to draw up rules or guidelines for fact-finders. The procedures and guidelines set forth in the following materials bear directly on investigations and reporting within the UN system. But they are also relevant to fact-finding by NGOs and by regional organs such as the Inter-American Commission on Human Rights (p. 877, *infra*).

In the following materials, Nicholas Valticos introduces some general issues. An excerpt from the State Department's annual Country Report on Human Rights Practices emphasizes the difficulty of getting to the truth of the matter. We then examine some attempts to codify international practice. The first such excerpt is from a detailed set of rules drawn up by the United Nations for a precedent-setting fact-finding mission to Chile in 1978. Despite attempts to do so, the UN has never agreed on a set of model rules. Hence the Memorandum of Understanding agreed upon with the Government of Chile remains an important benchmark. Then follows a set of Rules drawn up by the International Law Association, an NGO whose recommendations carry no formal weight but whose professional standing ensures that these Rules are considered seriously by the international community.[3]

NICHOLAS VALTICOS, FOREWORD

in B.G. Ramcharan (ed.), International Law and Fact-finding in the Field of
Human Rights (1982), at vii

[Fact-finding] is no longer a matter of ascertaining the facts in cases which merely involve the interests of two States. . . . [I]ssues of major importance to both the international community and the State concerned are often at stake. What type of action can be taken in such cases to meet the requirements of the international community while taking account of the susceptibilities of the State involved?
. . .

. . . [F]act-finding in the field of human rights has a special importance, and also encounters special difficulties, both because of the subject-matter and because of the importance attached to it by public opinion, which regards it as the acid test of the effectiveness of international organisations. [It] is however all the more difficult, because it frequently concerns the action and essential interests, if not indeed the very structure, of the States involved, who are therefore less inclined to accept international intervention in such matters. The issues often have political aspects and are the subject of discussion in political bodies, a factor which necessarily complicates their examination. Lastly, . . . fact-finding on questions concerning human rights has been undertaken by various organisations and bodies in differing contexts, and the methods used have not always been similar.
. . .

---

[3] Mention should also be made of a Declaration on Fact-finding by the United Nations in the Field of the Maintenance of International Peace and Security, adopted by General Assembly Resolution 46/59 in 1991. It is addressed not to human rights matters but to the field of international peace and security. Nevertheless, some of its principles are potentially as applicable to human rights inquiries. For a set of standard minimum terms of reference currently used by UN human rights missions, see UN Doc. E/CN.4/1999/104, Annex II.

Having myself taken part in such procedures, I should like to set out some general reflections on the problem.

In the first place, as we are on the frequently unstable terrain of international law, it is necessary, as has previously been recognized, not to confine oneself within unduly rigid categories or rules. In international law, functions intertwine—at times, indeed, too much—and judicial aspects cannot always be distinguished clearly from non-judicial ones. It is therefore not always possible, in international fact-finding, to transpose internal judicial procedures in full. Nor is it always possible—or even desirable—to establish unduly detailed rules which may turn out not to be applicable in practice. If procedures are too formal and judicial and rules too detailed, they may prove not to be adapted to the great variety of situations, to the susceptibilities and objections of the States concerned, or to practical needs.

One conclusion to be drawn from this is that it is necessary to have available a variety of procedures suited to different situations, ranging from quasi-judicial inquiries to methods involving a minimum of formality such as 'direct contacts'. . . .

. . .

The principles must be such that, having regard to the procedure followed and the persons entrusted with it, the fact-finding process enjoys the confidence of the international community as well as of the State concerned. It thus becomes possible more readily to obtain the co-operation of the latter, while not leaving the international community in any doubt about the integrity and reliability of the findings.

These principles must naturally be based on the principal concepts of *due process of law* in domestic procedures (such as the age-old rule 'auditur et altera pars'), but they must also make allowance for the special features of this kind of international action. Thus, in the event of on-the-spot visits, it will not normally be possible for a representative of the complainant to be present, nor will it be appropriate for a representative of the party complained against to take part in interviews with private individuals. The latter party should, however, be given an opportunity to comment on allegations received in the course of such visits. Similarly, precautions have sometimes to be taken to ensure the safety of witnesses and to protect them against intimidation or reprisals (or the mere fear of reprisals). . . .

A process as difficult as human rights fact-finding calls not only for procedural safeguards. In a divided and distrustful world, and on questions where there exist profound differences of views, fact-finding itself and the conclusions and recommendations emanating from it are more likely to find acceptance if it is entrusted to independent and impartial persons. Not only logic, but also several decades of experience lead to that conclusion.

NOTE

Issues of fact-finding necessarily figure in the annual country reports prepared by the United States. Note the following comments in US Department of State, *Country Reports on Human Rights Practices for 1998* (1999), Appendix A:

We base the annual Country Reports on Human Rights Practices on information available from all sources, including American and foreign government officials, victims of human rights abuse, academic and congressional studies, and reports from the press, international organizations, and [NGOs] concerned with human rights. We find particularly helpful, and make reference in most reports to, the role of NGO's, ranging from groups in a single country to those that concern themselves with human rights worldwide. While much of the information we use is already public, information on particular abuses frequently cannot be attributed, for obvious reasons, to specific sources.

. . .

We have attempted to make these country reports as comprehensive as space will allow, while taking care to make them objective and as uniform as possible in both scope and quality of coverage. . . .

It is often difficult to evaluate the credibility of reports of human rights abuses. With the exception of some terrorist organizations, most opposition groups and certainly most governments deny that they commit human rights abuses and often go to great lengths to conceal any evidence of such acts. There are often few eyewitnesses to specific abuses, and they frequently are intimidated or otherwise prevented from reporting what they know. On the other hand, individuals and groups opposed to a particular government sometimes have powerful incentives to exaggerate or fabricate abuses, and some governments similarly distort or exaggerate abuses attributed to opposition groups. . . . Many governments that profess to oppose human rights abuses in fact secretly order or tacitly condone them or simply lack the will or the ability to control those responsible for them. Consequently, in judging a government's policy, it is important to look beyond statements of policy or intent in order to examine what in fact a government has done to prevent human rights abuses, including the extent to which it investigates, tries, and appropriately punishes those who commit such abuses. We continue to make every effort to do that in these reports.

MEMORANDUM OF UNDERSTANDING WITH THE GOVERNMENT OF CHILE
UN Doc. A/33/331 (1978), Annex VII

1. This memorandum reflects the exchanges between the Ad Hoc Working Group and representatives of the Government of Chile at the meetings held in New York from 22 to 26 May 1978.

A. Visit of the Ad Hoc Working Group to Chile

2. The representatives of the Government of Chile informed the Group that conditions now existed which enabled the Government to agree to a visit by the Group to Chile in fulfilment of the Group's mandate. The Group recognized the unprecedented nature of the visit it would undertake to Chile and the Group expressed its determination to fulfil its mandate in an objective and impartial manner and, within the terms of its mandate, to take steps to that end in co-operation with the Government of Chile. Taking into consideration the Government's wish that

the visit take place in the near future and the need for adequate preparation it was agreed that the visit would begin on or about 12 July 1978 for an effective duration of two weeks, which the Group determined to be the minimum time necessary to carrying out adequately the visit as part of its mandate.

B. Facilities to be enjoyed by the Group during the visit

3. It was agreed that the Group would enjoy the following facilities during the visit which are necessary to the carrying out of its mandate:

(a) Freedom of movement

The members of the Group and the accompanying Secretariat staff will enjoy freedom of movement throughout the country.

(b) Freedom of investigation

The Group, its members and the accompanying Secretariat staff will have access to prisons, places of detention and interrogation centres, will be able to interview freely and privately persons, groups and representatives of entities and institutions and will have access to pertinent files and other documents or materials which it considers necessary to its inquiry. The Government will provide members of the Group and the Secretariat staff with official identity documents stipulating the above. The representatives of the Government of Chile noted that access to places, persons and files, documents or other materials under the jurisdiction of the judicial authorities is subject to the authorization of the competent officials and that access to places connected with national security is similarly subject to the authorization of the competent officials. The representatives of the Government of Chile undertook to make the necessary arrangements with the appropriate authorities prior to and during the visit to ensure the Group's freedom of investigation. Visits or interviews with private persons or institutions would take place with due respect for the normal rights of said persons or institutions.

C. Assurances given by the Government of Chile in connexion with the visit

4. The representatives of the Government of Chile assured the Group that no person who had been in contact with the Group would for that reason be subjected to coercion, sanctions, punishment or judicial proceedings. The Group attaches particular importance to these guarantees.

5. The representatives of the Government of Chile assured the Group that the required measures will be taken to ensure the privacy and unimpaired conduct of the activities of the Group and the security of the members of the Group, the Secretariat staff and the Group's records and documents while in Chile.

6. The freedoms and assurances mentioned in paragraphs 3, 4 and 5 would be officially communicated to the Group in writing by the Government of Chile.

D. Basic rules of procedure

7. The Group reiterated that it could not diminish or depart from its terms of reference as determined by the Commission on Human Rights and the General Assembly nor could it delegate or renounce its sole responsibility for the

interpretation of its mandate. Paragraphs 8 through 14 reflect the Group's understanding of certain aspects of its mandate.

. . .

9. Meetings and hearings of witnesses would, as provided for in rules 5 and 16 of the Group's rules of procedure, be held *in camera*.

E. *Exchange of information between the Group and the Government*

10. In order to facilitate collaboration between the Group and the Government of Chile the Group would communicate to the representatives of the Government of Chile in the measure possible the Group's views on areas of its concern relating to the situation of human rights in that country. The Group would also communicate to the Government of Chile information on testimonies, individual cases or events of concern to the Group relating to the situation of human rights in Chile insofar as such transmission of information is consistent with the Group's mandate and the Group's obligations to persons supplying information or mentioned therein. This would be done with a view to enabling the Government to submit information and views on these matters.

11. . . .Information or views from the Government of Chile will be taken into consideration by the Group in the preparation of its report and included therein as appropriate.

12. . . .The Group agreed that it would annex to its report the observations of the Government. . . .

F. *Information and evidence*

13. The Group will continue to carefully weigh the evidentiary value of all the information it receives taking into consideration, *inter alia*, the character of the source of the information, its direct and reliable nature, the potential motivations of the source and the concordant nature of other information. . . . The Group will take into consideration the relevant information and conclusions arrived at by the specialized agencies and other international bodies on matters within their respective competence.

14. The Group wishes to point out that the nature of its mandate and the task it is required to perform requires that it be responsible for the final decisions of the probative value of information and evidence in light of all the relevant circumstances.

15. In connexion with its visit to Chile the Group will transmit to the Government of Chile an indicative but not exhaustive list of persons and representatives of institutions the Group may wish to interview and the places and institutions it may wish to visit to enable the Government to take those steps necessary to facilitate the visit. In the exercise of its freedom of movement and investigation the Group will itself definitively decide on its programme and the persons it will interview and the places it will visit.

. . .

H. *Privileges and immunities of the members of the Group and Secretariat staff*

17. The Government of Chile agreed that the members of the Group and the

Secretariat staff would enjoy, in addition to the privileges and immunities to which they are entitled by virtue of the Convention on the Privileges and Immunities of the United Nations, full diplomatic privileges and immunities. This will be confirmed in writing by the Government of Chile.

...

INTERNATIONAL LAW ASSOCIATION, THE BELGRADE MINIMUM RULES OF PROCEDURE FOR INTERNATIONAL HUMAN RIGHTS FACT-FINDING MISSIONS
75 Am. J. Int. L. 163 (1981)

...

II. Selection of fact-finders

4. The fact-finding mission should be composed of persons who are respected for their integrity, impartiality competence and objectivity and who are serving in their personal capacities.

5. Where the mandate of the mission concerns one or several specific states, in order to facilitate the task of the mission, the government or governments concerned, whenever possible, should be consulted in regard to the composition of the mission.

6. Any person appointed a member of the fact-finding mission should not be removed from membership except for reasons of incapacity or gross misbehaviour.

...

8. Once a fact-finding mission has been established and its chairman and members appointed, no persons should be added to the mission as members except to fill a vacancy in the mission.

III. Collection of evidence

9. At the commencement of the mission, all material relevant to the purpose of the mission should be made available to it, with the assistance of the organization concerned.

10. Fact-finding missions should operate with staff sufficient to permit the independent collection of data and should be assisted by such independent experts as the mission may deem necessary.

...

13. Both the petitioners, such as states, non-governmental organizations, or groups of individuals, and the states concerned may present lists of witnesses to the fact-finding mission. The fact-finding mission should make its own determination as to which witnesses it will hear.

14. Petitioners ought ordinarily to be heard by the fact-finding mission in public session with an opportunity for questioning by the states concerned.

15. The fact-finding mission shall in advance require the state concerned to

provide adequate guarantee of non-retaliation against individual petitioners, witnesses and their relatives.

. . .

17. The fact-finding mission may withhold information which, in its judgement, may jeopardize the safety or well-being of those giving testimony, or of third parties, or which in its opinion is likely to reveal sources.

18. On the basis of data generated by its staff, written statements, and testimony of witnesses, the fact-finding mission should make its own determination as to whether it needs to conduct an on-site inspection.

IV. The on-site investigation

19. The fact-finding mission should draw up its programme of work, including the list of witnesses it wishes to interview at the site of the investigation, places it wishes to visit, and the sequence, timing and location of its activities on the site.

. . .

21. The fact-finding mission should insist on interviewing any persons it deems necessary, even if incarcerated.

V. Final stage

22. After conclusion of the on-site investigation, members of the fact-finding mission should draw up a set of preliminary findings and submit these, together with supplementary questions where appropriate, to the state concerned, giving it an opportunity, within a reasonable time, to present comments and/or to rectify the matter investigated.

23. A final report shall be prepared by the chairman reflecting the consensus of the fact-finding mission. In the absence of a consensus, the mission's report should contain the findings of the majority as well as any views of dissenting members.

24. In case a decision is made to publish the report, it should be published in its entirety.

25. The organization establishing the fact-finding mission should keep under review the compliance of states with their undertaking regarding non-reprisal against petitioners, witnesses, their relatives and associates.

NOTE

Any consideration of fact-finding with respect to human rights (or a great many other subjects) must keep in mind one pervasive, ongoing and transformative feature of the modern world. Electronic communication through fax, phone, e-mail or the internet makes possible the instant diffusion of information to a vast audience. These technologies have made it almost impossible to prevent the dissemination of at least some knowledge of new, serious human rights violations within any part of the world, however remote and isolated.

This recent revolution in communications puts the contemporary fact-finder in a radically different situation from her predecessor. As recently as the early decades of this century, horrific events within isolated parts of Europe such as the rural Balkans (during the 1912–13 wars preceding the First World War) became known only through difficult expeditions by investigators who brought their findings out with them.[4]

The contemporary fact-finder has a further powerful advantage over predecessors. The human rights researcher into a given country or problem has access to ever expanding and more efficient databases that apply search technologies to organized data and thereby yield detailed information about a vast range of matters from all parts of the globe.

Of course this vast expansion in the 'information' available to a broad public gives no assurance of accuracy. The problems of verification of allegations of human rights violations may be no less serious. But at a minimum the allegations are known, a large number of unrelated sources may have made them, and those receiving the information are able to make their decisions about how to proceed.

QUESTIONS

1. Does the formula in paragraph 3(b) of the Memorandum of Understanding between Chile and the UN strike a satisfactory balance? How might the wording be amended in order to promote a more human rights-friendly process?

2. If you were on a fact-finding mission investigating accusations of torture, disappearances, and political killings, what other sources of information would be available to you, and would it be appropriate for you to consult them and draw on them in the mission's report?

3. Suppose you were to visit a prison to determine the conditions in which prisoners lived. Taking into account these models, and bearing in mind the particular problems presented, what provisions would you attempt to negotiate for these visits?

4. Suppose the killing of 20 residents of a small village by hooded men takes place one night. The government denies responsibility, which it places on a guerrilla group seeking to prevent villagers from cooperating with the government. How does an investigator pursue her inquiry?

5. In light of the models considered above, is it plausible to argue that the purpose of on-site missions undertaken by the UN is fact-finding, while it remains for the UN Commission (to which the reports are delivered) to give meaning to those facts in the light of relevant human rights norms?

6. These models do not take account of the new information technologies. Should the developing technologies lead to significant changes in the approach reflected in, say, the ILA's Minimum Rules?

---

[4] See the account of the difficulties in getting a fact-finding Commission underway in G. Kennan, 'The Balkan Crises: 1913 and 1993', in *The Other Balkan War* (1993), at 3, 6–9.

D. THE UN COMMISSION'S MAIN PROCEDURES FOR RESPONDING TO VIOLATIONS

Although the terms of reference adopted for the Commission in 1946 included a general mandate to address any human rights matter, it spent most of its first 20 years engaged almost exclusively in standard-setting. This included the preparation of the first draft of the UDHR and the two Covenants, as well as a range of other instruments. Even today this standard-setting function continues to be important, as illustrated by efforts under way in 2000 to draft a 'declaration on indigenous rights', a draft convention on disappearances, and several optional protocols to treaties. Its role in responding to violations began only in 1967 when it effectively overturned a much-criticized statement it adopted in 1947 to the effect that it had 'no power to take any action in regard to any complaints concerning human rights'.

The early efforts to address serious violations were directed only to problems associated with racism and colonialism. In 1979, however, the Commission's work entered a third phase in which it began to apply the procedures it had developed in an increasingly creative fashion to an ever-widening range of countries and violations. For purposes of evaluating the Commission's work, one should bear in mind that it began to respond not much more than 20 years ago to violations in general.

In broad terms there are now three different procedures used by the Commission to address violations. They are: (1) confidential consideration of a situation under the 1503 procedure; (2) public debate under the 1235 procedure, which may lead to the appointment of a Special Rapporteur of the Commission, a Special Representative of the Secretary-General, or some other designated individual or group to investigate a situation; and (3) the designation of a 'thematic' rapporteur or Working Group to consider violations anywhere relating to a specific theme (such as torture, disappearances, or arbitrary detention).

In principle, each of these procedures is relatively distinct from the others in terms of its origins, the nature of its mandate, the steps to be followed and the types of outcome available. In practice, there is considerable overlap. It is conceivable that different aspects of a particular situation would be under review by all three procedures at the same time. Moreover, the same situation might be considered simultaneously by one or more of the treaty bodies (such as the ICCPR Human Rights Committee or the Committee Against Torture) to be considered in Chapter 9 (and as well by one of the regional organizations described in Chapter 10).

The following materials look at the functioning of each of these three procedures.

1. THE 1503 PROCEDURE: PROS AND CONS OF CONFIDENTIALITY

The 1503 procedure is named after Economic and Social Council Resolution 1503 (XLVIII) (1970). The resolution authorized the Commission to establish a procedure for the examination of communications (complaints) pertaining to 'situations which appear to reveal a consistent pattern of gross and reliably attested violations of human rights requiring consideration by the Commission'. Its origins lay in a dramatic change in the composition of the major UN organs by the mid-1960s as a result of the influx of new members, mainly newly independent African and Asian states. Membership of the Commission went from 18 in 1960 to 32 in 1967 (20 of which were from the Third World), en route to today's 53 members.

In 1965 a complaints procedure had been included in the Convention on the Elimination of All Forms of Racial Discrimination (CERD). The willingness of the Third World majority to develop new procedures for treaty bodies applied even though there was a significant 'risk' that the scope or reach of these procedures might eventually be extended to address a broader range of problems for which Third World governments might be responsible. And indeed this development cleared the way for an Optional Protocol to the Covenant on Civil and Political Rights to be adopted the following year.

At the same time, Third World countries, strongly supported by the Eastern Europeans, were pressing for a general, non-treaty-based, communications-type procedure as an additional means by which to pursue the struggle against racist and colonialist policies, particularly in southern Africa. These efforts resulted in the adoption of what eventually turned out to be two separate procedures, the scope of each of which was extended to include violations anywhere in the world. The first, established under ECOSOC Resolution 1235 (XLII), laid down the principle that violations could be examined by the Commission and responded to. It provided the necessary authorization for the Commission to engage in public debate on the issue each year. The second was the 1503 procedure. Although it was adopted after, and built upon, the 1235 procedure, it developed more rapidly than the latter, and has often been used as a precursor to action under it. Thus we consider the 1503 procedure first.

The UN Commission had previously (under Resolutions 75 (V) (1947) and 728 F (XXVIII) (1959)) used communications only as a means of identifying general trends, thus providing no response whatsoever to the particular violations at issue. The adoption of the 1503 procedure involved a typical horse-trading exercise in which governments with competing objectives sought to reconcile their goals through the use of open-ended and flexible language. Both the resolution itself and the subsequent Sub-Commission resolution that laid down the admissibility criteria for communications are perfect case studies in ambiguity.

ECOSOC RESOLUTION 1503 (XLVIII) (1970)

The Economic and Social Council,

. . .

1. *Authorizes* the Sub-Commission on Prevention of Discrimination and Protection of Minorities to appoint a working group consisting of not more than five
of its members, with due regard to geographical distribution, to meet once a year
in private meetings for a period not exceeding ten days immediately before the
sessions of the Sub-Commission to consider all communications, including replies
of Governments thereon, received by the Secretary-General under Council resolution 728F (XXVIII) of 30 July 1959 with a view to bringing to the attention of
the Sub-Commission those communications, together with replies of Governments, if any, which appear to reveal a consistent pattern of gross and reliably
attested violations of human rights and fundamental freedoms within the terms of
reference of the Sub-Commission;

. . .

4. *Further requests* the Secretary-General:

(a) To furnish to the members of the Sub-Commission every month a list of
communications prepared by him in accordance with Council resolution 728F
(XXVIII) and a brief description of them, together with the text of any replies
received from Governments;

(b) To make available to the members of the working group at their meetings
the originals of such communications listed as they may request . . . ;

. . .

5. *Requests* the Sub-Commission on Prevention of Discrimination and Protection of Minorities to consider in private meetings, in accordance with paragraph 1
above, the communications brought before it in accordance with the decision of a
majority of the members of the working group and any replies of Governments
relating thereto and other relevant information; with a view to determining
whether to refer to the Commission on Human Rights particular situations which
appear to reveal a consistent pattern of gross and reliably attested violations of
human rights requiring consideration by the Commission;

6. *Requests* the Commission on Human Rights after it has examined any situation referred to it by the Sub-Commission to determine:

(a) Whether it requires a thorough study by the Commission and a report and
recommendations thereon to the Council in accordance with paragraph 3 of
Council resolution 1235 (XLII);

[Eds. The other alternative is for the Commission to appoint an '*ad hoc* committee'
to investigate the situation. But that requires 'the express consent of the State
concerned and shall be conducted in constant co-operation with that State and
under conditions determined by agreement with it'. All 'available means at the
national level' must have been exhausted and the situation should not relate to a
matter being dealt with under other international procedures. Members of the
committee are appointed by the Commission but subject to the consent of the
government concerned. Its work is to be entirely confidential and it should 'strive

for friendly solutions' at all times. It then reports to the Commission 'with such observations and suggestions as it may deem appropriate'. This procedure has never been used.]

. . .

8. *Decides* that all actions envisaged in the implementation of the present resolution by the Sub-Commission [or Commission] shall remain confidential until such time as the Commission may decide to make recommendations to the Economic and Social Council;

. . .

10. *Decides* that the procedure set out in the present resolution for dealing with communications relating to violations of human rights and fundamental freedoms should be reviewed if any new organ entitled to deal with such communications should be established within the United Nations or by international agreement.

SUB-COMMISSION RESOLUTION 1 (XXIV) (1971)

The Sub-Commission on Prevention of Discrimination and Protection of Minorities,

. . .

Adopts the following provisional procedures for dealing with the question of admissibility of communications referred to above:

(1) Standards and criteria

(a) The object of the communication must not be inconsistent with the relevant principles of the Charter, of the Universal Declaration of Human Rights and of the other applicable instruments in the field of human rights.

(b) Communications shall be admissible only if, after consideration thereof, together with the replies of any of the Governments concerned, there are reasonable grounds to believe that they may reveal a consistent pattern of gross and reliably attested violations of human rights and fundamental freedoms, including policies of racial discrimination and segregation and of *apartheid*, in any country, including colonial and other dependent countries and peoples.

(2) Source of communications

(a) Admissible communications may originate from a person or group of persons who, it can be reasonably presumed, are victims of the violations referred to in subparagraph (1) (b) above, any person or group of persons who have direct and reliable knowledge of those violations, or non-governmental organizations acting in good faith in accordance with recognized principles of human rights, not resorting to politically motivated stands contrary to the provisions of the Charter of the United Nations and having direct and reliable knowledge of such violations.

(b) Anonymous communications shall be inadmissible; . . . ;

(c) Communications shall not be inadmissible solely because the knowledge of the individual authors is second-hand, provided that they are accompanied by clear evidence.

(3) Contents of communications and nature of allegations

(a) The communication must contain a description of the facts and must indicate the purpose of the petition and the rights that have been violated.

(b) Communications shall be inadmissible if their language is essentially abusive and in particular if they contain insulting references to the State against which the complaint is directed. Such communications may be considered if they meet the other criteria for admissibility after deletion of the abusive language.

(c) A communication shall be inadmissible if it has manifestly political motivations and its subject is contrary to the provisions of the Charter of the United Nations.

(d) A communication shall be inadmissible if it appears that it is based exclusively on reports disseminated by mass media.

(4) Existence of other remedies

(a) Communications shall be inadmissible if their admission would prejudice the functions of the specialized agencies of the United Nations system.

(b) Communications shall be inadmissible if domestic remedies have not been exhausted, unless it appears that such remedies would be ineffective or unreasonably prolonged. Any failure to exhaust remedies should be satisfactorily established.

(c) Communications relating to cases which have been settled by the State concerned in accordance with the principles set forth in the Universal Declaration of Human Rights and other applicable documents in the field of human rights will not be considered.

(5) Timeliness

A communication shall be inadmissible if it is not submitted to the United Nations within a reasonable time after the exhaustion of the domestic remedies as provided above.

COMMENT ON SAUDI ARABIA UNDER THE 1503 PROCEDURE

Until the mid-1980s the United Nations received around 25,000 complaints per year. In 1993 the number ballooned to around 300,000, but many of these complaints were identical as a result of letter-writing campaigns by groups with large and active memberships. It seems that, on average, about 50,000 complaints are still received each year. The processes involved are tedious and time-consuming. This is because the procedure was carefully designed to ensure that governments would not lightly be accused of violations and because it is concerned not with individual cases, but with 'situations'.

In statistical terms, the 1503 procedure has 'touched' an impressive number of countries. Between 1972 and 1999, 75 states have been subject to scrutiny. Of these, 20 were in Africa, 23 in Asia (including the Middle East), 15 in Latin America, 12 in Eastern Europe, and 5 in Western Europe.[5]

The entire 1503 procedure is shrouded in secrecy, with each of its stages being accomplished in confidential sessions by the bodies concerned. The only public statement is an indication provided by the Chairperson of the Commission each year of the names of the countries which are currently under consideration and those cases which have been discontinued. Nevertheless, the details have invariably been leaked to the media for one reason or another and the complete documentation on several country situations has been made available as a result of Commission decisions to release all relevant documentation in cases concerning Equatorial Guinea, Uruguay, Argentina, and the Philippines. Since those cases are now too old to provide a reliable guide to current practice, this case study on Saudi Arabia was compiled on the basis of 'confidential' but leaked UN documents as well as information gleaned from interviews with participants.

In April 1996 Amnesty International submitted a communication entitled 'Continuing Human Rights Violations in Saudi Arabia' to the UN, and sent a copy to the Saudi Government for information. It followed two previous communications submitted in April 1994 and April 1995. While the precise form of the ten-page report differed from Amnesty's published reports, the content reflected long-standing concerns published in various contexts by Amnesty and, according to the communication, repeatedly raised by Amnesty with the government without any response. The content was accurately reflected in Amnesty's public report issued in advance of the 1999 Commission session. A U.S. State Department assessment issued prior to the Commission's 1998 session spoke in similar terms. Excerpts from the two reports follow:

Amnesty International, 1999 UN Commission on Human Rights— Making Human Rights Work: Time to Strengthen the Special Procedures[6]

. . .

> Gross and systematic human rights violations continue in Saudi Arabia. Hundreds of people are detained indefinitely on political grounds. Although Saudi Arabia is a party to the Convention against Torture, torture and ill-treatment are widespread. Amputations, a form of torture, and floggings, amounting to torture or cruel, inhuman and degrading treatment, continue to be imposed and carried out as judicial punishments. Saudi Arabia has one of the highest execution rates per capita in the world. People continue to be executed, often in public, after summary and secret trials in blatant disregard of the most basic standards for fair trial.
>
> Contrary to international standards, defendants are denied access to lawyers. They are denied the basic right to bring witnesses in their defence or to cross examine those appearing for the prosecution. Appeals are conducted in total secrecy and the defendant is denied access to the proceedings and even knowledge of their progress.

[5] Source: <http://www.unhchr.ch/html/menu2/8/stat1.htm>.
[6] Report IOR 41/01/99, January 1999.

Prisoners are often held for indefinite periods without charge, in incommunicado detention, and there is no independent, impartial judicial supervision of arrest and detention. Such conditions foster torture and a climate of impunity for the perpetrators of torture and other gross human rights violations.

US Department of State, Saudi Arabia Country Report on Human Rights Practices for 1997, January 30, 1998[7]

. . .

The Government commits and tolerates serious human rights abuses. Citizens have neither the right nor the legal means to change their government. Security forces continued to abuse detainees and prisoners, arbitrarily arrest and detain persons, and facilitate incommunicado detention. Prolonged detention is a problem. Security forces committed such abuses, in contradiction of law, but with the acquiescence of the Government. . . . The Government disagrees with internationally accepted definitions of human rights and views its interpretation of Islamic law as its sole source of guidance on human rights.

In August 1996, the Sub-Commission agreed to forward the communication from Amnesty to the Commission under the 1503 procedure. The Saudi Government was then invited by the Commission to respond, which it did in a reply dated March 1998, just as the Commission session was getting under way. The 17-page reply alleged that the Amnesty figures relating to matters like execution, amputations and public floggings were inaccurate, but supplied no alternative figures on any of these issues. The Amnesty report was variously described as exaggerated, extreme, groundless, inaccurate, selective, ambiguous, and distorted. At one point the government questioned how Amnesty could characterize any Saudi trials as being unfair since its complaint lacked precise case details.

The two reports—one by Amnesty and the government's reply—were the principal documents before the UN Commission when it met in private session on 8 April 1998 under the 1503 procedure. In the course of about one hour the Commission disposed of the case. It first heard the Saudi representative affirm the government's faith in human rights and its confidence in the UN's human rights mechanisms. He also indicated that the government was considering contributing more money to a UN Trust Fund for the Victims of Torture, that it had respected international standards and had sought to improve the functioning of its judicial system. A succession of speakers—from Pakistan, Sri Lanka, Sudan, Morocco, Bangladesh, Malaysia, South Korea, the Philippines, China, Uganda, Indonesia and Tunisia—then welcomed the government's cooperative attitude and proposed that the Commission's 1503 examination of the situation in Saudi Arabia be discontinued. The US representative remained silent throughout, while speakers from Denmark and Germany posed some questions based on the government's report. After the Saudi representative indicated that note had been taken of the questions put, the Commission decided to discontinue the case. The Chairperson of the Commission provided neither reasons for the outcome nor details of the debate.

---

[7] <http://www.state.gov/www/global/human_rights/1997_hrp_report/saudiara.html>.

The documentation remained confidential. NGOs were highly critical of the decision and at a subsequent press conference, the US Permanent Representative to the UN in Geneva was asked to comment on the issue. Ambassador Moose replied as follows:

> I would say that indeed the issues of human rights in Saudi Arabia received intensive discussion and consideration in this Commission this year. In fact, one of the things we did see this year was a much greater readiness on the part of the Saudi government to respond to the concerns that have been raised in the Commission. Frankly it was on the basis of that responsiveness that the Commission determined to drop Saudi Arabia from the 1503 Procedures. On this issue, as on every other issue, I would simply say that we continue to look to the future, we will continue to monitor and to dialogue with the Saudis and with others to ensure that the responsiveness that we have seen is in fact the beginning of a process of ongoing dialogue and response.[8]

QUESTIONS

1. One way to grasp loopholes for governments in the 1503 procedure is to imagine a case and formulate arguments based on the procedure to the effect that the matter does not fit within the relevant guidelines and therefore should not be considered. Suppose that the government you represent is responding to a communication alleging that 100 members of a group have been arbitrarily detained for six months. The communication was submitted by a small NGO based in your country. The group's secretary is also the leader of a political party opposed to the government. The complaint, based upon newspaper reports and accounts provided by relatives of eleven detained persons, mentions that the government is widely considered to be both oppressive and exploitative. The communication notes that the state's courts have always done the government's bidding and that it would be a waste of time and resources to ask the courts to order the release of the detainees. What arguments would you make against admissibility?

2. Consider the following assessments of the 1503 procedure. In the mid-1970s, Amnesty International characterized the confidentiality of 1503 as 'an undisguised stratagem for using the United Nations, not as an instrument for promoting and protecting and exposing large-scale violations of human rights, but rather for concealing their occurrence'. In a similar vein the then Director of the UN's human rights Secretariat, Theo van Boven, made this thinly veiled allusion to the procedure in his opening statement to the Commission in 1980:

> Is it satisfactory to place so much emphasis on the consideration of situations in confidential procedures thereby shutting out the international community and oppressed peoples? Are certain procedures in danger of becoming, in effect, screens of confidentiality to prevent cases discussed thereunder from being aired in public? While there is probably no alternative to trying to co-

---

[8] Transcript of a press conference of 24 April 1998 at: <http://www3.itu.ch/MISSIONS/US/hrcom/0424bri.htm>.

operate with the Governments concerned, should we allow this to result in the passage of several years while the victims continue to suffer and nothing meaningful is really done?[9]

Some commentators have strongly defended the procedure on the grounds that: (1) 1503 review facilitates subsequent consideration of a country under the public procedures; and (2) it enables attention to be paid to situations that would otherwise be ignored. Others have commented that: 'While the 1503 process is painfully slow, complex, secret, and vulnerable to political influence at many junctures, it does afford an incremental technique for placing gradually increasing pressure on offending governments'.[10]

What criteria for effectiveness would you use in evaluating the 1503 procedure? Under what circumstances do you consider the use of confidentiality in such procedures to be justified? Would you suggest any reform in this procedure?

2. THE 1235 PROCEDURE: PROCESSES AND PARTICIPANTS

ECOSOC Resolution 1235 (XLII) (1967) established the procedure on the basis of which the Commission holds an annual public debate focusing on gross violations in a number of states. The pertinent parts of the resolution are as follows.

ECOSOC RESOLUTION 1235 (XLII) (1967)

The Economic and Social Council,
. . .

1. *Welcomes* the decision of the Commission on Human Rights to give annual consideration to the item entitled 'Question of the violation of human rights and fundamental freedoms, including policies of racial discrimination and segregation and of *apartheid*, in all countries, with particular reference to colonial and other dependent countries and territories. . . .'.

2. *Authorizes* the Commission on Human Rights and the Sub-Commission on Prevention of Discrimination and Protection of Minorities, . . . to examine information relevant to gross violations of human rights and fundamental freedoms, as exemplified by the policy of *apartheid* as practised in the Republic of South Africa and in the Territory of South West Africa . . . and to racial discrimination as practised notably in Southern Rhodesia. . . .

3. *Decides* that the Commission on Human Rights may, in appropriate cases, and after careful consideration of the information thus made available to it, in conformity with the provisions of paragraph 1 above, make a thorough study of situations which reveal a consistent pattern of violations of human rights, as exemplified by the policy of *apartheid* as practised in the Republic of South Africa

[9] T. van Boven, *People Matter: Views on International Human Rights Policy* (1982), at 65.
[10] F. Newman and D. Weissbrodt, *International Human Rights* (1990), at 122–3.

and in the Territory of South West Africa . . . and racial discrimination as practised notably in Southern Rhodesia, and report, with recommendations thereon, to the Economic and Social Council;

. . .

COMMENT ON THE 1235 PROCEDURE AND ITS POTENTIAL OUTCOMES

The provisions of Resolution 1235 provide a vivid illustration of the extent to which the Commission's mandate has evolved. The ways in which violations are now dealt with by the Commission under the rubric of the 1235 procedure bear only a passing resemblance to the Resolution. It was not until the late 1970s that the procedure began to fulfil its potential. In 1976–77 the Commission had notably failed to act publicly with regard to horrendous violations in Pol Pot's Democratic Kampuchea (Cambodia), Amin's Uganda, Bokassa's Central African Empire, Macias' Equatorial Guinea, the military's Argentina and Uruguay, and several other situations. Developing public opinion about these failures (almost by definition among the elites in the West and a limited number of Third World countries) combined with the higher profile given to human rights issues by the Carter Administration in the United States, and several of its allies, contributed to a political climate in which expansion of the Commission's work was almost an imperative. Starting with Equatorial Guinea and Cambodia in the late 1970s the UN Commission gradually widened the range of countries whose records were publicly scrutinized under the 1235 procedure.

That procedure now operates to provide the foundation for two types of activity. The first, in accordance with the mandate, involves the holding of an annual public debate during the Commission's annual session in which governments and NGOs are given an opportunity to identify publicly those country-specific situations that they consider to merit the Commission's attention. The second involves studying and investigating particular situations (or individual cases) through the use of whatever techniques the Commission deems appropriate. Such investigative activity is only authorized in relation to a small proportion of the situations identified during the annual debate. This does not mean that the remaining situations are entirely neglected, for the Commission can contribute in other ways to pressures on a government accused of violations. A broad range of outcomes might follow the identification of a serious country situation by a government or an NGO within the framework of the 1235 debate. They include:

- the mere mention of a situation in the debate might embarrass a country (sometimes referred to as the sanction of 'shaming'), generate media coverage, or influence another country's foreign policy;
- an NGO might use the occasion to pressure other governments to take up the issue on a bilateral or multilateral basis;
- a draft resolution might be circulated, and then withdrawn, perhaps after a strong lobbying effort by the government concerned or in response to concessions offered by that government; or

- the Chairperson of the Commission might issue a statement of exhortation, with the (either formal or *de facto*) approval of the Commission.

If the Commission does take up the matter it might:

- decide that the country concerned should be provided with 'advisory services', thus avoiding condemnation but making clear its concern;
- adopt a resolution calling for all available information to be submitted to it with a view to considering the matter at a later session;
- call upon the government to respond to the allegations in detail and in writing before its next session;
- adopt a resolution criticizing the government (for which purpose, language ranging from the diplomatic to the highly critical might be used) and calling upon the government to take specific measures;
- appoint a Special Rapporteur or other individual or group to examine the situation and submit a report to the Commission on the basis of a visit (if possible) to the country;
- call upon the Secretary-General to appoint a Special Representative to perform a similar function; or
- call upon the Security Council to take up the issue, with a view to considering the adoption of sanctions or some other punitive measure.

As later materials suggest, the impact of any of these measures will vary greatly depending on factors such as the nature of the violations and especially the extent to which their continuation is central to the government's strategy for retaining power, the relative influence of domestic pressure groups, the degree of support for the measure in the Commission, the openness of the country concerned to external influences, the vulnerability of the country to trade, aid or other pressures; and the attitude taken by the country's allies and its regional neighbours.

As of January 2000 the following 18 situations were being examined under the 1235 procedure: Afghanistan, Bosnia and Herzegovina, Burundi, Congo (Democratic Republic), Croatia, Cuba, Cyprus, East Timor, Equatorial Guinea, Federal Republic of Yugoslavia, Iran, Iraq, Israel (in relation to the Occupied Territories), Kosovo, Myanmar, Rwanda, Sierra Leone, and Sudan. In addition, Cambodia, Chad, Colombia, Haiti, Occupied Palestine, Somalia, and Western Sahara were under consideration under UN Commission agenda items other than that dealing with violations *per se*, such as self-determination issues and advisory services.

Together with the thematic procedures considered at p. 641, *infra*, these country examinations are known as the 'UN Special Procedures'. Their implementation is entrusted to a wide range of entities. While 'working groups' and 'special rapporteurs' were initially the favoured means of fact-finding, other designations have been added over the years, including 'rapporteurs', 'envoys', 'special representatives', 'independent experts' and 'delegations'. The Commission's creativity and inconsistency have blurred the significance of these distinctions. The Chairman of the Commission is expected to 'consult' with the regional groups before making an appointment. Those selected are generally prominent personalities from human rights-related backgrounds, including academics, lawyers, economists, and NGO leaders. Since 1994 when the first female expert was appointed the proportion of women has grown significantly. The experts receive no financial reward for their work, although their expences are covered. They rely upon the Office of the UN High Commissioner for Human Rights for secretariat services, but they have long complained of the gross inadequacy of the assistance available to them as a result of chronic staff shortages within the OHCHR.

The experts receive complaints from victims of violations, intervene with governments on their behalf, carry out country visits, research and study issues of concern, and report both orally and in writing to the UN Commission and sometimes also to the General Assembly. Depending on the terms of the resolution creating the position, most reports contain an analysis of the mandate, a section on methodology, a factual account of information gathered, conclusions, and recommendations.

There has been considerable unevenness in the quality of the reports produced by different experts. Some experts have been accused of being 'in the pockets' of the government being investigated, while the efforts of others have been deemed 'spineless' and 'needlessly apologetic'. But the overall quality of the reports has been strong.

The terms used to describe the formal mandates given to different experts have varied considerably. But whether they have been asked to 'study', 'inquire into', 'investigate', or 'examine', most experts have tended to assume considerable flexibility and to approach each situation as they see fit. The Commission, for its part, has generally not sought to impose any procedural straitjackets. Based on past practice it has been suggested that:

> . . .[T]hree principal approaches to country-reporting may be discerned. The first emphasizes the *fact-finding and documentation function.* In this view the function of reporting is to record the facts, to provide a reliable historical record, and to provide the necessary raw material against the background of which the political organs can determine the best strategy under the circumstances. In this approach, facts and their substantiation are the key. . . . The second approach assumes that the *prosecutorial/publicity function* is paramount. Thus the rapporteur's role is not to establish whether violations have occurred but to marshal as much evidence as possible to support a condemnation that, in many instances, will already have been made. Thus Bailey has described the Special Committee on southern Africa as a fact-finding body 'only in the sense that it collects and collates facts in pursuit of a predetermined political aim'. The goal in such cases is to mobilize world public opinion and to provide the basis on which the earlier conviction can be justified. The third approach is to emphasize the *conciliation function.* The rapporteur's role is not to confront the violators but to seek solutions which will improve, even if not necessarily resolve, the situation. The perceived challenge is to steer a middle course between the positions of the accused and their accusers and the emphasis is on dialogue and co-operation between the Commission and the government. . . .[11]

---

[11] Philip Alston, 'The Commission on Human Rights', in Alston (ed.), *The United Nations and Human Rights: A Critical Appraisal* (1992), at 163.

The preparedness of governments to cooperate with the procedures has varied significantly from one situation to another as well as over time. The factors that induce governmental cooperation seem to depend very much on a calculation, taking account of all of the relevant circumstances, as to the relative costs of co-operation versus non-cooperation. The costs of the latter are being steadily increased but they are still far from being consistently prohibitive. Reports are prepared even where permission to visit is denied.

Almost all the governments concerned have sought to defend themselves sys-tematically and vigorously within the Commission. Thus detailed rebuttals of country-specific reports are now very much the norm rather than the exception. *Ad hominem* criticisms are not uncommon, as illustrated by a statement by Iraq to mark the resignation in 1999 of former Dutch Foreign Minister Max Van der Stoel, after many years as Special Rapporteur for human rights in Iraq. His 'hostile' reports were said to have been 'marked by exaggeration of events, promotion of lies, distortion of facts, and stirring up sectarian and nationalistic sedition to fragment the unity of Iraq's people'. His departure made it possible to 'open up new horizons for cooperation' between Iraq and the UN Commission.[12]

QUESTIONS

Each year at the UN Commission session Amnesty International identifies a handful of countries it considers to be especially in need of attention by the Commission. In 1999 it named Algeria, Cambodia, Turkey and the Great Lakes Region of Africa. It also added the USA, 'where a persistent and widespread pattern of human rights violations appears to disproportionally affect people of racial or ethnic minority backgrounds' (AI Report IOR 41/08/99, June 1999). Not a single Western country appears in the list of countries currently under scrutiny under the 1235 procedure.

Is that a problem? Should the Commission take into account 'geographical balance' or representation of different cultural blocs in deciding which states should go on the 1235 list?

NOTE

The balance of the materials on the 1235 procedure consists of two case studies, one of Commission action in relation to Iran, and the other of Commission inaction in relation to China.

a. Case Study: Iran

In 1979 a revolution overthrew the government of the Shah who was succeeded by

[12] UN Wire, 16 November 1999, <http://www.unfoundation.org/unwire/archives/UNWIRE991116.cfm#19>.

Ayatollah Khomeini, with the title of Supreme Leader of the Islamic Revolution. In March 1984 the UN Commission appointed a Special Representative to undertake 'a thorough study of the human rights situation' in Iran. Reynaldo Galindo Pohl of El Salvador served through 1995, when he was succeeded by Maurice Copithorne of Canada. The latter visited Iran upon taking up his post, but as of January 2000, he had not been invited to return since 1996. The Government said his reports were biased and reflected 'an absence of accurate understanding of Islamic norms'. In its *World Report 2000*, Human Rights Watch noted that '[t]here were no independent human rights organizations active inside the country, and the government continued to obstruct visits by international monitors from [NGOs]. . . . Nevertheless, human rights monitoring and open debate of the government's human rights policies were a notable aspect of the activities of the independent press'. The Government did, however, permit visits in 1995 by UN thematic rapporteurs dealing respectively with religious intolerance, and freedom of expression and opinion.

The following materials compare two reports, one by each of the Special Representatives, from 1991 and 1999, respectively.

REPORT OF THE SPECIAL REPRESENTATIVE ON IRAN, 1991
UN Doc. E/CN.4/1991/35

. . .

II. Information Received by the Special Representative

29. The following paragraphs contain allegations of human rights violations received by the Special Representative and transmitted to the Government [as well as replies] . . . received from the Government. . . .

A. *Right to life*

30. According to a report by the daily *Abrar*, a man condemned for fornication was publicly executed in Mashad in early 1990. Agence France Presse reported on 16 January that a 31-year-old woman convicted of prostitution had been stoned to death in Bandar Anzali. On 31 January *Jomhouri Islami* published a declaration of the Komiteh Commander of the Province of West Azerbaijan, according to which five persons engaged in prostitution and corruption had been stoned to death. According to a report by *Ressalat* on 15 February 1990, Gholam Reza Masouri was hanged in Arak for pederasty.

31. *Jomhouri Islami* reported on 17 February 1990 that Bolouch Ismalel Zehi had been executed for drug-trafficking. On 10 January Radio Tehran announced that 31 persons convicted of drug-trafficking had been executed, 23 of them in Tehran, 3 at Shiraz, 3 at Sabzevar and 2 at Saveh. . . .

36. . . .Other sources reported directly to the Special Representative that Mr. Jamshead Amiry Bigvand, former Director of the Marodasht Shiraz Petrochemical Laboratory, and 13 other persons had allegedly been convicted on the charge of

espionage for the United States of America, an offence for which capital punishment might be applied. Reportedly these persons had been held for months in solitary confinement at Evin prison, and had not been allowed to avail themselves of legal assistance of their own choosing. It was further alleged that confessions had been extracted under torture and that some of them had been compelled to make extrajudicial confessions which were broadcast by Iranian television. The Special Representative requested the Government, by a letter dated 8 May 1990, to enable all 14 persons to benefit from all the procedural safeguards provided for in articles 6 and 14 of the International Covenant on Civil and Political Rights. . . .

. . .

38. By a letter dated 5 June 1990, the Permanent Representative of the Islamic Republic of Iran to the United Nations Office at Geneva forwarded to the Special Representative the following response of the judicial authorities of the Islamic Republic of Iran:

> According to the article 37 of the Constitution of the Islamic Republic of Iran, and as contained in the second paragraph of article 14 of the International Covenant on Civil and Political Rights, no person shall be considered guilty by law unless the accusation against him is proved by a competent court and the courts are naturally obliged to act accordingly;
>
> In the light of information received by the Islamic Revolutionary Court, those people were arrested and tried in accordance with the law. In addition, they were entitled to appoint a legal counsel and they duly and freely defended themselves during the trial;

. . .

42. It has further been reported that on 14 February 1990 a judicial panel sent to Hamadan on behalf of the Head of the Judiciary issued the following sentences:

. . .

(c) Reza Khanian, 23 years old, fruit and vegetable centre clerk: 74 lashes for committing robbery; 50 lashes for participation in a forbidden act; amputation of hand for committing assault and battery and hanging by scaffold.

. . .

53. It has also been widely reported that the Iranian Government has endorsed the death sentence against the British author Salman Rushdie. On 5 June 1990, the Leader of the Islamic Republic of Iran reportedly stated that the *fatwa* (religious verdict) of the late Imam Khomeini concerning the author was based on divine rulings and remained irrevocable. On 26 December 1990 the Leader of the Islamic Republic of Iran reiterated that the *fatwa* cannot be revised or repealed by anyone at any time.

54. By a letter of 22 January 1991, the Permanent Representative of the Islamic Republic of Iran also referred to the Rushdie case, as follows:

. . .

> . . . It should be pointed out that as a result of the criminal act of Mr. Rushdie which was a direct insult to the most sacred values of Muslims, tens of people lost their lives in different parts of the world. It is very surprising to note that the Special Representative addressed this political issue under the humanitarian mandate without making any reference whatsoever to those whose blood was

spilled in protest to this criminal act. The Special Representative is expected to show as much sensitivity to the right to life of those Muslims who lost their lives as that which he extends to the culprit.

. . .

59. It has been reported that as of January 1990 persons have been executed in the Islamic Republic of Iran for their homosexual or lesbian tendency.

60. In its reply of 22 January 1991, the Government of the Islamic Republic of Iran stated that 'according to the Islamic Shariat, homosexuals who confess to their acts and insist on that are condemned to death'.

. . .

B. Enforced or involuntary disappearances

73. The Special Representative wishes to refer to the report of the Working Group on Enforced or Involuntary Disappearances (E/CN.4/1991/20), which has transmitted to the Government of the Islamic Republic of Iran 451 cases of missing persons, 7 of which were reported to have occurred in 1990. So far only one case has been clarified by information received from non-governmental sources.

C. Right to freedom from torture or cruel, inhuman or degrading treatment or punishment

74. Reports on torture and ill-treatment during imprisonment have continued to be received since the first visit of the Special Representative to the Islamic Republic of Iran. It was also alleged that mutilations and corporal punishment are being applied. . . .

75. In the letter of 22 January 1991, the Government of the Islamic Republic of Iran stated that 'any physical abuse or torture under any name is denied in the prisons and they are totally baseless. But in regard to amputations, it is worth mentioning that the divine religion of Islam permits certain punishments for certain crimes and in the field of *Qesas* which entails amputations'.

. . .

IV. Conclusions and Recommendations

. . .

464. The Special Representative has expressed the view, which is also his belief, that, on the basis of existing international principles and known facts, a critical analysis should be made in order to arrive at some recommendations and conclusions in the light of criteria of probability. The aim is, of course, to base conclusions and recommendations not on findings similar to those of a court of justice, but, rather, on probability and reasonable belief. . . .

465. This exercise is particularly complex and complicated because of the specific circumstances which characterize the monitoring of human rights in the Islamic Republic of Iran. . . .Reports on international monitoring procedures may be used for political purposes and such use is beyond the scope of the competent United Nations bodies, but the aim of the exercise is not to support or destabilize Governments, but, rather, to encourage the fulfilment of international obligations relating to human rights. . . .

466. The mandate relating to Iran is one of the most controversial of all the mandates on which international monitoring has focused in particular countries in recent years. This is probably the result of the radical polarization of political forces, the conflict between opinions that have turned into pre-established, inflexible, intransigent credos and the struggle between national and international political interests. The situation is being followed attentively and even passionately in and outside the United Nations and in the media throughout the world.

. . .

468. The Special Representative has concentrated on objective consideration of the facts and the preparation of observations and recommendations on the basis of criteria of probability without giving in to the pressure and Manichaeism of persons or groups not connected with international monitoring. However, every voice which has expressed an opinion or criticism and drawn attention to procedures has been listened to. This task is one plagued by doubts, questions, conflicts of conscience and contradictory requests and it is a difficult one because the aim is to guarantee objective and independent international monitoring and compliance with international instruments, without complacency or fear.

. . .

471. During the second visit, information was received on the categories of acts which have been considered in previous reports, such as executions, the lack of a defence lawyer, failure to notify detainees of the charges against them immediately following arrest, difficulties in making trials public and ill-treatment and torture. Consistent information was also received on restrictions on freedom of the press, the publication of books and artistic creation, and delays and difficulties in exercising the right to freedom of association, including the right to form political parties. . . .

474. The positive measures adopted by the Government include: (a) the replies to many allegations which were communicated to it and which are reproduced *in extenso* in the present report; (b) the favourable outcome in a number of cases submitted by the Special Representative for consideration on humanitarian grounds; (c) the periodic adoption of clemency measures which benefit both ordinary prisoners and political prisoners; (d) the release of seven of the signers of the so-called 'Letter by the 90'; and (e) the decree of 31 December 1990, which requires a defence lawyer to be present at all stages in criminal proceedings. . . .

. . .

476. The Government acknowledged 113 executions between the first and second visits. Calculations based on the gathering of information broadcast on the official radio indicate that about 500 persons were executed between January and October 1990. The second visit had barely ended when Iranian radio reported further executions. . . .

477. According to the information received, most of the executions concern persons accused of drug trafficking and the others are for ordinary offences of various kinds and political offences. The study of Iranian legislation clearly indicates that, because there are no gradations in the penalties for various types of

criminal involvement and as a result of very general wording, the death penalty tends to be applied on a large scale. . . .

. . .

478. Executions in the Islamic Republic of Iran continue to go beyond the narrow limits within which the International Covenant on Civil and Political Rights allows the application of capital punishment.

. . .

483. The situation of followers of the Baha'i faith continues to be uncertain, given the unequal treatment they receive in different provinces and cities, depending on the ideas and temperament of individual officials. No reports of executions have been received in recent months. There do not appear to be any exceptions to the prohibition on admission to universities and there have been very few exceptions to refusals to grant legal recognition to inheritance rights . . .

484. During his second visit to the country, the Special Representative talked in private homes to people unconnected with the Government who lead a normal life and have no judicial or police problems. These people agreed to be interviewed after taking precautions to preserve their anonymity since they feared reprisals if it became known that they had given information about the human rights situation prevailing in the country. They said they feared mainly the activities of irregular groups and of Komiteh and Pasdarán agents who use intimidatory tactics. Other people interviewed at the United Nations Development Programme offices and the Esteghlal Hotel voiced the same fear.

. . .

492. The Special Representative is of the opinion and belief that there are arguments in favour of extending the international monitoring of the situation of human rights in the Islamic Republic of Iran with the objective of assuring, through co-operation, criticism, international public opinion and measures adopted by the Iranian authorities, that Iranian legislation, administration and practice are brought fully into line with the international instruments in force.

493. On the basis of the aforementioned information, the Special Representative, as in previous reports, ventures to make a number of recommendations. . . . The Special Representative states opinions and cannot act as a substitute for the Government, the General Assembly or the Commission on Human Rights, whose respective attributions include decision-making powers. It is for them to consider the recommendations and decide on them.

494. The Special Representative wishes to state that, in his view, it would be appropriate to adopt the following measures:

(a) The Government should take immediate action to reduce drastically the application of the death penalty . . . ;

(b) Just as the penalty of flogging is being gradually replaced by a fine or imprisonment, consideration should be given to replacing the penalties regarded by the international organizations as forms of torture, including stoning and amputation;

(c) The Government should be urged to initiate forthwith or to speed up the pace of legislative and administrative reform to make national institutions compatible with the international human rights instruments, beginning with the introduction of technical reforms to penal legislation, as well as to introduce remedies to make moral and economic redress effective and to assign responsibility for abuses or excesses of power;

(d) The Government should carefully supervise the enjoyment of equal rights and equal treatment for all citizens, regardless of their political opinions or their religious beliefs;

(e) The Government should be urged to take, immediately and urgently, effective measures to establish a climate of confidence and legal certainty in institutions to enable citizens to express themselves without fear or intimidation;

(f) The Government should take care to apply the rules of due process of law . . . ;

(g) A specific agreement should be concluded soon with the International Committee of the Red Cross so that prison visits may be carried out regularly and without exceptions;

(h) The legal functioning of independent organizations should be authorized, including political organizations and organizations that seek to defend human rights;

(i) The prior examination of books and forms of artistic creation in general should end;

(j) Measures should be adopted to guarantee genuine freedom for the media and journalists should enjoy full guarantees for their professional activities;

(k) Compensation should be granted to persons affected by violations of human rights or to members of their families.

. . .

REPORT OF THE SPECIAL REPRESENTATIVE ON IRAN, 1999
UN Doc. E/CN.4/1999/32

Introduction

1. In the period under review, from 1 September to 15 December 1998, progress continued to be made towards President Khatami's goal of a civil society, tolerant, diverse, and operating within the rule of law. Human rights—individual and group—were at the centre of this process. In the open atmosphere that now exists, it was not difficult to follow the progress as well as the failures.

2. For some, the progress is frustratingly slow. For others, it is proceeding in such a way as to threaten Islamic verities, the very basis of the Islamic Republic. The discourse is a remarkably open one which itself speaks for the enhancement of the freedom of expression in the country.

3. Indeed, this freedom is the terrain on which the debate, the struggle, is largely being waged. . . . [T]he trend is clear and said to be irreversible. . . .

. . .

5. Other areas, notably the status of women, are the subject of much attention.

The advocates of change became ever more outspoken and now include members of the political elite. However, the progress to date continues to be at the periphery; there is little sign so far of a willingness to tackle core issues.

6. The status of minorities continues to be an apparently forgotten one in the Government's plans and the full implications of the term 'diversity' appears yet to be fully recognized.

7. Overall, opposition to the President's plans does not seem to have diminished. Indeed, there is a fear that the struggle may be developing a raw, even violent, edge. A rash of unexplained disappearances and suspicious deaths of intellectual and political activists has set nerves on edge and reinforced fears for the further development of a law-abiding society.

8. With regard to cooperation with the Commission on Human Rights, the Special Representative [has not been invited] . . . to visit Iran since February 1996. On the other hand, he does acknowledge the issuance of an invitation to the Working Group on Enforced or Involuntary Disappearances to visit Iran.

. . .

9. . . . While in New York, [the Special Representative] held consultations with representatives of the Government of the Islamic Republic of Iran and representatives of several non-governmental organizations. . . .[H]is stay in Geneva included a number of consultations and meetings with senior officials from the Iranian Government. . . He also met with representatives of various non-governmental organizations, and he received representations from interested persons concerning alleged human rights violations in the Islamic Republic.

10. . . . In Geneva, the Special Representative had an opportunity to participate in an inter-agency informal consultation organized by OHCHR to discuss and exchange information among various United Nations and other intergovernmental agencies about the human rights and humanitarian situations in the Islamic Republic.

11. During the period under review, the Special Representative received written communications from the following non-governmental organizations: [The list includes international human rights and humanitarian NGOs as well as a number of NGOs and 'movements' concerned only with the situation in Iran.]

. . .

II. Freedom of Expression

13. [During the period under review] there was increased pressure on the press. A number of journals were banned or suspended for such offences as 'insulting the late Ayatollah Khomeini', 'altering remarks of the honoured Imam and publishing them in an insulting way', 'distorting news and insulting the war disabled', carrying out 'activities against national security', publishing 'lies and insults' and 'disturbing public opinion', and 'dissemination of fabrications and insults'. In some of these cases the officials of the journals concerned were detained; in some they were sentenced to such punishment as a one-year suspended jail sentence and a fine. In at least one case, a journal was shut down by court order and four of its journalists detained for a month, reportedly without access to family or lawyers.

. . .

14. .... Another [leader] declared 'these [newspapers] want to mislead the people. This is a cultural plot to overthrow our system'....

15. ...[T] he then press adviser to the President said that the ambiguity in the present regime was a major cause of the problem. There were significant differences of opinion between the executive and the judiciary over the interpretation of freedom of the press....

. . .

19. One task the new Government had set for itself was to strengthen the public's confidence in the press. Some success is now evident in the increase in circulation from 17 per 1,000 population to 35 per 1,000 over the 18 months. The number of provincial publications has grown considerably to 281 of which 12 are dailies....

. . .

21. Another important development has been the establishment of professional press associations. In 1997, the Professional Association of Journalists was established which now has about 1,000 members. The Association has been actively defending the rights of journalists and criticizing some procedures used against them....

. . .

22. The Special Representative, while accepting that significant progress has and is continuing to be made, believes that serious weaknesses remain particularly in the area of the press control regime....

. . .

24. With regard to books. . .[o]nly 100 titles have been rejected since the new Government took office; some 15,000 titles are now being published each year....

25. The Special Representative cannot conclude this section without reference to the chilling effect that the recent murders of intellectual and political figures immediately had on open discourse and freedom of expression in Iran. Those involved with efforts to reactivate the Writer's Association have become marked figures. There have been calls from outside the country for an international inquiry....

III. The Status of Women

[The Report concluded that the Khatami Government had so far achieved little improvement in the condition of Iranian women, although there had been favourable gradual change as in the literacy rate and steps toward equality with men in education. 'However, the construction of walls continues'. Violence against women in the family 'appears to be gaining more prominence'. Recent Government papers 'acknowledge that a major problem exists and outline a plan' that includes increasing public awareness of the problem, new laws to prevent violence, and establishing women's shelters. '[U]seful as many of these developments are, the various structural disabilities which Iranian women face are the heart of the problem. . . .[T]hese must be addressed squarely for there to be substantial, meaningful improvement. . . .']

IV. The Status of Minorities

[The Report described 'fresh reports on situations of discrimination and even of persecution' of Baha'is.]

41. In late September, the Special Representative was informed that the death sentences against two members of the Baha'i faith had been confirmed by prison authorities in Mashhad, despite the assurances to the contrary provided to him earlier by the Iranian authorities. In response to the written inquiry of the Special Representative, officials stated that 'the court found them guilty of charges of acting against national security and sentenced them to death', but 'the defendants can still resort to appeal and/or clemency'. The Special Representative is following this case closely. . . .

42. Reports suggest that in the middle of December 1998, 17 Baha'is remained in detention, 6 sentenced to death, 7 to imprisonment for periods ranging from 3 to 8 years, and for the rest, to sentences which are not yet known. The charges reportedly include holding meetings and teaching their faith, cooperating with Baha'i educational activities and engaging in espionage activities of one sort or another. . . .

. . .

45. . . . The Special Representative wishes to reiterate his appeal to the Government of the Islamic Republic to fulfil his outstanding recommendations as well as that of the Special Rapporteur on religious intolerance.

. . .

VI. C. Torture . . .

. . .

60. The most positive thing the Special Representative can say is to repeat the observations in his interim report to the General Assembly that for the first time some officials have been acknowledging the existence of torture, and secondly that its existence in Iran is now discussed in the press.

61. The Special Representative would urge the Government to move quickly to wipe out this inhuman and discreditable practice. As a first step, it might follow the same process it has used to address illegal detention centres, that is the appointment of a high-level inter-agency committee to examine the dimensions of the situation and recommend steps to be taken for its elimination. . . .

. . .

D. Executions

63. . . .[A]s reported in the Iranian press, there were probably some 155 executions from January to mid-December 1998, of which 60 were said to have taken place in public. These figures are generally regarded as being on the low side as it is widely assumed that many executions are not reported in the media.

64. The Special Representative again urges the Government to bring its policies in the matter of executions into line with Commission on Human Rights recommendations (resolution 1998/68).

VII. Democracy / A Civil Society

[Eds. Note: Relevant excerpts from the Iranian Constitution appear at pp. 459–464, *supra*.]

65. An important election held during the period under review, that for the Council of Experts, was held on 23 October amid controversy over the process of determining the eligibility of candidates. . . .

66. The Council has in theory very substantial power. It appoints the Supreme Leader who has the final say on all State matters. The Council also has the power to oversee the Leader's work and to dismiss him if he fails to perform his duties properly. The Council has reportedly become more active in recent years in the matter of oversight.

67. Eligibility to stand for election to the Council is determined by the Council of Guardians. The spokesman for the Council was quoted in Iranian papers as declaring that the 'most important criteria' were religious reputation and moral credibility, political and social insight and up-to-date knowledge of developments, loyalty to the Islamic Republic, and having 'no record of political or social mis-behaviour'. He denied that factional, i.e. political, preferences played any role in determining eligibility. However, stories persisted of the use of examinations to disqualify applicants. Judging by press accounts, many applicants who failed to qualify complained openly that politics had played a role.

. . .

72. Violence against politicians became more prominent. In September two reformist ministers of the Government were subjected to a public physical assault which was attributed to the extrajudicial group Ansar-i Hezbollah.

73. Two murders on 22 November by unknown assailants shocked many Irani-ans in the country and outside. The press estimated that 6,000 persons attended the funeral of Dariush Forouhar, the leader of the Iran Nation Party, and of his wife Parvanah. Mr. Forouhar was a veteran politician having among other roles served as Minister of Labour in the Bazargan Government. The Iran Nation Party was an unregistered but tolerated entity on Iran's political landscape. President Khatami termed the murders 'a repugnant crime' . . . Nine such activists have reportedly been killed in the last decade, half of them by the same method used in the deaths of the Foruhars. Reportedly, in none of the cases were the perpetrators known to have been found or brought to justice.

74. The Special Representative views these murders with regret and concern, concern that circumstances in Iran are not yet stable enough to permit dedicated politicians to serve their country without fear of physical attack and in some cases, for their lives. . . .

. . .

XI. Conclusions

. . .

87. The Government is now 18 months into its five-year mandate. Its plans for change as they are gradually becoming known, were and continue to be significant if not monumental. Progress has been uneven and objected to by many. The Government must find a way to establish the people's confidence in its plans in the face of attempts, including violent ones, to divert reform efforts. The Government must stay the course; it cannot afford to lose momentum.

QUESTIONS

1. On the basis of the various reactions by the Iranian authorities, how would you characterize the government's attitude to the Commission's investigation? Was it uniform?

2. What purposes did these reports likely serve? Did they advance dialogue between Iran and the UN or other groups of states? Do they constitute an authoritative report about Iranian violations of human rights?

3. Are the reports attentive to cultural relativism, to the distinctive role of religion in Iran, to tensions or contradictions between Islam and international human rights?

4. To what extent should an expert get involved in analyzing the overall political climate and offering interpretations thereon?

5. Do you agree that the aim of international monitoring 'is not to support or destabilize Governments' (1991 Report, para. 465)? Is this consistent with the views expressed in para. 492 of the same report?

6. Article 6 of the ICCPR, which applies to Iran, requires that the death penalty, if maintained, 'may be imposed only for the most serious crimes . . . and not contrary to the provisions of the present Covenant . . .'. Could Iran justify its use for crimes such as prostitution, pederasty, fornication outside marriage, or homosexuality?

7. In response to the 1999 report the UN Commission adopted a resolution (Res. 1999/13) by a vote of 23 in favour, 16 against and 14 abstentions, welcoming some recent developments but continuing to express concern. What is the significance for resolutions in general of such a split vote?

b. Case Study: China

COMMENTATORS ON CHINA BEFORE THE UN COMMISSION

Human Rights Watch, Chinese Diplomacy, Western Hyprocrisy and the U.N. Human Rights Commission (March 1997)

Background

A resolution on China at the Commission is a curiously potent tool for raising human rights issues, given that it is an unenforceable statement that carries no penalties or obligations. But as the product of the U.N., it has major implications for a country's international image, and even to table a resolution for discussion is considered by many countries, China among them, as a major loss of face. . . .

Interest in using the U.N. Human Rights Commission as a forum for criticizing China only emerged after the crackdown in Tiananmen Square in 1989. Beginning in 1990, the annual Geneva meetings were marked by efforts to table mildly worded resolutions urging China to improve its human rights practices and criticizing ongoing violations of international standards. These efforts were defeated before the resolutions could come up for debate by 'no-action' motions brought by one of China's friends on the commission—Pakistan could be counted on in this regard. A 'no-action' motion, if passed, meant that the resolution died a quick death before ever coming to debate and vote.

In March 1995, however, the 'no-action' motion failed for the first time. China's human rights record was debated, and a resolution sponsored by the U.S. and the European Union lost by only one vote when Russia unexpectedly cast its vote in opposition. It was the closest China had ever come to defeat. In April 1996, by contrast, China again successfully blocked a resolution through the 'no-action' procedure, by a vote of twenty-seven to twenty with six abstentions. In the year that elapsed between the two meetings, China's human rights record had worsened, but its lobbying had improved and the political will of its critics had weakened.

Visits between China and commission members between April 1996 and March 1997 resulted in more aid packages, new and expanded trade contracts including foreign investment and joint ventures, and promises of improved bilateral cooperation on projects ranging from agriculture to nuclear technology. While it is impossible to definitively document the direct relationship between each visit or aid package and the votes of individual commission members, an overall pattern emerged that may help to explain China's success at muzzling the commission. . . .

II. *The European Union and the United States*

. . .

. . . Overt Chinese pressure, of course, was not always needed: European leaders were well aware that the competitive edge with the Americans could be widened if human rights criticism was left to the latter, especially when the U.S. was already preoccupied with a struggle with China over intellectual property rights and the annual debate over Most Favored Nation status.

The first attempts to derail a resolution on China at the 1996 U.N. Human Rights Commission session took place in Bangkok on March 1 and 2, 1996 when Chinese Premier Li Peng met with German Chancellor Helmut Kohl and French President Jacques Chirac at the E.U.–Asia summit. With a US$2.1 billion Airbus contract hanging in the balance and a visit to France by Li Peng set for April, France took the lead in trying to work out a deal whereby in exchange for a few concessions from China, the E.U. and the U.S. would agree to drop the resolution.
. . .

The resolution was doomed by a failure of will on the American side as well. The United States was no more eager than its European counterparts to earn China's opprobrium by sponsoring a resolution, and, according to one source, a deliberate decision was made within the Clinton administration sometime in December 1995 to give the resolution less attention than the year before, with the result that lobbying was late, desultory and ultimately unsuccessful. . . .

**Statement by H.E. Ambassador Wu Jianmin, Head of the Chinese Delegation
to the UN Commission, April 8, 1997**

. . .

After the end of the Cold War, the East–West confrontation at the Commission
was replaced by the North–South confrontation which has lasted five years. It is
provoked by the North and imposed on the South.

. . . Since 1992, the Commission has adopted altogether seventy-two country
resolutions. Almost all of them are directed at the developing countries. This is no
coincidence. As the representative from a developing country, I cannot help asking,
are they qualified to pass judgment on the developing countries? The answer is
NO. Because:

First, the majority of these developed countries do not have a decent human
rights record in history. . . . The Western countries had been engaging in the trade
of black slaves for about four centuries. . . .

Since the fifteenth century, the Western countries had waged colonial wars for
several centuries. They massacred the people of the colonies and plundered their
wealth on a large scale. . . .

Secondly, the developed Western countries have the unshirkable responsibility
for the human rights problems the world faces today. . . . How come 1.3 billion
people are living in poverty? Does it have nothing to do with the aggression,
exploitation and plundering by the colonialists in the past? Isn't it the consequence
of the irrational international economic order established by the developed
countries? . . .

Thirdly, the human rights records of the developed countries are far from perfect. Let's take that largest developed country for an instance. . . . [w]e see racism
that plagued the country for hundreds of years still running amok.

. . .

A large number of developing countries are fed up with the atmosphere of
confrontation and politicization at this Commission. They have appealed time and
again for an end to it. Yet, some developed countries stubbornly cling to confrontation. Their statements under this item sound like indictments in a tribunal, and
are presented with intolerable arrogance. Why do they cling to confrontation?
There are at least three reasons.

First, to revive the old dream of colonialists. . . .

Secondly, to divert public attention. . . . In this way, the massive violation of
human rights in their own countries, such as racism, discrimination against
women, xenophobia and maltreatment of migrant workers could be cast to the
winds.

Thirdly, to shift the blame onto others. . . .

. . . [T]he Commission has squandered a great deal of time, resources and
energy on the North–South confrontation. It is high time we put an end to this
situation. For that purpose, the Chinese delegation would like to propose the
following:

I. The Commission should encourage cooperation and reject confrontation.
Confrontation intensifies mutual hostility and leads the Commission astray. . . .

II. The Commission should encourage democracy and oppose the practice of imposing on others by a few developed countries. . . .

III. The Commission should abide by the principle of equality and mutual respect and oppose the practice of the big oppressing the small, the strong bullying the weak. . . . This is a gross violation of the principle of equality which is not only the basic principle of human rights, but also the foundation for fruitful cooperation. Only when the principle of sovereign equality and mutual respect is sincerely adhered to and dialogue and cooperation encouraged, can the Commission make great achievements in promoting the human rights cause.

Remarks as Delivered by Mr Ross Hynes, Representative of Canada to the UN Commission (April 15, 1997)

. . .

On a purely procedural level, Canada agrees with those who have argued that there is no good reason that the Commission should not proceed—as it had done in any number of other situations—to direct action on the merits of this resolution. . . . China is the same as—and should be treated no differently from—any other country.

. . . If we are honest with ourselves . . . we have to admit that China is not the same as all other countries. China is . . . a major political and economic power, a permanent member of the United Nations Security Council, . . . justifiably proud of the crucial role [it plays] in today's world. . . . This is a reality that cannot be disputed.

. . . [There exists another reality that there exist . . . serious grounds for concerns about the actions of the Government of China in living up to its international human rights obligations . . . .

. . . Canada [has decided] that, in the current circumstances, instead of co-sponsoring the resolution, we would attempt this year to find other ways of working with China—ways of working both bilaterally and, ideally, with others as well to address the real differences we face, and to help bring about real, positive change towards improved respect for human rights.

Statement by John Shattuck, Assistant Secretary of State for Democracy, Human Rights, and Labor, to the UN Commission (April 15, 1997)

. . .

The proposed No Action Motion is sometimes cast as a North-South question. It is not. The North has no monopoly on virtue, while the South has many nations with strong human rights records. Indeed, the real question before us now is not whether a nation is from the North or South, whether it is developed or developing, but whether it is prepared to act on the principles that gave rise to the Commission itself.

A vote against the No Action Motion is more than a vote against censorship and intimidation. It is a vote to keep faith with thousands of citizens in China who have dared to stand up for human rights, democracy, and freedom and who have suffered as a result.

More than ever before, the eyes of the world are watching the way the Commission votes on this issue, Mr. Chairman. That's exactly the way it should be. If we cannot debate the human rights situation in China—or for that matter any other country—what will that say about this body and the members who agreed to silence themselves?

...

P. Shenon, U.S. Backs Away from Anti-China Vote

International Herald Tribune, March 16, 1998, p. 4

[The US administration gave China 'another important boost by dropping American sponsorship of an annual United Nations resolution condemning China's record on human rights'. The article reports that this move 'effectively kills' a resolution before the UN Commission. An administration official said that the decision was 'certainly not a reward' but as a calculation that it was 'the way to make progress in the future'. Human rights groups denounced the government's decision.]

Amnesty International, The 1999 Commission on Human Rights: A Parody of Human Rights Concerns

A1 Doc. 10R 41/07/99, 23 April 1999

... Despite the widely-acknowledged recent worsening of the human rights situation in China . . . members of the Commission, and in particular the EU, were passively looking the other way until the third week of the session. In a last minute, face-saving and half-hearted gesture, the United States announced then that it would table a resolution. The lateness of the decision eroded the probability of a strong unified approach, while reducing possibilities to reject the foreseeable no action motion. . . .

'It is appalling to note that members of the Commission gave in to Chinese pressure to create double standards. It is paradoxical that China—which has repeatedly criticized the Commission for its "selectivity and double standards"— was the only member of the Commission for years blatantly to misuse procedural motions to avoid any discussion of its human rights record', Amnesty International said.

ANN KENT, CHINA, THE UNITED NATIONS, AND HUMAN RIGHTS
(1999), at 74

It was in the 1997 Commission. . . . that China's political pressure on the West reached a climax. The pre-Commission politics and the politics of the session form a study in themselves. . . . Despite common expectation that the European Union would as usual table a draft resolution on China, France expressed its opposition to the draft prepared by the Dutch presidency and was quickly supported in its arguments by Germany, Italy, and Spain. The Dutch delegation decided not to present a draft resolution on China on behalf of the European Union unless its members could agree on a text. Finally, the Danish Minister for Foreign Affairs announced that Denmark would sponsor the resolution.

In response to this political imbroglio, China held out both stick and carrot. To those preparing to cosponsor the draft resolution, it openly threatened loss of trading and diplomatic opportunities; to those deciding to abandon their cosponsorship, it offered the promise of future dialogue, as well as the renewed possibility that China might sign the International Covenants. In particular, the Danish Ambassador was told that he 'would regret' his country's efforts; and China published a list of Danish corporations it intended to exclude from future contracts. . . . As it turned out, Australia, Canada, France, Germany, Italy, Spain, and Japan failed to cosponsor the resolution as they had in previous years, even though those that were members of the Commission subsequently voted against China's no-action motion. By a tactic of divide and rule, China had succeeded in bilateralizing a multilateral process. Consistent with its policy of open threats, China immediately announced measures of economic reprisal against Denmark and the Netherlands after the vote. Vice-Premier Zhu Rongji cancelled a planned trip to the Hague and traveled to Australia instead.

The result of the vote on the no-action motion on the 1997 China resolution—27 in favor, 17 against, and 9 abstentions—was not very different from the same vote in the 1996 Commission—27 in favor, 20 against, and 6 abstentions. Crucial to the abstentions was the swinging Latin American vote. Of eight Latin American states visited by Chinese Trade Minister Wu Yi and Premier Li Peng between June and November 1996, all but Peru were members of the 1997 Commission. Of these, only Chile eventually supported the West in the no-action motion. Cuba and Colombia (which in 1996 had abstained) voted with China, and five others, including Brazil (which in 1996 had voted with the West), abstained. Part of the Eastern European vote was also supportive of China, marking a partial swing back to the situation existing before the collapse of communism in Eastern Europe.

. . .

Conclusion

. . .

Nevertheless, three positive effects of China's interaction with the Commission and Sub-Commission should be reiterated. First, were the long-term socializing effects of the process of China's interaction at the international level that have already been discussed. Second, as Chinese dissident Wei Jingsheng has pointed out, the Commission and Sub-Commission resolutions on China indisputably served to strengthen the morale of those within China struggling for democracy and liberalization. Third, the effort to evade Commission and Sub-Commission censure involved China in activities effectively renegotiating its sovereignty, if only for short-term gains. Although its signature of the ICESCR and ICCPR and invitations to special rapporteurs and working groups do not necessarily reflect any long-term internalization of norms by China, they have effectively constituted China's acknowledgement of the importance of the International Covenants and of the international community's right to monitor its human rights conditions *in situ*.

However, it must be emphasized that the source of China's long-term learning has been the normative and structural robustness of these human rights bodies. Developments in the 1997 Commission undermined the resilience of both institutions and seriously set back this process of socialization. The decisions taken on the China resolution not only reflected a lack of Western unity, but, ironically, on the eve of a review by the Commission of progress in human rights in the five years since the UN World Human Rights Conference in Vienna, pressured the UN regime to the extent of imperiling some of its norms and procedures. The UN Secretary-General Kofi Annan and the UN High Commissioner for Human Rights, Mary Robinson, both expressed satisfaction that the Chinese government had invited Robinson to China and that it had signed the two Covenants. However, the question yet to be resolved is whether, by accepting this trade-off, the United Nations is more effectively incorporating China into the human rights regime, or merely facilitating the undermining of UN norms and procedures by China. The readiness of the international community to treat China as a club of one in the 1997 and 1998 meetings of the Commission will not necessarily provide a model for its subsequent treatment, as EU representatives and Mary Robinson have been at pains to point out. Yet the new emphasis on 'cooperation' has long-term implications for both bodies, undermining the important process of reintegrative shaming through country-situation resolutions which has been applied so effectively to China and many other states. . . .

NOTE

At the Commission's session in April 2000 a resolution proposed by the United States was shelved on the basis of a procedural motion not to take any action on the draft. That motion was adopted by a vote of 22 to 18, with 12 abstentions. Australia, Canada, the European Union, and Japan were all criticized by NGOs for opting not to co-sponsor the resolution.

QUESTIONS

1. Why does China fight so hard each year to avoid condemnation, or even discussion, by the Commission? What harm could China suffer as a result of a resolution condemning it? Why should it care?

2. Does China's general success in avoiding condemnation by the Commission confirm that human rights is merely a matter of politics as usual, lacking impartiality and objectivity? Powerful countries go free; smaller violators are condemned.

3. Are you critical of states that failed to support the resolution? How ought they to have voted in the Commission? Are other national interests irrelevant, so that rights trump all? Suppose for example a draft vital non-proliferation agreement on nuclear weapons, or a draft long-run trade agreement that will aid an export industry in a state of high unemployment; opposition to China before the Commission could weaken chances of such agreements becoming effective. Should such concerns be irrelevant, as if the Commission were a judicial body ignoring all but 'the law'? If they are not irrelevant to domestic politics and government legislative and executive decisions, why should they be irrelevant to decision-making in the Commission?

3. THE THEMATIC MECHANISMS

The first thematic mechanism—a mechanism devoted to a theme rather than a state or region, and hence that may have global reach rather than be restricted to a given state—to be established by the Commission was the 1980 Working Group on Disappearances. Its origins lay in efforts to respond to the massive 'disappearances' that took place during the 1970s in Argentina's 'dirty war' against leftist and other forces opposed to the military government. The government's strategy was effective in international human rights forums in avoiding condemnation. Even though the Inter-American Commission on Human Rights had issued a damning indictment of the situation in 1978, within the UN context many governments were ambivalent about 'naming' Argentina, for a variety of reasons ranging from trade interests to fear that they might be next on the list.

The means used by the Commission to get around this reluctance was to avoid a country-specific inquiry by establishing the first 'thematic' mechanism. Argentina hoped that the thematic approach would not single out any one country, would demonstrate that Argentina was only one of many countries that had problems, and would give a significant number of governments a strong incentive to ensure that the new mechanism would be kept under careful political control and thus remain ineffectual. But in the first few years of its existence, the Disappearances Working Group played an important role in developing techniques which were subsequently to serve as a model for a growing range of mechanisms dealing with other themes.

In 1985 there were three thematic mechanisms, in 1990 there were six, and in 1995 there were 14. By January 2000, this number had grown to 21. They dealt with: summary and arbitrary executions, torture, religious intolerance, mercenaries, sale of children, children in armed conflict, freedom of opinion and expression, xenophobia, contemporary forms of racism, independence of judges and lawyers, violence against women, internal displacement, enforced disappearances, arbitrary detention, the rights of migrants, toxic waste, foreign debt, the right to education, structural adjustment policies, extreme poverty, guidelines on restitution, and the right to development. Thus, in the two decades after the first mechanism was established the Commission created an average of slightly more than one new mechanism every year. This proliferation contributed to problems of inadequate financial and human resources, overlapping mandates, insufficient coordination, and a dilution of the pressures generated upon governments which have bedevilled the thematic mechanisms.

In general, the techniques used include: requests to governments for information on specific cases; an urgent action procedure involving a request that a government take immediate action to rectify or clarify a case; on-site visits for a more intensive examination of either specific cases or the overall situation; and submission to the UN Commission of detailed reports containing conclusions and recommendations for further action. The manner in which each technique is applied, if at all, varies considerably. The mechanisms also vary in the extent to which they have sought to develop the applicable normative framework, and to apply political pressure to individual governments. In recent years, as illustrated by the East Timor case below, joint missions by thematic mechanisms have become more common.

The following materials provide an overview of the different approaches adopted by two of the mechanisms—those dealing with arbitrary detention, and violence against women.

COMMENT ON THE WORKING GROUP ON ARBITRARY DETENTION

The Working Group was established in 1991 (Res. 1991/42) and its mandate revised in 1997 (Res. 1997/50). The current mandate is to investigate cases of arbitrarily imposed deprivation of liberty—provided that no final decision has been taken in such cases by local courts acting in conformity with domestic law, with the UDHR and with applicable international instruments. The Group is composed of five independent experts and its mandate has been renewed for three years at a time. Its activities are generally similar to those of other thematic mechanisms, except in relation to its distinctive communications (complaints) procedure that it took the initiative to establish from the outset. The principal activities are as follows.

1. **Communications.** The Group receives cases from the detained persons themselves, from members of their families or relatives, local, regional or international NGOs, or from other sources. It transmits them to governments with a request for a reply within 90 days. Thereafter it adopts an 'opinion' (previously a 'decision', but this characterization was resisted by governments). In 1998, for example, the Group adopted 21 opinions concerning 92 persons in 15 countries. In four of those cases, the relevant government advised that the individual concerned had been released. The Group classifies cases according to the following three categories:

I.   cases in which the deprivation of freedom is arbitrary, as it manifestly cannot be linked to any legal basis (such as continued detention beyond the execution of a criminal sentence, or detention despite an amnesty act); or

II. cases of deprivation of freedom when the facts giving rise to a prosecution or conviction of the detained person concern the exercise of individual rights and freedoms that are protected by Articles 7, 13–14, and 18–21 of the UDHR, and Articles 12, 18–19, 21–22, and 25–27 of the ICCPR; or

III. cases in which non-observance of the right to a fair trial is such that it confers on the deprivation of freedom, of whatever kind, an arbitrary character.

2. Issuance of urgent appeals. In 1998 the Group transmitted 83 urgent appeals to 37 Governments (as well as to the Palestinian Authority) concerning 763 individuals. Such appeals reflect a need for urgency but do not prejudge whether or not the detention is arbitrary. Thirteen of these governments replied.

3. Country missions. The Group seeks and accepts invitations to countries in which there are concerns. It has visited, *inter alia*, China, Peru, Romania, the United Kingdom, and Vietnam.

Illustration: The Use of the UDHR

In a Cuban case (Opinion 1/1998), the Group found that four dissidents had been arbitrarily detained. It noted that 'the criminal offence of "enemy propaganda" is extremely vague and may cover conduct which is lawful according to international human rights standards', and that, 'although Cuban internal law penalizes acts of political opposition', this is 'not in keeping with the relevant standards' in the UDHR (UN Doc. E/CN.4/1999/63/Add.1, para. 13). The Government of Cuba subsequently objected to the pre-eminence attached to the UDHR as a 'recommendatory document of the United Nations . . . over national legislation in force in any country'. It noted that the UN 'is still very far from being a universal parliament empowered to impose some kind of homogenizing standard on its Member States without their consent, in this or any other sphere' (UN Doc. E/CN.4/1999/128, para. 31).

In response the Working Group observed that the point is not whether the UDHR 'prevails over the legislation of a State or vice versa. It is simply that, according to the letter of the mandate of the Working Group, a case of deprivation of liberty ceases to be arbitrary if it is consistent both with domestic legislation and with the relevant international standards set forth in the Declaration and in other relevant international instruments accepted by the State concerned. It is only necessary for it to be inconsistent with one of those criteria . . . for the deprivation of liberty to be deemed arbitrary' (UN Doc. E/CN.4/1999/63, para. 60).

Illustration: Standards of Proof

In October 1997 the Group visited China. In a prison in Tibet it interviewed an inmate who had shouted pro-Dalai Lama slogans. The Group sought and received from the Chinese authorities assurances that the inmate would suffer no reprisals as a result. Having received information that he had subsequently been beaten and interrogated, the Group sought clarification from the government in March 1998. The latter denied that any inmate had been punished as a result of the Group's visit. In July the Group 'received precise and corroborated additional information confirming that the inmate [along with others] . . . had received extended prison sentences for their protests'. They sought additional clarification from the government, which indicated that the inmates' sentences had in fact been extended, but because they had committed new offences. The Group noted in its annual report (UN Doc. E/CN.4/1999/63):

> 24. . . . Given the gravity of the situation, the Working Group requested the Chinese authorities, on 18 September 1998, to provide specific information about the new offences . . . as well as a copy of the verdict . . . . By [4 December 1998], the Working Group had not received any response to its request for information.
> 25. In view of the foregoing, the Working Group finds the above-mentioned allegations to be sufficiently well-founded for the following reasons:
> (a) The fact that the three inmates in respect of whom the Working Group had obtained assurances should be the same as those whose prison terms were later extended is a regrettable coincidence that cannot, as such, be contested;
> (b) In this context, the Working Group strongly regrets that it was unable to obtain any reply from the Chinese authorities to its letter of 18 September 1998; it interprets this lack of a reply as being a consequence of the difficulty that the Chinese authorities have in persuading the Working Group in a credible manner that there was no causal relationship between the incident in question and the heavier prison sentences imposed on the three inmates;
> (c) The Working Group is all the more concerned because it has the feeling that this is not an isolated incident; . . . .

Illustration: Immigrants and Asylum Seekers

In 1997 the Commission extended the Group's mandate to cover the situation of 'immigrants and asylum seekers who are allegedly being held in prolonged administrative custody without the possibility of administrative or judicial remedy'. The Group excluded extradition cases and determinations of the 'lawfulness and conformity with international standards of procedures for granting asylum or conferring refugee status' from its work. In order to determine if the custody is arbitrary, the 'Group considers whether or not the alien is able to enjoy all or some of the following guarantees':

> Guarantee 1: To be informed, at least orally, when held for questioning at the border, or in the territory concerned if he has entered illegally, in a language which he understands, of the nature of and grounds for the measure refusing admission at the border, or permission for temporary residence in the territory, that is being contemplated with respect to him.
> Guarantee 2: Decision involving administrative custody taken by a duly authorized official with a sufficient level of responsibility in accordance with the criteria laid down by law and subject to guarantees 3 and 4.

Guarantee 3: Determination of the lawfulness of the administrative custody pursuant to legislation providing to this end for:

    (a) The person concerned to be brought automatically and promptly before a judge or a body affording equivalent guarantees of competence, independence and impartiality;

    (b) Alternatively, the possibility of appealing to a judge or to such a body.

Guarantee 4: To be entitled to have the decision reviewed by a higher court or an equivalent competent, independent and impartial body.

Guarantee 5: Written and reasoned notification of the measure of custody in a language understood by the applicant.

Guarantee 6: Possibility of communicating by an effective medium such as the telephone, fax or electronic mail, from the place of custody, in particular with a lawyer, a consular representative and relatives.

Guarantee 7: To be assisted by counsel of his own choosing . . . .

Guarantee 8: Custody effected in public premises intended for this purpose . . . .

. . .

Guarantee 10: Not to be held in custody for an excessive or unlimited period, with a maximum period being set, as appropriate, by the regulations.

. . .

Guarantee 13: Possibility for the alien to benefit from alternatives to administrative custody.

Guarantee 14: Possibility for the Office of the United Nations High Commissioner for Refugees, the International Committee of the Red Cross and specialized non-governmental organizations to have access to places of custody.

The Group observed that 'Where the absence of such guarantees or their violation, circumvention or non-implementation constitutes a matter of a high degree of gravity, [it] may conclude that the custody is arbitrary' (UN Doc. E/CN.4/1999/63, paras. 69–70).

QUESTIONS

1. Does the category II classification used by the Working Group effectively put it in the position of accepting substantive complaints based on any violations of the rights listed, provided only that the outcome was some form of detention? Do the Guarantees above put before the Group allow it to consider a broad range of due process arguments?

2. Is the Working Group's defence of its reliance upon the UDHR convincing, given that Cuba is not a party to the ICCPR? Could you fortify that defence with other arguments?

3. Reprisals against prisoners and others who give UN bodies information critical of a government are a common problem. Is the Group justified in using such a light standard of proof? Should the Commission make a major issue of such incidents?

4. What do you suppose is the effect of these opinions of the Group? As a member of the Group, how would you try to maximize their effect? How would you compare its effectiveness in bringing an end to violations or seeking relief for victims with, say, the 1235 procedure?

NOTE

The materials on CEDAW at p. 204, *supra*, reviewed some of the work carried out by the Special Rapporteur on Violence Against Women, especially her analytical contributions to the debate in that area. Her other activities have included a study on women's reproductive rights (UN Doc. E/CN.4/1999/68/Add.4), a survey of governments and NGOs to see what measures have been taken in relation to her earlier recommendations, and country visits to focus on specific issues. Consider the following excerpt from a report on her visit to the United States in 1998.

RADHIKA COOMARASWAMY (SPECIAL RAPPORTEUR ON VIOLENCE AGAINST WOMEN), REPORT OF THE MISSION TO THE UNITED STATES OF AMERICA ON THE ISSUE OF VIOLENCE AGAINST WOMEN IN STATE AND FEDERAL PRISONS
UN Doc. E/CN.4/1999/68/Add.2

. . . 1. At the invitation of the Government . . . the Special Rapporteur . . . visited Washington D.C. and the States of New York, Connecticut, New Jersey, Georgia, California, Michigan and Minnesota from 31 May to 18 June 1998 to study the issue of violence against women in the state and federal prisons in each of the states mentioned.

2. The Special Rapporteur would like to express her sincere appreciation for the cooperation and assistance extended to her by the Government . . . . [S]he met with high-level representatives from the Department of State, the Department of Justice, the Immigration and Naturalization Service (INS) and the Bureau of Prisons . . . .[She] also met members of the United States Senate . . . .

[The Rapporteur also met with state authorities, formerly incarcerated women, lawyers representing prison inmates, university professors and other experts on the issue and with NGO representatives.] . . .

9. Despite prior agreements with representatives of correction institutions in Virginia and Michigan, it was not possible for the Special Rapporteur to visit prisons in those two states. . . . [O]n the eve of her visit to Michigan, the Special Rapporteur received a letter dated 12 June 1998 from the Governor of Michigan informing her that she would not be allowed to meet state representatives or to

visit any of the women's prisons. . . . The Special Rapporteur found this refusal particularly disturbing since she had received very serious allegations of sexual misconduct . . . .

. . .

14. Wherever the Special Rapporteur went, officials asked her why she decided to visit the United States. She explained that based on information received from diverse sources, she was convinced that there were serious issues of custodial sexual misconduct in United States prisons that had to be investigated. Many felt nevertheless that special rapporteurs should concentrate on crisis situations around the world rather than focus on countries where human rights protection is more or less ensured. The Special Rapporteur maintains that the notion that human rights protections are only for societies that are in crisis should be contested. Human rights protections are not only applicable during emergencies, but are also required in societies perceived to be crisis-free. Although the United States has a comparatively high level of political freedom, some aspects of its criminal justice system pose fundamental human rights questions. Other special rapporteurs have also stressed this point.

15. A recent report based on Department of Justice statistics points out that the United States has the largest number of prisoners of any country in the world and that women constituted 6.3 per cent of the prison population in 1995. . . .

16. . . . Sixty-eight per cent of the women in federal prisons are there because of drug-related offences. Eighty per cent of incarcerated women have at least one child and the majority are not visited by their children. . . . [A] majority of women imprisoned for the killing of someone close to them had committed the killing while they were being abused. Eighty-five per cent of women in United States prisons have been physically or sexually abused at some time in their lives.

[The Special Rapporteur made lengthy findings, which related to issues like failure to maintain minimum standards, sexual misconduct, grievance procedures, privatization of prisons, and health care. She then made detailed recommendations, a selection of which follows.]

VI. Recommendations

A. *Federal Level*

205. The United States should ratify [CEDAW] and remove its reservations to [the ICCPR and the Convention against Torture]. It should enact implementing legislation so that these international treaties have a legal basis with regard to the national legal system.

206. The President's Inter-Agency Council on Women, the working group of women in prisons as well as the Violence against Women Office of the Department of Justice should be given resources to study key policy areas such as:

    (a) Drug laws and their severe impact on women;
    (b) A national mental health policy and the imprisonment of women with
        mental health problems;
    (c) Race policy in light of the intersection of race, poverty and gender and the

increase in the incarceration of African American women, the causes of this increase and the consequences for the African American family; and

    (d) Domestic violence and women in prisons.

207. Federal funding for state correctional facilities should require the following minimum conditions:

    (a) The states should criminalize all forms of sexual violence and sexual misconduct between staff and inmates, whether it occurs with the consent of the inmate or without;

    (b) There should be a prescreening of the backgrounds of those who apply to be corrections officers and any history of violence against women should disqualify individuals from being hired;

    (c) All corrections officers should be trained with regard to sexual misconduct issues as part of the mainstream training programme;

    (d) There should be external monitoring of prison management either by review boards, ombudsmen and/or special investigative units in corrections departments;

    (e) In consultation with the psychiatric, medical and human rights community, certain methods of restraint should be prohibited;

    (f) Minimum standards with regard to health care should be spelt out, including the presence of a qualified doctor on 24-hour call and easy access to gynaecologists;

    (g) All facilities, whether public or private, should have a minimum number of programmes, especially on parenting and vocational training;

    (h) Certain posts, such as corrections officers in housing units, and procedures, such as pat-frisks and body-searches should be based on same-sex guarding.

. . .

QUESTIONS

1. As a government lawyer instructed to draft an analysis rejecting many of these recommendations, what arguments would you make in relation to the scope of the Rapporteur's mandate, and the nature or scope of relevant international standards?

2. How do you evaluate the Rapporteur's answers to questions and objections about her visit? Would you have said more? What?

E. THE SECURITY COUNCIL: HUMANITARIAN INTERVENTION AND SANCTIONS

Those using the term 'humanitarian intervention' rarely specify precisely what it encompasses. This section understands the term in the sense of the use of force justified by reference to an overriding humanitarian emergency. Examples range from a brief, small-scale rescue operation to a limited military intervention to enable the delivery of food and other essential supplies to a region engaged in a civil war, to a prolonged military operation designed to end massive rights violations and restore order.

The Security Council consists of 15 members, five of which are permanent— China, France, Russia, the UK and the USA. Ten others are elected by the General Assembly for two-year terms. Each member has one vote. Substantive decisions require nine votes out of the 15, and must include the concurring votes (defined by the Council to include abstentions) of all five permanent members. This is the so-called 'veto' power. The Council is able to be convened at any time and non-members may be invited to participate, but without a vote, when their interests are affected.

The Council is given 'primary responsibility' for the maintenance of inter-national peace and security under the collective security system provided for in the UN Charter (Article 24), and member states are obligated to carry out its decisions (Article 25). It can act under *Chapter VI* of the Charter (Articles 33–38) to achieve the pacific settlement of 'any dispute, the continuance of which is likely to endanger the maintenance of international peace and security'. It is empowered to investigate any such dispute and to recommend 'appropriate procedures or methods of adjustment'. It can act under *Chapter VII* (Articles 39–51) whenever it determines 'the existence of any threat to the peace, breach of the peace, or act of aggression'. In such situations, the Council can call on states to apply sanctions of various kinds (Article 41) or to take such military action 'as may be necessary to restore international peace and security' (Article 42). Since all states are obligated by Article 2(4) of the Charter to 'refrain in their international relations from the threat or use of force against the territorial integrity or political independence of any state', except in the exercise of the right of self-defence against an armed attack (Article 51), the Council enjoys a legal monopoly over the use of force in all other circumstances. This monopoly extends to Article 53(1) which authorizes the Council to make use of 'regional arrangements or agencies for enforcement action under its authority'. But the latter are not permitted to act without the Council's authorization.

1. THE EVOLVING ROLE OF THE SECURITY COUNCIL WITH RESPECT TO HUMAN RIGHTS

COMMENT ON THE SIGNIFICANCE OF APARTHEID

Many procedures and techniques which were eventually developed by the General Assembly and the Security Council to deal with human rights were hammered out on the anvil of the South African apartheid system. The issue was first brought to the Assembly in 1946 by India which complained of the discriminatory treatment of persons of Indian origin. Very early on, India suggested that such conduct could be seen as a threat to international peace and thus as requiring the attention of the

Council. South Africa replied that most of those concerned were its nationals and that, in any event, the issue was exclusively a domestic affair.

The battle lines were thus set for a struggle continuing until today to clarify two key issues: (1) the relationship between the human rights provisions of the UN Charter and the domestic jurisdiction clause in Article 2(7) of the Charter (considered at pp. 588–91, *supra*); and (2) the circumstances under which gross human rights violations (and especially those with no significant international element such as the involvement of foreign nationals or the prompting of refugee flows) can be considered to threaten international peace and security and thus warrant Security Council measures under Chapter VII. While South Africa was the main focus of these debates, the situations in Southern Rhodesia (Zimbabwe) and the Portugese colonies in southern Africa (Angola and Mozambique) also figured in them.

With the influx of newly independent states into the United Nations from the late 1950s onwards, the South African case pitted a Security Council dominated by Western governments that were reluctant to act, against a General Assembly which was increasingly frustrated at the intransigence of the racist governments in southern Africa and the failure of the Assembly's barrage of resolutions to make any difference. In 1962 the Assembly tested the limits of its division of labour with the Security Council by itself calling upon member states to break off diplomatic relations with South Africa, to refuse entry to its ships and aircraft, to boycott its goods, and to impose an arms embargo. It also established what became the Special Committee against Apartheid to monitor developments and report, as appropriate, to either the Assembly or the Council. The resolution also called upon the Council to impose binding sanctions. In 1963 the Council characterized the South African situation as 'seriously disturbing international peace and security' and called for, but did not mandatorily impose, an arms embargo. The Assembly raised the stakes again in 1966 by condemning apartheid as 'a crime against humanity', an approach which was taken further by its adoption in 1973 of the Convention on the Suppression and Punishment of the Crime of Apartheid (GA Res. 3068 (XXVIII)). Three years later, the Assembly concluded that 'the continued brutal repression, including indiscriminate mass killings' by the apartheid regime left 'no alternative to the oppressed people of South Africa but to resort to armed struggle to achieve their legitimate rights', thus giving its imprimatur to the national liberation struggle.

It was not until 1977 that the Council (Res. 418) imposed a mandatory arms embargo under Chapter VII. In 1984, the Council rejected a new constitution that had been adopted by an exclusively white electorate as contrary to UN principles and thus 'null and void'. By 1989, as political movement within South Africa became evident, the Assembly adopted a different tack in its Declaration on Apartheid and Its Destructive Consequences in Southern Africa (GA Res. S-16/1), which called for a new constitutional order based on the UN Charter and the UDHR. After the South African transformation, the Council terminated the arms embargo and all other restrictions in May 1994.

The South African case thus showed a gradual but inexorable expansion of the definition of what constitutes a 'threat to the peace'. As Louis Sohn has observed, the Council moved from characterizing apartheid as a potential threat, to 'a social evil, to a repugnant practice, to a crime under international law, to a threat to the peace that must not be tolerated by the international community and which warranted the imposition of mandatory economic sanctions against the deviant government'.[13]

COMMENT ON THE POST-COLD WAR COUNCIL, ARMED CONFLICT, AND MASSIVE VIOLATIONS

Notwithstanding the important precedents set in relation to apartheid, the overall UN system for the maintenance of peace and security, and particularly the provisions for enforcement under Chapter VII, remained largely paralysed throughout the Cold War years. Statistics tell an important part of the story. Between 1946 and 1989 the Council held 2,903 meetings and adopted 646 resolutions. In the period from 1990–99 it held 1,182 meetings (plus innumerable consultations) and adopted 638 resolutions. In 1999 alone it held 122 meetings, adopted 64 resolutions, and 34 'Presidential Statements'.

Until 1986, the Council declared breaches of the peace only in Korea in 1950 and the Falklands/Malvinas in 1982. Its determinations during that period that a state had committed acts of 'aggression' reached only to Israel and South Africa, and it recognized the existence of a 'threat to international peace and security' only in relation to seven situations: Palestine in 1948, the Congo in 1961, Southern Rhodesia in 1966, Bangladesh in 1971, Cyprus in 1974, South Africa in 1977, and Israel's attack on the PLO headquarters in Tunis in 1985. Prior to 1990 the Council authorized the use of military force only three times (Korea, the Congo and Southern Rhodesia), and imposed sanctions only twice. In contrast, between 1990 and January 2000, the Council authorized the use of military force in five situations (Iraq, Somalia, the Former Yugoslavia, Rwanda and Haiti), and imposed sanctions in 11 situations (see pp. 662–72, *infra*).

Peacekeeping operations, however, show a different trend. At the end of 1990, the UN was involved in eight operations with a total of 10,000 troops. At the height of the early 1990s revival in UN peacekeeping there were 17 such operations involving more than 70,000 troops and costing over $3 billion a year. In March 2000, 26,700 troops and police were involved. Between April 1998 and November 1999 alone, five new operations were established (in the Central African Republic, Kosovo, Sierra Leone, East Timor, and the Democratic Republic of the Congo).[14] Also of immense importance are the steps since 1993 taken by the Council, acting under Chapter VII, to establish international criminal tribunals (see pp. 1143–92, *infra*).

At the beginning of the twenty-first century more than 90 per cent of armed conflicts are taking place within, rather than between, States. Yet the weight to be accorded to human rights considerations in the overall work of the Council remains unclear, as illustrated by the following Presidential Statement:

The Council emphasizes the need fully to respect and implement the principles

[13] Louis Sohn, 'Interpreting the Law', in O. Schachter and C. Joyner (eds.), *United Nations Legal Order* (1995), at 211.
[14] For details see: <www.un.org/Depts/DPKO?c_miss.htm>.

and provisions of the Charter . . . and norms of international law. . . . It affirms
its commitment to the principles of the political independence, sovereign equality and territorial integrity of all States. The Council also affirms the need for
respect for human rights and the rule of law. It will give special attention to the
humanitarian consequences of armed conflicts. The Council recognizes the
importance of building a culture of prevention . . . .[15]

It is not at all clear that this statement accords human rights the same importance as the 'principles' to which the Council affirms its commitment, and the
'special attention' to be given to 'humanitarian consequences' is intentionally
ambiguous. In essence, it appears to leave unfettered the Council's discretion as to
whether, and if so how, to respond to gross human rights violations. In part, this
ambiguity reflects the traumas of recent years when the Council was accused of
not having acted forcefully enough in response to massive violations in Rwanda
and Bosnia. In 1999 official investigations that were highly critical of the UN's
response in each case were published. The Rwanda report, for example, characterized the 1994 Rwandan genocide in which 800,000 people were killed in about 100
days as 'one of the most abhorrent events of the twentieth century'.

> The failure by the United Nations to prevent, and subsequently, to stop the
> genocide in Rwanda was a failure by the United Nations system as a whole. The
> fundamental failure was the lack of resources and political commitment devoted
> to developments in Rwanda and to the United Nations presence there. There was
> a persistent lack of political will by Member States to act, or to act with enough
> assertiveness. . . .[16]

Among its recommendations, the Independent Inquiry proposed, *inter alia*: an
action plan, involving the whole UN system, to prevent genocide; renewed efforts to
improve the UN's peacekeeping capacity; and preparedness on the part of the UN:

> and in particular the Security Council and troop contributing countries . . . to act
> to prevent acts of genocide or gross violations of human rights wherever they may
> take place. The political will to act should not be subject to different standards.

The controversial issue that remains is not whether the Security Council should
act to end massive violations. In principle, there appears to be agreement that it
should. The problem is the difficulty of obtaining the necessary consensus within
the Security Council in any given case. As the *Human Rights Watch World Report
2000* put it:

> [As the Council] functions today, with the five permanent members free to
> exercise their vetoes for the most parochial reasons, [it] cannot be counted on to
> authorize intervention even in dire circumstances. China and Russia seem pre-
> occupied by perceived analogies to Tibet and Chechnya. The United States is

---

[15] UN Doc. S/PRST/1999/34.
[16] Report of the Independent Inquiry into the
Actions of the United Nations During the 1994
Genocide in Rwanda, 15 December 1999. See:

<www.un.org/News/ossg/rwanda_report.htm>. For
the report of the Bosnia inquiry see: 'The Fall of
Srebrenica', UN Doc. A/54/549 (1999).

sometimes paralyzed by an isolationist Congress and a risk-averse Pentagon. Britain and France have let commercial or cultural ties stand in the way.

Concerns about the human and other costs of intervention, about the limited prospects of success, and about the conditions for ending humanitarian intervention are additional deterrents.

Three questions arise: (1) Is 'humanitarian intervention' by one state or a regional grouping of states, in the absence of a Security Council mandate, an acceptable option in order to put an end to gross and systematic violations of human rights? (2) If it is, how can it be reconciled with other principles upon which international law is based, such as the sovereign equality of states, non-interference in domestic affairs, and a Security Council monopoly on authorizing the use of force except in self-defence? (3) What safeguards might be imposed in order to limit the abuse of such an option by powerful states acting for their own ends? The current state of international disagreement is illustrated by the following summing up of the General Assembly's debate on this issue in 1999:

> On the notion of humanitarian intervention, there were those speakers who observed that respect for human rights has become more important than the sovereignty of States. Against this background, it was argued that the international community should intervene in the face of gross and systematic violations of human rights, with or without prior approval of the United Nations, particularly the Security Council.
>
> Other Member States expressed the view that the new notion of humanitarian intervention has the potential for destroying the Charter, undermining the sovereignty of States and overthrowing legitimate governments. They stressed that the protection of human rights is an obligation incumbent upon all governments within the context of the exercise of their sovereignty and constitutional order.
>
> Still, other delegations, recalling the spirit of the Charter of the world body, emphasizd that nations could not intervene in the internal affairs of others without a specific Security Council mandate. They observed that any massive violations of human rights leading to humanitarian emergencies required the coordinated action of the international community through the United Nations, and not by a fiat of unilateral action and creation of *faits accomplis* that would set bad precedents.[17]

The materials in Sections E and F examine these issues primarily through the lens of the two major intervention crises that occurred during 1999—Kosovo and East Timor.

2. THE CASE OF KOSOVO

Kosovo is a province of Serbia, itself part of the present Federal Republic of Yugoslavia (FRY). Until 1989, Kosovo had enjoyed an autonomous status within Serbia. From 1993 onwards a wealth of reports submitted to the UN Commission

---

[17] Statement by the President of the General Assembly, UN Press Release GA/SM/105, 2 October 1999.

documented a pattern of serious human rights abuses effectively by Serbia against Kosovo Albanians who made up 90 per cent of the province's population. In March 1998 the Security Council, acting under Chapter VII, imposed an arms embargo, and called for a political solution (Res. 1160). In September, as fighting intensified, it determined that there was 'a threat to peace and security in the region' and demanded a ceasefire (Res. 1199). Although these resolutions also threatened more drastic steps, Russia made clear that it would veto any Council resolution authorizing the use of force. In October, the North Atlantic Treaty Organization (NATO) announced that it would be prepared to launch military action if the FRY did not comply with the Council resolutions. The legal justification offered was 'humanitarian intervention'.

In October, the FRY signed agreements accepting the establishment of a verification mission of the Organization for Security and Cooperation in Europe (OSCE) in Kosovo, and a NATO air verification mission to complement the OSCE mission. These agreements were formally endorsed by the Council (Res. 1203) which reiterated that the situation constituted a continuing threat to peace and security. In late 1998, fighting again intensified in Kosovo with the burning of homes and destruction of villages by Serb forces and killings and disappearances carried out by the Kosovo Liberation Army (KLA). By March 1999, the United Nations High Commissioner for Refugees (UNHCR) estimated that there were some 260,000 displaced persons in Kosovo. When efforts to compel the parties to reach a negotiated agreement at Rambouillet failed, NATO carried out its threatened response in the form of air strikes in Kosovo and the FRY, which began on 24 March and continued until 9 June 1999. In the first eight days, UNHCR reported that some 220,000 persons were forcibly expelled from Kosovo to neighbouring states, principally Albania, by Serbian forces. The OSCE Verification Mission in Kosovo estimated that over 90 per cent of the Kosovo Albanian population—some 1.45 million people—had been displaced by the conflict by the time it ended.[18]

Although the Security Council had never authorized the intensive bombing campaign, it endorsed the political settlement that was reached and agreed to deploy an extensive 'international security presence' along with a parallel 'international civil presence'. The considerable responsibilities of each of these missions were spelled out in detail (Res. 1244 of 10 June 1999).

In his comments on legal perspectives on the use of force in Kosovo, Bruno Simma stated:[19]

. . .

> [W]hile the threat of armed force employed by NATO against the FRY in the Kosovo crisis since the fall of 1998 is illegal due to the lack of a Security Council authorization, the Alliance made every effort to get as close to legality as possible by, first, following the thrust of, and linking its efforts to, the Council resolutions which did exist, and, second, characterizing its action as an urgent measure to avert even greater humanitarian catastrophes in Kosovo, taken in a state of humanitarian necessity.
>
> The lesson which can be drawn from this is that unfortunately there do occur

---

[18] OSCE, Kosovo/Kosova: As Seen, As Told, Dec. 1999. See <www.osce.org/kosovo/reports/hr>.
[19] 'NATO, the UN and the Use of Force: Legal Aspects', 10 Eur. J. Int. L. 1, 22 (1999).

'hard cases' in which terrible dilemmas must be faced and imperative political and moral considerations may appear to leave no choice but to act outside the law. The more isolated these instances remain, the smaller will be their potential to erode the precepts of international law, in our case the UN Charter. As mentioned earlier, a potential boomerang effect of such breaches can never be excluded, but this danger can at least be reduced by indicating the concrete circumstances that led to a decision *ad hoc* being destined to remain singular. In this regard, NATO has done a rather convincing job. In the present author's view, only a thin red line separates NATO's action on Kosovo from international legality. But should the Alliance now set out to include breaches of the UN Charter as a regular part of its strategic programme for the future, this would have an immeasurably more destructive impact on the universal system of collective security embodied in the Charter. To resort to illegality as an explicit *ultima ratio* for reasons as convincing as those put forward in the Kosovo case is one thing. To turn such an exception into a general policy is quite another. . . .

The following readings explore further the relationship between legality and legitimacy, as well as reflect on the type of criteria that could be used in the future to assess humanitarian interventions.

ABDULLAHI AN-NA'IM, NATO ON KOSOVO IS BAD FOR HUMAN RIGHTS
17 Neths. Q. H. R. 229 (1999)

. . .

. . . [B]y violating the Charter of the United Nations and disregarding its system for the regulation of the use of force, NATO's actions have severely undermined the credibility of international law as the foundation of the universality of human rights. I also wish to emphasize that, even if these activities are justified on humanitarian, security or some other grounds, as some have argued, they are nevertheless seriously damaging for the rule of law in international relations, including the protection of universal human rights.

Moreover, I suggest, NATO's military activities should not qualify as 'humanitarian intervention' under international law because of the irresponsible manner in which this campaign was conducted. As openly acknowledged, military action was restricted to high-altitude 'remote-control' bombing in order to minimize political opposition for the self-proclaimed 'humanitarians' in their own countries. It is also clear, I believe, that this was done in the expectation of causing serious loss of life and severe hardship among the local, non-combatant civilian population. What should be equally openly conceded is that NATO's objectives in Kosovo cannot be achieved without a long-term occupation in an attempt to impose substantial political, economic and social changes in the country. When this 'colonial' project fails, as it is bound to, will NATO stay indefinitely or abandon the Albanian citizens of Kosovo to a worse fate than the one it claimed to redress through military intervention? Even by the unlikely scenario that NATO will stay and take matters to their logical conclusions, the outcome will hardly be a vindication of the human rights of purported beneficiaries of this adventure. In this light, I say that those who claim the high moral ground of pursuing the laudable objectives of humanitarian intervention must do so in morally credible and practically viable ways because good ends cannot be achieved through bad means.

A common rationalisation of the international lawlessness of the NATO Governments is that resort to the Security Council in this case would have been futile because Russia and China were expected to block any decisive action regarding Kosovo. But this is simply justifying taking the law into one's own hands by imposing one's own remedy to a conflict because the police are expected to be unable or unwilling to enforce it. It is true that the application of Chapter VII of the UN Charter has been frequently frustrated, not only this time, by the use of the veto power in the Security Council. But the proper response to such problems is surely to reform the system for all situations, instead of using it selectively to ensure specific outcomes whenever possible, and acting outside its framework when the results one wants cannot be achieved through the system.

. . .

I also wish to emphasize that the choice for the so-called international community is not between the Americanism of 'doing something' (read 'anything') or passively watching flagrant and systematic violations of basic human rights. Rather, it is between the principled and institutionalized application of the same standards everywhere, on the one hand, and self-help and vigilante justice, on the other. The 'something' that should be done in all crisis situations must be consistent with the systematic and institutionalized application of the same principles. Without the consistent application of clear principles, the actions of Western Governments will remain highly suspect, and ultimately ineffective.

. . .

MICHAEL IGNATIEFF, WHOSE UNIVERSAL VALUES? THE CRISIS IN HUMAN RIGHTS
(1999), at 19

. . . Since 1989, there has been a single human rights culture in the world, and nothing stands in the way to defy its moral imperium. Russia and China no longer have the power to do anything but deny Security Council approval to Western coalitions of the willing. Their veto power may deny legitimacy to actions by coalitions of the willing, but as the NATO operation in Kosovo shows, determined coalitions simply bypass the Security Council altogether. This momentous shift has combined with the coming of age of human rights advocacy from the grass roots in Western countries. As a result, the balance between state sovereignty and human rights claims has begun to shift towards the rights of the individual. But the impact of this shift has not necessarily been to the benefit of oppressed individuals, but rather to the benefit of the states which intervene in other states in the name of human rights.

Since 1989, there have been armed interventions to create a safe haven for the

Kurds in northern Iraq; to reverse a military overthrow of a democratically elected government in Haiti; to evict a dictator from Panama; to end a famine and factional war in Somalia; to attempt to prevent genocide in Rwanda; to end civil wars in Angola and Mozambique; to create a democratic transition in Cambodia; to force the Serbian government to sue for peace in Bosnia; to reverse ethnic cleansing in Kosovo and now, most recently, to re-establish peace and stability in East Timor. The armed forces of the Western powers have been busier since 1989 than they ever were during the Cold War and the legitimizing language for this activity has been the defence of human rights.

But the results are ambiguous: on the one hand, the language of human rights explicitly proscribes imperial adventurism; on the other, we seem to be behaving like imperial policemen. These interventions are supposed to be post-imperial, non-colonialist in intention and outcome. We are not intervening to take over territory, but to bring peace and stability and then get out; our mandate is to restore self-determination not to extinguish it. Yet we are now firmly ensconced in Bosnia, Kosovo and East Timor, with imperial obligations and no exit strategy in sight.

Some activists profess to be untroubled by these issues. They believe a profound and long term shift of the balance of power away from nation states is underway. For many human rights activists, state sovereignty is an anachronism in a global world. They wish to see ever more global oversight, ever more power to the international human rights community, ever more human rights protectorates. But is this wise? All unlimited forms of power are open to abuse, and there is no reason why power which legitimises itself in the name of human rights does not end up as tyrannous as any other. Those who will end up with more power may only be those who have power already: the coalitions of the willing, the Western nations with the military might necessary for any successful 'human rights' intervention.

. . .

There is a political crisis in human rights activism because we have failed to consider the conflict of principle between our commitment to individual human rights and our belief in self-determination. The first commits us to intervene; the second warns us against intervention. The one mandates 'outside' rescue missions; the second validates the sovereignty of states.

How are we to redress the balance? Instead of regarding state sovereignty as an outdated principle, . . . we need to appreciate the extent to which state sovereignty is both the principle of order in the international security system, but also the best guarantee of human rights that there is. This is an unfamiliar, even controversial principle within a human rights community which for 50 years has looked on the state as the chief danger to the human rights of individuals. And so it has often proved. But this need not always be the case, where the state in question at least observes the rule of law. For it can be said with certainty that the liberties of citizens are better protected by their own institutions than by the well-meaning interventions of outsiders. The right that a person has by virtue of membership in a law-abiding state are usually more valuable than the rights a person has by virtue of his membership in the human race, and the remedies which a citizen has by virtue of his citizenship are more effective than those which inhere in international human rights covenants.

So human rights might best be strengthened in today's world not by weakening already weak and overburdened states but by strengthening them wherever possible. The real human rights crisis of the last 15 years has followed from the collapse of states into civil war and ethnic conflict. These are the situations of war of all against all which produce most of the human rights abuses of the present day. These abuses cannot be stopped by international human rights activism alone, but by institution building—by creating states strong enough and legitimate enough to recover their monopoly over the means of violence, imposing order and creating the rule of law. And let us be explicit: democracy may not always be possible. Our best hope is for the rule of law. Authoritarian order which at least guarantees procedural fairness and due process is a good deal better than anarchy and civil war.

Where all order has disintegrated, it is fruitless to despatch human rights monitors or to expose the violators to international condemnation. The only effective action is intervention. But when we do so, we usually violate someone's sovereignty for the sake of someone else's self-determination. We violate one principle, in order to vindicate another. Moreover, we are then committed to staying in place—in a protectorate or an extended peacekeeping operation—which violates the principle of self-determination again.

. . .

KOFI ANNAN, IMPLICATIONS OF INTERNATIONAL RESPONSE TO EVENTS IN RWANDA, KOSOVO EXAMINED BY SECRETARY-GENERAL
UN Press Release GA/9595, 20 September 1999

[This is a report of a speech to the General Assembly by the UN Secretary-General, Kofi Annan.]

'While the genocide in Rwanda will define for our generation the consequences of inaction in the face of mass murder, the more recent conflict in Kosovo had prompted important questions about the consequences of action in the absence of unity on the part of the international community', he said. In the case of Kosovo, the inability of that community to reconcile the question of the legitimacy of an action taken by a regional organization without a United Nations mandate, on one side, and the universally accepted imperative of effectively halting gross and systematic violations of human rights, on the other, could only be viewed as a tragedy. It had revealed the core challenge to the Security Council and the United Nations in the next century: To forge unity behind the principle that massive, systematic violations of human rights—wherever they might take place—should not be allowed to stand.

He said that, to those for whom the greatest threat to the future of international order was the use of force in the absence of a Council mandate, one might ask—

not in the context of Kosovo, but in the context of Rwanda—if a coalition of States had been prepared to act in defence of the Tutsi population, but had not received prompt Council authorization, should such a coalition have stood aside and allowed the horror to unfold? To those for whom the Kosovo action heralded a new era when States and groups of States could take military action outside the established mechanisms for enforcing international law, one might ask: Was there not a danger of such intervention undermining the imperfect, yet resilient, security system created after the Second World War, and of setting dangerous precedents for future interventions?

. . .

. . . [I]n the Charter's own words, 'armed force shall not be used, save in the common interest'. What was the common interest, who should define it, who would defend it, and under whose authority and with what means of intervention? he asked. . . .

. . .

. . . In [Rwanda and Kosovo] Member States of the United Nations should have been able to find common ground in upholding the principles of the Charter, and acting in defence of 'our common heritage'. The Charter required the Council to be the defender of the 'common interest'. Unless it was seen to be so, there was a danger that others could seek to take its place.

HUMAN RIGHTS WATCH, WORLD REPORT 2000, THE CRITIQUE OF MILITARY INTERVENTION
(1999), at xviii

. . . [A] common concern is that military intervention might become a pretext for military adventures in pursuit of ulterior motives. Vigilance against such misuse of the human rights name is clearly warranted. Memories of the U.S. invasions of Grenada and Panama, for example, have not faded. But the interventions in East Timor and Kosovo gave fewer reasons for concern on this score than prior interventions.

. . .

In Kosovo, NATO's concern for its credibility may have contributed to its decision to begin bombing when Milosevic rejected the Rambouillet peace proposal. Worries about large refugee flows destabilizing Macedonia's delicate ethnic mix, producing cascading instability in the Balkans, and ultimately seeking entrance to the rest of Europe may also have driven NATO to seek the return of Kosovar refugees once Yugoslav and Serbian troops began forcibly expelling them in large numbers upon commencement of the bombing. Yet the common denominator in the multinational consensus behind NATO's action was fundamentally humanitarian, including fear that Milosevic would extend the sweep of genocide to Yugoslavia's southern province. Whatever mixed motives might have guided NATO's action, the desire to stop crimes against humanity was clearly a major goal.

. . . Human Rights Watch considers advocating nonconsensual military intervention only when it is the last feasible option to avoid genocide or comparable mass slaughter. Governments might well adopt other criteria. But given the risk to life inherent in any military action, only the most severe threats to life should warrant consideration of an international military response. And even then, as noted, strict compliance with international humanitarian law should be imperative.

Some critics challenge humanitarian action in Kosovo and East Timor on the grounds of selectivity. Why intervene in these situations, they ask, and not in Angola or Colombia, in Chechnya or Sudan? Again, legitimate concerns with equity lie behind this objection. Yet, the world should hardly deny a helping hand to people facing mass slaughter simply because it might not act to stop similar atrocities elsewhere.

. . .

. . . Not every human rights tragedy lends itself to military intervention. Indeed, Kosovo and East Timor may have been easier cases, because each had a colorable claim to self-determination and a local population that overwhelmingly favored intervention. . . .

ANTONIO CASSESE, *EX INIURIA IUS ORITUR* : IS INTERNATIONAL LEGITIMATION OF FORCIBLE HUMANITARIAN COUNTERMEASURES TAKING SHAPE IN THE WORLD COMMUNITY?
10 Eur. J. Int. L. 23 (1999), at 25

. . . [F]rom an *ethical* viewpoint resort to armed force was justified [in the Kosovo case]. Nevertheless, . . . this moral action is *contrary to current international law.*

I contend however that as legal scholars we must stretch our minds further and ask ourselves two questions. First, was the NATO armed intervention at least rooted in and partially justified by contemporary trends of the international community? Second, in this particular instance of use of force, were some parameters set that might lead to a gradual legitimation of forcible humanitarian countermeasures by a group of states outside any authorization by the Security Council?

[The author answers the first question in the affirmative based on various recent trends]. . . .

Based on these nascent trends in the world community, I submit that under certain strict conditions resort to armed force may gradually become justified even absent any authorization by the Security Council. These conditions may be enumerated as follows:

(i) gross and egregious breaches of human rights involving loss of life of hundreds or thousands of innocent people, and amounting to crimes against humanity, are carried out on the territory of a sovereign state, either by the central governmental authorities or with their connivance and support, or because the total collapse of such authorities cannot impede those atrocities;

(ii) if the crimes against humanity result from anarchy in a sovereign state, proof is necessary that the central authorities are utterly unable to put an end to those crimes, while at the same time refusing to call upon or to allow other states or international organizations to enter the territory to assist in terminating the crimes. If, on the contrary, such crimes are the work of the central authorities, it must be shown that those authorities have consistently withheld their cooperation with the United Nations or other international organizations, or have systematically refused to comply with appeals, recommendations or decisions of such organisations.

(iii) the Security Council is unable to take any coercive action to stop the massacres because of disagreement among the Permanent Members or because one or more of them exercises its veto power . . .;

(iv) all peaceful avenues which may be explored consistent with the urgency of the situation to achieve a solution based on negotiation, discussion and any other means short of force have been exhausted . . .;

(v) a group of states (not a single hegemonic Power, however strong its military, political and economic authority, nor such a Power with the support of a client state or an ally) decides to try to halt the atrocities, with the support or at least the non-opposition of the majority of Member states of the UN;

(vi) armed force is exclusively used for the limited purpose of stopping the atrocities and restoring respect for human rights, not for any goal going beyond this limited purpose. Consequently, the use of force must be discontinued as soon as this purpose is attained. Moreover, it is axiomatic that use of force should be commensurate with and proportionate to the human rights exigencies on the ground. The more urgent the situation of killings and atrocities, the more intensive and immediate may be the military response thereto. Conversely, military action would not be warranted in the case of a crisis which is slowly unfolding and which still presents avenues for diplomatic resolution aside from armed confrontation.

NOTE

Several of the preceding readings have referred to self-determination, a doctrine and concept of multiple meanings that Chapter 15 explores.

QUESTIONS

1. President Clinton told the UN General Assembly in September 1999 that 'By acting as we did, we helped to vindicate the principles and purposes of the U.N. Charter, to give the U.N. the opportunity it now has to play the central role in shaping Kosovo's future. In the real world, principles often collide, and tough choices must be made. The

outcome in Kosovo is hopeful'.[20] Has the Kosovo intervention seriously damaged the rule of law in international relations, as An-Na'im suggests? What do you understand to be the ingredients of this international rule of law?

2. (a) Is there any way to ensure 'the principled and institutionalized application of the same standards everywhere' or to give substance to the call by Human Rights Watch that 'Victims of atrocities deserve effective assistance wherever they' are?

(b) What reasons, if any, do you believe to have substance when a state argues against providing effective assistance in a given case?

(c) Suppose that the ideal of institutional regularity in responding to massive violations cannot be realized. Should individual states and IGOs simply then stay out of all situations to avoid the charge of selective, unprincipled intervention?

3. If the Charter approach is simply inadequate under today's circumstances, what alternative solutions might be considered: eliminating the veto power? Requiring two states to exercise their vetoes for it to be effective? Giving the General Assembly a significant role? Establishing an independent expert group to advise the Council?

4. Compare the criteria for justifying intervention put forward by Human Rights Watch with those suggested by Cassese. Is either approach helpful? What criteria would you propose?

5. Is Ignatieff's emphasis on state sovereignty and citizenship convincing in the context of a discussion of whether or not to intervene militarily in extreme cases?

3. SANCTIONS

Until 1990 the Security Council imposed sanctions only twice (Southern Rhodesia 1966–79, and South Africa 1977–94, see p. 650, *supra*). Between 1990 and January 2000, sanctions were applied in 11 situations (Iraq, Somalia, the Former Yugoslavia, Rwanda, Haiti, Liberia, Libya, Angola, the Federal Republic of Yugoslavia, Sudan, and Sierra Leone).[21] The scope and nature of these sanctions varied considerably from the comprehensive embargo placed on Haiti, through the arms embargo used in Sierra Leone, to the freezing of funds and assets linked to the UNITA rebel movement in Angola. At the national level, especially in the case of the United States, the popularity of unilaterally imposed sanctions also increased greatly during the 1990s. Thus, of 115 uses of sanctions by the United States between 1919 and 1996, 61 of them occurred between 1993 and 1996.[22]

Although human rights advocates have often proposed the imposition of sanctions against governments that are violating human rights, increasing doubts have been raised in recent years about both their effectiveness and their appropriateness. Reasons for concern include: the bluntness of the weapon, the porosity of

---

[20] See: <www2.whitehouse.gov/WH/New/html/19990921_1.html>.
[21] For details see: <www.un.org/News/ossg/sanction.htm>.
[22] See R. Haass, 'Sanctioning Madness', 76 For. Aff. 74 (1997).

most regimes, the ability of many elites to turn sanctions to their own advantage, and sanctions' disproportionate impact on the most vulnerable sectors of society. The most comprehensive and long-running set of UN-imposed sanctions has been applied to Iraq from 1991 until the present (January 2000). In response to Iraq's invasion of Kuwait, the Security Council (Res. 661 of 6 August 1990) imposed a full trade embargo barring all imports and exports except for medical supplies, foodstuffs and other items of humanitarian need as approved by the Council's sanctions committee (established by the same resolution). Lifting of the sanctions was made conditional upon compliance with a long list of demands, including full cooperation with the UN's mandated efforts to disarm Iraq of weapons of mass destruction. In 1995 a food-for-oil programme was authorized under which Iraq could sell limited quantities of oil and up to 66 per cent of the proceeds would be available to fund approved humanitarian purchases. Deliveries began by March 1997 and the programme was subsequently expanded.

In 1999 the Security Council established three expert panels in relation to Iraq, including one to examine humanitarian conditions. That panel concluded that the situation was dire and would continue to be so until there was a 'sustained revival of the Iraqi economy' (UN Doc. S/1999/356). It noted a grave deterioration in the state of public health and observed that communicable diseases, previously under control, 'had become part of the endemic pattern of the precarious health situation'. Similar reporting by UNICEF compared the 1984–89 and 1994–99 periods in the government-controlled centre and the south of Iraq. Infant mortality had more than doubled and under-five child mortality had increased by an even higher amount. The dramatic increase was due not only to insufficient food and medicine but also to the degradation of the water and sanitation systems, contributing to chronic intestinal and acute respiratory infections.

HUMAN RIGHTS WATCH, LETTER TO UN SECURITY COUNCIL
January 4, 2000, <www.hrp.org/hrw/press/2000/01/iraq-ltr.htm>

Dear Ambassador Holbrooke,

...

[Recent reports by the UN, UNICEF, the International Committee for the Red Cross and others] ... make clear that life-threatening conditions continue to prevail in Iraq, stemming from a pervasive and protracted public health emergency. This emergency is largely a consequence of the destruction of the civilian economic infrastructure in the 1991 Gulf war, repair of which has been severely impeded by the comprehensive embargo on Iraqi exports and imports. Restoration of the civilian economic infrastructure is essential to returning child mortality rates and other public health indicators to the levels and trajectories that existed prior to the embargo and war. Although the 'oil-for-food' humanitarian relief program authorized under Resolutions 986 (1995) and now expanded under Resolution 1284 (1999) provides materials for infrastructure repair, as a temporary relief program it does not encompass the planning and investment required to restore Iraq's infrastructure to a level needed to meet the most basic civilian necessities.

As an organization that has extensively documented war crimes and atrocities committed by the government of Iraq, Human Rights Watch is fully aware of the need for strong international measures to constrain and hold accountable those responsible for such crimes. We recognize, moreover, that the policies of the government—its failure to comply fully with Resolution 687, its refusal to implement any 'oil-for-food' arrangement between 1991 and 1996, its mixed record of cooperation since then, and its use of scarce available resources for non-humanitarian purposes in order to redirect the consequences of sanctions away from itself and onto vulnerable civilians—have greatly compounded and magnified the humanitarian crisis. It is apparent that the Iraqi government has not complied with its obligations under the [ICESCR] to use 'the maximum of its available resources', including 'international assistance', to provide an adequate standard of living and improve living standards.

The past ten years have made clear that the Iraqi government has no intention of making the humanitarian interests of the Iraqi people its first priority. The government's callous and manipulative disregard for its humanitarian obligations is not something the Council can reasonably expect will change. Rather, it is a reality the Council must take into account in deciding the appropriate means for securing the government's compliance with its disarmament demands.

Charges that Iraqi malfeasance and incompetence are entirely responsible for the severity and extent of the humanitarian crisis, moreover, are not credible. The Council should not use the high degree of Iraqi government culpability for the humanitarian crisis to obscure its own share of responsibility. The severe deprivations and widespread pauperization facing the great majority of Iraqis today cannot be dissociated from the unprecedentedly comprehensive and protracted character of the embargo. The Council should not continue the sanctions without substantial modification, in order to address the continuing humanitarian crisis and the inadequacy of the current humanitarian program. In trying to curtail Iraq's development of weapons of mass destruction, the Council must devise means that do not aggravate the poverty and suffering of ordinary Iraqis, suffering that the government appears to find tolerable, even useful. In deploying instruments of coercion, including non-military instruments such as an embargo, the Council must be governed by the core humanitarian principle of minimizing threats to life and bodily harm of innocent people who bear no responsibility for the government policies being sanctioned.

. . .

COMMITTEE ON ECONOMIC, SOCIAL AND CULTURAL RIGHTS, GENERAL COMMENT NO. 8 (1997)
UN Doc. E/1998/22, Annex V

The relationship between economic sanctions and respect for economic, social and cultural rights

. . .

3. While the impact of sanctions varies from one case to another, . . . they almost always have a dramatic impact on the rights recognized in the [ICESCR]. Thus, for example, they often cause significant disruption in the distribution of food, pharmaceuticals and sanitation supplies, jeopardise the quality of food and the availability of clean drinking water, severely interfere with the functioning of basic health and education systems, and undermine the right to work. In addition, their unintended consequences can include reinforcement of the power of oppressive elites, the emergence, almost invariably, of a black market and the generation of huge windfall profits for the priveleged elites which manage it, enhancement of the control of the governing elites over the population at large, and restriction of opportunities to seek asylum or to manifest political opposition. . . .

4. In considering sanctions, it is essential to distinguish between the basic objective of applying political and economic pressure upon the governing elite of the country to persuade them to conform to international law, and the collateral infliction of suffering upon the most vulnerable groups within the targeted country. For that reason, the sanctions regimes established by the Security Council now include humanitarian exemptions designed to permit the flow of essential goods and services destined for humanitarian purposes. It is commonly assumed that these exemptions ensure basic respect for economic, social and cultural rights within the targeted country.

5. However, [they do not]. . . . A 1996 study on the impact of armed conflict on children, stated that 'humanitarian exemptions tend to be ambiguous and are interpreted arbitrarily and inconsistently. . . . Delays, confusion and the denial of requests to import essential humanitarian goods cause resource shortages. . . . [Their effects] inevitably fall most heavily on the poor'. [A 1997 UN report concluded that the Council's review procedures] 'remain cumbersome and aid agencies still encounter difficulties in obtaining approval for exempted supplies. . . .'

. . .

7. The Committee considers that the provisions of the [ICESCR] . . . cannot be considered to be inoperative, or in any way inapplicable, solely because a decision has been taken that considerations of international peace and security warrant the imposition of sanctions. . . .

. . .

10. . . . While sanctions will inevitably diminish the capacity of the affected [target] State to fund or support some of the necessary measures, the State remains under an obligation to ensure the absence of discrimination in relation to the enjoyment of these rights, and to take all possible measures, including negotiations with other States and the international community, to reduce to a minimum the negative impact upon the rights of vulnerable groups within the society.

11. . . .[T]he party or parties responsible for the imposition, maintenance or implementation of the sanctions [also have obligations] . . . .

12. First, [economic, social and cultural] rights must be taken fully into account when designing an appropriate sanctions regime. Without endorsing any particular measures in this regard, the Committee notes proposals such as the creation of a United Nations mechanism for anticipating and tracking sanctions impacts, the elaboration of a more transparent set of agreed principles and procedures based on respect for human rights, the identification of a wider range of exempt goods and services, the authorisation of agreed technical agencies to determine necessary exemptions, the creation of a better resourced set of sanctions committees, more precise targeting of the vulnerabilities of those whose behaviour the international community wishes to change, and the introduction of greater overall flexibility.

13. Second, effective monitoring, which is always required under the terms of the Covenant, should be undertaken throughout the period that sanctions are in force. When an external party takes upon itself even partial responsibility for the situation within a country (whether under Chapter VII of the Charter or otherwise), it also unavoidably assumes a responsibility to do all within its power to protect the economic, social and cultural rights of the affected population.

14. Third, the external entity has an obligation 'to take steps, individually and through international assistance and co-operation, especially economic and technical' in order to respond to any disproportionate suffering experienced by vulnerable groups within the targeted country.

. . .

16. In adopting this General Comment the sole aim of the Committee is to . . . insist that lawlessness of one kind should not be met by lawlessness of another kind which pays no heed to the fundamental rights that underlie and give legitimacy to any such collective action.

JOY GORDON, A PEACEFUL, SILENT, DEADLY REMEDY: THE ETHICS OF ECONOMIC SANCTIONS
13 Ethics & Int. Affs 123 (1999)

. . .

. . . I assess the moral legitimacy of sanctions in the contexts of just war doctrine, Kantian ethics, and utilitarianism. I make the following arguments: sanctions are inconsistent with the principle of discrimination from just war doctrine [the need to distinguish between combatants and non-combatants, etc.]; sanctions reduce individuals to nothing more than means to an end by using the suffering of innocents as a means of persuasion, thereby violating the Kantian principle that human beings are 'ends in themselves'; and sanctions are unacceptable from a utilitarian perspective because their economic effectiveness necessarily entails considerable human damage, while their likelihood of achieving political objectives is low. Moreover, alternative goals such as punishment or the expression of resolve or moral outrage do not resolve these ethical dilemmas, but instead only offer an unpersuasive attempt to justify sanctions in the face of their failure to achieve their ostensible goals of preventing aggression and bringing about international governance.

...

Targeting Innocents: The Principle of Discrimination

... [S]anctions do not have to be identical to siege warfare in order to be subject to condemnation under just war principles. Indeed, if the intent of sanctions is peaceful rather than belligerent, then the usual justifications in warfare are unavailable. I am morally permitted to kill where my survival is at stake; and in war, I am morally permitted to kill even innocents, in some circumstances. But if one's goal is to see that international law is enforced or that human rights are respected, then the stakes and the justificatory context are quite different.

Lori Fisler Damrosch has argued that sanctions warrant a particularly high degree of tolerance because of the importance of the international norms they are intended to protect . . . .

Yet it is hard to make sense of the claim that 'collateral damage' can be justified in the name of protecting human rights; or that international law might be enforced by means that stand in violation of international laws, including the just war principle of discrimination. Thus, if sanctions are analogous to siege warfare, then they are problematic for the same reasons—both effectively violate the principle of discrimination. But if sanctions are not analogous to siege, then they are even more difficult to justify. If the goals of sanctions are the enforcement of humanitarian standards or compliance with legal and ethical norms, then extensive and predictable harm to civilians cannot be justified even by reference to survival or military advantage. Insofar as this is the case, sanctions are simply a device of cruelty garbed in self-righteousness.

The Suffering of Innocents as a Mechanism of Persuasion: A Kantian Analysis

...

... Where sanctions impose suffering on innocent sectors of the target country population for an objective other than preventing the deaths of other innocent persons, this is clearly incompatible with deontological ethics, since in these situations, to use Kantian language, human beings are reduced to nothing more than a means to an end, where that end is something less than the lives of other human beings.

It is sometimes argued that sanctions are defensible when the sanctioned population consents, or has leaders who consented, or can be deemed to have consented. If those harmed by sanctions were to consent, then arguably sanctions would be consistent with their autonomy. . . .

Actual consent

Within the history of sanctions, it is quite rare to find actual consent by those most affected by siege or by the sanctions. The sanctions against South Africa, and arguably Haiti, were perhaps the only instances in the twentieth century that could be defensible on deontological grounds. . . .

Damrosch and others have noted the importance of obtaining support for sanctions from 'authentic leaders' within the population that bears the brunt of the economic deprivation. But even that is quite different from actual consent—and from actual authorization. . . . Given the stakes, it would seem that a commitment to autonomy and the integrity of the person would require that those who would be most vulnerable to these injuries must provide actual, explicit, and informed consent. Where that is not the case—which is to say, in almost every case of sanctions in the twentieth century and before—then sanctions are simply the imposition of suffering upon the innocent, against their will.

Imputed consent

Damrosch frames the question of imputed consent as: 'Do we assume that people of the target state are innocent and passive bystanders, victims of their own rules and of sanctions? Or that they have the capacity to exercise free choice?' The question seems to invite the response that, of course, all persons have free will and are therefore accountable for their choices. But we know from the history of sanctions that this is not a realistic depiction of a nation under sanctions. Under sanctions, state control over the media is likely to increase, while nonstate parties have less access to equipment and materials needed to disseminate information. As families are forced to go to the black market for necessities, their savings are eroded and their energies are directed primarily toward meeting their immediate needs. The economic hardship to the middle class and the poor means that they will not have enough resources to consider emigrating. Even in a democratic society, the civilian population has no direct input into particular military and political decisions; and in an authoritarian society, this is even more true.

. . .

The shifting of moral agency

Walzer notes that siege warfare has historically been justified not only by the assumption of consent on the part of the civilian population, but also by the shifting of agency from the besieging nation to the recalcitrant leaders of the besieged. In Walzer's description of the siege of Jerusalem, Titus, commander of the besieging army, 'lamented the deaths of so many Jerusalemites, "and, lifting up his hands to heaven . . . called God to witness, that it was not his doing".' . . .

. . .

. . . [According to this position] the countries imposing sanctions are not 'causing' the harm; rather, the leadership of the target country is 'causing' the harm by failing to comply with political demands, or by failing to distribute domestic resources in the way that would most favor the vulnerable sectors of the population. . . . But the existence of wrongdoing does not somehow 'make' sanctions come about in a way that vitiates the moral agency of institutions imposing them. . . . [T]he nation or institution imposing sanctions is still the nation or institution that has imposed the deprivation—with choice, with intent, and in the face of other options, ranging from protest to inaction to military invasion.

. . .

Political Efficacy: The Utilitarian Justification of Sanctions

Since the formation of the League of Nations, those defending sanctions have justified them in part on the basis of utilitarian reasons: the argument is that the economic hardship of the civilian population of the target country entails less human harm overall, and less harm to the sanctioned population, than the military aggression or human rights violations the sanctions seek to prevent. Yet if this is so, then—as an ethical matter—we must look at the effectiveness of sanctions. . . .

. . .

The relation between economic effectiveness and political effectiveness is not at all clear; indeed, it may be an inverse relation. Many economists and historians hold that, generally, sanctions are politically ineffectual. . . .

Losman's study of long-term boycotts against Israel, Cuba, and Rhodesia notes that even where there was considerable economic damage, the only apparent political effect was increased political integration. The common (though not universal) result is that 'the morale-killing effects of economic sanctions often operate in the opposite fashion, stimulating xenophobia and strengthening the determination of the target country to maintain its stance'. . . .

. . .

Thus, . . . there is not a high likelihood that sanctions will succeed in stopping military aggression or human rights violations. . . .

. . .

Thus, sanctions offer themselves solely as mechanisms that strong nations with large economies, or international alliances including strong nations with large economies, can effectively use against countries with weak or import-dependent economies, or countries with unstable governments. The reverse is not true—sanctions are not a device realistically available to small or poor nations that can be used with any significant impact against large or economically dominant nations, even if the latter were to, say, engage in aggression or human rights violations, or otherwise offend the international community. . . .

. . .

Alternative Goals of Economic Sanctions

. . .

. . . A government may consider sanctions useful if they serve to 'declare its position to internal and external publics or help win support at home or abroad.' . . .

. . . [However, where] 'sending a message' or 'signaling resolve' or 'expressing outrage' is the purpose of sanctions, the sanctions patently entail the use of human beings as simply a means to an end; human suffering becomes merely a device of communication. Thus this purpose is unacceptable on deontological as well as utilitarian grounds.

The second major alternative justification of sanctions is punishment. . . . Yet it is not clear that the notion of 'good' and 'bad' nations is a plausible one, despite the ease with which terms like 'rogue nation' are used. Indeed, the notion of a 'rogue' nation is highly contrived, and rooted more in the institutional interests of political actors than in any fundamental concept of international ethics. Moralistic claims are deeply intertwined with geopolitical gamesmanship, with tendencies toward nationalistic self-congratulation, and with the tendency to mistake one's own political strength for moral superiority. . . .

But let us assume that particular acts, such as military aggression, are inherently wrong, and that it is appropriate for the international community to condemn these acts. Is it appropriate to view a nation as analogous to a person? Punishment—entirely aside from the issue of its ethical legitimacy or deterrent effect—is a coherent undertaking only when the wrongdoer is the same entity as the one who is punished. There is no 'punishment' when the person punished is separate from the wrongdoer and bears no responsibility for the wrongful acts.

. . .

Conclusion

. . .

Establishing criteria for the ethical use of sanctions does not resolve these contradictions, but instead masks them. To say that sanctions are ethical as long as we make sure to minimize civilian harm is to mask the fact that sanctions by their nature cause harm to civilians directly and primarily. It is like using a pick-axe for brain surgery: the nature of the instrument suggests that targeting certain areas with precision and effectiveness, without killing the patient in the process, is not going to happen. It is disingenuous to be surprised or apologetic when sanctions turn out to do no harm to a ruling elite, to achieve none of the ostensible goals of the sanctions regarding 'unacceptable behavior' or 'punishment of international outlaws', and to be generally ineffectual for much of anything besides rhetorical posturing and the psychological gratification of having done *something*.

GEORGE A. LOPEZ, MORE ETHICAL THAN NOT: SANCTIONS AS SURGICAL TOOLS
13 Ethics & Int. Affs 143 (1999)

. . .

My understanding of economic sanctions cases in the 1990s differs from Gordon's conclusions in three areas: the relationship between means and ends in sanctions cases, the extent of compliance of the targets (that is, the success of the imposition of sanctions), and the singular moral responsibility of sanctioners for the harms that result from sanctions. . . .

[Lopez then reviews some of the shortcomings of recent Security Council practice in the design and application of sanctions.]

. . .

That past behavior does not inspire confidence that attention will be paid to all the humanitarian needs of a sanctioned population may be clear, but being naive about issues of moral agency in the impact of sanctions compounds the problem. Specifically, Gordon takes the facts that harm comes to innocents and that sanctions are imposed by sanctioners and mistakenly makes the pain of the former the direct and singular responsibility of the latter. She refuses to deal with the intermediary and decision-making role that leadership in a target state plays in determining the impact of sanctions. While she blames the imposers of sanctions for treating a general population instrumentally, she appears not to acknowledge at all the moral responsibility of despicable leaders who victimize their own people instrumentally through the manipulation of sanctions.

While the impact of sanctions may be either immoral or moral, any judgment regarding their impact on innocent people must be assessed by examining the responses of the sanctioned country's leader, and in light of the international humanitarian relief effort mobilized on behalf of the innocent. Again here, the case of Iraq focuses the discussion on the burden of responsibility borne by Iraqi leaders.

. . .

A second area of disagreement concerns the Iraq case, where the claims have been so strong about the deaths of Iraqi children due to sanctions. Unspoken by critics of sanctions is the real possibility that an important positive ethic exists in the imposition of sanctions: we 'bystanders' have a moral obligation to ensure that Kurdish children, Saudi children, Israeli children (American children?) not be gassed or poisoned by Saddam's weapons of mass destruction that is *at least equivalent* to the obligation that we take all necessary steps to ensure life for Iraqi children. This is not meant to make Iraqi children instrumental, but rather to acknowledge a moral dilemma of the ethic of responsibility. And without question, sanctions have been instrumental, although not singular, in attaining the major (and moral) goal of reducing Iraq's capacity to build and maintain an unchecked storehouse of prohibited weapons.

. . .

Gordon dismisses much too quickly the possibility of 'smart sanctions' that can have minimal humanitarian impact and target elites responsible for the policies that generated the sanctions. . . .

. . .

NOTE

By the end of the 1990s there was general agreement with the view expressed by Kofi Annan that the results of UN sanctions had been 'ambiguous at best'. He noted that '[I]ntense debate continues, both within and outside the United Nations, on how effective the existing sanctions regimes have been, whether comprehensive, like those against Iraq, or more targeted, as in the case of [Libya]'.[23]

The Security Council responded to such questioning in its 1999 Presidential Statement on 'its role in the prevention of armed conflicts' by noting that, in

---

[23] UN Doc. A/54/1 (1999), paras. 62 and 125.

imposing 'targeted sanctions, in particular arms embargoes and other enforcement measures', it would in future 'pay special attention to their likely effectiveness in achieving clearly defined objectives, while avoiding negative humanitarian consequences as much as possible'.[24] It did not, however, go further than this, nor did it provide any further indications as to how future policies might change.

QUESTIONS

1. In light of these analyses, do sanctions remain a desirable or even viable option for use by the Security Council in responding to grave violations of human rights?

2. Do you agree with Gordon that attempts to establish criteria for the ethical use of sanctions are likely to do no more than mask the contradictions? Or would you see a need to persevere in efforts to establish both substantive and procedural criteria?

F. AN OVERVIEW OF UN PROCEDURES THROUGH THE LENS OF A SINGLE CASE: EAST TIMOR

For several reasons, the case of East Timor provides an excellent lens through which to gain an understanding of the various techniques and mechanisms used by the United Nations in the human rights area. First, unlike many human rights situations that have erupted in recent years, the UN has been the only major international organizational actor involved. Second, the entire gamut of UN procedures has been invoked, including those not traditionally directly linked to the human rights arena, such as the Security Council, the Special Committee on Decolonization, and the International Court of Justice. Third, it illustrates the current state of the art in various respects. And finally, it constitutes an important benchmark against which the responsiveness of the international community to comparable crises can be measured in the future.

The following materials present a highly selective chronology of key events in the 25 years up to 2000. They then examine excerpts from some of the principal documents detailing the measures taken by the UN. The objective is to facilitate some conclusions as to the strengths and weaknesses of the role played by different actors and as to the broader significance of these developments for the evolving international human rights regime.

[24] UN Doc. S/PRST/1999/34.

COMMENT ON SOME KEY EVENTS IN THE EAST TIMOR CASE IN THE UN[25]

1960—As a Portuguese colony, East Timor first appeared on the international agenda when the UN General Assembly listed it as a Non-Self-Governing Territory.

1974—After the collapse of Portugal's military dictatorship, the new Portuguese government sought to establish in East Timor a provisional government and a popular assembly which would determine the territory's status. Civil war there broke out between forces favouring independence and others advocating integration with Indonesia.

December 1975—Following Portugal's withdrawal, Indonesia intervened militarily. After a disputed act of self-determination involving an assertion of its sovereign independence, East Timor became by force Indonesia's 27th province in July 1976. The UN never recognized this purported act of self-determination, and the Security Council called for Indonesia's withdrawal (Security Council Res. 384 (1975) and 389 (1976)). Indonesia insisted that it enjoyed *de jure* as well as *de facto* sovereignty over the territory. Resistance to Indonesian rule was met in East TImor with a sustained and bloody campaign of repression.

12 November 1991—While the question of East Timor remained on the international agenda, it only regained great prominence after a massacre by Indonesian troops of East Timorese in the Santa Cruz cemetery in Dili, filmed footage of which was flashed around the world.

20 November 1992—The Indonesian army captured Xanana Gusmão, the leader of the East Timorese resistance.

May 1998—The Asian economic crisis, the re-election of President Suharto, and the killing of student demonstrators by troops in Jakarta led to days of rioting in which more than a thousand were killed. Suharto resigned on 21 May 1998 and Habibie became President of Indonesia.

5 May 1999—Amid continuing unrest and efforts by the government to defuse various crises, Indonesia signed a set of agreements with Portugal. The UN was asked to conduct a 'popular consultation' to ascertain whether the people of East Timor favoured autonomy within the framework of remaining part of Indonesia. Following the ballot the UN was to oversee a transition period in which the outcome of the vote would be implemented.

June 1999—The Security Council established the UN Mission in East Timor (UNAMET). It registered 451,792 potential voters among the population of over 800,000.

30 August 1999—98 per cent of those eligible voted. The autonomy proposal was rejected by 78.5 per cent of the voters, underscoring the popular will expressed through the referendum for self-determination in the sense of independence. Pro-integration militias, aided by the Indonesian military, immediately launched a campaign of violence, looting and arson. The Indonesian authorities response was slow and inadequate and hundreds of East Timorese were killed, while hundreds of thousands were displaced, many of whom fled the territory.

---

[25] For access to the key UN documentation, see <www.un.org/peace/etimor/docs>.

15 September 1999—With the agreement of Indonesia, the Security Council authorized a multinational force (INTERFET) under a unified command structure headed by Australia to restore peace and security in East Timor, to protect and support UNAMET, and to facilitate humanitarian assistance operations.

23–27 September 1999—a Session of the UN Commission was convened for the purpose of responding to the situation in East Timor.

19 October 1999—the Indonesian People's Consultative Assembly formally recognized the result of the referendum. Six days later the UN Transitional Administration in East Timor (UNTAET) was established with full responsibility for the territory during its lengthy transition to independence.

January 2000—The report of the UN Commission of Inquiry recommends the creation of an international war crimes tribunal for East Timor if the Indonesian investigation does not produce results within a matter of months.

COMMENT ON UN ACTORS INVOLVED IN THE DISPUTE OVER EAST TIMOR

Against this background, this Comment examines the role played by the various UN organs and mechanisms following the Indonesian takeover in 1975.

Throughout this period, the case was on the agenda of the *Special Committee on Decolonization*, which was set up to review implementation of the landmark Declaration on the Granting of Independence to Colonial Countries and Peoples (GA Res. 1514 (XV) (1960)). The Special Committee met annually to hear governmental, NGO, liberation movement, and other representatives. The matter was also regularly considered by the General Assembly's Fourth Committee (Special Political and Decolonization). The Assembly adopted resolutions on East Timor every year from 1976 to 1982.

The *UN Secretary-General* played a continuous role, although the intensity of his involvement waxed and waned, mainly as a function of the evolving political fortunes of the Indonesian Government. A Security Council resolution, adopted immediately after the Indonesian takeover, asked him to send a special representative to assist in resolution of the dispute. From 1982 onwards, at the General Assembly's request, successive Secretaries-General held regular talks with Indonesia and Portugal aimed at resolving the status of the territory. In February 1992, after the Santa Cruz cemetery massacre, the Secretary-General sent a Personal Envoy to 'obtain clarification on the tragic incident'. Numerous high-level diplomatic meetings were held under the auspices of both the Secretary-General himself and of his Special Representative throughout the 1990s. Prior to the May 1999 Agreements the Secretary-General prepared a detailed Memorandum on Security identifying the steps which were necessary.[26] In August and September 1999 the Secretary-General worked to rally support among Governments for the multinational force subsequently set up by the Security Council on 15 September.

The *International Court of Justice* was also involved in the issue when Portugal brought a case against Australia for having violated the right of the Timorese

[26] UN Doc. S/1999/513.

people to self-determination and permanent sovereignty over natural resources as a result of a 1989 treaty with Indonesia to exploit mineral resources in the area of the continental shelf between East Timor and Australia.[27] The Court's reluctance to take up the issue of self-determination was subsequently much criticized.

The *Sub-Commission on the Promotion and Protection of Human Rights* regularly took up the issue of East Timor. In 1982, for example, it deplored the neglect of the situation and called upon the Commission to act (Sub-Commission Res. 1982/20).

The *Commission on Human Rights* considered the situation in East Timor under all of its various procedures:

    (a) *1503*: Indonesia, including East Timor, was considered under the 1503 procedure during two periods: from 1978 to 1981 and from 1983 to 1985. On neither occasion was any information provided as to the outcome.

    (b) *1235*: The first and only resolution on East Timor was adopted in 1997. Beginning in 1992 a 'Chairperson's Statement' on East Timor was issued almost every year in the name of the Commission.

    (c) *Thematic Mechanisms*: Since 1982 the various mechanisms have frequently focused on East Timor, not as a result of any action by the Commission, but because of the submission of information by governments, NGOs or individuals that prompted a response by the experts in charge of the relevant mechanisms. In addition, on-site visits were undertaken, with the consent of the Indonesian Government, by the mechanisms on torture (1991), arbitrary executions (1994), violence against women (1998) and arbitrary detention (1999).

EXCERPTS TRACING THE PRINCIPAL DEVELOPMENTS IN UN ACTION CONCERNING EAST TIMOR

General Assembly Resolution 37/30, 23 November 1982 on the Question of East Timor

[When reading the following documents, bear in mind their temporal relationship to the preceding chronology of events.]

The General Assembly,

. . .

Having examined the chapter of the report of the Special Committee on [Decolonization] . . .,

Taking note of the report of the Secretary-General on the question of East Timor,

Taking note of resolution 1982/20 adopted by the Sub-Commission . . .,

Having heard the statement[s] of the representative of Portugal, as the administering Power, . . . of Indonesia, . . . of the [FRETILIN] and of various petitioners, as well as of [NGO] representatives . . .,

. . .

Concerned at the humanitarian situation prevailing in the Territory and believing that all efforts should be made by the international community to improve the

---

[27] *Case concerning East Timor (Portugal v. Australia)*, (1995) ICJ Reports 90.

living conditions of the people of East Timor and to guarantee to those people the effective enjoyment of their fundamental human rights,

1. Requests the Secretary-General to initiate consultations with all parties directly concerned, with a view to exploring avenues for achieving a comprehensive settlement of the problem and to report thereon to the General Assembly . . .;

2. Requests the Special Committee on [Decolonization] . . . to keep the situation in the Territory under active consideration . . .;

. . .

Statement by the Chairman of the Commission, UN Doc. E/CN.4/1992/84, para. 457

The Commission on Human Rights notes with serious concern the human rights situation in East Timor.

. . .

The Commission welcomes the early action of the Indonesian Government in setting up a national commission of inquiry . . . .

. . .

The Commission urges the Government of Indonesia to improve the human rights situation in East Timor; commends the report by its Special Rapporteur on the question of torture . . .; urges the Indonesian authorities to take the necessary steps to implement its recommendations . . .; and requests the Secretary-General to continue to follow closely the [situation] . . . .

Situation in East Timor: Report of the Secretary-General, UN Doc. E/CN.4/1993/49

I. Update on the good offices activities of the Secretary-General concerning the question of East Timor

. . .

2. [The Secretary-General's Personal Envoy] Mr. Wako visited Indonesia and East Timor from 9 to 14 February 1992. . . . On 24 March 1992, [his] conclusions and recommendations . . . were transmitted to the Government of Indonesia.

. . .

5. The Secretary-General has repeatedly discussed with the Indonesian Foreign Minister the possibility of dispatching a follow-up mission to Mr. Wako's first visit. While a date for such a visit has not yet been set, Indonesia in principle has accepted the idea and has promised to propose a date.

6. Since the arrest of Mr. Xanana Gusmão near Dili, on 20 November 1992, the Secretary-General has been following the situation of the detained FRETILIN leader. . . .

7. With respect to the search for an overall solution to the question of East Timor, the Secretary-General decided, as a result of his consultations at the highest level with the Governments of Indonesia and Portugal . . . to invite the Foreign

Ministers of the two countries to hold informal consultations under his auspices and without preconditions. . . .

II. Actions taken by Special Rapporteurs and Working Groups of the Commission on Human Rights concerning East Timor

. . .

8. [T]he Working Group on Enforced or Involuntary Disappearances . . . transmitted to the Government of Indonesia a total of 224 cases of disappearances related to the incident at the Santa Cruz cemetery . . . . Among those cases, 17 were transmitted on 10 December 1991 under the Working Group's urgent action procedure. The remaining 207 cases were transmitted by the Working Group on 15 December 1992. The Government of Indonesia informed the Working Group that 8 of the 17 persons . . . were alive and well . . . . [T]he Working Group considered these cases clarified since, after having communicated the reply of the Government to the sources, they did not contest the reply within a period of six months.

. . .

9. [T]he Special Rapporteur on extrajudicial, summary or arbitrary executions . . . [sent urgent messages] to the Government following the Dili incidents, calling on the authorities to investigate them, in conformity with the [relevant UN] Principles . . . and to ensure that those identified as responsible . . . would promptly be brought to justice. [He] also requested information about allegations to the effect that an additional number of persons, including witnesses to the events of 12 November 1991, had subsequently been executed by . . . the Indonesian Army. The Government [sent him] the findings of the National Commission of Inquiry and information on the subsequent prosecution of 10 members of the armed forces. . . .

. . .

11. [T]he Special Rapporteur on the question of torture [reported separately to the Commission] . . . on his visit to Indonesia and East Timor in November 1991 . . . .

12. . . . [He] also sent to the Government two urgent appeals on behalf of Xanana Gusmão . . . .

Annexes

Annex I Information provided by the Indonesian Government

[Details on the report of the Indonesian National Commission of Inquiry and the follow-up were provided.]

. . .

[Copy of a letter of 28 November 1992 from the Indonesian Foreign Minister to the UN Secretary-General]

'Thank you for your letter of 20 November 1992, in which you inquired about the recent arrest of Mr. Xanana Gusmão by the Indonesian security forces.

. . .

'At the present moment he is in safe custody and is being questioned in preparation for his court trial on the basis of the Indonesian criminal code and law on criminal procedures. I should like to assure you that he will be tried in strict accordance with those laws, i.e. in open, public court, and he will be provided with full legal assistance. I should also like to personally assure you of his good health and that he is not being ill-treated in any way.

'As regards access to him by the International Committee of the Red Cross, I am pleased to inform you that such access will be granted in due time in accordance with existing regulations.

(Signed): Ali Alatas[Foreign Minister]

Annex II Information provided by the Portuguese Government

. . .

'The Portuguese Government draws the attention of the international community to the trials of East Timorese arrested during the Santa Cruz massacre in November 1991. These trials are taking place without the minimum requirements of impartiality and legal defence. Two of the defendants have already been sentenced with heavy prison terms. There is a sharp contrast between the sentencing of the victims—who have been accused of engaging in non-violent political activity in favour of the internationally recognized rights of the East Timorese people—and the fact that there was no significant punishment at all for the officers responsible for the terrible violence.

. . .

Portugal protests vehemently against the trial of Xanana Gusmão which, apart from being unlawful, is clearly going to be carried out under circumstances offering no guarantees of impartiality and objectivity. There is a risk that the trial will develop into a sombre farce whose aim is to persuade world opinion that Indonesia's forcible annexation of East Timor is now a fait accompli, sacrificing the legitimate right to self-determination of the Timorese people.'

Annex III Material provided by Non-Governmental Sources

During the period covered by the present report (March 1992 to January 1993) [much] . . . material was provided by international non-governmental organizations, Indonesian human rights groups and groups concerned specifically with human rights in East Timor, based in most cases in Portugal. The Secretariat also received dozens of petitions from people in different countries, calling for the release of political prisoners in East Timor, and in particular the release of Xanana Gusmão.

The following is a summary of the allegations contained in the abovementioned information . . . [A]mong the above-mentioned organizations and groups which have provided the Secretariat with pertinent material during that period, Amnesty International is the only organization to have done so in a consistent and regular manner. . . .

**Comments by the Government of the Republic of Indonesia,
UN Doc. E/CN.4/Sub.2/1994/14/Add.1**

1. On 9 March 1994, at its fiftieth session, the Commission on Human Rights

adopted by consensus a statement by the Chairman on the human rights situation in East Timor.

2. Indonesia appreciates the non-confrontational approach that has led to the consensus regarding the statement. Throughout the process of consultation and negotiation, which has been characterized by goodwill and frankness, the interested delegations, namely the European Union Troika [the past, present and future Presidents of the EU], Portugal and Indonesia, have had opportunities to present cases and clarify points and hence to improve mutual understanding on the overall problem and on the crucial issues involved. . . .

3. The Chairman's statement is a consensus statement, which embodies a package of commitments of the membership of the Commission and all concerned government observers, in particular Portugal. The Government of the Republic of Indonesia is doing its best to respect the consensus, and it would only be fair to expect that all others, including Portugal, will also honour and sincerely observe the statement in its entirety.

4. Indonesia is encouraged by the recognition in the Chairman's statement of the positive measures it has taken . . . .

5. Being a collective expression of the Commission, the Chairman's statement represents a powerful and eloquent rebuttal of the unsubstantiated allegations made by some quarters who still deem fit to paint overdramatized pictures of the human rights situation in East Timor.

. . .

Statement by the Chairman of the Commission, UN Doc. E/CN.4/1995/176, para. 590

. . .

The Commission expresses its deep concern over the continuing reports of violations . . . .

. . .

A matter of preoccupation to the Commission is the incomplete information concerning the number of people killed and the persons still unaccounted for [in the Santa Cruz cemetery incident] . . . .

The Commission recognizes the greater access granted by the Indonesian authorities to East Timor and calls upon them to continue this policy, including the granting of access to human rights and humanitarian organizations and international media.

The Commission welcomes the undertaking of the Government of Indonesia to invite the [HCHR] to visit East Timor in 1995 and to submit his report to the Commission . . . . The Commission further takes note of the intention of the Government . . . to continue to cooperate with the relevant thematic special rapporteurs . . . .

. . . .

Report of the High Commissioner for Human Rights on his visit to Indonesia and East Timor, 3–7 December 1995, UN Doc. E/CN.4/1996/112

. . .

2. [The HCHR] met . . . the President of Indonesia, the Minister for Foreign Affairs, the Defence Minister, the Attorney-General, the Minister for Women's Affairs and the Secretary of the Minister for Welfare, as well as the President and the members of the National Human Rights Commission, and representatives of academic and research centres, non-governmental organizations and the media. The High Commissioner also met Mr. Xanana Gusmão . . . .

. . .

9. The Minister [for Foreign Affairs] appreciated the recognition of the efforts undertaken by his Government, particularly in terms of human rights education. . . . Mr. Alatas stated: 'Our advances in the field of human rights may be perceived as slow but they are certainly deliberate and will continue'.

10. The Minister indicated that he was rather disappointed by certain reports of mechanisms of the Commission, which could be considered as being unbalanced and lacking in objectivity, as well as by the attitude of some NGOs, which would appear to be waging a political campaign against Indonesia. As far as the ratification of human rights conventions was concerned, he said that the national human rights action plan would contain a timetable for ratification, starting with the Convention against Torture. Indonesia had certain difficulties with the two International Covenants, particularly the International Covenant on Civil and Political Rights.

11. The Minister stressed that East Timor was mainly a political problem . . . Responding to the High Commissioner's proposal to establish a United Nations human rights presence in East Timor, he pointed out that there were problems with the opening of a United Nations office in East Timor, but that a human rights presence could be established in Jakarta. The [HCHR] indicated that the staff concerned . . . should also be able to go to East Timor as often as necessary . . . .

. . .

Conclusions

23. The [HCHR] . . . recognized that progress has been made in the field of human rights in Indonesia, most notably through the establishment of the National Human Rights Commission. Furthermore, the Government of Indonesia expressed its determination to further the cooperation with the mechanisms of the Commission on Human Rights and to continue to implement their recommendations. The Government publicly indicated that it would extend invitations to United Nations human rights rapporteurs and working groups 'in due time'.

. . .

25. [The HCHR] publicly stated that there were violations of human rights which had to be corrected. This was particularly true with respect to East Timor.

. . .

27. It was agreed that . . . a human rights presence would be established in

Jakarta within the United Nations office there. The mandate of this human rights presence is currently under negotiation . . . .

. . .

29. The [HCHR] . . . will continue to do all he can for the better promotion and protection of human rights in Indonesia and East Timor. He will . . . recognize progress where progress is achieved and will continue to address the problems of human rights in the most constructive and objective manner, in keeping with his mandate and the effective realization of all human rights.

Observations by Indonesia on the Report of the Visit of [the HCHR], UN Doc. E/CN.4/1996/165, Annex

1. The Government of Indonesia highly values the visit of the High Commissioner . . . .

. . .

3. In general, the draft report is not overly critical. Nevertheless, it goes without saying that, for a report to be credible, it must entail a modicum of objectivity and balance as its foundation.

. . .

6. In conformity with General Assembly resolution 48/141 [establishing the Office of the HCHR], the thrust of the mandate of the [HCHR] is to pursue dialogue and promote cooperation with the Governments of Member States in the promotion and protection of human rights. This vividly demonstrates that this mandate is clearly and distinctly different from those of other United Nations human rights mechanisms and bodies, which are entrusted with purely monitoring tasks. To inject a new idea whereby part of the dialogue between the High Commissioner for Human Rights and the Member States consists of following up on the recommendations made by United Nations human rights mechanisms is a notion which, if not rejected, will compromise the mandate of the High Commissioner and in turn undermine his credibility.

. . .

8. [In relation to the discussion of establishing a UN presence in Jakarta] the intent of the Government of Indonesia is to utilize the technical cooperation and advisory services of the United Nations and not to seek some kind of 'human rights presence', which is factually related to crisis situations such as for example in Rwanda, Burundi or the former Yugoslavia. The fact that there are cases of human rights abuses in Indonesia is very much understood and well taken. However, the Government of Indonesia does not believe that the situation of human rights there warrants the establishment of a 'United Nations human rights presence' or of [a] 'field operation'.

9. The Government of Indonesia has never made any commitment nor has it agreed to the possibility of establishing 'a United Nations human rights presence' in the country in the first place. . . .

. . .

11. The Government of Indonesia remains fully committed to cooperating with

the relevant thematic special rapporteurs and/or working groups of the Commission . . . .

12. Any attempt to link the human rights situation with, and make it a prerequisite of, the resolution of the political question is considered both tenuous and indefensible. . . .

Commission on Human Rights Resolution 1997/63

The Commission on Human Rights,

. . .

2. Expresses its deep concern:

(a) At the continuing reports of violations of human rights in East Timor, including reports of extrajudicial killings, disappearances, torture and arbitrary detention, as contained in the reports of [each of the four relevant thematic mechanisms];

(b) At the lack of progress made by the Indonesian authorities towards complying with their commitments undertaken in statements agreed by consensus at previous sessions of the Commission;

(c) That the Government of Indonesia has not yet invited thematic rapporteurs and working groups of the Commission to East Timor, in spite of commitments undertaken to do so in 1997;

. . .

3. Calls upon the Government of Indonesia:

. . .

(b) To ensure the early release of East Timorese detained or convicted for political reasons . . . ;

(c) To ensure that all East Timorese in custody are treated humanely and in accordance with international standards, and that all trials in East Timor are conducted in accordance with international standards;

. . .

(f) To bring about the envisaged assignment of [an OHCHR] programme officer . . . to the Jakarta office of the [UNDP], as follow-up to the commitment undertaken, and to provide this officer with unhindered access to East Timor;

(g) To provide access to East Timor for human rights organizations.

4. Decides:

(a) To consider the situation in East Timor [in 1998] . . . on the basis of the reports of special rapporteurs and working groups and that of the Secretary-General;

(b) To encourage the Secretary-General to continue his good-offices mission . . . .

[Adopted by a roll-call vote of 20 votes to 14, with 18 abstentions.]

Report of the Working Group on Arbitrary Detention on its visit to Indonesia (31 January–12 February 1999), UN Doc. E/CN.4/2000/4/Add.2

[The Group had sought an invitation to visit Indonesia, and especially East Timor, since 1993. An invitation was part of the package reflected in the Commission Chairperson's Statement in 1998. Its recommendations included: (1) to 'intensify, on a non-discriminatory basis, measures consistent with the current policy of releasing all political prisoners'; (2) to 'reinforce the independence of the police'; (3) to 'reinforce the independence of the judges'; (4) 'information and education efforts should be intensified . . . . Priority should be given to: A campaign to sensitize lawyers, NGOs, prosecutors and judges to the procedure of habeas corpus'; (5) 'reform of the Code of Criminal Procedure'; (6) 'creation of a central detention register'; (7) 'legislation should be drafted and enacted promptly which would guarantee the independence of all activities of the' National Commission for Human Rights; (8) 'all emergency laws and measures should be abrogated'; (9) the competence of military tribunals 'should be limited strictly to offences committed under the Code of Military Justice by military personnel'; and (10) the Government should take initiatives to inform detained individuals of their rights and progressively put into place an effective legal aid system'.]

Statement by the Chairperson, 23 April 1999, UN Doc. E/1999/23, para. 243

The Commission on Human Rights, . . . expresses its deep concern at the serious human rights situation and at the outbreaks of violence in East Timor . . . .

The Commission takes into account that the talks under the auspices of the United Nations Secretary-General aimed at achieving a just, comprehensive and internationally acceptable solution to the question of East Timor taking place in New York are now at a crucial stage.

The Commission requests the Secretary-General to submit a report on the human rights situation in East Timor to it [in 2000].

Amnesty International Statement, AI Doc. IOR 41/07/99 23 April 1999

[T]he Commission failed to address the dramatic human rights situation in East Timor . . . . As talks on autonomy—with human rights conspicuously absent from the agenda—are taking place in New York, Commission members have proved unable to face up to the situation and to remind the Indonesian government of its responsibilities.

Security Council Resolution 1246 (11 June 1999)

The Security Council,

. . .

Noting with concern the assessment of the Secretary-General . . . that the security situation in East Timor remains 'extremely tense and volatile',

. . .

1. Decides to establish until 31 August 1999 the United Nations Mission in East Timor (UNAMET) to organize and conduct a popular consultation . . . ;

2. Authorizes until 31 August 1999 the deployment within UNAMET of up to 280 civilian police officers to act as advisers to the Indonesian Police in the discharge of their duties and, at the time of the consultation, to supervise the escort of ballot papers and boxes to and from the polling sites;

3. Authorizes until 31 August 1999 the deployment within UNAMET of 50 military liaison officers to maintain contact with the Indonesian Armed Forces . . . ;

4. Endorses the Secretary-General's proposal that UNAMET should also incorporate the following components:

> (a) a political component responsible for monitoring the fairness of the political environment, for ensuring the freedom of all political and other non-governmental organizations to carry out their activities freely and for monitoring and advising the Special Representative on all matters with political implications,
>
> (b) an electoral component responsible for all activities related to registration and voting,
>
> (c) an information component responsible for explaining to the East Timorese people, in an objective and impartial manner without prejudice to any position or outcome, the terms of the General Agreement and the proposed autonomy framework, for providing information on the process and procedure of the vote and for explaining the implications of a vote in favour or against the proposal.

[Eds. The Security Council (UN Doc. S/1999/972, 6 September 1999) decided to send a mission to Jakarta and East Timor composed of five senior New York-based diplomats. Except for the goal of pressing the government 'to ensure security and allow UNAMET to implement its mandate without hindrance', its terms of reference were vague and open-ended. The government's agreement to a multinational force was given on the day the mission concluded its visit.]

Letter [of 9 September 1999 from Portugal to the HCHR],
UN Doc. E/CN.4/S-4/21 September 1999

As you know, the situation in East Timor in the wake of the results of the referendum has developed dramatically, and the Timorese people, lacking any kind of protection, are now being systematically persecuted in what can only be defined as ethnic cleansing.

Principal responsibility for United Nations action in East Timor of course remains with the Security Council, and Portugal has indicated its support for an expanded effort by the Council. Nevertheless, Portugal believes effective action to prevent further human rights violations must be a central element of the overall United Nations response to the tragedy in East Timor.

Having this in mind, as well as the competence of the Commission on Human

Rights as the body with the main responsibility in addressing human rights violations in the United Nations system, Portugal requests the convening of a special session of the Commission.

My country has already started démarches with the States members of the Commission with a view to rallying support for the convening of the special session. We highly appreciate the efforts you have undertaken in the defence of the Timorese people and we ask for your support in promoting this special session.

Security Council Resolution 1264 (15 September 1999)

The Security Council,

. . .

Reiterating its welcome for the successful conduct of the popular consultation . . . ,

Deeply concerned by the deterioration of the security situation in East Timor . . .

. . .

Deeply concerned also at the attacks on the staff and premises of the United Nations Mission in East Timor (UNAMET) . . . ,

. . .

Appalled by the worsening humanitarian situation in East Timor, particularly as it affects women, children and other vulnerable groups,

Reaffirming respect for the sovereignty and territorial integrity of Indonesia,

Expressing its concern at reports indicating that systematic, widespread and flagrant violations of international humanitarian and human rights law have been committed in East Timor, and stressing that persons committing such violations bear individual responsibility,

Determining that the present situation in East Timor constitutes a threat to peace and security,

Acting under Chapter VII of the Charter of the United Nations,

1. Condemns all acts of violence in East Timor, calls for their immediate end and demands that those responsible for such acts be brought to justice;

. . .

3. Authorizes the establishment of a multinational force under a unified command structure, pursuant to the request of the Government of Indonesia conveyed to the Secretary-General on 12 September 1999, with the following tasks: to restore peace and security in East Timor, to protect and support UNAMET in carrying out its tasks and, within force capabilities, to facilitate humanitarian assistance operations, and authorizes the States participating in the multinational force to take all necessary measures to fulfil this mandate;

4. Welcomes the expressed commitment of the Government of Indonesia to cooperate with the multinational force . . . ;

. . .

9. Stresses that the expenses for the force will be borne by the participating Member States concerned and requests the Secretary-General to establish a trust fund through which contributions could be channelled to the States or operations concerned;

10. Agrees that the multinational force should collectively be deployed in East Timor until replaced as soon as possible by a United Nations peacekeeping operation. . . .

Security Council Resolution 1272 (25 Oct. 1999)

. . .

Determining that the continuing situation in East Timor constitutes a threat to peace and security,

Acting under Chapter VII of the Charter of the United Nations,

1. Decides to establish, in accordance with the report of the Secretary-General, a United Nations Transitional Administration in East Timor (UNTAET), which will be endowed with overall responsibility for the administration of East Timor and will be empowered to exercise all legislative and executive authority, including the administration of justice;

2. Decides also that the mandate of UNTAET shall consist of the following elements:

  (a) To provide security and maintain law and order throughout the territory of East Timor;
  (b) To establish an effective administration;
  (c) To assist in the development of civil and social services;
  (d) To ensure the coordination and delivery of humanitarian assistance, rehabilitation and development assistance;
  (e) To support capacity-building for self-government;
  (f) To assist in the establishment of conditions for sustainable development;

. . .

4. Authorizes UNTAET to take all necessary measures to fulfil its mandate;

. . .

6. Welcomes the intention of the Secretary-General to appoint a Special Representative who, as the Transitional Administrator, will be responsible for all aspects of the United Nations work in East Timor and will have the power to enact new laws and regulations and to amend, suspend or repeal existing ones;

. . .

8. Stresses the need for UNTAET to consult and cooperate closely with the East Timorese people in order to carry out its mandate effectively with a view to the development of local democratic institutions, including an independent East Timorese human rights institution, and the transfer to these institutions of its administrative and public service functions;

. . .

10. Reiterates the urgent need for coordinated humanitarian and reconstruction assistance, and calls upon all parties to cooperate with humanitarian and human rights organizations so as to ensure their safety, the protection of civilians, in particular children, the safe return of refugees and displaced persons and the effective delivery of humanitarian aid;

. . .

15. Underlines the importance of including in UNTAET personnel with appropriate training in international humanitarian, human rights and refugee law, including child and gender-related provisions, negotiation and communication skills, cultural awareness and civilian-military coordination;

16. Condemns all violence and acts in support of violence in East Timor, calls for their immediate end, and demands that those responsible for such violence be brought to justice;

. . .

Report of the United Nations High Commissioner for Human Rights 1999, UN Doc. A/54/36

East Timor

. . .

17. In response to the deteriorating human rights situation, the High Commissioner urged the Commission on Human Rights to consider holding a special session on the situation. From 11 to 13 September, she visited the area to carry out a first-hand assessment of the human rights situation in East Timor. In Darwin, Australia, the High Commissioner met East Timorese refugees and the staff of UNAMET who had been evacuated from the territory. In Jakarta, the High Commissioner met the President of Indonesia and the East Timorese leader Xanana Gusmão. (Unedited version)

Report of the High Commissioner for Human Rights on the Human Rights Situation in East Timor, UN Doc. E/CN.4/S-4/1999

. . .

4. It has become a widely accepted principle of contemporary international law and practice that wherever human rights are being grossly violated, the international community has a duty to do its utmost, as a matter of the greatest urgency, to help provide protection to those at risk; that the international community should help bring relief and assistance to those in need; that the facts must be gathered with a view to throwing light on what has taken place and with a view to bringing those responsible to justice; and that the perpetrators of gross violations must be rendered accountable and justice rendered to the victims. . . .

5. In a number of recent cases of gross violations of human rights and humanitarian law during internal or international armed conflicts, the various institutions of the United Nations and of regional organizations have sought to comply with these responsibilities and to act in tandem to respond to the situation. The cases of Angola, Rwanda, Democratic Republic of Congo, Kosovo, and Sierra Leone provide examples. . . .

. . .

IV. Conclusion

47. There is overwhelming evidence that East Timor has seen a deliberate,

vicious and systematic campaign of gross violations of human rights. I condemn those responsible in the strongest possible terms.

48. I have urged the Indonesian authorities to cooperate in the establishment of an international commission of inquiry into the violations so that those responsible are brought to justice. To end the century and the millennium tolerating impunity for those guilty of these shocking violations would be a betrayal of everything the United Nations stands for regarding the universal promotion and protection of human rights.

49. It is my intention to remain in contact with the Indonesian authorities on the establishment of an international commission of inquiry. As we have seen recently in a number of situations, the establishment of international commissions of inquiry into massive violations of human rights and humanitarian law is increasingly becoming standard practice—and even imperative. If needed, I am ready to take the initiative in launching such an international commission.

. . .

1999 Fourth Special Session of the UN Commission, Summary Record of the 2nd Meeting, 24 September 1999, UN Doc. E/CN.4/S-4/SR.2 (1999)

Chairperson: Ms. ANDERSON (Ireland)

1. Mr. ROWAN (Ireland) . . . The international community should use all the means at its disposal . . . . [T]he special session would bring a distinctive perspective to bear on the issue and augment and inform the discussions of the Security Council and the General Assembly.

. . .

12. [Mr. MORJANE (Tunisia)] The African Group considered that the special session should avoid confrontation and arrive at a negotiated and agreed outcome, in a spirit of cooperation and mutual understanding, since in that way the Commission would make an effective contribution to the desired reconciliation.

13. Lastly, the African Group found it regrettable that the international community continued to apply double standards in dealing with major issues, paying greater attention to some regions than to others.

. . .

17. Mr. MIRGHANI (Sudan) said that Sudan had had serious reservations concerning the special session . . . because . . . its objectives were not clear, given that both the Security Council and the General Assembly were considering or planning to consider the situation in East Timor.

. . .

20. [Mr. VOTO BERNALES (Peru)] The gravity of the situation in East Timor was compounded by the fact that the violence had flared up in reaction to the East Timorese people's exercise of their sovereign right to self-determination . . . . [T]here was no contradiction between the Security Council's provision for peacekeeping operations under the Charter of the United Nations and the Commission's duty to act within its own sphere of competence, namely human rights. . . . The fact that the Indonesian Government had requested the international force

added an element of consensus that would strengthen the moral force and legal coherence of that action. . . .

25. [Mr. MOOSE (United States)] The United States . . . welcomed the Indonesian Government's decision to set up a national commission of inquiry, but stressed that it was indispensable to have the backing of a credible international investigative mechanism. It would also be desirable to have the collaboration of the Indonesian Human Rights Commission, appropriate local non-governmental organizations (NGOs) and distinguished jurists of the region.

. . .

27. [T]he United States expected the Indonesian Government to honour its obligations, in keeping with national and international law, to protect East Timorese refugees and those forcibly displaced to West Timor, to disband and disarm the militias which threatened human life, to allow humanitarian organizations to have access to persons in need of assistance in West Timor, to facilitate the safe and speedy return of East Timorese to their homes and to cooperate in enabling the return of UNAMET staff and the resumption of their mission. . . .

. . .

41. [Mr. SALAMA (Egypt)] [A]ny recommendation ensuing from the session should be guided by specific criteria. [1] Any measures recommended should supplement domestic measures rather than replace them . . . . [2] Measures should be technical and not political in nature . . . . [3] It was essential for the Commission to employ existing mechanisms in order to strengthen human rights. [4] Human rights institutions should act without encroaching on other spheres of competence, so as to strengthen their credibility and avoid them being accused of politicization . . .

. . .

58. Mr. RAJA NUSHIRWAN (Malaysia) said his delegation fully associated itself with the statements made by Sri Lanka on behalf of the Asian Group and by the Philippines on behalf of the Association of South-East Asian Nations (ASEAN). Given the close, brotherly relations between Malaysia and Indonesia, the Malaysian Government felt compelled to speak as a concerned party.

59. The subject of East Timor had been dealt with comprehensively and usefully in the Security Council, and because the Indonesian Government had expressed its willingness to cooperate with that body, the matter would best be left there. Indonesia had demonstrated its willingness to work with various United Nations bodies, including those dealing with human rights, in addition to its commitment to domestic reform. Further insistence by the international community could only be counter-productive. In addressing the situation in East Timor, the international community must bear in mind its effect on regional stability and security, its impact on the democratic reforms under way in Indonesia and the views of the region concerned. . . . The outcome of the consultation must take into full consideration the views of the Indonesian Government, must be agreed by it and must respect the territorial integrity of that country.

61. Mr. [Bishop] BELO (Franciscans International) said that speaking as the apostolic administrator of the diocese of Dili, he wished to thank the Commission for its expression of solidarity with the people of East Timor.

62. Following the 30 August referendum, the militias and the military had immediately taken revenge on the population, after it had voted massively in favour of self-determination. In one such act of revenge, on 5 September 1999, his diocesan office housing displaced persons had been attacked and destroyed and 25 persons had been killed. The next day, his episcopal residence in Dili, in which some 4,000 persons had taken refuge, was attacked and destroyed by the militias and the army. . . .

64. Mr. ZOLLER (International Service for Human Rights) said that his organization was appalled by the debate . . . . Had the testimonies which NGOs had given to the Commission since 1982 been taken seriously, giving rise to effective and serious preventive measures, many lives would surely have been saved. The Indonesian Government had for years taken advantage of its position as a member of the Commission to deny the existence of concentration camps, to refute reports of massacres, to ignore its latest commitments and to repeat its lies, while the Commission itself had sought a consensus with the very people responsible for those crimes. . . .

Summary Record of the 5th Meeting, 27 September 1999, UN Doc. E/CN.4/S-4/SR.5 (1999)

. . .

7. Mr. WIRAJUDA (Indonesia) said that his Government questioned the legality and merit of holding the present special session . . .
. . .

9. Indonesian concern at human rights violations had prompted his Government to establish an independent Fact-Finding Commission [whose] . . . work would be open to international participation . . . The Indonesian Government was also considering the establishment of a Special Court for Human Rights within its criminal court system.

10. Furthermore, the magnitude of the human rights problems in East Timor needed to be placed in proportion. It was by no means certain that mass killings had occurred. His delegation appealed to all sides to refrain from introducing inflammatory rhetoric into the debate.

11. Paragraph 6 of [the] draft resolution . . . called upon the Secretary-General to establish an international commission of inquiry . . . . The Indonesian Government believed that the establishment of such a commission would in fact exacerbate the problems in East Timor. . . . It was important to go beyond political point-scoring and trying to look heroic in the eyes of domestic constituencies. There existed more effective and politically sensitive ways to secure accountability for human rights violations. In the case of Rwanda, for example, a Special Rapporteur had been appointed. The establishment of a Fact-Finding Commission by the Indonesian Government was therefore an appropriate response in the circumstances.

12. When discussing the issue of East Timor, the international community should also be aware of the extremely sensitive political transformation which was currently taking place in Indonesia. A high-handed, self-righteous and

blatantly intrusive approach could provoke a strong nationalist backlash in the country.

. . .

23. [Mr. KATSURA (Japan)] The draft resolution currently before the Commission did not enjoy wide support in the Asian region. In such circumstances, Japan had no choice but to abstain in the voting. It was also regrettable that the special session had been convened without wide support from Asian countries. . . .

. . .

27. At the request of the representative of Indonesia, a vote was taken by roll-call on the draft resolution.

. . .

In favour: Argentina, Austria, Canada, Cape Verde, Chile, Colombia, Congo, Czech Republic, Democratic Republic of the Congo, Ecuador, El Salvador, France, Germany, Guatemala, Ireland, Italy, Latvia, Luxembourg, Madagascar, Mauritius, Mexico, Mozambique, Norway, Peru, Poland, Romania, Rwanda, South Africa, United Kingdom . . ., United States of America, Uruguay, Venezuela.

Against: Bangladesh, Bhutan, China, India, Indonesia, Nepal, Pakistan, Philippines, Qatar, Russian Federation, Sri Lanka, Sudan.

Abstaining: Cuba, Japan, Morocco, Republic of Korea, Senegal, Tunisia.

29. The draft resolution was adopted by 32 votes to 12, with 6 abstentions.

. . .

31. Mr. WIRAJUDA (Indonesia) said that the convening of the special session and the substance of the resolution just adopted [see *infra*] had both been highly controversial. The moral authority of the Commission had been diminished. Indonesia had voted against the inclusion of paragraph 6 and the resolution as a whole, and hence neither decision was binding on his Government.

32. Mr. LIU Xinsheng (China) . . . . Article 12 of the Charter stated that, while the Security Council was exercising in respect of any dispute or situation the functions assigned to it in the Charter, the General Assembly must not make any recommendation with regard to that dispute or situation unless the Security Council so requested. The Security Council had already adopted a resolution mandating a multinational peacekeeping force to join Indonesian forces in East Timor with a view to guaranteeing peace and security in the region. China therefore believed that it was unduly precipitate to establish an international commission of inquiry. Such a commission would do nothing to solve the problem of East Timor. Moreover, it would constitute a serious violation of the Charter.

Commission on Human Rights Resolution 1999/S–4/1, UN Doc. E/CN.4/1999/167/Add.1

The Commission on Human Rights,

. . .

Recalling Security Council resolution 1264 (1999) [p. 685, *supra*] . . .,

Recalling also its previous resolutions and statements . . .,

Deeply concerned by the report of the [HCHR] and the information provided by the United Nations High Commissioner for Refugees and non-governmental organizations . . . ,

   1. Welcomes:

   (a) The decision of the Government of Indonesia to allow the exercise by the East Timorese of their right of self-determination . . . as well as [its] announcement . . . of its intention to honour and accept the result of the popular consultation;

   . . .

   (c) The invitation by the Government of Indonesia of an international force . . .;

   (d) The efforts of the United Nations High Commissioner for Human Rights in addressing the situation, including her visit to Darwin and Jakarta;

   (e) The assurances given by the Indonesian authorities that the displaced persons have the freedom to exercise their right to return voluntarily . . .;

   (f) The humanitarian response to the current crisis;

   (g) The establishment on 22 September 1999 of the independent [Indonesian] Fact-Finding Commission . . . and looks forward to the concrete results of its work in close cooperation with international bodies;

   2. Condemns [the widespread and gross violations of human rights, and activities of the militias in terrorizing the population];

   . . .

   3. Expresses its deep concern [at forced dislocations of East Timorese and violence against international agencies and media];

   . . .

   (d) At the lack of effective measures to deter or prevent militia violence and the reported collusion between the militias and members of the Indonesian armed forces and police in East Timor;

   4. Affirms that all persons who commit or authorize violations of human rights or international humanitarian law are individually responsible and accountable for those violations and that the international community will exert every effort to ensure that those responsible are brought to justice, while affirming that the primary responsibility for bringing perpetrators to justice rests with national judicial systems;

   5. Calls upon the Government of Indonesia:

   (a) To ensure, in cooperation with the Indonesian National Commission on Human Rights, that the persons responsible for acts of violence and flagrant and systematic violations of human rights are brought to justice;

   . . .

   6. Calls upon the Secretary-General to establish an international commission of inquiry, with adequate representation of Asian experts, in order, in cooperation with the Indonesian National Commission on Human Rights and thematic rapporteurs, to gather and compile systematically information on possible violations

of human rights and acts which may constitute breaches of international humanitarian law committed in East Timor since the announcement in January 1999 of the vote and to provide the Secretary-General with its conclusions with a view to enabling him to make recommendations on future actions, and to make the report of the international commission of inquiry available to the Security Council, the General Assembly and the Commission at its fifty-sixth session;

7. Decides:

    (a) To request the [thematic mechanisms on arbitrary executions, internally displaced persons, torture, violence against women, and disappearances] to carry out missions to East Timor and report on their findings to the Commission . . . ;

. . .

    (d) To request the High Commissioner to keep the Commission informed of developments.

[The Report of the Commission of Inquiry called for by the Commission on Human Rights is in UN Doc. 5/2000/59 (www.unhchr.org). Although the Report recommended the establishment of an 'international human rights tribunal', the Security Council has not acted, pending the outcome of the domestic prosecutions.]

QUESTIONS

1. While the Commission was very slow to take up the matter, the Sub-Commission played a catalytic role in 1982. Eventually the Assembly took the lead and relied mainly upon the Secretary-General. The role of the latter, and of the HCHR, were particularly significant. How would you characterize their involvement on a scale from low key/ineffectual to pushing the margins? Why can the HCHR do better than the Commission? Why in other respects not as well?

2. The Commission issued a 'Chairperson's Statement' almost every year in the 1990s. Like a resolution, it represented the outcome of detailed and protracted negotiations and in substance came increasingly to resemble a resolution. While no special procedure *per se* was activated, the reports which the Secretary-General was asked to prepare annually provided an important context in which to review developments, including the information provided by a wide range of NGO and other sources. Such reports also provided one of the backdrops against which the following Commission debate would take place. Note that the 'Statements' were usually a carefully balanced mixture of carrot and stick. Note Indonesia's attempt to put a favorable gloss on the Statement in 1994. Is the weakness of the 1999 Statement (p. 683, *supra*) justified in the circumstances?

3. How do you see the role played by the thematic mechanisms? Does overlapping or duplication seem to be a problem?

4. How much of the action taken by the Commission and Council involved human rights issues?

5. How do you explain the Asian regional coolness or hostility to these UN actions? Do you suspect that regional groups will always seek to protect one among them?

6. How would you describe the degree of cooperation shown by the Indonesian Government over the years? If it changed, why?

7. Note the significance attached by both sides to the establishment of a 'field presence' in Jakarta. Why is this issue so important?

8. Evaluate the role of the Security Council, and the ways in which the East Timor case could be considered to set important, novel precedents. What sort of precedent might that constitute for the future? To what extent do you believe it is now fair to say that human rights has become an integral component of the UN's overall approach as reflected in Resolution 1272?

9. What were the main reservations expressed by the relevant states during the Commission's Special Session? Note the ability of key actors, such as Dili's Bishop Belo, to participate.

10. How do you assess the entire process? Do you agree with the views of Zoller, p. 690, *supra*?

G. REFORM AND EVALUATION

A major issue arising from this Chapter is whether it is possible to eliminate some of the duplication among different procedures, and more broadly to re-design the architecture of the United Nations human rights regime as a whole. The reasons for some of the duplication have been explained in the following terms:

> . . . The system has grown 'like Topsy' and the boundaries between the different organs are often only poorly delineated. For the most part, this pattern has hardly been accidental. Rather, it is the inevitable result of a variety of actors seeking to achieve diverse, and perhaps sometimes even irreconcilable, objectives within the same overall institutional framework. If an existing body could not do a particular job, whether because of some intrinsic defects, sheer incompetence, or, more likely, political intransigence, the preferred response was to set up yet another. In a very short space of time States and individual actors would develop a vested interest in the maintenance of the new body in the same form. This pattern simply repeated itself when a new policy agenda, to which none of the existing bodies was sufficiently responsive, emerged.
>
> In general then, the evolution of the regime has reflected specific political developments. Its expansion has depended upon the effective exploitation of the opportunities which have arisen in any given situation from the prevailing mix

of public pressures, the cohesiveness or disarray of the key geopolitical blocks, the power and number of the offending state(s) and the international standing of their current governments, and a variety of other, often rather specific and ephemeral, factors. . . . [28]

Since the 1993 World Conference on Human Rights at Vienna, attempts have been made to reduce overlapping institutional competences. In 1998–99 a renewed push was made within the Commission on Human Rights to achieve reforms, but the outcome achieved in 2000 (CHR Decision 2000/109) reflected relatively minor adjustments to the existing arrangements. The proposals put forward do, however, offer useful insights into the concerns of different actors about such efforts.

HUMAN RIGHTS WATCH, HUMAN RIGHTS MECHANISMS UNDER ATTACK
HR/97/88, 16 December 1997

Human rights mechanisms of the United Nations have recently found themselves under threat from some U.N. member states which want to see them weakened and marginalized. . . .

. . .

[The various UN special procedures] add up to an increasingly effective and professional human rights system, capable of causing a considerable amount of discomfort and embarrassment for abusive governments and offering targeted recommendations that rallied the support of Commission members. Recently, however, many of these same abusive governments have taken steps aimed at weakening this machinery. . . . First, they have competed for election to the Commission, where they form powerful voting blocs. When their numbers could not collectively block attention to their abuses, they have made prodigious efforts to keep the human rights mechanisms of the UN weak, marginalized, distracted and ineffective, and to keep the information from reaching the public on a timely basis when it could still stop or prevent violations, or even from being disclosed at all.

In one procedural trick after another, the abuser-governments have tried to limit what can be investigated, where and how investigations are undertaken, and who receives the results. They have also sought to delay public reporting of findings, downgrade the relevance of conclusions reached by experts, and raise domestic law as a shield against intrusions by international human rights standards, another way of challenging the universality of human rights. The language used is often artful or even appealing on its surface, such as the call to 'rationalize' procedures and 'reduce duplication', or to be 'non-selective'. But the aim is simply to ensure that the UN does not develop the capacity to investigate, report publicly or respond effectively to stop violations.

For example, [two proposals have been made] . . . . The first one stipulates,

---

[28] Philip Alston, 'Appraising The United Nations Human Rights Regime', in P. Alston (ed.), *The United Nations and Human Rights: A Critical Appraisal* (1992), at 1, 2.

among other things, that when rapporteurs, representatives and working groups travel to a country, they should 'refrain from giving media publicity to their findings until these have been considered and deliberated upon by the Commission'. The effect would be to delay media coverage and resulting human rights pressure for up to a year, and often undermine that pressure altogether. . . . The second one would establish a thorough overall review of the Special Procedures and an open-ended working group that would elaborate specific proposals for rationalization of Special Procedures . . . .

In addition to these disturbing trends, there has also been an attempt to force the Commission to operate almost exclusively by consensus—a restriction which would severely limit its capacity and strength. Consensus, while useful in many other areas of U.N. activities, when applied to human rights issues usually means giving a veto power to the most abusive governments. It would also mean that there would be few if any country-specific resolutions at the Commission in the future and hence, few country-specific special rapporteur or country investigations.

. . .

REPORT OF THE BUREAU [ON] RATIONALIZATION OF THE WORK OF THE COMMISSION
UN Doc. E/CN.4/1999/104

[The Bureau of the Commission consists of the Chairperson, three vice-Chairpersons, and a Rapporteur, elected annually. It plays some role between the Commission's annual sessions, including preparation of these reform proposals.]

Executive Summary[29]

. . . [Reform] should be approached in dispassionate, technical terms, by organizing and managing the Commission's mechanisms on the basis of the highest standards of objectivity and professionalism, as free as possible of extraneous political influences; but it also requires political will, for the effectiveness of Commission mechanisms ultimately rests on the responsibility of all Governments to cooperate fully with them.

. . .

The special procedures have been one of the Commission's major achievements . . ., and should accordingly be preserved, strengthened, and provided all necessary support and cooperation.

In selecting mandates:

— There is some scope for rationalizing and strengthening the current network of thematic mechanisms

— The Commission also needs the capability to create appropriate country-specific mechanisms. . . . The Commission should also make

---

[29] [Eds]: Cross-references within the report have been eliminated.

full use of information and advice from its thematic mechanisms and other United Nations human rights institutions. More in-depth future consideration should be given to the appropriateness and possibilities of establishing additional or alternative procedures for initiating country-specific proceedings.

Regarding the roles and tasks of special procedures:

— The mandate of each mechanism can only be decided case-by-case in light of the requirements of the situation, but . . . objective monitoring and fact-finding . . . are an essential starting point and sine qua non for the work of the special procedures.
— The vital urgent appeals process should be strongly supported by OHCHR, and the Chair of the Commission should assist when necessary in securing governmental responses.
— Special procedures must also observe the Commission's guidance on cross-cutting issues, and need effective backing in this regard from OHCHR.

In selecting officeholders and setting their basic terms and conditions, the paramount considerations should be personal and technical qualifications, and the independence, objectivity and overall integrity of the mechanisms. With this in mind, it is suggested, inter alia:

— That appointments generally be made by the Commission's Chair assisted by a roster maintained by OHCHR;

. . .

— That the Secretary-General expedite work on an appropriate code of conduct;
— That measures be taken to ensure effective and timely compensation and administrative support of special procedures.

The effective discharge of the mandates of the special procedures mandates turns largely on their ability to work effectively with a range of actors. Key in this regard is the application and development of best practices, which should be reflected in the manual for special procedures mechanisms. Concerning the special procedures:

— In relation to non-governmental actors (media, NGOs, individuals, alleged victims of human rights violations), there is need for: grass-roots awareness about special procedures; protection against adverse consequences for dealings with special procedures; appropriate information verification efforts; and systematic acknowledgement of receipt of communications.
— Governments are encouraged to respond positively to requests from mechanisms to conduct missions when so requested, and to guarantee

the conditions necessary to ensure an effective visit. The Commission should conduct regular, focused and systematic reviews of serious incidents or situations involving a failure or denial of cooperation by Governments. . . .

— In dealings among special procedures and with other United Nations and international entities, every possible measure should be taken to strengthen and expand the exchange of information and coordination of activities. . . .

There is a crucial need for more timely, user-friendly special procedure reports. To this end, the report recommends:

. . .

— Preparation of structured executive summaries reflecting the key elements for the Commission's consideration . . .

There is an urgent need for more serious, focused and systematic utilization and follow up of the reports of special procedures, their recommendations and related Commission conclusions. With this in mind:

— The Commission should conduct a structured dialogue on each mechanism's report, organized around the elements of the executive summaries, and with the Governments concerned afforded full opportunity to explain their positions.

— A mid-cycle report on implementation and follow-up should be issued each fall, providing the focus for special Bureau review meetings to conduct dialogues with concerned Governments and consider how to assist in advancing the follow-through process.

— Every appropriate effort should be made to ensure effective dissemination of the results of the work of the special procedures, another principal responsibility of the High Commissioner.

. . .

COMMENTS ON THE REPORT OF THE BUREAU BY THE DELEGATIONS OF SEVERAL STATES[30]
UN Doc. E/CN.4/1999/WG.19/2

. . .

A. General comments

5. Ideally, the review process should have been a technical exercise aimed at enhancing the effectiveness of the mechanisms of the Commission on Human Rights by ensuring that they observe the ideals of objectivity, impartiality, univer-

---

[30] Algeria, Bhutan, China, Cuba, Egypt, India, the Islamic Republic of Iran, Malaysia, Myanmar, Nepal, Pakistan, Sri Lanka, the Sudan and Vietnam.

sality and depoliticization, as well as the indivisibility of all rights. However, the Bureau's overall approach has been to equate effectiveness exclusively with enhanced monitoring and compliance. For the Bureau, the right to raise country situations must remain sacrosanct. Further, under the Bureau's proposals, every mechanism will be utilized to monitor country situations. . . .

6. The Bureau . . . has failed to address the concern among developing countries regarding growing politicization, double standards and selectivity and the need to ensure that no country be allowed to use human rights to achieve political or any other non-human rights related objectives.

7. The 'effectiveness' of the Commission on Human Rights and its mechanisms is not derived from their capacity to coerce or pressurize countries through a narrow focus on monitoring and finger-pointing. It is a function of their capacity to engender confidence and cooperation through the identification of approaches that eschew politicization and selectivity, assist in the identification of solutions and facilitate the effective enjoyment of human rights at the grass-roots levels, particularly through building and strengthening national capacities. It should be recognized, in this regard, that enlarging and strengthening the role of the monitoring mechanisms of the Commission on Human Rights, expanding the scope of discussions on country situations and using the Commission on Human Rights and its Bureau as tools for forcing States to cooperate with human rights mechanisms are unlikely to genuinely promote the effectiveness of the Commission on Human Rights.

. . .

13. Moreover, there is also no reflection of 'particularities', as contained in the Vienna document which recognized 'the significance of national and regional particularities and various historical, cultural and religious backgrounds'. It appears from the report that it is intended to treat all countries alike, irrespective of their levels of development and their religious and cultural orientations.

14. The problem of non-cooperation of States with mechanisms cannot be simply reduced to a lack of political will. For the vast majority of States, cooperation with and acceptance of the mechanisms depend on objective elements, such as the sensitivity of the mechanisms to the specificities of the State concerned, their usefulness in addressing the problems encountered, as well as the level of encouragement that they can provide for progressive steps in the promotion and protection of human rights. It is in this connection that a code of conduct for the mechanisms becomes relevant and essential.

15. . . . Clearly, it is the Commission on Human Rights and not the United Nations Secretary-General who should determine the code of conduct for mechanisms and evaluate their performance on a regular basis.

. . .

18. According to the report, regional groups are one of the main causes of politicization and the North-South divide in the work of the Commission. It must be pointed out, however, that politicization is not the result of developing countries coalescing along regional lines. Rather, the principle of regionalism is regularly used by one regional group as a means of pointing fingers at others.

19. The report also attempts to give the High Commissioner and the secretariat

an intrusive monitoring capacity, to the extent of suggesting that the High Commissioner may be one of the initiators of the Commission's country specific decisions. Such recommendations will only bring to naught efforts to increase cooperation and decrease politicization among States.

. . .

C. Vision for the future

94. The turn of the century is an appropriate time to discard the cold-war mentality and further reflect on what should be the guiding principles of our future work in the field of human rights for the sake of their better protection and promotion. . . .

[What follows is a summary of the proposals of these states, which is also taken from the original document.]

. . .

(b) Need to strike a balance between collective and individual rights—civil and political as well as economic, social and cultural rights.

(c) Mainstreaming the right to development.

(d) Examining how the negative effects of globalization and trade liberalization affect human rights and their enjoyment.

(e) Need to respect cultural specificities in order to establish a genuine and fruitful dialogue and cooperation in the field of human rights.

(f) Evolving a consistent policy towards standard-setting.

(g) Balancing rights with responsibilities.

(h) Developing a 'code of conduct' for civil society on the model of similar efforts in the humanitarian field.

(i) Ensuring and guaranteeing official development assistance and technical cooperation to developing countries in the field of human rights.

. . .

(k) Ensure depoliticization and non-selectivity in the field of human rights by addressing non-human rights-related objectives.

(l) Developing further dialogue and cooperation in the field of human rights.

(m) Greater examination of the relationship between terrorism and human rights.

(n) Acknowledging the rule of consensus as the prerequisite for attaining universal human rights.

(o) Emphasis on national legislation, national institutions and the creation of a human rights culture.

(p) Maximum utilization of the expertise available in developing countries in all human rights activities.

(q) Shifting the focus of all field operations towards building national capacities.

(r) Intergovernmental bodies must approve any agreement entered into by OHCHR with individual Governments or their subsidiary bodies.

(s) Voluntary financial contributions should not skew priorities set by the intergovernmental bodies and aggravate existing imbalances between rights, based on donor priorities.

(t) Improving protection for the rights of minorities and migrants.

QUESTIONS

1. What are the main obstacles to reform of the various UN procedures as they emerge from these materials?

2. In the preceding Comments on the Report of the Bureau, how many of the proposals address work within the competence of the UN Commission? To which of these proposals might the United States or UK have objected, and why?

PHILIP ALSTON, APPRAISING THE UNITED NATIONS HUMAN RIGHTS REGIME,

in Alston (ed.), *The United Nations and Human Rights: A Critical Appraisal* (1992), at 14

. . .

What then are the key questions that need to be asked in evaluating the effectiveness of the UN regime. It is generally accepted in the academic literature that there are five such questions: When?, Where?, For Whom?, What?, and Why?. *When?* raises the issue of an appropriate time-frame. The 1993 World Conference, for example, has been asked 'to review and assess progress . . . since the adoption of the Universal Declaration' in 1948. It is indisputable that by almost any measure immense progress has been achieved since that time. But other time-frames could equally well have been chosen. Since the first World Conference in 1968, for example, or over the last decade, the results might look significantly different, although much would still depend on how the other questions were framed. . . .

Where? refers to the scope and focus of the evaluation. Donnelly, for example, in his analysis of the human rights regime looks specifically only at the Human Rights Committee and the Commission on Human Rights. From a feminist perspective this immediately biases the outcome by excluding the Commission on the Status of Women and CEDAW. Excluding the other treaty bodies as well as the Assembly and the Sub-Commission also ensures the presentation of only a partial picture. On the other hand, . . . attempting to cover the entire regime provides a potentially unmanageable focus.

The question *for whom?* poses an immediate problem in terms of the human rights regime. The outcome of the evaluation will be radically different depending on whether the standpoint adopted is primarily that of the victims of violations, human rights activists, governments, UN officials, or the press. The answer is by no means self-evident when the UN is asked to undertake the evaluation, since its approach in general seeks to balance the concerns of its different constituencies, while at the same time playing down any suggestion that trade-offs are being made. For this reason, another question is appropriately added in the present context: *by whom?* On occasion, the UN uses independent experts, but more often than not such people will be 'insiders' of one kind or another with strong vested interests in maintenance of the status quo. Should members of the expert committees, for example, be asked to evaluate their own activities . . . ? How objective, or out-spoken, can the Secretariat be in such a context? What weight should be placed on NGO evaluations? Presumably, evaluators from a range of backgrounds are required but then the frame of reference of each can still differ radically from those of others, thereby diminishing the comparability of the results.

What? adds another level of questions after *where?* Having determined, for example, that the focus will be on the Human Rights Committee it must still be decided whether its interstate complaints jurisdiction is best ignored as being certainly unproductive or is carefully examined in the hope of breathing life into a potentially important procedure. Similarly, should the task of developing a sophis-ticated jurisprudence based on the Covenant be treated as being of primary or only secondary importance? A focus on the Commission raises an even more complex array of issues, particularly the question of the importance attached to its function of responding to violations.

Finally, the question *why?* will be answered rather differently by an academic, an activist, a government minister, and an international official. The answers might range from a general quest to gain a better understanding of modes of inter-national co-operation, or a desire to increase efficiency defined in managerial terms, or a mandate 'to formulate concrete recommendations for improving [overall] effectiveness' (as in the case of the World Conference), through to a desire to ensure an immediate and productive response to all future reports of alleged violations.

A more formal or legalistic approach to evaluation, and one more consonant with the past practice of the UN, is to ignore most of these questions (implicitly dismissing them as practically or politically unanswerable) and to seek to compare existing practice with the stated objectives of the system. The problem, of course, is that the 'system' *per se* does not exist in such terms. Thus, the evaluator might turn either to the mandate provided in the UN Charter or to the more specific terms of reference outlined in the constituent instruments relating to each of the organs in question. But in the case of the principal Charter-based organs, the terms of the Charter provisions give little practical guidance for evaluation purposes and the constituent instruments may not be a great deal more helpful. In the case of the Commission, for example, its standard-setting mandate refers only to three specific issues, with respect to one of which (freedom of information) it has been able to achieve virtually nothing. . . . Similarly, the word 'protection' is only men-tioned in relation to 'minorities', but it is unthinkable that the Commission's success in providing 'protection' could be evaluated solely in that regard. In reality, most of the Commission's activities are justified by reference to the catch-all provision in its mandate referring to 'any other matter concerning human rights'. That hardly constitutes a meaningful yardstick for evaluation purposes, however.

PHILIP ALLOTT, EUNOMIA: NEW ORDER FOR A NEW WORLD
(1990), at 287

. . .

15.66. But, as so often in human social experience, the installation of human rights in the international constitution after 1945 has been paradoxical. The idea of human rights quickly became perverted by the self-misconceiving of international society. Human rights were quickly appropriated by governments, embodied in treaties, made part of the stuff of primitive international relations, swept up into the maw of an international bureaucracy. The reality of the idea of human rights has been degraded. From being a source of ultimate anxiety for usurping holders of public social power, they were turned into bureaucratic small-change. Human rights, a reservoir of unlimited power in all the self-creating of society, became a plaything of governments and lawyers. The game of human rights has been played in international statal organizations by diplomats and bureaucrats, and their appointees, in the setting and the ethos of traditional international relations.

15.67. The result has been that the potential energy of the idea has been dissipated. Alienation, corruption, tyranny, and oppression have continued wholesale in many societies all over the world. And in all societies governments have been reassured in their arrogance by the idea that, if they are not proved actually to be violating the substance of particularized human rights, if they can bring their willing and acting within the wording of this or that formula with its lawyerly qualifications and exceptions, then they are doing well enough. The idea of human rights should intimidate governments or it is worth nothing. If the idea of human rights reassures governments it is worse than nothing.

15.68. But, once again, there is room for optimism, on two grounds. (1) The idea of human rights having been thought, it cannot be unthought. It will not be replaced, unless by some idea which contains and surpasses it. (2) There are tenacious individuals and non-statal societies whose activity on behalf of the idea of human rights is not part of international relations but is part of a new process of international reality-forming.

. . .

QUESTIONS

1. Why do governments participate in the universal human rights system? Do they indeed have a choice?

2. How would you identify the major weaknesses in the institutional structures and processes for enforcement of human rights norms? Which of them do you believe can realistically be improved, and what such realistic improvements would you propose?

3. Should the criteria for effectiveness be the same in relation to all the procedures

and mechanisms considered in this Chapter? Or do they aim at different goals that imply different measures of effectiveness? Do they indeed change over time within the political limits of the possible?

ADDITIONAL READING

For a bibliography and chapters on each organ, see P. Alston (ed.), *The United Nations and Human Rights: A Critical Appraisal* (2nd ed., forthcoming 2000). For the history of UN efforts, see R. Russell and J. Muther, *A History of the United Nations Charter* (1958), and P.G. Lauren, *The Evolution of International Human Rights* (1998). On the Commission, see I. Guest, *Behind the Disappearances: Argentina's Dirty War against Human Rights and the United Nations* (1990), H. Tolley Jr., *The U.N. Commission on Human Rights* (1987), and M. Nowak, 'Lessons for the International Human Rights Regime from the Yugoslav Experience', VIII/2 *Collected Courses of the Academy of European Law* (forthcoming 2000). On fact-finding, see D. Orentlicher, 'Bearing Witness: The Art and Science of Human Rights Fact-Finding', 3 Harv. Hum. Rts Y.B. 83 (1990), T. Franck and H.S. Fairley, 'Procedural Due Process in Human Rights Fact-finding by International Agencies', 74 Am. J. Int'l L. 308 (1980), B.G. Ramcharan (ed.), *International Law and Fact-Finding in the Field of Human Rights* (1982), and T. Farer, 'Looking at Looking at Nicaragua', 10 Hum. Rts Q. 141 (1988).

On the Security Council, see I. Österdahl, *Threat to the Peace: The Interpretation by the Security Council of Article 39 of the UN Charter* (1998), Martti Koskenniemi, 'The Police in the Temple: A Dialectical View of the United Nations', 6 Eur. J. Int. L. 325 (1995), D. Sarooshi, *The United Nations and the Development of Collective Security* (1999), M. Byers (ed.), *The Role of Law in International Politics* (2000). On human rights in the context of UN peacekeeping, etc., see A. Henkin (ed.), *Honoring Human Rights: From Peace to Justice, Recommendations to the International Community* (1998), and I Martin, 'A New Frontier', 16 Neths Q. Hum. Rts 121 (1998). On apartheid, see *United Nations Action in the Field of Human Rights* (1994, UN Doc. ST/HR/2/Rev. 4, pp. 170–92), R. Massie, *Loosing the Bonds: The United States and South Africa in the Apartheid Years* (1997), and L. Sohn, *Rights in Conflict: The United Nations and South Africa* (1994).

More generally on the UN, see M. Schmidt, 'The Office of the UN High Commissioner for Human Rights', in R. Hanski and M. Suksi (eds.), *An Introduction to the International Protection of Human Rights: A Textbook* (2nd edn., 1999), A. Gallagher, 'Human Rights in the Wider UN System', in *ibid.*, and P. Alston, 'Neither Fish Nor Fowl: The Quest to Define the Role of the UN High Commissioner for Human Rights', 8 Eur. J. Int. L. 321 (1997).

On sanctions, see G. Lopez and D. Cortright, *The Sanctions Decade: Assessing UN Strategies in the 1990s* (2000), A. Winkler, 'Just Sanctions', 21 Hum. Rts Q. 133 (1999), N. Crawford and A. Klotz, *How Sanctions Work: Lessons from South Africa* (1999), A.C. Drury, 'Revisiting Economic Sanctions Reconsidered', 35 J. Peace Research 1 (1998), and R. Page, 'Why Economic Sanctions Do Not Work', 22 Int. Security 106 (1997).

On humanitarian intervention, see F. Teson, *Humanitarian Intervention* (2nd edn., 1997), S. Murphy, *Humanitarian Intervention* (1996), B. Roth, *Governmental Illegitimacy in International Law* (1999), A. Cassese, 'A Follow-Up: Forcible Humanitarian Countermeasures and *Opinio Necessitatis*', 10 Eur. J. Int. L. 791 (1999), F.K. Abiew, *The Evolution of the Doctrine and Practice of Humanitarian Intervention* (1999), 'Editorial Comments: NATO's Kosovo Intervention', 93 A.J.I.L. 824 (1999), and M. Reisman, 'Unilateral Action and the Transformations of the World Constitutive Process: The Special Problem of Humanitarian Intervention', 11 Eur. J. Int. L 3 (2000).

9

Treaty Organs: The ICCPR Human Rights Committee

Chapter 9 continues the inquiry into the structure, roles, functions and processes of international human rights bodies. We continue to emphasize the relationships among human rights norms, institutions and processes, as well as the reasons and techniques for 'institutionalization' of norms.

The Commission on Human Rights (UN Commission) created under the UN Charter (hence a 'Charter' organ) and examined in Chapter 8 remains the most complex and politically charged of the specifically human rights organs with universal reach. It differs markedly in organization, functions and powers, as well as notoriety, from the six organs (or bodies) related to six universal human rights treaties on civil and political rights, economic and social rights, racial discrimination, gender discrimination, torture and children's rights (hence 'treaty' organs). Each such body is distinctive in some respects; each has functions only with respect to the treaty creating it; each such treaty regime is now to some extent 'administered' or 'implemented' or 'developed' by that body.

Chapter 9 selects for systematic study one such treaty organ, the Human Rights Committee created by and functioning within one of the world's two principal human rights treaties, the International Covenant on Civil and Political Rights. We continue to use the abbreviation 'ICCPR Committee' to distinguish it from the 'UN Commission'.

No radical separation between the study of norms and institutions is possible. Thus prior chapters concentrating on treaties and norms have introduced aspects of the work of several treaty organs—for example, Chapter 3's materials on the ICCPR and CEDAW committees, Chapter 4's illustrations of the ICESCR Committee's work, and the discussion in Chapter 6 of the children's rights committee. By the same token, Chapter 9 cannot restrict itself to 'institutional processes and functions'. Through illustrations of the ICCPR Committee's work it inevitably describes the normative development of this Covenant. Nonetheless there is a large difference. The stress here is on institutional structure, functions, powers and efficacy; the substantive issues raised are secondary to this purpose, not a principal focus.

Similar questions to those in Chapter 8 arise. Why has the ICCPR Committee assumed the character, structure and functions that are here described and analysed? Should the structure and functions of the ICCPR Committee now be reconsidered, in the light of a half century of experience of the human rights movement and over two decades of experience with this Committee?

Two thoughts should be kept in mind: (1) The ICCPR Committee forms part of a complex of universal bodies concentrating on human rights issues, both Charter and treaty organs. Should it then be understood and evaluated not only as an isolated organ functioning under and within the ICCPR, but also as part of this larger complex? If so, it becomes relevant to assess the Committee's work in relation to the UN Commission's work, and indeed the work of NGOs. (2) Even when we examine the Committee's work only within the ICCPR, can we understand each of the Committee's three basic powers or functions in isolation from the others, or should each discrete function be seen as part of an ICCPR system, hence as potentially complementary while occupying different parts of a treaty scheme.

Section A examines the ICCPR Committee. Section B compares with the ICCPR Committee formal characteristics of the five other universal human rights treaties that create special organs.

A. POWERS, FUNCTIONS AND PERFORMANCE OF THE ICCPR COMMITTEE

1. INTRODUCTION

COMMENT ON THE FORMAL ORGANIZATION OF THE ICCPR COMMITTEE

You should now read the provisions bearing on the organization and functions of the ICCPR Committee, set forth in Articles 28–45 of the Covenant and in its First Optional Protocol. The following discussion incorporates some of those provisions.

Note the three dominant functions of the Committee: (1) Article 40 requires states parties to 'submit reports' on measures taken to 'give effect' to the undertakings of the Covenant and 'on the progress made' in the enjoyment of rights declared by the Covenant. The reports are transmitted to the Committee 'for consideration'. The Committee is to 'study' them. (2) The same article instructs the Committee to transmit 'such general comments as it may consider appropriate' to these states parties. (3) The Optional Protocol to the Covenant—a distinct agreement requiring separate ratification—authorizes the Committee to receive and consider 'communications' from individuals claiming to be victims of violations by states parties of the Covenant, and to forward its 'views' about communications to the relevant individuals and states. The materials in this chapter consider each of these activities.

Articles 28–31 of the Covenant provide the crucial information about the Committee's membership. The 18 members are to have 'high moral character and recognized competence in the field of human rights'. Consideration is to be given to the utility of including 'some persons having legal experience'. In fact, all members of the Committee have had such experience in some capacity: private practice, the academy, public interest work, diplomacy, judicial offices, or government. Note the characteristic provisions of Article 31(2) that consideration in elections 'shall be given to equitable geographical distribution of membership and to the representation of the different forms of civilization and of the principal legal systems'. As of January 2000, the 18 Committee members came from Argentina, Australia, Canada, Chile, Colombia, Finland, France, Germany, India, Israel, Italy, Japan, Lebanon, Mauritius, Poland, Tunisia, the United Kingdom, and the United States,

Under Article 28(3), all members are to be 'elected and shall serve in their personal capacity'. The UN term for such members is 'experts,' as opposed to the 'representatives' of states who sit on the UN Commission on Human Rights. If one links the reference to 'personal capacity' with references in the preceding paragraph to 'high moral character' and 'recognized competence' of members with an emphasis on their legal experience, the compelling inference is that Committee members are to act independently of the governments of their states, not under orders of their government—as does, for example, a state's representative (often with a rank of ambassador) on the UN Commission. This feature of independence of members characterizes each of the six treaty organs.

Generally this aspiration appears to have been realized, but in many contexts, 'independence' in the sense identified has been a relative rather than absolute concept. Consider members who are nationals of (and originally nominated for election by) states of an authoritarian character directed, say, by a single party, a military clique, or a personal dictator. Moreover, since membership on the Committee is a part-time business, a minority of members have continued to hold government (diplomatic and other) posts, again qualifying the degree of possible independence from their governments' positions on given issues.

The Committee meets for three sessions annually, each three weeks long, at UN headquarters in Geneva (twice) and New York. There is some intersessional work by individual members of by working groups, which may meet for one week prior to the start of each session. Since emoluments ($3,000 per year plus living expenses) paid by the UN are low and the work is part-time, members hold 'regular' jobs, closer to full time, and must fit the Committee's work into already busy schedules. Most meetings (the dominant exceptions being meetings considering 'communications' under the Optional Protocol or considering drafts of General Comments) are public, though generally poorly attended by outsiders and gathering little press coverage. Often representatives of international NGOs or national NGOs of the country at issue in e.g. a state report will attend. The ICCPR Committee has never enjoyed or indeed sought the publicity and notoriety of the UN Commission.

Decisions of the Committee should formally be by majority vote pursuant to Article 39(2). In fact, all decisions to date have been taken by consensus, although as a formal matter any member could demand a vote on any issue. This unbroken practice of reaching decisions by consensus (e.g., on decisions about the Committee's concluding observations on a state's report, p. 714, *infra*, or about the text of a General Comment, p. 731, *infra*) meets with varying reactions from Committee members. Its advantages in avoiding the factional battles that have dominated much of the life of the UN Commission and in permitting the Committee to move ahead as a unit are obvious. Its undoubted if indeterminate historical effects on the action taken by the Committee are as obvious: compromise, the blunting of positions, the failure to take the bolder step.

Committee members have said that the practice has had the general effect of not permitting an individual member to hold out for a different position from the large majority, but also has generated a lot of give-and-take while encouraging members holding minority views to go along with a clear trend or dominant opinion. In one activity, the writing of 'views' about communications discussed at p. 738, *infra*, Committee practice has allowed individual members to write concurring or dissenting opinions.

Like the UN Commission but not over so long a period (the Covenant entered into force only in 1976), the ICCPR Committee has witnessed vast changes in global politics. The early disputes and compromises, particularly those during the period of drafting of the ICCPR and Optional Protocol when the Committee's basic structure and functions were determined, have left a strong imprint on the Committee today. History's traces are indeed everywhere in the Committee's activities.

NOTE

Consider the following brief summaries by two authors of the nature of the earlier disputes and their continuing influence. The first is taken from Dominic McGoldrick, *The Human Rights Committee* (1991) at 13–14:

> 1.18 There was general agreement during the drafting that the primary obligation under the ICCPR would be implementation at the national level by States. There was continuing disagreement, however, on the question whether there should also be international measures of implementation. A minority of States, principally the Soviet bloc, insisted that there should be provisions to ensure implementation but that there should be no international measures of implementation. It was argued that such measures were a system of international pressure intended to force States to take particular steps connected with the execution of obligations under the Covenant. They were, therefore, contrary to the principle of domestic jurisdiction in article 2(7) of the United Nations Charter, would undermine the sovereignty and independence of States and would upset the balance of powers established by the UN Charter. Moreover, the establishment of petitions systems would transform complaints into international disputes with consequent effects upon peaceful international relations.
>
> 1.19 Against these views it was argued that the undertaking of international measures of implementation was an exercise of domestic jurisdiction and not an interference with it. International measures were essential to the effective observance of human rights, which were matters of international concern. However, even within those States that agreed that international measures were essential,

there were significant differences of opinion as to the appropriate types of measures. The proposals included an International Court of Human Rights empowered to settle disputes concerning the Covenant; settlement by diplomatic negotiation and, in default, by *ad hoc* fact-finding Committees; the establishment of an Office of High Commissioner (or Attorney-General) for Human Rights; the establishment of reporting procedures covering some or all of the provisions in the Covenant; empowering the proposed Human Rights Committee to collect information on all matters relevant to the observance and enforcement of human rights and to initiate an inquiry if it thought one necessary.

. . .

1.21 The lengthy drafting process of the ICCPR largely coincided with the depths of cold war confrontation, the explosive development of notions of self-determination and independence, the accompanying political tensions of large scale decolonization, and the consequential effects of a rapidly altering balance of diplomatic power within the United Nations. In retrospect then it must be acknowledged that it was much more difficult to agree on the text of a Covenant containing binding legal obligations and limited measures of international implementation than it had been to agree upon the statement of political principles in the Universal Declaration in 1948. . . .

The second summary is by Torkel Opsahl, '*The Human Rights Committee*', in Philip Alston (ed.), *The United Nations and Human Rights* (1992) at 371:

. . . The draft Covenant prepared in 1954 by the Commission envisioned a quasi-judicial Human Rights Committee quite different in its powers and functions from that which actually came into existence. It was another twelve years before the General Assembly's Third Committee debated the proposed implementation provisions, at which time they were drastically altered. The majority was opposed to making obligatory the procedure for interstate communications. . . .

All of the various positions, except that of dispensing with the Committee altogether, were taken into account by a formula worked out by the Afro-Asian group. According to this version, the Committee's only compulsory role would be to study and comment generally upon the reports of States Parties, a function originally intended for the Commission on Human Rights. Many of the details of this proposal were amended, which later caused doubts and disagreements about the proper role of the Committee in the reporting system. The functions relating to communications were made entirely optional, and arrangements providing for the consideration of individual complaints of violations were separated from the Covenant and put in the Optional Protocol. In other words, the result was a compromise between those States which favoured strong international measures and those which emphasized the primacy of national sovereignty and responsibility. As is inevitably the case with such compromises, many specific issues were left unresolved, perhaps intentionally. As a result the subsequent evolution of the arrangements has had to be shaped by a continuing give-and-take within the Committee over many years.

2. STATE REPORTING

COMMENT ON REPORTS OF STATES

Submission by states of reports to a human rights treaty organ about their implementation of that treaty has become a familiar requirement. But consider how revolutionary a practice this must have appeared at the time of the first proposals about 50 years ago. To many, it would have seemed nearly inconceivable that most of the world's states would periodically submit a report to an international body about their internal matters involving many politically significant aspects of relations between government and citizens, and then participate in a discussion about that report with members of that body drawn from all over the world.

The critical provision is Article 40, requiring states to 'submit reports on the measures they have adopted which give effect to the rights recognized herein and on the progress made in the enjoyment of those rights'. Reports shall 'indicate the factors and difficulties, if any, affecting the implementation of the present Covenant'. The ICCPR Committee is to 'study' the reports and transmit its 'general comments' to the states parties.

Discussions of reports are public proceedings, though attended by few persons other than Committee members and representatives of some NGOs or UN agencies. The proceedings amount less to a systematic 'study' (to use the term of Article 40) than to an examination of the report with members speaking individually, making comments and posing questions. The representative of the state responds to comments and questions. Reports are now presented by a state party every five years, though the Committee has exercised its authority to request reports at shorter intervals in cases such as national emergencies.

The General Comments at p. 73, *infra*, indicate some of the many problems that the Committee has encountered in the reports submitted to it: incomplete coverage, abstraction and formality that leads states to stress their formal constitutional or statutory provisions rather than to offer a realistic description of practices; and great delays in filing reports.

The Covenant makes no provision about the way in which a state should prepare a report, but the Committee has issued guidelines. The reporting process, from a report's preparation by a state through Committee proceedings, gets little publicity. In fact, only a few states include groups of their citizens—interest groups, particular lobbies, ethnic or gender groups or indigenous peoples, human rights NGOs and so on—in the process of the report's preparation or in the process of considering the Committee's reaction to the report.

The Committee is continuously considering its procedures for reports by formulating and implementing plans for improvement. For example, it submitted to the 1993 World Conference on Human Rights in Vienna several documents on its work and plans. One such document dealt with reports.[1] It reaffirmed that the purpose of the meetings to consider reports with state representatives was to

---

[1] Work of the Human Rights Committee under Article 40 of the Covenant on Civil and Political Rights, UN Doc. A/48/40 (1993), Part I, Annex X at 218.

establish a constructive dialogue between the Committee and the State party, and summarized several recent developments in the Committee's approach to reports:

1. The Committee listed the several times it had requested state parties to submit reports urgently about a new situation such as declarations of emergency or widespread violence, generally within three months of the request. The states included Iraq, Peru and parts of the former Yugoslavia.

2. The Committee has also given its support to the Secretary-General's proposal that ways should be explored of empowering human rights bodies to bring massive human rights violations to the attention of the Security Council.

3. In cases where it was unable to obtain required information, and to learn what had happened with respect to its recommendations in its concluding comments, the Committee was considering requesting the state party concerned to agree to receive a mission, consisting of one or two members of the Committee, with a view to collecting information the Committee needs to carry out its functions under the Covenant. Such a decision would only be taken after the Committee had satisfied itself that no adequate alternative approach was available. . . .

THOMAS BUERGENTHAL, THE HUMAN RIGHTS COMMITTEE
in Philip Alston (ed.), The United Nations and Human Rights (forthcoming 2000), Ch.10

[Thomas Buergenthal served several terms as a member of the Committee until he resigned in 1999 after his election as a judge of the International Court of Justice. These excerpts from his article consider state reports under ICCPR Article 40.]

. . .

. . . [W]hile states have tended to believe that inter-state and individual petition systems would threaten their freedom of action, reporting systems have on the whole not been seen by them as involving much of a risk in that regard. This explains why most of the human rights treaties adopted within the United Nations framework provide for a mandatory reporting system. Dispute resolution mechanisms are less common and usually optional, particularly those that give individuals a right of action, which states see as particularly threatening.

These same considerations entered into the drafting of the measures of implementation of the Covenant and explain why only the reporting requirement is mandatory. It should be emphasized, however, that the assumption that the reporting requirement is 'harmless' is not necessarily valid. Whether or not it is, will frequently depend upon the composition of the supervisory body, its commitment to the cause of human rights, its creativity and the larger political climate within which it exercises its functions. In fact, experience suggests that there is nothing inherently weaker about a reporting system when compared with other measures of implementation than the preconceived notion that quasi-judicial mechanisms of settlement or investigation are by their very nature better suited to achieve results in the human rights field. Whether one or the other implementation measure will produce the desired result in terms of improving a given country's human rights situation which, after all, is the object of the exercise, depends on a variety of factors. . . .

A. The Committee's role

. . .

The language of Article 40 indicates that those who drafted this provision did not wish to spell out very clearly what powers the Committee had in dealing with State reports. While the Committee was mandated 'to study' these reports, Article 40 fails to specify the object or purpose of the study. It provides that after studying the State reports, the Committee is to 'transmit its reports, and such general comments as it may consider appropriate, to the States Parties'. In other words, left unstated or vague is the function the Committee is to exercise in studying the State reports, what issues the Committee's reports may consider, and whether its comments may be addressed to individual states rather than to all States Parties in general.

. . .

In 1984 something of a compromise was reached when it was agreed that individual members could voice their own assessment or observations with regard to a State report at the conclusion of its review by the Committee. These individual observations were then summarized and reproduced in the Committee's annual report to the UN General Assembly. Finally, in 1992, after again reviewing its functions under Article 40(4), the Committee decided that 'observations or comments reflecting the views of the Committee as a whole at the end of the considerations of any State party report should be embodied in a written text, which would be dispatched to the State party concerned as soon as practicable'.

This is the current practice of the Committee. It consists of the adoption by the Committee of so-called 'Concluding Observations'. These observations consist of an assessment of the state's human rights situation in light of the information provided in the State report, the answers the Committee received to the questions posed by its members during the examination of the report, and information available to the members from other sources, all analyzed in terms of the country's obligations under the Covenant. The Committee transmits its concluding observations to the State Party concerned shortly after the hearing; they are also reproduced in the Committee's annual report to the General Assembly. . . .

Concluding observations are adopted by the Committee as a whole in closed meetings after a thorough paragraph-by-paragraph discussion of a draft text prepared by a country rapporteur. . . . [T]he findings set out in concluding observations must be viewed as authoritative pronouncements on whether a particular state has or has not complied with its obligations under the Covenant. What we have here is a type of Committee 'jurisprudence', which provides some insights about the manner in which the Committee interprets the Covenant.

B. Sources of information

. . .

. . . A dramatic change occurred in the early 1990s, when the Committee

> . . . modified its working methods so as to enable the specialized agencies and
> other United Nations organs to take an active part in its activities. The Commit-
> tee accordingly decided that a meeting would be scheduled at the beginning of
> each session of the pre-sessional working group so that it might suitably receive
> oral information provided by these organizations. Such information should thus
> relate to the reports to be considered during the Committee's session and, if need
> be, supplement the written information already provided.

This continues to be the Committee's practice, enabling it to receive valuable
information relating to the human rights situation in the reporting countries. The
Committee also draws with increasing frequency on the studies and resolutions of
various UN organs, particularly those prepared by country and thematic rapporteurs of the UN Commission on Human Rights.

In the past there was even greater controversy in the Committee regarding
information provided by non-governmental human rights organizations (NGOs).
. . . In recent years, Committee members increasingly refer by name to the NGO
source relied upon and even ask the State representative to confirm or deny the
information. Some NGOs even submit so-called 'alternative reports' in which the
information provided in the State report is contradicted. In 1995, moreover, the
Committee initiated a practice of giving NGOs an opportunity to meet with inter-
sessional working groups of the Committee prior to the Committee session to
exchange information on the human rights situation in countries whose reports
would be considered at that session. NGOs now also hold informal briefings for
members of the Committee.

C. Contents and examination of State reports

. . .

. . . [I]t should be noted that the nature of the dialogue between the States
Parties and the Committee has changed over the years. The questions of its members have become increasingly more probing and intrusive than in the past. Compared with the Committee's practice during the Cold War, when it was not
uncommon for certain states, regardless of their human rights record, to be treated
with 'kid gloves' during the examination of their reports, the Committee's current
practice is at once more honest, even-handed and certainly more inquisitorial in
style. The net result is a public review of a state's human rights situation that leaves
few relevant human rights issues unexplored. It also exposes, probably more than
other existing measures of implementation, the achievements and failures of a
State's human rights policies. This said, it must be emphasized that the great
weakness of the reporting system lies in the failure of certain states, frequently the
biggest violators of human rights, to submit their reports to the Committee in a
timely fashion. . . .

. . .

This discussion would be incomplete if it failed to call attention to the fact that the large number of overdue reports has made it possible for the Committee to avoid having to deal with a difficult problem: if all or almost all States Parties did submit their reports in a timely fashion , the Committee would face a serious backlog caused by its inability to process these reports within a reasonable period of time. The Committee now meets in three annual sessions of three weeks each. Experience indicates that the Committee cannot deal effectively with more than five to six State reports per session and complete its other work, especially the processing of the growing number of individual communications. Serious financial problems at the United Nations have reduced the Committee's professional support staff and resulted in substantial delays in the translation of State reports, all of which affects the Committee's ability to discharge its mandate expeditiously. . . .

NOTE

In its 1999 Annual Report to the General Assembly, A/54/40, 21 October 1999, the Committee included some observations on the review of state reports. Its combined Working Group on Communications and Article 40 had helped to prepare the Committee and the concerned state for Committee review of the state report. To obtain information on the reports to be examined at the coming three-week session, the Working Group met representatives from several NGOs, including Amnesty International, Equality Now, Human Rights Watch, the Lawyers Committee for Human Rights, and several local/national organizations. On the basis of the report and such additional information, the Working Group prepared for the Committee and the state a concise list of issues to be explored at the time of the review.

On the downside, the Report noted that 138 initial and periodic reports were overdue (sometimes several reports by a single state were overdue). Eighty-three of the ICCPR's states parties were in arrears, well over 50 per cent. Some periods of arrears were striking—for example, Syria (15 years), Kenya (13), Nicaragua (8), Rwanda (7), Czech Republic (5), Afghanistan (5).

ILLUSTRATIONS OF CONCLUDING OBSERVATIONS

[The following excerpts are taken from the Concluding Observations of the Committee that were prepared following the Committee's consideration of the initial or subsequent report of the state involved.[2] These excerpts do not present an

---

[2] The Concluding Observations appear in the section entitled 'Consideration of Reports Submitted by States Parties under Article 40 of the Covenant' in the Annual Reports of the Human Rights Committee submitted to the UN General Assembly. Except as otherwise indicated, all Concluding Observations denominated (1998) appear in the Committee's 22nd Annual Report, UN Doc. A/53/40, September 15, 1998, covering activities at its 61st–63rd sessions held in 1997 and 1998, while those denominated (1999) appear in the Committee's 23rd Annual Report, UN Doc. A/54/40, 21 October 1999, covering activities at its 64th–66th sessions held in 1998 and 1999. The paragraph numbers in these excerpts are those of the two Annual Reports in their entirety, not of the individual Concluding Observations.

accurate account of any one Concluding Observation. One can assume, for example, that every Committee comment on a state would refer to violations in that state like torture, arbitrary detention, censorship, discrimination, prison conditions, and so on. Rather, the purpose of these excerpts is to draw inquiries and comments selectively from the different reports in order to present the range of the observations and related purposes of the Committee in reviewing state reports.]

CHILE (1999)

2. Positive aspects

200. The Committee welcomes the progress made since considering the State party's third periodic report in re-establishing democracy in Chile after the military dictatorship. . . .

. . .

3. Factors and difficulties affecting implementation of the Covenant

202. The constitutional arrangements made as part of the political agreement that facilitated the transition from the military dictatorship to democracy hinder full implementation of the Covenant by the State party. While appreciating the political background and dimensions of these arrangements, the Committee stresses that internal political constraints cannot serve as a justification for non-compliance by the State party with its international obligations under the Covenant.

4. Principal areas of concern and recommendations

203. The Amnesty Decree Law, under which persons who committed offences between 11 September 1973 and 10 March 1978 are granted amnesty, prevents the State party from complying with its obligation under article 2, paragraph 3, to ensure an effective remedy to anyone whose rights and freedoms under the Covenant have been violated. The Committee reiterates the view, expressed in its general comment No. 20, that amnesty laws covering human rights violations are generally incompatible with the duty of the State party to investigate human rights violations, to guarantee freedom from such violations within its jurisdiction and to ensure that similar violations do not occur in the future.

204. The Committee is deeply concerned by the enclaves of power retained by members of the former military regime. The powers accorded to the Senate to block initiatives adopted by the Congress and the powers exercised by the National Security Council, which exists alongside the Government, are incompatible with article 25 of the Covenant. The composition of the Senate also impedes legal reforms that would enable the State party to comply more fully with its Covenant obligations.

205. The wide jurisdiction of the military courts to deal with all the cases involving prosecution of military personnel and their power to conclude cases that began in the civilian courts contribute to the impunity which such personnel enjoy from punishment for serious human rights violations. Furthermore, that Chilean military courts continue to have the power to try civilians violates article 14 of the

Covenant. Therefore: The Committee recommends that the law be amended so as to restrict the jurisdiction of the military courts to trials only of military personnel charged with offences of an exclusively military nature.

206. The Committee is deeply concerned at persistent complaints of torture and excessive use of force by police and other security personnel, some of which were confirmed in the State party's report, as well as at the lack of independent mechanisms to investigate such complaints. The sole possibility of resort to court action cannot serve as a substitute for such mechanisms. . . .

. . .

211. The criminalization of all abortions, without exception, raises serious issues, especially in the light of unrefuted reports that many women undergo illegal abortions which pose a threat to their lives. The legal duty imposed upon health personnel to report cases of women who have undergone abortions may inhibit women from seeking medical treatment, thereby endangering their lives. The State party has a duty to take measures to ensure the right to life of all persons, including pregnant women whose pregnancies are terminated. . . .

. . .

213. The absence of divorce under Chilean law may amount to a violation of article 23, paragraph 2, of the Covenant, according to which men and women of marriageable age have the right to marry and found a family. It leaves married women permanently subject to discriminatory property laws . . . even when a marriage has broken down irretrievably.

. . .

215. The Committee is concerned that the participation of women in political life, public service and the judiciary is quite inadequate. Therefore: The Committee recommends that steps be taken by the State party to improve the participation of women, if necessary by adopting affirmative action programmes.

216. The continuation in force of legislation that criminalizes homosexual relations between consenting adults involves violation of the right to privacy protected under article 17 of the Covenant and may reinforce attitudes of discrimination between persons on the basis of sexual orientation. Therefore: The law should be amended so as to abolish the crime of sodomy between adults.

. . .

218. . . . [T]he Committee is concerned that hydroelectric and other development projects might affect the way of life and the rights of persons belonging to the Mapuche and other indigenous communities. Relocation and compensation may not be appropriate in order to comply with article 27 of the Covenant. Therefore: When planning actions that affect members of indigenous communities, the State party must pay primary attention to the sustainability of the indigenous culture and way of life and to the participation of members of indigenous communities in decisions that affect them.

219. The Committee is concerned at the lack of comprehensive legislation that would prohibit discrimination in the public and private spheres, such as employment and housing. Under article 2, paragraph 3, and article 26 of the Covenant, the State party is under a duty to protect persons against such discrimination. Therefore: Legislation should be enacted to prohibit discrimination and provide

an effective remedy to those whose right not to be discriminated against is violated. . . .

220. The special status granted in public law to the Roman Catholic and
Orthodox Churches involves discrimination between persons on account of their
religion and may impede freedom of religion. Therefore: The State party should
amend the law so as to give equal status to all religious communities that exist in
Chile.

. . .

IRAQ (1998)

2. Factors and difficulties affecting the implementation of the Covenant

92. The Committee recognizes that eight years of war with the Islamic Republic
of Iran and the conflict following Iraq's invasion of Kuwait caused the destruction
of part of the country's infrastructure and considerable human suffering, and
produced a very difficult economic and social situation in Iraq.

93. The Committee notes that the effect of sanctions and blockades has been to
cause suffering and death in Iraq, especially to children. The Committee reminds
the Government of Iraq that, whatever the difficulties, the State party remains
responsible for implementing its obligations under the Covenant.

3. Positive aspects

94. The Committee welcomes the adoption of Revolutionary Command Council Decree No. 91 of 1996, which repeals the application of the death penalty and
amputation in certain cases.

. . .

4. Subjects of concern and the Committee's recommendations

96. The Committee is deeply concerned that all government power in Iraq is
concentrated in the hands of an executive which is not subject to scrutiny or
accountability, either politically or otherwise. It operates without any safeguards or
checks and balances designed to ensure the proper protection of human rights and
fundamental freedoms in accordance with the Covenant. This appears to be the
most significant factor underlying many violations of Covenant rights in Iraq,
both in law and in practice.

97. . . . [T]he Committee notes with grave concern reports from many sources
concerning the high incidence of summary executions, arbitrary arrests and detention, torture and ill-treatment by members of security and military forces, disappearances of many named individuals and of thousands of people in northern Iraq
and in the southern marshes, and forced relocations. In this respect, the Committee expresses its regret at the lack of transparency on the part of the Government
in responding to these concerns. . . . Therefore: The Committee recommends that
all allegations mentioned above be fully, publicly and impartially investigated, that
the results of such investigations be published and that the perpetrators of those
acts be brought to justice. . . .

. . .

99. The Committee also notes with great concern the increase in the categories of crimes punishable by the death penalty. . .and that the new categories include non-violent and economic infringements. These measures are incompatible with Iraq's obligations under the Covenant to protect the right to life. . . .

. . .

101. The Committee is deeply concerned that Iraq has resorted to the imposition of cruel, inhuman and degrading punishments, such as amputation and branding, which are incompatible with article 7 of the Covenant. Similarly, the Committee is deeply concerned by Revolutionary Command Council Decree No. 109 of 18 August 1994, which stipulates that any person whose hand has been amputated for a crime thus punishable by law shall be branded between the eyebrows with an 'X' symbol. . .

. . .

104. The Committee further notes with concern that special courts, which may impose the death penalty, do not provide for all procedural guarantees required by article 14 of the Covenant, and in particular the right of appeal. It also notes that in addition to the list of offences which are under the jurisdiction of the special courts, the Minister of the Interior and the Office of the President of the Republic have discretionary authority to refer any other cases to these courts. . . .

105. With respect to article 19 of the Covenant on the right to freedom of expression, the Committee is concerned about severe restrictions on the right to express opposition to or criticism of the Government or its policies. The Committee is also concerned that the law imposes life imprisonment for insulting the President of the Republic, and in certain cases death. It also imposes severe punishments for vaguely defined crimes which are open to wide interpretation by the authorities, such as writings detrimental to the President. . . .

. . .

ISRAEL (1998)

B. Factors and difficulties affecting the implementation of the Covenant

300. The Committee notes the security concerns of the State party, the frequent attacks on the civilian population, the problems linked to its occupation of territories and the fact that the State party is officially at war with a number of neighbouring States. However, the Committee draws attention to article 4 of the Covenant, which permits no derogation from certain basic rights even in times of public emergency.

C. Positive factors

301. The Committee notes with satisfaction that Israeli society is a democratic one in which sensitive issues are openly debated and that an active non-governmental community has taken firm root. It expresses appreciation for the wide dissemination of the initial report of Israel among professionals in the justice system who work directly in matters relating to the promotion and protection of human rights and among non-governmental organizations. . . .

. . .

D. *Principal subjects of concern and recommendations*

305. The Committee notes with regret that, although some rights provided for in the Covenant are legally protected and promoted through the Basic Laws, municipal laws, and the jurisprudence of the courts, the Covenant has not been incorporated in Israeli law and cannot be directly invoked in the courts. It recommends early action in respect of recent legislative initiatives aimed at enhancing the enjoyment of a number of the rights provided for in the Covenant, including proposals for new draft Basic Laws on due process rights and on freedom of expression and association. . . .

306. The Committee is deeply concerned that Israel continues to deny its responsibility to fully apply the Covenant in the occupied territories. In this regard, the Committee points to the long-standing presence of Israel in these territories, Israel's ambiguous attitude towards their future status, as well as the exercise of effective jurisdiction by Israeli security forces therein. In response to the arguments presented by the delegation, the Committee emphasizes that the applicability of rules of humanitarian law does not by itself impede the application of the Covenant or the accountability of the State under article 2, paragraph 1, for the actions of its authorities. The Committee is therefore of the view that, under the circumstances, the Covenant must be held applicable to the occupied territories and those areas of southern Lebanon and West Bekaa where Israel exercises effective control. The Committee requests the State party to include in its second periodic report all information relevant to the application of the Covenant in territories which it occupies.

307. The Committee expresses its deep concern at the continued state of emergency prevailing in Israel, which has been in effect since independence. It recommends that the Government review the necessity for the continued renewal of the state of emergency with a view to limiting as far as possible its scope and territorial applicability and the associated derogation of rights. In this regard, the Committee draws attention to article 4 of the Covenant, which permits no derogation from articles 6, 7, 8 (paras. 1 and 2), 11, 15, 16 and 18, and requires that permitted derogations be limited to the extent strictly required by the exigencies of the situation.

308. The Committee expresses serious concern about deeply imbedded discriminatory social attitudes, practices and laws against Arab Israelis that have resulted in a lower standard of living compared with Jewish Israelis, as is evident in their significantly lower levels of education, access to health care, access to housing, land and employment. It notes with concern that most Arab Israelis, because they do not join the army, do not enjoy the financial benefits available to Israelis who have served in the army, including scholarships and housing loans. The Committee also expresses concern that the Arabic language, though official, has not been accorded equal status in practice, and that discrimination against members of the Arab minority appears to be extensive in the private sector. In this regard, the Committee urges the State party to take steps without delay to ensure equality to Arabs and to proceed as soon as possible with the planned formulation of a draft law on discrimination in the private sector and to adopt it at an early date.

309. The Committee is concerned that Palestinians in the occupied territories who remain under the control of Israeli security forces do not enjoy the same rights and freedoms as Jewish settlers in those territories, in particular in regard to planning and building permits and access to land and water. The Committee is also concerned at the policies of confiscation of lands and settlement in the occupied territories. . . .

. . .

317. The Committee remains concerned that despite the reduction in the number of persons held in administrative detention on security grounds, persons may still be held for long and apparently indefinite periods of time in custody without trial. It is also concerned that Palestinians detained by Israeli military order in the occupied territories do not have the same rights to judicial review as persons detained in Israel under ordinary law. . . . The Committee considers the present application of administrative detention to be incompatible with articles 7 and 16 of the Covenant, neither of which allows for derogation in times of public emergency. . . .

. . .

320. The Committee deplores the demolition of Arab homes as a means of punishment. It also deplores the practice of demolitions, in part or in whole, of 'illegally' constructed Arab homes. The Committee notes with regret the difficulties imposed on Palestinian families seeking to obtain legitimate construction permits. The Committee considers the demolition of homes to conflict directly with the obligation of the State party to ensure without discrimination the right not to be subjected to arbitrary interference with one's home (art. 17), the freedom to choose one's residence (art. 12) and equality of all persons before the law and equal protection of the law (art. 26).

321. The Committee is also concerned that the Israel Lands Administration (ILA), responsible for the management of 93 per cent of land in Israel, includes no Arab members and that while ILA has leased or transferred land for the development of Jewish towns and settlements, few Arab localities have been established in this way until recent years. . . .

. . .

324. The Committee is concerned at the preference given to the Jewish religion in the allocation of funding for religious bodies, to the detriment of Muslims, Christians, Druze and other religious groups. The Committee recommends that regulations and criteria for funding be published and applied to all religious groups on an equal basis.

325. The Committee is concerned that the application of religious law to determine matters of personal status, including marriage and divorce, and the absence of provision for civil marriage effectively deny some persons the right to marry in Israel, and result in inequality between men and women. . . . The Committee urges early implementation of measures currently under consideration to facilitate civil marriages and civil burial for those who do not belong to a religion. . . .

. . .

JAPAN (1999)

2. Positive aspects

. . .

146. The Committee notes with satisfaction the establishment, at Cabinet level, of the Council for the Promotion of Gender Equality, aimed at investigating and developing policies for the achievement of a gender-equal society and its adoption of the Plan for Gender Equality 2000. The Committee also notes the measures being taken by the human rights organs of the Ministry of Justice to deal with the elimination of discrimination and prejudice against students at Korean schools in Japan, children born out of wedlock and children of the Ainu minority.

. . .

3. Principal subjects of concern and recommendations

. . .

152. . . . [T]he Committee is concerned that there is no independent authority to which complaints of ill-treatment by the police and immigration officials can be addressed for investigation and redress. The Committee recommends that such an independent body or authority be set up by the State party without delay.

. . .

154. The Committee continues to be concerned about discrimination against children born out of wedlock, particularly with regard to the issues of nationality, family registers and inheritance rights. It reaffirms its position that pursuant to article 26 of the Covenant, all children are entitled to equal protection. . . .

155. The Committee is concerned about instances of discrimination against members of the Japanese-Korean minority who are not Japanese citizens, including the non-recognition of Korean schools. The Committee draws the attention of the State party to general comment No. 23 (1994) which stresses that protection under Article 27 may not be restricted to citizens.

. . .

158. The Committee is concerned that there still remain in the domestic legal order of the State party discriminatory laws against women, such as the prohibition on women remarrying within six months following the date of the dissolution or annulment of their marriage and the different age of marriage for men and women. The Committee recalls that all legal provisions that discriminate against women are incompatible with articles 2, 3 and 26 of the Covenant and should be repealed.

. . .

164. The Committee is deeply concerned that the guarantees contained in articles 9, 10 and 14 are not fully complied with in pre-trial detention in that pre-trial detention may continue for as long as 23 days under police control and is not promptly and effectively brought under judicial control; the suspect is not entitled to bail during the 23-day period; there are no rules regulating the time and length of interrogation; there is no State-appointed counsel to advise and assist the suspect in custody; there are serious restrictions on access to defence counsel under

article 39 (3) of the Code of Criminal Procedure; and the interrogation does not take place in the presence of the counsel engaged by the suspect. The Committee strongly recommends that the pre-trial detention system in Japan should be reformed with immediate effect to bring it into conformity with articles 9, 10 and 14 of the Covenant.

. . .

172. The Committee continues to be gravely concerned about the high incidence of violence against women, in particular domestic violence and rape, and the absence of any measures to eradicate this practice. The Committee is troubled that the courts in Japan seem to consider domestic violence, including forced sexual intercourse, as a normal incident of married life.

. . .

POLAND (1999)

2. Positive aspects

. . .

338. The abolition of the death penalty, even during wartime, is welcomed.

. . .

3. Principal subjects of concern and recommendations

342. The Committee expresses its concern about the absence of any legal mechanism allowing the State party, on a systematic basis, to deal with views of the Committee under the Optional Protocol and to implement them.

. . .

344. The Committee notes with concern: (a) strict laws on abortion which lead to high numbers of clandestine abortions with attendant risks to the life and health of women; (b) limited accessibility for women to contraceptives owing to high prices and restricted access to suitable prescriptions; (c) the elimination of sexual education from the school curriculum; and (d) the insufficiency of public family planning programmes (arts. 3, 6, 9 and 26). The State party should introduce policies and programmes promoting full and non-discriminatory access to all methods of family planning and reintroduce sexual education at public schools.

345. The Committee is also concerned about the lack of gender equality (art. 3) in the employment sector. For example, the State party's figures and other information received show that: (a) the number of women holding high technical, managerial or political posts continues to be low while relatively large numbers occupy less well-rewarded positions; (b) average salaries earned by women amount to only 70 per cent of those earned by men; (c) women do not receive equal remuneration for work of equal value; and (d) employers continue to tend to require pregnancy testing. Further measures should be taken by the State party to counteract these forms of discrimination against women and to promote the equality of women in political and economic life.

. . .

351. The Committee expresses the view that the maximum length of pre-trial

detention (12 months), and especially the ability to extend this up to another 12 months, is incompatible with article 9, paragraph 3. . . .

. . .

SENEGAL (1998)

2. Factors and difficulties affecting the implementation of the Covenant

. . .

53. The Committee further notes the continued existence in the State party of laws and customs, in particular those affecting equality between men and women, which impede the full observance of the Covenant.

3. Positive aspects

54. The Committee observes with satisfaction that the State party has strengthened the status of the Senegalese Human Rights Committee (law of 10 March 1997), and in particular has ensured participation by non-governmental organizations, as well as its capacity to act as an advisory body for dialogue, consultation and promotion of human rights. The activities of the ombudsman (médiateur) are also welcomed.

. . .

58. . . . The Committee welcomes the willingness of the Government of Senegal to comply with the Views of the Committee in the case of Koné v. Senegal (Communication 386/1989) and to provide for a remedy acceptable to the author . . . , namely, an award of 500,000 francs, a plot of land and adequate medical treatment, all implemented just before the consideration of the report before the Committee.

. . .

4. Subjects of concern and the Committee's recommendations

60. In the context of events in Casamance, the Committee expresses concern at allegations it has received of indiscriminate killing of civilians by the army and police, of disappearances, and of ill-treatment and use of torture against persons suspected of being supporters of the Mouvement des forces démocratiques de Casamance (MFDC). . . .

61. The Committee regrets that certain traditional cultural attitudes with respect to women are not compatible with their dignity as human beings and continue to hamper their equal enjoyment of rights embodied in the Covenant. The practice of polygamy, which is incompatible with articles 2(1), 3 and 26 of the Covenant, is of particular concern. The Committee continues to be especially disturbed at the persistent custom of female genital mutilation, which violates articles 6 and 7 of the Covenant, and the high rate of maternal mortality which results from that practice, from early childbirth and from the strict prohibition of abortion. It recommends that judges and lawyers make use of ordinary criminal law provisions to deal with instances of female genital mutilation until a specific law for this offence, the adoption of which the Committee strongly supports, is enacted. In this regard: The Committee encourages the State party to launch a

systematic campaign to promote popular awareness of persistent negative attitudes towards women and to protect them against all forms of discrimination; it urges the State party to abolish practices prejudicial to women's health and to reduce maternal mortality. . . .

. . .

66. The Committee expresses its concern at the statement in the report that 'there are no minorities in Senegal', and at the failure of the State party to provide information on the recognition and protection of religious and ethnic minorities in Senegal. . . .

SUDAN (1998)

4. Subjects of concern and the Committee's recommendations

119. The imposition in the State party of the death penalty for offences which cannot be characterized as the most serious, including apostasy, committing a third homosexual act, illicit sex, embezzlement by officials, and theft by force, is incompatible with article 6 of the Covenant. . . .

120. Flogging, amputation and stoning, which are recognized as penalties for criminal offences, are not compatible with the Covenant. . . .

121. The Committee is concerned about the high maternal mortality rate in the Sudan, which may be the consequence of early marriage, clandestine abortions and female genital mutilation. The Committee is deeply concerned about the practice of female genital mutilation in the Sudan, particularly because it is practised on female minors, who may suffer the consequences throughout their lives. This practice constitutes cruel, inhuman and degrading treatment and violates articles 7 and 24 of the Covenant. Therefore: The State party should forbid, as a matter of law, the practice of female genital mutilation, making it a discrete criminal offence. Social and educational campaigns should be pursued to eliminate the practice.

. . .

123. The Committee is troubled by the number of reports of extrajudicial executions, torture, slavery, disappearances, abductions and other human rights violations from United Nations and non-governmental organizations sources, and by the delegation's assertions that such human rights violations are relatively infrequent. In this connection, the Committee's concern extends to reports of abduction by security forces of children, particularly in the South. . . . The Committee therefore recommends that: (a) Permanent and independent mechanisms be set up to investigate alleged abuses of power by police, security forces and the Popular Defence Forces. . . .

. . .

132. The Committee is concerned that in appearance as well as in fact the judiciary is not truly independent, that many judges have not been selected primarily on the basis of their legal qualifications, that judges can be subject to pressure through a supervisory authority dominated by the Government, and that very few non-Muslims or women occupy judicial positions at all levels. . . .

133. The Committee expresses concern at official enforcement of strict dress requirements for women in public places, under the guise of public order and morality, and at inhuman punishment imposed for breaches of such requirements. Restrictions on the liberty of women under the Personal Status of Muslims Act, 1992 are matters of concern under articles 3, 9 and 12 of the Covenant. Therefore: It is incumbent on the State party to ensure that all its laws, including those dealing with personal status, are compatible with the Covenant.

134. The Committee regrets the documented cases of official action which interferes with the rights of non-Muslim religious denominations and groups to practise their religion and to carry out peaceful educational activities. Therefore: A mechanism should be established to protect minority religious groups from discrimination and action seeking to impede their freedom to teach and practise their religious beliefs.

. . .

UNITED STATES OF AMERICA (1995)

U.N. Doc. CCPR/C/79/Add 50 (1995), 53rd Sess. of Committee

1. The Committee considered the initial report of the United States of America [in April 1995] and adopted the following comments.

A. Introduction

2. . . . The Committee regrets . . . that, while containing comprehensive information on the laws and regulations giving effect to the rights provided in the Covenant at the federal level, the report contained few references to the implementation of Covenant rights at the state level.

. . .

B. Factors and difficulties affecting the implementation of the Covenant

5. The Committee notes that, despite the existence of laws outlawing discrimination, there persist within society discriminatory attitudes and prejudices based on race or gender. Furthermore, the effects of past discriminations in society have not yet been fully eradicated. . . .

. . .

C. Positive aspects

7. . . . The Committee notes with satisfaction the rich tradition and the constitutional framework for the protection of human rights and freedoms in the United States.

. . .

9. The Committee welcomes the efforts of the Federal Government to take measures at the legislative, judicial and administrative levels to ensure that the States of the Union provide human rights and fundamental freedoms. . . .

. . .

D. Principal subjects of concern

. . .

16. The Committee is concerned about the excessive number of offences punishable by the death penalty in a number of States, the number of death sentences handed down by courts, and the long stay on death row which, in specific instances, may amount to a breach of article 7 of the Covenant. It deplores the recent expansion of the death penalty under federal law and the re-establishment of the death penalty in certain States. It also deplores provisions in the legislation of a number of States which allow the death penalty to be pronounced for crimes committed by persons under 18 and the actual instances where such sentences have been pronounced and executed. It also regrets that, in some cases, there appears to have been lack of protection from the death penalty of those mentally retarded.

17. The Committee is concerned at the reportedly large number of persons killed, wounded or subjected to ill-treatment by members of the police force in the purported discharge of their duties. It also regrets the easy availability of firearms to the public and the fact that federal and State legislation is not stringent enough in that connection to secure the protection and enjoyment of the right to life and security of the individual guaranteed under the Covenant.

. . .

20. The Committee is concerned about conditions of detention of persons deprived of liberty in federal or state prisons, particularly with regard to planned measures which would lead to further overcrowding of detention centres. . . . The Committee is particularly concerned at the conditions of detention in certain maximum security prisons which are incompatible with article 10 of the Covenant and run counter to the United Nations Standard Minimum Rules for the Treatment of Prisoners and the Code of Conduct for Law Enforcement Officials.

. . .

22. The Committee is concerned at the serious infringement of private life in some states which classify as a criminal offence sexual relations between adult consenting partners of the same sex carried out in private, and the consequences thereof for their enjoyment of other human rights without discrimination.

23. The Committee is concerned about the impact which the current system of election of judges may, in a few states, have on the implementation of the rights provided under article 14 of the Covenant and welcomes the efforts of a number of states in the adoption of a merit-selection system. . . .

24. The Committee welcomes the significant efforts made in ensuring to everyone the right to vote but is concerned at the considerable financial costs that adversely affect the right of persons to be candidates at elections.

25. The Committee is concerned that aboriginal rights of Native Americans may, in law, be extinguished by Congress. It is also concerned by the high incidence of poverty, sickness and alcoholism among Native Americans, notwithstanding some improvements achieved with the Self-Governance Demonstration Project.

26. The Committee notes with concern that information provided in the core document reveals that disproportionate numbers of Native Americans, African Americans, Hispanics and single parent families headed by women live below the poverty line and that one in four children under 6 live in poverty. It is concerned that poverty and lack of access to education adversely affect persons belonging to these groups in their ability to enjoy rights under the Covenant on the basis of equality.

E. Suggestions and recommendations

. . .

30. The Committee emphasizes the need for the government to increase its efforts to prevent and eliminate persisting discriminatory attitudes and prejudices against persons belonging to minority groups and women including, where appropriate, through the adoption of affirmative action. . . .

. . .

32. The Committee urges the state party to take all necessary measures to prevent any excessive use of force by the police. . . . Regulations limiting the sale of firearms to the public should be extended and strengthened.

. . .

QUESTIONS

1. What appears to be the legal nature of the recommendations in the Concluding Observations: collegial suggestions, formal and authoritative judgments, orders, something in between? What support does your answer find in the Covenant itself? In the practice of the Committee? As a state official, would you view such practice as sufficient by itself to ascertain the legal effect of the Concluding Observations on the states parties?

2. (a) Compare with the observations of the ICCPR Committee those made by Special Rapporteurs or Working Groups appointed by the UN Commission to investigate a particular state—for example, the Special Representatives' reports on Iran at pp. 624–33, *supra.* Do you view these two sources of critical observations about a state's human rights record as comparable in all important respects? If not, where and how do they differ? (b) Compare these ICCPR observations with a judgment of an international tribunal such as the International Court of Justice, if that court were to find a state in violation of human rights duties imposed by the ICCPR. What similarities and differences?

3. What pressures can be brought against a state, and by whom, to increase the probability of its compliance with the recommendations in Concluding Observations?

4. Does the Committee confine itself to a state's record with respect to the rights declared in the ICCPR, or does it range more broadly to embrace states' duties under other human rights and humanitarian instruments? If so, do you view this as appropriate?

5. Do the Concluding Observations (based on the preceding excerpts) develop the Covenant, interpret and elaborate its provisions, and provide general guidance to states and other international organs concerned with human rights? Or do they restrict themselves to stating the obvious, as by finding that a state that tortures political opponents violates the ICCPR? As a Committee member, which path would you follow?

6. To the extent that the Committee elaborates the Covenant, does it justify its conclusions that the particular types of state conduct that it describes violate (or 'may' violate) a given ICCPR article, or does it simply state the conclusion or raise the possibility? Consider illustrations like paras 211 and 215 (Chile), para. 325 (Israel), para. 344 (Poland), and paras 23, 24 and 26 (United States). Which ICCPR articles and what arguments would you employ to bear out the Committee's observations?

7. How do you assess the entire practice of state reporting? What consequences do you imagine it has had in states that differ with respect to their degree of observance of human rights? Even if recommendations are often ignored by some, most, or all states, is the process still worthwhile? Why?

DANIEL BODANSKY, REPORTING OBLIGATIONS IN ENVIRONMENTAL REGIMES: LESSONS FOR HUMAN RIGHTS SUPERVISION

in Philip Alston and J. Crawford (eds.), The Future of UN Human Rights Treaty Monitoring (2000), at 361

[Another excerpt from this article, comparing general characteristics of human rights and environmental regimes, appears at p. 570, *supra*.]

A. Introduction

. . .

Certainly, many of the problems that plague human rights reporting are present in international environmental regimes: national reports that are inaccurate, incomplete, tardy or not prepared at all; superficial reviews by international bodies; and a proliferation of reporting requirements, leading to fears of treaty congestion. . . . Even when reports are submitted, they may be inaccurate, even deliberately deceptive. . . .

Indeed, in some important respects, international environmental law lags far behind human rights law, particularly in creating individual complaint procedures, which are virtually non-existent in the environmental arena. In relation to climate change, the very idea of an obligation to 'report' was felt by some states to suggest an intrusive, heavy-handed process. Hence the more neutral phrase 'communication of information' was used instead.

. . .

C. An Overview of International Environmental Reporting

1. Functions of reporting

. . .

A second, related function of reporting is to bring about a change in the policies and ultimately the behaviour of states (the policy reform function). Reporting can promote such change in a range of more or less coercive ways. At the more coercive end of the spectrum, the evaluative process focuses pressure on states to perform better—peer pressure from other states, public pressure, and internal bureaucratic and political pressure. Less coercively, the process of preparing a report—by mobilising and empowering groups within and outside the government—may have a catalytic effect in promoting a process of internal policy reform. Finally, through the sharing of information in reports, states may learn about policy options (or, in the case of environmental reporting, technologies) not previously considered.

. . . Environmental reporting is also concerned to a substantial degree with the performance of individual states, although. . .in contrast to human rights reporting, verification has as its primary function the providing of assurance to the members of the regime that other states are fulfilling their end of the bargain. In this respect what counts is not so much a state's absolute efforts to protect the environment or to comply with existing norms as its efforts relative to other states, since this is what affects competitiveness.

. . .

3. Review of reports

Comparatively few international environmental agreements have specific arrangements for the review of national reports. Reports are typically processed and, in some cases, summarised by the treaty secretariat, and then forwarded to the conference of the parties. . . . As a result, reviews of reports [under many environmental agreeements] tend to focus on the aggregate performance of the parties in achieving treaty objectives, rather than on compliance by individual countries. Such reviews play a primarily legislative function. By indicating how countries are currently performing, they suggest whether adjustments or amendments are needed. For example, the statistical data in reports submitted under the Convention on International Trade in Endangered Species (CITES) can be used to calculate the total volume of trade in a species, which in turn can be used in assessments of the species' status and the need for additional conservation measures.

In a few cases, environmental regimes involve review of individual countries' performance. . . .

Until recently, practically the only other mechanism for focusing on an individual party's compliance with an environmental agreement was formal dispute settlement, which in practice was never used. Several recent agreements have attempted to fill the 'space between ... traditional reporting and dispute settlement articles' through two complementary mechanisms: in-depth reviews of individual country reports and non-compliance procedures. The climate change regime involves perhaps the most elaborate example of the former approach, although parties are currently considering whether to utilise the second mechanism as well, by establishing a 'multilateral consultative process to resolve questions regarding implementation'. . . .

. . .

D. Lessons for Human Rights Law

. . .

3. In-depth reviews of national reports

A frequent complaint about human rights supervision is that for a variety of reasons (lack of time, or money, or staff, or authority), human rights treaty bodies cannot meaningfully review national reports. While the same could be said of many international environmental regimes, one exception is the Climate Change Convention, which has a highly-developed review process that has been called 'one of the pillars of the Convention'. . . . The Climate Change review process begins with a number of advantages, which might not be replicable elsewhere. Most importantly, the regime is exceptionally well-funded and staffed, with a substantial budget and five full-time professional staff for the reporting and review process alone. Moreover, only industrialised countries have been required thus far to file reports and, with relatively few exceptions, they have done so in a timely manner, producing a much better record of compliance than under any other environmental treaty regime. . . .

. . .

The purpose of the review process is essentially the same as in the human rights arena, namely to enter into a constructive dialogue with the government concerned. A key means of promoting this dialogue has been the country visit. Although these visits were initially controversial and were dependent on an invitation from the state concerned, such invitations have been forthcoming (at least from industrialised states) and all the in-depth reviews to date have involved a country visit. In contrast to the reviews of national reports by human rights bodies, which last at most a couple of days (and in some cases only a few hours) and may involve the questioning of only a single official, country visits have typically been a week long and have involved meetings with a variety of government officials as well as NGOs. Each report is 10–20 pages long, and is reviewed and commented on by the country concerned before being finalised and made public.

The in-depth review procedure under the Climate Change Convention is still relatively new and untested and it remains to be seen whether it will yield significant results. Nevertheless, the early experience suggests several lessons for other review processes:

    (i) *Keep the review process flexible.* Compared to human rights review processes, the climate change reviews are highly flexible. Instead of holding one or two formal sessions where a single government representative is questioned, the review teams engage in an unofficial give-and-take with a number of government officials and with other important stakeholders (including industry representatives and environmentalists). This back-and-forth approach continues after the country visit. . . .

(ii) *Use ad hoc teams of experts, rather a single commission or committee.* The use of *ad hoc* teams rather than a single committee has allowed substantial time to be devoted to each in-depth review. A single committee or commission, even if it met year-round, would have had difficulty completing the 30-plus reviews undertaken thus far.

(iii) *Disseminate the results of the reviews widely.* The influence of the in-depth reviews is maximised through widespread distribution of the results. . . .

(iv) *Look beyond simple compliance and assess the effectiveness more generally of a country's policies and measures.* The more complex the international commitment, the greater the need to be able to assess whether a country is likely to comply in the future and not only whether it has complied in the past. This makes it possible to anticipate assistance needed, possible penalties, and adjustments to commitments. The Climate Change Convention in-depth review process examines not only present emissions but also national policies and forecasts of future emissions. . . .

QUESTIONS

1. Comparing purposes and functions of human rights and environmental international regimes, how would you explain these differences in the reporting mechanisms: (a) environmental regimes think more in terms of aggregate responses; (b) environmental regimes think more in terms of relative performance of different treaty parties; (c) environmental regimes think more of reports as part of a 'legislative' process?

2. What lessons do you think the ICCPR Committee, and other treaty bodies receiving periodic reports of treaty parties, should learn from reporting under environmental treaties?

3. GENERAL COMMENTS

The text of the ICCPR is characteristically terse and ambiguous about what is intended by 'general comments'. Article 40, after setting forth the undertaking of states to submit periodic reports to the Committee, provides in para. 4 that the Committee 'shall study the reports' submitted by states and 'shall transmit its reports, and such *general comments* as it may consider appropriate' to the states (emphasis added). Under para. 5, states 'may submit to the Committee observations on any comments that may be made' pursuant to para. 4.

So many possibilities existed for the elaboration of this opaque text, depending on how the Committee answered questions like: Are the general comments to be directed only to states' reports? Are they to vary with the report, addressing concretely this or that problem of this or that state? Alternatively, are they to remain truly 'general' in the sense that they do not pertain exclusively to one state but rather address issues of general relevance to all or many states? Are they to deal only with the processes of reporting or also with substantive provisions of the Covenant? Are they to elaborate those substantive provisions?

Consider the following comments on the evolution of general comments by Thomas Buergenthal, at p. 711, *supra*:

> ... It is also true that initially at least the Committee's practice in developing general comments was directly related to the reporting procedure and the debates that raged in the Committee on the scope of its authority to comment on the failure of individual states to live up to their obligations under the Covenant. But all that is ancient history because over time the general comment has become a distinct juridical instrument, enabling the Committee to announce its interpretations of different provisions of the Covenant in a form that bears some resemblance to the advisory opinion practice of international tribunals. These general comments or 'advisory opinions' are relied upon by the Committee in evaluating the compliance of states with their obligations under the Covenant, be it in examining State reports or 'adjudicating' individual communications under the Optional Protocol. ... General comments consequently have gradually become important instruments in the lawmaking process of the Committee, independent of the reporting system....
>
> ...
>
> ... The quality of general comments began to improve significantly in the late 1980's, in large measure because with the end of the Cold War it became increasingly easier within the Committee to reach the desired consensus on the manner in which different provisions of the Covenant should be interpreted. On the whole, general comments now became longer and more analytical, and they began to address difficult issues of interpretation. The more recent general comments tend as a rule to provide a thorough analysis of those provisions of the Covenant they seek to elucidate. But since consensus is still an inherent part of the drafting process of these instruments, they remain compromise instruments that on various occasions gloss over issues in need of clearer interpretative guidance. One of the problems here is that the Committee has not as yet developed a procedure enabling individual members to attach concurring or dissenting views to general comments. The absence of such a mechanism results in a stricter application of the consensus rule, since the majority is reluctant to impose its interpretation on a minority that has no outlet for the expression of opposing views.

ILLUSTRATIONS OF GENERAL COMMENTS

We here review excerpts from some General Comments (GCs) of the Committee from several perspectives: their functions, what they reveal about the Committee's understanding of the Covenant, the significance of GCs for the elaboration of the Covenant and for the human rights movement in general. It would be helpful to reread the articles of the Covenant that are referred to when you read the excerpts below from several GCs.[3] (Other GCs are described or set forth (1) at p. 157, *supra*, on a state's withdrawal from the Covenant, (2) at p. 465, *supra*, on freedom of religion, (3) at p. 1044, *infra*, on reservations to the ICCPR, and (4) at p. 851, *infra*, on the right to political participation.)

1. Aid to states in filing reports under Article 40

A prominent theme since the first GC of 1981 has been instructions to states about the reports to be filed under Article 40. The introduction to UN Doc. CCPR/C/21/ Rev.1, 19 May 1989, explains the purposes of GCs as follows:

> The Committee so far has examined 77 initial reports, 34 second periodic reports and, in some cases, additional information and supplementary reports. . . .
>
> The purpose of these general comments is to make this experience available for the benefit of all States parties in order to promote their further implementation of the Covenant; to draw their attention to insufficiencies disclosed by a large number of reports; to suggest improvements in the reporting procedure and to stimulate the activities of these States and international organizations in the promotion and protection of human rights. . . .

GC No. 2. 'Reporting Guidelines' (1981) (p. 3) provides in para. 3:

> 3. The Committee considers that the reporting obligation embraces not only the relevant laws and other norms relating to the obligations under the Covenant but also the practices and decisions of courts and other organs of the State party as well as further relevant facts which are likely to show the degree of the actual implementation and enjoyment of the rights recognized in the Covenant, the progress achieved and factors and difficulties in implementing the obligations under the Covenant.

A number of GCs underscore the Committee's frustration with the inadequacy of many reports. For example, *GC No. 13, 'Article 14'* (1984) (p. 14) concerned with procedures for a fair trial, states in para. 3:

> 3. The Committee would find it useful if, in their future reports, States parties could provide more detailed information on the steps taken to ensure that

---

[3] The GCs up to 1996 are set forth in UN Doc. HRI/GEN/1/Rev. 3 (15 Aug. 1997), 'Compilation of General Comments and General Recommendations Adopted by Human Rights Treaty Bodies,' at 1–54. Page references below are to this compilation. The General Comments also appear in Int. Hum. Rts. Reports. Later GCs here or elswhere in the course-book bear individual citations. All GCs are available at www.unhchr.ch/tbs/doc.nsf.

equality before the courts, including equal access to courts, fair and public hearings and competence, impartiality and independence of the judiciary are established by law and guaranteed in practice. In particular, States parties should specify the relevant constitutional and legislative texts which provide for the establishment of the courts and ensure that they are independent, impartial and competent, in particular with regard to the manner in which judges are appointed, the qualifications for appointment, and the duration of their terms of office; the condition governing promotion, transfer and cessation of their functions and the actual independence of the judiciary from the executive branch and the legislative.

————

Note the degree of detail about a system of implementation of a norm that is requested in para. 6 of *GC No. 21, 'Article 10,'* (1992) (p. 33), on conditions of detention.

> States parties should include in their reports information concerning the system for supervising penitentiary establishments, the specific measures to prevent torture and cruel, inhuman and degrading treatment, and how impartial supervision is ensured.

2. Clarification, interpretation and elaboration of provisions of the Covenant

Compare the following excerpts from the (frequently lengthy) GCs with the terse text of the articles subjected to commentary, in order to consider the methods and extent of elaboration and interpretation of the ICCPR.

————

GC No. 6, 'Article 6' (1982) (p. 6) and *GC No. 14, 'Article 6'* (1984) (p. 18). Both address the right to life, a phrase as central to the human rights corpus as it is open to a range of interpretations. Consider the following excerpt from *GC No. 6:*

> 1. The right to life enunciated in article 6 of the Covenant has been dealt with in all State reports. It is the supreme right from which no derogation is permitted even in time of public emergency which threatens the life of the nation (art. 4). However, the Committee has noted that quite often the information given concerning article 6 was limited to only one or other aspect of this right. It is a right which should not be interpreted narrowly.
> . . .
> 5. Moreover, the Committee has noted that the right to life has been too often narrowly interpreted. The expression 'inherent right to life' cannot properly be understood in a restrictive manner, and the protection of this right requires that States adopt positive measures. In this connection, the Committee considers that it would be desirable for States parties to take all possible measures to reduce infant mortality and to increase life expectancy, especially in adopting measures to eliminate malnutrition and epidemics.

Compare these provisions from the earlier GC with *GC No. 14,* two years later:

3. While remaining deeply concerned by the toll of human life taken by conventional weapons in armed conflicts, the Committee has noted that, during successive sessions of the General Assembly, representatives from all geographical regions have expressed their growing concern at the development and proliferation of increasingly awesome weapons of mass destruction, which not only threaten human life but also absorb resources that could otherwise be used for vital economic and social purposes, particularly for the benefit of developing countries, and thereby for promoting and securing the enjoyment of human rights for all.

4. The Committee associates itself with this concern. It is evident that the designing, testing, manufacture, possession and deployment of nuclear weapons are among the greatest threats to the right to life which confront mankind today. This threat is compounded by the danger that the actual use of such weapons may be brought about, not only in the event of war, but even through human or mechanical error or failure.

. . .

6. The production, testing, possession, deployment and use of nuclear weapons should be prohibited and recognized as crimes against humanity.

7. The Committee accordingly, in the interest of mankind, calls upon all States, whether Parties to the Covenant or not, to take urgent steps, unilaterally and by agreement, to rid the world of this menace.

———

GC No. 16. 'Article 17' (1988) (p. 21) elaborates the article's reference to interference with privacy. One illustration follows:

10. The gathering and holding of personal information on computers, databanks and other devices, whether by public authorities or private individuals or bodies, must be regulated by law. Effective measures have to be taken by States to ensure that information concerning a person's private life does not reach the hands of persons who are not authorized by law to receive, process and use it, and is never used for purposes incompatible with the Covenant. In order to have the most effective protection of his private life, every individual should have the right to ascertain in an intelligible form, whether, and if so, what personal data is stored in automatic data files, and for what purposes. Every individual should also be able to ascertain which public authorities or private individuals or bodies control or may control their files. If such files contain incorrect personal data or have been collected or processed contrary to the provisions of the law, every individual should have the right to request rectification or elimination.

———

GC No. 18. 'Non-discrimination' (1989) (p. 26) deals with several provisions of the Covenant—Articles 2, 3 and 26 among others—that state the principle of non-discrimination. Note the references to other human rights treaties.

7. . . . [T]he Committee believes that the term 'discrimination' as used in the Covenant should be understood to imply any distinction, exclusion, restriction or preference which is based on any ground such as race, colour, sex, language,

religion, political or other opinion, national or social origin, property, birth or other status, and which has the purpose or effect of nullifying or impairing the recognition, enjoyment or exercise by all persons, on an equal footing, of all rights and freedoms.

. . .

10. The Committee also wishes to point out that the principle of equality sometimes requires States parties to take affirmative action in order to diminish or eliminate conditions which cause or help to perpetuate discrimination prohibited by the Covenant. For example, in a State where the general conditions of a certain part of the population prevent or impair their enjoyment of human rights, the State should take specific action to correct those conditions. Such action may involve granting for a time to the part of the population concerned certain preferential treatment in specific matters as compared with the rest of the population. However, as long as such action is needed to correct discrimination in fact, it is a case of legitimate differentiation under the Covenant.

. . .

12. . . . In the view of the Committee, article 26 does not merely duplicate the guarantee already provided for in article 2 but provides in itself an autonomous right. . . . [T]he application of the principle of non-discrimination contained in article 26 is not limited to those rights which are provided for in the Covenant.

13. Finally, the Committee observes that not every differentiation of treatment will constitute discrimination, if the criteria for such differentiation are reasonable and objective and if the aim is to achieve a purpose which is legitimate under the Covenant.

———

GC No. 19. 'Article 23' (1990) (p. 29) concerns the protection of the family. Note the limited range of the comment on family planning, compared with CEDAW. What are its implications, for example, for the right to practice contraception or to abort?

4. . . . [T]he Committee wishes to note that. . . legal provisions must be compatible with the full exercise of the other rights guaranteed by the Covenant; thus, for instance, the right to freedom of thought, conscience and religion implies that the legislation of each State should provide for the possibility of both religious and civil marriages. . . .

5. The right to found a family implies, in principle, the possibility to procreate and live together. When States parties adopt family planning policies, they should be compatible with the provisions of the Covenant and should, in particular, not be discriminatory or compulsory. . . .

6. . . . During marriage, the spouses should have equal rights and responsibilities in the family. This equality extends to all matters arising from their relationship, such as choice of residence, running of the household, education of the children and administration of assets. Such equality continues to be applicable to arrangements regarding legal separation or dissolution of the marriage.

———

GC No. 20. 'Article 7' (1992) (p. 31) concerns torture and cruel or degrading treatment or punishment. Note the detail in the following provisions that bear on implementation.

> 11. ... To guarantee the effective protection of detained persons, provisions should be made for detainees to be held in places officially recognized as places of detention and for their names and places of detention, as well as for the names of persons responsible for their detention, to be kept in registers readily available and accessible to those concerned, including relatives and friends. To the same effect, the time and place of all interrogations should be recorded, together with the names of all those present and this information should also be available for purposes of judicial or administrative proceedings. Provisions should also be made against incommunicado detention. In that connection, States parties should ensure that any places of detention be free from any equipment liable to be used for inflicting torture or ill-treatment. The protection of the detainee also requires that prompt and regular access be given to doctors and lawyers and, under appropriate supervision when the investigation so requires, to family members.
>
> 12. It is important for the discouragement of violations under article 7 that the law must prohibit the use of admissibility in judicial proceedings of statements or confessions obtained through torture or other prohibited treatment.
> ...
>
> 15. The Committee has noted that some States have granted amnesty in respect of acts of torture. Amnesties are generally incompatible with the duty of States to investigate such acts; to guarantee freedom from such acts within their jurisdiction; and to ensure that they do not occur in the future. States may not deprive individuals of the right to an effective remedy, including compensation and such full rehabilitation as may be possible.

QUESTIONS

1. Many General Comments clearly go beyond the literal text of the ICCPR article under discussion. Using any illustrations above that you choose, how would you describe what the Committee is here doing? Working out reasonable inferences from that text—for example, how to make that text operational? Interpretation based on the larger internal context of all provisions of the ICCPR, or in light of the broad object and purpose of the ICCPR as a whole? Creative development in the light of changing world conditions and ideologies? Or working out the common understanding from time to time of representative states parties to the ICCPR of the meaning of various provisions?

2. If the last description is accurate, do the states parties participate in the preparation of General Comments? Should the procedures for drafting General Comments (including closed meetings) be changed, so that the Committee would make available to state parties, IGOs and NGOs a preliminary version of a proposed General Comment and solicit reactions thereto, perhaps at a formal hearing before the Committee? The Committee could then take those reactions into account as it thought appropriate when preparing the final form of the General Comment.

3. What authority do you believe that these General Comments should have before other institutions—say, a General Comment stating the content and reach of an ICCPR article (like the right to life) that might be relevant to (a) the UN Commission on Human Rights in a debate about whether a country was in violation of the ICCPR, (b) a national court of a state party that is applying the ICCPR to a case before it, (c) the International Court of Justice in a case where one state accuses another of violating that article? Does any other national or international institution have such a power of authoritative interpretation of the ICCPR? Should there be one such institution? Why?

4. Compare General Comments and Concluding Observations as means for the Committee to develop the ICCPR.

4. INDIVIDUAL COMMUNICATIONS

As of March 2000, 95 of the 144 states parties to the ICCPR were also parties to this First Optional Protocol. Note some of its critical provisions. The communications must be 'from individuals . . . who claim to be victims of a violation' by a state party to the Protocol 'of any of the rights set forth in the Covenant'. After being notified of the communication, the state party shall 'submit to the Committee written explanations or statements clarifying the matter . . .'. The Committee considers communications 'in the light of all written information made available to it by the individual and by the State Party concerned'. It will not consider a communication before ascertaining that the matter is 'not being examined under another procedure of international investigation or settlement'. Examination of the communications takes place at 'closed meetings'. The Committee is to forward 'its views' to the individual and state concerned.

Note some of the consequences or negative implications of these terse and ambiguous provisions, supplemented by the Committee's own procedural rules:

(1) The proceedings are in no sense a continuation of or appeal from judicial proceedings (if there were any) in the state in which the dispute originated. They are fresh, distinct proceedings that may involve the same two parties to prior proceedings, or different parties.

(2) Unlike the requirements for procedures 1235 and 1503 of the UN Commission on Human Rights, the communication to the ICCPR Committee need not allege that the violation complained of is systemic—that is, involves a consistent pattern in or practice of the state or some recurrent phenomenon. In theory, an isolated, atypical violation suffices to found the communication.

(3) There are no provisions for oral hearings, let alone confrontation between the parties, or for independent fact-finding (such as examination of the parties or witnesses or independent experts, or on-site visits) by the Committee. The Optional Protocol refers only to written proceedings.

(4) There are no hearings or debates of Committee members about how to deal with the communication that are open to the public.

(5) There is no provision setting forth the precise legal effect of 'views', surely no provision stating that the 'views' are binding, or setting forth what follow-up should take place if the Committee's views indicating that a state should take particular action (such as payment of compensation or release of a prisoner) are ignored by that state.

The Optional Protocol is one of only three human rights treaties of universal reach, the two others created by the conventions on racial discrimination and torture, that provide (some form of) an individual remedy at the international level. An Optional Protocol for the women's convention has been approved by the General Assembly and is now awaiting a sufficient number of state ratifications to become effective. Note that the optional provision in Article 41 of the ICCPR for the filing of a communication by one state party against another has never been utilized, although as of January 2000, 47 states had made the necessary declaration under that article.

TORKEL OPSAHL, THE HUMAN RIGHTS COMMITTEE
in Philip Alston (ed.), The United Nations and Human Rights (1992), at 421

More ambitious proposals for the handling of such complaints were discarded at an early stage. No private complaints system, to a Court or otherwise, could be made obligatory. Not even in an optional form was any such procedure allowed to become part of the Covenant itself. But a majority of the General Assembly decided at the eleventh hour to create a separate document, the Optional Protocol, allowing for 'communications from individuals claiming to be victims of violations of any of the rights set forth in the Covenant'. . . .

. . .

On some points, this system resembles those of the Council of Europe and the Organization of American States, but it is much simpler. The Committee is the only competent organ and its procedure is not very elaborate. Its 'views' are not to be understood as strictly binding in law and cannot be enforced. The Protocol itself seems to consider a case closed as soon as the views have been forwarded to the parties. There is no follow-up procedure leading, as in the European system, from the report of a Commission to binding decisions by other competent organs (such as the European Committee of Ministers or Court of Human Rights).

The consideration of communications takes place in closed meetings. The files and summary records of the Committee's deliberations remain confidential, but the texts of its final decisions, called 'views', have been made public from the beginning. . . .

. . .

. . . [D]espite the confidentiality of the proceedings under the Optional Protocol, ample material is now available. However, as a source of case law, the material is less developed than in, for instance, the European system, because the Committee does not go to the same lengths in its published reasoning.

. . .

The Committee has in many cases not only expressed its 'view' that there have been violations of specific rights, but also added what in its opinion should follow, stating as a separate conclusion a duty to provide individual reparation and take preventive measures for the future. This is now a settled interpretation of its role. The Committee could go further in seeking solutions in co-operation with the parties. Certainly it might, with their consent, develop its fact-finding role and allow oral pleadings.

. . .

. . . [M]onitoring *violations* of these rights through complaints procedures . . . should not be more than a secondary aim. Universality in such procedures is less necessary and more difficult to apply. It is true that complaints procedures, more than abstract inquiries, may throw specific light even over matters of general interest. Case law can also be more specific than general comments on how provisions ought to be understood. Nevertheless, the Committee will never be able to control violations in all parts of the world through complaints procedures. It would not be practical to develop its machinery to the extent which this control would require, since this would include hearings, fact-finding, visits, investigations, use of many languages, etc. Theoretically the procedures could become permanent and deal annually with thousands of cases rather than dozens. But there is a better alternative; building and strengthening regional complaints systems, like the European, American, and African ones, offers several advantages in the areas of logistics, local trust, and homogeneity. States Parties from the regions which have such systems in place have already shown their preference for them through reservations.

. . .

COMMENT ON THE COMMITTEE'S WORK UNDER THE OPTIONAL PROTOCOL

Growing caseload and dwindling resources

In its 1999 Annual Report, p. 714, *supra*, the Committee presented statistical information about the use of the Optional Protocol. Since 1977, 873 communications concerning 60 states parties had been registered with the Committee. Of that number, 328 communications were concluded by views of the Committee (including 253 views in which violations were found), 267 communications were declared inadmissible, 129 were discontinued, and 149 had not yet concluded (among which 38 had been declared admissible). 'In addition, the secretariat of the Committee has hundreds of communications on file in respect of which authors have been advised that further information would be needed before their communications could be registered for consideration by the Committee' (para. 286). (It should be noted that the number of registered communications is far lower than the number of individual complaints received under the ICCPR, many of which may be deemed insufficient in formal respects and discarded. The UNHCHR, in its Annual Appeal 2000, *Overview of Activities and Financial Requirements*, at 92, estimates that 'some 2,500 complaints' are received annually.)

During the three three-week sessions covered by the 1999 Annual Report, the Committee adopted views in 35 cases. Previous annual reports involve a similar number of newly adopted views, which has led some Committee members to suggest that, within the resources now available to it, about 30 views a year represents the maximum possible output under the Committee's current procedures.

The Report noted the growth of the Committee's caseload under the Optional Protocol, and commented that 'the increasing number of States parties to the Optional Protocol and better public awareness of the procedure have led to a growth in the number of communications submitted. . . . ' The number of pending cases had increased for each of the five years 1994–98, from 108 to 163. Indeed, the increase in communications was larger than the number formally registered under the Optional Protocol, since a shortage in staff has led to a backlog in processing communications to the point where they can be registered.

It had become the practice of the Committee to include the following paragraph in each view that finds a violation by a state:

> Bearing in mind that, by becoming a State party to the Optional Protocol, the State party has recognized the competence of the Committee to determine whether there has been a violation of the Covenant or not and that, pursuant to article 2 of the Covenant, the State party has undertaken to ensure to all individuals within its territory and subject to its jurisdiction the rights recognized in the Covenant and to provide an effective and enforceable remedy in case a violation has been established, the Committee wishes to receive from the State party, within ninety days, information about the measures taken to give effect to the Committee's Views.

The 1999 Report noted that the shortage in resources had also affected follow-up activities on views, through a Special Rapporteur created by the Committee who began in 1991 to request follow-up information about how states had responded to views finding that they had committed a violation. As of a recent date, the Committee had received follow-up information with respect to 152 of the 253 views that had found violations. No information had been received with respect to 84 views.

> 459. Attempts to categorize follow-up replies are necessarily imprecise. Roughly 30 per cent of the replies received could be considered satisfactory in that they display the State party's willingness to implement the Committee's Views or to offer the applicant an appropriate remedy. Many replies simply indicate that the victim has failed to file a claim for compensation within statutory deadlines and that no compensation can therefore be paid to the victim. Other replies cannot be considered satisfactory because they either do not address the Committee's recommendations at all or merely relate to one aspect of them. . . .
>
> 460. The remainder of the replies either explicitly challenge the Committee's

findings, on either factual or legal grounds, constitute much-belated submissions on the merits of the case, promise an investigation of the matter considered by the Committee or indicate that the State party will not, for one reason or another, give effect to the Committee's recommendations.

Sources of communications and drafting of views

The information under this heading is taken from an article of Elizabeth Evatt, a Committee member since 1992: 'Reflecting on the Role of International Communications in Implementing Human Rights', 5(2) Australian J. of Hum Rts. 20 (1999). Evatt noted that in recent years, Jamaica had become the 'most prolific source of communications', generating between 25 per cent and 30 per cent of the Committee's work on the Optional Protocol. In October 1997 it became the first country to denounce the Optional Protocol, partly because of the complications and delays growing out of the great amount of litigation involving the death penalty and claims of prisoners on death row. See, for example, *Errol Johnson v. Jamaica*, p. 28, *supra.*

The problem of concentration of states extended past Jamaica. By mid-1998, nearly 50 per cent of the 293 cases in which the Committee had adopted views were from Jamaica and Uruguay. Of the remaining views, about 45 per cent related to Western states, 30 per cent from Latin America, 20 per cent from Africa and 5 per cent from Asia and Eastern Europe. (Indeed, more than a few of the 95 states parties to the Optional Protocol have been persistent and systematic violators of basic human rights.) Evatt states:

> If cases from Uruguay and Jamaica are set to one side it may seem paradoxical that almost half the Committee's cases have come from States which apparently enjoy the rule of law and legal protection of human rights. . . . Take Peru, for example. The Committee has made determinations in only six cases from Peru and five of these are 10 years old. Yet there must be hundreds of potential cases the could be brought from that State. Perhaps the victims of abuse are reluctant to challenge their government in the Committee for fear of reprisals or perhaps they do not see the usefulness of the communications procedure unless their government has a basic respect for the rule of law. . . .
>
> It seems likely that. . .many of the victims have no knowledge of the international human rights procedures. . . . It is also likely that many possible complainants lack resources to seek legal advice. . . . .

Delays in considering and disposing of cases under the Optional Protocol have become more common, Evatt points out. By 1993, 'the average time taken from the initiation to the conclusion of a case was about three years' (p. 29). The growing number of states parties to the Optional Protocol, coupled with reduction in recent years of professional staff available to the Committee, are major causes of this situation.

Evatt stresses that in drafting views, the Committee is responsible for interpreting the ICCPR, a universal instrument, 'in a way which maintains its objectives and purposes and which commands respect throughout the world'.

The membership of the Committee, though somewhat imbalanced in favour of western States at present, nevertheless represents all regions and major legal systems. . . . The Committee insists that the standards of the ICCPR must apply in the same way to all States and to all groups. There is no room for relativity. . . .

. . . When dealing with communications, members. . .listen to each other, learn from each other, adjust their own prejudices and assumptions and try to reach an agreed position. But it is not always possible to agree. In the past few years, there has been a tendency. . .to adopt individual opinions. . . . Some decisions of the Committee appear rather obscure or brief because of amendments and deletions carried out in order to arrive at consensus. While consensus is desirable and maintains the collegial approach and the anonymity of decisions, in some cases the price of consensus is too high. . .In those cases it is better for different shades of opinion to be separately presented rather than to undermine or truncate the reasoning of the majority.

Finding of facts

Given only written submissions by the parties, and the fact that many cases come from states with questionable or clearly deficient systems of justice, the Committee faces obvious difficulties in resolving conflicting statements of fact by the individual author and the state. Such disputed allegations and statements of fact figured importantly in *Domukovsky v. Georgia,* Communications Nos. 623–624, 626–627/1995, Views of Committee, April 6, 1998, www1.umn.edu/humanrts/undocs/session 62. The authors' complaints concerned primarily alleged failures of criminal process. The excerpts below suggest one of the Committee's methods for resolving uncertainty.

18.1 The Human Rights Committee has considered the present communication in the light of all the information made available to it by the parties, as provided in article 5, paragraph 1, of the Optional Protocol.

. . .

18.4 Mr. Tsiklauri has claimed that he was arrested illegally in August 1992 without a warrant and that he was not shown a warrant for his arrest until after he had been in detention for a year. The State party has denied this allegation, stating that he was arrested in August 1993, but it does not address the claim in detail or provide any records. In the absence of information provided by the State party . . . and in the absence of an answer to the author's claim that he had been in custody for one year before the warrant was issued, the Committee considers that due weight must be given to the author's allegation. Consequently, the Committee finds that article 9, paragraph 2, has been violated in Mr. Tsiklauri's case.

. . .

18.6 Each of the authors have claimed that they have been subjected to torture and ill-treatment, including severe beatings and physical and moral pressure. . . . The State party has denied that torture has taken place, and stated that the judicial examination found that the claims were unsubstantiated. It has however, not indicated how the court has investigated the allegations, nor has it provided copies of the medical reports in this respect. In particular, with regard to the claim made by Mr. Tsiklauri, the State party has failed to address the allegation, simply referring to an investigation which allegedly showed that he had jumped from a moving vehicle and that he had spilled hot tea over himself. No copy of the investigation report has been handed to the Committee, and Mr. Tsiklauri has contested the outcome of the investigation, which according to him was conducted by police officers without a court hearing ever having been held. In the circumstances, the Committee considers that the facts before it show that the authors were subjected to torture and to cruel and inhuman treatment, in violation of articles 7 and 10, paragraph 1, of the Covenant.

COMMENT ON PROVISIONAL MEASURES

The problem of gaining a state's compliance with the Committee's action does not first arise when the Committee issues its views on a communication. In certain cases, it becomes important, indeed essential, for the state to suspend any action while the communication is being considered. Capital punishment is the prime example.

Consider the following illustration. A group of citizens of Sierra Leone submitted communications to the Committee in October 1998. The Committee, acting consistently with its internal rules through one its members, requested the government of Sierra Leone to stay executions of the authors of the communications as long as the communications were under consideration by the Committee. All such persons were nonetheless executed five days after the request. The Committee then sent an 'urgent' request to Sierra Leone to 'provide clarifications' about the executions, but received no reply. It later adopted a Decision, CCPR/C/64/D/839–841/1998, 4 November 1998, expressing 'its indignation' at the failure to grant the request for interim measures 'in the context of the consideration of the first cases submitted to the Committee since the Optional Protocol entered into force for Sierra Leone'. The Decision 'deplored' Sierra Leone's failure to clarify the circumstances of the execution.

Compare the Sierra Leone case with the *Breard* case in the United States, as recounted in Jonathan Charney and Michael Reisman, *Agora: Breard*, 96 Am. J. Int. L. 666 (1998). It arose in a different international context from the ICCPR Committee. Breard, a Paraguayan citizen, was tried and convicted of murder in Virginia state courts and sentenced to death. He did not at that time raise, nor did the state advise him of, provisions of the Vienna Convention on Consular Relations of 1963 to which the United States and Paraguay were parties. Article 36(1)(b) of that Convention provides that if an accused requests, state authorities shall notify the consular post of (in this case) Paraguay that one of its nationals has been arrested pending trial. 'The said authorities shall inform the person concerned without delay of his rights' under this provision.

After discussions between the United States and Paraguay and a series of further court actions seeking to postpone or upset the conviction, Paraguay filed an application in the International Court of Justice in the Hague, instituting proceedings against the United States and alleging a breach of the Vienna Convention. It sought a retrial, and also requested that the Court indicate provisional measures of protection to ensure that Breard would not be executed pending consideration and disposition of the case. After hearings, the ICJ indicated as a matter of urgency provisional measures that the United States should take to avoid the execution scheduled for that week.

The United States Secretary of State sent a letter to the Governor of Virginia requesting that the Governor suspend the execution. The letter noted that, on the merits, the United States supported Virginia's position. It expressed the State Department's view (i) that the ICJ lacked jurisdiction and (ii) that in any event the ICJ had no authority to issue a binding order on a provisional measure. Referring to 'unique and difficult foreign policy issues', the letter nonetheless requested of Virginia a stay of execution, particularly in view of the difficulties that an execution at this time could cause for the safety of Americans overseas who might wish to invoke the protections of international law but who might be denied those protections on grounds that the United States did not take seriously its obligations under the Convention. The Governor of Virginia replied:

> I am concerned that to delay Mr. Breard's execution so that the International Court of Justice may review this matter would have the practical effect of transferring responsibility from the courts of the Commonwealth and the United States to the International Court. Should the International Court resolve this matter in Paraguay's favour, it would be difficult, having delayed the execution so that the International Court could consider the case, to then carry out the jury's sentence despite the rulings [of] the International Court.
>
> The U.S. Department of Justice, together with Virginia's Attorney General, make a compelling case that the International Court of Justice has no authority to interfere with our criminal justice system. Indeed, the safety of those residing in the Commonwealth of Virginia is not the responsibility of the International Court of Justice. It is my responsibility and the responsibility of law enforcement and judicial officials throughout the Commonwealth. I cannot cede such responsibility to the International Court of Justice.
>
> ... I find no reason to interfere with his sentence.

Breard was then executed.

TOONEN V. AUSTRALIA
Communication No. 488/1992, Human Rights Committee
Views of Committee, March 31, 1994, UN Doc. CCPR/C/50/D/488/1992
1 Int. Hum. Rts. Reports 97 (No. 1994)

[The author of this communication was an Australian citizen resident in the Australian state of Tasmania, and a leading member of the Tasmanian Gay Law Reform Group. He claimed that he was a victim of violations by Australia of Articles 2(1), 17 and 26 of the ICCPR. Article 2(1) provides that each state party will ensure to all individuals the 'rights recognized in the present Covenant, without distinction of any kind, such as ... sex ... political or other opinion ... or other status'. Article 17 provides that no one shall be subjected 'to arbitrary or unlawful interference with his privacy . . .'. Article 26 provides that all persons 'are equal before the law and are entitled without any discrimination to the equal protection of the law'. Forbidden discriminations are similar to those in Article 2(1).

Toonen challenged in particular two provisions of the Tasmanian Criminal Code (Australia being internationally responsible for acts of a component state within its federal structure) which made criminal 'various forms of sexual conduct between men, including all forms of sexual contacts between consenting adult homosexual men in private'. The Tasmanian police had not charged anyone with violations of these statutes, such as 'intercourse against nature', but there remained a threat of enforcement. Moreover, the author alleged that the criminalization of homosexuality had nourished prejudice and 'created the conditions for discrimination in employment, constant stigmatization, vilification, threats of physical violence and the violation of basic democratic rights'. Tasmania alone among Australian jurisdictions continued to have such laws in effect, and the Federal Government's position before the Human Rights Committee was critical of those laws.

Excerpts from the Committee's view follow, starting with some of Australia's observations.]

6.5 The state party does not accept the argument of the Tasmanian authorities that the retention of the challenged provisions is partly motivated by a concern to protect Tasmania from the spread of HIV/AIDS, and that the laws are justified on public health and moral grounds. This assessment in fact goes against the Australian Government's National HIV/AIDS Strategy, which emphasizes that laws criminalizing homosexual activity obstruct public health programmes promoting safer sex. The State party further disagrees with the Tasmanian authorities's contention that the laws are justified on moral grounds, noting that moral issues were not at issue when article 17 of the Covenant was drafted.

6.6 None the less, the State party cautions that the formulation of article 17 allows for *some* infringement of the right to privacy if there are reasonable grounds, and that domestic social mores may be relevant to the reasonableness of an interference with privacy. The State party observes that while laws penalizing homosexual activity existed in the past in other Australian states, they have since been repealed with the exception of Tasmania. Furthermore, discrimination on the basis of homosexuality or sexuality is unlawful in three of six Australian states and the two self-governing internal Australian territories. The Federal Government has declared sexual preference to be a ground of discrimination that may be invoked under ILO Convention No. 111 (Discrimination in Employment or Occupation Convention), and created a mechanism through which complaints about discrimination in employment on the basis of sexual preference may be considered by the Australian Human Rights and Equal Opportunity Commission.

6.7 On the basis of the above, the State party contends that there is now a general Australian acceptance that no individual should be disadvantaged on the basis of his or her sexual orientation. Given the legal and social situation in all of Australia except Tasmania, the State party acknowledges that a complete prohibition on sexual activity between men is unnecessary to sustain the moral fabric of

Australian society. On balance, the State party 'does not seek to claim that the challenged laws are based on reasonable and objective criteria'.
. . .

Examination of the merits:

. . .

8.2 Inasmuch as article 17 is concerned, it is undisputed that adult consensual sexual activity in private is covered by the concept of 'privacy', and that Mr. Toonen is actually and currently affected by the continued existence of the Tasmanian laws. . . .

8.3 The prohibition against private homosexual behaviour is provided for by law, namely, Sections 122 and 123 of the Tasmanian Criminal Code. As to whether it may be deemed arbitrary, the Committee recalls that pursuant to its General Comment 16 on article 17, the 'introduction of the concept of arbitrariness is intended to guarantee that even interference provided for by the law should be in accordance with the provisions, aims and objectives of the Covenant and should be, in any event, reasonable in the circumstances'. The Committee interprets the requirement of reasonableness to imply that any interference with privacy must be proportional to the end sought and be necessary in the circumstances of any given case.

. . .

8.5 As far as the public health argument of the Tasmanian authorities is concerned, the Committee notes that the criminalization of homosexual practices cannot be considered a reasonable means or proportionate measure to achieve the aim of preventing the spread of AIDS/HIV. . . .

8.6 The Committee cannot accept either that for the purposes of article 17 of the Covenant, moral issues are exclusively a matter of domestic concern, as this would open the door to withdrawing from the Committee's scrutiny a potentially large number of statutes interfering with privacy. It further notes that with the exception of Tasmania, all laws criminalizing homosexuality have been repealed throughout Australia and that, even in Tasmania, it is apparent that there is no consensus as to whether Sections 122 and 123 should not also be repealed. Considering further that these provisions are not currently enforced, which implies that they are not deemed essential to the protection of morals in Tasmania, the Committee concludes that the provisions do not meet the 'reasonableness' test in the circumstances of the case, and that they arbitrarily interfere with Mr. Toonen's right under article 17, paragraph 1.

8.7 The State party has sought the Committee's guidance as to whether sexual orientation may be considered an 'other status' for the purposes of article 26. The same issue could arise under article 2, paragraph 1, of the Covenant. The Committee confines itself to noting, however, that in its view the reference to 'sex' in articles 2, paragraph 1, and 26 is to be taken as including sexual orientation.

9. The Human Rights Committee, acting under article 5, paragraph 4, of the Optional Protocol to the International Covenant on Civil and Political Rights, is of the view that the facts before it reveal a violation of articles 17, paragraph 1, *juncto* 2, paragraph 1, of the Covenant.

10. Under article 2(3)(a) of the Covenant, the author, victim of a violation of articles 17, paragraph 1, *juncto* 2, paragraph 1, of the Covenant, is entitled to a remedy. In the opinion of the Committee, an effective remedy would be the repeal of Sections 122 (a), (c) and 123 of the Tasmanian Criminal Code.

11. Since the Committee has found a violation of Mr. Toonen's rights under articles 17(1) and 2(1) of the Covenant requiring the repeal of the offending law, the Committee does not consider it necessary to consider whether there has also been a violation of article 26 of the Covenant.

12. The Committee would wish to receive, within 90 days of the date of the transmittal of its views, information from the State party on the measures taken to give effect to the views.

NOTE

In her article cited at p. 742, *supra*, at p. 24, Elizabeth Evatt commented on Australia's position in the *Toonen* case:

> Australians are only too well aware of the lack of domestic remedies to enforce ICCPR rights. For example, in *Toonen*, the Author's claim that Tasmania's anti-gay law violated his right to privacy could not be taken to the Australian courts. The only remedy available to Mr. Toonen was to take his case to the Committee under the Optional Protocol. . . . Australia had not fulfilled its obligations under Article 2(3) [of the ICCPR]. The Australian Government's response to the finding of violation . . . was to do what should have been done already, that is to introduce legislation to provide a remedy enforceable in the courts for any arbitrary interference with the privacy of sexual conduct between consenting adults [The Human Rights (Sexual Conduct) Act 1994 (Cth.)]. Had that remedy been available in the first place—as one might reasonably expect if Article 2(3) were taken seriously—the Committee might not have needed to consider Mr. Toonen's case. . . .

The reasons for the failure of a domestic Australian remedy are discussed at pp. 1014–1021, *infra*.

Discussion of homosexual acts and of other implications for gay and lesbian people of rights to privacy and equal protection continues at pp. 813–36, *infra*, in the framework of the European Convention on Human Rights.

QUESTIONS

1. Suppose that a communication comes from a state making sodomy between consenting adult males a criminal offence. The communication's author has been charged with this offence and faces trial. The state's defence before the Committee rests on biblical condemnation of such conduct and related moral views to the same effect held by a large majority of the state's population. What issues should be raised by the parties and discussed by the Committee? What relevance has the *Toonen* view to such a case?

2. How do you understand and assess para. 8.2? As a Committee member, would you have supported or opposed inclusion of this paragraph in its present form, or in any form? Was it necessary? What distinct issues are raised by inclusion of sexual orientation in the term 'sex' in Articles 2(1) and 26?

3. How do you assess the Committee's argument related to Article 17? Would you have taken a different approach?

4. What differences do you see between the Committee's expressing its understanding of Articles 17 and 2(1) in relation to homosexual acts through a view such as *Toonen*, or through a General Comment expressing the same ideas? Which route would you favor?

5. The United States is a party to the ICCPR, but not to the Optional Protocol. After the *Toonen* decision, is it likely to be in violation of the Covenant (Articles 2(1), 17) because the laws of certain states within the United States make sodomy between consenting adult males criminal? What are the obligations of the United States under Article 2(1) of the Covenant? How, to what institution and with what effect, might an individual in the United States who was adversely affected by a sodomy statute make the claim that the United States was in violation of the ICCPR?

ADDITIONAL READING

Laurence Helfer and Alice Miller, 'Sexual Orientation and Human Rights: Toward a United States and Transnational Jurisprudence', 9 Harv. Hum. Rts. J. 61 (1996); Douglas Sanders, 'Getting Lesbian and Gay Issues on the International Human Rights Agenda', 18 Hum. Rts Q. 67(1996) R. Wintemute, *Sexual Orientation and Human Rights* (1997); W. Morgan, 'Identfying Evil for what It Is: Tasmania, Sexual Perversity and the United Nations', 19 Melb. U. L. Rev 740 (1994); and *ibid.*, 'Protecting Rights or Just Passing the Buck? The Human Rights (Sexual Conduct) Bill 1994', 1 Aust. J. Hum. Rts 409 (1994). See also references under Additional Reading at p. 778, *infra*.

COMMENT ON HATE SPEECH

The view of the ICCPR Committee under the Optional Protocol that appears below, the *Faurisson* case, involves a so-called Holocaust-denial law that has a close affinity with laws making 'hate speech' a criminal offence (and that may also lead to civil sanctions). This Comment provides background on the general issue of hate speech, several definitions of which appear in the official texts below. The fundamental idea covers abusive, denigrating, harassing speech based on a group or individual's national, religious, racial, or ethnic identity. In some but not all definitions, such speech must incite to violence or discrimination.

These restrictive laws clearly impinge on freedom of speech, a core value of the human rights movement that is protected under the major universal and regional human rights instruments. Consider the universal instruments, which at once proclaim and qualify this freedom:

> **Article 19, UDHR:** Everyone has the right to freedom of opinion and expression; this right includes freedom to. . .impart information and ideas through any media and regardless of frontiers.
> **Article 19, ICCPR:** . . .
> (2) Everyone shall have the right to freedom of expression; this right shall include freedom to . . . impart information and ideas of all kinds, regardless of frontiers. . . .
> (3) The exercise of the right provided for in paragraph 2 of this article carries with it special duties and responsibilities. It may therefore be subject to certain restrictions, but these shall only be such as are provided by law and are necessary: (a) For respect of the rights or reputations of others; (b) For the protection of national security or of public order (*ordre public*), or of public health or morals.

Note also the following ICCPR articles, each of which has a comparable UDHR article: (1) the equal protection clause in Article 26; (2) the provision in ICCPR Article 5 that nothing in the Covenant should be interpreted as implying 'for any group or person any right to engage in any activity . . . aimed at the destruction of any of the rights and freedom recognized herein. . . . '; and (3) the provision in Article 17 that no one shall be subject to 'arbitrary or unlawful interference with his privacy . . . nor to unlawful attacks on his honour and reputation'.

The arguments in favour of free speech are broadly familiar, for example: the full realization of the individual human personality, the challenge to existing beliefs and the related stimulus to inquiry and debate and development of knowledge, the relation to principles of democratic government and pluralism, the close functional association with other human rights like freedoms of belief, religion, and association. But are these arguments sufficient to justify the protection of hate speech directed to particular racial, ethnic, religious, gender or other groups or their members? Such speech itself attacks basic premises of the human rights system, premises as deep as equal human dignity, respect for others, and equal protection. It may deny that the targeted group is entitled to benefit together with the rest of the population from human rights protections. It may advocate, indeed passionately urge, discriminatory or even violent action against members of the targeted group. It may pose threats of a greater or lesser immediacy of such violence.

The quoted provisions above of the ICCPR include qualifications to free speech that bear generally on these types of restrictive laws. Several human rights instruments are more explicit on these issues. Article 20(2) of the ICCPR doesn't simply 'permit' but 'requires' legal prohibition of certain kinds of hate advocacy. Note the ambiguous wording, providing that '[a]ny advocacy of national, racial or religious hatred that constitutes incitement to discrimination, hostility or violence shall be prohibited by law'. The ICCPR Committee has not issued a General Comment on Article 20. Manfred Nowak, in his *U.N. Covenant on Civil and Political Rights: CCPR Commentary* (1993), observes (p. 365) that the 'legal formulation of this provision is not entirely clear'. The wording of para. (2):

literally means that incitement to discrimination without violence must also be prohibited. ... Particularly inexplicable is the insertion of the word 'discrimination'. ... It is most difficult to conceive of an advocacy of national, racial or religious hatred that does not simultaneously incite discrimination. ... Art. 20(2). ..may be sensibly interpreted only in light of its object and purpose, i.e., taking into consideration its *responsive character* with regard to the Nazi racial hatred campaigns. ... Thus, despite its unclear formulation, States Parties are not obligated by Art. 20(2) to prohibit advocacy of hatred in private circles that instigates non-violent actions of racial or religious discrimination. What the delegates. ..had in mind was to. ...prevent the public incitement of racial hatred and violence within a State or against other States and peoples.

Note that Article 7 of the UDHR says in part: 'All are entitled to equal protection against any discrimination in violation of this Declaration and against any incitement to such discrimination'.

The United States ratified the ICCPR in 1992. In giving its consent to ratification, and acting consistently with proposals made to it by the Bush administration (see p. 1039, *infra*), the Senate entered a reservation to Article 20 that then qualified the US ratification. It reads: 'Article 20 does not authorize or require legislation or other action by the United States that would restrict the right to free speech and association protected by the Constitution and laws of the United States'.

Compare with Article 20 an equivalent provision, Article 4 of the Convention on Elimination of All Forms of Racial Discrimination. In that article, the states parties 'condemn all propaganda . . . based on ideas or theories of superiority of one race or group of persons or one colour or ethnic origin'. They undertake to declare a punishable offence 'all dissemination of ideas based on racial superiority or hatred, incitement of racial discrimination, as well as all acts of violence' against such a race or group. Article 1 defines 'racial discrimination' to mean any distinction based on 'race, colour, descent, or national or ethnic origin' that has the purpose or effect of impairing equal enjoyment of rights 'in the political, economic, social, cultural or any other field of public life'. When the United States ratified the Racial Convention, it reserved as to Article 4.

The primary constitutional provision referred to in these two reservations by the United States is the First Amendment: 'Congress shall make no law . . . abridging the freedom of speech. . . .'. The decisions of the US Supreme Court over recent decades have set stringent criteria for governmental restriction of denigrating or hate speech, whether directed to individuals or to groups, criteria that are described in the articles cited below in the section on Additional Reading.

The *Jersild* Decision

The United States reservations underscore the difference among countries in attitudes toward restrictive measures imposed by a state on hate speech. Canada, for example, 'has provided a rich jurisprudence on hate speech and has accepted a greater degree of limitation on expression than [the United States]'.[4]

Consider now the approach of the European Court of Human Rights in *Jersild v. Denmark*, Series A, No. A298 (1994). The question posed was whether Jersild, a Danish journalist, was criminally liable for aiding and abetting three youths who made racist remarks on interviews conducted by Jersild on a television programme on matters of public interest. The three young men were members of a group, the Greenjackets, that engaged in hate speech against particular groups—in this case people, particularly Danish residents, of African descent. In the course of the interview conducted by Jersild after he had located the men, and which had been sharply edited by Jersild from an initial length of hours to a few minutes, the men made numerous ugly and denigrating remarks about blacks. There was no allegation in the criminal charge that Jersild or the broadcasting station shared those views. On the other hand, since the point of the programme was to convey information to the Danish public about atypical, small racist groups, there was no effort by Jersild or the broadcasting station to challenge or oppose the racist views expressed.

A Danish penal statute, responsive to obligations of Denmark under the Convention on the Elimination of All Forms of Racial Discrimination, imposed a fine or imprisonment on '[a]ny person who, publicly or with the intention of disseminating it to a wide circle of people, makes a statement, or other communication, threatening insulting or degrading a group of persons on account of their race, colour, national or ethnic origin or belief . . .'. The three youths were found guilty of violating the statute, and did not appeal. Jersild was found guilty of aiding and abetting the three youths. His conviction was affirmed by the Danish appellate courts, and he then instituted proceedings before the European Commission on Human Rights, which ultimately referred the case to the European Court of Human Rights.

The Court decided that the conviction—that is, not the hate-speech statute abstractly, but the statute as here applied to Jersild for aiding and abetting—violated the free expression provisions (including freedom of media) of Article 10 of the European Convention on Human Rights. Its opinion stressed the need to protect freedom of the press, and that news reporting through interviews was an important means of informing the public. Conviction of a journalist in these circumstances could hamper discussion of matters of public interest. It concluded that the limitation on Jersild's freedom of expression was not 'necessary in a democratic society', a requirement of Article 10. The prosecution and conviction were disproportionate to the state's interest, also expressed in Article 10, of protecting the reputation or rights of others.

One of the dissenting opinions observed:

> . . . The applicant has cut the entire interview down to a few minutes, probably with the consequence or even the intention of retaining the most crude remarks.

---

[4] Dominic McGoldrick and T. O'Donnell, 'Hate-Speech Laws: Consistency with National and International Human Rights Law', 18 Leg. Studies 453 (1998), at 458.

That being so, it was absolutely necessary to add at least a clear statement of disapproval. The majority of the Court sees such disapproval in the context of the interview, but this is an interpretation of cryptic remarks. Nobody can exclude that certain parts of the public found in the television spot support for their racist prejudices.

And what must be the feelings of those whose human dignity has been attacked, or even denied, by the Greenjackets? Can they get the impression that seen in context the television broadcast contributes to their protection? A journalist's good intentions are not enough in such a situation, especially in a case in which he has himself provoked the racist statements.

Another dissenting opinion noted:

While appreciating that some judges attach particular importance to freedom of expression, the more so as their countries have largely been deprived of it in quite recent times, we cannot accept that this freedom should extend to encouraging racial hatred, contempt for races other than the one to which we belong, and defending violence against those who belong to the races in question. It has been sought to defend the broadcast on the ground that it would provoke a healthy reaction of rejection among the viewers. That is to display an optimism, which to say the least, is belied by experience. Large numbers of young people today, and even of the population at large, finding themselves overwhelmed by the difficulties of life, unemployment and poverty, are only too willing to seek scapegoats who are held up to them without any real word of caution; for—and this is an important point—the journalist responsible for the broadcast in question made no real attempt to challenge the points of view he was presenting, which was necessary if their impact was to be counterbalanced, at least for the viewers.

Hate Speech in Former Yugoslavia and Rwanda

The effect of years of intense Serbian-nationalist rhetoric under the rule of Milosevich on the internal and international wars in the Former Yugoslavia is well known. A news article reported in 1999 that the United States and its Western allies in the Bosnia peacekeeping operation were creating a tribunal with power to close radio and television stations and punish newspapers that issued propaganda undermining peace efforts. Western officials described the broadcasts that they wished to arrest as 'poisonous propaganda'. Groups of journalists and civil liberties groups expressed their concern about these efforts by democratic states to place restraints on the media. The Western officials avoided use of the term censorship, and explained 'that had no other option, given the venomous propaganda that they said often masquerades as news coverage in Bosnia and that can threaten the safety of the American-led NATO peacekeeping force there'. One spokesman said, 'Basically, there's a tradition here of propaganda in the class of Goebbels'. A State Department official said: 'There are obvious free-speech concerns, but we need to put in place something to deal with the abuses of the media—the hate, the racial epithets and ethnic slurs': *New York Times*, April 24, 1998, p. A8.

Consider the following observations about Rwanda by Bill Berkeley, 'Radio in Rwanda: The Sounds of Silence', *San Diego Union-Tribune*, August 18, 1994:

. . .

. . . Human rights groups, the United Nations and even, reluctantly, the U.S. State Department have described this systematic slaughter [In Rwanda] as 'genocide', yet no one has explained how thousands of peasants who say they had never killed before could have been lured, incited or coerced into participating in mass murder on par with this century's worst massacres. One answer, according to captive killers like Kiruhura and other moderate Hutus who were targeted by death squads but managed to escape, lies in the sinister propaganda broadcast by radio stations affiliated with the now-deposed Rwandan government. This was the match that started the fire, they say.

. . .

. . . The Tutsis were demonized . . . Radio Rwanda and a station owned by members of [the former Hutu President] Habyarimana's inner circle, Radio Milles Collines, had been terrorizing the Hutus with warnings about the evil Tutsi-led RPF and Hutu oppositionists, who were labeled 'enemies' or 'traitors' and who 'deserved to die'. Endless speeches, songs and slogans demonized the Tutsis. . . .

Throughout the terror, Radio Rwanda and Radio Milles Collines have systematically blurred the distinction between rebel soldiers and Tutsi civilians. On May 23, for example, Radio Rwanda warned its listeners of what it called the 'means and clues that the Inyenzi [cockroaches] use to infiltrate in a given zone'. It said RPF soldiers 'change their clothing appearance most of the time, trying to be confused with ordinary people who till the soil and go to the market'.

Hutus were urged to 'guard seriously the roadblock', a reference to the checkpoints where Tutsis were selected for slaughter. On June 1 Radio Milles Collines described the rebels as 'criminals' responsible for a series of harrowing massacres, a fact it claimed had been 'confirmed by international sources'. . . . [T]he broadcast concluded: 'This is the real face of the RPF. These people are not Rwandans, they are revengeful Ugandans. We hate them; we are disgusted with them, and nobody will accept that they take power. . . .'

. . .

'All the Westerners who come here ask us this question', says Sixbert Musangamfura, a Hutu journalist. 'They forget the evil of Hitler's propaganda. The propaganda heard here resembles the propaganda made by Joseph Goebbels. People received this propaganda all day long. It is the propaganda that is at the base of this tragedy.' . . .

NOTE

The *Faurisson* opinion that follows deals with 'Holocaust denial laws' that have been enacted by several states including Austria, Belgium, France, Germany, Israel, Lithuania, Spain, and Switzerland. As noted in McGoldrick and O'Donnell, *supra* n. 4, at 457, these laws vary a great deal:

The essential feature of the laws which attracts the label of holocaust denial is that they make it a criminal offence to deny certain things in a certain way. . . .

[F]or the French law it is 'crimes against humanity as defined by the Nuremberg International Military Tribunal'. The German law is wider, as it refers to 'persecution under National Socialism or any other form of despotism or tyranny'. The Israeli law is even wider again: 'acts committed in the period of the Nazi regime, which are crimes against the Jewish people or crimes against humanity'. The Austrian law extends to denial of the 'nationalist socialist genocide or other national socialist crimes against humanity'. The Austrian law extends to cover the gross trivialisation, approval or justification of the same. The German law is similar.

FAURISSON v. FRANCE
Communication No. 550/1993, Human Rights Committee
Views of Committee, November 8, 1996, UN Doc. A/52/40 (1999),
Vol. II, at 84

[Robert Faurisson, author of the communication and a former professor of literature, was removed from his university chair in 1991. He had expressed doubt about or denial of the accuracy of conventional accounts of the Holocaust, including (i) his conviction that there were no homicidal gas chambers for the extermination of Jews in Nazi concentration camps, (ii) his doubts over the number of people killed, and (iii) his disbelief in the records and evidence of the Nuremberg trial that were used to convict Nazis.

In 1990, the French legislature passed the so-called Gayssot Act. It amended the 1881 law on Freedom of the Press by adding Article 24 *bis*, which made it an offence to contest (*contestation*) the existence of the category of crimes against humanity as defined in the London Charter of 1945, on the basis of which Nazi leaders were convicted by the International Military Tribunal at Nuremberg in 1945–46. For the relevant provision of the Charter and excerpts from the Nuremberg judgment, see pp. 113–121, *supra*.

Faurisson attacked the 1990 law as a threat to academic freedom, including freedom of research and expression. He claimed that the Gayssot Act raised to the rank of infallible dogma the proceedings and verdict at Nuremberg, and endorsed forever the orthodox Jewish version of the Second World War. Arguing that the Nuremberg records could not be treated as infallible, he cited examples of historical revision such as the Katyn massacre in Poland of Polish army officers that was initially attributed to Germans but that was later shown to be of Soviet responsibility. Faurisson described as 'exorbitant' the 'privilege of censorship' from which the representatives of the Jewish community in France benefited.

The state party noted that anti-racism legislation adopted by France in the 1980s was considered insufficient to bring legal action against the trivialization of Nazi crimes. There was governmental concern over 'revisionism' by individuals justifying their writing through their status as historians. The French Government viewed these revisionist theses as a 'subtle form of contemporary anti-semitism'. The Gayssot Act was meant to fill a legal vacuum while defining the new criminal conduct as precisely as possible.

Associations of French resistance fighters and of deportees to German concentration camps filed a private criminal action against Faurisson, who was convicted in 1991 of violating the Gayssot Act. The Court of Appeal of Paris upheld the conviction and imposed a fine. Faurisson took the position that further appeal to the Court of Cassation would be futile and filed the present communication. He argued that the Act violated the ICCPR, although his communication did not invoke specific provisions.

The ICCPR Committee concluded in an earlier proceeding that the communication was admissible and that it raised issues under Article 19 of the Covenant. This proceeding led to the views of the Committee under Article 5(4) of the Optional Protocol, as well as five individual opinions signed by seven Committee members. Excerpts from the views of the Committee and several individual opinions follow.]

9.3 Although it does not contest that the application of the terms of the Gayssot Act . . . may lead, under different conditions than the facts of the instant case, to decisions or measures incompatible with the Covenant, the Committee is not called upon to criticize in the abstract laws enacted by States parties. The task of the Committee under the Optional Protocol is to ascertain whether the conditions of the restrictions imposed on the right to freedom of expression are met in the communications which are brought before it.

9.4 Any restriction on the right to freedom of expression must cumulatively meet the following conditions: it must be provided by law, it must address one of the aims set out in paragraph 3 (a) and (b) of article 19, and must be necessary to achieve a legitimate purpose.

9.5 . . . [T]he Committee concludes . . . that the finding of the author's guilt [in the French proceedings] was based on his following two statements: ' . . . I have excellent reasons not to believe in the policy of extermination of Jews or in the magic gas chambers . . . I wish to see that 100 per cent of the French citizens realize that the myth of the gas chambers is a dishonest fabrication'. His conviction therefore did not encroach upon his right to hold and express an opinion in general. Rather the court convicted Mr. Faurisson for having violated the rights and reputation of others. For these reasons the Committee is satisfied that the Gayssot Act, as read, interpreted and applied to the author's case by the French courts, is in compliance with the provisions of the Covenant.

9.6 To assess whether the restrictions placed on the author's freedom of expression by his criminal conviction were applied for the purposes provided for by the Covenant, the Committee begins by noting . . . that the rights for the protection of which restrictions on the freedom of expression are permitted by article 19, paragraph 3, may relate to the interests of other persons or to those of the community as a whole. Since the statements made by the author, read in their full context, were of a nature as to raise or strengthen anti-semitic feelings, the restriction served [sic] the respect of the Jewish community to live free from fear of an atmosphere of anti-semitism. The Committee therefore concludes that the restriction of the author's freedom of expression was permissible under article 19, paragraph 3 (a), of the Covenant.

9.7 Lastly the Committee needs to consider whether the restriction of the author's freedom of expression was necessary. The Committee noted the State party's argument contending that the introduction of the Gayssot Act was intended to serve the struggle against racism and anti-semitism. It also noted the statement of a member of the French Government, the then Minister of Justice, which characterized the denial of the existence of the Holocaust as the principal vehicle for anti-semitism. . . . [T]he Committee is satisfied that the restriction of Mr. Faurisson's freedom of expression was necessary within the meaning of article 19, paragraph 3, of the Covenant.

10. The Human Rights Committee, acting under article 5, paragraph 4, of the Optional Protocol to the International Covenant on Civil and Political Rights, is of the view that the facts as found by the Committee do not reveal a violation by France of article 19, paragraph 3, of the Covenant.

STATEMENT OF THOMAS BUERGENTHAL

As a survivor of the concentration camps of Auschwitz and Sachsenhausen whose father, maternal grandparents and many other family members were killed in the Nazi Holocaust, I have no choice but to recuse myself from participating in the decision of this case.

INDIVIDUAL OPINION BY NISUKE ANDO (CONCURRING)

. . . In my view the term 'negation' ('contestation'), if loosely interpreted, could comprise various forms of expression of opinions and thus has a possibility of threatening or encroaching the right to freedom of expression, which constitutes an indispensable prerequisite for the proper functioning of a democratic society. In order to eliminate this possibility it would probably be better to replace the Act with a specific legislation prohibiting well-defined acts of anti-semitism or with a provision of the criminal code protecting the rights or reputations of others in general.

INDIVIDUAL OPINION BY ELIZABETH EVATT AND DAVID KRETZMER, CO-SIGNED BY ECKART KLEIN (CONCURRING)

. . .

2. . . . The main issue is whether the restriction has been shown by the State party to be necessary, in terms of article 19, paragraph 3 (a), for respect of the rights or reputations of others.

3. . . . While we entertain no doubt whatsoever that the author's statements are highly offensive both to Holocaust survivors and to descendants of Holocaust victims (as well as to many others), the question under the Covenant is whether a restriction on freedom of expression in order to achieve this purpose may be regarded as a restriction necessary for the respect of the rights of others.

4. Every individual has the right to be free not only from discrimination on grounds of race, religion and national origins, but also from incitement to such discrimination. This is stated expressly in article 7 of the Universal Declaration of

Human Rights. It is implicit in the obligation placed on States parties under article 20, paragraph 2, of the Covenant to prohibit by law any advocacy of national, racial or religious hatred that constitutes incitement to discrimination, hostility or violence. The crime for which the author was convicted under the Gayssot Act does not expressly include the element of incitement, nor do the statements which served as the basis for the conviction fall clearly within the boundaries of incitement, which the State party was bound to prohibit, in accordance with article 20, paragraph 2. However, there may be circumstances in which the right of a person to be free from incitement to discrimination on grounds of race, religion or national origins cannot be fully protected by a narrow, explicit law on incitement that falls precisely within the boundaries of article 20, paragraph 2. This is the case where, in a particular social and historical context, statements that do not meet the strict legal criteria of incitement can be shown to constitute part of a pattern of incitement against a given racial, religious or national group, or where those interested in spreading hostility and hatred adopt sophisticated forms of speech that are not punishable under the law against racial incitement, even though their effect may be as pernicious as explicit incitement, if not more so.

. . .

6. The notion that in the conditions of present-day France, Holocaust denial may constitute a form of incitement to anti-semitism cannot be dismissed. . . .

7. The Committee correctly points out, as it did in its General Comment 10, that the right for the protection of which restrictions on freedom of expression are permitted by article 19, paragraph 3, may relate to the interests of a community as a whole. This is especially the case in which the right protected is the right to be free from racial, national or religious incitement. . . . It appears . . . that the restriction on the author's freedom of expression served to protect the right of the Jewish community in France to live free from fear of incitement to anti-semitism. . . .

8. The power given to States parties under article 19, paragraph 3, to place restrictions on freedom of expression, must not be interpreted as license to prohibit unpopular speech, or speech which some sections of the population find offensive. Much offensive speech may be regarded as speech that impinges on one of the values mentioned in article 19, paragraph 3(a) or (b) (the rights or reputations of others, national security, ordre public, public health or morals). The Covenant therefore stipulates that the purpose of protecting one of those values is not, of itself, sufficient reason to restrict expression. The restriction must be necessary to protect the given value. This requirement of necessity implies an element of proportionality. The scope of the restriction imposed on freedom of expression must be proportional to the value which the restriction serves to protect. . . .

9. The Gayssot Act is phrased in the widest language and would seem to prohibit publication of bona fide research connected with matters decided by the Nuremburg Tribunal. Even if the purpose of this prohibition is to protect the right to be free from incitement to anti-semitism, the restrictions imposed do not meet the proportionality test. They do not link liability to the intent of the author, nor

to the tendency of the publication to incite to anti-semitism. Furthermore, the legitimate object of the law could certainly have been achieved by a less drastic provision that would not imply that the State party had attempted to turn historical truths and experiences into legislative dogma that may not be challenged, no matter what the object behind that challenge, nor its likely consequences. In the present case we are not concerned, however, with the Gayssot Act, in abstracto, but only with the restriction placed on the freedom of expression of the author by his conviction for his statements in the interview in Le Choc du Mois. Does this restriction meet the proportionality test?

10. The French courts examined the author's statements in great detail. Their decisions, and the interview itself, refute the author's argument that he is only driven by his interest in historical research. In the interview the author demanded that historians 'particularly Jewish historians' who agree that some of the findings of the Nuremburg Tribunal were mistaken be prosecuted. The author referred to the 'magic gas chamber' ('la magique chambre à gaz') and to 'the myth of the gas chambers' ('le mythe des chambres à gaz'), that was a 'dirty trick' ('une gredinerie') endorsed by the victors in Nuremburg. The author has, in these statements, singled out Jewish historians over others, and has clearly implied that the Jews, the victims of the Nazis, concocted the story of gas chambers for their own purposes. While there is every reason to maintain protection of bona fide historical research against restriction, even when it challenges accepted historical truths and by so doing offends people, anti-semitic allegations of the sort made by the author, which violate the rights of others in the way described, do not have the same claim to protection against restriction. The restrictions placed on the author did not curb the core of his right to freedom of expression, nor did they in any way affect his freedom of research. ... It is for these reasons that we joined the Committee. . . .

Individual opinion by Rajsoomer Lallah (concurring)

. . .

11. I conclude, therefore, that the creation of the offence provided for in the Gayssot Act, as it has been applied by the Courts to the author's case, falls more appropriately, in my view, within the powers of France under article 20, paragraph 2, of the Covenant. The result is that there has, for this reason, been no violation by France under the Covenant.

. . .

13. Recourse to restrictions that are, in principle, permissible under article 19, paragraph 3, bristles with difficulties, tending to destroy the very existence of the right sought to be restricted. The right to freedom of opinion and expression is a most valuable right and may turn out to be too fragile for survival in the face of the too frequently professed necessity for its restriction in the wide range of areas envisaged under paragraphs (a) and (b) of article 19, paragraph 3.

. . .

QUESTIONS

1. As a legislator, would you have voted for the Gayssot Act? How would you have reacted to the following argument in general, or as applied to the passage of that Act?

> Freedom of expression is indeed a fundamental right. While its protection may sometimes be an end in itself, its exercise may not disturb the fundamental goals underlying human rights law. One of the most fundamental of those goals is achieving equality and non-discrimination. In fact, if there is any right which enjoys primacy among rights, it is arguably the principle of equality and non-discrimination. . . . The goal of hate mongers is to convince others that the members of the target group are not entitled to equal protection of the law; the hate mongers seek a society of discrimination. . . . They should not be entitled to claim protection under the right to freedom of expression for their abuse of speech rights to achieve that goal.[5]

2. Suppose that an author's statements leading to a prosecution under the Gayssot Act appeared in a periodical article that was the only writing by the author on the subject. The author concludes that the Nuremberg judgment, later judicial decisions describing the Holocaust, and 'official' accounts of the Holocaust were part of a conscious conspiracy among the victorious Allies to spur feelings of guilt by Germans and hatred of others toward them.

Would a conviction by French courts be likely to be upheld under the opinion above for the Committee? Under the concurring opinion by Elizabeth Evatt and David Kretzmer? How do these opinions differ, and which do you view as the better one?

3. Should the opinions have referred to arguments in favour of freedom of speech, or to the criteria in Section 19 for limiting speech, such as 'public order' or 'public morals'? What could have been the bases or events in France and French history for relying on such criteria to uphold the statute and affirm the conviction? Would comparable bases have been available in the United States to justify legislation similar to the Gayssot Act?

4. Do you think that the opinions as a whole succeed in illuminating the relevant aspects of the ICCPR, or indeed of human rights in general? Do they advance understanding of the value and limitations of free speech, and of the dilemmas of resolving conflicts among rights within the human rights instruments?

NOTE

Some states have forbidden political groups or parties that are based on racism, and hence that employ hate speech, from participating in elections. In Israel, for example, a system of proportional representation works by having a candidates'

---

[5] Stephanie Farrior, 'Moulding the Matrix: The Historical and Theoretical Foundations of International Law Concerning Hate Speech', 14 Berkeley J. of Int. L. 1 (1996), at 6, 98.

list from different parties or political formations presented to the electorate, which votes for a list as a whole. Amendment No. 9 to the Basic Law on the Knesset (Parliament) provides: 'A candidate's list shall not participate in elections to the Knesset if its objects or actions, expressly or by implication, include one of the following: ... (3) incitement to racism'.

ADDITIONAL READING

Sandra Coliver (ed.), *Striking a Balance: Hate Speech, Freedom of Expression and Non-Discrimination* (1992); Kent Greenawalt, *Fighting Words: Individuals, Communities, and Liberties of Speech* (1995); S. Douglas-Scott, 'The Hatefulness of Protected Speech: A Comparison of the American and European Approaches', 7 Wm. & Mary Bill of Rts. J. 305 (1999).

CHITAT NG V. CANADA
Communication No. 469/1991, Human Rights Committee
Views of Committee, November 5, 1993, UN Doc. A/49/40 (1994),
Vol. II, at 189

[Chitat Ng, a British subject born in Hong Kong and a resident of the United States, was convicted in Canada in 1985 for attempted theft and shooting a security guard. In 1987, the United States requested his extradition to stand trial in California courts on 19 criminal counts including kidnapping and 12 murders committed in 1984–85. If convicted, Chitat Ng faced the possibility of the death penalty. At the time of his submission of this communication to the Human Rights Committee, he was detained in Canada.

Canada effectively abolished the death penalty in 1976 (with a limited exception for certain military offences). It was not party at the time of this litigation to the Second Protocol to the ICCPR. Its extradition treaty with the United States provided that extradition could be refused where the relevant offence was punishable by death in the requesting state but not in the requested state, unless the requesting state gave adequate assurance that the death penalty would not be imposed. The power to seek such assurance was discretionary. After the Supreme Court of Canada decided in 1991 that extradition without assurance did not violate Canada's constitutional protection of human rights or standards of the international community, Chitat Ng was immediately extradited.

He claimed that the extradition violated the ICCPR, on grounds that execution by gas asphyxiation as provided by California statutes, after a conviction and imposition of the death penalty, would constitute cruel and inhuman treatment; that prison conditions on death row were cruel and inhuman; and that racial bias in the United States would influence imposition of the death penalty.

Among other responses, Canada argued that Chitat Ng could not be considered a 'victim' within the meaning of Article 1 of the Optional Protocol since his allegations rested on assumptions of what might happen in the United States, not on historical facts. The Committee concluded that he could be so considered, given the seriousness of the charges that were subject to the death penalty, statements by prosecutors involved in the case that they would seek the death penalty, and the failure of the State of California when intervening before the Supreme Court of Canada to disavow the prosecutors' position. Hence there was a 'real risk (a necessary and foreseeable consequence)' that Canada's extradition itself, the subject of the litigation, could be found to be a violation of the Covenant because of the fact of execution or the means of execution in the United States.

The materials at pp. 31–55, *supra*, consider the legality of capital punishment under national and international law. That broad issue is relevant to the excerpts that follow from the opinions of the Committee and several individual members.]

15.2 Counsel claims that capital punishment must be viewed as a violation of article 6 of the Covenant 'in all but the most horrendous cases of heinous crime; it can no longer be accepted as the standard penalty for murder'. Counsel, however, does not substantiate this statement or link it to the specific circumstances of the present case. . . . Mr. Ng was convicted of committing murder under aggravating circumstances; this would appear to bring the case within the scope of article 6, paragraph 2, of the Covenant. In this connection the Committee recalls that it is not a 'fourth instance' and that it is not within its competence under the Optional Protocol to review sentences of the courts of States. This limitation of competence applies a fortiori where the proceedings take place in a State that is not party to the Optional Protocol.

15.3 The Committee notes that article 6, paragraph 1, must be read together with article 6, paragraph 2, which does not prohibit the imposition of the death penalty for the most serious crimes. . . . Mr. Ng was extradited to stand trial on 19 criminal charges, including 12 counts of murder. If sentenced to death, that sentence, based on the information which the Committee has before it, would be based on a conviction of guilt in respect of very serious crimes. He was over eighteen years when the crimes of which he stands accused were committed. Finally, while the author has claimed . . . that his right to a fair trial would not be guaranteed in the judicial process in California, because of racial bias in the jury selection process and in the imposition of the death penalty, these claims have been advanced in respect of purely hypothetical events, and nothing in the file supports the contention that the author's trial in the Calaveras County Court would not meet the requirements of article 14 of the Covenant.
. . .

15.7 In the light of the above, the Committee concludes that Mr. Ng is not a victim of a violation by Canada of article 6 of the Covenant.

16.1 In determining whether, in a particular case, the imposition of capital punishment constitutes a violation of article 7, the Committee will have regard to the relevant personal factors regarding the author, the specific conditions of detention on death row, and whether the proposed method of execution is particularly abhorrent. In the instant case, it is contended that execution by gas asphyxiation is contrary to internationally accepted standards of humane treatment, and that it amounts to treatment in violation of article 7 of the Covenant. . . .

16.2 The Committee is aware that, by definition, every execution of a sentence of death may be considered to constitute cruel and inhuman treatment within the meaning of article 7 of the Covenant; on the other hand, article 6, paragraph 2, permits the imposition of capital punishment for the most serious crimes. Nonetheless, the Committee reaffirms . . . that, when imposing capital punishment, the execution of the sentence ' . . . must be carried out in such a way as to cause the least possible physical and mental suffering'.

16.3 . . . [T]he author has provided detailed information that execution by gas asphyxiation may cause prolonged suffering and agony and does not result in death as swiftly as possible, as asphyxiation by cyanide gas may take over 10 minutes. The State party had the opportunity to refute these allegations on the facts; it has failed to do so. Rather, the State party has confined itself to arguing that in the absence of a norm of international law which expressly prohibits asphyxiation by cyanide gas, 'it would be interfering to an unwarranted degree with the internal laws and practices of the Unites States to refuse to extradite a fugitive to face the possible imposition of the death penalty by cyanide gas asphyxiation'.

16.4 In the instant case and on the basis of the information before it, the Committee concludes that execution by gas asphyxiation, should the death penalty be imposed on the author, would not meet the test of 'least possible physical and mental suffering', and constitutes cruel and inhuman treatment, in violation of article 7 of the Covenant. Accordingly, Canada, which could reasonably foresee that Mr. Ng, if sentenced to death, would be executed in a way that amounts to a violation of article 7, failed to comply with its obligations under the Covenant, by extraditing Mr. Ng without having sought and received assurances that he would not be executed.

16.5 The Committee need not pronounce itself on the compatibility, with article 7, of methods of execution other than that which is at issue in this case.

17. The Human Rights Committee, acting under article 5, paragraph 4, of the International Covenant on Civil and Political Rights, is of the view that the facts as found by the Committee reveal a violation by Canada of article 7 of the Covenant.

18. The Human Rights Committee requests the State party to make such representations as might still be possible to avoid the imposition of the death penalty and appeals to the State party to ensure that a similar situation does not arise in the future.

. . .

INDIVIDUAL OPINION BY MR. FAUSTO POCAR (PARTLY DISSENTING, PARTLY CONCURRING AND ELABORATING)

. . .

. . . As the Committee pointed out in its General Comment 6(16), 'the article also refers generally to abolition in terms which strongly suggest that abolition is desirable'. Furthermore, the wording of paragraphs 2 and 6 clearly indicates that article 6 tolerates—within certain limits and in view of future abolition—the existence of capital punishment in States parties that have not yet abolished it, but may by no means be interpreted as implying for any State party an authorization to delay its abolition or, a fortiori, to enlarge its scope or to introduce or reintroduce it. Accordingly, a State party that has abolished the death penalty is in my view under the legal obligation, under article 6 of the Covenant, not to reintroduce it. This obligation must refer both to a direct reintroduction within the State party's jurisdiction, as well as to an indirect one, as is the case when the State acts—through extradition, expulsion or compulsory return—in such a way that an individual within its territory and subject to its jurisdiction may be exposed to capital punishment in another State. I therefore conclude that in the present case there has been a violation of article 6 of the Covenant.

Regarding the claim under article 7, I agree with the Committee that there has been a violation of the Covenant, but on different grounds. I subscribe to the observation of the Committee that 'by definition, every execution of a sentence of death may be considered to constitute cruel and inhuman treatment within the meaning of article 7 of the Covenant'. Consequently, a violation of the provisions of article 6 that may make such treatment, in certain circumstances, permissible, entails necessarily, and irrespective of the way in which the execution may be carried out, a violation of article 7 of the Covenant. . . .

INDIVIDUAL OPINION BY A. MAVROMMATIS AND W. SADI (DISSENTING)

We do not believe that, on the basis of the material before us, execution by gas asphyxiation could constitute cruel and inhuman treatment within the meaning of article 7 of the Covenant. A method of execution such as death by stoning, which is intended to and actually inflicts prolonged pain and suffering, is contrary to article 7.

Every known method of judicial execution in use today, including execution by lethal injection, has come under criticism for causing prolonged pain or the necessity to have the process repeated. We do not believe that the Committee should look into such details in respect of execution such as whether acute pain of limited duration or less pain of longer duration is preferable and could be a criterion for a finding of violation of the Covenant.

. . .

INDIVIDUAL OPINION BY BERTIL WENNERGREN (PARTLY DISSENTING, PARTLY CONCURRING)

. . .

By definition, every type of deprivation of an individual's life is inhuman. In practice, however, some methods have by common agreement been considered as acceptable methods of execution. Asphyxiation by gas is definitely not to be found among them. There remain, however, divergent opinions on this subject.

On 21 April 1992, the Supreme Court of the United States denied an individual a stay of execution by gas asphyxiation in California by a 7:2 vote. One of the dissenting justices, Justice John Paul Stevens, wrote: 'The barbaric use of cyanide gas in the Holocaust, the development of cyanide agents as chemical weapons, our contemporary understanding of execution by lethal gas, and the development of less cruel methods of execution all demonstrate that execution by cyanide gas is unnecessarily cruel. In light of all we know about the extreme and unnecessary pain inflicted by execution by cyanide gas', Justice Stevens found that the individual's claim had merit.

. . .

INDIVIDUAL OPINION BY KURT HERNDL (DISSENTING)

1. While I do agree with the Committee's finding that there is no violation of article 6 of the Covenant in the present case, I do not share the majority's findings as to a possible violation of article 7. . . .

Mr. Ng cannot be regarded as victim in the sense of article 1 of the Optional Protocol. . .

. . .

11. . . . The Committee's majority. . .attempts to make a distinction between various methods of execution.

. . .

13. No scientific or other evidence is quoted in support of this dictum. Rather, the onus of proof is placed on the defendant State which, in the majority's view, had the opportunity to refute the allegations of the author on the facts, but failed to do so. This view is simply incorrect.

14. As the fact sheets of the case show, the remarks by the Government of Canada on the sub-issue 'Death Penalty as a Violation of Article 7' total two and a half pages. In those remarks the Government of Canada states i.a. the following:

> While it may be that some methods of execution would clearly violate the Covenant, it is far from clear from a review of the wording of the Covenant and the comments and jurisprudence of the Committee, what point on the spectrum separates those methods of judicial execution which violate article 7 and those which do not.

. . .

17. It is also evident from the foregoing that the defendant State has examined the whole issue in depth and did not deal with it in the cursory manner suggested in paragraph 16.3 of the Committee's Views. . . . [T]he Minister of Justice of Canada stated as follows:

> You have argued that the method employed to carry out capital punishment in California is cruel and inhuman, in itself. I have given consideration to this issue. The method used by California has been in place for a number of years and has found acceptance in the courts of the United States.

. . .

19. . . . To attempt to establish categories of methods of judicial executions, as long as such methods are not manifestly arbitrary and grossly contrary to the moral values of a democratic society, and as long as such methods are based on a uniformly applicable legislation adopted by democratic processes, is futile, as it is

futile to attempt to quantify the pain and suffering of any human being subjected to capital punishment. . . .

. . .

INDIVIDUAL OPINION BY MR. NISUKE ANDO (DISSENTING)

. . .[T]he swiftness of death seems to be the very criterion by which the Committee has concluded that execution by gas asphyxiation violates article 7.

In many of the States parties to the Covenant where death penalty has not been abolished, other methods of execution such as hanging, shooting, electrocution or injection of certain materials are used. Some of them may take longer time and others shorter than gas asphyxiation, but I wonder if, irrespective of the kind and degree of suffering inflicted on the executed, all those methods that may take over ten minutes are in violation of article 7 and all others that take less are in conformity with it. . . .

. . .

. . .[I]t is impossible for me to specify which kind of suffering is permitted under article 7 . . . . What I can say is that article 7 prohibits any method of execution which is intended for prolonging suffering of the executed or causing unnecessary pain to him or her. As I do not believe that gas asphyxiation is so intended, I cannot concur with the Committee's view. . . .

. . .

NOTE

The electric chair was introduced in the United States in 1890 as a more humane form of execution. But over time it has been displaced by many states by other forms of execution, particularly lethal injection which is now viewed as more humane. In 1999, the US Supreme Court agreed to review a case from a state court raising the question of the constitutionality of execution by electric chair under the Eighth Amendment (cruel and unusual punishment) to the federal Constitution. *Bryan v. Moore*, 120 S.G. 394 (1999).

QUESTIONS

1. In light of the reasoning in the Committee opinion and individual opinions, what result would have been likely if the means of execution were the guillotine? Would it be relevant if execution were open, to the extent possible, to a public? What are the criteria that in fact emerge, and which if any of them do you find persuasive?

2. What guidance does the Committee opinion give to states in different parts of the world about the legality of their methods of execution? As a Committee member, what approach would you have suggested toward resolving the issue of the legality of a given means of execution in this multinational, multicultural world?

HENRY STEINER, INDIVIDUAL CLAIMS IN A WORLD OF MASSIVE VIOLATIONS: WHAT ROLE FOR THE HUMAN RIGHTS COMMITTEE?

in Philip Alston and James Crawford (eds.), The Future of UN Human Rights Treaty Monitoring 15 (2000), at 38

[In this article, Steiner considers what purposes the Committee might serve through the communications procedure. He concludes that the Committee cannot realistically serve the basic dispute-resolution function that informs adjudication by courts in many national legal systems. Nor can it effectively do justice in the individual case within the limits of its jurisdiction and to that extent vindicate the rule of law. Nor can it effectively protect rights under the ICCPR through deterrence. What remains a plausible and important purpose, Steiner concludes, is that of 'expounding (elucidating, interpreting and explaining) the Covenant so as to engage the Committee in an ongoing, fruitful dialogue with states parties, non-governmental and intergovernmental institutions, advocates, scholars and students'.]

The views written over two decades have created a considerable and important body of doctrine related to the ICCPR. But the doctrine is little reported or organised outside the Committee's internal documents such as Annual Reports, and a handful of scholarly articles and books. Only occasionally do views figure in a discursive way in judicial opinions of state courts. Only rarely do they summon attention and provoke comment outside formal legal circles. the production over two decades of views of this character, however valuable for the relatively small number of individual beneficiaries, has not mage a significant contribution to the normative development of the human rights movement.

Expounding a constitution or basic law-making treaty is a different business. It requires judges to use appropriate cases to elucidate the instrument that they are applying, to interpret and explain it. Committee members must employ such cases to probe the basic purposes of the Covenant, to show its significance for the life and needs of the peoples it is meant to serve. Such an understanding of the role of opinions will often require acknowledgement of the difficulties in reaching a judgment, the consideration of alternative grounds, and some form of justification for the decision reached. In the novel and vexing cases, it will always require reasoned argument rather than the terse and opaque application of norm to facts. The Committee must act as a deliberative body that is sensitive to the legitimate and immense possibilities of its role in the human rights movement.

Given the significance and complexity as well as range of the issues that come before it under the Protocol, The Committee is inevitably engaged in the development of the Covenant: confronting its ambiguities and indeterminacy, resolving conflicts among its principles and rights, working out meanings of its grand terms through consideration of the object and purposes of the Covenant, or through recourse to methods to interpretation other than the telelogical, such as *travaux préparatoires*, the contextual analysis of a provision within the broader structure of the treaty, or attention to trends in legal and moral thought.

To expound the ICCPR is to make this process explicit, to confront openly the dilemmas before the Committee in deciding the more troubling communications. The Committee fails to expound, and therefore to realise what should be a major purpose of the communications procedure, when its considerations in reaching a decision remain covert, secreted within formal opinions that merely state rather than argue towards conclusions. In so acting, the Committee wastes a unique opportunity to make the ICCPR a better known, more significant and persuasive instrument, and thereby to add strength to the universal human rights movement.

. . .

Despite its stark differences from courts, the Committee could contribute to the international adjudicatory processes that elaborate human rights law in the same manner as do opinions of the European and Inter-American Courts of Human Rights. . . . Its jurisdiction under the Protocol finds distant analogies in the human rights cases before the constitutional courts of states in Europe and elsewhere such as South Africa, and in the appellate courts with a broader jurisdiction that exercise the power of judicial review in countries like the United States. All these courts rule on the consistency of a state's executive and legislative action with the supreme law of a treaty or constitution. Of course the Committee lacks the formal authority and prestige of these other institutions and influences the general discourse of human rights correspondingly less. But that gap can be significantly narrowed.

To one or another degree, all these courts serve the two purposes earlier sketched: achieving justice in the individual case, and deterrence. But they do more. There can be no doubt of the significance for other courts, for legislatures and executive officials, for the legal profession and for the general public of their major opinions that expound the constitutions or law-making treaties before them. Such opinions are not put to the side as matters of dry law settling this or that dispute. Rather, they provoke discussion and reflection, praise and criticism. They inform and stimulate an ongoing legal, political, and moral debate on human rights issues. They become part of a rich and varied dialogue. They educate.

. . .

The institutional status of the Committee could enhance the influence of its views. . .[T]he ICCPR makes the Committee its exclusive organ. Each of the Committee's three principal activities concern only that instrument. No other international organ is as dedicated to the application and development of this vital treaty, and hence as well situated to assume a principal responsibility for expounding it. Courts in national legal systems that incorporated the ICCPR as domestic law could not make as strong an institutional claim for international attention to their interpretations.

Two significant changes in the Committee's mode of functioning under the Protocol would be necessary for realising these proposals: breaking with the historical pattern and style of writing views, and moving from a mandatory to a discretionary jurisdiction.

[In developing his first point, Steiner criticises the 'formulaic presentations' of the great majority of the Committee's views, particularly because of their lack of readability and the frequent terse, unelaborated statement of the Committee's conclusions following an exhaustive presentation of the parties' arguments. He offers several explanations for this form of presentation, including the observation that 'the very effort to reach consensus has sapped the views of strength. . . . The upshot is that views. . .hardly summon the human rights community to debate and dialogue. They fail to educate their readership adequately about the ICCPR in particular or about human rights in general'. He continues:]

The writing of views that possess the suggested characteristics requires that the Committee husband its energies under the Protocol, to allow more time to research and reflect on an issue, and to write. The Committee would have to allocate time to cases meriting exploration for the development of the Covenant, rather than depend on the flow of registered communications. These requirements would be difficult to satisfy in light of the overload of cases before the Committee and the prospects for its increase.

What then can be done to enable the Committee to establish some control over its caseload and the allocation of its time?. . .

Achieving [the necessary reduction in caseload] could then require amending the Protocol to make the jurisdiction of the Committee (in whole or in substantial part) discretionary rather than mandatory. . . .

Operating under a discretionary jurisdiction, the Committee might be able to issue 20 to 30 views a year, an ample number for making significant contributions to the understanding and development of the Covenant, and for stimulating thought and dialogue with diverse actors. In so different a system, the Committee would necessarily develop criteria for selection of communications. Such criteria might, for example, lead to rejection of cases where the case turned on contro-verted matters of fact that the Committee was not in a good position to resolve. They could disfavour cases raising issues that had been settled in prior views or that were not of general significance. The criteria might give priority to emergent issues affecting many states. The Committee might decide to handle a group of related problems, such as issues of criminal procedure or free speech, over several sessions.

. . . The Judicial Code of the United States gives the United States Supreme Court (with minor exceptions) discretion whether to review any case decided below by a federal or state court—even cases of the highest significance, involving the consti-tutionality of federal or state statutes, that had previously been subject to manda-tory jurisdiction. The Court's criteria for exercising discretion in favour of review include a decision by a state or federal court on 'an important question of federal law that has not been, but should be, settled by this Court'.

[This illustration from the United States involves] appeals relating to cases that . . . were decided by . . . a state or federal appellate court in the same country. If the Protocol provided for a discretionary jurisdiction, the Committee could have no such assurance that the decision below had been decided with integrity by a reputable court. The stakes are higher, in the sense that denial of review might quash the only hope of petitioners who lacked any possibility of achieving justice in their own state (a situation that might continue if a petitioner eventually benefited from a favourable view that the state refused to enforce).

Such an objection to a discretionary jurisdiction has considerable force. This article earlier referred to the strong sense of satisfaction of the Committee in doing justice in the individual case, and used as an illustration the invalidation of a conviction and sentence of death after a trial whose procedures violated the ICCPR. The surrender of automatic review, not simply in cases of capital punishment but also of torture and other gross and systematic abuses, in order to marshal the time and energy to expound the Covenant in appropriate cases might appear not only unjustified but heartless, remote, and sadly academic.

The proposal is less harsh than such an objection suggests. The present mandatory jurisdiction cannot realise the general purpose of providing justice in the individual case and vindicating the rule of law. Hence the Committee's historical approach to the communications procedure has veiled a more productive approach for the cause of human rights. Moreover, the proposed discretionary jurisdiction could take many forms. It could give the Committee discretion for the great range of cases but require decisions on the merits in a specific category of cases, perhaps capital punishment cases. Deciding on the precise criteria for review, including a decision whether any categorical exception to a discretionary jurisdiction could by its sheer volume undermine the new approach, requires deliberation by the Committee about substantive and statistical matters.

. . .

QUESTIONS

1. Why do you suppose Steiner rejects as impractical or otherwise unrealistic certain purposes or functions that the Committee might be thought to serve, particularly (a) general dispute resolution for the states parties to the Optional Protocol, (b) vindication of the rule of law by achieving justice in the individual case originating in those states parties, and (c) protecting ICCPR rights against violation by deterrence? Do you agree?

2. How do you assess the proposal that the major purpose of the communications procedures should be to expound the ICCPR in the way described in the article, even at the cost of abandoning mandatory jurisdiction for all communications that are found to be admissible under the Optional Protocol? What criteria would you suggest as guidelines for determination whether to hear on the merits a given communication? Where would a Committee view like *Errol Johnson v. Jamaica*, p. 28, *supra*, or *Chitat Ng* fall within those criteria?

3. From the perspective of the article's stress on expounding the ICCPR and writing views that promoted discussion within and dialogue among the different kinds of human rights actors, how do you assess the three preceding views of the Committee? What other purposes do they serve?

4. 'Each of the Committee's three functions can be found inadequate from different perspectives. But if we look at the Committee as a totality, and examine these functions not discretely but as complementary approaches toward the task of developing and protecting human rights, we reach a far more favourable judgment about the significance of the Committee's work for the human rights movement'. Do you agree? How would you develop this assertion?

5. EVALUATION

One of the perplexing questions about every international human rights institution (as well as about many national institutions) concerns the effect that it has had or may have on norms and practice in particular states, or more grandly on the human rights movement as a whole. For example, how does one go about assessing, let alone measuring, that effect? What would constitute proof, or at least reasonably persuasive evidence, that the ICCPR Committee's work has influenced the course of events in a given country, or the understandings and work of other human rights institutions?

At the end of his comprehensive scholarly account of the work of the Human Rights Committee during its initial 15 years, Dominic McGoldrick writes in *The Human Rights Committee* (1991), at 504:

> It is very difficult to provide positive evidence that the existence of the Covenant and the work of the HRC is having any concrete and positive effect on the human rights position in the States parties. However, many of the State representatives that have appeared before the HRC have stated that the Covenant and the work of the HRC have played an important role at the national level. It would be immensely helpful if the HRC could catalogue and reproduce those claims together with any more specific evidence of wholesale or partial national reviews of the implementation of the Covenant and of account being taken of the Covenant and the HRC, for example, in legislative assemblies, executive decision making, judicial or administrative decisions.

More generally, the question arises whether evaluation of the Committee should depend entirely on its actual or potential role *within* the Covenant, *independently* of all other human rights treaties and organs, or should also depend on its place and contribution within a more comprehensive framework of (at least the universal parts of) the human rights movement. That larger framework would include the Charter and its organs, as well as other universal human rights treaties and their organs. Within it, inquiry would be directed to the *complementary* nature of the functions that different organs fill or should fill under different treaties, with the goal of thereby maximizing the effectiveness of the human rights movement as a whole.

For example, comparison between the ICCPR Committee and UN Commission can inquire what the differences between these two institutions are, how they came about, what they say about the institutions and the political frameworks within which they were designed and now function, whether the differences make sense today, and, if not, how the institutions should be changed. The characteristics of the two organs that can be usefully compared include:

> do states participate in the work of each organ?
> what powers does each organ have to investigate?
> what powers does each organ have to evaluate, judge, condemn, or order particular action?
> what are the voting techniques and patterns?

what types of violations are examined?

are there marked influences by states on the agenda and how items are decided?

in what ways, if at all, have the mandates and powers of each organ evolved?

what role have NGOs in each organ?

Consider whether the answers that you bring to these questions would justify a characterization of the ICCPR Committee as the more 'legal' body, and of the UN Commission as the more 'political'. In responding, be clear about what meanings you are attributing to the two vital terms.

Consider the following excerpt from Dominic McGoldrick, *The Human Rights Committee* (1991), at 54:

... [O]n a number of occasions members of the HRC have indicated their perceptions of the institutional character and nature of the HRC and it is instructive to note some of these.

2.21 Mr Uribe-Vargas described it as a body whose work was of a 'judicial nature'. Mr Mora-Rojas said that 'The Committee was quite different in nature from other bodies and, even though it was not a court or a tribunal, it did hear testimony and had evidence presented to it'. Mr Tomuschat has commented that, 'The Committee was ... ruled by the Covenant and while it was true that members were not judges they had the task of applying the provisions laid down in the Covenant and therefore had to exercise judgement. It was the duty of the Committee to ensure that States parties fulfilled their obligations under the Covenant'. Mr Tomuschat has also said that 'The Committee was not an international court but was similar to one in certain respects, particularly in regard to its obligation to be guarded by exclusively legal criteria—which rightly distinguished it from a political body'. Mr Ermacora was concerned that the Committee should avoid giving the impression that it was 'a sort of advisory service, or had technical, assistance functions, whereas in fact its activities were based on legally binding instruments, with all the attendant consequences that that entailed'. Mr Aguilar commented that the Committee 'was not a judicial body' and 'its role was not to find fault'. Mr Bouziri commented that the 'Committee was not a court of law'. Mr Pocar commented that the Committee's function 'was not to judge and then either to condemn or congratulate States parties'. Mr Graefrath 'did not share the view that the work of the Committee could be compared to that of a court ... Unlike a court the Committee was not required to make judgements, but simply to consider and comment on reports and to act as a conciliatory body in dealing with complaints and communications'. Mr Opsahl has described the HRC as the 'executive organ' of the Covenant. Emphasis is often put on the HRC's role as a promoter, monitor, or supervisory body with respect to improved human rights performances. However, some members have expressed doubts as to whether the HRC can properly be called a 'supervisory body' or a 'parent organ'. Finally, Mr Suy (UN Legal Advisor) believed the HRC to be 'neither a legislative nor a judicial body but that every expert body was sui generis', and Mr Herndl, former Under Secretary-General of the United Nations, recently described the HRC as 'the guardian of the Covenant'.

B. COMPARISONS WITH OTHER U.N. HUMAN RIGHTS TREATY REGIMES

Chapter 9, which earlier examined the ICCPR Committee as a case study, concludes with comparisons with other treaty bodies. Not every universal human rights treaty—for example, the 1948 Genocide Convention and the 1956 Slavery Convention—has created a special organ to implement the treaty or monitor state conduct. In addition to the ICCPR Committee, there are now five other treaty bodies, three of which have figured in earlier materials:

- the Committee on Economic, Social and Cultural Rights (CESCR), established to monitor compliance with the ICESCR (see Chapter 4);
- the Committee on the Elimination of Racial Discrimination (CERD), established under the International Convention on the Elimination of All Forms of Racial Discrimination;
- the Committee on the Elimination of Discrimination against Women (CEDAW), established under the Convention on the Elimination of All Forms of Discrimination against Women (see Chapter 3);
- the Committee against Torture (CAT), established under the Convention against Torture and Other Cruel, Inhuman or Degrading Treatment or Punishment; and
- the Committee on the Rights of the Child (CRC), established under the Convention on the Rights of the Child (see Chapter 6).

COMMENT ON REPORTING AND COMPLAINTS PROCEDURES FOR THE SIX HUMAN RIGHTS TREATY BODIES

Although their mandates differ somewhat, reflecting the respective political climates in which the treaties were adopted and their subject-matters, the five treaty bodies listed above function essentially in ways similar to the ICCPR Committee. The following description notes salient differences among the reporting and complaints procedures, suggests common problems before these bodies, and sketches current proposals for reform within specific treaties or for the UN human rights treaty system as a whole.

States' Reports

The principal activity of all treaty bodies remains the consideration of state reports. For the most part, states must report within two years of becoming a party to the treaty and subsequently at five yearly intervals. On occasion, urgent *ad hoc* reports are sought by some of the committees. Initially, the reporting function was envisaged by most governments to be of a relatively *pro forma* nature, but it has since evolved into a much more demanding exercise.

Three examples illustrate how these committees initiated changes in procedures that have strengthened the reporting procedures. Perhaps the most significant is the practice, initiated by CERD in 1972, of 'inviting' states to send representatives to respond to questions by Committee members when the report by that state is being considered. This procedure was not foreseen in the treaty but it has since been adopted by all treaty bodies and is now an indispensable and fully accepted part of the process. A second example, initiated by the CESCR in 1991, is the practice of examining the situation in countries that have failed to report, even if no government-provided information is available and no representative is present. This practice removes the pre-existing reward to governments that ratified and never reported, thereby avoiding committee scrutiny. The third example is the move from a procedure that was restricted to the examination of 'official' information (i.e. produced by the government or an intergovernmental organization) to one that takes full account of all sources and invites NGOs to provide written, and in some cases oral, information.

Another indication of the extent to which reporting procedures have been broadened in scope appears in the following statement of the functions of reporting. It was adopted in relation to economic rights but has been generally accepted by the treaty bodies. The functions are:

[1] . . . to ensure that a comprehensive review is undertaken with respect to national legislation, administrative rules and procedures, and practices in an effort to ensure the fullest possible conformity with the Covenant . . .

[2] . . . to ensure that the State party monitors the actual situation with respect to each of the rights on a regular basis . . .

[3] . . . to provide the basis for the elaboration of clearly stated and carefully targeted policies, including the establishment of priorities which reflect the provisions of the Covenant. . . .

[4] . . . to facilitate public scrutiny of government policies . . . and to encourage the involvement of the various . . . sectors of society in the formulation, implementation and review of the relevant policies . . .

[5] . . . to provide a basis on which the State party itself, as well as the Committee, can effectively evaluate the extent to which progress has been made . . .

[6] . . . to enable the State party itself to develop a better understanding of [its] problems and shortcomings . . .

[7] . . . to develop a better understanding of the common problems faced by States . . . .[6]

Although reporting has achieved a great deal, critics have identified shortcomings in all aspects of the process. In relation to states, there is widespread non-reporting and significant tardiness. Reports are often superficial and governments are reluctant to facilitate domestic debate around the reports. In relation to the committees themselves, the level of expertise and independence of members has been questioned, the concluding observations on states reports are often excessively general, the approach adopted to different reports is not always consistent

---

[6] Committee on Economic, Social and Cultural Rights, General Comment No. 1 (1989), UN Doc. HRI/GEN/1/REV.3 (1997), p. 56.

within the same treaty body, and there is inadequate follow-up to recommendations made to governments.

Another pressing issue concerns the duplication of reporting obligations under the different treaty regimes. As originally conceived, the system was designed to enable a state to become a party to one treaty, even if it had no interest in any of the others. Now that the majority of states has ratified the majority of the six treaties, the overlapping reporting burden and the uncoordinated responses by the different committees are increasingly being challenged by governments. States are subject to the complex bureaucratic demands associated with a regular dialogue with as many as six separate committees. Identical reports might elicit different responses from different committees. NGOs with sparse resources must deal with the difficulties of monitoring states' compliance with each of these treaties and seeking to give adequate publicity to the work of each.

A report commissioned by the General Assembly has suggested three long-term options for reducing reporting burdens: (i) reducing the number of treaty bodies and hence the number of reports required; (ii) encouraging states to produce a single 'global' report to be submitted to all relevant treaty bodies; and (iii) replacing the requirement of comprehensive periodic reports with specifically-tailored reports.[7] Although there has been significant support, at least in the abstract, for reform, many observers have expressed concern about attempts to overhaul the entire reporting system. Committee members and NGOs fear that proposals for such systematic reform might be used to mask a significant downgrading of reporting, while governments worry that it might strengthen the system of reporting to a politically unacceptable extent.

On-site Visits

The Convention against Torture is distinctive among the six treaties in providing for a more intrusive procedure under which one or more of its members may be asked to undertake a confidential inquiry and to report urgently to the CAT Committee in cases in which it 'receives reliable information which appears to it to contain well-founded indications that torture is being systematically practised in the territory of a State Party' (Article 20). This procedure applies automatically to all states parties unless, at the time of ratification, they specifically exclude its application. With the agreement of the state concerned, an on-site visit may be undertaken, although all of the relevant proceedings are confidential. The Committee may, however, decide to include a summary account of the results in its annual report. This occurred in relation to Turkey in 1993, and the OHCHR indicated in January 2000 that 'there has been an extraordinary increase in the invocation of inquiries in recent years'.[8]

A similar procedure has also been provided for in an Optional Protocol to the CEDAW Convention which was adopted in October 1999.[9] Article 8 establishes an

---

[7] P. Alston, *Final Report on Enhancing the Long-Term Effectiveness of the United Nations Human Rights Treaty System*, UN Doc. E/CN.4/1997/74.

[8] Annual Appeal 2000, <www.unhchr.ch/html/menu2/9/fundrais/fundr.htm>, p.93.

[9] GA Res. 54/4 (1999). For the text see: <www.un.org/womenwatch/daw/cedaw/protocol/current.htm>.

inquiry procedure that allows the Committee to initiate a confidential investigation by one or more of its members where it has received reliable information of grave or systematic violations by a state party of rights established in the Convention. Where warranted and with the consent of the state party, the Committee may visit the country concerned. Any findings, comments or recommendations will be transmitted to the government, which has six months in which to respond. Thereafter, Article 9 provides that the government may be invited to provide the Committee with details of any remedial efforts it has taken. This procedure applies to all states accepting the Protocol, unless they specifically opt out of it.

Both CERD and the CESCR have undertaken on-site missions in order to pursue their dialogue with certain states, but these missions have been undertaken on the basis of the general monitoring provisions of the relevant treaties, rather than for specific investigations.

The most elaborate on-site human rights inspection procedure is to be found in the European Convention for the Prevention of Torture and Inhuman or Degrading Treatment or Punishment (see p. 795, *infra*). Since 1992, work has been under way to draft an optional protocol to CAT which would establish a comparable system of scheduled and unscheduled visits by the Committee to places of detention or other places where torture or cruel, inhuman or degrading treatment or punishment may be occurring (see UN Doc. E/CN.4/2000/58).

Interstate Complaints Procedures

Initially, an interstate complaints procedure was considered to be an important element in an effective monitoring system. Thus the first of the treaties adopted— CERD—provides for any state party to bring a complaint against another. By the following year, however, when the ICCPR was adopted, a comparable procedure was made dependent upon the specific, separate acceptance by a state of Article 41 of the Covenant. CAT has a similar optional provision. These procedures are determinedly 'statist' in nature in that they make no provision for involvement by NGOs or individuals, their emphasis is upon achieving a 'friendly solution', and the procedure is undertaken in closed meetings. The ICCPR also provides for the establishment of an *ad hoc* Conciliation Commission, in the event that an amicable solution cannot be found.

Despite the availability of the interstate complaint procedure to all of the 155 states parties to the CERD (as of February 2000) and the acceptance of Article 41 of the ICCPR by 47 of its 144 states parties (and the CAT procedure under Article 21 has been accepted by 44 states), no interstate complaint has ever been brought under any of the UN treaty-based procedures. The equivalent procedure under the European Human Rights Convention has been used a number of times, p. 804, *infra*.

Individual Complaints Procedures

Analogous procedures to individual complaints under the Optional Protocol of the ICCPR are also provided for under CAT (accepted by 40 states) and CERD (accepted by 27 states). Although this Chapter has demonstrated the significance of the communications procedure under the ICCPR, the similar procedures under the other two treaties have generated very few complaints. By February 2000 CAT had received 154 complaints, which had resulted in 33 Final Views, of which 16 found violations by the state concerned. CERD had received only nine complaints, in relation to three of which violations had been found. Compare the figures for the ICCPR Committee at p. 740, *supra.* One explanation for this discrepancy is that the ICCPR covers much of the same substantive territory as CAT and CERD, and its procedures are much better known to NGOs and other potential complainants.

A complaints procedure has also been included in the Optional Protocol to CEDAW adopted in 1999. It follows the general structure of the ICCPR Protocol. Communications may be submitted to the CEDAW Committee by or on behalf of individuals or groups of individuals 'claiming to be victims of a violation of any of the rights set forth in the Convention by that State Party'. It includes a number of matters absent from the ICCPR Protocol but developed by the practice of the lCCPR Committee—for example, requests for interim measures, and provision for reports by states parties of their compliance with views.[10] The Protocol was signed by 23 countries (all but one (Senegal) from Latin America or Western Europe) on 19 December 1999 and will enter into force upon being ratified by 10 states. The UN Secretary-General's Special Adviser on Gender Issues, Angela King, and the HCHR, Mary Robinson, noted at the time that:

> [l]n addition to providing an international remedy for violations of women's rights, the Optional Protocol will act as an incentive for Governments to take a fresh look at the means of redress that are currently available to women at the domestic level. This is perhaps the most important contribution of the Optional Protocol. It is action at the national level which will create the environment in which women and girls are able to enjoy all their human rights fully, and where their grievances will be addressed with the efficiency and speed they deserve.[11]

A draft Optional Protocol to the ICESCR, submitted by the ESCR Committee to the UN Commission on Human Rights in 1997 (UN Doc. E/CN.4/1997/105), remains on the Commission's agenda.[12] While NGOs and a few states have expressed support, some governments (notably Canada, Germany and Sweden) have rejected the proposal (See UN Docs. E/CN.4/1998/84 and Add.1; E/CN.4/1999/112 and Add.1; E/CN.4/2000/49).

---

[10] See A. Byrnes and J. Connors, 'Enforcing the Human Rights of Women: A Complaints Procedure for the Women's Convention?', 21 Brook. J Int. L. 679 (1996).

[11] <www.un.org/womenwatch/daw/news/ akop.htm>.

[12] P. Alston, 'Establishing a Right to Petition Under the Covenant on Economic, Social and Cultural Rights', 4/2 *Collected Courses of the Academy of European Law* (1995) 107.

QUESTION

The three states noted above which rejected a communications procedure for the ICE-SCR Committee are all parties to the ICCPR Optional Protocol. Does the ICESCR, relative to the ICCPR or CEDAW, raise particularly difficult problems for a committee deciding on individual complaints against a state? Suppose that an individual complainant alleges that state X has failed in its duty to provide (under Article 11 of the ICESCR) 'adequate food'. What kinds of issues could arise in the consideration and disposition of such a complaint? Are they radically different from the issues before the ICCPR Committee in cases involving equal protection, hate speech, or capital punishment?

ADDITIONAL READING

A. Byrnes, 'Using International Human Rights Law and Procedures to Advance Women's Human Rights', in K. Askin and D. Koenig, *Women and International Human Rights Law* (Vol. 2, 2000) 79; E. Tistounet, 'The Problem of Overlapping among Different Treaty Bodies', in P. Alston and J. Crawford (eds.), *The Future of UN Human Rights Treaty Monitoring* 383 (2000); C. Scott, 'Bodies of Knowledge: A Diversity Promotion Role for the UN High Commissioner for Human Rights', ibid., 403; E. Evatt, 'Ensuring Effective Supervisory Procedures: The Need for Resources', ibid., 461; M. Schmidt, 'Servicing and Financing Human Rights Supervision', ibid., 481; L. Helfer, 'Forum Shopping for Human Rights', 148 U. Penn. L. Rev. 285 (1999); I. Boerefijn, *The Reporting Procedure under the Covenant on Civil and Political Rights: Practice and Procedures of the Human Rights Committee* (1999); A. Bayefsky, 'The UN Human Rights Regime: Is it Effective?', 91 Proc. Ann. Mtg. Am. Soc. Int'l L. 1997 460 (1998); E. Klein (ed.), *The Monitoring System of Human Rights Treaty Obligations* (1998); M. Banton, *International Action Against Racial Discrimination* (1996); D. Harris and S. Joseph (eds.), *The International Covenant on Civil and Political Rights and United Kingdom Law* (1995).

10

Regional Arrangements

Part C's materials on intergovernmental institutions concludes with a look at the world's major regional human rights systems. After an introductory section comparing the advantages and disadvantages of a regional rather than universal system—in fact, in the case of human rights, of a regional system together with a universal system, rather than *only* a universal system—this chapter turns to the regional arrangements in Europe, the Americas and Africa.

The materials describe the norms, institutional structure and processes of the regional systems, and invite comparisons among them as well as with the UN system. The European and Inter-American systems have innovative institutions and processes; the African system has distinctive norms. Thus the regional arrangements add in important ways to knowledge derived from the United Nations and UN-related treaties like the ICCPR about possible avenues toward the protection and promotion of human rights. They illustrate the full range of the human rights movement's institutional architecture.

Chapter 10 concentrates on one distinctive aspect of each system. The remarkable feature of the European system is its productive and effective Court; the materials illustrate its work and the dilemmas of supranational adjudication through its decisions involving issues of homosexuality, blasphemy, and political democracy. In the Inter-American system, the materials look briefly at its Court but concentrate on its Commission on Human Rights, a powerful organ with tasks and functions not found in the European system. They examine the work of the Commission in a field of increasing importance for global and regional systems: defining and institutionalizing the practices of electoral democracy. The African system is the least developed institutionally. Part of Chapter 5 on cultural relativism looked at its distinctive stress on duties as well as rights; the present materials look primarily at the communications procedure of the African Commission on Human and Peoples' Rights.

A. COMPARISON OF UNIVERSAL AND REGIONAL SYSTEMS

The relationship between 'universal' (meaning, in this context, United Nations-sponsored) and regional human rights arrangements is a complex one. In addition to the three major systems, there is a largely dormant Arab system and a proposal for the creation of an Asian regional system. Although Chapter VIII of the United Nations Charter makes provision for regional arrangements in relation to peace and security, it is silent as to human rights cooperation at that level. Nevertheless, the Council of Europe moved as early as 1950 to adopt the European Convention on Human Rights. It was not until 1969 that the analogous American Convention was adopted. In the meantime, at least until the mid-1960s, the UN remained at best ambivalent about such developments. Vasak has noted some of the reasons for its reluctance:

> For a long time, regionalism in the matter of human rights was not popular at the United Nations: there was often a tendency to regard it as the expression of a breakaway movement, calling the universality of human rights into question. However, the continual postponements of work on the International Human Rights Covenants led the UN to rehabilitate, and to be less suspicious (less jealous, some would say) towards, regionalism in human rights, especially after the adoption of the Covenants in 1966.[1]

It was not then coincidental that the UN General Assembly began to contemplate the active encouragement of regional mechanisms only in 1966, when the two basic Covenants were finally adopted by the General Assembly. In 1977, it formally endorsed a new approach by appealing 'to States in areas where regional arrangements in the field of human rights do not yet exist to consider agreements with a view to the establishment within their respective regions of suitable regional machinery for the promotion and protection of human rights' (GA res. 32/127 (1977)). Four years later, the African Charter of Human and Peoples' Rights was adopted. Throughout this period the Communist states of Eastern Europe were strongly opposed to regional arrangements, and the Asian and Pacific countries generally argued that their region was much too heterogeneous to permit the creation of a regional mechanism.

Despite the UN General Assembly's annual adoption of a resolution calling upon the relevant regions to act, no significant regional or sub-regional systems has been created since 1981. Although states from the former Soviet Union adopted a Commonwealth of Independent States Convention on Human Rights in Minsk in 1995, the Convention has been much criticized and appears to have amounted to little in practice.[2] The current climate is somewhat more hospitable, in view of the desire of Eastern and Central European governments to become full partners in a united Europe, and even to join the European Union, which has prompted many of them to join the European human rights system. Moreover, the transformation of the Organization for Security and Co-operation in Europe (OSCE) from an East-West debating forum (or shouting match) into an organization designed to promote respect for a broadly defined range of human rights, has added another important dimension to regional human rights cooperation.

---

[1] In K. Vasak and P. Alston (eds.), *The International Dimensions of Human Rights* (Vol. 2, 1982), at 451.
[2] See text in 17 Hum. Rts L. J. 159 (1996) and critiques in *ibid.*, 164 and 181.

The successful example of the OSCE in promoting political cooperation, combined with the dramatically increased importance of the role of regional trading blocs—exemplified by the European Union Treaty in Europe, as well as the North American Free Trade Agreement between the United States, Canada and Mexico—and efforts to develop the Association of South-East Asian Nations (ASEAN) and the Asian-Pacific Economic Cooperation (APEC) initiative, have given renewed impetus to regional cooperation arrangements. Over time, this development may have important consequences for human rights.

——

The following readings develop some comparisons between universal and regional systems, both in general and with respect to human rights. Several themes suggested by these materials recur throughout the chapter: what are the relations between these systems—for example, are there hierarchical 'controls' between them; in what ways is it preferable from the perspective of observance of human rights to have a regional system complement a universal one; how do we explain the different institutional structures and differences in norms among these system; what can we learn from these differences about effective architecture for intergovernmental human rights organizations?

INIS CLAUDE, SWORDS INTO PLOWSHARES
(4th edn., 1984), at 102

Regionalism is sometimes put forward as an alternative to globalism, a superior substitute for the principle of universality. Emphasis is placed upon the bigness and heterogeneity of the wide world, and the conclusion is drawn that only within limited segments of the globe can we find the cultural foundations of common loyalties, the objective similarity of national problems, and the potential awareness of common interests which are necessary for the effective functioning of multilateral institutions. The world is too diverse and unwieldy; the distances—physical, economic, cultural, administrative, and psychological—between peoples at opposite ends of the earth are too formidable to permit development of a working sense of common involvement and joint responsibility. Within a region, on the other hand, adaptation of international solutions to real problems can be intelligently carried out, and commitments by states to each other can be confined to manageable proportions and sanctioned by clearly evident bonds of mutuality.

. . .

The advocacy of regionalism can be, and often is, as doctrinaire and as heedless of concrete realities as the passion for all-encompassing organization. It should be stressed that the suitability of regionalism depends in the first place upon the nature of the problem to be dealt with. Some problems of the modern world are international in the largest sense, and can be effectively treated only by global agencies. Others are characteristically regional, and lend themselves to solution by correspondingly delimited bodies. Still others are regional in nature, but require for their solution the mobilization of extra-regional resources.

...

The nature of a problem is significant not only for the determination of the most appropriate means of solution, but also for the measurement of the range of its impact. A problem may be regional in location, and susceptible of regional management, and yet have such important implications for the whole world that it becomes a fit subject for the concern of a general organization. The world-at-large cannot be disinterested in such 'regional' matters as the demographic problem in Asia or racialism in Southern Africa. Thus, the question of the ramifications of a problem as well as that of its intrinsic quality affects the choice between regional and universal approaches.

...

However, ... [t]he world does not in fact break easily along neatly perforated lines. Rational regional divisions are difficult to establish, boundaries determined for one purpose are not necessarily appropriate for other purposes, and the most carefully chosen dividing lines have a perverse way of changing or coming to require change, and of overlapping. It is true that brave universalist experiments tend to give way to sober regionalist afterthoughts, but it is equally true that carefully cut regional patterns tend to lose their shape through persistent stretching in the direction of universalism. In a sense, the adoption of the universal approach is the line of least resistance, since it obviates the difficulties of defining regions and keeping them defined.

... Intraregional affinities may be offset by historically rooted intraregional animosities, and geographical proximity may pose dangers which states wish to diminish by escaping into universalism, rather than collaborative possibilities which they wish to exploit in regional privacy. While global organization may be too large, in that it may ask states to be concerned with matters beyond the limited horizons of their interests, regional organization may be too small, in that it may represent a dangerous form of confinement for local rivalries. Global stretching, in short, may be no worse than regional cramping.

...

In a very general sense, it may be contended that regional organizations are particularly suitable for the cultivation of intensive cooperation among states, while global organizations have special advantages for dealing with conflict among states. If the goal is the development of linkages that bind states together in increasingly intimate collaboration and perhaps culminate in their integration, it would appear to be essential to restrict the enterprise to a few carefully selected states.

... On the other hand, the capacity of an organization to promote the control and resolution of conflicts may be enhanced by its inclusiveness. A global agency is inherently better equipped than a regional one to provide the mediatorial services of governments and individuals whose disinterested attitude toward any given pair of disputants is likely to be regarded as credible, and its potency as a mobilizer of pressure upon states engaged in conflict is a function of the broad scope of its membership and jurisdiction. The European Community may be treated as the model for international organization as a workshop for collaboration, and the United Nations as the model for international organization as an arena for conflict.

Regionalism and the United Nations

The atmosphere [during the 1945 Conference that drafted the UN Charter in] San Francisco was affected by the necessity of making the bow to regionalism which was demanded by those states that had already made heavy political investments in such arrangements as the Inter-American system, the Commonwealth, and the Arab League. . . .

. . .

The interaction between theoretical preference for universalism and political pressures for regionalism at San Francisco produced an ambiguous compromise. The finished Charter conferred general approval upon existing and anticipated regional organizations, but contained provisions indicating the purpose of making them serve as adjuncts to the United Nations and subjecting them in considerable measure to the direction and control of the central organization. The Charter reflected the premise that the United Nations should be supreme. . . .

. . .

REGIONAL PROMOTION AND PROTECTION OF HUMAN RIGHTS

Twenty-Eighth Report of the Commission to Study the Organization of Peace (1980), at 15

[In response to a 1968 UN study, the] Inter-American Commission on Human Rights supported those members of the Ad Hoc Study Group who favoured regional human rights commissions, noting four grounds: (1) the existence of geographic, historical, and cultural bonds among States of a particular region; (2) the fact that recommendations of a regional organization may meet with less resistence than those of a global body; (3) the likelihood that publicity about human rights will be wider and more effective; and (4) the fact that there is less possibility of 'general, compromise formulae', which in global bodies are more likely to be based on 'considerations of a political nature'.

. . .

Opposition to the establishment of regional human rights commissions has been expressed on numerous occasions by the Eastern European States and other Members of the United Nations, on several grounds. First, they argue that human rights, being global in nature and belonging to everyone, should be defined in global instruments and implemented by global bodies. 'The African and the Asian should have the same human rights as the European or the American'. Second, regional bodies in the human rights field would, at best, duplicate the work of United Nations bodies and, at worst, develop contradictory policies and procedures. . . . Third, the Eastern European States in particular object that any cooperation between regional commissions and the United Nations would add to the financial burdens of the latter. Fourth, several Western European States contend that preoccupation with regional arrangements might deflect official and public attention from the two International Covenants and delay their ratification.

It may be argued that the global approach and the regional approach to promotion and protection of human rights are not necessarily incompatible; on the contrary, they are both useful and complementary. The two approaches can be reconciled on a functional basis: the normative content of all international instruments, both global and regional, should be similar in principle, reflecting the Universal Declaration of Human Rights, which was proclaimed 'as a common standard of achievement for all peoples and all nations'. The global instrument would contain the minimum normative standard, whereas the regional instrument might go further, add further rights, refine some rights, and take into account special differences within the region and between one region and another.

Thus what at first glance might seem to be a serious dichotomy—the global approach and the regional approach to human rights—has been resolved satisfactorily on a functional basis. . . .

Implementation procedures may well vary even more from region to region, as the Governments therein desire. Indeed, they may vary within a region.

. . .

It may also be argued that the regional approach involves certain possible risks. First, a regional or sub-regional commission might serve to insulate the area from outside influences and encourage it to ignore the global standards and institutions of the United Nations system. Second, institutions of one region or sub-region might become involved in competition or conflict with those of another area. Given a modicum of good will and statesmanship on the part of any newly-established regional institutions, however, these risks should be minimal.

The further question arises whether if human rights commissions were established in certain regions, they might interpret international standards too narrowly and thus adversely affect the work of global bodies in this field. It might be necessary in such a case to establish the right of global institutions to consider a particular matter *de novo*.

Another difficulty might arise with respect to cases involving a 'consistent pattern of gross and reliably attested violations', which are subject to special procedures established by Resolution 1503 (XLVIII) of the Economic and Social Council (27 May 1970). It would delay the consideration of such questions if prior exhaustion of available regional remedies were required.

NOTE

Consider the following cautions of Vasak about conditions for the success of a regional human rights organization:

> The experience of the European Convention of Human Rights . . . tends to show
> that the regional protection of human rights can achieve full success only if it
> constitutes an element in a policy of integration on the part of the States of a

given region. Only at this price is it possible to permit the blow struck by regionalism in the matter of human rights against that necessary universalism which springs from the intrinsically identical nature of all human beings. The recent entry into force of the United Nations Covenants on Civil and Political Rights and on Economic, Social and Cultural Rights, which should be preserved as a legal expression of the universal character of the human being, should even lead us to be more exacting in the future in respect of regionalism than we were in the past when no universal system for the effective protection of human rights seemed feasible. In the last analysis, regional protection must come within the framework of regional organization in accordance with the Charter of the United Nations and become one aspect of the policy of integration. If, however, regional protection were but a *form of intergovernmental co-operation*, the parochial and perhaps even selfish attitudes of which it would also be the expression, would by no means justify the danger of such a serious blow to universalism.[3]

Note the flexibility of conceptions of what a 'region' consists in. For a range of purposes, such as caucuses among state representatives in the UN Commission on Human Rights, the UN divides the world into five geo-political regions: Asia, Africa, Eastern Europe, Latin America, and Western Europe and Others (including the United States). That classification need bear no relation whatsoever to appropriate definition of regions for purposes of a human rights regime. For example, the Pacific region (with or excluding Australia and New Zealand), South Asia, West Asia, Southeast Asia and possibly other groupings of states might all be considered appropriate units for the creation of a given type of joint human rights mechanism.

QUESTIONS

1. Consider the observation that '[r]egional and sub-regional blocs and groupings, whatever their purpose, are by their very nature inward-looking and designed to serve specific ends. Like the states of which they are composed, these blocs and groupings are more concerned with the exploitation of immediate advantages than with long-range world plans . . .'.[4] Is this view as appropriate for a human rights regime as for, say, a regional trading bloc?

2. To date, there have been no major conflicts (as opposed to minor differences) of interpretation, or formal decisions between the existing regional bodies and their UN counterparts, although the texts of the different regional treaties suggest on their face that serious conflicts with UN-related treaties could arise. In theory, such conflicts are to be avoided through the application of some basic guidelines or rules. How do you assess the following guidelines, and what alternatives might you propose to them?

   a. The standards in the Universal Declaration and in any other UN-related treaties accepted by the state or states concerned must be respected.

---

[3] *Ibid.*, 455.
[4] M. Moscowitz, *The Politics and Dynamics of Human Rights* (1968), at 48.

> b. Human rights standards forming part of general principles of international law
>   must also be respected.
> c. Where standards conflict, the one most favourable to the individual concerned
>   should prevail.
>
> 3. Should regional organizations provide an opening for cultural relativism—that is,
> for regionally specific norms that should be respected rather than superseded by the
> universal systems? How do the guidelines in the preceding question bear on that
> possibility?

ADDITIONAL READING

J. Burton, 'Regionalism, Functionalism and the United Nations', 15 Australian Outlook 73
(1961); B. Russett, *International Regions and the International System: A Study in Political
Ecology* (1967); R. Taylor, *International Organization in the Modern World: The Regional
and the Global Process* (1993); B. Weston, Lukes and Hnatt, 'Regional Human Rights
Regimes: A Comparison and Appraisal', 20 Vanderbilt J. Transnat'l L. 585 (1987); 'Chapter
VIII: Regional Arrangements', in B. Simma *et al.* (eds.), *The Charter of the United Nations:
A Commentary* 679 (1994).

B. THE EUROPEAN CONVENTION SYSTEM

1. INTRODUCTION

The European Convention for the Protection of Human Rights and Fundamental
Freedoms was signed in 1950 and entered into force in 1953. The ECHR is of
particular importance within the context of international human rights for several
reasons: it was the first comprehensive treaty in the world in this field; it established the first international complaints procedure and the first international court
for the determination of human rights matters; it remains the most judicially
developed of all the human rights systems; and it has generated a more extensive
jurisprudence than any other part of the international system. Our principal concern in this selective examination of the European Convention is with its evolving
institutional architecture, particularly with the European Court of Human Rights
and the manner in which it has performed the judicial function. Before turning to
the Court, however, this section locates the Convention within a broader European
framework of post-war initiatives and institutions.

COMMENT ON BACKGROUND TO THE CONVENTION

The impetus for the adoption of a European Convention came from three factors.
It was first a regional response to the atrocities committed in Europe during the

Second World War and an affirmation of the belief that governments respecting human rights are less likely to wage war on their neighbours. Secondly, both the Council of Europe, which was set up in 1949 (and under whose auspices the Convention was adopted), and the European Union (previously the European Community or Communities, the first of which was established in 1952) were partly based on the assumption that the best way to ensure that Germany would be a force for peace, in partnership with France, the United Kingdom and other Western European states, was through regional integration and the institutionalizion of common values. This strategy contrasted strongly with the punitive, reparations-based, approach embodied in the 1919 Versailles Treaty after the First World War.

Thus, the Preamble to the European Convention refers (perhaps somewhat optimistically at the time) to the 'European countries which are likeminded and have a common heritage of political traditions, ideals, freedom and the rule of law . . . '. But this statement also points to the third major impetus towards a Convention—the desire to bring the non-Communist countries of Europe together within a common ideological framework and to consolidate their unity in the face of the Communist threat. 'Genuine democracy' (to which the Statute of the Council of Europe commits its members) or the 'effective political democracy' to which the Preamble of the Convention refers, had to be clearly distinguished from the 'people's democracy' which was promoted by the Soviet Union and its allies.

The European Convention's transformation of abstract human rights ideals into a concrete legal framework followed a path which has characterized virtually all subsequent attempts. The initial enthusiasm was soon tempered by concerns over sovereignty and a reluctance to take the concept of a state's accountability too far. Thus a call by the Congress of Europe in 1948 for the adoption of a Charter of Human Rights to be enforced by a Court of Justice 'with adequate sanctions for the implementation of this Charter' went further than Western European governments were prepared to go. Instead, the final version of the Convention acknowledges in the Preamble that it constitutes only 'the first steps for the collective enforcement of certain of the Rights stated in the Universal Declaration'.

In recent years, major reforms of institutional provisions of the Convention have helped to move the system closer to that envisaged by the maximalists of the early 1950s. As with most systems for the protection of human rights, progress has required the gradual growth of popular expectations and an accumulation of experience in the functioning of the procedures that has served to assuage the worst fears of governments.

COMMENT ON THE RIGHTS RECOGNIZED BY THE CONVENTION

Although the initial moves to create a European Convention pre-dated the UN's adoption of the Universal Declaration, the text of the latter was available to those responsible for the final drafting of the Convention. Eventually the drafters defined rights in terms similar to the early version of the draft Covenant on Civil and Political Rights. (You should now read Articles 2–12 and 14 of the Convention in the Annex on Documents.) Since the Covenant went through numerous changes before adoption, the formulations used in the two treaties sometimes differ significantly. Several weighty provisions appear in only one or the other. For example, the European Convention contains no provision relating to self-determination or to the rights of members of minority groups (Articles 1 and 27 of the ICCPR). Each treaty limits freedoms of expression, association and religion in similar ways (criteria of public safety or national security, for example), but the European Convention consistently requires that a limitation be 'necessary in a democratic society' (Articles 8–11). The derogation clauses (Article 4 of the ICCPR, Article 15 of the Convention) differ with respect to the list of non-derogable provisions.

Article 1 requires the Parties to 'secure [these rights] to everyone within their jurisdiction', while Article 13 requires the state to provide 'an effective remedy before a national authority' for everyone whose rights are violated. Compare the more demanding Article 2 of the ICCPR, which refers to states' duty to adopt legislative and other measures to give effect to the recognized rights and to 'develop the possibilities of judicial remedy'.

When the Convention was adopted in 1950, there were several outstanding proposals on which final agreement could not be reached. It was therefore agreed to adopt Protocols containing additional provisions. Since 1952 11 protocols have been adopted. While the majority are devoted to procedural matters, others have recognized the following additional rights: the right to property ('the peaceful enjoyment of [one's] possessions'), the right to education, and the obligation to hold free elections (Protocol 1 of 1952); freedom from imprisonment for civil debts, freedom of movement and residence, freedom to leave any country, freedom from exile, the right to enter the country of which one is a national, and no collective expulsion of aliens (Protocol 4 of 1963); abolition of the death penalty (Protocol 6 of 1983); the right of an alien not to be expelled without due process, the right to appeal in criminal cases, the right to compensation for a miscarriage of justice, immunity of double prosecution for the same offence, and equality of rights and responsibility of spouses (Protocol 7 of 1984). Acceptance of each of the Protocols is optional.

By February 2000, all 41 member states of the Council of Europe were parties to the European Convention. Thirty states had ratified Protocol No. 1, 31 had ratified Protocol No. 4, 35 had ratified Protocol No. 6 and 26 had ratified Protocol No. 7. At the same time, drafting of a proposed Protocol 12 to the Convention was under way with a view to extending the right to non-discrimination in Article 14 of the Convention so that it would apply to 'any right set forth by law'.

2. THE BROAD EUROPEAN INSTITUTIONAL CONTEXT

Before examining the procedures and institutions through which the European system protects rights, it is necessary to consider the broader European institutional context within which the Convention is situated. The Convention is the creation of the Council of Europe, which is only one of three major regional mechanisms dealing with human rights within Europe. The other two are the European Union and the Organization (formerly termed Conference) for Security and Co-operation in Europe. None of the three is concerned exclusively with human rights. The Council of Europe has the longest and most significant track record in this field.

COMMENT ON THREE EUROPEAN ORGANIZATIONS

The Council of Europe

The Council was established in 1949 by a group of ten states, primarily to promote democracy, the rule of law, and greater unity among the nations of Western Europe. It represented both a principled commitment of its members to these values and an ideological stance against Communism. Over the years its activities have included the promotion of cooperation in relation to social, cultural, sporting and a range of other matters. Until 1990, the Council had 23 members, all from Western Europe. Post-Cold War developments, however, made a major impact upon the Council and by November 1996 it had 40 members, representing an increase of over 80 per cent in the space of less than eight years. With the addition of Georgia in April 1999, membership stood at 41.[5]

The conditions for the admission of a state to the Council of Europe are laid down in Article 3 of its Statute. The state must be a genuine democracy that respects the rule of law and human rights and must 'collaborate sincerely and effectively' with the Council in these domains. In practice, such collaboration involves becoming a party to the European Convention on Human Rights. An applicant state must satisfy the Council's Committee of Ministers that its legal order conforms with the requirements of Article 3. The opinion of the Parliamentary Assembly is sought and the Assembly in turn will appoint an expert group to advise it.

The opinion of the experts is based upon an on-site visit. For example, a 1994 expert report on the situation in Russia concluded that the requirements were not met. The report noted 'important shortcomings with regard to the rights to liberty and security of person and to fair trial' as well as the absence of the rule of law in view of the fact that the 'activities of public authorities are mainly decided upon according to general policy choices, personal allegiance and the effective power structure'.[6] Russia was admitted, nevertheless, in February 1996. This decision by the Council's Parliamentary Assembly, and another to admit Croatia, were strongly criticized by some human rights advocates.

---

[5] Albania, Andorra, Austria, Belgium, Bulgaria, Croatia, Cyprus, Czech Republic, Denmark, Estonia, Finland, France, Georgia, Germany, Greece, Hungary, Iceland, Ireland, Italy, Latvia, Liechtenstein, Lithuania, Luxembourg, Malta, Moldova, Netherlands, Norway, Poland, Portugal, Romania, Russian Federation, San Marino, Slovakia, Slovenia, Spain, Sweden, Switzerland, the former Yugoslav Republic of Macedonia, Turkey, United Kingdom and Ukraine.

[6] R. Bernhardt et al., 'Report on the Conformity of the Legal Order of the Russian Federation with Council of Europe Standards', 15 Hum. Rts. L.J. 249 (1994), at 287.

The importance attached by the states of Central and Eastern Europe to membership of the Council reflects not only a commitment to human rights but a determination to gain 'respectability' within Europe and, perhaps most importantly, to qualify for certain membership 'benefits' as well as for possible admission to the European Union. Although the process of becoming a party to the Convention is not required to be completed prior to obtaining membership in the Council, it is generally assumed that the domestic legislative and other measures required to enable the state to ratify or accede will be completed within a period of two years.

The European Union

The origins of the European Union (EU) lie in the Treaty of Paris of 1952 establishing the European Coal and Steel Community (ECSC) and subsequently in the two Treaties of Rome of 1957 creating the European Economic Community (EEC) and the European Atomic Energy Community. The entry into force on 1 November 1993 of the Treaty on Economic Union converted these communities into the European Union. Since 1 January 1995, the Union has consisted of 15 members: France, Germany, Italy, Belgium, Netherlands, Luxembourg (original EEC members in 1957), United Kingdom, Ireland, Denmark (since 1973), Greece (since 1981), Spain, Portugal (since 1986), Sweden, Finland and Austria (since 1995). In March 1998 the EU invited six countries to commence accession negotiations, five of which had been among the first to join the Council of Europe between 1990 and 1993: the Czech Republic, Estonia, Hungary, Poland and Slovenia.[7]

The impetus for the first step of creating the ECSC came essentially from a desire to ensure that the heavy industries of the Ruhr, which had underpinned Germany's military might in two World Wars, would be 'contained' within an intergovernmental structure bringing together West Germany and its former antagonists. The expansion into an EEC in 1957 was an attempt to promote closer economic integration within Europe for both federalist and economic reasons. While the adoption of a bill of rights had been proposed in the early 1950s, none of the subsequent treaties contained such a bill or a list of enumerated rights. The 1957 treaties were more concerned with protecting states' rights from Community encroachments than with the rights of individuals. The latter were seen to be appropriately protected at the national level.

Despite the absence of a bill of rights, the European Court of Justice (the judicial organ of the EU) began in 1969 to evolve a specific doctrine of human rights, the original motivation for which probably owed more to a desire to protect the competences of the Community than to any concern to provide extended protection to individuals. Over the years during which the human rights doctrine has evolved, the Court has identified several different normative underpinnings for it. They include certain provisions of the Treaty of Rome, the constitutional traditions of the member states, and international treaties accepted by member states. For the most part the European Court of Justice has applied this concept of human

---

[7] See <http://europa.eu.int/comm/enlargement.index.htm>.

rights to the actions of the Community itself, but not to actions of the member states.[8] The Court's jurisprudence was subsequently reflected in the amendments to the Treaty on European Union which came into force in 1999 in accordance with the Amsterdam Treaty. Article 6 provides that:

> 1. The Union is founded on the principles of liberty, democracy, respect for human rights and fundamental freedoms, and the rule of law, principles which are common to the Member States.
> 2. The Union shall respect fundamental rights, as guaranteed by the [ECHR] . . . and as they result from the constitutional traditions common to the Member States, as general principles of Community law.
> . . .

The Amsterdam Treaty also established a procedure (Article 7) whereby certain membership rights in the EU can be suspended if 'a serious and persistent breach' of human rights is deemed to exist within a member state. Despite these reforms, two different high-level expert groups have called for major reforms in EU human rights policies in order to make them 'coherent, balanced, substantive and professional'. The existing approach was said 'to be splintered in many directions, lacks the necessary leadership and profile, and is marginalized in policy-making'.[9]

While the ECHR (a Council of Europe treaty) has been accorded a privileged position within the Community legal order, various proposals that the European Community itself should adhere to the treaty have been unsuccessful. In 1996 the European Court of Justice (of the Community) held in its Opinion 2/94 on 'Accession by the Community to the ECHR' that such a step could not be taken in the absence of a specific treaty amendment to that effect.[10] The EU has since opted to move in a different direction by drafting its own 'Charter of Fundamental Rights', a process which could lead to the 'solemn proclamation' of the Charter by the European Council, the European Parliament and the Commission. According to the European Council 'it will then have to be considered whether and, if so, how the Charter should be integrated into the treaties'.[11] The ultimate legal effect of any such Charter thus remains unclear.

Although arrangements exist to facilitate consultation and coordination between the EU and the Council of Europe, they remain separate entities operating in very different settings despite the fact that the activities of each organization are very relevant to those of the other.

The Organization for Security and Co-operation in Europe (OSCE)

The Conference on Security and Co-operation in Europe (CSCE) opened in 1973 and concluded in August 1975 with the signing of the Final Act of Helsinki

---

[8] See P. Alston, M. Bustelo and J. Heenan (eds.) *The EU and Human Rights* (1999); and P. Craig and G. de Búrca, *EU Law: Text, Cases, and Materials* (2nd edn., 1998), Ch. 7.

[9] 'Leading by Example: A Human Rights Agenda for the European Union for the Year 2000', in Alston, *supra* n. 8 at 919; and European Commission,

Affirming Fundamental Rights in the European Union: Report of the Expert Group on Fundamental Rights (1999).

[10] [1996] ECR I-1759.

[11] Cologne Presidency, Conclusions, Annex IV: <http://db.consilium.eu.int/df/default.asp?lang=en>.

(known as the Helsinki Accord) by the 35 participating states (including all European States except Albania, plus Canada and the United States). The Soviet Union was motivated mainly by a desire to obtain formal recognition of its European frontiers, while the West took advantage of a period of East–West *détente* to obtain concessions primarily in relation to security matters. Human rights were of only secondary concern.

The CSCE process continued in the form of conferences designed to follow up and elaborate on the obligations contained in the Helsinki Accord. These agreements are reflected in various 'Concluding Documents', the most important of which in the human rights field ('the human dimension of the CSCE') are those adopted in Vienna and Paris in 1989, Copenhagen in 1990, Moscow in 1991 and Geneva in 1992.

Several characteristics distinguish the work of the CSCE from that of other entities in the human rights field. Its standards are all formally non-binding (in the sense that they are solemn undertakings, but are not in treaty form and thus not ratified or acceded to by states). Secondly, its membership is far broader than that of the European Union or even the Council of Europe. By 2000, it had grown to 55 states. Thirdly, until 1991 it had no more than a token institutional structure designed only to arrange its periodic meetings. It performed no operational tasks.

The non-binding diplomatic nature of the Helsinki Process led many observers to question its utility. Whatever contribution the process ultimately made to the demise of Communism, it clearly played an important role, especially in the second half of the 1980s and early 1990s, in legitimating human rights discourse within Eastern Europe, providing a focus for nongovernmental activities at both the domestic and international levels, and developing standards in relation to democracy, the rule of law, 'human contacts', national minorities and freedom of expression which went beyond those already in existence in other contexts such as the Council of Europe and the UN. To a large extent, its formally non-binding nature enabled the CSCE standard-setting process to yield more detailed and innovative standards than those adopted by its counterparts.

In 1995 the CSCE was officially transformed into the Organisation for Security and Co-operation in Europe (OSCE). Its official organs include the Parliamentary Assembly of the OSCE, the Ministerial Council (Foreign Ministers), the Permanent Council (which meets weekly), the 'Chairman-in-Office' which is a rotating post held by each member state Foreign Minister in turn, and Summit Meetings of Heads of State or Government (the sixth took place in Istanbul in December 1999). As of February 2000, the OSCE had over 250 officials, 2,500 field officers, and an annual budget of more than $100 million.

The OSCE's basic priorities today are: the consolidation of democratic institutions, civil society and the rule of law, conflict prevention and resolution, and the promotion of a cooperative security system. Its principal institutions are its Secretariat in Vienna, the Office for Democratic Institutions and Human Rights (ODIHR) in Warsaw, a Representative on Freedom of the Media, in Vienna, and a High Commissioner on National Minorities, based in The Hague. Since 1993 the latter post has been filled by a former Dutch Foreign Minister, Max van der Stoel.

He is assisted by 11 staff members and his role is to identify and resolve ethnic tensions that threaten peace and stability. The term 'national minority' has not been defined, although the High Commissioner has observed: 'I know a minority when I see one'. OSCE organs or the country concerned may request a mission, but the decision whether to make an on-site visit is his own. His recommendations address both short-term policy towards minorities and longer-term measures to encourage a continuing dialogue between the government and minority members.

The OSCE has played an important role in the field in a wide range of situations. One illustration of this is the work of the Verification Mission in Kosovo, described at p. 654, *supra.*

Throughout the 1990s there was significant evolution in the role played by the different international organizations functioning with a human rights mandate in Europe. Major issues of coordination of overlapping mandates have arisen. The Council of Europe, which once focused almost exclusively on protecting the rights of individuals through judicial and quasi-judicial mechanisms, has now developed a greater focus on broader rule of law issues, has established a European Commission for Democracy through Law, based in Venice, and has adopted a Framework Convention for the Protection of National Minorities (see *infra*). In addition to the ECHR's interstate complaints procedure and its provision for on-site fact-finding,[12] a confidential 'monitoring procedure' established by the Council of Europe's Committee of Ministers to survey member states' compliance with their human rights commitments has been operating since 1996.

While some of the relevant documentation is public, the most interesting documents remain confidential: 'distributed—in sealed envelopes—only to a limited number of persons who are directly involved'.[13] The actual and potential overlaps among this work, that of the OSCE, and that of various UN agencies with human rights responsibilities, are considerable. The reflections of Ian Martin, who has held high positions in a great variety of human rights field operations, on his experiences in Bosnia are telling in this regard:

> I believe that the configuration of international organisations in Bosnia is severely dysfunctional, and I find this view shared by the great majority of committed people working within any of them. Areas of work which should cooperate most closely are divided by boundaries between and within organisations: police supervision, human rights monitoring and rule of law institution-building. Areas of work which are best kept apart—human rights monitoring and election supervision—have been too closely related. Overlapping mandates produce an international presence which is both much more expensive and less effective than it needs to be, and a nightmare to attempt to coordinate.[14]

---

[12] See J. Frowein, 'Fact-Finding by the European Commission of Human Rights', in R. Lillich (ed.), *Fact-Finding before International Tribunals*, (1992), at 237.

[13] See <www.coe.fr/cm/reports/1998/note.htm>.

[14] I. Martin, 'Human Rights: The Role of Field Missions', paper presented to OSCE Human Dimension Seminar, Warsaw, 27–30 April 1999.

QUESTION

Is Europe blessed with too much of a good thing in the human rights area? Do you believe that consolidation of the functions performed by these organizations would be desirable? If so, what would be the best approach?

ADDITIONAL READING

The EU: P. Alston, M. Bustelo and J. Heenan (eds.), *The EU and Human Rights* (1999); J. Weiler and N. Lockhart, ' "Taking Rights Seriously": The European Court and Its Fundamental Rights Jurisprudence', 32 Common Market L. Rev. 51 (1995); B. Brandtner and A. Rosas, 'Human Rights in the External Relations of the European Community: An Analysis of Doctrine and Practice', 9 Eur. J. Int. L. 468 (1998); A. Toth, 'The European Union and Human Rights: The Way Forward', 34 Common Market L. Rev. 491 (1997); L. Betten and D. MacDevitt (eds.), *The Protection of Fundamental Social Rights in the European Union* (1996).

The OSCE: OSCE, CD-ROM Compilation of Documents 1973–1997 (1998); *OSCE Handbook* (3rd. edn., 1999); W. Zellner, *On the Effectiveness of the OSCE Minority Regime* (1999); D. Gottehrer, *Ombudsman and Human Rights Protection Institutions in OSCE Participating States* (1998); Bibliography on the OSCE High Commissioner on National Minorities (3rd ed., 1997); M. Bothe, N. Ronzitti, and A. Rosas, *The OSCE in the Maintenance of Peace and Security* (1997); W. Korey, *The Promises We Keep: Human Rights, The Helsinki Process, and American Foreign Policy* (1993); T. Buergenthal, 'The CSCE Rights System', 25 Geo. Wash. J. Int'l L. & Econ. 333 (1991); A. Bloed *et al.* (eds.), *Monitoring Human Rights in Europe: Comparing International Procedures and Mechanisms* (1993), at 45.

3. OTHER HUMAN RIGHTS CONVENTIONS ADOPTED BY THE COUNCIL OF EUROPE

COMMENT ON THREE CONVENTIONS

The European Social Charter

Although economic and social rights were reflected in the post-Second World War constitutions of France, Germany and Italy, they were not included in the European Convention. One of the key drafters, Pierre-Henri Teitgen, explained this decision in 1949 on the grounds that it was first necessary 'to guarantee political democracy in the European Union and then to co-ordinate our economies, before undertaking the generalisation of social democracy'. These rights were subsequently recognized in the European Social Charter of 1961.

The ESC system consists of: (1) the original Charter of 1961 (ratified by 24 states, as of February 2000), (2) an Additional Protocol of 1988 extending some of the rights (ten states), (3) an amending Protocol of 1991 which revises some of the original monitoring arrangements (16 states), (4) a revised (consolidated) Charter of 1996 which brings the earlier documents up to date and adds some new rights (eight states), and (5) a further Additional Protocol of 1995 which provides for a system of collective complaints (five states).[15] All but the 1991 Protocol have entered into force. The resulting picture is heavily fragmented since different states are governed by different regimes depending on which parts of the system they have ratified.[16] It is striking that, while every Council of Europe state has ratified the ECHR, 17 out of 41 have ratified none of the Social Charter instruments.

The Charter and its Additional Protocol of 1988 guarantee a series of 'rights and principles' with respect to employment conditions and 'social cohesion'. The former relate to: non-discrimination, prohibition of forced labour, trade union rights, decent working conditions, equal pay for equal work, prohibition of child labour, and maternity protection. Among the latter are: health protection, social security, and certain rights for children, families, migrant workers and the elderly. These rights are not legally binding *per se*. The legal obligations designed to ensure their effective exercise are contained in Part II, which details the specific measures to be taken in relation to each of the rights. Part III reflects the principle of progressive implementation tailored to suit the circumstances of individual states. Each contracting party must agree to be bound by at least five of seven rights which are considered to be of central importance. It must also accept at least five of the other rights as listed in Part II.

Part IV provides for a monitoring system based on the submission of regular reports by contracting parties. The reports are examined by the European Committee of Social Rights whose assessments of compliance and non-compliance are then considered by the Parliamentary Assembly and a Governmental Committee. Finally, on the basis of all these views, the Committee of Ministers may make specific recommendations to the state concerned. The Additional Protocol providing for collective complaints entered into force in July 1998, although by February 2000 only one case had been concluded.[17]

The European Convention for the Prevention of Torture

In 1987 the Council of Europe adopted the European Convention for the Prevention of Torture and Inhuman or Degrading Treatment or Punishment (ECPT). By comparison with the UN Torture Convention of 1984, the ECPT places a particular emphasis on prevention and is far more innovative and intrusive in its approach to supervision. As of February 2000 the ECPT had been ratified by 40

---

[15] See generally <www.coe.fr>.

[16] The European Social Charter should be distinguished from the European Community's Charter of Fundamental Social Rights of Workers and the 'social chapter' of the Amsterdam Treaty. See S. Sciarra, 'From Strasbourg to Amsterdam: Prospects for the Convergence of European Social Rights

Policy', in P. Alston, M. Bustelo and J. Heenan (eds.), *The EU and Human Rights* (1999), at 473.

[17] In a case brought by the International Commission of Jurists against Portugal concerning child labour, the Committee of Ministers confirmed in December 1999 that there had been a violation.

Member States of the Council of Europe and is also open to other states by invitation.[18]

The Convention establishes a Committee for the Prevention of Torture (CPT) which is composed of independent experts. Its function is 'to examine the treatment of persons deprived of their liberty with a view to strengthening, if necessary, the protection of such persons' from torture, inhuman or degrading treatment (Article 1). The Convention is not concerned solely with prisoners but with any 'persons deprived of their liberty by a public authority'. Each state party is required to permit the Committee to visit any such place within the state's jurisdiction (Article 2), unless there are exceptional circumstances (which will rarely be the case). Most visits are routine and scheduled well in advance, but there is also provision for *ad hoc* visits with little advance notice (Article 7).

As of January 2000 the CPT had made 67 periodic, and 29 *ad hoc* visits. It meets *in camera* and its visits and discussions are confidential as, in principle, are its reports. The latter, however, may be released, either at the request of the state concerned or if a state refuses to cooperate and the Committee decides by a two-thirds majority to make a public statement. This occurred in 1992 when the Committee concluded after three visits to Turkey that the government had failed to respond to its recommendations.[19] Since then, virtually all states have voluntarily agreed to the release of the Committee's report and (as of January 2000) 61 have been published.

Framework Convention for the Protection of National Minorities

Despite the importance of national minorities within Europe and discussions about appropriate measures since 1949, the issue had proven too controversial and complex for the Council of Europe to adopt specific standards until 1994, when the Framework Convention was adopted. In part, the impetus was the adoption of the 1992 UN Declaration on Rights of Persons Belonging to Minorities, p. 1298, *infra*, and the development of non-binding standards and promotional activities in this field by the CSCE. The Council sought to avoid longstanding controversies by, among other things, confining the Convention to programmatic obligations that are not directly applicable and that leave considerable discretion about implementation to the state concerned. International supervision is undertaken by the Committee of Ministers of the Council based upon periodic reports to be submitted by states parties. The Convention entered into force in February 1998 and as of January 2000 had been ratified by 28 states.

––––––

Note that even within one region, deep differences appear in the institutional structures of conventions adopted by the same body, as one compares these three

---

[18] See the Committee's website: <www.cpt.coe.int>; and M. Evans and R. Morgan, *Preventing Torture: A Study of the European Convention for the Prevention of Torture and Inhuman or Degrading Treatment or Punishment* (1998).

[19] Public Statement on Turkey, Doc. CPT/Inf (93)1 (15 December 1992).

conventions among themselves and with the European Convention on Human Rights to which the materials now turn.

QUESTION

Compare the powers and functions of the Committee for the Prevention of Torture with those of treaty organs under the UN-related conventions described in Chapter 9, particularly with the Committee formed under the Convention against Torture, p. 775, *supra.* In what respects is the European Committee 'innovative', as the text above states? Is it desirable to apply its innovative characteristics to a universal arrangement?

4. THE EUROPEAN COURT OF HUMAN RIGHTS: ARTICLE 34 INDIVIDUAL PETITIONS

The European Convention on Human Rights (ECHR) provides for two procedures by which member states (referred to in the Convention as the High Contracting Parties) may be held accountable by the European Court of Human Rights ('the Court') for violations of the recognized rights: the individual petition procedure pursuant to Article 34, and the interstate procedure under Article 33.

The Convention makes clear that the primary responsibility for implementation rests with the member states themselves. The implementation machinery of the Convention comes into play only after domestic remedies are considered to have been exhausted. The great majority of complaints submitted are deemed inadmissible, frequently on the grounds that domestic law provides an effective remedy for any violation that may have taken place. Recall the obligations of member states under Articles 1 and 13 of the Convention to 'secure to everyone' the Convention's rights and to provide 'an effective remedy before a national authority' for violations of those rights.

The remedy given by, say, a domestic court may be pursuant to provisions of domestic law that stand relatively independently of the Convention, although perhaps influenced by it: a code of criminal procedure or a constitutional provision on free speech that are consistent with the Convention, for example. Or a remedy may be given pursuant to the substantive provisions of the Convention itself after the Convention has been incorporated into domestic law automatically or by special legislation, a path examined at pp. 999–1006, *infra*.

This preference for domestic resolution is also reinforced by the requirement to seek a friendly settlement wherever possible and by the procedures for full government consultation in the examination of complaints. The confidentiality of part of the proceedings, the role accorded to the Committee of Ministers, and the provision for there to be a judge from every state party again underscore the state-centred nature of many of the Convention's procedures.

COMMENT ON THE COURT AND PROTOCOL NO. 11

The entry into force, in November 1998, of Protocol No. 11 to the Convention produced a more streamlined and efficient system than had previously been in operation. Under the old system, the main (and very often the final) stage in the examination of a complaint was undertaken by the European Commission of Human Rights, which ceased existence in October 1999 as a result of what has often been termed a merger or fusion of the old Court and Commission.

In the former system, the Commission included an expert elected from every state party to the Convention. Its findings as to whether a breach of the Convention had occurred were not *per se* legally binding on the states parties. Within three months of the Commission's report the case could have been referred to the Court by either the Commission or by a state concerned, but not by the complainant. If the case did not thereby reach the Court, the final verdict was pronounced by the Committee of Ministers. Rather than being able to determine which cases it would hear, the old Court was at the mercy of the Commission or the state concerned.

The Continuing Impetus for Reform

The impetus to reform the Convention system was essentially twofold, stemming from the inability of the old system to deal with the rapidly increasing workload and the need to accommodate a dramatic expansion in the Council's post-Cold War membership. The opportunity was also taken to strengthen the judicial rather than political character of the system.

Between 1980 and 1997, the annual number of applications received by the Commission rose from 2,000 to over 12,000, while the number accepted rose from below 500 to almost 5,000. The number of judgments handed down by the old Court went from less than 10 to over 200.[20] In an effort to deal with the backlog of cases, Protocol No. 8 was adopted by which the Commission was permitted to meet in Committees of Three and in Chambers, rather than always in plenary. But the entry into force of this reform coincided with the large increase in the Council's membership in the early 1990s, and the pressure of applications grew steadily. In 1998, the last year of operation of the old system, references by the Commission to the Court rose from 157 to 190 and decisions handed down by the Court rose from 206 to 216. Linked to this explosion was a blow-out in the time taken to resolve applications. In 1993 it took, on average, five years and eight months for a case to be finally decided. This was especially ironical in view of the Court's case law, which has often found states whose courts take equivalent periods of time to decide a case to be in breach of the right to a hearing 'within a reasonable time' under Article 6.

The new system has yet to radically change the picture. In 1999 the President of the new Court noted that:

> The continuing steep increase in the number of applications to the Court is

---

[20] Figures come from Council of Europe, *Human Rights Information Bulletin*, No. 42.

putting even the new system under pressure. Today we are faced with nearly 10,000 registered applications and more than 47,000 provisional files, as well as around 700 letters and more than 200 overseas telephone calls a day. The volume of work is already daunting but is set to become more challenging still . . . .[21]

In its first year (to October 1999) the new system attracted 8,396 applications compared with 5,981 in the last year of the old system, 2,040 in 1993, and 404 in 1981. The Court delivered 177 judgments, declared inadmissible or struck off 3,489 applications and declared admissible 658 applications.[22] These figures will continue to fuel the need for further reforms in how the ECHR system functions.

The Principal Elements of the Reform

Ratified by all 41 member states, the revised Convention brings 800 million people within the Court's jurisdiction. The Court is now permanent or full-time, rather than part-time; the right of individual petition is now mandatory rather than optional for states parties; virtually all interstate cases will now be considered by the Court, rather than only those referred to it from the Commission; the political role played by the Committee of Ministers is now confined to matters of enforcement, rather than the merits of cases; and applicants now have unrestricted access to the Court.

Under the new system, applications that are registered are reviewed by a three-judge Committee which may, by unanimous vote, declare cases inadmissible. Cases that go forward will, in the great majority of instances, be considered by a seven-judge Chamber (of which four now exist). Exceptionally, some cases will go to a Grand Chamber of 17 judges. The latter procedure is a consequence of the need for compromise between different models of reform that were put forward in the negotiation of Protocol No. 11. Under Article 30, in a case which 'raises a serious question affecting the interpretation of the Convention or the protocols thereto or where the resolution of a question . . . might have a result inconsistent with a judgment previously delivered by the Court', a Chamber may relinquish its jurisdiction to the Grand Chamber (unless one of the parties objects).

Under Article 43, any party to a case may request, within three months of a judgment by a Chamber, that the case be referred to the Grand Chamber. But this is said to apply only 'in exceptional cases' and a five-judge panel of the latter can only accept the case if it 'raises a serious question affecting the interpretation or application of the Convention or the protocols thereto, or a serious issue of general importance'. These re-hearing provisions are unusual by judicial standards, even though the Grand Chamber is to look at the matter anew and the judges from the Chamber that delivered the initial judgment (excepting the President of the Chamber and the judge coming from the state concerned) are excluded from the

---

[21] President of the Permanent European Court of Human Rights, quoted in 20/3 Hum. Rts L.J. 114 (1999).
[22] Opening of the Judicial Year, Address by The President of the European Court of Human Rights, Mr Luzius Wildhaber, Strasbourg, 25 January 2000.

new panel. The appropriateness of these arrangements has been questioned however, and in the view of some commentators they 'should be repealed'.[23] During the new Court's first year, no Article 43 referrals were made to the Grand Chamber.

The Judges

There are currently 41 judges, equal to the number of states parties. A state can nominate a national of another state party if it wishes, and the first Court saw a Swiss judge elected on the nomination of Liechtenstein and an Italian for San Marino. Each state is required to nominate three candidates, who are interviewed by a special sub-committee established for the purpose, before the Parliamentary Assembly of the Council of Europe proceeds to an election. Judges are elected for a six-year term, and cannot serve beyond their 70th birthday. Although the Committee of Ministers encouraged numerical gender equality, only eight (just under 20 per cent) of the judges are women.

The New System

Proceedings under the individual petitions procedure of Article 34 begin with a complaint by an individual, group or NGO against a state party. To be declared admissible a petition must not be anonymous, manifestly ill-founded, or constitute an abuse of the right of petition. Domestic remedies must have been exhausted, it must be presented within six months of the final decision in the domestic forum and it must not concern a matter which is substantially the same as one which has already been examined under the ECHR or submitted to another procedure of international investigation or settlement.

The first stage of the procedure is generally written, although the Chamber may decide to hold a hearing, in which case issues arising in relation to the merits will normally also be addressed. Hearings are adversarial in nature and usually public. Memorials and other documents filed in the case are also accessible to the public. Chamber decisions on admissibility, which are taken by majority vote, must contain reasons and be made public. Legal representation at all stages is recommended, and for hearings or once admissibility has been established, it is obligatory. The impact of this requirement is softened somewhat by the existence of a Council of Europe legal aid scheme for applicants who do not have sufficient means.

While the Court's official languages are English and French, applications may be drafted in any of the 21 official languages and, in practice, as many as 32 have been accepted. In hearings either English or French are used, unless exceptional authorization for the use of another language is given.

Decisions in Chambers are taken by a majority vote and each judge is entitled to give a separate opinion, whether concurring or dissenting. During the proceedings

---

[23] A. Drzemczewski, *The European Human Rights Convention: Protocol No. 11. Entry into Force and First Year of Application*, November 1999, p. 5, n. 3.

on the merits, negotiations aimed at securing a friendly settlement may be conducted. This technique was highly successful under the old system. Thus while only 15 such settlements were reached between 1980 and 1984, there were 242 between 1992 and 1997. The question arose in drafting Protocol No. 11 as to whether such a procedure was appropriate in the context of a wholly judicial system, in which the Chambers themselves would be required to give a provisional view on the merits in order to stimulate a settlement. Such proceedings are confidential and, in response to misgivings, the process has been defended both as historically very successful and as a 'triumph of pragmatism over principle'.[24]

The Court may, at the request of the Committee of Ministers, give advisory opinions on legal questions concerning the interpretation of the Convention and Protocols. Despite the proven success of this technique under the Inter-American system (see p. 873, *infra*) no request has yet been made.

The jurisprudence of the Court is explored in Section 7 below through illustrative cases. An excellent idea of the range of cases considered by the Court in the course of a year can be gained from its annual 'Survey of Activities', available on the Court's website (<www.echr.coe.int/eng>).

5. RESPONSES OF STATES TO FINDINGS OF VIOLATIONS

ANDREW DRZEMCZEWSKI AND MEYER-LADEWIG, PRINCIPAL CHARACTERISTICS OF THE NEW ECHR CONTROL MECHANISM, AS ESTABLISHED BY PROTOCOL NO. 11
15 Hum. Rts. L. J. 81 (1994), at 82

. . .

The Convention's achievements have been quite staggering, the case-law of the European Commission and Court of Human Rights exerting an ever deeper influence on the laws and social realities of the State parties. A few examples may be mentioned.

In Austria, where the Convention has the rank of constitutional law, the Code of Criminal Procedures has had to be modified as a result of case-law in Strasbourg; so too the system of legal aid fees for lawyers. In Belgium, amendments have been made to the Penal Code, its vagrancy legislation and its Civil Code to ensure equal rights to legitimate and illegitimate children. In Germany modifications that bring legislation better into line with the Convention's provisions have also been made, e.g. the Code of Criminal Procedure concerning pre-trial detention was amended. Various measures have been taken to expedite criminal and civil proceedings, and transsexuals have been given legal recognition.

In the Netherlands, where most of the Convention's self-executing substantive

---

[24] N. Bratza and M. O'Boyle, 'The Legacy of the Commission to the New Court under the Eleventh Protocol', in M. de Salvia and M. Villiger (eds.), *The Birth of European Human Rights Law: Essays in Honour of Carl Aage Nørgaard* (1998), at 388.

provisions are endowed with a hierarchically superior status to the Constitution itself, changes have been made in the Military Criminal Code and the law on detention of mental patients. In Ireland, court proceedings have been simplified and civil legal aid and advice schemes set up. Sweden has introduced rules concerning time-limits for expropriation permits and legislation enacted concerning the regulation of building permits. Switzerland has amended its Military Penal Code and completely reviewed its judicial organization and criminal procedure as applied to the federal army, as well as its Civil Code as regards deprivation of liberty in reformatory centres.

In France, the law relating to the secrecy of telephone communications had to be altered, while in Italy a new Code of Criminal Procedure was enacted to change the law concerning regulation of detention on remand. In the U.K., despite the fact that the Convention has not been incorporated into domestic law (as is also the case in Ireland, and for the time-being in Iceland, Norway and Sweden), its constitutional impact cannot be doubted, with changes in domestic law being made in the areas of freedom of information, privacy, prison rules, mental health legislation and payments of compensation for administrative miscarriages of justice, among others.

But the effects of the Convention are not limited to the follow-up given to judgments of the Court, decisions of the Commission and findings of violation by the Committee of Ministers. The procedure for friendly settlements under the Convention has also produced significant results in this respect. Indeed, over two hundred instances can be cited where settlements have been reached either formally or informally, often with the Commission's or the Court's approval, subsequent to concessionary measures taken by the governments concerned.

More generally, national courts in the States parties to the Convention increasingly turn to the Strasbourg case-law when deciding on a human rights issue, and apply the standards and principles developed by the Commission and Court. Many instances can also be cited of States modifying legislation and administrative practices prior to their ratification of the Convention, particularly in the case of those States which have recently joined the Organization.

CHRISTIAN TOMUSCHAT, QUO VADIS, ARGENTORATUM? THE SUCCESS STORY OF THE EUROPEAN CONVENTION ON HUMAN RIGHTS—AND A FEW DARK STAINS

13 Hum. Rts. L. J. 401 (1992)

... [Despite the system's successes] symptoms of a deep-seated crisis cannot be overlooked. As any mechanism for the protection of human rights, the Strasbourg system must be measured by the concrete results which it produces in favour of the aggrieved individual. It is not the legal perfection of its normative structure that matters in the last analysis, but its actual impact on the real enjoyment of human rights. In that respect, substantial reasons barring euphoria exist. However numerous and bold the decisions of the Strasbourg bodies may be, it has recently emerged that especially their implementation lacks sufficiently effective safeguards.

[One of Tomuschat's principal concerns was the failure of the Committee of Ministers to discharge its obligations under the Convention effectively. Since the entry into force of the revised Convention, that deficiency should have been remedied.]

a) *Reparation in individual cases*

As far as obligations to make specific payments are concerned, in the telephone tapping case of *Kruslin* France took more than one year and four months before it made the required payment to the applicant in respect of costs and expenses . . . and in the *Ezelin* case the period amounted to almost one year. . . . But the unfortunate top position is held by Italy. It appears that the *Colozza* case, in which Italy was ordered to pay to the victim's widow six million Lire by way of just satisfaction, [had still not been wound up seven years later].
. . .

b) *General amendment of legislation*

The most far-reaching challenge arises for a State when it has to modify its legislation following a judgment of the Court.
. . .

. . . It took Belgium roughly eight years to change its legislation on the status of illegitimate children after the judgment in the *Marckx* case had been delivered, whereas Ireland responded within one year to the Court's conclusion that certain aspects of the position of illegitimate children amounted to unlawful discrimination. The Federal Republic of Germany needed more than five years to comply with the judgment in the *Öztürk* case according to which provision of an interpreter free of charge for the accused is mandatory also with regard to regulatory offences (*Ordnungswidrigkeiten*). . . . Lastly, it is worth mentioning the judgment in *Norris v. Ireland* of 26 October 1988 . . . [see p. 814, *infra*. Four years later the legal position had remained unchanged].
. . .

More positive examples are the swift reaction of the Netherlands to the finding in the *Benthem* case that the system of review of administrative decisions was not in keeping with the required safeguards of a judicial procedure. . . . It is also with praiseworthy celerity that France responded to the *Huvig* and *Kruslin* judgments of 24 April 1990 which had passed a verdict of incompatibility with the Convention of the French system for telephone tapping in criminal proceedings. . . .

QUESTIONS

1. On what criteria or standards would you evaluate the effectiveness of the European Convention system? Should we examine the system in its own terms, primarily

through judicial decisions and state response thereto? Or should we compare the functions and powers of the organs in the Convention system with the different institutional structures and powers of other human rights systems, universal or regional, to make a broader judgement? Note the differences from the other systems examined in Chapters 8 and 9.

2. Lord Lester has called on the Court to resist 'the insidious temptation to resort to a "variable geometry" of human rights which pays undue deference to national or regional "sensitivities"'.[25] How seriously do you take the concern that the entry of countries such as Russia and various other Eastern European countries into the ECHR system will lead to a weakening of standards?

6. THE INTERSTATE PROCEDURE: ARTICLE 33

Article 33 of the revised Convention contains a procedure by which one or more states may allege breaches of the Convention by another state party. Unlike the traditional approach to such cases under the international law of state responsibility for injury to aliens, p. 81, *supra,* it is not necessary for an applicant state to allege that the rights of its own nationals have been violated.

As of February 2000, thirteen interstate applications had been lodged. They concern only seven different situations and are as follows:

(a) *Greece v. United Kingdom* (two cases, in 1956 and 1957) relating to Cyprus. The case concerned the declaration of a state of exception in Cyprus (then a British colony) and the introduction of emergency measures by the UK government. A political settlement was reached in 1959 before the Committee of Ministers had formulated its views.

(b) *Austria v. Italy* in 1960 related to the murder trial of six members of the German-speaking minority in the South Tyrol. The Committee of Ministers informed the parties of the Commission's view that clemency should be shown and sought to achieve a broader resolution of the issues surrounding the case.

(c) *Denmark, Netherlands, Norway and Sweden v. Greece* in 1967 and the same group, minus the Netherlands, again in 1970. This case is considered below.

(d) *Ireland v. the United Kingdom* (two cases, in 1971 and 1972) relating to a declared state of emergency in Northern Ireland. The three Commission delegates heard 118 witnesses before the Commission concluded that, although measures for detention without trial were 'strictly required by the exigencies of the situation', certain interrogation techniques used by the British forces did constitute torture and inhuman treatment. The Irish Government referred the case to the Court which found that, while the techniques involved 'inhuman and degrading treatment' (and thus violated Article 3), they did not amount to 'torture'.

(e) *Cyprus v. Turkey* (four cases in 1974, 1975, 1977 and 1996) after the Turkish intervention by armed forces in Cyprus. The Commission found in response to the last of these complaints that violations, including large-scale evictions, had

---

[25] Lester, 'The European Convention on Human Rights in the New Architecture of Europe', 38A *Yearbook of the European Convention on Human Rights* (1997), 223 at 226.

occurred. The Committee of Ministers requested Turkey to put an end to them, and urged the parties to resume intercommunal talks. The latest case was referred by the Commission to the new Court on 4 June 1999.

(f) *Denmark, France, the Netherlands, Norway and Sweden v. Turkey* in 1982, alleging violations, including torture, by the military government. Under the settlement approved by the Commission, the Turkish Government gave a number of vague undertakings such as a commitment to instruct 'the State Supervisory Council . . . to have special regard to the observance by all public authorities' of the Convention's prohibition against torture. In relation to the lifting of the state of emergency the settlement noted that 'special regard is given to the following declaration made by the Prime Minister of Turkey on 4 April 1985 in Washington D.C.: "I hope that we will be able to lift martial law from the remaining provinces within 18 months" '.[26] The settlement was widely criticised on the ground that it was not based on the respect for human rights required by the Convention.

(g) *Denmark v. Turkey* in 1997, in which the applicant alleged torture of a Danish citizen during detention by Turkish authorities. On 5 April 2000 a friendly settlement was reached and the case was struck from the Court's docket.

The Commission's response to the applications brought against Greece in 1967 and 1970 has been described as a model 'for demonstrating both the possibilities and the political limitations of the international protection of human rights'.[27] The case also provides an excellent illustration of fact-finding by the Commission. It should be noted, however, that this 'model' is in no sense representative of the outcome of the other interstate cases to date.

The background to the case involved the seizure of power by 'the Greek colonels' in a *coup d'état* in 1967. The military government proclaimed a state of emergency and notified various derogations under Article 15 of the Convention. The applications by Denmark, Netherlands, Norway and Sweden were declared admissible in January 1968. The Commission had to consider whether there was (under the criteria set for states of emergency under Article 15) an 'emergency threatening the life of the nation', and if so, whether the measures taken by the military government were 'strictly required by the exigencies of the situation'. The prohibition against torture as well as 11 other articles of the Convention were alleged to have been violated. The Commission initiated a fact-finding exercise. The story continues in the following reading.

A. H. ROBERTSON AND MERRILLS, HUMAN RIGHTS IN EUROPE: A STUDY OF THE EUROPEAN CONVENTION ON HUMAN RIGHTS
(3rd edn., 1993), at 278

. . . [A]fter hearing about thirty witnesses in Strasbourg in November and December 1968, the sub-commission 'fixed 6 February 1969 as the opening date

---

[26] Report of the Commission, 25 Int'l Legal Materials 308 (1986), at 314–15.
[27] Francis Jacobs, *The European Convention on Human Rights* (1975), at 27.

for its investigation in Greece'. In accordance with Article 28 of the Convention the Greek government was consulted about the arrangements, but not about the question whether the investigation should take place. At its request the date for the opening of the investigation was postponed until the beginning of March.

The sub-commission met in Athens on 9 March 1969 and began its investigation the following day. In the main, the Greek government cooperated and facilitated its work and the sub-commission expressed its appreciation of this. Between 10 and 20 March it heard thirty-four witnesses with regard to allegations of torture and twenty witnesses about the existence of a state of emergency. In addition it visited the police stations of the Security Police in Athens and Piraeus and delegated one of its members to visit the Hagia Paraskevi detention camp. When the sub-commission wanted a medical opinion on the condition of witnesses who alleged that they had been tortured, it summoned two forensic experts from the University of Geneva, who were provided with the necessary facilities. On the other hand, the government prevented the sub-commission from hearing thirteen witnesses whom it wished to examine in connection with allegations of torture and also prevented it from inspecting detention camps on the island of Leros and from visiting the Averoff prison in Athens. Since it considered the reasons for these refusals unjustified, the sub-commission terminated its visit and reported the facts to the plenary Commission.

Although some of the facilities it required were refused, the sub-commission succeeded in making a thorough investigation into the allegations of torture and the question of the existence of a state of emergency. This is demonstrated by the fact that, in addition to hearing many witnesses on the torture issue, it visited and photographed the notorious Bouboulinas station of the Security Police in Athens. Furthermore, during the hearings on the largely political question of the existence of a state of emergency, the witnesses included three former Prime Ministers, the Governor of the Bank of Greece, the chief of the armed forces and the Director General of Security at the Ministry of Public Order.

... [T]he full Commission, acting on the information obtained by its sub-commission, concluded that there was not a public emergency in Greece at the material time and, as a consequence, the Greek derogations were invalid. It also found that there was a practice of torture and ill-treatment by the Athens Security Police and, furthermore, that there had been violations of eight other articles of the Convention, together with Article 3 of Protocol No. 1. The Commission's conclusions were endorsed by the Committee of Ministers in April 1970 and thereby became decisions of the Committee under Article 32 of the Convention. In the meantime, however, while the Committee had been considering a recommendation from the Consultative Assembly on the situation in Greece, the Greek Minister for Foreign Affairs announced that his government had decided to denounce the Statute and withdraw from the Council of Europe, and also to denounce the European Convention.

. . .

[Eds. After the restoration of civilian government, Greece rejoined the Convention regime in 1974.]

NOTE

Consider the following observation in Laurence Helfer and Anne-Marie Slaughter, *Toward a Theory of Effective Supranational Litigation*, 107 Yale L. J. 273 (1997), at 296:

> The rate of compliance by states with the [European Court of Human Rights'] rulings is extremely high. Indeed, its judgments have been described as being 'as effective as those of any domestic court'. As with the [European Court of Justice], however, this record of success has occurred principally in cases brought by individuals against their national governments. By contrast, the effectiveness of the handful of interstate complaints filed with the European Commission and the [Court] is doubtful, again demonstrating the crucial role played by private parties in securing compliance with supranational court rulings.

A footnote after this quotation describes the view of several commentators on the European system who argue that states parties have been unwilling to expose violations in other states where their own interests are not involved, and where they run the risk of alienating the target state through what would be perceived as an unfriendly act of accusation or litigation. Some commentators argued that political considerations that might, for example, lead to a decision representing a compromise between the parties' positions, were far less likely to influence the Court in cases brought by individuals than in interstate cases.

QUESTIONS

1. Some of the largest European countries, including the United Kingdom, Germany and Spain, have never lodged an interstate complaint against another European government. Does this mean that this procedure is only likely to be invoked by small countries with limited political clout? If so, would that indicate a fundamental weakness of the procedure?

2. Under what circumstances might the lodging of an interstate complaint be most productive and when might it be considered counter-productive?

3. Although the interstate procedure has been used only in relation to seven situations under the European Convention, recall that a comparable procedure involving the Human Rights Committee under Articles 41–43 of the ICCPR has never been invoked. Why do you suppose this might be so?

ADDITIONAL READING

D. Harris, M. O'Boyle and C. Warbrick, *Law of the European Convention on Human Rights* (2nd edn., forthcoming 2000); R. Blackburn and J. Polakiewicz (eds.), *The European*

Convention on Human Rights 1950–2000 (2000); P. Mahoney *et al.* (eds.), *Studies in Honour of R. Ryssdal* (2000); P. Leuprecht, 'Minority Rights Revisited: New Glimpses of an Old Issue', in P. Alston (ed.), *Peoples' Rights* (2000), Ch. 4; A. Loux and W. Finnie, *Human Rights and Scots Law Comparative Perspectives on the Incorporation of the ECHR* (1999); L. Clements, N. Mole, and A. Simmons, *European Human Rights: Taking a Case under the Convention* (1999); R. Lawson and H. Schermers (eds.), *Leading Cases of the European Court of Human Rights* (2nd edn., 1999); T. Barkhuysen, M. van Emmerijk, and P. van Kempen, *The Execution of Strasbourg and Geneva Human Rights Decisions in the National Legal Order* (1999); P. Kempees, *A Systematic Guide to the Case-law of the European Court of Human Rights* (1998); P. van Dijk and G. van Hoof, *Theory and Practice of the European Convention on Human Rights* (3rd edn., 1998); P. Leuprecht, 'Innovations in the European System of Human Rights Protection: Is Enlargement Compatible with Enforcement?', 8 Transnat'l L. & Contemp. Probs 313 (1998); and A. Drzemczewski, 'A Major Overhaul of the European Human Rights Convention Control Mechanism: Protocol No. 11', VI/2 *Collected Courses of the Academy of European Law* 121 (1997).

7. THE EUROPEAN COURT IN ACTION: SOME ILLUSTRATIVE CASES

The role of the European Court is of particular importance for several reasons. Consider first the volume of cases. Until the early 1980s the Court dealt with an average of only five or six cases annually. By contrast, it delivered judgments in 177 cases in 1999. Secondly, many cases that are now brought are more complex and raise more complicated jurisprudential issues than those which tended to come before the Court in its earlier years. Thirdly, because the Court is the longest standing international human rights court (the Inter-American Court, p. 873, *infra*, being the only other international body fulfilling a comparable role), it is inevitably seen as the model against which to measure other regional courts or a possible universal human rights court.

Finally, the jurisprudence of the Court (as well as that of the Commission, although to a lesser extent) has been influential in the normative development of other parts of the international human rights system. Thus, the Inter-American Court and the ICCPR Human Rights Committee have frequently referred to judgments of the European Court. Its unacknowledged and perhaps unrecognized influence may have been even greater.

The frequency with which states have been before the Court differs considerably from country to country. In 1999, for example, 20.6 per cent of applications pending concerned Italy, and almost 40 per cent of the Court's findings of violations (44 cases) involved Italy. Fifteen per cent of findings (18 cases) involved Turkey; France with 16 cases and the UK with 12 cases were next. To some degree these figures reflect the extent to which adequate domestic remedies are available, which in turn is influenced by whether the Convention has been incorporated in domestic law. See pp. 1001–1006, *infra*.

Before examining some of the Court's case law consider the following description of its role.

J. G. MERRILLS, THE DEVELOPMENT OF INTERNATIONAL LAW BY THE EUROPEAN COURT OF HUMAN RIGHTS
(2nd edn., 1993), at 9

. . . Since there is no aspect of national affairs which can be said to be without implications for one or other of the rights protected by the Convention, there is no matter of domestic law and policy which may not eventually reach the European Court.

In terms of the character of the Court's work this has a double significance. In the first place, it means that the Court is required to investigate and pronounce on many issues which have not hitherto been regarded as appropriate subjects for international adjudication, which in turn raises the question of how far the Court is entitled to go in monitoring the laws and practices of the Contracting States. This is essentially a question about the impact of human rights law on national sovereignty and the role of international adjudication in establishing and enforcing uniform standards. The other way in which the nature of the Court's work is significant is that as a tribunal dealing with human rights, the Court is required to decide difficult and important questions concerning the proper relationship between the individual and the State. The issue here is what it means to have a particular right and how the balance is to be struck between such competing interests as, for example, privacy and national security, or prompt trial and the limitation of public expenditure.

. . . As a commentator has said of the Strasbourg [European Convention] institutions, 'Conceived as regional international organs with limited jurisdiction and even more limited powers, they have gradually acquired the status and authority of constitutional tribunals'. As we shall see, this transformation of the Convention and its institutions, which is still in progress, is the key to understanding the wider significance of the Court's decisions.
. . .

Although the Court is careful to avoid trespassing on what it sees as the function of the national authorities, investigating 'the international responsibility of the State' almost always calls for scrutiny of certain aspects of domestic law. Thus another feature of the Court's work is that the very nature of the obligations with which the Court is concerned makes the adequacy of the Contracting States' domestic law a matter for investigation.
. . .

The Court's decisions are binding on the Contracting States, which under Article 53 of the Convention, 'undertake to abide by the decision of the Court in any case to which they are parties'. When the Court concludes that the Convention has been violated, it is therefore incumbent on the respondent to take whatever steps may be needed to put matters right.
. . .

In each decision the Court is not just spelling out the obligations of the State which happens to be involved in the particular case.

. . . The common law, advancing from precedent to precedent, has a counterpart, then, in the developing law of the European Convention.

Judgments have this wider significance because the Court consistently seeks to justify its decisions in terms which treat its existing case-law as authoritative. In other words, it follows judicial precedent.

NOTE

The decisions below explore some of the characteristic problems that arise when international tribunals decide human rights issues that may deeply affect the internal order of states. They involve three fields in which the European Court has been active—rights of homosexuals, blasphemy, and electoral democracy—among the vast range of matters that have come before the Court. That range indeed approximates the breadth of issues that come before national constitutional courts or the US Supreme Court with respect to its constitutional decisions. Indeed, the United States offers a useful comparison: relationships between the European Court and the (judiciaries of the) member states of the European Convention, on the one hand; relationships between the US Supreme Court and the (judiciaries of the) component states of the American federalism, on the other.

The differences between, say, the work of the ICCPR Human Rights Committee and the European Court are striking. Of course deep and often disputed moral and political premises inform the work of the Court and sometimes enter into explicit debate . But its opinions take the traditional forms of the law—the facts of the dispute, argument about the interpretation of the text and related argument about the policies or principles involved, reflection on the institutional role of the Court in relation to national political orders, the ultimate decision applying the Convention in a decision binding the states parties, and possible recourse to a political body if a state does not comply with the Court's decision. From this point of view, a study of the European Court's decisions best illustrates the promise of an international (regional) *legal* order brought to bear on national human rights issues.

The question inevitably arises of how transferable this experience of the European human rights system may be—whether, for example, an equally effective judicial system functioning with so high a record of compliance by states could function under a universal human rights treaty such as the ICCPR, or in a different kind of regional regime such as the Americas or Africa.

The dominant jurisprudential and political theme that unifies the three groups of cases below is the doctrine (or theory, or principle) of margin of appreciation, critical to an understanding of the dilemmas before this international court and the ways in which it tries to come to terms with them. Following these decisions are excerpts from writings of scholars that probe the ways in which the Court has employed and developed this theme.

NOTE

The following materials deal with the rights of homosexual with respect to sexual relations and military service, principally within the context of the right to privacy.

The *Handyside* decision introduces those materials since it provides background for the European Court's decision in *Norris v. Ireland, infra.* The following excerpts consider only issues bearing directly on *Norris.*

HANDYSIDE CASE
European Court of Human Rights, 1976
Ser. A, No. 24, 1 EHRR 737

Handyside, a UK citizen who owned a publishing house, had advertised in 1971 and was en route to publishing 'The Little Red Schoolbook', an English translation of a Danish book published in a number of continental countries which was meant to serve as a reference work for schoolchildren. It treated education and teaching in general, advancing in many instances unorthodox, counter-cultural perspectives. About ten per cent of the book dealt with sexual matters, including 'reference' sections on masturbation, intercourse, contraceptives, homosexuality, pornography and venereal disease. Here too the advice offered was unorthodox: experiment, learn for yourself, don't fear disapproval. The publicity given the book drew adverse reactions from quarters such as schools, churches and parents' groups.

Before publication, government authorities acted under the Obscene Publications Acts 1959 and 1964, seizing all found copies of the book. Handyside was convicted of a violation of the Acts before a Magistrate's Court, which fined him and ordered that all books be destroyed. The appellate court affirmed, concluding that the book, seen as a whole, would tend to corrupt and deprave a significant portion of children who would read it, and that despite its virtues as an educational document, the book could not benefit from a statutory defence to the effect that on balance publication could be justified as being in the public good. A revised edition of the book was published later in 1971 and was not interfered with.

In 1972 Handyside filed an application against the United Kingdom before the European Commission of Human Rights, alleging several violations of the Convention but stressing Article 10. The Commission in effect concluded that there had been no breach of the Convention, and it referred the case to the European Court of Human Rights in 1976. The Court decided that no breach of Article 10 (or any other article) had been established. Article 10 provides:

> 1. Everyone has the right to freedom of expression. This right shall include freedom to hold opinions and to receive and impart information and ideas without interference by public authority and regardless of frontiers. This Article shall not prevent States from requiring the licensing of broadcasting, television or cinema enterprises.
> 2. The exercise of these freedoms, since it carries with it duties and responsibilities, may be subject to such formalities, conditions, restrictions or penalties as are prescribed by law and are necessary in a democratic society, in the interests of national security, territorial integrity or public safety, for the prevention of

disorder or crime, for the protection of health or morals, for the protection of
the reputation or rights of others, for preventing the disclosure of information
received in confidence, or for maintaining the authority and impartiality of the
judiciary.

After review of the book and the evidence before the English courts, the Court
concluded that the English judges had a basis, in the exercise of the discretion left
them by the Convention, for finding that the book would have a pernicious effect
on the morals of the likely readers between ages 12 and 18. The excerpts below
from the opinion treat matters relevant to a determination whether the UK
restrictions on publication were 'necessary in a democratic society' within the
meaning of Article 10(2).

48. . . . These observations apply, notably, to Article 10 § 2. In particular, it is not
possible to find in the domestic law of the various Contracting States a uniform
European conception of morals. The view taken by their respective laws of the
requirements of morals varies from time to time and from place to place, especially in our era which is characterised by a rapid and far-reaching evolution of
opinions on the subject. By reason of their direct and continuous contact with the
vital forces of their countries, State authorities are in principle in a better position
than the international judge to give an opinion on the exact content of these
requirements as well as on the 'necessity' of a 'restriction' or 'penalty' intended to
meet them. . . . [I]t is for the national authorities to make the initial assessment of
the reality of the pressing social need implied by the notion of 'necessity' in this
context.

Consequently, Article 10 § 2 leaves to the Contracting States a margin of
appreciation. This margin is given both to the domestic legislator ('prescribed by
law') and to the bodies, judicial amongst others, that are called upon to interpret
and apply the laws in force. . . .

49. Nevertheless, Article 10 § 2 does not give the Contracting States an
unlimited power of appreciation. The Court, which, with the Commission, is
responsible for ensuring the observance of those States' engagements (Article 19),
is empowered to give the final ruling on whether a 'restriction' or 'penalty' is
reconcilable with freedom of expression as protected by Article 10. The domestic
margin of appreciation thus goes hand in hand with a European supervision.
Such supervision concerns both the aim of the measure challenged and its
'necessity'. . . .

The Court's supervisory functions oblige it to pay the utmost attention to the
principles characterising a 'democratic society'. Freedom of expression constitutes
one of the essential foundations of such a society, one of the basic conditions for
its progress and for the development of every man. Subject to paragraph 2 of
Article 10, it is applicable not only to 'information' or 'ideas' that are favourably
received or regarded as inoffensive or as a matter of indifference, but also to those
that offend, shock or disturb the State or any sector of the population. Such are the
demands of that pluralism, tolerance and broadmindedness without which there is
no 'democratic society'. This means, amongst other things, that every 'formality',

'condition', 'restriction' or 'penalty' imposed in this sphere must be proportionate to the legitimate aim pursued.

From another standpoint, whoever exercises his freedom of expression undertakes 'duties and responsibilities' the scope of which depends on his situation and the technical means he uses. The Court cannot overlook such a person's 'duties' and 'responsibilities' when it enquires, as in this case, whether 'restrictions' or 'penalties' were conducive to the 'protection of morals' which made them 'necessary' in a 'democratic society'.

50. It follows from this that it is in no way the Court's task to take the place of the competent national courts but rather to review under Article 10 the decisions they delivered in the exercise of their power of appreciation.

. . .

NOTE

The judgment below of the European Court of Human Rights in *Norris v. Ireland* refers both to the *Handyside* case and to the *Dudgeon Case*, Ser. A, No. 45, 4 EHRR 149 (1981). Dudgeon, a homosexual resident of Northern Ireland, brought proceedings against the United Kingdom based on his complaint against laws of Northern Ireland that made certain sexual acts between consenting adult males criminal offences. The Court concluded that Dudgeon had suffered an unjustified interference with his right to respect for his private life and accordingly found a breach by the UK of Article 8 of the Convention. That same article was at issue in *Norris*.

Consider the following three provisions in human rights instruments on the right to privacy:

Article 8 of the European Convention

1. Everyone has the right to respect for his private and family life, his home and his correspondence.
2. There shall be no interference by a public authority with the exercise of this right except such as is in accordance with the law and is necessary in a democratic society in the interests of national security, public safety or the economic well-being of the country, for the prevention of disorder or crime, for the protection of health or morals, or for the protection of the rights and freedoms of others.

Article 12 of the Universal Declaration of Human Rights

No one shall be subjected to arbitrary interference with his privacy, family, home or correspondence, nor to attacks upon his honour or reputation. Everyone has the right to the protection of the law against such interference or attacks.

Article 17 of the ICCPR

The ICCPR provision is similar to the Universal Declaration, except that it refers to 'arbitrary *or unlawful* interference' with privacy and to '*unlawful* attacks' on honour (emphasis added). The ICCPR Human Rights Committee has issued a General Comment No. 16, see p. 735, *supra*, on Article 17 without mentioning questions of sexuality.

The United States Constitution makes no reference to a right to 'privacy' as such.

We turn to two judicial decisions interpreting and applying the European Convention and the US Constitution.

NORRIS v. IRELAND
European Court of Human Rights, 1989
Ser. A, No. 142, 13 EHRR 186

[The applicant, an Irish national and member of the Irish Parliament, was a homosexual and chairman of the Irish Gay Rights Movement. In 1977, he instituted proceedings in the High Court of Ireland, seeking a declaration that certain laws prohibiting homosexual relations were invalid under the Irish Constitution. Those laws included (i) section 62 of the Person Act 1861 to the effect that '[w]hosoever shall attempt to commit the said abominable crime [of buggery], or shall be guilty of any . . . indecent assault upon a male person', is guilty of a misdemeanor and subject to a prison sentence not exceeding ten years, and (ii) section 11 of the Criminal Law Amendment Act 1885 to the effect that any 'male person who, in public or in private, commits . . . any act of gross indecency with another male person', is guilty of a misdemeanor and subject to imprisonment not exceeding two years. The term 'gross indecency' was not statutorily defined and was to be given meaning by courts on the particular facts of each case. Later acts gave courts discretion to impose more lenient sentences.

At no time was the applicant charged with any offence in relation to his admitted homosexual activities, although he was continuously at risk of being so prosecuted on the basis of an indictment laid by the Director of Public Prosecutions. The Director made a statement in connection with this litigation to the effect that '[t]he Director has no *stated* prosecution policy on any branch of the criminal law. He has no unstated policy *not* to enforce any offence. Each case is treated on its merits'. Since the Office of the Director was created in 1984, no prosecution had been brought in respect of homosexual activities except where minors were involved or the acts were committed in public or without consent.

Mr Norris offered evidence of the ways in which this legislation had interfered with his right to respect for his private life, including evidence (i) of deep depression on realizing that 'any overt expression of his sexuality would expose him to criminal prosecution', and (ii) of fear of prosecution of him or of another man with whom he had a physical relationship.

The judge in the High Court found that '[o]ne of the effects of criminal sanctions against homosexual acts is to reinforce the misapprehension and general prejudice of the public and increase the anxiety and guilt feelings of homosexuals leading, on occasions, to depression . . .'. However, he dismissed the action on legal grounds, and his decision was upheld in 1983 by the Supreme Court of Ireland. That court concluded that the applicant had standing (*locus standi*) to bring an action for a declaration even though he had not been prosecuted, for the threat continued.

The Supreme Court rejected the applicant's argument that the Irish Constitution should be interpreted in the light of the European Convention on Human Rights, for the Convention was 'an international agreement [which] does not and cannot form part of [Ireland's] domestic law, nor affect in any way questions which arise thereunder'. Article 29(6) of the Irish Constitution declared: 'No international agreement shall be part of the domestic law of the State save as may be determined by the Oireachtas', and the Oireachtas (legislature) had not taken action to enact the Convention as domestic legislation.

The Supreme Court found the laws complained of to be consistent with the Constitution, since no right of privacy encompassing consensual homosexual activity could be derived from the 'Christian and democratic nature of the Irish State'. It observed (i) that homosexuality 'has always been condemned in Christian teaching as being morally wrong' and has been regarded for centuries 'as an offence against nature and a very serious crime', (ii) that '[e]xclusive homosexuality, whether the condition be congenital or acquired, can result in great distress and unhappiness for the individual and can lead to depression, despair and suicide', and (iii) that male homosexual conduct resulted in many states in 'all forms of venereal disease', which had become a 'significant public health problem'.

Mr Norris started proceedings before the European Commission of Human Rights, claiming that the Irish laws constituted a continuing interference with his right to respect for private life under Article 8 of the European Convention. In 1987, by six votes to five, the Commission expressed its opinion that there had been a violation of Article 8. The case was then referred to the European Court, which agreed with the conclusion in *Dudgeon* that the applicant could claim to be a victim of a violation of the Convention because of the risk of criminal prosecution that constituted a continuing interference with the applicant's right to respect for his private life. Excerpts from the judgment follow:]

39. The interference found by the Court does not satisfy the conditions of paragraph (2) of Article 8 unless it is 'in accordance with the law', has an aim which is legitimate under this paragraph and is 'necessary in a democratic society' for the aforesaid aim.

40. It is common ground that the first two conditions are satisfied. As the Commission pointed out in paragraph 58 of its report, the interference is plainly 'in accordance with the law' since it arises from the very existence of the impugned legislation. Neither was it contested that the interference has a legitimate aim, namely the protection of morals.

41. It remains to be determined whether the maintenance in force of the impugned legislation is 'necessary in a democratic society' for the aforesaid aim. According to the Court's case law, this will not be so unless, *inter alia*, the

interference in question answers a pressing social need and in particular is proportionate to the legitimate aim pursued.

. . .

42. . . . It was not contended before the Commission that there is a large body of opinion in Ireland which is hostile or intolerant towards homosexual acts committed in private between consenting adults. Nor was it argued that Irish society had a special need to be protected from such activity. In these circumstances, the Commission concluded that the restriction imposed on the applicant under Irish law, by reason of its breadth and absolute character, is disproportionate to the aims sought to be achieved and therefore is not necessary for one of the reasons laid down in Article 8(2) of the Convention.

. . .

44. . . . As early as 1976, the Court declared in its *Handyside* judgment of 7 December 1976 that, in investigating whether the protection of morals necessitated the various measures taken, it had to make an 'assessment of the reality of the pressing social need implied by the notion of 'necessity' in this context' and stated that 'every 'restriction' imposed in this sphere must be proportionate to the legitimate aim pursued'. It confirmed this approach in its *Dudgeon* judgment.

. . . [A]lthough of the three aforementioned judgments two related to Article 10 of the Convention, it sees no cause to apply different criteria in the context of Article 8.

. . .

46. As in the *Dudgeon* case, . . . not only the nature of the aim of the restriction but also the nature of the activities involved will affect the scope of the margin of appreciation. The present case concerns a most intimate aspect of private life. Accordingly, there must exist particularly serious reasons before interferences on the part of public authorities can be legitimate for the purposes of paragraph (2) of Article 8.

Yet the Government has adduced no evidence which would point to the existence of factors justifying the retention of the impugned laws which are additional to or are of greater weight than those present in the aforementioned *Dudgeon* case. At paragraph 60 of its judgment of 22 October 1981 the Court noted that

> As compared with the era when [the] legislation was enacted, there is now a better understanding, and in consequence an increased tolerance, of homosexual behaviour to the extent that in the great majority of the member States of the Council of Europe it is no longer considered to be necessary or appropriate to treat homosexual practices of the kind now in question as in themselves a matter to which the sanctions of the criminal law should be applied; the Court cannot overlook the marked changes which have occurred in this regard in the domestic law of the member States.

It was clear that 'the authorities [had] refrained in recent years from enforcing the law in respect of private homosexual acts between consenting [adult] males . . . capable of valid consent'. There was no evidence to show that this '[had] been injurious to moral standards in Northern Ireland or that there [had] been any public demand for stricter enforcement of the law'.

Applying the same tests to the present case, the Court considers that, as regards Ireland, it cannot be maintained that there is a 'pressing social need' to make such acts criminal offences. On the specific issue of proportionality, the Court is of the opinion that 'such justifications as there are for retaining the law in force unamended are outweighed by the detrimental effects which the very existence of the legislative provisions in question can have on the life of a person of homosexual orientation like the applicant. Although members of the public who regard homosexuality as immoral may be shocked, offended or disturbed by the commission by others of private homosexual acts, this cannot on its own warrant the application of penal sanctions when it is consenting adults alone who are involved'.

47. The Court therefore finds that the reasons put forward as justifying the interference found are not sufficient to satisfy the requirements of paragraph (2) of Article 8. There is accordingly a breach of that Article.

[The Court then considered the applicant's request for compensation under provisions of the Convention.]

49. The applicant requested the Court to fix such amount by way of damages as would acknowledge the extent to which he has suffered from the maintenance in force of the legislation.

[I]t is inevitable that the Court's decision will have effects extending beyond the confines of this particular case, especially since the violation found stems directly from the contested provision and not from individual measures of implementation. It will be for Ireland to take the necessary measures in its domestic legal system to ensure the performance of its obligation under [the Convention].

For this reason and notwithstanding the different situation in the present case as compared with the *Dudgeon* case, the Court is of the opinion that its finding of a breach of Article 8 constitutes adequate just satisfaction for the purposes of . . . the Convention and therefore rejects this head of claim.

. . .

NOTE

Consider the following observation of Andrew Clapham in *Human Rights in the Private Sphere* (1993), at 64:

> . . . [T]he courts, even when faced with a popular legitimate law, such as the law of the Isle of Man on birching [a form of whipping or spanking with a birch rod, used under the law referred to for discipline of children], may prefer to follow the Strasbourg lead. A parallel can be drawn between this case and the situation concerning homosexuality in Northern Ireland, where the Court of Human Rights, faced with another popular law (which prohibited sexual relations between men), found a breach of human rights: Dudgeon v. United Kingdom. It is in these types of situation involving unpopular minority interests that human

rights theory is really tested. Both laws were relatively popular in the Isle of Man and Northern Ireland respectively and it was the European Court of Human Rights in Strasbourg that held the laws to violate human rights. It may well be that such a court can bring a detachment to bear on domestic laws that national courts may find hard. It is for this reason that even if the United Kingdom were to adopt the European Convention in the form of a Bill of Rights, the right of individual petition to Strasbourg should still be kept open, so that the European Court of Human Rights has the chance to examine cases arising in the United Kingdom context and give authoritative judgments on the scope of the rights guaranteed by the Convention.

BOWERS v. HARDWICK
Supreme Court of the United States, 1986
478 U.S. 186 106 S. Ct. 2841

[A Georgia statute defined the crime of sodomy as 'any sex act involving the sex organs of one person and the mouth or anus of another'. Hardwick (who was under some surveillance by the police) was arrested in his home bedroom immediately after engaging in oral sex there with a consenting adult male. He was charged with the crime of sodomy and, before being tried, challenged the statute.

The Supreme Court, by a 5–4 vote, held that the statute was constitutional. Five opinions were written, including the opinion for the Court by Justice White, two separate concurring opinions and two dissents. The excerpts below from several opinions touch only on a few themes that provide comparisons with the opinion in *Norris*.]

OPINION OF JUSTICE WHITE FOR THE COURT

. . . The issue presented is whether the Federal Constitution confers a fundamental right upon homosexuals to engage in sodomy and hence invalidates the laws of the many States that still make such conduct illegal. . . .

We first register our disagreement with the [opinion of the Court of Appeals below] that the [Supreme] Court's prior cases have construed the Constitution to confer a right of privacy that extends to homosexual sodomy. . . .

[The opinion referred to prior decisions involving child rearing and education of children, to procreation and contraception, to marriage, and (*Roe v. Wade*) to abortion. Some of those decisions relied on a right to privacy not explicit in the Constitution but found to be within the protection provided by constitutional provisions such as the Due Process Clause of the Fourteenth Amendment.]

. . . [W]e think it evident that none of the rights announced in those cases bears any resemblance to the claimed constitutional right of homosexuals to engage in acts of sodomy that is asserted in this case. No connection between family, marriage, or procreation on the one hand and homosexual activity on the other has been demonstrated. . . .

. . .

. . . Proscriptions against [consensual sodomy] have ancient roots . . . Sodomy was a criminal offense at common law and . . . [i]n 1868, when the Fourteenth Amendment was ratified, all but 5 of the 37 States in the Union had criminal sodomy laws. In fact, until 1961, all 50 states outlawed sodomy, and today, 24 States and the District of Columbia continue to provide criminal penalties for sodomy performed in private and between consenting adults. . . . Against this background, to claim that a right to engage in such conduct is [quoting from prior decisions in unrelated cases seeking to give content to concepts like due process or basic rights] 'deeply rooted in this Nation's history and tradition' or 'implicit in the concept of ordered liberty' is, at best, facetious.

Nor are we inclined to take a more expansive view of our authority to discover new fundamental rights imbedded in the Due Process Clause. The Court is most vulnerable and comes nearest to illegitimacy when it deals with judge-made constitutional law having little or no cognizable roots in the language or design of the Constitution. . . .

. . .

Even if the conduct at issue here is not a fundamental right, respondent asserts that there must be a rational basis for the law and that there is none in this case other than the presumed belief of a majority of the electorate in Georgia that homosexual sodomy is immoral and unacceptable. This is said to be an inadequate rationale to support the law. The law, however, is constantly based on notions of morality, and if all laws representing essentially moral choices are to be invalidated under the Due Process Clause, the courts will be very busy indeed. . . .

CHIEF JUSTICE BURGER, CONCURRING

. . . Decisions of individuals relating to homosexual conduct have been subject to state intervention throughout the history of Western civilization. Condemnation of those practices is firmly rooted in Judeao-Christian moral and ethical standards. . . . To hold that the act of homosexual sodomy is somehow protected as a fundamental right would be to cast aside millennia of moral teaching.

. . .

JUSTICE BLACKMUN (JOINED BY JUSTICES BRENNAN, MARSHALL AND STEVENS), DISSENTING

This case is [not] about a 'fundamental right to engage in homosexual sodomy', as the Court purports to declare. . . . Rather, this case is about [quoting here and below from prior decisions of the Court] 'the most comprehensive of rights and the rights most valued by civilized men', namely, 'the right to be let alone'.

. . . I believe we must analyze respondent Hardwick's claim in the light of the values that underlie the constitutional right to privacy. If that right means anything, it means that, before Georgia can prosecute its citizens for making choices about the most intimate aspects of their lives, it must do more than assert that the choice they have made is an 'abominable crime not fit to be named among Christians'.

. . .

. . . We protect those rights [to family, procreation] not because they contribute, in some direct and material way, to the general public welfare, but because they form so central a part of an individual's life. . . . We protect the decision whether to have a child because parenthood alters so dramatically an individual's self-definition, not because of demographic considerations or the Bible's command to be fruitful and multiply. And we protect the family because it contributes so powerfully to the happiness of individuals, not because of a preference for stereotypical households. . . .

Only the most willful blindness could obscure the fact that sexual intimacy is 'a sensitive, key relationship of human existence, central to family life, community welfare, and the development of human personality'. The fact that individuals define themselves in a significant way through their intimate sexual relationships with others suggests, in a Nation as diverse as ours, that there may be many 'right' ways of conducting those relationships, and that much of the richness of a relationship will come from the freedom an individual has to choose the form and nature of these intensely personal bonds.

. . .

The assertion [in the State Attorney General's brief] that 'traditional Judeo-Christian values proscribe' the conduct involved cannot provide an adequate justification [for the Georgia statute]. That certain, but by no means all, religious groups condemn the behavior at issue gives the State no license to impose their judgments on the entire citizenry. The legitimacy of secular legislation depends instead on whether the State can advance some justification for its law beyond its conformity to religious doctrine. Thus, far from buttressing [the Attorney General's] case, invocation of Leviticus, Romans, St. Thomas Aquinas, and sodomy's heretical status during the Middle Ages undermines his suggestion that [the statute] represents a legitimate use of secular coercive power. A State can no more punish private behavior because of religious intolerance than it can punish such behavior because of racial animus. . . .

. . . [The State] and the Court fail to see the difference between laws that protect public sensibilities and those that enforce private morality. Statutes banning public sexual activity are entirely consistent with protecting the individual's liberty interest in decisions concerning sexual relations: the same recognition that those decisions are intensely private which justifies protecting them from governmental interference can justify protecting individuals from unwilling exposure to the sexual activities of others. But the mere fact that intimate behavior may be punished when it takes place in public cannot dictate how States can regulate intimate behavior that occurs in intimate places. . . .

. . . This case involves no real interference with the rights of others, for the mere knowledge that other individuals do not adhere to one's value system cannot be a legal cognizable interest, let alone an interest that can justify invading the houses, hearts, and minds of citizens who choose to live their lives differently.

. . .

NOTE

Compare Laurence Tribe, *American Constitutional Law* (2nd edn., 1987), at 1428:

... Therefore, in asking whether an alleged right forms part of a traditional liberty, it is crucial to define the liberty at a high enough level of generality to permit unconventional variants to claim protection along with mainstream versions of protected conduct. The proper question, as the dissent in Hardwick recognized, is not whether oral sex as such has long enjoyed a special place in the pantheon of constitutional rights, but whether private, consensual, adult sexual acts partake of traditionally revered liberties of intimate association and individual autonomy.

... It should come as no surprise that, in the kind of society contemplated by our Constitution, government must offer greater justification to police the bedroom than it must to police the streets. Therefore, the relevant question is not what Michael Hardwick was doing in the privacy of his own bedroom, but what the State of Georgia was doing there.

QUESTIONS

1. Do you believe that it was significant for the opinions that the European Convention is explicit about the right to 'respect' for 'private life' and the US Constitution is not? If there were no Article 8 in the European Convention, how would you as counsel for the applicants have argued your case? How might the Court have resolved it?

2. What are the salient differences between the opinions of the courts in *Norris* and *Bowers* with respect to trends in legislation and mores in European states (in *Norris*) or in states of the United States federalism (in *Bowers*)? Are the trends similar?

3. What method do you think the Court should explicitly follow in deciding a case like *Norris*, or the birching case from the Isle of Man, with respect to trends in European states? Should it survey the legislation and the practice under that legislation (whether or not to prosecute, nature of punishment, and so on) in all member states? What should it make of the survey? Would all states have equal 'weight' in the decision? What relevance would a 'trend' have—for example, 30 years ago 90 per cent of the states barred the practice at issue, but now only 60 per cent bar it (or the reverse, earlier permitted and now often barred)?

NOTE

The South African Constitution of 1996 includes the right to privacy and the right to dignity. The equal protection provision of Section 9 states:

(1) Everyone is equal before the law and has the right to equal protection and benefit of the law.

(2) Equality includes the full and equal enjoyment of all rights and freedoms. To promote the achievement of equality, legislative and other measures designed to protect or advance persons, or categories of persons, disadvantaged by unfair discrimination may be taken.

(3) The state may not unfairly discriminate directly or indirectly against anyone on one or more grounds, including race, gender, sex, pregnancy, marital status, ethnic or social origin, colour, sexual orientation, age, disability, religion, conscience, belief, culture, language and birth.

(4) No person may unfairly discriminate directly or indirectly against anyone on one or more grounds in terms of subsection (3). National legislation must be enacted to prevent or prohibit unfair discrimination.

(5) Discrimination on one or more of the grounds listed in subsection (3) is unfair unless it is established that the discrimination is fair.

Article 36 of the Constitution provides: 'The rights in the Bill of Rights may be limited only in terms of law of general application to the extent that the limitation is reasonable and justifiable in an open and democratic society based on human dignity, equality and freedom . . .'.

A number of decisions have involved challenges—based on the equal protection, privacy and dignity provisions of the Constitution—to laws concerning homosexuals. In *National Coalition for Gay and Lesbian Equality v. Minister of Justice*, CCT 11/98, 1999(1) SA6 (CC), 1998 (1) BCLR 1517 (CC), the Constitutional Court of South Africa declared the common law offences of sodomy between males and related statutory offences to be inconsistent with the Constitution because—as applied to consensual sexual relations in privacy between adult males—they breach the rights of equality, dignity and privacy.

QUESTION

In what ways does Article 9 of the South African Constitution differ from the analogous provisions in the ECHR and in the United States Constitution? Does it suggest that the advocate of gay and lesbian rights should rely on it alone, or is there reason to rely also on the right to privacy?

LUSTIG-PREAN AND BECKETT V. UNITED KINGDOM
European Court of Human Rights, 1999
www.echr.coe.int/eng/Judgments.htm

[The two applicants, British nationals, complained that 'investigations into their homosexuality and their discharge from the Royal Navy on the sole ground that they are homsexual' violated Article 8 of the European Convention taken alone and in conjunction with Article 14. Following entry into force of Protocol No. 11 in 1998, the applications were examined directly by a panel of the Court.

Lustig-Prean began his career in the Royal Navy in 1982. His evaluation in 1989 termed him an officer of 'great potential' and the 'sort of person that the Royal Navy needs to attract and retain'. A 1993 evaluation described him as an officer 'who enjoys my complete trust in all matters. He is an outstanding prospect for early promotion to commander'. In 1994, he became a lieutenant commander.

Since 1992, Lustig-Prean had been involved in a steady relationship with a civilian partner. In early 1994, he learned that the Royal Navy Special Investigations Branch (the 'service police') had been given anonymously an allegation of his homosexuality. He admitted to his commanding officer that he was homosexual. Interviews with service police followed, in which he was asked personal questions about his relationships, including whether he had a relationship with a serviceman and whether he was HIV-positive. His final evaluation in June 1994 by his commander noted his 'well-deserved reputation for outstanding professional ability and admirable personal qualities', as well as his 'loyal, dependable and always dignified service'. In December 1994, the Admiralty Board notified Lustig-Prean that he would be administratively discharged on grounds of his sexual orientation. His term of service would otherwise have ended in 2009, with possibility of renewal.

Beckett too had a successful career in the Royal Navy, with positive evaluations. He too admitted his homosexuality to the service police. The questions put to him were highly personal and detailed about his sexual life with his partner. His administrative discharge on grounds of homosexuality took place in 1993.

The applicants sought judicial review of the decisions to discharge them. The High Court dismissed their application, and the Court of Appeal later dismissed their appeal. The main opinion, written by the Master of the Rolls, concluded that

> the court may not interfere with the exercise of an administrative discretion on substantive grounds save where the court is satisfied that the decision is unreasonable in the sense that it is beyond the range of responses open to a reasonable decision-maker. But in judging whether the decision-maker has exceeded this margin of appreciation the human rights context is important. The more substantial the interference with human rights, the more the court will require by way of justification before it is satisfied that the decision is reasonable in the sense outlined above.

The opinion noted that the greater the policy content of the decision and the more remote the subject matter of a decision from ordinary judicial experience, the more hesitant the court had to be in holding a decision to be irrational. Stressing that the court was not the primary decision-maker and that it wasn't the court's role to regulate conditions of service in the armed forces, and taking into account its constitutional duty of ensuring rights of citizens, the opinion nonetheless stated that the court 'must properly defer to the expertise of responsible decision-makers, it must not shrink from its fundamental duty to "do right to all manner of people"'.

Commenting that the parties' submissions were 'of very considerable cogency', the Master of the Rolls nonetheless concluded that the armed forces policy could not be considered 'irrational'. With respect to the European Convention, the opinion stated that '[i]t is, inevitably, common ground that the United Kingdom's obligation, binding in international law, to respect and ensure compliance with [Article 8 of the Convention] is not one that is enforceable by domestic courts'.

Leave to appeal to the House of Lords was denied, and the applicants pursued other avenues of relief without success.

Britain had decriminalized homosexual acts in private between consenting adults in the Sexual Offenses Act 1967. The Criminal Justice and Public Order Act 1994 provided that nothing prevented a homosexual act from constituting a ground for discharging a member of the armed forces. In 1994, Armed Forces' Policy and Guidelines on Homosexuality were updated to state in part:

> Homosexuality, whether male or female, is considered incompatible with service in the armed forces. This is not only because of the close physical conditions in which personnel often have to live and work, but also because homosexual behaviour can cause offence, polarize relationships, induce ill-discipline and, as a consequence, damage morale and unit effectiveness. If individuals admit to being homosexual whilst serving and their Commanding Officer judges that this admission is well-founded they will be required to leave the services. . . .

A Homosexuality Policy Assesment Team (HPAT) was then established by the Ministry of Defence to make an internal assessment of the armed forces' policy.

> The starting-point of the assessment was an assumption that homosexual men and women were in themselves no less physically capable, brave, dependable and skilled than heterosexuals. It was considered that any problems to be identified would lie in the difficulties which integration of declared homosexuals would pose to the military system which was largely staffed by heterosexuals.

The following excerpts from the opinion of the European Court of Human Rights start with a discussion of the HPAT.]

47. The focus throughout the assessment was upon the anticipated effects on fighting power and this was found to be the 'key problem' in integrating homosexuals into the armed forces. It was considered well established that the presence of known or strongly suspected homosexuals in the armed forces would produce certain behavioural and emotional responses and problems which would affect morale and, in turn, significantly and negatively affect the fighting power of the armed forces.

These anticipated problems included controlling homosexual behaviour and heterosexual animosity, assaults on homosexuals, bullying and harassment of homosexuals, ostracism and avoidance, 'cliquishness' and pairing, leadership and decision-making problems including allegations of favouritism, discrimination and ineffectiveness . . ., privacy/decency issues, increased dislike and suspicions (polarized relationships), and resentment over imposed change especially if controls on heterosexual expression also had to be tightened.

. . .

55. The HPAT found that 'the key problem remains and its intractability has indeed been re-confirmed. The evidence for an anticipated loss in fighting power has been set out . . . and forms the centrepiece of this assessment . . . '.

Current service attitudes were considered unlikely to change in the near future. . . . [The HPAT] considered that it was not possible to draw any meaningful comparison between the integration of homosexuals and of women and ethnic minorities into the armed forces since homosexuality raised problems of a type and intensity that gender and race did not.

The HPAT considered that, in the longer term, evolving social attitudes towards homosexuality might reduce the risks to fighting power inherent in change but that their assessment could 'only deal with present attitudes and risks'. It went on:

> . . . [T]he Ministry must deal with the world as it is. Service attitudes, in as far as they differ from those of the general population, emerge from the unique conditions of military life, and represent the current social and psychological realities. They indicate military risk from a policy change . . .

. . .

60. The 1996 Select Committee [of Parliament] report (produced after that committee's review of the Armed Forces Act 1996) referred to evidence taken from members of the Ministry of Defence and from homosexual support groups and to the HPAT Report. Once again, the committee did not recommend any change in the Government's policy. It noted that, since its last report, a total of 30 officers and 331 persons of other rank had been discharged or dismissed on grounds of homosexuality. The committee was satisfied that no reliable lessons could as yet be drawn from the experience of other countries. It acknowledged the strength of the human rights arguments put forward, but noted that there had to be a balance struck between individual rights and the needs of the whole. It was persuaded by the HPAT summary of the strength of opposition throughout the armed services to any relaxation of the policy. It accepted that the presence of openly homosexual servicemen and women would have a significant adverse impact on morale and, ultimately, on operational effectiveness. The matter was then debated in the House of Commons and members, by 188 votes to 120, rejected any change to the existing policy.

61. Prior to September 1995, applicants to the armed forces were informed about the armed forces' policy as regards homosexuals in the armed forces by means of a leaflet entitled 'Your Rights and Responsibilities'. To avoid any mis-understanding and so that each recruit to each of the armed services received identical information, on 1 September 1995 the armed forces introduced a Service Statement to be read and signed before enlistment. Paragraph 8 of that statement is headed 'Homosexuality' and states that homosexuality is not considered compatible with service life and 'can lead to administrative discharge'.

AS TO THE LAW

1. Alleged Violation of Article 8 of the Convention

62. The applicants complained that the investigations into their homosexuality and their subsequent discharge from the Royal Navy ... constituted a violation of their right to respect for their private lives protected by Article 8 of the Convention. That Article, in so far as is relevant, reads as follows:

> 1. Everyone has the right to respect for his private ... life ...
> 2. There shall be no interference by a public authority with the exercise of this right except such as is in accordance with the law and is necessary in a demo-cratic society in the interests of national security, ... for the prevention of disorder ...

64. ... [T]he Court is of the view that the investigations by the military police ... constituted a direct interference with the applicants' right to respect for their private lives. Their consequent administrative discharge on the sole ground of their sexual orientation also constituted an interference with that right.

65. Such interferences can only be considered justified if the conditions of the second paragraph of Article 8 are satisfied. Accordingly, the interferences must be 'in accordance with the law', have an aim which is legitimate under this paragraph and must be 'necessary in a democratic society' for the aforesaid aim (see the *Norris v. Ireland* judgment of 26 October 1988, Series A no. 142, p. 18, § 39).

...

2. Legitimate aim

67. ... The Court finds no reason to doubt that the policy was designed with a view to ensuring the operational effectiveness of the armed forces or that investiga-tions were, in principle, intended to establish whether the person concerned was a homosexual to whom the policy was applicable. To this extent, therefore, the Court considers that the resulting interferences can be said to pursue the legitimate aims of 'the interests of national security' and 'the prevention of disorder'.

3. 'Necessary in a democratic society'

...

(a) The Government's submissions

...

70. ... [T]he Government emphasised, in the first place, the special British armed forces' context of the case. It was special because it was intimately connected with the nation's security and was, accordingly, central to a State's vital interests. Unit cohesion and morale lay at the heart of the effectiveness of the armed forces. ... Such cohesion and morale had to withstand the internal rigours of normal and corporate life, close physical and shared living conditions together with external pressures such as grave danger and war, all of which factors the Government

argued applied or could have applied to each applicant. In this respect, the armed forces were unique. . . .

In such circumstances, the Government, while accepting that members of the armed forces had the right to the Convention's protection, argued that different, and stricter, rules applied in this context. . . . Moreover, given the national security dimension to the present case a wide margin of appreciation was properly open to the State. Accordingly, the narrow margin of appreciation which applied to cases involving intimate private life matters could not be transposed unaltered to the present case.

In support of their argument for a broad margin of appreciation, the Government also referred to the fact that the issue of homosexuals in the armed forces has been the subject of intense debate in recent years in the United Kingdom, suggesting that the sensitivity and special context of the question meant that the decision was largely one for the national authorities. . . . The process of review was ongoing and the Government indicated their commitment to a free vote in Parliament on the subject after the next Parliamentary Select Committee review of the policy in 2001.

71. Secondly, the Government . . . considered that the observations and conclusions in the HPAT report of February 1996 . . . provided clear evidence of the risk to fighting power and operational effectiveness. . . .

The Government considered that the choice between establishing a code of conduct and maintaining the present policy lay at the heart of the judgment to be made in this matter. . . .

72. Thirdly, and as to the charge made by the applicants that the views expressed to the HPAT by the clear majority of serving personnel could be labelled as 'homophobic prejudice', the Government pointed out that these views represented genuine concerns expressed by those with first-hand and detailed knowledge of the demands of service life. Most of those surveyed displayed a clear difference in attitude towards homosexuality in civilian life. Conclusions could not be drawn from the fact that women and racial minorities were admitted while homosexuals were not because women and men were segregated in recognition of potential problems that might arise, whereas such arrangements were simply not possible in the case of same sex orientation. . . .

. . .

(b) The applicants' submissions

74. The applicants submitted that the interferences with their private lives . . . required particularly serious reasons by way of justification. . . .

. . .

76. [T]he applicants considered that the Government could not, consistently with Article 8, rely on and pander to the perceived prejudice of other service personnel. Given the absence of any rational basis for armed forces' personnel to behave any differently if they knew that an individual was a homosexual, the alleged risk of adverse reactions by service personnel was based on pure prejudice. It was the responsibility of the armed forces by reason of Article 1 of the Convention to ensure that those they employed understood that it was not acceptable for them to

act by reference to pure prejudice. However, rather than taking steps to remedy such prejudice, the armed forces punished the victims of prejudice. The applicants considered that the logic of the Government's argument applied equally to the contexts of racial, religious and gender prejudice; the Government could not seriously suggest that, for example, racial prejudice on the part of armed forces' personnel would be sufficient to justify excluding coloured persons from those forces.

. . .

78. . . . [T]he applicants submitted that the Government were required to substantiate their concerns about the threat to military discipline but had not produced any objective evidence to support their submission as to the risk to morale and operational effectiveness.

In this respect, they argued that the HPAT report was inadequate and fundamentally flawed. . . .

. . .

(c) The Court's assessment

(i) Applicable general principles

80. An interference will be considered 'necessary in a democratic society' for a legitimate aim if it answers a pressing social need and, in particular, is proportionate to the legitimate aim pursued (see the Norris judgment cited above, p. 18, § 41).

Given the matters at issue in the present case, the Court would underline the link between the notion of 'necessity' and that of a 'democratic society', the hallmarks of the latter including pluralism, tolerance and broadmindedness.

81. The Court recognizes that . . . [a] margin of appreciation is left open to Contracting States in the context of this assessment, which varies according to the nature of the activities restricted and of the aims pursued by the restrictions. . . .

82. Accordingly, when the relevant restrictions concern 'a most intimate part of an individual's private life', there must exist 'particularly serious reasons' before such interferences can satisfy the requirements of Article 8 § 2 of the Convention.

When the core of the national security aim pursued is the operational effectiveness of the armed forces, it is accepted that each State is competent to organise its own system of military discipline and enjoys a certain margin of appreciation in this respect. The Court also considers that it is open to the State to impose restrictions on an individual's right to respect for his private life where there is a real threat to the armed forces' operational effectiveness, as the proper functioning of an army is hardly imaginable without legal rules designed to prevent service personnel from undermining it. However, the national authorities cannot rely on such rules to frustrate the exercise by individual members of the armed forces of their right to respect for their private lives, which right applies to service personnel as it does to others within the jurisdiction of the State. Moreover, assertions as to a risk to operational effectiveness must be 'substantiated by specific examples'.

(ii) Application to the facts of the case

83. . . . In the case of the present applicants, the Court finds the interferences to have been especially grave for the following reasons.

84. In the first place, the investigation process was of an exceptionally intrusive character. . . .

85. Secondly, the administrative discharge of the applicants had. . .a profound effect on their careers and prospects. . . . The Court notes, in this respect, the unique nature of the armed forces (underlined by the Government in their pleadings before the Court) and, consequently, the difficulty in directly transferring essentially military qualifications and experience to civilian life. . . .

86. Thirdly, the absolute and general character of the policy which led to the interferences in question is striking. . . .

. . .

88. The core argument of the Government in support of the policy is that the presence of open or suspected homosexuals in the armed forces would have a substantial and negative effect on morale and, consequently, on the fighting power and operational effectiveness of the armed forces. The Government rely in this respect on the report of the HPAT. . . .

Although the Court acknowledges the complexity of the study undertaken by the HPAT, it entertains certain doubts as to the value of the HPAT report for present purposes. . . .

89. Even accepting that the views on the matter which were expressed to the HPAT may be considered representative, the Court finds that the perceived problems which were identified in the HPAT report as a threat to the fighting power and operational effectiveness of the armed forces were founded solely upon the negative attitudes of heterosexual personnel towards those of homosexual orientation. The Court observes, in this respect, that no moral judgment is made on homosexuality by the policy. . . .

90. . . . The Court observes from the HPAT report that these attitudes, even if sincerely felt by those who expressed them, ranged from stereotypical expressions of hostility to those of homosexual orientation, to vague expressions of unease about the presence of homosexual colleagues. To the extent that they represent a predisposed bias on the part of a heterosexual majority against a homosexual minority, these negative attitudes cannot, of themselves, be considered by the Court to amount to sufficient justification for the interferences with the applicants' rights outlined above, any more than similar negative attitudes towards those of a different race, origin or colour.

. . .

92. The Court notes the lack of concrete evidence to substantiate the alleged damage to morale and fighting power that any change in the policy would entail. . . .

93. However, in the light of the strength of feeling expressed in certain submissions to the HPAT and the special, interdependent and closely knit nature of the armed forces' environment, the Court considers it reasonable to assume that some difficulties could be anticipated as a result of any change in what is now a long-standing policy. Indeed, it would appear that the presence of women and racial minorities in the armed forces led to relational difficulties of the kind which the Government suggest admission of homosexuals would entail . . .

. . .

95. The Court considers it important to note, in the first place, the approach already adopted by the armed forces to deal with racial discrimination and with racial and sexual harassment and bullying The January 1996 Directive, for example, imposed both a strict code of conduct on every soldier together with disciplinary rules to deal with any inappropriate behaviour and conduct. This dual approach was supplemented with information leaflets and training programmes, the army emphasising the need for high standards of personal conduct and for respect for others.

The Government, nevertheless, underlined that it is 'the knowledge or suspicion of homosexuality' which would cause the morale problems and not conduct, so that a conduct code would not solve the anticipated difficulties. However, in so far as negative attitudes to homosexuality are insufficient, of themselves, to justify the policy, they are equally insufficient to justify the rejection of a proposed alternative. . . .

. . . [E]ven if it can be assumed that the integration of homosexuals would give rise to problems not encountered with the integration of women or racial minorities, the Court is not satisfied that the codes and rules which have been found to be effective in the latter case would not equally prove effective in the former. . . .

. . .

97. The Government, referring to the relevant analysis in the HPAT report, further argued that no worthwhile lessons could be gleaned from the relatively recent legal changes in those foreign armed forces which now admitted homosexuals. The Court disagrees. It notes the evidence before the domestic courts to the effect that the European countries operating a blanket legal ban on homosexuals in their armed forces are now in a small minority. It considers that, even if relatively recent, the Court cannot overlook the widespread and consistently developing views and associated legal changes to the domestic laws of Contracting States on this issue. . . .

98. Accordingly, the Court concludes that convincing and weighty reasons have not been offered by the Government to justify the policy against homosexuals in the armed forces or, therefore, the consequent discharge of the applicants from those forces.

[The Court then considered whether there were justification under Article 8 for the continuation of the investigation of the applicants after their 'early and clear' admissions of homosexuality. It concluded that the continuation of the investigation violated Article 8.]

104. In sum, the Court finds that neither the investigation conducted into the applicants' sexual orientation, nor their discharge on the grounds of their homosexuality . . . were justified under Article 8 § 2 of the Convention.

[The Court then considered the charge of violation of Article 14, which states that 'enjoyment of the rights and freedoms set forth in [the] Convention shall be secured without discrimination on any ground such as sex, race, colour, language, religion, political or other opinion, national or social origin, association with a national minority, property, birth or other status'.]

108. The Court considers that, in the circumstances of the present case, the applicants' complaints that they were discriminated against on grounds of their sexual orientation by reason of the existence and application of the policy of the Ministry of Defence, amounts in effect to the same complaint, albeit seen from a different angle, that the Court has already considered in relation to Article 8 of the Convention.

109. Accordingly, the Court considers that the applicants' complaints under Article 14 in conjunction with Article 8 do not give rise to any separate issue. [The formal, unanimous holding of the Court was that there was a violation of Article 8 and that 'no separate issue arises under Article 14 of the Convention taken in conjunction with Article 8'.]

[The Court agreed to provide further time to the parties to submit proposals for just satisfaction under Article 41, and held open the possibility of an agreement between the parties.]

JUDGE LOUCAIDES (PARTLY CONCURRING, PARTLY DISSENTING)

I agree with the majority on all points except as regards the finding that there has been a violation of Article 8 of the Convention by reason of the applicants' discharge from the armed forces on account of their homosexuality.

In this respect I have been convinced by the argument of the Government that particular problems might be posed by the communal accommodation arrangements in the armed forces. The applicants would have to share single-sex accommodation and associated facilities (showers, toilets, etc.) with their heterosexual colleagues. To my mind, the problems in question are in substance analogous to those which would result from the communal accommodation of male members of the armed forces with female members. What makes it necessary for males not to share accommodation and other associated facilities with females is the difference in their sexual orientation. It is precisely this difference between homosexuals and heterosexuals which makes the position of the Government convincing.

I find the answer given by the majority regarding this aspect of the case unsatisfactory. . . . The fact that separate accommodation is not 'warranted or wise' does not justify communal accommodation if such accommodation is really problematic. On the other hand, 'conduct codes and disciplinary rules' cannot change the sexual orientation of people and the relevant problems which . . . in the analogous case of women makes it incumbent to accommodate them separately from male soldiers. . . . I should add here that if homosexuals had a right to be members of the armed forces their sexual orientation could become known either through them disclosing it or manifesting it in some way.

. . .

. . . I agree with the Government that the narrow margin of appreciation which is applied to cases involving intimate private-life matters is widened in cases like the present, in which the legitimate aim of the relevant restriction relates to the operational effectiveness of the armed forces and, therefore, to the interests of national security. . . .

Regard must also be had to the principle that limitations incapable of being imposed on civilians may be placed on certain of the rights and freedoms of members of the armed forces . . .

I believe that the Court should not interfere simply because there is a disagreement with the necessity of the measures taken by a State. Otherwise the concept of the margin of appreciation would be meaningless. The Court may substitute its own view for that of the national authorities only when the measure is patently disproportionate to the aim pursued. . . .

NOTE

In 1996, the British Government submitted some proposals for improvement of the European Convention to the Council of Europe Secretary General.[28] The proposals stated in part:

> 7. There is widespread agreement that the common standards of the Convention have to be maintained. But equally it is widely recognized that differing circumstances and traditions in the way these standards are implemented in different countries have to be respected. The doctrine of the margin of appreciation has been developed by the Convention institutions to allow for diversity, particularly on those moral and social issues where the view of what is right may legitimately vary. For the support of the citizens of Council of Europe countries for the Convention and its mechanisms to be fully hearted, it is important the Strasbourg institutions give full weight to this principle and respect the decisions of local democratic institutions and tribunals, which are best placed to assess issues of this kind.
>
> 8. We would like to know whether others share our view that means should be sought for encouraging wider and more consistent application of the margin of appreciation. One possible approach might be a resolution in the Committee of Ministers, drawing *inter alia* on the following points:
>
> (a) account should be taken of the fact that democratic institutions and tribunals in Member States are best placed to determine moral and social issues in accordance with regional and national perspectives;
> (b) full regard should be paid to decisions by democratic legislatures and to differing legal traditions;
> (c) long-standing laws and practices should be respected, except where these are manifestly contrary to the Convention.

COMMENT ON NATIONAL AND INTERNATIONAL TRENDS

In deciding several cases concerning rights of homosexual parties, the European Court relied as in the *Lustig-Prean* case on Article 8 rather than Article 14, which it has not yet directly examined in this context. In its Report in *Sutherland v. United Kingdom*, Application 25986/94, adopted 1 July 1997, the European Commission

---

[28] 'European Court and Commission on Human Rights: Note on the Position of the British Government', 4 IHRR 260 (1997).

on Human Rights held that the 18 years age of consent to male homosexual acts in the United Kingdom criminal law, as compared with the 16 years age for heterosexual relations, violated the Convention. It stated in part:

50. The different minimum ages for lawful sexual relations between homosexuals and heterosexuals are a difference based on sexual orientation. In terms of Article 14 of the Convention, it is not clear whether this difference is a difference based on 'sex' or on 'other status'. The Commission notes that the Human Rights Committee set up under the International Covenant on Civil and Political Rights has considered that sexual orientation is included in the concept of 'sex' within the meaning of Article 26 of that Covenant, and that it did not therefore need to decide whether sexual orientation was included in the concept of 'other status' [*Toonen v. Australia*, p. 745, *supra*].

51. The Commission for its part considers that it is not required to determine whether a difference based on sexual orientation is a matter which is properly to be considered as a difference on grounds of 'sex' or of 'other status'. In either event, it is a difference in respect of which the Commission is entitled to seek justification.

. . .

58. The Government draw attention to the consistent series of decisions by the Commission recognising that the criterion of social protection justifies not only the imposition of restrictions on male homosexual activity but the setting of a higher minimum age than in the case of heterosexuals. . . .

59. The Commission, however, observes that its Report [referred to above] is now nearly 20 years old. . . . [M]ajor changes have in the meantime occurred in professional opinions—particularly those of the medical profession—on the subject of the need for the protection of young male homosexuals and on the desirability of introducing an equal age of consent. . . . It is further noted that equality of treatment in respect of the age of consent is now recognized by the great majority of member states of the Council of Europe.

60. The Commission, accordingly, considers it opportune to reconsider its earlier case-law in the light of these modern developments and, more especially, in the light of the weight of current medical opinion. . . .

. . .

66. [After consideration of the Government's arguments], the Commission finds that no objective and reasonable justification exists for the maintenance of a higher minimum age of consent to male homosexual, than to heterosexual, acts and that the application discloses discriminatory treatment in the exercise of the applicant's right to respect for private life under Article 8 of the Convention.

67. The Commission concludes, by fourteen votes to four, that in the present case there has been a violation of Article 8 of the Convention, taken in conjunction with Article 14 of the Convention.

In 1997, 15 member states of the Council of Europe signed the Treaty of Amsterdam, now in effect. It inserted a new Article 13 into the European Community Treaty that authorized the Council of the European Community, acting unanimously on the proposal of the Commission, to 'take appropriate action to combat discrimination based on . . . sexual orientation'.

In a 1999 submission to the Council of Europe,[29] the International Lesbian and Gay Association urged expansion of the categories now appearing in Article 14 to include 'sexual orientation'.

> Although sexual orientation arguably comes within 'sex' or 'other status', protection through the application of these grounds is not sufficient. . . .Only express inclusion of the ground 'sexual orientation' in the new Article 14 can provide specific, symbolic condemnation of this historic and ongoing form of discrimination, and the hatred, fear and ignorance that lie behind it.

Between the terms used by Article 14 of 'sex' or 'other status', the submission argued for inclusion of sexual orientation in the former so as to bring such discrimination within the Court's decisions on sex distinctions, which the Court had said could be justified only by 'very weighty reasons'. The category of 'other status', on the other hand, might not provide adequate protection because that category could embrace 'relatively trivial' and rare distinctions.

ROBERT PEAR, PRESIDENT ADMITS 'DON'T ASK' POLICY HAS BEEN FAILURE
New York Times, December 12, 1999, p. 1

President Clinton said today that the official policy toward gays in the military was 'out of whack' and that military leaders were not carrying it out as he intended and as they promised in 1993. Accordingly, Mr. Clinton said, the policy should be re-examined or at least carried out in a more humane way, to prevent the harassment of homosexuals in the armed forces.

. . .

Mr. Clinton said he hoped the beating death of a gay soldier at Fort Campbell, Ky., last July would 'give some sobering impetus to a re-examination about how this policy is implemented'. In the trial of the soldier charged in the slaying, witnesses described a casual culture in which gibes and taunts had been directed at the victim, Pfc. Barry Winchell, for months.

. . .

The president's initial efforts to make it easier for homosexuals to serve in the military, in 1993, touched off a political uproar. . . . The president later adopted the policy known as 'don't ask, don't tell'. Under this policy, the military may not inquire into a soldier's sex life unless there is clear evidence of homosexual conduct. But gays who volunteer this information can be discharged.

. . .

'Let me remind you', he said today, 'that the original intent was that people would not be rooted out, that they would not be questioned out, that this would be focused on people's conduct. If they didn't violate the code of conduct and they

---

[29] International Lesbian and Gay Association, 'Proposed Additional Protocol Broadening Article 14 of the European Convention', Submission to Steering Committee on Human Rights, Council of Europe, 13 May 1999.

didn't tell, their comings and goings, the mail they got, the associates they had—those things would not be sufficient to keep them out of the military, or subject them to harassment.

. . .

Secretary of Defense William S. Cohen has told all commanders that they should look at the climate on their bases to prevent harassment of gay and lesbian soliders. . . . In August the Pentagon reissued the statement on the 'don't ask, don't tell' policy, reminding the military that it focused on what gay and lesbian soliders could not do: disclose or act upon their sexuality.

. . .

Gay rights advocates say the policy is deeply flawed. Far from making life easier for gay men and lesbians in the armed forces, they say, it has left many to suffer in silence and has led to an increase in discharges of gay service members and an increase in complaints of harassment.

. . .

Mr. Clinton said today that his 1993 decision was the best he could do in the circumstances that existed then. 'The reason I went for "don't ask, don't tell" is that it's all I could do', Mr. Clinton said. If he had provided more protection to gays in the military, Mr. Clinton said, Congress would have reversed his decision by 'overwhelming majorities'.

. . .

QUESTIONS

1. 'At least with respect to dismissal from the armed forces, the Lustig-Prean decision could better have been decided under Article 14 alone, rather than (effectively) under Article 8 alone. The problem of discrimination is pervasive in many states with respect to activities in the public or private sectors—employment and housing, for example. Gender and race discrimination were stopped by anti-discrimination laws, the clearer and stronger path to follow with respect to sexual orientation also'. Do you agree? Would it be essential under Article 14 to involve Article 8 as well? Compare the *Toonen* decision, p. 745, *supra*, under Article 17 of the ICCPR.

2. How do you react to the proposal for a protocol to the European Convention that would include sexual orientation in Article 14, as opposed to developing protection for gay and lesbian people through case law as evidenced in the preceding materials? With respect to case law, what difficulties do you see in interpreting the term 'sex' in Article 14 to include 'sexual orientation'?

3. Does the *Lustig-Prean* opinion decide a case where a soldier, professionally competent in all respects, is conducting, to the knowledge of his fellow soldiers, a sexual relationship with another serviceman of equal rank during evenings off from base? What other factors might become relevant?

4. How do you assess the position taken by the British Government in its

recommendations to the Council of Europe, p. 832, *supra?* Should the democratic character of the state and its institutions have independent weight, so that (at the extreme) a law from an authoritarian state might be struck down whereas a similar law from a democratic state might be sustained?

ADDITIONAL READING

A. Clapham and K. Waaldijk (eds.) *Homosexuality: a European Community Issue* (1993); Eric Heinze, *Sexual Orientation: A Human Right* (1995); R. Wintemute, *Sexual Orientation and Human Rights* (1997); Janet Halley, 'Don't: A Reader's Guide to the Military's Anti-Gay Policy' (1999); *ibid.*, 'Reasoning about Sodomy: Act and Identity in and after *Bowers v. Hardwick*', 79 Va. L. Rev. 1721 (1993); *ibid.*, 'The Politics of the Closet: Towards Equal Protection for Gay, Lesbian, and Bisexual Identity', 36 U.C.L.A. L. Rev. 915 (1989). See also Additional Reading at p. 749, *supra*.

COMMENT ON BLASPHEMY CASES

In *Otto-Preminger-Institut v. Austria*,[30] the European Court of Human Rights decided in 1994 by 6 votes to 3 that the seizure and forfeiture of a blasphemous film did not violate the freedom of expression guaranteed by Article 10 of the European Convention. The applicant association had advertised the screening of the film, *Das Liebeskonzil*, based on an 1894 play, which:

> ... portrays the God of the Jewish religion, the Christian religion and the Islamic religion as an apparently senile old man prostrating himself before the devil with whom he exchanges a deep kiss and calling the devil his friend.... Other scenes show the Virgin Mary permitting an obscene story to be read to her and the manifestation of a degree of erotic tension between the Virgin Mary and the devil. The adult Jesus Christ is portrayed as a low grade mental defective and in one scene is shown lasciviously attempting to fondle and kiss his mother's breasts, which she is shown as permitting.

The film was presented by the association as a 'satirical tragedy'. 'Trivial imagery and absurdities of the Christian creed are targeted in a caricatural mode and the relationship between religious beliefs and worldly mechanisms of oppression is investigated'.

The Innsbruck Regional Court in Austria ordered seizure and forfeiture of the film under Section 188 of the Austrian Penal Code for the criminal offense of 'disparaging religious precepts'. The criminal proceedings against the association were eventually dropped.

Since there was no dispute that the seizure constituted an interference with the association's freedom of expression, the European Court considered whether the seizure was permissible under the conditions set by of Article 10, para. 2.

The Court concluded that the interference had the 'legitimate aim' of protecting

---

[30] Judgment of 20 September 1994, No. 11/1993/406/485, reprinted in 15 Hum. Rts. L. J. 371 (1994).

the rights of others to freedom of religion. Interpreting Article 9 of the Convention to include the right to respect for one's religious feelings, the Court found that such considerations outweighed the film's contribution to public debate. The Court reasoned:

> The respect for the religious feelings of believers as guaranteed in Article 9 can legitimately thought to have been violated by provocative portrayals of objects of religious veneration; and such portrayals can be regarded as malicious violation of the spirit of tolerance, which must also be a feature of democratic society. The Convention is to be read as a whole and therefore the interpretation and application of Article 10 in the present case must be in harmony with the logic of the Convention. (Para. 47). . . . [T]he Court accepts that the impugned measures pursued a legitimate aim under Article 10 para. 2, namely 'the protection of the rights of others'.

The Court stressed that freedom of expression applies not only to ideas that are favourably received, but also to those 'that shock, offend or disturb the State or any sector of the population. Such are the demands of that pluralism, tolerance and broadmindedness without which there is no "democratic society."' Nonetheless, people exercising their rights under Article 10 were subject to duties, among which could legitimately be included 'an obligation to avoid as far as possible expressions that are gratuitously offensive to others and thus an infringement of their rights, and which therefore do not contribute to any form of public debate capable of further progress in human affairs'.

The Court determined that the seizure could be considered 'necessary in a democratic society'. There was no 'uniform conception of the significance of religion in society' throughout Europe, 'even within a single country'. A 'certain margin of appreciation is therefore to be left to the national authorities in assessing the existence and extent of the necessity of such interference'. It is 'for the national authorities, who are better placed than the international judge, to assess the need for such a measure in the light of the situation obtaining locally'. Given that the Tyrolean population was 87 per cent Roman Catholic, the Court found that the Austrian authorities had acted within their margin of appreciation 'to ensure religious peace in that region and to prevent that some people should feel the object of attacks on their religious beliefs in an unwarranted and offensive manner'.

Three judges dissented. Given the precautions against offence to viewers taken by the association through a warning announcement, the showing of the film to a paid audience only, and the restriction of viewing to those over 17 years of age, the dissent found the seizure and forfeiture to be disproportionate to the aim pursued, and thus not necessary in a democratic society.

———

In *Wingrove v. United Kingdom,* European Court of Human Rights, 1996, www.echr.coe.int/eng/Judgments.htm, a film director who was a British national brought a complaint before the European Commission alleging that the United Kingdom had violated Article 10 by interfering with the director's freedom of expression through refusing to grant a distribution certificate for the director's 18-minute video work, *Visions of Ecstasy*. The video work involved visions of St. Teresa. about the crucified Christ, and in the view of the British Board of Film Classification, drew Christ graphically into the erotic desire of St. Teresa. The refusal to grant the certificate was based on the Board's conclusion that the video constituted blasphemy, defined in a recent case as 'any contemptuous, reviling, scurrilous or ludicrous matter related to God, Jesus Christ or the Bible'. The decision was upheld by the Video Appeals Committee.

The European Commission expressed the opinion in a 14–2 vote that there had been a violation of Article 10. The Commission and the United Kingdom brought the case before the European Court, which concluded by a 7–2 vote that there had been no violation of Article 10.

Some of its observations about the requirement in Article 10 that a restriction be 'necessary in a democratic society' follow:

> 57. The Court observes that the refusal to grant Visions of Ecstasy a distribution certificate was intended to protect 'the rights of others', and more specifically to provide protection against seriously offensive attacks on matters regarded as sacred by Christians. . . .
>
> . . . [B]lasphemy legislation is still in force in various European countries. It is true that the application of these laws has become increasingly rare and that several States have recently repealed them altogether. . . . Strong arguments have been advanced in favour of the abolition of blasphemy laws, for example, that such laws may discriminate against different faiths or denominations. . . . However, the fact remains that there is as yet not sufficient common ground in the legal and social orders of the member States of the Council of Europe to conclude that a system whereby a State can impose restrictions on the propagation of material on the basis that it is blasphemous is, in itself, unnecessary in a democratic society and thus incompatible with the Convention. . . .
>
> 58. Whereas there is little scope under Article 10 para. 2 of the Convention for restrictions on political speech or on debate of questions of public interest, . . . a wider margin of appreciation is generally available to the Contracting States when regulating freedom of expression in relation to matters liable to offend intimate personal convictions within the sphere of morals or, especially, religion. Moreover, as in the field of morals, and perhaps to an even greater degree, there is no uniform European conception of the requirements of 'the protection of the rights of others' in relation to attacks on their religious convictions. What is likely to cause substantial offence to persons of a particular religious persuasion will vary significantly from time to time and from place to place, especially in an era characterised by an ever growing array of faiths and denominations. By reason of their direct and continuous contact with the vital forces of their countries, State authorities are in principle in a better position than the international judge to give an opinion on the exact content of these requirements with regard to the rights of others as well as on the 'necessity' of a 'restriction' intended to protect from such material those whose deepest feelings and convictions would be seriously offended. . . .
>
> This does not of course exclude final European supervision. Such supervision is all the more necessary given the breadth and open-endedness of the notion of blasphemy and the risks of arbitrary or excessive interferences with freedom of

expression under the guise of action taken against allegedly blasphemous material. . . . Moreover the fact that the present case involves prior restraint calls for special scrutiny by the Court. . . .

The Court (para. 50) also considered the fact that the English law of blasphemy 'only extends to the Christian faith'. It was not, however, for the European Court 'to rule *in abstracto*' about the compatibility of British law with the Convention. 'The extent to which English law protects other beliefs is not in issue before the Court which must confine its attention to the case before it. . . . The uncontested fact that the law of blasphemy does not treat on an equal footing the different religions practised in the United Kingdom does not detract from the legitimacy of the aim pursued in the present context'. A concurring opinion of Judge Pettiti observed that the Convention left 'scope for review under Article 14. In the present case no complaint had been made to the European Court under that article'.

A dissenting opinion of Judge Lohmus noted that the law of blasphemy 'only protects the Christian religion and, more specifically, the established Church of England. . . . This in itself raises the question whether the interference was (in the language of Article 10) "necessary in a democratic society".'

QUESTIONS

1. How do these opinions resolve the question of who in the liberal state must show tolerance to whom? Must the majority put up with the minority's views and modes of expression (at least where those views and expressions are not 'forced' on the majority through unavoidable public acts)? Or is it the minority that must take account of the majority's sensibility and refrain from offending it?

2. During the colonial period, the British colonial government in India enacted several laws as part of the Indian Penal Code that defined offences including 'defiling a place of worship', 'acts insulting religion or religious beliefs', 'disturbing a religious assembly', 'trespassing on burial grounds', and 'utterances wounding religious feelings'. Punishments were a maximum of two years imprisonment, a fine, or both.

These laws were amended or supplemented by the Government of Pakistan. Section 295-B of the Pakistan Penal Code, added in 1982, provided:

Whoever willfully defiles, damages or desecrates a copy of the Holy Quran or an extract therefrom or uses it in any derogatory manner or for any unlawful purpose shall be punishable with imprisonment for life.

Section 295-C was enacted in 1986. It stated:

Whoever by words, either spoken or written, or by any visible representation, or by any imputation, innuendo, or insinuation, directly or indirectly, defiles the sacred name of the Holy Prophet Mohammed (peace be upon him) shall be punished with death, or imprisonment for life and shall also be liable to fine.

Compare the Pakistani statutes with the laws and action described in the *Otto-Preminger-Institut* and *Wingrove* cases. What are the salient differences? How would the Pakistani statutes be judged under the European Convention?

NOTE

The following materials concern political participation, elections and democratic government. They start with a decision of the European Court involving the electoral process in Turkey, and continue with some materials on questions of political participation and elections under the ICCPR. This theme of the relationships among human rights, political participation and democratic government recurs at pp. 888–919, *infra*, within a discussion of the Inter-American system of human rights.

UNITED COMMUNIST PARTY OF TURKEY V. TURKEY
European Court of Human Rights, 1998
www.echr.coe.int/eng/Judgments.htm

[The case originated in applications against the Republic of Turkey lodged with the Commission in 1992 by the United Communist Party of Turkey and two Turkish nationals, Nihat Sargin and Nabi Yagci. The Commission referred the case to the Court in 1996, requesting a decision whether the facts of the case disclosed a violation by Turkey of Article 11 of the European Convention, which reads in relevant part:

   1. Everyone has the right to freedom of . . . association with others, including the right to form and to join trade unions. . . .
   2. No restrictions shall be placed on the exercise of these rights other than such as are prescribed by law and are necessary in a democratic society in the interests of national security . . . or for the protection of the rights and freedoms of others.

The Commission concluded that there had been such a violation. The Chamber initially constituted by the Court to hear the case decided in 1997 to relinquish its jurisdiction in favour of a Grand Chamber. The following excerpts from the Court's opinion begin with a statement of the facts.]

7. The United Communist Party of Turkey ('the TBKP'), the first applicant, was a political party that was dissolved by the Constitutional Court. Mr Nihat Sargin and Mr Nabi Yagci, the second and third applicants, were respectively Chairman and General Secretary of the TBKP. They live in Istanbul.
8. The TBKP was formed on 4 June 1990. On the same day, its constitution and

programme were submitted to the office of Principal State Counsel at the Court of Cassation for assessment of their compatibility with the Constitution and Law no. 2820 on the regulation of political parties.

9. On 14 June 1990, when the TBKP was preparing to participate in a general election, Principal State Counsel at the Court of Cassation ('Principal State Counsel') applied to the Constitutional Court for an order dissolving the TBKP. He accused the party of having sought to establish the domination of one social class over the others (Articles 6, 10 and 14 and former Article 68 of the Constitution and section 78 of Law no. 2820), of having incorporated the word 'communist' into its name (contrary to section 96(3) of Law no. 2820), of having carried on activities likely to undermine the territorial integrity of the State and the unity of the nation (Articles 2, 3 and 66 and former Article 68 of the Constitution, and sections 78 and 81 of Law no. 2820) and of having declared itself to be the successor to a previously dissolved political party, the Turkish Workers' Party (section 96(2) of Law no. 2820).

[These excerpts from the opinion concern almost exclusively the principal charge of undermining the unity of the nation. In omitted portions, the opinion found the other three grounds inadequate to justify interference with the right of association under Article 11.]

In support of his application Principal State Counsel relied in particular on passages from the TBKP's programme, mainly taken from a chapter entitled 'Towards a peaceful, democratic and fair solution for the Kurdish problem'; that chapter read as follows:

> The existence of the Kurds and their legitimate rights have been denied ever since the Republic was founded, although the national war of independence was waged with their support. The authorities have responded to the awakening of Kurdish national consciousness with bans, oppression and terror. Racist, militarist and chauvinistic policies have exacerbated the Kurdish problem. That fact both constitutes an obstacle to the democratization of Turkey and serves the interests of the international imperialist and militaristic forces seeking to heighten tension in the Middle East, set peoples against each other and propel Turkey into military adventures.
>
> The Kurdish problem is a political one arising from the denial of the Kurdish people's existence, national identity and rights. It therefore cannot be resolved by oppression, terror and military means. Recourse to violence means that the right to self-determination, which is a natural and inalienable right of all peoples, is not exercised jointly, but separately and unilaterally. The remedy for this problem is political. If the oppression of the Kurdish people and discrimination against them are to end, Turks and Kurds must unite.
>
> The TBKP will strive for a peaceful, democratic and fair solution of the Kurdish problem, so that the Kurdish and Turkish peoples may live together of their free will within the borders of the Turkish Republic, on the basis of equal rights and with a view to democratic restructuring founded on their common interests.
>
> The solution of the Kurdish problem must be based on the free will of the Kurds and take into account the common interests of the Turkish and Kurdish

nations and contribute to the democratisation of Turkey and peace in the Middle East.

A solution to the Kurdish problem will only be found if the parties concerned are able to express their opinions freely, if they agree not to resort to violence in any form in order to resolve the problem and if they are able to take part in politics with their own national identity.

The solution of the Kurdish problem will require time. In the immediate future, priority must be given to ending military and political pressure on the Kurds, protecting the lives of Kurdish citizens, bringing the state of emergency to an end, abandoning the 'village guards' system and lifting bans on the Kurdish language and Kurdish culture. The problem should be freely discussed. The existence of the Kurds must be acknowledged in the Constitution.

Without a solution of the Kurdish problem, democratic renewal cannot take place in Turkey. Any solution will entail a fight for the democratization of Turkey.

[Another passage] relied on by Principal State Counsel read as follows:

. . .

The cultural revival will be fashioned by, on the one hand, the reciprocal influence of contemporary universal culture and, on the other, Turkish and Kurdish national values, the heritage of the Anatolian civilizations, the humanist elements of Islamic culture and all the values developed by our people in their effort to evolve with their times.

10. On 16 July 1991 the Constitutional Court made an order dissolving the TBKP, which entailed ipso jure the liquidation of the party and the transfer of its assets to the Treasury, in accordance with section 107(1) of Law no. 2820. . . . As a consequence, the founders and managers of the party were banned from holding similar office in any other political body.

. . .

As to the allegation that the TBKP's constitution and programme contained statements likely to undermine the territorial integrity of the State and the unity of the nation, the Constitutional Court noted, inter alia, that those documents referred to two nations: the Kurdish nation and the Turkish nation. But it could not be accepted that there were two nations within the Republic of Turkey, whose citizens, whatever their ethnic origin, had Turkish nationality. In reality the proposals in the party constitution covering support for non-Turkish languages and cultures were intended to create minorities, to the detriment of the unity of the Turkish nation.

Reiterating that self-determination and regional autonomy were prohibited by the Constitution, the Constitutional Court said that the State was unitary, the country indivisible and that there was only one nation. It considered that national unity was achieved through the integration of communities and individuals who, irrespective of their ethnic origin and on an equal footing, formed the nation and founded the State. In Turkey there were no 'minorities' or 'national minorities' . . . and there were no constitutional or legislative provisions allowing distinctions to be made between citizens. Like all nationals of foreign descent, nationals of Kurdish origin could express their identity, but the Constitution and the law precluded them from forming a nation or a minority distinct from the Turkish nation. Consequently, objectives which, like those of the TBKP, encouraged separatism and the division of the Turkish nation were unacceptable and justified dissolving the party concerned.

II. *Relevant domestic law*

11. At the material time the relevant provisions of the Constitution read as follows:

> ARTICLE 2: The Republic of Turkey is a democratic, secular and social State based on the rule of law, respectful of human rights in a spirit of social peace, national solidarity and justice, adhering to the nationalism of Atatürk and resting on the fundamental principles set out in the Preamble.
>
> ARTICLE 3 § 1: The State of Turkey constitutes with its territory and nation, an indivisible whole. The official language is Turkish.
>
> ARTICLE 6: Sovereignty resides unconditionally and unreservedly in the nation.
>
> . . .
>
> ARTICLE 10 § 1: All individuals shall be equal before the law without any distinction based on language, race, colour, sex, political opinion, philosophical belief, religion, membership of a religious sect or other similar grounds.
>
> ARTICLE 14 § 1: None of the rights and freedoms referred to in the Constitution shall be exercised with a view to undermining the territorial integrity of the State and the unity of the nation, jeopardising the existence of the Turkish State or Republic, abolishing fundamental rights and freedoms . . . introducing discrimination on the grounds of language, race, religion or membership of a religious sect, or establishing by any other means a political system based on any of the above concepts and opinions.
>
> ARTICLE 66 § 1: Everyone linked to the Turkish State by nationality shall be Turkish.
>
> (Former) ARTICLE 68: Citizens shall have the right to form political parties and to join them or withdraw from them in accordance with the lawful procedure laid down for the purpose . . . Political parties shall be an indispensable part of the democratic political system.
>
> Political parties may be formed without prior permission and shall carry on their activities in accordance with the Constitution and the law.
>
> The constitutions and programmes of political parties shall not be inconsistent with the absolute integrity of State territory and of the nation, human rights, national sovereignty or the principles of a democratic secular Republic. . . .
>
> (Former) ARTICLE 69: Political parties shall not engage in activities other than those referred to in their constitutions and programmes, nor shall they disregard the restrictions laid down by Article 14 of the Constitution, on pain of permanent dissolution.
>
> . . .
>
> The decisions and internal running of political parties shall not be contrary to democratic principles.
>
> . . .
>
> Political parties may be dissolved by the Constitutional Court, on application by Principal State Counsel.

Founding members and managers, at whatever level, of political parties which have been permanently dissolved may not become founding members, managers or financial controllers of any new political party, nor shall a new party be formed if a majority of its members previously belonged to a party which has been dissolved . . .

12. The relevant provisions of Law no. 2820 on the regulation of political parties read as follows:

SECTION 78: Political parties (a) shall not aim, strive or incite third parties to

change: the republican form of the Turkish State; the . . . provisions concerning the absolute integrity of the Turkish State's territory, the absolute unity of its nation, its official language, its flag or its national anthem; . . . the principle that sovereignty resides unconditionally and unreservedly in the Turkish nation; . . . the provision that sovereign power cannot be transferred to an individual, a group or a social class . . . ;

jeopardize the existence of the Turkish State and Republic, abolish fundamental rights and freedoms, introduce discrimination on grounds of language, race, colour, religion or membership of a religious sect, or establish, by any means, a system of government based on any such notion or concept.

. . .

SECTION 80: Political parties shall not aim to change the principle of the unitary State on which the Turkish Republic is founded, nor carry on activities in pursuit of such an aim.

SECTION 81: Political parties shall not

(a) assert that there exist within the territory of the Turkish Republic any national minorities based on differences relating to national or religious culture, membership of a religious sect, race or language; or

(b) aim to destroy national unity by proposing, on the pretext of protecting, promoting or disseminating a non-Turkish language or culture, to create minorities on the territory of the Turkish Republic or to engage in similar activities . . .

SECTION 101: The Constitutional Court shall dissolve a political party where (a) the party's programme or constitution . . . is contrary to the provisions of Chapter 4 of this Law . . .

AS TO THE LAW

I. Alleged Violation of Article 11 of the Convention

1. Submissions of those appearing before the Court

(a) The Government

19. The Government submitted that Article 11 did not in any event apply to political parties. . . .

Even a cursory examination of the Convention showed that neither Article 11 nor any other Article made any mention of political parties or referred to the

States' constitutional structures. It was significant that the only Article containing a reference to political institutions was in Protocol No. 1 (Article 3) and did not confer any right on individuals as it was worded so as to create an obligation on the States.

. . .

21. Furthermore, if the TBKP were able to achieve its political aims, Turkey's territorial and national integrity would be seriously undermined. By drawing a distinction in its constitution and programme between Turks and Kurds, referring to the Kurds' 'national' identity, requesting constitutional recognition of 'the existence of the Kurds', describing the Kurds as a 'nation' and asserting their right to self-determination, the TBKP had opened up a split that would destroy the basis of citizenship, which was independent of ethnic origin. . . .

In the Government's submission, the States Parties to the Convention had at no stage intended to submit their constitutional institutions, and in particular the principles they considered to be the essential conditions of their existence, to review by the Strasbourg institutions. For that reason, where a political party such as the TBKP had called those institutions or principles into question, it could not seek application of the Convention or its Protocols.

. . . In a context of vicious terrorism such as Turkey was experiencing, the need to preclude improper use of the Convention by applying Article 17 was even more obvious, as the Turkish authorities had to prohibit the use of 'expressions' and the formation of 'associations' that would inevitably incite violence and enmity between the various sections of Turkish society.

2. The Court's assessment

24. The Court considers that the wording of Article 11 provides an initial indication as to whether political parties may rely on that provision. It notes that although Article 11 refers to 'freedom of association with others, including the right to form . . . trade unions . . '., the conjunction 'including' clearly shows that trade unions are but one example. . .

25. . . . [P]olitical parties are a form of association essential to the proper functioning of democracy. In view of the importance of democracy in the Convention system, there can be no doubt that political parties come within the scope of Article 11.

. . .

27. . . . [A]n association, including a political party, is not excluded from the protection afforded by the Convention simply because its activities are regarded by the national authorities as undermining the constitutional structures of the State. . . .

[W]hile it is in principle open to the national authorities to take such action as they consider necessary to respect the rule of law or to give effect to constitutional rights, they must do so in a manner which is compatible with their obligations under the Convention and subject to review by the Convention institutions.

28. The Preamble to the Convention refers to the 'common heritage of political traditions, ideals, freedom and the rule of law', of which national constitutions are in fact often the first embodiment. Through its system of collective enforcement of

the rights it establishes, the Convention reinforces, in accordance with the principle of subsidiarity, the protection afforded at national level, but never limits it (Article 60 of the Convention).

. . .

30. The political and institutional organization of the member States must accordingly respect the rights and principles enshrined in the Convention. It matters little in this context whether the provisions in issue are constitutional or merely legislative. . . .

. . .

32. It does not, however, follow that the authorities of a State in which an association, through its activities, jeopardizes that State's institutions are deprived of the right to protect those institutions. In this connection, the Court points out that it has previously held that some compromise between the requirements of defending democratic society and individual rights is inherent in the system of the Convention. For there to be a compromise of that sort any intervention by the authorities must be in accordance with paragraph 2 of Article 11, which the Court considers below. . . .

. . .

37. Such an interference [by Turkey with Article 11] will constitute a breach of Article 11 unless it was 'prescribed by law', pursued one or more legitimate aims under paragraph 2 and was 'necessary in a democratic society' for the achievement of those aims.

. . .

(b) Legitimate aim

39. The Government maintained that the interference pursued a number of legitimate aims: ensuring national security, public safety and territorial integrity and protecting the rights and freedoms of others.

. . .

41. Like the Commission, the Court considers that the dissolution of the TBKP pursued at least one of the 'legitimate aims' set out in Article 11: the protection of 'national security'.

(c) 'Necessary in a democratic society'

42. The Court reiterates that notwithstanding its autonomous role and particular sphere of application, Article 11 must also be considered in the light of Article 10. The protection of opinions and the freedom to express them is one of the objectives of the freedoms of assembly and association as enshrined in Article 11.

43. That applies all the more in relation to political parties in view of their essential role in ensuring pluralism and the proper functioning of democracy.

As the Court has said many times, there can be no democracy without pluralism. It is for that reason that freedom of expression as enshrined in Article 10 is applicable, subject to paragraph 2, not only to 'information' or 'ideas' that are favourably received or regarded as inoffensive or as a matter of indifference, but also to those that offend, shock or disturb. The fact that their activities form part of a collective exercise of freedom of expression in itself entitles political parties to seek the protection of Articles 10 and 11 of the Convention.

44. .... [T]he Court [has[described the State as the ultimate guarantor of the principle of pluralism. In the political sphere that responsibility means that the State is under the obligation, among others, to hold, in accordance with Article 3 of Protocol No. 1, free elections at reasonable intervals by secret ballot under conditions which will ensure the free expression of the opinion of the people in the choice of the legislature. Such expression is inconceivable without the participation of a plurality of political parties representing the different shades of opinion to be found within a country's population. By relaying this range of opinion . . . political parties make an irreplaceable contribution to political debate, which is at the very core of the concept of a democratic society.

45. Democracy is without doubt a fundamental feature of the European public order. That is apparent, firstly, from the Preamble to the Convention, which establishes a very clear connection between the Convention and democracy by stating that the maintenance and further realization of human rights and fundamental freedoms are best ensured on the one hand by an effective political democracy and on the other by a common understanding and observance of human rights. The Preamble goes on to affirm that European countries have a common heritage of political tradition, ideals, freedom and the rule of law. The Court has observed that in that common heritage are to be found the underlying values of the Convention; it has pointed out several times that the Convention was designed to maintain and promote the ideals and values of a democratic society.

In addition, Articles 8, 9, 10 and 11 of the Convention require that interference with the exercise of the rights they enshrine must be assessed by the yardstick of what is 'necessary in a democratic society'. The only type of necessity capable of justifying an interference with any of those rights is, therefore, one which may claim to spring from 'democratic society'. Democracy thus appears to be the only political model contemplated by the Convention and, accordingly, the only one compatible with it.

The Court has identified certain provisions of the Convention as being characteristic of democratic society. Thus in its very first judgment it held that in a 'democratic society within the meaning of the Preamble and the other clauses of the Convention', proceedings before the judiciary should be conducted in the presence of the parties and in public and that that fundamental principle was upheld in Article 6 of the Convention. . . .[T]he Court has on many occasions stated, for example, that freedom of expression constitutes one of the essential foundations of a democratic society and one of the basic conditions for its progress and each individual's self-fulfilment; . . . it noted the prime importance of Article 3 of Protocol No. 1, which enshrines a characteristic principle of an effective political democracy.

46. Consequently, the exceptions set out in Article 11 are, where political parties are concerned, to be construed strictly; only convincing and compelling reasons can justify restrictions on such parties' freedom of association. In determining whether a necessity within the meaning of Article 11 § 2 exists, the Contracting States have only a limited margin of appreciation, which goes hand in

hand with rigorous European supervision embracing both the law and the decisions applying it, including those given by independent courts. . . .

47. When the Court carries out its scrutiny, [it does not have] to confine itself to ascertaining whether the respondent State exercised its discretion reasonably, carefully and in good faith; it must look at the interference complained of in the light of the case as a whole and determine whether it was 'proportionate to the legitimate aim pursued' and whether the reasons adduced by the national authorities to justify it are 'relevant and sufficient'. In so doing, the Court has to satisfy itself that the national authorities applied standards which were in conformity with the principles embodied in Article 11 and, moreover, that they based their decisions on an acceptable assessment of the relevant facts.

2. Application of the principles to the present case

. . .

49. The Government pointed out that . . . [t]he margin of appreciation had to be gauged in the light of the legitimate aim pursued by the interference and the background to the facts of the case. . . .

. . . [A] pressing need to impose the impugned restriction in circumstances in which territorial integrity and national security were threatened would be found not just in the case of Turkey, but also in that of each of the Council of Europe's member States. What was at stake was the essential conditions for a State's existence in the international order, conditions which were even guaranteed by the Charter of the United Nations.

Further, it was apparent from the case-law that where the interference pursued as a legitimate aim the protection of public order, territorial integrity, the public interest or democracy, the Convention institutions did not require that the risk of violence justifying the interference should be real, current or imminent. . . .

. . .

In short, faced with a challenge to the fundamental interests of the national community, such as national security and territorial integrity, the Turkish authorities had not in any way exceeded the margin of appreciation conferred on them by the Convention.

. . .

51. The Court notes at the outset that the TBKP was dissolved even before it had been able to start its activities and that the dissolution was therefore ordered solely on the basis of the TBKP's constitution and programme, which . . . contain nothing to suggest that they did not reflect the party's true objectives and its leaders' true intentions. Like the national authorities, the Court will therefore take those documents as a basis for assessing whether the interference in question was necessary.

. . .

55. The second submission accepted by the Constitutional Court was that the TBKP sought to promote separatism and the division of the Turkish nation. . . .

56. The Court notes that although the TBKP refers in its programme to the Kurdish 'people' and 'nation' and Kurdish 'citizens', it neither describes them as a 'minority' nor makes any claim—other than for recognition of their existence—

for them to enjoy special treatment or rights, still less a right to secede from the rest of the Turkish population. On the contrary, the programme states: 'The TBKP will strive for a peaceful, democratic and fair solution of the Kurdish problem, so that the Kurdish and Turkish peoples may live together of their free will within the borders of the Turkish Republic, on the basis of equal rights and with a view to democratic restructuring founded on their common interests'. With regard to the right to self-determination, the TBKP does no more in its programme than deplore the fact that because of the use of violence, it was not 'exercised jointly, but separately and unilaterally', adding that 'the remedy for this problem is political' and that '[i]f the oppression of the Kurdish people and discrimination against them are to end, Turks and Kurds must unite'.

. . .

The TBKP also said in its programme: 'A solution to the Kurdish problem will only be found if the parties concerned are able to express their opinions freely, if they agree not to resort to violence in any form in order to resolve the problem and if they are able to take part in politics with their own national identity'.

57. The Court considers one of the principal characteristics of democracy to be the possibility it offers of resolving a country's problems through dialogue, without recourse to violence, even when they are irksome. Democracy thrives on freedom of expression. From that point of view, there can be no justification for hindering a political group solely because it seeks to debate in public the situation of part of the State's population and to take part in the nation's political life in order to find, according to democratic rules, solutions capable of satisfying everyone concerned. . . .

. . .

59. The Court is also prepared to take into account the background of cases before it, in particular the difficulties associated with the fight against terrorism. . . .

60. Nor is there any need to bring Article 17 into play as nothing in the constitution and programme of the TBKP warrants the conclusion that it relied on the Convention to engage in activity or perform acts aimed at the destruction of any of the rights and freedoms set forth in it .

61. Regard being had to all the above, a measure as drastic as the immediate and permanent dissolution of the TBKP, ordered before its activities had even started and coupled with a ban barring its leaders from discharging any other political responsibility, is disproportionate to the aim pursued and consequently unnecessary in a democratic society. It follows that the measure infringed Article 11 of the Convention.

[The Court noted that the facts supporting the alleged violation of Article 3 of Protocol No. 1 on elections 'were incidental effects of the TBKP's dissolution', and that in view of the decision on violation of Article 11, it was unnecessary to consider Article 3 separately.

The Court then considered the damages claimed by the applicants under the Convention. It dismissed a claim for damages by the party, held that its judgment 'constitutes sufficient just satisfaction in respect of any damage sustained by Mr.

Sargin and Mr. Yagci', and held that Turkey should pay a stated sum to these two applicants in respect of costs and expenses.]

STEPHEN KINZER, TURKS' HIGH COURT ORDERS DISBANDING OF WELFARE PARTY
New York Times, January 17 1998, p. A1

Turkey's highest court placed an immediate ban on the country's largest political party today, ruling that it harbored a subversive agenda and was working to replace the nation's secular order with one based on Islam. 'This court has decided to close the Welfare Party because of evidence confirming its actions against the principles of the secular republic', Ahmet Necdet Sezer, Chief Judge of the Constitutional Court, said in announcing the ruling.

The court also ruled that seven leaders of the party would be barred from political activity for five years. Among them is the party leader, Necmettin Erbakan, 71, who was Prime Minister from June 1996 until June 1997. Six, including Mr. Erbakan, are currently members of Parliament, and the seventh is a mayor. Today, Mr. Erbakan . . . said he would appeal the decision to the European Court of Human Rights.

. . .

. . . [T]he British Embassy in Ankara issued a statement saying, 'We are concerned with the implications for democratic pluralism and freedom of expression, and will be discussing the closure of Welfare urgently with our E.U. partners'.

. . .

In making its decision, the court acted under a series of laws, including one that prohibits efforts 'to change the secular character of the Turkish Republic' and another that bans political parties from seeking political advantage 'through the use or misuse of religion or religious beliefs'. Turkey's Constitution defines secularism as one of the nation's basic principles and forbids repeal, or even discussion of repealing, that definition. Military commanders and other secularists say these restrictions are necessary to preserve what they describe as the world's only Muslim democracy. . . .

. . .

Mr. Savas [the State Prosecutor] said Welfare leaders were working to 'destroy the Turkish Republic' and 'establish a state based on religious principles'. 'The assumption that political parties cannot be closed in democratic regimes is not correct', Mr. Savas asserted. 'The Turkish Constitution accepts the understanding of "combative democracy", which permits the closure of political parties if their programs or activities threaten the existence of the state'.

. . .

. . . [Welfare leaders] declared that they were 'against any sort of religious or political fanaticism' and 'on the side of pluralist democracy, reconciliation and tolerance'. Military commanders scoffed at such assertions, calling them part of Welfare's duplicity. . . .

. . .

One American scholar who has closely studied the Welfare Party, Jenny B. White of Boston University, wrote before today's ban that the party's 'ultimate direction is still unclear'. 'Despite Welfare's pragmatism and modern image, there is concern that more radical religious zealots are riding into power on its coattails', Ms. White wrote....

NOTE

Both the Universal Declaration of Human Rights and the ICCPR include articles on the individual right to political participation. ICCPR Article 25, similar to UDHR Article 21, reads in part:

> Each citizen shall have the right and the opportunity ... (a) To take part in the conduct of public affairs, directly or through freely chosen representatives; (b) To vote and to be elected at genuine periodic elections which shall be by universal and equal suffrage and shall be held by secret ballot, guaranteeing the free expression of the will of the electors; ...

Bear in mind the general categories of rights in the ICCPR as described at p. 145, *supra*.

GENERAL COMMENT NO. 25 OF HUMAN RIGHTS COMMITTEE (1996)
UN Doc. HRI/GEN/1/Rev. 3 (1997)

[At its 57th session in 1996, the ICCPR Committee adopted General Comment No. 25 under Article 40 of the ICCPR. The Comment concerned Article 25 of the ICCPR. Excerpts follow:]

1. ... Article 25 lies at the core of democratic government based on the consent of the people and in conformity with the principles of the Covenant.

2. The rights under article 25 are related to, but distinct from, the right of peoples to self determination. By virtue of the rights covered by article 1(1), peoples have the right to freely determine their political status and to enjoy the right to choose the form of their constitution or government. Article 25 deals with the right of individuals to participate in those processes which constitute the conduct of public affairs....

...

5. The conduct of public affairs, referred to in paragraph (a), is a broad concept which relates to the exercise of political power, in particular the exercise of legislative, executive and administrative powers....The allocation of powers and the means by which individual citizens exercise the right to participate in the conduct of public affairs protected by article 25 should be established by the constitution and other laws.

6. Citizens participate directly in the conduct of public affairs when they exercise power as members of legislative bodies or by holding executive office. . . . Citizens also participate directly in the conduct of public affairs when they choose or change their constitution or decide public issues through a referendum or other electoral process conducted in accordance with paragraph (b). Citizens may participate directly by taking part in popular assemblies which have the power to make decisions about local issues or about the affairs of a particular community and in bodies established to represent citizens in consultation with government. . . .

. . .

7. Where citizens participate in the conduct of public affairs through freely chosen representatives, it is implicit in article 25 that those representatives . . . are accountable through the electoral process for their exercise of that power. . . .

8. Citizens also take part in the conduct of public affairs by exerting influence through public debate and dialogue with their representatives or through their capacity to organize themselves. This participation is supported by ensuring freedom of expression, assembly and association.

. . .

11. States must take effective measures to ensure that all persons entitled to vote are able to exercise that right. Where registration of voters is required, it should be facilitated and obstacles to such registration should not be imposed. . . . Voter education and registration campaigns are necessary to ensure the effective exercise of article 25 rights by an informed community.

12. Freedom of expression, assembly and association are essential conditions for the effective exercise of the right to vote and must be fully protected. Positive measures should be taken to overcome specific difficulties, such as illiteracy, language barriers, poverty or impediments to freedom of movement which prevent persons entitled to vote from exercising their rights effectively. Information and materials about voting should be available in minority languages. . . .

. . .

19. . . . Reasonable limitations on campaign expenditure may be justified where this is necessary to ensure that the free choice of voters is not undermined or the democratic process distorted by the disproportionate expenditure on behalf of any candidate or party. . . .

20. An independent electoral authority should be established to supervise the electoral process and to ensure that it is conducted fairly, impartially and in accordance with established laws which are compatible with the Covenant. . . . There should be independent scrutiny of the voting and counting process and access to judicial review or other equivalent process so that electors have confidence in the security of the ballot and the counting of the votes. . . .

21. Although the Covenant does not impose any particular electoral system, any system operating in a State party must be compatible with the rights protected by article 25 and must guarantee and give effect to the free expression of the will of the electors. The principle of one person, one vote must apply, and within the framework of each State's electoral system, the vote of one elector should be equal to the vote of another. The drawing of electoral boundaries and the method of

allocating votes should not distort the distribution of voters or discriminate against any group. . . .

. . .

26. In order to ensure the full enjoyment of rights protected by article 25, the free communication of information and ideas about public and political issues between citizens, candidates and elected representatives is essential. This implies a free press and other media able to comment on public issues without censorship or restraint and to inform public opinion. . . .

27. The right to freedom of association, including the right to form and join organizations and associations concerned with political and public affairs, is an essential adjunct to the rights protected by article 25. Political parties and membership in parties play a significant role in the conduct of public affairs and the election process. States should ensure that, in their internal management, political parties respect the applicable provisions of article 25 in order to enable citizens to exercise their rights thereunder.

. . .

QUESTIONS

1. Based on the preceding cases and other materials in this Chapter, how would you describe the core elements of democratic government in the contemporary world as perceived by human rights institutions? How many of those elements are set forth in or necessarily implied by the basic human rights instruments? Are comprehensive human rights instruments (with respect to civil and political rights) like the ICCPR or the European Convention simply another form of describing contemporary liberal democracies? Could one then call the ICCPR or the European Convention a 'charter for democracy'? Or are most of the rights declared in those instruments consistent with other, distinct forms of government. [The materials at pp. 888–919, *infra*, shed further light on these questions.]

2. Suppose that the Communist Party platform had urged the government to consider seriously the claim of some Kurdish factions for sovereign independence, a claim which (assume) the Communist Party found just and desirable. In what respects would the argument of the opinion have been different? Would the outcome have likely been different?

3. Suppose that the Welfare Party leaders had indicated that they would work through democratic, electoral means to increase state recognition and financial support of Islamic institutions, to remove bans on certain forms of religious observance and dress, and in general to change the emphatically and formally secular character of the state. How should the European Court evaluate this situation with respect to the Convention and its commitment to democratic government?

NOTE

Discussion of the doctrine of the margin of appreciation has figured in most of the preceding court decisions. One analysis of the European Court asserts that this concept lies 'at the heart of virtually all major cases that come before the Court, whether the judgments refer to it expressly or not'.[31] There follows a summary of views of several commentators about the meaning and relevance of this concept.

VIEWS OF COMMENTATORS ON THE MARGIN OF APPRECIATION

Paul Mahoney, Marvellous Richness of Diversity or Invidious Cultural Relativism

19 Hum. Rt's L. J. 1 (1998)

Mahoney observes at the start that in any system of international enforcement of human rights, 'some interpretational tool is needed to draw the line between what is properly a matter for each community to decide at a local level and what is so fundamental that it entails the same requirement for all countries whatever the variations in traditions and culture. In the European system that function is served by the doctrine of the margin of appreciation'. That doctrine is much maligned; some fear that through this doctrine the Court has 'diluted' many strict conditions in the Convention.

Mahoney stresses the principle of subsidiarity in Article 1, which puts primary responsibility for protection of human rights on national authorities. Because the Convention speaks in terms of standards rather than detailed prescriptions, those authorities will inevitably have much choice about how to proceed, much discretion. The international machinery is 'subsidiary' to human rights protection at the local level, and the international authorities are not intended to 'substitute themselves for the national authorities in exercising discretion'.

Moreover, the Convention deals with protection of human rights in democratic societies, where elected, representative bodies have the main responsibility. Judges with over-broad discretion, or government by judiciary, are 'quite alien to our conception of 'law' in democracy'. It inheres in the Convention that judges have this limited function of interpretative law-making, for they must 'give due recognition to the democratic processes' of member states. The doctrine of margin of appreciation addresses this question of 'what in the instant context is the area of retained democratic discretion'. 'Where societal values are still the subject of debate and controversy at national level, they should not easily be converted by the Court into protected Convention values allowing of only one approach'.

Although the Convention aims at establishing a legal community 'with a

---

[31] R. Macdonald, 'The Margin of Appreciation in the Jurisprudence of the European Court of Human Rights', in *Essays in Honor of Roberto Ago* (Vol. III, 1987), at 208.

common ethos' in human rights matters, Europe itself shows 'an inexhaustible cultural and ideological variety'. The Court should aim at preservation of this diversity, or 'at least, should not undermine it by seeking to impose rigidly uniform solutions'. Seen from this perspective, '[r]ecognition of legitimate cultural variety is not the same as cultural relativism'.

Franz Matscher, Methods of Interpretation of the Convention

in R. St. J. Macdonald, Matscher and Petzold (eds.), *The European System for the Protection of Human Rights* (1993), at 75

Matscher argues that Convention institutions 'are not entitled to dictate uniformity' but 'are obliged to respect, within certain bounds, the cultural and ideological variety, and also the legal variety, which are characteristic of Europe'. He refers to remarks of Hallstein, a former President of the European Community Commission, to the effect that:

> what we need is not a streamlined Europe; rather, the preservation of the marvellous richness and inexhaustible variety of our continent must remain a goal as important as integration. It is precisely this insight which forms the ideological background to the theory of the so-called 'margin of appreciation' of discretion, which is also a characteristic of the case-law of the Convention institutions.

Matscher notes that the Convention does not expressly allow member states any discretion in relation to the protected rights but 'merely defines the extent of those rights'. He emphasizes the number of general, undefined terms in the Convention that states must apply—terms like 'family life', 'protection of morals', necessary in a democratic society', and so on. But the Court:

> has adopted a more realistic attitude here and de facto has allowed the States a certain discretion in their legislative and executive functions. The Court merely examines whether the States have used the discretion allowed them in a reasonable fashion. . . .

He sums up the 'theory' of margin of appreciation as 'the expression of a realistic "judicial self-restraint"'.

R. St. J. Macdonald, The Margin of Appreciation

in Macdonald, Matscher and Petzold (eds.), *The European System for the Protection of Human Rights* (1993), at 122

Macdonald sees the task of the Court 'to reconcile' the political, economic, social and cultural diversity of the member states with the 'development of an effective and reasonably uniform standard of protection for Convention rights'.

The margin of appreciation, 'more a principle of justification than interpretation', helps the Court to show 'the proper degree of respect' for member states' objectives while 'preventing unnecessary restrictions' on the Conventions's rights. It is this 'flexibility' that has enabled the Court 'to avoid any damaging dispute' with states over authority of the Court and Convention on one hand, and the states and their legislatures on the other.

The margin of justification has then a 'pragmatic' justification. Progress toward the goal of a European-wide uniform standard of protection must be gradual.

> [T]he gradual refining of an originally expansive margin of appreciation reflects the increasing legitimacy of the Convention organs in the European legal order. As that legitimacy has increased, an obvious way of reducing the amount of discretion to which national authorities should consider themselves entitled is to hold them to standards which are observed Europe-wide.

This pragmatism is not without its costs, for it 'prevents the emergence of a coherent vision of the Court's function . . . . But perhaps the Convention system is now sufficiently mature to be able to move beyond the margin of appreciation and grapple more openly with the questions of appropriateness which that device obscures'.

J. G. Merrills, The Development of International Law by the European Court of Human Rights

(1988) at 146

Merrills criticizes the views of a commentator on the *Handyside* decision who suggested that it might appropriately be the function of the Court to develop a 'European conception of morals' to displace the variations among the Convention's member states. 'To this the answer is surely no. The Court's function is not to decree uniformity wherever there are national differences, but to ensure that fundamental values are respected'. Where there are 'clear differences of view' among member states, there must be 'room for a significant margin of appreciation'.

> [I]n any democratic society there are situations in which the rights set out in the Convention may be limited. The question which then arises is how and by whom the need for a disputed limitation is to be judged. No one, of course, would wish to argue that the matter should be wholly in the hands of the respondent State. The difficulty, however, is that the limitations are permitted for reasons which on the face of it only the State can properly assess. There is a great deal to be said for the view that 'If it is accepted that the State has a valid interest in the prevention of corruption and in the preservation of the moral ethos of its society, then the State has a right to enact such laws as it may reasonably think necessary to achieve these objects . . . . ' The result [of reviewing a number of the Court's judgments] is not so much an inconsistency in the Court's jurisprudence, as a

demonstration . . . that decisions about human rights are not a technical exercise in interpreting texts, but judgments about political morality.

VIEWS OF COMMENTATORS ABOUT DYNAMIC INTERPRETATION AND CONSENSUS

The preceding views of commentators about the margin of appreciation also considered the question of the significance of consensus among European states on a question before the Court. In fact, these two issues are complexly intertwined, as the opinions in *Dudgeon, Norris* and *Lustig-Prean* demonstrate. All refer to the changing laws and morals of European states, and consider the relevance of those changes for the Court's judgments. Consider two commentators' views.

Laurence Helfer, Consensus, Coherence and The European Convention on Human Rights

26 Cornell Int. L. J. 13 (1933), at 134

Helfer asserts that the Commission and Court, far from 'being bound by the intention of the drafters . . . interpret the Convention as a modern document that responds to and progressively incorporates changing European social and legal developments'. When 'rights-enhancing' practices among member states 'achieve a certain measure of uniformity, a "European consensus", so to speak, the Court and Commission raise the standard of rights-protection to which all states must adhere'. In this way, these institutions have extended the Convention's protection to groups not within the drafters' intentions.

Helfer warns that the 'failure to articulate with precision the scope and function of the consensus inquiry poses a potentially grave threat to the tribunals' authority as the arbiters of European human rights'. They must develop 'a more comprehensive and rigorous methodology for applying the European consensus inquiry'. To the present, these institutions have relied on three factors as 'evidence of consensus': legal consensus expressed through statutes or regional agreements; expert consensus; and European public consensus. But the tests lack specificity. Helfer asks, for example, what percentage of member states must alter their laws 'before a right-enhancing norm will achieve consensus status'.

P. Van Dijk, The Treatment of Homosexuals under The European Convention on Human Rights

in Waaldijk and Clapham (eds.), *Homosexuality: A European Community Issue* (1993), at 198

Van Dijk refers to a decision of the Court of Human Rights to the effect that the Convention's right to marry guaranteed by Article 12 refers to 'traditional' heterosexual marriage as the basis of a family. Even conceding such a link between marriage and procreation was intended by the Convention's drafters, he questions whether Article 12 should have been interpreted decades later to refer to such 'traditional' marriage in view of the dynamic interpretation of 'family'.

Van Dijk discusses a later case involving a transsexual, in which the Court held that developments in the member states did not evidence a departure from the traditional concept of marriage.

> It is submitted that by requiring such evidence of a general abandonment the Court sets a limitation to its powers to adopt a dynamic approach in its case-law.... After all, in the Dudgeon case and the Norris case there was also no general abandonment of the penalisation of homosexual acts between adults. Application of the 'European consensus inquiry' in its extreme would exclude the possibility of finding any national legislation in violation of the ECHR.

Van Dijk refers to a dissenting opinion in that decision, which argued that in cases involving family law and sexuality, the Court adapts its interpretation of the Convention to societal changes (quoting here from the dissenting opinion)

> only if almost all member States have adopted the new ideas. In my opinion this caution is in principle not consistent with the Court's mission to protect the individual against the collectivity and to do so by elaborating common standards. ... [I]f a collectivity oppresses an individual because it does not want to recognize societal changes, the Court should take care not to yield too readily to arguments based on a country's cultural and historical particularities.

QUESTION

1. Based on the several opinions in this Chapter, what meaning(s) or methods or premises do you attach to invocation by a judge of the margin of appreciation? Does that doctrine or principle appear to have the same meaning in all the decisions, or does its meaning change with the context?

2. With which of the following assertions do you agree? Would you add a better formulation?

a. 'The margin of appreciation is simply a fancy name given to an inevitable concern of an international tribunal. It tells the Court not to overstep its role and to be respectful of the sovereign states that created and submitted to the Court in the first instance. Else the Court and the Convention could get into deep trouble. It is a rule of prudence'.

b. 'The margin of appreciation is another name for cultural relativism. It respects difference, and cautions the Court not to compress the varied European states and cultures into one juridical and moral form'.

c. 'The margin of appreciation is less an application than a perversion of cultural relativism. Europe possesses an important unity vis-à-vis the rest of the world. We are not talking of a universal system embracing the United States as well as Yemen, Russia as well as Bolivia, where indeed one can find strong arguments for a degree of cultural relativism. Here the differences are relatively slight. The effect of invocation of this principle is to permit ongoing oppression of the culturally deviant within a country, of the minorities that characteristically have had to resort to *universal* human rights norms to challenge their states' laws and practice'.

d. 'The margin of appreciation is consistent with the principle of subsidiarity in European Community Law, a principle expressed in the Treaty on European Union whose Preamble declares that decisions will be taken 'as closely as possible to the citizen in accordance with the principle of subsidiarity'. The local population, provided it expresses itself through the forms of democracy, knows what is best for it'.

e. 'The margin of appreciation is an empty, redundant concept that adds nothing to a court's discussion. It is subject, and frequently subjected, to the greatest manipulation. It is a bundle of contradictions. The European Court would do much better to hande an issue directly, without this obfuscating rhetoric, by going straight to the question whether a state-imposed limitation on a right or freedom can be viewed as "necessary in a democratic society"'.

COMMENT ON POWERS AND JURISDICTION OF INTERNATIONAL TRIBUNALS

Consider some comparisons and contrasts between the European Court of Human Rights and other international tribunals.

(1) *International arbitral tribunals.* Recall the discussion of arbitral tribunals and the *Chattin* case, pp. 81–92, *supra*, decided by the United States–Mexican Claims Commission under the 1923 General Claims Convention between the two states. Frequently these tribunals were tripartite, one member appointed by each party to the dispute and the third pursuant to a stated procedure. In most instances, as in *Chattin*, the states themselves were the parties to the arbitration, with the complainant state frequently acting on behalf of (extending diplomatic protection to) an allegedly injured national. In a few instances, the individuals alleging injury by another state could themselves initiate proceedings before the arbitral tribunal. The governing agreement between the states generally required that the individual involved had exhausted the respondent state's local remedies. The tribunal or claims commission could provide whatever relief (generally, not invariably, the award of damages) that the governing instrument (a general arbitration treaty, an *ad hoc* agreement to create the tribunal for a given controversy, and so on) provided. As in the United States–Mexican General Claims Convention, the governing agreement generally spelled out the applicable law, often through terse references to principles of justice or international law.

(2) *International Military Tribunal*, p. 115, *supra*. This Tribunal, whose Charter was annexed to the London Agreement of 1945 among the Allied powers, was created for the trial of the Nazi war criminals at Nuremberg. The Charter spelled

out the governing norms. The IMT's four judges were drawn from each of the four major Allied powers. The punishments imposed by the IMT on the individual defendants included the death penalty. (Chapter 14 examines the contemporary International Criminal Tribunals for the former Yugoslavia and for Rwanda, which again exercises criminal jurisdiction over individual defendants. They were created pursuant to decisions of the UN Security Council.)

(3) *The International Court of Justice*: The opinion in the *Minority Schools in Albania* case of the Permanent Court of International Justice, the predecessor court under the League of Nations, appears at p. 96, *supra*. The contemporary ICJ is provided for in Article 92 of the UN Charter. It has both a contentious and advisory jurisdiction. Under Article 94, each member state of the UN agrees to comply with a decision of the ICJ against it. The Court's jurisdiction depends on states' consent, and under its Statute, only states may be parties before it. The Statute defines the governing law in very general terms (see Article 38 of the Statute, p. 58, *supra*). The Court may order the payment of damages by a respondent state as well as provide other forms of relief.

(4) The *Court of Justice* under the Treaty Establishing the European Community, p. 790, *supra*, is to 'ensure that in the interpretation and application of this Treaty the law is observed'. (Article 220, ex 164). Generally that application will in the first instance be by the courts of member states. The Court of Justice exercises different types of jurisdiction—for example, in cases brought against a state by another institution of the European Community (such as the Commission) (Article 226, ex 169), or brought by one member state against another (Article 227, ex 170). States are 'required to take the necessary measures to comply with the judgment' of the Court (Article 228, ex 171). Depending on its precise jurisdictional base, the Court may enter judgment against a party, annul an administrative act, award money damages, or afford other relief.

Article 234 (ex 177) grants the Court jurisdiction to give 'preliminary rulings' on matters including the Treaty's interpretation, and the validity and interpretation of acts of Community institutions.[32]

> Where such a question is raised before any court or tribunal of a member state, that court or tribunal may, if it considers that a decision on the question is necessary to enable it to give judgment, request the Court of Justice to give a ruling thereon.
>
> Where any such question is raised in a case pending before a court of tribunal of a member state, against whose decisions there is no judicial remedy under national law, that court or tribunal shall bring the matter before the Court of Justice.

Article 234 is not an 'appeals' procedure leading to affirmance, reversal, remand with instructions, and so on. The Court does not 'decide' the case. Rather, the Court must 'interpret' the relevant Treaty provision, not 'apply' it. (In these

---

[32] For analyses of the problems that have arisen under Article 234 (ex 177), see P. Craig and G. de Búrca, *EU Law* (2nd edn., 1998) 407–52; and T. de la Mare, 'Article 177 in Social and Political Context', in P. Craig and G. de Búrca (eds.), *The Education of EU Law* (1999) 215–60.

respects, Article 234 is analogous to the jurisdiction of appellate courts in a number of civil law countries.) The state court suspends proceedings and itself (rather than a party to the state court proceeding) certifies questions of interpretation to the Court of Justice, which renders its opinion in the form of an abstract interpretation. The state court then continues the proceedings in light of that opinion. At the start, the primary purpose of Article 234 was to assure a uniform application of Community law by the courts of the member states. Over the decades, most of the Court's major rulings deciding basic principles about the Community grew out of Article 234.

Article 234 involves then mutual cooperation and a shared jurisdiction of both a state and Community court. Predictable problems have arisen with respect to the responsibility of state courts (the conditions under which that responsibility arises) to certify a question to the Court of Justice rather than resolve the question themselves, and with respect to the duty of the state court to decide the case consistently with the interpretation of the Court of Justice. Attitudes of judiciaries in the several member states have varied.

QUESTIONS

Compare the situation of international tribunals as described in the preceding Comment with procedures and powers of appellate courts in relation to lower courts in the domestic law of some states like the United States. In such countries, a typical procedure would involve (a) the certification to the appellate court of a record of proceedings in the lower court; (b) a decision by the appellate court to affirm or reverse the lower court, perhaps with a remand ordering the lower court to enter judgment for one or the other party (in which event, the case is terminated if the decision is by the highest appellate court); or (c) a remand by the appellate court to the lower court with instructions to proceed in other stated ways (to hold a new trial, modify an injunction, order release of a prisoner, dismiss or reinstate the case, and so on).

1. Would you view it as desirable to have an international human rights tribunal linked to the highest court in a state judiciary in this way?

2. Would you view such an arrangement as politically feasible? In what respects does it go beyond existing arrangements for, say, the ICCPR Human Rights Committee or the European Court of Human Rights?

3. What argument would you make for or against a Protocol to the European Convention that would introduce a process similar to Article 234?

LAURENCE HELFER AND ANNE-MARIE SLAUGHTER, TOWARD A THEORY OF EFFECTIVE SUPRANATIONAL LITIGATION
107 Yale L.J. 273 (1997), at 298

[The authors develop a 'checklist for effective supranational adjudication' by 'distilling commentary and analysis by judges, lawyers, and political scientists who have closely observed the workings of the [European Court of Justice and European Court of Human Rights, and] supplementing these findings with our own analysis'. They divide the checklist into several categories of factors 'that plausibly affect the effectiveness of supranational tribunals'. The items on the list under each category appear in descending order of importance and applicability across regimes. The following excerpts from the article's checklist omit numerous qualifications and details.]

1. Factors Within the Control of States Party to an Agreement Establishing a Supranational Tribunal

a. Composition of the Tribunal

... [T]he experience of the ECJ and ECHR suggests that they should give careful consideration to the background and experience of jurists who serve on it. . ... The implicit point is that where a supranational tribunal depends on acceptance of its judgments by national tribunals, it will wield greater authority if its members are known and respected by national judges.

...

b. Caseload or functional capacity of the Court

... The trick is to build a sufficiently high-profile caseload at the outset to attract a steady stream of claimants. The material and financial resources that states devote to the tribunal, together with the degree of complexity they impose regarding its procedures and operations, can assist or hamper this endeavor.

...

... [State-provided]resources can help to: (1) ensure that judges on the tribunal can educate potential constituencies of litigants concerning both the existence of the tribunal and the law it is charged to apply; (2) dispatch quickly and efficiently the complaints that the tribunal receives; and (3) publicize the results. ...

c. Independent fact-finding capacity

... A guaranteed capacity to generate facts that have been independently evaluated, either through a third-party factfinding process or through the public contestation inherent in the adversary system, helps counter the perception of self-serving or 'political' judgments. [The authors note the special problems for fact-finding of appellate tribunals, or tribunals like the European Court of Justice to which general questions of law may be certified by national courts.]

...

d. Formal authority or status as law of the instrument that the Tribunal is charged with interpreting and applying

Also relevant to effectiveness is whether the instrument that the tribunal is charged with interpreting and the tribunal's decisions themselves are regarded as binding and hence accorded formal status as law.... [Such] provisions establish the authority of these bodies as legal tribunals, a factor to which commentators assessing their effectiveness give considerable weight.

. . .

2. Factors Within the Control of the Judiciary

. . .

In [the cases of the two European Courts], the question remains: why have national actors listened and responded? More precisely, how did these two tribunals manipulate factors within their control to maximize their impact on the relevant national actors? . . .

a. Awareness of Audience

. . . [The two] tribunals have recognized an audience beyond the parties to the case at hand and have crafted their opinions to encourage additional cases by appealing to both the material interests and professional ideals of prospective litigants. . . . They have also used these appeals to penetrate the surface of the state, linking up to different domestic political actors with actually or potentially divergent interests.

. . .

b. Neutrality and demonstrated autonomy from political interests

Commentators have emphasized the link between a supranational tribunal's authority and its neutrality, here defined not only in terms of equidistance between litigants but also with regard to a tribunal's ability to explicate a decision based on generally applicable legal principles. The alternative is 'political' dispute resolution, in which the dispute resolver seeks above all to satisfy or reconcile the parties' competing interests. The challenge for a court seeking to present itself as a judicial rather than a political body is thus to demonstrate its independence from both political authorities and political modes of dispute resolution. The judicial selection and tenure process are obviously key factors here. . . . As the history of supranational adjudication in Europe makes plain, both the ECJ and the ECHR have been willing to decide against governments in big cases.

. . .

. . . 'Court-ness' does not rule out incrementalism or strategic decisionmaking. . . . It does, however, mandate decisionmaking premised (at least formally) on principle rather than power. As studies of 'legalization' of international decisionmaking suggest, secrecy and compromise are the hallmarks of diplomacy, not law. Thus, tribunals must be willing to brave political displeasure, searching always for generalizable principles, even as they search for formulations or procedural mechanisms to render the principles more palatable to the states concerned.

c. Incrementalism

Bold demonstrations of judicial autonomy by judgments against state interests and appeals to constituencies of individuals must be tempered by incrementalism and awareness of political boundaries. . . .

. . .

The ECHR has also demonstrated an acute awareness of the tension between the preferences of national decisionmakers and the requirements of the European Convention. To address this tension, the ECHR has developed the concept of a 'margin of appreciation', acknowledging an area of discretion for national governments when applying and interpreting the treaty. . . . It has also stressed, however, that any discretion to national decisionmakers is limited by a 'European supervision' that 'empower[s the ECHR] to give the final ruling' on whether a challenged practice is compatible with the Convention.

. . .

In striking the balance between deference and independent judicial review, the ECHR looks to the degree of consensus or harmony among the national laws of signatory states in deciding how wide or narrow a margin to afford the respondent state in the case before it. This approach allows the court to narrow the margin of discretion allotted to national governments in an incremental fashion, finding against state respondents according to the underlying treatment of the right at issue within other European nations. . . . The conjunction of the margin of appreciation doctrine and the consensus inquiry thus permits the ECHR to link its decisions to the pace of change of domestic law, acknowledging the political sovereignty of respondent states while legitimizing its own decisions against them.

. . .

d. Quality of legal reasoning

. . .

The ECHR has also benefited substantially from the quality of its reasoning, at least according to experienced observers. Polakiewicz and Jacob-Foltzer conclude their study by noting that, with a few rare exceptions, the ECHR has 'never been openly defied by national courts'. They attribute this 'persuasive authority' in large part to 'the weight of the Court's arguments'. Francois Ost concurs, finding 'the judgments of the Court [to be] exceptionally well reasoned. . . . Each of the questions it seeks to answer . . . is scrupulously examined as to the facts, the law and the practice. . . .' And for J.G. Merrills, looking ahead, the factor that 'will ultimately determine the importance of the European Court's contribution is the quality of the work. . . .'

. . . Merrills, for instance, attributes the 'wider significance' of the Court's judgments to its consistent efforts 'to justify its decisions in terms which treat its existing case-law as authoritative. In other words, it follows judicial precedent'. Adherence to precedent, even when used only as authoritative guidepost and not as binding obligation, ensures a minimum degree of both temporal and systemic consistency.

. . .

We search thus for a set of more fundamental attributes of sound legal reasoning, the qualities that Weiler encompasses when he refers to 'reasoned interpretation' and 'logical deduction'. Yet, it is here that assessments of quality diverge, based on the type of legal reasoning and the logical mode a particular author prefers. . . . Ost points to 'the injection . . . of certain indeterminate elements (. . . elastic criteria, methods of balancing conflicting interests, proportionality)' that forsake binary logic in favour of the flexible evolution of a few general principles. Mary Ann Glendon highlights the ECHR's 'searching and tentative style . . . , its open wrestling with the weaknesses as well as the strength of [its] positions'. In short, and not surprisingly, scholarly evaluation of the ECJ and ECHR reflects many of the same debates about the distinctive and effective attributes of legal reasoning found in any national or international jurisprudential literature. . . .

. . .

. . . A supranational court, in particular, is essentially in the business of constructing its own polity, defining the boundaries of a legal community constituted by adherence to an international instrument. A mode of judicial decisionmaking that acknowledges competing values while emphasizing dignity and democratic participation has a particular value in this context.

e. *Judicial cross-fertilization and dialogue*

The ECJ and the ECHR enhance each other's authority by referring to one another's decisions. The ECHR (or individual judges writing for it) periodically refers to ECJ decisions both to assert its primary authority in a case of potentially conflicting jurisdiction and to bolster its own power over national courts by referring to a similar power of the ECJ. . . .

f. *Form of opinions*

. . . The principal issue with respect to form is whether the opinion should be written as if the judgment were unanimous or if dissents and concurring opinions should be allowed. Opinions differ substantially on this question as do the two courts themselves. . . .

. . .

It is possible to reconcile these two views if we note that the ECJ talks primarily to national courts, whereas the ECHR depends more directly on the reactions of national bureaucrats and politicians. Addressing an audience of national judges, themselves accustomed to handing down 'the law', the ECJ may be right in its calculation that unanimity enhances authority. In addition, this audience was initially relatively small and uniform—judges from six civil law countries at the core of Western Europe. The ECHR, by contrast, has found itself seeking to persuade government officials from fifteen countries, adding the Austrian, British, Irish, Scandinavian, Greek, and Turkish legal systems to the original mix. In this context, evidence that a number of judges could reach the same conclusion, albeit on different grounds, and that contrary arguments had been thoroughly ventilated, as demonstrated by dissenting opinions, could well enhance persuasive power. Indeed, as the number of countries subject to the jurisdiction of the ECJ grows, pressure has mounted on the Court to drop the unanimity rule.

. . .

3. Factors Often Beyond the Control of States or Judges

a. Nature of violations

A principal factor that has contributed to the success of the European human rights system is the limited nature of complaints brought before the ECHR. Menno Kamminga directly attributes the success of the ECHR to the minor and unintentional nature of most violations found under the Convention, which requires few concessions from the offending state. . . . Indeed, Torkel Opsahl draws a contrast between the kinds of cases typically heard by the ECHR and those often submitted to the U.N. Human Rights Committee by noting the difference in the percentage of cases declared admissible—'almost 50 percent [in the U.N. system] as against less than 3 percent [in the European system]'. He attributes much of this difference to the 'serious facts of many cases [going to the UNHRC]'.

. . .

b. Autonomous Domestic Institutions Committed to the Rule of Law and Responsive to Citizen Interests

The European experience of supranational adjudication is the experience of two supranational tribunals operating within a community of liberal democracies with strong domestic commitments to the rule of law. This dimension of the European experience provides the subtext for much of the analysis of factors discussed in this section, such as the nature of violations or cultural homogeneity. . . .

The burgeoning literature on the 'democratic peace', seeking to explain why liberal democracies rarely if ever go to war with one another, has spurred scholars to explore other ways in which attributes of a domestic regime-type affect international behavior. Of particular interest here are hypotheses, as yet unproved, concerning the positive impact of liberal democracy on compliance with international commitments, including the judgments of international and supranational tribunals. As defined in this literature, 'liberal democracy' combines representative government with a commitment to the rule of law, itself defined to include both an independent judiciary and protection of basic civil and political rights. . . .

. . .

. . . [W]e conclude that the existence . . . of domestic government institutions committed to the rule of law, responsive to the claims of individual citizens, and able to formulate and pursue their interests independently from other government institutions, is a strongly favourable precondition for effective supranational adjudication. . . .

. . .

c. Relative cultural and political homogeneity of states subject to a supranational tribunal

Many observers of the ECJ, the ECHR, and the Inter-American system have contrasted the relative homogeneity of the states participating in these systems with the diversity of universal regimes such as the International Covenant on Civil and Political Rights. . . .

. . . [H]omogeneity is not a constant. As the experience of the Council of Europe's expanding membership into Eastern Europe and former Soviet states demonstrates, even nations with very different social and political histories may seek to join a treaty regime with a dynamic and powerful supranational court. . . .

. . .

QUESTIONS

1. In what respects, if any, would your list (based upon discussion of the ICCPR Committee in Chapter 9 and the European Court) differ in basic concept or structure, priorities, or detail? How would you assess the ICCPR Committee under the proposed checklist?

2. Do you agree with the authors' understanding of the margin of appreciation in relation to the Court's attention to consensus?

3. Do the preceding opinions of the European Court fall within a category of relatively minor deviations, often unintentional, from a society's broad observance of human rights norms, or within a category of intentional, structural departures from what the opinions conclude are basic human rights requirements? If the latter, does that undermine the authors' point about factors beyond the control of the state?

ADDITIONAL READING

D. Harris, M. O'Boyle and C. Warbrick, *Law of the European Convention on Human Rights* (2nd edn., forthcoming 2000); M. Janis, R. Kay and A. Bradley, *European Human Rights Law: Text and Materials* (2nd edn., 2000); R. Singh, M. Hunt and M. Demetriou, 'Is there a Role for the "Margin of Appreciation" in National Law after the Human Rights Act?', [1999] Eur. Hum. Rts. L. Rev. 15; T. Barkhuysen *et al.*, *The Execution of Strasbourg and Geneva Human Rights Decisions in the National Legal Order* (1999); *Yearbook of the European Convention on Human Rights* (annual, vol. 41, 1999); P. Van Dijk and G.J.H. Van Hoof, *Theory and Practice of the European Convention on Human Rights* (3rd edn., 1998); P. Kempees, *A Systematic Guide to the Case-Law of the European Court of Human Rights* (3 vols., 1996–98); Special Issue: 'The Doctrine of the Margin of Appreciation under the European Convention on Human Rights', 19 Hum. Rts. L. J. 1 (1998); C. Gearty (ed.), *European Civil Liberties and the European Convention on Human Rights* (1997); R. St J. Macdonald, F. Matscher and H. Petzold (eds.), *The European System for the Protection of Human Rights* (1993); Council of Europe, *Collected Edition of the 'Travaux Préparatoires' of the European Convention on Human Rights* (8 vols., 1975–85).

C. THE INTER-AMERICAN SYSTEM: PROMOTING DEMOCRACY

Section C selects two aspects of the Inter-American system to illustrate its structure and work: an institution, the Inter-American Commission on Human Rights (IACHR); and a topic, political participation and democracy. At the same time, although less extensively than with respect to the European human rights system, the materials describe the rights protected by the American Convention on Human Rights and the complex institutional arrangements that result from the parallel existence of organs based on both the Charter of the Organization of American States (OAS) and the Convention. The section illustrates the work of the Inter-American Court of Human Rights through one of its prominent decisions.

1. BACKGROUND AND INSTITUTIONS

COMMENT ON DEVELOPMENT OF THE INTER-AMERICAN SYSTEM

In May 1948 the ninth Inter-American Conference, held in Bogotá, established the Organization of American States (OAS). Its predecessor organizations date back to the International Union of American Republics of 1890. The 1948 Charter entered into force in December 1951 and has since been amended by the Protocol of Buenos Aires of 1967, the Protocol of Cartagena de Indias of 1985, the Protocol of Washington of 1992, and the Protocol of Managua of 1993. The purposes of the OAS are:

> to strengthen the peace and security of the continent; to promote and consolidate representative democracy, with due respect for the principle of nonintervention; to prevent possible causes of difficulties and to ensure the pacific settlement of disputes that may arise among the member states; to provide for common action on the part of those States in the event of aggression; to seek the solution of political, juridical and economic problems that may arise among them; to promote by cooperative action, their economic, social and cultural development, and to achieve an effective limitation of conventional weapons that will make it possible to devote the largest amount of resources to the economic and social development of the member states. (*Annual Report of the Inter-American Commission on Human Rights 1994* (1995), at 347.)

Its principal organs are the General Assembly that meets annually and in additional special sessions if required, the Meeting of Consultation of Ministers of Foreign Affairs that considers urgent matters, the Permanent Council and the General Secretariat. The latter two organs are based in Washington DC.

The Bogotá Conference of 1948 also adopted the American Declaration of the Rights and Duties of Man. The Inter-American system thus had a human rights declaration seven months before the United Nations had adopted the Universal

Declaration and two and a half years before the European Convention was adopted. Nevertheless, the development of a regional treaty monitored by an effective supervisory machinery was to take considerably longer. The Inter-American Commission on Human Rights was created in 1959 and the American Convention on Human Rights was adopted in 1969. It entered into force in 1978.

The development of the Inter-American system followed a different path from that of its European counterpart. Although the institutional structure is super-ficially very similar and the normative provisions are in most respects very similar, the conditions under which the two systems developed were radically different. Within the Council of Europe, military and other authoritarian governments have been rare and short-lived, while in Latin America they were close to being the norm until the changes that started in the 1980s.

The major challenges confronting the European system are epitomized by issues such as the length of pre-trial detention and the implications of the right to privacy. Cases involving states of emergency have been relatively few. The Euro-pean Commission and Court have rarely had to deal with completely unresponsive or even antagonistic governments or national legal systems, or with deep struc-tural problems that led to systematic and serious human rights violations. (That situation, as noted earlier, began to change with the expansion of membership in the European Convention to many recently authoritarian states in Central and East Europe and to Turkey.) By contrast, states of emergency have been common in Latin America, the domestic judiciary has often been extremely weak or cor-rupt, and large-scale practices involving torture, disappearances and executions have not been uncommon. Many of the governments with which the Inter-American Commission and Court have had to work have been ambivalent towards those institutions at best and hostile at worst.

In March 2000 there were 35 member states of the OAS, of which 25 had ratified the American Convention on Human Rights and 20 had recognized the jurisdic-tion of the Court. Peru recently renounced its earlier recognition of the Court's jurisdiction. Although the United States signed the Convention in 1978, it has yet to ratify. Cuba remains, technically, a member of the OAS, but the Government of Fidel Castro has been excluded from participation in its work since 1962. This has not prevented the OAS from scrutinizing the human rights record of Cuba.

COMMENT ON RIGHTS RECOGNIZED IN THE AMERICAN DECLARATION AND CONVENTION

You should now become familiar with these two instruments, excerpts from which appear in the Document Annex.

In terms of rights, the American Declaration on the Rights and Duties of Man is similar in content to the Universal Declaration, including the economic and social rights therein. What distinguishes it are ten articles setting out the duties of the citizen: the duty 'so to conduct himself in relation to others that each and every one may fully form and develop his personality'; to 'aid support, educate and protect his minor children', to 'acquire at least an elementary education', to vote in

popular elections, to 'obey the law and other legitimate commands of the authorities', to 'render whatever civil and military service his country may require for
its defence and preservation', to cooperate with the state with respect to social
security and welfare; to pay taxes; and to work.

The process of drafting an Inter-American treaty began in 1959. The result was
the American Convention on Human Rights of 1969 (also known as the Pact of
San José, Costa Rica) which contains 26 rights and freedoms, 21 of which are
formulated in similar terms to the provisions of the ICCPR. Consider some
comparisons:

1. Article 27 of the ICCPR, which recognizes the rights of members of
   minority groups, has no counterpart in the American Convention.
2. The five provisions which are in that Convention but not in the ICCPR are
   the right of reply (Article 14), the right to property (Article 21), freedom
   from exile (Article 22(5)), the right to asylum (Article 22(7)), and
   prohibition of 'the collective expulsion of aliens' (Article 21(9)).
3. Some provisions in the American Convention express the same general
   idea as in other human rights treaties but give it a distinctive
   specification—for example, Article 4 on the right to life that provides in
   para. 1 that the right 'shall be protected by law and, in general, from the
   moment of conception'.
4. Article 23 on participation in government, which figures in the later
   materials, contains the same rights and requirements as the analogous
   Article 21 of the UDHR and Article 25 of the ICCPR.

When the Convention was adopted in 1969 it was decided not to have a separate
treaty relating to economic, social and cultural rights but rather to include a
general provision (Article 26) in the following terms:

> The States Parties undertake to adopt measures, both internally and through
> international cooperation, especially those of an economic and technical nature,
> with a view to achieving progressively by legislation or other means, the full
> realization of the rights implicit in the economic, social, educational, scientific
> and cultural standards set forth in the Charter of the Organization of American
> States as amended by the Protocol of Buenos Aires.

The OAS Charter, as amended, sets up an Inter-American Council for Education, Science and Culture, as well as an Economic and Social Council, both of
which are supposed to set standards, consider reports made by States, and make
recommendations. That machinery has, however, achieved very little indeed in
relation to economic, social and cultural rights, although the Inter-American
Commission on Human Rights has carried out occasional reviews of states'
reports. In 1988 the OAS adopted an Additional Protocol to the American Convention on Human Rights in the Area of Economic, Social and Cultural Rights
(known as the Protocol of San Salvador). It obliges parties to adopt measures, 'to
the extent allowed by their available resources, and taking into account their

degree of development', for the progressive achievement of the rights listed. The Protocol became effective in 1999 and had, as of January 2000, 11 states parties.

The rights recognized in the Protocol are similar to those in the International Covenant on Economic, Social and Cultural Rights, although the formulations differ significantly. The Protocol does not recognize the rights to adequate clothing and housing or to an adequate standard of living (Article 11 of the ICESCR), but it does include the right to a healthy environment, the right to special protection in old age, and the rights of persons with disabilities, none of which are explicitly recognized in the ICESCR.

NOTE

Compare the individual duties expressed in the American Declaration with the ICCPR, in which duties are only referred to in the preamble that paraphrases Article 29(1) of the Universal Declaration ('Everyone has duties to the community in which alone the free and full development of his personality is possible'). The conception and nature of the duties expressed in the African Charter on Human and Peoples' Rights, p. 354, *supra*, is radically different.

CECILIA MEDINA, THE INTER-AMERICAN COMMISSION ON HUMAN RIGHTS AND THE INTER-AMERICAN COURT OF HUMAN RIGHTS: REFLECTIONS ON A JOINT VENTURE

12 Hum. Rts. Q. 439 (1990), at 440

[When the Inter-American Commission was established in 1959, the assumption was that it would confine itself to 'abstract investigations'. When complaints immediately flowed in, the Commission was compelled to respond in some way.]

. . .

A significant part of the Commission's work was addressing the problem of countries with gross, systematic violations of human rights, characterized by an absence or a lack of effective national mechanisms for the protection of human rights and a lack of cooperation on the part of the governments concerned. The main objective of the Commission was not to investigate isolated violations but to document the existence of these gross, systematic violations and to exercise pressure to improve the general condition of human rights in the country concerned. For this purpose, and by means of its regulatory powers, the Commission created a procedure to 'take cognizance' of individual complaints and use them as a source of information about gross, systematic violations of human rights in the territories of the OAS member states.

The Commission's competence to handle individual communications was formalized in 1965, after the OAS reviewed and was satisfied with the Commission's work. The OAS passed Resolution XXII, which allowed the Commission to 'examine' isolated human rights violations, with a particular focus on certain rights. This procedure, however, provided many obstacles for the Commission. Complaints could be handled only if domestic remedies had been exhausted, a requirement that prevented swift reactions to violations. Also, the procedure made the Commission more dependent on the governments for information. This resulted in the governments' either not answering the Commission's requests for information or answering with a blanket denial that did not contribute to a satisfactory solution of the problem.

Furthermore, once the Commission had given its opinion on the case, there was nothing else to be done; the Commission would declare that a government had violated the American Declaration of the Rights and Duties of Man and recommend the government take certain measures, knowing that this was unlikely to resolve the situation. . . . [I]n order not to lose the flexibility it had, the Commission interpreted Resolution XXII as granting the Commission power to 'examine' communications concerning individual violations of certain rights specified in the resolution without diminishing its power to 'take cognizance' of communications concerning the rest of the human rights protected by the American Declaration. The Commission preserved this broader power for the purposes of identifying gross, systematic human rights violations.

The procedure to 'take cognizance' of communications evolved and became the general case procedure and was later used in examining the general human rights situation in a country. . . . [T]he Commission could publicize its findings in order to put pressure upon the governments. Finally, the report resulting from the investigation could be sent to the political bodies of the OAS, thereby allowing for a political discussion of the problem which, at least theoretically, could be followed by political measures against the governments involved.

Since financial and human resources were limited, the Commission concentrated all its efforts on the examination of the general situation of human rights in each country. The examination of individual cases clearly took a secondary place. . . .

In short, the Commission was the sole guarantor of human rights in a continent plagued with gross, systematic violations, and the Commission was part of an international organization for which human rights were definitely not the first priority, and these facts made an imprint on the way the Commission looked upon its task. . . .. Apparently, the Commission viewed itself more as an international organ with a highly political task to perform than as a technical body whose main task was to participate in the first phase of a quasi-judicial supervision of the observance of human rights. The Commission's past made it ill-prepared to efficiently utilize the additional powers the [American] Convention subsequently granted it.

A. *The system under the American Convention on Human Rights*

The Convention vested the authority to supervise its observance in two organs: the Inter-American Commission, which pre-existed the Convention, and Inter-American Court of Human Rights, which was created by the Convention.

The Inter-American Commission is composed of seven members elected in a nongovernmental capacity by the OAS General Assembly and represents all the OAS member states. The entry into force of the Convention in 1978 invested the Commission with a dual role. It has retained its status as an organ of the OAS, thereby maintaining its powers to promote and protect human rights in the territories of all OAS member states. In addition, it is now an organ of the Convention, and in that capacity it supervises human rights in the territories of the states parties to the Convention.

The Commission's functions include: (1) promoting human rights in all OAS member states; (2) assisting in the drafting of human rights documents; (3) advising member states of the OAS; (4) preparing country reports, which usually include visits to the territories of these states; (5) mediating disputes over serious human rights problems; (6) handling individual complaints and initiating individual cases on its own motion, both with regard to states parties and states not parties to the Convention; and (7) participating in the handling of cases and advisory opinions before the Court.

The Inter-American Court consists of seven judges irrespective of the number of states that have recognized the jurisdiction of the Court. Although the Court is formally an organ of the Convention and not of the OAS, its judges may be nationals of any member state of the OAS whether or not they are parties to the Convention.

The Court has contentious and advisory jurisdiction. In exercising its contentious jurisdiction, the Court settles controversies about the interpretation and application of the provisions of the American Convention through a special procedure designed to handle individual or state complaints against states parties to the Convention. Under its advisory jurisdiction, the Court may interpret not only the Convention but also any other treaty concerning the protection of human rights in the American states.

. . . The advisory jurisdiction of the Court may be set in motion by any OAS member state, whether or not it is a party to the Convention, or by any OAS organ listed in Chapter X of the OAS Charter, which includes the Commission.

The procedure for handling individual or state complaints [under the Convention] begins before the Commission. The procedure resembles those set forth in the European Convention and in the Additional Protocol to the International Covenant on Civil and Political Rights. It is a quasi-judicial mechanism which may be started by any person, group of persons, or nongovernmental entity legally recognized in one or more of the OAS member states, regardless of whether the complainant is the victim of a human rights violation. This right of individual petition is a mandatory provision in the Convention, binding on all states parties. Inter-state communications, however, are dependent upon an explicit recognition of the competence of the Commission to receive and examine them. In addition, the Commission may begin processing a case on its own motion.
. . .

The Commission has powers to request information from the government concerned and, with the consent of the government, to investigate the facts in the complaint at the location of the alleged violation. If the government does not cooperate in the proceedings by providing the requested information within the time limit set by the Commission, Article 42 of the Commission's Regulations allows the Commission to presume that the facts in the petition are true, 'as long as other evidence does not lead to a different conclusion'. Following this, the Commission need investigate the case no further.

. . .

The Court may consider a case that is brought either by the Commission or by a state party to the Convention. For the Commission to refer a case to the Court, the case must have been admitted for investigation and the Commission's draft report sent to the state party. In addition, the state must recognize the Court's general contentious jurisdiction or a limited jurisdiction specified by a time period or case. For a state party to be able to place a case before the Court, the only requirement is that both states must have recognized the Court's contentious jurisdiction.

. . .

If a state does not comply with the decision of the Court, the Court may inform and make recommendations to the OAS General Assembly. There is no reference in the Convention to any action that the General Assembly might take; the assembly, being a political body, may take any political action it deems necessary to persuade the state to comply with its international obligations.

. . .

In addition to the problems posed by the Commission's status as part of a political organization and by the lack of cooperation among the states, financial limitations are also potentially troublesome. The OAS does not provide the Commission with the necessary means to carry out all its various activities.

. . . Under these circumstances, the Commission inevitably makes a choice as to what it can accomplish and places a priority on tasks it perceives as most likely to increase the general respect for human rights. In this ordering, the handling of individual complaints does not rank very high.

. . .

DAVID HARRIS, REGIONAL PROTECTION OF HUMAN RIGHTS: THE INTER-AMERICAN ACHIEVEMENT
in David Harris and S. Livingstone (eds.), The Inter-American System of Human Rights (1998), at 1

. . .

The inter-American system differs in many ways from the other well established regional system for the protection of human rights, namely that under the European Convention on Human Rights. . . . The inter-American system is more complex than that of the European Convention in that it is based upon two overlapping instruments, namely the American Declaration on the Rights and Duties of Man and the American Convention. . . . It also has more than one dimension in that the Inter-American Commission not only hears petitions but also conducts *in loco* visits, leading to the adoption of country reports on the human rights situation in OAS member states. This second, very important dimension to the Inter-American Commission's work has no counterpart in the European system.

Another crucial difference is the political context within which the two systems operate. Whereas the European system has during its forty year history generally regulated democracies with independent judiciaries and governments that observe the rule of law, the history of much of the Americas since 1960 has been radically different, with military dictatorships, the violent repression of political opposition and of terrorism and intimidated judiciaries for a while being the order of the day in a number of countries. The result is that human rights issues in the Americas have often concerned gross, as opposed to ordinary, violations of human rights. They have been much more to do with the forced disappearance, killing, torture and arbitrary detention of political opponents and terrorists than with particular issues concerning, for example, the right to a fair trial or freedom of expression that are the stock in trade of the European Commission and Court. This difference is apparent both in the country reports of the Inter-American Commission and in its decisions on individual petitions. A remarkable feature of the Commission's annual reports has been the long sequences of cases of forced disappearances on the street and extra-judicial killings by state agents in which the Commission, in the absence of any government response, finds a breach of the right to life on the basis of the petitioner's credible allegations.

. . .

A final difference exists at the stage of enforcing final decisions and judgments. The inter-American system provides no counterpart to the supervisory role of the Committee of Ministers of the Council of Europe. Related to this is the fact that the outcome of proceedings in the inter-American system is not necessarily a legally binding decision. The judgments of the Inter-American Court are legally binding upon the parties. But very few cases as yet go on to the Court, and the conclusions and recommendations of the Commission, which are the end result in the great majority of cases that are completed on the merits, are not legally binding. Although there would not appear to have been any comprehensive study of the record of states in responding to the recommendations of the Commission, such indications as there are suggest that they have not been followed in the many cases of gross violations by military regimes.

One further introductory comment that may be made about the inter-American system is that it applies to the whole of a region that has a certain dislocation within it, between the United States and Canada and the rest. As one reads the annual reports of the Commission and the judgments of the Court, one has the sense that the system is essentially a Latin American one, with the United States and, more recently, Canada making an occasional appearance.[33]

. . .

There have been few signs that the Commission or the Court are overtly following national law standards common to the Americas. To the contrary, it is noticeable that the Court has stated that a 'certain tendency to integrate the regional and

---

[33] A small number of individual petitions have been brought under the Declaration against the US and, in a few cases, Canada (neither are bound by the Convention) and the Commission has made *in loco* visits to the US. But otherwise, outside of the political organs, and despite the active participation of US nationals on the Commission and the Court, the impression is very much one of Latin American concerns and priorities. . . .

universal system for the protection of human rights can be perceived in the Convention'. In accordance with such an approach, both the Court and the Commission have referred to, and generally followed, the jurisprudence of the European Court and Commission of Human Rights where appropriate.

. . .

This contrasts with the approach of the European Commission and Court which tend to set their standards quite openly by reference to the law in the great majority of European states. Moreover, on matters touching upon public morality (for example, obscenity, blasphemy), where values vary from one European state or group of European states to another, the tendency of the European Court has been to permit particular states a measure of discretion through the use of the 'margin of appreciation' doctrine. The European system has also had to accommodate the differences between common and civil law judicial systems, generally allowing each to operate in their own ways provided that justice can be seen to be done overall.

Given that most of the cases that reach the Inter-American Commission and Court involve gross violations of basic human rights upon which all legal systems and societies would agree, there has yet been little occasion for the application of specifically American standards or for cultural relativism otherwise to become an issue. Nor has the question whether a change in social values has been sufficiently generally acknowledged throughout the region for the Commission or the Court, applying a dynamic approach to interpretation, to recognise a new social standard arisen in practice. It may be anticipated that, as the American system evolves, with the number and percentage of ordinary, as opposed to gross, human rights violations increasing, these kinds of issues will arise for the Inter-American Commission and Court. Certainly, there are varying conceptions of morality and honour and kinds of legal systems in different parts of South and North America.

. . .

In the first fifteen or so years of its history, the Commission made *in loco* visits and country reports the central part of its work, not the examination of individual petitions. Faced with gross violations of human rights by military regimes that would be unlikely to respond to rulings against them of the European kind, the Commission prioritised the need to establish and publicise what was happening and to seek change by negotiation, and possibly by pressure through the General Assembly of the OAS, rather than through adverse ruling in petition cases. Consequently, the Commission focused on visiting states and talking with governments and on the publication of country reports and their presentation to the General Assembly for debate. The Commission's work in this regard parallels that of the UN Commission on Human Rights. On occasions, the Inter-American Commission's reports have acted as a catalyst or had some other beneficial effect. A vivid example was the 1980 report that brought home to people in Argentina the record of their military government on disappeared persons in the late 1970s. Such effect as the Commission's reports have achieved has not been with the backing of the General Assembly of the OAS. Apart from a short period in the late 1970s when pressure from the Carter Government in Washington led the Assembly to discuss the Commission's reports and generally support its work, the noninterventionalist tradition within the OAS has led other states largely to ignore the evidence presented to them, with such criticism as has been mounted in the Assembly being addressed against the Commission by the state that it has dared to attack, rather than by other states against the delinquent state.

While *in loco* visits and country reports remain an important and necessary part of the Commission's work, the consideration of individual petitions has come to play an increasing role in its activities in recent years. This has been prompted by the entry into force of the American Convention in 1979, which introduced the possibility of cases being referred to the Inter-American Court for a final, legally binding decision, and the return to democracy and law and order in South and Central American states since then, which has reduced the number of instances of gross violations of human rights for which *in loco* visits are particularly appropriate.

. . .

TOM FARER, THE RISE OF THE INTER-AMERICAN HUMAN RIGHTS REGIME: NO LONGER A UNICORN, NOT YET AN OX
in David Harris and S. Livingstone (eds.), The Inter-American System of Human Rights (1998), at 32

[The author was a member of the Inter-American Commission on Human Rights from 1976–83 and served as its President from 1980–82.]

Introduction: the birth of a big surprise

. . .

Some six years after creating the Commission and providing it with a vaguely-worded mandate to assist in the defense of human rights, the OAS had given the Commission explicit authority to investigate individual instances of alleged human rights violations. . . . Armed with its new mandate, the Commission could have concentrated on individual cases, futilely but respectably pursuing an endless paper trail of victims' complaints and official denials. . . . Instead, focusing upon the investigation of the facts and the preparation of country reports on the actual conditions that it found, the Commission converted itself into an accusatory agency, a kind of Hemispheric Grand Jury, storming around Latin America to vacuum up evidence of high crimes and misdemeanors and marshaling it into bills of indictment in the form of country reports for delivery to the political organs of the OAS and the court of public opinion.

Western Europe's human rights institutions, the Commission and the Court, also charged governments with violations of human rights. But the violations almost invariably involved actions undertaken openly on the thinly marked border between the legitimate exercise of public authority on behalf of the community and the irreducible claims of individual liberty. The various European governments employing challenged acts no doubt regarded them as useful but hardly as means essential to the preservation of order or the execution of any other important public function. Moreover, both competitive elections and, in most if not all the countries then subject to the regime, constitutional restraints enforced by independent courts broadly limited their ends and means to those generally consistent in fact with internationally recognized human rights. Thus the European human rights regime largely reinforced national restraints on the exercise of executive and legislative power rather than adding on strong additional ones.

Latin American constitutions also contained long lists of protected rights and corresponding checks on government action. But few, if any, countries had effectively independent judiciaries available and committed to enforcing them. Furthermore, on close inspection constitutional restraints were often riddled with specific exceptions and were for the most part subject to derogation in times of emergency. And the region's constitutional courts had shown little zeal for auditing executive branch claims that the required emergency existed and that the particular suspension of guarantees was reasonably necessary to protect public order. Their determined passivity may not have been entirely unconnected to the fact that judges, certainly judges of the courts with powers of constitutional review, came from the same middle and upper classes suffused with anxiety about Leftist threats to the established order of things. Serving in the midst of what luminaries of that order (in the United States no less than in Latin America) declared to be a global Cold War and in ideologically polarized societies, judges would be naturally inclined to concede to governments a very large margin of appreciation about the requirements of domestic security. In actual fact, however, governments rarely tested the full measure of that inclination, since they committed the most flagrant human rights delinquencies secretly or at least behind the often thin veil of official denial.

So although the norms invoked by the inter-American human rights institutions often mirrored those of national constitutions, the conjunction of multiple exceptions with an auto-restrained judiciary and a secretive state made constitutional norms ineffective. In actual fact, therefore, the Commission, unlike its European counterpart, was attempting to impose on governments restraints without domestic parallel. It was trying to do this, moreover, in the face of the conviction held by many regimes and their class supporters that grave violations of human rights were a regrettable but absolutely necessary means, if not for survival altogether, then at least for the restoration of their domestic tranquillity.

. . .

Whither the Commission in a democratic era?

At the end of the 1980s even Central America began to step back from remorseless civil war. Throughout Latin America, then, the grosser human rights violations subsided from the old torrent to a trickle, and elected—if not always liberal—democratic regimes began to seem normal. The end of the Hemispheric state of emergency and the proliferation of credible investigating agencies, some with greater competence and drive than the Commission, provided two reasons for it to consider shifting a *modest* proportion of its human and financial resources to individual cases, which continued to arrive. For as an official institution, it had a role denied to the NGOs, namely building a body of doctrine interpreting the American Declaration and Convention.

As long as governments were simply torturing and maiming, interpretation was hardly necessary. But with governments striving with varying degrees of effort to establish the rule of law, the Commission naturally began to receive more cases from the gray borderland where the state's authority to promote the general interest collides with individual rights. From such governments, moreover, one might expect at least a measure of cooperation with the Commission, substituting for brazen denial open legal defense of their position on questions of fact and law.

Unlike the Buenos Aires Protocol with its broad grant of authority to the Commission, the Convention deals in some detail with individual petition cases and, being modeled on the European Convention, arguably envisions a modestly formal presentation of evidence by petitioner and the accused state. . . .

. . . But with an exiguous staff, numerous cases and a continuing commitment to general reports, the Commission continued to handle cases casually. In doing so, it came under increasing criticism not only from some governments, but from human rights lawyers as well. Like any good lawyers, they wanted to feel that technical competence in the accumulation and presentation of evidence mattered. And they wanted deadlines, so that decisions came predictably and with reasonable dispatch. In addition, they wanted formal precedents that could then be deployed in arguments with governments. And finally, they wanted more than a Commission conclusion in favor of their clients. They wanted injunctions and reparations which they could secure only from the Inter-American Court. And they could not get to that Court until the Commission had finished processing the case and, even then, only if the Commission or the target state decided to invoke the Court's jurisdiction.

. . .

The Commission's seeming indifference to the Court, even reluctance send it business, had two sources . . . [U]ntil the mid-1980s the main inhibitor was continuing emphasis on reports; and thereafter it was in part limited time and resources. Preparation for and the conduct of formal hearings for many cases made huge demands on a staff very poorly equipped to respond, not to mention the demands on Commissioners who functioned as it were in their spare time. Nevertheless, pressured by commentators, lawyers and governments, the Commission has gradually begun to move toward a more case-oriented existence and correspondingly to generate much more business for the Court.

Yet there remains a great need for country reports. Despite the spread of elected governments and great improvement in the condition of human rights, indisputable and grave violations continued to occur in many countries, albeit with less international hue and cry, since once again almost all of the victims are drawn from the only episodically visible and relatively mute lower classes. And given an enduring culture of impunity for public security agencies, weak judicial systems, a tradition of broad executive discretion in the exercise of power and a continuing tendency of elites to dismiss non-governmental human rights activists as 'Leftists,' grave violations of basic rights are likely to continue as a feature of life in many countries. Reports, in part because they bring together many cases of abuse and reveal a pattern of delinquency by public officials, attract far more attention than conclusions in individual cases. In addition, they provide members of the target country and the international community with a far more accurate appreciation of the extent and endemic character of human rights violations. *Therefore they must continue to be the central preoccupation of the Commission and its most important contribution to the mitigation of officially inflicted pain and humiliation in the Western Hemisphere.*

Reports must continue. However, the altered and enhanced but not transformed conditions of life in the Western Hemisphere call for additional dimensions to the Commission's reporting efforts. Beyond its traditional single-country focus, peculiarly appropriate where gross violations are epidemic or a country has undergone what appear to be dramatic changes, the Commission should attempt occasional thematic reports. For instance, it might look cross-nationally at the access of the poor to the civil courts or at the output of justice systems in a number of countries. Equally challenging and important would be reports on economic and social rights. The Commission has construed the single reference to them in the Declaration and Convention as creating two obligations for states. One is to develop a serious plan for mitigating extreme poverty. The other is to begin implementing such a plan giving priority to health and nutrition. Compliance with those minimal obligations is measurable.

Human rights lawyers were not the Commission's only critics. As a kind of peace settled over Latin American societies, democratic governments began lashing out at the one organ of the OAS which had battled with their authoritarian predecessors, battled to create the space in which democracy could grow. This was ironic but not really anomalous. For where in a democratic era is one likely to find greater self righteousness than in the offices of elected leaders? To be elected is to enjoy the Peoples' mandate which, in an age also secular, is as close to heaven's mandate as one can get.

When you accuse an authoritarian government of human rights violations, you arguably accuse only the people who run it. Accuse a democratic one, and you slander the Nation; for what is a nation but the people who comprise it and democratic leaders are their chosen voice. That at least is how some of the newly elected regimes appeared to feel when confronted with adverse Commission rulings.

Two kinds of issues have excited the greatest irritation. One concerns the legality of various sorts of legal immunity coerced from their elected successors by military establishments as they withdrew. In the case of Uruguay, where an electorate threatened with the restoration of military rule had endorsed immunity, the Commission inevitably found that popular majorities could not for any reason deny remedies to the victims of human rights delinquencies, any more than popular majorities could legitimate the denial of due process to or the torture of some despised individual or group. The other issue concerned elections, more particularly the Commission's claim of right to hear and resolve claims that elections had not been conducted fairly. Despite the proliferation of official monitoring missions all over the globe, regimes formed by the winners in contested cases claimed that Commission review constituted an unauthorized interference in their internal affairs, claimed that despite the clear language of the Convention giving to every person a right to 'vote and to be elected in genuine periodic elections, which shall be by universal and equal suffrage and by secret ballot that guarantees the free expression of the will of the voters . . .' In these final years of the Millennium, a time of triumph for liberalism in politics hardly less than economics, elected governments moot projects to discipline the Commission, to clip its jurisdictional wings. Hopefully those projects will come to nothing. For surely it is a little early to conclude either that authoritarian government has forever abandoned the Hemisphere or that elected governments are incapable of terrible acts. What greater irony if, having survived intact the time of night and fog, the Commission were maimed in full daylight by the democracies it struggled to produce.

. . .

2. THE COURT IN ACTION

In the Inter-American system, the Court plays a more restricted and modest role than does its equivalent in the European system. Its governing provisions bear a close relationship to those for the European Court of Human Rights. Hence the following materials illustrate its work through a single decision, to be understood within the framework for the Court's work that was described in the preceding articles by Medina, Harris and Farer.

In the mid-1980s, a cooperative relationship began to evolve between the Commission and Court, commencing with the referral by the Commission of three contentious cases to the Court, each involving instances of disappearances in Honduras. The principal case, *Velásquez Rodríguez*, appears below. It was the first contentious case initiated by an individual that involved systemic state violence, and was one of three cases leading to decisions by the Court on the question of disappearances in Honduras. Outside as well as inside the Inter-American system, it has also proved to be one of the most influential and cited decisions of an international human rights tribunal.

The three cases placed in a judicial setting the same issues that occupied the UN Commission on Human Rights and its Working Group on Disappearances, p. 641, *supra*, and the Inter-American Commission in its function of investigating and reporting on systemic violations. Indeed, one of the striking aspects of the *Velásquez Rodríguez* decision is how effectively it links the individual and systemic aspects of a violation.

After this decision, the Commission started to generate a small but steady flow of cases for the Court.

VELÁSQUEZ RODRÍGUEZ CASE
Inter-American Court of Human Rights, 1988
Ser. C No. 4, 9 Hum. Rts L. J. 212 (1988).

[This case arose out of a period of political turbulence, violence and repression in Honduras. It originated in a petition against Honduras received by the Inter-American Commission on Human Rights in 1981. The thrust of the petition was that Angel Manfredo Velásquez Rodríguez was arrested without warrant in 1981 by members of the National Office of Investigations (DNI) and the G-2 of the Armed Forces. The 'arrest' was a seizure by seven armed men dressed in civilian clothes who abducted him in an unlicensed car. The petition referred to eyewitnesses reporting his later detention, 'harsh interrogation and cruel torture'. Police and security forces continued to deny the arrest and detention. Velásquez had disappeared. The petition alleged that through this conduct, Honduras violated several articles of the American Convention on Human Rights.

In 1986, Velásquez was still missing, and the Commission concluded that the Government of Honduras 'had not offered convincing proof that would allow the Commission to determine that the allegations are not true'. Honduras had recognized the contentious jurisdiction of the Inter-American Court of Human Rights, to which the Commission referred the matter. The Court held closed and open hearings, called witnesses and requested the production of evidence and documents. The statement of facts below is taken from the Court's opinion and consists both of its independent findings and its affirmation of some findings of the Commission.

The Commission presented witnesses to testify whether 'between the years 1981 and 1984 (the period in which Manfredo Velásquez disappeared) there were numerous cases of persons who were kidnapped and who then disappeared, these actions being imputable to the Armed Forces of Honduras and enjoying the acquiescence of the Government of Honduras', and whether in those years there were effective domestic remedies to protect such kidnapped persons. Several witnesses testified that they were kidnapped, imprisoned in clandestine jails and tortured by members of the Armed Forces. Explicit testimony described the severity of the torture—including beatings, electric shocks, hanging, burning, drugs and sexual abuse—to which witnesses had been subjected. Several witnesses indicated how they knew that their captors and torturers were connected with the military. The Court received testimony indicating that 'somewhere between 112 and 130 individuals were disappeared from 1981 to 1984'.

According to testimony, the kidnapping followed a pattern, such as use of cars with tinted glass, with false licence plates and with disguised kidnappers. A witness who was President of the Committee for the Defense of Human Rights in Honduras testified about the existence of a unit in the Armed Forces that carried out the disappearance, giving details about its organization and commanding personnel. A former member of the Armed Forces testified that he had belonged to the battalion carrying out the kidnapping. He confirmed parts of the testimony of witnesses, claiming that he had been told of the kidnapping and later torture and killing of Velásquez, whose body was dismembered and buried in different places. All such testimony was denied by military officers and the Director of Honduran Intelligence.

The Commission also presented evidence showing that from 1981–1984 domestic judicial remedies in Honduras were inadequate to protect human rights. Courts were slow and judges were often ignored by police. Authorities denied detentions. Judges charged with executing the writs of habeas corpus were threatened and on several occasions imprisoned. Law professors and lawyers defending political prisoners were pressured not to act; one of the two lawyers to bring a writ of habeas corpus was arrested. In no case was the writ effective in relation to a disappeared person.

In view of threats against witnesses it had called, the Commission asked the Court to take provisional measures contemplated by the Convention. Soon thereafter, the Commission reported the death of a Honduran summoned by the Court to appear as a witness, killed 'on a public thoroughfare [in the capital city] by a group of armed men who . . . fled in a vehicle'. Four days later the Court was informed of two more assassinations, one victim being a man who had testified before the Court as a witness hostile to the Government. After a public hearing, the Court decided on 'additional provisional measures' requiring Honduras to report within two weeks (1) on measures that it adopted to protect persons connected with the case, (2) on its judicial investigations of threats against such persons, and (3) on its investigations of the assassinations.

The Court's opinion refers to several articles of the American Convention. *Article 4* gives every person 'the right to have his life respected. . . . No one shall be arbitrarily deprived of his life'. *Article 5* provides that no one 'shall be subjected to torture or to cruel, inhuman, or degrading punishment or treatment'. *Article 7* gives every person 'the right to personal liberty and security', prohibits 'arbitrary arrest or imprisonment', and provides for such procedural rights as notification of charges, recourse of the detained person to a competent court, and trial within a reasonable time or release pending trial. There follow excerpts from the opinion. (Other excerpts at p. 212, *supra*, discuss the liability of Honduras for the disappearance, whether the actual abductors were state or nonstate actors.)

[VII]

. . .

123. Because the Commission is accusing the Government of the disappearance of Manfredo *Velásquez*, it, in principle, should bear the burden of proving the facts underlying its petition.

124. The Commission's argument relies upon the proposition that the policy of disappearances, supported or tolerated by the Government, is designed to conceal and destroy evidence of disappearances. When the existence of such a policy or practice has been shown, the disappearance of a particular individual may be proved through circumstantial or indirect evidence or by logical inference. Otherwise, it would be impossible to prove that an individual has been disappeared.

. . .

126. . . . If it can be shown that there was an official practice of disappearances in Honduras, carried out by the Government or at least tolerated by it, and if the disappearance of Manfredo *Velásquez* can be linked to that practice, the Commission's allegations will have been proven to the Court's satisfaction, so long as the evidence presented on both points meets the standard of proof required in cases such as this.

127. The Court must determine what the standards of proof should be in the instant case. Neither the Convention, the Statute of the Court nor its Rules of

Procedure speak to this matter. Nevertheless, international jurisprudence has recognized the power of the courts to weigh the evidence freely, although it has always avoided a rigid rule regarding the amount of proof necessary to support the judgment.

. . .

130. The practice of international and domestic courts shows that direct evidence, whether testimonial or documentary, is not the only type of evidence that may be legitimately considered in reaching a decision. Circumstantial evidence, indicia, and presumptions may be considered, so long as they lead to conclusions consistent with the facts.

131. Circumstantial or presumptive evidence is especially important in allegations of disappearances, because this type of repression is characterized by an attempt to suppress any information about the kidnapping or the whereabouts and fate of the victim.

. . .

134. The international protection of human rights should not be confused with criminal justice. States do not appear before the Court as defendants in a criminal action. The objective of international human rights law is not to punish those individuals who are guilty of violations, but rather to protect the victims and to provide for the reparation of damages resulting from the acts of the States responsible.

135. In contrast to domestic criminal law, in proceedings to determine human rights violations the State cannot rely on the defense that the complainant has failed to present evidence when it cannot be obtained without the State's cooperation.

136. The State controls the means to verify acts occurring within its territory. Although the Commission has investigatory powers, it cannot exercise them within a State's jurisdiction unless it has the cooperation of that State.

. . .

138. The manner in which the Government conducted its defense would have sufficed to prove many of the Commission's allegations by virtue of the principle that the silence of the accused or elusive or ambiguous answers on its part may be interpreted as an acknowledgment of the truth of the allegations, so long as the contrary is not indicated by the record or is not compelled as a matter of law. This result would not hold under criminal law, which does not apply in the instant case . . .

. . .

[IX]

147. The Court now turns to the relevant facts that it finds to have been proven. They are as follows:

    a. During the period 1981 to 1984, 100 to 150 persons disappeared in the Republic of Honduras, and many were never heard from again. . . .

    b. Those disappearances followed a similar pattern. . . .

    c. It was public and notorious knowledge in Honduras that the kidnappings were carried out by military personnel, police or persons acting under their orders. . . .

d. The disappearances were carried out in a systematic manner, regarding which the Court considers the following circumstances particularly relevant:

    i. The victims were usually persons whom Honduran officials considered dangerous to State security. . . . [Omitted paragraphs deal with arms used, details of the kidnappings and interrogations, denials by officials of any knowledge about the disappeared person, and the failure of any investigative committees to produce results.]

e. On September 12, 1981, between 4:30 and 5:00 p.m., several heavily armed men in civilian clothes driving a white Ford without license plates kidnapped Manfredo *Velásquez* from a parking lot in downtown Tegucigalpa. Today, nearly seven years later, he remains disappeared, which creates a reasonable presumption that he is dead. . . .

f. Persons connected with the Armed Forces or under its direction carried out that kidnapping. . . .

g. The kidnapping and disappearance of Manfredo *Velásquez* falls within the systematic practice of disappearances referred to by the facts deemed proved in paragraphs a–d.

. . .

[X]

149. Disappearances are not new in the history of human rights violations. However, their systematic and repeated nature and their use, not only for causing certain individuals to disappear, either briefly or permanently, but also as a means of creating a general state of anguish, insecurity and fear, is a recent phenomenon. Although this practice exists virtually worldwide, it has occurred with exceptional intensity in Latin America in the last few years.

150. The phenomenon of disappearances is a complex form of human rights violation that must be understood and confronted in an integral fashion.

151. The establishment of a Working Group on Enforced or Involuntary Disappearances of the United Nations Commission on Human Rights by Resolution 20(XXXVI) of February 29, 1980, is a clear demonstration of general censure and repudiation of the practice of disappearances. . . . The reports of the rapporteurs or special envoys of the Commission on Human Rights show concern that the practice of disappearances be stopped, the victims reappear and that those responsible be punished.

152. Within the inter-American system, the General Assembly of the Organization of American States (OAS) and the Commission have repeatedly referred to the practice of disappearances and have urged that disappearances be investigated and that the practice be stopped. . . .

153. International practice and doctrine have often categorized disappearances as a crime against humanity, although there is no treaty in force which is applicable to the States Parties to the Convention and which uses this terminology. . . .

. . .

155. The forced disappearance of human beings is a multiple and continuous violation of many rights under the Convention that the States Parties are obligated

to respect and guarantee. The kidnapping of a person is an arbitrary deprivation of liberty, an infringement of a detainee's right to be taken without delay before a judge and to invoke the appropriate procedures to review the legality of the arrest, all in violation of Article 7 of the Convention. . . .

156. Moreover, prolonged isolation and deprivation of communication are in themselves cruel and inhuman treatment, harmful to the psychological and moral integrity of the person and a violation of the right of any detainee to respect for his inherent dignity as a human being. Such treatment, therefore, violates Article 5 of the Convention. . . .

157. The practice of disappearances often involves secret execution without trial, followed by concealment of the body to eliminate any material evidence of the crime and to ensure the impunity of those responsible. This is a flagrant violation of the right to life, recognized in Article 4 of the Convention. . . .

158. The practice of disappearances, in addition to directly violating many provisions of the Convention, such as those noted above, constitutes a radical breach of that treaty in that it implies a crass abandonment of the values which emanate from the concept of human dignity and of the most basic principles of the inter-American system and the Convention. . . .

. . .

[The part of the Court's opinion examining the obligation of a state not only to respect individual rights (such as by not 'disappearing' the government's opponents), but also to ensure free exercise of rights (such as by protecting those expressing political opinions against violence by private, non-governmental actors), appears at p. 212, *supra.*]

[XII]

189. Article 63(1) of the Convention provides:

> If the Court finds that there has been a violation of a right or freedom protected by this Convention, the Court shall rule that the injured party be ensured the enjoyment of his right or freedom that was violated. It shall also rule, if appropriate, that the consequences of the measure or situation that constituted the breach of such rights or freedom be remedied and that fair compensation be paid to the injured party.

Clearly, in the instant case the Court cannot order that the victim be guaranteed the enjoyment of the right or liberty violated. The Court, however, can rule that the consequences of the breach of the rights be remedied and rule that just compensation be paid.

190. During this proceeding, the Commission requested the payment of compensation, but did not offer evidence regarding the amount of damages or the manner of payment. Nor did the parties discuss these matters.

191. The Court believes that the parties can agree on the damages. If an agreement cannot be reached, the Court shall award an amount. The case shall, therefore, remain open for that purpose. The Court reserves the right to approve the agreement and, in the event no agreement is reached, to set the amount and order the manner of payment.

[In the concluding paragraphs, the Court unanimously declared that Honduras violated Articles 4, 5 and 7 of the Convention, all three read in conjunction with Article 1(1); and unanimously decided that Honduras was required to pay fair compensation to the victim's next-of-kin.]

NOTE

Note several aspects of this opinion. (1) The petition was brought against Honduras in 1981. The decision of the Court is dated 1988. (2) The Commission is active in the Court proceedings, arguing on behalf of the individual seeking relief. (3) The proceedings include varied participants such as witnesses and nongovernmental organizations. The Court itself acts as a blend of trial and appellate court.

The *Velásquez Rodríguez* decision was followed by two related judgments of the Inter-American Court of Justice that also involved disappearances in Honduras alleged to be the government's responsibility: the *Godínez* Judgment, (Ser. C) No. 5 (1989), and the *Fairen Garbi and Solis Corrales* Judgment, (Ser. C) No. 6 (1989). The *Godínez* case was substantially similar to *Velásquez Rodríguez* and the Court reached a similar decision. In the *Fairen Garbi* case, the Court concluded that Honduras was not responsible for the disappearances there relevant. As far as was known, neither of the disappeared persons were involved in activities considered dangerous by the government. The Court said that there was insufficient evidence 'to relate the disappearance ... to the governmental *practice* of disappearances. There is no evidence that Honduran authorities had [the disappeared persons] under surveillance or suspicion of being dangerous persons, nor that [they] were arrested or kidnapped in Honduran territory'.

QUESTIONS

1. The facts are contested. What method does the Court employ to resolve them? Does it employ such traditional notions of the law of evidence in systems of national law as burdens of proof (burdens of persuasion) or presumptions? For example:

a. What is the relevance to the Court's finding of Honduran responsibility of the Court's use of terms like (the Honduran) 'practice' or 'policy', or the characterization of disappearances as 'systemic'?

b. What is the significance of the Court's observation that the state 'controls the means to verify acts occurring within its territory'? Is the Court threatening the state with an adverse finding if it fails to make that effort?

2. 'It is wrong to contend that contentious cases before the Court can effectively handle only individual situations and violations, while the Commission must expose structural and systemic violations of human rights through its state reports. The *Velásquez Rodríguez* case shows that the two tasks can be accomplished effectively at the same time. The Court is an adequate alternative to the Commission'. Comment.

3. In relation to the European Convention the argument in favour of having a judge from every state party is twofold: to ensure confidence in the European organs on the part of each state, and to ensure expertise in relation to each state legal system. In relation to the Inter-American system the argument in favour of having only seven judges and commissioners is that their independence is thereby assured. Which approach would you opt for and why?

3. THE COMMISSION AT WORK: COMPLAINTS AND STATE REPORTS ON DEMOCRATIC GOVERNMENT

a. Background on the Human Rights Movement and Contemporary Forms of Democracy

The following materials, as well as the complaints before and state reports of the Commission, develop the theme of human rights, elections, and democratic government that was introduced at pp. 840–853, *supra*, within the discussion of the European human rights system.

COMMENT ON RELATIONSHIPS BETWEEN THE HUMAN RIGHTS MOVEMENT AND DEMOCRATIC GOVERNMENT

This Comment briefly notes some theories or ideologies or historical realizations of democracy that figure in the human rights debates and that underlie arguments about democracy that are based on the human rights instruments. An awareness of what are understood to be indispensable or significant components of a democratic system of government, and of divergent conceptions of democracy, will permit a more probing analysis of the Commission's work.

It is indeed difficult to bypass a discussion of democracy in relation to human rights in the contemporary world. Many will argue that democracy—often an unspecified form or realization thereof that may consist of no more than the essential element of periodic, genuine, contested elections—is now becoming or has indeed become a global norm. Hence, an article in this sub-section is entitled an 'emerging right to democratic governance'.[34] The conception of democracy in much of the ongoing debate concentrates on, and sometimes does not go beyond, the fundamental premise of 'rule by the people' (or related expressions of this premise such as popular sovereignty, or government as expressive of the will of the people) through one or another form of representative government that elections are meant to achieve. Needless to say, the degree to which the contemporary observer detects a significant trend toward democratic governance will depend on the observer's conception of democracy and its essential characteristics.

---

[34] See Franck, p. 900, *infra*. See also Gregory Fox, 'The Right to Political Participation in International Law', 17 Yale J. Int. L. 539 (1992).

Other observers, at least in the context of universal human rights rather than of a regional system like the Inter-American or European, raise questions about the content of this 'emerging right' in terms of ideals and components of democracy other than genuine elections. Contested conceptions today of the nature of democratic government range from (1) the classical democracy of a century ago with limited powers and activity of government and a sharp division between the state and civil society, to (2) the different types of liberal and social democracies of recent decades in which governments assume a larger responsibility for social and economic welfare and are attentive to forms of inequality of wealth, power and opportunity in a society. They range, to employ another example, from (1) a notion of moderate and sporadic political participation by the citizenry primarily through elections to choose between the options offered, to (2) a notion of ongoing and active citizen participation in governance and in the related institutions of civil society.

The debate raises vital issues of the relationship, necessary or contingent, between political democracy and an economic system characterized by private property and a market subject to one or another degree of governmental regulation. Though history has resolved certain ideological issues about democratic government, such as an inclusive franchise that has eliminated past discriminations, the notion of democracy remains sharply contested in a world in which democracy, capitalism, and globalization have for many become linked phenomena or goals, and in which many countries in East Europe, Latin America and elsewhere have moved from authoritarian to 'democratic' regimes.

Constitutions of a particular character have become characteristic of the new democracies, a character that has been captured in the rubric 'constitutionalism' that distinguishes such instruments from, for example, the constitutions of authoritarian states. Constitutionalism itself then becomes complexly related to conceptions of democracy, a relationship stressed in Section A of Chapter 12, *infra*, that describes the horizontal spread among states of liberal constitutions characteristic of Western democracies since the period of decolonization but particularly since the collapse of the Soviet empire. Those readings raise questions both of the adaptability of Western-style constitutionalism to regions and cultures of radically different histories and structures, and of the aspects of constitutionalism apart from elections that might be said to inhere in or be required by democratic government—for example, the separation of powers and particularly judicial independence; the related notion of the Rule of Law; protection of pluralism; and the protection against majority will offered by constitutionally entrenched individual rights and by judicial review of legislative as well as executive action.

In broad terms, one can pose two questions—perhaps two sides of the same question—about the relationships between the human rights movement and democratic governance, questions that have become more vital and pertinent since the end of the Cold War: (1) Do the fundamental norms of the human rights instruments point toward, or indeed require, democratic government? Will observance of those norms inevitably lead to such government, or are they consistent with other forms of government—say, a monarchy, theocracy, military junta, or ideology requiring one ruling and guiding party? (2) Does political democracy require the protection and observance of the fundamental norms of the human rights movement—for example, physical security of citizens, due process, equal protection, freedoms of speech and association? Can democratic government be realized without that full array of norms? Are current understandings of the basic human rights declared in the major instruments and of democracy simply two sides of the same coin?

Such questions rest on premises that must be clarified before one can attempt answers. Those premises involve both the conception of democracy and the conception of fundamental human rights norms. To use a graphic example, the norms include those recognized in the International Covenant on Economic, Social and Cultural Rights. But much of the discussion about human rights in relation to democracy stresses or considers only the fundamental civil and political rights noted in the preceding paragraph. From the perspective of the human rights movement and of much contemporary theory of democracy, the relationships between civil/political rights and economic/social rights must inform discussion about the contemporary practice and ideal of democratic government.

———

The two readings in this sub-section develop and clarify some aspects of the preceding discussion. Steiner examines theories of democratic participation that could inform the provisions of the basic human rights documents on political participation and democracy, and underscores the fundamental choices about such participation that those provisions leave open. Written four years later, after the collapse of the Soviet Union had started, and in the midst of a trend from authoritarian government to electoral democracy in a number of developing countries, Franck's article argues on the basis of both human rights texts and state practice for an emerging norm of democratic governance.

HENRY STEINER, POLITICAL PARTICIPATION AS A HUMAN RIGHT
1 Harv. Y'bk Int. L. 77 (1988), at 78

The article . . . examines the norms expressing this right [to political participation] that are included in two principal international instruments of universal scope: the Universal Declaration of Human Rights, and the International Covenant on Civil and Political Rights. . . . My discussion emphasizes two different ways in which the international norms express citizens' right to political participation: the relatively vague and abstract right to take part in the conduct of public affairs or government, and the relatively specific right to vote in elections. It builds upon that distinction to explore different modes of political participation. . . .

. . .

II. The Texts: Their Making and Interpretation

. . .

What emerged from the periods of drafting and debates were norms that expressed an important ideal of political participation. But they gave little indication of the different ways of institutionalizing that ideal. It cannot have been by chance that their language was sufficiently confined—with respect to the 'elections' clause—and sufficiently abstract and porous—with respect to the 'take part' clause—to permit democratic and nondemocratic states to assert that they satisfied the norms' demands. More specific norms would have put at risk the goal of achieving broad support for the human rights instruments as a whole.

Article 25 of the International Covenant, the principal treaty declaring a right to political participation, states:

> Every citizen shall have the right and the opportunity, without . . . unreasonable restrictions:
>
> (a) To take part in the conduct of public affairs, directly or through freely chosen representatives;
> (b) To vote and to be elected at genuine periodic elections which shall be by universal and equal suffrage and shall be held by secret ballot, guaranteeing the free expression of the will of the electors. . . .

Alone among the International Covenant's provisions, this article restricts a right to citizens. It distinguishes between direct and representative participation, but validates both. The article does not indicate how citizens are to 'take part in the conduct of public affairs', other than by identifying periodic and 'genuine' elections as an ingredient of the right to participate.

. . .

The provisions of Article 25 are unusual among human rights norms in that they do more than declare a right. They articulate a political ideal inspiring that right. Though not invoking a particular political tradition such as democracy, Article 25 affirms that the popular vote is meant to guarantee 'the free expression of the will of the electors'.

The Universal Declaration, an inspiration and important model for the International Covenant and similar in content to it, contains the analogous provision in its Article 21:

> (1) Everyone has the right to take part in the government of his country, directly or through freely chosen representatives. . . .
> (3) The will of the people shall be the basis of the authority of government; this will shall be expressed in periodic and genuine elections which shall be by universal and equal suffrage and shall be held by secret vote or by equivalent free voting procedures.

This earlier instrument, influenced to a greater degree than the International Covenant by the tradition of liberal democracy, gives more emphasis to the role of the 'will of the people' as the 'basis of the authority of government'. But like the International Covenant, Article 21 neither employs the term 'democracy', nor makes explicit whether plural political parties and contested elections must be permitted.

The influence of the Universal Declaration on the International Covenant extends to the internal structure of Article 25. It too begins with, and thereby gives an apparent priority and emphasis to, the 'take part' clause, and continues with the 'elections' clause . . . . Generally I shall use the two clauses to refer, respectively, to non-electoral and electoral (voting) participation in political processes.

. . .

Notwithstanding its mixed ancestry and ambiguities, the Covenant gives some internal guidance for an understanding of Article 25. In view of their essential role in most political activities, the expressive rights to free speech, press, assembly and association must in some way inform any theory of participation. Their prominence in the International Covenant reminds us that Article 25 should not be approached as an isolated provision, detached from the larger structure of rights in the Covenant. That larger structure here suggests that the 'take part' and 'elections' clauses assume some degree of public political debate and of citizens' participation in political groups expressing their beliefs or interests.

. . .

III. Treaty Provisions in Relation to Contemporary Debate About Participation in the Liberal Democracies

An attempt to formulate a universal norm about political participation confronts mutually antagonistic theories and practices among the liberal democracies, communist states, military dictatorships and a range of third world governments. Consensus over a norm limited to West European, North American and Commonwealth democracies should then be easier to achieve. Basic obstacles to agreement about reasonably specific provisions fall away when, for example, none of the proposed signatories is a one-party state or imposes strict censorship.

Even among the democracies, however, a norm about political participation must leave significant matters open. To gain adoption, a regional norm embracing West European and North American countries would have to be understood as consistent with distinct theories of participation informing these countries' political systems. It would have to accommodate important variations in forms of government and in related practices institutionalizing political participation.

. . .

A. *Political participation in the large: competing conceptions*

All regimes, including over time the most repressive, permit or encourage or even require some institutionalized modes of political participation. Reasons additional to the need to be informed of popular discontent argue for a government's inviting political participation. The government may thereby enlist popular support and gain international as well as domestic legitimacy. It may reduce the risks accompanying efforts to rule exclusively by force.

In nondemocratic societies, such participation will reach beyond the ruling elite, however defined, to include broader elements of the population. It may stop shy even of controlled elections, and involve no more than informal consultations or legally approved ways to express grievances. It may be relatively self-generated or mobilized and manipulated, relatively genuine and effectual or ceremonial and insubstantial. Like the forms of popular political participation in all societies, it will represent some combination of institutionalized ideals, practical functions, public ritual, and legitimating myth.

Liberal democracies, then, are not distinctive in institutionalizing modes of political participation, but the modes which they stress are. The traditional negative rights and expressive rights of liberalism protect the environment of political pluralism. Political processes culminating in a popular and contested election are meant to yield a representative legislature, and a chief executive or government elected directly (presidential system) or elected indirectly by such legislature (parliamentary system).

Elections serve a variety of purposes for both the voters and the polity. So do the less common forms of citizens' political activities in liberal societies. No one ideal of political participation succeeds in rationalizing these diverse purposes. Therefore, no single scale can measure political participation comparatively. . . . Scales calibrated to different values would weigh different phenomena, or give varying weights to phenomena like elections. . . .

. . . [I]t is useful to concentrate on the divide between theories in which elections constitute a near-sufficient form of political participation for the great majority of the people, and theories urging more. Within this article's framework, that divide could be expressed in terms of the 'elections' clause and 'take part' clause of the international norms. While recognizing that elections are indispensable, the more demanding theories argue for a continuing rather than episodic experience of participation, for a broad conception of a right to 'take part' in the conduct of public affairs. They involve varied and flexible modes of non-electoral participation that supplement rather than substitute for voting. This dispute about the sufficiency of electoral democracy reflects deeper disagreement over the ends of participation. . . .

Permeating these writings is a distinction between notions of participation as an instrumental and as an inherent good. . . . Like most such contrasts, it wrenches apart elements in the psychology and practice of political participation that may usefully complement each other and comfortably coexist for most citizens. But understanding one or the other as a dominant justification for political participation helps to elucidate some underlying themes.

Emphasis on participation's instrumental character suggests that the function of political participation must be to influence public policy, to gain governmental recognition of individual or group interests. The value of participation lies in its instrumental efficacy. It is a means toward a goal rather than an end in itself. Elections are the paramount means for influencing governmental action. They give the electorate some degree of control over and thereby impose some degree of responsibility on those exercising power. Of all modes of political participation, elections enlist the largest number of citizens, including the largest number of those toward the bottom of the socio-economic ladder.

Other more demanding political activities, engaged in by relatively small percentages of the population, are oriented toward and culminate in elections: active membership in a political party, raising campaign funds, soliciting votes for a candidate. They form part of a complex electoral process which is itself part of the larger political process. Some activities which continue between election campaigns require greater devotion from their participants and longer-run planning—for example, the work of the interest groups which have become endemic to liberal societies. Lobbying and other strategies of those groups supplement the electoral process.

Within this prevalent justification for political participation—influencing public policy and governmental action—citizens' votes play a role as vital as it is confined. Theorists emphasize that, in modern mass society, elections cannot convey with any clarity to elected officials the preferences of citizens which they are meant to take into account . . . . Contested elections mean that the people have a choice, but political elites rather than the people decide what that choice is between.

. . .

Despite the indirect and limited control that it exercises, electoral participation does establish boundaries for governmental action. It rules out policies that meet wide opposition, at least if groups with a political voice are among that opposition. Elections thereby serve a vital protective function, one also served by courts in societies where judicial review vindicates constitutional norms. By periodically subjecting elected officials to the approval of the electorate, they help to arrest governmental violations of widely valued rights, or to counter threats to the interests of sufficiently important groups among the electorate. . . .

Other theorists, faulting a solely functional approach to political participation, hold that participation constitutes an inherent as well as an instrumental good. They do not claim that influencing governmental policies and checking governmental abuses are mythical or trivial consequences of the vote. Rather, they argue that elections and political activities closely related to the electoral process are indispensable, but themselves insufficient to realize the democratic ideal of the citizenry's continuing involvement in public life. Within the framework of the international norms on participation, these theorists could be said to elaborate the 'take part' clause.

Such theorists criticize exclusively instrumental views of participation because of their tendency to value only liberal premises of individualism, of the hegemony of private rights, and of limited government whose primary function is to honor those rights. A nearly exclusive reliance on elections heightens the sense of powerlessness of the many to act other than passively by reacting to choices formulated by others. Most citizens, at least those who even choose to vote, treat that act as meeting their full responsibility for participating in public affairs. Voting satisfies that responsibility in an undemanding and individualistic way without need for collegial discussion or group action. Reducing the participation of most citizens to the periodic vote denies them the benefits of a continuing experience of involvement in public life, of 'taking part' in the conduct of public affairs.

Recognizing the impossibility of extensive participation in the central government of modern states, theorists of direct or strong or participatory democracy emphasize other contexts. Inevitably they advocate decentralization of authority, and direct attention toward local governments of a size and functions more conducive to continuing and active public involvement. That participation can, and in many states now does, take various forms: citizen representation on governmental boards, public meetings and discussions, formally structured relationships between the managers of public enterprises and their consumers or the general citizenry, more extensive functions of city government responsive to citizens' needs.

In effect, these theorists urge the further development of established trends in the legislation of many liberal democracies increasing citizen participation in local government units, ranging from school or zoning boards and consumer protection agencies to environmental agencies. The character of the participation becomes vital. Active involvement in a neighborhood group addressing local concerns would be favored over a passive dues-paying membership in a political party or interest group.

Such proposals reach beyond the involvement of citizens in local government. They urge active participation in the formulation of policies of nongovernmental institutions like churches or clubs. That is, they challenge the traditional distinction between public and private in the organization of social life. All institutions which exert significant social influence are in that sense political and public. The conception of political participation therefore expands to embrace activities in a broad range of institutional settings. . . . .

Theorists of direct and strong democracy apply these arguments with particular force to greater participation of workers in union government and in decision-making in the workplace. . . .

The purposes of this extensive popular involvement in an enlarged domain of public life are at once greater self-government and self-realization. The two are interrelated. By taking responsibility for public life and committing their personal resources to it, citizens experience differently their relationship to society. Through increased participation in the institutions affecting their lives, they develop a sense of their worth and significance. That is, the benefits of participation are at once material and psychological. More citizens will feel empowered to act rather than only react. This heightened sense of responsibility and competence strengthens an ethic of civic virtue which points toward participation for reasons additional to the advancement of self-interest. The inherent good of political participation stems from this possibility of self-realization through development of the social self as a member of the polity.

B. Electoral systems: their range and effects

. . .

Elections may offer relatively accessible or relatively closed avenues, real or sham avenues, toward the people's participation in governance. The factors determining which of these avenues is opened by a given country's electoral system largely escape consideration or regulation by the international norms. . . .

Article 25 of the International Covenant and Article 21 of the Universal Declaration require periodic and genuine elections. . . . [T]he international norms leave to the states decisions which carry important consequences for the quality of participation and the distribution of political power.

Consider the alternative systems for election of a legislature: proportional representation ('PR' system), under which the legislature is divided among parties according to the percentage vote received by each party list in the popular election; and single-member constituencies, in which the winner in an electoral district, the first past the post, takes all ('district' system). A choice between these systems or among their many variations will not be determined by the logic of a broadly shared theory of representation, participation or democracy. No such choice will be detached from practical politics.

In a given context, it will generally be clear which groups will benefit from a proposed change in an electoral system. It is not, for example, surprising that suggestions in the United Kingdom for a form of PR come from the smaller parties that have been underrepresented by the district system. On the other hand, PR's structural problems, namely the party fragmentation often caused by PR and the related politics of coalition governments that may give disproportionate strength to small parties, have led to proposals in countries like Israel for significant modifications.

Electoral systems, including the nominating or selection processes through which parties' candidates are chosen, thus both reflect and mold political power. Each system will favour some interests at the expense of others by defining the avenues and strategies through which political power must be gained. Electoral participation can then be arranged consistently with human rights norms to yield many different arrangements of power.

. . .

. . . [H]uman rights law offers no guidelines for the selection of an electoral system in a given political and socio-economic context, no theory of broad or fair electoral participation or access which might influence the contextual choice by a state among the many possibilities. By its terms and in view of the debates during its drafting period, the 'elections' clause remains neutral about these choices.

C. Elections as the paramount mode of political participation in liberal democracies

. . .

The question here considered is not then *why* Article 25 of the International Covenant specifies elections, but why it specifies *only* elections and leaves the 'take part' clause suggestive and unelaborated. An answer to that question lies in part in the conceptual structure of the human rights instruments and in ideological premises to liberal society. Those instruments impose on governments, not on individuals or nongovernmental institutions, most of the duties that correspond to the individual rights which they declare. Their requirements address principally state action: respect by government for individuals' integrity, governmental protection of individuals against lawless behavior, provision of fair trials, equal protection in the making and enforcement of law. This observation holds for the right to political participation as well. A government's correlative duty requires it to permit, foster or arrange for such participation.

In liberal democracies, most political participation stems from the initiatives of individuals or of institutions that are not formally part of government. Consider, for example, the International Covenant's declaration of rights to free speech and association, rights related to the electoral process. Under the traditional under-standings of liberal democratic theory, the correlative duties of government do not obligate it to create the institutional frameworks for political debate and action, or to assure all groups of equal ability to propagate their views. Rather, those trad-itional understandings require governments to protect citizens in their political organizations and activities: forming political parties, mobilizing interest groups, soliciting campaign funds, petitioning and demonstrating, campaigning for votes, establishing associations to monitor local government, lobbying.

Such governmental duties of tolerance and equal protection for all political activities could be viewed as a minimum, essential elaboration of the 'take part' clause. They respond to the liberal commitment to guarantee citizens their political and legal equality. . . . Choices about types and degrees of participation may depend on citizens' economic resources and social status. But it is not government's responsibility to alleviate that dependence, to open paths to political participation which lack of funds or education or status would otherwise block.

Emphasis upon a right to vote, without elaboration of companion rights to other ways of taking part in public affairs, therefore fits traditional liberal concep-tions of public and private spheres of competence. . . . Limiting governmental duty to what only governments can do, the construction of an electoral system, leaves the rest of the participatory framework to private initiative. Although Article 25 imposes no such limitation on governmental action, neither does it impose specific obligations other than the conduct of elections.

These understandings do not, however, constitute the whole of the tradition of liberal democracy. Changing ideologies and practices—those associated with the classical and contemporary theorists of direct, strong and participatory democracy—have blurred older lines between private and public spheres. Many states no longer treat the establishment of electoral machinery and the protection of citizens' political speech and association as the outer boundary of a government's duty to honor citizens' right to participate. Governmental functions in liberal democracies have expanded in ways that heighten popular participation. . . .

[Discussion of regulation of political parties, primaries, campaign funding and access to media; of devolution and consultative arrangements; and of worker representation and related matters is omitted.]

Such developing involvement of government in the institutionalization of polit-ical participation within and outside electoral processes stems from a theory which my prior discussion of liberal democracy has characterized as participatory and strong rather than representative and thin. . . . That theory is, however, more com-plex and contentious than one which aims only at justifying elections. Difficulties lie not only in its formulation but also in assessing compliance with an inter-national norm embodying it. Suppose, for example, that such theory were under-stood to inform the 'take part' clause of Article 25, and thereby to give coherent direction to its elaboration. Problems would arise in reaching a judgment whether a government had satisfied its duty to enact legislation extending opportunities for citizens—for all citizens, powerful and powerless—to 'take part in the conduct of public affairs'.

As generally understood, the 'elections' clause poses no comparable difficulty. A government's violation of that clause, like torture or mock trials, is relatively easy to determine. Elections either take place or they don't; they are or are not contested; fact finders can make judgments about the integrity of the casting and counting of ballots; those elected do or do not take and hold office.[35] The expression 'genuine elections' in the human rights instruments is generally understood to cover these formal, even measurable criteria. By meeting those criteria elections are understood to comply with the human rights norms.

One can imagine the use of a more complex criterion than procedural correctness to determine whether an election satisfies Article 25—for example, the criterion whether it constitutes, in the article's language, the 'free expression of the will of the electors'. That phrase, if interpreted to require more than a non-coerced and secret ballot, could make relevant those considerations which a concentration on the formal integrity of an electoral process enables one to ignore: the distribution of political and economic power, its effect on differential access of classes and ethnic groups to the electoral process and political power, the obstacles to greater access, the power of elected officials relative to other centers of power in the society. What escapes analysis in the contemporary understanding of international norms on political participation is the quality and significance of electoral participation itself.

. . .

V. Political Participation as a Programmatic Right

. . . Do the human rights norms about participation express any ideal common to diverse nations? Are they more than indeterminate prescriptions which, in a fractious world, were fated or even meant to be understood in dramatically different ways? Do they serve any useful purpose?

The answers which I propose turn on the suggestion that the right to political participation be viewed as a programmatic right, one responsive to a shared ideal but to be realized progressively over time in different ways in different contexts through invention and planning that will often have a programmatic character. . . .

At first look, political participation falls within the . . . immediately effective category of international human rights. It figures in the International Covenant as

---

[35] Farer, 'Human Rights and Human Wrongs: Is the Liberal Model Sufficient?', 7 Hum. Rts. Q. 189 (1985). Farer, a former Chairman of the Inter-American Commission on Human Rights, comments on a report of the Commission on Colombia, prepared during his tenure. He criticizes the Commission for not attempting 'to peer behind the form of party competition to determine whether . . . the right to participate in government was inhibited' by such factors as limited access to the media by left-wing parties, and an agreement between leaders of the two major parties 'to keep certain potentially popular programs off the political agenda' (at 199).

Farer observes that nothing in the text of the governing convention (the American Convention on Human Rights) 'compels [or] precludes deep analysis of the political process as a condition for assessing compliance with the right to participate'. He points to the deep liberal assumption informing such inquiries of human rights groups 'that in a state where associational rights are reasonably well protected, the right of political participation is realized in all cases where formal political power coincides with electoral achievement. As long as the franchise is not arbitrarily restricted and the ballots are accurately counted, traditional liberal criteria are satisfied'.

a right so fundamental that the realization of many others depends upon it. Nothing in Article 25 or in other text of the Covenant justifies a distinction between the clarity or immediacy of a state's duties under that article and, say, its duty to refrain from torture. Citizens of a party to the Covenant would have a valid claim under international law if their government had seized power and abolished elections.

Nonetheless, I argue that the right to political participation can be better understood as sharing the programmatic character of many economic and social rights. So understood, it nourishes a vital ideal and serves important purposes. I mean, to be sure, a programmatic right of a distinct character from the typical economic rights. Moreover, my characterization applies to the 'take part' clause of the international norms rather than to the 'elections' clause. . . .

. . .

The clearer if still open-textured character of the 'elections' clause, together with the programmatic character of the 'take part' clause, nourish the argument that Article 25 now expresses some 'positive law', but also contains an aspirational or hortatory element which distinguishes it from most provisions of the International Covenant. The aspirations that it expresses are of course shaped by the different strands of political theory and the different national practices with which the world is familiar. But this rich historical deposit of ideas and practices cannot exhaust the ways of understanding or institutionalizing an ideal of political participation.

. . .

Although the practice of participation may be severely suppressed in a given state, the norm stands as an invitation to the disenfranchised or repressed to draw on the example of other societies where it is better appreciated. Its recognition in national and universal instruments legitimates inquiry and may spur protest. Dormant or imprisoned within a hostile environment—as lay dormant for many decades the ideal of equality expressed in the Equal Protection Clause of the Fourteenth Amendment of the United States Constitution—the norm retains its subversive potential.

. . .

. . . Fresh understandings and different institutionalizations of the right in different cultural and political contexts may reveal what an increasing number of states believe to be a necessary minimum of political participation for all states. That minimum should never require less of a government than provision for meaningful exercise of choice by citizens in some form of electoral process permitting active debate on a broad if not unlimited range of issues. But it could require much more.

THOMAS FRANCK, THE EMERGING RIGHT TO DEMOCRATIC GOVERNANCE
86 Am. J. Int. L. 46 (1992), at 53

[Franck refers to two notions: governments derive their just powers from consent of the governed, and the international legitimacy of a state needs to be acknowledged by 'mankind'. These two notions form a 'radical vision' which, he contends, 'is rapidly becoming, in our time, a normative rule of the international system'. We see the 'emergence of a community expectation' that 'those who seek the validation of their empowerment patently govern with the consent of the governed. Democracy, thus, is on the way to becoming a global entitlement, one that will be increasingly promoted and protected by collective international process'.

This 'democratic entitlement' is gradually being transformed 'from moral prescription to international legal obligation'. In support of this claim, 'data will be marshaled from three related generations of rule making and implementation.]

. . . The oldest and most highly developed is that subset of democratic norms which emerged under the heading of 'self-determination'. The second subset—freedom of expression—developed as part of the exponential growth of human rights since the mid-1950s and focuses on maintaining an open market-place of ideas. The third and newest subset seeks to establish, define and monitor a right to free and open elections.

These three subsets somewhat overlap, both chronologically and normatively. Collectively, they do not necessarily penetrate every nook and cranny of democratic theory. For example, the three subsets do not yet address normatively the thorny issue of the right of a disaffected portion of an independent state to secede; nor, as we shall see, is it conceptually or strategically helpful—at least at this stage of its evolution—to treat the democratic entitlement as inextricably linked to the claim of minorities to secession. Still, these three increasingly normative subsets are large building stones, gradually reinforcing each other and assuming the shape of a coherent normative edifice. . . .

[The author interprets the right to self-determination—as expressed in the UN Charter, several General Assembly resolutions and declarations, and Article 1 of the ICCPR and ICESCR; and as developed by state practice—to refer to the right of citizens of all nations to determine their collective political status through democratic means. 'The right now entitles peoples in all states to free, fair and open participation in the democratic process of governance freely chosen by each state'.

Franck then refers to the right of free political expression, and (his third strand) 'the emerging normative entitlement of a participatory *electoral* process' which, despite its infancy, is 'rapidly evolving toward that determinacy which is essential to being perceived as legitimate'. He draws on Article 21 of the UDHR and Article 25 of the ICCPR, and discusses the evolution in the UN and in regional systems such as the European and the OAS of insistence on a state's duty to promote representative democracy, primarily through elections.

Franck notes that this 'evolution of textual determinacy with respect to the electoral entitlement is a relatively recent development', and traces the recent trend toward election monitoring by the UN, by regional organizations, by states, and by NGOs. He stresses, however, that problems abound about the degree to which the international community can insist on standards that involve concrete forms of intervention, given the residual force of notions like domestic jurisdiction in Charter Article 2(7).]

. . . To proclaim a general right to free elections is less intrusive than monitoring any particular election in an independent state. Effective monitoring is even more intrusive than the mere observation of balloting. And collective action to compel states to adhere to a standard is the most intrusive of all. Thus, the conflict of principles needs to be recognized, made explicit, and reconciled to the general satisfaction of the large preponderance of states before the democratic entitlement's global legitimacy is demonstrated by real, as opposed to formulaic, coherence. That will require action to meet the practical concerns of states that still regard the nonintervention principle as of overriding importance to their national well-being.

Also unclear is the extent to which the various parts of the democratic entitlement can yet claim the legitimacy that derives from 'treating like cases alike'. Are virtually all states, for example, ready to have their elections monitored by a credible global process? This and other issues need to be examined in detail before the democratic entitlement can be said to have achieved universal coherence.

A bright line links the three components of the democratic entitlement. The rules, and the processes for realizing self-determination, freedom of expression and electoral rights, have much in common and evidently aim at achieving a coherent purpose: creating the opportunity for all persons to assume responsibility for shaping the kind of civil society in which they live and work. There is a large normative canon for promoting that objective: the UN Charter, the Universal Declaration of Human Rights, the International Covenant on Civil and Political Rights, the International Convention on the Elimination of All Forms of Racial Discrimination, the International Convention on the Suppression and Punishment of the Crime of Apartheid, the Declaration on the Elimination of All Forms of Intolerance and of Discrimination Based on Religion or Belief, and the Convention on the Elimination of All Forms of Discrimination against Women. These universally based rights are supplemented by regional instruments such as the European Convention for the Protection of Human Rights and Fundamental Freedoms, the American Convention on Human Rights, the African Charter on Human and Peoples' Rights, the Copenhagen Document and the Paris Charter.

Each of these instruments recognizes related specific entitlements as accruing to individual citizens. These constitute internationally mandated restraints on governments. As we have seen, they embody rights of free and equal participation in governance, a cluster within which electoral rights are a consistent and probably necessary segment. The result is a net of participatory entitlements. The various texts speak of similar goals and deploy, for the most part, a similar range of processes for monitoring compliance, several of which have already become common usage in connection with the democratic entitlement. One can convincingly argue that states which deny their citizens the right to free and open elections are violating a rule that is fast becoming an integral part of the elaborately woven human rights fabric. Thus, the democratic entitlement has acquired a degree of legitimacy by its association with a far broader panoply of laws pertaining to the rights of persons vis-à-vis their governments.

. . .

There are . . . no legal impediments to institutionalizing voluntary international election monitoring as one way to give effect to the emerging right of all peoples to free and open electoral democracy, but this is not to say that states as yet have a *duty* to submit their elections to international validation . . . .

[Franck then relates the democratic entitlement to the central concern of the UN (as evidenced by the reversal of Iraq's attack on Kuwait) in stopping aggression and maintaining peace.]

If that principle indeed stands at the apex of the global normative system, the democratic governance of states must be recognized as a necessary, although certainly not a sufficient, means to that end. Peace is the consequence of many circumstances: economic well-being, security, and the unimpeded movement of persons, ideas and goods. States' nonaggressiveness, however, depends fundamentally on domestic democracy. Although the argument is not entirely conclusive, historians have emphasized that, in the past 150 years, 'no liberal democracies have ever fought against each other'. It has been argued persuasively that 'a democratic society operating under a market economy has a strong predisposition towards peace'. This stands to reason: a society that makes its decisions democratically and openly will be reluctant to engage its members' lives and treasure in causes espoused by leaders deluded by fantasies of grievance or grandeur.

. . .

Thus, it appears with increasing clarity, in normative text and practice, that compliance with the norms prohibiting war making is inextricably linked to observance of human rights and the democratic entitlement. . . . A distinction needs to be noted here. As we have observed, some governments have argued that the international community's jurisdiction to intervene in the domestic affairs of states to secure compliance with the democratic entitlement is (or should be) limited to cases where its violation has given rise to breaches of the peace. Others have disagreed, claiming that the jurisdiction to intervene is also based on broader human rights law, which authorizes various intrusive forms of monitoring and even envisages sanctions against gross violators. One can prefer this latter view, while still agreeing that the democratic entitlement does have a connection to the United Nations' 'peace' role, that the *legitimacy* of any collective international intervention to support a democratic entitlement is augmented by the entitlement's intimate link to peace. The substance of that link, however, is not merely the role of democracy in *making* or *restoring* peace after conflict has arisen but also—indeed preeminently—its role in *maintaining* peace and *preventing* conflict.

. . .

The democratic entitlement's newness and recent rapid evolution make it understandable that important problems remain. We have considered these primarily under the rubric of coherence, indicating that this entitlement is not yet entirely coherent. The key to solving these residual problems is: (1) that the older democracies should be among the first to volunteer to be monitored in the hope that this will lead the way to near-universal voluntary compliance, thus gradually transforming a sovereign option into a customary legal obligation; (2) that a credible international monitoring service should be established with clearly defined parameters and procedures covering all aspects of voting, from the time an election is called until the newly elected take office; (3) that each nation's duty to be monitored should be linked to a commensurate right to nonintervention by states acting unilaterally; and (4) that legitimate governments should be assured of protection from overthrow by totalitarian forces through concerted systemic action after—and only the community has recognized that such an exigency has arisen. In the longer term, compliance with the democratic entitlement should also be linked to a right of representation in international organs, to international fiscal, trade and development benefits, and to the protection of UN and regional collective security measures.

Both textually and in practice, the international system is moving toward a clearly designated democratic entitlement, with national governance validated by international standards and systematic monitoring of compliance. The task is to perfect what has been so wondrously begun.

b. The Commission, Political Participation and Democracy

Until the late 1980s the Inter-American Commission, like its UN counterparts, had rarely grappled with issues relating directly to the right to political participation. The following statement, taken from the Inter-American Commission's Annual Report for 1971, p. 35, illustrates the pre-occupation at that time with military dictatorships rather than the finer points of democratic theory.

> . . . [W]ith each passing day, more and more people in this part of the world are denied the opportunity to take part in the affairs of the governments of the states in which they live. Terrorism and guerrilla action have led to de facto governments in a number of states, where the activities of political parties have been suspended . . . and elections have been postponed. Thus, fundamental human rights can no longer be exercised . . . [T]his Commission considers it to be its duty to point out that . . . cultural development is not furthered by the people's belief that they will be better off by turning away from politics, political parties, politicians, and political institutions and practices. . . .

By the late 1980s, however, the world had changed. Democratic governments had been established or restored in many Latin American countries, while in

Europe the Berlin Wall had fallen and communism was in its death throes. These developments created a climate that was more conducive to the elaboration of international legal norms relating to democracy. A group of cases from Mexico on elections that appear below provided the Commission with an important opportunity to elucidate through its Reports some fundamental notions about democracy. As background for these Reports of the Commission, the section begins with a review of references to democracy in the basic Inter-American documents.

COMMENT ON PROVISIONS ON DEMOCRACY IN INTER-AMERICAN DOCUMENTS

This Comment describes provisions that refer to democracy in the OAS Charter, a Protocol thereto, the American Declaration and the American Convention.[36]

The Charter is distinctive among comparable instruments in the attention that it gives to democratic theory and practice. Its Preamble declares that 'representative democracy is an indispensable condition for the stability, peace and development of the region'. Article 2(b) states that one of the 'essential purposes' of the OAS is '[t]o promote and consolidate representative democracy. . . .'. Article 3(d) affirms the 'principle' that the 'solidarity of the American States and the high aims which are sought through it require the political organization of those States on the basis of the effective exercise of representative democracy'.

A 1992 Protocol of Washington amended the Charter to provide in a new Article 9 that an OAS member 'whose democratically constituted government has been overthrown by force may be suspended from the exercise of the right to participate in the sessions of' any organs of the OAS, including the General Assembly and the IACHR.

The 1948 American Declaration of the Rights and Duties of Man declares in Article 20 that every person has a right to 'participate in the government of his country', and spells out some requirements of voting and elections. Article 32 converts the right to vote into a 'duty of every person to vote in the popular elections of the country of which he is a national, when he is legally capable of doing so'. Article 28 states: 'The rights of man are limited by the rights of others, by the security of all, and by the just demands of the general welfare and the advancement of democracy'.

The American Convention itself contains strong affirmations of democracy. Its Preamble declares the intention of the states parties 'to consolidate in this hemisphere, within the framework of democratic institutions, a system of personal liberty and social justice based on respect for the essential rights of man'. Article 23, close in wording to Article 21 of the UDHR and Article 25 of the ICCPR, does

---

[36] This Comment draws on a section of a seminar paper at Harvard Law School by A. James Vázquez-Azpiri, 'The Determinacy of the Democratic Entitlement in the Inter-American System', 3 May 1995.

not employ the term 'democracy' in its statement of the right to political participation. Citizens enjoy the right under para. 1:

a.   to take part in the conduct of public affairs, directly or through freely chosen representatives;
b.   to vote and to be elected in genuine periodic elections, which shall be by universal and equal suffrage and by secret ballot that guarantees the free expression of the will of the voters. . . .

This provision is made non-derogable 'in time of war, public danger, or other emergency' by Article 27. Contrast the analogous Article 25 of the ICCPR, which does not figure in the list of non-derogable provisions in that instrument that is set forth in ICCPR Article 4.

Article 29(c) of the Convention, a provision dealing with interpretation of the instrument, provides that no Convention provision shall be interpreted as precluding other rights that are 'derived from representative democracy as a form of government'.

FINAL REPORT ON CASES 9768, 9780 AND 9828 OF MEXICO
Annual Report of the Inter-American Commission on Human Rights 1989–90 (1990), at 98

[These cases before the Commission involved electoral processes in two Mexican states in 1985–86. The petitioners belonged to the National Action Party (PAN). They claimed that members of the ruling Institutional Revolutionary Party (PRI) committed fraud in the elections, including forgeries of voter rolls, cancellation of polling place, stuffing of ballot boxes, and the use of government-controlled police and the military on election day. As a consequence, petitioners alleged violations of their free exercise of political rights set forth in Article 23 of the American Convention.

The Mexican Government argued on several related grounds that the Commission lacked competence to consider these cases. (1) Under federal and state constitutions in Mexico, rulings of domestic electoral bodies are 'final' or 'irrevocable' and thus cannot be subjected to international review. (2) If electoral processes were subjected to international jurisdiction, 'a State would cease to be sovereign'. (3) An adverse finding by the Commission would infringe upon the political autonomy of the Mexican state and violate the principle of the self-determination of peoples. (4) The American Convention did not limit 'the sovereign powers of the States to elect their political bodies', and when it ratified the Convention, Mexico did not imagine that an international body could review elections of political bodies.

Excerpts from the Commission's Final Report on these cases follow:]

44. In short, the exercise of political rights is an essential element of representative democracy, which also presupposes the observance of other human rights.

Furthermore, the protection of those civil and political rights, within the framework of representative democracy, also implies the existence of an institutional control of the acts of the branches of government, as well as the supremacy of the law.

45. Since popular will is the basis for the authority of government, according to the terms of the Universal Declaration, it is consistent with a method for naming public officials through elections. Both the Universal Declaration and the American Declaration, the International Covenant on Civil and Political Rights and the American Convention on Human Rights coincide in that elections must have certain specific characteristics: they must be 'authentic' ('genuine' in the American Declaration), 'periodic', 'universal' and be executed in a manner that preserves the freedom of expression of the will of the voter.

. . .

48. The different pronouncements which the Inter-American Commission on Human Rights has made on the subject . . . show that the authenticity of elections covers two different categories of phenomena: on one hand, those referring to the general conditions in which the electoral process is carried out and, on the other hand, phenomena linked to the legal and institutional system that organizes elections and which implements the activities linked to the electoral act, that is, everything related in an immediate and direct way to the casting of the vote.

49. As to the *general conditions* in which the electoral contest takes place, from the concrete situations considered by the Commission we can deduce that they must allow the different political groups to participate in the electoral process under equal conditions, that is, that they all have similar basic conditions for conducting their campaign. . . .

. . .

57. With respect to Chile, in its 1987–1988 Annual Report, the Inter-American Commission noted that the mature and reasoned exercise of the right to vote during the 1988 plebiscite demanded a series of conditions in effect for a sufficiently long period before the aforementioned electoral act. Those conditions were the lifting of the states of exception, a sufficient number of registered voters, equitable access by the different political positions to communications media and the absence of any form of pressure on voters.

58. After verifying the existence of the first two conditions, the Commission analyzes the situation of the communications media to point out that:

> The presentation makes it possible to draw the conclusion that access to communications media, during the period covered by the present Annual Report and with reference to the plebiscite's campaign, has been characterized by a disproportionate presence of the government, which has used all the resources at its disposal to promote messages and images that favour its position in the next plebiscite. To that, numerous restrictions, legal and *the de facto*, must be added, those affecting independent organs of expression and journalists and political leaders. Also, it must be pointed out that the authorization to broadcast political programs constitutes progress that, nevertheless, does not compensate the

unequal access to communications media derived from the aforementioned circumstances.

. . .

62. Another aspect linked to the authenticity of elections is the *organization of the electoral process* and the actual casting of votes. . . .

63. [In its 1978 report on El Salvador the Commission noted:] There is a generalized skepticism on the part of citizens with regard to the right to vote and participation in government. In particular, opposition political parties go as far as doubting the possibility of having pure and free elections. . . .

. . .

65. In the Seventh Report on the Situation of Human Rights in Cuba, in 1983, the Commission deems that one of the elements that determines the limited political participation of the population in important matters is the result of electoral mechanisms and control exercised over it by the Government and the Cuban Communist Party. After analyzing the principal characteristics of the Cuban electoral system, it points out as a 'counterproductive' element the preponderance of that political party, whose leaders intervene 'in a decisive manner in the operation of mechanisms to select candidates to occupy free elective offices'.

. . .

72. With respect to the exercise of the right to freedom of expression, the Commission has considered the manner in which the government uses its power both for disseminating messages in its favour as well as restricting the possibility of the opposition to broadcast its message. . . .

73. With respect to the freedom of assembly, the experience of the Commission has led it to examine the restrictions of this right resulting from states of exception or other legal restrictions (police permits, for example) or the use of indirect control such as the obligatory participation of public employees in demonstrations.

. . .

77. . . . [T]he Commission has examined aspects of practical operations such as electoral rolls and registration requirements; the composition of polling stations; the composition of the electoral tribunal and its powers, and the existence of understandable ballots, devoid of any influence on voters.

. . .

81. The Commission considers that the act of ratifying the American Convention presupposes acceptance of the obligation of not only respecting the observance of rights and freedoms recognized in it, but also guaranteeing their existence and the exercise of all of them . . . . [The Commission then cites with approval passages from the *Velásquez Rodríguez* decision expounding states' obligations under Articles 1 and 2 of the Convention to respect and guarantee the recognized rights and, pursuant thereto, 'to organize all the State apparatus and, in general, all the structures through which the exercise of public power is manifested, in such a manner that they are able to legally insure the free and full exercise of human rights'. The Commission applied those statements of the Court in the instant case to Mexico's obligations to guarantee rights under Article 23.]

. . .

84. .... [When Mexico] contracted the obligations derived from the Convention, it also accepted that the Inter-American Commission exercise the functions and attributions conferred by the Convention; no reservations or limitations were recorded in the instruments deposited when the Convention was ratified.

. . .

86. [In relation to the Government's characterization of the right to legitimate elections as a 'progressively achievable right'] several observations are in order. . . .In order for this interpretive distinction between individual rights of immediate enforceability (the right to vote and to be elected) and collective rights to be developed progressively (the right to elections with particular characteristics) to have validity in the cases under consideration, it would have been necessary for Mexico, at one time or another, to have advanced this interpretation of the article

. . .

87. No reference to such a distinction can be found in [any Mexican Government document] . . .

88. From the normative point of view, the structure of Article 23.1.b makes reference to certain features that should be present in order for the right to be recognized to be valid in practice. Indeed, any mention of the right to vote and to be elected would be mere rhetoric if unaccompanied by a precisely described set of characteristics that the elections are required to meet. . . .

89. The [Mexican] comments also contain the argument that ' . . . the need for the elections to be legitimate imposes upon the State an obligation to act: To progressively develop, in accordance with circumstances and conditions in each country, the guarantee that the voters may freely express their will'. This argument would condition the existence of human rights on 'the circumstances and situation of each country' leaving the whole legal system in a precarious state.

90. With respect to the argument contained in the Mexican Government's comments which holds that any opinion issued by the Commission on an electoral process on the basis of individual complaints constitutes a violation of the principle of nonintervention, it should be stated here once again that the Mexican State, by virtue of having signed and ratified the Convention, has consented to allow certain aspects of its internal jurisdiction to be a subject of judgments on the part of the organs instituted to protect the rights and guarantees recognized by the Convention. . . .

91. Moreover, as stated in Article 18 of the OAS Charter, the principle of nonintervention is a rule of conduct that governs the acts of States or groups of States. . . . The Inter-American Juridical Committee, in its 'Draft Instrument' on cases of violations of the principle of nonintervention (1972), indicated that one of the basic criteria followed preparing it was that 'only States can be subjects of intervention'.

. . .

93. The principle of nonintervention is therefore linked to the right of peoples to self-determination and independence and is described as a principle to be practiced in suitable harmony with human rights and fundamental freedoms. This important interrelation of principles of international law is formalized as a rule of law in Article 16 of the OAS Charter, which reads as follows:

Each State has the right to develop its cultural, political, and economic life freely and naturally. In this free development, the State shall respect the rights of individuals and the principles of universal morality.

94. According to this rule, the right of the State to develop its internal life freely has a counterpart in its obligation to respect the rights of individuals. And in inter-American law these rights are formally recognized in the American Convention on Human Rights. The correct interpretation of the principle of nonintervention is, therefore, one based on protecting the right of States to self-determination provided that right is exercised in a manner consistent with respect for the rights of individuals.

95. The above leads to the conclusion that the Commission, based on its regulatory instruments, is empowered to examine and evaluate the degree to which the internal legislation of the State party guarantees or protects the rights stipulated in the Convention and their adequate exercise and, obviously, among these, political rights. The IACHR is also empowered to verify, with respect to these rights, if the holding of periodic, authentic elections, with universal, equal, and secret suffrage takes place, within the framework of the necessary guarantees so that the results represent the popular will, including the possibility that the voters could, if necessary, effectively appeal against an electoral process that they consider fraudulent, defective, and irregular or that ignores the 'right to access, under general conditions of equality, to the public functions of their country'.

. . .

Issues in this case

. . .

100. In relation with the internal remedies and guarantees in Mexico, the matter to be examined is whether Mexican law offers adequate means or a simple and quick remedy or of 'any other effective remedy before competent judges or independent and impartial courts' that protect those who petition against 'acts that violate their fundamental rights', as is the case with political rights. The Commission has been able to perceive that no such remedy [exists] in Mexico.

101. In view of the aforementioned . . . the Commission deems it advisable to remind the Government of Mexico of its duty to adopt measures of internal law, in accordance with its constitutional procedures and the provisions of the Convention, whether legislative or of another character, necessary to make effective the rights and liberties which the Convention recognizes.

102. . . . [T]he Commission . . . has been informed that there is underway an active process of reform of the electoral laws. The Commission hopes that these reforms will lead to the adoption of standards that will adequately protect the exercise of political rights and create a rapid and effective process assuring the protection of the same . . .

INTER-AMERICAN COMMISSION ON HUMAN RIGHTS, ANNUAL REPORT 1990–91
(1991), at 514

[This Annual Report of the IACHR included a section examining 'areas in which steps need to be taken' toward full observance of the human rights recognized in the American Declaration and the American Convention. Part III of that section is entitled 'Human Rights, Political Rights and Representative Democracy in the Inter-American System'. Excerpts from Part III below start by tracing the 'most important milestones' in the Inter-American system's development of democracy-related ideas.]

1. Representative democracy and human rights in the inter-American system

Later, the postulate of the relationship between representative democracy and human rights was further refined in the Declaration of Santiago, adopted in 1959 by the Fifth Meeting of Consultation of Ministers of Foreign Affairs [of the OAS]. . . .

> 1. The principle of the rule of law should be assured by the separation of powers, and by the control of the legality of governmental acts by competent organs of the state.
>
> . . .
>
> 4. The governments of the American states should maintain a system of freedom for the individual and of social justice based on respect for fundamental human rights.
>
> . . .
>
> 7. Freedom of the press, radio, and television, and, in general, freedom of information and expression, are essential conditions for the existence of a democratic regime.
>
> . . .

The last of the General Assembly resolutions that should be cited is AG/RES. 890 (XVII-0/87), wherein it decides:

> To reiterate to those governments that have not yet reinstated the representative democratic form of government that it is urgently necessary to implement the pertinent institutional machinery to restore such a system in the shortest possible time, through free and open elections held by secret ballot, since democracy is the best guarantee of the full exercise of human rights and is the firm foundation of the solidarity among the states of the hemisphere.
>
> . . .
>
> . . . [T]he observance of these rights and freedoms calls for a legal and institutional order wherein the law takes precedence over the will of the governing and where certain institutions exercise control over others so as to preserve the integrity of the expression of the will of the people—a constitutional state or a state in which the rule of law prevails.

On numerous occasions the Commission has made reference to several aspects associated with the exercise of political rights in a representative democracy and their relationship to the other fundamental rights of the individual. For the sake of brevity, only those texts that best illustrate this point will be cited. And so, the Inter-American Commission has said the following in this regard:

. . .

The right to political participation leaves room for a wide variety of forms of government; there are many constitutional alternatives as regards the degree of centralization of the powers of the state or the election and attributes of the organs responsible for the exercise of those powers. However, a democratic framework is an essential element for establishment of a political society where human values can be fully realized.

The right to political participation makes possible the right to organize parties and political associations, which through open discussion and ideological struggle, can improve the social level and economic circumstances of the masses and prevent a monopoly on power by any one group or individual. At the same time it can be said that democracy is a unifying link among the nations of this hemisphere. (Annual Report of the IACHR, 1979–80, p. 151).

. . .

In this context, governments have, in the face of political rights and the right to political participation, the obligation to permit and guarantee: the organization of all political parties and other associations, unless they are constituted to violate human rights; open debate of the principal themes of socio-economic development; the celebration of general and free elections with all the necessary guarantees so that the results represent the popular will.

As demonstrated by historical experience, the denial of political rights or the alteration of the popular will may lead to a situation of violence. (Annual Report of the IACHR, 1980–81, pp. 122–123).

The analysis of the human rights situation in the States to which the Commission has made reference in the foregoing chapter, as well as in others where the human rights situation has been considered by the Commission in recent years, enables the Commission to affirm that only by means of the effective exercise of representative democracy can the observance of human rights be fully guaranteed.

. . . The Commission's factual experience has been that serious human rights violations that have occurred or that are occurring in some countries of the Americas are primarily the result of the lack of political participation on the part of the citizenry, which is denied by the authorities in power. . ..The result has been that both the government and the more extreme opposition sectors have shown a preference for the use of violence as the sole means of resolving conflicts in the face of a lack of peaceful and rational options.

This experience confirms, therefore, the authentic social peace and respect for human rights can only be found in a democratic system. It is the only system that allows for the harmonious interaction of different political tendencies and within which, by means of the inter institutional equilibrium it establishes, the necessary controls can be invoked to correct errors or abuses by the authorities. (Annual Report of the IACHR, 1985–1986, p. 191).

Finally, in its 1987 Report on the Situation of Human Rights in Paraguay, after analyzing the most relevant legal texts produced in the hemisphere, the Commission [stated]. . . .

. . .

This hemispheric vision of the exercise of political rights within the context of a democratic system of government is completed by the requisite development and promotion of economic, social and cultural rights. Without them, the exercise of political rights is severely limited and the very permanence of the democratic regime is seriously threatened.

. . .

QUESTIONS

1. In what respects, if any, do the Final Report on the Mexican cases and the 1990–91 Annual Report elucidate the requirements of democratic government beyond the specific requirements of elections in Article 23(1)(b)? Does any larger 'theory' of democracy emerge?

2. Can you identify a coherent conception of sovereignty or domestic jurisdiction that the Commission develops to respond to Mexico's challenges to its competence? What content does the Commission give to the broad principle of non-interference in states' domestic affairs?

3. In the light of these cases, is there any aspect of a state's electoral system with which the Commission should not, from either a legal or policy (hortatory) perspective, concern itself? If so, which aspects, and why?

REPORT ON THE SITUATION OF HUMAN RIGHTS IN MEXICO

Inter-American Commission on Human Rights, 1998
OEA/Ser.L/V/ll.100, Doc. 7 rev. 1, Sept. 24, 1998

Introduction

. . .

2. . . . [T]he IACHR has been analyzing the general situation of human rights in Mexico. The decision to carry out an on-site visit, in order to evaluate the situation first hand, was based on the invitation extended by President Ernesto Zedillo Ponce De Leon. . . . The visit itself took place from 15 to 24 July 1996, under the legal framework of the American Convention on Human Rights. . . .

. . .

II. Institutional Framework

4. In recent years, Mexico has made considerable efforts to reform its institutions and adapt them to the demands of a modern democratic State governed by its Constitution and the rule of law. In that respect, emphasis must be placed on the significant political reforms that have been implemented in Mexico, which

have brought about improvements in the electoral system through impartial regulatory bodies that are independent of the Government. . . .

5. This process was put to the test in the recent elections held on July 6, 1997, which were noted for their competitiveness, transparency, large voter turnout, and normalcy, as well as for the fact that the results were accepted by the majority of the participants. It is worth mentioning that the opposition obtained a majority in the Chamber of Deputies, and that it won the elections to head the Federal District, and the gubernatorial elections in Querétaro and Nuevo León. . . . Regardless of the outcome of the elections, the importance of the reforms and the need for the people to have a more open and transparent electoral system are apparent.

6. The subject of human rights has been a key element in these reforms. A National Human Rights Commission (CNDH) was established by the Presidential Decree of 5 June 1990 as an independent agency within the Ministry of the Interior. . . .

. . .

10. During its stay in Mexico, the Commission visited the Federal District and the states of Chiapas, Guerrero and Baja California in order to meet with state authorities and representatives of civil society. At all times during the visit, the Commission enjoyed complete freedom and members were able to travel about the country and to meet with representatives of all sectors, individuals and groups.

. . .

12. During its visit, the Commission had the opportunity to meet with the President of Mexico, Dr. Ernesto Zedillo, and with other high-level federal, state and district officials, as well as with church dignitaries, businessmen, representatives of the media and non-governmental human rights organizations and other representatives of civil society.

. . .

Chapter I Structure of the State of Mexico

. . .

20. The United Mexican States is a federal, representative, democratic Republic made up of states that are free and sovereign in all internal matters but which are joined in a Federation that was established in conformity the principles of its Basic Law. . . .

21. The Government of Mexico is divided into its legislative, executive, and judicial branches. . . .

. . .

32. A presidential system of government has been established in most political constitutions in Latin America. In the case of Mexico, this system is accentuated, possibly because of the interest initially in consolidating the achievements of the Mexican Revolution by putting in place an executive branch with powers that outweighed those of the other branches of government.

33. The executive branch is clearly at the centre of the political system and the political life of Mexico. In this connection, a number of authors . . . have noted that among the reasons for this predominance of the executive branch are the following: the President is the leader of the predominant party, whose

membership includes the principal trade unions and peasant and professional organizations; the weakness of the legislative branch derives from the fact that the vast majority of legislators are members of the predominant party who are aware that should they oppose the President their chances of success would be virtually nil and that they would doubtlessly be jeopardizing their own political careers; . . . the marked influence which decentralized State agencies and State-owned enterprises have on the economy, through the operations of the central bank, and the broad powers of the Executive in matters relating to the economy; . . . the broad constitutional and extra-constitutional powers of the Executive, such as the power to designate the candidate of the ruling party, the PRI, and to appoint state governors; . . .

. . .

35. . . . [T]he Commission has taken note of and acknowledges the significant institutional changes which have taken place in Mexico and which have led to a deepening of multi-party politics and the strengthening of democracy. . . .The various changes noted, however, have not brought about any significant alteration of the marked presidential character of the Mexican political system.

. . .

63. In recent years, Mexico has witnessed an alternation of political parties in a number of states of the Union and in the Federal District, which has contributed to the evolution and further development of its democratic institutions. In that context, mention must be made of the victory of Ernesto Ruffo Appel, candidate of the PAN, in the elections for Governor of Baja California in 1989. The importance of this event lies in the fact that it was the first time an opposition politician was declared the winner in a governatorial race since the PRI came to power in 1929. The process was consolidated in the 1997 elections. . . .This evolution has led to the emergence of an important mechanism for the division and control of power in Mexico, where no longer one but several political parties exist, depending on the particular territorial political entity in question. . . .

. . .

Chapter VI Political Rights

423. The effective exercise of political rights has been one of the issues in Mexico of greatest interest to the IACHR over the years. During a considerable period of time, reports on Mexico received by the Commission mostly had to do with the elections and other rights protected by Article 23 of the American Convention. In the corresponding reports on individual cases, the Commission issued recommendations which to some extent helped give impetus to the important electoral reform process undertaken by the State. . . . Of the reforms carried out in the past few years, reference should be made to the new method of registration, the strengthening and independence of the Federal Electoral Institute (IFE), and the electoral court. As a result of all the reforms, the latest general elections, held in July 1997, were regarded by Mexican observers and the international community as the cleanest and most correct ever held in Mexico.

. . .

427. Article 35 of the Constitution states that the prerogatives of citizens are:

(1) to vote at popular elections; to be voted for, for all offices subject to popular election . . . and to assemble to discuss the political affairs of the country. Article 36, for its part, establishes that the obligations of citizens of the Republic are: to vote in popular elections in the electoral district to which they belong. . . .

[The Report describes several of the recent and ongoing flaws in the electoral system. It describes reforms in the Federal Electoral Institute that give this body more autonomy and integrity and inspire more confidence in the outcome of elections, and reforms in other related governmental bodies as well. It describes typical complaints about the electoral system that had been received by the Commission over years: blocks to registration of voters, inadequate legal processes for individuals to protest what they believed to be denial of voting rights, improper annulment of elections, and so on. It then turns to a description of recent reforms.]

451. The Mexican electoral system has thus been the focus of a reform effort that has affected its basic institutions of organization, management, and government, to such an extent that the system can now be said to have shifted from party control of the electoral process to a gradual hand-over to citizens themselves. Within a framework of national dialogue, the Commission must acknowledge the progress that is beginning to be manifest towards enacting a new electoral law with regard to the following aspects in particular: autonomy and independence of electoral organs; greater fairness of the conditions under which electoral competition takes place; greater control over the sources of funding of political parties to ensure more fairness, transparency and equity; and guarantees to achieve greater equality of access by political parties to the communications media. . . .

[The following excerpts describe a few of these reforms and a few of the remaining problems.]

460. One of the principal weaknesses of the electoral system was the fact that voting districts were the same as those that had been drawn up in 1977 on the basis of the 1970 census. The outdated information meant that there were significant imbalances in the value of a vote, thereby violating the principle of an equal vote.

461. As a result, the new 'districting' was aimed at achieving a better distribution of districts as well as better political representation of citizens. The new boundaries of the 300 electoral districts . . . were based on the general population census of 1990. . . .
. . .

463. It is also important to note that, despite the progress made, certain issues of great importance have not yet been subject to reform. Among them, it is possible to mention a clear and conclusive definition of electoral offences and measures to effectively guarantee their punishment; measures to punish all forms of coercion or inducement to vote, based on relationship of employment, union membership or enjoyment of a public service or public asset; and guarantees and

mechanisms to ensure that public programs are not identified in any way with party programs or used for electoral purposes.

[There follow a few sections of the Report that analyse specific problems in the Mexican political system bearing on elections.]

[*Campaign financing*]

470. Two of the factors that undoubtedly define a democratic electoral contest are fairness and transparency in the use of financial resources. In this regard, political parties are today one of the hubs around which any democratic system turns. In order to achieve their objectives, political parties need increasingly larger quantities and more costly material and organizational resources.

471. Some significant reforms have been enacted in Mexico, such as a limit on individual contributions, the imposition of ceilings on anonymous donations and the setting of a limit on campaign spending for the first time in the country. . . . [U]nder the rules for the allocation of public funds for campaign spending in 1997: Political parties will be entitled to public financing for their activities, and so this type of financing will take precedence over other types that have existed in the past.

472. Under the new system, the mechanism for financing has been simplified. There is to be a specific allocation for spending on election campaigns. This will lend greater transparency to election budgets, since expenditures for ordinary transactions will be distinguished from campaign expenditures. . . .
. . .

474. . . . Thanks to the changes, parties can be guaranteed enough funds for their normal activities and for financing their campaigns. The increased financing also gives parties greater independence and helps to ensure greater transparency with regard to the sources of funding.

475. Moreover, these reforms are intended to ensure greater equity in public financing. For example, the new laws provide that 30 per cent of the total resources allocated should be distributed equally among all the parties. The remaining 70 per cent is allocated in accordance with the percentage of votes received by each party in the most recent elections. The parties not represented in the legislature will receive public financing equivalent to 4 per cent of the total.

476. It should not be forgotten, however, that, despite the recent reforms, the system has been characterized thus far by the absence of specific regulations that provide for political parties to be audited; by the absence of mechanisms for determining how much each party spends; and by the fact that current laws do not provide for punishment for the violation of spending limits. The potential for inequality in election campaigning is therefore great in the areas of infrastructure, logistics, payroll, access to and time purchased in the media, public advertising and material resources and, in general, the sum total of resources devoted to events of all types.
. . .

478. . . . Private contributions are limited and anonymous donations prohibited, except for special collections. Moreover, 25 per cent of private contributions

to political parties are deductible. The electoral auditing body may order audits of parties to be conducted either by that body itself or by third parties.

479. Financing for the strengthening of political parties, for which provision was made in the 1996 reforms, should also be viewed as a valuable complement to earlier methods of financing. The equal treatment accorded to all political groups must be viewed as a positive factor. . . .

480. The IACHR believes that this measure promotes the emergence of new political groups and strengthens the smaller ones that are already in existence, which will in turn promote political pluralism.

[*Access to communications media*]

481. Establishing a culture of respect for human rights depends to a great extent on respect for the right to information and to freedom of expression. . . . [T]he communications media must transmit in an objective and balanced manner the various points of view that are expressed in a society.

482. . . . [T]he responsible presentation of information facilitates the full and conscious exercise of political rights. This means that adequate guarantees must be provided that not only would there be objectivity and impartiality but also that information relating to party political figures and to candidates for election will not be manipulated.

. . .

484. In order for an election to take place democratically, citizens must receive free and timely information about the election process and about the various candidates participating in it. This is guaranteed by article 6 of the Mexican Constitution, by the Federal Law on Radio and Television and by the Press Law.

485. The partiality of the mass media allows certain political figures to unilaterally present to citizens their political platforms, positions, proposals, and points of view on national issues or events of general interest, in contrast to what other political candidates are able to do. This unequal treatment of candidates in the media prevents the public from having a complete basis on which to decide their vote.

486. This could have an adverse effect on political rights . . . since the necessary conditions are not being met for ensuring a competitive, open, and transparently democratic contest.

. . .

488. In the case of Mexico, private media houses dominate over public corporations in the communications sector. However, since the public has an inherent interest in television, the State authorizes its exploitation by granting concessions to the owners of television stations. In this connection, the Mexican Human Rights Academy has noted that . . . Mexican legislation is based on the need for mechanisms to monitor the information activity of the electronic media and establishes as guiding principles objectivity, timeliness and truthfulness. . . .

489. . . . [T]he Mexican laws which have been in force since November 1996 allow for more time for political campaigns to be conducted in the communications media. It is hoped that the use of public financing will help to improve both the quantity and fairness of the distribution of information. It has thus been

decided that preference will be given to time slots for political advertising by parties during general programming hours. In addition to these time slots, a special radio and television program will be aired twice a month and additional time will be provided during political campaigns.

. . .

499. . . . [I]n order to increase the fairness of future electoral contests and of the financing of such contests and to guarantee a minimum base period for all participants, the time granted to parties will be divided into two parts in accordance with the new legislation: one part will be distributed equally and the other will be allotted according to the [number representing] each party. . . .The IACHR acknowledges the advances achieved toward electoral reform and clarifies that it has not yet received any specific complaints regarding lack of access to the media during the campaigns that preceded the 1997 elections.

. . .

VI. Recommendations

501. In light of the situation reviewed above, the IACHR makes the following recommendations to the Mexican State:

502. To adopt the necessary measures so that the right to vote and to be elected provides for the most ample and participatory access of candidates to the electoral process, as an element of consolidation for democracy.

503. To monitor compliance by local entities with the provisions of article 115 of the Constitution, which provides that 'for their internal government, the States shall adopt the popular, representative, republican form of government, with the free Municipality as the basis of their territorial division and political and administrative organization. . . .'.

504. To clearly define electoral crimes and establish mechanisms to guarantee their effective punishment.

505. To adopt the necessary legislation with a view to effectively auditing the finances of political parties.

QUESTIONS

1. 'It is obvious that matters like electoral fraud, or failure to provide adequate remedies for citizens claiming that their political rights have been denied, violate the American Convention. But what of the other issued discussed by the IACHR, like campaign financing and access to media? The American Convention provides no "answers" to these issues; the Commission seems to be interpreting or elaborating the Convention in its comments on such issues. Such occasional, contingent, discretionary features of different democratic states have no foundation in human rights instruments'. Comment.

2. Is the European Convention or the ICCPR, or the Human Rights Committee's General Comment on ICCPR Article 25 at p. 85, *supra*, more precise or helpful on these issues?

3. What relationship do the 'recommendations' at the end of the Report bear to the analysis of particular problems and the comments of the Commission throughout the Report?

4. Whatever your conclusions about the formal effect of the Commission's comments, what are the image and components of political democracy that emerge from this Report? For example: (a) Do you read the Report to suggest that the President exercises excessive power that should in part be allocated to the legislature within a democratic separation of powers? (b) Do you read the Report, in its comments on electoral districts, to suggest that a principle like 'one person one vote' is expressed by the American Convention, or that the Convention prefers or requires one type of voting system—first-past-the-post in electoral districts, or proportional representation, for example?

5. Based on the materials in this section, how do you assess the significance of final reports or state reports by the Commission for possible reform within the criticized states? If you were a citizen of a state criticized by such an IACHR report, and sought to increase the report's effectiveness, what action would you take? What action could the Commission take to give a report greater effect?

6. Recall the suggestion in Steiner that the right to political participation be viewed in some respects as programmatic, thus subject to progressive realization. Do the three documents about Mexico in this section lend support for that view? Would it have been appropriate for the Commission in its Final Report on the Mexican cases or in its Report on Mexico to have viewed Mexico as in compliance with the American Convention because it was in the process of gradual realization of the right to political participation and was proceeding at a reasonable pace of reform? Note the Mexican argument in para. 86 of the Final Report, which was not responded to on its merits by the Commission.

ADDITIONAL READING

On the Inter-American system see: A.A. Cançado Trindade, 'The Inter-American Human Rights System at the Dawn of the New Century: Recommendations for Improvement of its Mechanisms of Protection', in D. Harris and S. Livingstone (eds.), *The Inter-American System of Human Rights* 395 (1998); ibid, 'Reporting in the Inter-American System of Human Rights Protection', in P. Alston and J. Crawford (eds.), *The Future of UN Human Rights Treaty Monitoring* 333 (2000); D. Shelton, *Remedies in International Human Rights Law* (1999); S. Davidson, *The Inter-American Human Rights System* (1996); ibid., *The Inter-American Court of Human Rights* (1992); C. Cerna, 'The Structure and Functioning of the Inter-American Court of Human Rights (1979–1992)', 63 Brit. Y.B. Int'l L. 135 (1992); C. Medina Quiroga, *The Battle of Human Rights: Gross, Systematic Violations and the Inter-American System* (1988); T. Buergenthal, 'The Inter-American System for the Protection of Human Rights', in T. Meron (ed.), *Human Rights in International Law: Legal and Policy Issues* 439 (1984).

On democracy and international law see: S. Marks, *The Riddle of All Constitutions: International Law, Democracy, and the Critique of Ideology* (2000); C. Hesse and R. Post (eds.), *Human Rights in Political Transitions: Gettysburg to Bosnia* (1999); L. Diamond, *Developing Democracy: Toward Consolidation* (1999); T. Carothers, *Aiding Democracy Abroad: The Learning Curve* (1999); B. Roth, *Governmental Illegitimacy in International Law* (1998); A. de Brito, *Human Rights and Democratization in Latin America* (1997); L. Whitehead (ed.), *The International Dimensions of Democratization: Europe and the Americas* (1996).

D. THE AFRICAN SYSTEM

The newest, the least developed or effective (in relation to the European and Inter-American regimes), the most distinctive and the most controversial of the three established regional human rights regimes involves African states. In 1981 the Assembly of Heads of States and Government of the Organization of African Unity adopted the African Charter on Human and Peoples' Rights. It entered into force in 1986. As of March 2000, 53 African states were parties.

In Chapter 5's discussion of rights and duties, at pp. 324–361, *supra*, the Charter itself served as an important illustration of a human rights regime that was more duty-oriented than the universal human rights system or the two other regional systems. This present section examines only institutional aspects of the African system; the substantive problems that occupy the African Commission on Human and Peoples' Rights in the following materials are incidental to the description of how the Commission functions. The examination is brief, since the system's sole implementing organ, the Commission, has had only 15 years of experience, has few powers, and for the most part has been hesitant in exercising those powers or creatively interpreting and developing them. Moreover, the basic structure and tasks of the Commission do not introduce novel themes to Part D's examination of the architecture of intergovernmental human rights institutions.

It follows that the African system has not yet yielded anywhere near the same amount of information and 'output' of recommendations or decisions—state reports and reactions thereto, communications (complaints) from individuals about state conduct, studies of 'situations' or investigations of particular violations—as have the other systems. In comparison with those systems, the states parties and Commission have taken few forceful or persuasive actions within the structure of the Charter to attempt to curb serious human rights violations, although recent years have shown promise of a more insistent and active stance. Moreover, recent years have seen peacekeeping actions within the Organization of African Unity or by individual African states, both outside the framework of the Human Rights Charter, to respond to violence and slaughter in states like Liberia.

This examination of institutional aspects of the African system begins with a brief description of the Organization of African Unity. You should be familiar with the provisions of the African Charter set forth in the Documents Annex.

COMMENT ON THE ORGANIZATION OF AFRICAN UNITY

The OAU is the official regional body of all African states. It was inspired by the anti-colonial struggles of the late 1950s, and was primarily dedicated to the eradication of colonialism. The emergent African states created through it a political bloc to facilitate intra-African relations and to forge a regional approach to Africa's relationships with external powers. The OAU's Charter was adopted in 1963 by a conference of Heads of State and Government. Today, all African states are members of the OAU.

Unlike the UN Charter, that of the OAU makes no provision for the enforcement of its principles. It emphasizes cooperation among member states and peaceful settlement of disputes, and includes among its purposes in Article II(1) the promotion of the 'unity and solidarity' of African states, as well as defence of 'their sovereignty, their territorial integrity and independence'. This inviolability of territorial borders, expressed through the principle of non-interference in the internal affairs of member states, has been one of the OAU's central creeds.

This creed has contributed to the reluctance of member states to promote human rights aggressively. The most visible failure in this regard has been the reluctance of member states to criticize one another about human rights violations. A prominent case in point was the failure of most African states, the single exception being Tanzania, to denounce the abusive regime of Ugandan dictator Idi Amin. Over the last decade, there have been several peacekeeping (as well as overtly aggressive) interventions by African states, independently or through a joint force, into states of systematic, serious human rights violations, particularly states caught up in insurgencies and civil war. Congo and the Great Lakes region offer recent illustrations.

The single prominent exception with respect to general human rights policy has been the adoption by the OAU in 1981 of the African Charter on Human and Peoples' Rights. The formal, legal basis for that act is found in Article II(1)(b) of the OAU Charter, which requires member states to 'coordinate and intensify their collaboration and efforts to achieve a better life for the peoples of Africa', and Article II(1)(e), which asks member states to 'promote international co-operation, having due regard to the Charter of the United Nations and the Universal Declaration of Human Rights'.

COMMENT ON INSTITUTIONAL IMPLEMENTATION: THE AFRICAN COMMISSION

The 11 members of the Commission, elected by secret ballot by the Assembly of Heads of State and Government from a list of persons nominated by parties to the Charter, are to serve (Article 31) 'in their personal capacity'. Article 45 defines the mandate or functions of the Commission to be (1) to 'promote Human and Peoples' Rights', (2) to 'ensure the protection of human and peoples' rights' under conditions set by the Charter, (3) to 'interpret all the provisions of the Charter' when so requested by states or OAU institutions; and (4) to perform other tasks that may be committed to it by the Assembly. So the three dominant functions appear to be promotion, ensuring protection, and interpretation.

The Commission's task of 'promotion' includes (Article 45) undertaking 'studies and researches on African problems in the field of human and peoples' rights', as well as organizing seminars and conferences, disseminating information, encouraging 'local institutions concerned with human and peoples' rights', giving its views or making recommendations to governments, and formulating principles and rules 'aimed at solving legal problems related to human and peoples' rights . . . upon which African Governments may base their legislation'. Article 46 states tersely that the Commission 'may resort to any appropriate method of investigation'. In general, the 'Charter gives pre-eminence to the promotion of human rights and vests a wide range of responsibility on the Commission. In this regard, it has functions that are not directly vested in the . . . American Commission'.[37] Several steps have been taken to implement the task of promotion—for example, resolutions by the Commission to the effect that states should include the teaching of human rights at all levels of the educational curricula, should integrate the Charter's provisions into national laws, and should establish committees on human rights.

Communications (complaints) and state reports are the most significant functions or processes involving the Commission that are identified in the Charter. Thus far, the procedures in the Charter involving communications by a state party concerning another state party have not been used. Individuals and national and international institutions can also send communications to the Commission, as provided in Articles 55–59. These provisions recall, but differ significantly from, the First Optional Protocol of the ICCPR examined at pp. 738–770, *supra*.

The Charter refers tersely to reports. Under Article 62, each party 'shall undertake to submit every two years . . . a report on the legislative or other measures taken with a view to giving effect to the rights' under the Charter. Compare the more elaborate provisions in Article 40 of the ICCPR about the role of the ICCPR Committee in reviewing states' reports under that Covenant.

Although there is some irony in the observation that the Commission, addressing a continent rife with state-imposed abuses, should have promotion as its primary function, that concentration of energy makes some sense in view of Africa's large uneducated population that is ignorant of its rights or lacks organization and capacity for mobilization to vindicate them. Creating a 'rights awareness' could understandably be considered to be a primary function.

But in the long run, promotion alone will not be sufficient. This human rights regime governs states that have committed rampant violations, and that lack experience in and institutions for curbing the abuse of governmental power. Such a regime must depend on the effectiveness of intervention and protection of individuals, in order to effect long-term change. The African system—in part through the work of the Commission—must raise the costs to states of violations

---

[37] U.O. Umozurike, 'The African Commission on Human and Peoples' Rights', 1 Rev. Afr. Comm. Hum. & Peoples' Rts 5 (1991), at 8.

through one or another of the sanctions with which other human rights regimes are familiar.

CHIDI ANSELM ODINKALU, THE INDIVIDUAL COMPLAINTS PROCEDURES OF THE AFRICAN COMMISSION ON HUMAN AND PEOPLES' RIGHTS: A PRELIMINARY ASSESSMENT
8 Transnat'l L. & Contemp. Probs 359 (1998), at 365

. . .

II. The African Commission on Human and Peoples' Rights: A brief background to its composition and structure

The African Commission on Human and Peoples' Rights (Commission or African Commission) was created under Article 30 of the African Charter, which declares that it is 'established within the Organization of African Unity to promote human and peoples' rights and ensure their protection'. The Commission is comprised of eleven persons 'chosen from amongst African personalities of the highest reputation, known for their high morality, integrity, impartiality, and competence in matters of human and peoples' rights; particular consideration being given to persons having legal experience'. Since its inception in 1987, a total of nineteen persons have at different times been elected to the Commission, of which only one has been a nonlawyer and two have been women. . . .

Members of the Commission are elected by the Assembly of Heads of States and Governments of the OAU for a renewable term of seven years. From among themselves, in turn, the Commissioners elect a Chairman and Vice-Chairman every two years. Members of the Commission are elected to serve in their individual capacities and are, therefore, expected to act independently while serving as Commissioners. In practice, as with other international institutions and mechanisms, the process of nomination and election to the Commission minimizes the likelihood of the body being composed of persons who may be substantially or rigorously impervious to state pressure. Of the ten persons presently serving on the Commission, two are diplomats, three are judges, two are university professors, two others are the heads of the national human rights institutions in their respective countries, while another is a legal practitioner presently living in exile. The independence of the members of the African Commission impacts very much on its credibility. . . . The credibility of the Commission, in turn, is strengthened if it is perceived to be constituted in a way that enhances its impartiality and independence.

The Commission . . . meets in bi-annual Ordinary Sessions in Spring and Fall respectively. . . . lasting mostly ten days each. Until relatively recently, however, very little was known about the tasks and initiatives undertaken by the Commission to protect human rights in specific cases or countries, due substantially to the strict interpretation the Commission had placed on Article 59 (1) of the African Charter which prohibits disclosure of 'all measures' taken in respect of protective activities by the Commission 'until such a time as the Assembly of Heads of State and Governments shall otherwise decide'. This provision ensured that very little was known or learned about the Commission relative to such recent African tragedies as the conflicts in Burundi, Rwanda, and Liberia. It also confirmed the subordination of the Commission to the political organs of the OAU. By late 1993, this confidentiality principle was undermining the reputation of the Commission. . . .

Therefore, by 1994, the Commission was ready to begin to disclose information on its protective work on individual communications through the medium of its annual activity reports. When its Tenth Annual Activity Report was published in June 1997, the Commission had recorded 200 individual cases and complaints of which 101 cases had been decided, 75 were pending, and another 24 had been closed without consideration. Of the 101 decided cases, 45 had been declared inadmissible, 24 were irreceivable, one was declared by the Commission to have merit, while the Commission decided that another had been satisfactorily resolved. In three cases, the Commission welcomed the continuing efforts of the member state concerned to remedy the violations complained of. The Commission found that six more cases had been amicably resolved and it has decided 21 cases on the merits.

. . . [W]hile Articles 47–54 of the Charter provide for interstate complaints, thus far there have been no such complaints recorded by the Commission. . . .

III. The legal basis of the individual communications procedure under the African Charter

Unlike the African Charter's provisions concerning the promotional mandate of the African Commission, its provisions concerning the Commission's protective mandate are not notable for their clarity or precision. As a result, the legal basis of the individual communications procedure of the Commission is somewhat controversial, having been called into question by some commentators. . . .

Article 30 of the African Charter requires the Commission to 'promote human and peoples' rights and ensure their protection'. Subsequently, in Article 45, it empowers the Commission to 'ensure the protection of human and peoples' rights under conditions laid down by the present Charter'. The Commission also is charged to interpret the Charter, monitor state party compliance with the provisions of the Charter by receiving and considering reports concerning the measures that they have instituted to implement the Charter, and 'perform any other tasks which may be entrusted to it by the Assembly of Heads of State and Government'. In fulfilling these functions, the Charter also empowers the commission to 'resort to any appropriate method of investigation'.

Concerning non-state communications, Article 55 of the Charter, titled 'other communications', reads as follows:

> 1. Before each session, the Secretary of the Commission shall make a list of the communications other than those of States parties to the present Charter and transmit them to the members of the Commission, who shall indicate which communications should be considered by the Commission.

2. A communication should be considered by the Commission if a simple majority of its members so decide.

Each of the individual cases dealt with by the Commission has been received under these provisions of Article 55. However, in some cases the Commission has received 'one or more communications that apparently relate to special cases that reveal the existence of a series of serious or massive violations of human and peoples' rights'. [Article 58(1)] Article 58 of the Charter requires the Commission to draw such cases to the attention of the Assembly of Heads of State and Government of the OAU who 'may then request the Commission to undertake an in-depth study of these cases and make a factual report, accompanied by its finding and recommendations'. . . .

. . .

The summary of [positions taken by commentators that were described by the author] is twofold. First, they call into question the legal basis of the individual communications procedure under the African Charter. Second, to the extent that they recognize the Commission as having any responsibility to act on complaints of violations brought to its attention by non-state actors, they claim that the ability of the Commission to act on such complaints is dependent on prior authorization by the Assembly of Heads of State and Governments of the OAU and limited only to carrying out in-depth studies. While shortcomings in the drafting of the Charter are clear and conceded, this section will show that it is nonetheless obvious that the decision of the Commission to develop procedures for individual communications is well founded under the Charter . . .. [Discussion of Charter provisions omitted.]

. . .

. . . [A broad interpretation by the Commission of its mandate to 'consider' communications] is consistent with the Commission's responsibility to promote human rights and ensure their protection in Africa. The promotion and protection of human rights are two interrelated and indistinguishable functions because the objective of promoting human rights is to reduce the likelihood of their being violated. When it examines a particular situation and issues specific recommendations to the state party concerned to remedy the violations, the Commission fulfills a protective role in relation to the specific cases before it. In addition, its jurisprudence forms part of international law and, as such, contributes to norm clarification and awareness raising, both of which are ends of a promotional character.

. . .

IV. Objective of the individual complaints procedure

The African Charter does not expressly define an objective for the individual complaints procedure. In the Free Legal Assistance Group Case [a 1996 decision involving Zaire], the Commission established that the objective of the communications procedure is 'to initiate a positive dialogue, resulting in an amicable resolution between the complainant and the state concerned, which remedies the prejudice complained of'. The attainment of this objective, the Commission continued, was dependent on 'the good faith of the parties concerned, including their willingness to participate in a dialogue'. The Commission thus recognizes that the bottom line of the communications procedure is the redress of violations complained of. To enable it to reach this objective, it is prepared to seek an amicable settlement between the parties, which must fulfill a two-pronged, subjective and objective criteria. Subjectively, the parties must be satisfied with the result, a difficult standard to meet given that the interests and aims of the victims and perpetrators of violations are often at odds. Objectively, both parties are called upon to act in good faith so as to bring about a resolution which 'remedies the prejudice complained of'.

. . .

Another limitation of the objectives established by the Commission for the communications procedure is that it is dependent on the volition and good faith of the state party, respondent in the case, and thus may not be entirely consistent with the obligation of the states parties under Article 1 of the African Charter to recognize the rights, duties, and freedoms enshrined in it and to 'undertake to adopt legislative and other measures to give effect to them'. Where efforts to reach an amicable resolution fail, the Commission is then forced to reach a decision on the merits. [A footnote refers to the 1994 decision in the Mekongo communication against Cameroon.]

In a series of communications, the Commission was presented with serious and massive allegations of violations of human rights against the state of Malawi. The Commission sent several requests and reminders to the state party which were neither answered nor acknowledged. The Commission designated a member of the Commission, the Late Chief Justice Moleleki Mokama of Botswana, to undertake a mission to Malawi and report back to it, but the Malawi authorities refused to admit him into their territory or to co-operate with him. At its 14th Ordinary Session in Addis Ababa, Ethiopia, on December 3, 1993, the Commission took the then-unprecedented step of adopting and publishing a strongly worded resolution deploring the attitude of the Malawi government in apparently ignoring the Commission's inquiries and finding Malawi 'guilty of massive and serious violations of human rights'. Following this experience, the Commission decided in 1994 that 'where allegations of human rights abuse go uncontested by the government concerned, even after repeated notifications, the Commission must decide on the facts provided by the complainant and treat those facts as given'. . . .

V. Admissibility requirements

The African Charter prescribes certain conditions that must be fulfilled by any communications submitted for the consideration of the Commission. [See Article 56 in the Documents Annex. The author's observations on a few of these conditions follow.]

[Identity of the Authors and Victims] The Charter requires that the authors of the communication give their names 'even if they desire to be anonymous with respect to the state involved'. However, the authors need not be the victims or members of the victims' families, an interpretation that the Commission justifies as being 'a clear response to the practical difficulties that face individuals in Africa and, in particular, where there are serious or massive violations that may preclude individual victims from pursuing national or international legal remedies on their behalf'. . . .

. . .

[Exhaustion of Domestic Remedies] . . . In practice, the Commission has been willing to allow wide margins of exception to this requirement, especially in situations in which massive violations of human rights are alleged. As the Commission stated in one leading case, it:

> must read Article 56.5 in the light of its duty to ensure the protection of the human and peoples' rights under conditions laid down by the Charter. The Commission cannot hold the requirement of exhaustion of local remedies to apply literally in cases where it is impractical or undesirable for the complainant to seize the domestic courts in the case of each individual complainant. This is the case where there are a large number of individual victims. Due to the seriousness of the human rights situation as well as the great numbers of people involved, such remedies as might theoretically exist in the domestic courts are, as a practical matter unavailable or, in the words of the Charter, unduly prolonged. [Free Legal Assistance Case, *supra*].

Thus, where it finds that a communication or set of communications disclose serious and massive violations, the Commission routinely grants an exception to the rule on exhaustion of local remedies . . . The Commission also has granted an exception to the exhaustion of local remedies rule where an appeal remained undecided for more than twelve years after it was initiated and where it concluded that the domestic legal procedures were 'willfully obstructed'.
. . .

VI. Fact-finding and representation

Article 46 of the African Charter enables the commission to adopt methods of investigation (including fact-finding) appropriate to the complaints before it. A major innovation by the Commission is its recent charge to initiate and deploy fact-finding missions as part of its communications procedure. Until 1995, states parties, most notably Zaire and Malawi, had repeatedly turned down requests from the Commission to conduct fact-finding missions in their territories. This changed when the Government of Togo agreed to receive a mission of the Commission in 1995. Since then the Commission has conducted missions to Mauritania, Nigeria, Sudan, and Senegal. The reports of the Mauritania and Senegal missions were issued in 1997. . . .

Since its sixteenth Ordinary Session, the Commission has routinely issued notices to all the parties to attend or be represented at the hearing of the merits. . . . The Commission will proceed to consider and decide on the case even if the parties are unable to attend the hearing. . . . The Commission takes oral arguments from the parties if they are necessary. . . . To date it has not yet registered any dissenting opinion.

VII. Relationship with non-governmental organizations (NGOs)

The development of the African Commission and its procedures has been facilitated by an active collaboration which it has forged over the years with non-governmental organizations from within and outside Africa. Two examples illustrate the nature of this relationship. Since 1991, each of the Commission's bi-annual sessions has been preceded by a forum of the non-governmental organizations organized jointly by the Commission and the International Commission of Jurists (ICJ). The conclusions of these NGO forums, which are routinely attended by NGOs and other independent observers of the Commission and by members of the Commission, usually are forwarded to the formal sessions of the Commission for adoption and action as the Commission sees fit.

Unlike other regional human rights institutions in the Americas and in Europe, the Rules of Procedure of the Commission expressly authorize it to grant observer status to NGOs who thereby are entitled to be consulted by the Commission 'either directly or through several committees set up for this purpose. These consultations may be held at the invitation of the Commission or at the request of the organization'. NGOs that have observer status with the Commission can also propose items for the agenda of the Commission. As of the end of 1997, there were some two hundred and twenty-three NGOs with observer status with the Commission.

The NGOs have been most active in collaborating with the Commission on promotional activities and in the creation and deployment of its special procedures; working with it in undertakings such as conferences, seminars, workshops; and the preparation of missions. With respect to its protective activities, the Commission has been more circumspect, although there are signs that it is also now beginning to offer opportunities for NGOs to participate in some aspects of its protective work. . . . For instance, its mission to Senegal was undertaken on the basis of a complaint filed by a Senegalese NGO. . . .

. . .

IX. Problems encountered by the African Commission

Foremost among the problems that the Commission has encountered is the very text of the African Charter itself, which, like the Rules of Procedure, is opaque and difficult to interpret.

. . .

Another set of problems is found in what a former member of the Commission has bluntly described as 'a lack of money, lack of funds, lack of ability to act'. The resource and personnel problems of the Commission are endemic. The severity of the budgetary and resource limitations faced by the Commission is captured in its interim report to the sixty-seventh Ordinary Session and the OAU Council of Ministers in February 1998, in which the Commission complained that it:

> could not carry out quite a number of activities despite their importance, owing to the paucity of the human, financial and material resources needed to ensure its smooth running. As a matter of fact, the Commission has in its staff only two (2) jurists, notwithstanding the technical nature and volume of work it is

expected to do. In the budgetary appropriations for the commission, there is no provision for human rights protection and promotion activities which constitute the cornerstone of its mandate ... Communication between the Commission members on the one hand, and between these members and the Secretariat, on the other, as well as contacts between the Commission, States Parties and other partners, were seriously hampered by lack of financial resources. These constraints have been faced by the Commission throughout its ten years of existence.

. . .

X. Conclusion: What prospects for the Commission?

In an interview with the present author in 1993, then Chairman of the Commission, Dr. Ibrahim Baddawi El-Sheikh, cautioned against comparing 'the Commission with the Human Rights Committee [under the first Optional Protocol to the International Covenant on Civil and Political Rights] which for almost 16 or 17 years had been operating with a huge staff and a very sophisticated system'. Writing around the same time, Makau Wa Mutua dismissed the Commission as 'a facade, a yoke that African leaders have put around our necks', and called on human rights advocates in Africa to 'cast it off and reconstruct a system that we can proudly proclaim as ours'. More recently, the Commission seems to have begun to earn more measured, sometimes positive, reviews. Writing in 1995, Joe Oloka-Onyango describes its evolution as 'steady, but unremarkable' ... In my view, however, any conclusions or opinions about the work of the Commission, especially as they concern individual petitions, must remain tentative and probably lie somewhere between the extremes of opinions represented by these different assessments.

. . .

The [slow] development of the individual petition procedure [reflects] possibly, a low level of awareness about the mechanism or cynicism about the utility of adjudication mechanisms generally in addressing the kinds of violations of human rights that are witnessed in many parts of Africa. Jurisprudentially, the Commission has tilted the balance of its conciliation efforts in favour of the states parties by appearing too ready to affirm the existence of amicable settlements without clarifying their terms or setting accompanying compliance and verification guidelines. . . . Given the gravity of the complaints that it receives, the enthusiasm of the African Commission for amicable settlements that are not capable of either compliance or verification can only damage its credibility. To avoid this result, the Commission must evolve better principles and practice for negotiating settlements and inducing states parties to respect them.

On its interpretation of the Charter, the Commission has been mostly positive and sometimes even innovative. . . . In cases where it has proceeded to the merits, it has interpreted the rights in the Charter effectively, although its application of the principles thus established has not always been consistent. . . .

One question that I am often asked is whether the decisions of the Commission are effective. . . . [A]ny temptation to dismiss [the Commission] as a worthless institution today must be regarded as premature, ill-informed, or both. The individual petition procedure of the Commission offers a point of pressure which, if used creatively, can make a difference, as exemplified by a case involving capital punishment [in which the Commission's and NGOs' interventions ultimately led the Nigerian government to free prisoners whose convictions rested on procedures violating due process.] . . .

At the age of five years in 1992, the Commission had registered only 76 communications—an average of just about 15 communications per year—of which 34 were pending and all but two of the remainder were either irreceivable or inadmissible. Five years later in 1997, the number of communications received had risen to 200, an increase of 48 communications or just under 69 per cent when compared with the first five years, translating into an average during this five year period of nearly 25 communications per year or an increase over the first five year period of nearly 67 percent. Whereas in 1992 the Commission had reached no firm decision on the merits, by 1997 it had concluded and handed down decisions on the merits of 21 decisions, undertaken five fact-finding missions, and organized one Extraordinary Session on the situation of human rights in Nigeria, an event that was almost certainly unthinkable when the Commission was inaugurated in 1987. These figures could be evidence of a positive, if marginal, growth in the confidence and capacity of the Commission, and in public awareness about the mechanism and its level of credibility. However, in putting these figures into context, it is important to remember that there are 51 states parties to the Charter. In effect, taking the best average of 25 communications over the last five years, these statistics approximate at best to an average of one communication for every two states parties in a year!

These statistics indicate that the Commission is very much under-capacitated and under-utilized. The responsibility for changing this situation must be shared between the Commission and its interlocutors, including the states parties, victims and their representatives, and the NGO community. In the context of its individual petition procedures in particular, the most effective avenue for positively transforming the Commission's procedure is to confront it with actual cases and problems. With the imminent creation of an African Court of Human Rights, the likelihood is that the number of individual petitions brought to the attention of the Commission will continue to increase as will the burden on the institution. The proposed Court will not replace the Commission but will complement and reinforce its mandate. . . .

. . .

CIVIL LIBERTIES ORGANIZATION V. NIGERIA

African Commission on Human and Peoples' Rights, Communication No. 129/94, 2 Int. Hum. Rts R. 616 (1995)

Facts

1. The Communication is filed by the Civil Liberties Organization, a Nigerian NGO. The Commission alleges that the military government of Nigeria has enacted various decrees in violation of the African Charter, specifically the Constitution (Suspension and Modification) Decree No. 107 of 1993, which not only

suspends the Constitution but also specifies that no decrees promulgated after December 1993 can be examined in any Nigerian Court; and the Political Parties (Dissolution) Decree No. 114 of 1993, which, in addition to dissolving political parties, ousts the jurisdiction of the Courts and specifically nullifies any domestic effect of the African Charter.

Complaint

2. The Communication complains that the ousting of the jurisdiction of the Courts in Nigeria to adjudicate the legality of any decree threatens the independence of the Judiciary and violates Article 26 of the African Charter.

3. The Communication also complains that this ouster of the jurisdiction of the Courts deprives Nigerians of their right to seek redress in the Courts for government acts which violate their fundamental rights, in violation of article 7(1)(a) of the African Charter.

...

The Merits of the Case

9. Article 7 of the African Charter provides:

> 1. Every individual shall have the right to have his cause heard. This comprises: a) the right to an appeal to competent national organs against acts violating his fundamental rights as recognized and guaranteed by conventions, law, regulations and customs in force.
>
> ...

12. The reference in Article 7(1)(a) to 'fundamental rights as recognized and guaranteed by conventions ... in force' signifies the rights in the Charter itself, among others. Given that Nigeria ratified the African Charter in 1983, it is presently a Convention in force in Nigeria. If Nigeria wished to withdraw its ratification it would have to undertake an international process involving notice, which it has not done. Nigeria cannot negate the effects of its ratification of the Charter through domestic action. Nigeria remains under the obligation to guarantee the rights of Article 7 to all of its citizens. The ousting of jurisdiction of the Courts of Nigeria over any decree enacted in the past ten years, and those to be subsequently enacted, constitutes an attack of incalculable proportions on Article 7. The Complaint refers to a few examples of decrees which violate human rights but which are now beyond the review of the Courts. An attack of this sort on the jurisdiction of the Courts is especially invidious, because while it is a violation of human rights itself it permits other violations of rights to go unredressed.

13. Article 26 of the African Charter reiterates the right enshrined in Article 7 but is even more explicit about States Parties' obligations to guarantee the independence of the Courts and '... allow the establishment and improvement of appropriate national institutions entrusted with the protection and promotion of the rights and freedoms guaranteed by the present Charter'. While Article 7 focuses on the individual's right to be heard, Article 26 speaks of the institutions which are essential to give meaning and content to that right. This Article clearly

envisages protection of the Courts which have traditionally been the bastion of protection of the individual's rights against abuses of State power.

14. The Communication notes that Nigeria fully incorporated the African Charter upon ratification in 1983. . . .

. . .

. . . Any doubt that may exist as to Nigeria's obligations under the African Charter is dispelled by reference to Article 1 of the Charter which reads:

> The member States . . . parties to the present Charter shall recognize the rights, duties and freedoms enshrined in this Charter and shall undertake to adopt legislative or other measures to give effect to them.

15. The African Commission has to express its approval of Nigeria's original incorporation of the Charter, an incorporation that should set a standard for the whole of Africa, and its sadness at the subsequent nullification of this incorporation . . .

FOR THE ABOVE REASONS THE COMMISSION:

1. *holds* that the Decrees in question constitute a breach of Article 7 of the Charter, the right to be heard
2. *holds* the ouster of the Courts' jurisdiction constitutes a breach of Article 26, the obligation to establish and protect the Courts
3. *finds* the act of the Nigerian Government to nullify the domestic effect of the Charter constitutes an affront to the African Charter on Human and Peoples' Rights.

CONSTITUTIONAL RIGHTS PROJECT V. NIGERIA
African Commission on Human and Peoples' Rights, Communication No. 87/93, 3 Int. Hum. Rts R. 137 (1996)

The Facts

1. Communication 87/93 was brought on behalf of seven men Zamani Lekwot, James Atomic Kude, Yohanna Karau Kibori, Marcus Mamman, Yahaya Duniya, Julius Sarki Zamman Dabo and Iliya Maza—sentenced to death under the Civil Disturbances (Special Tribunal) Decree No. 2 of 1987 from Nigeria. This decree does not provide for any judicial appeal against the decisions of the special tribunals and prohibits the courts from reviewing any aspect of the operation of the tribunal.

2. The communication also alleges that the accused and their counsel were constantly harassed and intimidated during the trial, ultimately forcing the withdrawal of the defense counsel. Despite the lack of defense, the tribunal condemned the accused to death for culpable homicide unlawful assembly and breach of the peace.

Argument

3. The communication argues that the prohibition on judicial review of the special tribunals and lack of judicial appeals of judgments of these tribunals violates the right to an appeal to competent national organs against acts violating fundamental rights, guaranteed by Article 7, paragraph 1(a) of the African Charter.

4. The communication complains that the conduct of the trials before these tribunals, which included harassment of defense counsel, and deprivation of defense counsel, violated the right to be defended by counsel of one's choice, guaranteed by Article 7, paragraph 1(c).

5. The communication finally complains that the practice of setting up special tribunals, composed of members of the armed forces and police in addition to judges, violates the right to be tried by an impartial tribunal guaranteed by Article 7, paragraph 1(d).

. . .

The Merits of the Case

7. The Civil Disturbances (Special Tribunal) Act, Part IV, Section 8(1) provides:

> The validity of any decision, sentence, judgment . . . or order given or made, . . . or any other thing whatsoever done under this Act shall not be inquired into in any court of law.

8. . . . While punishments decreed as the culmination of a carefully conducted criminal procedure do not necessarily constitute violations of [fundamental] rights, to foreclose any avenue of appeal to 'competent national organs' in criminal cases bearing such penalties clearly violates Article 7.1(a) of the African Charter, and increases the risk that even severe violations may go unredressed.

9. The communication alleges that during the trials the defense counsel for the complainants was harassed and intimidated to the extent of being forced to withdraw from the proceedings. In spite of this forced withdrawal of counsel, the tribunal proceeded to give judgment in the matter, finally sentencing the accused to death. The Commission finds that defendants were deprived of their right to defense, including the right to be defended by counsel of their choice, violation of Article 7.1(c) as cited above.

10. The Civil Disturbances (Special Tribunal) Act, Part II, Section 2(2) says that the tribunal shall consist of one judge and four members of the Armed Forces. As such, the tribunal is composed of persons belonging largely to the executive branch of government, the same branch that passed the Civil Disturbances Act.

Article 7.1(d) of the African Charter requires the court or tribunal to be impartial. Regardless of the character of the individual members of such tribunals, its composition alone creates the appearance, if not actual lack of impartiality. It thus violates Article 7.1(d).

FOR THE ABOVE REASONS, THE COMMISSION

> *declares* that there has been a violation of Article 7(a), (c) and (d) of the African Charter; and
> *recommends* that the Government of Nigeria should free the complainants. At the 17th Session the Commission decided to bring the file to Nigeria for a planned mission in order to make sure that the violations have been repaired.

COMMISSION NATIONALE DES DROITS DE L'HOMME ET DES LIBERTÉS V. CHAD

African Commission on Human and Peoples' Rights, Communication No. 74/92, 4 Int. Hum. Rts R. 94 (1997)

The Facts

1. The communication is brought by *La Commission Nationale des Droits de l'Homme et des Libertés de la Fédération Nationale des Unions de Jeunes Avocats de France.* The complaint alleges several massive and severe violations in Chad.

2. The complaint alleges that journalists are harassed, both directly and indirectly. These attacks are often by unidentified individuals who the complainants claim to be security service agents of the Government. The Government denies responsibility.

. . .

4. There are several accounts of killings, disappearance and torture. 15 people are reported killed, 200 wounded, and several persons tortured as a result of the civil war between the security services and other groups.

5. The communication alleges the assassination of Bisso Mamadou, who was attacked by armed individuals. The Minister responsible was warned of the danger to Mr. Bisso, but he refused to issue protection. Subsequently, the Minister did not initiate investigation into the killing.

. . .

The Law

17. Article 1 of the African Charter reads:

> The Member States of the Organizations of African Unity parties to the present Charter shall recognize the rights, duties and freedoms enshrined in this Charter and shall undertake to adapt legislative or other measures to give effect to them.

18. In this case, the complainant claims that not only did the Government agents commit violations of the African Charter, but that the State failed to protect the rights in the Charter from violation by other parties.

19. The Government claims that no violations were committed by its agents, and that it had no control over violations committed by other parties, as Chad is in a state of civil war.

20. The Charter specifies in Article 1 that the States Parties shall not only recognize the rights and duties and freedoms adopted by the Charter, but they should also 'undertake . . . measures to give effect to them'. In other words, if a State neglects to ensure the rights in the African Charter, this can constitute a violation, even if the State or its agents are not the immediate cause of the violation.

21. The African Charter, unlike other human rights instruments, does not allow for States Parties to derogate from their treaty obligations during emergency situations. Thus, even a civil war in Chad cannot be used as an excuse by the State violating or permitting violations of rights in the African Charter.

22. In the present case, Chad has failed to provide security and stability in the country, thereby allowing serious and massive violations of human rights. The national armed forces are participants in the civil war and there have been several instances in which the Government has failed to intervene to prevent the assassination and killing of specific individuals. Even where it cannot be proved that violations were committed by Government agents, the Government had a responsibility to secure the safety and the liberty of its citizens, and to conduct investigations into murders. Chad therefore is responsible for the violations of the African Charter.

23. The complainant claims that the events in Chad constitute violations of Articles 4 (right to life), 5 (prohibition of torture, inhuman and degrading treatment), 6 (right to life and security of persons), 7 (right to a fair trial), and 10 (right to freedom of expression).

24. In the present case, there has been no substantive response from the Government of Chad, only a blanket denial of responsibility.

25. The African Commission, in several previous decisions, has set out the principle that where allegations of human rights abuse go uncontested by the Government concerned, the Commission must decide on the facts provided by the complainant and treat those facts as given. This principle conforms with the practice of other international human rights adjudicatory bodies and the Commission's duty to protect human rights. Since the Government of Chad does not wish to participate in a dialogue, the Commission must, regrettably, continue its consideration of the case on the basis of the facts and opinions submitted by the complaints alone.

26. Thus in the absence of a substantive response by the Government, in keeping with its practice, the Commission will take its decisions based on the events alleged by the complainants.

FOR THESE REASONS, THE COMMISSION

Finds that there have been serious and massive violations of human rights in Chad.

Finds that there have been violations of Articles 4, 5, 6, 7.

COMMENT ON PROTOCOL ON AFRICAN COURT ON HUMAN AND PEOPLES' RIGHTS

In 1998 the Assembly of Heads of State and Government of the OAU adopted a Protocol, reproduced in 20 Hum. Rts L. J. 269 (1999), to the African Charter on Human and Peoples' Rights that would establish a Court to complement the Commission in the African human rights regime. The Protocol is to become effective when 15 states parties to the Charter have ratified it. The Preamble recites that the states parties to the Charter are 'firmly convinced that the attainment of the objectives' of the Charter 'requires the establishment of an African court' to 'complement and reinforce the functions' of the Commission.

The Court consists of 11 judges 'elected in an individual capacity'; no two judges may be nationals of the same state. (Article 11). Its membership is to include 'representation of the main regions of Africa and of their principal legal traditions', and in the election of judges the Assembly 'shall ensure that there is adequate gender representation'. (Article 14) Judicial independence is to be fully ensured. (Article 17).

The Court's jurisdiction extends to cases and disputes 'concerning the interpretation and application' of the Charter, Protocol, 'and any other relevant human rights instrument ratified by the States concerned' (Article 3). At the request of a member state of the OAU or the OAU, the Court may give its advisory opinion 'on any legal matter related to the Charter or any other relevant human rights instruments', provided that the matter is not then being examined by the Commission (Article 4).

To invoke the Court's contentious jurisdiction, the Commission, a state party that has brought a complaint before the Commission or against whom a complaint has been brought, a state party whose citizen is a victim of a violation, and African intergovernmental organizations can submit a case to the Court (Article 5). On the other hand, the capacity of individuals and NGOs to bring a complaint against a state depends both on a special declaration by the state and on the discretion of the Court (Articles 5 and 34). This double barrier represents a sharp contrast with the access of individuals to the other two regional courts.

The Commission continues to play an important role under the Protocol. The provisions on admissibility provide that the Court 'may consider cases or transfer them to the Commission' (Article 6). The Court's Rules of Procedure are to state the conditions under which the Court shall consider cases, 'bearing in mind the complementarity between the Commission and the Court' (Article 8). The communications procedure itself of the Commission is not reconciled with the new Court; it remains unclear when one or the other path should be followed by an institution or individual intending to submit a complaint against a state. Thus the two organs appear to be in competition with each other, without any clear hierarchy, posing a large risk of duplication of effort.

If the Court finds a violation, 'it shall make appropriate orders to remedy the violation' (Article 27). States parties to the Protocol 'undertake to comply with the judgment in any case to which they are parties . . . and to guarantee its execution'

(Article 30). The OAU Council of Ministers is to 'monitor' a judgment's execution (Article 29).

QUESTION

Given the provisions of the Protocol and the present circumstances of the Commission and of the African human rights regime in general, would you as an African human rights advocate have urged the present creation of a court? What plausible arguments could be made for or against such a move at this time?

ADDITIONAL READING

M. Mutua, *The African Human Rights Court: A Two-Legged Stool?*, 21 Hum. Rts Q. 342 (1999); E.K. Quashigah and O.C. Okafor (eds.), *Legitimate Governance in Africa: International and Domestic Legal Perspectives* (1999); N. Krisch, 'The Establishment of an African Court on Human and Peoples' Rights', 58 Zeitschrift für ausländisches öffentliches Recht und Völkerrecht 713 (1998); G. Naldi and K. Magliveras, *Reinforcing the African System of Human Rights: The Protocol on the Establishment of a Regional Court of Human and Peoples' Rights*, 16 Neth. Q. of Hum. Rts 431 (1998); C.A. Odinkalu and C. Christensen, 'The African Commission on Human and Peoples' Rights: The Development of Non-State Communication Procedures', 20 Hum. Rts Q. 235 (1998); U.O. Umozurike, *The African Charter on Human Peoples' Rights* (1997); E. Ankumah, *The African Commission on Human and Peoples' Rights* (1996).

11

Civil Society: Human Rights NGOs and Other Groups

A. NGOs, INGOs, AND CIVIL SOCIETY

COMMENT ON TYPES AND ACTIVITIES OF NONGOVERNMENTAL ORGANIZATIONS

Nongovernmental organizations (NGOs)—both domestic and international (INGOs)—have figured prominently in many preceding Chapters. This Chapter explores their character, constitution, functions, methods of work and effects.

NGOs pervade and are a vital part of the overall human rights regime. Above all, human rights NGOs bring out the facts. They also contribute to standard-setting as well as to the promotion, implementation and enforcement of human rights norms. They provoke and energize. They spread the message of human rights and mobilize people to realize that message. Decentralized and diverse, they proceed with a speed, decisiveness and range of concerns impossible to imagine in relation to most of the work of bureaucratic and politically constrained intergovernmental organizations.

NGOs operate on the basis of differing mandates, each responding to its own priorities and methods of action, bringing a range of viewpoints to the human rights movement. It is inconceivable that the state of human rights in the world, whatever its shortcomings, could have progressed as much since the Second World War without the spur and inventiveness of NGOs.

Human rights NGOs are only a part of a much broader range of nongovern-mental actors whose activities are part of what are now commonly referred to by such terms as 'civil society', 'transnational advocacy networks', and 'social move-ments'. Until the fall of the Berlin Wall, the concept of civil society was little more than a heading in the history of ideas, addressed by those looking at the work of Hegel, Locke and Adam Ferguson. Today, the term is everywhere, even if its defin-ition remains contested. One major study defines it as 'a sphere of social inter-action between economy and state, composed above all of the intimate sphere (especially the family), the sphere of associations (especially voluntary associ-ations), social movements, and forms of public communication'. This definition excludes political parties and those actors of 'political and economic society [which] are directly involved with state power and economic production, which they seek to control and manage'.[1]

Transnational advocacy networks, a term used by political scientists, have been defined even more broadly so as to encompass: '(1) international and domestic nongovernmental research and advocacy organizations; (2) local social movements; (3) foundations; (4) the media; (5) churches, trade unions, consumer organizations, and intellectuals; (6) parts of regional and international intergovernmental organizations; and (7) parts of the executive and/or parliamentary branches of governments'.[2] Commercial economic actors are about the only group clearly excluded from that definition. Finally, in definitional terms, 'social movements' are said to 'have no definite memberships or authority structures; they consist of as many people, as much territory and as many issues as seems appropriate to the people involved; they have no central headquarters and are spread across numerous locales; and they are all inclusive, excluding no one and embracing anyone who wishes to be part of the movement'.[3] It is in this latter sense that the term 'human rights movement' is sometimes used, including in this book.

To add to the terminological complexity, a great many acronyms have been coined to describe different categories of groups. In addition to NGOs and INGOs (international NGOs) they include: CSOs (civil society organizations), CBOs (community-based organizations), PVOs (private voluntary organizations), GROs (grassroots organizations), QUANGOs (quasi-NGOs), GONGOs (government organized NGOs), BINGOs (business and industry NGOs), DONGOs (donor organized NGOs), and DNGDOs (domestic nongovernmental development organizations).

This book uses the term NGO partly because of its consistent historical usage in the human rights domain, partly because its use in Article 71 of the UN Charter has discouraged any alternative terminology in that context, and partly because a 'nongovernmental' character remains a defining element in the make-up of any such human rights group. Nevertheless, the term NGO, standing alone, still reaches too broadly for our purposes. It includes myriad types of organizations that are (more-or-less, depending on the state) independent of the state: economic interest groups like labour unions, consumer unions or industrial associations; racial, gender and religious groups; issue-oriented groups like educational, environmental or animal welfare organizations; groups representing those with disabilities or the elderly or the young; public interest groups that are anti-corruption or pro-universal health care; and so on—the many types of associations of citizens and of non-state institutions that some theorists view as the essential ingredients of the concept of civil society.

This Chapter is concerned with that subset of NGOs which is involved with human rights issues, although that category is rapidly expanding. Post-Cold War efforts to make human rights an integral part of the mainstream in a wide range of

---

[1] Cohen and Arato, *Civil Society and Political Theory* (1992), ix.
[2] Keck and Sikkink, *Activists Beyond Borders: Advocacy Networks in International Politics* (1998), 9.

[3] J. Rosenau, 'Governance and Democracy in a Globalizing World', in Archibugi, Held and Köhler (eds.), *Re-Imagining Political Community: Studies in Cosmopolitan Democracy* (1998), 28 at 42.

activities have highlighted that expansion by bringing a significant number of development and humanitarian NGOs into the picture, by urging businesses and other private actors to accept human rights responsibilities, and by underscoring the relevance of human rights considerations in areas such as trade, environment, or labour.

Within individual states, it is often the domestic human rights NGOs that call governments to account and compel reconsideration of policies and programmes that have been designed in disregard or violation of human rights norms. It is not only the domestic policies of a state that figure in NGO reporting and advocacy. The development in a few states of a foreign economic policy that takes into account human rights violations in other states owes much to the information provided and pressures exerted by NGOs.

At the international level, and particularly in the United Nations context, the frequent reluctance of governmental actors to criticize their counterparts from other countries and the limited supply of independent sources of information have contributed to making NGOs the lynchpins of the system as a whole. In situations in which NGO information is not available or where the NGOs are either unable or unwilling to generate political pressures upon the governments concerned, the chances of a weak response by the international community, or of none at all, are radically increased. A high proportion of the most significant initiatives to draft new international instruments, to establish new procedures and machinery, and to identify specific governments as violators have come as a result of concerted NGO campaigns designed to mobilize public opinion and lobby governmental support. As noted in Chapter 8, well over half of the 3,240 persons who participated in the 1999 session of the UN Commission on Human Rights were NGO representatives. At the Beijing World Conference on Women in 1995, 40,000 persons attended the NGO forum. According to UN estimates the number of international NGOs grew from around 1,300 in 1960 to more than 36,000 in 1995, and the number has increased significantly since then.

But numerical indicators tell only a small part of the overall story. Human rights NGOs have experienced a quantum leap in their professionalism from the days of the 'amiable amateurs' importuning delegates for a brief chat to the high level of professionalism of many groups today. By comparison with the situation even as recently as 15 years ago, the output of the major international NGOs is more visible and better marketed, their strategies are more clearly mapped out, their level of technical expertise is greater, and their funding more adequate to the task. The communications revolution has assisted them in gathering timely and com-pelling information, in disseminating it, in running well coordinated campaigns, and in enlisting public opinion.

Moreover, their impact is often more obvious and tangible than it was in an earlier era. The 1997 Ottawa Conference to draft a Landmines Treaty, the 1998 Rome Conference to draft the Statute of an International Criminal Court, and the 1999 Seattle Ministerial Meeting of the World Trade Organization represent a high water mark in terms of NGO involvement and influence. Perhaps most significant is the blurring of the distinction between the insiders and the outsiders as NGO representatives have become part of governmental delegations. They have also increasingly become key partners in the delivery of humanitarian and other forms of development assistance, partners with government in performing a variety of functions such as human rights education, the monitoring of voluntary codes of conduct and even the delivery of basic social services, and even partners with businesses and labour unions in various areas.

THE NON-GOVERNMENTAL ORDER
The Economist, 18 December 1999, at 23

[This analysis was published after the failure of a WTO Ministerial Meeting in Seattle in November 1999 which had aimed to launch a new round of negotiations to further liberalize world trade. Commentators attributed much of the responsibility to a highly visible NGO campaign.]

. . . [The NGOs] that descended on Seattle were a model of everything the trade negotiators were not. They were well organized. They built unusual coalitions (environmentalists and labour groups, for instance, bridged old gulfs to jeer the WTO together). They had a clear agenda—to derail the talks. And they were masterly users of the media.

The battle of Seattle is only the latest and most visible in a string of recent NGO victories. The watershed was the Earth Summit in Rio de Janeiro in 1992, when the NGOs roused enough public pressure to push through agreements on controlling greenhouse gases. In 1994, protesters dominated the World Bank's anniversary meeting with a 'Fifty Years is Enough' campaign, and forced a rethink of the Bank's goals and methods. In 1998, an ad hoc coalition of consumer-rights activists and environmentalists helped to sink the Multilateral Agreement on Investment (MAI), a draft treaty to harmonize rules on foreign investment under the aegis of the OECD. In the past couple of years another global coalition of NGOs, Jubilee 2000, has pushed successfully for a dramatic reduction in the debts of the poorest countries.

The NGO agenda is not confined to economic issues. One of the biggest successes of the 1990s was the campaign to outlaw landmines, where hundreds of NGOs, in concert with the Canadian government, pushed through a ban in a year. Nor is it confined to government agendas. Nike has been targeted for poor labour conditions in its overseas factories, Nestlé for the sale of powdered baby milk in poor countries, Monsanto for genetically modified food. In a case in 1995 that particularly shocked business, Royal Dutch/Shell, although it was technically in the right, was prevented by Greenpeace, the most media-savvy of all NGOs, from disposing of its Brent Spar oil rig in the North Sea.

. . . Are citizens' groups, as many of their supporters claim, the first steps towards an 'international civil society' (whatever that might be)? Or do they represent a dangerous shift of power to unelected and unaccountable special-interest groups?

. . . Although organizations like these have existed for generations (in the early

1800s, the British and Foreign Anti-Slavery Society played a powerful part in abolishing slavery laws), the social and economic shifts of this decade have given them new life. The end of communism, the spread of democracy in poor countries, technological change and economic integration—globalization, in short—have created fertile soil for the rise of NGOs. Globalization itself has exacerbated a host of worries: over the environment, labour rights, human rights, consumer rights and so on. Democratization and technological progress have revolutionized the way in which citizens can unite to express their disquiet.

It is, by definition, hard to estimate the growth of groups that could theoretically include everything from the tiniest neighbourhood association to huge international relief agencies, such as CARE, with annual budgets worth hundreds of millions of dollars. One conservative yardstick of international NGOs (that is, groups with operations in more than one country) is the Yearbook of International Organizations. This puts the number of international NGOs at more than 26,000 today, up from 6,000 in 1990.

Far more groups exist within national borders. A recent article . . . suggested that the United States alone has about 2m NGOs, 70% of which are less than 30 years old. India has about 1m grass-roots groups, while another estimate suggests that more than 100,000 sprang up in Eastern Europe between 1988 and 1995. Membership growth has been impressive across many groups, but particularly the environmental ones. . . .

. . . As a group, NGOs now deliver more aid than the whole United Nations system. Some of the biggest NGOs, such as CARE or Médecins Sans Frontières, are primarily aid providers. Others, such as Oxfam, are both aid providers and campaigners . . .
. . .

New coalitions can be built online. . . . [T]he Internet allows new partnerships between groups in rich and poor countries. Armed with compromising evidence of local labour practices or environmental degradation from southern NGOS, for example, activists in developed countries can attack corporations much more effectively.

This phenomenon—amorphous groups of NGOs, linked online, descending on a target—has been dubbed an 'NGO swarm' . . . [which has] no 'central leadership or command structure; it is multi-headed, impossible to decapitate'. And it can sting a victim to death.

Less dramatic, but just as important, is the rise of NGOs that are dubbed . . . 'technical' groups. These specialize in providing highly sophisticated analysis and information, and they can be crucial to the working of some treaties. . . . In the campaign to cut third-world debt, a handful of NGOs, including Oxfam, have become as expert in the minutiae of debt-reduction procedures as the bureaucrats at the IMF and World Bank. Increasingly, they have been co-opted into making policy. . . .

If the power of NGOs has increased in a globalized world, who has lost out? . . . Certainly national governments no longer have a monopoly of information, or an unequalled reach, compared to corporations and civil society. But the real losers in this power shift are international organizations.

Inter-governmental institutions such as the World Bank, the IMF, the UN agencies or the WTO have an enormous weakness in an age of NGOs: they lack political leverage. No parliamentarian is going to face direct pressure from the IMF or the WTO; but every policymaker faces pressure from citizens' groups with special interests. . . .

Less obvious is whether NGO attacks will democratize, or merely disable, these organizations. At first sight, Seattle suggests a pessimistic conclusion: inter-governmental outfits will become paralysed in the face of concerted opposition. History, however, suggests a different outcome. Take the case of the World Bank. The Fifty Years is Enough campaign of 1994 was a prototype of Seattle (complete with activists invading the meeting halls). Now the NGOs are surprisingly quiet about the World Bank. The reason is that the Bank has made a huge effort to co-opt them.

James Wolfensohn, the Bank's boss, has made 'dialogue' with NGOs a central component of the institution's work. More than 70 NGO specialists work in the Bank's field offices. More than half of World Bank projects last year involved NGOs. Mr Wolfensohn has built alliances with everyone, from religious groups to environmentalists. His efforts have diluted the strength of 'mobilization networks' and increased the relative power of technical NGOs (for it is mostly these that the Bank has co-opted).

. . .

B. HUMAN RIGHTS NGOs

In the readings that follow we first take up the issue of how, if at all, a 'human rights' NGO might be distinguished from other NGOs. We then look at some of the obstacles that governments place in the way of domestic NGOs and examine the mandate of some of the most prominent of the INGOs.

HENRY STEINER, DIVERSE PARTNERS: NON-GOVERNMENTAL ORGANIZATIONS IN THE HUMAN RIGHTS MOVEMENT
(1991), at 5

[These excerpts are from the report of a retreat for human rights NGO activists from around the world.]

. . .

[*A. What makes a group a 'Human Rights' NGO?*]

Participants distinguished between 'national' NGOs limiting their activities to their home country, and 'international' NGOs (INGOs) that act in two or more countries. . . .

Our discussions about threshold definitions underscored how diverse were the participants' understandings of the human rights movement. Certain questions recurred. For a public interest group to qualify as a 'human rights' NGO, must it base its criticism of state conduct on international human rights law—the Universal Declaration of Human Rights (UDHR), the Civil-Political Rights Covenant, and so on? Most participants thought not. They were more persuaded by the nature of the claims made and the goals advanced by a group than by the formal source of the norms that it invoked to criticize state conduct.

In fact, some participants noted, the choice between relying on a national legal system or on international law norms to support advocacy before national institutions often amounts to a question of strategy. Employing domestic standards rather than international law might be politically expedient—more political clout, less risk that an NGO will be viewed as inspired by alien doctrine. On the other hand, international law has strategic advantages in countries whose domestic legal norms are of little assistance. . . .

Participants suggested other reasons for national NGOs to rely on domestic law. In countries that have ratified few covenants, NGOs arguing before national courts can criticize domestic law or conduct as violating international norms only by invoking the less determinate customary international law. . . . [P]ublic interest groups in the U.S. that vindicate civil and political rights—for example, the American Civil Liberties Union (ACLU), or the NAACP Legal Defense and Education Fund (LDF), an NGO committed to ending discrimination against blacks—base their advocacy on domestic constitutional law and only rarely refer to international human rights. Nonetheless, from an international perspective, these groups are as much 'human rights' NGOs as, say, Tutela Legal in El Salvador, which invokes primarily international standards and has close links with INGOs.

Public interest groups in fields like consumer or environmental protection or workers' safety regulation fall within more ambiguous categories. Whether they are classified as 'human rights' organizations does not, however, appear to have operational significance.

. . .

Many participants concluded that self-perception and self-definition by NGOs constitute the only sensible method of identifying human rights organizations. It would be impractical and unwise to maintain a protective boundary around some core or traditional preserve of human rights work, such as the protection of individuals against violence or discrimination. Who would define and monitor such a boundary, and what sanctions could be imposed on organizations crossing it but still claiming to be human rights NGOs? An attempt at authoritative definition could block a natural and important growth of the human rights movement, such as its earlier evolution toward economic and social rights, or its present initiatives toward linking human rights concerns with developmental and environmental issues. Other participants, however, stressed that to be effective, it was important for NGOs to hold to clearly defined mandates based on consensual legal norms.

Like the human rights movement itself, NGOs are in a state of flux. The costs of such change and uncertainty—a threat to the human rights movement's core identity, a blurring of fields, disagreements about whether employing the rhetoric of 'human rights' for certain goals will strengthen or hurt the movement as a whole—inhere in a dynamic, decentralized, multicultural, universal movement.

PERSPECTIVES ON DOMESTIC NGOs

The following three comments of participants in and observers of the non-governmental movement raise issues of (1) assessing NGOs in terms of their 'genuine efforts to promote human rights', (2) governmental control of NGO activities, and (3) broad participation in NGO activities.

Aryeh Neier, Not all Human Rights Groups are Equal

Letter to Editor, *New York Times*, May 27, 1989, p. 22

. . .

A phenomenon that has concerned the human rights movement is the proliferation of groups claiming to speak in the name of the human rights cause but actually engaged in efforts to promote one or another side in a civil conflict. Nowhere has this been more of a factor than in Nicaragua. On both sides, the human rights issue has been a weapon to use against the enemy.

It may be useful, accordingly, to suggest a few questions to raise in distinguishing partisan efforts from genuine efforts to promote human rights. These include:

- Is the organization funded by or otherwise linked to any party to the conflict?
- Is it impartial? If it is an international group, does it regularly criticize abuses by governments of all political persuasions and geopolitical alignments? In situations of sustained armed conflict, does it criticize violations of the laws of war by both sides according to the same criteria?
- Does it engage in systematic field research and does it avoid sweeping comments, except to the degree that these are sustained by its detailed findings through field research?
- Does it exercise care in the use of language? For example, does it refer to 'torture' when the word 'mistreatment' would be more appropriate? When does it allege 'atrocities' as a 'strategy'?
- Does it acknowledge contradictory evidence, such as a government's prosecutions of its own personnel for abuses, or the statements of one witness that cast doubt on the statements of another?

Above all, of course, it is the record that an organization has compiled over time that indicates whether it deserves credence when it reports on human rights . . .

Peter van Tuijl, NGOs and Human Rights: Sources of Justice and Democracy

52 J. Int'l Affs 493 (1999), at 503

. . .

To maintain . . . control, governments use different means to hamper, disturb or stop NGO activities. They may challenge the credibility or legitimacy of an NGO or its actions by using legal or sometimes illegal means to ban NGOs from operating in the country or to intimidate or arrest NGO personnel. Governments that neglect or violate human rights are more inclined to try to control NGOs by repressing them or denying their right to exist. Where a state prohibits the operation of independent NGOs, such as in China, politically sensitive NGO activities can often be conducted by falling back on more informal methods. Collecting information on human rights violations or environmental degradation can be done using rudimentary forms of organization or individual action.

Under such severe governmental pressure, NGOs have found creative ways to survive using their organization's structure or mutual relationships vis-à-vis the prevailing legal and political regime. In Egypt, NGOs have been able to evade the impact of restrictive laws by registering as non-profit companies under the general Egyptian law on corporations. As a consequence, nearly all human rights NGOs in Egypt are registered as 'civil companies'. In Indonesia most NGOs are registered as foundations so they can avoid being subject to the restrictive law on mass organizations. NGOs may also exist and operate in an undefined institutional space created by lengthy legal or bureaucratic procedures. The Malaysian chapter of Amnesty International has been awaiting approval of its registration for five years. Nevertheless, it has been active ever since it applied for registration by operating in an undefined, gray area, thus not violating state laws.

Moreover, coalition building among NGOs has been an effective means of protection against government interference. In some cases NGOs have opted for national NGO coalitions or networks in order to build consensus and to present a unified front to authorities. In other cases NGOs have decided to stay away from centralized coalitions to avoid becoming visible targets for control-driven authorities.

Chidi Anselm Odinkalu, Why More Africans Don't Use Human Rights Language

Hum. Rts. Dialogue, Winter 2000, p. 3 at 4

. . .

The current human rights movement in Africa—with the possible exception of the women's rights movement and faith-based social justice initiatives—appears almost by design to exclude the participation of the people whose welfare it purports to advance. Most human rights organizations are modeled after Northern watchdog organizations, located in an urban area, run by a core management without a membership base (unlike Amnesty International), and dependent solely on overseas funding. The most successful of these organizations only manage to achieve the equivalent status of a public policy think-tank, a research institute, or a specialized publishing house. With media-driven visibility and a lifestyle to match, the leaders of these initiatives enjoy privilege and comfort, and progressively grow distant from a life of struggle.

In the absence of a membership base, there is no constituency-driven obligation or framework for popularizing the language or objectives of the group beyond the community of inward-looking professionals or careerists who run it. Instead of being the currency of a social justice or conscience-driven movement, 'human rights' has increasingly become the specialized language of a select professional cadre with its own rites of passage and methods of certification. Far from being a badge of honor, human rights activism is, in some of the places I have observed it, increasingly a certificate of privilege.

COMMENT ON INTERNATIONAL NGOs

Human rights INGOs span an increasingly wide spectrum. For the most part, their activities focus on the preparation of reports on specific countries throughout the world (including a broad range of issues within any one country), as well as on generic problems involving many countries like censorship or prison conditions. They distribute these reports, provide the information in them to the media, and use the information to engage in lobbying or other forms of advocacy before national executive officials or legislatures and international organizations. That lobbying or advocacy may, for example, urge particular forms of pressure against offending countries. Sometimes INGOs initiate or (as *amicus curiae*) join in litigation before national or international tribunals.

Their other activities include the drafting of proposed legislation and of international standards, human rights education, active participation in conferences and other forms of promotion, grassroots mobilization on particular issues, leading popular protests and demonstrations, letter-writing and urgent action campaigns, monitoring and critiquing the work of governmental and intergovernmental human rights agencies, and working with and strengthening their local affiliates. In addition to INGOs focused on specific issues such as the rights of women, minorities, children, indigenous peoples, media freedom, and economic and social rights,[4] there are several especially prominent ones with which students should be familiar.

Amnesty International. Established in 1961, Amnesty (website: www. amnesty.org) had over one million members by 1999 in more than 160 countries, including national sections in 56 countries. Its International Secretariat in London employs 320 official and 95 volunteers. It is governed by a nine-member International Executive Committee elected every two years by an International

---

[4] The University of Minnesota's Human Rights Library contains a wide-ranging list of NGO websites at <www1.umn.edu/humanrts/links/ngolinks.html>.

Council comprising representatives of the worldwide movement. The main focus of its campaigning has been to: free all prisoners of conscience (people detained for their beliefs or because of their ethnic origin, sex, colour, language, etc. and who have not used or advocated violence); ensure fair and prompt trials for political prisoners; abolish the death penalty, torture and other cruel, inhuman or degrading treatment of prisoners; and end extrajudicial executions and 'disappearances'. In 1998 it issued 93 major human rights reports on 49 countries and sent 132 delegations to 82 countries.

The International Secretariat's annual budget of over US$25 million in 1998–99 came from membership fees, private donations and donations from trusts, foundations and companies. Amnesty neither seeks nor accepts governmental funds for its investigative and campaigning work.

Human Rights Watch. HRW (website: www.hrw.org) is the largest US-based INGO. It began in 1978 as Helsinki Watch. Americas Watch was added in 1981 and Asia Watch in 1985. The HRW umbrella was adopted in 1988. It is not a membership-based organization. As of 2000 it was organized into divisions covering Africa (sub-Saharan Africa), Americas (Latin America and the Caribbean), Asia, Europe and Central Asia, and the Middle East (Middle East and North Africa), as well as thematic divisions on Arms, Children's Rights, and Women's Rights. It has also maintained 'special initiatives' relating to academic freedom, corporations and human rights, drugs and human rights, free expression, prison conditions, and the United States. It has a staff of over 100 in New York and has a number of other offices worldwide. Its annual budget is over $16 million. It describes its mandate in the following terms:

> Human Rights Watch conducts regular, systematic investigations of human rights abuses in some seventy countries around the world. Our reputation for timely, reliable disclosures has made us an essential source of information for those concerned with human rights. We address the human rights practices of governments of all political stripes, of all geopolitical alignments, and of all ethnic and religious persuasions. Human Rights Watch defends freedom of thought and expression, due process and equal protection of the law, and a vigorous civil society; we document and denounce murders, disappearances, torture, arbitrary imprisonment, discrimination, and other abuses of internationally recognized human rights. Our goal is to hold governments accountable if they transgress the rights of their people (*Human Rights Watch World Report 2000*, vii).

The Lawyers Committee for Human Rights. In existence since 1978, the LCHR (website: www.lchr.org) describes its work as 'impartial, holding all governments accountable to [human rights] standards. . . . Its programs focus on building the legal institutions and structures that will guarantee human rights in the long term. Strengthening independent human rights advocacy at the local level is a key feature of its work'. It also 'seeks to influence the US government to promote the rule of law in both its foreign and domestic policy, and presses for greater integration of human rights into the work of the UN and the World Bank' and 'works to protect refugees through the representation of asylum seekers and by challenging legal restrictions on the rights of refugees in the United States and around the world'. Its funding comes from foundations and law firms.

The International Committee of the Red Cross. The ICRC (website: www.cicr.org/eng) was established in 1863. It describes itself as 'an impartial, neutral and independent organization whose exclusively humanitarian mission is to protect the lives and dignity of victims of war and internal violence and to provide them with assistance. It directs and coordinates the international relief activities conducted by the [Red Cross] Movement [consisting of national Red Cross and Red Crescent societies] in situations of conflict. It also endeavours to prevent suffering by promoting and strengthening humanitarian law and universal humanitarian principles'. It is funded largely by the Swiss Government.

Médecins sans Frontières. MSF (website: www.msf.org) was set up in 1971 and was awarded the Nobel Peace Prize in 1999. Its mandate focuses principally on emergency medical relief but in recent years human rights issues have assumed greater prominence. 'In carrying out humanitarian assistance, we act as a witness and will speak out, either in private or in public, about the plight of populations in danger for whom we work. In doing so, [MSF] seeks to alleviate human suffering, to protect life and health and to restore and ensure respect for . . . human beings and their fundamental human rights' (www.msf.ca).

QUESTIONS

1. Neier talks of 'genuine efforts' to promote human rights. Which if any of the following characteristics or tasks of NGOs would you view as potentially raising questions about such genuineness of NGOs and their activities: types of funding sources, participation or not by broad dues-paying membership, appointment of NGO members by government?

2. Recall Question (3) at p. 157, *supra*, which raised the issue of how human rights NGOs should allocate their scarce resources. Consider this question again in the context of Part C's analysis of human rights organizations, and this Chapter's concentration on NGOs. If you were the director of an INGO, how would you decide about what issues to examine? You might, for example, explore a given problem across a few or many countries—perhaps gender discrimination or press censorship. You might concentrate on offences within a given state, or devise some other approach to your work. Under what criteria would you select among countries, topics, or strategies? What priorities would you establish?

C. NGOs AND INGOs: CHARACTERISTICS AND CRITICISMS

1. REPRESENTATIVENESS, CONSTITUENCIES AND ACCOUNTABILITY

KENNETH ANDERSON, THE OTTAWA CONVENTION BANNING LANDMINES, THE ROLE OF INTERNATIONAL NON-GOVERNMENTAL ORGANIZATIONS AND THE IDEA OF INTERNATIONAL CIVIL SOCIETY
11 Eur. J. Int. L. 92 (2000)

. . . The Ottawa Convention [on the Prohibition of the Use, Stockpiling, Production and Transfer of Anti-Personnel Mines and on their Destruction] represents the first time in over a century in which a major, traditional weapon system has been banned outright and not simply regulated in its use. . . .

. . .

3. The Romance Between NGOs and International Organizations

A. Seven lessons from the Landmines Ban Campaign

[The author recalls the origin of the international campaign to ban landmines in the form of efforts by the ICRC. These were subsequently overtaken by a coalition of INGOs with diverse standpoints and coming together to form the International Campaign to Ban Landmines (ICBL). The groups that came together in 1992 included HRW, Handicap International (France), Medico International (Germany), Mines Awareness Group (UK), Physicians for Human Rights (US), and Vietnam Veterans of America Foundation (US). The campaign eventually numbered more than 1,200 NGOs in 60 countries. For mandate reasons, the ICRC was not a formal part of the coalition but actively supported the process leading to the Ottawa Convention.]

Second, governments were initially entirely uninterested; it was regarded by governments everywhere as pie-in-the-sky, even if they were not actively hostile to the idea. . . .

Third, the ban campaign had a simple, easily understood message—a complete and comprehensive ban, nothing more, nothing less. . . .

Fourth, although . . . the world's militaries [felt threatened, the campaign] did not represent an overwhelming economic threat to arms makers. . . . As a consequence, no industrial and private sector groups had a strong incentive within the NATO countries to contribute money to a counter-campaign.

. . .

Fifth, . . . largely in response to [INGO] pressures [consensus was not the rule for negotiations. Instead] sympathetic governments adopted a new principle of negotiating a treaty among 'like-minded' states . . .

Sixth, governments eventually began to come on board the landmines ban cause for three principal reasons. NGO pressure, first, brought them to an awareness of the genuine extent of the problem and put it on their policy agendas. . . .

Seventh, . . . the ban campaign [came to be seen as] a genuine partnership between NGOs, international organizations and sympathetic states. . . .

B. The partnership between 'international civil society', sympathetic states, and international organizations

. . .

The central assumption underlying the idea that the landmines campaign is a new and better way of doing international lawmaking is that international NGOs are somehow 'international civil society'. . . .

. . . [INGOs] are therefore a force for democratizing international relations and international institutions and, moreover, the authoritative bearers of 'world opinion'. They are therefore the legitimate representatives in the international sphere of 'people' in the world, in a way in which their states, even democratic states, and their state representatives, are not. . . . As [Canadian] Foreign Minister Axworthy put it in an address to NGOs in the midst of the Ottawa process:

> One can no longer relegate NGOs to simple advisory or advocacy roles in this process. They are now part of the way decisions have to be made. They have been the voice saying that government belongs to the people, and must respond to the people's hopes, demands and ideals.

. . .

C. But who elected the International NGOs?

. . .

. . . [The international bureaucracy] has adopted this theory of politics, of the legitimacy of the independent international NGO sector . . . [because] public international organizations *themselves* are in desperate need of legitimacy. . . . [I]nternational organizations have volunteered and been volunteered for a variety of tasks that, in a word, require forms of legitimacy that international organizations have never had.

By 'legitimacy' in this context I mean merely that institutions act and be understood to act with authority that is accepted as proper and moral and just. . . . [W]e call this apperception 'democracy' and the consent of the governed.

. . . [I]nternational lawyers . . . fundamentally believe that international organizations, and their underlying concept of 'world government'—what is today taken as the vision of Grotius—*are* legitimate, and deserve to be understood as the world's constitutionally supreme sources of authority and the exercise of power. . . .

. . . [They] tend to form a church of those converted to belief in supranationalism . . . .

. . .

. . . [But] the brutal fact remains that international organizations as they exist

today do not have the perception of legitimacy to carry out the functions that international elites would assign to them . . . .
. . .

. . . Yet now it is urgently needed, and where to get it?

. . . International organizations claim to have overcome the democratic deficit as an impediment to their legitimacy by having as their partners, and having the moral and political approval of, international NGOs, the voice of 'world opinion', and the loud and incessant invocation of 'international civil society'. . . .
. . .

. . . International NGOs, for their part, are happy to accept the accolade of 'international civil society', the voice of the people, and so on, for the obvious reason that it increases their power and authority within international organizations, international elites, and beyond. . . .
. . .

[The author suggests that some legitimacy might inhere in INGOs if they could claim to be] authentic intermediaries of the 'people'. . . . But this is implausible, for at least two reasons.

First, [INGOs] are not very often connected, in any direct way, to masses of 'people'. International NGOs, in virtue of their role to operate globally rather than locally, are fundamentally elite organizations. There are exceptions, to be sure, but they are prototypically large religious affiliations. . . . There are certain large secular exceptions, as well; Amnesty International is perhaps one, in that at least it has a large base membership. But that membership comes mostly from wealthy countries, and its membership even in those countries tends to be educated and at least middle class . . . [T]he far more typical 'international' NGO of the kind whose approval and favour international organizations seek is much closer to the model of Human Rights Watch—a relatively small, highly professional, entirely elite organization funded by foundations and wealthy individuals in the Western democracies, and having no discernible base outside international elites. This is not to denigrate Human Rights Watch or the vital work it does, but it would be the first to declare that its legitimacy is not based on democratic roots among the masses but on its fidelity to its own conception of the meaning of international human rights. . . .

International NGOs collectively are not conduits from the 'people' or the 'masses' or the 'world citizenry' from the 'bottom up'. They are, rather, a vehicle for international elites to talk to other international elites about the things—frequently of undeniably critical importance—that international elites care about. The conversation is not vertical, it is horizontal. It has a worthwhile, essential function in making the world—sometimes at least, a better place—but it does not reduce the democratic deficit.

Second, if the idea of 'international civil society' is drawn by an analogy to civil society in domestic society, then it bears noting that at least in the United States, with its vigorous and diverse civil society, civil society is *not* conceived of as being a substitute for democratic processes, let alone conveying democratic legitimacy. On the contrary, the glory of civil society is precisely that it is something different from democracy and democratic processes. . . .

Put bluntly, the glory of organizations of civil society is not democratic legitimacy, but the ability to be a pressure group. . . .

NOTE

Compare the following views of Reginald Dale in 'The NGO Specter Stalks Trade Talks', *International Herald Tribune*, March 5, 1999, p. 11. The author focuses on the opposition of various INGOs to the WTO's trade liberalization agenda:

. . .

Trade diplomats, however, are split between those who think it wise to accommodate the NGOs and those who want to keep them far out of the way. Accommodating them creates many problems.

One senior trade diplomat in Geneva quite rightly points out that the NGOs often display none of the transparency they seek in others, hide the sources of their funding and represent only narrow special interests, not the wider public. Some of the more aggressive NGOs are more interested in confrontation than in consensus and are out to kill rational debate through biased, if not erroneous, scare-mongering. Their holier-than-thou tactics are often clearly undemocratic.

But they are not going to go away.

The challenge will be to satisfy the NGOs, or at least the more reasonable among them, that their opinions are being taken into account without letting them interfere in the actual negotiating process. That must remain between governments. . . .

But greater openness should not mean giving away commercially valuable information, revealing privileged governmental or legal communications or compromising ongoing negotiations. And the same standards should apply to the NGOs themselves. Their privacy should not be free from the scrutiny they seek to impose on others.

QUESTIONS

1. How do you assess the following responses to the critique that NGOs are unrepresentative and unaccountable:

'[T]he issues the NGOs take up are more important than their own democratic representativeness'.[5]

'Perhaps the best that can be hoped for may be a kind of crude balance at the local, national and international levels in which a mixture of governmental, intergovernmental and nongovernmental voices more closely reflects reality than a state-dominated framework with only a smattering of intergovernmental input'.[6]

---

[5] P. Baehr, 'Mobilization of the Conscience of Mankind: Conditions of Effectiveness of Human Rights NGOs', in E. Denters and N. Schrijver (eds.), *Reflections on International Law from the Low Countries* (1998), at 147.

[6] L. Gordenker and T. Weiss, 'NGO Participation in the International Policy Process', in Weiss and Gordenker (eds.), *NGOs, the UN, and Global Governance* (1996), at 219.

'If numbers are the benchmark of legitimacy, the NGO community easily passes the test. However imperfect the mechanisms of representation, environmental and human rights NGOs collectively speak for many times over the numbers represented by even medium-size states in the UN and even narrowly defined NGOs would outrank the microstates.... Funding more often follows success than the other way around, and the greater part of NGO coffers is filled by member contributions'.[7]

'As Robert D. Putnam explains: "Networks of civic engagement are an essential form of social capital: The denser such networks in a community, the more likely that its citizens will be able to cooperate for mutual benefit". This insight could also be applied at the international level. That is, transnational NGOs can improve IGOs [intergovernmental organizations] and promote peace not only by the merit of their ideas, but also by promoting social cohesion within our global village'.[8]

'Because [INGOs] can use the process of stigmatization only against the backdrop of broadly shared values, and because the stigmatization process must be highly visible to be effective, human rights NGOs cannot stray far from the basic values of the human rights cause without either losing their effectiveness or subjecting themselves to public criticism. Indeed, this highly public form of accountability is arguably stronger than the theoretical accountability exerted on a classic NGO by its members, many of whom may not have the time, inclination or knowledge to scrutinize lower-profile activities'.[9]

How do you assess the critiques put forward by Anderson and Dale? Are any of the responses above persuasive?

2. How do other prominent actors on the international stage, such as the media or transnational corporations, measure up in terms of criteria of representativeness and accountability? Are they fundamentally different in their character or situation from human rights NGOs? If so, how, and with what consequences for these criteria? If not, why should NGOs be held to more demanding standards than they are?

2. PROBLEMS OF RELATIONSHIPS, PRIORITIES, FUNDING, AND TASKS

The relationship between NGOs at national and international levels (which has of course been in an ongoing process of evolution in the last two decades) is problematic in several respects. We consider below problems of setting agendas, the capacity of external actors (INGOs) to distort and perhaps disrupt efforts by domestic human rights NGOs, the related issues of funding, and the question of distinctive tasks and strategies among different types of NGOs.

[7] P. Spiro, 'New Global Communities: Nongovernmental Organizations in International Decision-Making Institutions', 18 Wash. Q. (Winter 1995), 45 at 52.

[8] S. Charnowitz, 'Two Centuries of Participation: NGOs and International Governance', 18 Mich. J. Int. L. 184, (1997), at 272.

[9] K. Roth Executive Director of HRW, 'Human Rights Organizations: A New Force for Social Change', lecture at Harvard University, 4 November 1998.

Some have argued that the policies promoted by INGOs and other civil society actors at the international level and directed in part to the South reflect political struggles in the North rather than consideration of appropriate priorities for the South. Consider the following analysis.

PETER BAEHR, AMNESTY INTERNATIONAL AND ITS SELF-IMPOSED LIMITED MANDATE
12 Neths Q.H.R. 5 (1994)

. . .

5.3. Homosexuality

For many years the issue was debated, whether Amnesty should work for the release of persons imprisoned or detained for their homosexual identity or orientation or for homosexual acts committed in private and between consenting adults. This issue even threatened to split up the organization along multicultural lines. While members in Western Europe and North America tended to consider it rather obvious that Amnesty should work for such persons, many people in Asian, African as well as some Latin American countries thought otherwise.

Agreement existed only to work for (a) persons imprisoned or detained for advocating equality for homosexuals, (b) persons charged with homosexuality as a pretext, while the real reason for their imprisonment was the expression of their political, religious or other conscientiously held beliefs, (c) persons subjected to medical treatment while in prison with the aim of modifying their homosexual orientation without their agreement.

The issue was hotly debated for a number of years, resulting in various voluminous studies of the matter. The differences of view can be roughly summarized as follows. Those in favour of working for imprisoned homosexuals argued that '(homo)sexual orientation' and '(homo)sexual identity' are attributes similar or subordinate to the category of 'sex', which has for many years been in the mandate and that it would only be logical to add this category of persons to the mandate. The opponents felt that in societies where homosexuality is considered a physical ailment or a reflection of socially deviant behaviour, activities on behalf of such individuals would be seen as not related to human rights and make Amnesty look ridiculous; moreover, if Amnesty were to work for imprisoned homosexuals, this would risk to involve it in having to deal with all sorts of other sexual practices.

. . . The International Council adopted by consensus a simple resolution deciding 'to consider for adoption as prisoners of conscience persons who are imprisoned solely because of their homosexuality, including the practice of homosexual acts in private between consenting adults'. The resolution expressed the realization that this decision would increase the difficulty of the development of Amnesty in many parts of the world and instructed the International Executive Committee to draft guidelines regarding action on behalf of imprisoned homosexuals, 'taking into consideration the cultural background of various areas where we have sections and groups or countries in which AI is proposing development'.

Thus ended the major internal debate on the issue of homosexuality. The result had certain features of a political compromise. It was not explicitly decided how the position taken related to the text of the Statute. There is nothing in the Statute, except for a broad interpretation of the word 'sex', which would cover such activities. The issue of whether the consequence of the decision on homosexuality would indeed open the debate on other sexual practices, was never faced. Nor was a fundamental debate held on the issue of whether Amnesty's new stand on homosexuality meant a departure from its emphasis on universal human rights values. Politically, it was also a matter of attracting one constituency (the gay community) at the risk of possibly losing another (potential Amnesty International-members in the Third World).

. . .

VIEWS OF COMMENTATORS ON RELATIONSHIPS, FUNDING, TASKS AND STRATEGIES

Larry Cox, Reflections on Human Rights at Century's End

Human Rights Dialogue, Winter 2000, p. 5

Where once there were scores of national human rights groups around the world, now there are thousands operating in every region and in almost every country. The implications for promoting human rights are profound and positive. National and local groups are far better placed to understand the social and political context in which violations are occurring and to devise appropriate strategies. They have a legitimacy that external actors lack. Particularly when they are rooted in local communities, domestic groups are in a position to mobilize social forces to ensure that human rights laws and policies are put not only in place but also into practice.

None of this means that there is no longer a need for international work. For myriad reasons, external pressure to uphold international norms is still vital and in some cases can be even more powerful than pressure from within. Moreover, because external actors are usually removed from partisan domestic battles, they can have a legitimacy and an authority of their own. Groups in the North, of course, also retain access to other powerful external forces that can be an important part of an overall strategy, such as wealthy governments, multinational institutions, and citizen action groups that can effectively organize boycotts and other forms of consumer pressure. Most important of all, international work upholds the notion that human rights are a matter of human and universal, not national and particular, concern, thus reaffirming in practice precisely what gives human rights norms their power.

The problem is that . . . [i]nternational work is still for the most part the domain of groups located in the North. Groups in the South are still seen largely as domestic partners or as 'human rights defenders' who are protected by those doing international work. The possibility for groups outside Western Europe and the United States either to set the international agenda for human rights or even to influence, as equal partners, the strategies set by international groups for their countries is still very limited. To change this would take a much deeper commitment than currently exists on the part of either donors or NGOs to invest in travel, discussions, and the alteration of old patterns.

Nevertheless, there are some hopeful signs. New global movements—around such issues as globalization, land mines, and women's rights—are successfully addressing barriers associated with colonial legacies and the excessive professionalization of human rights. More Southern groups are developing institutional mechanisms that will amplify their voices and increase their capacity to provide leadership on international strategies and agendas. . . .

Bahey El Din Hassan, The Credibility Crisis of International Human Rights in the Arab World

Human Rights Dialogue, Winter 2000, p. 9

. . .

. . . [Problems arise] when international human rights groups, which operate away from the political, social, and cultural context in which Arab human rights violations occur, fail to consult with local human rights organizations. In the preparation of their reports, international human rights organizations often rely on foreign sources. They are based in the centers of international power—London, Washington, New York, Paris, Geneva—that many Arabs associate with double-dealing, double standards, and the use of human rights in the service of narrow interests. When international human rights organizations ignore these realities, their standing in the local Arab context is damaged. But the moral standing of local Arab organizations, along with our ability to mobilize public opinion in support of human rights, suffers even greater setbacks.

To illustrate, . . . [i]n 1992, Human Rights Watch released a report on torture in Egypt. It recommended that the United States and the European Community suspend all bilateral aid and loans until torture and prolonged arbitrary detention ended. Such a demand was not acceptable to the Egyptian public, especially because it perceived that the same criterion was not applied to Israel . . . .

In 1994, Amnesty International published a report entitled 'Human Rights Defenders under Threat', which documented the arrest and torture of a small group of lawyers who were known for defending Islamic political prisoners and accused of having various other connections to armed Islamic groups. Although this was accurate, the government was not specifically threatening any local human rights organizations, despite the implications of the report's title. It was at that point that our movement in Egypt started to be subjected to 'threat' [by the government]. . . .

Considerable progress could have been made on human rights issues in Egypt during these years had international human rights groups formulated a common strategy with local organizations. International groups did rely upon local organizations for collecting, verifying, and documenting information. However, with few exceptions, we were not further consulted on their many reports or campaigns. For instance, we were not included in the formulation of their policies that escalated confrontation with the Egyptian government. This occurred despite the fact that the international groups knew there would be negative repercussions for us because the authorities consider local groups to be the source of information for international groups. International groups also failed to use their position of influence to create dialogue between the concerned government authorities and our local movement.

Lawyers Committee for Human Rights

www.lchr.org/devintro.htm (1999)

Today hundreds, if not thousands, of local human rights groups are putting pressure on their governments to uphold basic human rights protections. They operate in countries where the rule of law is tenuous at best, where judicial systems lack credibility, and where past abuses have yet to be redressed.

These groups have a whole range of needs that we—as the largest legally oriented human rights group in the US—take on.

> We arm local activists with facts about international human rights law to strengthen their own legal systems.
> We can help them make their concerns and problems heard at the United Nations and the World Bank, powerful institutions that wield influence over their governments.
> We can equip them with the tools of mass communication so that they can alert the world to the abuses they witness.
> And when they are put on trial, we can mobilize international pressure for a release or fair trial.

[Eds. The range of activities that can be undertaken by NGOs, whether based in the North or the South, is often dependent upon the availability of funds beyond those that might in a few instances be generated by membership fees. In the human rights area, foundations have played a very important role. Their funding has been supplemented over recent years by grants from both governmental and NGO development programmes. In addition, the humanitarian crises of the 1990s in conjunction with other post Cold War developments have led to great sums being channelled through development and humanitarian aid groups, which themselves have been increasingly involved in human rights activities. Northern funding—whether from governments, foundations, businesses, professional groups, or transnational coalitions—to support NGO activities in the South and to facilitate their more active involvement in the international arena is seen as helpful but by no means adequate to overcome the essential inequality of the relationship. The readings that follow raise a range of questions both as to funding and the appropriate nature of the relationships between domestic and international NGOs.]

Chidi Anselm Odinkalu, Why More Africans Don't Use Human Rights Language

Human Rights Dialogue, Winter 2000, p. 4

Part of the responsibility for [the elitist nature of much of the human rights movement in Africa] lies with the overseas sponsors of our human rights organizations. Unlike the groups they support, donor agencies and philanthropies that fund human rights work are accountable to their trust deeds and the laws of the countries (in the North) where they are incorporated. While exhorting national human rights groups in Africa to think globally and act locally, these agencies think locally and act globally. With overseas donors as sources of reference and accountability, the only obligations local human rights groups have are reporting requirements arising under grant contracts where these exist. The raison d'être of the African human rights movement is primarily to fulfill such contracts rather than to service a social obligation or constituency. Local human rights groups exist to please the international agencies that fund or support them. Local problems are only defined as potential pots of project cash, not as human experiences to be resolved in just terms, thereby delegitimizing human rights language and robbing its ideas of popular appeal.

Alan Fowler, Civil Society, NGDOs and Social Development: Changing the Rules of the Game

UN Research Institute for Social Development, Geneva 2000: Occasional Paper No. 1 (2000)

Today's rule of thumb in international development is that everybody wants to be a partner with everyone, on everything, everywhere. . . . Consequently, the phrase 'partnership in development' has become virtually meaningless and discredited. The more so because too often it camouflages aid-related relationships that are unbalanced, dependency-creating and based on compromise in favour of the powerful. Frequently, these dis-empower NGDOs [nongovernmental development organizations] (and others) on the receiving end of the aid system. This can occur in many circumstances, for example, when:

- aid conditions and procedures undermine an NGDO's own governance and local accountability, or work against applying good practice and achieving comparative advantages;
- donors do not accept mutual responsibility for performance, loading everything onto the NGDO;

- NGDO attention to financiers is at the cost of attention to and the influence of local constituencies;
- NGDO local knowledge and rootedness is discounted by external, comparative knowledge and imported models;
- external development policies become fashions to be followed and only questioned at the risk of being financially excluded—in other words, when NGDO self-censorship becomes an organizational way of life;
- the 'lottery' aspect of funding generates insecurity in an NGDO's organizational behaviour, as well as 'short-termism';
- patron-client behaviour becomes the norm; and
- local NGDOs are 'captured' by foreign agencies, eroding or compromising their autonomy, local credibility and identity by becoming extensions of those—'the foreign masters'—that they serve.

Harvard Law School Human Rights Program and Center for the Study of Developing Countries at Cairo University, International Aspects of the Arab Human Rights Movement (2000)

[The following excerpts are taken from an interactive roundtable discussion in Cairo among 21 participants.]

Mustapha K. Al-Sayyid

It's my impression that the relationship between the international human rights movement and its counterparts in the Arab world, Latin America, or Africa, reflects generally the problems of North–South relations in all their aspects. Decisions are adopted in the North and implemented in the South. Funding, setting programs and agendas are elements of power which the countries in the North possess in all fields, be they economic, political, or social matters and also human rights ... [Through educating donors about our perspective], we can hope to escape from historical North–South relations and create ties of true partnership.

It is interesting to compare these issues with the general context of government-provided foreign aid. The OECD Development Assistance Committee (DAC) is intended to coordinate the aid policies of all its members—the advanced industrial states. One of the items on its agenda is human rights, which means that it is one component of the big powers' foreign policies. Thus, the international human rights organizations actually implement the member states' policies. There should be no doubt about that. Naturally, we hope that relations between the international human rights organizations, and their Arab and regional counterparts, would not reflect all the negative aspects of North–South relations.

In order to avoid such risk, the human rights agendas of these organizations, their priorities and their understanding of human rights should not be identical to those of their governments. Western governments make much noise about human rights violations in Iraq, but they say almost nothing about human rights violations in Saudi Arabia or other Gulf countries. We in the Arab movement do not approve of the human rights policies of the Iraqi government, but we find economic sanctions imposed on Iraq to be a gross violation of the economic rights of Iraqi people. Collective rights are important for Arab peoples, but they do not figure much in the human rights discourse of Western governments. On all these issues, we would like human rights organizations operating at the international level to distinguish themselves from their governments.

We also do not like to see international human rights organizations assume a lecturing posture when they address human rights groups in other countries—telling them what they should or should not care about, using funding as leverage to reward or punish local organizations depending on whether or not they behave. If international organizations take a stand on human rights issues and abandon lecturing to human rights organizations in our countries, relations within the world human rights movement will avoid replicating North–South relations in other realms.

. . .

As a general matter, even if necessary for a short period, foreign funding should not be the rule. Funding reflects on the relations between the local organization and its community. If these organizations have strong relations with a community that is aware of their role and importance, it will fund them. In Egypt, private sector organizations fund many activities, but not human rights. That is because Egyptian donors are not yet convinced of the importance of human rights work.

Dependence on foreign funds turns Egyptian and other Arab organizations away from developing means of mobilizing funds locally. I have proposed to Egyptian organizations that they seek help from performing and vocal artists. A number of film stars and singers are known to be supporters of human rights organizations. I urged that these groups organize concerts, invite leading artists and direct the revenues to human rights. But no one was interested because foreign aid was too easily available. All you have to do is fill in an application and get the desired sums. If foreign funding continues, local organizations will lose the ability to mobilize the local community, or to find new methods to achieve that aim.

Another point I would like to stress is the transformation of human rights organizations into a popular movement. The only hope, for Egyptian and other Arab human rights organizations to advance, is to engage the masses. So long as there is excessive dependence on foreign funding, the human rights movement will never become a people's movement.

Peter Rosenblum

Frankly, I think that most of the significant funding issues are the same whether we are talking about international NGOs or local NGOs in the developing world. Funding has been delicate for the human rights movement both because of the real influence exerted by funders and because of the perceived threat to objectivity, particularly from certain—though not all—government funders.

. . .

In my view, the difference between local funding and foreign funding has less to do with reality than perceptions. An organization that relies on local funding may appear more legitimate, more authentic, but that isn't necessarily true. Why would local donors be less manipulative than foreign donors? If the issue is public legitimacy, measured by the breadth of local support, there are other ways to achieve it. Many legitimate human rights groups in the West rely for the bulk of their funds on a narrow range of institutional and wealthy donors—often the same organizations who fund NGOs in the developing world. Of the significant international human rights organizations, only Amnesty International relies on funding through membership. As a result, it has to devote huge amounts of its resources to managing its constituency. Other organizations can raise the essential funds from a small group of donors and demonstrate legitimacy through other channels, for example, participatory activities, consultations, public outreach and press work.

QUESTIONS

1. Opposition by many groups from the South to the inclusion of homosexuality within Amnesty's mandate was, in effect, outvoted by groups in the North with more members and thus more votes. As you see it, what issues does that raise for an INGO?

2. How far does the type of programme put forward by the LCHR go in responding to the concerns expressed by Larry Cox and Bahey El Din Hassan? Can you think of more effective policies on the part of INGOs to respond to the perceived problems?

3. Is it desirable for INGOs to seek to identify a joint strategy with their domestic counterparts, in the way Hassan suggests? Should indeed INGOs follow the directions (what is to be investigated, what are the priorities, what strategies should be followed) set by local NGOs in each country? Are there some issues—strategies, priorities, others—on which local NGOs have a stronger claim to be followed?

4. A proposal is put to a foundation that provision of funds to a local NGO with no strings attached represents a better model by virtue of leaving local groups unfettered discretion in determining policy priorities. As a member of the foundation's executive committee, how do you react? Do you have other proposals responsive to complaints of the NGO?

5. Local NGOs hardly fall into one homogenous mass of human rights advocates. Some may work at monitoring and reporting, some at producing research, some at networking with INGOs, some at mobilization of popular support and other grassroots activities such as popular human rights education. What kinds of relationships would you believe to be profitable from the perspective of the human rights movement between the elite, top-down approaches of many INGOs, and the local grassroots organizations that follow a bottom-up approach? Do the top-down organizations 'need' the grassroots bottom-up organizations, and vice versa? What does each type of organization gain from the other? Does cooperation between them raise the probability of realizing a given human rights goal that they hold in common? If so, why?

NOTE

One can draw a boundary line—to be sure, an uncertain and porous one—between the traditional human rights NGOs performing the functions discussed in this Chapter, and 'humanitarian' organizations, a category that embraces several kinds of mandates. At the simplest level, such organizations may provide relief—food, shelter, clothing, medical supplies for refugees, for those internally displaced by violent conflict. Organizations like CARE, OXFAM, and local Red Cross groups are examples. Or such organizations may have more complex missions related particularly to violent conflict with its massive civilian casualties. The International Committee for the Red Cross (ICRC), described at p. 949, *supra*, is a classic illustration, with its distinctive claims to neutrality and its strategy of confidentiality with respect to what its missions observe in order to maintain relationships with and to be granted future access by the state or insurgent group in question.

Should these tasks be kept discrete, in order to allow each kind of NGO to perform its distinct and valuable function? Or are the 'neutrality' and 'confidentiality' characteristics of some humanitarian NGOs open to serious question? Consider the following report.

SYDNEY MORNING HERALD, DUTY OF CARE
February 5, 2000, www.smh.com.au/news/0002/05/text/review3.html

When Jim Carlton, the secretary-general of the Red Cross in Australia, was recently asked to act as an observer in the Sri Lankan elections, he refused. Not because the task was unimportant, but because he felt it could compromise the Red Cross's binding mandate to remain politically neutral at all times, in all situations.

. . .

Carlton recalls too that 'when NATO started putting up tents for Kosovo refugees they wanted the Red Cross to take those facilities over. We refused. We didn't want to be seen to be running NATO camps'. Indeed, says Carlton, the Red Cross even refuses to appear before war crimes tribunals. 'Nobody would ever admit us to a battlefield again if we disclosed everything we saw'.

Honourable adherence to principle? Or impractical idealism? Surely, argue the ultra pragmatists, the fact that a huge and growing proportion of aid money comes from governments must necessitate compromise for all sides—host regimes, recipients, donors and deliverers? Or as their opponents maintain, does humanitarian work become jeopardized the minute you try to harness it to other tasks?

It's a debate which has been going on vigorously within the aid community for a while, but it was dramatically flushed into the open [in] SBS's Dateline program .... Pratt and Wallace, two aid workers for CARE Australia, were tried and imprisoned for espionage by Yugoslav authorities at the height of NATO's bombing campaign.

The spy charges were vigorously denied. However, Dateline revealed that CARE Canada, CARE Australia's sister organization, had at the time entered into a contract with a Canadian government agency to recruit observers for what was in effect a quasi-military monitoring program in Kosovo. This 'peace monitoring' operation, run by the Organization for Security and Co-operation in Europe (OSCE)—of which Canada is a member—was later said to have passed data to NATO.

. . .

In a revealing interview, CARE Australia's chairman, former prime minister Malcolm Fraser, told SBS he'd been unaware of CARE Canada's contract at the time, though he remained convinced it had not been a factor in Wallace and Pratt's arrest. However, he made plain his strong disapproval of the deal. . . .

. . .

Said one leading agency boss: 'The future of humanitarian action depends on the degree to which it is impartial and independent. If you keep blurring the lines between aid and advocacy and political action you compromise that'.

. . .

The Nobel-prize winning MSF was the most outspoken, with its Australian president, Fiona Terry, describing the CARE Canada deal as one which would shock and disappoint most in the aid community.

Terry, who is completing a doctoral thesis on ethical dilemmas in humanitarian action, says there's a lot of pressure on aid organisations to agree to 'mission creep'. As well, she told the Herald, the aid community was prone to a 'culture of justification'.

'It derives from the fact that the money comes from donors, and that skews accountability away from the people you are trying to assist, towards the donors whether private or government'.

. . .

World Vision's Beris Gwynne points out that non-government organizations are hugely diverse, and for some it's appropriate to work more closely with official briefs. She puts organizations involved in 'democracy building' (an American favourite) at one end of the spectrum and the Red Cross, with its adherence to absolute neutrality, at the other.

. . .

QUESTION

Should humanitarian aid groups collaborate with human rights monitoring groups such as the OSCE? Is it desirable to put in place a strict rule in humanitarian NGO mandates either prohibiting or mandating such cooperation?

D. ISSUES ABOUT HUMAN RIGHTS INGOs

STANLEY COHEN, GOVERNMENT RESPONSES TO HUMAN RIGHTS REPORTS: CLAIMS, DENIALS, AND COUNTERCLAIMS
18 Hum. Rts Q. 517 (1996)

. . .

There are no mandatory guidelines about how to write a human rights report. Nevertheless, the genre has developed a recognizable standard style and format of its own. Most organizations feel constrained to follow certain rules, cover certain subjects and use a particular terminology. We find a language of objectivity, references to how sources are checked, standard ways of documentation and citation of testimonies, obligatory references to appropriate international human rights standards, avoidance of taking sides in the conflict or expressing political views, and references to previous reports.

These traditional self-imposed rules have good justifications. Adherence to a standard format, however, allows for a predictable set of government responses. There is a ritualistic pattern to the sequence of claim, counter-claim, and repeated claim.

There are variations by subject, scope, and type of organization, but the basic report contains the following seven fixed elements:

1. Expressing concern

The first paragraph, introduction, briefing, executive summary, or press release states the organization's position about the situation (for example, torture in Turkey or political killings in Colombia). The organization 'is concerned', 'remains concerned', 'is deeply troubled', 'strongly condemns', 'has grounds to believe that . . .'.

2. Stating the problem

Then follows an introductory statement about the problem—either the overall human rights position in the country or the specific abuse in question (press censorship, unfair trials, prison conditions, etc.).

3. Setting the context

Some attempt is made to set out the context of the alleged abuses with the length and detail varying between book-length reports to ten page briefings. A brief political history gives the background to the conflict.

4. Sources and methods

There is an account (usually rather inadequate) of where, when, from whom, and how the organization obtained its information.

5. Detailed allegations

The largest section of the report is devoted to a detailed description of the violations in question. Statistics are given where appropriate. More often, individual cases are presented: conditions in a particular prison, testimonies of ex-detainees alleging torture, eyewitness accounts, and affidavits given to lawyers.

6. International and domestic law

The contents and applicability of relevant international legal provisions—covenants, conventions, standards—are set out. The target country's obligations according to international law, as well as details of domestic laws and enforcement procedures, are explained.

7. Required action

The report ends by 'calling on', 'urging', or 'demanding' the government to do something. The required action might be: (1) intervention on a particular case (release this political prisoner, reopen this newspaper, unban this organization); (2) changing a policy (repeal this law, end deportations, ensure fair trials); (3) conformity to international law; (4) implementing accountability (prosecutions or disciplinary actions against those responsible for violations); (5) investigation (an independent inquiry, access to human rights observers); (6) merely asking the government to condemn the violations in question.

. . .

NOTE

Consider the following protest against reports by a leading INGO. Letter to Pierre Sané, Secretary-General of Amnesty International, from Permanent Representative of Republic of Indonesia to the UNHCHR, 2 November 1994, UN Doc. E/CN.4/1995/108:

> I wish to voice my strong protest against the contents of a series of publications that Amnesty International issued in succession this year [concerning East Timor and Indonesia]. . . .

. . .

> Of the three publications in question, the booklet, 'Power and Impunity—Human Rights under the New Order' is the most virulent and malicious for it not only falsely attributes a 'persistent pattern' of human rights violations to the Indonesian Government but also misrepresents the present New Order of Indonesia as the product of a bloody coup d'état. This is worse than mere distortion of history. By misrepresenting the origin of the New Order which was the vantage around which the Indonesian people rallied to save themselves from chaos in the middle 1960s, you would deprive us of one of the defining moments in the history of modern Indonesia. . . .
>   . . . [I]n your desire to blacken the reputation of Indonesia, you have resorted to the dissemination of falsehoods, misrepresentations and innuendos without any factual basis. The second victim is the avowed noble mission of Amnesty

International, for by waging this political campaign, you have in fact abandoned the objective of promoting and protecting human rights and adopted a political agenda as well as a political objective. . . . You have also unmasked your Organization for what it really is, and which we have all along described it to be: an organization waging a political campaign against Indonesia under the banner of human rights.

For if Amnesty International were really interested in promoting human rights, it should not begrudge Indonesia the recognition given it by other countries and the United Nations Commission on Human Rights for its efforts to improve the human rights situation in East Timor. . . .

. . . [I]t should not, in its evaluation of the human rights situation in Indonesia, studiously ignore the enhanced social and economic rights that the Indonesian people, including the people of East Timor, Aceh and Irian Jaya, are now enjoying. A balanced and fair assessment of the human rights situation in any country should at least consider these factors. . . .

QUESTIONS

1. Cohen suggests that the format of NGO human rights reports and the range of responses elicited from governments have become ritualistic and calls for a re-examination of the style, format and genre of such reports. What sort of options might be considered?

2. What are the strategies reflected in the Indonesian response to the Amnesty reports? Do you find them effective?

3. It has been said that the effectiveness of groups such as Amnesty and HRW 'depends absolutely on their moral fervor and political nonpartisanship, which combine with their rational voluntaristic character to make them a sort of 'voice of humanity' to which states must listen'.[10] Do you agree?

DAVID RIEFF, THE PRECARIOUS TRIUMPH OF HUMAN RIGHTS
New York Times Magazine, August 8, 1999, p. 8

. . .

. . . [Human rights advocates] routinely claim that there can be no peace without justice. But the evidence suggests that often that isn't true. Consider the eight-year civil war in Sierra Leone, during which Revolutionary United Front guerrillas committed the most unspeakable atrocities and war crimes—routinely mutilating children and raping and murdering civilians. When they were defeated by a

[10] J. Boli, 'Conclusion: World Authority Structures and Legitimations', in J. Boli and G. Thomas (eds.), *Constructing World Culture: International Nongovernmental Organizations since 1875* (1999), at 293.

Nigerian-led regional intervention force in 1998, their leader, Foday Sankoh, was tried and sentenced to death. To have executed Sankoh would have been justice. But the reality in Sierra Leone was that there could be no peace without a deal between the rebels and the Government. The guerrillas would not sign until Sankoh and other detained rebels were pardoned and set free. In the name of peace, the Government agreed not to prosecute—rightly, in my view. In order to seize what was almost certainly Sierra Leone's only chance, justice had to be sacrificed. And as a result, a fragile peace reigns in Freetown for the first time since 1991.

But the outrage of the human rights movement knew no bounds. Mary Robinson, the United Nations High Commissioner for Human Rights, declared that the United Nations did not accept the deal. There could be no impunity for human rights violations, she insisted. And in a letter to the United Nations Security Council, Human Rights Watch denounced the agreement. Its advocacy director, Reed Brody, announced that his group would lobby to get the blanket amnesty for Sankoh and his comrades annulled.

. . . Closer to home, we have different standards. At the same time Western leaders were welcoming Slobodan Milosevic's indictment for war crimes and insisting that the days of the 'culture of impunity' were numbered, the Blair Government in Britain was releasing paramilitary prisoners in Northern Ireland to further the peace process there. 'Justice and peace are often not the same thing', Holmes has said. 'Actually, they can be contradictory'.

Examples of this tension can be found around the globe. An obvious example is Algeria. In 1992, faced with the threat of Islamic fundamentalists taking power after free elections, the Algerian Government annulled that vote and imposed a state of emergency. Human rights groups were quick to respond. Amnesty International issued a special report denouncing the Government. The counterargument—namely, that had the fundamentalists been allowed to take over this might have been the last free election to be held in Algeria—cut no ice with them. Norms were norms, and violators were violators. In a similar display of orthodoxy, Human Rights Watch recently accused the United States Government of making drugs rather than human rights 'the centerpiece of U.S. policy' in Colombia. The message was plain: it is immoral *ever* to fail to uphold human rights.

I would say that there is a case to be made for what the Algerian generals did— and that it's understandable that the United States has concluded that Colombian drug interdiction is at least as important a concern, and as morally reputable a one, as human rights. This is not to say that human rights advocates are wrong to point out abuses; in the Algerian case, there was ample evidence of systematic and barbarous behavior on the part of the authorities. But there is a danger in turning human rights principles into dogma.

Imagine if Human Rights Watch were confronted not with contemporary Algeria but with Germany circa 1932. Wouldn't the world have been better off had there been a German Government with the courage to annul Hitler's victory at the polls? Seen through the tunnel vision of today's human rights leadership, such a move would have been unacceptable. A violation, after all, is a violation. It may be stacking the deck to use an analogy with Nazi Germany, but it illustrates the hard questions about the assumptions of the human rights movement that are not being asked. What if you are a secular Algerian citizen? What is the relative moral weight of the human rights imperative versus your well-founded fear of fundamentalism? At the very least, the picture becomes cloudier, and the transcendent insights of human rights suddenly seem less transcendent.

Even the Kosovo conflict points to a problem with the human rights movement's absolutist stance. Most activists, though not all, privately hoped for and initially welcomed NATO's action. But consternation and self-doubt began almost from the moment the first bomb fell. Human Rights Watch even issued a report denouncing NATO military tactics like dropping cluster bombs on civilian areas. And yet it seems that it was *precisely* this bombing of civilian targets in Serbia—which may well have been illegal under international law, just as Human Rights Watch has asserted—that eventually forced the Milosevic regime to give in. The battle-damage assessments have shown that Serb forces in Kosovo came through largely unscathed. Once again: do human rights norms provide an adequate guide to what the right thing to do is in a hard case like Kosovo?

. . .

NOTE

Consider the following observations in Henry Steiner, *Diverse Partners: Non-Governmental Organizations in the Human Rights Movement* (1991), at 19. The excerpt is taken from the report of a retreat for human rights NGO activists from around the world, held in Crete in 1989. It is part of a debate between some of the Third World NGOs and INGOs present at the retreat about the nature of INGO human rights reports. The proposal made was that INGOs reach beyond their attention to (enumerated, individual) violations, ranging from torture to censorship, by emphasizing and analyzing issues of political, social and economic structures that underlie the violations—issues like land reform, or the role of the military. The excerpt responds to such proposals.

> Even though conceptions of right are surely relevant to broad-ranging advocacy for social change, proposals that NGOs challenge basic political and economic structures of a society differ dramatically from the NGO work of two decades. Where, it was asked, could a mandate for so enveloping a task be found within the corpus of human rights law? Was not the strength and success of the human rights movement attributable partly to the fact that norms were relatively discrete, set only basic ground rules, expressed no final vision of the good or just society, and rested largely on consensus?
>
> . . .
>
> To the extent that NGOs base their prescriptions for society not solely on a body of human rights norms but on broader social analysis, how are they to be distinguished from other institutions in the vast and controverted world of social analysis—think tanks, academics, government policy makers? As one commentator among many on political choices, an NGO might repel or enlist our sympathies. But it would shed the objectivity that traditional human rights groups

claim in their reporting of facts and judgments about violations. A claim of 'accurate' analysis, of accurate diagnosis and prognosis, could not be supported in the way that, say, Amnesty International could support its account of violations and its condemnation of governmental action under a widely acknowledged norm prohibiting torture. The public interest sector of the human rights movement could lose its character as a defender of legality and readily merge into the broad political process.

QUESTION

Is it the task, or even the responsibility, of human rights NGOs to come up with a comprehensive balance sheet of the various concerns that need to be taken into account in a given situation and base their advocacy on that calculus, rather than to undertake a human rights analysis and then leave the political weighing of different considerations and structural or causal analysis to others?

PHILIP ALSTON, THE FORTIETH ANNIVERSARY OF THE UNIVERSAL DECLARATION

in J. Berting et al. (eds.), Human Rights in a Pluralist World, Individuals and Collectivities (1990), at 1, 12

... [It] is my contention that the result, albeit not the intention, of Amnesty's efforts is the widespread dissemination of a conception of human rights which is partial (in the sense of being incomplete) and is not a faithful reflection of the Universal Declaration and the assumptions underpinning that document (from which the Declaration derives its strength and standing). I would suggest that the great majority of Amnesty members and activists would, if pressed, provide a rather distorted list of basic human rights which would reflect the list of core 'mandate' issues pursued by Amnesty and little more. This distortion is essentially a consequence of the enormous success of the organization's determination not to be diverted from the core issues as it sees them. If that consequence could be characterized as intentional then Amnesty should not claim fidelity to the Universal Declaration and should concede that its concerns, far from being a reflection of universal minorities, mirror more closely values associated with the Western liberal tradition. In that case, any pretense to ideological blindness or neutrality should be abandoned. I believe, however, that for the most part that consequence is entirely unintended. If that is the case, it is time for the organization squarely and openly to address the issue of how it can best combat the risk of being perceived to endorse an unduly selective conception of human rights, while at the same time maintaining its core focus which can be justified in terms of manageability, legal specificity and operational potential.

I would not suggest that this will be an easy task, and there will be some among its membership who will resist it fiercely (for reasons of both effectiveness and ideology). Nevertheless, there are some relatively straightforward and painless first steps which could be taken by way of an expanded public information and education campaign. . . . [A] very widely distributed booklet entitled *What Does Amnesty International Do?* notes that Amnesty's 'work is based on principles set forth in the . . . Universal Declaration'. It states that while the organization's focus on prisoner's rights leads it to concentrate 'on a specific program in the human rights field' this 'does not imply that the rights it does not deal with are less important'. But at no point in the twenty-five-page booklet is any indication given as to what those other rights are. It is hard to believe that a brief educational reference to those other rights would in any way impair Amnesty's need to maintain a limited range of concerns.

The principal retort to my objection is likely to be that Amnesty, like all other human rights NGOs, is entitled to be specific in its focus and that other groups can better fill the gaps that Amnesty leaves. But this argument overlooks the fact that Amnesty, whether it likes it or not, is the single dominant force in the entire field. It is bigger, richer, better organized, more representative and more influential than most of the other groups put together. As a result, it is precluded from taking refuge in a justification which, when proffered by smaller NGOs, must (reluctantly) be accepted. As the great powers themselves often need to be reminded, with power and influence comes responsibility. Much of that responsibility may be unwanted, but it cannot simply be shrugged off.

NOTE

Compare the following observations in Amnesty International *Annual Report 1998*, www.amnesty.org/ailib/aireport/ar98:

> Addressing the imbalance between economic rights and other human rights is vital at a time when the debate over human rights is increasingly played out in the economic sphere. When governments fail to protect their citizens from the negative consequences of globalization, the need to protect and enhance economic rights becomes evident. The parallel imperative of ensuring that economic rights are not divorced from other human rights is shown each time that people are harassed, tortured and killed in the name of economic progress.
>
> Amnesty International, with a mandate geared primarily to civil and political rights, has been a part of this imbalance. The very success of the organization in building a worldwide membership and raising its concerns among a wide public has been a factor in focusing attention on civil and political rights. Amnesty International is now engaging in broader human rights debates and seeks to promote the full spectrum of human rights in its campaigning and human rights education activities. However, this side of its work has remained relatively underdeveloped. Decisions taken by the 1997 International Council Meeting affirmed the need to explore ways of raising awareness of the full range of human rights, to provide more economic and social context in Amnesty International's reporting, and to make greater efforts to promote international standards and mechanisms protecting economic and social rights.

E. NGOs IN THE UNITED NATIONS SETTING

1. ILLUSTRATION: UNITED NATIONS-RELATED ACTIVITIES OF WOMEN'S RIGHTS NGOS

ABOUT IWRAW AND THE CONVENTION
www.igc.org/iwraw/about/overview/

The International Women's Rights Action Watch (IWRAW) was organized in 1985 at the World Conference on Women in Nairobi, Kenya to monitor implementation of the ... CEDAW Convention .... It was founded on the belief that women's human rights—established through legal, political, and educational systems—are an essential component of development, and that governments and NGOs can be encouraged to understand and apply the Convention's principles to achieve equality. . . .

. . .

... NGOs have a very important role in making the [CEDAW] Convention an instrument of women's empowerment, through advocacy and monitoring their government's implementation of the treaty. Because the Convention's enforcement mechanism is based on a reporting system, it is imperative that NGOs understand and use the reporting mechanism to maintain government accountability both inside the country and at the United Nations.

These procedural and format guidelines are designed to assist NGOs in producing shadow reports for the CEDAW Committee . . . .

. . .

NGO reporting. Governments' assessments of their efforts to comply with the Convention frequently are incomplete and tend to minimize problems and maximize accomplishments. Recognizing this, the CEDAW Committee asks governments whether they have involved NGOs in preparing the government report. The Committee has invited direct NGO input, in the form of independent or 'shadow' reports and informal presentations, to bring women's real concerns to national and international attention.

Coordinating the contributors. It is entirely possible for a single organization to prepare a helpful shadow report. However, many NGOs have chosen to collaborate with other national and international NGOs in preparing reports. Collaboration can enhance the impact of the report on the government, as it can demonstrate a consensus voice and existence of broad constituencies in favor of positions taken in the report. Coordination also helps the Committee use NGO information effectively, as the experts cannot be expected to give adequate attention to multiple reports, especially if they arrive in the last few days before the session. . . .

Organizing the report for maximum impact. The following suggestions are based on seven years of NGO experience in submitting NGO information:

1. Organize the information according to articles of the CEDAW Convention, not by issue. . . . 2. Try to limit the report to no more than 30 pages. . . . 3. Provide an executive summary with specific language that the Committee could use in asking questions and drafting concluding observations . . . . 4. Analyze rather than simply describe . . . . 5. Prioritize issues. . . .

. . .

Recommendations for action should be concrete, suggesting specific action.

. . .

The Committee holds one meeting during the first week of each CEDAW session to hear country-specific information directly from NGOs. This is an opportunity to make your points to a number of the experts at once. Simultaneous interpretation is provided. Many of the CEDAW experts are readily approachable individually before and after the working sessions to talk informally about the issues that concern NGOs. Some will be willing to have a full-length meeting before a working session or at midday. Most will be approachable to at least have a few words. BE PREPARED for these meetings by having your specific points of concern ready to be conveyed in a few words and on a single sheet of paper.

A. CLARK, E. FRIEDMAN, AND K. HOCHSTETLER, THE SOVEREIGN LIMITS OF GLOBAL CIVIL SOCIETY
51 World Politics 1 (1998) at 15

[Starting with the Teheran Human Rights Conference in 1968 and the 1972 Stockholm Conference on the Human Environment, the United Nations has organized a series of world conferences on different themes. Conferences on women were held in Mexico City in 1975, Copenhagen in 1980, Nairobi in 1985 and Beijing in 1995. The Rio Conference on Environment and Development was held in 1992 and the Vienna Human Rights Conference in 1993.]

. . .

[Women] had been frustrated at conferences during the United Nations Decade for Women (1975–85) because NGOs were neither involved in the crucial drafting of the conference documents nor sufficiently organized at the conferences themselves. Women improved their lobbying in three ways between Nairobi and Beijing. First, they built coalitions through a caucus mechanism. Second, they participated early and often in preparatory meetings and in the development of new preparatory strategies. Third, they increased contact with the media and national delegations.

Women developed many of those innovations at the UN conferences on other issues. . . .

Before the Vienna human rights conference, women's NGOs and human rights organizations formed the Global Campaign for Women's Human Rights. This group of ninety NGOs focused on violence against women as a global human rights issue, working to make it a special theme of the conference. The Global Campaign's efforts culminated at the NGO forum with a Tribunal on Violations of Women's Human Rights, where women presented testimony of human rights abuses to a distinguished panel of judges. The Women's Caucus coordinated lobbying on women at Vienna and was able to make six plenary presentations at the official conference.

In advance of Beijing, the women's own conference, women's NGOs used strategies developed at earlier conferences: large numbers participated in preparatory meetings, formed new caucus structures, and negotiated with national delegations. WEDO [Women's Environment and Development Organization] coordinated a Linkage Caucus to advance gains made by women at prior UN conferences and circulated three advocacy documents that served as the basis for NGO lobbying efforts. In Beijing up to fifty caucuses met daily on conference grounds to discuss lobbying strategies. A group called the *Equipo* ('Team'), which represented the major caucuses, coordinated a daily NGO briefing session. Despite their inability to make statements, NGOs were allowed to attend most of the meetings of the governmental Working Groups that debated the text remaining to be negotiated. Since NGOs were still kept out of many of the smaller, more sensitive negotiations, most lobbying was done in the halls, with more organized caucuses circulating draft language. Longtime working relationships with delegates, particularly NGO members who belonged to official delegations, facilitated communication. In addition, NGOs made fully one-third of the plenary speeches. One area where NGOs led the way was in fulfilling their promise to make Beijing a 'Conference of Commitments'. Although governments refused to hold themselves accountable in the official document for promises made at the conference, NGOs did so by publicizing every promise made by an official delegate.

. . .

D. OTTO, A POST-BEIJING REFLECTION ON THE LIMITATIONS AND POTENTIAL OF HUMAN RIGHTS DISCOURSE FOR WOMEN

in K. Askin and D. Koenig (eds.), Women and International Human Rights Law (Vol. 1, 1999), at 115

There have been many glowing feminist assessments of the official outcomes from the 1995 Fourth World Conference on Women (Beijing Conference). . . .

. . .[T]his author's overall assessment of the Beijing outcomes is considerably less glowing. While the language of equality and human rights, which dominates the Beijing Declaration and Platform For Action (Beijing Platform), proved extremely effective in resisting moves by fundamentalist forces to claw back the advances that women have made since the adoption of the U.N. Charter in 1945, it also functioned to prevent transformative outcomes.

. . .

. . . The affirmation in the Vienna Declaration, that 'women's rights are human rights', has proved to be a hollow victory. While the Beijing Declaration makes the same assertion, it was not repeated in the section on human rights in the Platform because states had agreed not to recognize any *new* human rights in Beijing. Consequently, the Platform's text is careful to make a distinction between human rights, which are universal, and women's rights, which are not.

This distinction is clearest in the priority areas of health and violence against women, which deal largely with rights that are specific to women. For example, paragraph 95 states that 'reproductive rights embrace certain human rights' that are 'already recognized' in human rights instruments. Also, violence against women is recognized as 'impairing' or 'nullifying' women's enjoyment of human rights, *not* as a violation of women's human rights in itself. . . .

The result is that the gendered hierarchy of human rights orthodoxy remains intact. Where the experience of women and men is commensurable, women are granted access to human rights in the same way as men. But female-specific violations, which often result from gendered social practices and institutions, remain outside the heavily policed human rights heartland. Instructively, the language of 'power' used in the section on violence against women, in a repeat of language from the Declaration Against Violence, is not used elsewhere in the Platform. The effect is to confine the transformative challenges of the global campaign against gendered violence to a single issue that is firmly positioned outside the human rights mainstream.

. . .

Missing from the feminist human rights agenda were the important issues of the post-Cold War globalization of capital and the devastating reshaping of the development paradigm. Also absent was a class-based awareness of the importance of economic and social rights. Without actively and coherently addressing *all* human rights as indivisible and interdependent, the women's-rights-are-human-right-strategy is in danger of being co-opted by the institutions of global capital, in the same way that the women's development agenda was turned to the service of the development establishment by the end of the Decade for Women.

. . .

NOTE

Compare Philip Alston, 'The U.S. and the Right to Housing: A Funny Thing Happened on the Way to the Forum', 1 Eur. Hum. Rts. L. Rev. 120 (1996), at 133:

> Views differ greatly as to the [value of UN world conferences]. Their supporters point to their roles in assisting the formulation of appropriate global policies, facilitating the exchange of experiences, bringing activists and

policy-makers together, compelling governmental attention to key issues, providing an occasion to launch new international promotional endeavours or reinvigorate existing ones, mobilising additional resources, and stimulating public debate.

The critics see a large-scale waste of resources that would be better spent on action rather than talk, a torrent of policy statements and commitments which are not worth the cost of the many languages into which they must be translated, thinly veiled and largely self-serving efforts to promote one bureaucratic agenda at the expense of another, unnecessary dislocation of local populations to put on a good show for the visitors, and an effort to conceal rather than expose or debate the fundamental disagreements which are at the root of the international community's policy and programmatic paralysis. There is some truth in all of these views and any portrayal of the conferences either as an unqualified success or a total waste of time simply overlooks the complexity of the exercises themselves and of the contexts in which they take place. But the example of the right to housing [at the Habitat II conference in Istanbul in 1996] demonstrates both the potential for these conferences to take major steps backwards and their ability to provide a forum in which more progressive and constructive outcomes can find agreement.

QUESTIONS

1. Should a government offer to include NGO perspectives within its national report to a treaty body like the ICCPR Committee or CEDAW? Should NGOs accept any such invitation?

2. Is it inappropriate for NGOs to be lobbying and even 'spoon-feeding' independent expert members of the CEDAW Committee in the ways suggested by IWRAW?

3. Are the UN world conferences inevitably a double-edged sword from the perspective of human rights activists, in the sense that although offering a progressive forum they also follow a statist agenda which will inevitably be limited in its commitment to change?

2. THE UN DECLARATION ON HUMAN RIGHTS DEFENDERS OF 1998

LAWYERS COMMITTEE FOR HUMAN RIGHTS, PROTECTING HUMAN RIGHTS DEFENDERS

(1999), www.lchr.org/media/chr/defdecanalysis.htm

. . .

The international community has repeatedly acknowledged the vital role of human rights defenders in the implementation of human rights on the domestic level. International monitoring mechanisms . . . often rely heavily on the findings of local and national human rights activists in their assessment of domestic human rights conditions. . . .

However, precisely because of their critical role in promoting human rights awareness and debate on the national and international level, many human rights defenders find their own rights flagrantly violated by repressive governments. In recent years, the number of reported attacks on human rights defenders has increased dramatically. . . . Attacks on human rights defenders frequently include intimidation and harassment, arbitrary arrest and detention, disappearances, torture, and other physical violence. Those involved in such attacks often enjoy complete impunity.

. . . National laws and regulations frequently infringe upon the right to freedom of association by imposing lengthy and burdensome registration procedures or discriminatory restrictions on the right to obtain funding for human rights activities—particularly from outside the country. Other forms of restriction include denial of freedom of movement and assembly, and crippling limitations on human rights publications.

[A Working Group of the UN Commission on Human Rights took 13 years to draft the Declaration. It was finally adopted by the General Assembly.]

The slow process in finalizing the Declaration can be attributed to two major factors: 1) from its inception, there has been friction between those governments genuinely interested in strengthening the position of human rights defenders, and those who used this drafting exercise to further restrict and hamper their work; and 2) the need for consensus allowed a small group of participating governments to veto any real progress in the finalization of the Declaration. Key contentious issues in the Working Group were; (i) the role of national law in the implementation of the Declaration; (ii) the extent to which human rights defenders have special responsibilities or duties; (iii) the right of human rights defenders to obtain resources for their work; (iv) the right to observe trials; (v) the right to act on behalf of victims; and (vi) the ability of human rights defenders to freely choose which human right issues to work on. . . .

In reviewing the Declaration . . . , our overall assessment is a very positive one. The Declaration is the first UN instrument to emphasize that everyone has the right to promote, protect, and defend human rights, on the national and international levels.

DECLARATION ON THE RIGHT AND RESPONSIBILITY OF INDIVIDUALS, GROUPS AND ORGANS OF SOCIETY TO PROMOTE AND PROTECT UNIVERSALLY RECOGNIZED HUMAN RIGHTS AND FUNDAMENTAL FREEDOMS
GA Res. 53/144, Annex

. . .

Article 1

Everyone has the right, individually and in association with others, to promote and to strive for the protection and realization of human rights and fundamental freedoms at the national and international levels.

...

Article 3

Domestic law consistent with the Charter of the United Nations and other international obligations of the State in the field of human rights and fundamental freedoms is the juridical framework within which human rights and fundamental freedoms should be implemented and enjoyed, and within which all activities referred to in this Declaration for the promotion, protection and effective realization of those rights and freedoms should be conducted.

...

Article 5

For the purpose of promoting and protecting human rights and fundamental freedoms, everyone has the right, individually and in association with others, at the national and international levels:

    (a) To meet or assemble peacefully;
    (b) To form, join and participate in non-governmental organizations, associations or groups;
    (c) To communicate with non-governmental or intergovernmental organizations.

...

Article 9

   1. In the exercise of human rights ... everyone has the right, individually and in association with others, to benefit from an effective remedy and to be protected in the event of violation of these rights.

...

   3. To the same end, everyone has the right, individually and in association with others, inter alia:

    (a) To complain about the policies and actions of individual officials and governmental bodies with regard to violations of human rights and fundamental freedoms by petitions or other appropriate means to competent domestic judicial, administrative or legislative authorities or any other competent authority provided for by the legal system of the State, which should render their decision on the complaint without undue delay;
    (b) To attend public hearings, proceedings and trials, to form an opinion on their compliance with national law and applicable international obligations and commitments;
    (c) To offer and provide professionally qualified legal assistance or other relevant advice and assistance in defending human rights and fundamental freedoms.

   4. To the same end, and in accordance with applicable international instruments and procedures, everyone has the right, individually and in association with

others, to unhindered access to and communication with international [human rights] bodies. . . .

5. The State shall conduct a prompt and impartial investigation or ensure that an inquiry takes place whenever there is reasonable ground to believe that a violation of human rights and fundamental freedoms has occurred in any territory under its jurisdiction.

. . .

Article 11

. . . Everyone who, as a result of his or her profession, can affect the human dignity, human rights and fundamental freedoms of others should respect those rights and freedoms and comply with relevant national and international standards of occupational and professional conduct or ethics.

. . .

Article 13

Everyone has the right, individually and in association with others, to solicit, receive and utilize resources for the express purpose of promoting and protecting human rights and fundamental freedoms, through peaceful means, in accordance with article 3 of this Declaration.

Article 14

1. The State has the responsibility to take legislative, judicial, administrative or other appropriate measures to promote the understanding by all persons under its jurisdiction of their civil, political, economic, social and cultural rights.

. . .

QUESTIONS

1. How much protection from hostile national legislation does Article 3 afford to a human rights NGO?

2. As Attorney-General in a repressive government, can you outline a national policy which complies with all of the provisions of the Declaration that are excerpted above?

3. Does the formulation reflected in Article 9 represent significant progress when compared with, for example, the provisions of the ICCPR?

4. Why might Article 13 have been so strongly contested by governments? From an NGO perspective, how satisfactory is the outcome?

3. NGOs' ACCESS TO THE UNITED NATIONS

Article 71 of the UN Charter provides that the Economic and Social Council (ECOSOC) may make suitable arrangements for consultation with NGOs. No such provision exists in relation to the Security Council or the General Assembly. While the UN Commission on Human Rights, as a subsidiary of ECOSOC, is covered by the ECOSOC arrangements, the UN human rights treaty bodies are not and have tended to be rather less formal in their dealings with NGOs. As of mid-2000, close to 2,000 NGOs hold consultative status, 400 of which were admitted in 1999–2000. Details can be found on the UN's website, www.un.org. The relevant groups may request that items be placed on the agenda of the relevant body, attend meetings, submit written statements, and make oral presentations in meetings. Ironically, as their numbers grow, the value of consultative status can actually diminish because there is simply not enough meeting time to permit all to be heard. Thus, 'the right to make oral statements at the [UN Commission] is often rendered virtually useless because of the fact that the debate is so crowded, with so many governments and NGOs wanting to speak, that NGOs are frequently allotted the least popular time, late at night, when there are few government delegates to hear or respond to them'.[11]

CONSULTATIVE RELATIONSHIP BETWEEN THE UNITED NATIONS AND NON-GOVERNMENTAL ORGANIZATIONS
ECOSOC Res. 1996/31

. . .

The following principles shall be applied in establishing consultative relations with non-governmental organizations:

1. The organization shall be concerned with matters falling within the competence of the Economic and Social Council and its subsidiary bodies.

2. The aims and purposes of the organization shall be in conformity with the spirit, purposes and principles of the Charter of the United Nations.

3. The organization shall undertake to support the work of the United Nations . . . in accordance with its own aims and purposes. . . .

. . .

5. Consultative relationships may be established with international, regional, subregional and national organizations. . . . The [ECOSOC NGO] Committee, in considering applications for consultative status, should ensure, to the extent possible, participation of non-governmental organizations from all regions, and particularly from developing countries, in order to help achieve a just, balanced, effective and genuine involvement. . . .

. . .

8. Regional, subregional and national organizations . . . may be admitted provided that they can demonstrate that their programme of work is of direct relevance to the aims and purposes of the United Nations and, in the case of national organizations, after consultation with the Member State concerned. . . .

. . .

10. The organization shall have an established headquarters, with an executive

---

[11] M. Posner and C. Whittome, 'The Status of Human Rights NGOs', 25 Colum. Hum. Rts. L. Rev. 269 (1994), at 28.

officer. It shall have a democratically adopted constitution . . . which shall provide for the determination of policy by a conference, congress or other representative body, and for an executive organ responsible to the policy-making body.

. . .

12. The organization shall have a representative structure and possess appropriate mechanisms of accountability to its members, who shall exercise effective control over its policies and actions through the exercise of voting rights or other appropriate democratic and transparent decision-making processes. Any such organization that is not established by a governmental entity or intergovernmental agreement shall be considered a non-governmental organization for the purpose of these arrangements, including organizations that accept members designated by governmental authorities, provided that such membership does not interfere with the free expression of views of the organization.

13. The basic resources of the organization shall be derived in the main part from contributions of the national affiliates or other components or from individual members. Where voluntary contributions have been received, their amounts and donors shall be faithfully revealed to the Council Committee on Non-Governmental Organizations. Where, however, the above criterion is not fulfilled and an organization is financed from other sources, it must explain to the satisfaction of the Committee its reasons for not meeting the requirements laid down in this paragraph. Any financial contribution or other support, direct or indirect, from a Government to the organization shall be openly declared to the Committee . . . and shall be devoted to purposes in accordance with the aims of the United Nations.

. . .

NOTE

Compare the recommendation in the Report of the Fifth Meeting of Persons Chairing the Human Rights Treaty Bodies, UN Doc. A/49/537 (1994):

> The chairpersons recommend that each treaty body examine the possibility of changing its working methods or amending its rules of procedure to allow non-governmental organizations to participate more fully in its activities. Non-governmental organizations could be allowed, in particular, to make oral interventions and to transmit information relevant to the monitoring of human rights provisions through formally established and well-structured procedures. In order to facilitate the participation of non-governmental organizations, the chairpersons recommend that information about States parties' reporting, including scheduling and document numbers of the reports, be made available at a single point in the Centre for Human Rights. Similarly, advance information on the topics of proposed general comments should be made available to encourage non-governmental organizations to provide input to the drafts and to promote further discussion. Attention should be given by treaty bodies and non-governmental organizations to securing a stronger, more effective and coordinated participation of national non-governmental organizations in the consideration of States parties' reports.

. . .

QUESTIONS

1. Should the member state concerned be given a de facto veto over the granting of status to a national NGO?

2. Is the emphasis on NGO democratic decision-making, representativity, accountability, and transparency warranted? Are such requirements put on member states?

3. It has often been suggested that the UN should adopt far less restrictive policies in relation to NGOs and begin to treat them as authentic partners. One such approach would involve the establishment of a consultative popular assembly to be elected on a global basis—a global civil society forum. Could such an approach be workable in practice? On what basis, and with what functions?

ADDITIONAL READING

For a detailed bibliography see: A. Fowler, *Civil Society, NGDOs and Social Development: Changing the Rules of the Game (2000)* (website: www.unrisd.org/cgi-bin/dnld1). See generally on NGOs: H. Ranjeva, 'Non-Governmental Organizations and the Implementation of International Law', 270 *Collected Courses of the Hague Academy of Int. L.* 1 (1997); M. Keck and K. Sikkink, *Activists Beyond Borders: Advocacy Networks in International Politics* (1998); T. Risse, S. Ropp and K. Sikkink (eds.), *The Power of Human Rights: International Norms and Domestic Change* (1999); A. Donini, 'The Bureaucracy and the Free Spirits: Stagnation and Innovation in the Relationship between the UN and NGOs', in T. Weiss and L. Gordenker (eds.), *NGOs, the UN, and Global Governance* (1996), at 83; P. Uvin, 'Scaling Up the Grassroots and Scaling Down the Summit: The Relations between Third World NGOs and the UN', *ibid.*, at 159; P. Uvin, *Aiding Violence: The Development Enterprise in Rwanda* (1998); and D. Shelton, 'The Participation of Nongovernmental Organizations in International Judicial Proceedings', 88 Am. J. Int'l L. 611 (1994).

On human rights NGOs: R. Brett, 'Non-Governmental Actors in the Field of Human Rights', in R. Hanski and M. Suksi (eds.), *An Introduction to the International Protection of Human Rights: A Textbook* (2nd. edn., 1999); D. Otto, 'Nongovernmental Organizations in the United Nations System: The Emerging Role of International Civil Society', 18 Hum. Rts Q. 107 (1996); F. Gaer, 'Reality Check: Human Rights NGOs Confront Governments at the UN', in T. Weiss and L. Gordenker (eds.), *NGOs, the UN, and Global Governance* (1996) at 51; R. Maran, 'The Role of Nongovernmental Organizations', in B. Dunér (ed.), *An End to Torture: Strategies for its Eradication* (1998), at 222; Howard Tolley Jr., *The International Commission of Jurists: Global Advocates for Human Rights* (1994); Manfred Nowak, *World Conference on Human Rights: The Contribution of NGOs, Reports and Documents* (1994); D. Weissbrodt and J. McCarthy, 'Fact-Finding by International Nongovernmental Human Rights Organizations', 22 Va. J. Int'l L. (1981); Theo van Boven, 'The Role of Non-Governmental Organizations in International Human Rights Standard-Setting: A Prerequisite of Democracy', 20 Calif. Western Int'l L. J. 207 (1990).

On women's rights: B. A. Ackerly and S. Moller Okin, 'Feminist Social Criticism and the International Movement for Women's Rights as Human Rights', in I. Shapiro and C. Hacker-Cordón, *Democracy's Edges* (1999), at 134; M.A. Chen, 'Engendering World Conferences: The International Women's Movement and the UN', in T. Weiss and L. Gordenker (eds.), *NGOs, the UN, and Global Governance* (1996), at 139; N. Rodley, 'The Work of Non-Governmental Organizations in the World-Wide Promotion and Protection of Human Rights', 90/1 U.N. Bulletin of Human Rights 84 (1991).

On the ICRC see: C. Moorehead, *Dunant's Dream: War, Switzerland and the History of the Red Cross* (1998); J. Hutchinson, *Champions of Charity: War and the Rise of the Red Cross* (1996); M. Finnemore, 'Rules of War and Wars of Rules: The International Red Cross and the Restraint of State Violence', in J. Boli and G. Thomas (eds.), *Constructing World Culture: International Nongovernmental Organizations since 1875* (1999), at 149; and generally see *The International Review of the Red Cross* (quarterly).

On NGOs in the UN see: S. Charnowitz, 'Two Centuries of Participation: NGOs and International Governance', 18 Michigan J. Int'l L. 183 (1997); J. Mertus, 'Considering Nonstate Actors in the New Millennium: Toward Expanded Participation in Norm Generation and Norm Application', 32 N.Y.U. J. Int'l L. & Pol. 567 (2000); R. Lagoni, 'Article 71', in B. Simma *et al.* (eds.), *The Charter of the United Nations: A Commentary* 902–15 (1994), at 902; P. Chiang, *Non-Governmental Organizations at the United Nations* (1981); D. Bienen, V. Rittberger, and W. Wagner, 'Democracy in the United Nations System: Cosmopolitan and Communitarian Principles', in D. Archibugi, D. Held and M. Köhler (eds.), *Re-Imagining Political Community: Studies in Cosmopolitan Democracy* (1998), at 287; R. Falk, 'The United Nations and Cosmopolitan Democracy: Bad Dream, Utopian Fantasy, Political Project', *ibid.*, at 309.

PART D
STATES AS PROTECTORS AND ENFORCERS
OF HUMAN RIGHTS

Part D completes the basic structure of this coursebook. We first examined in Part A the processes for the creation of international human rights norms and the basic categories of civil-political and economic-social rights. Our attention then turned in Part C to the relations between norms and institutions, particularly to the significance of international institutions and processes for the development and enforcement of norms.

Those parts gave primary attention to the international dimensions of the human rights movement. Of course, states—the creators of the norms, the designers and members of the institutions, the participants in the processes, as well as the primary duty-bearers under international human rights law—figured prominently in these earlier materials. They appeared frequently as the violators, the defendants, the entities being monitored, investigated and reported on by intergovernmental and nongovernmental organizations.

Part D shifts focus. Here we observe primarily the internal processes of the states themselves, particularly the decisions and acts of governments bearing on human rights issues. Our perspective is that of the state rather than the international community. For the most part, we examine executive, legislative and judicial action looking toward the observance and protection of human rights, rather than state action violating rights. In short, we here imagine states as the first-line enforcers of the international human rights system that they have created. Such is indeed the primary focus of the entire human rights movement. In a state-organized world, the highest human rights aspiration would imagine states as fully adequate protectors of human rights, to the point where an international enforcement machinery would become redundant.

Part D has two chapters, both of which involve the interpenetration of national legal-political orders and the international system. Chapter 12 examines ways in which states observe and protect human rights. Chapter 13 inquires into the ways in which a state acts internationally as an enforcer of international human rights by applying pressure against violator states.

In both chapters, as in the entire coursebook, the materials view the state primarily *in its relationships* to the international system. That is, these chapters do not examine state politics, history, or culture *independently* of that system. In both chapters, states draw from and work to increase the efficacy of the international standards. The chapters draw their illustrations particularly from the United States and Europe, to permit a more contextual examination of the issues posed.

12

Interpenetration of International and National Systems: Internal Protection of Human Rights by States

Human rights violations occur *within* a state, rather than on the high seas or in outer space outside the jurisdiction of any one state. Ultimately, effective protection must come from within the state. The international human rights system does not typically place delinquent states in political bankruptcy and through some form of receivership take over the administration of a country in order to assure the enjoyment of human rights—although the measures implemented by the international community in Bosnia-Herzegovina after the 1995 Dayton Peace Agreement and especially in Kosovo (see p. 653, *supra*) represent steps in that direction. Rather the international system seeks to persuade or pressure states to fulfil their obligations through one or another method—either observing national law (constitutional or statutory) that is consistent with the international norms, or making the international norms themselves part of the national legal and political order.

Such is the focus of Chapter 12, which falls into three sections. *Section A* describes the adoption by many states during the last half of the twentieth century, and especially the recent decades, of constitutions informed by liberal political (and often economic) premises and frequently declaring human rights. It notes the many relationships between such state constitutions and the international human rights regime. These themes are surely familiar, in the light of the many illustrations of state constitutions and constitutional litigation in this coursebook's earlier chapters. *Section B* inquires how states 'internalize' *treaty* norms—that is, how they absorb the provisions of human rights treaties within the state's legal and political order so that they can be implemented and enforced by state authorities. *Section C* then turns to the use of state judiciaries to provide remedies to victims of human rights violations that took place in other countries, and in the process to draw on customary international law. It stresses the role of distinctive legislation in the United States, the Alien Tort Statute.

A. THE SPREAD OF STATE CONSTITUTIONS IN THE LIBERAL MODEL

This section looks at one of the important phenomena of the past 50 years or so: the spread among many states of constitutions expressing the principles of political (and sometimes economic) liberalism, and often recognizing human rights.[1] Although 82 per cent of constitutions adopted between 1788 and 1948 contained provisions of some sort dealing with human rights,[2] the subsequent period is of particular importance because of the convergence of the formulae used (with the Constitutions of the United States, France and Germany, as well as the Universal Declaration, being especially influential) and the expanded emphasis upon judicial and other remedies for violations. Of course other states have adopted constitutions that have involved neither liberal principles nor the embrace of human rights.

One can approach this phenomenon from two perspectives. First, the adoption of liberal-style constitutions (or at least constitutions with a significant liberal component) can be seen as a *horizontal* trend among states, a consequence of the influence and pressures exerted by powerful countries in the liberal constitutional tradition like the United States. For the states achieving independence upon decolonization and adopting constitutions in the liberal model, the primary influence may have been the internal constitutional and political orders of the former colonial powers.

A second perspective stresses the links between the spread of such types of constitutions and the achievements of the human rights movement in constructing an international system of norms, institutions and processes. One could describe these links and the related influence and pressure as *vertical* rather than horizontal in character, since they come from international law and institutions 'above' the state rather than from other states.

Both horizontal and vertical influences and pressures were simultaneously at work in this process of states' drafting constitutions. They were indeed complexly intertwined, for the very states exerting a 'horizontal' influence were simultaneously creators and members of the international system exerting pressure from above. International human rights figured ever more pervasively in the discourse of international relations and made demands on states that in many respects could best be met through constitutions assuring the conduct required by the treaties to the citizens of the state. Those constitutions both 'borrowed' from other states and revealed, through their governmental structure and declarations of rights, the influence on them of the UDHR and the two basic Covenants.

---

[1] Many decisions of courts of these states, including the new constitutional courts, that interpret and apply these constitutions are set forth in Vicki Jackson and M. Tushnet, *Comparative Constitutional Law* (1999).

[2] H. van Maarseveen and G. van der Tang, *Written Constitutions: A Computerized Comparative Study* (1978), at 191.

COMMENT ON CONSTITUTIONS AND CONSTITUTIONALISM

The range of constitutions

Most states of the world (the United Kingdom being the most striking exception) have a formal, written constitution. By itself, that statement says very little. A 'constitution' refers simply to a basic state document that organizes a political system by, for example, setting forth the basic institutions of government. It need not follow any particular structure, impose or reflect any particular political or economic system or ideology, or prescribe any particular form of government. It may be democratic or authoritarian, oriented to private property and markets or to collective ownership and central direction, multi-party or one-party, attentive or not to individual rights, and so on.

Constitutions vary radically in their practical significance and symbolism as well as content. At one extreme, entire instruments or particular provisions may be meant to be hortatory and aspirational rather than to form part of the state's legal system. Those aspirations may represent genuine goals to be worked toward, or amount to sham and pretence, a shallow disguise of radically different and less admirable state purposes and methods. At the other extreme, constitutional provisions may be judicially enforceable against the government in actions brought by private parties, even to the extent of judicial review—that is, testing legislation against constitutional norms, and invalidating legislation found to violate them.

From a different perspective, a constitution may be broadly understood by the people to be insignificant, a document freely manipulated by government. Consider, for example, the People's Republic of China which, since 1949, has had five constitutions, each of which has:

> . . . signaled a change in power or a change in the economic or political objectives of the Chinese leadership. . . . The judiciary had virtually no significant role in this constitutional evolution. . . . [E]ach constitution has been premised on the belief that rights are granted to citizens by the state. Rights are not derived from human personhood, nor are they enshrined or fixed within the constitution itself. This premise or belief allows the state to change both the quality and quantity of a citizen's rights whenever it is believed necessary because the existence of such rights does not limit the power of the state. Consequently, each constitution has either implicitly or explicitly permitted the state to define the nature of a citizen's rights by legislation. . . . [T]he U.S. constitutional principle of checks and balances between the traditional branches of government (executive, judicial, and legislative) is absent.[3]

Alternatively, a constitution may be understood as an authoritative charter, or a solemn covenant, between the government and people. If so, it will tend to be more stable and resistant to change; the amendment process will be correspondingly complex, demanding and time-consuming.

---

[3] R. Folsom, J. Minan and L.A. Otto, *Law and Politics in the People's Republic of China* (1992), at 56.

Constitutionalism

Scholars frequently use the term 'constitutionalism' to describe a particular genus of constitutional system. This fluid term is put to many different uses, although many scholars would agree on the core meaning. Constitutionalism here refers to a constitutional system that falls within the liberal tradition (see the Comment on liberalism at p. 361, *supra*) and possesses many characteristics of the democratic state. Often constitutionalism in this sense is implied when one speaks of the spread of constitutions among states as a part of the human rights movement—for example, the post-apartheid South African constitution.

Constitutionalism refers broadly to the following characteristics of a constitution, found among many states to a greater or lesser degree, in different combinations and with different emphases. Often based on a conception of popular sovereignty, the constitution assures accountability to the people through a range of techniques and institutions, the most important being the requirement of periodic and genuine elections in a multi-party system. Consistent with the liberal tradition, the constitution would control and limit the powers of government in several different ways, including a scheme of checks and balances through a separation of powers that must include an independent judiciary. That judiciary becomes the essential guardian of the rule of law, in the sense that the executive (or 'government') must act within established legal frameworks and according to established processes. The legality and legitimacy of that action must be subject to judicial review.

Constitutionalism implies that the constitution is a 'real' rather than merely hortatory instrument, truly the fundamental law or charter—in the words of the United States Constitution, 'supreme law'. It thus possesses a distinctive solemnity and force. It may come to symbolize the nation itself.

Constitutionalism generally involves a declaration of the individual rights associated with the liberal tradition, in the manner of the Bill of Rights of (the first ten amendments to) the US Constitution, and of many European constitutions as well as constitutions in a broad range of African, Asian and Latin American states. These rights are indispensable to setting limits to governmental action, particularly when they are coupled with judicial review of the constitutionality of legislation. Such judicial review itself could be seen as a desired but not essential element of the constitutional scheme.

The list of rights declared will vary among states. For example, in the constitutional history of the United States, the property right protected by the Fifth and Fourteenth Amendments to the Constitution has played a large and influential role. That has been much less the case in many states whose constitutions now fall within the liberal tradition, and indeed in the major human rights treaties.

Since the end of the Cold War new constitutions, including bills of rights, have been adopted in a great many countries. In Central and Eastern Europe alone, there have been more than 25 new or revised constitutions in that time. Developments in Africa have been characterized as a prolonged fit of 'constitutional fever'; a 1998 compilation included 20 constitutions published in French since 1990.

One of the most notable success stories of this period is South Africa's transition from a racist regime to constitutionalism. Perhaps no change in regime and principles has been as sudden and dramatic. After the collapse of apartheid came various interim arrangements which in turn were followed by the 1996 Constitution of the Republic of South Africa. Chapter 1 (sec. 1) of the Constitution is entitled Founding Provisions and reads like a textbook on constitutionalism:

> The Republic of South Africa is one sovereign democratic state founded on the following values:
>
> (a) Human dignity, the achievement of equality and the advancement of human rights and freedoms.
> (b) Non-racialism and non-sexism.
> (c) Supremacy of the constitution and the rule of law.
> (d) Universal adult suffrage, a national common voters roll, regular elections and a multi-party system of democratic government, to ensure accountability, responsiveness and openness.

Section 2 provides that the 'Constitution is the supreme law of the Republic'. Chapter 2 contains a Bill of Rights which is described as 'a cornerstone of democracy' and 'enshrines the rights of all people in our country and affirms the democratic values of human dignity, equality and freedom'. 'The state must respect, protect, promote and fulfil' these rights. The Constitutional Court here plays a vital role.[4]

The key question raised by such developments is: Under what circumstances will provisions designed to establish a system of constitutionalism succeed? Are there any indispensable ingredients? Are there preconditions, in the absence of which an otherwise splendid constitution will remain as a façade or an illusion? Compare the analyses which follow. Ghai paints a bleak picture of the experience in post-colonial Kenya, but retains an element of optimism. Several authors who survey recent developments within Africa see cause for considerable satisfaction. The assessments of post-1989 developments in Eastern and Central Europe are less sanguine.

YASH GHAI, THE KENYAN BILL OF RIGHTS: THEORY AND PRACTICE
in Philip Alston (ed.), Promoting Human Rights through Bills of Rights: Comparative Perspectives (1999), at 187

I. Introduction: The Background to the Bill of Rights

... During the colonial period, there were no restrictions, stemming from a fundamental law, on the legislative or executive power of the government. The colonial administration established and maintained by means of the law a governmental and social system characterized by authoritarianism, and racial

---

[4] The decision of the South African Constitutional Court in the *Makwanyane* case p. 39, *supra*, offers an apt illustration.

discrimination. . . . Several features of this system may be mentioned. First, for a long time there was no local or popular participation in law making. . . .

Second, in general the law conferred wide discretion on officials. . . .

. . .

. . . [T]he colonial laws and administration . . . fashioned official attitudes and behaviour and the submissiveness of the people to authority. Not only have these attitudes and behaviour continued, but so have most of the laws. . . . The result of these laws and practices was the growth of a powerful administration which had scant regard for the rights of the people. . . .

However, European settler and commercial communities could not face with equanimity the prospects of such a legal and administrative system continuing into the era of African rule. . . . Under their pressure, Britain agreed upon a fundamental reversal of policy. This involved political and administrative decentralisation . . . [and] the inclusion of a Bill of Rights in the Constitution for independence. Britain had in fact extended the [European Convention on Human Rights (ECHR)] to Kenya in 1953, but it was not incorporated in local laws and therefore had little impact in the country. . . .

Equally ineffective was the first domestic Bill of Rights which made its appearance in 1960. It is not possible to trace a single case in which the Bill was successfully invoked. It was succeeded by another one . . . [which] was entrenched in the independence Constitution (December 1963). The 1960 Bill was closely modelled on the ECHR, although for subsequent Bills inspiration was drawn from the Nigerian and Ugandan constitutions. This made little difference since the latter two countries had drawn upon the ECHR (or rather the [British] Colonial Office had drawn on it for them).

It should be stated that the decision to include the Bill of Rights was that of Britain. By this time it was becoming normal (but by no means universal. . .) for a colony to adopt a Bill of Rights on independence, but the need to protect Kenya's minorities, particularly the white settlers, was upper-most in the decision. There is no evidence of any enthusiasm on the part of African parties for the Bill (although it would have been hard for them to oppose it, given their anti-colonial stance).

. . .

V. Conclusion: The Reason for the Ineffectiveness of the Bill of Rights

Most African states adopted shortly before or at independence a Bill of Rights, very similar in form and content to that in Kenya. In the large majority of instances, the Bill of Rights was no more effective than in Kenya. How is one to explain the ineffectiveness of the Bill of Rights?

[The author adopts a dichotomy used by Max Weber to distinguish between legal-rational (rule of law-related) and patrimonial systems of governance. Over time, Kenya moved to the latter system, under which an] apparatus of coercion and oppression (. . . a mixture of the legal and the illegal) is established to deal with those who resist the arbitrary exercise of patrimonialism, while the resources of the state provide a ready source of patronage to keep others in line.

The explanation for this shift lies in the nature and purposes of the state in Africa. The state is an imposition, and stands in a relationship of antagonism to civil society. . . . Independence facilitated the access to state power of leaders who had only a weak hold in the economy. . . . As the state is the primary instrument of accumulation, corruption is endemic, woven into the very fabric of the apparatus of the state. The pressures towards corruption arise not only from economic greed, but also from the imperatives of political survival, since the main basis of a politician's support is generally not the party or another political platform, but clientelism, sustained by regular favours to one's followers. Public control and accountability over that apparatus are unacceptable; resistance on the part of the exploited is met with coercion. The role of constitutions and laws becomes totally instrumental, unmediated by autonomous processes and procedures. Law itself becomes a commodity that only the state may mobilize and manipulate. . . . In these circumstances it becomes impossible to secure the enforcement of rights and freedoms.

The domestic and international environment was not unpropitious to the centralisation of power. The leitmotif of the time was 'nation building' and economic development, and African leaders managed to present the independence constitutions (with the diffusion of power and checks and balances) as obstacles towards these goals. Arguments were also presented as to the failure of the constitutions to reflect the 'African personality' and understandings of authority and power. Thus from the very beginning the legitimacy of these constitutions was undermined, the ideology of legality replaced by that of developmentalism. (The legal system was allowed to atrophy; law reports ceased to be published, law libraries were run down, the system of filing in courts became the twin victim of inefficiency and corruption). The fact that this was merely a cover for the aggrandisement and consolidation of personal power did not become obvious until later. There were few domestic groups with a genuine commitment to human rights (for the truth is that anti-colonialism was not about human rights but about black power). . . .

. . .

In these circumstances . . . the Bill of Rights became largely irrelevant. . . . Even if a judicial decision favourable for human rights could be secured, it seems to have little impact on administrative or police practice, or indeed on subsequent litigation. However, this assessment needs a qualification. The experience of the 80s shows that the Bill is not without effect in other ways. The skilful use of it by a few lawyers tied the government in litigation of key political issues. Courts became the only venue where these issues could be aired. They exposed the inconsistencies and malpractices of the government and raised public consciousness of rights and politics. . . . The Bill established standards by which the conduct of the government and the courts could be judged. It inspired the establishment and work of some NGOs. It helped to produce a sense of solidarity among disparate persons working for social and political reform. For a time it provided the only alternative coherent ideology to that of tribalism and one partyism of the government. It also enabled democratic struggles in Kenya to be linked to the growing international concern with rights and democracy, and being focused on rights which by now were proclaimed as universal rather than on specifics of local politics, it facilitated the engagement of foreign private and official institutions.

. . .

The authoritarianism of African rulers and the bankruptcies of their policies have raised a consciousness of the value of human rights. A number of NGOs, with a commitment to human rights, have arisen. There is greater awareness of the procedures to secure human rights (and a growing number of lawyers willing to risk the use of them). The international environment is supportive. The role of the state is being downgraded. There are growing demands for public accountability. . . .

ANALYSES OF CONTEMPORARY MOVES TOWARD CONSTITUTIONALISM IN DIVERSE STATES

Mpazi Sinjela, Constitutionalism in Africa: Emerging Trends
60 The Review, Int'l Commission of Jurists 2 (1998)

[At] independence most African countries adopted a 'Westminster' or a 'Gaullist' constitution model . . . [Subsequently, however, a] multiparty democracy was considered to encourage tribal division and conflict, and was, therefore, undesirable. . . .

. . .

Where a peaceful transition to a one party rule was not possible, civilian governments were overthrown by force and were replaced by military rule.

The political changes in Eastern Europe signalling the end of the Cold War meant that African totalitarian [states] were no longer needed by the West by virtue of their strategic or geographical location. No longer supported but condemned for gross violations of human rights, these dictatorial regimes had to succumb and give way to a new order. A hurricane of political change in Sub-Saharan Africa ensued. . . .

. . .

[The author then refers to the 1990s constitutions of South Africa, Namibia, Tanzania and Malawi, all of which contain extensive human rights provisions.] . . . By the beginning of the 1990s, multiparty systems had been introduced in almost all Francophone countries. The constitutional reforms accompanying the political reforms have also signalled a return to the independence constitutions modelled after that of France. Like in Anglophone African countries, the new Constitutions include an array of human rights provisions. A mechanism for safeguarding human rights has been established. This includes the establishment of Constitutional Courts or the office of an Ombudsman. . . .

. . .

Bertrand Ramcharan, The Evolving African Constitutionalism
60 The Review, Int'l Commission of Jurists 23 (1998)

. . . [African states] are engaged in a determined effort to address conflicts in the continent and to promote African solutions to African problems. . . .

...

The national constitutions bring out one point forcefully: the evolving African constitutionalism is a constitutionalism of human rights and liberty. In all the constitutions discussed, the themes of democracy and respect for human rights are emphasised prominently. There is experimentation in new forms of governance, sure enough, but the thread running through these experiments is an insistence on democratic legitimacy—with the meaning of democracy left open as the experiments unfold. . . .

Amedou Ould-Abdallah, The Rule of Law and Political Liberation in Africa
60 The Review, Int'l Commission Jurists 29 (1998)

. . . The mere existence of a constitution, however comprehensive, will do little to create a stable environment for democracy and development unless people know and understand its provisions, have faith that their governments will not overrule it, and believe that their rights as promulgated within it, will indeed be upheld. Therefore, the existence of an independent judiciary and legislature, a free and competent press, and a vibrant civil society are all necessary to ensure that constitutional provisions are translated into reality.
. . .

. . . An unfortunate legacy of single-party politics in some countries is that most people have little faith in either the legal system or the judiciary, and public confidence has to be re-built if the rule of law is to be institutionalised.
. . .

. . . [A]s experience has shown, freedoms can easily be reversed and repression reintroduced. There is no guarantee that the current process of democratisation in Africa will continue or be sustained. . . .

Abdullahi An-Na'im, Eritrean Independence and African Constitutionalism: A Sudanese Perspective
in Tekle (ed.), *Eritrea and Ethiopia: From Conflict to Cooperation* (1994), at 115

. . .

. . . Constitutions by themselves cannot transform political, economic and social reality; at best, they can only seek to regulate it and direct its energy in the desired direction. In essence, constitutions represent the legal expression of underlying principles and institutions which should be firmly embedded in and supported by norms and values regarding the incidence, exercise, sharing and transfer of political power which are accepted and practiced by the population at large. For better or worse, constitutions and constitutionalism should therefore be the product of the historical evolution of the culture of the particular society.
. . .

. . . I argue that the need and cultural resources for developing commitment to constitutionalism are present in African societies. The need is due to the fact that the nation-state is now the primary form of large scale political organization. Both domestic and international political and economic relations are predicated on this fact, Africans must develop and learn to operate their own nation-states in order to exercise their right to self-determination in the modern world. In my view, the necessary resources for this already exist in African cultural traditions, albeit in somewhat rudimentary form. To the extent that one can speak of African culture in general, there are certainly rich traditions of political consultation or government by consensus and communitarian welfare which can now be utilized to promote African constitutional models.

I am not suggesting that traditional African cultures are in full accord with modern constitutionalism. On the contrary, I can see that certain aspects of that tradition, such as the status of women and outsiders to the clan or tribe, are certainly at odds with constitutional principles of equality and non-discrimination.

. . .

Igor Petrukhin, The Judicial Protection of the Constitutional Rights and Freedoms in Russia: Myths and Reality

in Gibney and Frankowski (eds.), *Judicial Protection of Human Rights: Myth or Reality?* (1999), at 25

[This analysis focuses on the role of the judiciary under the 1993 Russian Constitution which proclaims in Article 2 that 'Man, his rights and freedoms shall be the supreme value. It shall be a duty of the state to recognize, respect and protect the rights and liberties of man and citizen'. The Constitution contains a comprehensive listing of civil and political rights and enumerates a significant range of economic, social and cultural rights. Human rights are judicially enforceable and a Constitutional Court is established.]

The 1993 Russian Constitution is a good basis for the democratization of justice and the protection of citizens' rights. Many important laws have been adopted in its implementation. These laws govern various aspects of the market economy, they allow the authorities to fight crime more effectively and they also protect citizens' rights and freedoms. But the process of legal reform is far from over. . . .

The judicial profession has become less attractive. The courts are badly financed, receiving only about one third of the funds allocated to them by the state. In some regions, one may speak of the virtual paralysis of justice. Owing to high court costs, many people cannot afford to turn to the judiciary to vindicate their rights. The judiciary is generally distrusted. Defense attorneys have found themselves in a difficult situation because most of them handle 50 percent of their cases free of charge or for a low payment from the government while acting as appointed defense attorneys.

The judiciary is still under pressure from prosecutors, the Ministry of Internal

Affairs and the Federal Security Service. These agencies are dissatisfied with the number of not-guilty verdicts (although they amount to only 0.5 percent of the verdicts), with the judicial supervision over pre-trial detention and with the remand by the judiciary of many cases for additional investigation. Finally, a series of laws on operational investigatory activities have legalized highly questionable methods and techniques typical of oppressive political regimes. All of these phenomena raise serious concerns regarding the future of judicial legal reform in Russia.

. . .

Istvan Pogany, Constitution Making or Constitutional Transformation in Post-Communist Societies?

in Bellamy and Castiglione (eds.), *Constitutionalism in Transformation: European and Theoretical Perspectives* (1996), at 157

    . . . Amongst many of the post-Soviet states, in particular, the absence of established national political cultures (other than Communism), the stresses and dislocation resulting from transition to a quasi-market economy (characterized by corruption and incompetence) and the general absence of ethnic, linguistic or religious homogeneity (a factor which was frequently exacerbated by the policies pursued during the Soviet era) have combined to create conditions in which many of the new state structures remain vulnerable and fragile. In such circumstances, even if a general collapse of state authority can be avoided (or recovered from), the alternative may not be liberal democracy. It is altogether more probable that authoritarian governments, drawing on ethnic, religious or other loyalties, will provide a more credible basis for the preservation and continuation of central authority in these states.

. . .

    Constitution making and constitutional transformation may go hand in hand. However, there is no logical reason why this should always be so. Indeed, there are numerous reasons why governments engage in spates of constitution making, apart from the wish to transform the way in which a society is governed. These include the desire for international (or national) legitimacy, a need to encourage foreign aid or investment, or even the wish to avoid genuine transformation. Constitution making may, thus, constitute a form of political deception, helping cynical and manipulative regimes to pursue policies which are the reverse, or merely a parody, of the principles enshrined in the constitution (this is at least partially the case in Slovakia, Romania and in some of the post-Soviet states).

. . .

    . . . It surely cannot be a coincidence that the four most successfully transforming political democracies and market economies—the Czech Republic, Slovenia, Poland and Hungary—are strikingly homogeneous in ethnic, religious and linguistic terms. They are truly 'nation' states. . . . By contrast, in Romania, Slovakia, Bulgaria, Ukraine, the Russian Federation, the Baltic states and the former Yugoslavia, tensions over minorities have undoubtedly complicated a possible transition to democracy and constitutionalism.

This is, in many respects, a depressing conclusion. It suggests that democracy and constitutionalism will be slow to develop, or may never develop, in many of the post-Communist states. Even if these countries succeed in overcoming the legacy of the Communist era—political, social and economic infantilization, economic backwardness, pollution etc., they must continue to wrestle with the ghosts of their pre-Communist pasts. For some, these may prove to be altogether more formidable adversaries. Thus, 'the more fundamental trend may be a return to indigenous political traditions'.

. . .

QUESTIONS

1. Where civil society remains both weak and repressed in many countries, should reformers put liberal constitutionalism low on their priorities?

2. An-Na'im concludes that if constitutionalism is to succeed it should be 'the product of the historical evolution of the culture of the particular society'. Is this true historically in any of the cases with which you are familiar? Germany? Japan? Kenya? What are the difficulties of 'transplanting' constitutions in the liberal model from countries in which they grew over time organically (even if the process started by violent revolution) to states of a radically different ethnic, cultural, religious, economic and political character?

3. Does it make sense to promote a single model of constitutionalism both for countries which have major ethnic, religious, linguistic or other minorities, and for those whose populations are relatively homogeneous? If a standard model should be modified for countries with mutually antagonistic minorities, what should the modifications consist of?

4. Is constitutionalism synonymous with human rights? All the rights of the UDHR and the two Covenants? If not all, which? Can you imagine a state characterized by constitutionalism that was at the same time a systematic and gross violator of basic rights in the UDHR?

ADDITIONAL READING

M. Tushnet, 'The Possibilities of Comparative Constitutional Law', 108 Yale L. J. 1225 (1999); M. Tushnet and V. Jackson (eds.), _Comparative Constitutional Law: Cases and Materials_ (1999); P. Alston, 'Lessons Relating to Bills of Rights from Pre-Twentieth Century Experience' in F Coomans _et al._ (eds.), _Rendering Justice to the Vulnerable_ (forthcoming 2000); D. Nelken, _Comparing Legal Cultures_ (1997); W. Twining, 'Globalization and Comparative Law', 6 Maastricht J. Eur. & Comp. L. 217 (1999); G. Teubner (ed.), _Global Law without a State_ (1997); F. Azzam, _Arab Constitutional Guarantees of Civil and Political Rights_

(1996); D. Beatty (ed.), *Human Rights and Judicial Review: A Comparative Perspective* (1994); R. Bellamy and D. Castiglione (eds.), *Constitutionalism in Transformation: European and Theoretical Perspectives* (1996); T. Buergenthal, 'Modern Constitutions and Human Rights Treaties', 36 Columbia Journal of Transnational Law 211 (1997); Symposium, 'Rights in New Constitutions', 26 Columbia Human Rights Law Review 1 (1994); D. Greenberg *et al.* (eds.), *Constitutionalism and Democracy: Transitions in the Contemporary World* (1993); M. Lacey and K. Haakonssen (eds.), *A Culture of Rights: the Bill of Rights in Philosophy, Politics and Law* (1991); and L. Henkin and A. Rosenthal (eds.), *Constitutionalism and Rights: The Influence of the United States Constitution Abroad* (1990).

B. HUMAN RIGHTS TREATIES WITHIN STATES' LEGAL AND POLITICAL ORDERS

While the many new constitutions have been deeply influenced by the Western models and by the basic international human rights instruments, they are nonetheless emphatically *national* instruments, created and shaped and instituted by each state.

Section B shifts attention to international instruments, specifically to human rights treaties. It examines the interpenetration of the international and national systems, the significance of treaties within states. The broad questions explored are: how do these treaties influence the national legal and political systems of states parties? Are they automatically absorbed into a state legal system, or reproduced in state legislation, and with what effects on the different branches of government such as the executive and judiciary? Or do they remain distinct from the state system, 'above' it as part of international law? The readings draw on the techniques and experiences of a range of countries in this excursion into comparative constitutional law.

1. BASIC NOTIONS: ILLUSTRATIONS FROM DIFFERENT STATES

VIRGINIA LEARY, INTERNATIONAL LABOUR CONVENTIONS AND NATIONAL LAW
(1982) at 1

[The efficacy of human rights treaties] depends essentially on the incorporation of their provisions in national law. . . .

. . .

International law determines the validity of treaties in the international legal system, i.e., when and how a treaty becomes binding upon a state as regards other State Parties. It also determines the remedies available on the international plane for its breach. But it is the national legal system which determines the status or force of law which will be given to a treaty within that legal system, i.e., whether national judges and administrators will apply the norms of a treaty in a specific case.... When the treaty norms become domestic law, national judges and administrators apply them, and individuals in the ratifying states may receive rights as a result of the treaty provisions. Thus, developed municipal legal systems supplement the more limited enforcement system of international law.

While the international legal system does not reach *directly* into the national systems to enforce its norms it attempts to do so *indirectly*. States are required under international law to bring their domestic laws into conformity with their validly contracted international commitments. Failure to do so, however, results in an international delinquency but does not change the situation within the national legal systems where judges and administrators may continue to apply national law rather than international law in such cases....

The status of treaties in national law is determined by two different constitutional techniques referred to in this study as 'legislative incorporation' and 'automatic incorporation'. In some states the provisions of ratified treaties do not become national law unless they have been enacted as legislation by the normal method. The legislative act creating the norms as domestic law is an act entirely distinct from the act of ratification of the treaty. The legislative bodies may refuse to enact legislation implementing the treaty. In this case the provisions of the treaty do not become national law. This method, referred to as 'legislative incorporation', is used, inter alia, in the United Kingdom, Commonwealth countries and Scandinavian countries. In other states, which have a different system, ratified treaties become domestic law by virtue of ratification. This method is referred to as 'automatic incorporation' and is the method adopted, inter alia, by France, Switzerland, the Netherlands, the United States and many Latin American countries and some African and Asian countries.... Even in such states, however, some treaty provisions require implementing legislation before they will be applied by the courts. Such provisions are categorized as 'non-self-executing'.
. . .

International law does not dictate that one or the other of the methods of legislative or automatic incorporation must be used. Either is satisfactory assuming that the norms of treaties effectively become part of national law. Conversely, neither method is *ipso facto* satisfactory under international law, if, in practice, the norms of ratified treaties are not applied by national judges and administrators. The method by which treaties become national law is a matter in principle to be determined by the constitutional law of the ratifying state and not a matter ordained by international law. The international community, lacking more effective means of enforcement, is often dependent on the constitutional system of particular states for the effective application of treaties intended for internal application.

Some national constitutions provide for automatic incorporation of treaty provisions. In other states, judicial decisions have determined that treaties are to be automatically incorporated. A correlation appears to exist between legislative consent to ratification and automatic incorporation. In states with the system of automatic incorporation, legislative consent by at least one house of the legislature is generally required before the executive may ratify treaties. In states with the system of legislative incorporation, ratification of treaties is frequently a purely executive act not requiring prior approbation of the legislature. In the United Kingdom, and other common law countries which have followed UK precedent in this regard, parliamentary consent to ratification is normally not required and express legislative enactment of treaty provisions is necessary before they become domestic law.

. . .

An individual may invoke the provisions of a treaty before national courts in automatic incorporation states in the absence of implementing legislation only when its provisions are considered to be self-executing and when he has standing to do so. . . . [I]n general, treaty provisions are considered by national courts and administrators as self-executing when they lend themselves to judicial or administrative application without further legislative implementation. . . .

. . .

NOTE

As of March 2000, there were 41 Member States of the Council of Europe, all of which are parties to the European Convention on Human Rights. Chapter 10 examined the international organ of the ECHR, the European Court of Human Rights; these materials examine the internal application by member states of the Convention's rules.

All but three states parties have incorporated the Convention into domestic law. Of those three, the United Kingdom (see p. 1008, *infra*) and Norway are in the process of creating a new relationship between the Convention and domestic law. In Ireland the Convention continues to have only the status of international law within the domestic legal system, although a move to incorporate is under active review.

There follow brief studies of treaties within the domestic law of several countries.

JÖRG POLAKIEWICZ, THE APPLICATION OF THE EUROPEAN CONVENTION ON HUMAN RIGHTS IN DOMESTIC LAW
17 Hum. Rts. L. J. 405 (1996), at 406

. . .

II. The status of the Convention in the domestic law of States Parties

Since there is no formal obligation for member States to incorporate the substantive provisions of the Convention into their domestic law their status varies from one country to another. . . .

. . .

The experience of Nordic countries is rather interesting. . . . The Convention was already ratified by the Nordic countries during the 1950s. . . . Even before formally incorporating the Convention, courts in these countries referred regularly to the Convention when applying domestic law. In a judgment of 22 March 1989, the Swedish Supreme Court [said]. . . . even though the Convention does not form part of Swedish law it is natural that its position in questions of rights influences the interpretation of the Instrument of Government [Constitution]. . . .

The benefits of incorporation are obvious. Incorporation gives national authorities the opportunity to afford redress in cases of human rights violations before the case is taken to Strasbourg. Protracted proceedings in a forum that is both remote from and unfamiliar to the claimant can be spared. The settlement of litigations [sic] on the national level, saving both time and money, always remains the preferable solution.

. . .

As far as the States which have incorporated the Convention in their domestic law are concerned, two different situations have to be distinguished. In States with a monist tradition like Belgium, Luxembourg or the Netherlands, the rights and freedoms of the Convention were applied by the courts immediately after ratification. In States favouring a dualist approach to international law such as Germany, Italy and most of the States of Eastern and Central Europe, the Convention had to be 'transformed' into domestic law. It is usually the parliamentary act of ratification. i.e. the law approving the treaty and authorizing the deposit of the instrument of ratification which makes the Convention's provisions applicable in domestic law. . . .

III. Application of the Convention in domestic law

In the past, a direct application of the Convention had sometimes been objected to with the argument that the rights and freedoms contained therein were too abstract and vague to be of any help for the national judge or lawyer. Lord Denning MR once went so far as considering the Convention to be 'indigestible':

> The convention is drafted in a style very different from the way which we are used to in legislation. It contains wide general statements of principle. They are apt to lead to much difficulty in application because they give rise to much uncertainty. They are not the sort of thing which we can easily digest. Article 8 [of the ECHR] is an example. It is so wide as to be incapable of practical application. So it is much better for us to stick to our own statutes and principles and only to look to the convention for guidance in case of doubt.

Today, such a reasoning appears anachronistic. The Convention and its Protocols are not only a mere catalogue of basic fundamental rights and freedoms. They constitute a body of law which bas been tested, developed and applied by the Court and Commission for more than forty years. . . .

. . .

The main responsibility for ensuring the observance of the Convention in domestic law lies with the legislature and the judiciary. In the first place. it is for the legislature to ensure that national legislation is in conformity with the rules of the Convention. Prior to ratification, a number of States which have recently become Parties to the Convention went, with the assistance of the Council of Europe, through a 'compatibility exercise'. In Finland, Hungary, Lithuania, Estonia and Latvia, inter-ministerial committees or working groups were set up in order to analyse and assess the domestic legislation and its compatibility with the Convention.

. . .

Secondly, it is for the national judiciary to take the Convention seriously and to use it in the interpretation of statutory law. It is a usual practice in many countries to interpret statutes in a manner consistent with treaties. This practice is sometimes referred to as the rule of presumption. . . .

IV. The position of the Convention with regard to the rights and freedoms of national constitutions

All ten countries of Eastern and Central Europe have incorporated the Convention into their domestic law. Prior to this and sometimes even in parallel, most of them have embarked on a process of far-reaching constitutional reform which has resulted in the adoption of a whole series of new constitutions. . . .

. . . [Most] countries adopted a detailed catalogue of fundamental rights and freedoms often inspired by the provisions of the European Convention on Human Rights. . . .

. . .

V. How to overcome possible conflicts between the provisions of the Convention and domestic legislation?

. . .

. . . It is common practice in many countries that the courts give statutes, wherever possible, an interpretation which is in line with the Convention. National courts are indeed required to ensure that international responsibility of their country arising from wrongful application of or disrespect for rules of public international law be avoided.

There may, however, be cases of a clear-cut conflict between domestic legislation and the Convention. Here, the national judge has to decide. Where, according to the constitutional law of the State concerned, the provisions of the Convention take precedence over domestic legislation, the national judge must disregard the national law and apply the Convention instead.

This is the situation in a certain number of countries. The Dutch Constitution generally gives pre-eminence to the self-executing norms of international treaties. Austria has formally accorded constitutional rank to all the rights and freedoms contained in the Convention. Their precedence over conflicting legislation, both prior and subsequent to the ratification of the Convention, is in principle recognised in Belgium, Cyprus, the Czech Republic, France, Greece, Lithuania, Luxembourg, Malta, Portugal, Romania, Spain and Switzerland.

In other countries, the Convention's provisions can theoretically be overridden by subsequent legislation according to the well known *lex posterior derogat legi priori* rule. Fortunately, such a result which would constitute a violation of the

Convention is practically always avoided by using [techniques including broadening the presumption of the supremacy of the Convention by requiring that the legislature be explicit when a later-in-time statute is intended to deviate from the Convention (as the German Constitutional Court has done), and treating the Convention as *lex specialis* so that even subsequent statutes need not necessarily take precedence.]

. . .

COMMENT ON MONISM AND DUALISM

The preceding article refers to monist and dualist (or pluralist) theories about the relationship between international and national law, thereby tapping into a longstanding jurisprudential, legal and political debate. Monist theories imagine a unitary world legal system in which national and international law have 'comparable, equivalent, or identical subjects, sources, and substantive contents'.[5] Monists argue for the supremacy of international law in relation to national law. In its classical formulation, monism asserts that all activity of states is regulated by the superior international law. Thus the so-called 'domestic affairs' of a state are not affairs unregulated by international law, but rather affairs which a state has exclusive competence to regulate pursuant to and under international law.

Dualist theories distinguish between the system or public order of international law and of national law. Each has 'its own distinguishable subjects, distinguishable structures and processes of authority, and distinguishable substantive content'. Thus the subjects of international law are only states, its sources lie only in treaties and custom made by states, and its content involves only relations between states. Neither international law nor national law can *per se* create or invalidate the other. Of course a state may by its own custom or national law adopt rules of international law as the law of the land, through practices and theories of incorporation, transformation, adoption and so on.

Hans Kelsen has stressed the different perspectives on institutions and world values and order that these two theories express:

> . . . It may be that our choice . . . is guided by ethical or political preferences. A person whose political attitude is that of nationalism and imperialism may be inclined to accept as a hypothesis the basic norm of his own national law. A person whose sympathy is for internationalism and pacifism may be inclined to accept as a hypothesis the basic norm of international law and thus proceed from the primacy of international law. From the point of view of the science of law, it is irrelevant which hypothesis one chooses. But from the point of view of politics, the choice [between dualism and monism] may be important since it is tied up with the ideology of sovereignty.[6]

---

[5] All quotations in this Note are taken from Myres McDougal, 'The Impact of International Law upon National Law: A Policy-Oriented Perspective', 4 S. Dak. L. Rev. 25, (1959) at 27–31.

[6] *Principles of International Law* (1952), at 446, quoted in McDougal, *supra* n. 5.

The monist theory is clearly illustrated by the Dutch Constitution of 1983, discussed in the following excerpts:[7]

> ... Art. 93 of the Constitution provides that provisions of treaties and decisions of international organisations, the contents of which may be binding on everyone, shall have this binding effect as from the time of publication. The words 'the contents of which may be binding on everyone' are generally understood to refer to the self-executing character which is required for their application by Dutch Courts. The rights contained in the ECHR are considered self-executing by the courts and are therefore directly applicable.
>
> . . .
>
> ... [Pursuant to Art. 94 of the Dutch Constitution, Dutch courts must] give precedence to self-executing treaty provisions over domestic law that is not in conformity therewith, be it antecedent or posterior, statutory or constitutional law.... But the courts have no competence to nullify, repeal or amend the legislation in question. The provision remains in force, but will not be applied.
>
> . . .
>
> **3. Case-law**
>
> . . .
>
> [The earlier] reticent attitude of Dutch courts towards the ECHR has changed quite dramatically during the 1980s. The statistical survey recently given by Van Dijk shows a considerable increase of references to the ECHR. The percentage of cases, however, in which the Supreme Court has found a violation of the Convention remains small (an average of 9%). When confronted with a conflict between a provision of the ECHR and a provision of Dutch law, the Supreme Court tends to circumvent it by giving to the latter an interpretation or scope different from its original meaning and from the anterior legal practice, or by inserting a new principle into Dutch law derived from the treaty provision. . . .

Dualist theories are illustrated in the practice and constitutional norms of several of the states described below.

BRUNO SIMMA ET AL., THE ROLE OF GERMAN COURTS IN THE ENFORCEMENT OF INTERNATIONAL HUMAN RIGHTS
in B. Conforti and F. Francioni (eds.), Enforcing International Human Rights in Domestic Courts (1997), at 107

Our review of the jurisprudence of German courts on international human rights will probably leave the observer with mixed feelings. On the one hand, the implementation of human rights treaties and customary human rights law in the German legal order, combined with the extensive jurisdiction and broad powers of review available to the judiciary, would offer a good starting-point for German courts to take an active part in the formation of an extensive body of case law on

---

[7] Jörg Polakiewicz and V. Jacob-Foltzer, 'The European Human Rights Convention in Domestic Law', 12 Hum. Rts. L. J. 65 (1991), at 125.

international human rights. The demand of the Bundesverfassungsgericht [Federal Constitutional Court] to pursue an interpretation in favour of public international law . . . grants German courts further possibilities to apply international human rights indirectly in their jurisprudence. Unfortunately, however, the number of cases in which German courts deal with international human rights is rather meagre except in some areas like expulsion and extradition, where domestic statutes explicitly require the consideration of international human rights standards.

Why do German courts apply international human rights norms so rarely? In part at least, practical reasons can explain this reluctance of German courts:

1. International human rights norms are not part of the core curricula in the legal education and practical training of lawyers and judges.
2. Some courts may have difficulties in obtaining German translations. . . .
3. Access to the texts of international norms sometimes proves to be difficult. . . .

The most plausible explanation for the reluctance of German courts to consider international human rights norms in their case law, however, seems to be the far-reaching *prime facie* parallelism of some international rights and domestic constitutional and statutory rights. Whenever courts can enforce an individual right simply on the basis of a constitutional or statutory provision they will do so, simply because they can rely on an elaborate case law, commentaries and other secondary literature. . . . In addition, German courts, and German jurists in general, seem convinced that the German legal system establishes such a high standard of protection for individual rights guaranteed in the Basic law that international human rights law could hardly offer any improvement. Thus, it is not surprising that courts often refer to international human rights only in the way of stating briefly that the application of these rights would not lead to a different result in the specific case. Judgments of the European Court of Human Rights which found a violation of the Convention by German authorities have proved that this general assumption is erroneous. In the long run, these decisions had quite considerable impact insofar as they changed the general attitude of German courts towards the European Convention. . . .

. . .

YUJI IWASAWA, INTERNATIONAL LAW, HUMAN RIGHTS LAW AND JAPANESE LAW: THE IMPACT OF INTERNATIONAL LAW ON JAPANESE LAW
(1998) at 288–306

A. The Relationship between International Law and Japanese Law

. . .

International law is accorded high formal authority in Japan; both treaties and customary international law have the force of law and override statutes, even if the statutes were enacted later in time.

. . .

B. Impact of International Law on Japanese Law

. . .

(a) *Tendency of the courts to ignore arguments based on international human rights law*

. . .

[T]he courts are generally reluctant to adjudicate on the basis of international human rights law. Japanese courts often restrict their interpretation to the Japanese Constitution, ignoring arguments based on international human rights law.
. . .

(b) *Tendency of the courts to summarily dismiss arguments based on international human rights law*

Japanese courts tend to dismiss arguments based on international human rights law without detailed analysis of their substance. The courts often interpret the Japanese Constitution and then apply the same reasoning to a comparable provision in a human rights treaty. Japanese courts assume that the meaning, scope, and effect of human rights provisions under international human rights law are the same as those under the Japanese Constitution. Accordingly, if a governmental action is found to be lawful under the Japanese Constitution, it is automatically regarded as lawful under international human rights law as well.

. . .

. . . To justify restrictions of human rights, the courts have preferred to rely on the familiar Japanese concept of 'public welfare' rather than the international concepts of 'national security, public order (*ordre public*), public health or morals'. . . .

. . .

(c) *Reluctance of the courts to find violations of international human rights law*

. . . In recent years, more and more individuals and attorneys have come to invoke international human rights law, particularly the International Covenants on Human Rights, before the courts. Yet, the courts have so far applied the ICCPR directly in only a few instances. Occasionally, the courts have used international human rights law as an aid in the interpretation of domestic law to hold in favour of the individual who had invoked it.

. . .

(d) *Japanese courts and the practice of judicial restraint*

. . .

. . . Japanese courts are highly restrained in judicial review and generally reluctant to invalidate legislation on constitutional grounds. Even when Japanese courts sympathize with the plaintiff, they hesitate to find a government action to be unconstitutional, preferring instead to dispose of the case by statutory interpretation. . . .

. . . In the five decades since the enactment of the Constitution, statutes have been found to be unconstitutional on only five occasions.

. . .

2. Revision of Domestic Law in Accordance with International Law

(a) *Revision of domestic law upon ratification of treaties*

Since treaties have the force of law and override domestic laws in Japan, when the Japanese Government decides to enter into a treaty, it makes scrupulous efforts to bring Japanese law into conformity with the treaty. . . . Thus, upon ratification of treaties, Japanese law significantly improves through revision of laws. The most conspicuous such changes have occurred in the area of human rights—in the treatment of aliens and women.

. . .

K.D. EWING, THE HUMAN RIGHTS ACT AND PARLIAMENTARY DEMOCRACY
62 Modern L. Rev. 79 (1999)

The UK Human Rights Act 1998 . . . represents an unprecedented transfer of political power from the executive and legislature to the judiciary, and a funda-mental re-structuring of our 'political constitution'. As such it is unquestionably the most significant formal redistribution of political power in this country since 1911, and perhaps since 1688 . . . .

. . .

The nature and extent of incorporation

The Human Rights Act 1998 does not incorporate the ECHR into domestic law in the way that the European Communities Act 1972 incorporates the EC Treaty. Rather what it does is to give effect to certain provisions of the Convention and some of its protocols by providing that these so-called 'Convention rights' are to have a defined status in English law. There is no question of the Convention rights in themselves 'becoming part of our substantive domestic law': rather, certain defined provisions of the Convention enjoy a defined legal status. The terms of the Convention which are given effect to in this way by section 1 of the Act are articles 2 to 12 and 14, as well as articles 1 to 3 of the First Protocol and . . . articles 1 and 2 of the Sixth Protocol. The major omissions here are articles 1 and 13 of the Convention, the former providing that 'The High Contracting Parties shall secure to everyone within their jurisdiction the rights and freedoms defined in Section 1 of [the] Convention'; and the latter providing that 'Everyone whose rights and freedoms as set forth in this Convention are violated shall have an effective remedy before a national authority'. There was little objection to the omission of article 1, which was properly excluded on the ground that it was an inter-state obligation.

. . .

In giving effect to Convention rights in this way, by section 2 the Act also directs the courts to have regard to the jurisprudence of the different enforcement and supervisory bodies in Strasbourg. For this purpose the Act refers expressly to the

European Court of Human Rights, the European Commission of Human Rights, and the Committee of Ministers. As we have seen, the Commission and the Committee of Ministers will have been abolished or removed from questions of adjudication by the time the Act comes into force, though the jurisprudence of these bodies will continue to be relevant. It is to be noted, however, that the courts are required simply to take into account the jurisprudence of the Strasbourg bodies, but are not bound by it, and that the government rejected an amendment in the Lords which would have imposed the stronger obligation. . . .

. . .

The fact remains that the Convention is meaningful only because of the principles of interpretation developed in the case law, and the decisions on points of substance, issues which are of universal application. As a text the Convention is meaningless without the jurisprudence, as is true of any other legal text: to sever the jurisprudence from the treaty is like severing the limbs from a torso. But whatever the reasons for refusing to be bound by Strasbourg jurisprudence, it should be clear that the nature and extent of judicial power under the Act are greater than may be realised. Convention rights are now free standing and autonomous (even if not 'substantive') rights of British law which the judges are empowered to develop as they wish, guided but unconstrained by the Convention jurisprudence.

What this in fact confirms is that what we have incorporated is not the European Convention on Human Rights, but a number of principles which happen to be included in the Convention. We have something much closer to a distinctively British Bill of Rights than is sometimes imagined: not perhaps in terms of the structure of the rights themselves; but certainly in terms of their interpretation and application, with British judges having the same [un]'fetter'[ed] (the word is Lord Browne-Wilkinson's) discretion as their counterparts in Canada and elsewhere.

Statutory interpretation

The first way by which the Convention will impact upon domestic law is through the obligations in respect of statutory interpretation in section 3. This provides that 'so far as possible to do so', both primary legislation and delegated [subordinate, secondary] legislation are to be read and given effect to in a way which is compatible with Convention rights. . . .

. . . Parliament has also been careful to point out in section 3, however, that the duty of construction which it embraces does not 'affect the validity, continuing operation or enforcement of any incompatible primary legislation'. Nor does it affect the continuing operation or enforcement of any incompatible subordinate legislation 'if primary legislation prevents removal of the incompatibility'.

But what happens if legislation—primary or subordinate—is incompatible with Convention rights, and it is not possible to construe the former to meet the demands of the latter? The answer lies in section 4 which empowers the courts to make a declaration of incompatibility . . . [Discussion of secondary legislation omitted.]

The power to grant a declaration of incompatibility is limited to the higher courts. . . . The duty to construe legislation to comply with Convention rights is one which in contrast is imposed on all courts. The granting of a declaration of incompatibility is discretionary even where a 'mismatch' has been found, and the government resisted an amendment that it should be mandatory. If granted, a declaration of incompatibility has 'no operative or coercive effect', and 'does not prevent either party relying on, or the courts enforcing, the law in question': it does not affect the validity, continuing operation or enforcement of the legislation in question; nor is it binding on the parties in the proceedings in which it is made. This in itself may serve to ensure that there is little incentive for litigants to appeal where they have lost under legislation which may infringe a Convention right, but which the lower court has no authority to determine. It is in any event unclear at this stage whether there would always be grounds to appeal where a case has been decided clearly and unequivocally under legislation which may prove to breach Convention rights.

. . .

Liability of public authorities

The second way by which the Act gives effect to the Convention is by imposing an obligation on public authorities to comply with Convention rights, an obligation which is directly enforceable in the courts. Section 6 provides that it is unlawful for a public authority to act in a way which is incompatible with one or more of the Convention rights, with a 'public authority' being widely defined to include a court; a tribunal which exercises functions in relation to legal proceedings; and any person certain of whose functions are functions of a public nature. The definition is fluid and open ended. . . . But the intention clearly is that they should apply to central government (including executive agencies), local government, the police, immigration officers, and the prison service, as well as to others. One of the most difficult questions under the Act relates to the inclusion of courts and tribunals within the definition of a public authority. The precise meaning and implications of this are unclear . . . .

According to the Lord Chancellor, the government 'believe that it is right as a matter of principle for the courts to have the duty of acting compatibly with the Convention not only in cases involving other public authorities but also in developing the common law in deciding cases between citizens'. But what does this mean, given the government's belief that 'full horizontal effect' would be 'a step too far in a Bill which . . . is designed to allow the Convention rights to be invoked in this country by people who would have already a case in Strasbourg', and given also the rejection by the Lord Chancellor of the view that the courts will be required to legislate by way of judicial decision 'whenever a law cannot be found either in the statute book or as a rule of common law to protect a convention right'? The answer it seems is that Convention rights may be relied upon in litigation between private parties, but cannot themselves be the basis of a cause of action. So although a worker dismissed for a reason incompatible with the Convention may not sue his or her employer for breach of a Convention right, the worker in question may be able to sue for wrongful dismissal, claiming that a dismissal for a reason incompatible with a Convention right is wrongful.

. . .

Remedial action

As we have seen, section 4 of the Act permits the courts to declare an Act of Parliament to be incompatible with Convention rights, though they are required still to enforce and apply it until such time as the legislation has been amended. The government considered but rejected the option of giving the courts the power to set aside an Act of Parliament believed to be incompatible with Convention rights, 'because of the importance the Government attaches to Parliamentary sovereignty'. The White Paper continues in powerful and convincing terms, as follows:

> In this context, Parliamentary sovereignty means that Parliament is competent to make any law on any matter of its choosing and no court may question the validity of any Act that it passes. In enacting legislation, Parliament is making decisions about important matters of public policy. The authority to make those decisions derives from a democratic mandate because they are elected, accountable and representative.

Concern was expressed that to permit the courts to set aside Acts of Parliament 'would confer on the judiciary a general power over the decisions of Parliament', and 'would be likely on occasions to draw the judiciary into serious conflict with Parliament'. Crucially there 'is no evidence to suggest that they desire this power, nor that the public wish them to have it'.

So why give the courts the power to rule on the compatibility of an Act of Parliament with Convention rights? How can this be reconciled with the authority of the mandate? The answer is that it is open to the government to decide how to deal with the decision of the courts, and to refuse to take steps to remedy the incompatibility if it deems it appropriate to do so. This after all is the position currently with decisions of the European Court of Human Rights which do not change domestic law but require amending legislation, which the government cannot be compelled to introduce and Parliament cannot be compelled to pass. But although these are weighty and logical considerations, we should be careful about distinguishing form from substance, principle from practice. As a matter of constitutional legality, Parliament may well be sovereign, but as a matter of constitutional practice it has transferred significant power to the judiciary.

. . .

QUESTIONS

1. It has often been observed that respect for human rights begins and ends at home and that international organizations have little more than a catalytic or intermediary role. On the basis of the preceding descriptions of states' relationships to international human rights norms, how satisfactory have the efforts of each of the states been to ensure that its legal order respects the relevant norms?

2. Is the *de facto* preference for applying domestic constitutional rather than inter-

national human rights norms desirable, neutral, or dangerous from the perspective of realizing international human rights?

3. Some commentators have suggested that Articles 1 and 13 of the European Convention, taken together, create a legal obligation upon states' parties to make the provisions of the Convention applicable in domestic law. What are arguments for and against such an approach, which stands in clear contradiction to the approach of the UK?

4. Should future international human rights treaties require ratifying states to guarantee the full incorporation in and enforcement by domestic law of their provisions?

5. Compare the approach reflected in the UK Human Rights Act with the statement of the UK Government at p. 832, *supra*. Are they two versions of the same theme? What do they tell you of the status in the UK of the debate over state sovereignty and the supremacy of international human rights norms?

NOTE

The preceding readings have focused primarily on the extent to which courts in different states are required to apply international human rights norms in domestic cases. But regardless of any such legal requirements, there are important ways referred to in those readings in which both the judiciary and the executive have a role in giving domestic effect to applicable human rights standards. Murray Hunt has observed that the international human rights law regime has tended, in a variety of ways, to blur the old distinctions between incorporated and unincorporated norms:

> The language of 'incorporation' presupposes a dualist position derived from an uncompromising premise of the sovereignty of Parliament. The question of the domestic status of international law in that binary framework is an 'in/out' question: has the international norm been made 'part of' domestic law or not? The concepts and the language lack the sophistication to capture the more nuanced reality that there are many different ways in which international law may be of relevance to an issue before a domestic court. A norm of international treaty law may not be 'part of' domestic law in the sense that it gives rise to a right or obligation which is directly enforceable in domestic courts and on which individuals may therefore found their case, but, insofar as judicial recourse to it is permitted by the treaty presumption, to assist in the interpretation of domestic statute law, or its customary or near-customary status provides guidance in the development of domestic common law, it is clearly of legal relevance.[8]

This argument could also be extended (although Hunt explicitly does not do so) to ground a presumption that the executive branch of government will not act inconsistently with treaty norms even if domestic law does not formally obligate

---

[8] M. Hunt, *Using Human Rights Law in English Courts* (1998), at 41–42.

the executive to apply those standards. This issue is of particular relevance in countries such as the United Kingdom, Australia, and New Zealand, which follow a system of legislative incorporation that leaves unclear the status or significance of treaties which have been ratified but have not been given effect in domestic law by legislation.

The following materials examine from international and national perspectives some of the difficulties in reaching a general understanding among states of the nature of their obligation to give domestic effect to their treaty commitments.

COMMITTEE ON ECONOMIC, SOCIAL AND CULTURAL RIGHTS, GENERAL COMMENT NO. 9
Domestic Application of the Covenant, UN Doc. E/1999/22, Annex IV, 1998

A. The duty to give effect to the Covenant in the domestic legal order

. . .

2. [The Covenant requires] each State Party to use *all* the means at its disposal to give effect to the rights recognized in the Covenant. . . . Thus the norms themselves must be recognised in appropriate ways within the domestic legal order, appropriate means of redress, or remedies, must be available to any aggrieved individual or group, and appropriate means of ensuring governmental accountability must be put in place.

. . .

B. The status of the Covenant in the domestic legal order

4. In general, legally binding international human rights standards should operate directly and immediately within the domestic legal system of each State party, thereby enabling individuals concerned to seek enforcement of their rights before national courts and tribunals. The rule requiring the exhaustion of domestic remedies reinforces the primacy of national remedies in this respect. . . .

5. The Covenant itself does not stipulate the specific means by which its terms are to be implemented in the national legal order. And there is no provision obligating its comprehensive incorporation or requiring it to be accorded any specific type of status in national law. Although the precise method by which Covenant rights are given effect in national law is a matter for each State Party to decide, the means used should be appropriate in the sense of producing results which are consistent with the full discharge of its obligations by the State Party. The means chosen are also subject to review as part of the Committee's examination of the State Party's compliance with its Covenant obligations.

. . .

C. The role of legal remedies

. . .

11. The Covenant itself does not negate the possibility that the rights may be considered self-executing in systems where that option is provided for. Indeed,

when it was being drafted, attempts to include a specific provision in the Covenant providing that it be considered 'non-self-executing' were strongly rejected. In most States the determination of whether or not a treaty provision is self-executing will be a matter for the courts, not the executive or the legislature. In order to perform that function effectively the relevant courts and tribunals must be made aware of the nature and implications of the Covenant and of the important role of judicial remedies in its implementation. . . . [W]hen Governments are involved in court proceedings, they should promote interpretations of domestic laws which give effect to their Covenant obligations. . . .

. . .

D.   The treatment of the Covenant in domestic courts

. . .

13. . . . [S]ome courts have applied the provisions of the Covenant either directly or as interpretive standards. Other courts are willing to acknowledge, in principle, the relevance of the Covenant for interpreting domestic law, but in practice, the impact of the Covenant on the reasoning or outcome of cases is very limited. Still other courts have refused to give any degree of legal effect to the Covenant in cases in which individuals have sought to rely on it. . . .

14. Within the limits of the appropriate exercise of their functions of judicial review, courts should take account of Covenant rights where this is necessary to ensure that the State's conduct is consistent with its obligations under the Covenant. Neglect by the courts of this responsibility is incompatible with the principle of the Rule of Law which must always be taken to include respect for international human rights obligations.

. . .

MICHAEL KIRBY, THE ROLE OF INTERNATIONAL STANDARDS IN AUSTRALIAN COURTS
in P. Alston and M. Chiam (eds.), Treaty-Making and Australia: Globalization versus Sovereignty (1995), at 82

The Bangalore Principles

The traditional view of most common law countries has been that international law is not part of domestic law. Blackstone in his Commentaries, suggested that:

> The law of nations (whenever any question arises which is properly the object of its jurisdiction) is here [in England] adopted in its full extent by the common law, and is held to be part of the law of the land.

Save for the United States, where Blackstone had a profound influence, this view came to be regarded, virtually universally, as being 'without foundation'. . . .

More recently, however, a new recognition has come about of the use that may be made by judges of international human rights principles and their exposition by the courts, tribunals and other bodies established to give them content and effect. This reflects both the growing body of international human rights law and the instruments, both regional and international, which give effect to that law. It furthermore recognizes the importance of the content of those laws. An expression that seems to encapsulate the modern approach was given [at a meeting among jurists from many states] in February 1988 in Bangalore, India in the so-called *Bangalore Principles.*

The Bangalore Principles state, in effect, that:

(1) International law, whether human rights norms or otherwise, is not, as such, part of domestic law in most common law countries;

(2) Such law does not become part of domestic law until Parliament so enacts or the judges, as another source of law-making, declare the norms thereby established to be part of domestic law;

(3) The judges will not do so automatically, simply because the norm is part of international law or is mentioned in a treaty, even one ratified by their own country;

(4) But if an issue of uncertainty arises, as by a lacuna in the common law, obscurity in its meaning or ambiguity in a relevant statute, a judge may seek guidance in the general principles of international law, as accepted by the community of nations; and

(5) From this source material, the judge may ascertain and declare what the relevant rule of domestic law is. It is the action of the judge, incorporating the rule into domestic law, which makes it part of domestic law.

. . .

High judicial pronouncements

In the seven years since Bangalore, . . . something of a sea change has come over the approach of courts in Australia, as well as in New Zealand and England.

The clearest indication of the change in Australia can be found in the remarks of Brennan J (with the concurrence of Mason CJ and McHugh J) in *Mabo v Queensland (No 2).* In the course of explaining why a discriminatory doctrine, such as that of *terra nullius* (which refused to recognize the rights and interests in land of the indigenous inhabitants of a settled colony such as Australia) could no longer be accepted as part of the law of Australia, Brennan J said:

> The expectations of the international community accord in this respect with the contemporary values of the Australian people. The opening up of the international remedies to individuals pursuant to Australia's accession to the *Optional Protocol* to the *International Covenant on Civil and Political Rights* brings to bear on the common law the powerful influence of the *Covenant* and the international standards it imports. The common law does not necessarily conform with international law, but international law is a legitimate and important influence on the development of the common law, especially when international law declares the existence of universal human rights.

. . .

NOTE

Justice Kirby has commented further on the developments noted in his preceding article:[9]

...

> Critics of [these] developments ... list a number of considerations which need to be kept in mind by judges as they venture upon this new source of principle for judicial law-making. The expressed concerns include:
>
> 1. Treaties are typically negotiated by the executive government. They may, or may not, reflect the will of the people as expressed in parliament. . . .
> 2. The processes of ratification are often defective. . . .
> 3. In federal countries, such as Australia, Canada, Malaysia, and others, special concern may be expressed that the ratification of international treaties could be used as a means to undermine the constitutional distribution of powers . . .
> 4. Judicial introduction of human rights norms may sometimes divert the community from the more open, principled and democratic adoption of such norms in constitutional or statutory amendments which have the legitimacy of popular endorsement.
> 5. Some commentators have also expressed scepticism about the international courts, tribunals and committees which pronounce upon human rights. They argue that often they are composed of persons from legal regimes very different from our own.
> 6. To similar effect, critics have pointed to the broad generality of the expression of the provisions contained in international human rights instruments. Of necessity, these are expressed in language that lacks precision. This means that those who use them may be tempted to read into their broad language what they hope, expect or want to see. Whilst the judge of the common law tradition has a creative role, such creativity must be in the minor key. The judge must proceed in a judicial way. He or she must not undermine the primacy of democratic law-making by the organs of government directly or indirectly accountable to the people.
> 7. Finally, some critics warn against undue, premature undermining of the sovereignty of a State by judicial *fiat* without the authority of the State's democratically accountable law-makers. The latter is, generally, the proper institution to develop human rights in the State's own way.

...

MINISTER OF STATE FOR IMMIGRATION AND ETHNIC AFFAIRS v. AH HIN TEOH
High Court of Australia, 1995 183 CLR 273

[Mr Teoh, a Malaysian citizen, entered Australia in May 1988 on a temporary entry permit. In July he married an Australian citizen who had been the *de facto* spouse of his deceased brother. In November 1990 he was convicted on charges of heroin importation and possession and sentenced to six years imprisonment. The

---

[9] 'Domestic Implementation of Human Rights Norms', 5 Aust. J. Hum. Rts. 109 (1999), at 119.

offences were clearly related to Mrs Teoh's heroin addiction. In 1991 Teoh was ordered to be deported on the grounds that he had committed a serious crime. At that time Mrs Teoh had six of her children living with her, all under ten years old, and three of them had been fathered by Teoh. The deportation order was appealed to the Federal Court, which upheld the appeal partly on the grounds that the requirement in the Convention on the Rights of the Child, that the child's best interests be considered in such matters, had not been taken into account. The Minister appealed that decision to the High Court.]

MASON CJ AND DEANE J:

. . .

25. It is well established that the provisions of an international treaty to which Australia is a party do not form part of Australian law unless those provisions have been validly incorporated into our municipal law by statute. . . .

26. But the fact that the Convention [on the Rights of the Child] has not been incorporated into Australian law does not mean that its ratification holds no significance for Australian law. Where a statute or subordinate legislation is ambiguous, the courts should favour that construction which accords with Australia's obligations under a treaty or international convention to which Australia is a party, at least in those cases in which the legislation is enacted after, or in contemplation of, entry into, or ratification of, the relevant international instrument. That is because Parliament, *prima facie*, intends to give effect to Australia's obligations under international law.

27. . . . If the language of the legislation is susceptible of a construction which is consistent with the terms of the international instrument and the obligations which it imposes on Australia, then that construction should prevail. So expressed, the principle is no more than a canon of construction and does not import the terms of the treaty or convention into our municipal law as a source of individual rights and obligations.

28. Apart from influencing the construction of a statute or subordinate legislation, an international convention may play a part in the development by the courts of the common law. The provisions of an international convention to which Australia is a party, especially one which declares universal fundamental rights, may be used by the courts as a legitimate guide in developing the common law. But the courts should act in this fashion with due circumspection when the Parliament itself has not seen fit to incorporate the provisions of a convention into our domestic law. Judicial development of the common law must not be seen as a backdoor means of importing an unincorporated convention into Australian law. A cautious approach . . . would be consistent with the approach which the courts have hitherto adopted. . . .

. . .

34. . . . [R]atification by Australia of an international convention . . . is a positive statement by the executive government of this country to the world and to the Australian people that the executive government and its agencies will act in accordance with the Convention. That positive statement is an adequate foundation

for a legitimate expectation, absent statutory or executive indications to the contrary, that administrative decision-makers will act in conformity with the Convention and treat the best interests of the children as 'a primary consideration'. . . .

. . .

36. . . . To regard a legitimate expectation as requiring the decision-maker to act in a particular way is tantamount to treating it as a rule of law. It incorporates the provisions of the unincorporated convention into our municipal law by the back door. . . .

37. But, if a decision-maker proposes to make a decision inconsistent with a legitimate expectation, procedural fairness requires that the persons affected should be given notice and an adequate opportunity of presenting a case against the taking of such a course.

. . .

TOOHEY J:

27. In *Reg. v. Home Secretary; Ex parte Brind* the House of Lords rejected the broad proposition that the Secretary of State should exercise a statutory discretion in accordance with the terms of the [ECHR], which was not part of English domestic law. That decision was considered by the New Zealand Court of Appeal in *Tavita v. Minister of Immigration* where a deportee argued that those concerned with ordering his deportation were bound to take into account the Convention and the [ICCPR], both of which had been ratified by New Zealand. In the end the Court did not have to determine the point. But it said of the contrary proposition: 'That is an unattractive argument, apparently implying that New Zealand's adherence to the international instruments has been at least partly window-dressing . . . there must at least be hesitation about accepting it'.

. . .

MCHUGH J:

. . .

37. . . . The people of Australia may note the commitments of Australia in international law, but, by ratifying the Convention, the Executive government does not give undertakings to its citizens or residents. The undertakings in the Convention are given to the other parties to the Convention. How, when or where those undertakings will be given force in Australia is a matter for the federal Parliament. . . .

38. If the result of ratifying an international convention was to give rise to a legitimate expectation that that convention would be applied in Australia, the Executive . . . would have effectively amended the law of this country. . . . The consequences for administrative decision-making in this country would be enormous. . . . Australia is a party to about 900 treaties. Only a small percentage of them has been enacted into law. Administrative decision-makers would have to ensure that their decision-making complied with every relevant convention or

inform a person affected that they would not be complying with those conventions.

39. I do not think that it is reasonable to expect that public officials will comply with the terms of conventions which they have no obligation to apply or consider merely because the federal government has ratified them. . . . Total compliance with the terms of a convention may require many years of effort, education and expenditure of resources. For these and similar reasons, the parties to a convention will often regard its provisions as goals to be implemented over a period of time rather than mandates calling for immediate compliance. . . .

ILLUSTRATIONS OF NATIONAL EXECUTIVE VIEWS ABOUT METHODS OF COMPLIANCE

(1) In response to the Teoh judgment the Australian Government issued a statement. While opposition in the Senate to the statement had, as of February 2000, prevented its enactment into law, it is nonetheless of obvious importance for administrative law.[10]

(3) . . . The High Court in the Teoh case . . . gave treaties an effect in Australian law . . . which they did not previously have. The Government is of the view that this development is not consistent with the proper role of Parliament in implementing treaties in Australian law. . . . It is for Australian parliaments . . . to change Australian law to implement treaty obligations.

(4) The purpose of this statement is to ensure that the executive act of entering into a treaty does not give rise to legitimate expectations in administrative law.

(5) . . . The prospect was left open by the Teoh case of decisions being challenged on the basis of a failure sufficiently to advert to relevant international obligations including where the decision-maker and person affected had no knowledge of the relevant obligation at the time of the decision. This is not conducive to good administration.

(6) Therefore, we indicate on behalf of the Government that the act of entering into a treaty does not give rise to legitimate expectations in administrative law which could form the basis for challenging any administrative decision made from today. This is a clear expression by the Executive Government of the Commonwealth of a contrary indication referred to by the majority of the High Court in the Teoh Case.

. . .

(2) Consider the following problem about international human rights and federalism. In February 2000 a 15-year-old Aboriginal boy in the Northern Territory of Australia committed suicide in his prison cell. He had been jailed for 28 days for stealing pencils and stationery and breaking a window, under Territory legislation which mandates imprisonment for property offences. In 1997 the UN Committee on the Rights of the Child expressed concern at the legislation and suggested that it

---

[10] Joint Statement, The Minister for Foreign Affairs and the Attorney-General and Minister for Justice: http:// /law.gov.au/aghome/agnews/1997news/attachjs.htm, 25 February 1997.

was inconsistent with Article 37(b) of the Convention, which requires that detention of a child should only be 'used as a measure of last resort'. The issue was complicated by the reluctance of Australia's Federal Government to use its powers to overrule criminal laws adopted by the Territory legislature. When asked about Australia's compliance with its treaty obligations, Prime Minister John Howard replied:[11]

> Australia decides what happens in this country through the laws and the parliaments of Australia. I mean in the end we are not told what to do by anybody. We make our own moral judgments. . . . Australia's human rights reputation compared with the rest of the world is quite magnificent. We've had our blemishes and we've made our errors and I'm not saying we're perfect. But I'm not going to cop this country's human rights name being tarnished in the context of a domestic political argument. Now this is a difficult issue. Traditionally these matters are the prerogative of States. And if you have Federal governments seeking to overturn laws of this kind you really are remaking the rule book.

(3) Compare the following 1998 Presidential Executive Order in the United States:[12]

> By the authority vested in me as President . . . it is hereby ordered as follows:
> Sec. 1. Implementation of Human Rights Obligations.
>
> (a) It shall be the policy and practice of the Government of the United States, . . . fully to respect and implement its obligations under the international human rights treaties to which it is a party, including the ICCPR, the CAT, and the CERD. . . .
>
> Sec. 2. Responsibility of Executive Departments and Agencies.
>
> (a) All executive departments and agencies . . . shall maintain a current awareness of United States international human rights obligations that are relevant to their functions and shall perform such functions so as to respect and implement those obligations fully. . . .
>
> Sec. 3. Human Rights Inquiries and Complaints.
> Each agency shall take lead responsibility, in coordination with other appropriate agencies, for responding to inquiries, requests for information, and complaints about violations of human rights obligations that fall within its areas of responsibility . . . .
> . . .
> Sec. 6. Judicial Review, Scope, and Administration.
>
> (a) Nothing in this order shall create any right or benefit, substantive or procedural, enforceable by any party against the United States, its agencies or instrumentalities, its officers or employees, or any other person.

---

[11] <www.pm.gov.au/media/pressrel/2000/AM1802.htm>, 18 February 2000.
[12] US Executive Order 13107 on Implementation of Human Rights Treaties, *Federal Register*, Dec. 15, 1998, Vol. 63, No. 240, pp. 68991–93.

(b) This order does not supersede Federal statutes and does not impose any justiciable obligations on the executive branch.

(c) The term 'treaty obligations" shall mean treaty obligations as approved by the Senate pursuant to Article II, section 2, clause 2 of the United States Constitution.

(d) To the maximum extent practicable and subject to the availability of appropriations, agencies shall carry out the provisions of this order.

QUESTIONS

1. To what extent does the Economic and Social Committee's General Comment go beyond the position about international law's requirements for state incorporation described by Leary at p. 999, *supra*? How would you justify its position?

2. How would you respond to the concerns enumerated by Kirby about the approach reflected in the Bangalore Principles?

3. Do the political and administrative consequences of the Teoh decision go beyond what can reasonably be expected of a state party to a human rights treaty? What are the implications of the Government's subsequent 'Joint Statement'?

4. Should the approach reflected in the US Executive Order be the norm for all states? Does it matter that, in ratifying various international human rights treaties, the US Government has declared that it considers the substantive provisions to be non-self-executing and thus unable to be invoked by US courts to decide cases?

5. As a member of the Committee on the Rights of the Child how would you respond to the statement by the Australian Prime Minister, bearing in mind the sensitivity of federal-state issues in countries such as Canada, the United States and Australia.

ADDITIONAL READING

H. Knop, 'Here and There: International Law in Domestic Courts,' 32 N.Y.U. J. Int'l L. & Pol. 501 (2000); J. Doyle and B. Wells, 'How Far Can the Common Law Go in Protecting Human Rights', in P. Alston (ed.), *Promoting Human Rights Through Bills of Rights* (1999), at 17; T. Schweisfurth and R. Alleweldt, 'The Position of International Law in the Domestic Legal Orders of Central and Eastern European Countries', in 40 German Yearbook of International Law 164 (1997); E. Stein, 'International Law in Internal Law: Toward Internationalisation of Central-Eastern European Constitutions', 88 American Journal of International Law 427 (1994); E. Benvenisti, 'The Influence of International Human Rights Law on the Israeli Legal System: Present and Future', 28 Israel Law Review 136 (1994); K. Port, 'The Japanese International Law "Revolution": International Human Rights Law and its Impact in Japan', 28 Stanford Journal of International Law 139 (1991).

COMMENT ON TREATIES IN THE UNITED STATES

Read the references to 'treaties' in the following provisions of the Constitution: Article I, Section 10; Article II, Section 2; Article III, Section 2; and Article VI. The term 'treaty' has a special constitutional significance in the United States. The following materials speak of *treaties* in this constitutional sense, as opposed to another form of international agreement (so-called executive agreements) into which the United States enters. The information below complements the Comment on Treaties at p. 103, *supra*, which describes treaties from an international-law rather than national perspective. Like the other materials in Chapter 12, this Comment ignores the distinctive issues about treaties' relations to domestic legal orders that are posed by a federalism such as the United States. That is, these materials concern only the central, 'federal' government of such a federalism.

The conclusion of a treaty binding on the United States normally involves three stages. (1) Negotiation of the treaty is usually conducted by an agent of the Executive, although members of the Senate have occasionally been brought into the process at an early stage as observers and advisers. (2) The President submits the treaty to the Senate for the advice and consent required by Article II, Section 2. If the treaty fails to receive the required two-thirds vote of those present, no further action may be taken on it. If it receives that vote, the President may ratify it. (3) Ratification takes place by an exchange of instruments or, in the case of multi-lateral agreements, by deposit with a designated depositary. The President then proclaims the treaty, making it a matter of public notice and often effective as of that time.

Of course the United States has had to resolve the same issues as other countries about the internal status and effect of treaties. Constitutional decisions have brought reasonably clear answers to some basic questions. For example, treaties that have become part of the internal legal order have the same domestic effect as federal statutes. A treaty thus supersedes earlier inconsistent legislation. Just as a statute can be superseded by a later inconsistent statute, so can a treaty be super-seded, although maxims of interpretation encourage a judicial effort to construe the later-in-time statute so as not to violate the treaty. If that effort fails, the legislative rule prevails internally, although as a matter of international law the United States has broken its obligations to the other treaty party.

Perhaps the most vital question about a treaty effective as domestic law is its status *vis-à-vis* the Constitution. Will a treaty provision—perhaps one requiring a government to ban certain types of 'hate' speech—be given effect internally even if legislation to the same effect that was independent of any treaty commitment would be judged to be unconstitutional? The US Supreme Court considered this question in the following decision.

REID v. COVERT
Supreme Court of the United States, 1957
354 U.S. 1, 77 S. Ct. 1222

[Mrs Covert and Mrs Smith killed their husbands, who were then performing military service in England and Japan, respectively. They were each tried by courts-martial convened under Article 2(11) of the Uniform Code of Military Justice, which provided:

> The following persons are subject to this code:
>   (11) Subject to the provisions of any treaty or agreement to which the United States is or may be a party or to any accepted rule of international law, all persons serving with, employed by, or accompanying the armed forces without the continental limits of the United States. . . .

After conviction, each woman sought release on a writ of habeas corpus, which was granted in the case of Mrs Covert and denied in the case of Mrs Smith. On direct appeal the Court affirmed Mrs Covert's case and reversed Mrs Smith's. There were four opinions. Six members of the Court agreed that civilian dependents of members of the armed forces overseas could not constitutionally be tried by a court-martial in time of peace for capital offences, even if committed abroad. Justice Black (in an opinion joined by the Chief Justice, Justice Douglas and Justice Brennan) concluded that military trial of civilians was inconsistent with the Constitution—particularly with those provisions of Article III, Section 2 and of the Fifth and Sixth Amendments which assure indictment by grand jury and trial by jury. Justice Frankfurter and Justice Harlan, in concurring opinions, limited their holdings to capital cases. There was a dissenting opinion.

The excerpts below from the opinion of Justice Black refer to 'executive agreements'. For present purposes, they can be considered to be the equivalent of treaties.]

At the time of Mrs Covert's alleged offense, an executive agreement was in effect between the United States and Great Britain which permitted United States' military courts to exercise exclusive jurisdiction over offenses committed in Great Britain by American servicemen or their dependants.[13]

---

[13] Executive Agreement of July 27, 1942, 57 Stat. 1193. The arrangement now in effect in Great Britain and the other North Atlantic Treaty Organization nations, as well as in Japan, is the NATO Status of Forces Agreement, 4 U.S. Treaties and Other International Agreements 1792, T.I.A.S. 2846, which by its terms gives the foreign nation primary jurisdiction to try dependants accompanying American servicemen for offences which are violations of the law of both the foreign nation and the United States: Article VII, 1(b), 3(a). The foreign nation has exclusive criminal jurisdiction over dependants for offences which only violate its laws; Article VII, 2(b). However, the Agreement contains provisions which require that the foreign nations provide procedural safeguards for US nationals tried under the terms of the Agreement in their courts: Article VII, 9. Generally, see Note, 70 Harv. L. Rev. 1043.

Apart from those persons subject to the Status of Forces and comparable agreements and certain other restricted classes of Americans, a foreign nation has plenary criminal jurisdiction, of course, over all Americans—tourists, residents, businessmen, government employees and so forth—who commit offences against its laws within its territory.

For its part, the United States agreed that these military courts would be willing and able to try and to punish all offenses against the laws of Great Britain by such persons. In all material respects, the same situation existed in Japan when Mrs. Smith killed her husband. Even though a court-martial does not give an accused trial by jury and other Bill of Rights protections, the Government contends that article 2(11) of UCMJ, insofar as it provides for the military trial of dependents accompanying the armed forces in Great Britain and Japan, can be sustained as legislation which is necessary and proper to carry out the United States' obligations under the international agreements made with those countries. The obvious and decisive answer to this, of course, is that no agreement with a foreign nation can confer power on the Congress, or on any other branch of Government, which is free from the restraints of the Constitution.

. . .

   . . . There is nothing in [the language of Article VI of the Constitution] which intimates that treaties and laws enacted pursuant to them do not have to comply with the provisions of the Constitution. Nor is there anything in the debates which accompanied the drafting and ratification of the Constitution which even suggests such a result. These debates as well as the history that surrounds the adoption of the treaty provision in Article VI make it clear that the reason treaties were not limited to those made in 'pursuance' of the Constitution was so that agreements made by the United States under the Articles of Confederation, including the important peace treaties which concluded the Revolutionary War, would remain in effect. It would be manifestly contrary to the objectives of those who created the Constitution, as well as those who were responsible for the Bill of Rights—let alone alien to our entire constitutional history and tradition—to construe Article VI as permitting the United States to exercise power under an international agreement without observing constitutional prohibitions. In effect, such construction would permit amendment of that document in a manner not sanctioned by Article V. The prohibitions of the Constitution were designed to apply to all branches of the National Government and they cannot be nullified by the Executive or by the Executive and the Senate combined.

   There is nothing new or unique about what we say here. This Court has regularly and uniformly recognized the supremacy of the Constitution over a treaty. . . .

   This Court has also repeatedly taken the position that an Act of Congress, which must comply with the Constitution, is on a full parity with a treaty, and that when a statute which is subsequent in time is inconsistent with a treaty, the statute to the extent of conflict renders the treaty null. It would be completely anomalous to say that a treaty need not comply with the Constitution when such an agreement can be overridden by a statute that must conform to that instrument.

   There is nothing in State of Missouri v. Holland, 252 U.S. 416, 40 S.Ct. 382, 64 L.Ed. 641, which is contrary to the position taken here. There the Court carefully noted that the treaty involved was not inconsistent with any specific provision of the Constitution. The Court was concerned with the Tenth Amendment which reserves to the States or the people all power not delegated to the National Government. To the extent that the United States can validly make treaties, the people and the States have delegated their power to the National Government and the Tenth Amendment is no barrier.

In summary, we conclude that the Constitution in its entirety applied to the trials of Mrs. Smith and Mrs. Covert. Since their court-martial did not meet the requirements of Article III, 2, or the Fifth and Sixth Amendments we are compelled to determine if there is anything *within* the Constitution which authorizes the military trial of dependents accompanying the armed forces overseas. . . .

[The opinion concluded that the Constitution did not authorize such trials.]

COMMENT ON SELF-EXECUTING TREATIES

A question that frequently arises in the United States, as in the European states earlier examined, is whether a treaty is 'self-executing', in the sense that it creates rights and obligations for individuals that are enforceable in the courts without legislative implementation of the treaty. The concept of 'self-executing' is close to the concept of 'automatic incorporation' in the excerpts from Virginia Leary, p. 999, *supra*.

Each country here faces distinctive problems. In the United States, the answer to the question posed is bound up in constitutional text and in the allocation of powers over treaties among the Executive Branch, the Senate and the Congress as a whole. For example, note the status of 'supreme law' that is accorded the treaty under Article VI of the Constitution (the Supremacy Clause), and the relationship of that clause to the self-executing character of treaties.

Consider the following excerpts from Section 111 of the *Restatement (Third), Foreign Relations Law of the United States* (1987):

> (3) Courts in the United States are bound to give effect to international law and to international agreements of the United States, except that a 'non-self-executing' agreement will not be given effect as law in the absence of necessary implementation.
>
> (4) An international agreement of the United States is 'non-self-executing' (a) if the agreement manifests an intention that it shall not become effective as domestic law without the enactment of implementing legislation, (b) if the Senate in giving consent to a treaty, or Congress by resolution, requires implementing legislation, or (c) if implementing legislation is constitutionally required.

Comment (h) to Section 111 provides:

> In the absence of special agreement, it is ordinarily for the United States to provide how it will carry out its international obligations. Accordingly, the intention of the United States determines whether an agreement is to be self-executing in the United States or should await implementation by legislation or by appropriate executive or administrative action. If the international agreement is silent as to its self-executing character and the intention of the United States is

unclear, account must be taken of ... any expression by the Senate or by Congress in dealing with the agreement.

... Whether an agreement is to be given effect without further legislation is an issue that a court must decide when a party seeks to invoke the agreement as law .... Some provisions of an international agreement may be self-executing and others non-self-executing. If an international agreement or one of its provisions is non-self-executing, the United States is under an international obligation to adjust its laws and institutions as may be necessary to give effect to the agreement.

Certain types of treaties have traditionally been understood to be self-executing and have been applied by courts without any implementing legislation. Consider bilateral treaties giving (reciprocally) rights to nationals of each party to establish residence for certain purposes in the territory of the other party, establish corporations, conduct business there, and so on, frequently on national-treatment terms. Courts have long entertained actions by nationals of a treaty party seeking to enforce one or another of the rights provided for in the treaty.

Under US law (as developed through constitutional decisions of the courts), certain types of treaties cannot be self-executing but require implementing legislation to have domestic effects. Note Section 111(4)(c) above of the *Restatement.* For example, a treaty obligating the United States to make certain conduct criminal, even if it closely defined that conduct and stated its penalty, would nonetheless require such legislation. A treaty obligating the United States to pay funds to another state may require an appropriation of funds by the Congress.

Generally it is not relevant from an international-law perspective whether a treaty is self-executing, since a state is obligated under international law to do whatever may be required under its internal law (such as legislative enactment) to fulfil its treaty commitments. The state can follow either path.

The question of the attributes of a self-executing treaty has assumed a new prominence in recent years through a number of human rights treaties ratified by the United States—the ICCPR, for example—that were approved by the Senate and ratified subject to a declaration that the treaties were not self-executing. The terms of the declaration have varied among treaties. The precise effect of some of these declarations on courts remains a matter of dispute—for example, whether the treaty could be invoked defensively by a defendant in a prosecution, even if it could not be used by a plaintiff as the foundation for an action. See p. 1041, *infra.*

SEI FUJII v. STATE
Supreme Court of California, 1952
38 Cal.2d 718, 242 P.2d 617

[In this litigation, Fujii, a Japanese who was ineligible for citizenship under the United States naturalization laws then in effect, brought an action to determine whether an escheat of certain land that he had purchased had occurred under provisions of the California Alien Land Law. That Law (1 Deering's Gen. Laws, Act 261, as amended in 1945) provided in part:

1. All aliens eligible to citizenship under the laws of the United States may acquire, possess, enjoy, use, cultivate, occupy, transfer, transmit and inherit real property, or any interest therein, in this state, and have in whole or in part the beneficial use thereof, in the same manner and to the same extent as citizens of the United States except as otherwise provided by the laws of this state.

2. All aliens other than those mentioned in section one of this act may acquire, possess, enjoy, use, cultivate, occupy and transfer real property, or any interest therein, in this state, and have in whole or in part the beneficial use thereof, in the manner and to the extent, and for the purposes prescribed by any treaty now existing between the government of the United States and the nation or country of which such alien is a citizen or subject, and not otherwise.

7. Any real property hereafter acquired in fee in violation of the provisions of this act by any alien mentioned in section 2 of this act, . . . shall escheat as of the date of such acquiring, to, and become and remain the property of the state of California.

The Superior Court of Los Angeles County concluded that the property purchased by Fujii had escheated to the State. This decision was reversed by the District Court of Appeals. That court held that the Alien Land Law was unenforceable because contrary to the letter and spirit of the Charter of the United Nations, which as treaty was superior to state law. That decision was reviewed by the California Supreme Court. Excerpts from its opinion by Chief Justice Gibson appear below.]

It is first contended that the land law has been invalidated and superseded by the provisions of the United Nations Charter pledging the member nations to promote the observance of human rights and fundamental freedoms without distinction as to race. Plaintiff relies on statements in the preamble and in Articles 1, 55 and 56 of the Charter, 59 Stat. 1035.

It is not disputed that the charter is a treaty, and our federal Constitution provides that treaties made under the authority of the United States are part of the supreme law of the land and that the judges in every state are bound thereby. U.S. Const., art. VI. A treaty, however, does not automatically supersede local laws which are inconsistent with it unless the treaty provisions are self-executing. In the words of Chief Justice Marshall: A treaty is 'to be regarded in courts of justice as equivalent to an act of the Legislature, whenever it operates of itself, without the aid of any legislative provision. But when the terms of the stipulation import a contract—when either of the parties engages to perform a particular act, the treaty addresses itself to the political, not the judicial department; and the Legislature must execute the contract, before it can become a rule for the court'. *Foster v. Neilson*, 1829, 2 Pet. 253, 314, 7 L.Ed. 415.

In determining whether a treaty is self-executing courts look to the intent of the signatory parties as manifested by the language of the instrument, and, if the instrument is uncertain, recourse may be had to the circumstances surrounding its execution. . . . In order for a treaty provision to be operative without the aid of implementing legislation and to have the force and effect of a statute, it must appear that the framers of the treaty intended to prescribe a rule that, standing alone, would be enforceable in the courts. . . .

It is clear that the provisions of the preamble and of Article 1 of the charter which are claimed to be in conflict with the alien land law are not self-executing. They state general purposes and objectives of the United Nations Organization and do not purport to impose legal obligations on the individual member nations or to create rights in private persons. It is equally clear that none of the other provisions relied on by plaintiff is self-executing. . . . Although the member nations have obligated themselves to cooperate with the international organization in promoting respect for, and observance of, human rights, it is plain that it was contemplated that future legislative action by the several nations would be required to accomplish the declared objectives, and there is nothing to indicate that these provisions were intended to become rules of law for the courts of this country upon the ratification of the charter.

The language used in Articles 55 and 56 is not the type customarily employed in treaties which have been held to be self-executing and to create rights and duties in individuals. For example, the treaty involved in *Clark v. Allen*, 331 U.S. 503, 507–508, 67 S.Ct. 1431, 1434, 91 L.Ed. 1633, relating to the rights of a national of one country to inherit real property located in another country, specifically provided that 'such national shall be allowed a term of three years in which to sell the [property] . . . and withdraw the proceeds . . .' free from any discriminatory taxation. . . . In other instances treaty provisions were enforced without implementing legislation where they prescribed in detail the rules governing rights and obligations of individuals or specifically provided that citizens of one nation shall have the same rights while in the other country as are enjoyed by that country's own citizens. . . .

. . .

The provisions in the charter pledging cooperation in promoting observance of fundamental freedoms lack the mandatory quality and definiteness which would indicate an intent to create justiciable rights in private persons immediately upon ratification. Instead, they are framed as a promise of future action by the member nations. . . .

. . . We are satisfied . . . that the charter provisions relied on by plaintiff were not intended to supersede existing domestic legislation, and we cannot hold that they operate to invalidate the alien land law. . . .

[The Court then upheld plaintiff's alternative allegation that the Alien Land Law was invalid since it violated the Equal Protection Clause of the Fourteenth Amendment.]

QUESTIONS

1. What advantages do you see in the UK system (legislation) and in the US system (self-executing treaties) for giving treaty provisions internal effect? If you were drafting the US Constitution freshly, which of the constitutional arrangements in the prior readings for giving treaties internal effect would you select?

2. What relation do you see between the conception of self-executing treaties in the United States and the provision of Article VI of the Constitution that treaties consistent with the Constitution form part of the 'supreme law' of the land?

3. 'The path of self-executing treaty can frustrate fundamental democratic principles. It would be satisfactory if the House of Representatives, the more popular and representative House in Congress, participated in giving consent to ratification, but only the Senate does. If two-thirds of that body will go along with treaty provisions that might bring about deep internal change in U.S. law, the treaty has the force of "supreme law". But there has been no full legislative process and debate, and that's not how laws should be made in the U.S.' Comment. Can you give realistic illustrations for the argument made? Are they apt to be common in treaty making?

ADDITIONAL READING

L. Henkin, *Foreign Affairs and the United States Constitution* (2nd edn. 1996); H. Koh, 'Why Do Nations Obey International Law?', 106 Yale L. J. 2599 (1997); D. Sloss, 'The Domestication of International Human Rights', 24 Yale J. Int'l L. 129 (1999); K. Starmer, *European Human Rights Law: The Human Rights Act 1998 and the European Convention on Human Rights* (1999); D. Kinley (ed.), *Human Rights in Australian Law* (1968).

2. RATIFICATION BY THE UNITED STATES OF THE ICCPR: THE QUESTION OF RESERVATIONS

In comparison with other democratic states, and even with many one-party and authoritarian states that are persistent and cruel violators of basic human rights, the United States has a modest record of ratification of human rights treaties. That comparison cuts both ways. One might say that the United States has a lesser commitment to and concern with developing international human rights than do many (say, European and Commonwealth) states of a roughly similar political and economic character. As the world's leading power, its lesser commitment necessarily weakens the human rights movement. *Or*, one might say that the United States does not engage in the hypocrisy of many states in ratifying and then ignoring treaties. If it ratifies, it means to comply, and hence will take a careful look to be certain that full compliance is possible.

One can be certain that neither of these 'pure' explanations captures the complexity of the arguments within the Executive Branch and the Senate about ratification of these treaties. This section examines aspects of the ratification process of the ICCPR to illustrate that complexity.

As background to the materials on the ICCPR, the introductory readings below describe earlier attitudes within the United States about involvement in the international human rights system, and indicate the reasons why the United States effectively withdrew from participation in human rights treaties in the early 1950s. Recall the significant role played by the United States just a few years earlier in helping to launch the International Bill of Rights through the drafting of the Universal Declaration.

LOUIS SOHN AND THOMAS BUERGENTHAL, INTERNATIONAL PROTECTION OF HUMAN RIGHTS
(1973) at 961

1. In 1945, during the Senate Foreign Relations Committee's hearings on the U.N. Charter, a principal Department of State expert on the Charter, Dr. Leo Pasvolsky, was questioned extensively on the relationship between Article 2(7) and the human rights provisions of the Charter. The following is an excerpt from his testimony:

> Senator Millikin. I notice several reiterations of the thought of the Charter that the Organization shall not interfere with domestic affairs of any country. How can you get into these social questions and economic questions without conducting investigations and making inquiries in the various countries?
>
> Mr. Pasvolsky. Senator, the Charter provides that the Assembly shall have the right to initiate or make studies in all of these economic or social fields. . . .
>
> Senator Millikin. Might the activities of the Organization concern themselves with, for example, wage rates and working conditions in different countries?
>
> Mr. Pasvolsky. The question of what matters the Organization would be concerned with would depend upon whether or not they had international repercussions. This Organization is concerned with international problems. International problems may arise out of all sorts of circumstances. . . .
>
> Senator Millikin. Could such an Organization concern itself with various forms of discrimination which countries maintain for themselves, bloc currency, subsidies to merchant marine, and things of that kind?
>
> Mr Pasvolsky. I should think that the Organization would wish to discuss and consider them. It might even make recommendations on any matters which affect international economic or social relations. The League of Nations did. The International Labor Office has done that. This new Organization being created will be doing a great deal of that. . . .
>
> Senator Millikin. Would the investigation of racial discriminations be within the jurisdiction of this body?
>
> Mr. Pasvolsky. Insofar, I imagine, as the Organization takes over the function of making studies and recommendations on human rights, it may wish to make studies in those fields and make pronouncements.
>
> Senator Vandenberg. At that point I wish you would reemphasize what you read from the Commission Report specifically applying the exemption of domestic matters to the Social and Economic Council.
>
> Mr. Pasvolsky. I will read that paragraph again.

Senator Vandenberg. Yes, please.

Mr. Pasvolsky. (reading): The members of Committee 3 of Commission II are in full agreement that nothing contained in chapter IX can be construed as giving authority to the Organization to intervene in the domestic affairs of Member states . . .

Senator Millikin. Is there any other international aspect to a labor problem or a racial problem or a religious problem that does not originate domestically? . . .

Mr. Pasvolsky. Well, Senator, I suppose we can say that there is no such thing as an international problem that is not related to national problems, because the word 'international' itself means that there are nations involved. What domestic jurisdiction relates to here, I should say, as it does in all of these matters, is that there are certain matters which are handled internally by nations which do not affect other nations or may not affect other nations. On the other hand, there are certainly many matters handled internally which do affect other nations and which by international law are considered to be of concern to other nations.

Senator Millikin. For example, let me ask you if this would be true. It is conceivable that there are racial questions on the southern shores of the Mediterranean that might have very explosive effects under some circumstances; but they originate locally, do they not, Doctor?

Mr Pasvolsky. Yes.

Senator Millikin. And because they might have explosive effects, this Organization might concern itself with them; is that correct?

Mr. Pasvolsky. It might, if somebody brings them to the attention of the Organization.

Senator Millikin. And by the same token, am I correct in this, that in any racial matter, any of these matters we are talking about, that originates in one country domestically and that has the possibility of making international trouble, might be subject to the investigation and recommendations of the Organization?

Mr. Pasvolsky. I should think so, because the Organization is created for that.

2. A number of different versions of a proposal to amend the treatymaking power under the U.S. Constitution were considered by the Congress in the course of the so-called 'Bricker Amendment' debate, which lasted roughly from 1952 to 1957.[14]

. . .

4. It is generally acknowledged that the defeat of the proposed constitutional amendment was due in large measure to the vigorous lobbying by the Eisenhower Administration and its concomitant undertaking, articulated in the above-quoted testimony by Secretary of State John Foster Dulles, not to adhere to human rights treaties. This undertaking was also embodied in a policy statement issued by Mr. Dulles in the form of a letter addressed to Mrs. Oswald B. Lord, the United States Representative on the United Nations Commission on Human Rights. 28 DSB 579–80 (1953); 13 M. M. Whiteman, Digest of International Law 667–68 (Washington, D.C., 1970). This letter read in part:

---

[14] [Eds.] The Bricker Amendment, a series a proposals for constitutional amendments, would have significantly limited executive power over treaties and correspondingly increased the power of the Senate or the Congress as a whole. Different versions of the amendments would have curtailed the use of self-executing treaties rather than treaties followed by legislation, and redrawn the boundary line between treaties and executive agreements so as to require larger Senate participation.

In the light of our national, and recently, international experience in the matter of human rights, the opening of a new session of the Commission on Human Rights appears an appropriate occasion for a fresh appraisal of the methods through which we may realize the human rights goals of the United Nations. These goals have a high place in the Charter as drafted at San Francisco and were articulated in greater detail in the Universal Declaration of Human Rights. . . .

Since the establishment of these goals, much time and effort has been expended on the drafting of treaties, that is, Covenants on Human Rights, in which it was sought to frame, in mutually acceptable legal form, the obligations to be assumed by national states in regard to human rights. We have found that such drafts of Covenants as had a reasonable chance of acceptance in some respects established standards lower than those now observed in a number of countries.

While the adoption of the Covenants would not compromise higher standards already in force, it seems wiser to press ahead in the United Nations for the achievement of the standards set forth in the Universal Declaration of Human Rights through ways other than the proposed Covenants on Human Rights. This is particularly important in view of the likelihood that the Covenants will not be as widely accepted by United Nations members as initially anticipated. Nor can we overlook the fact that the areas where human rights are being persistently and flagrantly violated are those where the Covenants would most likely be ignored.

In these circumstances, there is a grave question whether the completion, signing and ratification of the Covenants at this time is the most desirable method of contributing to human betterment particularly in areas of greatest need. Furthermore, experience to date strongly suggests that even if it be assumed that this is a proper area for treaty action, a wider general acceptance of human rights goals must be attained before it seems useful to codify standards of human rights as binding international legal obligations in the Covenants.

With all these considerations in mind, the United States Government asks you to present to the Commission on Human Rights at its forthcoming session a statement of American goals and policies in this field; to point out the need for reexamining the approach of the Human Rights Covenants as the method for furthering at this time the objectives of the Universal Declaration of Human Rights; and to put forward other suggestions of method, based on American experience, for developing throughout the world a human rights conscience which will bring nearer the goals stated in the Charter. . . .

. . . By reason of the considerations referred to above, the United States Government has reached the conclusion that we should not at this time become a party to any multilateral treaty such as those contemplated in the draft Covenants on Human Rights, and that we should now work toward the objectives of the Declaration by other means. While the Commission continues, under the General Assembly's instructions, with the drafting of the Covenants, you are, of course, expected to participate. This would be incumbent on the United States as a loyal Member of the United Nations.

NOTE

A 1953 memorandum prepared within the State Department[15] listed the pros and cons of US support for the then draft international covenants. The arguments noted in the memorandum for changing the present policy of support included: (1) It was doubtful that a covenant on civil and political rights could gain the necessary Senate consent. (2) It was 'by no means clear' that many countries ratifying the covenants would 'actually give effect to their provisions'. (3) The Covenants:

> could work to the disadvantage of United States interests, whether this country becomes a party or not. The Covenants would be a source of propaganda attack on positions taken by the United States and on conditions within this country. The Covenants might contain provisions on economic self-determination and the right of nationalization which would be detrimental to United States interests in certain areas abroad.

(4) US support appeared to some critics as 'inconsistent with the Administration's policy on civil rights in the United States, where the emphasis is now on persuasion as against any new federal civil rights legislation'.

COMMENT ON BACKGROUND TO SUBMISSION OF ICCPR TO SENATE

In the years following the decision to withdraw from participation in the two major Covenants, the United States did ratify a few human rights treaties, including the Slavery Convention, the Protocol Relating to the Status of Refugees, the Convention on the Political Rights of Women, and the four Geneva Conventions on the laws of war. But it was not until the Carter administration in the late 1970s that a President sought the Senate's consent for ratification of a number of major treaties (including the two Covenants).

In recent years, the record of the United States has substantially improved, for it has become a party not only to the ICCPR but also to the Convention on the Prevention and Punishment of the Crime of Genocide; the Convention against Torture and other Cruel, Inhuman or Degrading Treatment or Punishment; and the International Convention on the Elimination of All Forms of Racial Discrimination. But there has never been sustained debate in the Senate or broader political debate in the country about participation in three major and widely ratified treaties: the Convention on the Elimination of All Forms of Discrimination against Women, the American Convention on Human Rights, or the International Covenant on Economic, Social and Cultural Rights.

The following materials deal with aspects of the ratification process of the International Covenant on Civil and Political Rights. Given the similarities between the provisions of that Covenant and the US tradition of liberal

---

[15] United States Policy Regarding Draft International Covenants on Human Rights, Foreign Relations of the United States 1952–1954, Vol. III (1979), p. 1550.

constitutionalism and a Bill of Rights, no opponents of ratification then expressed doubt about the broad consistency between the principles of the Covenant and the US Constitution. There were statements from civil liberties groups stressing significant if more limited ways in which the United States, were it to become a party without making numerous legislative and policy changes, would be in violation of several ICCPR provisions.[16]

One of the recurrent issues before the Executive Branch and the Senate in deciding whether the United States should become a party to the ICCPR was whether the Covenant, or salient parts of it, should be understood to be self-executing. Note that the ICCPR itself makes no reference to its self-executing or non-self-executing character but provides in Article 2(2):

> Where not already provided for by existing legislation or other measures, each State Party to the present Covenant undertakes to take the necessary steps, in accordance with its constitutional processes and with the provisions of the present Covenant, to adopt such legislative or other measures as may be necessary to give effect to the rights recognized in the present Covenant.

Article 2(3) bears out this obligation by stating the further undertaking to 'ensure that any persons whose rights . . . are violated shall have an effective remedy', and to 'ensure that any person claiming such a remedy shall have his right thereto determined by competent judicial, administrative or legislative authorities . . . and to develop the possibilities of judicial remedy'. How the states fulfil these obligations lies within their discretion; they are not obligated to incorporate the treaty *as such* within their domestic legal order, whether through automatic incorporation (self-executing treaty) or legislative incorporation. Consider the following comments on the ICCPR:

> In practice, differences in the domestic status of the Covenant are substantial. . . . In its examination of individual communications and State reports, the [ICCPR Human Rights Committee] has confirmed that the States Parties may implement the Covenant domestically as they see fit. There is, however, a certain tendency to promote the *direct applicability* of the Covenant.[17]

SENATE HEARINGS ON INTERNATIONAL HUMAN RIGHTS TREATIES

S. Comm. For. Rel., 96th Cong., 1st Sess. (1979)

[In 1977, President Carter signed four human rights treaties on behalf of the United States and soon thereafter submitted them to the Senate for its consent to ratification. The Carter Administration proposed that the Senate adopt a number of reservations, understandings and declarations as part of its consent.

---

[16] See, e.g., *Human Rights Watch and American Civil Liberties Union, Human Rights Violations in the United States: A Report on U.S. Compliance with the International Covenant on Civil and Political Rights* (1993).

[17] Manfred Nowak, *U.N. Covenant on Civil and Political Rights: CCPR Commentary* (1993), at 54.

The following excerpts from the 1979 Senate hearings on the treaties concern only one of them, the International Covenant on Civil and Political Rights. The treaties were never brought to vote in the Senate, and the matter effectively died until the Bush Administration revived in 1991 the question of US participation in this Covenant. It submitted the Covenant afresh to the Senate, together with modestly amended proposals for reservations, understandings and declarations that are set forth at p. 1039, *infra*.

There follow some brief excerpts from the lengthy Senate hearings.]

Statement of Charles Yost, Former Ambassador to United Nations

. . .

There are, in my judgment, few failures or omissions on our part which have done more to undermine American credibility internationally than this one. Whenever an American delegate at an international conference, or an American Ambassador making representations on behalf of our Government, raises a question of human rights, as we have in these times many occasions to do, the response public or private, is very likely to be this: If you attach so much importance to human rights, why have you not even ratified the United Nations' conventions and covenants on this subject? . . .

Our refusal to join in the international implementation of the principles we so loudly and frequently proclaim cannot help but give the impression that we do not practice what we preach, that we have something to hide, that we are afraid to allow outsiders even to inquire whether we practice racial discrimination or violate other basic human rights. Yet we constantly take it upon ourselves to denounce the Soviet Union, Cuba, Vietnam, Argentina, Chile, and many other states for violating these rights. . . .

Many are therefore inclined to believe that our whole human rights policy is merely a cold war exercise or a display of self-righteousness directed against governments we dislike. . . .

. . .

Prepared Statement of Robert Owen, Legal Adviser, Department of State

. . .

. . . [Objections to the human rights treaties] tend to fall into three categories. First, it is said that the human rights treaties could serve to change our laws as they are, allowing individuals in courts of law to invoke the treaty terms where inconsistent with domestic law or even with the Constitution. The second type of objection is that the treaties could be used to alter the jurisdictional balance between our federal and state institutions. . . . The third type of objection is that the relationship between a government and its citizens is not a proper subject for the treaty-making powers at all, but ought to be left entirely to domestic legislative processes. . . .

. . . [T]he treaties do diverge from our domestic law in a relatively few instances. Critics fear that this divergence will cause changes in that domestic law outside the normal legislative process, or at least will subject the relations between the government and the individual to conflicting legal standards.

This fear is not well-founded, in our judgment, for two reasons. First, the President has recommended that to each of the four treaties there is appended a declaration that the treaties' substantive provisions are not self-executing.

. . .

. . . This does not mean that vast new implementing legislation is required, as the great majority of the treaty provisions are already implemented in our domestic law. It does mean that further changes in our laws will be brought about only through the normal legislative process. This understanding as to the non-self-executing nature of the substantive provisions of the treaties would not derogate from or diminish in any way our international obligations under the treaties; it touches only upon the role the treaty provisions will play in our domestic law.

A second reason why we need not fear a confusion of standards due to possible conflicts between the treaty provisions and domestic law rests in this Administration's recommended reservations and understandings. In the few instances where it was felt that a provision of the treaties could reasonably be interpreted to diverge from the requirements of our constitution or from federal or state law presently in force, the Administration has suggested that a reservation or understanding be made to that provision. In our view, these reservations do not detract from the object and the purpose of the treaties—that is, to see to it that minimum standards of human rights are observed throughout the world—and they permit us to accept the treaties in a form consonant with our domestic legal requirements.

. . .

. . . The primary objective is the fostering of international commitments to erect and observe a minimum standard of rights for the individual as set forth by the treaties. This standard is met by our domestic system in practice, although not always in precisely the same way that the treaties envision. By ratification, we would commit ourselves to maintain the level of respect we already pay to the human rights of our people; we would commit ourselves not to backslide, and we would be subjecting this commitment and our human rights performance as a whole to international scrutiny.

. . .

Another reason why the Administration has proposed a number of reservations, understandings and declarations is pragmatic. We believe these treaties to be important and necessary, and we are anxious to secure the advice and consent of the Senate to their ratification. It is our judgment that the prospects for securing that ratification would be significantly and perhaps decisively advanced if it were to be clear that, by adopting these treaties, the United States would not automatically be bringing about changes in its internal law without the legislative concurrence of the federal or state governments.

———

Senator Pell. Do you think by affixing reservations we may be making an error in that we would be permitting other nations also to affix reservations and reinterpret the covenants according to their own ideologies?

Mr. Owen. The reservations that we have recommended in some cases are absolutely essential in order to avoid conflicts with our own Constitution.

As to the other reservations, if the Senate should decide that they are not necessary, I think the administration would be willing to dispense with them. Then we would be, in effect, bringing about a more rigorous civil rights regime and there would be no possible criticism that we were not fulfilling the treaties as a whole.

. . .

Senator Pell. Where do you think the opposition has been to the passage of these treaties? Why is it we have had to delay for 20 years or more?

. . .

Mr. Farer. . . . I think that race relations have been one factor, if we will be perfectly frank. A lot of opposition came from representatives of States where law or practice were crudely discriminatory.

But I also think that like most other countries, particularly large countries, we tend to react instinctively with some belligerence to the idea that other countries and peoples can assess for themselves what we are doing, and the idea that they may fault the level of achievement that we have managed to reach.

. . .

Senator Pell. What would you think, Professor Sohn?

Mr. Sohn. I agree with the two other speakers that the fears have been exaggerated and that it is simply part of the general feeling that the United States knows better about various things and therefore should not be subject to other peoples' judgments. It reminds me of what happened in the United Kingdom when they finally ratified the European Convention on Human Rights. The Foreign Minister made a statement in the House of Commons saying of course we are willing to ratify it because nobody can find anything wrong with the British laws on human rights. Well, of course, two weeks later all of the cases relating to immigration from Kenya to the United Kingdom by people nominally British citizens and the restrictions on them by immigration authorities immediately were taken to the European Commission. The United Kingdom had to admit that its administrative procedures were not in accordance with the standards of the Convention.

I think on the one hand we always say to everybody else that our standards are higher than those of anyone else; but we will discover, if we are subject to international supervision, that there are some skeletons in our closet and they will be paraded in public, and we do not like that idea.

. . .

Statement of Phyllis Schlafly, Alton, III

. . .

I oppose Senate ratification of these international human rights treaties for the following reasons.

First, the treaties do not give Americans any rights whatsoever. They do not add a minuscule of benefit to the marvelous human rights proclaimed by the Declaration of Independence, guaranteed by the U.S. Constitution, and extended by our Federal and State laws.

Second, the treaties imperil or restrict existing rights of Americans by using treaty law to restrict or reduce U.S. constitutional rights, to change U.S. domestic Federal or State laws, and to upset the balance of power within our unique system of federalism.

Third, the treaties provide no tangible benefit to peoples in other lands and, even if they did, that would not justify sacrificing American rights.

. . .

This covenant sets up a Human Rights [Committee] of 18 members on which the United States would have at most one or perhaps no representative at all. It would have the competence to hear complaints against us, and who knows what they would do.

. . .

QUESTIONS

Based on the prior readings, how would you identify the principal concerns that a President who believed it important to ratify a given human rights treaty should be aware of when seeking the Senate's consent? Can you think of ways in which the President might seek to alleviate or dispose of those concerns before submitting the treaty to the Senate?

NOTE

The following description of the ratification process of the ICCPR stresses the problem of treaty reservations. You should review the Comment on Treaty Reservations at p. 439, *supra*, up to the part of that Comment that specifically concerns CEDAW.

* * * *

President Bush sent a letter to the Senate Foreign Relations Committee in 1991,[18] urging the Senate to give its advice and consent to ratification of the ICCPR. It stated in part:

> The end of the Cold War offers great opportunities for the forces of democracy and the rule of law throughout the world. I believe the United States has a special responsibility to assist those in other countries who are now working to make the transition to pluralist democracies. . . .
>
> United States ratification of the Covenant on Civil and Political Rights at this moment in history would underscore our natural commitment to fostering democratic values through international law. . . . Subject to a few essential

---

[18] Rep. of S. Comm. for For. Rel. to Accompany Exec. E, 95–2 (1992), at 25.

reservations and understandings, it is entirely consonant with the fundamental principles incorporated in our own Bill of Rights. U.S. ratification would also strengthen our ability to influence the development of appropriate human rights principles in the international community. . . .

. . .

PROPOSALS BY BUSH ADMINISTRATION OF RESERVATIONS TO INTERNATIONAL COVENANT ON CIVIL AND POLITICAL RIGHTS
Rep. of S. Comm. For. Rel. to Accompany Exec. E, 95–2 (1992) at 10

[In 1978, the Carter Administration had proposed a list of reservations, understandings and declarations when it put four human rights treaties, including the ICCPR, to the Senate for its consent to ratification. In 1991, when the Bush Administration revived the ICCPR alone among the four treaties, it submitted a revised list to the Senate Foreign Relations Committee. The following excerpts from this 1991 submission set forth the Bush Administration's reasons for proposing several of the reservations, understandings and declarations.]

General Comments

. . .

In a few instances, however, it is necessary to subject U.S. ratification to reservations, understandings or declarations in order to ensure that the United States can fulfill its obligations under the Covenant in a manner consistent with the United States Constitution, including instances where the Constitution affords greater rights and liberties to individuals than does the Covenant. Additionally, a few provisions of the Covenant articulate legal rules which differ from U.S. law and which, upon careful consideration, the Administration declines to accept in preference to existing law. . . .

Formal Reservations

1. Free Speech (Article 20)

Although Article 19 of the Covenant specifically protects freedom of expression and opinion, Article 20 directly conflicts with the First Amendment by requiring the prohibition of certain forms of speech and expression which are protected under the First Amendment to the U.S. Constitution (i.e., propaganda for war and advocacy of national, racial or religious hatred that constitutes incitement to discrimination, hostility or violence). The United States cannot accept such an obligation.

Accordingly, the following reservation is recommended:

> Article 20 does not authorize or require legislation or other action by the United States that would restrict the right of free speech and association protected by the Constitution and laws of the United States.

. . .

2. *Article 6 (capital punishment)*

Article 6, paragraph 5 of the Covenant prohibits imposition of the death sentence for crimes committed by persons below 18 years of age and on pregnant women. In 1978, a broad reservation to this article was proposed in order to retain the right to impose capital punishment on any person duly convicted under existing or future laws permitting the imposition of capital punishment. The Administration is now prepared to accept the prohibition against execution of pregnant women. However, in light of the recent reaffirmation of U.S. policy towards capital punishment generally, and in particular the Supreme Court's decisions upholding state laws permitting the death penalty for crimes committed by juveniles aged 16 and 17, the prohibition against imposition of capital punishment for crimes committed by minors is not acceptable. Given the sharply differing view taken by many of our future treaty partners on the issue of the death penalty (including what constitutes 'serious crimes' under Article 6(2)), it is advisable to state our position clearly.

Accordingly, we recommend the following reservation to Article 6:

> The United States reserves the right, subject to its Constitutional constraints, to impose capital punishment on any person (other than a pregnant woman) duly convicted under existing or future laws permitting the imposition capital punishment, including such punishment for crime committed by persons below eighteen years of age.

. . .

4. *Article 15(1) (post-offense reductions in penalty)*

Article 15, paragraph 1, precludes the imposition of a heavier penalty for a criminal offense than was applicable at the time the offense was committed, and requires States Party to comply with any post-offense reductions in penalties: '[i]f, subsequent to the commission of the offense, provision is made by law for the imposition of the lighter penalty, the offender shall benefit thereby.' Current federal law, as well as the law of most states, does not require such relief and in fact contains a contrary presumption that the penalty in force at the time the offense is committed will be imposed, although post-sentence reductions are permitted (see 18 U.S.C. 3582 (c)(2) and the Federal Sentencing Guidelines) and are often granted in practice when there have been subsequent statutory changes. Upon consideration, there is no disposition to require a change in U.S. law to conform to the Covenant. [A reservation was proposed.]

Understandings

1. *Article 2(1), 4(1) and 26 (non-discrimination)*

The very broad anti-discrimination provisions contained in the above articles do not precisely comport with long-standing Supreme Court doctrine in the equal protection field. In particular, Articles 2(1) and 26 prohibit discrimination not only on the bases of 'race, colour, sex, language, religion, political or other opinion, national or social origin, property, birth' but also on any 'other status.' Current U.S. civil rights law is not so open-ended: discrimination is only prohibited for specific statuses, and there are exceptions which allow for discrimination. For example, under the Age Discrimination Act of 1975, age may be taken into account in certain circumstances. In addition, U.S. law permits additional distinctions, for example between citizens and non-citizens and between different categories of non-citizens, especially in the context of the immigration laws.

. . .

Notwithstanding the very extensive protections already provided under U.S. law and the Committee's interpretive approach to the issue, we recommend [an understanding that expresses the preceding concerns.] [Eds. The text of that understanding is here omitted.]

4. Article 14 (right to counsel, compelled witness, and double jeopardy)

In a few particular aspects, this Article could be read as going beyond existing U.S. domestic law. . . . Under the Constitution, double jeopardy attaches only to multiple prosecutions by the same sovereign and does not prohibit trial of the same defendant for the same crime in, for example, state and federal courts or in the courts of two states. See *Burton v. Maryland*, 395 U.S. 784 (1969).

To clarify our reading of the Covenant with respect to these issues, we recommend the following understanding, similar to the one proposed in 1978:

> . . . The United States understands the prohibition upon double jeopardy in paragraph 7 to apply only when the judgment of acquittal has been rendered by a court of the same governmental unit, whether the Federal Government or a constituent unit, as is seeking a new trial for the same cause.

Declarations

1. Non-self-executing Treaty

For reasons of prudence, we recommend including a declaration that the substantive provisions of the Covenant are not self-executing. The intent is to clarify that the Covenant will not create a private cause of action in U.S. courts. As was the case with the Torture Convention, existing U.S. law generally complies with the Covenant; hence, implementing legislation is not contemplated.

We recommend the following declaration . . .

> The United States declares that the provisions of Articles 1 through 27 of the Covenant are not self-executing.

. . .

3. Article 41 (state-to-state complaints)

Under Article 41, States Party to the Covenant may accept the competence of the Human Rights Committee to consider state-to-state complaints by means of a formal declaration to that effect. . . .

Accordingly, we recommend informing the Senate of our intent, subject to its approval, to make an appropriate declaration under Article 41 at the time of ratification, as follows:

> The United States declares that it accepts the competence of the Human Rights

Committee to receive and consider communications under Article 41 in which a State Party claims another State Party is not fulfilling its obligations under the Covenant.

. . .

QUESTIONS

1. Several NGOs participating in the Senate hearings on ratification of the ICCPR opposed the proposed (and later adopted) declaration to the effect that the substantive provisions of the Covenant would not be self-executing. Note the following comments in a report by the largest domestic civil liberties organization and the largest US-based international human rights organization in the United States:[19]

> . . . Americans would have been able to enforce the treaty in U.S. courts either if it had been declared to be self-executing or if implementing legislation had been enacted to create causes of action under the treaty. The Bush administration rejected both routes. The result was that ratification became an empty act for Americans: the endorsement of the most important treaty for the protection of civil rights yielded not a single additional enforceable right to citizens and residents of the United States.
>
> We issue this report to demonstrate the inaccuracy of the view that Americans do not need the protection of the ICCPR. As we show, the Bush administration was wrong in its assessment that the United States is already complying with all the treaty's obligations, even after the administration nullified some of the rights through its reservations, declarations and understandings. In the areas of racial and gender discrimination, prison conditions, immigrants' rights, language discrimination, the death penalty, police brutality, freedom of expression and religious freedom, we show that the United States is now violating the treaty in important respects. As a result, the Clinton administration is under an immediate legal obligation to remedy these human rights violations at home, through specific steps that we outline.
>
> Moreover, to ensure that these remedies are sufficient, we believe the U.S. government is obligated to grant Americans the right to invoke the protections of the treaty in U.S. courts, at least through specific legislation enabling them to do so, but preferably through a formal declaration that the treaty is self-executing, and thus invocable in U.S. courts without further legislation. . . .

Do you agree with these observations about the need for a self-executing Covenant? What arguments would you make against this position?

2. What remedial path has a US citizen who plausibly claims that the government has violated his rights under the ICCPR, but who lacks any plausible claim under US law? What steps could he realistically take to pressure the US government to accept his position?

---

[19] Human Rights Watch and American Civil Liberties Union, *Human Rights Violations in the United States: A Report on U.S. Compliance with the International Covenant on Civil and Political Rights* (1993), at 2.

3. Ratification by the United States of the ICCPR Optional Protocol does not seem to have been discussed. No such proposal was put to the Senate. (a) Why do you suppose this to have been the case? (b) As a member of the State Department, would you have argued for or against joining the Optional Protocol? (c) 'Ratification of the Optional Protocol would have been the correct solution, preferable to making the ICCPR self-executing.' Comment.

COMMENT ON EFFECTS OF RESERVATIONS

With respect to the reservation covering Article 20, note the ambiguous wording of para. 2 of that article, providing that '[a]ny advocacy of national, racial or religious hatred that constitutes incitement to discrimination, hostility or violence shall be prohibited by law'. The ICCPR Committee has not issued a General Comment on Article 20. Manfred Nowak, in his *U.N. Covenant on Civil and Political Rights: CCPR Commentary* (1993), observes (at 365) that the 'legal formulation of this provision is not entirely clear'. The wording of para. (2):

> literally means that incitement to discrimination without violence must also be prohibited. . . . Particularly inexplicable is the insertion of the word 'discrimination'. . . . It is most difficult to conceive of an advocacy of national, racial or religious hatred that does not simultaneously incite discrimination. . . . Art. 20(2) as well may be sensibly interpreted only in light of its object and purpose, i.e., taking into consideration its *responsive character* with regard to the Nazi racial hatred campaigns. . . . Thus, despite its unclear formulation, States Parties are not obligated by Art. 20(2) to prohibit advocacy of hatred in private circles that instigates non-violent actions of racial or religious discrimination. What the delegates . . . had in mind was to . . . prevent the public incitement of racial hatred and violence within a State or against other States and peoples.

The Senate consented to ratification subject to the described (and other) reservations, understandings and declarations. In the Senate debate preceding the approving vote, Senator Moynihan noted that '[o]thers have raised the legitimate concern that the number of reservations in the administration's package might imply to some that the United States does not take the obligations of the covenant seriously'. He stressed how few and selective the package was, in the context of the entire covenant, and argued that 'a wholly different interpretation' could be placed on it—namely, as an indication of the seriousness with which the United States approached its new obligations, unlike 'nations of the totalitarian block [that] ratified obligations without reservation—obligations that they had no intention of carrying out'. He observed that 'a Senator might well conclude that it is in the interests of the United States to ratify the covenant with this package of reservations even if that Senator disagrees strongly with a particular domestic practice which has prompted a reservation'. Efforts to change that domestic practice through legislation could continue (138 Cong. Rec. S4781, April 2, 1992).

The United States then ratified the Covenant. A number of states parties to the ICCPR objected to one or more of the reservations.[20] Several states—including Belgium, Denmark, Finland, France, Germany, Italy, Netherlands, Norway, Portugal, Spain and Sweden—objected to the reservation regarding Article 6, para. 5, prohibiting the imposition of the death sentence for crimes committed by persons below 18 years of age, and found that reservation incompatible with the ICCPR's provisions and with its object and purpose. Most of these states also objected to other reservations (or to understandings), particularly the one relating to Article 7. The objections, however, stressed that (to take one illustration) the state's position on the relevant reservations 'does not constitute an obstacle to the entry into force of the Covenant between the Kingdom of Spain and the United States of America'.

In objecting to three reservations and three understandings, Sweden observed that under international treaty law, the name 'assigned to a statement' that excluded or modified the effect of certain treaty provisions:

> does not determine its status as a reservation to the treaty. Thus, the Government considers that some of the understandings made by the United States in substance constitute reservations to the Covenant.
>
> A reservation by which a State modifies or excludes the application of the most fundamental provisions of the Covenant, or limits its responsibilities under that treaty by invoking general principles of national law, may cast doubts upon the commitment of the reserving State to the object and purpose of the Covenant. The reservations made by the United States of America include both reservations to essential and non-derogable provisions, and general references to national legislation. Reservations of this nature contribute to undermining the basis of international treaty law. All States parties share a common interest in the respect for the object and purpose of the treaty to which they have chosen to become parties.

GENERAL COMMENT NO. 24 OF HUMAN RIGHTS COMMITTEE
CCPR/C/21/Rev.1/Add.6, 2 Nov. 1994.

[At its 52nd session in 1994, the ICCPR Committee adopted General Comment No. 24 entitled: 'General comment on issues relating to reservations made upon ratification of accession to the Covenant or the Optional Protocols thereto, or in relation to declarations under article 41 of the Covenant'. (Earlier General Comments (GCs) of the Committee appear at p. 732, *supra*). This GC was adopted after the ratification of the ICCPR by the United States described above, and preceded the Committee's consideration of the first periodic report submitted by the United States in 1995. It refers to the judicial decision and to the provisions of the Vienna

---

[20] The objections are set forth in alphabetical order of the states involved, starting at 47 in CCPR/C/2/ Rev. 4, 24 August 1994, entitled 'Reservations, Declarations, Notifications and Objections Relating to the International Covenant on Civil and Political Rights and the Optional Protocols Thereto'.

Convention on the Law of Treaties described in the Comment on Treaty Reservations at p. 439, *supra*.

The GC notes that as of its date, 46 of the 127 states parties to the ICCPR had entered a total of 150 reservations, ranging from exclusion of the duty to provide particular rights, to insistence on the 'paramountcy of certain domestic legal provisions' and to limitation of the competence of the Committee. Those reservations 'tend to weaken respect' for obligations and 'may undermine the effective implementation of the Covenant'. The Committee felt compelled to act, partly under the necessity of clarifying for states parties just what obligations had been undertaken, a clarification that would require the Committee to determine 'the acceptability and effects' of a reservation or unilateral declaration.

The GC observed that the ICCPR itself makes no reference to reservations (as is true also for the First Optional Protocol; the Second Optional Protocol limits reservations), and that the matter of reservations is governed by international law. It found in Article 19(3) of the Vienna Convention on the Law of Treaties 'relevant guidance'. Therefore, that article's 'object and purpose test . . . governs the matter of interpretation and acceptability of reservations'. The GC continues:]

8. Reservations that offend peremptory norms would not be compatible with the object and purpose of the Covenant. Although treaties that are mere exchanges of obligations between States allow them to reserve *inter se* application of rules of general international law, it is otherwise in human rights treaties, which are for the benefit of persons within their jurisdiction. Accordingly, provisions in the Covenant that represent customary international law (and *a fortiori* when they have the character of peremptory norms) may not be the subject of reservations. Accordingly, a State may not reserve the right to engage in slavery, to torture, to subject persons to cruel, inhuman or degrading treatment or punishment, to arbitrarily deprive persons of their lives, to arbitrarily arrest and detain persons, to deny freedom of thought, conscience and religion, to presume a person guilty unless he proves his innocence, to execute pregnant women or children, to permit the advocacy of national, racial or religious hatred, to deny to persons of marriageable age the right to marry, or to deny to minorities the right to enjoy their own culture, profess their own religion, or use their own language. And while reservations to particular clauses of Article 14 may be acceptable, a general reservation to the right to a fair trial would not be.

9. Applying more generally the object and purpose test to the Covenant, the Committee notes that, for example, . . . a State [may not] reserve an entitlement not to take the necessary steps at the domestic level to give effect to the rights of the Covenant (Article 2(2)).

10. . . . [I]t falls for consideration as to whether reservations to the non-derogable provisions of the Covenant are compatible with its object and purpose. While there is no hierarchy of importance of rights under the Covenant, the operation of certain rights may not be suspended, even in times of national emergency. This underlines the great importance of non-derogable rights. But not all rights of profound importance, such as articles 9 and 27 of the Covenant, have in fact been made non-derogable. One reason for certain rights being made

non-derogable is because their suspension is irrelevant to the legitimate control of the state of national emergency (for example, no imprisonment for debt, in article 11). Another reason is that derogation may indeed be impossible (as, for example, freedom of conscience). At the same time, some provisions are non-derogable exactly because without them there would be no rule of law. . . .

11. . . . The Committee's role under the Covenant, whether under article 40 or under the Optional Protocols, necessarily entails interpreting the provisions of the Covenant and the development of a jurisprudence. Accordingly, a reservation that rejects the Committee's competence to interpret the requirements of any provisions of the Covenant would also be contrary to the object and purpose of that treaty.

12. . . . Domestic laws may need to be altered properly to reflect the requirements of the Covenant; and mechanisms at the domestic level will be needed to allow the Covenant rights to be enforceable at the local level. Reservations often reveal a tendency of States not to want to change a particular law. And sometimes that tendency is elevated to a general policy. Of particular concern are widely formulated reservations which essentially render ineffective all Covenant rights which would require any change in national law to ensure compliance with Covenant obligations. No real international rights or obligations have thus been accepted. And when there is an absence of provisions to ensure that Covenant rights may be sued on in domestic courts, and, further, a failure to allow individual complaints to be brought to the Committee under the first Optional Protocol, all the essential elements of the Covenant guarantees have been removed.

. . .

17. . . . [Human rights] treaties, and the Covenant specifically, are not a web of inter-State exchanges of mutual obligations. . . . Because the operation of the classic rules on reservations is so inadequate for the Covenant, States have often not seen any legal interest in or need to object to reservations. The absence of protest by States cannot imply that a reservation is either compatible or incompatible with the object and purpose of the Covenant. . . .

18. It necessarily falls to the Committee to determine whether a specific reservation is compatible with the object and purpose of the Covenant. . . . Because of the special character of a human rights treaty, the compatibility of a reservation with the object and purpose of the Covenant must be established objectively, by reference to legal principles, and the Committee is particularly well placed to perform this task. The normal consequence of an unacceptable reservation is not that the Covenant will not be in effect at all for a reserving party. Rather, such a reservation will generally be severable, in the sense that the Covenant will be operative for the reserving party without benefit of the reservation.

19. Reservations must be specific. . . . States should not enter so many reservations that they are in effect accepting a limited number of human rights obligations, and not the Covenant as such. So that reservations do not lead to a perpetual non-attainment of international human rights standards, reservations should not systematically reduce the obligations undertaken only to the presently existing in less demanding standards of domestic law. Nor should interpretative declarations

or reservations seek to remove an autonomous meaning to Covenant obligations, by pronouncing them to be identical, or to be accepted only insofar as they are identical, with existing provisions of domestic law.

. . .

NOTE

The United States submitted observations to the ICCPR Committee on General Comment No. 24,[21] which it said 'appears to go much to far'. It noted that the ICCPR did not 'impose on States Parties an obligation to give effect to the Committee's interpretations or confer on the Committee the power to render definitive interpretations of the Covenant'.

The observations stated that paras 16–20 of the GC 'appear to reject the established rules of interpretation of treaties' in the Vienna Convention and in customary international law. It criticized the GC's condemnation of the types of reservations that the United States had entered. The observations were particularly critical of para. 18, which stated that in the indicated circumstances, 'the Covenant will be operative for the reserving party without benefit of the reservations'. This conclusion is 'completely at odds with established legal practice and principles. . . .'. If it were determined that any one or more of the US reservations were ineffective, the consequence would be that the ratification as a whole could thereby be nullified, and the United States would not be party to the Covenant.

QUESTIONS

1. Why was there near unanimity among the states parties to the ICCPR that objected to the reservations by the United States about the particular reservation concerning Article 6, para. 5 (death sentence)? Did that reservation raise a special problem under the Covenant? On the other hand, was there special reason for the United States to reserve as to that provision?

2. In the light of General Comment No. 24, if you were a Senator committed to US ratification of the major human rights instruments, would you have voted for *any* reservation? Did any one of the reservations have a special justification?

3. Is General Comment No. 24 consistent with the spirit of the *Genocide Convention* case described in the Comment on Treaty Reservations, p. 440, *supra*? Using that decision, how would you argue that the reservations of the United States should be accepted in their entirety as valid under international law?

---

[21] These observations of the United States, as well as those of the United Kingdom, are set forth in 16 Hum. Rts L. J. 422 (1995).

COMMENT ON US RATIFICATION OF THE CONVENTION ON ELIMINATION OF RACIAL DISCRIMINATION

In 1994, the United States ratified the International Convention on the Elimination of All Forms of Racial Discrimination (CERD) subject to three reservations, one understanding, and one declaration (stating that the Convention is not self-executing).

One reservation was addressed to Article 4 of CERD, which is the equivalent of Article 20 of the ICCPR. States Parties 'condemn all propaganda . . . based on ideas or theories of superiority of one race or group of persons of one colour or ethnic origin'. They undertake to declare a punishable offence 'all dissemination of ideas based on racial superiority or hatred, incitement to racial discrimination, as well as all acts of violence' against such a race or group. Article 1 defines 'racial discrimination' to mean any distinction based on 'race, colour, descent, or national or ethnic origin' that has the purpose or effect of impairing equal enjoyment of rights 'in the political, economic, social, cultural or any other field of public life'.

Another reservation concerned the extent to which CERD reaches beyond state discrimination to prohibit certain private or nongovernmental conduct.

> *Article 2. Para. 1:* 'States Parties condemn racial discrimination and undertake to pursue by all appropriate means . . . a policy of eliminating racial discrimination in all its forms . . . and, to this end: . . . (d) Each State Party shall prohibit and bring to an end, by all appropriate means, including legislation . . . , racial discrimination by any persons, group or organization; . . .

> *Article 5:* States Parties undertake to guarantee the right of everyone to the enjoyment of stated rights, including . . . (e) Economic and social rights, in particular: . . . (iii) the right to housing; (f) The right of access to any place or service intended for use by the general public, such as transport, hotels, restaurants, cafes, theatres and parks.

The reservation noted that the US Constitution and laws reached 'significant areas of non-governmental activity' in protecting against discrimination. It continued:

> Individual privacy and freedom from governmental interference in private conduct, however, are also recognized as among the fundamental values which shape our free and democratic society. The United States understands that the identification of the rights protected under the Convention by reference in Article 1 to fields of 'public life' reflects a similar distinction between spheres of public conduct that are customarily the subject of governmental regulation, and spheres of private conduct that are not. To the extent, however, that the Convention calls for a broader regulation of private conduct, the United States does not accept any obligation under this Convention to enact legislation or take other measures under [designated provisions, including para. (1) and subpara. 1(d) of Article 2, and Article 5] with respect to private conduct except as mandated by the Constitution and laws of the United States.[22]

---

[22] 140 Cong. Rec. S 7643, 103rd Cong. 2nd Sess., June 7, 1994.

C. STATE JUDICIAL ENFORCEMENT OF HUMAN RIGHTS THROUGH ACTIONS BASED ON FOREIGN VIOLATIONS

Courts, especially in common law jurisdictions, are increasingly confronted with cases seeking to establish the civil or criminal liability of individuals for human rights violations committed in foreign countries. Such cases constitute a bridge between Chapters 12 and 13. Although they are decided in domestic courts and domestic law plays a vital role, they may impose a liability for activities occurring in other countries that did not involve local citizens, and their decrees may impose remedies which affect officials or other citizens of those countries. This Section C examines questions of individual civil liabiltiy, while Chapter 14 examines individual criminal liability.

The most important line of civil cases involves the US Alien Tort Statute (ATS), legislation dating back to 1789 but given new life by the *Filartiga* decision of 1980. That decision has been used as a reference point for over 100 cases. The US Torture Victim Protection Act of 1992, p. 1069, *infra*, has added another dimension to the opportunities afforded by the ATS. In addition, courts in other countries have begun to entertain private law causes of action as a means for seeking redress for human rights violations. One result is that the central concerns of private international law (jurisdiction, including *forum non conveniens*[23] and state immunity; choice of law, including 'act of state'; and enforcement of judgments) are now increasingly relevant to litigation based on human rights law.

The Alien Tort Statute decisions, though resting on a federal statute, involve themes about customary international law that were first explored in Chapter 2; the statute by its terms requires courts to refer to such law. Recall *The Paquete Habana*, p. 59, *supra*, and its illustration of earlier, traditional approaches to identifying international customary norms. Recall also Section C of Chapter 3 on the continuing role of custom. Compare the approach to customary law in the *Filartiga* decision that follows, in terms of (i) the court's method and argument, and (ii) the kinds of legal and other materials drawn on by the court as it decides whether a given norm has been established at customary international law.

FILARTIGA v. PENA-IRALA
United States Court of Appeals, Second Circuit, 1980
630 F.2d 876

[The plaintiffs, Paraguayan citizens who arrived in the United States in 1978, were Dr. Joel Filartiga, a physician and longstanding opponent of the then military government, and his daughter, Dolly. They brought suit in New York against Americao Pena-Irala (Pena), who in March 1976 was Inspector General of Police in Asuncion, Paraguay. Plaintiffs alleged that he was responsible for kidnapping and torturing to death Dr. Filartiga's 17-year-old son, Joelito, in retaliation for his

---

[23] A common law doctrine which allows, or may even require, courts to decide not to take jurisdiction over a case because another country's court system is better suited to hear the case.

father's political activities and beliefs. Dr. Filartiga had initiated a criminal action in Paraguay against Pena. His attorney was arrested, shackled to a wall, threatened with death by Pena, and then disbarred without just cause.

In July 1978, Pena entered the United States under a visitor's visa, and remained in Brooklyn after its expiry. Dolly Filartiga, then living in Washington, DC, learned of his presence, and requested that he be arrested by the Immigration and Naturalization Service. He was subsequently ordered to be deported on 5 April, 1979. The Filartigas then served a summons on Pena at the Brooklyn Navy Yard, where he was being held pending deportation, alleging that Pena had wrongfully caused Joelito's death by torture and seeking compensatory and punitive damages of $10,000,000. They also sought to enjoin Pena's deportation to ensure his availability for testimony at trial. The cause of action was stated as arising under 'wrongful death statutes; the U.N. Charter; the Universal Declaration on Human Rights; the U.N. Declaration Against Torture; the American Declaration of the Rights and Duties of Man; and other pertinent declarations, documents and practices constituting the customary international law of human rights and the law of nations'.

Jurisdiction was claimed principally under the Alien Tort Statute. Two federal jurisdictional statutes are relevant to the opinion's discussion of the issue of jurisdiction:

> 28 U.S.C. §1331: The district courts shall have original jurisdiction of all civil actions arising under the Constitution, laws, or treaties of the United States.
> 28 U.S.C. §1332: 'The district courts shall have original jurisdiction of all civil actions where the matter in controversy exceeds [$50,000] and is between: [citizens of different states of the United States; or citizens of such a state and citizens of a foreign state] . . .

Pena moved to dismiss the complaint for lack of subject matter jurisdiction and because of *forum non conveniens*. There was no suggestion of diplomatic immunity from suit. Pena claimed that Paraguayan law provided a full and adequate civil remedy, but Dr. Filartiga justified not having commenced such an action on the grounds that it would be futile. On 22 May, 1979, the appellant's applications for further stays of deportation were denied and Pena returned to Paraguay. Judge Nickerson dismissed the complaint for want of subject matter jurisdiction, so that the motion to dismiss on *forum non conveniens* grounds was not before the appellate court.]

IRVING R. KAUFMAN, CIRCUIT JUDGE

[I]

. . .

Implementing the constitutional mandate for national control over foreign relations, the First Congress established original district court jurisdiction over 'all causes where an alien sues for a tort only [committed] in violation of the law of nations'. Judiciary Act of 1789, ch. 20, 9(b), 1 Stat. 73, 77 (1789), *codified at 28*

U.S.C. §1350. Construing this rarely-invoked provision, we hold that deliberate torture perpetrated under color of official authority violates universally accepted norms of the international law of human rights, regardless of the nationality of the parties. Thus, whenever an alleged torturer is found and served with process by an alien within our borders, §1350 provides federal jurisdiction. Accordingly, we reverse the judgment of the district court dismissing the complaint for want of federal jurisdiction.

. . .

[II]

Appellants rest their principal argument in support of federal jurisdiction upon the Alien Tort Statute, 28 U.S.C. §1350, which provides: 'The district courts shall have original jurisdiction of any civil action by an alien for a tort only, committed in violation of the law of nations or a treaty of the United States'. Since appellants do not contend that their action arises directly under a treaty of the United States, a threshold question on the jurisdictional issue is whether the conduct alleged violates the law of nations. In light of the universal condemnation of torture in numerous international agreements, and the renunciation of torture as an instrument of official policy by virtually all of the nations of the world (in principle if not in practice), we find that an act of torture committed by a state official against one held in detention violates established norms of the international law of human rights, and hence the law of nations.

The Supreme Court has enumerated the appropriate sources of international law. The law of nations 'may be ascertained by consulting the works of jurists, writing professedly on public law; or by the general usage and practice of nations; or by judicial decisions recognizing and enforcing that law'. *United States v. Smith*, 18 U.S. (5 Wheat.) 153, 160–61, 5 L.Ed. 57 (1820). . . . In *Smith*, a statute proscribing 'the crime of piracy [on the high seas] as defined by the law of nations', 3 Stat. 510(a) (1819), was held sufficiently determinate in meaning to afford the basis for a death sentence. The *Smith* Court discovered among the works of Lord Bacon, Grotius, Bochard and other commentators a genuine consensus that rendered the crime 'sufficiently and constitutionally defined'.

[The Court then discussed *The Paquete Habana*, p. 59, *supra*, stressing its lesson that 'courts must interpret international law not as it was in 1789, but as it has evolved and exists among the nations of the world today'].

The requirement that a rule command the 'general assent of civilized nations' to become binding upon them all is a stringent one. Were this not so, the courts of one nation might feel free to impose idiosyncratic legal rules upon others, in the name of applying international law. Thus, in *Banco Nacional de Cuba v. Sabbatino*, 376 U.S. 398, 84 S.Ct. 923, the Court declined to pass on the validity of the Cuban government's expropriation of a foreign-owned corporation's assets, noting the sharply conflicting views on the issue propounded by the capital-exporting, capital-importing, socialist and capitalist nations. Id. at 428–30, 84 S.Ct. at 940–41.

The case at bar presents us with a situation diametrically opposed to the conflicted state of law that confronted the *Sabbatino* Court. Indeed, to paraphrase that Court's statement, id. at 428, 84 S.Ct. at 940, there are few, if any, issues in international law today on which opinion seems to be so united as the limitations on a state's power to torture persons held in its custody.

The United Nations Charter . . . makes it clear that in this modern age a state's treatment of its own citizens is a matter of international concern [Articles 55 and 56 of the UN Charter are then cited].

. . .

While this broad mandate has been held not to be wholly self-executing, Hitai v. Immigration and Naturalization Service, 343 F.2d 466, 468 (2d Cir.1965), this observation alone does not end our inquiry. For although there is no universal agreement as to the precise extent of the 'human rights and fundamental freedoms' guaranteed to all by the Charter, there is at present no dissent from the view that the guaranties include, at a bare minimum, the right to be free from torture. This prohibition has become part of customary international law, as evidenced and defined by the Universal Declaration of Human Rights, General Assembly Resolution 217 (III)(A) (Dec. 10, 1948) which states, in the plainest of terms, 'no one shall be subjected to torture'. The General Assembly has declared that the Charter precepts embodied in this Universal Declaration 'constitute basic principles of international law'. G.A.Res. 2625 (XXV) (Oct. 24, 1970).

Particularly relevant is the [General Assembly] Declaration on the Protection of All Persons from Being Subjected to Torture [which provides, inter alia] that '[w]here it is proved that an act of torture or other cruel, inhuman or degrading treatment or punishment has been committed by or at the instigation of a public official, the victim shall be afforded redress and compensation, in accordance with national law'.

. . .

. . . [A] U.N. Declaration is, according to one authoritative definition, 'a formal and solemn instrument, suitable for rare occasions when principles of great and lasting importance are being enunciated'. . . . Accordingly, it has been observed that the Universal Declaration of Human Rights 'no longer fits into the dichotomy of 'binding treaty' against 'nonbinding pronouncement,' but is rather an authoritative statement of the international community.' *E. Schwelb, Human Rights and the International Community* 70 (1964). Thus, a Declaration creates an expectation of adherence, and 'insofar as the expectation is gradually justified by State practice, a declaration may by custom become recognized as laying down rules binding upon the States'. 34 U.N. ESCOR supra. Indeed, several commentators have concluded that the Universal Declaration has become, *in toto*, a part of binding, customary international law. . . .

. . . The international consensus surrounding torture has found expression in numerous international treaties and accords. . . . The substance of these international agreements is reflected in modern municipal—i.e. national—law as well. Although torture was once a routine concomitant of criminal interrogations in many nations, during the modern and hopefully more enlightened era it has been universally renounced. According to one survey, torture is prohibited, expressly or implicitly, by the constitutions of over fifty-five nations, including both the United States and Paraguay. . . . We have been directed to no assertion by any contemporary state of a right to torture its own or another nation's citizens. Indeed, United States diplomatic contacts confirm the universal abhorrence with which torture is viewed:

> In exchanges between United States embassies and all foreign states with which the United States maintains relations, it has been the Department of State's general experience that no government has asserted a right to torture its own nationals. Where reports of torture elicit some credence, a state usually responds by denial or, less frequently, by asserting that the conduct was unauthorized or constituted rough treatment short of torture.[24] (Memorandum of the United States as *Amicus Curiae* at 16 n. 34.)

Having examined the sources from which customary international law is derived—the usage of nations, judicial opinions and the works of jurists—we conclude that official torture is now prohibited by the law of nations. The prohibition is clear and unambiguous, and admits of no distinction between treatment of aliens and citizens. Accordingly, we must conclude that the dictum in *Dreyfus v. von Finck*, [534 F.2d 24 (2d Cir.1976), at 31] to the effect that 'violations of international law do not occur when the aggrieved parties are nationals of the acting state', is clearly out of tune with the current usage and practice of international law. The treaties and accords cited above, as well as the express foreign policy of our own government, all make it clear that international law confers fundamental rights upon all people vis-a-vis their own governments. While the ultimate scope of those rights will be a subject for continuing refinement and elaboration, we hold that the right to be free from torture is now among them. We therefore turn to the question whether the other requirements for jurisdiction are met.

[III]

. . .

It is not extraordinary for a court to adjudicate a tort claim arising outside of its territorial jurisdiction. A state or nation has a legitimate interest in the orderly resolution of disputes among those within its borders, and where the *lex loci delicti commissi* is applied, it is an expression of comity to give effect to the laws of the state where the wrong occurred. . . .

. . . Here, where *in personam* jurisdiction has been obtained over the defendant, the parties agree that the acts alleged would violate Paraguayan law, and the

---

[24] The fact that the prohibition of torture is often honoured in the breach does not diminish its binding effect as a norm of international law. As one commentator has put it, 'The best evidence for the existence of international law is that every actual State recognizes that it does exist and that it is itself under an obligation to observe it. States often violate international law, just as individuals often violate municipal law; but no more than individuals do States defend their violations by claiming that they are above the law': J. Brierly, *The Outlook for International Law* (1944) at 4–5.

policies of the forum are consistent with the foreign law,[25] state court jurisdiction would be proper. Indeed, appellees conceded as much at oral argument.

... [W]e proceed to consider whether the First Congress acted constitutionally in vesting jurisdiction over 'foreign suits', ... alleging torts committed in violation of the law of nations. A case properly 'aris[es]' under the ... laws of the United States' for Article III purposes if grounded upon statutes enacted by Congress or upon the common law of the United States.... The law of nations forms an integral part of the common law, and a review of the history surrounding the adoption of the Constitution demonstrates that it became a part of the common law *of the United States* upon the adoption of the Constitution. Therefore, the enactment of the Alien Tort Statute was authorized by Article III.

During the eighteenth century, it was taken for granted on both sides of the Atlantic that the law of nations forms a part of the common law. 1 Blackstone, Commentaries 263–64 (1st Ed. 1765–69); 4 id. at 67....

...

As ratified, the judiciary article contained no express reference to cases arising under the law of nations. Indeed, the only express reference to that body of law is contained in Article I, sec. 8, cl. 10, which grants to the Congress the power to 'define and punish ... offenses against the law of nations'. Appellees seize upon this circumstance and advance the proposition that the law of nations forms a part of the laws of the United States only to the extent that Congress has acted to define it. This extravagant claim is amply refuted by the numerous decisions applying rules of international law uncodified in any act of Congress. E.g. [... *The Paquete Habana*, and *Sabbatino*, supra.] ...

The Filartigas urge that 28 U.S.C. §1350 be treated as an exercise of Congress's power to define offenses against the law of nations. While such a reading is possible ... we believe it is sufficient here to construe the Alien Tort Statute, not as granting new rights to aliens, but simply as opening the federal courts for adjudication of the rights already recognized by international law. The statute nonetheless does inform our analysis of Article III, for we recognize that questions of jurisdiction 'must be considered part of an organic growth—part of an evolutionary process', and that the history of the judiciary article gives meaning to its pithy phrases. *Romero v. International Terminal Operating Co.*, 358 U.S. 354, 360, 79 S.Ct. 468, 473 (1959). The Framers' overarching concern that control over international affairs be vested in the new national government to safeguard the standing of the United States among the nations of the world therefore reinforces the result we reach today.

... The paucity of suits successfully maintained under the section is readily attributable to the statute's requirement of alleging a '*violation* of the law of nations' (emphasis supplied) at the jurisdictional threshold. Courts have, accordingly, engaged in a more searching preliminary review of the merits than is required, for example, under the more flexible 'arising under' formulation.... Thus, the narrowing construction that the Alien Tort Statute has previously

---

[25] Conduct of the type alleged here would be actionable under 42 U.S.C. 1983 or, undoubtedly, the Constitution, if performed by a government official.

received reflects the fact that earlier cases did not involve such well-established, universally recognized norms of international law that are here at issue.

[Discussion omitted of prior decisions under the Alien Tort Statute involving different fact situations and distinct claims such as suits for fraud or for wilful negligence leading to an accident.]

Since federal jurisdiction may properly be exercised over the Filartigas' claim, the action must be remanded for further proceedings. Appellee Pena, however, advances several additional points that lie beyond the scope of our holding on jurisdiction. Both to emphasize the boundaries of our holding, and to clarify some of the issues reserved for the district court on remand, we will address these contentions briefly.

[IV]

Pena argues that the customary law of nations, as reflected in treaties and declarations that are not self-executing, should not be applied as rules of decision in this case. In doing so, he confuses the question of federal jurisdiction under the Alien Tort Statute, which requires consideration of the law of nations, with the issue of the choice of law to be applied, which will be addressed at a later stage in the proceedings. The two issues are distinct. Our holding on subject matter jurisdiction decides only whether Congress intended to confer judicial power, and whether it is authorized to do so by Article III. The choice of law inquiry is a much broader one, primarily concerned with fairness, see *Home Insurance Co. v. Dick*, 281 U.S. 397, 50 S.Ct. 338, 74 L.Ed. 926 (1930); consequently, it looks to wholly different considerations. See *Lauritzen v. Larsen*, 345 U.S. 571, 73 S.Ct. 921, 97 L.Ed. 1254 (1954). Should the district court decide that the *Lauritzen* analysis requires it to apply Paraguayan law, our courts will not have occasion to consider what law would govern a suit under the Alien Tort Statute where the challenged conduct is actionable under the law of the forum and the law of nations but not the law of the jurisdiction in which the tort occurred.

Pena also argues that '[i]f the conduct complained of is alleged to be the act of the Paraguayan government, the suit is barred by the Act of State doctrine'. This argument was not advanced below, and is therefore not before us on this appeal. We note in passing, however, that we doubt whether action by a state official in violation of the Constitution and laws of the Republic of Paraguay, and wholly unratified by that nation's government, could properly be characterized as an act of state. Paraguay's renunciation of torture as a legitimate instrument of state policy, however, does not strip the tort of its character as an international law violation, if it in fact occurred under color of government authority. . . .

. . .

In the twentieth century the international community has come to recognize the common danger posed by the flagrant disregard of basic human rights and particularly the right to be free of torture. Spurred first by the Great War, and then the Second, civilized nations have banded together to prescribe acceptable norms of international behavior. From the ashes of the Second World War arose the United Nations Organization, amid hopes that an era of peace and cooperation had at last begun. Though many of these aspirations have remained elusive goals, that circumstance cannot diminish the true progress that has been made. In the modern age, humanitarian and practical considerations have combined to lead the nations of the world to recognize that respect for fundamental human rights is in their individual and collective interest. Among the rights universally proclaimed by all nations, as we have noted, is the right to be free of physical torture. Indeed, for purposes of civil liability, the torturer has become—like the pirate and slave trader before him—*hostis humani generis*, an enemy of all mankind. Our holding today, giving effect to a jurisdictional provision enacted by our First Congress, is a small but important step in the fulfillment of the ageless dream to free all people from brutal violence.

NOTE

Following remand, the defendant took no part in the action and a default judgment was entered. The district court, 577 F. Supp. 860 (E.D.N.Y. 1984), awarded punitive damages of $5,000,000 to each plaintiff, so that the total judgment amounted to $10,385,364. The judgment was never collected.

Like many cases under the ATS, *Filartiga* was undefended throughout, and the case ended in a default judgment. The appellate courts in these cases have frequently been required to rule on motions by defendants to dismiss for want of subject matter jurisdiction or for failure to state a cause of action. For purposes of their decisions on these matters, they have therefore taken plaintiffs' allegations as true. That is, such trial and appellate court decisions do not involve fact finding.

Filartiga and the following decisions under the ATS take different positions about the statute's purpose and effect and the bases for jurisdiction. Bear in mind some of the possible positions: (1) The only question before a court (as in the *Filartiga* decision) is subject matter jurisdiction. This is all that the ATS purports to do. It does not create a cause of action, point toward resolution of the merits, and so on. (2) The ATS creates a federal cause of action. The court fills in the remedial provisions. (3) The court can assert general federal question jurisdiction under 28 U.S.C. §1331, for the civil action is one 'arising under the . . . laws . . . of the United States'.

QUESTIONS

1. Describe the court's argument in concluding that torture is a violation of customary international law, a part of the 'law of nations' under §1350. Compare and contrast the approach of the Supreme Court in *The Paquete Habana*. Specifically:

  (a) What use is made in *Filartiga* of UN resolutions and declarations and of human rights treaties? What relevance to this case have those treaties?

(b) Does the court's conception of custom stress consensus over norms or over practice? What is the relation between the two?

(c) How would you criticize the court's resort to practice about torture within states to support its finding of an international custom?

(d) What relevance to this decision has the classical notion of *opinio juris*?

2. Note the difficulty in drawing on the 'law of nations' to support civil cases like those under the ATS rather than criminal cases.

(a) What relevance to this decision has, for example, the Nuremberg precedent, p. 115, *supra*?

(b) Do the universal and regional human rights treaties provide for civil remedies against individuals who commit human rights violations?

(c) What relevance to this issue has Article 8 of the UDHR or Article 2(3) of the ICCPR?

COMMENT ON THE TEL-OREN CASE

In 1978, in a few violent hours, members of the Palestine Liberation Organization (PLO) entered Israel for a terrorist raid, killing 24 people and wounding 77 more. With few exceptions, the victims were Israeli civilians. Plaintiffs in *Tel-Oren v. Libyan Arab Republic*, 726 F. 2d 774 (D.C. Cir. 1984), included most of the wounded and survivors of most of the killed. Plaintiffs alleged that the PLO had trained the terrorists and planned the raid, and that Libya had participated. Jurisdiction was claimed under 28 U.S.C. §1331 and under the Alien Tort Statute, 28 U.S.C. §1350. The court of appeals affirmed *per curiam* a dismissal by the district court for want of subject matter jurisdiction. Each of the three judges wrote a separate opinion. The description below of two of the opinions deals only with the claim under the Alien Tort Statute and only with the PLO as defendant.

In his opinion, *Judge Edwards* drew on the *Filartiga* decision, *supra*, stressing its observation that the law of nations was not stagnant but should be construed 'as it exists today among the nations of the world', and its conclusion that §1350 opened federal courts for 'adjudication of rights already recognized by international law'. Plaintiffs were not required to point to a specific right to sue under the law of nations in order to establish jurisdiction under §1350. That section requires only that the action rest upon a violation of the law of nations. This permits countries 'to meet their international obligations as they will'—or as a treaty (no such treaty being relevant to this case) might specifically provide.

One could infer from *Filartiga*, said Judge Edwards, that persons could be subject to civil liability under §1350 either by (i) committing a crime that traditionally warranted universal jurisdiction (such as the criminal prosecution of a pirate or slave trader) or (ii) committing an offence comparably violating contemporary international law. Commentators had begun to identify 'a handful of heinous actions—each of which violates definable, universal and obligatory norms—and in the process are defining the limits of section §1350's reach'. Judge Edwards referred to a then current draft of the *Restatement of the Law of Foreign Relations* that included as violations of customary international law murder and torture, both of which were within plaintiffs' allegations.

Nonetheless, Judge Edwards affirmed the dismissal on grounds that the PLO was not a recognized state, and that (unlike *Filartiga*) the case did not therefore involve 'official torture' or persons acting under color of state law. He was unwilling to extend the notion of the law of nations (and hence §1350) to include conduct of non-state actors. Nor, alternatively, was he willing to view terrorism (by analogy to piracy) as a violation itself of the law of nations that, without any state's involvement, led to individual responsibility of those committing terrorist acts.

Judge Bork took a very different position. He argued that §1350 was no more than a grant of jurisdiction to federal courts, and criticized the opinion in *Filartiga* for its failure to inquire whether international law created a cause of action enforceable by private parties in municipal (national) courts. Recalling that there was no concept of international human rights in 1789, Judge Bork stressed that neither was there any recognition of a right of private parties to recover under customary international law. 'That problem is not avoided by observing that the law of nations evolves'. Contemporary customary international law should not be construed to create such a civil action, for international law is fundamentally a law among states in which individuals have no direct enforcement or other role.

In these types of cases, Judge Bork continued, the understanding of international law argued for by §1350 plaintiffs would require that 'our courts must sit in judgment of the conduct of foreign officials in their own countries with respect to their own citizens'. To recognize such an action would amount to 'judicial interference with nonjudicial functions, such as the conduct of foreign relations'. Adjudication 'would present grave separation of powers problems'. A different conclusion might be reached if §1350 'had been adopted by a modern Congress that made clear its desire that federal courts police the behavior of foreign individuals and governments'.

Drawing on Blackstone, Judge Bork concluded that the 1789 Congress enacting the Alien Tort Statute might have been thinking of the then principal offences by individuals against the law of nations: violation of safe-conducts, infringement of rights of ambassadors, and piracy. This modest list of civil actions based on the law of nations continues in effect today. Nor should the contemporary human rights treaties be construed to create private causes of action, except where (as with respect to the European Human Rights Convention) they specifically do so.

COMMENT ON THE ACT-OF-STATE DOCTRINE AND SOVEREIGN IMMUNITY

The Act-of-State Doctrine

In his observations about potential judicial interference with the conduct of foreign relations, Judge Bork drew on a strand of Supreme Court decisions dealing with the so-called act-of-state doctrine. That doctrine has figured prominently in recent decisions under the Alien Tort Statute (together with other doctrines and principles such as sovereign immunity and the political question defence).

Bypassing the complexities in the act-of-state doctrine and its exceptions, this Comment sketches some of its characteristics that are relevant to litigation under §1350. An early statement of the doctrine appears in *Underhill v. Hernandez*, 168 U.S. 250 (1897). An American citizen in Venezuela was operating under contract a local water system. Over a period of several months, a Venezuelan general effect-ively exercising governmental power denied him the necessary documents to per-mit him to leave, thus coercing him to continue his operations. That citizen later brought an action against the general in a US federal court to recover damages for unlawful detention. The Supreme Court affirmed a judgment for the defendant, stating in part:

> Every sovereign state is bound to respect the independence of every other sover-eign state, and the courts of one country will not sit in judgment on the acts of the government of another, done within its own territory. Redress of grievances by reason of such acts must be obtained through the means open to be availed of by sovereign powers as between themselves.

It agreed with the conclusion of the lower court that 'the acts of the defendant were the acts of the government of Venezuela, and as such are not properly the subject of adjudication in the courts of another government'.

The principal decision launching the act-of-state doctrine on its modern career is *Banco Nacional de Cuba v. Sabbatino*, 376 U.S. 398 (1964), a case involving a Cuban expropriation of sugar properties owned by US residents. The act-of-state issue arose in the context of deciding whether a US court would examine the legality of the Cuban expropriation and, if it were found illegal, would deny it effect.

It was the contention of the US commercial interests involved in the litigation that the doctrine did not apply to acts of state violating international law. Such a violation was claimed to have occurred in this case, since the compensation offered by Cuba did not meet an alleged customary international law standard of prompt, adequate and effective compensation for takings by a state of alien-owned prop-erty. The Supreme Court, however, pointed out that this standard was disputed among states. 'There are few if any issues in international law today on which opinion seems to be so divided as the limitations on a state's power to expropriate the property of aliens'.

In finding the act-of-state-doctrine applicable (thus leading to the presumed legitimacy of the Cuban expropriation), Justice Harlan wrote for the Court:

> [The doctrine's] continuing vitality depends on its capacity to reflect the proper distribution of functions between the judicial and political branches of the Gov-ernment on matters bearing upon foreign affairs. It should be apparent that the greater the degree of codification or consensus concerning a particular area of international law, the more appropriate it is for the judiciary to render decisions regarding it, since the courts can then focus on the application of an agreed

principle to circumstances of fact rather than on the sensitive task of establishing a principle not inconsistent with the national interests or with international justice. It is also evident that some aspects of international law touch more sharply on national nerves than do others; the less important the implications of an issue are for our foreign relations, the weaker the justification for exclusivity in the political branches. . . . Therefore, rather than laying down or reaffirming an inflexible and all-encompassing rule in this case, we decide only that the Judicial Branch will not examine the validity of a taking of property within its own territory by a foreign sovereign government . . . in the absence of a treaty or other unambiguous agreement regarding controlling legal principles, even if the complaint alleges that the taking violates customary international law.

The *Sabbatino* decision, together with later decisions in this field, stress the relevance to the doctrine's application of several other factors, including whether the Executive Branch (generally the Department of State) informs a court that it opposes judicial examination of the legality of the foreign government's act on the ground of the act-of-state doctrine.

Sovereign Immunity

Recall Judge Edward's opinion in the *Tel-Oren* case dismissing the $1350 action because the PLO was not a recognized state and thus could not commit 'official torture' or take action under color of state law. However, had the PLO been a recognized state, a judicial action would have been barred under the doctrine of sovereign immunity, as indeed was the case with the Government of Libya, the second defendant in *Tel-Oren*. This question of sovereign immunity has frequently arisen in cases under the Alien Tort Statute, sometimes in a close relation to the act-of-state doctrine.

The Foreign Sovereign Immunities Act of 1976 (FSIA), codified principally at 22 U.S.C.A. 1602–11, provides a comprehensive legislative framework for deciding on claims of foreign defendants for immunity. Foreign states, including 'an agency or instrumentality' thereof, are immune from judicial jurisdiction, subject to enumerated exceptions. Those exceptions include court actions growing out of a state's commercial activities occurring in the United States, and actions involving property expropriated by the foreign government in violation of international law.

Argentine Republic v. Amerada Hess Shipping Corp., 488 U.S. 428 (1989) involved a $1350 action growing out of the Falklands (Malvinas) war between the UK and Argentina. It was based on the damage to plaintiff's ship by an attack of Argentinian aircraft. Plaintiff claimed that the attack was in violation of international law. The Supreme Court refused to draw an exception to the rule of immunity for suits under the Alien Tort Statute because of Argentina's alleged violation of international law. It drew from the FSIA 'the plain implication that immunity is granted in those cases involving alleged violations of international law that do not come within one of the FSIA's exceptions'.

Saudi Arabia v. Nelson, 507 U.S. 349 (1993), involved tort claims based on alleged human rights violations. The Supreme Court held that alleged acts of unlawful detention and torture by the defendant state did not fall within any of the

FSIA's exceptions. It concluded that '[t]he conduct [complained of by plaintiff] boils down to abuse of the power of its police by the Saudi Government, and however monstrous such abuse undoubtedly may be, a foreign state's exercise of the power of its police has long been understood . . . as peculiarly sovereign in nature'. Sovereign immunity was granted Saudi Arabia.

In *Siderman de Blake v. Republic of Argentina*, 965 F.2d 699 (9th Cir. 1992), the court of appeals agreed with the plaintiff's argument that official acts of torture attributed to Argentina constituted a violation of a *jus cogens* norm of the 'highest status within international law'. Nonetheless, taking its lesson from the *Amareda Hess* decision in which the Supreme Court was so specific, the court concluded that it was Congress that would have to make any further exceptions to sovereign immunity. 'The fact that there has been a violation of *jus cogens* does not confer jurisdiction under the FSIA.'

In *Al-Adsani v. Government of Kuwait* (1996) 107 I.L.R. 536, the English Court of Appeal reached the same conclusion when it dismissed an action for damages in tort by the plaintiff who claimed to have been tortured in Kuwait. In holding that Kuwait was entitled to immunity, the court rejected the argument that the prohibition of torture is a *jus cogens* norm which overrides even the principle of sovereign immunity.

In view of the FSIA and the decisional law described above, US plaintiffs in §1350 actions have sought to avoid the issue of sovereign immunity by suing not the state itself but individual perpetrators—as indeed occurred in *Filartiga*. Courts required to sort out the relevance of sovereign immunity when individual defendants are before it have taken different approaches in characterizing the relationship between the individual and the state.

Consider *In re Estate of Ferdinand Marcos*, 25 F.3d 1467 (9th Cir. 1994). The court held that the FSIA did not bar jurisdiction under §1350 over the estate of former President Ferdinand Marcos for alleged acts of torture and wrongful death, since those were not official acts perpetrated within the scope of his official authority in the Philippines but rather acts outside the scope of his authority as President.[26] Quoting from a prior related case, the court said that '[o]ur courts have had no difficulty in distinguishing the legal acts of a deposed ruler from his acts for personal profit that lack a basis in law'. At the same time, the requirement of state action under the definition of official torture (recall Judge Edward's discussion of this issue in *Tel-Oren*) could still be met by an official acting under colour of authority, though not within an official mandate. That is, such an official could violate international law for purposes of the Alien Tort Statute.

All these issues are raised by the *Suarez-Mason* decision that follows.

---

[26] Subsequently the court awarded almost $2 billion in compensatory and corrective damages against Marcos, but no payment had been made as of February 2000. See *Hilao v. Estate of Marcos*, 103 F.3d 767 (9th Cir. 1996).

FORTI v. SUAREZ-MASON
United States District Court, Northern District California, 1987
672 F. Supp. 1531

MEMORANDUM DECISION AND ORDER, JENSEN, DISTRICT JUDGE.

. . .

[I] Facts

This is a civil action brought against a former Argentine general by two Argentine citizens currently residing in the United States. Plaintiffs Forti and Benchoam sue on their own behalf and on behalf of family members, seeking damages from defendant Suarez-Mason for actions which include, *inter alia*, torture, murder, and prolonged arbitrary detention, allegedly committed by military and police personnel under defendant's authority and control. . . .

. . .

Plaintiff's action arises out of events alleged to have occurred in the mid to late 1970s during Argentina's so-called 'dirty war' against suspected subversives. In 1975 the activities of terrorists representing the extremes of both ends of the political spectrum induced the constitutional government of President Peron to declare a 'state of siege' under Article 23 of the Argentine Constitution. President Peron also decreed that the Argentine Armed Forces should assume responsibility for suppressing terrorism. The country was accordingly divided into defense zones, each assigned to an army corps. In each zone the military was authorized to detain suspects and hold them in prison or in military installations pursuant to the terms of the 'state of siege'. Zone One—which included most of the Province of Buenos Aires and encompassed the national capital—was assigned to the First Army Corps. From January 1976 until January 1979 defendant Suarez-Mason was Commander of the First Army Corps.

On March 24, 1976 the commanding officers of the Armed Forces seized the government from President Peron. The ruling military junta continued the 'state of siege' and caused the enactment of legislation providing that civilians accused of crimes of subversion would be judged by military law. In the period from 1976 to 1979, tens of thousands of persons were detained without charges by the military, and it is estimated that more than 12,000 were 'disappeared', never to be seen again. *See generally Nunca Mas: The Report of the Argentine National Commission on the Disappeared* (1986).

In January 1984 the constitutionally elected government of President Raul Alfonsin assumed power. The Alfonsin government commenced investigations of alleged human rights abuses by the military, and the criminal prosecution of certain former military authorities followed. The government vested the Supreme Council of the Armed Forces with jurisdiction over the prosecution of military commanders. Summoned by the Supreme Council in March 1984, defendant failed to appear and in fact fled the country. In January of 1987 Suarez-Mason was arrested in Foster City, California pursuant to a provisional arrest warrant at the request of the Republic of Argentina. While defendant was in custody awaiting an extradition hearing he was served with the Complaint herein.

[The court described the allegations in the Complaint about acts committed in the zone under the defendant's command. Those acts included (a) the torture, killing and continued disappearance of several family members of the plaintiffs, (b) harsh imprisonment without judicial process of one plaintiff for four years, (c) abduction and seizure of family members without charge, and (d) the seizure of personal property.]

Although the individual acts are alleged to have been committed by military and police officials, plaintiffs allege that these actors were all agents, employees, or representatives of defendant acting pursuant to a 'policy, pattern and practice' of the First Army Corps under defendant's command. Plaintiffs assert that defendant 'held the highest position of authority' in Buenos Aires Province; that defendant was responsible for maintaining the prisons and detention centers there, as well as the conduct of Army officers and agents; and that he 'authorized, approved, directed and ratified' the acts complained of.

... Although both plaintiffs retain their Argentine citizenship, both reside currently in Virginia. Plaintiffs predicate federal jurisdiction principally on the 'Alien Tort Statute', 28 U.S.C. §1350, and alternatively on federal question jurisdiction, 28 U.S.C. 1331. Additionally, they assert jurisdiction for their common-law tort claims under principles of pendent and ancillary jurisdiction.

Based on these above allegations, plaintiffs seek compensatory and punitive damages for violations of customary international law and laws of the United States, Argentina, and California. They press eleven causes of action. Both allege claims for torture; prolonged arbitrary detention without trial; cruel, inhuman and degrading treatment; false imprisonment; assault and battery; intentional infliction of emotional distress; and conversion. Additionally Forti claims damages for 'causing the disappearance of individuals', and Benchoam asserts claims for 'murder and summary execution', wrongful death, and a survival action.
...

[II] Subject Matter Jurisdiction

As a threshold matter, defendant argues that the Court lacks subject matter jurisdiction under 28 U.S.C. §1350, the 'Alien Tort Statute'. Defendant urges the Court to follow the interpretation of §1350 as a purely jurisdictional statute which requires that plaintiffs invoking it establish the existence of an independent, private right of action in international law. Defendant argues that the law of nations provides no tort cause of action for the acts of 'politically motivated terrorism' challenged by plaintiffs' Complaint. Alternatively, defendant argues that even if §1350 provides a cause of action for violations of the law of nations, not all of the torts alleged by plaintiffs qualify as violations of the law of nations. For the reasons set out below, the Court rejects defendant's construction of §1350 and finds that plaintiffs allege sufficient facts to establish subject matter jurisdiction under both the Alien Tort Statute and 28 U.S.C. §1331. ...

A. *The Alien Tort Statute*

[The court agreed with the views of Judge Edwards in *Tel-Oren v. Libyan Arab Republic*, 726 F.2d (D.C. Cir. 1984), *supra*. Plaintiffs are not required to 'establish the existence of an independent express right of action' under the law of nations, for that law doesn't create or define civil actions. Hence such a requirement 'would effectively nullify' a vital portion of §1350. That section provides both for jurisdiction and for a federal cause of action arising by recognition of certain 'international common law torts'. As indicated in Judge Edward's opinion, such an international tort must be 'definable, obligatory (rather than hortatory) and universally condemned .... The requirement of international consensus is of paramount importance. ... ']

B. *Analysis under 28 U.S.C. §1350*

In determining whether plaintiffs have stated cognizable claims under Section §1350, the Court has recourse to 'the works of jurists, writing professedly on public law; ... the general usage and practice of nations; [and] judicial decisions recognizing and enforcing that law'. *United States* v. *Smith*, 18 U.S. (5 Wheat.) 153, 160–61, 5 L.Ed. 57 (1820). . . .

1. *Official torture*

In Count One, plaintiffs both allege torture conducted by military and police personnel under defendant's command. The Court has no doubt that official torture constitutes a cognizable violation of the law of nations under §1350. . . . The claim would thus allege torture committed by *state officials* and so fall within the international tort first recognized in *Filartiga*.

2. *Prolonged arbitrary detention*

. . .

There is case law finding sufficient consensus to evince a customary international human rights norm against arbitrary detention. . . .

The consensus is even clearer in the case of a state's *prolonged* arbitrary detention of its own citizens. *See, e.g., Restatement (Revised) of the Foreign Relations Law of the United States* 702 (Tenth Draft No. 6, 1985) (prolonged arbitrary detention by state constitutes international law violation). The norm is obligatory, and is readily definable in terms of the arbitrary character of the detention. The Court finds that plaintiffs have alleged international tort claims for prolonged arbitrary detention.

3. *Summary execution*

. . .

The proscription of summary execution or murder by the state appears to be universal, is readily definable, and is of course obligatory. The Court emphasizes that plaintiff's allegations raise no issue as to whether or not the execution was within the lawful exercise of state power; rather, she alleges murder by state officials with neither authorization nor recourse to any process of law. Under these circumstances, the Court finds that plaintiff Benchoam has stated a cognizable claim under §1350 for the 1977 murder/summary execution of her brother by Argentine military personnel.

4. Causing disappearance

. . .

Sadly, the practice of 'disappearing' individuals—i.e., abduction, secret detention, and torture, followed generally by either secret execution or release—during Argentina's 'dirty war' is now well documented in the official report of the Argentine National Commission on the Disappeared *Nunca Mas.* Nor are such practices necessarily restricted to Argentina. With mounting publicity over the years, such conduct has begun to draw censure as a violation of the basic right to life. Plaintiff cites a 1978 United Nations resolution and a 1980 congressional resolution to this effect. U.N.G.A.Res. /173 (1978); H.R.Con.Res. 285, 96th Cong., 2d Sess. The Court notes, too, that the proposed Restatement of the Law of Foreign Relations lists 'the murder or causing the disappearance of individuals', where practiced, encouraged, or condoned by the state, as a violation of international law. However, plaintiffs do not cite the Court to any case finding that causing the disappearance of an individual constitutes a violation of the law of nations.

Before this Court may adjudicate a tort claim under §1350, it must be satisfied that the legal standard it is to apply is one with universal acceptance and definition; on no other basis may the Court exercise jurisdiction over a claimed violation of the law of nations. Unfortunately, the Court cannot say, on the basis of the evidence submitted, that there yet exists the requisite degree of international consensus which demonstrates a customary international norm. Even if there were greater evidence of universality, there remain definitional problems. It is not clear precisely what conduct falls within the proposed norm, or how this proscription would differ from that of summary execution. . . . For instance, plaintiffs have not shown that customary international law creates a presumption of causing disappearance upon a showing of prolonged absence after initial custody.

For these reasons the Court must dismiss Count Four for failure to state a claim upon which relief may be grounded.

. . .

5. Cruel, inhuman and degrading treatment

Finally, in Count Five plaintiffs both allege a claim for 'cruel, inhuman and degrading treatment' based on the general allegations of the Complaint and consisting specifically of the alleged torture, murder, forcible disappearance and prolonged arbitrary detention.

This claim suffers the same defects as Count Four. Plaintiffs do not cite, and the Court is not aware of, such evidence of universal consensus regarding the right to be free from 'cruel, inhuman and degrading treatment' as exists, for example, with respect to official torture. Further, any such right poses problems of definability. . . . Accordingly, the Court dismisses Count Five of the Complaint for failure to state a claim upon which relief may be granted.

. . .

[The court also found jurisdiction under 28 U.S.C. 1331, which covers claims based on federal common law. It cited cases including *The Paquete Habana* for the proposition that federal common law incorporated international law.

The court, after describing decisions such as *Underhill* and *Sabbatino*, p. 1059 *supra*, next concluded that the act of state doctrine, which if applicable would block adjudication of the legality of defendant's conduct, did not apply. It said in part:]

. . . Defendant maintains that all of the challenged acts were taken pursuant to the 'state of siege' declared by the constitutional government and reaffirmed by the military junta. Thus, defendant argues, he was a government official acting under policies promulgated by the junta, and this Court cannot adjudicate the question of his liability without also passing on the question of the legality of the acts of the Argentine government. This, he concludes, is precisely the sort of case which the act of state doctrine removes from the courts' scrutiny.

. . .

Here, by contrast [with prior discussed decisions], plaintiffs allege acts by a subordinate government official in violation not of economic rights, but of fundamental human rights lying at the very heart of the individual's existence. These are not the public official acts of a head of government, nor is it clear at this stage of the proceedings to what extent defendant's acts were 'ratified' by the *de facto* military government. . . .

. . . [F]or purposes of §1350 a plaintiff must allege 'official' (as opposed to private) action—but this is not necessarily the governmental and public action contemplated by the act of state doctrine. That is, a police chief who tortures, or orders to be tortured, prisoners in his custody fulfills the requirement that his action be 'official' simply by virtue of his position and the circumstances of the act; his conduct may be wholly unratified by his government and even proscribed by its constitution and criminal statutes. . . .

. . . Inasmuch as this is a Rule 12(b)(6) motion, the Court must accept as true the allegations of the Complaint, and may not dismiss the Complaint unless plaintiffs can prove no set of facts to establish their claims. The Court cannot say at this stage of the proceedings that adjudication of plaintiffs' claims will necessarily entail considering the legality of the official acts of a foreign sovereign. [Defendant's motion to dismiss denied.]

. . .

NOTE

Plaintiffs in the above case filed a motion for reconsideration of the court's order dismissing the claims for 'disappearance' and 'cruel, inhuman or degrading treatment'. In *Forti v. Suarez-Mason*, 694 F. Supp. 707 (N.D. Cal. 1988), Judge Jensen denied reconsideration of the second claim. 'Plaintiffs' submissions fail to establish that there is anything even remotely approaching universal consensus as to what constitutes 'cruel, inhuman or degrading treatment.' He granted, however, plaintiffs' motion with respect to disappearance and reinstated that claim, stating in part:

> The legal scholars whose declarations have been submitted in connection with this Motion are in agreement that there is universal consensus as to the two essential elements of a claim for 'disappearance'. In Professor Franck's words:
>
>> The international community has also reached a consensus on the definition of a 'disappearance'. It has two essential elements: (a) abduction by a state official or by persons acting under state approval or authority; and (b) refusal by the state to acknowledge the abduction and detention.
>
> Plaintiffs cite numerous international legal authorities which support the assertion that 'disappearance' is a universally recognized wrong under the law of nations. For example, United Nations General Assembly Resolution 33/173 recognizes 'disappearance' as violative of many of the rights recognized in the [UDHR]. . . .
>
> Other documents support this characterization of 'disappearance' as violative of universally recognized human rights. The United States Congress has denounced 'prolonged detention without charges and trial' along with other 'flagrant denial[s] of the right to life, liberty, or the security of person'. 22 U.S.C. 2304 (d)(I). The recently published Restatement (Third) of the Foreign Relations Law of the United States 702 includes 'disappearance' as a violation of the international law of human rights. The Organization of American States has also denounced 'disappearance' as 'an affront to the conscience of the hemisphere and . . . a crime against humanity'. Organization of American States, Inter-American Commission on Human Rights, General Assembly Resolution 666 (November 18, 1983).

. . .

QUESTIONS

1. What differences do you see between the positions on the ATS of the opinions in *Filartiga* and *Suarez-Mason*?

2. Do you agree with the court's resolution of the defense of act of state? Does this case present a stronger argument than *Filartiga* for such a defense?

3. Suppose that the former dictatorial president of a state that continues to be governed by an authoritarian elite supported by the military is sued for wrongful death damages under the Alien Tort Statute when he is in the United States (where he owns valuable real property). The plaintiff produces convincing evidence of the torture and murder of his parents, political opponents of the defendant, on the orders of the defendant. Torture and killing (or forcing flight from the state through threats) were and continue to be the government's strategy for dealing with potentially threatening political opponents. The presidential successor to the defendant protests to the State Department this civil suit in the United States, which he views as an insult to the state's sovereignty. How should the court rule on the defences of act of state and sovereign immunity? How, for example, might the defendant distinguish the *Filartiga* decision?

4. The plaintiff, a citizen of state X now in the United States, brings an ATS action against a visiting official from X for categorically denying the plaintiff in X a permit to hold a parade in X's capital city. The parade's purpose was to publicize the programme of the opposition party in X (to which plaintiff belongs). X is a tightly controlled state in which opposition parties are permitted to operate within severe limits. Elections are sham, the press is censored, the jails hold some political prisoners. Assume that there is no issue of sovereign or diplomatic immunity. What problems do you see in such an action? How does the action differ from *Filartiga* and *Suarez-Mason*?

5. How do you assess the significance of ATS actions and decisions, given that the collection of damages in most (not all) cases is unlikely? From the perspective of the human rights movement or the development of that movement within the United States, are ATS actions helpful? Why? Can you see any disadvantages in them?

6. Following the *Pinochet* litigation (pp. 1198–1213, *supra*), one commentator suggested that:

> while states and state officials would continue to be held immune in civil proceedings in the United Kingdom for acts of torture . . ., as regards criminal proceedings they might be held accountable and no plea of immunity might be available to them. To the present writer this creates a manifest inconsistency which ought to be remedied by denying immunity also to state and state officials in civil proceedings.[27]

Is the argument for consistency a compelling reason to reject the reasoning in cases like *Al-Adsani* and *Nelson*, pp. 1060–61, *supra*?

NOTE

The prior judicial decisions have all examined customary international law in the context of applying the Alien Tort Statute. The statute demands such an examination. The ATS litigation has indeed been the principal occasion in recent years for US courts to explore that law in the field of human rights.

Absent some statutory foundation or reference, the customary international law of human rights has an uncertain status, influence or even relevance in US courts, particularly in federal courts concerned with issues of federal law, when it is relied on to challenge legislation or action by branches, agencies, or officials of the US government. In such contexts, the dispute may be entirely internal; a US citizen relies on customary international law to challenge the application, meaning or constitutionality of a federal statute or regulation. A contemporary illustration can be found in a criminal defendant's possible reliance on customary international law to challenge the legality of capital punishment in the United States in a case where, as applied, capital punishment would meet the US constitutional test. See pp. 31–9, *supra*.

---

[27] A. Bianchi, 'Immunity versus Human Rights: The *Pinochet* Case', 10 *Eur. J. Int. L.* 237 (1999), at 264.

This uncertainty about the significance of customary international law, relative to the formal constitutional status and significance of treaties, is not distinctive to the United States, as references to other states at pp. 999–1021, *supra*, suggest. Neither the decisional law of the US courts nor the *Restatement (Third), Foreign Relations Law of the United States* provides clear responses to a number of basic questions that claims by plaintiffs based on customary international law would pose. Of course that body of law is subject, like treaties and statutes, to the Constitution. But other questions abound, on which scholars too are in deep dispute.[28] For example:

relative rank within the US constitutional order of customary international law, and federal statutes, regulations or indeed common law;

when a customary norm becomes established in time, relative to an inconsistent federal statute's enactment;

the significance for courts of executive disavowal or interpretation of an asserted customary norm;

the relationship of customary international law to federal common law.

TORTURE VICTIM PROTECTION ACT
106 Stat. 73 (1992), 28 U.S.C.A. §1350 Notes

. . .

Section 2. Establishment of Civil Action

(a) LIABILITY.—An individual who, under actual or apparent authority, or color of law, of any foreign nation —

(1) subjects an individual to torture shall, in a civil action, be liable for damages to that individual; or

(2) subjects an individual to extrajudicial killing shall, in a civil action, be liable for damages to the individual's legal representative, or to any person who may be a claimant in an action for wrongful death.

(b) EXHAUSTION OF REMEDIES.—A court shall decline to hear a claim under this section if the claimant has not exhausted adequate and available remedies in the place in which the conduct giving rise to the claim occurred.

(c) STATUTE OF LIMITATIONS.—No action shall be maintained under this section unless it is commenced within 10 years after the cause of action arose.

Section 3. Definitions.

(a) EXTRAJUDICIAL KILLING.—For the purposes of this Act, the term 'extrajudicial killing' means a deliberated killing not authorized by a previous judgment pronounced by a regularly constituted court affording all the judicial guarantees which are recognized as indispensable by civilized peoples. Such term, however,

---

[28] See Additional Reading references at p. 1081, *infra*.

does not include any such killing that, under international law, is lawfully carried out under the authority of a foreign nation.

(b) TORTURE.—For the purposes of this Act —

(1) the term 'torture' means any act, directed against an individual in the offender's custody or physical control, by which severe pain or suffering (other than pain or suffering arising only from or inherent in; or incidental to; lawful sanctions), whether physical, or mental, is intentionally inflicted on that individual for such purposes as obtaining from that individual or a third person information or a confession, punishing that individual for an act that individual or a third person has committed or is suspected of having committed, intimidating or coercing that individual or a third person, or for any reason based on discrimination of any kind; and

(2) mental pain or suffering refers to prolonged mental harm caused by or resulting from —

(A) the intentional infliction or threatened infliction of severe physical pain or suffering;

(B) the administration or application, or threatened administration or application,of mind altering substances or other procedures calculated to disrupt profoundly the senses or the personality;

(C) the threat of imminent death; or

(D) the threat that another individual will imminently be subjected to death, severe physical pain or suffering, or the administration or application of mind altering substances or other procedures calculated to disrupt profoundly the senses or personality.

SENATE REPORT ON THE TORTURE VICTIM PROTECTION ACT
S. Rep. 102–249, Committee on the Judiciary, 102nd Cong., 1st Sess., 1991

. . . This legislation will carry out the intent of the Convention Against Torture and Other Cruel, Inhuman or Degrading Treatment or Punishment, which was ratified by the U.S. Senate on October 27, 1990. The convention obligates state parties to adopt measures to ensure that torturers within their territories are held legally accountable for their acts. This legislation will do precisely that—by making sure that torturers and death squads will no longer have a safe haven in the United States.

. . .

The TVPA would establish an unambiguous basis for a cause of action that has been successfully maintained under an existing law, section 1350 of title 28 of the U.S. Code. . . .

. . .

The TVPA would . . . enhance the remedy already available under section 1350 in an important respect: while the Alien Tort Claims Act provides a remedy to aliens only, the TVPA would extend a civil remedy also to U.S. citizens who may have been tortured abroad.

. . .

Congress clearly has authority to create a private right of action for torture and extrajudicial killings committed abroad. Under article III of the Constitution, the Federal judiciary has the power to adjudicate cases 'arising under' the 'laws of the United States'. The Supreme Court has held that the law of the United States includes international law. In *Verlinden B.V.* v. *Central Bank of Nigeria* 461 U.S. 480, 481 (1983), the Supreme Court held that the 'arising under' clause allows Congress to confer jurisdiction on U.S. courts to recognize claims brought by a foreign plaintiff against a foreign defendant. Congress' ability to enact this legislation also drives from article I, section 8 of the Constitution, which authorizes Congress 'to define and punish . . . Offenses against the Laws of Nations'.

IV. Analysis of Legislation

. . .

D. Who can be sued

First and foremost, only defendants over which a court in the United States has personal jurisdiction may be sued. In order for a Federal court to obtain personal jurisdiction over a defendant, the individual must have 'minimum contacts' with the forum state, for example through residency here or current travel. Thus, this legislation will not turn the U.S. courts into tribunals for torts having no connection to the United States whatsoever.

The legislation uses the term 'individual' to make crystal clear that foreign states or their entities cannot be sued under this bill under any circumstances: only individuals may be sued. Consequently, the TVPA is not meant to override the Foreign Sovereign Immunities Act (FSIA) of 1976, which renders foreign governments immune from suits in U.S. courts, except in certain instances.

The TVPA is not intended to override traditional diplomatic immunities which prevent the exercise of jurisdiction by U.S. courts over foreign diplomats. . . .

. . .

Similarly, the committee does not intend the 'act of state' doctrine to provide a shield from lawsuit for former officials. In *Banco Nacional de Cuba* v. *Sabbatino*, 376 U.S. 398 (1964), the Supreme Court held that the 'act of state' doctrine is meant to prevent U.S. courts from sitting in judgment of the official public acts of a sovereign foreign government. Since this doctrine applies only to 'public' acts, and no state commits torture as a matter of public policy, this doctrine cannot shield former officials from liability under this legislation.

E. Scope of liability

. . .

The legislation is limited to lawsuits against persons who ordered, abetted, or assisted in the torture. It will not permit a lawsuit against a former leader of a country merely because an isolated act of torture occurred somewhere in that country. However, a higher official need not have personally performed or ordered the abuses in order to be held liable. Under international law, responsibility for torture, summary execution, or disappearances extends beyond the person or persons who actually committed those acts—anyone with higher authority who authorized, tolerated or knowingly ignored those acts is liable for them. . . .

Finally, low-level officials cannot escape liability by claiming that they were acting under orders of superiors. Article 2(3) of the Torture Convention explicitly states that 'An order from a superior official or a public authority may not be invoked as a justification for torture'.

. . .

VII. Minority Views of Messrs. Simpson and Grassley

. . .

The executive branch, through the Department of Justice, has expressed a most serious concern with S. 313, which we share. Senate bill 313 could create difficulties in the management of foreign policy. For example, under this bill, individual aliens could determine the timing and manner of the making of allegations in a U.S. court about a foreign country's alleged abuses of human rights.

There is no more complex and sensitive issue between countries than human rights. The risk that would be run if an alien could have a foreign country judged by a U.S. court is too great. Judges of U.S. courts would, in a sense, conduct some of our Nation's foreign policy. The executive branch is and should remain, we believe, left with substantial foreign policy control.

In addition the Justice Department properly notes that our passage of this bill could encourage hostile foreign countries to retaliate by trying to assert jurisdiction for acts committed in the United States by the U.S. Government against U.S. citizens. For example, if this bill's principles were adopted abroad, Saddam Hussein could try a United States citizen police officer who happened to be present in Iraq, in an Iraqi court, for alleged human rights abuses against any United States citizen that the policeman happened to arrest while performing his duties in the United States.

. . .

COMMENT ON CRIMINAL PROSECUTION UNDER CONVENTION AGAINST TORTURE

Although the preceding Senate Report states that the TVPA 'will carry out the intent' of the Torture Convention, it does so only with respect to *civil liability*. Article 14 of that Convention provides that each State Party 'shall ensure in its legal system that the victim of an act of torture obtains redress and has an enforceable right to fair and adequate compensation . . . '.

Compare the provisions for *criminal prosecution* under Article 1 of the Convention, which applies (with respect to torture, as there defined) to pain and suffering that is 'inflicted by or at the instigation of or with the consent or acquiescence of a public official or other person acting in an official capacity'. Article 2 provides that States Parties 'shall take effective . . . measures to prevent acts of torture' in their territory. But the Convention reaches beyond this traditional territorial base for a state's criminal jurisdiction. Under Article 4, each State Party 'shall ensure that all acts of torture are offences under its criminal law', and 'shall make these offences punishable by appropriate penalties'. Under Section (1) of Article 5, each Party 'shall take such measures as may be necessary to establish its jurisdiction over the offences referred to in article 4':

  (a) when offences are committed in the state's territory;
  (b) when 'the alleged offender is a national of that State'; and
  (c) when 'the victim is a national of that State if that State considers it appropriate'.

In addition, jurisdiction is to be established under Section (2) of Article 5, where the alleged offender is present in the state's territory and the state does not extradite him pursuant to the Convention to other indicated and involved states for criminal prosecution there.

  In 1990, the Senate Committee on Foreign Relations reported favourably on the Convention and recommended that the Senate give its consent to ratification. With respect to Section (1) of Article 5, the Committee report states:[29]

> A major concern in drafting Article 5 ... was whether the Convention should provide for possible prosecution by any State in which the alleged offender is found—so-called universal jurisdiction.[30] The United States strongly supported the provision for universal jurisdiction, on the grounds that torture, like hijacking, sabotage, hostage-taking, and attacks on internationally protected persons, is an offense of special international concern, and should have similarly broad, universal recognition as a crime against humanity, with appropriate jurisdictional consequences. Provision for 'universal jurisdiction' was also deemed important in view of the fact that the government of the country where official torture actually occurs may seldom be relied on to take action. . . . [E]xisting federal and state law appears sufficient to establish jurisdiction when the offense has allegedly been committed in any territory under U.S. jurisdiction. . . . Implementing legislation is therefore needed only to establish Article 5(1)(b) jurisdiction over offenses committed by U.S. nationals outside the United States, and to establish Article 5(2) jurisdiction over foreign offenders committing torture abroad who are later found in territory under U.S. jurisdiction. . . . Similar legislation has already been enacted to implement comparable provisions of the Conventions on Hijacking, Sabotage, Hostages, and Protection of Diplomats.

  In 1990, the Senate consented to ratification of the Convention, provided that the criminal legislation required by the Convention first be enacted by Congress. The Torture Convention Implementing Legislation was enacted in 1994, 18 U.S.C.A. 2340–2340B. Section 2340A gives courts jurisdiction for torture (as defined) committed 'outside the United States' where the alleged offender is a US national or 'is present in the United States, irrespective of the nationality of the victim or alleged offender'. The United States then ratified the Convention.

---

[29] Sen. Comm. For. Relations, Report on Convention against Torture, 100th Cong., 2d Sess. (1990).
[30] [Eds.] A discussion and illustrations of general bases for jurisdiction including universal jurisdiction appear at pp. 1132–1142, *infra*.

QUESTIONS

Compare the TVPA with the prior §1350 decisions. What are the differences with respect to coverage and parties in civil actions under the two statutes? What are the differences with respect to the bearing on the civil actions of international law?

NOTE

The following opinion considers the relationship between the Alien Tort Statute and the Torture Victim Protection Act. This ATS case involves allegations other than torture, particularly of genocide and war crimes growing out of the savage fighting in Bosnia. It thereby highlights the role of the ATS in providing civil remedies while the International Criminal Tribunal for the Former Yugoslavia, pp. 1150–1, *infra*, adjudicated criminal prosecutions based on similar events. Note the holding about the civil liability of 'private' individuals for war crimes and other violations of humanitarian law. The definitions of war crimes for purposes of criminal liability under the International Criminal Tribunal and under the proposed International Criminal Court are set forth at pp. 1150 and 1193, *infra*.

KADIC V. KARADZIC

70 F. 3d 232 (2d Cir. 1995)

[This suit under the Alien Tort Statute was brought in a federal district court by victims of atrocities committed in Bosnia. The suit was against the leader of insurgent Bosnian-Serb forces. Defendant Karadzic came to the United States in 1993 as an invitee of the United Nations, to discuss the situation in Bosnia. He was served with summons and complaint in New York City, outside the UN head-quarters district. The appellate court's opinion concluded that Karadzic was not immune from service as an invitee of the UN, and hence that the service gave the district court personal jurisdiction.

The district court dismissed the action for lack of subject matter jurisdiction. The opinion on appeal, written by Chief Judge Newman, held that such jurisdiction existed, and reversed and remanded the case for further proceeding.

The plaintiffs were Croat and Muslim citizens of the new state of Bosnia-Herzegovina, a republic in the former Yugoslavia. Their complaints, whose facts and allegations were accepted as true for purposes of the appeal, alleged systematic acts of great cruelty by the Bosnian-Serb military forces: rape, torture, summary execution. Defendant Karadzic was President of a three-man presidency of the self-proclaimed Bosnian-Serb republic within Bosnia referred to as 'Srpska'. In that capacity he exercised authority and actual control over large parts of Bosnian territory, and held ultimate command authority over his military forces. The complaints alleged that the injuries suffered by plaintiffs were committed as part of a pattern of systematic human rights violations by military forces commanded by Karadzic, and that Karadzic acted in an official capacity either as the titular head of Srpska or in collaboration with the government of the former Yugoslavia and its dominant constituent republic, Serbia.

The plaintiffs asserted causes of action including genocide, rape, torture, summary execution, and wrongful death, and sought compensatory and punitive damages. They based subject matter jurisdiction on the ATS, the Torture Victim Protection Act, and 28 U.S.C. §1331. Excerpts from the part of the opinion discussing subject matter jurisdiction follow.]

. . . Karadzic contends that appellants have not alleged violations of the norms of international law because such norms bind only states and persons acting under color of a state's law, not private individuals. In making this contention, Karadzic advances the contradictory positions that he is not a state actor even as he asserts that he is the President of the self-proclaimed Republic of Srpska. . . .

. . .

. . . [W]e hold that certain forms of conduct violate the law of nations whether undertaken by those acting under the auspices of a state or only as private individuals. . . .

. . .

. . . The Executive Branch has emphatically restated in this litigation its position that private persons may be found liable under the Alien Tort Act for acts of genocide, war crimes, and other violations of international humanitarian law.

. . .

Karadzic also contends that Congress intended the state-action requirement of the Torture Victim Act to apply to actions under the Alien Tort Act. We disagree. Congress enacted the Torture Victim Act to codify the cause of action recognized . . . in Filartiga, and to further extend that cause of action to plaintiffs who are U.S. citizens. At the same time, Congress indicated that the Alien Tort Act 'has other important uses and should not be replaced', because claims based on torture and summary executions do not exhaust the list of actions that may appropriately be covered [by the Alien Tort Act]. . . . The scope of the Alien Tort Act remains undiminished by enactment of the Torture Victim Act.

. . . [I]t will be helpful to group the appellants' claims into three categories: (a) genocide, (b) war crimes, and (c) other instances of inflicting death, torture, and degrading treatment.

(a) Genocide. In the aftermath of the atrocities committed during the Second World War, the condemnation of genocide as contrary to international law quickly achieved broad acceptance by the community of nations. . . .

The Convention on Genocide . . . provides a more specific articulation of the prohibition of genocide in international law. The Convention . . . makes clear that 'persons committing genocide . . . shall be punished, whether they are constitutionally responsible rulers, public officials or private individuals'. . . .

. . .

Appellants' allegations that Karadzic personally planned and ordered a campaign of murder, rape, forced impregnation, and other forms of torture designed to destroy the religious and ethnic groups of Bosnian Muslims and Bosnian Croats clearly state a violation of the international law norm proscribing genocide, regardless of whether Karadzic acted under color of law or as a private individual. . . .

(b) War crimes. Plaintiffs also contend that the acts of murder, rape, torture, and arbitrary detention of civilians, committed in the course of hostilities, violate the law of war. . . . [I]nternational law imposes an affirmative duty on military commanders to take appropriate measures within their power to control troops under their command for the prevention of such atrocities.

. . .

The offenses alleged by the appellants, if proved, would violate the most fundamental norms of the law of war embodied in common article 3 [of the Geneva Conventions, pp. 1135 and 1177, *infra*], which binds parties to internal conflicts regardless of whether they are recognized nations or roving hordes of insurgents. The liability of private individuals for committing war crimes has been recognized since World War I and was confirmed at Nuremberg after World War II. . . . and remains today an important aspect of international law. The District Court has jurisdiction pursuant to the Alien Tort Act over appellants' claims of war crimes and other violations of international humanitarian law.

(c) Torture and summary execution. . . . [T]orture and summary execution— when not perpetrated in the course of genocide or war crimes—are proscribed by international law only when committed by state officials or under color of law. . . .

In the present case, appellants allege that acts of rape, torture, and summary execution were committed during hostilities by troops under Karadzic's command and with the specific intent of destroying appellants' ethnic-religious groups. Thus, many of the alleged atrocities are already encompassed within the appellants' claims of genocide and war crimes. . . . It suffices to hold at this stage that the alleged atrocities are actionable under the Alien Tort Act, without regard to state action, to the extent that they were committed in pursuit of genocide or war crimes, and otherwise may be pursued against Karadzic to the extent that he is shown to be a state actor. . . .

[Discussion omitted about the dispute over characterization of Srpska as a state and of Karadzic as a state actor. One of the court's conclusions follows.]

Appellants' allegations entitle them to prove that Karadzic's regime satisfies the criteria for a state, for purposes of those international law violations requiring state action. Srpska is alleged to control defined territory, control populations within its power, and to have entered into agreements with other governments. It has a president, a legislature, and its own currency. These circumstances readily appear to satisfy the criteria for a state in all aspects of international law. Moreover, it is likely that the state action concept, where applicable for some violations like 'official' torture, requires merely the semblance of official authority. The inquiry, after all, is whether a person purporting to wield official power has exceeded internationally recognized standards of civilized conduct, not whether statehood in all its formal aspects exists.

. . .

[Most of the discussion of the justiciability of this dispute, in relation to the political question doctrine, is here omitted. The opinion recognized that 'suits of this nature can present difficulties that implicate sensitive matters of diplomacy historically reserved to the jurisdiction of the political branches'. Its approach was to 'weigh carefully the relevant considerations on a case-to-case basis'. It concluded that the present litigation did not present nonjusticiable political cases within the meaning of *Baker v. Carr*, 389 U.S. 186 (1982), and stressed that the *Filartiga* decision 'established that universally recognized norms of international law provide judicially discoverable and manageable standards for adjudicating' ATS suits. Hence there was no need 'to make initial policy decisions of the kind normally reserved for nonjudicial discretion'. It further concluded that decision in these cases would not contradict prior decisions taken by a political branch and thereby 'seriously interfere with important governmental interests'. The opinion continued:]

As to the act of state doctrine, the doctrine was not asserted in the District Court and is not before us on this appeal. Moreover, the appellee has not had the temerity to assert in this Court that the acts he allegedly committed are the officially approved policy of a state. Finally, as noted, we think it would be a rare case in which the act of state doctrine precluded suit under section 1350. *Banco Nacional* [*v. Sabbatino*, p. 1059, *supra*] was careful to recognize the doctrine 'in the absence of . . . unambiguous agreement regarding controlling legal principles', such as exist in the pending litigation, and applied the doctrine only in a context— expropriation of an alien's property—in which world opinion was sharply divided.

Finally, we note that at this stage of the litigation no party has identified a more suitable forum, and we are aware of none. Though the Statement of the United States suggests the general importance of considering the doctrine of forum non conveniens, it seems evident that the courts of the former Yugoslavia, either in Serbia or war-torn Bosnia, are not now available to entertain plaintiffs' claims, even if circumstances concerning the location of witnesses and documents were presented that were sufficient to overcome the plaintiffs' preference for a United States forum.

. . .

NOTE

The United States is distinctive in having legislation in effect that explicitly permits tort actions by foreign victims against foreign human rights violators for violations that occurred in foreign states. As a result, the phenomenon of transnational human rights litigation in national courts has largely been an American one, and much of the ensuing literature has focused on the implications for the US legal system. But the *Pinochet* litigation in the UK (pp. 1198–1216, *infra*) and the increasing number of national prosecutions in criminal cases based on human rights violations that occurred elsewhere have compelled a re-thinking.

Two issues arising out of the US experience are whether the ATS and TVPA approaches should be emulated by other legal systems, and whether such emulation may be accomplished by judicial initiative alone. Various contributors to a symposium on this issue[31] have argued either that transnational human rights litigation is not (always) a good idea or that its conceptual and doctrinal foundations are not as strong as is commonly taken for granted in ATS discourse. The counter arguments include:

- such litigation is dubious because it involves intervention by judges in politics and by foreign states in the affairs of other societies;
- the assertion of jurisdiction over a foreign case might undermine domestic mechanisms (such as the courts or truth and reconciliation commissions) that seek to address the same violations;
- the danger of involving foreign courts in ideologically motivated goals that they may not be well placed to deal with; and
- such litigation may undermine the ability of multilateral anti-torture regimes, such as the European Convention on Torture (p. 795, *supra*), to persuade states to accept inspection visits since any resulting reports might subsequently be used as evidence to sustain cases in foreign courts.

QUESTIONS

How do you assess these arguments? Is it problematic for the U.S. to be alone in offering such opportunities for victims everywhere to seek remedies in U.S. courts for foreign violations?

NOTE

Another way in which national courts are becoming increasingly involved in legal actions designed to obtain a remedy for alleged human rights violations committed in other states is through lawsuits brought against transnational corporations for harms caused, directly or indirectly, by their activities.

---

[31] Craig Scott (ed.), *Torture as Tort: Comparative Perspectives on the Development of Transnational Human Rights Litigation* (2000).

CRAIG SCOTT, MULTINATIONAL ENTERPRISES AND
EMERGENT JURISPRUDENCE ON VIOLATIONS OF
ECONOMIC, SOCIAL AND CULTURAL RIGHTS

in A. Eide, C. Krause, A. Rosas and M. Scheinin (eds.), *Economic, Social and
Cultural Rights: A Textbook* (2nd edn., 2000, forthcoming)

. . .

In the famous *Bhopal* case, the pesticide plant run by Union Carbide India Limited
(U.C.I.L.), a subsidiary of U.S.-based Union Carbide (U.C.), malfunctioned and
clouds of toxic gas were released, killing thousands and crippling many more.[32] . . .
India promptly filed a civil suit before a federal court in the United States against
the parent company, Union Carbide, claiming that specific decisions and conduct
taken in the United States by U.C. justified holding the parent company liable. . . .
India's theory of the case, which it called 'multinational enterprise liability', was
that Union Carbide was liable both because . . . U.C. and U.C.I.L. functioned in all
material respects as a single 'enterprise' regardless of formal separations of corporate personality and because, beyond this general relationship, conduct specifically connected to the causes of the Bhopal disaster had occurred in the United
States. . . . However, the trial judge, Judge Keenan, accepted U.C.'s jurisdictional
argument of *forum non conveniens*. The appropriate forum, in his view, was India
whose judges were urged to 'stand tall before the world' and show that they could
handle this kind of litigation. . . . According to the judge, U.S. citizens had limited
'interest' in hearing a case like this which would inconvenience local jury members
and crowd an already-congested court docket. Subject to one condition left standing after appeal (that U.C. must accept jurisdiction of the Indian courts), the
Bhopal litigation was sent back to India. In relatively short order after the case was
dismissed in the U.S., the Indian Supreme Court had brokered a $500 million
settlement, relatively large by previous Indian standards (even given the number of
plaintiffs, it seems) but paltry when compared to what monetary awards would
likely have been given if a U.S. civil jury had heard the case and had found U.C.
liable. . . .

. . . A decade later a new series of forays began as foreign plaintiffs sought to take
a run at the *Bhopal* precedent in various state and federal district courts around
the United States. The majority of these cases have been against natural resource
extraction companies, most notably oil companies but also mining companies.
The alleged harms have ranged from harm to the environment to harm to human
health to corporate complicity in physical brutality (such as forced labour, torture
and slavery). The early results before a series of trial judges in the various cases
suggested that *Bhopal* was alive and well. . . . Three separate actions against Texaco
were dismissed, two of which had been brought for harm in Ecuador (one before a
Texas federal court and one before a New York federal court) and one for harm
caused to Peruvians by the cross-border effects of harm originating in Ecuador

---

[32] *In re. Union Carbide Corporation Gas Plan Disaster at Bhopal, India, in December 1984*, 634 F.Supp. 842
(S.D. New York, Keenan J.); upheld on appeal: 809 F.2d 195 (2d Cir. 1987).

from Texaco's alleged activities.[33] As well, an action against Southern Peru Copper Corporation (SPCC) brought in Texas for harm caused by toxic emissions in Peru was also dismissed, like the Texaco cases, on *forum non conveniens* grounds.[34] . . .

However, [in a reversal of this trend, in] 1998, a federal court of appeal . . . overturned [the] lower court dismissals in *Aguinda v. Texaco* (jointly decided on appeal with *Ashanga*) . . . .[35] And, in mid-1997, the first major breakthrough in a trial-level judgment occurred in *Doe v. Unocal,* a case dealing with an oil pipeline construction project linked to serious human rights abuses in Burma.[36] [The court upheld the causes of actions in US courts against corporations for some human rights violations].

[Australia]

[In the *Ok Tedi* case] proceedings were brought by four groups of plaintiffs living in an area of Papua New Guinea.[37] They alleged harms caused by toxic pollution into a river and a flood plain stemming from a copper mine run by a major Australian mining [company] (BHP and its subsidiary OTML). The defendants corporations sought to have the actions brought in Australia dismissed for want of jurisdiction over the subject matter of the claims. However, the significance of *Ok Tedi* resides in the fact that the judge held that he *did* have jurisdiction over certain causes of action related to negligence. . . .

. . . BHP agreed to settle the claims. The settlement was significant, including $400 million (Australian dollars) for the construction of a tailings containment system and up to $150 million as compensation for environmental damage. BHP did not even follow up its failed motion to dismiss for want of jurisdiction with a *forum non conveniens* application. . . .

. . .

QUESTIONS

The corporation's failure in the *Ok Tedi* case to press the argument of *forum non conveniens* has been explained on the grounds that Australian companies must demonstrate that the use of the local jurisdiction is so unreasonable as to amount to harassment by the foreign plaintiff.

> Thus it acts as an incentive for companies based in Australia to adopt similar industrial safety and environmental standards in their overseas activities as they are required to domestically. . . . [F]oreign environmental damage cases

---

[33] *Sequihua v. Texaco, Inc.,* 847 F.Supp. 61 (S.D. Tex. 1994); *Aguinda v. Texaco, Inc.* 945 F.Supp. 625 (S.D.N.Y. 1996); *Ashanga v. Texaco,* S.D.N.Y. Dkt. No. 94 Civ. 9266 (August 13, 1997).

[34] *Torres v. Southern Peru Copper Corporation,* 965 F.Supp. 895 (S.D. Tex. 1995).

[35] The combined *Aguinda* and *Ashanga* appeals took on the new name of *Jota v. Texaco, Inc.,* 157 F.3d 153 (2nd Cir. 1998).

[36] *Doe I v. Unocal,* 963 F. Supp. 880 (Cent. Dist. Cal., 1997); *Doe I v. Unocal,* 27 F. Supp 2d 1174 (Cent. Dist. Cal., 1998).

[37] *Dagi; Shackles; Ambetu; Maun and Others v. The Broken Hill Proprietary Company Ltd. and Ok Tedi Mining Limited (No. 2),* [1997] 1 Victoria Reports [V.R.] 428.

have done much to create the perception that the law of the United States allows its multinationals to avoid US legal standards when operating overseas. Apart from ensuring a peaceful resolution of the *Ok Tedi* case through legal means, the willingness of the Australian courts to hear the case meant BHP could not escape the application of Australian legal standards in its mining operations in Papua New Guinea.[38]

Is it desirable for Australian courts to compel respect for domestic standards in relation to economic and social rights in foreign states and situations that may be very different from anything prevailing locally?

ADDITIONAL READING

A. Byrnes, 'Civil Remedies for Torture Committed Abroad: An Obligation Under the Convention Against Torture?', in C. Scott (ed.), *Torture as Tort: Comparative Perspectives on the Development of Transnational Human Rights Litigation* (2000); L. Garnett, 'The Defence of State Immunity for Acts of Torture', 18 Aust. YB Int. L. 99 (1998); J. Walker Jr., 'Domestic Adjudication of International Human Rights Violations Under the Alien Tort Statute', 41 St. Louis U. L. J. 539 (1997); M. Byers, 'Al-Adsani v. Government of Kuwait and others', [1996] British YB Int. L. 67; A. Bianchi, 'Denying State Immunity to Violators of Human Rights', 46 Austrian J. Pub. Int. L. 195 (1994); R. Steinhardt, 'Fulfilling the Promise of Filartiga: Litigating Human Rights Claims against the Estate of Ferdinand Marcos', 20 Yale J. Int. L. 65 (1995); R. Steinhardt and A. D'Amato (eds.), *The Alien Tort Claims Act: An Analytical Anthology* (1999); B. Stephens, 'Expanding Remedies for Human Rights Abuses: Civil Litigation in Domestic Courts', in K. Askin and D. Koenig (eds.), *Women and International Human Rights* 119 (Vol. 2, 2000).

Customary law in the United States: C. Bradley and J. Goldsmith, 'Customary International Law as Federal Common Law: A Critique of the Modern Position', 110 Harv. L. Rev. 815 (1997); C. Bradley and J. Goldsmith, 'The Current Illegitimacy of International Human Rights Litigation', 66 Fordham L. Rev. 319 (1997); G. Neuman, 'Sense and Nonsense about Customary International Law', 66 Fordham L. Rev. 371 (1997).

---

[38] P. Prince, 'Bhopal, Bougainville and Ok Tedi: Why Australia's Forum Non Conveniens Approach is Better', (1998) 47 Int. & Comp. Law Qu. 573 at 595.

13

Enforcement by States Against Violator States

Chapter 12 offered the promise or ideal. States will take the necessary measures to assure internal compliance with international human rights. In many states their own constitutions, whether predating or instituted during the human rights movement, will achieve broad compliance. In other contexts, states will internalize the international norms so that their courts apply those norms directly.

Our concern of course is with states that fall short of this ideal, sometimes far short. We have seen principally in Chapter 8, but also in the regional systems of Chapter 10, the efforts of intergovernmental institutions and their organs to secure compliance by violator states. Such modes of enforcement can be understood as *vertical*, in the sense that pressures are exerted and perhaps sanctions applied by international organs 'above' the state. Such organs apply international law. From the perspective of that law, those international bodies exercise authority over all member states in accordance with the terms of the treaties creating them.

Of course international organizations' decision-making about what action, if any, to take is not divorced from the decisions of their member states. To the contrary, the international bodies attempting to ensure, or at least to heighten the probability of, compliance are often 'intergovernmental' in two sense. First, the treaties creating them were ratified by their member states. Second, within the UN Charter system (apart from the International Court of Justice), the decision-making bodies for compliance and enforcement measures are composed of representatives of such states. Their decisions are not then 'divorced' from these states' separate decisions, for each member of a given body must decide how to vote—say, within the UN Commission on Human Rights or General Assembly or Security Council. Nonetheless, the organ's vote (say, to pass a resolution, make an investigation, authorize or order sanctions or intervention, or to refuse to take any of these actions) is a collective vote, an organizational decision, which may in the end impose obligations on many states individually. The organization, however influenced in its decision it may be by a few member states, is in a formal and vital sense the acting party.

Here, in Chapter 13, we consider entirely *horizontal* modes of implementing and enforcing human rights. Although there may be coordination with international bodies, the action or policy here at issue is rooted in the state. Acting singly or as part of a consortium, states may apply a range of pressures against a violator state. Their possible action includes exhortations and threats of future action, encouragement/incentives and sanctions, carrots and sticks. They may rely importantly on damaging the reputation of the state involved, on 'shaming', to use a term commonly invoked as one of a range of strategies. They may impose boycotts or embargoes, suspend trading or investment relationships. They may impose conditions on bilateral or multilateral security assistance, development aid, or trade advantages such as a most-favored-nation clause—conditions that require the recipient or trading state to comply with stated human rights norms. Within such a 'horizontal' (state-to-state) application of sanctions and pressures, the state imposing human rights conditions—so-called 'conditionality'—as part of its foreign policy becomes part of a multi-layered system of enforcement of international human rights.

The debate within the United States about the relevance of human rights to foreign policy—excluding in this chapter internal US debate about policies of the UN bearing on human rights—has been active and contentious for decades. It has ranged from security assistance and development aid to trade and foreign investment. The contexts in which these issues have been argued include the central crises of American foreign policy since the early 1970s—for example, US security or economic aid to, investment in, or trade with regimes in El Salvador, Nicaragua, Chile, South Africa, Nigeria, Burma, China and other states. The economic importance of aid and trade has involved major sectors of the US economy— defense industries anxious to export their products, manufacturing and service-oriented firms fearful of losing foreign markets in retaliation for elimination by the United States of other states' advantages in trade, consumer groups fearful of losing cheaper imported products, and so on. Such strong consequences raise the stakes for a politics of conditionality.

The chapter starts with a general discussion of the 'national interest' in relation to human rights enforcement, continues with illustrations of US policy toward violator states and its experience in aid conditionality, gives particular attention to United States–China trade relations, and concludes with descriptions of analogous policies in the European Union.

A. NATIONAL INTEREST AND HUMAN RIGHTS

The clash of positions in the debate over conditionality evokes similar clashes throughout US history about the actual or necessary or desired character of foreign policy. The clash can be defined in various ways, including such broad notions as: idealism versus realism, altruism versus self-interest, moral ideals versus national interest, principles versus power.

The first term (in a human rights context, the more 'interventionist') in each of these pairs could be characterized in most instances as favoring conditionality in US aid and trade legislation. The second term could be understood as tending to oppose human rights conditions, for they frustrate aid or trade policies that are believed to be in the national interest. Often the debate has had a more ambiguous and contextual character, in which the dominant questions have been instrumental ones like the effectiveness of aid-trade sanctions as compared with alternative paths to achieve human rights goals.

Why indeed should a country like the United States take human rights considerations into account in its bilateral relations with other states? If it is in the 'national interest' to provide a given country with security (military) assistance or with development aid, does not making such aid dependent on the recipient's compliance with human rights norms impair that 'interest'? Is not the United States (or any other country following similar policies) surrendering its practical and ideological concerns in order to act as a global policeman, to enforce human rights norms at a cost to its own interests? Is not a purpose of the human rights movement to lift the problem of enforcement from the level of states to that of international organizations in which many states participate?

Such are the issues debated in the following readings.

HANS MORGENTHAU, HUMAN RIGHTS AND FOREIGN POLICY

reprinted in Kenneth Thompson (ed.), Moral Dimensions of American Foreign Policy (1984), at 344

[Morgenthau was a leading realist among political scientists in the decades following the Second World War, when this article originally appeared.]

. . .

[The preceding discussion] brings me to the popular issue with which the problem of morality in foreign policy presents us today, and that is the issue of what is now called human rights. That is to say, to what extent is a nation entitled and obligated to impose its moral principles upon other nations? To what extent is it both morally just and intellectually tenable to apply principles we hold dear to other nations that, for a number of reasons, are impervious to them? It is obvious that the attempt to impose so-called human rights upon others or to punish others for not observing human rights assumes that human rights are of universal validity—that, in other words, all nations or all peoples living in different nations would embrace human rights if they knew they existed and that in any event they are as inalienable in their character as the Declaration of Independence declares them to be.

I'm not here entering into a discussion of the theological or strictly philosophic nature of human rights. I only want to make the point that whatever one's conception of that theological or philosophical nature, those human rights are filtered through the intermediary of historic and social circumstances, which will lead to different results in different times and under different circumstances. One need only look at the unique character of the American polity and at these very special, nowhere-else-to-be-found characteristics of our protection of human rights within the confines of America. You have only to look at the complete lack of respect for human rights in many nations . . . to realize how daring . . . an attempt it is to impose upon the rest of the world the respect for human rights or in particular to punish other nations for not showing respect for human rights. . . .

It is quite wrong to assume that this has been the American tradition. . . . I think it was John Quincy Adams who made the point forcefully that it was not for the United States to impose its own principles of government upon the rest of mankind, but, rather, to attract the rest of mankind through the example of the United States. And this has indeed been the persisting principle the United States has followed. . . . This has been the great difference between the early conception of America and its relations to the rest of the world on the one hand and what you might call the Wilsonian conception on the other.

For Wilson wanted to make the world safe for democracy. He wanted to transform the world through the will of the United States. The Founding Fathers wanted to present to the nations of the world an example of what man can do and called upon them to do it. So there is here a fundamental difference. . . . [T]he dedication to human rights as an example to be offered to other nations . . . is, I think, a better example of the American tradition than the Wilsonian one.

There are two other objections that must be made against the Wilsonian conception. One is the impossibility of enforcing the universal application of human rights. We can tell the Soviet Union, and we should from time to time tell the Soviet Union, that its treatment of minorities is incompatible with our conception of human rights. But once we have said this we will find that there is very little we can do to put this statement into practice. . . . There are other examples where private pressure—for example, the shaming of public high officials in the Soviet Union by private pressure—has had an obvious result. But it is inconceivable . . . to expect that the Soviet Union will yield to public pressure . . . and will thereby admit its own weakness in this particular field . . .

There is a second weakness of this approach, which is that the United States is a great power with manifold interests throughout the world, of which human rights is only one and not the most important one, and the United States is incapable of consistently following the path of the defense of human rights without maneuvering itself into a Quixotic position. This is obvious already in our discriminating treatment of, let me say, South Korea on the one hand and the Soviet Union on the other. Or you could mention mainland China on the one hand and the Soviet Union on the other. We dare to criticize and affront the Soviet Union because our relations, in spite of being called détente, are not particularly friendly. We have a great interest in continuing the normalization of our relations with mainland China, and for this reason we are not going to hurt her feelings. On the other hand South Korea is an ally of the United States, it is attributed a considerable military importance, and so we are not going to do anything to harm those relations.

In other words, the principle of the defense of human rights cannot be consistently applied in foreign policy because it can and it must come in conflict with other interests that may be more important than the defense of human rights in a particular instance. And to say . . . that the defense of human rights must be woven into the fabric of American foreign policy is, of course, an attempt to conceal the actual impossibility of consistently pursuing the defense of human rights. And once you fail to defend human rights in a particular instance, you have given up the defense of human rights and you have accepted another principle to guide your actions. And this is indeed what has happened and is bound to happen if you are not a Don Quixote who foolishly but consistently follows a disastrous path of action.

. . .

SAMUEL HUNTINGTON, AMERICAN IDEALS VERSUS AMERICAN INSTITUTIONS

in G. Ikenberry (ed.), American Foreign Policy (1989), at 239

In the eyes of most Americans not only should their foreign-policy institutions be structured and function so as to reflect liberal values, but American foreign policy should also be substantively directed to the promotion of those values in the external environment. This gives a distinctive cast to the American role in the world. In a famous phrase Viscount Palmerston once said that Britain did not have permanent friends or enemies, it only had permanent interests. Like Britain and other countries, the United States also has interests, defined in terms of power, wealth, and security, some of which are sufficiently enduring as to be thought of as permanent. As a founded society, however, the United States also has distinctive political principles and values that define its national identity. These principles provide a second set of goals and a second set of standards—in addition to those of national interest—by which to shape the goals and judge the success of American foreign policy.

This heritage, this transposition of the ideals-versus-institutions gap into foreign policy, again distinguishes the United States from other societies. Western European states clearly do not reject the relevance of morality and political ideology to the conduct of foreign policy. They do, however, see the goal of foreign policy as the advancement of the major and continuing security and economic interests of their state. Political principles provide limits and parameters to foreign policy but not to its goals. . . .

. . .

The effort to use American foreign policy to promote American values abroad raises a central issue. There is a clear difference between political action to make American political practices conform to American political values and political action to make *foreign* political practices conform to American values. Americans can legitimately attempt to reduce the gap between American institutions and American values, but can they legitimately attempt to reduce the gap between other people's institutions and American values? The answer is not self-evident.

The argument for a negative response to this question can be made on at least four grounds. First, it is morally wrong for the United States to attempt to shape the institutions of other societies. Those institutions should reflect the values and behavior of the people in those societies. To intrude from outside is either imperialism or colonialism, each of which also violates American values. Second, it is difficult practically and in most cases impossible for the United States to influence significantly the institutional development of other societies. The task is simply beyond American knowledge, skill, and resources. To attempt to do so will often be counterproductive. Third, any effort to shape the domestic institutions of other societies needlessly irritates and antagonizes other governments and hence will complicate and often endanger the achievement of other more important foreign-policy goals, particularly in the areas of national security and economic well-being. Fourth, to influence the political development of other societies would require an enormous expansion of the military power and economic resources of the American government. This in turn would pose dangers to the operation of democratic government within the United States.

A yes answer to this question can, on the other hand, also be justified on four grounds. First, if other people's institutions pose direct threats to the viability of American institutions and values in the United States, an American effort to change those institutions would be justifiable in terms of self-defense. . . .

Second, the direct-threat argument can be generalized to the proposition that authoritarian regimes in any form and on any continent pose a potential threat to the viability of liberal institutions and values in the United States. A liberal democratic system, it can be argued, can only be secure in a world system of similarly constituted states. In the past this argument did not play a central role because of the extent to which the United States was geographically isolated from differently constituted states. The world is, however, becoming smaller. Given the increasing interactions among societies and the emergence of transnational institutions operating in many societies, the pressures toward convergence among political systems are likely to become more intense. . . .

Third, American efforts to make other people's institutions conform to American values would be justified to the extent that the other people supported those values. Such support has historically been much more prevalent in Western Europe and Latin America than it has in Asia and Africa. . . . Americans could well feel justified in supporting and helping those individuals, groups, and institutions in other societies who share their belief in these values. At the same time it would also be appropriate for them to be aware that those values could be realized in other societies through institutions significantly different from those that exist in the United States.

Fourth, American efforts to make other people's institutions conform to American values could be justified on the grounds that those values are universally valid and universally applicable, whether or not most people in other societies believe in them. For Americans not to believe in the universal validity of American values could indeed lead to a moral relativism: liberty and democracy are not inherently better than any other political values; they just happen to be those that for historical and cultural reasons prevail in the United States. This relativistic position runs counter to the strong elements of moral absolutism and messianism that are part of American history and culture, and hence the argument for moral relativism may not wash in the United States for relativistic reasons. In addition the argument can be made that some element of belief in the universal validity of a set of political ideals is necessary to arouse the energy, support, and passion to defend those ideals and the institutions modeled on them in American society.

Historically Americans have generally believed in the universal validity of their values. At the end of World War II, when Americans forced Germany and Japan to be free, they did not stop to ask if liberty and democracy were what the German and Japanese people wanted. Americans implicitly assumed that their values were valid and applicable and that they would at the very least be morally negligent if they did not insist that Germany and Japan adopt political institutions reflecting those values. Belief in the universal validity of those values obviously reinforces and reflects those hypocritical elements of the American tradition that stress the United States's role as a redeemer nation and lead it to attempt to impose its values and often its institutions on other societies. . . .

NOTE

Consider the following observations of Owen Harries, '*Virtue by Other Means*', *New York Times*, October 26, 1997, p. WK 15:

. . . Many, perhaps most, Americans of all political persuasions believe profoundly that it is their nation's right and duty—indeed its destiny—to promote freedom, justice and democracy in the world. . . . It is a noble and powerful impulse, one not casually to be ridiculed or dismissed. But acting on it—if one is concerned to be effective and not merely to feel virtuous—is more complicated and difficult than many human rights activists will allow.

Typically, the proponents of human rights see things in straightforward terms. They regard those rights as absolute, and demand consistency in their application, denouncing anything less as hypocrisy and cynicism. These denunciations are given some plausibility by the failure of administrations to live up to inflated official rhetoric on the subject. But the truth is that while individuals and special-interest groups are free to give human rights absolute and unqualified priority, governments are not.

For the activist, human rights are a cause. But when they are incorporated into a government's foreign policy, they become an interest, one among many. Their claims have to be balanced against those other interests, many of which—apart from having a compelling practical importance—have moral content and moral claims of their own (for example, peace, security, order, prosperity). The place that human rights will occupy in the hierarchy of interests will necessarily vary from occasion to occasion.

Sometimes, as when the violation of rights is horrendous and no other vital interest is at risk, they will rank very high; sometimes they will have to give way to other compelling interests. America's wartime alliance with Stalin's Soviet Union is a striking example of such a subordination. It would be convenient if all one's interests always pointed in the same direction, but they don't. . . .

The other factor that complicates the application of human rights policy—what makes it not a simple matter of consistency but a complicated one of judgment and discrimination—is the variability and particularity of circumstance. 'The circumstances', insisted Edmund Burke, 'are what render every civil and political scheme beneficial or noxious to mankind'. What makes good sense in one set of circumstances may well be futile in another—and positively disastrous in a third. . . .

. . .

B. INTERNATIONAL HUMAN RIGHTS POLICIES IN U.S. FOREIGN POLICY

LOUIS HENKIN, THE AGE OF RIGHTS
(1990), at 77

Ch. 5. Human Rights and United States Foreign Policy

. . .

. . . For the most part, however, Congress did not attend seriously to the condition of human rights in other countries during the first twenty-five years of the postwar era and generally acquiesced in what the executive branch did. Congress had little occasion for formal involvement in the development of United States human rights policy. . . . The Senate, whose advice and consent is constitutionally required to human rights treaties as to others, had few occasions to consider agreements that aimed at the condition of rights in other countries. . . .

An independent Congressional initiative to shape United States human rights policy developed in the early 1970s. Under influence of concerned liberal members of the House of Representatives, and responding to inadequacies in United Nations and other multilateral responses to human rights violations, Congress enacted a series of statutes declaring the promotion of respect for human rights to be a principal goal of United States foreign policy, and denying foreign aid, military assistance, and the sale of agricultural commodities to states guilty of gross violations of internationally recognized human rights. In addition, United States representatives were directed to act in international financial institutions so as to prevent or discourage loans to governments guilty of such violations. Congress also established a human rights bureau in the Department of State, and directed the department to report annually on the condition of human rights in every country in the world.

The Congressional program, it should be clear, was directed not at deviations from democratic governance as practiced by the United States (and by its European allies) but against 'consistent patterns of gross violations of internationally recognized human rights', those that nations publicly decried and that none claimed the right to do or admitted doing. Congress specified clearly the violations at which it aimed—'torture or cruel, inhuman or degrading treatment or punishment, prolonged detention without charges, causing the disappearance of persons by the abduction and clandestine detention of those persons, or other flagrant denial of the right to life, liberty or the security of person'. Also, it should be clear, this general legislation was not aimed at Communism and the Communist states since they received neither arms nor aid from the United States, but at the non-Communist Third World. In addition, Congress addressed human rights in particular countries, e.g., denying various aid to Chile, Argentina, South Africa, Uganda and others, when the condition of human rights in those countries was particularly egregious. Later, Congress imposed various human rights conditions on assistance to particular countries in Central America. In 1986, Congress enacted the Comprehensive Anti-Apartheid Act.

The Congressional program was never popular with the executive branch (regardless of political party), particularly with those who reflected the dominant, traditional attitudes in the Department of State. That program limited executive autonomy in the conduct of foreign policy. It required embassies to collect information often critical of the countries in which they 'lived'; it required the Department of State to publish information often critical of countries with which the United States had friendly relations. It injected into foreign policy elements that foreign governments, and many in the State Department, thought not to be United States business. It sometimes disturbed alliances and alignments, base agreements or trade arrangements, and friendly relations generally.

Congress made some concessions to executive branch resistance. It gave the Aid Administrator authority to disregard the statutory limitation when assistance 'will directly benefit the needy people in such country'. It authorized security assistance to a country guilty of gross violations if the President certified that 'extraordinary circumstances exist warranting provision of such assistance', or if the President finds that 'such a significant improvement in its human rights record has occurred as to warrant lifting the prohibition on furnishing such assistance in the national interest of the United States'.

...

In the main, the tension between Congress and the executive branch reflected not partisan or political differences, but the different positions and perspectives of the two branches. Congress was closer to popular sentiment in the United States, which was responsive to the human condition in other countries, and wished to do something about it or at least to dissociate the United States from repressive regimes in general or in particular countries. The executive branch, more removed from constituent influence in the United States, was closer to official sentiment in other countries with which it had to deal; it was not indifferent to, but less swayed by, moral concerns, more attuned to international political and diplomatic needs and mores. . . .

...

I have described tensions within the executive branch and differences between the two branches. There have also been differences between Presidents and between presidential administrations, reflecting some partisan or ideological differences and some personal differences.

...

In sum, human rights legislation in the United States does not govern as other law does. Although gross violations of human rights are rampant in many countries, including some that are important beneficiaries of United States aid and arms trade, there have been virtually no cases in which military assistance or foreign aid was in fact cut off on human rights grounds. But the law is hardly a dead letter and Congress is not a toothless tiger. The existence of the law, the constitutional posture of Congress and President, establish a political context and generate a process that have important human rights consequences. Sometimes they deter Presidents from asking for aid for blatant violators, as in Guatemala. Sometimes they compel the President to press would-be beneficiary governments to act to improve the human rights condition in these countries, so that the President could certify to Congress at least significant improvement. . . .

...

Prospect

The human rights policy of the United States is part of a larger foreign policy in the national interest broadly conceived. National interest is not a simple, single concern, and United States foreign policy has often struggled with competing national interests. But the ambiguities, ambivalences, and contradictions of United States human rights policy have been particularly glaring. . . .

No one in the United States suggests that the United States should end human rights violations in other countries by war and conquest; that would be a violation of international law and would bring more human suffering than it would cure. Some favor economic sanctions such as boycotts but most knowledgeable Americans recognize that such measures are generally ineffective and might damage other United States interests, though it may sometimes be necessary to make a political-moral statement as Congress did in enacting the Comprehensive Anti-Apartheid Act of 1986. But human rights advocates insist that the United States is fully entitled to withhold its foreign aid and deny arms to regimes that are guilty of consistent patterns of gross violations of human rights, as it has denied them to Communist countries. . . .

. . .

US DEPARTMENT OF STATE, 1999 COUNTRY REPORTS ON HUMAN RIGHTS PRACTICES

2000, http://www.state.gov/www/global/human_rights/99hrp_index.html

This report is submitted to the Congress by the Department of State in compliance with sections 116(d) and 502(b) of the Foreign Assistance Act of 1961 (FAA), as amended, and section 504 of the Trade Act of 1974, as amended. The law provides that the Secretary of State shall transmit to the Speaker of the House of Representatives and the Committee on Foreign Relations of the Senate, by February 25 'a full and complete report regarding the status of internationally recognized human rights, within the meaning of subsection (A) in countries that receive assistance under this part, and (B) in all other foreign countries which are members of the United Nations and which are not otherwise the subject of a human rights report under this Act'. We have also included reports on several countries that do not fall into the categories established by these statutes and that thus are not covered by the congressional requirement.

. . . The first reports, in 1977, covered only countries receiving U.S. aid, numbering 82; this year 194 reports are submitted.

In August 1993, the Secretary of State moved to strengthen further the human rights efforts of our embassies. All sections in each embassy were asked to contribute information and to corroborate reports of human rights violations, and new efforts were made to link mission programming to the advancement of human rights and democracy. In 1994 the Bureau of Human Rights and Humanitarian Affairs was reorganized and renamed as the Bureau of Democracy, Human Rights, and Labor, reflecting both a broader sweep and a more focused approach to the interlocking issues of human rights, worker rights, and democracy. The 1999 human rights reports reflect a year of dedicated effort by hundreds of State Department, Foreign Service, and other U.S. Government employees.

Our embassies, which prepared the initial drafts of the reports, gathered information throughout the year from a variety of sources across the political spectrum, including government officials, jurists, military sources, journalists, human rights monitors, academics, and labor activists. . . .

After the embassies completed their drafts, the texts were sent to Washington for careful review by the Bureau of Democracy, Human Rights, and Labor, in cooperation with other State Department offices. . . . Department officers drew on their own sources of information. These included reports provided by U.S. and other human rights groups, foreign government officials, representatives from the United Nations and other international and regional organizations and institutions, and experts from academia and the media. Officers also consulted with experts on worker rights issues, refugee issues, military and police matters, women's issues, and legal matters. The guiding principle was to ensure that all relevant information was assessed as objectively, thoroughly, and fairly as possible.

The reports in this volume will be used as a resource for shaping policy, conducting diplomacy, and making assistance, training, and other resource allocations. They also will serve as a basis for the U.S. Government's cooperation with private groups to promote the observance of internationally recognized human rights.

The Country Reports on Human Rights Practices cover internationally recognized individual, civil, political, and worker rights, as set forth in the Universal Declaration of Human Rights. . . .

US LEGISLATION ON MILITARY AID: HUMAN RIGHTS PROVISIONS
Human Rights and Security Assistance
Sec. 502B of the Foreign Assistance Act of 1961, as amended, 22 U.S.C.A. 2304

(a) Observance of human rights as principal goal of foreign policy; Implementation requirements

(1) The United States shall, in accordance with its international obligations as set forth in the Charter of the United Nations and in keeping with the constitutional heritage and traditions of the United States, promote and encourage increased respect for human rights and fundamental freedoms throughout the world without distinction as to race, sex, language, or religion. Accordingly, a principal goal of the foreign policy of the United States shall be to promote the increased observance of internationally recognized human rights by all countries.

(2) Except under circumstances specified in this section, no security assistance may be provided to any country the government of which engages in a consistent pattern of gross violations of internationally recognized human rights. Security assistance may not be provided to the police, domestic intelligence, or similar law enforcement forces of a country ... the government of which engages in a consistent pattern of gross violations of internationally recognized human rights unless the President certifies in writing ... that extraordinary circumstances exist warranting provision of such assistance. . . .

(3) In furtherance of paragraphs (1) and (2), the President is directed to formulate and conduct international security assistance programs of the United States in a manner which will promote and advance human rights and avoid identification of the United States, through such programs, with governments which deny to their people internationally recognized human rights and fundamental freedoms, in violation of international law or in contravention of the policy of the United States as expressed in this section or otherwise.

(4) In determining whether the government of a country engages in a consistent patern of gross violations of internationally recognized human rights, the President shall give particular consideration to whether the government—

(A) has engaged in or tolerated particularly severe violations of religious freedom, as defined in section 3 of the International Religious Freedom Act of 1998[1]; or

(B) has failed to undertake serious and sustained efforts to combat particularly severe violations of religious freedom when such efforts could reasonably have been undertaken.

(b) Report by Secretary of State on practices of proposed recipient countries; considerations

The Secretary of State shall transmit to the Congress, as part of the presentation materials for security assistance programs proposed for each fiscal year, a full and complete report, prepared with the assistance of the Assistant Secretary of State for Democracy, Human Rights, and Labor, and with the assistance of the Ambassador at Large for International Religious Freedom, with respect to practices regarding the observance of and respect for internationally recognized human rights in each country proposed as a recipient of security assistance. Wherever applicable, such report shall include information on practices regarding coercion in population control, including coerced abortion and involuntary sterilization. Such report shall also include, wherever applicable, information on violations of religious freedom, including particularly severe violations [as defined in the International Religious Freedom Act of 1998.] . . . In determining whether a government falls within the provisions of subsection (a)(3) of this section and in the preparation of any report or statement required under this section, consideration shall be given to—

(1) the relevant findings of appropriate international organizations, including nongovernmental organizations, such as the International Committee of the Red Cross; and

(2) the extent of cooperation by such government in permitting an unimpeded investigation by any such organization of alleged violations of internationally recognized human rights.

(c) Congressional request for information; information required; 30-day period; failure to supply information; termination or restriction of assistance

(1) Upon the request of the Senate or the House of Representatives by resolution of either such House, or upon the request of the Committee on Foreign Relations of the Senate or the Committee on Foreign Affairs of the House of Representatives, the Secretary of State shall, within thirty days after receipt of such request, transmit to both such committees a statement, prepared with the assistance of the Assistant Secretary of State for Democracy, Human Rights, and Labor, with respect to the country designated in such request, setting forth—

(A) all the available information about observance of and respect for human rights and fundamental freedom in that country, and a detailed description of practices by the recipient government with respect thereto;

(B) the steps the United States has taken to —

---

[1] [Eds.]Paragraph (4) was added pursuant to the International Religious Freedom Act of 1998.

   (i) promote respect for and observance of human rights in that country
       and discourage any practices which are inimical to internationally
       recognized human rights, and
  (ii) publicly or privately call attention to, and disassociate the United
       States and any security assistance provided for such country from,
       such practices;
 (C) whether, in the opinion of the Secretary of State, notwithstanding any
     such practices—
   (i) extraordinary circumstances exist which necessitate a continuation
       of security assistance for such country, and, if so, a description of
       such circumstances and the extent to which such assistance should
       be continued (subject to such conditions as Congress may impose
       under this section), and
  (ii) on all the facts it is in the national interest of the United States to
       provide such assistance; and
 (D) such other information as such committee or such House may request.

  (3) In the event a statement with respect to a country is requested pursuant to
paragraph (1) of this subsection but is not transmitted in accordance therewith
within thirty days after receipt of such request, no security assistance shall be
delivered to such country except as may thereafter be specifically authorized by law
from such country unless and until such statement is transmitted.

. . .

(d) Definitions

  For the purposes of this section—
  (1) the term 'gross violations of internationally recognized human rights'
includes torture or cruel, inhuman, or degrading treatment or punishment, prolonged detention without charges and trial, causing the disappearance of persons
by the abduction and clandestine detention of those persons, and other flagrant
denial of the right to life, liberty, or the security of person. . . .

. . .

(e) Removal of prohibition on assistance

  Notwithstanding any other provision of law, funds authorized to be appropriated under subchapter I of this chapter may be made available for the furnishing of
assistance to any country with respect to which the President finds that such a
significant improvement in its human rights record has occurred as to warrant
lifting the prohibition on furnishing such assistance in the national interest of the
United States.

STEPHEN COHEN, CONDITIONING U.S. SECURITY ASSISTANCE ON HUMAN RIGHTS PRACTICES
76 Am. J. Int. L. 246 (1982)

. . .

The principal (although not exclusive) legislative enactment on human rights and military ties has been section 502B of the Foreign Assistance Act of 1961. . . .

. . .

In 1974, when Congress originally enacted section 502B, it also began to pass legislation to limit military aid and arms sales to designated countries. The country-specific legislation was contained in bills authorizing or appropriating funds for military aid, and it named, at various times, Argentina, Brazil, Chile, El Salvador, Guatemala, Paraguay, the Philippines, South Korea, Uruguay, and Zaire. The legislation usually mentioned only military aid and was effective for a single year, although in two cases it expressly prohibited arms sales as well and was of indefinite duration.

Congress has successfully attached country-specific legislation to bills authorizing or appropriating military aid for every fiscal year since 1975. For example, Chile was prohibited from receiving any military aid in fiscal 1975 and the amount requested for South Korea was substantially reduced. . . .

. . .

Perhaps the most remarkable evidence of the Carter administration's conservative approach to section 502B was its policy never to determine formally, even in a classified decision, that a particular government was engaged in gross abuses. The primary reason for this policy was the belief that such a determination, even if classified, would inevitably be leaked to the press and become generally known. It was feared that each country named would then consider itself publicly insulted, with consequent damage to our bilateral relationship. In addition, there was concern that once such a finding was revealed, the freedom to alter it might be severely constrained by public political pressures.

. . .

In practice, the Secretary of State had to resist pressures both from Congress and within his own Department to make such findings. Administration representatives repeatedly refused congressional requests for a list of governments considered to be engaged in gross abuses, stating that it was administration policy not to draw up such a list. Within the Department, the Secretary of State sought to avoid explaining the reason for decisions on security assistance either in writing or even informally. When he resolved a dispute, he often communicated simply whether the request was approved or disapproved and little more. Particularly in cases of disapproval, the Secretary strenuously avoided ever stating that it was required by section 502B since such a statement would have meant that the government in question was considered to be engaged 'in a consistent pattern of gross violations of human rights'.

. . .

. . . The major issues of interpretation [of section 502B] are discussed below. The three key questions were:

(1) When was a foreign government considered to be engaged 'in a consistent pattern of gross violations of internationally recognized human rights'?
(2) What U.S. interests constituted 'extraordinary circumstances'?
(3) What was encompassed by the category 'security assistance'?

1. Gross Violations. . . . [T]he issue never arose with respect to many governments that appear to have practiced gross abuses. The question whether section 502B might apply to them was never raised because they were never seriously considered for security assistance for a variety of reasons other than human rights. . . .

After these countries were eliminated, approximately 70 remained that were seriously considered for military aid and arms sales. A narrow reading of the 'gross violations' language was adopted, so that, in the end, only about 12 of the 70 were thought to fall within it. While in some respects the narrow reading was consistent with the congressional purpose, in others it appeared to subvert the intended meaning of the statute. The narrow reading was derived from the way that the four basic elements of the category were interpreted. First, there must be violations of 'internationally recognized human rights'. Second, the violations must be 'gross'. Third, the frequency of violations must result in a 'consistent pattern'. Fourth, the government itself must be engaged, which is to say, responsible for the violations.
. . .

The Carter administration . . . decisions on security assistance [went] no further than required by the abuses specifically listed in subsection (d)(1). A government was considered to fall within it only when it practiced arbitrary imprisonment, torture, or summary execution of relatively large numbers of its own people. That a government was authoritarian, denied basic civil and political liberties, or failed to promote basic economic and social rights was not, by itself, enough to invoke the statutory prohibition on military ties.

The second element, that the violations must be 'gross', was read to mean that they must be significant in their impact. . . .

Third, the element of a 'consistent pattern' was held to mean that abuses had to be significant in number and recurrent. Isolated instances of torture or summary execution, while certainly gross abuses, would not trigger termination of security assistance under section 502B. For example, the reported imprisonment and torture of several dozen labor leaders in Tunisia was considered not to be sufficient by itself to constitute a 'consistent pattern'. . . .
. . .

2. Extraordinary Circumstances. The Carter administration always gave considerable weight to arguments that other U.S. interests might require continuation of security assistance, even when the government in question was thought to be a 'gross violator'. Thus, the charge that its pursuit of human rights was 'single-minded' and to the exclusion of other interests was far wide of the mark. If anything, the administration gave excessive credence to claims that some specific foreign policy objective would and could be promoted only if security assistance were provided, and often failed to subject such claims to rigorous analysis.
. . .

. . . In the end, human rights concerns resulted in the termination of security assistance to only eight countries, all in Latin America: Argentina, Bolivia, El Salvador, Guatemala, Haiti, Nicaragua, Paraguay, and Uruguay.

Extraordinary circumstances were found for all of the other countries considered to be gross violators. Thus, Indonesia (although technically not on the list) was a key member of ASEAN (the pro-Western association of Southeast Asian countries) and important to countering Soviet and Vietnamese influence in the region. Iran was judged critical because it shared a long border with the Soviet Union, was a major supplier of oil to the West, and defended our strategic interests in the Persian Gulf. Military ties with South Korea were deemed essential to deterring the threat of an invasion from the north. Military bases in the Philippines were judged critical to the United States and a security assistance relationship essential to keeping the bases. Finally, Zaire, the third largest country by area in Africa, was the source of nearly all the West's cobalt, a material crucial to the performance of high-performance jet engines.

. . .

IV. Conclusions

. . . The history of section 502B is a case study of executive frustration of congressionally mandated foreign policy and underlines the need, particularly with this kind of legislation, for clearer directives, less discretion, and more assiduous congressional oversight. While these observations emerge from experience in the human rights area, they are . . . especially apt when congressional objectives may require decisions that displease particular governments and that will therefore be resisted by the Foreign Service bureaucracy whose paramount interest is maintaining cordial relations. For example, conclusions about the effectiveness of legislation conditioning security assistance on human rights practices are likely to be highly relevant to legislation conditioning nuclear exports on practices with respect to nuclear proliferation.

Congress has the most decisive impact when its directives allow the Executive no discretion at all, as in the country-specific legislation stating precisely which governments are to be denied military aid and arms sales on human rights grounds. . . .

. . .

There are, perhaps, some drawbacks to statutes that deny all discretion, such as the country-specific legislation. Once such a provision is enacted, the Executive lacks the flexibility to respond quickly to changed conditions. While Congress has a legitimate role to play in setting basic foreign policy goals, it may be less well equipped to make day-to-day decisions about how best to fulfill those goals in specific cases. . . .

. . .

This examination . . . suggests another important issue: whether withholding is an effective instrument for enforcing adherence to international human rights law. A definitive answer to this question is far from easy to obtain. It may be difficult to determine whether a government has taken positive steps to improve human rights conditions. Changes that are merely 'cosmetic' must be distinguished from those which indicate real improvement. When positive changes do occur, it may be difficult to say whether U.S. actions or other factors were decisive. But the fact that positive changes are lacking does not mean that U.S. actions have been ineffective. Although a targeted government may not have altered current practices, it may be deterred from worse violations. Moreover, regimes other than the immediate target may be influenced by the risk of being denied United States security assistance if they engage in repression. While the impact of withholding security assistance on human rights practices is beyond the scope of this article, it is the logical next question for scholars interested in international human rights.

. . .

QUESTIONS

1. 'The U.S. legislation imposing human rights conditions on security aid arbitrarily carves out from the human rights corpus certain types of violations and ignores other vital ones. There is no justification in the human rights movement for making these distinctions.' Comment, bearing in mind:

a. What kinds of human rights violations are included in the statutory definitions? Is there any unity among them?

b. Would a bare reference to 'gross violations of internationally recognized human rights' have been preferable? If a selective list is preferable, do you agree with the present inclusions/exclusions?

2. 'What long-run purposes does this legislation serve, even assuming it is effective with respect to its short-term goals? A country is asked to stop a given practice, like arbitrary detentions. It does so. All bad structures—military control, repression of speech and association, economic control by a small elite, and so on—may very well stay in place. As soon as the practice is relaxed, as soon as it's on a downward curve, aid can be resumed. Of course the practice itself will be reinstated in its prior vigor when politically necessary. What has been accomplished?' Comment.

3. Given the pattern of executive-legislative relationships and the broad use of waivers as described by Cohen, would you locate the power to impose sanctions fully in the Congress? Or do you believe that the Congress should continue to write executive waivers into its legislation? Why?

NOTE

Human rights became an important concern in the US Congress in the early 1970s, and became a significant element of US foreign policy under President Carter at the end of that decade. It was in the early years of his administration that Secretary of State Vance delivered the following speech.

SECRETARY OF STATE CYRUS VANCE, SPEECH ON HUMAN RIGHTS AND FOREIGN POLICY
76 Dep't of State Bull. 505 (1977)

. . . Let me define what we mean by 'human rights'.

First, there is the right to be free from governmental violation of the integrity of the person. Such violations include torture; cruel, inhuman, or degrading treatment or punishment; and arbitrary arrest or imprisonment. And they include denial of fair public trial and invasion of the home.

Second, there is the right to the fulfilment of such vital needs as food, shelter, health care, and education. We recognize that the fulfillment of this right will depend, in part, upon the stage of a nation's economic development. But we also know that this right can be violated by a government's action or inaction—for example, through corrupt official processes which divert resources to an elite at the expense of the needy or through indifference to the plight of the poor.

Third, there is the right to enjoy civil and political liberties: freedom of thought, of religion, of assembly; freedom of speech; freedom of the press; freedom of movement both within and outside one's own country; freedom to take part in government.

Our policy is to promote all these rights. They are all recognized in the Universal Declaration of Human Rights, a basic document which the United States helped fashion and which the United Nations approved in 1948. There may be disagreement on the priorities these rights deserve. But I believe that, with work, all of these rights can become complementary and mutually reinforcing.

. . .

In pursuing a human rights policy, we must always keep in mind the limits of our power and of our wisdom. A sure formula for defeat of our goals would be a rigid, hubristic attempt to impose our values on others. A doctrinaire plan of action would be as damaging as indifference.

We must be realistic. Our country can only achieve our objectives if we shape what we do to the case at hand. . . .

. . .

A second set of questions concerns the prospects for effective action:

Will our action be useful in promoting the overall cause of human rights?

Will it actually improve the specific conditions at hand? Or will it be likely to make things worse instead?

Is the country involved receptive to our interest and efforts?

Will others work with us, including official and private international organizations dedicated to furthering human rights?

Finally, does our sense of values and decency demand that we speak out or take action anyway, even though there is only a remote chance of making our influence felt?

3. We will ask a third set of questions in order to maintain a sense of perspective:

Have we steered away from the self-righteous and strident, remembering that our own record is not unblemished?

Have we been sensitive to genuine security interests, realizing that outbreak of armed conflict or terrorism could in itself pose a serious threat to human rights?

Have we considered *all* the rights at stake? If, for instance, we reduce aid to a government which violates the political rights of its citizens, do we not risk penalizing the hungry and poor, who bear no responsibility for the abuses of their government?

If we are determined to act, the means available range from quiet diplomacy in its many forms, through public pronouncements, to withholding of assistance. Whenever possible, we will use positive steps of encouragement and inducement. Our strong support will go to countries that are working to improve the human condition. We will always try to act in concert with other countries, through international bodies.

. . .

Our policy is to be applied within our own society as well as abroad. We welcome constructive criticism at the same time as we offer it.

No one should suppose that we are working in a vacuum. We place great weight on joining with others in the cause of human rights.

The U.N. system is central to this cooperative endeavor. . . .

. . .

We can nourish no illusions that a call to the banner of human rights will bring sudden transformations in authoritarian societies.

. . .

We seek these goals because they are right—and because we, too, will benefit. Our own well-being, and even our security, are enhanced in a world that shares common freedoms and in which prosperity and economic justice create the conditions for peace. And let us remember that we always risk paying a serious price when we become identified with repression.

Nations, like individuals, limit their potential when they limit their goals. The American people understand this. I am confident they will support foreign policies that reflect our traditional values. To offer less is to define America in ways we should not accept.

. . .

MAKAU MUTUA AND PETER ROSENBLUM, ZAIRE: REPRESSION AS POLICY
(1990), at 187

United States Human Rights Policy Towards Zaire

The United States has been closely involved in Zairian politics since its independence. In 1960, the United States actively opposed the country's first elected leader, Patrice Lumumba. It supported the rise of Mobutu to the Presidency in 1965; and intervened with military support to protect the Mobutu government during the second invasion of Shaba in 1978. When the government of Zaire has been threatened with economic crisis and internal insurgency, the United States has stepped in to support it.

. . .

Throughout the last 25 years, the United States has provided significant bilateral economic and military assistance to Zaire. It has supported Zaire in international lending institutions such as the World Bank, the International Monetary Fund (IMF) and the African Development Bank. . . .

The United States is perceived by many Zairians as being responsible, at least in part, for Mr. Mobutu's continuation in power. Robert Remole, a former Political Counselor at the U.S. Embassy in Kinshasa and a retired 28-year veteran of the State Department, testified before the Subcommittee on Africa on this subject in 1980. 'I have heard this innumerable times,' he said, 'from educated Zairians, members of the Legislative Council, lawyers, other people who will be of import-ance when the Mobutu regime does finally collapse'. Mr. Remole emphasized that blaming the United States was 'of course irrational, unreasonable', but he argued that the policy of U.S. support for and identification with the government of Zaire 'bears great risk'. 'The risk', he testified, 'is one that has been alluded to obliquely; that is, another Iran'.

U.S. support for the government of Zaire has created considerable resentment among Zairians. As one American-educated Zairian told the Lawyers Committee, 'When Mobutu goes, and he is going to go one day, the United States may find it extremely difficult to make friends in this country, because of its support for Mobutu'. . . .

Nevertheless, though fully informed about President Mobutu's tactics and unpopularity, Congress and the Administration have repeatedly accepted the same justification for support to his government, namely, Zaire's strategic importance and its support for U.S. policies in the region. . . .

. . .

. . . Elliot Abrams, Assistant Secretary of State for Human Rights and Humani-tarian Affairs under the Reagan Administration, articulated a similar justification for U.S. support for the government of Zaire:

> As you are well aware, Zaire has long been a friend and key regional partner of the United States and the West. It has consistently worked with us. . . . Zairian minerals, notably copper and cobalt, are important to the West. Zaire's strategic relevance, which is due to its large size and population as well as its common borders with nine African countries, has never been more important than now, as we work towards political solutions in southern Africa.

. . .

In 1982, as criticism of Zaire's human rights record mounted, the United States Congress reduced assistance to Zaire from $70 million to $20 million. In response, President Mobutu announced in May 1982 that he would no longer accept U.S. aid. The following month UN Ambassador Jeanne Kirkpatrick travelled to Kin-shasa, in an effort to mend fences with President Mobutu. Following her visit, aid was delivered.

Two years later, President Mobutu was treated as an honored guest by the President of the United States. In an August 1984 visit to the White House, he received a 'warm welcome' from President Reagan. Mr. Reagan praised President Mobutu as 'a faithful friend for some 20 years'. . . .

President Mobutu has effectively used Ambassador Kirkpatrick's visit, his meetings with U.S. presidents and other symbolic gestures of support to sustain the perception that the United States condones his conduct, and will stand by his government.

. . .

Despite the continued intransigence of the government of Zaire, and the ongoing pattern of human rights abuses, the Bush Administration continues to press for continued U.S. aid to that country. The Administration is using virtually the same language it has in the past to justify its request. . . .

. . .

NOTE

For a decade, Human Rights Watch has issued a World Report reviewing the prior year's human rights practices around the globe. This HRW World Report 1999 refers to practices in 1998. The excerpts below, from the Report's Introduction, comment on US Foreign Policy.

> The Clinton administration's efforts to promote human rights around the world were subject to large blind spots. Major parts of Africa, the Middle East and the former Soviet Union never made it to the administration's human rights agenda. As has become common in recent years, the State Department accurately reported on human rights abuses in its annual Country Reports on Human Rights Practices. But for many countries, this one-shot commentary was never repeated in other fora, let alone allowed to influence U.S. policy. Human rights concerns rarely ranked with the administration's other interests.

> [The Report spoke favourably of US foreign policy with respect to 'the pariah countries' such as Burma, Sierra Leone and Sudan; noted that it had 'performed well' on other pivotal countries like Croatia, Malaysia and Algeria; and termed its record 'mixed' for countries like Colombo and China. It continued:]

> Most troubling were the vast swaths of the globe that were exempt from U.S. pressure on human rights. In South Asia, the administration condemned nuclear tests by India and Pakistan but said little about their dismal human rights records. In the Middle East, Saudi Arabia and its oil-rich or strategically useful neighbors faced no public pressure on their own records of repression. Nor did Israel, Egypt, or Syria. Israeli abuses, if mentioned at all, were treated as 'obstacles to peace' rather than human rights violations. . . .
> The petroleum-rich states of Central Asia were also courted without reference to their repressive conduct. Typically, President Saparmurat Niyazov of Turkmenistan was welcomed at the White House even though he denies his citizens virtually all civil liberties. . . . It also rewarded him with $96 million in investments backed by the Export-Import Bank. Human rights similarly took a back seat to energy interests in Azerbaijan, Kazakstan, and Uzbekistan.
> In Africa, where the United States hoped to promote stability, it favored strategic alliances with new leaders rather than overtly addressing their human rights problems. . . . In Uganda, Washington firmly supported President Museveni, whose help it needs to contain Sudan. . . .

QUESTIONS

1. The materials make clear how variable US foreign policy about aid and human rights has been, and how large the gap has been between an ideal as stated by Vance and strategic decisions.

   a. Do you view inconsistency as such to be a substantial criticism of human rights conditionality or other aspects of US military or economic aid? Is it possible for a great power like the United States to act consistently on these matters? Is it desirable?

   b. Is there some grand principle that you believe could be developed that would embrace and guide the many difficult decisions, and that could locate human rights considerations within a broader scheme of other considerations germane to a foreign policy decision?

   c. Is it sufficient that whenever questions of military or economic assistance or particular trade or investment relationships involve states committing serious human rights violations, the issue of human rights be raised and seriously considered at top-level discussions?

   d. What factors should, in your view, properly influence considerations about suspensions of aid—say, in a case like Zaire? What factors that have been historically relevant in such types of cases do you view as improper? Why?

2. If a suspension of economic aid is being considered, what steps could realistically be taken to assure that the cut-off will not severely hurt the poor and needy in the target country, the very groups that may be the primary victims of human rights violations?

3. What value do you see in the annual State Department country reports? What difficulties? Do they necessarily have some effect on US foreign policy toward the states involved?

COMMENT ON THE INTERNATIONAL RELIGIOUS FREEDOM ACT OF 1998

After months of intense political debate within the United States and of expression of strong concerns by several governments, Congress enacted the International Religious Freedom Act of 1998.[2] The compromise Act took account of several of the criticisms of its earlier draft forms, thereby allaying to some degree earlier concerns.

Congressional findings in section 2(a) stated in part:

   (1) The right to freedom of religion undergirds the very origin and existence of the United States. . . .
   (2) Freedom of religious belief and practice is a universal human right and fundamental freedom articulated in numerous international instruments. . . .

. . .

---

[2] This Comment describes and quotes from the Act as it was enacted in 1998, 112 Stat. 2787. Technical amendments followed a year later. The Act, as amended, is set forth in 22 U.S.C. §6401 *et seq.*

(4) The right to freedom of religion is under renewed and, in some cases, increasing assault in many countries around the world. More than one-half of the world's population lives under regimes that severely restrict or prohibit the freedom of their citizens to study, believe, observe, and freely practice the religious faith of their choice. Religious believers and communities suffer both government-sponsored and government-tolerated violations of their rights to religious freedom. Among the many forms of such violations are state-sponsored slander campaigns, confiscations of property, surveillance by security police, including by special divisions of 'religious police', severe prohibitions against construction and repair of places of worship, denial of the right to assemble and relegation of religious communities to illegal status through arbitrary registration laws, prohibitions against the pursuit of education or public office, and prohibitions against publishing, distributing, or possessing religious literature and materials.

(5) Even more abhorrent, religious believers in many countries face such severe and violent forms of religious persecution as detention, torture, beatings, forced marriage, rape, imprisonment, enslavement, mass resettlement, and death merely for the peaceful belief in, change of or practice of their faith. . . .

Section 3 sets forth some vital definitions:

. . .

(11) The term 'particularly severe violations of religious freedom' means systematic, ongoing, egregious violations of religious freedom, including violations such as—

(A) torture or cruel, inhuman, or degrading treatment or punishment;
(B) prolonged detention without charges;
(C) causing the disappearance of persons by the abduction or clandestine detention of those persons; or
(D) other flagrant denial of the right to life, liberty, or the security of persons.

. . .

(13) The term 'violations of religious freedom' means violations of the internationally recognized right to freedom of religion and religious belief and practice, as set forth in the international instruments referred to in section 2(a)(2) . . . including violations such as—

(A) arbitrary prohibitions on, restrictions of, or punishment for.—
    (i) assembling for peaceful religious activities such as worship, preaching, and prayer, including arbitrary registration requirements;
    (ii) speaking freely about one's religious beliefs;
    (iii) changing one's religious beliefs and affiliation;
    (iv) possession and distribution of religious literature, including Bibles; or
    (v) raising one's children in the religious teachings and practices of one's choice; or
(B) any of the following acts if committed on account of an individual's religious belief or practice: detention, interrogation, imposition of an onerous financial penalty, forced labor, forced mass resettlement,

> imprisonment, forced religious conversion, beating, torture, mutila-
> tion, rape, enslavement, murder, and execution.

The Act established an office on International Religious Freedom, based in the Department of State and headed by an Ambassador at Large appointed by the President with the advice and consent of the Senate. His responsibility is to denounce violations of the right to freedom of religion and to recommend responses by the US government. He serves as adviser to the President with respect to policies advancing that right. The Ambassador assists the Secretary of State in preparing the Secretary's Annual Report on International Religious Freedom, which is to contain (section 102) a description of religious freedom in each foreign country, and a detailed assessment and description of violations including:

> persecution of one religious group by another religious group, religious persecu-
> tion by governmental and nongovernmental entities, persecution targeted at
> individuals or particular denominations or entire religions, the existence of gov-
> ernment policies violating religious freedom, and the existence of government
> policies concerning—
>   (i) limitations or prohibitions on, or lack of availability of, openly conducted,
>   organized religious services. . . .

In compiling data and assessing the degree of observance of the right, US mission personnel abroad:

> shall, as appropriate, seek out and maintain contacts with religious and human
> rights nongovernmental organizations, with the consent of those organizations,
> including receiving reports and updates from such organizations and, when
> appropriate, investigating such reports.

The Secretary of State is to maintain lists of persons believed to be imprisoned or detained for their religious faith.

Section 201 establishes a United States Commission on International Religious Freedom of ten members. Its duties, under section 202, include reviewing all information generated by other reports and giving policy options to the President with respect to violator states committing particularly severe violations of religious freedom. It also suggests policy options for states taking deliberate steps to improve respect for this right. The Commission submits an annual report.

Section 301 establishes a Special Adviser to the President within the National Security Council, who also submits policy options and serves as liaison among different bodies.

Section 401 concerns presidential actions responding to violations. The President is either to take one or more of the actions described in section 405(a), or enter into a binding agreement with a country's government, as described in section 405(b). The President is to seek to target action 'as narrowly as practicable with respect to the agency or instrumentality of the foreign government, or specific officials thereof, that are responsible . . . '. In determining what action to take, the President:

shall seek to minimize any adverse impact on—

> (A) the population of the country whose government is targeted by the Presidential action or actions; and
> (B) the humanitarian activities of United States and foreign nongovernmental organizations in such country.

The President is to designate states that have engaged in or tolerated 'particularly severe violations of religious freedom' as countries 'of particular concern for religious freedom'. For the government of each such country, the President is to seek to determine the precise agency or instrumentality and the specific officials 'that are responsible for the particularly severe violations . . .'.

After deciding to take action against a country, the President is to consult a number of parties, including consultation with the government of the violator state. The President is also to consult with foreign governments to explore the possibility of a coordinated international policy.

The contemplated Presidential actions are set forth in section 405(a). They include a private demarche, official public demarche, a public condemnation, condemnation within multilateral fora, canceling scientific or cultural changes or state visits, suspension or withdrawal of development assistance or security assistance, directions to international financial organizations not to approve specified loans or guarantees of credit, ordering US agencies not to issue specific licences, prohibiting US financial institutions from making loans or extending credits over $10 million, or prohibiting US agencies from entering into particular contracts. In the case of countries with 'particularly severe violations', the President is to impose the stricter among these sanctions, involving suspension of security assistance, development aid or loans or issuance of licences.

The President may also, under section 405(c):

> negotiate and enter into a binding agreement with a foreign government that obligates such government to cease . . . the act, policy, or practice constituting the violation of religious freedom. The entry into force of a binding agreement for the cessation of the violations shall be a primary objective for the President in responding to a foreign government that has engaged in or tolerated particularly severe violations of religious freedom.

Section 407 authorizes a presidential waiver of the application of some of the actions described in section 405(a) above—those actions involving suspension of military assistance or economic aid or suspension of loans and credits. The President must then report to the appropriate Congressional committee and justify the waiver on one of the following grounds: that the foreign government has ceased the violations, the waiver would further the purposes of the Act, or 'the important national interest of the United States requires' the waiver.

NOTE

Changes responding to earlier criticism that were made in the final version of this legislation include the following. (1) The President would not be required to impose automatic sanctions but would have a waiver power. There had been concern that automatic sanctions would hurt countries viewed as allies in basic policies, such as Saudi Arabia. Business groups remained concerned that the Act could alienate important trading partners. (2) An independent Commission expressing its views about religious freedom elsewhere would be created to act as a check on the executive. (3) The legislation originated in efforts by a number of groups, including prominently a Christian Coalition and other conservative religious group. As it broadened and changed character, it drew support from a wide range of religious groups.

In 1999, the State Department submitted to Congress its first Annual Report on International Religious Freedom, required by the 1998 Act. The Department's 1999 Country Report on Human Rights Practices, p. 1092, *supra*, describes that Report. Excerpts follow:

> The Report demonstrates that violations of religious freedom, including religious persecution, are not confined to any one country, religion, or nationality. Throughout the world, Baha'is, Buddhists, Christians, Hindus, Jews, Muslims, and other believers continue to suffer for their faith.
>
> . . .
>
> The International Religious Freedom Act also required [that the Annual Report] identify those countries where the government has engaged in or tolerated 'severe' or 'particularly severe' violations of religious freedom. In October Secretary Albright informed Congress that she was designating five 'Countries of Particular Concern': Burma, China, Iran, Iraq, and Sudan. The Secretary also informed Congress that she was identifying as particularly severe violators the Taliban regime in Afghanistan and the Government of Serbia. This last action was not taken under the auspices of the International Religious Freedom Act because the United States does not regard the Taliban as a government or Serbia as a country as envisioned by the act.

QUESTIONS

1. In what important respects does this Act differ either from the legislation on security assistance or the controversy with China over the most favored nation clause? Is one or the other among these more 'interventionist'? More likely to arouse concerns and opposition in other states? Why?

2. How do you assess the potential effectiveness of this legislation in achieving its goal of religious freedom, compared with the other legislation noted above?

C. CASE STUDY: MOST FAVORED NATION TREATMENT AND THE PEOPLE'S REPUBLIC OF CHINA

COMMENT ON MOST FAVORED NATION TREATMENT

The following materials about the bearing of human rights considerations on trade with China draw on human rights conditions to trade that were stated in legislation, proposed legislation and an Executive Order. Neither of the statutory provisions previously considered—section 502B and section 116 of the Foreign Assistance Act of 1961, as amended—are here relevant, for the United States has provided neither security assistance nor development assistance to the PRC.

The so-called Jackson-Vanik Amendment to the Trade Act of 1974 (Sec. 402, 19 U.S.C. 2432) at once authorizes the granting of trade benefits to designated categories of states and qualifies its authorization by stating:

> To assure the continued dedication of the United States to fundamental human rights . . . products from any nonmarket economy country shall not be eligible to receive nondiscriminatory treatment (most-favoured-nation treatment) . . . during the period beginning with the date on which the President determines that such country —
>
>> (1) denies its citizens the right or opportunity to emigrate;
>> (2) imposes more than a nominal tax on emigration . . . ; or
>> (3) imposes more than a nominal tax . . . or other charge on any citizen as a consequence of the desire of such citizen to emigrate to the country of his choice. . . .

This provision is subject to Presidential waiver under stated conditions noted below.

The most favored nation (MFN) treatment to which the amendment refers is a familiar clause and concept regulating many types of relationships among states. In general, a MFN clause (in, say, a treaty) grants a state benefiting from it (state 'X') the same treatment (say, with respect to the ability of X's citizens to do business in state 'Y', the other party to the treaty) as has been given by Y to some other 'most-favored' state. In other words, X and its citizens benefit from the most favored treatment that Y has granted to any other state on this matter.

For example, suppose that state 'Z' had previously entered into a treaty with Y giving Z's citizens extensive rights to do business in Y, rights that are as favorable as or more favorable than those given by Y to any other state. By virtue of the MFN clause in its treaty with Y, X is assured that its citizens doing business in Y will be treated as favorably as the nationals of Z.

In the case of the Jackson-Vanik Amendment, the MFN clause appears in domestic legislation (not a treaty) and affects tariffs, a field highly regulated both by multilateral arrangements such as the General Agreement on Tariffs and Trade (GATT) and World Trade Organization (WTO) and by national legislation.

Special categories of states may fall within special treaty or statutory regimes, such as the System of Generalized Preferences covering a range of exports from less developed countries. In the case of the PRC, which the United States did not view as a party to GATT and which is not a party to the WTO, MFN treatment plays a vital role. If such treatment were withdrawn by the United States, statutory tariff rates that are often much higher than MFN rates would apply to imports from the PRC.

The Jackson-Vanik Amendment was enacted primarily in response to bars erected by the Soviet Union to emigration. Those bars particularly affected members of several groups anxious to leave, including principally Soviet Jews. After the (ongoing) transformation and disintegration of the former Soviet Union, the question of MFN treatment has been dominated by issues other than a state's denial of the right of its citizens to emigrate. That has surely been the case with respect to decisions about MFN treatment for China. Conditions other than those stated in the Jackson-Vanik Amendment have become relevant to tariffs on imports from the PRC. The same is true for other states—including Afghanistan, Cuba and North Korea—which have been denied 'normal' MFN trading status under the Amendment.

The following materials look at selective illustrations over a decade of the Chinese–American conflict, and at the related Congressional–Executive conflict, over human rights conditions to MFN treatment for tariffs on trade from China, an issue further complicated in recent years by China's quest for admission to the World Trade Organization.

ROBERT DRINAN AND TERESA KUO, THE 1991 BATTLE FOR HUMAN RIGHTS IN CHINA
14. Hum. Rts. Q. 21 (1992), at 22

. . .

While [President Bush] believes that the unconditional extension of MFN is the best way to advance US ideals of freedom and democracy in China, the majority of lawmakers disagree. . . .

. . . [T]he President recognized in 1991 that an overwhelming majority of the House of Representatives likely will not support unconditional MFN renewal. Therefore, from the initial stages of the 1991 MFN debate, the administration focused its efforts on garnering the thirty-four Senate votes needed to sustain a presidential veto of conditional MFN renewal.

. . .

The Jackson-Vanik Amendment allows the President to waive the emigration requirement only when it would 'substantially promote' the goals of the Amendment *and* the President has received assurances that the country's emigration practices will 'lead substantially' to such objectives. Since 1980 three presidents have used the waiver method to grant MFN status to China.

. . .

In 1991 both the Senate and the House took early action to disapprove the presidential waiver renewing China's MFN status. In addition to voicing its increasing dissatisfaction over China's human rights abuses, Congress also expressed growing concerns both over China's unfair trade practices toward the United States and with regard to the sales of nuclear weapons to developing nations. . . .

. . .

Despite the long list of human rights violations, the issue which captured the attention of many members of Congress last year was China's $10.4 billion trade [surplus] with the United States in 1990. The Treasury, along with the Central Intelligence Agency, attributed the trade imbalance to China's use of protectionist policies toward US imports. . . .

. . .

[Description omitted of Congressional bills providing for extension of MFN trade status in 1991 for another year with condition that President must certify as to certain matters for the renewal in 1992. The matters included certification that China had released certain political prisoners, and had made 'significant' progress in allowing human rights groups to have access to prisoners and trials, and in 'taking action to stop human rights violations'. Amendments to one bill would have required, as a condition to renewal, that China not contribute to proliferation of missiles and prohibit export of prison-made goods. These bills were defeated for varied reasons, including 'the desire to protect US farmers from possible Chinese retaliation at MFN revocation', and a big impact made by pro-MFN lobby groups on the Senate. 'Key players', US companies doing business in China, also did effective lobbying, as did public relations firms and law firms employed by the Chinese government. Human rights watch groups and labor organizations argued that MFN status should be revoked or should be renewed only with conditions attached.]

Although some have argued that MFN status should not be used as a tool to advance the cause of human rights in China, the United States has had a history of denying MFN status to other countries with similar human rights violations. . . . The United States also has steadfastly refused to grant MFN status to countries such as Afghanistan, Albania, Cambodia, Cuba, and North Korea, all run by tyrannical rulers. From 1982 to 1987, while Poland was under martial law, the United States refused to renew Poland's MFN status in order to protest the government's mass arrests and imprisonment of people connected with the Solidarity Movement. . . .

. . .

COMMENT ON PROPOSED LEGISLATION AND EXECUTIVE ORDER

In September 1992, Congress passed the United States China Act of 1992, 138 Cong. Rec. H. 8841, 102nd Cong. 2d Sess. It provided that the President could not recommend from July 1993 the continuation of a waiver related to nondiscriminatory MFN treatment for China unless he reported that China had taken 'appropriate actions' to 'begin adhering' to the UDHR in China and Tibet; allowed emigration for reasons of political or religious persecution; accounted for and released political prisoners' and prevented export to the United States of goods made by prison labour. Moreover, the President's report had to state that China had 'made overall significant progress' in other respects, including ending unfair trade practices against US business.

Even if the President could not report as required, nondiscriminatory MFN treatment was still to apply to goods manufactured by a business venture 'that is not a state-owned enterprise' of China, provided that such goods were not marketed or exported by a state-owned enterprise.

President Bush vetoed the Act. The House of Representatives overrode the veto by a vote of 345–74, but the Senate vote of 59–40 fell short of the required two-thirds majority for an override and hence sustained the veto.

Consider the following observations in Roger Sullivan, 'Discarding the China Card', 86 For. Pol. 3 (1992), at 8:

> ... [B]efore the 1989–91 worldwide collapse of communism, few questioned two key assumptions guiding Washington's China policy: first, that communist regimes cannot be fundamentally reformed or overthrown; and, second, that the Chinese communist government was firmly in control and that it enjoyed the support of the Chinese people. Events in Eastern Europe and the Soviet Union have done much more to undercut these assumptions than has the massacre at Tiananmen.
>
> ...
>
> ... The annual process of renewing non-discriminatory (so-called 'most-favored-nation', or MFN) tariff treatment for China became the outlet for congressional frustration and the vehicle for engaging the administration in a general policy debate. Renewal had been routine every year since MFN treatment was first extended to China in 1980 because Congress was well aware that MFN treatment is not a special benefit but is considered standard for almost all trading partners. . . . But when Congress saw no change in administration China policy, despite the collapse of communism in Eastern Europe and the Soviet Union and the clear evidence that China was becoming more repressive, congressional opposition to China's MFN status mounted.

In May 1993, President Clinton issued Executive Order 12850, Conditions for Renewal of Most Favored Nation Status for the People's Republic of China in 1994 (56 Fed. Reg. 31327, June 1, 1993). The Order continued the waiver for China for an additional 12 months to June 1994, so as to assure it of most favoured nation treatment during this period, but made renewal after June 1994 subject to stated conditions.

Those conditions included a determination that further extension of the waiver would promote 'freedom of emigration objectives', and that China was complying with the 1992 agreement on prison labour. Further determinations were required to the effect that China had made 'overall, significant progress' with respect to matters including: 'taking steps to begin adhering' to the UDHR, giving an accounting of and releasing political prisoners, ensuring humane treatment of prisoners, 'protecting Tibet's distinctive religious and cultural heritage', and permitting international radio and television broadcasts into China.

COMMENT ON SUBSEQUENT DEVELOPMENTS ABOUT MFN STATUS AND CHINA–US TRADE

This Comment notes a few illustrative events in the subsequent six years that indicate the considerations and forces at work with respect to US action bearing on trade with China and human rights violations in that country.[3]

1. US demands that China improve its human rights record or lose trade privileges were rejected by Chinese officials who complained of intereference in their internal affairs. The Chinese Prime Minister states that 'China will never accept the U.S. human rights concept. . . . History has already proven that it is futile to apply pressure on China' (*New York Times*, March 13, 1994, p. A1).

2. The Boeing Company led a lobbying campaign against a change in China's trade status. It stressed the existing orders of China for planes that had a value of $3.9 billion. It also argued that US trade was contributing to the rapid decentralization and transformation of China's economy, increasing freedom. Its corporate vice president stated: 'As in Taiwan and South Africa, the development of a vigorous middle class will bring the development of social and political freedom for all Chinese more than any other factor' (*New York Times*, March 21, 1994, p. D1). Other business leaders stressed the large number of jobs dependent on trade with China. The president of a footwear association said that denial of MFN status to China would lead to higher shoe prices for Americans, given that Chinese-made shoes were almost 50 per cent of the US market.

3. The Clinton Administration explored with Beijing the concessions necessary to lead the US to abandon the annual threat of trade sanctions. The present policy, the Administration stated, is outmoded, for withdrawing MFN benefits would cost thousands of American jobs and billions of dollars. Moreover, leaving MFN status in place for China would promote the rule of law there. Renewal of MFN status in 1994 had almost no conditions attached, and the President stated that he would abandon his efforts to use trade as a lever for human rights improvement. 'Thus Mr. Clinton cast aside the executive order issued last year' (*New York Times*, May 27, 1994, p. A1). He signalled as reasons China's role in putting pressure on North Korea to abandon its nuclear weapons programme, and China's significance as the world's most populous country and third-largest economy. Business groups strongly approved; the US Chamber of Commerce compared tying human rights issues to trade policy to 'using a blunt instrument for brain surgery'. Spokesmen for several human rights group strongly disapproved, pointing out that the United States had sacrificed its strongest point of pressure for improvement in China's human rights record. Critics stressed that the US policy toward China encouraged

---

[3] Except as otherwise noted, the accounts and the quotations are taken from *New York Times* articles over this period.

other violator states to assume they could do as they wished internally; US economic interests would block any serious pressures against them.

4. On the other hand, US policy was strong and threatening (as with respect to possible punitive tariffs) on other Chinese practices that, for example, tolerated widespread piracy in China of US-made software, movies and music. A 1995 controversy on that issue led to a trade agreement between the two countries that avoided announced trade sanctions that were soon to become effective. Violations by China of that agreement led to renewed threats in 1996 that tariffs could reach 100 per cent on Chinese imports of an aggregate value of over $1 billion.

5. Chinese–American relations suffered from the mid-1990s on for other reasons as well. The United States took the prominent role in proposing and lobbying for a resolution criticizing China's human rights practices in the UN Commission (see p. 634, *supra*). Such resolutions, which sometimes would have required the Commission to investigate human rights in China and sometimes also praised China in fields like economic and social rights, had repeatedly been defeated, but the United States approached the effort with a new strength and energy. The effort (narrowly defeated in 1995) continued in most of the subsequent years, though China's statement that it would sign the ICCPR—it has yet to ratify that Covenant—led the sponsors to withdraw the resolution in 1998.

6. The dispute over the possible productive or counterproductive effects of US trade sanctions, as through withdrawal of MFN status, continued to rage. The major human rights NGOs strongly advocated sanctions. Wei Jingsheng, among the most prominent of China's outspoken political dissidents, was convicted in 1996 of conspiracy to subvert the government and sentenced to 14 years in prison. An edited translation of his defense statement (China Rights Forum, Spring 1996, at 24) said in part:

> . . . . In relation to the harm the revocation of MFN status might do to the Chinese economy, my views differ from those of my friends abroad. I don't believe this to be the best method, because the direct victims of such measures are the already poverty-stricken Chinese people. Greater poverty will not constitute any threat to the bureaucrats and corrupt officials in control of the government because they do not care whether people live or die. On the contrary, they will put the blame for all the hardships on the 'imperialists' interference in our domestic affairs' and seize the opportunity to incite extreme nationalism which, instead of promoting China's democracy and reform, is likely to constitute a threat to world peace. Therefore, while supporting continuing efforts to impel the Chinese government to improve the human rights situation, I also hope for alternatives other than economic sanctions—alternatives that are safer and less likely to hurt the Chinese people. . . .

Other critics of economic sanctions feared that, unless European states joined in the Sanctions, their principal effect would be significant diversion of Chinese trade from the United States to Europe.

7. During 1998 and 1999, serious human rights violations led to a number of sharp rebukes by the United States accompanied by claims that China had broken

clear promises to improve its record on issues like political dissent. Other events contributed to a worsening relationship: bombing of the Chinese embassy in Belgrade, a worsening economic situation in China, Chinese campaign contributions and alleged spying in the United States, Chinese threats to Taiwan of possible use of force to achieve reunification. More broadly, discussions about and renewals of MFN status were drawn into the larger issue of China's admission to the World Trade Organization, whose rules would require permanent MFN status for China as a member. Nonetheless, the Clinton Administration held to its policy of 'constructive engagement', and generally was favorable to China's effort to join the WTO even as it sought concessions from China on trade and investment issues (such as allowing market access to China) as a condition to its support. China insisted that the United States end its annual MFN review and that it be granted 'permanent normal trading relations' with the United States, but the Administration faced serious opposition in Congress on that issue, partly because of the human rights violations. In the end, Congress granted permanent normal trading relations and brought annual review to an end in 2000.

US DEPARTMENT OF STATE, 1999 COUNTRY REPORTS ON HUMAN RIGHTS PRACTICES
2000, http://www.state.gov/www/global/human_rights/99hrp_index.html

CHINA

. . .

The Government's poor human rights record deteriorated markedly throughout the year, as the Government intensified efforts to suppress dissent, particularly organized dissent. A crackdown against a fledgling opposition party, which began in the fall of 1998, broadened and intensified during the year. . . . Tens of thousands of members of the Falun Gong spiritual movement were detained after the movement was banned in July; several leaders of the movement were sentenced to long prison terms in late December and hundreds of others were sentenced administratively to reeducation through labor in the fall. . . . The Government continued to commit widespread and well-documented human rights abuses, in violation of internationally accepted norms. These abuses stemmed from the authorities' extremely limited tolerance of public dissent aimed at the Government, fear of unrest, and the limited scope or inadequate implementation of laws protecting basic freedoms. The Constitution and laws provide for fundamental human rights; however, these protections often are ignored in practice. Abuses included instances of extrajudicial killings, torture and mistreatment of prisoners, forced confessions, arbitrary arrest and detention, lengthy incommunicado detention, and denial of due process. Prison conditions at most facilities remained harsh. In many cases, particularly in sensitive political cases, the judicial system denies criminal defendants basic legal safeguards and due process because authorities attach higher priority to maintaining public order and suppressing political opposition than to enforcing legal norms. The Government infringed on citizens' privacy rights. The Government tightened restrictions on freedom of speech and of the press, and increased controls on the Internet; self-censorship by journalists also increased. The Government severely restricted freedom of assembly, and continued to restrict freedom of association. The Government continued to restrict freedom of religion, and intensified controls on some unregistered churches. The Government continued to restrict freedom of movement. The Government does not permit independent domestic nongovernmental organizations (NGOs) to monitor publicly human rights conditions. Violence against women, including coercive family planning practices—which sometimes include forced abortion and forced sterilization; prostitution; discrimination against women; trafficking in women and children; abuse of children; and discrimination against the disabled and minorities are all problems. The Government continued to restrict tightly worker rights, and forced labor in prison facilities remains a serious problem. Child labor persists. Particularly serious human rights abuses persisted in some minority areas, especially in Tibet and Xinjiang, where restrictions on religion and other fundamental freedoms intensified.

. . .

Despite intensified suppression of organized dissent, some positive trends continued. Nongovernmental-level village committee elections proceeded, giving citizens choices about grassroots representatives, as well as introducing the principle of democratic elections. Additional experiments with higher level township elections were conducted without fanfare (or official approval by the central Government). Social groups with economic resources at their disposal continued to play an increasing role in community life. As many as 8.9 million citizens had access to the Internet, although the Government increased its efforts to try to control the content of material available on the Internet. Most average citizens went about their daily lives without significant interference from the Government, enjoying looser economic controls, increased access to outside sources of information, greater room for individual choice, and more diversity in cultural life. . . .

. . .

NOTE

The Report on China was characterized in the *New York Times*[4] as:

> using the toughest terms since the pro-democracy movement was crushed in Beijing [Tiananmen Square] more than a decade ago. . . . The tougher language and the detail of today's report on China were warmly received by human rights groups and members of Congress who have complained in the past that the State Department's annual report was not sufficiently critical of rights abuses in China. . . . [T]he report was released as the administration tried to garner support in Europe for a resolution condemning China's practices at the United Nations Human Rights Commission's annual conference in Geneva. . . .

[4] Jane Perlez, 'U.S. Report Harshly Criticizes China for Deterioration of Human Rights; Russia Also Faulted', *New York Times*, February 27, 2000, p. A7.

QUESTIONS

1. 'Trying to enforce human rights against other countries by threatening withdrawal of MFN status is a losing battle. Too many constituencies are involved, too many pressure groups both domestic and foreign have a keen interest in the outcome. Instead of maintaining a sharp and single moral purpose, the threat of withdrawal becomes enmeshed in a great power struggle involving many different economic interests and actors.' Comment. Is the situation notably different from threats of suspending military aid?

2. Note the catalogue of conditions that were talked of within the United States or imposed on MFN renewal during the early 1990s. What coherence does it have? Why were these conditions chosen and other more significant issues overlooked?

3. If China had accepted all these conditions and made the necessary changes, would something substantial have been accomplished? Or was it not the purpose of this legislation to achieve something basic, structural?

D. A COMPARISON: THE EUROPEAN COMMUNITY (UNION)

Inducements or sanctions, carrots or sticks, often pose vexing choices for governments seeking to change policies and practices in other states—in this context, human rights policies and practices. The preceding illustrations from US foreign policy stressed sanctions, the suspension or elimination of military or economic aid, favorable trade provisions, and so on. Of course overall US foreign policy has a significant 'carrot' side, offering help to states that are willing to attempt certain changes, such as a move toward democratic government or the rule of law. Various US or US-funded agencies provide foreign states with a range of assistance in such efforts—expert consultants, training government branches (particularly the judiciary) to observe basic principles of the rule of law, and so on. Such aid programmes, stressing relationships between democracy and the rule of law on the one hand, and market economies and free trade on the other, form part of the current globalization debate, discussed in Chapter 16.

The following materials look at such issues of human rights conditionality, carrots and sticks, and links between economic development and democracy from the perspective of other states, those assembled in the European Community (European Union), discussed at p. 790, *supra*.

BRUNO SIMMA, J. B. ASCHENBRENNER AND C. SCHULTE, HUMAN RIGHTS CONSIDERATIONS IN THE DEVELOPMENT OF CO-OPERATION ACTIVITIES OF THE EC
in Philip Alston (ed.), The EU and Human Rights (1999), at 571

Introduction

The Community[5] launched its development policy in 1958, but, until the Maastricht Treaty, there was no explicit legal basis for conducting such a policy. . . . [T]he Community and its Member States together provide more than half of all development assistance given in the world today. The Community has a widespread system of co-operation agreements with countries all over the world, and grants preferential trade relations and other forms of autonomous assistance to developing countries. Because the Community deals with many developing countries, with a broad range of needs, no single strategy can be applied to all of them. Strategies differ based on the needs of the developing country receiving the aid. These needs range from open access to the markets of the Community to technical and financial assistance, and even to substantial food aid. This chapter discusses the Community development policy of granting such assistance to developing states with the aim of promoting human rights and democracy. . . .

I. Development Co-operation and Positive Ways of Promoting Human Rights

. . . .

A. The Community's development co-operation

In contrast to Community policy in 1958, when preferential treatment and development assistance were restricted to associated countries, the successive Lomé Conventions (Nos. I–IV)[6] increased the number of recipient countries from the original 18 of the Yaoundé Convention to 71 developing countries, including countries without ties to the Community as former colonies. The EC and the Mediterranean countries launched co-ordinated co-operation in 1972 and amended the bilateral agreements . . . already concluded in order to integrate these countries into the Community's system of preferential treatment. In 1976 the Community started its ALA Programme of financial and technical co-operation with Asian and Latin American countries. Thus, Community assistance spanned the globe by the early 1980s.

. . .

The vast majority of Community assistance, no less than 84%, goes to developing countries. . . . The Community grants the remaining 16% to economies in transition [as in Central and Eastern Europe]. In regional terms, almost half of all Community assistance goes to the ACP countries. . . .

---

[5] The relationship between the European Community and the European Union is a very complex one. For a detailed analysis see P. Craig and G. de Búrca, EU Law (2nd edn., 1998).

[6] [Eds.] Since 1975, the Community adopted four Lomé Conventions governing the links related to development cooperation among the Community, its member states, and the so-called ACP group of sates—i.e., states of the African, Caribbean and Pacific group that receive a high percentage of the Community's total aid to the developing world.

The instruments of Community assistance can be classified as follows: [primarily progamme aid, food aid, humanitarian assistance, and project aid].

The Community usually defines positive measures to promote human rights and democracy in third states as project aid, under the titles 'governance and civil society' or 'social infrastructure projects in education and training'. Less often the Community classifies these measures as 'assistance to NGOs'. Positive measures of Community assistance include the promotion of civil society as such, of human rights, support for electoral processes and the rule of law, as well as the independence of the media. The Community channels this assistance to the third states through relevant Programmes in the form of financial and technical grants. This type of operation, the focal point of this paper, only accounts for 2% of total assistance given by the Community.

B. The original emphasis of development co-operation activities

In the development policy of the early days, the Community failed to take into account the potential political dimension of development, the possibility of influencing the political system of the recipient country. The role of human rights in development policy only concerned humanitarian relief (the basic needs approach). . . . The international community believed that increases in economic wealth and industrialization, brought about by development assistance in the form of single (*ad hoc*) projects, would be sufficient to stimulate growth even among the poorest sectors of society. However, after several years of implementation of this policy, the situation of the poor was not improving.

. . .

. . . [I]n the 1980s, the prevailing concerns of aid donors were crisis management and eco-political reform in recipient countries. . . . Macro-economic structural adjustment Programmes, which centre around currency, trade liberalization and stable public finances, were considered by many donors to be a panacea. . . .

. . .

C. The change in community policy: development related to democracy and human rights

. . . [T]he Community took almost 20 years [after its economic development policy started] to begin to make serious efforts to include human rights considerations in its general development policy. A [European] Commission memorandum to the Council and the Parliament [of the European Community, or European Union] on human rights, democracy and development co-operation policy, dated March 1991, paved the way in this direction, followed by a June 1991 European Council resolution which pronounced its dedication to the relationship between human rights and development. The foregoing advances culminated in the Council resolution of 28 November 1991, which officially included issues of human rights and democracy, and their observance in the recipient country, as an essential element in the overall development policy-making process, relying primarily on positive measures. . . .

. . . The Lomé Convention IV of 1989 recognized the importance of human rights for development. . . . [It dealt] mainly with economic and social rights probably because the drafters perceived these rights as more closely related to 'economic development'. In contrast, the November 28 Council Resolution explicitly puts equal emphasis on economic, social and cultural rights and civil and political rights.

The Resolution elevates democracy to a prominent place in development policy, in that the minimum requirement for democracy requires the observance of certain civil and political rights, which fall under the broader category of human rights. . . . [T]he international community was discovering that there can be no development without a certain degree of democracy, no democracy without respect for human rights, and, finally, no democracy without development. . . .

The Community attaches equal importance to the promotion of the rule of law in the recipient country, based on the realization that the rule of law is also closely related to development. . . .

The Maastricht Treaty affirms the Community's course taken regarding development policy, consolidation of democracy, the rule of law and respect for human rights and fundamental freedoms. . . . What is interesting, however, is that the notion of human rights, although a firm component of development policy, rarely appears in express terms. . . . Altogether, the Community refers to human rights as part of a 'larger set of requirements'; it builds human rights into a triptych consisting of human rights, democracy and the rule of law, and seems to regard the term of 'good governance' as the primary, all-embracing principle.

. . .

D. The new emphasis on positive measures

. . . [T]he Commission's March 1991 memorandum still followed traditional policy by emphasizing sanctions as a means of responding to human rights violations and disrespect for democratic principles. . . . [The change was] elaborated in the 28 November 1991 Resolution, which clearly emphasizes positive measures in general development policy towards all recipient states. According to this Resolution 'the Community and its Member States will give high priority to a positive approach that stimulates respect for human rights and encourages democracy'. Nevertheless, negative measures are still considered appropriate responses in the 'event of grave and persistent human rights violations or serious interruptions of the democratic process'. Hence, along with the emphasis of positive measures, the so-called second generation conditionality in aid was brought to the forefront of Community policy.

The Community can implement the positive approach . . . through active support for useful initiatives and through an open and constructive dialogue. The emphasis of the positive approach is on creating an environment conducive to respect for human rights, supported by increased assistance to countries respecting these values.

Economic sanctions . . . have been the subject of many comprehensive studies, most of which have been critical of the success of such sanctions. Positive measures, on the other hand, display important advantages. . . .

Whereas negative measures are generally considered to be promising due to their capacity to exert pressure on governments and to express clear limits for state behaviour in the international context, it is exactly this component of negative measures which also leads to their first drawback: their infringement on state sovereignty. States, especially the newly independent states of the 1960s, were extremely reluctant to accept outside interference in their internal affairs because domestic policy was considered out of reach of other states. Therefore, strong interference by one state in issues the target state considers part of its domestic policy could likely lead to a breakdown of communication between the states. Undeniably, such infringements of sovereignty (ranging from appeals to observe human rights to the cessation of aid and trade) are usually considered permissible in international human rights literature; nevertheless, the danger of deteriorating relations with the target state remains an obstacle to sanctions. Positive measures, on the other hand, generally do not infringe upon the sovereignty of the state concerned since they constitute measures of support and are increasingly based on consensus and co-operation through policy-dialogue. This is not always the case, as exceptions can be found in which outside support of an anti-regime NGO, whose aim is to enhance the democratization of the country, can strongly infringe upon the sovereignty of the recipient country. The recent Mexican elections present just such an example. There the EU wanted to support a specific NGO before the elections, but was prevented in doing so by resistance of the Mexican government which felt the Community was infringing upon its sovereignty. . . .

Another disadvantage of negative measures is that they do not address the actual causes of human rights violations but only scratch the surface of much deeper issues. Moreover, the victims of such measures are the members of the population of the state concerned, not its political leaders. Accordingly, sanctions often mobilize the affected population to unite with the oppressive regime against the state imposing sanctions, contrary to the aim of negative measures. However, the Community continues humanitarian assistance during the suspension of aid to counter the effect of sanctions on the poorest members of the population. In comparison to negative measures, positive initiatives centred on humanitarian concerns are not targeted at governments, but are determined by the needs of the people. This focus on the individual underlies the belief that change must come from within, not imposed from outside solely through coercive measures.

Furthermore, negative measures, as applied by Western donors, usually promote the enforcement of civil and political rights only. Sanctions such as withdrawal of aid or the termination of preferential trade arrangements have an undesirable effect on social and economic rights because a government's respect for these rights will not improve without outside assistance. Therefore, when the community applies negative measures, they are unable to meet the objective of promoting both sets of rights equally, given the declared interdependence of these right. . . . Community Programmes, in practice, still closely connect social and economic rights to the basic needs approach, especially in the lesser developed countries, and consequently these rights still lack equal standing with civil and political rights in Community Programmes.

Another important factor in a critical assessment of negative measures is their close relationship to foreign policy considerations, which encourages more arbitrary action towards countries which range low on the 'foreign policy scale'. Since self-interest determines a state's external relations, a decision to apply economic sanctions can be a sign of low interest in the target country. Positive measures remain more distinct from foreign policy considerations, enabling the donor governments to act more rationally and less arbitrarily. It is also easier to find common ground of action for a positive measure than for a negative one. In the case of Nigeria, France granted visas to several members of the Nigerian government despite the imposed EU sanctions and thus contradicted a negative measure established by the Community.

However, positive measures can have dangerous consequences if the donor fails to consider foreign policy interests. . . . The 'philosophy' of the positive approach was also maintained in Algeria when the European Community decided to continue to support the Algerian authorities in their fight against terrorism, despite ongoing violence and killings within the country, by pushing the early conclusion of a partnership agreement (but including a human rights clause). In Albania, the EC uncritically supported the oppressive regime of Sali Berisha with $560 million since 1990, and thus the European Community indirectly fuelled the violent political upheaval there in 1997. The EC granted preferential trade status as well as a new aid package to the Federal Republic of Yugoslavia in the spring of 1997 without regard to the human rights violations that were still going on there at that time. Human Rights Watch claimed that leverage, which could have been used to ensure compliance with the Dayton Agreement, was lost because of the European Community's actions.

Finally, sanctions will only have their intended effect if the target government is willing and capable to respond to pressure. Sanctions will have little effect on strong, undemocratic regimes and no effect on countries that do not have suitable institutions which can react to a situation and improve it. In sum, although negative measures may help in very specific situations, sanctions are usually a sign of previous failure of aid to promote human rights and democratic institutions. The promotion of human rights in a positive 'system' of measures adopts a preventive approach, addressing the roots of the problem instead of waiting for undesired results and then trying to 'repair' them.

. . .

. . . The Council listed examples of positive measures in its November 28 Resolution:

- support for countries which are attempting to institute democracy and improve their human rights performance;
- the holding of elections, the setting-up of new democratic institutions and the strengthening of the rule of law;
- the strengthening of the judiciary, the administration of justice, crime prevention and the treatment of offenders;
- promoting the role of NGOs and other institutions which are necessary for a pluralist society;
- the adoption of a decentralized approach to co-operation;
- ensuring equal opportunities for all.

. . .

... The Council of Development Ministers has suggested broadening the scope of development policy by including such issues as freedom of the press, protection of minorities, and return of political exiles.

...

IV. Positive Initiatives in Development Co-operation: A Thematic Perspective

A. *Support for democratic transition processes*

...

... The proposed definition [of democracy] consists of two elements: a procedural and a substantive one. The first element deals with procedures and institutions of democracy (especially multi-party elections). The second concerns the degree of participation of the people in political life, the actual sharing of power among different groups in society, the possibilities to exert control over the government, and in general influence on the situation in which citizens live (room for civil society Programmes).

... Operations which the Community/European Union supported between 1990 and 1995 concerned 44 countries being given mainly technical assistance through specialized bodies in the pre- and post-election phase. ... [T]he Community is increasingly involved in projects to strengthen the role of the media especially with a view to ensure their independence and the quality of election coverage.

...

... [T]he wave of democratic change has ... directed international attention towards the issue of election-monitoring. The dispatch of observers and the disposal of technical assistance are no longer seen as an interference in internal affairs and breach of sovereignty. As regards donors' budgets, elections are a relatively inexpensive technical tool and offer an easy option to develop a political surrounding conducive to the respect of human rights. The number of countries that have become 'democracies', and the measurable success of this type of operations seem to present another incentive for electoral assistance. It is far more difficult to assess the impact of long-term human rights activities, and to predict their possible outcome, let alone the immense costs related to them, than the result of elections, it is often argued. Finally, the assumption that democracies do not wage war against each other provides another argument for increased democracy activities, including election observation.

...

'Free elections and multi-party systems', Amnesty International states, 'cannot guarantee human rights on their own'. Moreover, they are only a first step in the transition process to democracy. It is therefore essential that assistance in this field also focuses on the substantial understanding of democracy. This form of operations ... focuses on the strengthening of civil society. Initiatives include the promotion of the independence of the media, support for the freedom of expression and of the press, human rights education and public awareness-raising, promotion of equal opportunities for all members of society, funding of NGOs. ...

...

Surely, one important point is to provide people with the means of existence before they can think of democracy: that is, to fulfil basic needs first. But the enjoyment of basic economic and social needs and the transfer of technology and financial means alone are not sufficient and do not lead to sustainable development. Development cannot be decoupled from observance of (all) human rights, and democracy and development are closely interrelated. . . . [D]emocracy forms an important condition of the lasting realization of economic and social rights, but is certainly not the panacea. . . .

. . . [T]o impose western democratic models from the outside without respecting the country's background is no solution. The promotion of democracy has to be affected on a case-by-case basis, taking account of its stabilizing function in reaching equitable and sustainable development. Civic education and confidence building have to remain an essential part of democratic activities to ensure the active participation of the people.

There is a danger in donors' initiatives in that they seem inclined to equate democracy with multi-party elections. . . . [C]ountries are judged democratic as soon as they have conducted multi-party elections. The sustainability of elections can only be guaranteed if substantive democracy remains the focus of donor activity and if elections are seen only as a first step. The Community appears to make a considerable effort not only to promote free and fair elections, but also to promote civil society. However, it is not enough only to accompany elections with democratic assistance to guarantee the success of election monitoring. . . .

. . .

. . . [D]emocracy, despite its successes, has its own considerable weaknesses. The Council of Europe has acknowledged that 'democracies consolidated by decades of existence are suffering from the growing indifference of citizens to political life and the decline in the rate of citizens' participation in elections'. Whoever seeks to export such a system has to be aware of the unforeseeable consequences this model can have in an unknown environment. The other problem concerns the outcome of elections. The results of majority votes and the leaders elected do not always reflect the donors' views of a 'good government'.

. . .

C. Promoting equal opportunities for all and support for vulnerable groups

Initiatives under this heading include not only those focused specifically on vulnerable groups in society, but also all means to foster equal rights and equal dignity generally. Legal assistance as well as prevention through education and long-term measures are important tools for the implementation of both kinds of operations. Target groups include women, younger generations, certain social groups, refugees, victims of torture, and prisoners. [Certain] democracy programmes have placed growing emphasis on increasing the involvement of national minorities and women in civil, social and political life. . . .

. . .

BARBARA BRANDTNER AND A. ROSAS, TRADE PREFERENCES AND HUMAN RIGHTS

in Philip Alston (ed.), The EU and Human Rights (1999), at 698

I. Introduction

. . .

. . . [T]rade and human rights have also become linked in a way which suggests *conditionality* of trade preferences and other trade measures on respect for human rights and fundamental freedoms in general, including rights and principles which go beyond property rights, such as the principle of democracy and political rights and freedoms.

At the universal level, and in the context of the World Trade Organization (WTO) in particular, the issue of conditionality is controversial. Existing WTO law, notably Article XX of the General Agreement on Tariffs and Trade (GATT), seems to enable trade restrictions prompted by human rights concerns only to a very limited extent, if at all. The question of a 'social clause', or 'core labour standards' has been discussed in the WTO context, but the Singapore Ministerial Conference of 9–13 December 1996 could only agree on a general statement noting that the International Labour Organization (ILO) is 'the competent body to set and deal with these standards' and affirming its support for the ILO's work in promoting them. In a recent Declaration on Fundamental Principles and Rights at Work, the International Labour Conference advanced the normative foundation of core labour standards but avoided establishing any conditionality between their respect and trade rules.

This has not prevented the major traders, notably the European Community (EC) and the United States (US), from introducing linkages between trade preferences and human rights in their bilateral and unilateral trade policy instruments adopted outside the WTO framework. . . .

. . .

The present paper will focus on trade preferences provided in both *unilateral* Community instruments and in *bilateral agreements*, especially the 'human rights clause' included in such agreements. A basic theme running through the paper is to analyze whether, and to what extent, the development of the Community's recent practice corresponds to a development from a 'stick' towards a 'carrot' approach, as exemplified by the concept of 'Conditionality' (notably with respect to the countries of former Yugoslavia) and the 'special incentive arrangements' introduced through amendments to the EC Generalized System of Preferences (GSP) of May 1998.

This will be linked to the human rights standards involved and the question will be asked whether the 'stick' approach has been limited to what is sometimes called the 'first generation' of human rights, that is, mainly civil and political rights, and in this context whether it is conceived as applying to 'serious' human rights violations only, while the 'carrot' might be considered more appropriate for 'second generation' human rights, notably economic and social rights. . . .

. . .

II. The Human Rights Clause

The 'human rights clause' that the EC has been including in its bilateral trade and co-operation agreements since the early 1990s ... will be seen in the specific context of trade preferences. ...

More than 50 Community agreements negotiated during the 1990s have a clause stipulating that respect for democratic principles and fundamental human rights (often by reference to the Universal Declaration of Human Rights of 1948 and, in a European context, the Helsinki Final Act of 1975 and the Charter of Paris for a New Europe of 1990) inspire the internal and external policies of the Parties and constitute an 'essential element' of the agreement. In the more recent agreements, a final clause (non-execution clause) spells out the possibility to take 'appropriate measures' (including suspension of the agreement) if a Party considers that the other Party has not fulfilled its obligations under the agreement.

So far, the human rights clause has never been used as a ground for suspending or otherwise not executing trade preferences granted by a Community agreement. Does this mean that the human rights clause is simply an act of window-dressing? We believe such a conclusion would be premature, and this for several reasons.

First of all, the human rights clause is a child of the 1990s, and many of the agreements providing for such a clause have not even entered into force. Secondly, recent Community practice seems to suggest that the EC is not foreclosing taking measures when human rights are violated. While this has mainly occurred with respect to *unilateral* trade preferences or financial or development *assistance,* one cannot rule out that this practice might also be extended to the formal suspension of bilateral trade arrangements.

...

Nevertheless, there are some reasons why the non-execution of bilateral trade arrangements seems less likely to occur than the suspension of unilateral trade preferences or the suspension of development assistance. ...

As to the legal instrument involved, it should be recalled that the non-execution of an agreement (treaty) always poses a problem of international law, notably the fundamental principle of *pacta sunt servanda.* [The discussion refers to litigation on suspension of trade concessions brought before the European Court of Justice. It also notes other problems, including possible conflicts between some trade agreements and suspensions thereof with rules of the WTO, and questions posed under some of the constitutive treaties of the EC.]

...

The only initiative for the formal suspension of a Community agreement based on the human rights clause which exists to date, the request for consultations with Togo of July 1998, concerns alleged irregularities in general elections, that is political rights and 'internal self-determination' as a 'right to democracy'. The 1991 suspension of the Co-operation Agreement with Yugoslavia (which did not contain an express human rights clause) was based on a fundamental change of circumstances, including 'war' (or at least, serious internal armed conflict) and the dissolution of the former SFRY. Finally, the 'conditionality' applied in the context of unilateral trade preferences seems mainly to focus on basic civil and political rights. ...

While it can thus be surmised that the suspension of trade preferences based on the human rights clause would be likely to concern violations of the 'right to democracy' and basic civil and political rights (military coups, genocide, crimes against humanity, etc.), it should be underlined that the human rights clause is not, in principle, limited to civil and political rights. The Universal Declaration as well as the Community's human rights policy is based on the principle of indivisibility of human rights. In many cases, it is difficult to draw the line between civil rights on the one hand and economic and social rights on the other. . . .

. . .

V. Conclusion

. . . [T]rade benefits are more likely to be suspended by the Community (the 'stick') if . . . they are based on unilateral rather than bilateral instruments and if they go beyond obligations stemming from the WTO. . . .

. . . [T]he 'stick', whether used in the context of bilateral agreements (*ex*-Yugoslavia in 1991) or in the context of unilateral acts (Myanmar in 1996), is more likely to be resorted to if fundamental rights and values are at stake—and if there has been a *serious* human rights violation. However, the combination of 'sticks and carrots' ('*conditionality*' in *ex*-Yugoslavia) or emphasis on 'more carrots' (the '*special incentive arrangements*' in the context of the GSP) make it easier to bring in a wider range of human rights . . .

. . .

. . . The WTO dimension provides further restraints, particularly between WTO Members and as regards trade concessions covered by the WTO. Nevertheless, it is the authors' impression that the substantive and procedural limitations inherent in its 'sticks' will not prevent the Community from using trade *sanctions* for *human rights goals*. The 'stick' will certainly not be in daily use, however. While trade sanctions may sometimes fulfil an important symbolic function and may be reasonably effective (as the prospect of economic loss does have a dissuasive effect), they should not be resorted to lightly. Resorting to 'carrots' may well prove to be a more attractive way of 'forcing people to be free'.

QUESTION

'Serious and systemic human rights violations of the type that may lead to suspension of aid or trade will not change overnight. Transformation to participatory regimes respectful of human rights will require time, many forms of foreign assistance and encouragement, and the development of internal movements in a nascent civil society of the violator states. Dialogue, assistance, and constructive engagement are the essentials. Sticks like suspensions of economic aid or trade preferences won't help.' Based on the readings in Chapter 13, do you agree, or if not, how would you qualify this statement? Could it serve as a general guiding principle?

ADDITIONAL READING

On human rights and foreign policy see: D. Forsythe (ed.), *Comparative Foreign Policy and International Human Rights* (forthcoming, 2000); United Kingdom, Department for International Development, *Strategies for Achieving the International Development Targets: Human Rights for Poor People,* <http://www.dfid.gov.uk/public/what/strategy_papers/ target_strategy.html>; K. Tomaševski, *Between Sanctions and Elections: Aid Donors and their Human Rights Performance* (1997); P. Baehr, *The Role of Human Rights in Foreign Policy* (2nd edn., 1996); J. Donnelly, *International Human Rights* (2nd edn., 1998); Ministry of Foreign Affairs of the Netherlands, *Human Rights and Foreign Policy* (1979).

On US foreign policy see: D. Price and J. Hannah, 'The Constitutionality of United States State and Local Sanctions', 39 Harv. Int'l L. J. 443 (1998); A. Schlesinger Jr., 'Human Rights and the American Tradition', 57 For. Affs. 503 (1979); J. Muravchik *The Uncertain Crusade: Jimmy Carter and the Dilemmas of Human Rights Policy* (1986); D. Forsythe, 'Human Rights and US Foreign Policy', XLIII Political Studies 111 (1995); S. Poe *et al.*, 'Human Rights and US Foreign Aid Revisited: The Latin American Region', 16 Hum. Rts Q. 539 (1994); S. Steinmetz, *Democratic Transition and Human Rights: Perspectives on U.S. Foreign Policy* (1994); K. Sikkink, 'The Power of Principled Ideas: Human Rights Policies in the United States and Western Europe', in J. Goldstein and R. Keohane (eds.), *Ideas and Foreign Policy: Beliefs, Institutions, and Political Change* (1995).

On China and Human Rights see: R. Foot, *Rights Beyond Borders: The Global Community and the Struggle over Human Rights in China* (2000); A. Kent, *China, the United Nations, and Human Rights* (1999).

On the EU's human rights foreign policy see: Council of the European Union, *European Union Annual Report on Human Rights 1998–1999* (1999); K. Arts, *Integrating Human Rights into Development Cooperation: The Case of the Lomé Convention* (2000); A. Clapham, 'Where is the EU's Human Rights Common Foreign Policy, and How is it Manifested in Multilateral Fora?', in P. Alston, M. Bustelo and J. Heenan (eds.), *The EU and Human Rights* 627 (1999); E. Riedel and M. Will, 'Human Rights Clauses in External Agreements of the EC', in ibid. 723; M. Lister, The European Union and the South: relations with Developing Countries (1997); N. Neuwahl and A. Rosas (eds.), *The European Union and Human Rights* (1995); O. A. Babarinde, *The Lomé Conventions and Development* (1994); P. J. Kuyper, 'Trade Sanctions, Security and Human Rights and Commercial Policy', in M. Maresceau (ed.), *The European Community's Commercial Policy after 1992: The Legal Dimension* 387 (1993).

PART E
CURRENT TOPICS

Drawing on the framework created by Parts A–D, the chapters in Part E examine three broad topics of great signfiicance for the human rights movement—three among the larger number of current and vital human rights themes that could as well have been selected. Chapters 14–16 examine consequences of massive human rights tragedies, particularly individual criminal prosecutions and truth commissions; self-determination and autonomy regimes; and relationships between globalization and human rights.

14

Massive Human Rights Tragedies: Prosecutions and Truth Commissions

The topics and documents in this chapter grow out of massive human rights tragedies. The illustrations below include the Holocaust, Bosnia, Rwanda, the apartheid regime of South Africa, and the earlier years of the Pinochet government in Chile. Most of these tragedies had powerful underlying ethnic components—religion, race, ethnic tradition—and involved savage dehumanization and hatred, often stimulated by an oppressor state.

The theme of the chapter can be stated simply: what have been the nature and effects of two types of legal and political reactions to such systematic, massive and cruel violations: criminal prosecutions before international or national tribunals, and truth commissions? How do we understand them, how do we assess them, in what directions do or should they now point?

To approach such questions, the chapter explores a number of related themes: international crimes and universal jurisdiction, the *ad hoc* international criminal tribunals for the former Yugoslavia and for Rwanda, the permanent International Criminal Court whose Statute was adopted in 1998 and that is yet to enter into force, the Pinochet judgment in the UK in 1999, and the use of truth commissions, particularly in South Africa. With some exceptions, the emphasis in the earlier sections is on prosecutions before international tribunals, and in the concluding sections on national tribunals and truth commissions.

Several of the chapter's illustrations of systemic violations grow out of contexts of armed conflict, whether principally international in character or principally internal to a state. Others took place in periods of severe internal repression that, despite its violence, stopped shy of internal armed conflict—Chile, for example. For the first category, the *humanitarian laws of war* with their deep historical roots become particularly relevant. Hence the chapter builds on the earlier discussions of laws of war in connection with the Nuremberg Judgment and on that Judgment itself, pp. 112–122, *supra.* In cases like Chile and much (though not all) of the South African experience, mainstream *international human rights law* that has developed over the last half century has been the source of criticism and judgment.

Nonetheless, the trends since the 1940s in both bodies of law have brought them into a closer, intertwined relationship—a relationship vividly illustrated by the statutes of the two international criminal tribunals and the judgments of those

tribunals. Each field retains a near exclusive interest in a large number of important issues—the laws of war, say, with respect to aspects of *jus in bello* such as
military necessity or proportionality in the waging of war; human rights law, say,
with respect to free speech, gender equality, or political participation. But on
numerous issues that are germane to the international crimes and criminal prosecutions described below, the boundary lines are blurring.

The post-Nuremberg growth of the humanitarian laws of war—particularly
through the Geneva Conventions and their two Additional Protocols, and the
statutes and judicial decisions of the two international criminal tribunals—as well
as the striking success in standard-setting of the human rights movement, have
greatly expanded the number of crimes defined by international law that are based
on those bodies of law and that impose individual responsibility. Today's international crimes are both conventional and customary in character. Issues of punishment, impunity or immunity, amnesty and pardon of those involved in the
most serious violations of human rights have become endemic to the resolution of
today's major conflicts.

A. UNIVERSAL JURISDICTION AND
INTERNATIONAL CRIMES

As used in this chapter, 'international crimes' refer to crimes committed not by
states as such but by individuals who bear a personal criminal responsibility for
commission of crimes defined (at least in the first instance) by international law.
The meaning of the term is not self-evident. For example, is a crime 'international'
simply by virtue of being within the subject-matter jurisdiction of an international
tribunal? Or by virtue of having been defined by a treaty (such as the Torture
Convention) that obligates states parties to take the necessary measures (such as
legislation) to make that crime applicable to individuals within its territory? Or by
virtue of being subject to universal jurisdiction?

Section A reviews basic jurisdictional principles on which states prescribe (make
law), particularly prescribe criminal laws imposing individual responsibility, and
the basic jurisdictional principles on which a state's courts try criminal cases.
Some of these principles are also germane to cases brought before an international
tribunal.

COMMENT ON JURISDICTIONAL PRINCIPLES FOR
CRIMINAL LAWS AND LITIGATION

Criminal litigation, unlike civil litigation, ordinarily requires that the state whose
courts are trying a case have custody of the defendant. Holding criminal trials *in
absentia* is rare. Choice of law, so vital an element of many civil cases, generally
does not figure in criminal litigation; the court applies only the law of the state

from which it derives its authority, almost always the one in which it sits, even if the conduct occurred or the effects were felt in other states. The principle of universal jurisdiction, below, constitutes a major exception to this generalization.

The bases on which states enact the criminal laws to which their courts look therefore becomes a critical issue. There are certain conventional categories, some of which are more broadly accepted internationally than others. Several of these categories appear in the following description, based on the American Law Institute, *Restatement (Third), The Foreign Relations Law of the United States* (1987), section 402.

> (1) *Territorial principle*, or prescribing with respect to conduct taking place within a state's territory. This principle is surely the most common and the most readily accepted throughout the world. (2) *Effects principle*, prescribing with respect to conduct outside the territory that has effects within it. (3) *Nationality principle*, prescribing with respect to acts, interests or relations of a state's nationals within and outside its territory. (4) *Protective principle*, prescribing with respect to certain conduct of non-nationals outside a state's territory that is directed against the security of the state or against a limited class of state interests that threaten the integrity of governmental functions (such as counterfeiting). (5) *Passive personality principle*, or prescribing with respect to acts committed outside a state by a non-national where the victim was a national. This principle is surely the least recognized among states as a valid basis for criminal legislation.

These principles are bounded by a number of qualifications and competing considerations, some of which are sketched in section 403 of the Restatement. There follow the Restatement's provision on universal jurisdiction.

> 404. Universal jurisdiction to Define and Punish Certain Offenses
> A state has jurisdiction to define and prescribe punishment for certain offenses recognized by the community of nations as of universal concern, such as piracy, slave trade, attacks on or hijacking of aircraft, genocide, war crimes, and perhaps certain acts of terrorism. . . .
>
> COMMENT:
> a. *Expanding class of universal offenses.* . . . [I]nternational law permits any state to apply its laws to punish certain offenses although the state has no links of territory with the offense, or of nationality with the offender (or even the victim). Universal jurisdiction over the specified offenses is a result of universal condemnation of those activities and general interest in cooperating to suppress them, as reflected in widely-accepted international agreements and resolutions of international organizations. These offenses are subject to universal jurisdiction as a matter of customary law. Universal jurisdiction for additional offenses is provided by international agreements, but it remains to be determined whether universal jurisdiction over a particular offense has become customary law for states not party to such an agreement. . . .

. . .

REPORTERS' NOTES

1. *Offenses subject to universal jurisdiction.* Piracy has sometimes been described as 'an offense against the law of nations'—an international crime. Since there is no international penal tribunal, the punishment of piracy is left to any state that seizes the offender. . . . Whether piracy is an international crime, or is rather a matter of international concern as to which international law accepts the jurisdiction of all states, may not make an important difference.
. . .

That genocide and war crimes are subject to universal jurisdiction was accepted after the Second World War. . . .

The [Genocide] Convention provides for trial by the territorial state or by an international penal tribunal to be established, but no international penal tribunal with jurisdiction over the crime of genocide has been established. Universal jurisdiction to punish genocide is widely accepted as a principle of customary law. . . .

International agreements have provided for general jurisdiction for additional offenses, e.g., the Hague Convention for the Suppression of Unlawful Seizure of Aircraft . . . and the International Convention against the Taking of Hostages.

. . . These agreements include an obligation on the parties to punish or extradite offenders, even when the offense was not committed within their territory or by a national. . . . An international crime is presumably subject to universal jurisdiction.
. . .

The description at p. 1072, *supra,* of the Torture Convention and the enactment by the United States Congress of implementing legislation before the United States became a party to that Convention illustrate the principle of universal jurisdiction at work.

COMMENT ON INTERNATIONAL CRIMES

Recall the following observation in the Nuremberg Judgment, p. 117, *supra*:

That international law imposes duties and liabilities upon individuals as well as upon States has long been recognized . . . Crimes against international law are committed by men, not by abstract entities, and only by punishing individuals who commit such crimes can the provisions of international law be enforced.

Both that Judgment and the Restatement provisions above refer to customary international law , whose rules long ago imposed criminal sanctions on individual pirates. The Comment at p. 112, *supra,* and the Judgment describe the slow development of war crimes, which turned out to be the single most important component of the crimes defined in the Charter of the International Military Tribunal (IMT) at Nuremberg. That development, spurred by the Nuremberg Judgment, has since continued in the forms of both customary and conventional international law, as evidenced in codified form by the statutes of the three international criminal tribunals described in this chapter. So has the development of crimes against humanity, a category so highly limited by the Nuremberg Judgment in view of its then novelty that it played little independent role in those proceedings. During the last few decades, such crimes have gained both clarity and number. Genocide, not a category of international crimes at Nuremberg, rapidly became one through UN resolutions and the early UN approval of the Genocide Convention, which soon entered into force.

Other institutions played an important role over these decades in the development of international crimes. Foremost among them was the International Law Commission, created by the UN General Assembly (GA Res. 174 (II), 1947). Its 25 members, 'persons of recognized competence in international law' under its Statute, examine subjects at the ILC's own initiative or at the request of the General Assembly. The ILC worked throughout this period on a draft code of offences, and in 1996 completed a Draft Code of Crimes against the Peace and Security of Mankind. Its work figured in the arguments of advocates in this field that were based on the developing customary law.

The evolution of war crimes was stimulated by the four Geneva Conventions of 1949 for the protection of victims of war. The four conventions contain common articles defining so-called 'grave breaches' of the conventions for injuries to protected persons or property. The parties to the Conventions are required to search for persons alleged to have committed grave breaches and, upon arresting such persons, either to try them criminally (no matter what their nationality or the nationality of the victim or where the acts causing the injuries occurred) or extradite them. Like the Torture Convention, the Conventions thereby establish a universal jurisdiction for grave breaches.

The definitions of grave breaches vary among the four conventions. Article 147 of the Fourth Geneva Convention Relative to the Protection of Civilian Persons in Time of War is the most extensive. It includes willful killing, torture or inhuman treatment, willfully causing great suffering or serious injury, extensive destruction of property not justified by military necessity and carried out unlawfully and wantonly, unlawfully deporting or transferring or confining a protected person, willfully depriving a protected person of the right to a fair trial, and taking hostages. The First Protocol to the Geneva Conventions—the 1977 Additional Protocol Relating to the Protection of Victims of International Armed Conflict, which entered into force in 1978—added several grave breaches, including: medical experimentation on protected persons, transfer by an occupying power of part of its own population into territory it occupies, deporting part of the population of occupied territory, and racial discrimination.

Other international crimes, unrelated to armed conflict whether international or internal and not necessarily related to traditional human rights themes, have been created by treaties on enslavement and slave trade, on traffic in persons for prostitution, on the production or distribution or sale of narcotic drugs, on aircraft hijacking, and on a few other selected activities.

When treaties define criminal offences, they use a range of formulae. (1) Sometimes the international agreement will both define and directly establish the crime underlying prosecutions (before an international tribunal), as in the London Charter for the Nuremberg trials held before the IMT, or in the statutes for the three international criminal tribunals discussed in this chapter. (2) Sometimes treaties provide in very general terms that a forbidden act, such as genocide, constitutes an international crime that, in absence of an international penal tribunal, must be tried before specified national courts. (3) Sometimes they impose a duty on treaty parties to prosecute those who commit the defined acts on the basis of universal jurisdiction, as with respect to the provisions for grave breaches in the Geneva Conventions or the provisions in the Torture Convention.

The juristic techniques by which states comply with their obligations under such treaties will vary, depending either or both on the precise treaty provisions and on states' constitutional or traditional ways of dealing with internal obligations under treaties or customary law—issues discussed at pp. 999–1029, *supra*. For example, in the United States criminal laws cannot be self-executing. That is, the treaty's criminal provision standing alone cannot provide a basis for criminal prosecution. Normal legislation that reproduces (and sometimes changes) the treaty definition of a crime must be enacted, thereby 'incorporating' the treaty's criminal provision into US law. A prosecution would then rest directly on the statute rather than on the treaty animating it (which might, however, serve as a source of interpretation of or justification for the statute). As a formal matter, state rather than international criminal law is applied to the defendant. Nonetheless, the crime has a fundamental international character, which is indeed an important basis for subjecting it to universal jurisdiction. Consider the following observations of Yoram Dinstein, 'International Criminal Law', 5 Israel Y'bk on Hum. Rts. 55 (1975) 73:

> ... [A]s long as no penal tribunal has been established on the international plane, the trial of persons charged with offences defined by international law must take place in the national courts of States. . . . These courts may be regarded, for this purpose, as organs of the international community applying international criminal law and bringing it home to the individual, who is directly subjected to international obligations . . .
>
> While this situation lasts, international criminal law is admittedly beclouded by doubts: from the viewpoint of the offender facing a regular judge in a domestic court, the criminal trial looks like ordinary municipal proceedings: and from the standpoint of the national judge, that judge does not apply international law unless it is incorporated into the national legal system and to the extent of its incorporation. If and when a permanent international criminal court comes into being, it will be possible to distinguish between real international offenses (namely, international duties incurred directly by the individual, who is criminally liable for their infraction) over which the court will have jurisdiction, and national offences originating in international treaties (that is, international obligations imposed on the State, which is required to take measures to suppress the forbidden acts. . .). But as long as no such court exists, the distinction is not easy to draw.

Note the great range of treaties or customary laws and of conduct that figures in the contemporary categories of international crimes:

> (1) Most international crimes have a clear basis in treaty law, even though, like war crimes and genocide, they may have a substantial foundation in

customary law as well. Others, such as crimes against humanity, have developed since the Nuremberg Judgment primarily through customary law, although they have taken codified form in statutes of the two current international criminal tribunals.

(2) Some crimes growing out of the humanitarian laws of war require a context of armed conflict, such as many defined under the Geneva Conventions or a later Additional Protocol. Certain treaties, or articles in treaties, require that the conflict be international in character; others cover internal conflict. The definition of conflict itself varies among such treaties. On the other hand, treaties such as the Genocide Convention or Torture Convention that form part of mainstream human rights law do not require a context of armed conflict (although that context will often exist).

(3) The major international crimes involve unjustified violence, primarily to persons but also to property, whether within or outside contexts of armed conflict. But other crimes such as those related to airplane hijacking or drug trafficking demand no such violence as a condition to prosecution. Indeed, such crimes express serious state and international interests and concerns that are at some level related to but that are distinct from mainstream human rights norms.

(4) Some treaties such as the Torture Convention that impose criminal liability require an important relationship—employment, public office or function, and so on—between the individual defendant and the state. Other crimes such as hijacking or genocide do not demand a state nexus, although genocide will ordinarily involve one. Such other crimes can then involve entirely 'private' defendants without any state links (the traditional pirate, airplane hijacking, drug trafficking), as well as members of organized military or other nonstate groups that may, for example, be insurgents in armed conflict against the state. Nonetheless, it is true that the principal international crimes like genocide or war crimes or crimes against humanity are likely to occur within a state plan or in implementation of state policy.

(5) Some crimes can be discrete occurrences, not part of a systematic plan or policy of the state—for example, the war crime of rape committed by an individual soldier, or a violation of the Torture Convention by an official acting against orders but under color of law. Other crimes have an implicit mass or systemic character that may enter into their definition, such as crimes against humanity and genocide.

These and other variations among international crimes require a close attention in legal argument to the texts of relevant treaties and to the political, ideological and formal developments that have pushed customary law so far in this field. The opinions below of international criminal tribunals evidence that close attention.

It is well to keep this expanding but bounded domain of international crimes distinct from the many situations in the human rights corpus where states are required by treaty to regulate the conduct of nonstate parties, whether individuals or groups/associations. That regulation *may* involve a state's resort to criminal laws and prosecutions that are independent of any international crime. Consider, for example, Article 2 of the ICCPR. A state party 'undertakes to respect and to ensure to all individuals within its territory. . .the rights recognized in the present covenant'. As emphasized in the materials at pp. 180–184, *supra*, such a provision requires the state to take reasonable action to protect people from conduct of other (nonstate) individuals or associations—action that might include murder, rape, interference with the right to practice religion, or interference with the right to vote. The treaty duty to protect requires the state to develop bodies of law like tort (civil liability) or the criminal law, as well as to establish police, courts, prisons. But the individual defendant in a criminal action based on murder or physical assault is not necessarily the subject of an international duty or international crime, as are the defendants described above in this Comment who commit crimes against humanity or a crime like hijacking. The husband physically abusing his wife will have broken the criminal law of the state, which here serves (among other functions) to fulfil the state's obligation under Article 2 to 'ensure' the Covenant's rights to all within its jurisdiction. But he is not a subject of international law.

Consider another illustration. Article 11 of CEDAW requires states parties to 'take all appropriate measures' to eliminate discrimination against women in employment. A state may proceed through only civil regulation by creating judicial or administrative remedies for the victims of any such discrimination—damages, injunctive relief, and so on. It may enact criminal legislation that covers certain acts of discrimination of corporations and of individuals. But the individual who is convicted of illegal sex discrimination under such legislation is not (today) within the scope of international crimes.

COMMENT ON THE *EICHMANN* TRIAL

The Eichmann trial and conviction in 1961 illustrate themes in the preceding Comments at an early stage of the post-Nuremberg evolution of human rights law.

Adolf Eichmann, operationally in charge of the mass murder of Jews in Germany and German-occupied countries, fled Germany after the war. He was abducted from Argentina by Israelis, and brought to trial in Israel under the Nazi and Nazi Collaborators (Punishment) Law, enacted after Israel became a state. Section 1(a) of the Law provided:

> A person who has committed one of the following offences—(1) did, during the period of the Nazi regime, in a hostile country, an act constituting a crime against the Jewish people; (2) did, during the period of the Nazi regime, in a hostile country, an act constituting a crime against humanity; (3) did, during the period of the Second World War, in a hostile country, an act constituting a war crime; is liable to the death penalty.

The Law defined 'crimes against the Jewish people' to consist principally of acts intended to bring about physical destruction. The other two crimes were defined similarly to the like charges at Nuremberg. The 15 counts against Eichmann involved all three crimes. The charges stressed Eichmann's active and significant participation in the 'final solution to the Jewish problem' developed and administered by Nazi officials. Eichmann was convicted in 1961 and later executed. There appear below summaries of portions of the opinions of the trial and appellate courts.

The Attorney-General of the Government of Israel v. Eichmann[1]

Eichmann argued that the prosecution violated international law by inflicting punishment (1) upon persons who were not Israeli citizens (2) for acts done by them outside Israel and before its establishment, (3) in the course of duty, and (4) on behalf of a foreign country. In reply, the Court noted that, in event of a conflict between an Israeli statute and principles of international law, it would be bound to apply the statute. However, it then concluded that 'the law in question conforms to the best traditions of the law of nations. The power of the State of Israel to enact the law in question or Israel's 'right to punish' is based . . . from the point of view of international law, on a dual foundation: The universal character of the crimes in question and their specific character as being designed to exterminate the Jewish people'.

Thus the Court relied primarily on the universality and protective principles to justify its assertion of jurisdiction to try the crimes defined in the Law. It held such crimes to be offences against the law of nations, much as was the traditional crime of piracy. It compared the conduct made criminal under the Israeli statute (particularly the 'crime against the Jewish people') and the crime of genocide, as defined in Article 1 of the Convention for the Prevention and Punishment of Genocide.

> The Contracting Parties confirm that genocide, whether committed in time of peace or in time of war, is a crime under international law which they undertake to prevent and to punish.[2]

The Court also stressed the relationship between the Law's definition of 'war crime' and the pattern of crimes defined in the Nuremberg Charter. It rejected arguments of Eichmann based upon the retroactive application of the legislation, and stated that 'all the reasons justifying the Nuremberg judgments justify *eo ipse* the retroactive legislation of the Israeli legislator'.

The Court then discussed another 'foundation' for the prosecution—the offence specifically aimed at the Jewish people.

> [This foundation] of penal jurisdiction conforms, according to [the] acknowledged terminology, to the protective principle . . . The 'crime against the Jewish people,' as defined in the Law, constitutes in effect an attempt to exterminate the Jewish people. . . . If there is an effective link (and not necessarily an identity)

---

[1] District Court of Jerusalem, Judgment of 11 December 1961. This summary and the selective quotations are drawn from 56 Am. J. Int. L. 805 (1962) (unofficial translation).

[2] Article 6 of the Convention, the meaning and implications of which were viewed differently by the parties, states: 'Persons charged with genocide or any of the other acts enumerated in Article III shall be tried by a competent tribunal of the State in the territory of which the act was committed, or by such international penal tribunal as may have jurisdiction with respect to those Contracting Parties which shall have accepted its jurisdiction'.

between the State of Israel and the Jewish people, then a crime intended to exterminate the Jewish people has a very striking connection with the State of Israel. . . . The connection between the State of Israel and the Jewish people needs no explanation.

Eichmann v. The Attorney-General of the Government of Israel[3]

After stating that it fully concurred in the holding and reasoning of the district court, the Supreme Court proceeded to develop arguments in different directions. It stressed that Eichmann could not claim to have been unaware at the time of his conduct that he was violating deeply rooted and universal moral principles. Particularly in its relatively underdeveloped criminal side, international law could be analogized to the early common law, which would be similarly open to charges of retroactive law making. Because the international legal system lacked adjudicatory or executive institutions, it authorized for the time being national officials to punish individuals for violations of its principles, either directly under international law or by virtue of municipal legislation adopting those principles.

Moreover, in this case Israel was the most appropriate jurisdiction for trial, a *forum conveniens* where witnesses were readily available. It was relevant that there had been no requests for extradition of Eichmann to other states for trial, or indeed protests by other states against a trial in Israel.

The Court affirmed the holding of the district court that each charge could be sustained. It noted, however, much overlap among the charges, and that all could be grouped within the inclusive category of 'crimes against humanity'.

PNINA LAHAV, JUDGMENT IN JERUSALEM
1997, at 150

[In this portion of her biography of Simon Agranat, Justice and later Chief Justice of the Israeli Supreme Court, Lahav analyses his role in the Supreme Court's affirmance of Eichmann's conviction and death sentence. The Court delivered its judgment in a *per curiam* opinion. Justice Agranat had prepared the section of that opinion dealing with jurisdictional challenges to the trial.]

Agranat also understood that more than appearance was at stake: the soul of the Zionist project was reshaped by the brutal confrontation with the Holocaust. The old tension within Zionism between universalism and particularism now tilted in favor of particularism. Israelis were perceiving themselves as special: a special target for genocide and special in their right to ignore international norms in pursuit of justice. Popular hubris was growing, nurturing a victim mentality, a

---

[3] Supreme Court sitting as Court of Criminal Appeals, 29 May 1962. This summary is based upon an English translation of the decision appearing in 36 Int'l. L. Rep. 14–17, 277 (1968).

sense of self-righteousness and excessive nationalism, threatening to weaken the already shaky foundations of universalism in Israeli political culture.

. . .

Agranat understood that the legal reasoning he chose would affect the resolution of the tension between particularism and universalism. The Supreme Court could either let the conviction stand on the basis of crimes against the Jewish people, thereby lending force to the contention that Israel operated by its own rules, impervious to the laws developed by the community of nations, or it could try to show that Eichmann's trial was compatible with international norms of justice and fairness.

Most of the legal arguments advanced by Eichmann were designed to prove that Israel lacked jurisdiction to try him. Two of these arguments received extensive attention from the international community. The first was that the 1950 Israeli Law against the Nazis and Nazi Collaborators, which vested jurisdiction in the Israeli courts, was an ex post facto criminal law and as such could not apply to foreign nationals; the second was that, because the crimes were 'extra-territorial offenses' committed by a foreign national, Israel could not prosecute Eichmann according to the territoriality principle of international law.

In rejecting these arguments, the district court stressed the superiority of Israeli law in the sovereign state of Israel. The Law against the Nazis and Nazi Collaborators, the district court held, was a part of Israeli positive law and, as such, was binding on the courts of the land. It did hold that the law agreed with international norms, but emphasized the impact of the Holocaust on the evolution of the law of nations. This holding contained a symbolic message: Jewish national pride and self-assertion ruled the day. There was poetic justice in this interpretation. If the Final Solution was about the lawless murder of Jews, the *Eichmann* case was about the subjection of the perpetrators to Jewish justice, conceived and applied by the very heirs of those murdered.

There was ambivalence in Agranat's handling of this theme. On one hand, he endorsed the district court's analysis; on the other, his own reasoning went in a different direction. He sought to prove that the validity of the Law against the Nazis and Nazi Collaborators stemmed not from its superiority to the law of nations but from its compatibility with international law. Jewish justice was thereby not different from or superior to the law of nations; rather, it was a part of it.

. . .

. . . Citing scholarly works and judicial opinions, he asserted that international law did not prohibit ex post facto laws and was not dogmatic about the territoriality principle. Thus Israel's decision to prosecute, far from being a violation of international law, was simply a perfectly legitimate reluctance to recognize principles not fully endorsed by the community of nations. . . . He wanted to show that Israel's law was not an aberration but an affirmation of the law of nations.

The Law against the Nazis and Nazi Collaborators created a new category of crimes: crimes against the Jewish people. As such, it was a unique ex post facto law. The crime was specific to Jews and created a category hitherto unknown in any legal system. It was precisely for this reason that the crime formed a coherent part of Zionism. . . . Zionism portrayed the Holocaust less as the vile fruit of totalitarianism and more as the culmination of two millennia of anti-Semitism. The Jews had been defenseless because they did not possess political power. Even in Nuremberg the Allies refused to recognize that the Jews as a nation were especially targeted by the Nazis. The offense, 'crimes against the Jewish people', was designed to correct that myopia and to assert, ex post facto and forever, the Jewish point of view. . . .

Speaking for the Supreme Court, Agranat raised a different voice. He reviewed the four categories of the indictment, and he concluded that they had a common denominator, a 'special universal characteristic'. About 'crimes against the Jewish people' he had this to say: 'Thus, the category of "crimes against the Jewish people" is nothing but . . . "the gravest crime against humanity". It is true that there are certain differences between them . . . but these are not differences material to our case'. Therefore, he concluded, in order to determine whether international law recognized Israeli jurisdiction stemming from this ex post facto statute, the Court could simply collapse the entire indictment into 'the inclusive category of "crimes against humanity"'. This 'simple' technique enabled Agranat to devote the bulk of his opinion to the universal aspects of the *Eichmann* case.

QUESTIONS

1. Consider the alternatives to trial of Eichmann by the Israeli court. Would any international tribunal have been competent? What would have been involved in an effort to establish another *ad hoc* international criminal tribunal like Nuremberg, and would that effort have been likely to succeed? Would trial before the courts of another state have been preferable? Which state?

2. What problems, if any, do you see in reliance on 'crimes against the Jewish people'? How would you distinguish it from, for example, legislation by an African state defining 'crimes against the black people' that could reach persons in Western or other states who are accused of violence against black people? Are both types of statutes good ideas?

ADDITIONAL READING

Theodor Meron, *Human Rights and Humanitarian Norms as Customary Law* (1989); Roy Gutman, D. Rieff and K. Anderson (eds.), *Crimes of War: What the Public Should Know* (1999); Hans-Peter Gasser, *International Humanitarian Law* (1993); Timothy McCormack and G. Simpson (eds.), *The Law of War Crimes* (1997); L. C. Green, *The Contemporary Law of Armed Conflict* (1993); Adam Roberts, *Humanitarian Action in War* (1996); Chris Jochnick and R. Normand, 'The Legitimation of Violence: A Critical History of the Laws of War', 35 Harv. Int'l L. J. 49 (1994); Robert Kolb, 'The Relationship between International Humanitarian Law and Human Rights', 324 Int'l Rev. of the Red Cross 409 (1998).

B. INTERNATIONAL CRIMINAL TRIBUNALS FOR THE FORMER YUGOSLAVIA AND RWANDA

MARTHA MINOW, BETWEEN VENGEANCE AND FORGIVENESS
(1998), at 25

To respond to mass atrocity with legal prosecutions is to embrace the rule of law. This common phrase combines several elements. First, there is a commitment to redress harms with the application of general, preexisting norms. Second, the rule of law calls for administration by a formal system itself committed to fairness and opportunities for individuals to be heard both in accusation and in defense. Further, a government proceeding under the rule of law aims to treat each individual person in light of particular, demonstrated evidence. In the Western liberal legal tradition, the rule of law also entails the presumption of innocence, litigation under the adversary system, and the ideal of a government by laws, rather than by persons. No one is above or outside the law, and no one should be legally condemned or sanctioned outside legal procedures. . . .

A trial in the aftermath of mass atrocity, then, should mark an effort between vengeance and forgiveness. It transfers the individuals' desires for revenge to the state or official bodies. The transfer cools vengeance into retribution, slows judgment with procedure, and interrupts, with documents, cross-examination, and the presumption of innocence, the vicious cycle of blame and feud. The trial itself steers clear of forgiveness, however. It announces a demand not only for accountability and acknowledgment of harms done, but also for unflinching punishment. At the end of the trial process, after facts are found and convictions are secured, there might be forgiveness of a legal sort: a suspended sentence, or executive pardon, or clemency in light of humanitarian concerns. Even then, the process has exacted time and agony from, and rendered a kind of punishment for defendants, while also accomplishing change in their relationships to prosecutors, witnesses, and viewing public. Reconciliation is not the goal of criminal trials except in the most abstract sense. We reconcile with the murderer by imagining he or she is responsible to the same rules and commands that govern all of us; we agree to sit in the same room and accord the defendant a chance to speak, and a chance to fight for his or her life. But reconstruction of a relationship, seeking to heal the accused, or indeed, healing the rest of the community, are not the goals in any direct sense. . . .

. . .

Justice Jackson's own defense of the prosecutorial effort at Nuremberg was more modest than the assertion of deterrence offered by others since. He called for modest aspirations especially because wars are usually started only in the confidence that they can be won. Therefore, he acknowledged, '[p]ersonal punishment, to be suffered only in the event the war is lost, is probably not to be a sufficient deterrent to prevent a war where the war-makers feel the chances of defeat to be negligible'. Does the risk of punishment for human rights violations make the leaders of authoritarian regimes reluctant to surrender power in the first place? Individuals who commit atrocities on the scale of genocide are unlikely to behave as 'rational actors', deterred by the risk of punishment. Even if they were, it is not irrational to ignore the improbable prospect of punishment given the track record of international law thus far. A tribunal can be but one step in a process seeking to ensure peace, to make those in power responsible to law, and to condemn aggression.

. . .

THEODOR MERON, THE CASE FOR WAR CRIMES TRIALS IN YUGOSLAVIA
72 Foreign Affairs 122 (No. 3, 1993), at 123

. . . Except in the case of a total defeat or subjugation—for example, Germany after World War II—prosecutions of enemy personnel accused of war crimes have been both rare and difficult. National prosecutions have also been rare because of nationalistic, patriotic or propagandistic considerations.

The Versailles Treaty after World War I illustrates the case of a defeated but not wholly occupied state. Germany was obligated to hand over to the allies for trial about 900 persons accused of violating the laws of war. But even a weak and defeated country such as Germany was able to effectively resist compliance. The allies eventually agreed to trials by German national courts of a significantly reduced number of Germans. The sentences were both few and clement. The Versailles model proved to be clearly disappointing.

On the other hand, after the four principal victorious and occupying powers established an international military tribunal (IMT) following World War II, several thousand Nazi war criminals were tried either by national courts under Allied Control Council Law No. 10 or by various states under national decrees. Nuremberg's IMT, before which about 20 major offenders were tried, and the national courts functioned reasonably well; the Allies had supreme authority over Germany and thus could often find and arrest the accused, obtain evidence and make arrangements for extradition.

Despite the revolutionary development of human rights in the U.N. era, no attempts have been made to bring to justice such gross perpetrators of crimes against humanity or genocide as Pol Pot, Idi Amin or Saddam Hussein, perhaps because the atrocities in Cambodia, Uganda and Iraq (against the Kurds) did not occur in the context of international wars. Internal strife and even civil wars are still largely outside the parameters of war crimes and the grave breaches provisions of the Geneva conventions.

The Persian Gulf War, as an international war, provided a classic environment for the vindication of the laws of war so grossly violated by Iraq by its plunder of Kuwait, its barbaric treatment of Kuwait's civilian population, its mistreatment of Kuwaiti and allied prisoners of war and during the sad chapter of the U.S. and other hostages. Although the Security Council had invoked the threat of prosecutions of Iraqi violators of international humanitarian law, the ceasefire resolution did not contain a single word regarding criminal responsibility. Instead, the U.N. resolution promulgated a system of war reparations and established numerous obligations for Iraq in areas ranging from disarmament to boundary demarcation.

This result is not surprising, for the U.N. coalition's war objectives were limited, and there was an obvious tension between negotiating a ceasefire with Saddam Hussein and demanding his arrest and trial as a war criminal. A historic opportunity was missed to breathe new life into the critically important concept of individual criminal responsibility for the laws of war violations. At the very least, the Security Council should have issued a warning that Saddam and other responsible Iraqis would be subject to arrest and prosecution under the grave breaches provisions of the Geneva conventions whenever they set foot abroad.

. . .

Warnings of war crimes trials have been unsuccessful deterrents in past wars and may prove no more effective in the case of the former Yugoslavia. The precedent and moral considerations for the establishment of the tribunal require action in any event. Furthermore, several factors may yet strengthen deterrence. First, modern media ensures that all actors in the former Yugoslavia know of the steps being taken to establish the tribunal. Second, the tribunal will probably be established while the war is still being waged. Even the worst war criminals involved in the present conflict know that their countries will eventually want to emerge from isolation and be reintegrated into the international community. Moreover, they themselves will want to travel abroad. Normalization of relations and travel would depend on compliance with warrants of arrest. A successful tribunal for Yugoslavia will enhance deterrence in future cases; failure may doom it.

. . .

The establishment of an ad hoc tribunal should not stand alone, however, as a sole or adequate solution. The world has failed to prosecute those responsible for egregious violations of international humanitarian law and human rights in Uganda, Iraq and Cambodia. To avoid charges of Eurocentrism this ad hoc tribunal for the former Yugoslavia should be a step toward the creation of a permanent criminal tribunal with general jurisdiction. The drafting of a treaty on a permanent tribunal, on which work has begun by the U.N. International Law Commission, should be expedited, providing an opportunity to supplement the substantive development of international law by an institutional process.

. . .

SECURITY COUNCIL RESOLUTIONS ON ESTABLISHMENT OF AN INTERNATIONAL TRIBUNAL FOR THE FORMER YUGOSLAVIA
reprinted in 14 Hum. Rts. L. J. 197 (1993)

Resolution 808, 22 February 1993

. . .

Recalling paragraph 10 of its resolution 764 (1992) of 13 July 1992, in which it reaffirmed that all parties are bound to comply with the obligations under international humanitarian law and in particular the Geneva Conventions of 12 August 1949, and that persons who commit or order the commission of grave breaches of the Conventions are individually responsible in respect of such breaches,

. . .

Expressing once again its grave alarm at continuing reports of widespread violations of international humanitarian law occurring within the territory of the former Yugoslavia, including reports of mass killings and the continuance of the practice of 'ethnic cleansing',

Determining that this situation constitutes a threat to international peace and security,

Determined to put an end to such crimes and to take effective measures to bring to justice the persons who are responsible for them,

Convinced that in the particular circumstances of the former Yugoslavia the establishment of an international tribunal would enable this aim to be achieved and would contribute to the restoration and maintenance of peace.

. . .

1. *Decides* that an international tribunal shall be established for the prosecution of persons responsible for serious violations of international humanitarian law committed in the territory of the former Yugoslavia since 1991;

2. *Requests* the Secretary-General to submit for consideration by the Council . . . a report on all aspects of this matter, including specific proposals and where appropriate options for the effective and expeditious implementation of the decision contained in paragraph 1 above, taking into account suggestions put forward in this regard by Member States;

. . .

Resolution 827, 25 May 1993

. . .

Acting under Chapter VII of the Charter of the United Nations,

1. Approves the report of the Secretary-General;

2. Decides hereby to establish an international tribunal for the sole purpose of prosecuting persons responsible for serious violations of international humanitarian law committed in the territory of the former Yugoslavia between 1 January 1991 and a date to be determined by the Security Council upon the restoration of peace and to this end to adopt the Statute of the International Tribunal annexed to the above-mentioned report;

. . .

4. Decides that all States shall cooperate fully with the International Tribunal and its organs in accordance with the present resolution and the Statute of the International Tribunal and that consequently all States shall take any measures necessary under their domestic law to implement the provisions of the present resolution and the Statute, including the obligation of States to comply with requests for assistance or orders issued by a Trial Chamber under Article 29 of the Statute;

. . .

7. Decides also that the work of the International Tribunal shall be carried out without prejudice to the right of the victims to seek, through appropriate means, compensation for damages incurred as a result of violations of international humanitarian law;

. . .

REPORT OF THE SECRETARY-GENERAL UNDER SECURITY COUNCIL RESOLUTION 808
Doc. S/2504, 3 May 1993, reprinted in 14 Hum. Rts. L. J. 198 (1993)

. . .

I. The Legal Basis for the Establishment of the International Tribunal

. . .

18. Security Council resolution 808 . . . [does not] indicate how such an international tribunal is to be established or on what legal basis.

19. The approach which, in the normal course of events, would be followed in establishing an international tribunal would be the conclusion of a treaty by which the States parties would establish a tribunal and approve its statute. This treaty would be drawn up and adopted by an appropriate international body (e.g., the General Assembly or a specially convened conference), following which it would be opened for signature and ratification. Such an approach . . . would allow the States participating in the negotiation and conclusion of the treaty fully to exercise their sovereign will, in particular whether they wish to become parties to the treaty or not.

20. . . . [T]he treaty approach incurs the disadvantage of requiring considerable time to establish an instrument and then to achieve the required number of ratifications for entry into force. Even then, there could be no guarantee that ratifications will be received from those States which should be parties to the treaty if it is to be truly effective.

21. . . . The involvement of the General Assembly in the drafting or the review of the statute of the International Tribunal would not be reconcilable with the urgency expressed by the Security Council in resolution 808 (1993). The Secretary-General believes that there are other ways of involving the authority and prestige of the General Assembly in the establishment of the International Tribunal.

22. In the light of the disadvantages of the treaty approach in this particular case . . . the Secretary-General believes that the International Tribunal should be

established by a decision of the Security Council on the basis of Chapter VII of the Charter of the United Nations. Such a decision would constitute a measure to maintain or restore international peace and security, following the requisite determination of the existence of a threat to the peace, breach of the peace or act of aggression.

23. This approach would have the advantage of being expeditious and of being immediately effective as all States would be under a binding obligation to take whatever action is required to carry out a decision taken as an enforcement measure under Chapter VII.

. . .

25. . . . [T]he Security Council has already determined that the situation posed by continuing reports of widespread violations of international humanitarian law occurring in the former Yugoslavia constitutes a threat to international peace and security. The Council has also decided under Chapter VII of the Charter that all parties and others, concerned in the former Yugoslavia, and all military forces in Bosnia and Herzegovina, shall comply with the provision of resolution 771 (1992), failing which it would need to take further measures under the Charter. Furthermore, the Council has repeatedly reaffirmed that all parties in the former Yugoslavia are bound to comply with the obligations under international humanitarian law. . . .

26. Finally, the Security Council stated in resolution 808 (1993) that it was convinced that in the particular circumstances of the former Yugoslavia, the establishment of an international tribunal would bring about the achievement of the aim of putting an end to such crimes and of taking effective measures to bring to justice the persons responsible for them, and would contribute to the restoration and maintenance of peace.

27. The Security Council has on various occasions adopted decisions under Chapter VII aimed at restoring and maintaining international peace and security, which have involved the establishment of subsidiary organs for a variety of purposes. Reference may be made in this regard to Security Council resolution 687 (1991) and subsequent resolutions relating to the situation between Iraq and Kuwait.

28. In this particular case, the Security Council would be establishing, as an enforcement measure under Chapter VII, a subsidiary organ within the terms of Article 29 of the Charter, but one of a judicial nature. This organ would, of course, have to perform its functions independently of political considerations; it would not be subject to the authority or control of the Security Council with regard to the performance of its judicial functions. As an enforcement measure under Chapter VII, however, the life span of the international tribunal would be linked to the restoration and maintenance of international peace and security in the territory of the former Yugoslavia, and Security Council decisions related thereto.

29. It should be pointed out that, in assigning to the International Tribunal the task of prosecuting persons responsible for serious violations of international humanitarian law, the Security Council would not be creating or purporting to 'legislate' that law. Rather, the International Tribunal would have the task of applying existing international humanitarian law.

30. On the basis of the foregoing considerations, the Secretary-General proposes that the Security Council, acting under Chapter VII of the Charter establish the International Tribunal. . . .

II. Competence of the International Tribunal

. . .

33. According to paragraph 1 of resolution 808 (1993), the international tribunal shall prosecute persons responsible for serious violations of international humanitarian law committed in the territory of the former Yugoslavia since 1991. This body of law exists in the form of both conventional law and customary law. While there is international customary law which is not laid down in conventions, some of the major conventional humanitarian law has become part of customary international law.

34. In the view of the Secretary-General, the application of the principle *nullum crimen sine lege* requires that the international tribunal should apply rules of international humanitarian law which are beyond any doubt part of customary law so that the problem of adherence of some but not all States to specific conventions does not arise. This would appear to be particularly important in the context of an international tribunal prosecuting persons responsible for serious violations of international humanitarian law.

35. The part of conventional international humanitarian law which has beyond doubt become part of international customary law is the law applicable in armed conflict as embodied in: the Geneva Conventions of 12 August 1949 for the Protection of War Victims; the Hague Convention (IV) Respecting the Laws and Customs of War on Land and the Regulations annexed thereto of 18 October 1907; the Convention on the Prevention and Punishment of the Crime of Genocide of 9 December 1948; and the Charter of the International Military Tribunal of 8 August 1945.

. . .

Grave breaches of the 1949 Geneva Conventions

37. The Geneva Conventions constitute rules of international humanitarian law and provide the core of the customary law applicable in international armed conflicts. . . .

. . .

39. The Security Council has reaffirmed on several occasions that persons who commit or order the commission of grave breaches of the 1949 Geneva Conventions in the territory of the former Yugoslavia are individually responsible for such breaches as serious violations of international humanitarian law.

40. The corresponding article of the statute would read: [see Article 2 of the Statute, *infra.*]

Violations of the laws or customs of war

41. The 1907 Hague Convention (IV) Respecting the Law and Customs of War on Land and the Regulations annexed thereto comprise a second important area of

conventional humanitarian international law which has become part of the body of international customary law.

. . .

44. These rules of customary law, as interpreted and applied by the Nürnberg Tribunal, provide the basis for the corresponding article of the statute which would read as follows: [see Article 3 of the Statute, *infra*.]

Genocide

45. The 1948 Convention on the Prevention and Punishment of the Crime of Genocide . . . is today considered part of international customary law. . . .

46. The relevant provisions of the Genocide Convention are reproduced in the corresponding article of the statute, which would read as follows: [see Article 4 of the Statute, *infra*.]

Crimes against humanity

47. Crimes against humanity were first recognized in the Charter and Judgement of the Nürnberg Tribunal, as well as in Law No. 10 of the Control Council for Germany. Crimes against humanity are aimed at any civilian population and are prohibited regardless of whether they are committed in an armed conflict, international or internal in character.

48. . . . In the conflict in the territory of the former Yugoslavia, such inhumane acts have taken the form of so-called 'ethnic cleansing' and widespread and systematic rape and other forms of sexual assault, including enforced prostitution.

49. The corresponding article of the statute would read as follows: [see Article 5 of the Statute, *infra*.]

STATUTE OF THE INTERNATIONAL TRIBUNAL FOR THE FORMER YUGOSLAVIA
reprinted in 14 Hum. Rts. L. J. 211 (1993)

Article 1—Competence of the International Tribunal

The International Tribunal shall have the power to prosecute persons responsible for serious violations of international humanitarian law committed in the territory of the former Yugoslavia since 1991 in accordance with the provision of the present Statute.

Article 2—Grave breaches of the Geneva Conventions of 1949

The International Tribunal shall have the power to prosecute persons committing or ordering to be committed grave breaches of the Geneva Conventions of 12 August 1949, namely the following acts against persons or property protected under the provisions of the relevant Geneva Convention:

    (a) wilful killing;
    (b) torture or inhuman treatment, including biological experiments;
    (c) wilfully causing great suffering or serious injury to body or health;

(d) extensive destruction and appropriation of property, not justified by military necessity and carried out unlawfully and wantonly;

(e) compelling a prisoner of war or a civilian to serve in the forces of a hostile power;

(f) wilfully depriving a prisoner of war or a civilian of the rights of fair and regular trial;

(g) unlawful deportation or transfer or unlawful confinement of a civilian;

(h) taking civilians as hostages.

Article 3—Violations of the laws or customs of war

The International Tribunal shall have the power to prosecute persons violating the laws or customs of war. Such violations shall include, but not be limited to:

(a) employment of poisonous weapons or other weapons calculated to cause unnecessary suffering;

(b) wanton destruction of cities, towns or villages, or devastation not justified by military necessity;

(c) attack, or bombardment, by whatever means, of undefended towns, villages, dwellings, or buildings;

(d) seizure of, destruction or wilful damage done to institutions dedicated to religion, charity and education, the arts and sciences, historic monuments and works of art and science;

(e) plunder of public or private property.

Article 4—Genocide

1. The International Tribunal shall have the power to prosecute persons committing genocide as defined in paragraph 2 of this article or of committing any of the other acts enumerated in paragraph 3 of this article.

2. Genocide means any of the following acts committed with intent to destroy, in whole or in part, a national, ethnical, racial or religious group, as such:

(a) killing members of the group;

(b) causing serious bodily or mental harm to members of the group;

(c) deliberately inflicting on the group conditions of life calculated to bring about its physical destruction in whole or in part;

(d) imposing measures intended to prevent births within the group;

(e) forcibly transferring children of the group to another group.

3. The following acts shall be punishable:

(a) genocide;

(b) conspiracy to commit genocide;

(c) direct and public incitement to commit genocide;

(d) attempt to commit genocide;

(e) complicity in genocide.

Article 5—Crimes against humanity

The International Tribunal shall have the power to prosecute persons responsible for the following crimes when committed in armed conflict, whether international or internal in character, and directed against any civilian population:

    (a) murder;
    (b) extermination;
    (c) enslavement;
    (d) deportation;
    (e) imprisonment;
    (f) torture;
    (g) rape;
    (h) persecutions on political, racial and religious grounds;
    (i) other inhumane acts.

. . .

Article 7—Individual criminal responsibility

    1. A person who planned, instigated, ordered, committed or otherwise aided and abetted in the planning, preparation or execution of a crime referred to in articles 2 to 5 of the present Statute, shall be individually responsible for the crime.

    2. The official position of any accused person, whether as Head of State or Government or as responsible Government official, shall not relieve such person of criminal responsibility nor mitigate punishment.

    3. The fact that any of the acts referred to in articles 2 to 5 of the present Statute was committed by a subordinate does not relieve his superior of criminal responsibility if he knows or had reason to know that the subordinate was about to commit such acts or had done so and the superior failed to take the necessary and reasonable measures to prevent such acts or to punish the perpetrators thereof.

    4. The fact that an accused person acted pursuant to an order of a Government or of a superior shall not relieve him of criminal responsibility, but may be considered in mitigation of punishment if the International Tribunal determines that justice so requires.

. . .

Article 9—Concurrent jurisdiction

    1. The International Tribunal and national courts shall have concurrent jurisdiction to prosecute persons for serious violations of international humanitarian law committed in the territory of the former Yugoslavia since 1 January 1991.

    2. The International Tribunal shall have primacy over national courts. At any stage of the procedure, the International Tribunal may formally request national courts to defer to the competence of the International Tribunal in accordance with the present Statute and the Rules of Procedure and Evidence of the International Tribunal.

Article 10—Non-bis-in-idem

    1. No person shall be tried before a national court for acts constituting serious violations of international humanitarian law under the present Statute, for which he or she has already been tried by the International Tribunal.

2. A person who has been tried by a national court for acts constituting serious violations of international humanitarian law may be subsequently tried by the International Tribunal only if:

  (a) the act for which he or she was tried was characterized as an ordinary crime; or
  (b) the national court proceedings were not impartial or independent, were designed to shield the accused from international criminal responsibility, or the case was not diligently prosecuted.

. . .

Article 18—Investigation and preparation of indictment

1. The Prosecutor shall initiate investigations ex-officio or on the basis of information obtained from any source . . .

2. The Prosecutor shall have the power to question suspects, victims and witnesses, to collect evidence and to conduct on-site investigation . . .

3. If questioned, the suspect shall be entitled to be assisted by counsel of his own choice, including the right to have legal assistance assigned to him without payment by him in any case if he does not have sufficient means to pay for it, as well as to necessary translation into and from a language he speaks and understands.

4. Upon a determination that a prima facie case exists, the Prosecutor shall prepare an indictment containing a concise statement of the facts and the crime or crimes with which the accused is charged under the Statute. The indictment shall be transmitted to a judge of the Trial Chamber.

Article 19—Review of the indictment

1. The judge of the Trial Chamber to whom the indictment has been transmitted shall review it. If satisfied that a prima facie case has been established by the Prosecutor, he shall confirm the indictment. If not so satisfied, the indictment shall be dismissed.

2. Upon confirmation of an indictment, the judge may, at the request of the Prosecutor, issue such orders and warrants for the arrest, detention, surrender or transfer of persons, and any orders as may be required for the conduct of the trial.

Article 20—Commencement and conduct of trial proceedings

1. The Trial Chambers shall ensure that a trial is fair and expeditious and that proceedings are conducted in accordance with the rules of procedure and evidence, with full respect for the rights of the accused and due regard for the protection of victims and witnesses.

. . .

4. The hearings shall be public unless the Trial Chamber decides to close the proceedings in accordance with its rules of procedure and evidence.

Article 21—Rights of the accused

1. All persons shall be equal before the International Tribunal.

2. In the determination of charges against him, the accused shall be entitled to a fair and public hearing. . . .

3. The accused shall be presumed innocent until proved guilty according to the provisions of the present Statute.

4. In the determination of any charge against the accused pursuant to the present Statute, the accused shall be entitled to the following minimum guarantees, in full equality: [provisions for a fair trial omitted]

Article 22—Protection of victims and witnesses

The International Tribunal shall provide in its rules of procedure and evidence for the protection of victims and witnesses. Such protection measures shall include, but shall not be limited to, the conduct of *in camera* proceedings and the protection of the victim's identity.

Article 23—Judgement

1. The Trial Chambers shall pronounce judgments and impose sentences and penalties on persons convicted of serious violations of international humanitarian law.

2. The judgment shall be rendered by a majority of the judges of the Trial Chamber, and shall be delivered by the Trial Chamber in public. It shall be accompanied by a reasoned opinion in writing, to which separate or dissenting opinions may be appended.

Article 24—Penalties

1. The penalty imposed by the Trial Chamber shall be limited to imprisonment. In determining the terms of imprisonment, the Trial Chambers shall have recourse to the general practice regarding prison sentences in the courts of the former Yugoslavia.

. . .

Article 25—Appellate proceedings

1. The Appeals Chamber shall hear appeals from persons convicted by the Trial Chambers or from the Prosecutor on the following grounds:

    (a) an error on a question of law invalidating the decision; or
    (b) an error of fact which has occasioned a miscarriage of justice.

2. The Appeals Chamber may affirm, reverse or revise the decisions taken by the Trial Chambers.

. . .

Article 27—Enforcement of sentences

Imprisonment shall be served in a State designated by the International Tribunal from a list of States which have indicated to the Security Council their willingness to accept convicted persons. Such imprisonment shall be in accordance with the applicable law of the State concerned, subject to the supervision of the International Tribunal.

. . .

Article 29—Cooperation and judicial assistance

1. States shall cooperate with the International Tribunal in the investigation and prosecution of persons accused of committing serious violations of international humanitarian law.

2. States shall comply without undue delay with any request for assistance or an order issued by a Trial Chamber, including, but not limited to:

    (a) the identification and location of persons;

    (b) the taking of testimony and the production of evidence;

    (c) the service of documents;

    (d) the arrest or detention of persons;

    (e) the surrender or the transfer of the accused to the International Tribunal.

. . .

Article 32—Expenses of the International Tribunal

The expenses of the International Tribunal shall be borne by the regular budget of the United Nations in accordance with Article 17 of the Charter of the United Nations.

. . .

NOTE

The establishment of the International Criminal Tribunal for the Former Yugoslavia—the first such tribunal since the International Military Tribunal at Nuremberg, whose membership was indeed limited to the four major victorious powers—was an historic event holding considerable promise and inescapable risk. This Comment notes several aspects of the ICT and its work.

1. Observers have read different motivations into the Security Council's decision to establish the Tribunal. Some understand the ICT to be an essential response by the Council to the public outcry after exposure by the media of the outrages in the conflict—a minimum response, an effort to do 'something' that could prove to be significant and that was politically manageable (unlike the failures in efforts at negotiation or in discussions of types of intervention). Others understand the Tribunal to be a slave to conscience for the West, a way of responding to ethnic cleansing and the accompanying brutality without taking effective action. Whatever the motivations—and they were surely complex—the fact remains that a tribunal has been created, and the arguments for or against its establishment are now irrelevant.

2. The ICT is in a radically different situation from a court in a state observing fundamental principles of the Rule of Law in the sense that the state's executive and legislative branches comply with and execute court judgments. The Security Council has created an independent organ, as must be the case. Nonetheless, the ICT remains dependent on an uncertain and changing political context; it lacks the relative autonomy of a court in a state with a strong tradition of an independent judiciary. The Tribunal depends for funds on a UN General Assembly whose

members hold different views about it and who may judge its work differently. It must receive support from states and from the Security Council with respect to such basic matters as putting pressure on states to comply with its orders. There is no equivalent to a 'national tradition' for the Tribunal to draw on.

3. Beyond its fundamental mission of bringing a sense of justice and reconciliation to the combatants and civilians in the area, the ICTY (and the ICT for Rwanda, *infra*) possess an exceptional opportunity to develop international law in the field of individual criminal responsibility in an authoritative way. The Prosecutor and judges have confronted and will continue to confront numerous vexing issues, some of ancient lineage and some bred by the developments over the last half century in international humanitarian law including the crimes defined at Nuremberg.

QUESTIONS

1. In what respects does the Statute on its face reveal changes in the definitions of war crimes and crimes against humanity from the Nuremberg Charter? What is the direction of those changes?

2. Why do you suppose the Statute lacks a provision for crimes against peace similar to that at Nuremberg?

COMMENT ON BACKGROUND TO THE TADIC LITIGATION BEFORE THE INTERNATIONAL CRIMINAL TRIBUNAL FOR FORMER YUGOSLAVIA

The Broad Context:

The 1997 opinion of a Trial Chamber of the ICTY in *Prosecutor v. Tadic, infra,* was the first determination of individual guilt or innocence in connection with serious violations of international humanitarian law by this tribunal. This Comment sketches the context in which this and similar cases arose. For this sketch, it draws on the opinion of the Trial Chamber, which relied on expert witnesses called by the Prosecution and Defence. Where conflict emerged between witnesses, the Trial Chamber sought to resolve it 'by adopting appropriately neutral language.' It did not turn to any other sources. The area stressed by the opinion was northwestern Bosnia and Herzegovina (hereafter Bosnia), particularly Prijedor Opstina (the Prijedor district).

For centuries the population of Bosnia, more than any other republic of the former Yugoslavia, had been mulit-ethnic: Serbs (Eastern Orthodox), Bosnian Muslims, and Croats (Roman Catholic), all indeed Slav peoples within a broader conception of ethnicity. In the nineteenth century, a concept of a state of the south

Slavs, with a common language and ethnic origin, had developed, together with the growth among Serbs of the concept of a Greater Serbia including within its borders all ethnic Serbs. The collapse of the Ottoman Empire (it withdrew from the former Yugoslavia by 1912) and the Austro-Hungarian Empire after the First World War led to the creation of such a state of the south Slavs, Yugoslavia. The Axis occupation of Yugoslavia during the Second World War left bitter memories: Croatia's status as a puppet state of the Axis powers, the massacres it committed against Serbs and others, the fighting that occurred between the various Serb factions including the partisans under Marshal Tito (as he became later known), the retaliations after the war ended. Much of the fighting and many atrocities against civilians took place in Bosnia.

Nonetheless until about 1991, the different ethnic groups in Bosnia lived 'happily enough together,' though particularly in rural areas such as those in the outlying parts of the Prijedor district the three populations tended to live separately. As the opinion stated:

> Many witnesses speak of good inter-communal relations, of friendships across ethnic and coincident religious divides, of intermarriages and of generally harmonious relations. It is only subsequent events that may suggest that beneath that apparent harmony always lay buried bitter discord, which skilful propaganda readily brought to the surface, with terrible results.

Tito and his Communist regime acted sternly to suppress nationalist tendencies. The country consisted of six republics: Serbia (with its autonomous regions, Vojvodina and Kosovo), Slovenia, Croatia, Bosnia, Macedonia and Montenegro. Bosnia alone had no single majority ethnic grouping. During the latter part of Tito's rule from the mid-1960s on, there was a trend toward devolution of power to the republics, a trend which after Tito's death became useful to the overt resurgence of nationalist sentiment.

Economic and political crises developed simultaneously in the late 1980s. Slowly Yugoslavia fell apart as secessionist sentiment grew. A 1990 plebiscite in Slovenia voted overwhelmingly for independence from Yugoslavia, as did one in 1991 in Croatia. Slovenia effectively withdrew from Yugolsavia after brief fighting, but fierce hostilities broke out in Croatia. Both declared their independence, which was ultimately recognized by the European Union. The Bosnian Parliament declared Bosnia sovereign in 1991, and following a 1992 referendum, Bosnia declared itself independent. The United States and European Union states recognized the independence of the three new states in 1992.

With the encouragement and direction of Slobodan Milosevic, the Serbian president, the Serbian media stirred up nationalist feelings. With the break-up of Yugoslavia, the objectives of Serbia, including the Serbian-controlled JNA (Yugoslav People's Army) became the creation of a Serb-dominated western extension of Serbia to include Serb-dominated portions of Croatia and Bosnia, so as to form a new Yugoslavia with a substantially Serb population. But the large Muslim and Croat populations of Bosnia stood in the way. Hence it was necessary to adopt the practice of ethnic cleansing. The media propaganda intensified and began to accuse non-Serbs of plotting genocide against Serbs. Serbs were told that they had to protect themselves against a fundamentalist Muslim threat. The message from the government of Serbia was, as the tribunal's opinion put it, 'relentless,' 'cogent and potent.'

By the end of 1991, Serb autonomous regions in Bosnia had been formed. Serb leadership, the JNA and paramilitary organizations, and special police units began to establish physical and political control over municipalities, sometimes by rigged plebiscites. In March 1992, a Serb Republic of Bosnia (*Republika Srpska*) was formed as a distinct republic. The JNA, once a multi-ethnic national army although with a disproportionately Serb officer corps, became the instrument of policy of the new rump Federal Republic of Yugoslavia (consisting of Serbia and Montenegro). Gradually only ethnic Serbs were recruited into the armed forces. In late 1991, military units were formed in Serb-populated villages in Bosnia and supplied with weapons. Bosnian Serbs joined such distinct units as well as the JNA. More reliance came to be put on Serb paramilitary forces recruited in Serbia and Montenegro, and used to control non-Serb communities in Bosnia. Such forces acted in conjunction with the JNA.

By mid-1992 there were substantial international demands, including a Security Council resolution, that the JNA quit Bosnia. Serbia responded by ordering all non-Bosnian Serbs in the JNA to serve elsewhere, and by directing to Bosnia all Bosnian Serbs who served in the JNA elsewhere. The eventual new army of Republika Srpska retained close contacts with and received weapons and funding from the JNA and its successor in the Former Yugoslavia, the VJ (Vojska Jugoslavije, Armed Forces of Yugoslavia).

As the Serb take-over of Serb-dominated areas continued, shelling and round-ups of non-Serbs intensified, leading to many civilian deaths and the flight of non-Serbs, who were forced to meet in stated assembly areas for expulsion from the area. The Prijedor district was important because of its location as part of a land corridor between Serb-dominated areas. Before the fighting and expulsions, Bosnia Muslims were a slight majority in the area. Careful Serbian planning preceded the take-over of the town of Prijedor, and the joining of Prijedor to an autonomous Serb region that was part of Republika Srpska. An attack on the nearby town of Kozarac, also in Prijedor municipality and with a concentrated Muslim population, led to great destruction and many deaths. The non-Serb population was effectively expelled. Severe restrictions were imposed on the movement of non-Serbs throughout the region, and forms of economic discrimination were instituted. Massive destruction of Muslim religious and cultural sites began. The population of Bosnian Muslims in the Prijedor district fell from about 50,000 to 6,000.

Thousands of Muslim and Croat civilians were confined to camps in Omarska and other locations, and were subjected to severe mistreatment. The Trial Chamber heard testimony from about 30 witnesses who survived the brutality, and who reported the frequent killings and torture. Up to 3,000 prisoners were at Omarska at any one time. They were held in very confined space, and forced to live in filth and stifling heat. They received one inadequate meal a day, if that. There was rampant sickness. Frequent interrogations included severe beatings and injuries. Prisoners were summoned to be attacked with sticks and iron bars with nails.

Bodies were slashed with knives. Many prisoners who were summoned never returned. Women were routinely summoned at night and raped. Dead bodies were a not infrequent sight. Prisoners heard bursts of machine gun fire in one situation, and were called the next morning to load over 150 bodies on a truck.

Tadic

Tadic was born in 1955 in Kozarac, to a prominent Serb family. He joined the Serb nationalist party in 1990. After the ethnic cleansing of Kozarac was completed, he became a political leader of the town. The military tried several times to enlist him, and he was indeed arrested or threatened with arrest several times by the military police. In June 1993 he was mobilized and posted to the war zone. He managed to escape several times, and ultimately fled to Germany, where he was arrested by German authorities in 1994 on suspicion of having committed offences at the Omarska camp that constituted crimes under German law. The ICT then issued a formal request to Germany (as contemplated by the Statute and Rules of the ICT) for deferral of its intended prosecution and surrender of Tadic to the tribunal. Germany enacted the necessary legislation for his surrender (distinct from normal extradition to another state), and Tadic was transferred in 1995 to a UN detention unit in the Hague.

   The indictment by the Prosecutor against Tadic and a co-accused charged them with 132 counts involving grave breaches of the Geneva Conventions, violations of the laws or customs of war, and crimes against humanity. The defence filed a motion challenging the jurisdiction of the ICT. It disputed the legality of the establishment of the ICT by the Security Council, and challenged the tribunal's subject matter jurisdiction. The Trial Chamber dismissed the motion. An inter-locutory appeal was brought. The opinion in that appeal follows.

PROSECUTOR V. TADIC

Appeals Chamber, International Criminal Tribunal for the Former Yugoslavia, 1995 Case No. IT-94–1-AR72, 2 October 1995, http://www.un.org/icty/tadic/appeal/decision-e/51002.htm

[At the outset of his criminal prosecution in the Trial Chamber, Tadic moved to dismiss the case on three grounds, including unlawful establishment of the ICT, and lack of jurisdiction *ratione materiae*. The Trial Chamber denied the motion, and defendant-appellant brought this interlocutory appeal on jurisdiction. The following excerpts from the opinion of the Appeals Chamber (Presiding Judge Cassese, and Judges Li, Deschênes, Abi-Saab, and Sidhwa) examine a few of Tadic's arguments.]

II. Unlawful Establishment of the International Tribunal

. . .

   11. . . . International law, because it lacks a centralized structure, does not pro-vide for an integrated judicial system operating an orderly division of labour

among a number of tribunals, where certain aspects or components of jurisdiction as a power could be centralized or vested in one of them but not the others. In international law, every tribunal is a self-contained system (unless otherwise provided). This is incompatible with a narrow concept of jurisdiction, which presupposes a certain division of labour. Of course, the constitutive instrument of an international tribunal can limit some of its jurisdictional powers, but only to the extent to which such limitation does not jeopardize its 'judicial character'. . . .

12. . . . The plea based on the invalidity of constitution of the International Tribunal goes to the very essence of jurisdiction as a power to exercise the judicial function within any ambit. . . .This issue is preliminary to and conditions all other aspects of jurisdiction.

[In the Trial Chamber, the Prosecutor had argued that the ICT lacked authority to review its establishment by the Security Council, and that in any event the question whether the Council complied with the UN Charter when it created the ICT raised a non-justiciable 'political question'. The Trial Chamber agreed with this argument. The Appeals Chamber disagreed. It drew on the precedent of the UN Administrative Tribunal (UNAT) established by the General Assembly, whose governing Statute provided that, in event of a dispute as to whether the Tribunal had competence to decide in a given case, the Tribunal would decide the matter. This power of 'jurisdiction to determine its own jurisdiction' was part of the inherent jurisdiction of any judicial tribunal, and no text limiting this principle appears in the Statute of the ICT. Hence the ICT could examine the legality of its establishment by the Council solely for the purpose of determining its jurisdiction over the case before it. In so doing, it was not acting as a constitutional tribunal reviewing the acts of the Council against the Charter. The opinion continued:]

24. The doctrines of 'political questions' and 'non-justiciable disputes' are remnants of the reservations of 'sovereignty', 'national honour', etc. in very old arbitration treaties. They have receded from the horizon of contemporary international law, except for the occasional invocation of the 'political question' argument before the International Court of Justice in advisory proceedings and, very rarely, in contentious proceedings as well.

. . .On this question, the International Court of Justice declared in its advisory opinion on Certain Expenses of the United Nations:

> [I]t has been argued that the question put to the Court is intertwined with political questions, and that for this reason the Court should refuse to give an opinion. It is true that most interpretations of the Charter of the United Nations will have political significance, great or small. In the nature of things it could not be otherwise. The Court, however, cannot attribute a political character to a request which invites it to undertake an essentially judicial task, namely, the interpretation of a treaty provision (1962 I.C.J. Reports 151, at 155 (Advisory Opinion of 20 July)).

This dictum applies almost literally to the present case.

[The opinion then quoted from the Trial Chamber's summary of Tadic's claims and arguments with respect to the the the constitutionality of the establishment of the ICT.]

27. . . . These arguments . . . turn on the limits of the power of the Security Council under Chapter VII of the Charter. . . .[T]hey can be formulated as follows:

1. was there really a threat to the peace justifying the invocation of Chapter VII as a legal basis for the establishment of the International Tribunal?
2. assuming such a threat existed, was the Security Council authorized, with a view to restoring or maintaining peace, to take any measures at its own discretion, or was it bound to choose among those expressly provided for in Articles 41 and 42 (and possibly Article 40 as well)?
3. in the latter case, how can the establishment of an international criminal tribunal be justified, as it does not figure among the ones mentioned in those Articles, and is of a different nature?

28. Article 39 opens Chapter VII of the Charter . . . :

> The Security Council shall determine the existence of any threat to the peace, breach of the peace, or act of aggression and shall make recommendations, or decide what measures shall be taken in accordance with Articles 41 and 42, to maintain or restore international peace and security.

It is clear from this text that the Security Council plays a pivotal role and exercises a very wide discretion under this Article. But this does not mean that its powers are unlimited. The Security Council is an organ of an international organization, established by a treaty which serves as a constitutional framework for that organization. . . .

In particular, Article 24, after declaring, in paragraph 1, that the Members of the United Nations 'confer on the Security Council primary responsibility for the maintenance of international peace and security' . . . provides, more importantly, in paragraph 2, that:

> In discharging these duties the Security Council shall act in accordance with the Purposes and Principles of the United Nations. The specific powers granted to the Security Council for the discharge of these duties are laid down in Chapters VI, VII, VIII, and XII.

The Charter thus speaks the language of specific powers, not of absolute fiat.

29. What is the extent of the powers of the Security Council under Article 39 and the limits thereon, if any?

The Security Council plays the central role in the application of both parts of the Article. It is the Security Council that makes the determination that there exists one of the situations justifying the use of the 'exceptional powers' of Chapter VII. And it is also the Security Council that chooses the reaction to such a situation: it either makes recommendations (i.e., opts not to use the exceptional powers but to continue to operate under Chapter VI) or decides to use the exceptional powers by ordering measures to be taken in accordance with Articles 41 and 42 with a view to maintaining or restoring international peace and security. The situations justifying resort to the powers provided for in Chapter VII are a 'threat to the peace', a 'breach of the peace' or an 'act of aggression.' While the 'act of aggression' is more amenable to a legal determination, the 'threat to the peace' is more of a political concept. But the determination that there exists such a threat is not a totally unfettered discretion, as it has to remain, at the very least, within the limits of the Purposes and Principles of the Charter.

30. It is not necessary for the purposes of the present decision to examine any further the question of the limits of the discretion of the Security Council in determining the existence of a 'threat to the peace'. . . . [A]n armed conflict (or a series of armed conflicts) has been taking place in the territory of the former Yugoslavia since long before the decision of the Security Council to establish this International Tribunal. If it is considered an international armed conflict, there is no doubt that it falls within the literal sense of the words 'breach of the peace'. . . .

But even if it were considered merely as an 'internal armed conflict', it would still constitute a 'threat to the peace' according to the settled practice of the Security Council and the common understanding of the United Nations member-ship in general. Indeed, the practice of the Security Council is rich with cases of civil war or internal strife which it classified as a 'threat to the peace' and dealt with under Chapter VII, with the encouragement or even at the behest of the General Assembly, such as the Congo crisis at the beginning of the 1960s and, more recently, Liberia and Somalia. It can thus be said that there is a common under-standing, manifested by the 'subsequent practice' of the membership of the United Nations at large, that the 'threat to the peace' of Article 39 may include, as one of its species, internal armed conflicts.
. . .

31. . . . A question arises in this respect as to whether the choice of the Security Council is limited to the measures provided for in Articles 41 and 42 of the Charter (as the language of Article 39 suggests), or whether it has even larger discretion. . . . [Articles 41 and 42] leave to the Security Council such a wide choice as not to warrant searching, on functional or other grounds, for even wider and more general powers than those already expressly provided for in the Charter.

These powers are coercive vis-à-vis the culprit State or entity. But they are also mandatory vis-à-vis the other Member States, who are under an obligation to cooperate with the Organization (Article 2, paragraph 5, Articles 25, 48) and with one another (Articles 49), in the implementation of the action or measures decided by the Security Council.
. . .

32. . . . Appellant has attacked the legality of this decision . . . on at least three grounds:

> (a) that the establishment of such a tribunal was never contemplated by the framers of the Charter as one of the measures to be taken under Chapter VII; . . .

(b) that the Security Council is constitutionally or inherently incapable of creating a judicial organ, as it is conceived in the Charter as an executive organ, hence not possessed of judicial powers which can be exercised through a subsidiary organ;

(c) that the establishment of the International Tribunal has neither promoted, nor was capable of promoting, international peace, as demonstrated by the current situation in the former Yugoslavia.

33. . . . Obviously, the establishment of the International Tribunal is not a measure under Article 42. . . . Nor can it be considered a 'provisional measure' under Article 40. . . .

34. Prima facie, the International Tribunal matches perfectly the description in Article 41 of 'measures not involving the use of force.' Appellant, however, has argued . . . : before both the Trial Chamber and this Appeals Chamber, that:

. . . [I]t is clear that the establishment of a war crimes tribunal was not intended. The examples mentioned in this article focus upon economic and political measures and do not in any way suggest judicial measures.

It has also been argued that the measures contemplated under Article 41 are all measures to be undertaken by Member States, which is not the case with the establishment of the International Tribunal.

35. . . . It is evident that the measures set out in Article 41 are merely illustrative examples which obviously do not exclude other measures. All the Article requires is that they do not involve 'the use of force.' It is a negative definition.
. . .

[N]othing in the Article suggests the limitation of the measures to those implemented by States. The Article only prescribes what these measures cannot be. . . .
. . .

38. The establishment of the International Tribunal by the Security Council does not signify, however, that the Security Council has delegated to it some of its own functions or the exercise of some of its own powers. Nor does it mean, in reverse, that the Security Council was usurping for itself part of a judicial function which does not belong to it but to other organs of the United Nations according to the Charter. The Security Council has resorted to the establishment of a judicial organ in the form of an international criminal tribunal as an instrument for the exercise of its own principal function of maintenance of peace and security. . . .

The General Assembly did not need to have military and police functions and powers in order to be able to establish the United Nations Emergency Force in the Middle East ('UNEF') in 1956. Nor did the General Assembly have to be a judicial organ possessed of judicial functions and powers in order to be able to establish UNAT. . . .
. . .

[Tadic argued that human rights treaties require that a court be 'established by law', and that no 'law' established the ICT.]

43. . . . It is clear that the legislative, executive and judicial division of powers which is largely followed in most municipal systems does not apply to the international setting nor, more specifically, to the setting of an international organization such as the United Nations. Among the principal organs of the United Nations the divisions between judicial, executive and legislative functions are not clear cut. Regarding the judicial function, the International Court of Justice is clearly the 'principal judicial organ' (see United Nations Charter, art. 92). There is, however, no legislature, in the technical sense of the term, in the United Nations system and, more generally, no Parliament in the world community. That is to say, there exists no corporate organ formally empowered to enact laws directly binding on international legal subjects.

. . . [T]he separation of powers element of the requirement that a tribunal be 'established by law' finds no application in an international law setting. The aforementioned principle can only impose an obligation on States concerning the functioning of their own national systems.

44. In addition, the establishment of the International Tribunal has been repeatedly approved and endorsed by the 'representative' organ of the United Nations, the General Assembly: this body not only participated in its setting up, by electing the Judges and approving the budget, but also expressed its satisfaction with, and encouragement of the activities of the International Tribunal in various resolutions.

. . .

IV. Lack of Subject-Matter Jurisdiction

[This third ground of appeal argued that Articles 2, 3 and 5 of the ICT's Statute, on which the charges against Tadic rested, were limited to crimes 'committed in the context of an international armed conflict', whereas even if proven, Tadic argued, the crimes were committed in the context of *internal* armed conflict. The Prosecutor argued in the alternative that the conflicts in the former Yugoslavia should be characterized as an international armed conflict, and that even if internal, Articles 3 and 5 of the Statute gave the Tribunal jurisdiction to adjudicate. He further argued that the Security Council, by adopting the Statute, had determined that the conflicts were international and thereby gave the ICT jurisdiction.]

. . .

77. On the basis of the foregoing [description of the development of the conflicts in the Former Yugoslavia over several years], we conclude that [they] have both internal and international aspects, that the members of the Security Council clearly had both aspects of the conflicts in mind when they adopted the Statute of the International Tribunal, and that they intended to empower the International Tribunal to adjudicate violations of humanitarian law that occurred in either context. To the extent possible under existing international law, the Statute should therefore be construed to give effect to that purpose.

78. With the exception of Article 5 dealing with crimes against humanity, none of the statutory provisions makes explicit reference to the type of conflict as an element of the crime. . . . Since customary international law no longer requires any

nexus between crimes against humanity and armed conflict, Article 5 was intended to reintroduce this nexus for the purposes of this Tribunal. . . . [A]lthough Article 2 does not explicitly refer to the nature of the conflicts, its reference to the grave breaches provisions [of the Geneva Conventions of 1949] suggest that it is limited to international armed conflicts. . . . It would however defeat the Security Council's purpose to read a similar international armed conflict requirement into the remaining jurisdictional provisions of the Statute. Contrary to the drafters' apparent indifference to the nature of the underlying conflicts, such an interpretation would authorize the International Tribunal to prosecute and punish certain conduct in an international armed conflict, while turning a blind eye to the very same conduct in an internal armed conflict. . . .
. . .

82. The above interpretation [of Article 2 of the ICT's Statute] is borne out by. . . the Report of the Secretary-General. There, in introducing and explaining the meaning and purport of Article 2 and having regard to the 'grave breaches' system of the Geneva Conventions, reference is made to 'international armed conflicts'.

83. We find that our interpretation of Article 2 is the only one warranted by the text of the Statute and the relevant provisions of the Geneva Conventions, as well as by a logical construction of their interplay as dictated by Article 2. However, we are aware that this conclusion may appear not to be consonant with recent trends of both State practice and the whole doctrine of human rights which tend to blur in many respects the traditional dichotomy between international wars and civil strife. In this connection the Chamber notes with satisfaction the statement in the amicus curiae brief submitted by the Government of the United States, where it is contended that 'the "grave breaches" provisions of Article 2 of the International Tribunal Statute apply to armed conflicts of a non-international character as well as those of an international character'.

This statement, unsupported by any authority, does not seem to be warranted as to the interpretation of Article 2 of the Statute. Nevertheless, seen from another viewpoint, there is no gainsaying its significance: that statement articulates the legal views of one of the permanent members of the Security Council on a delicate legal issue; on this score it provides the first indication of a possible change in opinio juris of States. Were other States and international bodies to come to share this view, a change in customary law concerning the scope of the 'grave breaches' system might gradually materialize. Other elements pointing in the same direction can be found in [citations to a national military manual, a national court decision, and an agreement among conflicting parties in Bosnia are omitted.]

[The Appeals Chamber specified four requirements for the application of Article 3, including that the violation must infringe 'a rule of international humanitarian law' and that the violation must be 'serious'. The opinion examined more closely the two remaining requirements: that the Prosecution show that customary international rules exist governing internal strife, and that violation of such rules may entail individual criminal responsibility.]

97. Since the 1930s, however, the [distinction between international and

internal conflict] has gradually become more and more blurred, and international legal rules have increasingly emerged or have been agreed upon to regulate internal armed conflict. There exist various reasons for this development. First, civil wars have become more frequent, not only because technological progress has made it easier for groups of individuals to have access to weaponry but also on account of increasing tension, whether ideological, inter-ethnic or economic; as a consequence the international community can no longer turn a blind eye to the legal regime of such wars. Secondly, internal armed conflicts have become more and more cruel and protracted, involving the whole population of the State where they occur: the all-out resort to armed violence has taken on such a magnitude that the difference with international wars has increasingly dwindled (suffice to think of the Spanish civil war, in 1936–39, of the civil war in the Congo, in 1960–68, the Biafran conflict in Nigeria, 1967–70, the civil strife in Nicaragua, in 1981–1990 or El Salvador, 1980–1993). Thirdly, the large-scale nature of civil strife, coupled with the increasing interdependence of States in the world community, has made it more and more difficult for third States to remain aloof: the economic, political and ideological interests of third States have brought about direct or indirect involvement of third States in this category of conflict, thereby requiring that international law take greater account of their legal regime in order to prevent, as much as possible, adverse spill-over effects. Fourthly, the impetuous development and propagation in the international community of human rights doctrines, particularly after the adoption of the Universal Declaration of Human Rights in 1948, has brought about significant changes in international law, notably in the approach to problems besetting the world community. A State-sovereignty-oriented approach has been gradually supplanted by a human-being-oriented approach. . . .

98. The emergence of international rules governing internal strife has occurred at two different levels: at the level of customary law and at that of treaty law. Two bodies of rules have thus crystallized, which are by no means conflicting or inconsistent, but instead mutually support and supplement each other. Indeed, the interplay between these two sets of rules is such that some treaty rules have gradually become part of customary law. This holds true for common Article 3 of the 1949 Geneva Conventions. . . .

. . .

126. The emergence of the aforementioned general rules on internal armed conflicts does not imply that internal strife is regulated by general international law in all its aspects. . . . [T]he general essence of those rules, and not the detailed regulation they may contain, has become applicable to internal conflicts. . . .

127. Notwithstanding these limitations, it cannot be denied that customary rules have developed to govern internal strife. These rules, as specifically identified in the preceding discussion, cover such areas as protection of civilians from hostilities, in particular from indiscriminate attacks, protection of civilian objects, in particular cultural property, protection of all those who do not (or no longer) take active part in hostilities, as well as prohibition of means of warfare proscribed in international armed conflicts and ban of certain methods of conducting hostilities.

Individual criminal responsibility in internal armed conflict

128. . . . [C]ommon Article 3 of the Geneva Conventions contains no explicit reference to criminal liability for violation of its provisions. Faced with similar claims with respect to the various agreements and conventions that formed the basis of its jurisdiction, the International Military Tribunal at Nuremberg concluded that a finding of individual criminal responsibility is not barred by the absence of treaty provisions on punishment of breaches. The Nuremberg Tribunal considered a number of factors relevant to its conclusion that the authors of particular prohibitions incur individual responsibility: the clear and unequivocal recognition of the rules of warfare in international law and State practice indicating an intention to criminalize the prohibition, including statements by government officials and international organizations, as well as punishment of violations by national courts and military tribunals. . . .

129. Applying the foregoing criteria to the violations at issue here, we have no doubt that they entail individual criminal responsibility, regardless of whether they are committed in internal or international armed conflicts. Principles and rules of humanitarian law reflect 'elementary considerations of humanity' widely recognized as the mandatory minimum for conduct in armed conflicts of any kind. No one can doubt the gravity of the acts at issue, nor the interest of the international community in their prohibition.

130. Furthermore, many elements of international practice show that States intend to criminalize serious breaches of customary rules and principles on internal conflicts. . . .

. . .

133. Of great relevance to the formation of opinio juris to the effect that violations of general international humanitarian law governing internal armed conflicts entail the criminal responsibility of those committing or ordering those violations are certain resolutions unanimously adopted by the Security Council. Thus, for instance, in two resolutions on Somalia, where a civil strife was under way, the Security Council unanimously condemned breaches of humanitarian law and stated that the authors of such breaches or those who had ordered their commission would be held 'individually responsible' for them. (See S.C. Res. 794 (3 December 1992); S.C. Res. 814 (26 March 1993).)

. . .

137. In the light of the intent of the Security Council and the logical and systematic interpretation of Article 3 as well as customary international law, the Appeals Chamber concludes that, under Article 3, the International Tribunal has jurisdiction over the acts alleged in the indictment, regardless of whether they occurred within an internal or an international armed conflict. . . .

Article 5

. . .

141. It is by now a settled rule of customary international law that crimes against humanity do not require a connection to international armed conflict. Indeed, as the Prosecutor points out, customary international law may not require

a connection between crimes against humanity and any conflict at all. Thus, by requiring that crimes against humanity be committed in either internal or international armed conflict, the Security Council may have defined the crime in Article 5 more narrowly than necessary under customary international law. There is no question, however, that the definition of crimes against humanity adopted by the Security Council in Article 5 comports with the principle of nullum crimen sine lege.

142. We conclude, therefore, that Article 5 may be invoked as a basis of jurisdiction over crimes committed in either internal or international armed conflicts. In addition. . . we conclude that in this case there was an armed conflict. Therefore, the Appellant's challenge to the jurisdiction of the International Tribunal under Article 5 must be dismissed.

[Either unanimously or by votes of 4–1, the Appeals Chamber rejected each of the three grounds on which the appeal was based and dismissed the appeal. The separate opinions are omitted.]

COMMENT ON THE TADIC CASE BEFORE THE TRIAL CHAMBER

After dismissal of the interlocutory appeal, the case continued in the Trial Chamber: *Prosecutor v. Tadic*, No. IT-94–1-T, Opinion and Judgment of 7 May 1997.[4]

Findings of Fact

The Trial Chamber considered separately each count of the indictment. It discussed the events alleged, the role of Tadic in those events, and the case for the defence. It then made findings of fact, leaving legal issues such as interpretation of the relevant articles of the Tribunal's Statute for the end of the opinion.

Paragraph 7 of the indictment, for example, concerned events in Omarska prison camp. The cruel conduct alleged in some of the many counts in this paragraph included:

> A prisoner was frequently summoned for severe beatings. On one occasion, he was made to go on a hangar floor 'and there for up to half an hour was kicked and beaten by a group of soldiers armed with metal rods and metal cables. Then he was suspended upside down from an overhead gantry for some minutes.' As a result he suffered head fractures, a wasted hand, an injured spine and damage to his kidneys.
>
> A prisoner was struck as he entered the hangar floor. Another prisoner saw him being slashed with a knife and having black liquid poured over him. A third witness saw him being beaten with an iron bar and falling to the floor. This prisoner was never seen again.
>
> Two prisoners were forced to jump into an inspection pit with a third prisoner

---

[4] http://www.un.org/icty/tadic/trialc2/jugement-e/tad-tj970507e.htm

who was naked and bloody from beatings. One prisoner was ordered 'to suck his penis and then to bite his testicles. Meanwhile a group of men in uniform stood around the inspection pit watching and shouting to bite harder'. One prisoner was made to bite the other's testicles until he bit one testicle off and spat it out. He was then told that he was free to leave.

The opinion reviewed in detail the testimony of each of the witnesses. The defence of the accused to these counts was principally by way of alibi. Tadic said that he never visited the Omarska camp and on the day in question was living in Prijedor and working as a traffic policeman.

In its findings of fact, the tribunal considered all elements of the defence position, and pointed out where prosecution witnesses were vague or seriously inconsistent with each other. Nevertheless, there was 'much evidence from many witnesses' that Tadic was indeed in the Omarska camp on the relevant day. The Trial Chamber was 'satisfied beyond reasonable doubt' that Tadic was among the group beating several of the named prisoners, and that he attacked another prisoner with a knife; and that Tadic was present on the hangar floor on the occasion of the sexual assault on and mutilation of a prisoner. But it 'is not satisfied that [Tadic] took any active part' in that assault and mutilation. Moreover, the Prosecution had 'failed to elicit clear and definitive evidence from witnesses' about the condition of four prisoners after they were assaulted, 'let alone that they died or that death resulted from the assault upon them. . . . There must be evidence to link injuries received to a resulting death'.

Paragraph 4 of the indictment covered events at different locations in the Prijedor district. Several counts alleged that Serb forces including Tadic destroyed and plundered Muslim and Croat residential areas, imprisoned thousands under brutal conditions, and deported or expelled the majority of Muslim and Croat residents of the district. Muslims and Croats inside and outside the camp were subjected to a 'campaign of terror which included killings, torture, sexual assaults, and other physical and psychological abuse'. There was abundant testimony of systematic rape, often repetitive rape of the same victim, attended by great humiliation and cruelty, and sometimes followed by killing.

The Trial Chamber found beyond reasonable doubt that Tadic had participated in many of these events, and that he killed two Muslim policemen in Kozarac. All these events occurred 'within the context of an armed conflict'. Again the legal issues were reserved.

The Trial Chamber described the policy of discrimination instituted against non-Serbs, of which the camps were the most striking illustration. Those remaining were often required to wear white armbands and were continuously subject to beatings and terror tactics. Derogatory, denigrating curse words were common, and non-Serbs were forced to sing Serb nationalist songs. On various counts, the Trial Chamber found beyond a reasonable doubt that Tadic committed acts falling within this pattern of discrimination on religious and political grounds.

Legal Issues Relating to the Offences Charged

Armed conflict. The Trial Chamber examined Articles 2, 3 and 5 of the Statute. It stressed that each of these articles, 'either by its terms of by virtue of the customary rules which it imports, proscribes certain acts when committed "within the context of" an "armed conflict"'. Article 2 (grave breaches) applied only to armed conflicts of an international character. Article 3 absorbed violations of rules contained in Article 3 common to the Geneva Conventions, applicable to armed conflicts in general, while Article 5 (crimes against humanity proscribed by customary law) required a context of armed conflict whether national or international in character. Hence it was necessary to show that an armed conflict existed at all relevant time in Bosnia and that Tadic's acts were committed within such a context. In the case of Article 2, it was necessary to find both an international conflict and that offences were committed against 'protected persons.'

The Trial Chamber drew on the test stated by the Appeals Chamber for 'armed conflict'—namely, a resort to armed force between states or protracted armed violence between a government and organized armed groups of between such groups. It observed that Tadic's acts were connected to the armed conflict in two ways: (1) acts during the take-over of Kozarac and other villages that took place within 'an ethnic war and the strategic aim of the *Republika Srpska* to create a purely Serbian State,' and (2) acts within the camps as part of an accepted policy toward prisoners that furthered the objective of ethnic cleansing by means of terror and killings.

Article 2. The opinion referred to the view of the Appeals Chamber that the Statute restricted prosecution of grave breaches to those committed against 'persons . . . protected under the provisions of the relevant Geneva Conventions.' The Fourth Geneva Convention dealing with civilian populations was specifically in point. Protected persons are those who find themselves in the hands of a party to the conflict or of an occupying power of which they are not nationals. That requirement led the Trial Chamber to inquire whether, and to what degree, the armed Serbian groups in Bosnia were under such control from the Federal Republic of Yugoslavia that acts of such groups could be imputed to Yugoslavia's government. That the JNA played a role of 'vital importance' in establishing, supplying, maintaining and staffing local Serbian military groups was in itself 'not enough'. It was necessary to show that the Yugoslavian government continued to exercise effective control over the operations of such groups.

The Trial Chamber concluded that there was 'no evidence' on which it could state that the armed forces of the *Republika Srpska* 'were anything more than mere allies, albeit highly dependent allies', of the Yugoslavian Government. Hence the non-Serb civilian population of Bosnia, although it enjoyed the protection of prohibitions contained in Common Article 3 of the Geneva Conventions which were applicable to all armed conflict, did not benefit from the grave breaches regime of Article 2. It could not be said that the civilian victims 'were at any relevant time in the hands of a party to the conflict of which they were not nationals.' Hence the Trial Chamber found Tadic not guilty with respect to all charges based on Article 2.

Article 3. With respect to application of the rules of customary international humanitarian law expressed in Article 3, the Trial Chamber found that an armed conflict existed at all relevant times, that the victims were persons protected by that article, and that the offences charged were committed within that armed conflict.

Article 5. The opinion traced the development of the concept of crimes against humanity from Nuremberg to the present, and underscored such crimes' status as part of customary law. It repeated the statement in the decision of the Appeals Chamber that it was now a 'settled rule of customary international law that crimes against humanity do not require a connection to international armed conflict.' The conditions of applicability, as summarized in the opinion, included a nexus between the relevant acts and an armed conflict, that the acts be undertaken on a widespread and systematic basis in furtherance of a policy, that (in light of the Report of the Secretary General, p. 1147, *supra*) all relevant acts be undertaken on discriminatory grounds, and that the perpetrators have knowledge of the wider context in which their acts occur.

With respect to the need for discriminatory intent, the Trial Chamber described the law as 'quite mixed.' Many commentators and national courts had found the requirement of such intent to be inherent in crimes against humanity, necessary for the inhumane acts described in Article 5 as well as for persecution. The acts had to be taken against victims because of their membership in a group targeted by the perpetrator. The Tribunal's Statute did not include a requirement of discriminatory intent for all crimes against humanity, as did the Statute for the ICT for Rwanda. Nonetheless, in light of the Secretary General's report and comments of several Security Council members, the Trial Chamber adopted the requirement of discriminatory intent. It noted that the requirement was satisfied by the evidence that only the non-Serb part of the population was attacked precisely because they were non-Serb.

With respect to the requirement of a 'policy', the Trial Chamber rejected the notion at Nuremberg that the policy must be that of a state (as opposed to, for example, nonstate forces such as the organized groups of Bosnian Serbs). It observed that, as the 'first international tribunal to consider charges of crimes against humanity alleged to have occurred after the Second World War', the ICT 'is not bound by past doctrine but must apply customary international law as it stood at the time of the offences'.

After analyzing other components of the charges, such as the nature of the participation in events that was necessary for individual criminal liability, the Trial Chamber found Tadic guilty on numerous counts, but not guilty with respect to charges under Article 2 and with respect to several other counts.

NOTE

The Appeals Chamber in its Judgment of 15 July 1999[5] affirmed the convictions of Tadic while reversing several holdings of the Trial Chamber, thereby rendering Tadic liable for additional crimes. Two illustrations follow.

---

[5] http://www.un.org/icty/tadic/appeal/judgement/main.htm

1. Contrary to the Trial Chamber, the Appeals Chamber concluded that Article 5 of the Statute did not require all crimes against humanity to have been committed with a discriminatory intent. Such an intent was necessary only for 'persecutions' provided for in Article 5(h). It stated:

> 285. . . . [T]he interpretation of Article 5 in the light of its object and purpose bears out the above propositions. . . . In light of the humanitarian goals of the framers of the Statute, one fails to see why they should have seriously restricted the class of offences coming within the purview of 'crimes against humanity', thus leaving outside this class all the possible instances of serious and widespread or systematic crimes against civilians on account only of their lacking a discriminatory intent. For example, a discriminatory intent requirement would prevent the penalization of random and indiscriminate violence intended to spread terror among a civilian population as a crime against humanity. . . . The experience of Nazi Germany demonstrated that crimes against humanity may be committed on discriminatory grounds other than those enumerated in Article 5(h), such as physical or mental disability, age or infirmity, or sexual preference. Similarly, the extermination of 'class enemies' in the Soviet Union during the 1930s . . . and the deportation of the urban educated of Cambodia under the Khmer Rouge between 1975–1979, provide other instances which would not fall under the ambit of crimes against humanity based on the strict enumeration of discriminatory grounds suggested by the Secretary-General in his Report.

2. Again contrary to the Trial Chamber, the Appeals Chamber concluded that, with respect to the provisions of Article 2 of the Statute on grave breaches, it had been proven that the victims were 'protected persons' under applicable provisions of the Fourth Geneva Convention. For Article 2 to be applicable, it was necessary to show that the conflict was international. The Appeals Chamber so found. It concluded that the many relationships between the army of the FRY and the Bosnian Serb forces amounted to one force under the direction of the FRY rather than two separate armies in any genuine sense. With respect to the issue of 'protected persons,' the Appeals Chamber stated:

> 167. In the instant case the Bosnian Serbs, including the Appellant, arguably had the same nationality as the victims, that is, they were nationals of Bosnia and Herzegovina. However, it has been shown above that the Bosnian Serb forces acted as de facto organs of another State, namely, the FRY. Thus the requirements set out in Article 4 of Geneva Convention IV are met: the victims were 'protected persons' as they found themselves in the hands of armed forces of a State of which they were not nationals.
>
> . . .
>
> 170. It follows from the above that the Trial Chamber erred in so far as it acquitted the Appellant on the sole ground that the grave breaches regime of the Geneva Conventions of 1949 did not apply.
>
> 171. The Appeals Chamber accordingly finds that the Appellant was guilty of grave breaches . . . .

Sentencing of Tadic raised a range of issues that led to two judgments of the

Trial Chamber and a judgment of the Appeals Chamber in 2000[6] which put the long litigation to an end.

QUESTIONS

1. What are the significant interpretations or changes in the bodies of law relevant to these international crimes that these opinions introduce? Do they have a common characteristic? From these excerpts, how do you understand these opinions' methodological approaches to the ongoing development of customary international law?

2. Are you persuaded by the opinion on the interlocutory appeal? Or would you have preferred (a) the approach of the Trial Chamber to the issue of jurisdiction, or (b) a less deferential and more independent approach of the Appeals Chamber?

3. 'It is clear that Tadic, a mere foot soldier in these sordid events, was selected for prosecution because the Tribunal did not have custody of a higher ranking, more significant figure. There were hundreds or thousands of people like Tadic, starting with his close companions in perpetrating the horrors described in the opinion. What is the point of convicting one among them in what seems to be a mere lottery?' Comment.

4. 'It is wrong to imagine the prosecution of Tadic as serving the goal of individualizing guilt, so as to overcome notions of collective guilt and allow peoples like the Serbs to get on with their lives after the war. Tadic is part of a system. His guilt is deeply linked to the guilt of the larger bloody scheme in which he played a role. The opinion indicts an entire leadership and those who executed its plans. These are not the isolated, deviant crimes of murder or torture or rape that occur within all countries and that are sensibly punished as such.' Comment.

5. Observers have described the aims of the international criminal tribunals in ways that evoke traditional notions of the aims of the criminal law generally, but that also address specific characteristics of this conflict. Consider:

a. *Deterrence.* Whom is the Tribunal attempting to deter: the present leaders in this conflict, or those who might instigate and commit crimes in future conflicts? Should different strategies be at work to achieve one or the other goal? Who indeed can be deterred in an ethnic conflict stirring such deep hatreds and cruel actions—only the leaders, or also the foot soldiers who commit many of the atrocities? Is a court the most effective instrument of deterrence, or does the Tribunal play this role because of failure of other means of addressing the conflict?

b. *Punishment-retribution.* How can the Tribunal best serve this function? Is symbolic justice through the conviction and imprisonment of a small number of people (in relation to the number of people committing the international crimes defined by the Statute) sufficient to create a broad sense of justice among the conflict's victims? What other means (shy of forceful intervention) are available to help build this sense of justice?

---

[6] http://www.un.org/icty/tadic/appeal/judgement/tad-asj000126e.htm

c. *Reconciliation*, long-term peace and stability. Can reconciliation and a 'true' lasting peace be achieved partly through the work of the Tribunal? What role are convictions and imprisonment likely to play in this process of reconciliation in comparison with, for example, a Serbian–Bosnian settlement on issues like territorial control and resettlement, about an international agreement on compensation of victims that may permit them to get on with their lives, and so on?

6. 'Some have argued that the ICTY serves no important function in a context where the territorial aims of the aggressors have in good part been met, indeed to some extent ratified by the Dayton accords. Consider how different were the trials at Nuremberg, which followed the total defeat of Germany and left it with none of its spoils of war. Nuremberg ratified a victory in legal terms. The ICTY follows a defeat.[7] But this is a mistaken argument. To have rejected the idea of an international criminal tribunal in the case of the Former Yugoslavia would have been to acquiesce in the argument of those who understand Nuremberg only as 'victor's law.' It was essential to make the point through the ICTY that international standards (at least of *jus in bello* if not *jus ad bellum*) must be vindicated independently of whether there was or would ever be a military victory to roll back the illegal gains. International law was more than an afterthought at Nuremberg after the crucial military victory was won. It made its independent point. This Tribunal too provides a golden opportunity for international law to demonstrate its autonomy from international military force as a means of protecting human rights. The differences between the two situations are irrelevant.' Comment.

7. How do you understand the savage cruelty shown by the Serbian captors to their prisoners? (The same question can be put to many parties to ethnic and other conflicts (such as the Rwandan conflict), as well as to members of majority or powerful groups that behave in physically cruel ways to the despised and dehumanized minority or powerless groups.) Is encouragement or condoning of such behaviour by those in charge meant to serve a purpose, like ethnic cleansing? Meant to humiliate? Does the context of weapons and force and killing encourage release of this base side of human nature, in the sense that violence dissolves all bonds and restraints? Is such mass conduct in the context of mass violence deterrable?

JOSÉ ALVAREZ, CRIMES OF STATES/CRIMES OF HATE: LESSONS FROM RWANDA
24 Yale J. Int'l L. 365 (1999), at 443

Attention to the ethnic divisions that underlie the 1994 genocide and the continuing violence in that country should make us skeptical as well about how the ICTR handles evidentiary issues. The difficulties in this regard have been raised most clearly in the ICTY's Tadic case. . . . [T]he vast bulk of the evidence in the Tadic case came not in the form of physical evidence, such as contemporaneous written records of atrocities (as at Nuremberg), but rather through the oral testimony of self-interested, live witnesses who replicated inside the courtroom the ethnic

---

[7] Compare the argument of Kenneth Anderson in 'Nuremberg Sensibility: Telford Taylor's Memoir of the Nuremberg Trials', 7 Harv. Hum. Rts. J. 281 (1994).

divides of the society at large. In the Tadic case, there were only Serbian witnesses for the defense, while the prosecution relied entirely on non-Serbs (mostly Muslim victims). For Tadic's judges, the situation posed considerable difficulties. How does a tribunal generate confidence in its neutral conclusions when the primary source for these must be conflicting testimony that is subject to the challenge that Muslim witnesses will say anything against those who they believe are at war with them and that Serbian witnesses will do the same against non-Serbs? How does a tribunal's treatment of the inevitable conflict between the biases of Serb and non-Serb witnesses avoid replicating among trial observers in the region the prevalent ethnic and religious tensions that gave rise to the Balkan conflict in the first place?

Tadic's judges reacted to these challenges in the time-honored fashion of judges in liberal states—they pretended such strains did not exist. . . . The Tadic judges' curt response to the politically explosive defense claim that all the Muslim witnesses were inherently biased because they would say anything against their perceived oppressors, is revealing:

> The reliability of witnesses, including any motive they may have to give false testimony, is an estimation that must be made in the case of each individual witness. It is neither appropriate, nor correct, to conclude that a witness is deemed to be inherently unreliable solely because he was the victim of a crime committed by a person [of another] creed, ethnic group, armed force or any other characteristic of the accused. That is not to say that ethnic hatred . . . can never be a ground for doubting the reliability of any particular witness. Such a conclusion can only be made, however, in the light of the circumstances of each individual witness, his individual testimony, and such concerns as the Defence may substantiate either in cross-examination or through its own evidence-in chief.

Similarly, that chamber generally avoided casting aspersions on the veracity of defense witnesses due to their pro-Serb sympathies. Occasionally, however, the judgment indicates, without comment, certain background facts with respect to such witnesses, presumably letting these speak for themselves. The Tadic chamber papered over these difficult issues presumably to elicit confidence in the ICTY's neutrality.

Did the Tadic judges' efforts to generate confidence in their verdict succeed among significant segments of local communities within the former Yugoslavia? While it is difficult to judge success in this regard and impossible to predict how perceptions of success are likely to change over time, there is reason for skepticism. The immediate reaction to the Tadic judgment remained strongly divided along ethnic lines within the former Yugoslavia. Local governments in the Balkans remain highly suspicious, incredulous, skeptical, or, in some cases, even hostile towards international trials.

QUESTIONS

How do you assess Alvarez's criticism of the tribunal's handling of this issues of credibility, or indeed of the issue of deep ethnic conflict? What were the alternative approaches to enhance the Tribunal's claim to neutrality? Would that claim have been stronger if prosecutions were before national courts?

NOTE

By Resolution 955 (1994), the Security Council established an International Tribunal for Rwanda to prosecute persons 'responsible for genocide and other serious violations of international humanitarian law' committed principally in that country in 1994. The new tribunal (ICTR) had the same Prosecutor and appellate judges as the ICTY, but had separate trial judges.

The preamble to the resolution stated that the Council was convinced that prosecution of those responsible for serious violations 'would contribute to the process of national reconciliation and to the restoration and maintenance of peace', and would contribute to 'ensuring that such violations . . . are halted and effectively redressed'.

The Council, 'acting under Chapter VII of the Charter', adopted the annexed Statute of the ICTR, excerpts from which appear below.

STATUTE OF THE INTERNATIONAL TRIBUNAL FOR RWANDA
reprinted in 33 I.L.M. 1590 (1994)

Article 1—Competence of the International Tribunal for Rwanda

The International Tribunal for Rwanda shall have the power to prosecute persons responsible for serious violations of international humanitarian law committed in the territory of Rwanda and Rwandan citizens responsible for such violations committed in the territory of neighbouring States between 1 January 1994 and 31 December 1994, in accordance with the provisions of the present Statute.

Article 2—Genocide

1. The International Tribunal for Rwanda shall have the power to prosecute persons committing genocide as defined in paragraph 2 of this article or of committing any of the other acts enumerated in paragraph 3 of this article

2. [The definition of genocide is identical with Article 4 of the Statute of the ICTY, p. 1151, *supra.*]
. . .

Article 3—Crimes against Humanity

The International Tribunal for Rwanda shall have the power to prosecute persons responsible for the following crimes when committed as part of a widespread or systematic attack against any civilian population on national, political, ethnic, racial or religious grounds:

    (a) Murder;

    (b) Extermination;
    (c) Enslavement;
    (d) Deportation;
    (e) Imprisonment;
    (f) Torture;
    (g) Rape;
    (h) Persecutions on political, racial and religious grounds;
    (i) Other inhumane acts.

Article 4—Violations of Article 3 common to the Geneva Conventions and of Additional Protocol II

The International Tribunal for Rwanda shall have the power to prosecute persons committing or ordering to be committed serious violations of Article 3 common to the Geneva Conventions of 12 August 1949 for the Protection of War Victims, and of Additional Protocol II thereto of 8 June 1977. These violations shall include, but shall not be limited to:

    (a) Violence to life, health and physical or mental well-being of persons, in particular murder as well as cruel treatment such as torture, mutilation or any form of corporal punishment;
    (b) Collective punishments;
    (c) Taking of hostages;
    (d) Acts of terrorism;
    (e) Outrages upon personal dignity, in particular humiliating and degrading treatment, rape, enforced prostitution and any form of indecent assault;
    (f) Pillage;
    (g) The passing of sentences and the carrying out of executions without previous judgment pronounced by a regularly constituted court, affording all the judicial guarantees which are recognized as indispensable by civilized peoples;
    (h) Threats to commit any of the foregoing acts.

[Many articles in the ICTR Statute are identical with the equivalent articles in the ICTY Statute, p. 1150, *supra*, including articles on personal jurisdiction, individual criminal responsibility, concurrent jurisdiction, non-*bis-in-idem*, investigation and preparation of indictment, review of the indictment, commencement and conduct of trial proceedings, rights of the accused, protection of victims and witnesses, judgment, penalties, appellate proceedings, enforcement of sentences, cooperation and judicial assistance, and expenses of the tribunal.]

NOTE

One of the important novel features of the indictments and opinions of the ICTY and ICTR has been the strong attention to sexual crimes, particularly systematic sexual violence against women. Mass rape and other organized forms of sexual violence and humiliation have been frequent, and often used as instruments of fear, shame, and ethnic cleansing. Rape itself, long unmentioned in definitions of crimes in the humanitarian law of war, is included in the definition of several crimes in the two statutes. Note the attention to sexual violence against women in the *Akayesu* opinion below.

PROSECUTOR V. AKAYESU

Trial Chamber, International Criminal Tribunal for Rwanda, 1998
Case No. ICTR-96-4-T, www.ictr.org/ENGLISH/judgements/
AKAYESU/akay001.htm

[The indictment against Akayesu a Hutu, charged him with genocide, crimes against humanity, and violations of Article 3 common to the Geneva Conventions, punishable under Articles 2–4 of the Statute of the ICT for Rwanda. All alleged acts took place in Rwanda during 1994. The country is divided into 11 prefectures, which are subdivided into communes placed under the authority of bourgmestres. Akayesu had served as bourgmestre, 'the most powerful figure in the commune,' of the Taba commune from April 1993 to June 1994. He was charged in that office with the maintenance of public order and had exclusive control over the communal police. Subject to the prefect's authority, he was responsible for the execution of the laws and administration of justice.

There were 15 counts in the indictment. Some illustrative charges follow: (1) A least 2,000 Tutsis were killed in Taba from April to June 1994. Killings were so open and widespread that the defendant 'must have known about them,' but despite his authority and responsibility, he never attempted to prevent the killings. (2) Hundreds of displaced Tutsi civilians sought refuge at the bureau communal. Females among them were regularly taken by the armed local militia and subjected to sexual violence, including multiple rapes. Civilians were frequently murdered on or near the communal premises. Akayesu knew of these events and at times was present during their commission. That presence and his failure to attempt to prevent 'encouraged these activities.' (3) At meetings, Akayesu urged those present to kill accomplices of Tutsis, and on one occasion named three Tutsis who had to be killed. Two killings soon followed. (4) Akayesu ordered and participated in the killing of three brothers, and took eight detained men from the bureau communal and ordered militia members to kill them. (5) He ordered local people to kill intellectuals and influential people. On his instructions, five secondary school teachers were killed.

During the 43 trial days, the Prosecutor called 28 witnesses and the defence called 13 witnesses. All eye-witnesses requiring protection benefited from measures guaranteeing the confidentiality of their testimony. Pseudonyms and screens shielded such witnesses' identities from the public, but not from the accused and his counsel.

The opinion notes that Akayesu, before the events in question, was a broadly liked and respected member of the community who seemed to be doing his job well. A witness said that a bourgmestre is considered the 'parent' of the entire population 'whose every order would be respected.' Another witness stated that 'the people could not disobey the orders of the bourgmestre.'

As bourgmestre, Akayesu had ultimate authority over the communal police, a civilian police not subject to the military penal code but to administrative law sanctions. His sanctions against the police reached no further than reprimand or suspension. He also had control over any gendarmes (part of a military force) put at his disposal. Nonetheless, it was 'far from clear' that in such circumstances Akayesu would have 'command authority over a military force.'

The Trial Chamber found it 'necessary to say, however briefly, something about the history of Rwanda, beginning from the pre-colonial period up to 1994'. Prior to and during colonial rule (first under Germany, and from 1917 until independence under Belgium), Rwanda was an advanced monarchy ruled by the monarch's representatives drawn from the Tutsi nobility. The demarcation line between Hutus and Tutsis was then blurred, and clear ethnic categories had not developed. Colonizers favoured the Tutsis, who were lighter colour, taller, looked more like them, 'and were, therefore, more intelligent and better equipped to govern.' In the 1930s, Belgian authorities introduced a permanent distinction by dividing the population into three 'ethnic' groups, with the Hutu composing about 84 per cent of the population and the Tutsi about 15 per cent. Mandatory identity cards noted ethnicity. The Tutsi were more willing to be converted to Chrisianity; hence the church too supported their monopoly of power. Alison Desforges, an expert witness, testified at the trial:

> The primary criterion for [defining] an ethnic group is the sense of belonging to that ethnic group. It is a sense which can shift over time. . . . But, if you fix any given moment in time, and you say, how does this population divide itself, then you will see which ethnic groups are in existence in the minds of the participants at that time. . . . [R]eality is an interplay between the actual conditions and peoples' subjective perception of those conditions. In Rwanda, the reality was shaped by the colonial experience which imposed a categorization which was probably more fixed, and not completely appropriate to the scene. . . . The categorisation imposed at that time [by the Belgians] is what people of the current generation have grown up with. They have always thought in terms of these categories, even if they did not in their daily lives have to take cognizance of that. . . . [T]his division into three ethnic groups became an absolute reality.

When the Tutsi led campaigns for independence, the allegiance of the colonizer shifted to the Hutu. In the 1950s, elections were held and political parties were formed. The Hutu held a clear majority in voting power. Violence broke out between Hutu and Tutsi. Independence was attained in 1962. In 1975, a one-party system was instituted under (Hutu) President Habyarimana, whose policies became increasingly anti-Tutsi through discriminatory quota systems and other methods. In 1991, following violence and growing pressures, Habyarimana accepted a multi-party system.

Many Tutsi in exile formed a political organization and a military wing, the Rwandan Patriotic Army (RPA). Their aim was to return to Rwanda. Violence, negotiations and accords led to the participation of the Tutsi political organization (RPF) in the government institutions. Hard-line Hutu formed a radical political party, more extremist than Habyarimana. There were growing extremist calls for elimination of the Tutsi.

The Arusha accords between the government and the RPF in 1993 brought temporary relief from the threat of war. The climate worsened with assassinations, and the accords were denounced. Habyarimana died in an air crash, of unknown cause, in April 1994. The Rwandan army, Presidential Guard and militia immediately started killing Tutsi, as well as Hutu who were sympathetic to the Arusha accords and to power-sharing between Tutsi and Hutu. Belgian soldiers and a small UN peacekeeping force were withdrawn from the country. RPF troops resumed open war against Rwandan armed forces. The killing campaign against the Tutsi reached its zenith in a matter of weeks, and continued to July. The estimated dead in the conflict at that time, overwhelmingly Tutsi, ranged from 500,000 to 1,000,000.

The following excerpts from the opinion are taken from the text of the above-referenced website in 1999. Subsequent changes may have been made. The excerpts (Presiding Judge Kama, Judge Aspegren and Judge Pillay) begin with a discussion of the charge of genocide.]

As regards the massacres which took place in Rwanda between April and July 1994, . . . the question before this Chamber is whether they constitute genocide. Indeed, it was felt in some quarters that the tragic events which took place in Rwanda were only part of the war between the Rwandan Armed Forces (the RAF) and the Rwandan Patriotic Front (RPF).

. . .

The second requirement is that these killings and serious bodily harm. . . be committed with the intent to destroy, in whole or in part, a particular group targeted as such. In the opinion of the Chamber, there is no doubt that considering their undeniable scale, their systematic nature and their atrociousness, the massacres were aimed at exterminating the group that was targeted. . . . In this connection, Alison Desforges, an expert witness, . . . stated as follows:

> On the basis of the statements made by certain political leaders, on the basis of songs and slogans popular among the Interahamwe, I believe that these people had the intention of completely wiping out the Tutsi from Rwanda so that—as they said on certain occasions—their children, later on, would not know what a Tutsi looked like, unless they referred to history books.

. . . Dr. Zachariah also testified that the Achilles' tendons of many wounded persons were cut to prevent them from fleeing. In the opinion of the Chamber, this demonstrates the resolve of the perpetrators of these massacres not to spare any Tutsi. . . . [E]ven newborn babies were not spared. Even pregnant women, including those of Hutu origin, were killed on the grounds that the foetuses in their wombs were fathered by Tutsi men, for in a patrilineal society like Rwanda, the child belongs to the father's group of origin. . . .

In light of the foregoing, it is now appropriate for the Chamber to consider the issue of specific intent that is required for genocide (*mens rea* or *dolus specialis*). In other words, it should be established that the above-mentioned acts were targeted at a particular group as such. In this respect also, many consistent and reliable testimonies . . . agree on the fact that it was the Tutsi as members of an ethnic group [who were targeted during the massacres.] . . . [I]n the context of the period in question, [the Hutu and Tutsi] were, in consonance with a distinction made by the colonizers, considered both by the authorities and themselves as belonging to two distinct ethnic groups. . . . [T]he Tutsi were not the sole victims of massacres. Many Hutu were also killed, though not because they were Hutu, but simply because they were, for one reason or another, viewed as having sided with the Tutsi.

. . . [T]he propaganda campaign conducted before and during the tragedy by the audiovisual media . . . or the print media, like the Kangura . . . overtly called for the killing of Tutsi, who were considered as the accomplices of the RPF and accused of plotting to take over the power lost during the revolution of 1959. . . . Clearly, the victims were not chosen as individuals but, indeed, because they belonged to said group. . . . Consequently, the Chamber concludes from all the foregoing that genocide was, indeed, committed in Rwanda in 1994 against the Tutsi as a group. Furthermore, in the opinion of the Chamber, this genocide appears to have been meticulously organized. . . .

. . . [A]s to whether the tragic events that took place in Rwanda in 1994 occurred solely within the context of the conflict between the RAF and the RPF, the Chamber replies in the negative, since it holds that the genocide did indeed take place against the Tutsi group, alongside the conflict. The execution of this genocide was probably facilitated by the conflict, in the sense that the fighting against the RPF forces was used as a pretext for the propaganda inciting genocide against the Tutsi. . . . The Chamber's opinion is that the genocide was organized and planned not only by members of the RAF, but also by the political forces who were behind the 'Hutu-power', that it was executed essentially by civilians including the armed militia and even ordinary citizens, and above all, that the majority of the Tutsi victims were non-combatants, including thousands of women and children, even foetuses. . . .

. . . [T]he fact that genocide was indeed committed in Rwanda in 1994 and more particularly in Taba, cannot influence [the Tribunal] in its decisions in the present case. Its sole task is to assess the individual criminal responsibility of the accused for the crimes with which he is charged, the burden of proof being on the Prosecutor. . . .

4. Evidentiary matters

. . .

. . . The Chamber notes that it is not restricted under the Statute of the Tribunal to apply any particular legal system and is not bound by any national rules of evidence. In accordance with Rule 89 of its Rules of Procedure and Evidence, the Chamber has applied the rules of evidence which in its view best favour a fair determination of the matter before it and are consonant with the spirit and general principles of law.

. . .

[The Chamber discussed a number of issues, including whether there was need to have corroboration by other persons of testimony of a single witness before that testimony could be relied on, the problem of delay in the collection of evidence, and the impact of trauma on the testimony of witnesses. It turned to the problem of interpretation from Kinyarwanda, in which most witnesses testified, into French and English, and stressed the great difficulties of translation. The problem arose in pre-trial interviews and during court proceedings, and interpretation often moved from Kinyarwanda into French and then into English. Experts pointed out that certain words relevant to the prosecution had to be contextualized in time and place, for their meaning changed among groups and in different historical periods.]

The terms *gusambanya, kurungora, kuryamana* and *gufata ku ngufu* were used interchangeably by witnesses and translated by the interpreters as 'rape'. The Chamber has consulted its official trial interpreters to gain a precise understanding of these words and how they have been interpreted. . . . The word *kuryamana* means 'to share a bed' or 'to have sexual intercourse', depending on the context. It seems similar to the colloquial usage in English and in French of the term 'to sleep with'. The term *gufata ku ngufu* means 'to take (anything) by force' and also 'to rape'. The context in which these terms are used is critical to an understanding of their meaning and their translation. . . . Having reviewed in detail with the official trial interpreters the references to 'rape' in the transcript, the Chamber is satisfied that the Kinyarwanda expressions have been accurately translated.

5. Factual findings

[The Chamber noted that in addition to testimony of witnesses, it would take 'judicial notice' of UN reports extensively documenting the massacres of 1994. Its listing included reports of a Commission of Experts established by a Security Council resolution, of a special rapporteur of the Secretary General, and of the High Commissioner for Human Rights. Note that the 'factual findings' *infra* are relevant to determining whether the conditions stated in several articles of the ICTR Statute were here met.]

Paragraph 8 of the indictment alleges that the acts set forth in each paragraph of the indictment charging crimes against humanity, i.e. paragraphs 12–24, 'were committed as part of a widespread or systematic attack against a civilian population on national, political, ethnic or racial grounds'. . . . For [reasons given in earlier parts of the opinion], the Chamber finds beyond a reasonable doubt that a widespread and systematic attack began in April 1994 in Rwanda, targeting the civilian Tutsi population and that the acts referred to in paragraphs 12–24 of the indictment were acts which formed part of this widespread and systematic attack.

Paragraph 9 of the indictment states, 'At all times relevant to this indictment, a state of internal armed conflict existed in Rwanda'. The Chamber notes the testimony of General Dallaire, a witness called by the Defence, that the FAR was and the RPF were 'two armies' engaged in hostilities. . . . Based on the evidence presented, the Chamber finds beyond a reasonable doubt that armed conflict existed in Rwanda during the events alleged in the indictment, and that the RPF was an organised armed group, under responsible command, which exercised control over territory in Rwanda and was able to carry out sustained and concerted military operations. Paragraph 10 of the indictment reads, 'The victims referred to in this indictment were, at all relevant times, persons not taking an active part in the hostilities' . . . [T]he Chamber finds beyond a reasonable doubt that all the other victims referred to in the indictment were civilians, not taking any active part in the hostilities that prevailed in 1994. . . .

. . .

The Chamber now considers paragraph 12 of the indictment, which alleges the responsibility of the Accused, his knowledge of the killings which took place in Taba between 7 April and the end of June 1994, and his failure to attempt to prevent these killings or to call for assistance from regional or national authorities. . . .

. . .

The Chamber finds that the allegations set forth in paragraph 12 cannot be fully established. The Accused did take action between 7 April and 18 April to protect the citizens of his commune. It appears that he did also request assistance from national authorities at the meeting on 18 April 1994. . . . Nevertheless, the Chamber finds beyond a reasonable doubt that the conduct of the Accused changed after 18 April 1994 and that after this date the Accused did not attempt to prevent the killing of Tutsi in the commune of Taba. In fact, there is evidence that he not only knew of and witnessed killings, but that he participated in and even ordered killings. . . .

. . . [M]any witnesses, including Witnesses E, W, PP, V and G, testified to the collaboration of the Accused with the Interahamwe in Taba after this date. . . . The Accused contends that he was overwhelmed. Witness DAX and Witness DBB, both witnesses for the Defence, testified that the Interahamwe threatened to kill the Accused if he did not cooperate with them. The Accused testified that he was coerced by the Interahamwe. . . . The Chamber recognises the difficulties a bourgmestre encountered in attempting to save lives of Tutsi in the period in question. Prosecution witness R, who was the bourgmestre of another commune . . . averred that a bourgmestre could do nothing openly to combat the killings after that date or he would risk being killed; what little he could do had to be done clandestinely. The Defence case is that this is precisely what the accused did.

The Accused contends that he was subject to coercion, but the Chamber finds this contention greatly inconsistent with a substantial amount of concordant testimony from other witnesses. . . . [T]he Chamber does not accept the testimony of the Accused regarding his conduct after 18 April, and finds beyond a reasonable doubt that he did not attempt to prevent killings of Tutsi after this date. Whether he had the power to do so is not at issue, as he never even tried and as there is evidence establishing beyond a reasonable doubt that he consciously chose the course of collaboration with violence against Tutsi rather than shielding them from it.

. . .

[Paragraph 18 alleges that defendant took steps to stop the flight of three brothers, and then ordered and participated in their killing. After reciting the detailed testimony of witnesses, the Chamber pointed out similarities or contradictions among the narrative accounts offered. It then made its findings of fact.]

. . .

. . . The brothers of Karangwa tried to flee, and the police officers blew their whistles and said stop those 'Inyenzi' [a pejorative term] from running away. A mob of people took up the call, chased after the brothers and brought them back. The brothers were bleeding from open wounds and their clothing was torn. They were made to sit on the ground about 2 metres from the entrance to the courtyard. The bourgmestre of Musambira asked the Accused if he knew the men and what should be done with them. The Accused said they came from his commune and said we need to finish these people off—they need to be shot. All three brothers were then shot dead at close range in the back of their heads by two policemen from Musambira, in the Accused's presence. . . .

[The Chamber continued in its examination of each count of the indictment and, after presenting testimony of witnesses, made findings of fact. Several counts dealt with sexual violence. Some of the Chamber's findings follow.]

. . . [T]he Chamber finds that there is sufficient credible evidence to establish beyond a reasonable doubt that during the events of 1994, Tutsi girls and women were subjected to sexual violence, beaten and killed on or near the bureau communal premises, as well as elsewhere in the commune of Taba. Witness H, Witness JJ, Witness OO, and Witness NN all testified that they themselves were raped, and all, with the exception of Witness OO, testified that they witnessed other girls and women being raped. Witness J, Witness KK and Witness PP also testified that they witnessed other girls and women being raped in the commune of Taba. Hundreds of Tutsi, mostly women and children, sought refuge at the bureau communal during this period and many rapes took place on or near the premises of the bureau communal. . . . Witness JJ was also raped repeatedly on two separate occasions in the cultural center on the premises of the bureau communal, once in a group of fifteen girls and women and once in a group of ten girls and women. Witness KK saw women and girls being selected and taken by the Interahamwe to the cultural center to be raped. . . . Witness PP saw three women being raped at Kinihira, the killing site near the bureau communal, and Witness NN found her younger sister, dying, after she had been raped at the bureau communal. . . .

Witness KK and Witness PP also described other acts of sexual violence which took place on or near the premises of the bureau communal—the forced undressing and public humiliation of girls and women. The Chamber notes that much of the sexual violence took place in front of large numbers of people, and that all of it was directed against Tutsi women. . . .

There is no suggestion in any of the evidence that the Accused or any communal policemen perpetrated rape. . . . On the basis of the evidence set forth herein, the Chamber finds beyond a reasonable doubt that the Accused had reason to know and in fact knew that sexual violence was taking place on or near the premises of the bureau communal, and that women were being taken away from the bureau

communal and sexually violated. There is no evidence that the Accused took any measures to prevent acts of sexual violence or to punish the perpetrators of sexual violence. In fact there is evidence that the Accused ordered, instigated and otherwise aided and abetted sexual violence. . . . On the two occasions Witness JJ was brought to the cultural center of the bureau communal to be raped, she and the group of girls and women with her were taken past the Accused, on the way. On the first occasion he was looking at them, and on the second occasion he was standing at the entrance to the cultural center. On this second occasion, he said, 'Never ask me again what a Tutsi woman tastes like'.
. . .

[Part 6 of the opinion turned to legal issues. The Chamber first addressed the problem of cumulative charges relating to the same sets of facts—for example, genocide, complicity in genocide, and crimes against humanity. It stated criteria for deciding when it was acceptable to convict the accused of two offenses in relation to the same set of facts. It then considered some issues of individual criminal responsibility as set forth in Article 6 of the Tribunal's Statute—for example, the necessary kind and degree of participation in the described events that ran a range from planning and incitement to ordering, or aiding and abetting. It examined the liability of civilians as well as state officials, and the complex questions of delegation of state authority to others. The opinion next turned to the charges of genocide and crimes against humanity. A few of its observations follow.]

The Chamber holds that it is necessary to recall that criminal intent is the moral element required for any crime and that, where the objective is to ascertain the individual criminal responsibility of a person accused of crimes falling within the jurisdiction of the Chamber, such as genocide, crimes against humanity and violations of Article 3 Common to the Geneva Conventions and of Additional Protocol II thereto, it is certainly proper to ensure that there has been malicious intent, or, at least, ensure that negligence was so serious as to be tantamount to acquiescence or even malicious intent. As to whether the form of individual criminal responsibility referred to Article 6(3) of the Statute applies to persons in positions of both military and civilian authority, it should be noted that during the Tokyo trials, certain civilian authorities were convicted of war crimes under this principle. . . .
. . .

The Chamber therefore finds that in the case of civilians, the application of the principle of individual criminal responsibility, enshrined in Article 6(3), to civilians remains contentious. Against this background, the Chamber holds that it is appropriate to assess on a case by case basis the power or authority actually devolved upon the Accused in order to determine whether or not he had the power to take all necessary and reasonable measures to prevent the commission of the alleged crimes or to punish the perpetrators thereof.
. . .

[Genocide]

The Genocide Convention is undeniably considered part of customary international law . . . . Thus, punishment of the crime of genocide did exist in

Rwanda in 1994, at the time of the acts alleged in the Indictment, and the perpetrator was liable to be brought before the competent courts of Rwanda to answer for this crime. . . .

. . .

The Chamber holds that the expression [in the Statute's definition of genocide] deliberately inflicting on the group conditions of life calculated to bring about its physical destruction in whole or in part, should be construed as the methods of destruction by which the perpetrator does not immediately kill the members of the group, but which, ultimately, seek their physical destruction. . . . [The methods include for purposes of Article 2(2)(c) of the Statute] subjecting a group of people to a subsistence diet, systematic expulsion from homes and the reduction of essential medical services below minimum requirement.

. . .

For purposes of interpreting Article 2(2)(d) of the Statute, the Chamber holds that the measures intended to prevent births within the group, should be construed as sexual mutilation, the practice of sterilization, forced birth control, separation of the sexes and prohibition of marriages. In patriarchal societies, where membership of a group is determined by the identity of the father, an example of a measure intended to prevent births within a group is the case where, during rape, a woman of the said group is deliberately impregnated by a man of another group, with the intent to have her give birth to a child who will consequently not belong to its mother's group. Furthermore, the Chamber notes that measures intended to prevent births within the group may be physical, but can also be mental. For instance, rape can be a measure intended to prevent births when the person raped refuses subsequently to procreate, in the same way that members of a group can be led, through threats or trauma, not to procreate.

. . .

[Crimes against Humanity] . . .

The Chamber considers that Article 3 of the Statute confers on the Chamber the jurisdiction to prosecute persons for various inhumane acts which constitute crimes against humanity. . . .

The Chamber considers that it is a prerequisite that the act must be committed as part of a wide spread or systematic attack and not just a random act of violence. The act can be part of a widespread or systematic attack and need not be a part of both. . . .

. . .

The Chamber considers that an act must be directed against the civilian population if it is to constitute a crime against humanity. Members of the civilian population are people who are not taking any active part in the hostilities, including members of the armed forces who laid down their arms and those persons placed hors de combat by sickness, wounds, detention or any other cause. Note that this definition assimilates the definition of 'civilian' to the categories of person protected by Common Article 3 of the Geneva Conventions; an assimilation which would not appear to be problematic. . . .

The Statute stipulates that inhumane acts committed against the civilian population must be committed on 'national, political, ethnic, racial or religious grounds.' Discrimination on the basis of a person's political ideology satisfies the requirement of 'political' grounds as envisaged in Article 3 of the Statute. . . . The perpetrator must have the requisite intent for the commission of crimes against humanity. . . .

Article 3 of the Statute sets out various acts that constitute crimes against humanity . . . The Chamber notes that the accused is indicted for murder, extermination, torture, rape and other acts that constitute inhumane acts. The Chamber in interpreting Article 3 of the Statute, shall focus its discussion on these acts only.
. . .

[Rape]

. . . While rape has been defined in certain national jurisdictions as non-consensual intercourse, variations on the act of rape may include acts which involve the insertion of objects and/or the use of bodily orifices not considered to be intrinsically sexual. The Chamber considers that rape is a form of aggression and that the central elements of the crime of rape cannot be captured in a mechanical description of objects and body parts. . . . Like torture, rape is used for such purposes as intimidation, degradation, humiliation, discrimination, punishment, control or destruction of a person. Like torture, rape is a violation of personal dignity, and rape in fact constitutes torture when inflicted by or at the instigation of or with the consent or acquiescence of a public official or other person acting in an official capacity. The Chamber defines rape as a physical invasion of a sexual nature, committed on a person under circumstances which are coercive. Sexual violence which includes rape, is considered to be any act of a sexual nature which is committed on a person under circumstances which are coercive. This act must be committed (a) as part of a wide spread or systematic attack; (b) on a civilian population; (c) on certain catalogued discriminatory grounds, namely: national, ethnic, political, racial, or religious grounds.

[With respect to Article 4 of the Statute—violations of Common Article 3 of the Geneva Conventions and of the 1997 Additional Protocol No. 2—the Chamber had concluded that there was in Rwanda an armed conflict not of an international character between the government of Rwanda and the RPF. Thus one requirement of Article 4 was met. But to hold the defendant criminally responsible under that article, the Prosecutor had to prove that he acted for the government or for the RPF. The Chamber concluded that it had not been proved beyond a reasonable doubt that acts of the defendant were committed in conjunction with an armed conflict, or that he was a member of the armed forces or expected as a public official to support the war effort. Hence Akayesu was not criminally liable under Article 4.]

[Sexual violence]

. . . In considering the extent to which acts of sexual violence constitute crimes against humanity under Article 3(g) of its Statute, the Tribunal must define rape, as there is no commonly accepted definition of the term in international law. . . .

The Tribunal defines rape as a physical invasion of a sexual nature, committed on a person under circumstances which are coercive. The Tribunal considers sexual violence, which includes rape, as any act of a sexual nature which is committed on a person under circumstances which are coercive. Sexual violence is not limited to physical invasion of the human body and may include acts which do not involve penetration or even physical contact. The incident described by Witness KK in which the Accused ordered the Interahamwe to undress a student and force her to do gymnastics naked in the public courtyard of the bureau communal, in front of a crowd, constitutes sexual violence. The Tribunal notes in this context that coercive circumstances need not be evidenced by a show of physical force. Threats, intimidation, extortion and other forms of duress which prey on fear or desperation may constitute coercion, and coercion may be inherent in certain circumstances, such as armed conflict or the military presence of Interahamwe among refugee Tutsi women at the bureau communal. Sexual violence falls within the scope of 'other inhumane acts', set forth in Article 3(i) of the Tribunal's Statute, 'outrages upon personal dignity', set forth in Article 4(e) of the Statute, and 'serious bodily or mental harm', set forth in Article 2(2)(b) of the Statute. . . .

The Tribunal finds, under Article 6(1) of its Statute, that the Accused, having had reason to know that sexual violence was occurring, aided and abetted the following acts of sexual violence, by allowing them to take place on or near the premises of the bureau communal and by facilitating the commission of such sexual violence through his words of encouragement in other acts of sexual violence which, by virtue of his authority, sent a clear signal of official tolerance for sexual violence, without which these acts would not have taken place:

. . .

[In its verdict, the Chamber unanimously found Akayesu guilty of several counts of genocide, of direct and public incitement to commit genocide, and of several crimes against humanity (extermination, murder, torture, rape, and other humane acts). It found him not guilty of certain other counts, particularly of violations of Article 3 common to the Geneva Conventions and of Article 4(2)(e) of Additional Protocol No. 2. As of March 2000, the decision was on appeal.]

QUESTIONS

1. Consider, as applied to the ICTR and the Akayesu decision, question 5 at p. 1173, *supra*.

2. This case was decided before the Tadic litigation, *supra*, came to an end. Do you find inconsistencies or contradictions in the interpretation of these international crimes between these two cases? If so, are they traceable to differences between the two Statutes

in definition of these crimes? (Recall that as of March 2000, the Akayesu decision was on appeal, and that the Appeals Chamber consists of the same judges for the ICTY and the ICTR.)

3. Does the Akayesu opinion (as presented in these excerpts) broaden the crimes defined in the Statute to any considerable degree? How? In particular, how does the ICTR respond to the sexual cruelty to which Tutsi women were subjected?

4. Suppose that evidence made clear that Akayesu had been threatened by Hutus committing the genocide and told that unless he assisted in the round-up of Tutsi he would be treated as a Tutsi sympathizer and, like other such persons, would be killed. Such evidence also shows that Akayesu then started to participate in the genocide by revealing the whereabouts of about 30 Tutsi, who were caught by Hutu and murdered. What result should the Trial Chamber reach on the charges of genocide and crimes against humanity?

BARBARA CROSSETTE, INQUIRY SAYS U.N. INERTIA IN '94 WORSENED GENOCIDE IN RWANDA
New York Times, December 17, 1999, p. A1

A strongly worded report issued today by an international panel of experts holds both the United Nations and leading member countries, primarily the United States, responsible for failing to prevent end the genocide in Rwanda in 1994, which cost hundreds of thousands of lives.

The report, commissioned by Secretary General Kofi Annan, who was then head of the peacekeeping department, spares no one, naming those in the highest reaches of the United Nations who were running the operation in Rwanda, including Mr. Annan and his predecessor, Secretary General Boutros Boutros-Ghali.

Mr. Annan and others in his department made weak and equivocal decisions in the face of mounting disaster, the panel found. At the same time the Clinton administration . . . persistently played down the problem, setting the tone for a Security Council generally lacking the political will for a tougher response.

Both the United Nations and the United States sent the wrong message to militias bent on genocide, the report concluded. Today Mr. Annan called the report 'thorough and objective.' 'On behalf of the United Nations, I acknowledge this failure and express my deep remorse,' he said, calling the events in Rwanda 'genocide in its purest and most evil form'. . . .

. . . [T]he leader of the investigation, Ingvar Carlsson, a former Swedish prime minister, said it would 'always be difficult to explain' why the Security Council— managed by the world's major powers and not the United Nations bureaucracy— drastically cut the peacekeeping force in Rwanda, reducing it to a few hundred from 2,500 when the genocide began, and then increasing it to 5,500 when the weeks of massacres were over. The United States, . . . effectively blocked the Security Council in 1993 and 1994 from authorizing significant action in Rwanda. . . .

Today Mr. Carlsson repeated the Clinton administration's explanation that the loss of 18 American Rangers in Somalia in 1993 had scared the United States off peacekeeping, particularly in Africa, for domestic political reasons. . . . On a trip to Rwanda last year, President Clinton apologized for Washington's inaction.

. . .

The Rwanda report follows by several weeks the release of an internal United Nations inquiry into problems in the Bosnia peacekeeping operation that led to thousands of deaths in Serbian attacks on Bosnian Muslims in Srebrenica and other towns. That report also found fault with both the organization and Security Council members.

The report issued today shows a pattern of ignored warnings and missed signs of the genocide to come in Rwanda. . . . 'Information received by a United Nations mission that plans are being made to exterminate any group of people requires an immediate and determined response', the panel said.

. . .

In the bloody melee that followed [the very first steps in the genocide], groups of United Nations peacekeepers were rounded up by Rwandan Hutu troops and 10 Belgians were executed. The remaining Belgians, the best-qualified soldiers among the peacekeepers, were then abruptly withdrawn.

In the report, Belgium was criticized for this and for abandoning 2,000 civilians hiding in a technical school after telling them they would be protected. They were savagely attacked. The Belgian withdrawal prompted others to pull out, an action supported by the United States, the panel said.

. . .

JOSÉ ALVAREZ, CRIMES OF STATES/CRIMES OF HATE: LESSONS FROM RWANDA
24 Yale J. Int'l L. 365 (1999), at 400

. . . [T]he West's complicity in the 1994 killings in Rwanda is a discomforting fact. The scale and seriousness of that complicity take various forms. At one level, certain European powers, namely the colonizers of Rwanda who imported their racist notions of 'superior races' to Rwanda, need to accept their responsibility for creating the 'tribalism without tribes' that helped make genocide possible and continues to characterize Rwanda today. Much greater blame can be attributed to those, like the French, who, in the 1990s and through the 1994 killings themselves, continued to befriend and arm the Habyarimana [Hutu] government. But the circle of blame extends much wider and includes Kofi Annan, who ignored warnings of the impeding genocide; all members of the U.N., and particularly the Security Council, who, in the wake of the fiasco of Somalia, failed to send the 5000 troops that, it is estimated, might have prevented the vast majority of the killings; and the international community as a whole, which, in the wake of the emergence of a new government in Rwanda after the genocide, ignored that new government's pleas for assistance but came to the aid of the Hutu killers in exile while failing to prevent their ongoing incursions into Rwanda to continue the genocide.

For all their attention to the attribution of individual blame for these crimes, international lawyers have not been attentive to these wider circles of guilt. In surreal fashion, international lawyers have argued that judges from some of the very countries that are regarded as partly 'to blame' for these crimes will be readily accepted as neutral arbitrators simply because they do not come from Rwanda. Blind to the colonial-era racism that helped to make the Rwandan genocide possible, and equally blind to the continuing insensitivities of the U.N. and its patrons since the genocide, international lawyers pin their hopes for verdicts that will be accepted as impartial on a U.N.-approved bench, simply because it does not contain a Hutu or a Tutsi. This seems a slim reed on which to rely. To the extent that the U.N., as an organization, was itself derelict in enforcing international humanitarian law, that fact is surely detrimental to the credibility of the ICTR's judgments.

. . . Knowledge of what led to the Rwandan killings as well as who is to blame in this wider sense strengthens the very premise that individuals must be held responsible In addition, sensitivity to colonial-era racism and what has occurred in its wake prompts scrutiny of the policies now being touted by the U.N.'s Security Council with respect to Rwanda. . . . Those who were blind once to the important consequences of acting on the basis of ethnic prejudices could be wrong a second time when they insist that international trials should proceed as if the prejudices they helped to instill can be ignored.

. . . Knowledge of the West's complicity should make us skeptical of a scheme that would deny to the Rwandan government what each Western state has for centuries enjoyed, namely the right to try its own war criminals.

QUESTIONS

1. Accepting the report of the panel appointed by Kofi Annan and Alvarez's analysis, what follows from them? Do they lessen, or strengthen, the argument for individual punishment of those committing the genocide on the ground? Should they lead to criminal liability under international law of non-Rwandans who are implicated in some other way in the genocide? Against whom, and under what charges?

2. Does this analysis delegitimate the ICTR and its judgments if a panel of the Trial Chamber or the Appeal Chamber consists dominantly of non-African judges, particularly judges from the states that are alleged to bear responsibility? Does it point to resort to the Rwandan judiciary rather than to an international tribunal—a small judiciary in a country where tens of thousands of prisoners have been long awaiting trial for the genocide? Would analogous problems to those described by Alvarez arise in constituting a judicial bench in state criminal proceedings in countries that have suffered massive tragedies in civil conflict or severe repression? Does the fact that a conflict or political represssion has a strong ethnic dimension in addition to its deep political divisions complicate such issues?

ADDITIONAL READING

In addition to the readings noted at p. 1142, *supra,* see: Theodor Meron, *War Crimes Law Comes of Age* (1998); Stephen Ratner and J. Abrams, *Accountability for*

Human Rights Atrocities in International Law (1997); Michael Scharf, *Balkan Justice: The Story Behind the First International War Crimes Tribunal since Nuremberg* (1997); Virginia Morris and M. Scharf, *The International Criminal Tribunal for Rwanda* (1998); Antonio Cassese, 'On the Current Trends towards Criminal Prosecution and Punishment of Breaches of International Humanitarian Law', 9 EJIL 2 (1998); Jose Alvarez, 'Rush to Closure: Lessons of the Tadic Judgment', 96 Mich. L. Rev. 2031 (1998); Steven Ratner, 'New Democracies: Old Atrocities; An Inquiry in International Law', 87 Georgetown L.J. 707 (1999); Cherif Bassiouni, 'Strengthening the Norms of International Humanitarian Law to Combat Impunity', in Burns Weston and S. Marks (eds.), *The Future of International Human Rights* (1999), at 245; Symposium, 'Genocide, War Crimes, and Crimes against Humanity', 23 Fordham Int'l L. J. 275–488 (1999).

C. THE INTERNATIONAL CRIMINAL COURT

The idea of a permanent international criminal court has been a part of the human rights movement since 1948, when the General Assembly instructed the International Law Commission to study the possibility of establishing one. In 1992, the General Assembly requested the ILC to draft a statute for such a court. Four years later, it decided that a diplomatic conference should be held on establishing the court. That conference among states took place in Rome in 1998. It culminated in the overwhelming adoption of a Statute for the International Criminal Court (ICC) by a vote of 120 to 7, with 21 abstentions. The Statute will enter into force after 60 states have ratified it.

The following excerpts from the Statute state the crimes that are within the jurisdiction of the Court.

ROME STATUTE OF THE INTERNATIONAL CRIMINAL COURT
37 I.L.M. 999 (1998)

Article 5—Crimes within the jurisdiction of the Court

1. . . . The Court has jurisdiction in accordance with this Statute with respect to the following crimes: (a) The crime of genocide; (b) Crimes against humanity; (c) War crimes; (d) The crime of aggression.

2. The Court shall exercise jurisdiction over the crime of aggression once a provision is adopted in accordance with articles 121 and 123 defining the crime and setting out the conditions under which the Court shall exercise jurisdiction with respect to this crime. Such a provision shall be consistent with the relevant provisions of the Charter of the United Nations.

Article 6—Genocide

[This section repeats Article 2 of the Genocide Convention, as did the Statutes for the ICTY and ICTR.]

Article 7—Crimes against humanity

1. For the purpose of this Statute, 'crime against humanity' means any of the following acts when committed as part of a widespread or systematic attack directed against any civilian population, with knowledge of the attack:

    (a) Murder;

    (b) Extermination;

    (c) Enslavement;

    (d) Deportation or forcible transfer of population;

    (e) Imprisonment or other severe deprivation of physical liberty in violation of fundamental rules of international law;

    (f) Torture;

    (g) Rape, sexual slavery, enforced prostitution, forced pregnancy, enforced sterilization, or any other form of sexual violence of comparable gravity;

    (h) Persecution against any identifiable group or collectivity on political, racial, national, ethnic, cultural, religious, gender as defined in paragraph 3, or other grounds that are universally recognized as impermissible under international law, in connection with any act referred to in this paragraph or any crime within the jurisdiction of the Court;

    (i) Enforced disappearance of persons;

    (j) The crime of apartheid;

    (k) Other inhumane acts of a similar character intentionally causing great suffering, or serious injury to body or to mental or physical health.

. . .

3. For the purpose of this statute, it is understood that the term 'gender' refers to the two sexes, male and female, within the context of society. The term 'gender' does not indicate any meaning different from the above.

Article 8—War crimes

1. The Court shall have jurisdiction in respect of war crimes in particular when committed as part of a plan or policy or as part of a large-scale commission of such crimes.

2. For the purpose of this Statute, 'war crimes' means:

    (a) Grave breaches of the Geneva Conventions of 12 August 1949 namely, any of the following acts against persons or property protected under the provisions of the relevant Geneva Convention:

        (i) Wilful killing;

        (ii) Torture or inhuman treatment, including biological experiments;

        (iii) Wilfully causing great suffering, or serious injury to body or health;

        (iv) Extensive destruction and appropriation of property, not justified by military necessity and carried out unlawfully and wantonly;

        (v) Compelling a prisoner of war or other protected person to serve in the forces of a hostile Power;

        (vi) Wilfully depriving a prisoner of war or other protected person
              of the rights of fair and regular trial;
       (vii) Unlawful deportation or transfer or unlawful confinement;
     (viii) Taking of hostages.
    (b) Other serious violations of the laws and customs applicable in inter-
        national armed conflict, within the established framework of inter-
        national law, namely, any of the following acts: [the designated acts
        include intentionally directing attacks against a civilian population as
        such, against civilian objects that are not military objectives, or against
        a humanitarian assistance or peacekeeping mission in accordance with
        the UN Charter; killing or wounding combatants who have sur-
        rendered; transfer by an Occupying Power of part of its own civilian
        population into territory it occupies, or deporting the population of
        the occupied territory outside the territory; employing poisonous gases
        or weapons that cause superfluous injury or unnecessary suffering;
        committing rape, sexual slavery, or forced pregnancy.]

[Section (c), concerning armed conflict not of an international character, is
omitted.]

. . .

Article 9—Elements of Crimes

    1. Elements of Crimes shall assist the Court in the interpretation and applica-
tion of articles 6, 7 and 8. They shall be adopted by a two-thirds majority of the
members of the Assembly of States Parties.

    2. Amendments to the Elements of Crimes may be proposed by:

    (a) Any State Party;
    (b) The judges acting by an absolute majority;
    (c) The Prosecutor.

    Such amendments shall be adopted by a two-thirds majority of the members of
the Assembly of States Parties.

    3. The Elements of Crimes and amendments thereto shall be consistent with
this Statute.

Article 21—Applicable law

    1. The Court shall apply:

    (a) In the first place, this Statute, Elements of Crimes and its Rules of
        Procedure and Evidence;
    (b) In the second place, where appropriate, applicable treaties and the prin-
        ciples and rules of international law, including the established principles
        of the international law of armed conflict;
    (c) Failing that, general principles of law derived by the Court from national
        laws of legal systems of the world including, as appropriate, the national

laws of States that would normally exercise jurisdiction over the crime, provided that those principles are not inconsistent with this Statute and with international law and internationally recognized norms and standards.

2. The Court may apply principles and rules of law as interpreted in its previous decisions.

3. The application and interpretation of law pursuant to this article must be consistent with internationally recognized human rights, and be without any adverse distinction founded on grounds such as gender as defined in article 7, paragraph 3, age, race, colour, language, religion or belief, political or other opinion, national, ethnic or social origin, wealth, birth or other status.

KENNETH ROTH, THE COURT THE US DOESN'T WANT
N.Y. Rev. Books, November 19, 1998, at 45

. . . In favor of the [International Criminal] court were most of America's closest allies, including Britain, Canada, and Germany. But the United States was isolated in opposition, along with such dictatorships and enemies of human rights as Iran, Iraq, China, Libya, Algeria, and Sudan. . . .

. . .

The Clinton administration's opposition to the ICC stemmed in part from its fear, a plausible one, that hostile states like Cuba, Libya, or Iraq might try to convince the court to launch a frivolous or politically motivated prosecution of US soldiers or commanding officers. The Rome delegates adopted several safeguards against this possibility, most importantly the so-called principle of complementarity. This gives the ICC jurisdiction over a case only if national authorities are 'unwilling or unable' to carry out a genuine investigation and, if appropriate, prosecution. The complementarity principle also reflects the widely shared view that systems of national justice should remain the front-line defense against serious human rights abuse, with the ICC serving only as a backstop. (By contrast, the Yugoslav and Rwandan tribunals are empowered to supersede local prosecutorial authorities at their discretion and have done so repeatedly.)

According to the principle of complementarity, if an American soldier were to commit a serious war crime—say, by deliberately massacring civilians—he could be brought before the ICC only if the US government failed to pursue his case. Indeed, even a national decision not to prosecute must be respected so long as it is not a bad faith effort to shield a criminal from justice. Because of the strength of the US judicial system, an ICC prosecutor would have a hard time dismissing a US investigation or prosecution as a sham. And, under the treaty, any effort to override a nation's decision not to prosecute would be subject to challenge before one panel of international judges and appeal before another.

Much would still depend on the character and professionalism of the ICC prosecutor and judges. The record of the International Criminal Tribunals for

Rwanda and the former Yugoslavia suggests that faith in them would be well placed. . . .

There is every reason to believe that the ICC will be run by jurists of comparable stature. . . .

But the Pentagon and its congressional allies were not satisfied with the principle of complementarity as protection against unjustified prosecutions. . . .

Efforts by the US to exempt its nationals from the ICC's jurisdiction contributed to four points in contention during the Rome conference. . . . The resulting concessions [by other states] weakened the court significantly; still the Clinton administration ended up denouncing it.

The first controversy concerned whether and, if so, how the UN Security Council should be permitted to halt an ICC prosecution. The US proposed that before the ICC could even begin an investigation the Security Council would have to expressly authorize it. Because the United States, as a permanent Council member, could single-handedly block Council approval by exercising its veto, this proposal would have allowed Washington to prevent any investigation, including of its own soldiers and those of its allies. The other four permanent Council members— Britain, France, China, and Russia—would necessarily have had the same veto power. As a result, only criminals from a handful of pariah states would have been likely to face prosecution. . . .

Singapore offered a compromise to the veto problem which ultimately prevailed. It granted the Security Council the power to halt an ICC prosecution for a one-year period, which could be renewed. But the Security Council would act in its usual manner—by the vote of nine of its fifteen members and the acquiescence of all five permanent members. Therefore no single permanent Council member could use its veto to prevent a prosecution from being initiated.

. . .

The third major controversy involved what restrictions should be placed on the ICC's definition of war crimes. . . .

. . .

. . . Of special concern was the so-called rule of proportionality under international law, which prohibits a military attack causing an incidental loss of civilian life that is 'excessive' compared to the military advantage gained. This less precise rule could implicate activity that US military commanders consider lawful but the ICC might not. For example, the Gulf War bombing of Iraq's electrical grid was claimed to have killed a disproportionate number of civilians, including the thousands said to have died because of the resulting loss of refrigeration, water purification, and other necessities of modern life. What if the ICC had been in existence and had found such claims well founded?. . .

To avoid prosecution in such borderline situations, US negotiators successfully redefined the proportionality rule to prohibit attacks that injure civilians only when such injury is 'clearly excessive' in relation to the military advantage. . . .

The United States, joined by France, also proposed that governments be allowed to join the ICC while specifying that their citizens would be exempted from war crimes prosecutions. . . . [A]s a compromise, the treaty allows governments to exempt their citizens from the court's war crimes jurisdiction for a period of seven years. That would allow a hesitant government to reassure itself about the court's treatment of war crimes without permanently denying the court jurisdiction over its citizens. . . .

The most divisive issue delegates faced was deciding how—once the ICC treaty was ratified by sixty countries—the court would get jurisdiction over a case that was referred by an individual government or initiated by the prosecutor. (This issue does not arise when the Security Council refers a matter for prosecution, since the Council has the power to impose jurisdiction.)

. . .

South Korea put forward a more limited proposal which gained broad support. It would have granted the ICC jurisdiction when any one of four governments concerned with a crime had ratified the ICC treaty or accepted the court's jurisdiction over the crime. These were: (1) the government of the suspect's nationality; (2) the government of the victims' nationality; (3) the government on whose territory the crime took place; or (4) the government that gained custody of the suspect. In any given case, some and perhaps all of these governments would be the same, but each separate category increases the possibility that the court could pursue a particular suspect.

Speaking for the Clinton administration, Ambassador Scheffer vehemently insisted that the court should be empowered to act only if the government of the suspect's nationality had accepted its jurisdiction. . . .

Clinton administration officials were not mollified by the fact that, under the doctrine of universal jurisdiction, American soldiers are already vulnerable to prosecution in foreign courts. The US government has many ways of dissuading governments from attempting to try an American—from diplomatic and economic pressure to the use of military force. But the administration fears such dissuasion would be less effective against the ICC. After all, the Pentagon could hardly threaten to bomb The Hague.

. . . Facing these extraordinary threats [from the United States], the Rome delegates gave in, but only partially. They got rid of two of Korea's proposed conditions for ICC jurisdiction: that the treaty would have to be ratified by the state of the victim's nationality or it would have to be ratified by the state that gained custody of the suspect.

This concession was damaging. Because a state could not give the ICC jurisdiction just by arresting a suspect, a leader who commits atrocities against his own country's citizens, such as a future Pol Pot or Idi Amin, could travel widely without being brought before the ICC—so long as his own government had not ratified the treaty (and assuming the Security Council does not act). . . . And if the victims' nationality cannot be used as grounds for ICC jurisdiction, then the ICC could not take action against the leader of a nonratifying government that slaughters refugees from a ratifying state who seek shelter on its territory (again, assuming the Security Council fails to act). . . .

But the Rome delegates did not accept the Clinton administration's demands entirely. They retained two grounds for the ICC's jurisdiction: not only that the government of the suspect's nationality had ratified the treaty (the only ground acceptable to the US) but also that the government on whose territory the crime took place had ratified it. In the case of a tyrant who commits crimes at home, these two governments would be the same. But the territorial 'hook' could catch, for example, Saddam Hussein for committing war crimes during a new invasion of Kuwait. . . .The United States, however, feared that the territorial hook might catch American troops, or their commanders, for alleged crimes committed while they were abroad. If the country where US troops are present has ratified the treaty, the ICC could pursue a case against them even though the United States had not joined the court.

. . .

Can the ICC survive without US participation? The Clinton administration is betting that it cannot. Already Jesse Helms, having declared the ICC treaty 'dead on arrival' in the Senate, has vowed to sponsor legislation forbidding the US government to fund the court or do anything to give it legitimacy. The State Department said publicly it might put pressure on governments not to join the court; and it is considering renegotiating the bilateral treaties that govern the stationing of US forces overseas in order to protect them from the ICC.

The Clinton administration . . . also contends that, small as the risk is of an American being brought before the court, the ICC will undermine humanitarian goals by making the United States reluctant to deploy troops in times of need.

ADDITIONAL READING

David Scheffer, 'The United States and the International Criminal Court', 93 AJIL 12 (1999); Mahnoush Arsanjani, 'The Rome Statute of the International Criminal Court', 93 AJIL 22 (1999); Darryl Robinson, 'Defining "Crimes against Humanity" at the Rome Conference', 93 AJIL 43 (1999).

D. THE PINOCHET LITIGATION

Until the International Criminal Court becomes operational, no international tribunal exists to try individuals for alleged international crimes that do not fall within the jurisdiction of the ICTY and ICTR. There is always, of course, the possibility of criminal trial in the country where the acts took place, particularly if the perpetrators are citizens and residents of that country. Such trials have taken place in numbers of European countries, particularly Germany with respect to Nazi war criminals. In very few instances, they have also taken place with respect to post-Second World War events, such as the trials in Argentina in the 1970s of members of the military junta who were in charge during that country's 'dirty war'.

But these have been rare phenomena. Often the terms of transfer from a government in charge during a period of massive violations to a successor elected civilian government have precluded trial of those responsible for the violations. Such was the case in Chile. Other ways of dealing with the prior period have been utilized in a growing number of countries, such as the truth commissions in Chile,

Guatemala, South Africa and elsewhere that are examined in Section E of this chapter.

What then of trying such alleged criminals in the courts of other states in which they may be present at the time of arrest? The *Eichmann* trial, p. 1138, *supra*, offers an early precedent—although in that case the defendant was abducted from Argentina and brought to Israel. What are the advantages in such an approach, what are the risks or dangers? What legal and political barriers are there to such trials of, say, X, a former leader or high official of Y during the period in which gross human rights violations occurred there, who is temporarily in Z when arrested and charged with the commission of international crimes? Does the Alien Tort Statute in the United States (see pp. 1049–1068, *supra*), which permits a civil action for damages by one alien against another alien based on a tort constituting a violation of the law of nations that took place in a foreign state, provide a helpful analogy?

The path-breaking Pincohet case in the United Kingdom explores this topic.

REGINA v. BARTLE
House of Lords, 24 March 1999
[1999] 2 All ER 97, [1999] 2 WLR 827

[General Pinochet resigned as head of state of Chile in 1990 and became a Senator for life. In 1998, he travelled to the United Kingdom for medical treatment. Judicial authorities in Spain sought to extradite him to stand criminal trial in Spain on several charges, including torture, during his period as head of state that were related to the military, right-wing overthrow of President Allende and the subsequent extreme political repression that included several thousand murders, systematic use of torture, and disappearances. An international warrant for his arrest was issued in Spain, and a magistrate in London issued a provisional warrant under the UK Extradition Act of 1989. He was arrested and detained in England. None of the conduct alleged by the Spanish authorities was committed against UK citizens or in the UK.

Seeking to return to Chile, Pinochet started proceedings for habeas corpus and for judicial review of the warrant. The Divisional Court quashed the warrant on the ground that Pinochet, as a former head of state, was entitled to state immunity in respect of the acts with which he was charged. The Crown Prosecution Service, acting on behalf of the Government of Spain, appealed to the House of Lords. The Divisional Court certified as the relevant point of law 'the proper interpretation and scope of the immunity enjoyed by a former head of state from arrest and extradition proceedings in the United Kingdom in respect of acts committed while he was head of state'.

The appeal, heard by a five-member Appellate Committee of the House of Lords, was allowed by a vote of three to two on the ground that Pinochet was not entitled to immunity in relation to crimes under international law. However, this judgment of the House of Lords was set aside because of a conflict of interest of a member of the Appellate Committee, such that the Committee was held not to have been properly constituted. A differently constituted seven-member Appellate Committee reheard the appeal in 1999. In the meantime, the British Home Secretary had authorized the magistrate to proceed with the extradition request under a 1989 Act on all charges except genocide. In this rehearing, Chile was granted leave to intervene as a party. Amnesty International also argued as an intervener, and Human Rights Watch made a written submission.

Throughout this process, the Spanish government several times revised and clarified the charges underlying the extradition request. The Crown Prosecution Service prepared for the rehearing a schedule of 32 UK criminal charges which corresponded to the allegations against Senator Pinochet under Spanish law (excluding the allegation of genocide). In the rehearing, the opinion of Lord Hope of Craighead summarized the charges to include principally conspiracy to torture between 1972 and 1990; conspiracy to take hostages between 1973 and 1990; conspiracy to torture in furtherance of which murder was committed between 1972 and 1990 in countries including Italy, France, Spain and Portugal; and conspiracy to murder in Spain and Italy in 1975–76.

The excerpts below from four of the seven individual opinions of the members of the Appellate Committee examine the principal charge of torture. Six of the seven Lords of Appeal allowed the appeal, but (in the majority of their opinions) only with respect to a small number of the charges. The effect of the judgment of the House of Lords was that extradition proceedings could continue with respect to such charges. In proposing a range of outcomes, the seven opinions not only differed on the particular issues to be resolved, but presented a range of perspectives on the broader development of international law and human rights since Nuremberg.]

LORD BROWNE-WILKINSON

. . .

Outline of the law

In general, a state only exercises criminal jurisdiction over offences which occur within its geographical boundaries. If a person who is alleged to have committed a crime in Spain is found in the United Kingdom, Spain can apply to the United Kingdom to extradite him to Spain. The power to extradite from the United Kingdom for an 'extradition crime' is now contained in the Extradition Act 1989. That Act [requires] that the conduct complained of must constitute a crime under the law both of Spain and of the United Kingdom. This is known as the double criminality rule.

Since the Nazi atrocities and the Nuremberg trials, international law has recognised a number of offences as being international crimes. Individual states have taken jurisdiction to try some international crimes even in cases where such crimes were not committed within the geographical boundaries of such states. The most important of such international crimes for present purposes is torture which is regulated by the International Convention Against Torture and other Cruel, Inhuman or Degrading Treatment or Punishment, 1984. The obligations placed

on the United Kingdom by that Convention . . . were incorporated into the law of
the United Kingdom by section 134 of the Criminal Justice Act 1988. That Act
came into force on 29 September 1988. Section 134 created a new crime under
United Kingdom law, the crime of torture. As required by the Torture Convention
'all' torture wherever committed world-wide was made criminal under United
Kingdom law and triable in the United Kingdom. No one has suggested that before
section 134 came into effect torture committed outside the United Kingdom was a
crime under United Kingdom law. Nor is it suggested that section 134 was
retrospective so as to make torture committed outside the United Kingdom
before 29 September 1988 a United Kingdom crime. Since torture outside the
United Kingdom was not a crime under UK law until 29 September 1988, the
principle of double criminality which requires an Act to be a crime under both
the law of Spain and of the United Kingdom cannot be satisfied in relation to
conduct before that date if the principle of double criminality requires the conduct to be criminal under United Kingdom law *at the date it was committed.* If,
on the other hand, the double criminality rule only requires the conduct to be
criminal under UK law *at the date of extradition* the rule was satisfied in relation
to all torture alleged against Senator Pinochet whether it took place before or after
1988. The Spanish courts have held that they have jurisdiction over all the crimes
alleged.

. . .

. . . [I]n my view only a limited number of the charges relied upon to extradite
Senator Pinochet constitute extradition crimes since most of the conduct relied
upon occurred long before 1988. In particular, I do not consider that torture
committed outside the United Kingdom before 29 September 1988 was a crime
under UK law. It follows that the main question discussed at the earlier stages of
this case—is a former head of state entitled to sovereign immunity from arrest or
prosecution in the UK for acts of torture—applies to far fewer charges. But the
question of state immunity remains a point of crucial importance since . . . [certain
conduct of Senator Pinochet, 'albeit a small amount'] does constitute an
extradition crime. . . .

. . .

. . . The background to the case is that to those of left-wing political convictions
Senator Pinochet is seen as an arch-devil: to those of right-wing persuasions he is
seen as the saviour of Chile. It may well be thought that the trial of Senator
Pinochet in Spain for offences all of which related to the state of Chile and most of
which occurred in Chile is not calculated to achieve the best justice. But I cannot
emphasise too strongly that that is no concern of your Lordships. Although others
perceive our task as being to choose between the two sides on the grounds of
personal preference or political inclination, that is an entire misconception. Our
job is to decide two questions of law: are there any extradition crimes and, if so, is
Senator Pinochet immune from trial for committing those crimes. If, as a matter
of law, there are no extradition crimes or he is entitled to immunity in relation to
whichever crimes there are, then there is no legal right to extradite Senator Pinochet to Spain or, indeed, to stand in the way of his return to Chile. If, on the other
hand, there are extradition crimes in relation to which Senator Pinochet is not

entitled to state immunity then it will be open to the Home Secretary to extradite him. The task of this House is only to decide those points of law.

. . .

[The opinion quoted Section 2 of the 1989 Act, defining an 'extradition crime' for which an accused person could be arrested and sent to the state requesting extradition. Section 2(1)(a) referred to conduct in a foreign state 'which, if it occurred in the United Kingdom, would constitute an offence punishable with imprisonment' for at least 12 months, and which is so punishable under the foreign law.]

My Lords, if the words of section 2 are construed in isolation there is room for two possible views. . . . [I]f read in isolation, the words 'if it occurred . . . would constitute' read more easily as a reference to a hypothetical event happening now, i.e. at the request date, than to a past hypothetical event, i.e. at the conduct date. But in my judgment the right construction is not clear. The word 'it' in the phrase 'if it occurred . . . ' is a reference back to the actual conduct of the individual abroad which, by definition, is a past event. The question then would be 'would that past event (including the date of its occurrence) constitute an offence under the law of the United Kingdom.' The answer to that question would depend upon the United Kingdom law at that date.

But of course it is not correct to construe these words in isolation and your Lordships had the advantage of submissions which strongly indicate that the relevant date is the conduct date. The starting point is that the Act of 1989 regulates at least three types of extradition.

[The opinion construed particular provisions in the 1989 Act and the predecessor Extradition Act 1870, and concluded that the double criminality rule referred to the time of conduct rather than request. Hence the charges of torture and conspiracy to torture covering conduct that occurred before Section 134 became effective on September 29, 1988 did not provide a basis for extradition. Only those charges related to conspiracy to torture and to torture that covered the later period (post September 29, 1988) could lead to extradition. Moreover, the charge relating to hostage-taking did not disclose any offence under UK law. The opinion then turned to consideration of the 'modern law of torture.']

Apart from the law of piracy, the concept of personal liability under international law for international crimes is of comparatively modern growth. The traditional subjects of international law are states not human beings. But consequent upon the war crime trials after the 1939–45 World War, the international community came to recognise that there could be criminal liability under international law for a class of crimes such as war crimes and crimes against humanity. Although there may be legitimate doubts as to the legality of the Charter of the Nuremberg Tribunal, in my judgment those doubts were stilled by the Affirmation of the Principles of International Law recognised by the Charter of Nuremberg Tribunal adopted by the United Nations General Assembly on 11 December 1946. . . . At least from that date onwards the concept of personal liability for a crime in international law must have been part of international law. In the early years state torture was one of the elements of a war crime. In consequence torture, and various other crimes against humanity, were linked to war or at least to hostilities of some kind. But in the course of time this linkage with war fell away and torture, divorced from war or hostilities, became an international crime on its own. . . . Ever since 1945, torture on a large scale has featured as one of the crimes against humanity. . . . Moreover, the Republic of Chile accepted before your Lordships that the international law prohibiting torture has the character of jus cogens or a peremptory norm. . . .

The jus cogens nature of the international crime of torture justifies states in taking universal jurisdiction over torture wherever committed. International law provides that offences jus cogens may be punished by any state because the offenders are 'common enemies of all mankind and all nations have an equal interest in their apprehension and prosecution'. . . .

. . . In the light of the authorities to which I have referred (and there are many others) I have no doubt that long before the Torture Convention of 1984 state torture was an international crime in the highest sense.

But there was no tribunal or court to punish international crimes of torture. Local courts could take jurisdiction: see *Attorney-General of Israel v. Eichmann* (1962) 36 I.L.R.S. But the objective was to ensure a general jurisdiction so that the torturer was not safe wherever he went. For example, in this case it is alleged that during the Pinochet regime torture was an official, although unacknowledged, weapon of government and that, when the regime was about to end, it passed legislation designed to afford an amnesty to those who had engaged in insti-tutionalised torture. If these allegations are true, the fact that the local court had jurisdiction to deal with the international crime of torture was nothing to the point so long as the totalitarian regime remained in power. . . . Hence the demand for some international machinery to repress state torture which is not dependent upon the local courts where the torture was committed. In the event, over 110 states (including Chile, Spain and the United Kingdom) became state parties to the Torture Convention. . . . The Torture Convention was agreed not in order to create an international crime which had not previously existed but to provide an inter-national system under which the international criminal—the torturer—could find no safe haven. . . .

Article 1 of the Convention defines torture as the intentional infliction of severe pain and of suffering with a view to achieving a wide range of purposes 'when such pain or suffering is inflicted by or at the instigation of or with the consent or acquiesence of a public official or other person acting in an official capacity.' Article 2(1) requires each state party to prohibit torture on territory within its own jurisdiction and Article 4 requires each state party to ensure that 'all' acts of torture are offences under its criminal law. Article 2(3) outlaws any defence of superior orders. Under Article 5(1) each state party has to establish its jurisdiction over torture (a) when committed within territory under its jurisdiction (b) when the alleged offender is a national of that state, and (c) in certain circumstances, when the victim is a national of that state. Under Article 5(2) a state party has to take jurisdiction over any alleged offender who is found within its territory. Article 6 contains provisions for a state in whose territory an alleged torturer is found to detain him, inquire into the position and notify the states referred to in Article 5(1) and to indicate whether it intends to exercise jurisdiction. Under Article 7 the state in whose territory the alleged torturer is found shall, if he is not extradited to any of the states mentioned in Article 5(1), submit him to its authorities for the purpose of prosecution. Under Article 8(1) torture is to be treated as an extraditable offence and under Article 8(4) torture shall, for the purposes of extradition, be treated as having been committed not only in the place where it occurred but also in the state mentioned in Article 5(1).

. . .

. . . The crucial question is not whether Senator Pinochet falls within the definition in Article 1: he plainly does. The question is whether, even so, he is procedurally immune from process. . . .

. . .

. . . The purpose of the Convention was to introduce the principle aut dedere aut punire—either you extradite or you punish . . . . . :

I gather the following important points from the Torture Convention:

. . .

(4) There is no express provision dealing with state immunity of heads of state, ambassadors or other officials.

(5) Since Chile, Spain and the United Kingdom are all parties to the Convention, they are bound under treaty by its provisions whether or not such provisions would apply in the absence of treaty obligation. Chile ratified the Convention with effect from 30 October 1988 and the United Kingdom with effect from 8 December 1988.

State immunity

. . .

It is a basic principle of international law that one sovereign state (the forum state) does not adjudicate on the conduct of a foreign state. The foreign state is entitled to procedural immunity from the processes of the forum state. This immunity extends to both criminal and civil liability. State immunity probably grew from the historical immunity of the person of the monarch. In any event, such personal immunity of the head of state persists to the present day: the head of state is entitled to the same immunity as the state itself. The diplomatic representative of the foreign state in the forum state is also afforded the same immunity in recognition of the dignity of the state which he represents. This immunity enjoyed by a head of state in power and an ambassador in post is a complete immunity . . . granted ratione personae.

What then when the ambassador leaves his post or the head of state is deposed? The position of the ambassador is covered by the Vienna Convention on Diplomatic Relations, 1961. . . .

The continuing partial immunity of the ambassador after leaving post is of a different kind from that enjoyed ratione personae while he was in post. Since he is no longer the representative of the foreign state he merits no particular privileges or immunities as a person. However in order to preserve the integrity of the activities of the foreign state during the period when he was ambassador, it is necessary to provide that immunity is afforded to his *official* acts during his tenure in post. If this were not done the sovereign immunity of the state could be evaded by calling in question acts done during the previous ambassador's time. . . . This limited immunity, ratione materiae, is to be contrasted with the former immunity ratione personae which gave complete immunity to all activities whether public or private.

In my judgment at common law a former head of state enjoys similar immunities, ratione materiae, once he ceases to be head of state. He too loses immunity ratione personae on ceasing to be head of state. . . . As ex head of state he cannot be sued in respect of acts performed whilst head of state in his public capacity. . . .

. . .

. . . Senator Pinochet as former head of state enjoys immunity ratione materiae in relation to acts done by him as head of state as part of his official functions as head of state.

The question then which has to be answered is whether the alleged organisation of state torture by Senator Pinochet (if proved) would constitute an act committed by Senator Pinochet as part of his official functions as head of state. It is not enough to say that it cannot be part of the functions of the head of state to commit a crime. Actions which are criminal under the local law can still have been done officially and therefore give rise to immunity ratione materiae. The case needs to be analysed more closely.

Can it be said that the commission of a crime which is an international crime against humanity and jus cogens is an act done in an official capacity on behalf of the state? I believe there to be strong ground for saying that the implementation of torture as defined by the Torture Convention cannot be a state function. This is the view taken by Sir Arthur Watts ['The Legal Position in International Law of Heads of States, Heads of Government and Foreign Ministers'] who said (at p. 82):

> While generally international law . . . does not directly involve obligations on individuals personally, that is not always appropriate, particularly for acts of such seriousness that they constitute not merely international wrongs (in the broad sense of a civil wrong) but rather international crimes which offend against the public order of the international community. States are artificial legal persons: they can only act through the institutions and agencies of the state, which means, ultimately through its officials and other individuals acting on behalf of the state. For international conduct which is so serious as to be tainted with criminality to be regarded as attributable only to the impersonal state and not to the individuals who ordered or perpetrated it is both unrealistic and offensive to common notions of justice.
>
> . . .
>
> It can no longer be doubted that as a matter of general customary international law a head of state will personally be liable to be called to account if there is sufficient evidence that he authorised or perpetrated such serious international crimes.

It can be objected that Sir Arthur was looking at those cases where the international community has established an international tribunal in relation to which the regulating document *expressly* makes the head of state subject to the tribunal's jurisdiction: see, for example, the Nuremberg Charter Article 7; the Statute of the International Tribunal for former Yugoslavia; the Statute of the International Tribunal for Rwanda and the Statute of the International Criminal Court. It is true that in these cases it is expressly said that the head of state or former head of state is subject to the court's jurisdiction. But those are cases in which a new court with no existing jurisdiction is being established. The jurisdiction being established by the Torture Convention and the Hostages Convention is one where existing domestic courts of all the countries are being authorised and required to take jurisdiction internationally. The question is whether, in this new type of jurisdiction, the only possible view is that those made subject to the jurisdiction of each of the state courts of the world in relation to torture are not entitled to claim immunity.

I have doubts whether, before the coming into force of the Torture Convention, the existence of the international crime of torture as jus cogens was enough to justify the conclusion that the organisation of state torture could not rank for immunity purposes as performance of an official function. At that stage there was no international tribunal to punish torture and no general jurisdiction to permit or require its punishment in domestic courts. Not until there was some form of universal jurisdiction for the punishment of the crime of torture could it really be talked about as a fully constituted international crime. But in my judgment the Torture Convention did provide what was missing: a worldwide universal jurisdiction. Further, it required all member states to ban and outlaw torture: Article 2. How can it be for international law purposes an official function to do something which international law itself prohibits and criminalises? Thirdly, an essential feature of the international crime of torture is that it must be committed 'by or with the acquiesence of a public official or other person acting in an official capacity.' As a result all defendants in torture cases will be state officials. Yet, if the former head of state has immunity, the man most responsible will escape liability while his inferiors (the chiefs of police, junior army officers) who carried out his orders will be liable. I find it impossible to accept that this was the intention.

Finally, and to my mind decisively, if the implementation of a torture regime is a public function giving rise to immunity ratione materiae, this produces bizarre results. Immunity ratione materiae applies not only to ex-heads of state and ex-ambassadors but to all state officials who have been involved in carrying out the functions of the state. . . . They would all be entitled to immunity. It would follow that there can be no case outside Chile in which a successful prosecution for torture can be brought unless the State of Chile is prepared to waive its right to its officials' immunity. Therefore the whole elaborate structure of universal jurisdiction over torture committed by officials is rendered abortive. . . .

For these reasons in my judgment if, as alleged, Senator Pinochet organised and authorised torture after 8 December 1988, he was not acting in any capacity which gives rise to immunity ratione materiae because such actions were contrary to international law, Chile had agreed to outlaw such conduct and Chile had agreed with the other parties to the Torture Convention that all signatory states should have jurisdiction to try official torture (as defined in the Convention) even if such torture were committed in Chile.

As to the charges of murder and conspiracy to murder, no one has advanced any reason why the ordinary rules of immunity should not apply and Senator Pinochet is entitled to such immunity.

For these reasons, I would allow the appeal so as to permit the extradition proceedings to proceed on the allegation that torture in pursuance of a conspiracy to commit torture, including the single act of torture which is alleged in charge 30, was being committed by Senator Pinochet after 8 December 1988 when he lost his immunity.

. . .

LORD GOFF OF CHIEVELEY

. . .

Before the Divisional Court, and again before the first Appellate Committee, it was argued on behalf of the Government of Spain that Senator Pinochet was not entitled to the benefit of state immunity basically on two grounds, viz. first, that the crimes alleged against Senator Pinochet are so horrific that an exception must be made to the international law principle of state immunity; and second, that the crimes with which he is charged are crimes against international law, in respect of which state immunity is not available. . . . [A] majority of the first Appellate Committee [sitting in the earlier first hearing before the House of Lords] accepted the second argument. The leading opinion was delivered by Lord Nicholls of Birkenhead, whose reasoning was of great simplicity. . . .

. . .

Lord Slynn of Hadley and Lord Lloyd of Berwick, however, delivered substantial dissenting opinions. In particular, Lord Slynn (see [1998] 3 W.L.R. 1456 at pp. 1471F–1475G) considered in detail 'the developments in international law relating to what are called international crimes.' . . .

> It does not seem to me that it has been shown that there is any state practice or general consensus let alone a widely supported convention that all crimes against international law should be justiciable in national courts on the basis of the universality of jurisdiction. Nor is there any jus cogens in respect of such breaches of international law which requires that a claim of state or head of state immunity, itself a well-established principle of international law, should be overridden.

He went on to consider whether international law now recognises that some crimes, and in particular crimes against humanity, are outwith the protection of head of state immunity. . . .

> . . . except in regard to crimes in particular situations before international tribunals these measures did not in general deal with the question as to whether otherwise existing immunities were taken away. Nor did they always specifically recognise the jurisdiction of, or confer jurisdiction on, national courts to try such crimes.

He then proceeded to examine the Torture Convention of 1984, the Genocide Convention of 1948 and the Taking of Hostages Convention of 1983, and concluded that none of them had removed the long established immunity of former heads of state.

I wish to record my respectful agreement with the analysis, and conclusions, of Lord Slynn set out in the passages from his opinion to which I have referred. . . .

. . .

There can be no doubt that the immunity of a head of state, whether ratione personae or ratione materiae, applies to both civil and criminal proceedings. . . .

However, a question arises whether any limit is placed on the immunity in respect of criminal offences. Obviously the mere fact that the conduct is criminal does not of itself exclude the immunity, otherwise there would be little point in the immunity from criminal process; and this is so even where the crime is of a serious character. It follows, in my opinion, that the mere fact that the crime in question is torture does not exclude state immunity. It has however been stated by Sir Arthur Watts [p. 1205, *supra*] that a head of state may be personally responsible:

. . .

. . . [I]t is evident from this passage that Sir Arthur is referring not just to a specific crime as such, but to a crime which offends against the public order of the international community, for which a head of state may be *internationally* (his emphasis) accountable. The instruments cited by him show that he is concerned here with crimes against peace, war crimes and crimes against humanity. Originally these were limited to crimes committed in the context of armed conflict, as in the case of the Nuremberg and Tokyo Charters, and still in the case of the Yugoslavia Statute. . . . Subsequently, the context has been widened to include (inter alia) torture 'when committed as part of a widespread or systematic attack against a civilian population' on specified grounds. A provision to this effect appeared in the International Law Commission's Draft Code of Crimes of 1996 . . . and also appeared in the Statute of the International Tribunal for Rwanda (1994), and in the Rome Statute of the International Court (adopted in 1998). . . . [T]hese instruments are all concerned with international responsibility before international tribunals, and not with the exclusion of state immunity in criminal proceedings before national courts. . . .

It follows that, if state immunity in respect of crimes of torture has been excluded at all in the present case, this can only have been done by the Torture Convention itself.

[The opinion, noting that the Convention does not mention state immunity, states that the argument for concluding that nonetheless no immunity is available turns on an 'implied term', which Lord Goff argues against. He develops several reasons for refusing to find in the Convention any such implied term, including:]

Furthermore, if immunity ratione materiae was excluded, former heads of state and senior public officials would have to think twice about travelling abroad, for fear of being the subject of unfounded allegations emanating from states of a different political persuasion. In this connection, it is a mistake to assume that state parties to the Convention would only wish to preserve state immunity in cases of torture in order to shield public officials guilty of torture from prosecution elsewhere in the world. . . . State immunity ratione materiae . . . can therefore be effective to preclude any such process in respect of alleged crimes, including allegations which are misguided or even malicious—a matter which can be of great significance where, for example, a former head of state is concerned and political passions are aroused. Preservation of state immunity is therefore a matter of particular importance to powerful countries whose heads of state perform an executive role, and who may therefore be regarded as possible targets by governments of states which, for deeply felt political reasons, deplore their actions while in office. But, to bring the matter nearer home, we must not overlook the fact that it is not only in the United States of America that a substantial body of opinion supports the campaign of the I.R.A. to overthrow the democratic government of Northern Ireland. It is not beyond the bounds of possibility that a state whose government is imbued with this opinion might seek to extradite from a third country, where he or she happens to be, a responsible Minister of the Crown, or even a more humble public official such as a police inspector, on the ground that he or she has acquiesced in a single act of physical or mental torture in Northern Ireland. . . .

. . .

For the above reasons, I am of the opinion that by far the greater part of the charges against Senator Pinochet must be excluded as offending against the double criminality rule; and that, in respect of the surviving charges—charge 9, charge 30 and charges 2 and 4 (insofar as they can be said to survive the double criminality rule)—Senator Pinochet is entitled to the benefit of state immunity ratione materiae as a former head of state. I would therefore dismiss the appeal. . . .

LORD HOPE OF CRAIGHEAD

. . .

The Torture Convention is an international instrument. As such, it must be construed in accordance with customary international law and against the background of the subsisting residual former head of state immunity. Article 32.2 of the Vienna Convention, which forms part of the provisions in the Diplomatic Privileges Act 1964 which are extended to heads of state by section 20(1) of the Sovereign Immunity Act 1978, subject to 'any necessary modifications', states that waiver of the immunity accorded to diplomats 'must always be express'. . . . The Torture Convention does not contain any provision which deals expressly with the question whether heads of state or former heads of state are or are not to have immunity from allegations that they have committed torture.

. . .

. . . There is no requirement [in the Convention's definition of torture that torture] should have been perpetrated on such a scale as to constitute an international crime in the sense described by Sir Arthur Watts . . . that is to say a crime which offends against the public order of the international community. A single act of torture by an official against a national of his state within that state's borders will do. The risks to which former heads of state would be exposed on leaving office of being detained in foreign states upon an allegation that they had acquiesced in an act of official torture would have been so obvious to governments that it is hard to believe that they would ever have agreed to this. . . .

Nevertheless there remains the question whether the immunity can survive Chile's agreement to the Torture Convention if the torture which is alleged was of such a kind or on such a scale as to amount to an international crime. . . .

The allegations which the Spanish judicial authorities have made against Senator Pinochet fall into that category. . . . We are dealing with the remnants of an allegation that he is guilty of what would now, without doubt, be regarded by customary international law as an *international* crime. . . . This is because he is said to have been involved in acts of torture which were committed in pursuance of a policy to commit systematic torture within Chile and elsewhere as an instrument of government. . . .

Despite the difficulties which I have mentioned, I think that there are sufficient signs that the necessary developments in international law were in place by [September 29 1998].

. . .

I would not regard this as a case of waiver. Nor would I accept that it was an implied term of the Torture Convention that former heads of state were to be deprived of their immunity ratione materiae with respect to all acts of official torture as defined in article 1. It is just that the obligations which were recognised by customary international law in the case of such serious international crimes by the date when Chile ratified the Convention are so strong as to override any objection by it on the ground of immunity ratione materiae to the exercise of the jurisdiction over crimes committed after that date which the United Kingdom had made available.

. . .

LORD MILLETT

. . .

The charges brought against Senator Pinochet are concerned with his public and official acts, first as Commander-in-Chief of the Chilean army and later as head of state. . . . As international law stood on the eve of the Second World War, his conduct as head of state after he seized power would probably have attracted immunity ratione materiae. . . .

. . . Even before the end of the Second World War, however, it was questionable whether the doctrine of state immunity accorded protection in respect of conduct which was prohibited by international law. As early as 1841, according to Quincy Wright (see (1947) 41 A.J.I.L at p. 71), many commentators held the view that 'the Government's authority could not confer immunity upon its agents for acts beyond its powers under international law'.

Thus state immunity did not provide a defence to a crime against the rules of war [citations to scholarly writing omitted].

Article 7 of the Charter of the Nuremberg Tribunal provided:

> The official position of defendants, *whether as heads of state or responsible officials in government departments*, shall not be considered as freeing them from responsibility or mitigating punishment. (my emphasis)

...

The great majority of war criminals were tried in the territories where the crimes were committed. As in the case of the major war criminals tried at Nuremberg, they were generally (though not always) tried by national courts or by courts established by the occupying powers. The jurisdiction of these courts has never been questioned and could be said to be territorial. But everywhere the plea of state immunity was rejected in respect of atrocities committed in the furtherance of state policy in the course of the Second World War. . . .

The principles of the Charter of the International Military Tribunal and the Judgment of the Tribunal were unanimously affirmed by Resolution 95 of the General Assembly of the United Nations in 1946. Thereafter it was no longer possible to deny that individuals could be held criminally responsibility for war crimes and crimes against peace and were not protected by state immunity from the jurisdiction of national courts. Moreover, while it was assumed that the trial would normally take place in the territory where the crimes were committed, it was not suggested that this was the only place where the trial could take place.

. . .

[The opinion considered the 'landmark decision' of the Supreme Court of Israel in *Attorney General of Israel v. Eichmann*, p. 1138, *supra*.]

The case is authority for three propositions:

(1) There is no rule of international law which prohibits a state from exercising extraterritorial criminal jurisdiction in respect of crimes committed by foreign nationals abroad.

(2) War crimes and atrocities of the scale and international character of the Holocaust are crimes of universal jurisdiction under customary international law.

(3) The fact that the accused committed the crimes in question in the course of his official duties as a responsible officer of the state and in the exercise of his authority as an organ of the state is no bar to the exercise of the jurisdiction of a national court.

. . .

In my opinion, crimes prohibited by international law attract universal jurisdiction under customary international law if two criteria are satisfied. First, they must be contrary to a peremptory norm of international law so as to infringe a jus cogens. Secondly, they must be so serious and on such a scale that they can justly be regarded as an attack on the international legal order. Isolated offences, even if committed by public officials, would not satisfy these criteria. . . .

. . .

In my opinion, the systematic use of torture on a large scale and as an instrument of state policy had joined piracy, war crimes and crimes against peace as an international crime of universal jurisdiction well before 1984. I consider that it had done so by 1973. For my own part, therefore, I would hold that the courts of this country already possessed extra-territorial jurisdiction in respect of torture and conspiracy to torture on the scale of the charges in the present case and did not require the authority of statute to exercise it. . . .

. . .

For my own part, I would allow the appeal in respect of the charges relating to the offences in Spain and to torture and conspiracy to torture wherever and whenever carried out. . . .

NOTE

Note several aspects of the Pinochet decision: (1) The Appellate Committee was bound to apply the UK Immunity Act to resolve the issue. But it drew broadly on international law to interpret that statute. (2) The basis for the extradition proceedings was the European Convention on Extradition, to which the UK and Spain were parties. The UK had incorporated its terms into domestic law in the Extradition Act 1989 and the European Convention on Extradition Order 1990.

After the decision, the extradition case continued while Pinochet remained under house arrest. France, Belgium and Switzerland also made extradition requests. A decision of the Metropolitan Magistrate in the Bow Street Magistrates' Court in 1999, reproduced in 38 ILM 135 (2000), concluded that the conduct alleged against Pinochet would be extraditable offences under English law. The Magistrate further concluded that he was bound by the Spanish representation in the request for extradition that the offences alleged would also be punishable under Spanish law. Hence the double criminality rule was satisfied. He stressed that he was not concerned in these proceedings with proof of facts or any possible defence, for these were matters for the trial court (in Spain). He then committed Pinochet to await decision about extradition.

In January 2000, the British Home Secretary stated that results of a medical examination of Pinochet by four specialists were leading him to conclude that the 84-year-old general was incapable of standing trial and should be released to return to Chile. In March, Pinochet was allowed to fly home, to a radically different political context in which he was an isolated, far less influential and potent figure. Judicial steps were underway toward intense investigation into Pinochet's connection with the killings and torture. But as of that date, the parliamentary immunity that accompanied his position as senator for life precluded prosecution.

QUESTIONS

1. 'The disagreeement among the Law Lords . . . attests to the fact that the current state of evolution of international law is the object of divergent evaluations. This discrepancy and relatively rapid consolidation of both human rights and international criminal law has deeply affected, but not decisively altered, the structure and process of international law. The understandable [resistance] of states to accepting a moving away from a strictly "State-centered order of things" creates a strain between yet unsystematized notions of international public order and the traditional precepts of international law, largely based on the sovereignty paradigm. . . . In strictly positivistic terms it would have been equally difficult to demonstrate conclusively on the basis of state practice either that former heads of states enjoy immunity or that they do not. Between two legally plausible solutions, the House of Lords faced a policy choice. . . . Although one may doubt that this was intended by the Law Lords, the House of Lords' final finding against immunity provided the result which best conforms with the ends and values of the international legal system.'[8] In what respects do you agree or disagree with this analysis?

2. Assuming the conclusion that there is no immunity for Pinochet with respect to some of the charges, was the UK then *permitted* to extradite him or *required* to extradite? What were its obligations, if any?

3. What links exist among several categories or concepts: international law crimes, obligations *erga omnes* or *jus cogens*, and universal jurisdiction? Are they necessary links, in the sense that each category or concept implies the other two? Would you distinguish among international law crimes (that range from hijacking or drug trafficking to crimes against humanity)?

4. 'The outcome was essential, inevitable. It would be the deepest contradiction to allow an immunity based on international law to shield one from a crime defined under that same body of law.' Comment.

5. Article 27 of the Rome Statute of the International Criminal Court, p. 1192, *supra*, is entitled the 'irrelevance of official capacity'.

> 1. This Statute shall apply equally to all persons without any distinction based on official capacity. In particular, official capacity as a Head of State or Government, a member of a Government or parliament, an elected representative or a government official shall in no case exempt a person from criminal responsibility under this Statute, nor shall it, in and of itself, constitute a ground for reduction of sentence.
> 2. Immunities or special procedural rules which may attach to the official capacity of a person, whether under national or international law, shall not bar the Court from exercising its jurisdiction over such a person.

Would such a provision be appropriate for legislation by a state?

---

[8] Andrea Bianchi, 'Immunity versus Human Rights: The Pinochet Case', 10 EJIL 237 (1999), at 271.

COMMENT ON IMPLICATIONS OF PINOCHET DECISION

The decision of the House of Lords brought cheer to many, surely including the victims of the Pinochet regime and human rights advocates. It brought concern to others about the possibilities that it opened to broader use by a state judiciary of criminal trials based on international law for crimes allegedly committed by former leaders or high officials of other states who, for one or another reason (tourism, official mission, business, kidnapping), were in that state's territory. Different governments had different worries. Among Western governments, for example, this concern addressed the possibility that a high military or government official, present or former, involved in the planning of military actions like the Gulf War or in Kosovo might be placed on trial in states like Iraq or Yugoslavia on charges of having committed crimes under international law such as those defined in the Statutes of the ICTY and ICTR and the proposed ICC.

Consider the following events that followed soon after the denial of immunity to Pinochet.

(1) Iraqui and Indonesian leaders

Barbara Crosette, 'Dictators Face the Pinochet Syndrome', *New York Times*, August 22, 1999, p. WK 3

The Austrian case involved Izzat Ibrahim al-Duri, regarded as the No. 2 man in Iraq after Saddam Hussein. A Vienna city councilman, Peter Pilz, discovered that Mr. Ibrahim, who is accused of directing the mass murder of Kurds in 1988 and torturing and killing other Iraqi citizens, was in a Vienna hospital for treatment. . . . Mr. Pilz filed a criminal complaint with Austrian authorities on Monday. Less than 48 hours later, Mr. Ibrahim made a hasty exit and Austria, to the consternation of human rights groups, let him go. So did Jordan, since Mr. Ibrahim had to pass through Amman. . . .

In Jakarta, a leading newspaper said the Pinochet Syndrome also haunts President Suharto of Indonesia, who was forced from office last year after three decades of autocratic rule. Mr. Suharto, who is under investigation by the new Indonesian Government, . . . is 78 years old and seriously ill. . . .

Like other strongmen who tolerate inferior health care for everyone but themselves, Mr. Suharto had been expected to seek medical treatment in Germany, as he has done in the past. Not likely, people close to his family told The Jakarta Post. A host of people would be waiting with warrants.

Human Rights Watch has compiled a list of ex-tyrants who have fled their battered countries for what they thought were safer addresses. Idi Amin of Uganda is still in Saudi Arabia; Jean-Claude Duvalier of Haiti is in France and one of his successors, Raul Cedras, is in Panama; Paraguay's Alfredo Stroessner is in Brazil, and Hissan Habre of Chad is in Senegal.

(2) Chad leader

Norimitsu Onishi, 'An African Dictator Faces Trial in His Place of Refuge', *New York Times*, March 1, 2000, p. A3

... [T]he former president of Chad is expected to stand trial later this year on charges of torture. The case against the former president, Hissene Habre, is being watched closely in Africa, where brutal rulers have engaged in widespread human rights violations with impunity. ...

...

'This is a message to other African leaders that nothing will be the same any longer,' said Delphine Djiraibe, president of a human rights group working on the case. 'It shows that Africa can also play a role in the fight for human rights and can fight on its own soil.'

... Mr. Habre, 57, ... has lived in exile in Dakar since being toppled from power in 1990. ... [S]everal human rights organizations have worked quietly for months to collect evidence against Mr. Habre, drawing on the legal precedent established in the Pinochet case. ...

In the case of Mr. Habre, the human rights groups say they have documented 97 cases of political killings, 142 cases of torture and 100 cases of people who have disappeared in Chad, an impoverished, desert nation in central Africa.

... [Habre] has been in Dakar under house arrest since being indicted on torture charges by the court.

...

Senegal is regarded as having one of the few independent judiciaries in Africa, and that is one of the main reasons that international human rights organizations, including Human Rights Watch and the International Federation of Human Rights, have joined in the case against Mr. Habre.

... Reed Brody, advocacy director of the New York-based Human Rights Watch, [said]: 'The case has profound implications in a way that it would not if it were being held in a European country, particularly a colonial country. That's one of the things that Latin Americans were saying about the Pinochet case—that it was Europe imposing its laws'. ...

... In 1982, Mr Habre, a rebel chieftain, seized power and ingratiated himself with France and the United States for being a staunch opponent of Col. Muammar el-Qaddafi of Libya.

During Mr. Habre's eight-year reign, his American and French backers often portrayed him positively, describing him as a charismatic leader and intellectual who genuinely cared about issues facing the developing world. But the French eventually tired of Mr. Habre. ... [I]n December 1990, after a French-supported invasion from Sudan, Idriss Deby—who had been Mr. Habre's military commander and the country's No. 2 leader—overthrew Mr. Habre and sent him into exile.

In Dakar, several Senegalese intellectuals said it was hypocritical of Western human rights organizations to pursue Mr. Habre now, given their governments' previous support. 'Hissene Habre was received and honored in Paris as a head of state and ally,' said Babacar Sine, one of Senegal's most famous intellectuals. 'France never regarded him as a dictator'.

Mr. Sine, who has known Mr. Habre for 40 years, added: 'This case is much more complex than the role of Habre. There is the role of France that supported him. There is the role of the United States that supported him. If we are to judge Hissene Habre, we have to also judge those who supported him'.

. . .

. . . Human rights organizations behind the case are pushing for the trial to take place in Senegal. If Mr. Habre were extradited to Chad, they say, a fair trial would be unlikely because his testimony would implicate members of the current government, including President Deby.

. . .

QUESTIONS

1. The concern that universal jurisdiction could be abused by states against leaders of their current or former enemies (and military opponents) was expressed in the *Pinochet* opinions. How serious a problem do you take this to be? What steps could be taken to control the problem? What significance do you attach to the fact that acts that are alleged to constitute an international law crime may have taken place in the framework of UN-authorized action under Chapter VII of the Charter, or in the framework of direction by a regional organization like NATO?

2. The article on Rwanda by Alvarez at p. 1190, *supra*, also refers to the responsibility of other states, particularly Western powers, for serious and systemic violations of human rights by leaders of third-world states. Based on the definitions of international law crimes in the Statutes for the ICTY, ICTR and ICC, what charges could be brought—and realistically, in what states?

ADDITIONAL READING

Andrea Bianchi, 'Immunity *versus* Human Rights: The Pinochet Case', 10 EJIL 1 (1999); Richard Wilson, 'Prosecuting Pinochet: International Crimes in Spanish Domestic Law', 21 Hum. Rts. Q. 927 (1999); Curtis Bradley and Jack Goldsmith, 'Pinochet and International Human Rights Litigation', 97 Mich. L. Rev. 2129 (1999).

E. TRUTH COMMISSIONS

Sections B–D examined the role of international and national courts in the prosecution of individuals accused of committing international crimes (whether defined by customary international law, by Statutes of tribunals that were adopted by the Security Council or were parts of a treaty to be ratified by states, or by state statutes incorporating the international definitions of the crime). The issues to be explored in Section E, like those in earlier sections, arise when systematic and gross human rights violations are committed internally by a controlling state regime (and in some cases by opposition groups or forces as well). At a certain stage, whether because of a strengthening internal opposition, international pressures, economic deterioration, or special international circumstances such as a war, negotiations between opposing forces or movements may start to displace the authoritarian regime in power by a popularly elected government that is committed to human rights. Alternatively, the (often military) regime in power may simply collapse.

The question then arises how the new regime should act toward those suspected or accused of serious human rights violations in the prior period. Should there be trial and punishment of individuals, and, if so, of all violators or only of leaders? Should there be a general amnesty?[9] Should other paths be followed? Section E examines one other path, that of truth commissions.

HENRY STEINER, INTRODUCTION TO TRUTH COMMISSIONS

Harvard Law School Human Rights Program and World Peace Foundation, **Truth Commissions: A Comparative Assessment** (1997), at 7

The cause of the Irish problem, suggested William Gladstone, is that the Irish never forget, while the English never remember. Is there then a golden mean, some 'proper' degree of collective memory appropriate for bearing in mind the cruelties and lessons of a troubled past, while not so consuming as to stifle the possibilities of reconciliation and growth? How might one imprint such a memory on a people's or state's conscience? What kinds of institutions or processes would be appropriate? What purposes might be served by a detailed recording of gross abuses, not only for the collectivity but also for the individuals involved as victims or perpetrators?

. . .

In a brief fifteen years, 'truth commission' has become a familiar conception and institution for a state emerging from a period of gross human rights abuses and debating how to deal with its recent past. The term serves as the generic designation of a type of governmental organ that is intended to construct a record of this tragic history, and that has borne different titles in the many countries over several continents that have resorted to it. These commissions offer one among many ways of responding to years of barbarism run rampant, of horrific human rights violations that occurred while countries were caught up in racial, ethnic, class, and ideological conflict over justice and power. They may be alternative or

---

[9] In general, *amnesties* foreclose prosecutions for stated crimes (often by reference to crimes or conduct that took place before a stated date), whereas *pardons* release convicted human rights offenders from serving their sentences (or the remainders thereof if they are prisoners at the time of pardon). Nonetheless, usage often views these terms as interchangeable, so that persons not yet tried are 'pardoned' and prisoners serving sentences are granted an 'amnesty'.

complementary to other national responses, including the poles of amnesty and criminal prosecution.

The contemporary surge of truth commissions . . . started in Argentina after the country's defeat in the Falkland Islands war and the military's related retreat from political power. Other prominent examples of commissions that have effectively completed their work include Chile and El Salvador. In some countries such as Uruguay, commissions did not achieve a great deal. In others such as Uganda, hampered by a lack of political will and funds, they have been unable to complete their mission and issue a report. Among the commissions functioning today, the most discussed and—given the degree of reconstruction that will be necessary—potentially the most significant for a country's future operates in South Africa. . . .

The truth commission has been a protean organ, not only in the many institutional forms it has assumed, but also in its varying membership, in the diverse functions that it serves, and in its range of powers, methods, and processes. Each country—as time progressed from the early 1980s to the present, with ever more precedents as guides—has given its commission a distinctive architecture. The mandates imposed on commissions by executive or legislative measures could be spread over many points along a spectrum moving from strong to weak powers and functions.

Although the general purposes and methods of truth commissions properly figure in a critical discussion of what they have achieved, what rapidly becomes apparent is that concrete examples drawn from different countries must inform abstract description. No architect of these institutions has proceeded by deduction from general principles. The effect of specific historical contexts on the kind of commission created is inconcealable. Consider, for example, one important explanation for the variations among commissions' mandates. When the military continues to hold considerable power as part of a negotiated move toward civilian rule (as in Chile where it retained its commander, the former political leader), severe constraints influence what a truth commission may be empowered to do, or the possibility of prosecution of military personnel. The Argentinian transition following a military disgrace enjoyed greater, though still limited, possibilities.

Commissions are official organs that are generally but not always staffed by citizens. They are organized for a time certain and for the specific purpose of examining through one or another method serious violations of personal integrity. Frequently, victims of gross violations testify before them, and alleged or confessed violators may testify as well. Invariably, the commissions receive or gather evidence of violations committed by state actors, and in some instances also of violations by nonstate actors such as insurgent groups. The investigative capacity given commissions has ranged from extensive staffs armed with legal powers, to reliance principally on voluntary testimony that may or may not be verified. Hearings have been both private and public. The reports of proceedings—including graphic evidence of abuses, sometimes the naming of victims and less frequently of perpetrators, summaries and conclusions, on occasion recommended changes in state institutions or structures—ultimately become public documents. . . .

. . . [T]ruth commissions have addressed state conduct that raises the most politically and morally sensitive issues facing the country as a whole.

Commission's reports have implicated high reaches of state authority in raw and systematic violations of law that claimed victims into the many tens of thousands. This slaughter, rape, torture, imprisonment, and disappearance of victims occurred in the setting of consuming conflicts, sometimes decades long, over a country's basic nature and structure: ethnic hierarchy or equality, military or democratic rule, dictation or participation, repression or expression, mass murder or the rule of law, concentration of wealth and power within a given elite or broader distribution. . . .

. . . [G]overnments have created these commissions principally at the time of a state's transition toward more participatory government expressing ideals of democracy, power bounded by law, formal legal equality, and social justice. Even when the moment of political change has been non-violent—as in Chile where the structural and substantive features of the change were discussed between an opposition and a government, or in South Africa where those features were submitted to the people for its approval—the term 'transition' may understate how radically the successor regime has departed from its predecessor with respect to moral principle and political ideology.

Realization of (or at least the aspiration toward) fundamental change appears to be an almost constant companion to the use of truth commissions. A repressive regime succeeding as repressive a government that it has ousted from power is unlikely to explore prior misdeeds that may be ideally suited to its own malign purposes. The movement toward democratic rule and associated human rights in the years since the Argentinean experiment has become more common in a world informed by the powerful ideals of the international human rights movement. Hence truth commissions have become more likely.

Second, the rules and principles drawn on by commissions in determining what is relevant testimony, in reaching conclusions about criminal conduct, or in making recommendations may be found directly in the international human rights movement. Or they may be found in a state's own internal law, a law that was violated by those holding power in the prior period. Even when the latter is the case, the impact on the national proceedings of such international norms (on murder, torture, disappearances, repression, ethnic discrimination, and so on) seems evident. South Africa offers a striking illustration of the powerful effect on a state of the international system's norms and pressures. Indeed, the term 'human rights' has figured as part of some commissions' titles.

. . .

Any assessment of truth commissions must involve comparisons between them and other approaches toward dealing with a tragic period of national history. At one extreme, a state may grant amnesty to those who committed defined crimes—say, crimes with a political objective—during a prior regime. At another, it may criminally prosecute (as did Argentina) a limited number of leading figures who are viewed as ultimately responsible. Despite recent and massive efforts in Ethiopia and Rwanda, in no instance has a new government succeeded in prosecuting a large number of political figures and military or police personnel involved in serious abuses. Surely the most dramatic and widely known of contemporary efforts to prosecute involves the International Criminal

Tribunal in the Hague with respect to the conflicts in the former Yugoslavia and Rwanda.

Except where barred by amnesty provisions, victims' civil suits for compensatory damages first become possible as the repression lifts. The new government may develop a public program of systematic compensation or restitution. It may make public apology without fresh investigative proceedings—as, for example, the Czech and German governments have done in a recent joint declaration bearing on stated abuses during and after World War II. The so-called process of lustration (purification) may by law dismiss people from or make them ineligible for government or other positions because of their involvement in the criticized conduct of the prior regime.

Truth commissions can stand apart from all these approaches to dealing with the past, or they may be closely linked to one among them, perhaps to amnesty or to prosecution. In South Africa, for example, confession before a commission may lead to a grant of amnesty. . . .

Some possibilities and purposes of truth commissions are distinctive to them; others characterize several of the alternative or complementary processes that have been noted. . . .

[The author then notes some major issues about truth commissions.]

(1) Why should a state deal in some official way with its past? If it selects the path of truth commissions, what assurance can it have that major goals such as reconciliation among groups or catharsis for victims will be realized? For example, will the findings of a truth commission promote reconciliation without companion policies like compensation? Can the goal of deterrence of massive violations of human rights be realized through selective prosecutions of leaders, or through the narratives of truth commissions? (Consider in this respect the title, *Nunca Mas*, used for several reports of commissions.)

(2) What criteria and conditions should lead a state to resort to a truth commission rather than to alternative ways of dealing with the past like prosecution or lustration?

(3) Should commissions restrict themselves to recording facts developed through voluntary testimony or through investigative procedures? Should they also engage in broader causal analysis, as by advancing historical explanations of the sources of a conflict? Should a report include recommendations of structural and substantive changes in government with the purpose of avoiding mass recidivism?

(4) Can such questions be answered in general, or will answers necessarily depend on the particular close context for decision?

. . .

JOSÉ ZALAQUETT, INTRODUCTION

Report of the Chilean National Commission on Truth and Reconciliation (1993), Vol. 1, p. xxiii

This report is the core of Chile's earnest response to a major ethical and political dilemma of our time. The problem may be summarized as follows: How can a country overcome a legacy of dictatorial rule and massive human rights violations if the new government is subject to significant institutional and political constraints? How, in those circumstances, can the equally necessary but often conflicting objectives of justice and social peace be harmonized? What are the moral tenets which should guide the politician's actions in such ambiguous situations?

Chile came to confront this dilemma after the inauguration of elected President Patricio Aylwin on March 11 of 1990, which put an end to more than sixteen years of military rule. . . .

. . .

Defining a policy involved first establishing ultimate objectives. These made themselves evident: to repair the damage caused by human rights violations both to individual victims and to the society as a whole; and to prevent such atrocities from ever happening again. The crux of the matter, however, was to decide on the means to achieve such objectives and on the likely extent to which they could be accomplished. These questions could not be answered in a void. At least four major considerations had to be duly weighted: the nature and extent of the human rights violations committed and the measure of investigation of the truth and justice for which they called; the restrictions imposed by the existing laws and institutions and by the likely reaction of the Chilean armed forces; the relevant experience of other countries; and the duties dictated by international human rights norms . . . .

On September 11 of 1973 the Chilean armed forces attacked La Moneda, the presidential palace in the center of Santiago. Within hours Chile's elected president, Salvador Allende, lay dead (this report concludes that he committed suicide), and a military junta presided by General Augusto Pinochet took power.

There followed an intense political repression which resulted in political killings and 'disappearances', the imprisonment or exile of countless Chileans, and the widespread use of torture. These massive human rights violations shocked the world.

. . .

The military government always insisted that it had been waging a war, albeit an unorthodox one, against an insidious, subversive enemy. Yet under no accepted definition of armed conflict could such an allegation be sustained. As established in this report, except for isolated acts of resistance on the day of the coup d'état and in its immediate aftermath, the military government exerted effective control over the country. It was able to suppress any opposition, whether peaceful or not. . . .

These realities dictated that the human rights policy of the Aylwin government should focus, as a priority, on revealing the truth about the fatal victims of political violence: victims of assassinations and 'disappearances' committed by agents of the government (the vast majority) but also political assassinations committed by rebel groups. The practice of torture by the government also had to be accounted for.

A second factor the Aylwin administration had to take into account was the set of institutional and political constraints it inherited. Among the most salient was an amnesty law decreed by the military government in 1978. . . . The worst and most systematic human rights violations perpetrated by the military government occurred in the period covered by the amnesty. . . .

. . . [T]he thinking about dealing with State crimes was largely framed by the foremost precedent of our time: the Nüremberg and Tokyo trials. This precedent emphasized the duty, imposed by the conscience of humankind and by several international legal norms, to prosecute and punish certain crimes and the necessity of such measures in order to preserve the collective memory and to build up an effective deterrent. . . .

However, the postwar model rested on a necessary material condition: the war criminals who were brought to trial did not lose power through political means but through a complete military defeat. The victors did not have to wrestle with questions of correlation of forces.

[A]fter the rapid succession of political transitions . . . , in all regions of the world (from the Americas, to Eastern and Central Europe, to Africa) the whole array of complex ethical, legal, and political issues involved in the change from dictatorship to democracy became fully apparent. In most of these countries the successor governments did not come to power as a result of military victories but through tortuous political paths. The perpetrators and their supporters were still a force to be reckoned with. Often before they left power they managed to impose institutional and legal arrangements to limit the scope of action of the incoming government. In some cases there had been an internal armed conflict, but it ended in a negotiated peace, with no clear victor; or else, one of the parties did emerge victorious, but feared to antagonize the rival ethnic or national groups through widespread prosecutions, lest the conflict be reignited.

. . .

In what concerned Chile, President Aylwin could draw from recent examples in Argentina and Uruguay. These countries were not only Chile's South American neighbors. Like Chile they had been ruled by military regimes, following a similar process of political polarization. Human rights violations in all three countries were of comparable gravity.

Argentina emphasized truth telling, through an official commission which produced a thorough report on disappearances. It also annulled an amnesty law passed by the military. But eventually the Alfonsin government felt compelled to back off from its initial stance and passed, under pressure, legislation to preclude further prosecutions. . . .

The lesson for the Aylwin administration was that it should stake out a policy it could sustain. Reparation and prevention were defined as the objectives of the policy. Truth and justice would be the primary means to achieve such objectives. The result, it was expected, would be to achieve a genuine reconciliation of the divided Chilean family and a lasting social peace.

The truth was considered as an absolute, unrenounceable value for many reasons: In order to provide for measures of reparation and prevention, it must be clearly known what it is that ought to be repaired and prevented. Further, society cannot simply black out a chapter of its history, however differently the facts may be interpreted. The void would be filled with lies or with conflicting versions. The unity of a nation depends on a shared identity, which, in turn, depends largely on a shared memory. The truth also brings a measure of social catharsis and helps to prevent the past from reoccurring. In addition, bringing the facts to light is, to some extent, a form of punishment, albeit mild, in that it provokes social censure against the perpetrators or the institutions or groups they belonged to. But although the truth cannot really in itself dispense justice, it does put an end to many a continued injustice—it does not bring the dead back to life, but it brings them out from silence; for the families of the 'disappeared', the truth about their fate would mean, at last, the end to an anguishing, endless search. . . .

Based on these considerations, the Aylwin administration promised 'the whole truth, and justice to the extent possible'. Responsibility dictated that during the transition this was the most that could be aimed for. In fact, if the government had made an attempt (however futile, given Chile's existing legality) to expand the possibilities for prosecutions, most likely it would have provoked tensions and reactions resulting in that neither truth nor justice could be achieved.

The human rights policy, therefore, rested mainly on disclosing the truth. The government was conscious that for the truth to achieve the expected purposes it had to be established in a manner that elicited the respect of all Chileans. That is how President Aylwin came to appoint the National Commission for Truth and Reconciliation, a panel of eight people from across the political spectrum, which produced this report.

. . .

The establishment of the Commission was strenuously objected to by the armed forces. However, in the end, they abided by the President's authority to do so and responded (mostly in form rather than in substance) to the Commission's many inquiries. Political parties which had also objected to the establishment of the Commission finally accepted its need and lent to it their cooperation.

On February 9 of 1991 the Commission delivered its report to the President. On March 4 in a televised address to the nation President Aylwin presented the findings of the Commission and, as the head of State, atoned for the crimes committed by its agents. The report was then widely disseminated. Congress passed a unanimous resolution commending it. All political parties acknowledged the truth of the facts investigated, although some disputed the historical interpretations contained in it. . . .

The Commission named the victims but not the perpetrators. It mentions the branch of the armed forces or police responsible for the acts and even the specific unit, but it does not attribute guilt to individuals. However, it sent to the courts the incriminating evidence it could gather. The Commission was not a tribunal and was not conducting trials. To name culprits who had not defended themselves and were not obliged to do so would have been the moral equivalent to convicting someone without due process. This would have been in contradiction with the spirit, if not the letter, of the rule of law and human rights principles.

. . .

Those who worked to produce this report became keenly aware of the cleansing power of the truth. Interviewing thousands of relatives of victims and other witnesses nationwide was a necessarily rigorous method. But, as the interviewers soon discovered, it was at the same time a means to heal the wounds, one by one, and thus to contribute to the building of a lasting peace. They were also humbled by the generosity shown by the relatives of the victims they met. Certainly, many of them asked for justice. Hardly anyone, however, showed a desire for vengeance. Most of them stressed that in the end, what really mattered to them was to know the truth, that the memory of their loved ones would not be denigrated or forgotten, and that such terrible things would never happen again.

REPORT OF THE CHILEAN NATIONAL COMMISSION ON TRUTH AND RECONCILIATION
(1993), Vol. 1, p. 13

Chapter 1: Methodology and Work of the National Commission on Truth and Reconciliation in Preparing this Report

A. Objectives of the Commission

. . .

As it began to operate, the Commission believed that its primary duty was to determine what really had happened in every case in which human rights had been seriously violated. . . .

. . . The president judged that in order to meet its objectives the Commission should complete its task in a relatively short period of time. Accordingly, only the most grave violations could be considered and investigated. The decree [establishing the Commission] defined such violations as disappearances of people who had been arrested, executions, torture leading to death when committed by agents of the government or people in its service, and those kidnappings and attempts on peoples' lives committed by private citizens for political purposes. . . .

. . .

In order to achieve its purposes the Commission was empowered to carry out whatever inquiry and measures it judged appropriate, including requesting reports, documents, or evidence from government authorities and agencies. The same decree obligated government officials and bodies to offer their full collaboration within their own specific area of competence. The Commission did not have the authority to oblige anyone to appear before it and testify.

. . .

B. Knowledge of the Truth
1. Deciding which cases the Commission should consider
After approving an overall work plan and by-laws, and hiring the first staff

members, the Commission sought to invite all the relatives of the victims of these events to register their cases. . . .

. . .

Through registration by family members and information presented by [the armed forces, the police, and other sources such as labour organizations], the Commission was able to decide on the overall body of cases it should examine. After duplications and errors had been eliminated, a little more than 3,400 cases remained.

. . .

3. *Testimony from family members*

. . .

Each session lasted from forty-five minutes to an hour, although some lasted much longer. The Commission sought to obtain from relatives any information they could supply about the events. It particularly wanted any evidence that might serve to advance the investigation, such as the names of witnesses, and any information concerning proceedings initiated in the courts, human rights organizations, and other agencies. Relatives were also asked to explain the impact of these events on the family so that this aspect of the truth could be made known. This information was also intended to help provide the basis for devising policies for making reparation. The families were amazingly willing to put their trust in our group. For many of them, this was the first gesture made by the Chilean government to acknowledge their situation.

. . .

4. *Subsequent investigations*

. . .

In practically all cases in which the evidence gathered indicated that agencies of the armed forces or police might have been involved, the head of the respective branch was consulted as well as the chief of staff when appropriate, and they were asked for any evidence their institution might have on those events. The Chilean Army replied to more than two-thirds of these requests. In most of its replies it pointed out that in keeping with the legislation in force and its own by-laws, the evidence on such events that might have existed had been burned or destroyed when the legal period for doing so had passed. . . .

The Chilean Police almost always responded to such requests by indicating that the documents from that period had been legally burned. . . .

. . .

When information on the involvement of their security agencies was requested, the army, the navy, and the air force pointed out that they were legally prohibited from providing information having to do with intelligence activities.

. . .

In almost every case in which the evidence gathered made it possible to pick out a particular person [in the armed forces or police], the Commission asked that person to give testimony. . . . After explaining that the individual member had been mentioned in a document the Commission had received, noting that such testimony was voluntary and could be made confidentially, and that it was not the Commission's role to determine whether individuals were guilty of crimes, these officers were asked to inform the individual members how important their testimony was considered to be. The Commission requested the testimony of one hundred and sixty members of the armed forces and the police. . . . With the exception of a few cases, . . . those who were on active duty refused to offer testimony to this Commission. . . .

. . .

5. Individual decision on each case

. . .

The first cases were presented to the Commission at the end of October 1990. In sessions lasting until mid-January 1991, the Commission individually examined about 3,400 cases, until it had reached agreement over how it was going to present each case in which human rights had been gravely violated or in which people had been killed as a result of political violence. In other cases it concluded that it had not been able to come to such a determination or that the case was beyond its competence. . . .

. . .

D. Acknowledgement of harm inflicted and proposals for reparation and prevention

. . .

In addition to examining what the relatives of the victims of grave human rights violations had suffered, the Commission consulted with relevant experts and persons who could offer guidance on proposals for reparation and prevention such as the decree had urged it to prepare. The Commission consulted with a large number of national and international organizations. . . . [T]hey were asked about measures that might strengthen the legal order and institutional framework, or promote a culture more respectful of human rights in order to assure that such events never again take place in our country. One hundred and nine organizations were consulted in this fashion, including those of the victims' family members, human rights agencies, the main universities and centers of learning, the political parties, the churches, and other moral authorities. Internationally, the request was sent primarily to those intergovernmental and private bodies with the greatest experience in protecting and promoting human rights. . . .

. . .

VIEWS ON FUNCTIONS AND UTILITY OF TRUTH COMMISSIONS

Consider the following excerpts from the roundtable discussion in Truth Commissions: A Comparative Assessment, p. 1217, supra.

Bryan Hehir

I think that truth commissions function at three levels. The first entails catharsis. . . . The second level involves the process of moral reconstruction. . . . Society must pass judgment on what has been heard. It must establish a moral account of the historical record. The third level verges on the political—what is done with the process of truth telling? A number of options are available. A society may [even] choose to 'forget' or ignore the truth.

Tina Rosenberg

I am struck by how many comments outline the parallels between truth commissions and the therapeutic process of dealing with victims of post-traumatic stress disorder. The similarities are striking. People need to tell their story, but this is not all. Two other levels are important. People need to tell their stories to someone who is listening to them seriously and validating them. This is official acknowledgment. More importantly, victims must be able to reintegrate that narrative into their whole life story.

Lawrence Weschler (Staff Writer, *New Yorker*)

Furthermore, as the victims put their own lives together, they also pull the whole country together.

I detect three overlapping metaphors in our discussion—the realms of law, art and therapy. The most effective truth commissions carry on elements of the theatric, by being broadcast to the public on television for example. Artfulness of presentation makes the commission more effective. The public responds like an audience of a Greek tragedy. People must organize their lives in an artful way that lends them a cathartic life experience at the end.

[Use of truth commissions in the context of particular international disputes:]

Yael Tamir

Should Israel and Palestine establish a truth commission? . . . I can think of three kinds of justifications, which I have ordered from the most to the least convincing.

The first presupposes that we have a moral obligation to know and remember the wrongs that have occurred. If we ignore the injustice that has been done or forget it, we become in some sense accomplice to it. This implies that we have an obligation to know what has happened regardless of the social effects that this knowledge might produce. A truth commission contributes to our ability to reach this goal and is therefore welcome. It signals that no harm will go unnoticed and that those who bear responsibility will not go unpunished.

The second justification is instrumental. It is grounded in the psychological needs of the victims and their relatives: the need to talk about their harsh experiences and to have their suffering publicly acknowledged. . . . I am skeptical about the ability of truth commissions to serve this goal. I also have a deeper doubt about the psychological assumptions—for example, whether victims are better off if they are allowed to recount their experiences.

Truth commissions are also seen as instrumental in promoting reconciliation. I find this claim doubtful. In my experiences in Israeli-Palestinian workshops, I have found that an attempt to expose the facts is not particularly useful. It is often better to assume that injustices have been committed by both sides, and then focus on how to solve the conflict.

The most convincing justifications are then of the first kind, for the arguments for commissions that rest on instrumental justifications are very contingent on detailed contexts. I believe that a truth commission is unlikely to be helpful in the Israeli-Palestinian case.

. . .

To summarize, if the peace process is to move forward it cannot proceed on the basis of an investigation of the past. Rather, we must disassociate ourselves from the past and build a future based on an abstract acknowledgment of the injustice done by both sides, an injustice grounded in the fact that we share the same small piece of land for which both sides make claims of right. We must therefore reach an agreement regardless of past injustices. Peace cannot be grounded in competition over past suffering.

Fateh Azzam

Basically I agree with Yael Tamir's assessment of the situation and the potential for a truth commission. At the same time, I cannot help but note the urgency of dealing with issues of past injustices.

What should emerge from this strange animal called the peace process? I have some disagreement with Yael. Unless we acknowledge what happened in the past, it will continue to come up. Israelis and Palestinians must redefine their relationship, but not necessarily deny it. We must acknowledge one another in a way that lays a proper foundation for our future. This will take a very long time. The Palestinians need to hear some acknowledgment in order for them to admit that co-existence is possible.

For these reasons, I had thought a truth commission might be a useful exercise. But further reflection has made me realize how much the outcome of the peace process depends on politics and political desires. Our societies need to accept one another, and this has not yet happened. Perhaps it is a question of timing.

QUESTIONS

1. What do you view as the advantages and disadvantages of a truth commission in the Chilean model as an alternative to prosecutions? Is it always a 'second best', to be employed when the political and military context makes prosecutions impossible? Are truth commissions and prosecutions compatible?

2. Some commentators have argued that a decision to 'name names' in a truth commission's report of those (in armed forces, police) accused of committing serious human rights violations, as was done in the Report on El Salvador, is justified in part by

the fact that the state's justice system is incapable of honest investigation and impartial judgment. Do you agree? Are there other reasons pointing toward including names of violators? What form and methods of investigation would you recommend for a truth commission that intended to publish such names?

3. 'Truth commissions are particularly useful where the people involved—violators, victims, those just standing by—will (indeed must) live in close proximity to each other as members of the same state and society. Hence they are less necessary and less effective in many types of international conflicts where the peoples involved, the violators and the victims, will live separately after some accord and end to the conflict.' Do you agree?

ABDULLAH OMAR, INTRODUCTION TO TRUTH AND RECONCILIATION COMMISSION

http://www.truth.org.za/legal/justice.htm

[The author, Minister of Justice of South Africa, was active in the planning of the South African Truth and Reconciliation Commission. He wrote this description as the debate in Parliament over the TRC ended and the scene was 'finally set' for appointment of its commissioners. Several provisions of the legislation governing the TRC that are referred to below were subsequently amended.]

. . .

. . . The Commission is based on the final clause of the Interim Constitution which reads as follows:

> This Constitution provides a historic bridge between the past of a deeply divided society characterised by strife, conflict, untold suffering and injustice, and a future rounded on the recognition of human rights, democracy and peaceful co-existence and development opportunities for all South Africans, irrespective of colour, race, class, belief or sex.
>
> . . .
>
> . . . [T]here is a need for understanding but not for vengeance, a need for reparation but not retaliation, a need for ubuntu but not for victimisation.
>
> In order to advance such reconciliation and reconstruction, amnesty shall be granted in respect of acts, omissions and offences associated with political objectives and committed in the course of the conflicts of the past. To this end, Parliament under this Constitution shall adopt a law . . . providing for the mechanisms, criteria and procedures, including tribunals, if any, through which such amnesty shall be dealt with at any time after the law has been passed.

. . .

I could have gone to Parliament and produced an amnesty law—but this would have been to ignore the victims of violence entirely. We recognised that we could not forgive perpetrators unless we attempt also to restore the honour and dignity of the victims and give effect to reparation.

The question of amnesty must be located in a broader context and the wounds of our people must be recognized. I do not distinguish between ANC [African National Congress] wounds, PAC [Pan African Congress] wounds and other wounds—many people are in need of healing, and we need to heal our country if we are to build a nation which will guarantee peace and stability.

. . .

. . . President [Mandela] supports the setting up of a Commission of Truth and Reconciliation. The democratic government is committed to the building up of a human rights culture in our land.

. . .

Objectives of the Commission

The objectives of the Commission will be to promote national unity and reconcili-ation in a spirit of understanding which transcends the conflicts and divisions of the past by:

- establishing as complete a picture as possible of the causes, nature and extent of the gross violations of human rights which were committed during the period from 1 March 1960 to the cut-off date including the antecedents, circumstances, factors and context of such violations, as well as the perspectives of the victims and the motives and perspectives of the persons responsible for committing such violations, by conducting investi-gations and holding hearings;
- facilitating the granting of amnesty to persons who make full disclosure of all the relevant facts relating to acts associated with a political objective and which comply with the requirements of the Act (Promotion of National Unity and Reconciliation Act);
- establishing and making known the fate or whereabouts of victims and restoring the human and civil dignity of such victims by granting them an opportunity to relate their own accounts of the violations of which they are the victims, and recommending reparation measures in respect of them;
- compiling a report providing as comprehensive an account as possible of the activities and findings of the Commission and containing recom-mendations of measures to prevent the future violations of human rights.

Functions of the Commission

The function of the Commission will be to achieve its objectives and to that end the Commission shall:

- facilitate, and where necessary initiate or coordinate, inquiries into:
- gross violations of human rights, including violations which were part of a systematic pattern of abuse;
- the nature, causes and extent of gross violations of human rights, including the antecedents, circumstances, factors, context, motives and perspectives which led to such violations;
- the identity of all persons, authorities, institutions and organizations involved in such violations;

- the question whether such violations were the result of deliberate planning on the part of the State or a former state or any of their organs, or of any political organisation, liberation movement or other group or individual;
- accountability, political or otherwise, for any such violation;
- facilitate, and initiate or coordinate, the gathering of information and the receiving of evidence from any person, including persons claiming to be victims of such violations or the representatives of such victims, which establish the identity of victims of such violations, their fate or present whereabouts and the nature and extent of the harm suffered by such victims;
- facilitate and promote the granting of amnesty in respect of acts associated with political objectives . . . .

  . . .

- make recommendations to the President with regard to the creation of institutions conducive to a stable and fair society and the institutional, administrative and legislative measures which should be taken or introduced in order to prevent the omission of human rights violations.

Constitution of the Commission

- The Commission shall consist of not fewer than 11 and not more than 17 commissioners, as may be determined by the President in consultation with the Cabinet.
- The President shall appoint the commissioners in consultation with the Cabinet.
- The commissioners shall be fit and proper persons who are impartial and who do not have a high political profile, provided that not more than two persons who are not South African citizens may be appointed as commissioners.

. . .

Structure of the Commission

Committee on Human Rights Violations

[Reference to powers and duties referred to under Functions of the Commission]

The Committee will exercise the powers of investigation granted to the Commission in Chapter Six and Chapter Seven of the Act. This entails the establishment of an Investigating Unit . . .

Committee on Amnesty

This Committee will facilitate and promote the granting of amnesty in respect of acts associated with political objectives by receiving from persons desiring to make a full disclosure of all the relevant facts relating to such acts applications for the granting of amnesty in respect of such acts and by publishing decisions granting amnesty in the *Government Gazette.*

. . . The hearings of the Amnesty Committee, which will have a Judge of the Supreme Court as its chairperson, will be held in public unless, in the judgment of the chairperson and the committee, this may jeopardise life or limb, or contradict a process of fundamental human rights. . . .

If . . . a hearing is necessary the Committee will inform the person of the place and time when the application will be heard and considered. The Committee then will deal with the application by granting or refusing amnesty. One of the provisions laid down is that the applicant must make a full disclosure of all relevant facts. The Committee shall be guided by the consideration of certain laid-down criteria:

- the motive of the person who committed the act, omission or offence;
- the context in which the act, omission or offence took place, and in particular whether the act, omission or offence was committed in the course of or as part of a political uprising, disturbance or event, or in reaction thereto;
- the legal and factual nature of the act, omission or offence, including the gravity of the act, omission or offence;
- the object or objective of the act, omission or offence, and in particular whether the act, omission or offence was primarily directed at a political opponent or State property or personnel or against private property or individuals;
- whether the act, omission or offence was committed in the execution of an order of, or on behalf of, or with the approval of, the organisation, institution, liberation movement or body of which the person who committed the act was a member, an agent or a supporter; and
- the relationship between the act, omission or offence and the political objective pursued, and in particular the directness and proximity of the relationship and the proportionality of the act, omission or offence to the objective pursued.

However, this does not include any act, omission or offence committed by any person referred to in subsection (2) of the Act who acted:

- for personal gain . . . ; or
- out of personal malice, ill-will or spite, directed against the victim of the acts committed.

Committee on Reparation and Rehabilitation of Victims

. . .

The Committee may:

- make recommendations which may include urgent interim measures as to appropriate measures of reparation to victims;
- make recommendations relating to the creation of institutions conducive to a stable and fair society and the measures which need to be taken to prevent the commission of human rights violations;

. . .

Applications for reparation

Any person who is of the opinion that he or she has suffered harm as a result of a gross violation of human rights may apply to the Committee for reparation. The Committee shall consider any such application and may exercise any of the powers conferred on it, as outlined above.

. . .

Victims of Human Rights Violations

When dealing with victims, the actions of the Commission shall be guided by the following principles:

- Victims shall be treated with compassion and respect for their dignity;
- Victims shall be treated equally and without discrimination of any kind . . . ;
- Procedures for dealing with applications by victims shall be expeditious, fair, inexpensive and accessible;
- Victims shall be informed through the press and any other medium of their rights in seeking redress through the Commission . . . ;
- Appropriate measures shall be taken in order to minimise inconvenience to victims and, when necessary, to protect their privacy, to ensure their safety as well as that of their families and of witnesses testifying on their behalf and to protect them from intimidation;
- Appropriate measures shall be taken to allow victims to communicate in the language of their choice;
- Informal mechanisms for the resolution of disputes, including mediation, arbitration and any procedure provided for by customary law and practice shall be applied, where appropriate, to facilitate reconciliation and redress for victims.

REPORT OF TRUTH AND RECONCILIATION COMMISSION OF SOUTH AFRICA
1998, 5 vols

[There appear below excerpts from the Report. They are identified by volume, chapter number of volume, and paragraph number of chapter. The Report is available through *www.truth.org.za*.]

Volume 1
Chapter 4: The Mandate

- *Why the South African Commission is different from other Commissions*

. . .

25. The most important difference between the South African Commission and others was that it was the first to be given the power to grant amnesty to individual perpetrators. No other state had combined this quasi-judicial power with the investigation tasks of a truth-seeking body. More typically, where amnesty was introduced to protect perpetrators from being prosecuted for the crimes of the

past, the provision was broad and unconditional, with no requirement for individual application or confession of particular crimes. . . .

26. Another significant difference can be found in the Commission's powers of *subpoena,* search and seizure, which are much stronger than those of other truth commissions. This has led to more thorough internal investigation and direct questioning of witnesses, including those who were implicated in violations and did not apply for amnesty. . . .

27. The very public process of the South African Commission also distinguishes it from other commissions. . . . The Latin American truth commissions heard testimony only in private, and information only emerged with the release of the final reports.

. . .

29. The South African Commission was the first to create a witness protection programme. This strengthened its investigative powers and allowed witnesses to come forward with information they feared might put them at risk.

30. Finally, the South African Commission was several times larger in terms of staff and budget than any commission before it.

. . .

• *Interpreting the mandate*

. . .

34. It was recognised at the outset that the Commission could not carry out all the tasks required of it simultaneously. Thus, it first gave attention to the question of the restoration of the human and civil dignity of (individual) victims of past gross human rights violations. It did so by creating opportunities for victims 'to relate their own accounts' of the violations they had suffered by giving testimony at public hearings across the length and breadth of South Africa between April 1996 and June 1997. These highly publicised hearings were coupled with an extensive statement-taking drive, investigations, research and so-called 'section 29' hearings (where witnesses and alleged perpetrators were *subpoenaed*) in order to 'establish the fate or whereabouts of victims' and the identity of those responsible for human rights violations.

35. During the second half of the Commission's life (from approximately the middle of 1997), the Commission shifted its focus from the stories of individual victims to an attempt to understand the individual and institutional motives and perspectives which gave rise to the gross violations of human rights under examination. It enquired into the contexts and causes of these violations and attempted to establish the political and moral accountability of individuals, organisations and institutions. The goal was to provide the grounds for making recommendations to prevent future human rights violations. Features of this phase were public submissions by, and questioning of, political parties, and a range of institutional, sectoral and special hearings that focused on the health and business sectors, the legal system, the media and faith communities, prisons, women, children and youth, biological and chemical warfare and compulsory national service. It was also during this period that the majority of amnesty hearings took place.

. . .

- *Who were victims of gross violations of human rights?*

...

51. It is this systemic and all-pervading character of apartheid that provides the background for the present investigation. During the apartheid years, people did many evil things. Some of these are the gross violations of human rights with which this Commission had to deal. But it can never be forgotten that the system itself was evil, inhumane and degrading for the many millions who became its second and third class citizens. Amongst its many crimes, perhaps the greatest was its power to humiliate, to denigrate and to remove the self-confidence, self-esteem and dignity of its millions of victims. Mtutuzeli Matshoba expressed it thus:

> For neither am I a man in the eyes of the law,
> Nor am I a man in the eyes of my fellow man.

55. ... [T]he Commission resolved that its mandate was to give attention to human rights violations committed as specific acts, resulting in severe physical and/or mental injury, in the course of past political conflict. As such, the focus of its work was not on the effects of laws passed by the apartheid government, nor on general policies of that government or of other organisations, however morally offensive these may have been. This underlines the importance of understanding the Commissions as but one of several instruments responsible for transformation and bridge-building in post-apartheid South Africa.

...

57. But bodily integrity rights are not the only fundamental rights. When a person has no food to eat, or when someone is dying because of an illness that access to basic health care could have prevented—that is, when subsistence rights are violated—rights to political participation and freedom of speech become meaningless.

58. Thus, a strong argument can be made that the violations of human rights caused by 'separate development'—for example, by migrant labour, forced removals, bantustans, Bantu education and so on—had, and continue to have, the most negative possible impact on the lives of the majority of South Africans. The consequences of these violations cannot be measured only in the human lives lost through deaths, detentions, dirty tricks and disappearances, but in the human lives withered away through enforced poverty and other kinds of deprivation.

...

- *Just ends, just means and crimes against humanity*

64. In making judgments in respect of the above requirements, the Commission was guided by criteria derived from just war theory . . . , international human rights principles and the democratic values inherent in the South African Constitution. By using these criteria, the Commission was able to take clear positions on the evils of apartheid, while also evaluating the actions of those who opposed it.

...

74. The Commission's confirmation of the fact that the apartheid system was a crime against humanity does not mean that all acts carried out in order to destroy

apartheid were necessarily legal, moral and acceptable. The Commission concurred with the international consensus that those who were fighting for a just cause were under an obligation to employ just means in the conduct of this fight.

75. As far as justice in war is concerned, the framework within which the Commission made its findings was in accordance with international law and the views and findings of international organisations and judicial bodies. The strict prohibitions against torture and abduction and the grave wrong of killing and injuring defenceless people, civilians and soldiers 'out of combat' required the Commission to conclude that not all acts in war could be regarded as morally or legally legitimate, even where the cause was just.

76. It is for this reason that the Commission considered the concept of crimes against humanity at both a systemic level and at the level of specific acts. Apartheid as a system was a crime against humanity, but it was also possible for acts carried out by any of the parties to the conflicts of the past to be classified as human rights violations.

77. Thus, the Commission adopted the view that human rights violations could be committed by any group or person inside or outside the state: by persons within the Pan Africanist Congress (PAC), the IFP, the South African Police (SAP), the South African Defence Force (SADF), the ANC or any other organisation.

78. It is important to note, however, that this wider application of human rights principles to non-state entities is a relatively recent international development. . . .

79. The Act establishing the Commission adopted this more modern position. In other words, it did not make a finding of a gross violation of human rights conditional on a finding of state action. . . .

. . .

• *Political context and motivation*

121. To implement its mandate, the Commission had, furthermore, to determine the 'political motive' of the acts of torture, abduction, killing and severe ill treatment which 'emanated from the conflicts of the past' (section 1(1)(X), the Act). . . .

122. In interpreting this part of the definition of gross human rights violations, the Commission was guided by the definition of an 'act associated with a political objective' (section 20(2) and (3)). However, it also went further and employed the less restrictive notion of 'political motive' (section 1(1)(X)).

123. The framework applied in implementing the political requirement was that a violation of human rights within the prescribed period was found to constitute a gross violation of human rights if it was advised, planned, directed, commanded, ordered or committed by:

> a any member or supporter of a publicly known political organisation or liberation movement on behalf of or in support of that organisation or movement, in furtherance of a political struggle waged by that organisation or movement (section 20(2)(a)). This included not only membership of or support for political organisations like the PAC or the ANC, but also

    membership of youth and community-based organisations. Trade unions were also included in this description (given the suppression of purely political organisations and the resultant political role that unions played), as was general resistance to the previous state through, for example, rent boycotts.

  b any employee of the state (or any former state) or any member of the security forces of the state (or any former state) in the course and scope of his or her duties and directed against a publicly known political organisation or liberation movement engaged in a political struggle against the state (or former state) or against any members or supporters of such organisation or movement or any person in furtherance of a political struggle. The act in question must have been committed with the objective of countering or otherwise resisting the said struggle (section 20(2)(b)).

. . .

Racism

127. There were cases in which people were victims of racist attack by individuals who were not involved with a publicly known political organisation and where the incident did not form part of a specific political conflict. Although racism was at the heart of the South African political order, and although such cases were clearly a violation of the victim's rights, such violations did not fall within the Commission's mandate.

128. Cases which were interpreted as falling inside the Commission's mandate included instances where racism was used to mobilise people through a political organisation as part of their commitment to a political struggle, or where racism was used by a political organisation to incite others to violence. Examples of these were instances when white 'settlers' or farmers were killed by supporters of the PAC or the ANC, or where black people were killed by supporters of white right-wing organisations.

. . .

Naming

152. The Act required the publication of the names of those who received amnesty in the Government Gazette. These individuals had already identified themselves as perpetrators by applying for amnesty. The Commission had therefore, to resolve which of the other perpetrators identified in the course of its work should be named in accordance with its mandate—to enquire into 'the identity of all persons, authorities, institutions and organisations' involved in gross human rights violations, as well as the 'accountability, political or otherwise, for any such violation' (section 4(a)(iii), (V), the Act).

153. In fulfilling this part of its mandate, the Commission was again required to walk a tightrope. This time, it was faced with the tension between the public interest in the exposure of wrongdoing and the need to ensure fair treatment of individuals in what was not a court of law; between the rights of victims of gross violations of human rights to know who was responsible and the fundamentally

important question of fairness to those who are accused of crimes or serious wrongdoing.

155. Given the investigative nature of the Commission's process and the limited legal impact of naming, the Commission made findings on the identity of those involved in gross violations of human rights based on the balance of probability. This required a lower burden of proof than that required by the conventional criminal justice system. It meant that, when confronted with different versions of events, the Commission had to decide which version was the more probable, reasonable or likely, after taking all the available evidence into account.

Volume 5

Chapter 6: Findings and conclusions

. . .

The Commission's position on responsibility and accountability

. . .

66. In the light of the above and of the evidence received, the Commission is of the view that gross violations of human rights were perpetrated or facilitated by all the major role-players in the conflicts of the mandate era. These include:

    a The state and its security, intelligence and law-enforcement agencies, the SAP, the SADF and the NIS.

    b Groups and institutions which, to a greater or lesser extent, were affiliated or allied to the state in an official capacity. These include homeland governments and their security forces as well as groups and institutions informally allied to the state. . . .

    c White right-wing organizations which, while actively opposing the state, actively and violently took action to preserve the *status quo* in the 1990s. . . .

    d Liberation movements and organizations which sought to bring about change through armed struggle and which operated outside South Africa and by covert and underground means inside the country.

    e Organizations which sought to bring about change by non-violent means prior to and post-1990, including the United Democratic Front; and

    f Non-state paramilitary formations such as the ANC's self-defence units and the IFP's self-protection units (SPUs).

. . .

68. At the same time, the Commission is not of the view that all such parties can be held to be equally culpable for violations committed in the mandate period. Indeed, the evidence accumulated by the Commission and documented in this report shows that this was not the case. The preponderance of responsibility rests with the state and its allies.

. . .

71. . . . [T]he evidence shows that the perpetration of gross violations of human rights by non-state actors often took place in circumstances where they were acting in opposition to the official state ideology and the policy of apartheid. In this sense, it was the state that generated violent political conflict in the mandate

period—either through its own direct action or by eliciting reactions to its policies and strategies.

72. . . . A state has powers, resources, obligations, responsibilities and privileges that are much greater than those of any group within that state. It must therefore be held to a higher standard of moral and political conduct than are voluntary associations. . . .

. . .

74. It would, however, be misleading and wrong to assign blame for the gross violation of human rights only to those who confronted each other on the political and military battlefields, engaged in acts of commission. Others, like the church or faith groups, the media, the legal profession, the judiciary, the magistracy, the medical/health, educational and business sectors, are found by the Commission to have been guilty of acts of omission in that they failed to adhere or live up to the ethics of their profession and to accepted codes of conduct.

75. It is also the view of the Commission that these sectors failed not so much out of fear of the powers and wrath of the state—although those were not insignificant factors—but primarily because they were the beneficiaries of the state system. They prospered from it by staying silent. By doing nothing or not enough, they contributed to the emergence of a culture of impunity within which the gross violations of human rights documented in this report could and did occur.

[The balance of this section on Findings and Conclusions states detailed findings against each of the state organs, government leaders, internal allies of the state, regional groups, liberation movements, and sectors of civil society to which the earlier parts of this section refer.]

DECISIONS OF AMNESTY COMMITTEE, TRUTH AND RECONCILIATION COMMISSION
http://www.truth.org.za/amnesty

Ntamo, VS (4734/97); Peni, NA (5188/97); Nofemela, EM (5282/97); Manqina, MC (0669/96) (Heard in July 1997)

The Applicants were convicted and sentenced to imprisonment for 18 years for the murder of Amy Biehl. . . . The offence was committed on the NY1 Road in the Gugulethu Township, in Cape Town on the 25th August 1993. The applicants are young men whose ages, at the time of the commission of the offence ranged between 18 and 22 years. Except for Ntamo, whose education had not progressed beyond Std 4, the others were high school students.

They have applied for amnesty in terms of section 18 of the Promotion of National Unity and Reconciliation Act No. 34 of 1995.

Amy Biehl their victim was an American Citizen. She was on a Fulbright Scholarship and was affiliated to the Community Law Centre at the University of the Western Cape where she was pursuing her studies for a Ph.D in Political Science. On that fateful afternoon, she was conveying three colleagues in her car.

She was on her way to drop some of them off in Gugulethu, when her vehicle came under attack by people who were running towards it and throwing stones at it. The stones smashed the windscreen and windows of the car. One of the stones hit Amy Biehl on her head, causing her to bleed profusely. She could not continue driving. She got out of her car and ran towards a garage across the road. Her attackers did not relent. They pursued her and continued throwing stones at her. Manqina tripped her, causing her to fall. She was surrounded by between 7 and 10 people and while she was being stoned, one of her attackers stabbed her. She died as a result of the injuries they inflicted on her.

According to the evidence of the applicants they were among those who were involved in the attack on Amy Biehl. Peni admitted throwing stones at his victim when he was three to four metres from her. Manqina stabbed her with a knife in addition to throwing stones at her. Nofemela threw stones at her and stabbed at her 3 or 4 times. Ntamo threw many stones at her head when he was only a metre away. They stopped attacking her when the police arrived on the scene.

The attack on the car driven by Amy Biehl was one of many incidents of general lawlessness in NY1 that afternoon. Bands of toyi-toying youths threw stones at delivery vehicles and cars driven by white people. One delivery vehicle was toppled over and set alight and only the arrival of the police prevented more damage. . . .

The applicants explained their behavior by saying that earlier that day they had attended a meeting at the Langa High School where a Pan African Student organization (PASO) unit was relaunched. Peni was elected Chairperson at the meeting. Manqina was Vice Chairperson of the PASO unit at the Gugulethu Comprehensive School and Nofemela was a PASO organizer at the Joe Slovo High School.
. . .

The applicants said that speakers dealt with:

- the strike by Teachers in the Western Cape who demanded recognition for the South African Democratic Teachers Union (SADTU);
- the struggles of the Azanian Peoples Liberation Army (APLA) for the return of the land to the African People;
- APLA had declared 1993 as the 'Year of the Great Storm'. Reference was also made to the launching of 'OPERATION BARCELONA' to stop all deliveries into the townships.

The speakers urged the members of PASO to take an active part in the struggle of APLA by assisting APLA operators on the ground by making the country ungovernable.

The speeches were militant and punctuated by shouting the slogan 'ONE SETTLER ONE BULLET'.

Applicants said that they were all inspired by the speakers to such an extent that they left the meeting with many others in a militant mood. They marched through the township toyi-toying and shouting ONE SETTLER ONE BULLET, determined to put into effect what they had been urged to do. This is how they got involved in the activities briefly described above which led to the killing of Amy Biehl.
. . .

Although they did not act on the orders or instructions of APLA or PAC [Pan African Congress] on that day, they believed they owed loyalty to the same cause.
. . .

As members of PASO, which was a known political organization of students, they were active supporters of the PAC and subscribed to its political philosophy and its policies. By stoning company delivery vehicles and thereby making it difficult for deliveries into the townships, they were taking part in a political disturbance and contributing towards making their area ungovernable. To that extent, their activities were aimed at supporting the liberation struggle against the State. But Amy Biehl was a private citizen, and the question is why was she killed during this disturbance. Part of the answer may be that her attackers were so aroused and incited, that they lost control of themselves and got caught up in a frenzy of violence. One of the applicants said during his evidence that they all submitted to the slogan of ONE SETTLER, ONE BULLET. To them that meant that every white person was an enemy of the Black people. At that moment to them, Amy Biehl, was a representative of the white community. They believed that by killing civilian whites, APLA was sending a serious political message to the government of the day. By intensifying such activity the political pressure on the government would increase to such an extent that it would demoralize them and compel them to hand over political power to the majority of the people of South Africa.

When the conduct of the applicants is viewed in that light, it must be accepted that their crime was related to a political objective.

The PAC regarded the killing of Amy Biehl as a mistake committed by young people who were misguided. They nevertheless supported the application for amnesty.

The parents of Amy Biehl had come from America to attend the hearing. At the conclusion of the evidence Mr Biehl addressed the Amnesty Committee. Part of his speech reads as follows:

> . . . We have the highest respect for your Truth and Reconciliation Commission and process. We recognise that if this process had not been a pre-negotiated condition your democratic free elections could not possibly have occurred. Therefore, and believing as Amy did in the absolute importance of those democratic elections occurring we unabashedly support the process which we recognize to be unprecedented in contemporary human history.
>
> At the same time we say to you it's your process, not ours. We cannot, therefore, oppose amnesty if it is granted on the merits. In the truest sense it is for the community of South Africa to forgive its own and this has its basis in traditions of ubuntu and other principles of human dignity. Amnesty is not clearly for Linda and Peter Biehl to grant.
>
> . . .
>
> . . . We, as the Amy Biehl Foundation are willing to do our part as catalysts for social progress. All anyone need do is ask. Are you, the community of South Africa, prepared to do your part?

The applicants have made a full disclosure of all the relevant facts as required by section 20(1) of the Act. On a consideration of all the evidence placed before us, we have come to the conclusion that they be granted amnesty for the murder of Amy Biehl. . . .

Dirk Coetzee (0063/96), David Tshikalange (0065/96), and Butana Almond Nofomela (0064/96) (Heard in November 1996 and January 1997)

. . .

We are dealing now with the applications for amnesty made by the three Applicants in respect of the murder of Griffiths Mxenge. The three Applicants, who were at all relevant times serving members of the South African Police Force, have applied for amnesty in respect of many acts committed by them. [The three applicants had been convicted for one of the offences stated in their application, the murder of Mxenge.]

. . .

The evidence led before us disclosed that the three Applicants were stationed at a place called Vlakplaas, which was a base established in the country where the police stationed what could perhaps fairly be described as hit squads. . . .

At the relevant time all four groups from Vlakplaas were in Durban for various purposes. The First Applicant who was the commander reported, so he said, daily to Brigadier Van der Hoven, the regional security commander at about 7.30 am and again at 4 pm. On one such occasion, a few days before the 19th of November 1981, Brigadier Van der Hoven called him to make a 'plan' with Mxenge. He understood this to mean that he was to make arrangements to eliminate Mxenge. He was told in very brief terms that Mxenge, who was the victim in this application, was an ex-Robben Island prisoner and was an attorney practising in Durban. He acted on behalf of members of the liberation movement and others who were charged with criminal offences arising out of the struggle against apartheid, and a large amount of money was known to have gone through his account. There was no suggestion in the evidence before us that this money was improperly used in any way. . . .

He was told that the security police had been unable to bring any charges against Mxenge and that he had accordingly become a thorn in their flesh by enabling persons charged with political offences to obtain the protection of the courts.

The First Applicant said that Brigadier Van der Hoven told him that they must not shoot or abduct Mxenge but that they should make it look like a robbery. He was then taken to Captain Taylor who gave him certain information about Mxenge. This information related to where his office was, where his house was, what car he drove and matters of that nature. . . .

The First Applicant took charge of arrangements and set up a squad which was to be responsible for killing Mxenge, consisting of the Second and Third Applicants, [a certain] Mamasela, and a certain Brian Ngulunga, because he was from the Umlazi area and knew the vicinity well. The First Applicant took charge of the general planning of the murder. . . . He however left the details as to the actual killing to the four members of the squad he had appointed. . . . They intercepted the car in which Mxenge was travelling and dragged him out of it. While Brian Ngulunga stood by with a pistol in his hand, the others commenced to stab their victim. . . . The stabbing continued until he was dead. He had been disemboweled; his throat had been cut and his ears had been practically cut off. His body was found to have 45 lacerations and stab wounds.

It is quite clear from his evidence and from the evidence of the other two Applicants, that they considered this to be an act performed as part of their duties as policemen on the instructions of senior officers who would undoubtedly have satisfied themselves as to the necessity for it.

In this regard the First Applicant said the following during the course of his evidence before us:

. . .

> 'Do you still today believe that those were necessary or lawful orders?'
> 'Absolutely not.'
> 'Why do you think differently today?'
> 'Well, at the time, yes, but with hindsight absurd and absolutely—I mean unjustifiable.'

On the evidence before us we are satisfied that none of the Applicants knew the deceased, Mxenge, or had any reason to wish to bring about his death before they were ordered to do so. We are satisfied that they did what they did because they regarded it as their duty as policemen who were engaged in the struggle against the ANC and other liberation movements. It is, we think clear, that they relied on their superiors to have accurately and fairly considered the question as to whether the assassination was necessary or whether other steps could have been taken. . . .

. . .

. . . With regard to the First Applicant, there was no direct evidence to confirm that he acted on the orders of Van der Hoven or Taylor. In fact, it is a matter of public knowledge that Van der Hoven and Taylor denied any involvement; they did so during their recent trial in which they were co-accused with the Applicants on a criminal charge in respect of this very incident. While there may be some doubt about the identity of the person or persons on whose advice, command or order, the First Applicant acted, the fact that he acted on the advice, command or order of one or more senior members of the security branch, admits of no doubt. . . .

. . .

We are accordingly of the view that the three Applicants are entitled to amnesty in respect of this offence, that is the murder of Griffiths Mxenge on the 19th of November 1981, and it will accordingly not be necessary for the Trial Court to proceed with the question of sentence.

NOTE

The Interim Report of the Amnesty Committee of the TRC (*Truth and Reconciliation Commission of South Africa Report* (1998), vol. 5, Ch. 3) noted that a 'considerable part' of the Committee's workload remained incomplete. Hence the Committee's life span was extended, while the rest of the Commission was suspended on 31 October 1998. The Committee's executive secretary announced that the Committee had to deal in public with over 1,000 amnesty applications.

Most applications to the Committee came from prisoners. The Committee made efforts to achieve some balance by receiving applications from 'role players in the conflict' as well—that is, government officials, security police, and so on.

The Interim Report stressed the role of the Commission in communicating to a relevant public the nature of amnesty and the process for submitting applications through visits of its members and staff to institutions such as prisons and through public talks. The amnesty hearings were open to all media, and television coverage became standard.

With respect to the procedure of the hearings, the Committee took care to 'avoid overly formalising the process' and to retain flexibility. It took the view of the Commission (TRC) that 'process should not be equated to that of a court of law and should not be overly regulated.' Nonetheless, the proceedings 'are largely judicial in nature' and included such rights as cross-examination 'within reasonable bounds.' Proceedings were recorded, and the Committee gave 'reasoned decisions' on all issues to be decided. All decisions were published.

Several legal challenges to the legislation underlying the amnesty provisions and the procedure governing the hearings were brought in the courts. The Constitutional Court resolved one such challenge in *Azanian Peoples Organisation (AZAPO) v. President of the Republic of South Africa*, CCT 17/96 (1996), www.law.wits.ac.za/judgements/azapo.html. The applicants claimed that certain provisions on amnesty of the Promotion of National Unity and Reconciliation Act 34 of 1995 were unconstitutional, since if amnesty were granted, a perpetrator would not be criminally or civilly liable in respect of the acts subject to the amnesty.

The Court upheld the constitutionality of these provisions that limited applicants' right set forth in the Constitution to 'have justiciable disputes settled by a court of law.' The interim Constitution's epilogue on national unity and reconciliation sanctioned this limitation on the applicants' right of access to courts to bring a suit for damages. Absent such provisions, there would be no incentive for offenders to disclose the truth. Moreover, the amnesty provisions were a crucial part of the negotiated settlement leading to the Constitution. Parliament could always act to provide systematic reparations for victims of past abuses, and to provide for individualized reparations taking account of the claims of all victims, rather than preserving civil liability of the state and its officials for provable acts of wrongdoing. The Court also concluded that the amnesty provisions did not violate any international norms.

DESMOND TUTU, NO FUTURE WITHOUT FORGIVENESS
(1999), at 260

[Archbishop Tutu was chairperson of the Truth and Reconciliation Commission.]

. . . The world had expected that the most ghastly blood bath would overwhelm South Africa. It had not happened. Then the world thought that, after a democratically elected government was in place, those who for so long had been denied their rights, whose dignity had been trodden underfoot, callously and without compunction, would go on the rampage, unleashing an orgy of revenge and retribution that would devastate their common motherland. Instead there was this remarkable Truth and Reconciliation Commission to which people told their heartrending stories, victims expressing their willingness to forgive and perpetrators telling their stories of sordid atrocities while also asking for forgiveness from those they had wronged so grievously.

. . .

It is crucial, when a relationship has been damaged or when a potential relationship has been made impossible, that the perpetrator should acknowledge the truth and be ready and willing to apologize. It helps the process of forgiveness and reconciliation immensely. It is never easy. We all know just how difficult it is for most of us to admit that we have been wrong. It is perhaps the most difficult thing in the world—in almost every language the most difficult words are, 'I am sorry'. Thus it is not at all surprising that those accused of horrendous deeds and the communities they come from, for whom they believed they were committing these atrocities, almost always try to find ways out of even admitting that they were indeed capable of such deeds. They adopt the denial mode, asserting that such-and-such has not happened. When the evidence is incontrovertible they take refuge in feigned ignorance. The Germans claimed they had not known what the Nazis were up to. White South Africans have also tried to find refuge in claims of ignorance. The former apartheid cabinet member Leon Wessels was closer to the mark when he said that they had not wanted to know, for there were those who tried to alert them. For those with eyes to see there were accounts of people dying mysteriously in detention. For those with ears to hear there was much that was so disquieting and even chilling . . . .

We do not usually rush to expose our vulnerability and our sinfulness. But if the process of forgiveness and healing is to succeed, ultimately acknowledgment by the culprit is indispensable—not completely so but nearly so. Acknowledgment of the truth and of having wronged someone is important in getting to the root of the breach. . . .

. . .

If the wrongdoer has come to the point of realizing his wrong, then one hopes there will be remorse, or at least some contrition or sorrow. This should lead him to confess the wrong he has done and ask for forgiveness. . . .

The victim, we hope, would be moved to respond to an apology by forgiving the culprit. . . . [W]e were constantly amazed in the commission at the extraordinary magnanimity that so many of the victims exhibited. Of course there were those who said they would not forgive. That demonstrated for me the important point that forgiveness could not be taken for granted; it was neither cheap not easy. As it happens, these were the exceptions. Far more frequently what we encountered was deeply moving and humbling.

In forgiving, people are not being asked to forget. On the contrary, it is important to remember, so that we should not let such atrocities happen again. Forgiveness does not mean condoning what has been done. It means taking what happened seriously and not minimizing it; drawing out the sting in the memory that threatens to poison our entire existence. It involves trying to understand the perpetrators and so have empathy, to try to stand in their shoes and appreciate the sort of pressures and influences that might have conditioned them.

. . .

Once the wrongdoer has confessed and the victim has forgiven, it does not mean that is the end of the process. Most frequently, the wrong has affected the victim in tangible, material ways. Apartheid provided the whites with enormous benefits and privileges, leaving its victims deprived and exploited. If someone steals my pen and then asks me to forgive him, unless he returns my pen the sincerity of his contrition and confession will be considered to be nil. Confession, forgiveness, and reparation, wherever feasible, form part of a continuum.

. . .

. . . [U]nless houses replace the hovels and shacks in which most blacks live, unless blacks gain access to clean water, electricity, affordable health care, decent education, good jobs, and a safe environment—things which the vast majority of whites have taken for granted for so long—we can just as well kiss reconciliation goodbye.

. . .

If we are going to move on and build a new kind of world community there must be a way in which we can deal with a sordid past. . . . It may be, for instance, that race relations in the United States will not improve significantly until Native Americans and African Americans get the opportunity to tell their stories and reveal the pain that sits in the pit of their stomachs as a baneful legacy of dispossession and slavery. We saw in the Truth and Reconciliation Commission how the act of telling one's story has a cathartic, healing effect.

. . .

. . . With all its imperfections, what we have tried to do in South Africa has attracted the attention of the world. This tried, disillusioned, cynical world, hurting so frequently and so grievously, has marveled at a process that holds out considerable hope in the midst of much that negates hope. People . . . see in this flawed attempt a beacon of hope. . . . At the end of their conflicts, the warring groups in Northern Ireland, the Balkans, the Middle East, Sri Lanka, Burma, Afghanistan, Angola, the Sudan, the two Congos, and elsewhere are going to have to sit down together to determine just how they will be able to live together amicably, how they might have a shared future devoid of strife, given the bloody past that they have recently lived through. They see more than just a glimmer of hope in what we have attempted in South Africa.

. . .

QUESTIONS

1. Do you view either the Chilean or South African model as abstractly a 'superior' one, and if so, superior from what perspectives? Or do you conclude that there is no 'one' model, that the design—purposes, functions, powers, methods—of truth commissions is highly context-dependent?

2. Assuming that there were no serious political constraints in South Africa on one or another plan, what changes would you have made in the provisions for the TRC, including amnesty?

3. What is your estimate of the long or short term consequences/effects of the hearings, other processes and Report of the TRC for South African democracy, growth, political stability, and acceptance of each other by the different racial and ethnic groups so as to permit cooperation and peace? Do you view other factors as equally or more important to achieve these goals? How would you assess the significance of the TRC among those other factors?

4. Given the conditions for amnesty in the relevant legislation, do you agree with the decisions in the two amnesty cases? Do you agree with the Amnesty Committee's approach to the notion of a 'political motive', as applied in the Amy Biehl case?

5. Recall that the TRC's provisions for amnesty do not require that the person seeking amnesty apologize, or seek forgiveness. That person must make a full disclosure of the conduct that has led to the request for amnesty. Is apology implicit in full disclosure of violations? Is repentance implicit? Should one or the other have been required by the TRC as a condition to a grant of amnesty with respect to the disclosed conduct?

6. Is forgiveness by the victim, or by relatives of a tortured and murdered victim, in your view essential to the individual and social healing to which Archbishop Tutu refers? Or would apology by the victim be sufficient?

7. What would you imagine forgiveness (understood by Archbishop Tutu in explicitly religious, Christian terms) to entail or represent for a victim—say, with respect to acts of deliberate cruelty directed to the victim and the victims's family with permanent serious consequence? Can a person—say, children of a murdered victim—forgive a perpetrator for the torture and murder of another?

ADDITIONAL READING

N. Kritz (ed.), *Transnational Justice: How Emerging Democracies Reckon with Former Regimes* (3 Vols. 1995); N. Roht-Arriaza (ed.), *Impunity and Human Rights in International Law and Practice* (1995); M. Minow, *Between Vengeance and Forgiveness* (1998).

15

Self-Determination and Autonomy Regimes

The vital concept or right or ideal or vision of self-determination continues to play a major role in political and legal debate. Its place of honor as Article 1 of the two major Covenants itself suggests its status as a 'super rule,' as a concept that stands apart from the normal discourse of rights and directly affects political power and organization within and among states. No one can deny its deep historical significance for several phases of the human rights movement, starting with decolonization and continuing to the contemporary focus on democratization and prominence of ethno-separatist movements. It is a protean concept, rich in meanings that may be appropriated by diverse and even antagonistic actors on the world stage, each for its own purposes. It can represent a grand and noble ideal; it can serve as a weapon in an unadorned and brutal fight for political power. Consider the following comments of Rodolfo Stavenhagen;[1]

> It does not help matters that 'self-determination' means different things to different persons. It is, as one international lawyer asserts, 'one of those unexceptionable goals that can be neither defined nor opposed'. Is it then, a goal, an aspiration, an objective? Or is it a principle, a right? And if the latter, is it only a moral and political right, or is it also a legal right? Is it enforceable? Should it be enforceable? Or is it none of these, or all of these at the same time, and more? . . . [S]elf-determination has become, indeed *is*, a social and political fact in the contemporary world, which we are challenged to understand and master for what it is: an *idee-force* of powerful magnitude, a philosophical stance, a moral value, a social movement, a potent ideology, that may also be expressed, in one of its many guises, as a legal right in international law. Whereas for some the 'self' in self-determination can only be the singular, individual human being, for others the right of collective self-determination, that is, the claim of a group of people to choose the form of government under which they will live, must be treated as a myth in the Levi-Straussian sense (that is, as a blueprint for living); not as an enforceable or enforced legal, political or moral right.

Section A of this Chapter presents readings that offer different perspectives on self-determination and on the 'peoples' that enjoy a right to it. The readings trace the history of the concept, and raise issues that are as contemporary as the conflicts around the globe in the former Yugoslavia, in India and Sri Lanka, in China (Tibet), in Israel and Palestine, in the United Kingdom, in Canada and elsewhere

---

[1] 'Self-Determination: Right or Demon?', IV Law and Society Trust (Issue No. 67, November 1993), at 12.

in the Americas. Many of those conflicts have an ethnic character, involving minorities and indigenous peoples. Many raise an urgent and ultimate question about the principle of self-determination: if, and if so under what conditions, it legitimates secession and creation of a new state or adherence to another existing one.

Three of the readings in Section A are advisory opinions of different types of tribunals: commissions established to advise the Council of the League of Nations on the Aaland Islands dispute after the Second World War, and the 1998 Supreme Court of Canada to which the question of the Quebec secession was referred. The conflicts almost span the last century, from the period of birth of the law and rhetoric of self-determination as we have come to know it, to our own time. One can question whether such 'legal' institutions and opinions provide the best insight into questions so informed by the deepest issues of sovereignty, political power, and democratic government. But the three opinions—surrounded by other diverse readings—sharply illustrate the problems of a court in seeking to separate from its turbulent political context a relatively discrete 'legal' dimension of a self-determination controversy that it can address with some authority. Even assuming that the necessary procedural and jurisdictional understandings were in place, imagine submitting to a court the self-determination issue presented by most of the world's current conflicts involving claims of separation or substantial autonomy by and for a minority group.

Section B briefly examines trends in the human rights movement toward recognition of rights of ethnic minorities and their members within the framework of what some call 'internal self-determination'—that is, forms of self-government and separateness within a state rather than separation (so-called 'external' self-determination) from the state. Those materials stress the character and significance of autonomy regimes—political systems or subsystems organized within a state for purposes of political participation and self-government by ethnic minorities. Together with other related human rights norms, the notion of self-determination continues in these situations to influence the debate over and possible forms of realization of these autonomy regimes.

A. EXTERNAL SELF-DETERMINATION: SOME HISTORY, COMMENTARY, AND DISPUTES

DIANE ORENTLICHER, SEPARATION ANXIETY: INTERNATIONAL RESPONSES TO ETHNO-SEPARATIST CLAIMS
23 Yale J. Int. L. 1 (1998)

[The article explores separatist movements basing their claims on ethnic identity, within the framework of international law's heightened attention to and affirmation of democratic theory and government. The following excerpts introduce the article's themes by sketching the doctrinal background for the nation-state and self-determination in international law.]

I. Introduction

Remapping Europe with explosive force, national movements in the former Yugoslavia dispelled hopes that the liberal peace would replace communism in Eastern Europe and reversed decades of progress in affirming universal principles of humanity. . . . The volcanic fury of ethnic assertion has been global, ranging from Liberia to Sri Lanka, from Chechnya to Rwanda, from Northern Ireland to Kashmir.

Flouting international law's bedrock principle of established states' territorial integrity, national movements from Slovenia to Eritrea have forced international institutions and governments to reckon with, ratify, and in some respects even defend their separatist claims. But while responding in piecemeal fashion, the international community has failed to develop a principled response to secessionist movements. When, if ever, should international law and institutions support separatist claims? When, instead, should the international community defend a state's right to suppress internal movements bent on its dismemberment?. . .

. . .

International law has long been ambivalent in its treatment of national identity as a basis for statehood. . . . In large perspective, international law has in recent decades embraced a cosmopolitan, liberal vision of states, their relationships with their citizens, and their relations with each other. While respect for pluralism within states is part of that vision, liberal internationalists have largely disdained ethnic particularity as an organizing principle of political legitimacy, emphasizing instead liberal republican virtues of civic equality. In similar fashion, global adherence to human rights principles in the postwar decades has affirmed a cosmopolitan faith in universal norms that would displace the parochial values of an obsolete nationalism.

The fulcrum of international law's embrace of liberal values has been its affirmation of democratic governance as a universal entitlement . . . [Its] embrace of democracy fairly raises the question, does the internationally protected right to governance by the consent of the governed include the right to determine the boundaries of political commitment? . . .

. . .

II. The Nation State in History

Two claims dominate arguments in support of separatist claims based on national identity. One rests upon proponents' belief that states whose citizens comprise a national group are relatively stable. This claim tends to support an 'objective' principle of self-determination, which holds that, to the extent possible, the borders of states should correspond with the boundaries of national communities. The second claim asserts the right of groups to control their common destiny by determining the political community to which they owe paramount allegiance. This claim is sometimes associated with a 'subjective' principle of self-determination, which emphasizes groups' right to determine their political community through the exercise of collective will—notably through plebiscite.

. . .

A. Nations and nationalism

. . .

Although problematic, Joseph Stalin's definition provides an instructive point of departure: 'A nation is a historically evolved, stable community of language, territory, economic life, and psychological make-up manifested in a community of culture.' The chief problem with this definition is that it assumes what is often an article of faith on the part of national groups: that the essence of a nation can be captured in objective terms, in which the factual data of history loom large. Yet as chroniclers of nationalism have so often reminded us, attempts to define nations solely in objective terms inevitably fall short. Central to any adequate definition of a nation is a shared sense of communal solidarity—a sentimental identification with the group.

But if subjective will is essential to any definition of nations, it is scarcely possible to define nations solely in subjective terms. An exclusive emphasis on subjectivity would, as E. J. Hobsbawm cautions, 'lead the incautious into extremes of voluntarism which suggests that . . . if enough inhabitants of the Isle of Wight wanted to be a Wightian nation, there would be one.' National consciousness may be a modern artifact, but nationalists cannot invent their histories out of whole cloth.

What features, then, are peculiar to national identity? Are Serbs a nation because of the importance they attach to their Slavic ethnicity? Or is it principally their Eastern Orthodox Christianity that constitutes them as a nation and distinguishes them from ethnically similar Croats and Slavic Muslims?

In this Article, I use the term 'nation' to connote groups that share a sense of group solidarity based on language, lineage, ethnicity, culture, and/or religion and a sense of political community rooted in their group identity. While such a common political identity does not necessarily entail a sense of entitlement to independent statehood, it is of course a necessary basis for the separatist claims. . . .

. . .

. . . In this Article, I use the term 'nationalism' to signify the principle that nations are a proper unit—or, in the doctrine's extreme version, the proper unit—of political organization and also to refer to social movements that are committed to this principle or that act in accordance with it, whether or not pursuant to a well-formulated ideology. This range of meanings is intended to include national movements seeking a political status, such as local autonomy within an established state or independent statehood, regardless of whether the claimants believe that other nations deserve a similar status.

. . .

III. The Nation-State in International Law

While nationalism had a profound influence in political discourse and on the cartography of Europe during the nineteenth and early twentieth centuries, its principles registered only at the margins of international legal doctrine until the interwar period. More particularly, issues of national identity remained largely—though not wholly—irrelevant to determinations of statehood under international law until 1919, when the 'principle of national self-determination' became the touchstone for peacemakers at Versailles.

Pursuant to that principle, the boundaries of new and reconfigured states in Central and Eastern Europe would, to the extent possible, be drawn along national lines, and in that respect the predominantly ethnic strand of nineteenth-century nationalism seemed finally to have triumphed in the peace of Versailles. Further, to the extent that this application of an 'objective' principle of self-determination necessarily relies upon groups' subjective identification of themselves as nations, the vindication of national claims entailed an element of 'subjective' self-determination as well. Finally, by resolving that the fate of some territories would be determined by plebiscite, the Versailles peacemakers explicitly affirmed the strand of self-determination that emphasized popular sovereignty.

But if statesmen were willing to apply the principle of self-determination to the territories they configured at Versailles, states were not yet prepared to recognize self-determination as a legal right. That would have to wait until after the next world war. . . .

. . .

A. The (virtual) irrelevance of nations in international law before 1919

. . . Before 1919, if international law enforced any conception of self-determination, it meant one thing: Established states had a right to be left alone by other states. This principle was the very linchpin of international law from its inception, and it could not have been otherwise. For that law arose, with the advent of sovereign states, as a means of regulating relations among them. . . .

. . .

It was during this period that the statist orientation of international law reached its zenith. A 'fortress-like conception of state sovereignty' formed the basic pillar of international law. . . . This noninterference paradigm of sovereignty served to prevent international law from concerning itself with individuals' right to shape their government within an existing state; much less did it support any people's right to secede from an established state. Accordingly, while international law assured the independence of states—itself a key dimension of self-determination—that right vested only after states already had achieved independence.[2]

Far from legitimizing national aspirations to statehood, international law

---

[2] While postwar law recognizing a right to self-determination has established an important exception, it is still the general rule that entities are entitled to statehood by virtue of acquiring its attributes. The prevailing view in contemporary international law is that statehood is a function of objective conditions, and established states must treat an entity that possesses these qualities as a state regardless of whether they formally recognize it as such. See *Restatement of the Foreign Relations Law of the United States* (1987), at 202(1). In the words of the *Restatement*, 'a state is an entity that has a defined territory and permanent population, under the control of its own government, and that engages in, or has the capacity to engage in, formal relations with other such entities'. *Ibid*. 201. The *Restatement* follows the widely accepted definition set forth in the Montevideo Convention on the Rights and Duties of States, December 26, 1933, Art. I, 49 Stat. 3097, 3100, 165 L.N.T.S. 19, 25.

refused even to address such claims until they had succeeded. . . . [W]hen it came to changes in territory occasioned by the emergence of a new state, international law was essentially indifferent to the mode by which sovereignty was established.

. . . That same [fortress-like] conception of sovereignty also meant that international law would allow governments virtually unfettered sway over . . . questions relating to secession, a process deemed a domestic matter beyond the province of international regulation. Once a separatist movement succeeded in achieving effective independence, the international community would recognize the established facts of statehood, but would not intercede earlier to help secure them.

. . .

C. Dependent territories

A full-blown principle of national self-determination would in fact have been anathema to the major European powers, which retained extensive colonial holdings well into the twentieth century. And so they reconciled their insistence on the principle of noninterference by one state in the affairs of another with their colonial incursions in Africa, Asia, and Latin America by contriving into international law such categories as 'dependent' territories.

Although classical international law had not discriminated on grounds of race or continent, nineteenth-century positivism introduced a distinction between 'civilized nations'—principally the same European powers that created and shaped international law—and others. Importantly, international law bound and protected only the former. This doctrinal move conveniently advanced Europe's acquisition of sovereignty over African territory.

. . .

Finally, international law's insistence on independence as a precondition of statehood served to perpetuate the exclusion of Europe's colonies from the community of states that are full subjects of international law. In effect, subordination of colonial territories by European powers became its own justification. . . . Recognition of the principle of self-determination at the Versailles peace conference did little to change this.

D. The Treaty of Versailles: enthroning the principle of national self-determination . . . ?

. . .

But if the Versailles conference did more in the way of ratifying established facts than fashioning states out of whole cloth, the Western powers nonetheless came to the peace table officially committed to the principle of national self-determination. Outlining the Allies' war aims in his Fourteen Points address, President Woodrow Wilson declared that the 'evident principle . . . of justice to all peoples and nationalities' ran through the 'whole programme.' Soon after, he proclaimed national self-determination to be 'an imperative principle of action,' and indeed that principle became the capstone of the peace settlement. . . .

At Versailles, as at past peace conferences, power politics and strategic considerations played a significant role. . . . [But h]owever much the goal of national self-determination might have been compromised in the face of competing considerations . . . the peacemakers at Versailles officially adopted the principle as their North Star when they set out to remap postwar Europe.

. . .

1. Legal status of the principle of national self-determination

. . . As Wilson readily conceded, there was no attempt to universalize the principle of self-determination to apply, for example, to the Allies' dependent territories. This, Wilson explained, would have to wait for another day. . . .

Wilson hoped to universalize the principle applied in the postwar settlements by incorporating it into the Covenant of the League of Nations, an integral part of the Treaty of Versailles. He proposed a draft provision of article III of the Covenant that would commit the Contracting Powers to effect 'such territorial readjustments, if any, as may in the future become necessary by reason of changes in present racial conditions and aspirations or present social and political relationships, pursuant to the principle of self-determination . . . '. But the proposal encountered powerful opposition, not least among some of Wilson's own advisors, and was defeated.

But if this outcome denied Wilson's principle the immediate force of positive law, it would be a mistake to dismiss the framework established at Versailles as merely a case-specific disposition of territorial issues that left no imprint on international legal doctrine. [To do so obscures] the paradigms of international institutional competence that [the peace settlements] generated—paradigms that continue to influence international responses to nationalism.

2. The principle of self-determination: what did it mean?

While the principle of self-determination had several distinct renderings in the Treaty of Versailles, it meant above all that the new borders of Europe would, to the extent possible, be drawn along national lines. Thus the 'objective' principle of self-determination that had been such a robust force in nineteenth-century Europe became, in the early twentieth century, a principle for state-making, at least in the context of a peace settlement. . . . In this respect the Paris peace conference inverted the state-to-nation progression that had been characteristic of the formation of Western European nation-states.[3]

. . .

More consequentially, in several important respects the Treaty of Versailles gave explicit effect to the 'subjective' principle of self-determination. In some disputed regions, such as Upper Silesia and Schleswig, the fate of a territory and its population would be determined by an internationally supervised plebiscite. Still, the plebiscite principle played only a supporting role in the peace settlement; despite the importance President Wilson had attached earlier to the subjective principle of

---

[3] To the extent that congruence between nationality and state territory could not be fully achieved, national groups that consequently would form a minority in a new or reconfigured state received special protections through minority rights undertakings, whose implementation would be supervised by various organs of the League of Nations. [Eds. The minorities regime created in Central and East Europe after the First World War is described at pp. 93–103, *supra*.]

self-determination, the peace treaties provided for plebiscites only to resolve the fate of several disputed border regions.

. . .

. . . [T]he question [of self-determination] is even more complex . . . Who are the members of the 'race' or 'community,' and how is membership determined? How does one establish the relationship between a group and territory when there have been significant transfers of population? In these situations, how does one establish the appropriate baseline date for distinguishing between inhabitants entitled to participate in an exercise of self-determination and those deemed 'settlers' who are to be excluded? How, in any case, should a population's wishes be ascertained? Should there be plebiscites in every case? Who may vote—just those who might secede, or also other inhabitants of a territory from which the former might secede? Where plebiscites are held, should their results have lasting effect, or should the relevant population be allowed to change its mind in light of changes in its identity and desires over time?. . .

Several participants and observers voiced more fundamental concerns. Even if narrowly defined to sidestep some of these conundrums, a principle of self-determination could prove endlessly destabilizing if validated by international law. [A United States official at the Versailles conference] evoked a specter that continues to influence international responses to separatist claims: 'No tribal entity was too small to have ambitions for self-determination.'

. . .

As Nathaniel Berman's scholarship has elucidated, the interwar period was one of extraordinary experimentalism in international institutional and legal responses to these and other dilemmas presented by nationalist claims. . . .

[The author then discusses the Aaland Islands dispute, examined at p. 1257, *infra*.]

. . .

E. Self-determination: decolonization

. . .

. . . In many respects, international law experienced a fundamental disruption with the onset of World War II, and the principle of self-determination might have seemed a leading candidate for entombment as a manifest failure of the interwar system. Yet it was impossible to contain the concept's mobilizing power in the ensuing years and decades. The principle (later 'right') reappeared across decades in a raft of international instruments, the legitimacy of its inclusion no longer subject to serious challenge—but its meaning periodically subject to renewed contention.

The Charter of the United Nations gave a prominent place to the 'principle of self-determination,' yet the sponsoring countries could not agree on the meaning of this conveniently ambiguous phrase. . . .

. . .

. . . The 'principle of self-determination of peoples' was a natural banner for the decolonization movement that swept the globe in the early decades of the United Nations's life, and it took little time for this principle, previously associated with the right of subject nationalities to form their own state, to metamorphose into a right of colonial territories to break free of the metropolitan state.

In 1950, the General Assembly adopted the first of what would be many resolutions recognizing 'the right of peoples and nations to self-determination' as fundamental. . . . [Eds. Excerpts from several resolutions, declarations and treaties that refer to self-determination are set forth at p. 1265, *infra*.]

. . .

It was not just established states that were eager narrowly to define the right of self-determination as a right end colonial status. The newly independent states of Africa were keen to erect a breakwater against the spread of secessionist proclivities to subgroups in their territories. And so, with the dawning of decolonization in its continent, the Organization of African Unity adhered to the principle of *uti possidetis*, developed a century earlier when Latin American states acquired independence from Spain. That principle 'upgraded former administrative delimitations, established during the colonial period, to international frontiers', thereby assuring their sanctity as state borders. It also provided a bright line test for assessing claims to self-determination—one that could be rationalized more readily in terms of international stability concerns than of political philosophy.

. . .

In the postwar era, then, international law finally elevated self-determination to the status it had been denied by the League of Nations—a rule of international law. . . .

But if these aspects of postwar law seemed to augment both the status and compass of the principle of self-determination, its coupling with the principle of *uti possidetis* severely contracted its reach. If anything, *uti possidetis* reinforced the ultrastatist view of nineteenth-century law, which regarded the state as a virtually impenetrable fortress. More fundamentally, by defining the 'self' entitled to exercise the right in strictly territorial terms, the postwar rendering of self-determination drained the principle of its rich interwar meaning Self-determination thus was transformed from a principle for state-making into a corrective to the historical injustice of alien subjugation. Through this legal alchemy, international law could claim to preserve a principle that had acquired a potent symbolic power while simultaneously depriving that principle of its power to threaten established states' territorial boundaries.

Yet even the postwar rendering of self-determination is more complex doctrinally than is suggested in its common characterization as a right of 'external' self-determination—that is, a right of territorially defined peoples to emancipation from imperial rule. As elaborated by the United Nations, peoples entitled to self-determination could not only cast off their metropolitan overlords but also determine their political status through the exercise of collective will. General Assembly Resolution 1541 (XV) notes that available options in this regard include independent statehood, free association with an independent state, and integration with an independent state. . . . In an important opinion on the postwar law of decolonization [Western Sahara, 1975 I.C.J. 12, 25 (January 1)], the International Court of Justice defined the principle of self-determination as 'the need to pay regard to the expressed will of peoples' after first making clear that the right was, in essence, a right of decolonization.

In its postwar incarnation, the principle of self-determination has now largely accomplished its assigned task. Yet an array of scholars and advocates are reluctant to retire the right and have earnestly sought to find it new work. A significant measure of scholarly support has begun to coalesce around the view that self-determination should once again be invested with new meaning, this time emphasizing its internal dimension—democratic governance.

. . . But as I argue in Part IV, the implications of international law's recent validation of democratic rights cannot readily be confined to those relating to internal self-determination. For the right to choose one's government inevitably raises the question, may people choose—or reject—the state in which they will exercise the right to govern themselves?

. . .

REPORT OF INTERNATIONAL COMMISSION OF JURISTS ON LEGAL ASPECTS OF THE AALAND ISLANDS QUESTION
League of Nations Official Journal, Spec. Supp. No. 3, at 3 (1920)

[At the end of the First World War (referred to below as the Great War), Finland and Sweden, both members of the League of Nations, were engaged in a dispute over the Aaland Islands. Article 15 of the Covenant of the League provides that disputes between members of the League should in certain circumstances be submitted to the Council of the League, which could hear the facts and make recommendations. Under paragraph 8 of that article, if the Council found the dispute to arise out of a matter that by international law was solely within the 'domestic jurisdiction' of a party to the dispute, the Council should so report and therefore make no recommendation.[4]

In 1920 the Council of the League adopted a resolution to the effect that an International Commission of Jurists should be appointed to submit to the Council its advisory opinion whether the dispute presented to it by Sweden dealt with a question that under international law should be left to the 'domestic jurisdiction' of Finland. Three professors (from France, the Netherlands and Switzerland) were appointed as the jurists. Finland's claim of domestic jurisdiction would, if found valid, deprive the League of jurisdiction to entertain the merits of Sweden's claim that the inhabitants of the Aaland Islands should be authorized to determine by plebiscite whether the archipelago should remain under Finnish jurisdiction or be incorporated into the Kingdom of Sweden.

Excerpts from the Report of the Commission of Jurists to the Council follow:]

---

[4] The Comment at p. 588, *supra*, examines the concept of domestic jurisdiction in its later incarnation in Article 2(7) of the UN Charter, and describes its erosion over recent decades.

The question really takes this form: can the inhabitants of the Aaland Islands, as at present situated, and taking as a basis the principle that peoples must have the right of self-determination, request to be united to Sweden? Can Sweden, on her side, claim that a plebiscite should take place in order to give the inhabitants of the Islands the opportunity of recording their wish with regard to their union with Sweden or continuance under Finnish rule?

Although the principle of self-determination of peoples plays an important part in modern political thought, especially since the Great War, it must be pointed out that there is no mention of it in the Covenant of the League of Nations. The recognition of this principle in a certain number of international treaties cannot be considered as sufficient to put it upon the same footing as a positive rule of the Law of Nations.

On the contrary, in the absence of express provisions in international treaties, the right of disposing of national territory is essentially an attribute of the sovereignty of every State. Positive International Law does not recognize the right of national groups, as such, to separate themselves from the State of which they form part by the simple expression of a wish, any more than it recognizes the right of other States to claim such a separation. Generally speaking, the grant or refusal of the right to a portion of its population of determining its own political fate by plebiscite or by some other method, is, exclusively, an attribute of the sovereignty of every State which is definitively constituted. A dispute between two States concerning such a question, under normal conditions therefore, bears upon a question which International Law leaves entirely to the domestic jurisdiction of one of the States concerned. Any other solution would amount to an infringement of sovereign rights of a State and would involve the risk of creating difficulties and a lack of stability which would not only be contrary to the very idea embodied in the term 'State,' but would also endanger the interests of the international community. If this right is not possessed by a large or small section of a nation, neither can it be held by the State to which the National group wishes to be attached, nor by any other State.

The Commission, in affirming these principles, does not give an opinion concerning the question as to whether a manifest and continued abuse of sovereign power, to the detriment of a section of the population of a State, would, if such circumstances arose, give to an international dispute, arising therefrom, such a character that its object should be considered as one which is not confined to the domestic jurisdiction of the State concerned, but comes within the sphere of action of the League of Nations. Such a supposition certainly does not apply to the case under consideration, and has not been put forward by either of the parties to the dispute.

[The Report then stated that its prior observations about sovereignty applied only to a nation 'definitively constituted' as a sovereign state and thus 'an independent member of the international community'. Often this condition to sovereignty is lacking. Revolutions and wars bring about the 'formation, transformation and dismemberment' of states. They thereby create 'situations of fact' to which the 'normal rules of positive law' cannot apply. When in such situations the essential basis of 'territorial sovereignty' is lacking or confused, 'the situation is obscure and uncertain from a legal point of view'. Clarity must await the establishment of a new situation that is 'normal in respect to territorial sovereignty'.]

This transition from a *de facto* situation to a normal situation *de jure* cannot be considered as one confined entirely within the domestic jurisdiction of a State. It tends to lead to readjustments between the members of the international community and to alterations in their territorial and legal status; consequently, this transition interests the community of States very deeply both from political and legal standpoints.

Under such circumstances, the principle of self-determination of peoples may be called into play. New aspirations of certain sections of a nation, which are sometimes based on old traditions or on a common language and civilization, may come to the surface and produce effects which must be taken into account in the interests of the internal and external peace of nations.

The principle recognizing the rights of peoples to determine their political fate may be applied in various ways; the most important of these are, on the one hand the formation of an independent State, and on the other hand the right of choice between two existing States. This principle, however, must be brought into line with that of the protection of minorities; both have a common object—to assure to some national Group the maintenance and free development of its social, ethnical or religious characteristics.

The protection of minorities is already provided for, to a very varying extent, in a fairly large number of constitutions. This principle appears to be one of the essential characteristics of liberty at the present time. Under certain circumstances, however, it has been thought necessary to go further, and to guarantee, by international treaties, some particular situation to certain racial or religious minorities. Thus, in some recent treaties a special legal régime, under the control and guarantee of the League of Nations, has been established for certain sections of the population of a State.

The fact must, however, not be lost sight of that the principle that nations must have the right of self-determination is not the only one to be taken into account. Even though it be regarded as the most important of the principles governing the formation of States, geographical, economic and other similar considerations may put obstacles in the way of its complete recognition. Under such circumstances, a solution in the nature of a compromise, based on an extensive grant of liberty to minorities, may appear necessary according to international legal conception and may even be dictated by the interests of peace.

[The two preceding paragraphs, in their mention of a 'special legal régime' of treaties under the 'guarantee of the League of Nations' and 'an extensive grant of liberty to minorities', refer to the minority treaties and declarations set up after the First World War in Central and Eastern Europe and discussed at pp. 93–103, *supra.*

The Report went on to summarize the complex recent history of the area involving the people of the Aaland Islands, Sweden, Russia, and the turbulent military and political events of the First World War. The Aaland Islands had earlier belonged to Sweden but were absorbed by Russia, as was Finland, by conquest in the early nineteenth century. During this period of Russian rule, the Aaland Islands were viewed as part of Finland. Finland declared its independence from Russia at the time of the Russian revolution in 1917, when a Bolshevik manifesto proclaimed the right of self-determination (deciding their own future) of all peoples not of the Russian race. Finland attained independence in 1918, and argued that the Aaland Islands had been incorporated into it. At the Paris Peace Conference, representatives of the Aaland Islands invoked President Wilson's argument for the right of peoples to self-determination and sought annexation to Sweden.

After reviewing these events, the International Commission stressed the transformations in territory and sovereignty which they brought about, and the interests of several states in such matters.]

The Commission, after consideration of the arguments set out and developed in the preceding report, have arrived at the following conclusions:—

(1) The dispute between Sweden and Finland does not refer to a definitive established political situation, depending exclusively upon the territorial sovereignty of a State.

(2) On the contrary, the dispute arose from a *de facto* situation caused by the political transformation of the Aaland Islands, which transformation was caused by and originated in the separatist movement among the inhabitants, who quoted the principle of national self-determination, and certain military events which accompanied and followed the separation of Finland from the Russian Empire at a time when Finland had not yet acquired the character of a definitively constituted State.

(3) It follows from the above that the dispute does not refer to a question which is left by International Law to the domestic jurisdiction of Finland.

(4) The Council of the League of Nations, therefore, is competent, under paragraph 4 of Article 15, to make any recommendations which it deems just and proper in the case.

. . .

REPORT OF COMMISSION OF RAPPORTEURS ON THE AALAND ISLANDS QUESTION
League of Nations Doc. B7 21/68/106 (1921)

NOTE

[After receiving the Report of the International Commission of Jurists, the Council of the League then appointed a second body, a Commission of Rapporteurs, to examine Sweden's petition. That Commission submitted to the Council its own Report on The Aaland Islands Question. The Reports of the two Commissions, while agreeing that self-determination of peoples was not a general rule of international law and while showing similar sensibilities to the claims of the local population, differed in basic respects in their approach to the issues. The few excerpts below from the Report of the Commission of Rapporteurs address themes that figure in the excerpts above from the Report of the earlier Commission.]

The enquiry which we have made, by virtue of this mandate, has given us the absolute conviction that the only method to adopt in order to obtain a solution of the question in accordance with these lofty views, is to entrust it to impartial examination by the Council. It is therefore within its rights in declaring its competence. Although we cannot share the opinion stated by the Commission of Jurists on all points, we agree with their declaration that the Aaland question is one that extends beyond the sphere of domestic policy. But, in our opinion, it is because it had acquired such considerable international importance that it was necessary to submit it to the high authority which the League of Nations represents in the eyes of the world. On its equitable settlement depend, not only the re-establishment of the spirit of peace where feeling has been running high among this interesting Baltic population, and the resumption of the good relations which should exist between two nations which have all the conditions for a mutual understanding, Sweden and Finland, but also the consolidation of the peace which the population of this part of Europe need as much as others to efface the deep traces left by the war, to reconstitute their forces of production and to establish their economic development upon solid foundations.

. . .

Before discussing the right of the Aalanders to have recourse to a plebiscite, we must review the motives which have aroused their intense desire for re-incorporation with Sweden.

. . .

It would, however, be a grave mistake to assign purely political grounds for the wish of the Aalanders: that would be a misconception of its true character. For them reunion with their former mother-country is above all a question of nationality. In Sweden they see the natural guardian of their language, their customs, their immemorial traditions, of which they are proud and to which they are attached above everything else. Even more than Russian domination they fear Finnish domination, which would lead to their gradual denationalisation, the absorption of their population, which has remained free from all ethnical mixture, by a race of whose language they are ignorant and whose invasion they abhor. Statistics, which are very suggestive, have been shown us regarding the expansion of the Finnish race, which advances regularly towards the west, towards the coast and the neighbouring island groups where there is a shortage of labour. In Finland the Finns to-day form nine-tenths of the population, and as compared with their Swedish fellow-citizens they have the advantage of a higher birth-rate, with the result that the disproportion between the two races becomes yearly more accentuated in favour of the Finns. In 1885 the Finns comprised 85% and the Swedes 14% of the total population: in 1900 the proportion was 87% of the former to 12½% of the latter: in 1910 89% to 11%. When we add that Sweden is nearer Aaland than the mainland of Finland, it is quite easy to understand the part played by the instinct of self-preservation, as well as a genuine attachment sprung from memories of the past, their Swedish extraction and their constant relations. They have caused these peasants and sailors, confined at the extremity of Finnish territory in an isolation well calculated to develop a pronouncedly insular mentality and an essentially local patriotism, to look towards Sweden.

. . .

[The principle of self determination] is not, properly speaking a rule of international law. . . . It is a principle of justice and of liberty, expressed by a vague and general formula which has given rise to the most varied interpretations and differences of opinion. . . .

. . .

. . . Is it possible to admit as an absolute rule that a minority of the population of a State, which is definitely constituted and perfectly capable of fulfilling its duties as such, has the right of separating itself from her in order to be incorporated in another State or to declare its independence? The answer can only be in the negative. To concede to minorities, either of language or religion, or to any fractions of a population the right of withdrawing from the community to which they belong, because it is their wish or their good pleasure, would be to destroy order and stability within States and to inaugurate anarchy in international life; it would be to uphold a theory incompatible with the very idea of the State as a territorial and political entity.

The idea of justice and of liberty, embodied in the formula of self-determination, must be applied in a reasonable manner to the relations between States and the minorities they include. It is just that the ethnical character and the ancient traditions of these minorities should be respected as much as possible, and that they should be specially authorised to practise freely their religion and to cultivate their language. This postulate marks one of the most noble advances of modern civilisation and, as it is clear that there can be no lasting peace apart from justice, constitutes one of the most powerful means of strengthening peace and combating hatred and dissensions both within the State and in international relations. But what reasons would there be for allowing a minority to separate itself from the State to which it is united, if this State gives it the guarantees which it is within its rights in demanding, for the preservation of its social, ethnical or religious character? Such indulgence, apart from every political consideration, would be supremely unjust to the State prepared to make these concessions.

The separation of a minority from the State of which it forms a part and its incorporation in another State can only be considered as an altogether exceptional solution, a last resort when the State lacks either the will or the power to enact and apply just and effective guarantees.

In the case of the Aalanders, the important question is the protection of their language—the Swedish language. Its language is the very soul of people. We appreciate the ardent desire, the resolute wish of the Aaland population, proud in its democratic simplicity and eager for independence, to preserve intact the Swedish language and culture—their heritage from their ancestors. . . .

In spite of the lively sympathy with which the Aalanders inspired us, we yet cannot, in view of the heavy responsibility which is laid on us, accede to their request.

. . . If it were true that incorporation with Sweden was the only means of preserving its Swedish language for Aaland, we should not have hesitated to consider this solution. But such is not the case. Thee is no need for a separation. The Finnish State is ready to grant the inhabitants satisfactory guarantees and faithfully to observe the engagement which it will enter into with them: of this we have no doubt. To take the Aaland Islands away from Finland in these circumstances would be the more unjust inasmuch as from the point of view of history, geography and politics, all the arguments militate in favour of the *status quo*.

. . .

[The Report had suggested certain protections for the Aaland Island population, to be guaranteed by the League of Nations, that would assure their cultural autonomy as part of Finland. It stated that a different situation with respect to self-determination would arise if Finland refused to grant that population the detailed guarantees. In such circumstances, the Rapporteurs would advise the separation of the islands from Finland if this wish were freely expressed by the population by means of a plebiscite. In so stating, the Report of Rapporteurs went well beyond the earlier Report.]

NATHANIEL BERMAN, 'BUT THE ALTERNATIVE IS DESPAIR': EUROPEAN NATIONALISM AND THE MODERNIST RENEWAL OF INTERNATIONAL LAW
106 Harv. L. Rev. 1792 (1993), at 1872

[This excerpt compares the preceding opinions of the two Commissions in the Aaland Islands dispute.]

The Jurists and the Rapporteurs presented two versions of the new international law. . . . Both commissions expanded the competence of international law at the expense of sovereignty, but their emphases lay in opposed directions. The Jurists' innovation lay in their stress on the movement 'downward,' according legal recognition to those forces emerging 'from below the surface.' The Rapporteurs, by contrast, emphasized the augmentation of international law through the unprecedented powers given to the 'high authority' of the organized community.

The Jurists would accord previously legally nonexistent groups the right, under certain circumstances, to displace territorial sovereigns. They limited this opening of the international legal forum to nonstate groups in three ways, however. First, such access could only be provided in the face of extraordinary historical disruption. Moreover, the international tribunal, though deriving its authority from nationalist disruptions, could balance the claims of such groups with other considerations; in particular, it could grant minority protection instead of self-determination. Finally, this process was teleologically directed toward the restoration of the 'normal' situation: a system grounded in sovereignty.

Nevertheless, the Jurists implicitly envisioned a repeatedly renewed oscillation between the traditional and innovative jurisprudential maps. Each exercise of self-determination would be an extraordinary, one-time affair, after which the veil of sovereignty would regain its immunity from critical international legal scrutiny. However, new cases could continually arise, provoking new shifts from one jurisprudential map to the other. Thus, the history of international law would henceforth consist of an alternation between two 'incompatible' conceptions.

By contrast, the Rapporteurs were loath to countenance any attack on the system of sovereignty by nationalist desires bubbling up from below. Rather, the Rapporteurs attenuated the privileges of sovereignty primarily in favor of the international community. International society, under this conception, consisted of a newly organized system of sovereigns subordinate to the 'high authority' of the League; the sub-sovereign strata could not be granted extraordinary powers of initiative. The power of the community did not derive spasmodically from the vagaries of popular passion but from its constant, self-evident 'high authority.'

This conception of the augmented power of the community worked a profound transformation in the notion of sovereignty, a transformation seen in the system of minority protection favored by the Rapporteurs. In such a system, sovereigns would generally be maintained on the land they effectively controlled. However, their conduct would be subject to ongoing regulation and supervision by the community. Minority protection was no one-shot affair like a plebiscite; it effected the permanent embroidering of the sovereign into the fabric of the international legal community. The sovereign would not be divested of control, except in extreme circumstances; yet its exercise of that control, would be subject to substantial restrictions.

Although the Rapporteurs stressed the 'upward' movement of the expansion of international law, the 'downward' movement was also crucial to their conception. The system of minority protection consisted precisely in the international community's ability to intervene in matters concerning groups formerly invisible behind the veil of sovereignty. Moreover, the Rapporteurs asserted the community's right to grant a group's wish to secede from its state, should circumstances demand. Secession is thus a policy tool of the community, not an inherent right of the separatist group.

. . .

QUESTIONS

1. In the Report of the Commission of Jurists, 'normal' international law (that is, in 'normal circumstances of state sovereignty') would leave the issue before the Commission to states. What is the function of international law in situations that are not 'normal'? Could bodies charged with applying international law then take account of the self-determination principle? If so, what significance would desires of a local ethnic group have? What other considerations become relevant to a decision based on international law?

2. In the view of this Commission, what facts and factors must underlie the claim of a local population to some form of self-determination in order to give that claim credibility and formal significance?

3. In the Report of the Commission of Rapporteurs, why does this dispute raise issues of international law rather than remain a matter of domestic jurisdiction of Finland? What gives the claim of the Aaland Islanders legal and political significance? To what extent, and under what conditions, is their claim recognized?

UNITED NATIONS RELATED TEXTS ON SELF-DETERMINATION

[The opinions in the Aaland Islands dispute explored general principles of international law and customary law. They did not rely on authoritative texts. There were none. Current debate (generally, not invariably) proceeds from and argues on the basis of the following texts, even if recourse to later practice and to motivations for that practice is indispensable for the interpretation and elaboration of these texts.]

United Nations Charter

Article 1(2): [The Purposes of the United Nations are to] develop friendly relations among nations based on respect for the principle of equal rights and self-determination of peoples, and to take other appropriate measures to strengthen universal peace.

Article 55: With a view to the creation of conditions of stability and well-being which are necessary for peaceful and friendly relations among nations based on respect for the principle of equal rights and self-determination of peoples, the United Nations shall promote [higher standards of living; solutions of economic-social problems; and universal respect for and observance of human rights].

[1960] Declaration on the Granting of Independence to Colonial Countries and Peoples

G.A. Res. 1514 (XV), Dec. 14, 1960

The General Assembly . . . Declares that:

1. The subjection of peoples to alien subjugation, domination and exploitation constitutes a denial of fundamental human rights, is contrary to the Charter of the United Nations and is an impediment to the promotion of world peace and co-operation.

2. All peoples have the right to self-determination; by virtue of that right they freely determine their political status and freely pursue their economic, social and cultural development.

. . .

4. All armed action or repressive measures of all kinds directed against dependent peoples shall cease in order to enable them to exercise peacefully and freely their right to complete independence, and the integrity of their national territory shall be respected.

. . .

7. All States shall observe faithfully and strictly the provisions of the Charter of the United Nations, the Universal Declaration of Human Rights and the present Declaration on the basis of equality, noninterference in the internal affairs of all States, and respect for the sovereign rights of all peoples and their territorial integrity.

[1970] Declaration on Principles of International Law Concerning Friendly Relations and Co-operation among States in Accordance with the Charter of the United Nations

G.A. Res. 2625 (XXV), Oct. 24, 1970

The General Assembly . . .

. . .

1. Solemnly proclaims the following principles:

. . .

The principle concerning the duty not to intervene in matters within the domestic jurisdiction of any State, in accordance with the Charter

. . .

> The use of force to deprive peoples of their national identity constitutes a violation of their inalienable rights and of the principle of non-intervention. Every state has an inalienable right to choose its political, economic, social and cultural systems, without interference in any form by another State.

. . .

The principle of equal rights and self-determination of peoples

> By virtue of the principle of equal rights and self-determination of peoples enshrined in the Charter of the United Nations, all peoples have the right freely to determine, without external interference, their political status and to pursue their economic, social and cultural development, and every State has the duty to respect this right in accordance with the provisions of the Charter. Every State has the duty to promote, through joint and several action, realization of the principle of equal rights and self-determination of peoples, in accordance with the provisions of the Charter . . . .
>
> . . .
>
> The establishment of a sovereign and independent State, the free association

or integration with an independent State or the emergence into any other political status freely determined by a people constitute modes of implementing the right of self-determination by that people.

. . .

Nothing in the foregoing paragraphs shall be construed as authorizing or encouraging any action which would dismember or impair, totally or in part, the territorial integrity or political unity of sovereign and independent States conducting themselves in compliance with the principle of equal rights and self-determination of peoples as described above and thus possessed of a government representing the whole people belonging to the territory without distinction as to race, creed or colour.

Every State shall refrain from any action aimed at the partial or total disruption of the national unity and territorial integrity of any other State or country.

. . .

3. Declares further that:

The principles of the Charter which are embodied in this Declaration constitute basic principles of international law, and consequently appeals to all States to be guided by these principles in their international conduct and to develop their mutual relations on the basis of the strict observance of these principles.

International Covenant on Civil and Political Rights

(Approved by General Assembly in 1966, entered into force 1976)

Article 1:

1. All peoples have the right of self-determination. By virtue of that right they freely determine their political status and freely pursue their economic, social and cultural development.

2. All peoples may, for their own ends, freely dispose of their natural wealth and resources without prejudice to any obligations arising out of international economic co-operation, based upon the principle of mutual benefit, and international law. In no case may a people be deprived of its own means of subsistence.

3. The States Parties to the present Covenant . . . shall promote the realization of the right of self-determination, and shall respect that right, in conformity with the provisions of the Charter of the United Nations.

International Covenant on Economic, Social and Cultural Rights

(Approved by General Assembly in 1966, entered into force 1976)

Article 1 is identical with Article 1 of the ICCPR.

NOTE

The precise term 'self-determination', absent from the Covenant of the League of Nations and other major international instruments in the interwar period, achieved prominence from the time of its mention in the UN Charter. The remaining materials in Section A refer to other important documents on self-determination, such as the Vienna Declaration emerging from the 1993 UN World Conference on Human Rights.

Several features of the declarations and treaties following the Charter should be noted.

(1) Although they elaborate to some degree the conception of self-determination simply stated in the Charter, none of them expounds the vital term, 'peoples'.

(2) The tension between peoples' right to self-determination and states' right to territorial integrity figures in all these instruments.

(3) The 1970 Declaration alone among these instruments raises the basic issue of conditions that may legitimate a claim for self-deteremination, even one taking the form of secession. This question of legitimating conditions, if any, remains central to current debate about self-determination.

(4) One continuing dilemma about self-determination, noted at the end of the *Quebec* opinion below, came early to the surface, during the period of decolonization. The ICCPR and ICESCR reach beyond the earlier 1960 Declaration's stress on decolonization to imagine self-determination as an ongoing phenomenon—one that could, in principle, affect a part or parts of the varied populations of all states, including post-colonial states that had drawn on that very concept in the struggle for their own sovereign independence.

Consider in this connection the Indian reservation to Article 1 of the ICCPR and ICESCR:

> ... [T]he Government of India declares that the words 'the right of self-determination' appearing [in Article 1 of both Covenants] apply only to the peoples under foreign domination and that these worlds do not apply to sovereign independent States or to a section of a people or nation—which is the essence of national integrity.

Several states objected to this reservation. Germany stated in its formal objection:

> The right of self-determination. . .applies to all peoples and not only to those under foreign domination. . . . [A]ny limitation of [these provisions'] applicability to all nations is incompatible with the object and purposes of the Covenants.

MARTTI KOSKENNIEMI, NATIONAL SELF-DETERMINATION TODAY: PROBLEMS OF LEGAL THEORY AND PRACTICE
43 Int. & Comp. L.Q. 241 (1994), at 245

In the first place, national self-determination acts as a *justification* of a State-centred international order. . . . As the 1970 Friendly Relations Declaration puts it, all peoples have the right freely to determine, without external interference, their political status. A people choosing to live as a State has the perfect right to do so and in such case 'every State has the duty to respect this right'. Without a principle that entitles—or perhaps even requires—groups of people to start minding their own business within separately organized 'States', it is difficult to think how state-hood and everything that we connect with it—political independence, territorial integrity and legal sovereignty—can be legitimate. As a background principle, self-determination expresses the political phenomenon of State patriotism and explains why we in general endow acts of foreign States with legal validity even when we do not agree with their content and why we think there is a strong argument against intervening in other States' political processes.

This idea of national self-determination as a patriotic concept, a justification of statehood, has not always been apparent. Much of the classical positivist writing has simply accepted States as the factual foundation of international law. The need to look behind States—into self-determination—however, becomes necessary when statehood itself is or becomes uncertain.

. . .

. . . A Hungarian writer has claimed that national self-determination 'is the most important basic ideological principle of the 1990s'. But it is more: it is a legal-constitutional principle that claims to offer a principal (if not the only) basis on which political entities can be constituted, and among which international rela-tions can again be conducted 'normally'. The centrality of the State to the political order becomes comprehensible only if we regard it as the formal, political shell for which nationhood provides the substance.

But of course there is another sense of national self-determination which far from supporting the formal structures of statehood provides a *challenge* to them. According to this sense, true self-determination is not expressed in the normal functioning of existing participating processes and in the duty of other States not to interfere but in the existence and free cultivation of an authentic communal feeling, a togetherness, a sense of being 'us' among the relevant group. If, in extreme cases, this may be possible only by leaving the State, then the necessity turns into a right.

. . .

National self-determination, then, has an ambiguous relationship with state-hood as the basis of the international legal order. On the one hand, it supports statehood by providing a connecting explanation for why we should honour exist-ing *de facto* boundaries and the acts of the State's power-holders as something other than gunman's orders. On the other hand, it explains that statehood *per se* embodies no particular virtue and that even as it is useful as a presumption about the authority of a particular territorial rule, that presumption may be overruled or its consequences modified in favour of a group or unit finding itself excluded from those positions of authority in which the substance of the rule is determined.

The extraordinary difficulties into which an attempt at a *consistent* application of the principle leads stem from the paradox that it both supports and challenges statehood and that it is impossible to establish a general preference between its patriotic and secessionist senses.

. . .

FREDERIC KIRGIS, JR., THE DEGREES OF SELF-DETERMINATION IN THE UNITED NATIONS ERA
88 Am. J. Int. L. 304 (1994), at 306

. . .

[The disclaimer in the 1970 Declaration on Friendly Relations] referred only to a government representing the whole people belonging to the territory without distinction as to race, creed or color. The disclaimer was reiterated in the Vienna Declaration emanating from the 1993 UN World Conference on Human Rights, with one significant change. The Vienna Declaration exempted only 'a Government representing the whole people belonging to the territory without distinction *of any kind*'. These disclaimers are a far cry from the General Assembly's formulation in 1960, when it said: 'Any attempt aimed at the partial or total disruption of the national unity and the territorial integrity of a country is incompatible with the purposes and principles of the Charter of the United Nations'.

Of course, these are non binding instruments. Nevertheless, they purport to, and probably do, reflect an *opinio juris*. In the human rights field, a strong showing of *opinio juris* may overcome a weak demonstration of state practice to establish a customary rule. . . .

An arguable, limited right of secession is only one of the numerous faces of self-determination. Mentioned below are the more prominent ones that have appeared. Of course, some of them remain quite controversial because of disagreement either over what is meant by 'peoples' or over what is meant by self-determination itself. The many faces include:

(1) The established right to be free from colonial domination, with plenty of well-known examples in Africa, Asia and the Caribbean.
(2) The converse of that—a right to remain dependent, if it represents the will of the dependent people who occupy a defined territory. . . .
(3) The right to dissolve a state, at least if done peacefully, and to form new states on the territory of the former one, as in the former Soviet Union and Czechoslovakia. The breakup of the former Yugoslavia except for Serbia and Montenegro might even be considered an example of this, after the initial skirmish in Slovenia ended and the Yugoslav federal forces ceased operating as such in Croatia and Bosnia-Hercegovina. The

later fighting in Croatia and Bosnia-Hercegovina could be seen as efforts not so much to hold the old state of Yugoslavia together as to define the territories and ethnic composition of the new states, including possible new states within Bosnia-Hercegovina.

(4) The disputed right to secede, as in the case of Bangladesh and Eritrea.

(5) The right of divided states to be reunited, as in Germany.

(6) The right of limited autonomy, short of secession, for groups defined territorially or by common ethnic, religious and linguistic bonds—as in autonomous areas within confederations.

(7) Rights of minority groups within a larger political entity, as recognized in Article 27 of the Covenant on Civil and Political Rights and in the General Assembly's 1992 Declaration on the Rights of Persons Belonging to National or Ethnic, Religious and Linguistic Minorities.

(8) The internal self-determination freedom to choose one's form of government, or even more sharply, the right to a democratic form of government, as in Haiti.

. . . Clearly, the right to be free from alien colonial control is an established rule of international law. One cannot categorically say the same about the other manifestations. Their juridical status varies. Nevertheless, we can make some headway toward evaluating each claim. . . . [W]e can try to identify key variables that reduce the vast complexity of the problem to a manageable form and can serve as rough predictors for normative assessment of claims as they are made.

The key variables can be found in the [General Assembly's 1970 Declaration and the 1993 Vienna Declaration]. . . . Dismemberment is at the end of a scale of claims, ranging from modest to extremely destabilizing, that includes all of those listed above. Moreover, as there are degrees of claim, there are degrees of representative government, with absolute dictatorship and all-inclusive democracy at the opposite extremes.

One can thus discern degrees of self-determination, with the legitimacy of each tied to the degree of representative government in the state. The relationship is inverse between the degree of representative government, on one hand, and the extent of destabilization that the international community will tolerate in a self-determination claim, on the other. If a government is at the high end of the scale of democracy, the only self-determination claims that will be given international credence are those with minimal destabilizing effect. If a government is extremely unrepresentative, much more destabilizing self-determination claims may well be recognized.

In this schema, a claim of right to secede from a representative democracy is not likely to be considered a legitimate exercise of the right of self-determination, but a claim of right by indigenous groups within the democracy to use their own languages and engage in their own noncoercive cultural practices is likely to be recognized—not always under the rubric of self-determination, but recognized nevertheless. Conversely, a claim of a right to secede from a repressive dictatorship *may* be regarded as legitimate. Not all secessionist claims are equally destabilizing. The degree to which a claimed right to secede will be destabilizing may depend on

such things as the plausibility of the historical claim of secessionist group to the
territory it seeks to slice off.

. . .

GREGORY FOX, SELF-DETERMINATION IN THE POST-COLD WAR ERA: A NEW INTERNAL FOCUS?
16 Mich. J. Int'l L. 733 (1995), at 743

[These excerpts consider a fundamental question about the legal status of self-
determination (with respect to secession) as a matter of customary international
law, as a matter of state practice. The decision following this article of the Supreme
Court of Canada confronts in its closing paragraphs a similar issue.]

The dissolutions of the Soviet Union and the Socialist Federal Republic of Yugoslavia, despite giving birth to a myriad of new states ultimately recognized by the
international community, have made only uncertain contributions to a substate
conception of the self. The strongest *opinio juris* that could have emerged from
either break-up would have been statements of an entitlement to self-
determination before *the fact* of independent statehood was clearly evident. Established conceptions of the self have followed this pattern. Resolution 1514 [The
1960 Declaration on Colonial Independence] was such a general statement regarding colonial territories, as was the General Assembly's recognition of [the African
National Congress and the Palestine Lilberation Organization] as 'legitimate' representatives of peoples well before independence (or majoritarian elections) were
presented to the Assembly as a *fait accompli*. . . . Recognition after statehood has
been achieved, or after the state resisting independence finally acquiesces, does not
necessarily affirm a prior right to seek independence. It may simply constitute a
recognition by states or international organizations that according to the prevailing declarative theory, a new state has come into existence and must be dealt with
as such.

   International reaction to the break-up of the Soviet Union—and in particular
the Baltic states, whose departure precipitated its dissolution—generally fell into
this second weaker category. While the United States had, in principle, never
recognized the incorporation of the Baltics into the Soviet Union, this was mostly
a status of symbolic significance. In the aftermath of the August 1991 coup, President Bush announced not that preexisting relations with the Baltics would continue in some heightened fashion but that the United States was 'prepared
immediately to *establish* diplomatic relations with their governments'. More
importantly, prior to President Yeltsin's decree of August 24, 1991 recognizing the
independence of Latvia and Estonia (Russia had recognized Lithuania in 1990),
only Iceland had established diplomatic relations with a Baltic state, and that was
with Lithuania. The European Community waited until August 27 to call for the
establishment of relations. The United States extended recognition on September
2. The CSCE and the United Nations waited still longer—until after independence

had been affirmed by the State Council of the Soviet Union on September 6—to admit the Baltics to membership.

Recognition of the former Yugoslav republics unfolded in a similar fashion. . . .

. . .

. . . The United States repeatedly opposed early recognition of the republics, a position it maintained through mid-December 1991. In December the Coordinating Bureau of the Non-Aligned Countries denounced 'all attempts aimed at undermining the sovereignty, territorial integrity and international legal personality of Yugoslavia'. Also in December—at a time when Germany had begun making clear its intention to offer early recognition—Secretary-General Boutros-Ghali urged forbearance until an overall peace settlement could be reached. Germany and Italy recognized Slovenia and Croatia on December 23; other states and international organizations followed over the next five months, culminating in the admission of Croatia, Slovenia, and Bosnia-Herzegovina to membership in the United Nations on May 22, 1992.

. . . Formal recognition came at a time when any right to secede (if it indeed existed) had already been exercised. The establishment of relations is more plausibly attributable to states' realistic assessment that diplomatic relations with the republics could only be carried out through their newly established governments . . . Alternatively, some states may have judged that the republics would be better protected against external aggression if they were Member States of the United Nations. . . . The former republics were, in fact, states and had to be dealt with as such. . . .

. . .

NOTE

Whenever state practice is at issue in determining the status in international law of a given doctrine or principle, much will depend on the eyes of the beholder. Fox takes a clear position in his historical illustrations of the distinction between recognition by other states of a 'right' to self-determination *ex ante*, and recognition of the 'fact' of secession and of a new state *ex post*. Different parties to a dispute, different judges on a court (compare the opinion for the US Supreme Court and the dissenting opinion in *The Paquete Habana*, p. 59, *supra*), different scholars, may view the relevant historical record differently: the conduct or practice of states, let alone the motivations underlying them (for example, *opinio juris*). The very boundaries of what is historically relevant may be disputed. From this perspective, compare with the preceding article of Fox the following observations of Falk.

RICHARD FALK, THE RIGHT OF SELF-DETERMINATION UNDER INTERNATIONAL LAW: THE COHERENCE OF DOCTRINE VERSUS THE COHERENCE OF EXPERIENCE
in Wolfgang Danspeckgruber and A. Watts (eds.), Self-Determination and Self-Administration 47 (1997), at 55

... [T]he whole history of the right of self-determination is, for better and worse, the story of adaptation to the evolving struggles of peoples variously situated to achieve effective control over their own destinies. For a period, states agreed that self-determination would not have secessionist implications except in colonial settings, and even here, it was more a matter of changed status and only secessionist in relation to the colonial empire. This attitude was acceptable to the Soviet Union, appreciating the explosive danger of encouraging either captive nationalities within its sovereign boundaries or the various captive peoples restive within its East European bloc of countries to assert claims of independence as a matter of right. . . . [T]he former colonial peoples were in general agreement that opening up the colonial boundaries for revision could contribute to political disarray and widespread warfare, especially in Africa. . . . There was thus a political and moral consensus among governments that shaped the legal conception of the right of self-determination during the Cold War, but it was a historically conditioned conception that has not held in the period since 1989.

In the last five years, the practice of states, the transnational assertiveness of indigenous peoples, and the moral force of groups rights in various situations have expanded the scope of the legal right of self-determination . . . . The more flexible international law approach that is sensitive to context and the trends in official practice give a more realistic picture of the relevance of law to current discussions of self-determination than does its restrictive counterpart, which purports a clarity and definiteness that seems increasingly out of touch with the ways in which self-determination claims have been validated by diplomatic recognition and UN admissions procedures. Arguably, criticisms can be made of this variable legal content accorded self-determination, but to deny such a content is to attempt by legalistic sleight-of-hand to keep the self-determination genie in the doctrinal box of a statist world. Yet such a world has been eroded, and to pretend otherwise is to place an unacceptable strain on the descriptive and prescriptive character of international law, as well as to finesse the need for a politically effective way to recapture the genie of self-determination, or even to admit that recapture is only partially possible at this stage.

. . .

. . . Even in [the Cold War] period, the secession in 1972 of East Pakistan from Pakistan to form Bangladesh, in the wake of atrocities perpetrated by the armies of the central government, was widely and quickly recognized by other states. Not long afterwards, Bangladesh became a UN member, although its emergence altered the external boundaries of the former Pakistan, as well as generated a second sovereign state. Such an outcome was substantively an exercise of the right of self-determination by the peoples involved, even if not so described at the time. The quest for a national homeland by the Palestinians, the various Kurdish national movements, and the various struggles of ethnic groups in the former Soviet Union are appropriately treated as part of the subject matter of self-determination, whether the outcome is consummated internally through autonomy arrangements or through the establishment of a new state. . . .

The disintegration of the Soviet Union and Yugoslavia in 1991 involved establishing a series of new, sovereign states that sought diplomatic recognition and full membership in international institutions. In effect, these emergent states shattered the territorial unity of the former federated entities and departed from the apparent UN guidelines premised on always exercising the right of self-determination *within* existing states, being inapplicable at the level of the federal units that together constitute a state. This recent practice is a significant confirmation of the extent to which the effective political outcomes that are welcomed by important countries produce *legal* results incompatible with earlier conceptions of legal doctrine. Community responses to such state-shattering practice are registered by way of recognition and admission to international institutions, which are diplomatic rituals of legitimizing impact quite inconsistent with earlier efforts to reject self-determination claims of a state-shattering variety. . . .

. . .

A crucial point here is that the unconditionality of respect for territorial unity has been decisively breached in relation to the former Yugoslavia and that the movements of separation launched by these developments were operationally invoking their right of self-determination even if the specific language was not emphasized. . . . In effect, what is accepted as valid by organized international society cannot be adequately understood by consulting abstract legal guidelines. The fact that the claims of independent statehood have generally corresponded with prior internal boundaries [that is, the boundaries of the constituent republics of the former Yugoslavia] does not alter the breach of the fundamental effort of international law during the Cold War era to reconcile the territorial unity of existing states with the exercise of the right of self-determination . . . .

. . .

REFERENCE RE SECESSION OF QUEBEC
Supreme Court of Canada, 1998
[1998] 2 S.C.R. 217, 37 Int'l Leg. Mat. 1342 (1998)

[Pursuant to Canadian legislation, the Governor in Council referred several questions to the Supreme Court, including:

1. Under the Constitution of Canada, can the National Assembly, legislature or government of Quebec effect the secession of Quebec from Canada unilaterally?
2. . . . [I]s there a right to self-determination under international law that would give the National Assembly, legislature or government of Quebec the right to effect the secession of Quebec from Canada unilaterally? . . .

The Judgment by the Court noted that the Reference 'requires us to consider momentous questions that go to the heart of our system of constitutional government', and that it was not here performing its traditional adjudicative function but rather acting in an advisory capacity. It rejected the contention of an *amicus curiae* brief that the questions were not justiciable because they were too theoretical or speculative and were 'political in nature'. The questions posed in the Reference 'may clearly be interpreted as directed to legal issues, and, so interpreted, the Court is in a position to answer them'.

The Court then addressed Question 1. It reviewed the history of Canada that led to confederation.

> The federal-provincial division of powers was a legal recognition of the diversity that existed among the initial members of Confederation, and manifested a concern to accommodate that diversity within a single nation by granting significant powers to provincial governments. The Constitution Act, 1867, was an act of nation-building.... Federalism was the political mechanism by which diversity could be reconciled with unity.

Canada gradually evolved from colony to independent state. The Constitution Act, 1982, 'removed the last vestige of British authority' and re-affirmed the country's commitment to the protection of its minority, to equality, and to fundamental freedoms as declared in the Canadian Charter of Rights and Freedoms. The 1982 amendments did not alter the division of powers set forth in the Constitution Act, 1867, 'which is the primary textual expression of the principle of federalism in our Constitution'.

Excerpts from the opinion follow:]

(3) Analysis of the Constitutional Principles

(a) Nature of the Principles

49. .... The following discussion addresses the four foundational constitutional principles that are most germane for resolution of this Reference: federalism, democracy, constitutionalism and the rule of law, and respect for minority rights. These defining principles function in symbiosis. No single principle can be defined in isolation from the others, nor does any one principle trump or exclude the operation of any other.

...

(b) Federalism

...

58. The principle of federalism recognizes the diversity of the component parts of Confederation, and the autonomy of provincial governments to develop their societies within their respective spheres of jurisdiction. The federal structure of our country also facilitates democratic participation by distributing power to the government thought to be most suited to achieving the particular societal objective having regard to this diversity. ....

...

59. The principle of federalism facilitates the pursuit of collective goals by cultural and linguistic minorities which form the majority within a particular province. This is the case in Quebec, where the majority of the population is French-speaking, and which possesses a distinct culture. This is not merely the result of chance. The social and demographic reality of Quebec explains the existence of the province of Quebec as a political unit and indeed, was one of the essential reasons for establishing a federal structure for the Canadian union in 1867. . . .

. . .

(c) Democracy

61. Democracy is a fundamental value in our constitutional law and political culture. While it has both an institutional and an individual aspect, the democratic principle was also argued before us in the sense of the supremacy of the sovereign will of a people, in this case potentially to be expressed by Quebecers in support of unilateral secession. . . .

. . .

64. Democracy is not simply concerned with the process of government. On the contrary, . . . democracy is fundamentally connected to substantive goals, most importantly, the promotion of self-government. Democracy accommodates cultural and group identities. Put another way, a sovereign people exercises its right to self-government through the democratic process. . . .

65. In institutional terms, democracy means that each of the provincial legislatures and the Parliament is elected by popular franchise. These legislatures, we have said, are 'at the core of the system of representative government'. . . .

66. It is, of course, true that democracy expresses the sovereign will of the people. Yet this expression, too, must be taken in the context of the other institutional values we have identified as pertinent to this Reference. The relationship between democracy and federalism means, for example, that in Canada there may be different and equally legitimate majorities in different provinces and territories and at the federal level. No one majority is more or less 'legitimate' than the others as an expression of democratic opinion, although, of course, the consequences will vary with the subject matter. A federal system of government enables different provinces to pursue policies responsive to the particular concerns and interests of people in that province. At the same time, Canada as a whole is also a democratic community in which citizens construct and achieve goals on a national scale through a federal government acting within the limits of its jurisdiction. The function of federalism is to enable citizens to participate concurrently in different collectivities and to pursue goals at both a provincial and a federal level.

67. . . . [D]emocracy in any real sense of the word cannot exist without the rule of law. It is the law that creates the framework within which the 'sovereign will' is to be ascertained and implemented. To be accorded legitimacy, democratic institutions must rest, ultimately, on a legal foundation. That is, they must allow for the participation of, and accountability to, the people, through public institutions created under the Constitution. Equally, however, a system of government cannot survive through adherence to the law alone. A political system must also possess legitimacy, and in our political culture, that requires an interaction between the

rule of law and the democratic principle. The system must be capable of reflecting the aspirations of the people. But there is more. Our law's claim to legitimacy also rests on an appeal to moral values, many of which are imbedded in our constitutional structure. It would be a grave mistake to equate legitimacy with the 'sovereign will' or majority rule alone, to the exclusion of other constitutional values.

68. Finally, we highlight that a functioning democracy requires a continuous process of discussion. The Constitution mandates government by democratic legislatures, and an executive accountable to them, 'resting ultimately on public opinion reached by discussion and the interplay of ideas'. . . . At both the federal and provincial level, by its very nature, the need to build majorities necessitates compromise, negotiation, and deliberation. . . .

69. The Constitution Act, 1982 gives expression to this principle, by conferring a right to initiate constitutional change on each participant in Confederation. In our view, the existence of this right imposes a corresponding duty on the participants in Confederation to engage in constitutional discussions in order to acknowledge and address democratic expressions of a desire for change in other provinces. . . .

(d) Constitutionalism and the Rule of Law

. . .

72. . . . The essence of constitutionalism in Canada is embodied in s. 52(1) of the Constitution Act, 1982, which provides that '[t]he Constitution of Canada is the supreme law of Canada, and any law that is inconsistent with the provisions of the Constitution is, to the extent of the inconsistency, of no force or effect'. Simply put, the constitutionalism principle requires that all government action comply with the Constitution. The rule of law principle requires that all government action must comply with the law, including the Constitution. This Court has noted on several occasions that with the adoption of the [Canadian Charter of Rights and Freedoms], the Canadian system of government was transformed to a significant extent from a system of Parliamentary supremacy to one of constitutional supremacy. . . .

73. An understanding of the scope and importance of the principles of the rule of law and constitutionalism is aided by acknowledging explicitly why a constitution is entrenched beyond the reach of simple majority rule. There are three overlapping reasons.

74. First, a constitution may provide an added safeguard for fundamental human rights and individual freedoms which might otherwise be susceptible to government interference. . . . Second, a constitution may seek to ensure that vulnerable minority groups are endowed with the institutions and rights necessary to maintain and promote their identities against the assimilative pressures of the majority. And third, a constitution may provide for a division of political power that allocates political power amongst different levels of government. . . .

75. The argument that the Constitution may be legitimately circumvented by resort to a majority vote in a province-wide referendum is superficially persuasive, in large measure because it seems to appeal to some of the same principles that underlie the legitimacy of the Constitution itself, namely, democracy and

self-government. In short, it is suggested that. . . the same popular sovereignty that originally led to the present Constitution must (it is argued) also permit 'the people' in their exercise of popular sovereignty to secede by majority vote alone. . . .

76. . . . Constitutional government is necessarily predicated on the idea that the political representatives of the people of a province have the capacity and the power to commit the province to be bound into the future by the constitutional rules being adopted. These rules are 'binding' not in the sense of frustrating the will of a majority of a province, but as defining the majority which must be consulted in order to alter the fundamental balances of political power (including the spheres of autonomy guaranteed by the principle of federalism), individual rights, and minority rights in our society. . . .

77. In this way, our belief in democracy may be harmonized with our belief in constitutionalism. . . .

. . .

(e) Protection of minorities

79. The fourth underlying constitutional principle we address here concerns the protection of minorities. There are a number of specific constitutional provisions protecting minority language, religion and education rights. Some of those provisions are, as we have recognized on a number of occasions, the product of historical compromises. . . .

. . .

(4) The Operation of the Constitutional Principles in the Secession Context

83. Secession is the effort of a group or section of a state to withdraw itself from the political and constitutional authority of that state, with a view to achieving statehood for a new territorial unit on the international plane. . . . [T]he legality of unilateral secession must be evaluated, at least in the first instance, from the perspective of the domestic legal order of the state from which the unit seeks to withdraw. As we shall see below, it is also argued that international law is a relevant standard by which the legality of a purported act of secession may be measured.

84. The secession of a province from Canada must be considered, in legal terms, to require an amendment to the Constitution, which perforce requires negotiation. The amendments necessary to achieve a secession could be radical and extensive. . . . [A]lthough the Constitution neither expressly authorizes nor prohibits secession, an act of secession would purport to alter the governance of Canadian territory in a manner which undoubtedly is inconsistent with our current constitutional arrangements. . . .

85. . . . It lies within the power of the people of Canada, acting through their various governments duly elected and recognized under the Constitution, to effect whatever constitutional arrangements are desired within Canadian territory, including, should it be so desired, the secession of Quebec from Canada. . . .

. . .

86. . . . [W]hat is claimed by a right to secede 'unilaterally' is the right to effectuate secession without prior negotiations with the other provinces and the federal

government. At issue is not the legality of the first step but the legality of the final act of purported unilateral secession. . . .

87. Although the Constitution does not itself address the use of a referendum procedure, and the results of a referendum have no direct role or legal effect in our constitutional scheme, a referendum undoubtedly may provide a democratic method of ascertaining the views of the electorate on important political questions on a particular occasion. . . . [A]n expression of the democratic will of the people of a province carries weight, in that it would confer legitimacy on the efforts of the government of Quebec to initiate the Constitution's amendment process in order to secede by constitutional means. In this context, we refer to a 'clear' majority as a qualitative evaluation. The referendum result, if it is to be taken as an expression of the democratic will, must be free of ambiguity both in terms of the question asked and in terms of the support it achieves.

88. The federalism principle, in conjunction with the democratic principle, dictates that the clear repudiation of the existing constitutional order and the clear expression of the desire to pursue secession by the population of a province would give rise to a reciprocal obligation on all parties to Confederation to negotiate constitutional changes to respond to that desire. . . .

89. What is the content of this obligation to negotiate? . . .

90. . . . [We] reject two absolutist propositions. One of those propositions is that there would be a legal obligation on the other provinces and federal government to accede to the secession of a province, subject only to negotiation of the logistical details of secession. . . .

91. . . . [I]t would be naive to expect that the substantive goal of secession could readily be distinguished from the practical details of secession. The devil would be in the details. . . .

92. However, we are equally unable to accept the reverse proposition, that a clear expression of self-determination by the people of Quebec would impose no obligations upon the other provinces or the federal government. . . . The rights of other provinces and the federal government cannot deny the right of the government of Quebec to pursue secession, should a clear majority of the people of Quebec choose that goal, so long as in doing so, Quebec respects the rights of others. Negotiations would be necessary to address the interests of the federal government, of Quebec and the other provinces, and other participants, as well as the rights of all Canadians both within and outside Quebec.

93. . . . The negotiation process precipitated by a decision of a clear majority of the population of Quebec on a clear question to pursue secession would require the reconciliation of various rights and obligations by the representatives of two legitimate majorities, namely, the clear majority of the population of Quebec, and the clear majority of Canada as a whole, whatever that may be. There can be no suggestion that either of these majorities 'trumps' the other. . . .

. . .

95. Refusal of a party to conduct negotiations in a manner consistent with constitutional principles and values would seriously put at risk the legitimacy of that party's assertion of its rights, and perhaps the negotiation process as a whole. . . .

96. No one can predict the course that such negotiations might take. The possibility that they might not lead to an agreement amongst the parties must be recognized. . . . After 131 years of Confederation, there exists, inevitably, a high level of integration in economic, political and social institutions across Canada. . . . [W]hile there are regional economic interests, which sometimes coincide with provincial boundaries, there are also national interests and enterprises (both public and private) that would face potential dismemberment. There is a national economy and a national debt. Arguments were raised before us regarding boundary issues. There are linguistic and cultural minorities, including aboriginal peoples, unevenly distributed across the country who look to the Constitution of Canada for the protection of their rights. . . .

97. . . . While the negotiators would have to contemplate the possibility of secession, there would be no absolute legal entitlement to it and no assumption that an agreement reconciling all relevant rights and obligations would actually be reached. . . .

. . .

100. . . . The Court has no supervisory role over the political aspects of constitutional negotiations. Equally, the initial impetus for negotiation, namely a clear majority on a clear question in favour of secession, is subject only to political evaluation, and properly so. . . .

101. . . . The reconciliation of the various legitimate constitutional interests outlined above. . . can only be achieved through the give and take of the negotiation process. . . .

. . .

103. To the extent that a breach of the constitutional duty to negotiate in accordance with the principles described above undermines the legitimacy of a party's actions, it may have important ramifications at the international level. Thus, a failure of the duty to undertake negotiations and pursue them according to constitutional principles may undermine that government's claim to legitimacy which is generally a precondition for recognition by the international community. Conversely, violations of those principles by the federal or other provincial governments responding to the request for secession may undermine their legitimacy. . . . Both the legality of the acts of the parties to the negotiation process under Canadian law, and the perceived legitimacy of such action, would be important considerations in the recognition process. In this way, the adherence of the parties to the obligation to negotiate would be evaluated in an indirect manner on the international plane.

. . .

B. QUESTION 2

. . . [I]s there a right to self-determination under international law that would give the National Assembly, legislature or government of Quebec the right to effect the secession of Quebec from Canada unilaterally?

. . .

(1) Secession at International Law

111. It is clear that international law does not specifically grant component parts of sovereign states the legal right to secede unilaterally from their 'parent' state.... [P]roponents ... are therefore left to attempt to found their argument ... (ii) on the implied duty of states to recognize the legitimacy of secession brought about by the exercise of the well-established international law right of 'a people' to self-determination. ...

. . .

(b) The Right of a People to Self-determination

114. The existence of the right of a people to self-determination is now so widely recognized in international conventions that the principle has acquired a status beyond 'convention' and is considered a general principle of international law. ...

[The opinion quoted relevant portions of many international documents, including: Articles 1 and 55 of the UN Charter; Article 1 of the ICCPR and of the ICESCR; and the 1970 UN Declaration on Friendly Relations, p. 1266. *supra*. It also quoted from the UN Declaration on the Occasion of the Fiftieth Anniversary of the United Nations, GA Res. 50/6, 9 November 1995, which provides in Article 1 that UN member states will:

> Continue to reaffirm the right of self-determination of all peoples, taking into account the particular situation of peoples under colonial or other forms of alien domination or foreign occupation, and recognize the right of peoples to take legitimate action in accordance with the Charter of the United Nations to realize their inalienable right of self-determination. This shall not be construed as authorizing or encouraging any action that would dismember or impair, totally or in part, the territorial integrity or political unity of sovereign and independent States conducting themselves in compliance with the principle of equal rights and self-determination of peoples and thus possessed of a Government representing the whole people belonging to the territory without distinction of any kind. ...

Finally the Court drew on the Final Act of the Conference on Security and Co-operation in Europe, 14 I.L.M. 1292 (1975) (Helsinki Final Act), of which Canada was a member. Chapter VIII of the Helsinki Final Act provides:

> The participating States will respect the equal rights of peoples and their right to self-determination, acting at all times in conformity with the purposes and principles of the Charter of the United Nations and with the relevant norms of international law, including those relating to territorial integrity of States.

The opinion continued:]

123. International law grants the right to self-determination to 'peoples'. ...
124. It is clear that 'a people' may include only a portion of the population of

an existing state. The right to self-determination has developed largely as a human right, and is generally used in documents that simultaneously contain references to 'nation' and 'state'. The juxtaposition of these terms is indicative that the reference to 'people' does not necessarily mean the entirety of a state's population. . . .

125. While much of the Quebec population certainly shares many of the characteristics (such as a common language and culture) that would be considered in determining whether a specific group is a 'people', as do other groups within Quebec and/or Canada, it is not necessary to explore this legal characterization to resolve Question 2 appropriately. Similarly, it is not necessary for the Court to determine whether, should a Quebec people exist within the definition of public international law, such a people encompasses the entirety of the provincial population or just a portion thereof. Nor is it necessary to examine the position of the aboriginal population within Quebec. . . .

126. The recognized sources of international law establish that the right to self-determination of a people is normally fulfilled through internal self-determination—a people's pursuit of its political, economic, social and cultural development within the framework of an existing state. A right to external self-determination (which in this case potentially takes the form of the assertion of a right to unilateral secession) arises in only the most extreme of cases and, even then, under carefully defined circumstances. . . .
. . . .

127. The international law principle of self-determination has evolved within a framework of respect for the territorial integrity of existing states. . . .
. . .

130. . . . There is no necessary incompatibility between the maintenance of the territorial integrity of existing states, including Canada, and the right of a 'people' to achieve a full measure of self-determination. A state whose government represents the whole of the people or peoples resident within its territory, on a basis of equality and without discrimination, and respects the principles of self-determination in its own internal arrangements, is entitled to the protection under international law of its territorial integrity.
. . .

133. The other clear case [in addition to colonial domination] where a right to external self-determination accrues is where a people is subject to alien subjugation, domination or exploitation outside a colonial context. This recognition finds its roots in the Declaration on Friendly Relations: . . .

134. A number of commentators have further asserted that the right to self-determination may ground a right to unilateral secession in a third circumstance . . .—when a people is blocked from the meaningful exercise of its right to self-determination internally, it is entitled, as a last resort, to exercise it by secession. The Vienna Declaration requirement that governments represent 'the whole people belonging to the territory without distinction of any kind' adds credence to the assertion that such a complete blockage may potentially give rise to a right of secession.

135. . . . Even assuming that the third circumstance is sufficient to create a right

to unilateral secession under international law, the current Quebec context cannot be said to approach such a threshold. . . .
. . .

136. The population of Quebec cannot plausibly be said to be denied access to government. Quebecers occupy prominent positions within the government of Canada. Residents of the province freely make political choices and pursue economic, social and cultural development within Quebec, across Canada, and throughout the world. The population of Quebec is equitably represented in legislative, executive and judicial institutions. In short, to reflect the phraseology of the international documents that address the right to self-determination of peoples, Canada is a 'sovereign and independent state conducting itself in compliance with the principle of equal rights and self-determination of peoples and thus possessed of a government representing the whole people belonging to the territory without distinction'.
. . .

139. We would not wish to leave this aspect of our answer to Question 2 without acknowledging the importance of the submissions made to us respecting the rights and concerns of aboriginal peoples in the event of a unilateral secession, as well as the appropriate means of defining the boundaries of a seceding Quebec with particular regard to the northern lands occupied largely by aboriginal peoples. However, the concern of aboriginal peoples is precipitated by the asserted right of Quebec to unilateral secession. In light of our finding that there is no such right applicable to the population of Quebec, either under the Constitution of Canada or at international law, but that on the contrary a clear democratic expression of support for secession would lead under the Constitution to negotiations in which aboriginal interests would be taken into account, it becomes unnecessary to explore further the concerns of the aboriginal peoples in this Reference.

(2) Recognition of a Factual/Political Reality: the 'Effectivity' Principle

140. As stated, an argument advanced by the *amicus curiae* on this branch of the Reference was that, while international law may not ground a positive right to unilateral secession in the context of Quebec, international law equally does not prohibit secession and, in fact, international recognition would be conferred on such a political reality if it emerged, for example, via effective control of the territory of what is now the province of Quebec.

141. It is true that international law may well, depending on the circumstances, adapt to recognize a political and/or factual reality, regardless of the legality of the steps leading to its creation. However, as mentioned at the outset, effectivity, as such, does not have any real applicability to Question 2, which asks whether a right to unilateral secession exists.

142. No one doubts that legal consequences may flow from political facts, and that 'sovereignty is a political fact for which no purely legal authority can be constituted . . . '. Secession of a province from Canada, if successful in the streets, might well lead to the creation of a new state. Although recognition by other states is not, at least as a matter of theory, necessary to achieve statehood, the viability of a would-be state in the international community depends, as a practical matter,

upon recognition by other states. That process of recognition is guided by legal norms. However, international recognition is not alone constitutive of statehood and, critically, does not relate back to the date of secession to serve retroactively as a source of a 'legal' right to secede in the first place. Recognition occurs only after a territorial unit has been successful, as a political fact, in achieving secession.

143. As indicated in responding to Question 1, one of the legal norms which may be recognized by states in granting or withholding recognition of emergent states is the legitimacy of the process by which the de facto secession is, or was, being pursued. The process of recognition, once considered to be an exercise of pure sovereign discretion, has come to be associated with legal norms. . . . [A]n emergent state that has disregarded legitimate obligations arising out of its previous situation can potentially expect to be hindered by that disregard in achieving international recognition, at least with respect to the timing of that recognition. On the other hand, compliance by the seceding province with such legitimate obligations would weigh in favour of international recognition. . . .

. . .

ROSALYN HIGGINS, COMMENTS
in Catherline Brölmann, R. Lefeber and M. Zieck (eds.), Peoples and Minorities in International Law (1993), at 30

[Higgins contends that 'it is one of the great myths that the UN Charter provided for and required self-determination in the form in which it evolved'. The concept developed in ways 'quite *un*intended' by the Charter, whose Articles 1(2) and 55 referred in context only to 'rights of the peoples of one state to be protected from interference by other states or governments'. But ideas develop, and the growing identification of self-determination with independence from colonial rule 'has long since been regarded on all sides as legitimate and desirable'.

Higgins then inquires into what the concept has come to mean since the 1960 Declaration on Colonial Independence.]

. . . Can terms be invoked to mean whatever the user finds it convenient for them to mean? I am aware that I here approach the dangerous waters of linguistics and the current controversies on deconstructionism. My position is that I believe that legal ideas develop, and that that is proper. But that is not to say that they can mean simply whatever those using them want them to mean. The degree of change from a given normative understanding, that we should as lawyers tolerate, must depend in large part upon the policy implications.

. . .

. . . The concept of the self-determination of peoples requires us to answer not only what self-determination means, but the 'peoples' to whom it applies. Minority rights are the rights held by minorities. . . . But the right of self-determination is the right of *peoples*. The Political Covenant gives entirely discrete rights to minorities on the one hand (minority rights, as elaborated in Article 27) and to peoples (self-determination rights, as provided in Article 1). One cannot—though many today try, lawyers as well as politicians—assert that minorities are *peoples* and that therefore minorities are entitled to the right of self-determination. This is simply to ignore the fact that the Political Covenant provides for two discrete rights. It also, more insidiously, denies the right of self-determination to those to whom it was guaranteed—the peoples of a state *in their entirety.*

. . .

It follows that international law provides no right of secession, in the name of self-determination, to minorities. . . .

Quebec has no legal right to secede on the alleged ground that it is composed of a linguistic minority within a state in which the majority are of a different linguistic grouping. Francophone Quebecois *are*, of course, fully entitled to use their own language. . . . Croatia and Bosnia-Hercegovina had no automatic legal right to secede by invocation of a right of self-determination of ethnic or religious groups who formed a minority in the larger federal state of Yugoslavia. The perceived need of secession is understandable when minorities are denied their rights as minorities or where they cannot participate, as part of the entire peoples of a country, in the political and economic life of the country. But I am less sure . . . that even this entails a legal right to secession, in contra-distinction to a compelling political imperative. Where I certainly agree . . . is that, even if international law does not authorise secession, it will eventually recognise the reality once it has occurred and been made effective.

. . .

So I return to the importance of using concepts with some care. Looking at the ideas behind this current battle of the words, I am of course very aware that there are those who use the armory of words in full knowledge of what they do. What, they ask, is wrong with secession/self-determination for every minority that wants it? Why shouldn't this be their right? And what is so wrong with the prospect of a world of two thousand states? I can only give my own answer. . . . There is, quite simply, no end to the disintegrative processes that are encouraged. . . .

Because I believe in diversity, and plurality, and tolerance, and mutual respect, I favour multilateralism and multinationalism. The use of force is appalling, indiscriminate barbarity unforgivable. But the move to uninational and unicultural states that constitutes postmodern tribalism is profoundly illiberal. The attempt to legitimate these tendencies by the misapplication of legal terms runs the risk of harming the very values that international law is meant to promote.

ALAN BUCHANAN, SELF-DETERMINATION, SECESSION, AND THE RULE OF LAW

in Robert McKim and J. McMahan (eds.), The Morality of Nationalism 301 (1997), at 310

From the standpoint of developing principles for secession under the rule of international law, then, the second major task is to articulate and gain consensus on the primary justifying grounds for secession—the conditions under which a group may be said to have a right to secede, assuming that the just terms of secession will be observed in the exercise of the right (fair procedures for dividing the national debt will be followed, credible guarantees of the rights of minorities will be offered, et cetera).

In a recent book on the morality of secession, I rejected the idea that anything so general and open-ended as a right of self-determination (of all 'peoples' or 'nationalities') could serve as a primary justifying ground for secession. I argued instead that there is a limited set of special conditions under which a group can be said to have a right to secede.

The approach I began to develop there construes the right to secede as a remedial right. More precisely, the right to secede is seen as a remedy of last resort for serious injustices, not as a general right of groups or even of certain kinds of groups ('nations', 'peoples', et cetera, as such). Chief among the grievances I identify as providing primary justifying grounds for secession are these: (1) persistent and serious violations of individual human rights and (2) past unredressed unjust seizure of territory. If a state persists in serious violations of the human rights of a minority within its borders, it is permissible for that group to attempt to establish its own state as a sanctuary from persecution if no other recourse is available. Or if, as in the case of the Baltic Republics, a sovereign state was unjustly annexed, secession can be viewed as a legitimate rectification of that injustice.

A third and more controversial primary justifying ground for secession is discriminatory redistribution (or, as it is sometimes called, internal colonialism or regional exploitation). Discriminatory redistribution occurs wherever the state implements taxation schemes, property rights systems, regulatory policies, or economic development programs that systematically work to the disadvantage of some groups while benefiting others in morally arbitrary ways. More simply, discriminatory redistribution occurs when a group is subjected to unequal economic treatment without sound justification for this inequality. Examples would include the state imposing higher taxes on one group while spending less on it or placing special economic restrictions on one region without just cause. In most, if not all, cases of secessionist movements of which there is any record, the charge of discriminatory redistribution has been at the forefront of the grievances cited to justify separation.

. . .

The case of secession to rectify a past unjust seizure of territory may seem the least controversial because secession in this instance is simply a matter of taking back what was unjustly taken. Nevertheless, thorny problems lurk here as well. The most serious is what I have elsewhere dubbed 'the moral statute of limitations problem.' Just how far back may we or must we go in determining the rightful owners of a territory and how clear must the title be?

Given that virtually every state in existence originally acquired all or some of its territory by theft, genocide, or fraud (or acquired it from those who gained it by such methods), this is no minor issue. Nevertheless, there are situations in which this justification for a right to secede is compelling. The case of the Baltic Republics is perhaps the most obvious instance. The Soviet annexation was recent, well documented, and clearly unjust, and the Republics' claims to territory were at least as valid as those of most, if not all, states that are now recognized as sovereign under international law.

In such cases, the most difficult problem seems to lie not with whether there is a right to secede but rather with determining the just terms of secession. . . .

. . .

A less obvious difficulty with both the consent and democratic theories of the right to secede is that they legitimize the secession of the rich from the poor, thus threatening to undercut the functioning of the state as an instrument of distributive justice. They would allow the citizens of a richer region to secede (if a majority within it so chose) simply to make themselves even better off by divesting themselves of the burden of sharing part of their wealth with their less fortunate countrymen. (There are, in fact, several recent instances of secessionist movements that might be said to fit this description—for example, the secession of Slovenia from Yugoslavia and the separatist movement in Northern Italy, as well as the earlier case of the secession of Katanga Province from the Congo.) At least for those who, unlike the most extreme libertarians, believe that the state should engage in some redistribution of wealth from the better-off to the worse-off, this is a troubling prospect.

. . .

QUESTIONS

1. Suppose that the Canadian Supreme Court had concluded that international law did indeed grant a right of secession to the 'people' of Quebec if they clearly expressed their preference for secession. What issues then would the Court have had to examine?

2. Based on Section A's full materials, how do you evaluate the Court's understanding of the international law of self-determination, at least with respect to the question of secession? As a law clerk, would you have advised changes in the Court's analysis?

3. How do you react to the analyses of the break-up of the Soviet Union and the former Yugoslavia by Fox and Falk? What historical evidence would you demand before concluding that international law recognized or was moving toward recognition of a right to self-determination that could take the form of secession? What procedures or conditions would you read the historical evidence to require?

4. If recognition of independent statehood and admission to international organizations will often be granted by states *ex post* when a seceding group succeeds, as with Bangladesh or Croatia or Georgia, why is it significant whether or not a 'right' was recognized *ex ante* by other states?

5. Is the internal political character of a new state, or of a proposed new state, relevant to the question of the right of the 'people' involved to self-determination? Suppose, for example, that the seceding population (the dominant population of the new state) will impose religious law that denies basic human rights like freedom of

religious observance or gender equality. Suppose that it will take the form of an authoritarian leadership and will, based on historical evidence, impose harsh controls on political pluralism and dissent. What if any text of the human rights instruments would you draw on to limit a right to self-determination in such circumstances?

6. How would you handle the problem of 'nesting'—that is, the seceding population will find in its new state minority groups that themselves may wish to secede, or to remain attached to the original state? The Canadian Supreme Court refers to such problems in its brief discussion of indigenous peoples within Quebec. What of the Russian minorities in the former Soviet republics? Is the process one of endless decomposition and fragmentation, and if not, what general principle could bring it to an end?

ADDITIONAL READING

J. Crawford, 'The Right of Self-determination in International Law: Its Development and Future', in P. Alston (ed.), *Peoples' Rights* (forthcoming, 2000); B. Kingsbury, 'Reconciling Five Competing Conceptual Structures of Indigenous People's Claims in International and Comparative Law', in *ibid.*; J. Oloka-Onyango, 'Heretical Reflections on the Right to Self-determination: Prospects and Problems for a Democratic Global Future in the New Millennium', 15 *Am. U. Int'l L. Rev.* 151–208 (1999); D. Fottrell and B. Bowring, *Minority and Group Rights in the New Millennium* (1999); A. Bloed and P. van Dijk (eds.), *Protection of Minority Rights through Bilateral Treaties: The Case of Central and Eastern Europe* (1999); D. Wippman (ed.), *International Law and Ethnic Conflict* (1998); S.J. Anaya, *Indigenous Peoples in International Law* (1996); A. Cassese, *Self-Determination of Peoples. A Legal Appraisal* (1995); C. Tomuschat (ed.), *The Modern Law of Self-determination* (Nijhoff, 1993).

B. AUTONOMY REGIMES

Section B turns to rights and protections of ethnic minorities and their members within a state—that is, independently of any possible right to secession. It examines political arrangements relevant to such groups that the materials refer to as autonomy regimes (defined below). Such regimes may be bargained for, created, administered and governed by ethnic minorities. The materials explore the degree to which international law has recognized or is moving toward recognition of a 'right' of minorities to autonomy regimes, referred to by some advocates and scholars as a right to 'internal' (as opposed to 'external') self-determination (that is, a form and degree of self-determination achieved within the boundaries rather than through secession, and within the overriding political system of the state).

The special regimes for a number of minorities in Central and East Europe that grew out of the First World War (pp. 93–103, *supra*) fell into disfavor because of their ineffectiveness and the malign uses to which some of their concepts were put. As a consequence, and in the belief that observance by states of individually based norms would solve the historical problems of oppression and brutality that many minorities had confronted, the UN Charter, the Universal Declaration on Human Rights and the International Covenant on Civil and Political Rights paid scant attention to minorities as such or (subject to the major exception of the self-determination clauses, and to the very conception of the state) to collective rights as such. Not until 1992, when the General Assembly adopted the Declaration on Minorities, p. 1298, *infra*, did the human rights movement produce a universal instrument dedicated to the problems and rights of minorities and their members.

In a general sense, the full range of the classical and individually based human rights norms become relevant to the rights and protections of minorities and indigenous peoples, from rights to personal security or due process or equal protection to rights of speech or association and the right to political participation. Three ICCPR provisions, however, are particularly pertinent to the discussion in this section of autonomy regimes: Article 1 on self-determination, Article 25 on political participation (discussed at pp. 840–853 and 903–919, *supra*), and Article 27 that is discussed below.

COMMENT ON CHARACTERISTICS OF MINORITY GROUPS

These materials concern minority groups that are typically ethnic, racial, religious, linguistic, or national origin in character. The text below uses the term 'ethnic' as a shorthand reference to all such minorities, whatever their distinctive characteristic. Hence that term embraces groups as diverse as Muslims of North African background in France, blacks and Jews in the United States, the Roma people in Hungary, Kurds in Iraq or Turkey, Russians in Georgia, Tamils in Sri Lanka, Copts in Egypt, and Turks in Germany. Frequently these ethnic minorities bear two or more of the defining characteristics, such as Basques in Spain, the Francophone population in Canada, or Arabs in Israel.

To characterize a group within a state as a minority tells us little about its political, economic or cultural situation. Relations with a dominant majority or with other minority groups may be amicable or hostile. The minority may be well integrated, indeed moving towards a voluntary assimilation, or may be both rejected by dominant groups and intent on maintaining its own distinctive character. The differences in religion, culture and so on between majority and minority may be formal and inconsequential, or dramatic and stemming from basic world-views.

Two world wars, and many savage conflicts during the last half century of the human rights movement, have made evident the ways in which ethnic conflicts deeply affect international politics. Third-party countries become involved in such conflicts, particularly when their co-religionists or other groups with which they identify are involved—India in Sri Lanka, Turkey and Greece in Cyprus, several Muslim states in Bosnia, and so on. Conflicts spill across frontiers, as the violence in the Former Yugoslavia and in Rwanda have shown. Refugee flows involve other countries in serious ways. Universal or regional security systems observe and sometimes act, effectively or ineffectively. Hence steps to alleviate tensions between ethnic minorities and a state, or among such minorities, and to assure a necessary minimum of protection for minorities, would contribute not only to the well being of countless individuals but also to international peace and stability.

These materials are concerned with the degree to which and the ways in which minority issues have become 'internationalized'—that is, are now subject to regulation by international law and particularly human rights norms. What indeed are 'minorities' within the discourse of international law? No authoritative instrument like a treaty or declaration answers the question by a definition. Hence the term remains to some degree politically disputed, a subject of debate among scholars, spokespersons for minorities or indigenous peoples, and governments. There appears to be a consensus over two broad parts of a definition, sometimes expressed in terms of objective and subjective criteria. *Objectively*, the group at issue must constitute a non-dominant minority of the population (often a relatively small percentage of the population, even if a substantial number of people), and its members must share distinctive characteristics such as race, religion or language. Some of those characteristics will be natural, immutable; others (subject to cultural constraints) may be open to change. *Subjectively*, (most) members of this group must hold or evidence a sense of belonging to the group, and evidence the desire to continue as a distinctive group.

The present discussion is concerned only with the universal human rights system. Minority issues have figured as well in regional settings, particularly within the European system which has generated bolder instruments. The problems are most intense in a global setting, where profound differences among groups, cultures and political systems burden the task of developing standards and living in peace.

COMMENT ON AUTONOMY REGIMES

[This Comment appears at p. 491, *supra*. It is followed there by a discussion of systems of personal religious law in Israel and India that offer illustrative studies of the workings and dilemmas of that type of autonomy regime. The Comment, the discussion of the two regimes, and the questions addressed to those materials bear directly on the themes of this Section B, although they include personal law regimes for the majority as well as minority populations.]

NOTE

Article 27 of the ICCPR, the preeminent human rights norm for discussion of rights and protections of minorities and their members, provides:

> In those States in which ethnic, religious or linguistic minorities exist, persons belonging to such minorities shall not be denied the right, in community with the other members of their group, to enjoy their own culture, to profess and practise their own religion, or to use their own language.

This terse provision (1) refers to 'minorities' rather than, as does ICCPR Article 1, to 'peoples'; and (2) protects 'persons belonging to' minorities rather than the minorities themselves, although (3) the right is to be exercised 'in community with the other members' of a minority.

In 1994, the ICCPR Committee on Human Rights adopted General Comment No. 23 on Article 27 of the Covenant.[5] A summary of and selective quotations from several of its provisions follow:

> *Para. 3.2*: Enjoyment of rights under Article 27 'does not prejudice the sovereignty and territorial integrity of a State party'. Nonetheless, aspects of rights of individuals protected under that article, such as enjoyment of a particular culture, 'may consist of a way of life which is closely associated with territory', particularly for members of indigenous communities.
>
> *Para. 6.1*: A state party is 'under an obligation to ensure that the existence and the exercise of [the right declared by Article 27] are protected against their denial or violation. Positive measures of protection are, therefore, required . . . also against the acts' of non-state actors.
>
> *Para. 6.2*: Although the rights protected are individual, they depend on the ability of the minority group to maintain its culture. 'Accordingly, positive measures by States may also be necessary to protect the identity of a minority' and the rights of its members. Such positive measures must respect the non-discrimination clauses of the Covenant with respect to treatment among minorities and between minorities and the rest of the population. 'However, as long as those measures are aimed at correcting conditions' impairing enjoyment of the guaranteed rights, they may 'constitute a legitimate differentiation . . . [if] based on reasonable and objective criteria'.
>
> *Para. 7*: Cultural rights under Article 27 extend to ways of life 'associated with the use of land resources, especially in the case of indigenous peoples . . . . The enjoyment of those rights may require positive legal measures of protection and measures to ensure the effective participation of members of minority communities in decisions which affect them'.
>
> Para. 8: None of the protected rights under Article 27 may be exercised 'to an extent inconsistent with the other provisions of the Covenant'.

HENRY STEINER, IDEALS AND COUNTER-IDEALS IN THE STRUGGLE OVER AUTONOMY REGIMES FOR MINORITIES
66 Notre Dame L. Rev. 1539 (1991), at 1547

[This article examines autonomy regimes, in the sense described in the above-noted Comment, from the perspective of norms and ideals in the human rights movement. The excerpts below assess such regimes against those ideals as expressed primarily in the Universal Declaration and in the International Covenant on Civil and Political Rights.]

---

[5] CCPR/C/21/Rev. 1/Add.5, 26 April 1994. For a description of General Comments, see pp. 731–738, *supra*.

IV. Ideals and counter-ideals

... We now inquire whether [autonomy] schemes tend to realize vital ideals pervasive to the entire human rights movement, and paradoxically threaten at the same time to subvert those very ideals.

Let us first consider how autonomy schemes reinforce a basic human rights ideal. The Universal Declaration and Civil-Political Rights Covenant accept and, indeed, encourage many forms of diversity. They insist on respect for difference, an insistence expressed only in part through the particular attention given ethnic minorities in article 27. The value placed on the survival (and creation) of diversity in cultural, religious, political, and other terms permeates human rights law, which evidences throughout its hostility to imposed uniformity.

...

Other rights declared in basic human rights instruments complement the ideal of equal respect and confirm the value placed on diversity. Everyone has a right to adopt 'a religion or belief of his choice' and has freedom 'either individually or in community with others and in public or private' to manifest belief or religion in practice and teaching. Rights to 'peaceful assembly' and 'freedom of association with others', in each case qualified by typical grounds for limitation like public order or national security, further commit the human rights movement to the protection of people's ongoing capacity to form, develop, and preserve different types of groups.

We have noted that such provisions of the Universal Declaration and Civil-Political Rights Covenant are expressed in terms of individuals' freedom and choice of action, but that their individual and collective characters are nonetheless inextricably linked. This must be so. Groups and communities, not isolated individuals, transmit culture from one generation to the next. They embody and give significance to cultural and social differences in a society. Hence we see the link between autonomy regimes and an ideal of maintaining diversity. Since those regimes protect, indeed entrench, diversity in group terms, they must constitute an effective means to realize this fundamental human rights ideal.

...

By valuing diverse cultural traditions, and by its related protection of groups, human rights law evidences what must be a basic assumption—namely that differences enrich more than endanger the world. They contribute to a fund of human experience on which all individuals and groups can draw in the ongoing processes of change and growth. Ethnic groups nourish that fund. ... The survival of distinctive characteristics of ethnic minorities guards against the trend toward homogenization. ... Autonomy regimes of ethnic minorities defend cultural survival rights in counteracting this trend. In given contexts, they may be useful or essential to the preservation of a culture.

...

... The ideal in the human rights movement of preserving difference cannot [however] so readily be bent to support the creation of autonomy regimes. To the contrary, a further elaboration of that ideal prompts a deep criticism of such regimes and their fragmenting effects.

Consider at the outset the relation of autonomy schemes to the norm of equal protection. We noted earlier that these schemes in some ways complement one purpose of a nondiscrimination norm of preserving differences. Institutionalized separateness, however, also violates the spirit and perhaps the letter of that norm.

A state must give all its citizens equal protection. Power-sharing schemes proceed on a contradictory premise. They are cast in ethnic terms (group X is assured of x% of the legislature or cabinet or judiciary or military, group Y of y%) and thus explicitly discriminate among groups on grounds like religion, language, race or national origin. Separate voting rolls or application forms for civil service positions drive home the lesson that socioeconomic life and career turn on ethnic bonds. Separate personal laws for each religious community, particularly if enforced within a mandatory assignment system permitting no escape by community members to a nationwide secular law, dramatize citizens' particular rather than shared characteristics.[6]

. . .

To a lesser or greater degree, autonomy schemes frustrate a major objective of the human rights movement of assuring that societies remain open to challenge and change. That movement institutionalizes no one ideal of social order. To the contrary, it explicitly allows for many faiths and ideologies while denying to any one among them the right or power to impose itself by force. It expresses a humanistic commitment to ongoing inquiry and diversity. . . . To the extent that autonomy regimes protect historical differences but inhibit the creation, as it were, of fresh differences, they would convert the human rights movement's framework of protection of open inquiry and advocacy into the protection of static traditions. A state composed of segregated autonomy regimes would resemble more a museum of social and cultural antiquities than any human rights ideal.

. . .

Two deep characteristics of human rights law are here relevant. The first characteristic involves the relation between groups and individuals. Communities have a right to guard their own integrity, but only within the constraints imposed by human rights norms on governments' treatment of individuals, including the equal respect due to all members of a society. The central government of a state must respect individual conscience and choice. So then must ethnic communities within a state when they exercise (constitutionally based or statutorily delegated) governmental power over their members by applying a personal law or exercising a territorial authority or administering a power-sharing scheme in the central government.

In wielding governmental power, ethnic minorities may violate human rights norms in numerous ways—for example, by discriminating among their members on grounds forbidden by those norms, except to the extent that disadvantaged members can be understood to 'accept' the discriminatory treatment as part of

---

[6] See the discussion of the Israeli and Indian systems of personal religious law at pp. 493–510, *supra.*

their cultural tradition.[7] Within practical and cultural constraints, which may indeed be so deep and powerful as to block individuals from exercising any choice, all persons should be seen as empowered by human rights norms to decide whether to remain on one side of a cultural boundary, to shift to another side, or to seek a life not committed to one or the other community.

A second characteristic of human rights law pointing toward open boundaries within a state concentrates on the polity as a whole rather than on individuals. Strong ethnic consciousness and concentration may stamp out the desire or even capacity for broader political or cultural associations. Formal legal barriers reinforce the natural tendencies of a group's members to look inward and assume only a particular identity, rather than to experience the tension between the particular and a more diffuse or broader identity as a citizen or human being.

As the sense of a common humanity weakens, alliances among people that shatter ethnic boundaries become more unlikely. Polyethnic political formations resting on generic interests like economic class or political ideology will confront decisive obstacles. Demonization of 'the other' may become part of an ethnic group's credo and stamp out the possibility of developing empathy for others. . . . Enforced ethnic separation both inhibits intercourse among groups, and creative development within the isolated communities themselves. It impoverishes cultures and peoples.

The distinctions between the ideals or pictures of social life that inhere in the human rights movement as a whole and those that point toward autonomy regimes can be stated with different degrees of contrast. Much turns on the strength and exclusivity of the autonomy regimes. For example, advocates of these regimes may argue that the inclusive ideals of the human rights movement are ultimately desirable for a state, but that autonomy is necessary for a transitional period. Such an argument may be based on circumstances of necessity, such as the incidence of violence . . . , or on the view that some degree of autonomy is essential for maintenance of the group's culture against the onslaught of the modern state. On the other hand, those advocates may decisively reject human rights ideals as alien and evil since they risk the subversion from within or without of a religious or other tradition that binds a community together.

Autonomy regimes differ in other salient ways. The regime may involve relatively slight group differentiation and barely affect outsiders (a personal, religious law of marriage and divorce), or it may separate groups with respect to political matters of vital significance for all members of the polity (separate voting rolls, quotas, and so on). Within a federal state, an autonomy scheme for a geographically concentrated ethnic minority may grant that minority modest self-government and retain vital powers for the central government, or grant it extensive powers that border on self-rule. Those administering an autonomy regime may invite popular participation or may subject a population to decision-making powers of, say, religious officials.

---

[7] . . . A group's treatment of its own members within an autonomy regime poses issues about cultural relativism and universalism in human rights norms, and about the degree to which cultural survival for many communities may be understood to require practices violating human rights instruments . . . .

For purposes of clarity and emphasis, the following list of ideals or pictures of social life bypasses these important distinctions, assumes strong and exclusive autonomy regimes, and hence states the differences in terms of stark contradictions.

Human rights ideals and pictures of social life	*Strong autonomy regime ideals and pictures of social life*
Self and others, intercourse with strangers	Self versus others, avoid strangers
Ethnic identity in tension with human identity and potential	Ethnic identity as total identity
Relevance of both particular and universal identity	Stress on the particular, what is exclusive rather than shared
Open, pluralism of spirit	Closed, separate lives within boundaries
Learn from own tradition and from others	Learning only within own tradition
Forward looking, potential for change in cultural tradition	History (myth) looking, stability-oriented
Attention to individual choice in affiliation with ethnic group	Affiliation as identity, a given that is not subject to individual choice

V. The need for autonomy regimes

One way of testing the preceding observations is to inquire whether justifications as deep as those supporting, for example, rights to personal security or freedoms of conscience or expression, also support autonomy schemes for ethnic minorities. . . .

The question raised is whether autonomy regimes express respect for difference or express despair over the possibility that diverse peoples can live with difference. Their widespread use in diverse countries and their potential effectiveness in realizing important goals indicate that these arrangements, if not ideal, are not anathema. They may rest on genuine acceptance by all affected communities. They may grow out of concrete and agonizing histories, frequently involving authoritarian and abusive rule over a minority that has been denied a fair share of power, resources, and opportunities. Often the product of negotiations between hostile communities seeking to contain discord that may have led to violence, they appear to be justified in such circumstances as the best available solution to otherwise unyielding problems.

Separation of ethnic communities through power-sharing arrangements, regional governments, and personal laws may then constitute a practical necessity, a 'least worst' solution that is surely preferable to ongoing violence and systemic oppression. The solutions that they bring to ethnic conflict may improve chances for pacific co-existence and provide the only realistic alternative not only to continuing oppression, but to a split of the contending ethnic groups into two states. Internal self-determination through autonomy schemes may blunt a minority's demands for external self-determination.

The distinction that I have drawn is a vital one: recognizing that autonomy regimes in given contexts may be preferable to other arrangements, or alternately characterizing autonomy regimes as a 'right' to be declared in international norms. The rhetoric of rights legitimates claims and mobilizes support for groups demanding autonomy. That rhetoric empowers and encourages. It goes beyond the welfare maximizing, contextual justification for autonomy regimes as 'least worst' solutions to pressing situations.

. . .

Despite these problems, the argument for recognizing in certain circumstances the justice or legitimacy of minority claims for some form of autonomy regime deserves support. The high incidence of ethnic conflicts and the particular dangers that they pose for the ethnic minorities require that the United Nations and regional institutions examine the possibility of international regulation. International attention to the systemic, structural aspects of ethnic conflict must be given a chance to show what it is capable of achieving, including achievement through the development of international law in this field. Given the reluctance of a government to support the development of international law principles favorable to autonomy schemes that may be relied on by dissident ethnic groups in its own state, or its reluctance to intervene in ethnic conflicts in foreign states and thereby risk others' intervention in its own internal disputes, the effort to achieve progress at the start through a United Nations declaration confronts dramatic obstacles. But the effort must be made.

. . .

NOTE

A proposal in 1978 for commencing work in the UN Commission on Human Rights on a declaration on minorities and their members initiated a 14-year process that came to fruition in 1992 with the adoption of the declaration by the General Assembly. It is a supreme irony that the Government of Yugoslavia, a country in dissolution in 1992 when gripped by an intensifying violence among its ethnic groups, was the author of the original proposal.

As initially introduced, the draft concerned the 'rights of national, ethnic, linguistic and religious minorities'. A later draft referred to the 'rights of persons belonging to' such minorities. The tension between these two formulations of the project, with their significantly different implications, continued until the end. The ultimate resolution of that tension by the Commission led to the following title of the declaration:

DECLARATION ON THE RIGHTS OF PERSONS BELONGING TO NATIONAL OR ETHNIC, RELIGIOUS OR LINGUISTIC MINORITIES
GA Res. 47/135, 18 December 1992

The General Assembly

. . .

Inspired by the provisions of article 27 of the International Covenant on Civil and Political Rights concerning the rights of persons belonging to ethnic, religious or linguistic minorities,

Considering that the promotion and protection of the rights of persons belonging to national or ethnic, religious and linguistic minorities contribute to the political and social stability of States in which they live.

. . .

Considering that the United Nations has an important role to play regarding the protection of minorities.

. . .

Proclaims this Declaration on the Rights of Persons Belonging to National or Ethnic, Religious and Linguistic Minorities:

Article 1

1. States shall protect the existence and the national or ethnic, cultural, religious and linguistic identity of minorities within their respective territories and shall encourage conditions for the promotion of that identity.

2. States shall adopt appropriate legislative and other measures to achieve those ends.

Article 2

1. Persons belonging to national or ethnic, religious and linguistic minorities (hereinafter referred to as persons belonging to minorities) have the right to enjoy their own culture, to profess and practise their own religion, and to use their own language, in private and in public, freely and without interference or any form of discrimination.

2. Persons belonging to minorities have the right to participate effectively in cultural, religious, social, economic and public life.

3. Persons belonging to minorities have the right to participate effectively in decisions on the national and, where appropriate, regional level concerning the minority to which they belong or the regions in which they live, in a manner not incompatible with national legislation.

. . .

Article 3

1. Persons belonging to minorities may exercise their rights, including those set forth in the present Declaration, individually as well as in community with other members of their group, without any discrimination.

2. No disadvantage shall result for any person belonging to a minority as the consequence of the exercise or non-exercise of the rights set forth in the present Declaration.

Article 4

1. States shall take measures where required to ensure that persons belonging to minorities may exercise fully and effectively all their human rights and fundamental freedoms without any discrimination and in full equality before the law.

2. States shall take measures to create favourable conditions to enable persons belonging to minorities to express their characteristics and to develop their culture, language, religion, traditions and customs, except where specific practices are in violation of national law and contrary to international standards.

3. States should take appropriate measures so that, wherever possible, persons belonging to minorities may have adequate opportunities to learn their mother tongue or to have instruction in their mother tongue.

4. States should, where appropriate, take measures in the field of education, in order to encourage knowledge of the history, traditions, language and culture of the minorities existing within their territory. Persons belonging to minorities should have adequate opportunities to gain knowledge of the society as a whole.

5. States should consider appropriate measures so that persons belonging to minorities may participate fully in the economic progress and development in their country.

. . .

Article 8

. . .

2. The exercise of the rights set forth in the present Declaration shall not prejudice the enjoyment by all persons of universally recognized human rights and fundamental freedoms.

3. Measures taken by States to ensure the effective enjoyment of the rights set forth in the present Declaration shall not *prima facie* be considered contrary to the principle of equality contained in the Universal Declaration of Human Rights.

4. Nothing in the present Declaration may be construed as permitting any activity contrary to the purposes and principles of the United Nations, including sovereign equality, territorial integrity and political independence of States.

. . .

NOTE

Note that the Declaration does not use the term 'peoples'—nor the terms 'self-determination' or 'autonomy'. Note also its traditional reference to territorial integrity.

Consider the clauses in the Declaration on Minorities that refer to 'participation'. Article 2(2) provides that '[p]ersons belonging to minorities have the right to participate effectively in cultural, religious, social, economic and public life'. Article 2(3) gives such persons the right 'to participate effectively' in national or regional decisions concerning the minority, 'in a manner not incompatible with national legislation'. Under Article 4(5), states are to consider 'appropriate measures' so that such persons 'may participate fully in the economic progress and development in their country'.

What might constitute the appropriate forms of 'participation' to realize the goals of the Declaration? Various options have been suggested, including the representation of minorities on advisory and decision-making bodies in fields like religion, education or cultural activities; self-administration ('functional autonomies') by the minority on matters essential to its particular identity such as development of language or religious rituals; local forms of self-government; and measures to assure representation of minorities in national legislatures.

QUESTIONS

1. The preamble to the Declaration on Minorities states that it was 'inspired' by Article 27. What major differences appear between the two?

a. As a spokesperson of a minority, does the Declaration strengthen your hand (relative to your relying on Article 27 alone) in advancing claims of right for the minority or claims for protection of the minority by the state? For example, does it better support a claim for an autonomy regime that would assure the minority of, say, 20 per cent of the seats in a national legislature, or of extensive self-government in the region where the minority is concentrated? Does it better support a claim for financial support by the state for a minority's religious schools or for cultural activities like theater, art or music?

b. Does the Declaration implicitly rely on the right to self-determination or on the related individual right to political participation to support its provisions?

c. 'Individual rights take the form of the abstract and universal. Collective rights take the form of the concrete and local. To reach the goals of cultural survival and preservation of differences, collective rights are essential. Article 27 goes only half way toward meeting that goal, and is patently inadequate'. Comment.

2. How do you react to Steiner's assessment of autonomy regimes for ethnic minorities? Would you support, say, a supplementary declaration or convention that would to some extent authorize such regimes? If, as Steiner suggests, 'rights language' is not an appropriate way to express arguments in favor of such regimes, what alternative language would you propose for an instrument extending the provisions of the Declaration on Minorities?

3. Power-sharing arrangements are not necessarily restricted to ethnic groups. Recall the materials in Chapter 3 (p. 195, *supra*) on political participation of women, and the proposals for allocating to women stated percentages of seats in, say, a local or national legislative body. Would you view such proposals more or less favourably than the same form of power-sharing for an ethnic minority?

4. 'Autonomy regimes (such as local government within a federalism, or a personal law regime governing marriage and divorce) should be accepted as legitimate within the

Declaration on Minorities, or accepted by human rights law in general, only if they observe basic human rights, including popular participation in the formation of local government, freedoms of expression and association, and non-discrimination norms. International law should not legitimate any state or people's reliance on self-determination to create a new internal regime or new state that violates basic human rights norms'. Comment.

COMMENT ON INDIGENOUS PEOPLES

This comment briefly discusses analogous issues of indigenous peoples, issues that have assumed considerable global importance over the last two decades and achieved a new prominence in the human rights movement. Although there are important similarities between the categories of ethnic minorities and indigenous peoples, there are also significant differences. It has been important for strategic and other reasons for indigenous peoples to emphasize these differences and therefore to argue for a separate regulatory regime under international law. In fact, the United Nations has addressed the rights and protections of ethnic minorities and indigenous peoples in two separate contemporary standard-setting processes. One led to the 1992 Minorities Declaration appearing above, while the other is now in mid-stream en route toward a declaration.

The developing international legal and political significance of the claims of indigenous peoples owes much to the human rights movement. In the last 15 years or so that movement acted vigorously to recognize interests of indigenous peoples. Over that period, international law has given increased recognition to indigenous peoples as distinctive communities meriting a special international law regime distinct from both the general regime of individual rights and the regime for minorities and members thereof.

There now exist two binding universal instruments dealing specifically with indigenous peoples: a 1957 International Labor Organization (ILO) Convention No. 106, and ILO Convention No. 169 effective in 1991. Over the last 15 years, a Draft Declaration on the Rights of Indigenous Peoples has been prepared within the UN system. Work on it began in 1977. In 1982, the UN created a Working Group on Indigenous Populations of the UN Sub-Commission on Prevention of Discrimination and Protection of Minorities, a body subordinate to the UN Commission that consists of independent expert members. The Working Group started to draft a declaration in 1985, and it soon became the pre-eminent world forum for discussion of issues related to indigenous peoples among representatives of indigenous peoples, of states, and of a broad range of NGOs and scholars. The annual August meetings were considered among the most broadly participatory in the entire UN system.

A Draft Declaration appearing below was agreed upon by members of the Working Group and was submitted to the UN Sub-Commission, which adopted the draft in 1994 and submitted it soon thereafter to the UN Commission on Human Rights for its consideration. The UN Commission created an open-ended inter-sessional working group charged with the mission of elaborating a draft declaration. This working group has met several times to discuss provisions of the 1994 draft.[8] But that draft remains the last formulation of the entire draft Declaration. The process continues of discussing and amending it in the Commission which, it is important to bear in mind, is a body of state representatives rather than independent experts. The underlying economic, political, and sovereignty issues will come to the surface the more clearly as the contending forces seek to work toward the law-like formulation of a Declaration to be approved by the General Assembly.

UN DRAFT DECLARATION ON THE RIGHTS OF INDIGENOUS PEOPLES
UN Doc. E/CN.4/Sub.2/1994/2/Add.1, 20 April 1994

. . .

Article 3: Indigenous peoples have the right of self-determination. By virtue of that right they freely determine their political status and freely pursue their economic, social and cultural development.

Article 4: Indigenous peoples have the right to maintain and strengthen their distinct political, economic, social and cultural characteristics, as well as their legal systems, while retaining their rights to participate fully, if they so choose, in the political, economic, social and cultural life of the State.

. . .

Article 16: . . . States shall take effective measures, in consultation with the indigenous peoples concerned, to eliminate prejudice and discrimination and to promote tolerance, understanding and good relations among indigenous peoples and all segments of society.

. . .

Article 19: Indigenous peoples have the right to participate fully, if they so choose, at all levels of decision-making in matters which may affect their rights, lives and destinies through representatives chosen by themselves in accordance with their own procedures, as well as to maintain and develop their own indigenous decision-making institutions.

Article 20: Indigenous peoples have the right to participate fully, if they so choose, through procedures determined by them, in devising legislative or administrative measures that may affect them. States shall obtain the free and informed consent of the peoples concerned before adopting and implementing such measures.

. . .

Article 25: Indigenous peoples have the right to maintain and strengthen their distinctive spiritual and material relationship with the lands, territories, waters and coastal seas and other resources which they have traditionally owned or otherwise

---

[8] See, for example, the Report of the Working Group set forth in 'Commission on Human Rights, Indigenous Issues', UN Doc. E/CN.4/2000/84, 6 December 1999.

occupied or used, and to uphold their responsibilities to future generations in this regard.

Article 26: Indigenous peoples have the right to own, develop, control and use the lands and territories, including the total environment of the lands, air, waters, coastal seas, sea-ice, flora and fauna and other resources which they have traditionally owned or otherwise occupied or used. This includes the right to the full recognition of their laws, traditions and customs, land-tenure systems and institutions for the development and management of resources, and the right to effective measures by States to prevent any interference with, alienation of or encroachment upon these rights.

Article 27: Indigenous peoples have the right to the restitution of the lands, territories and resources which they have traditionally owned or otherwise occupied or used, and which have been confiscated, occupied, used or damaged without their free and informed consent. Where this is not possible, they have the right to just and fair compensation. Unless otherwise freely agreed upon by the peoples concerned, compensation shall take the form of lands, territories and resources equal in quality, size and legal status.

. . .

Article 30: Indigenous peoples have the right to determine and develop priorities and strategies for the development or use of their lands, territories and other resources, including the right to require that States obtain their free and informed consent prior to the approval of any project affecting their lands, territories and other resources, particularly in connection with the development, utilization or exploitation of mineral, water or other resources. Pursuant to agreement with the indigenous peoples concerned, just and fair compensation shall be provided for any such activities and measures taken to mitigate adverse environmental, economic, social, cultural or spiritual impact.

Article 31: Indigenous peoples, as a specific form of exercising their right to self-determination, have the right to autonomy or self-government in matters relating to their internal and local affairs, including culture, religion, education, information, media, health, housing, employment, social welfare, economic activities, land and resources management, environment and entry by non-members, as well as ways and means for financing these autonomous functions.

Article 32: Indigenous peoples have the collective right to determine their own citizenship in accordance with their customs and traditions. Indigenous citizenship does not impair the right of indigenous individuals to obtain citizenship of the States in which they live. Indigenous peoples have the right to determine the structures and to select the membership of their institutions in accordance with their own procedures.

. . .

Article 34: Indigenous peoples have the collective right to determine the responsibilities of individuals to their communities.

. . .

Article 36: Indigenous peoples have the right to the recognition, observance and enforcement of treaties, agreements and other constructive arrangements concluded with States. . . . Conflicts and disputes which cannot otherwise be settled should be submitted to competent international bodies agreed to by all parties concerned.

NOTE

Consider the following comments of Richard Falk, p. 1274, *supra*, at 61:

> Another recent development of some consequence is the insistence by indigenous peoples . . . on a core right of self-determination that befits their generally shared avowal of sovereignty and nationhood. The degree to which such a right of self-determination is currently part of international law remains uncertain and controversial. There is, to be sure, no binding formal instrument that establishes such a right, or for that matter clarifies its scope, particularly in relation to . . . sovereign states within whose territory or territories such indigenous peoples and nations are situated.
>
> At the same time, there has been a notable evolution of political consciousness with respect to such a claim, as well as a process of acknowledgement to a degree within the United Nations and on the part of existing states. It can be argued that the right of self-determination inheres in a people, and need not be established on its own, or that the path of customary international law has been cleared to a sufficient degree to admit of the legal existence of a right of self-determination. Such matters are embedded in a gray sector of controversy and indefiniteness and are likely to remain so for the next decade, at the very least.
>
> What seems evident is that the emergence of an array of potential claims by indigenous peoples around the world related to the right of self-determination adds to the current confusion as to the status of the right and contributes to nervousness on the part of many diplomats about the persistence of a right of self-determination in this post-colonial era. . . .

QUESTIONS

1. What are the fundamental distinctions between the 1992 Minorities Declaration and the 1994 Draft Declaration? As a representative of indigenous peoples, why would you have preferred a separate track through the UN and a separate declaration, rather than to have the 1992 Declaration embrace both categories?

2. What significance do you attach to the use in the title and text of the word 'peoples'?

3. What understanding of the right to self-determination does this Draft Declaration express?

4. What issues would you expect to arise in the ongoing debates over the Draft Declaration in the Working Group, and thereafter in the UN Commission itself? As a representative of an indigenous people, what legal-political arguments would you stress to support the present formulation of the Draft Declaration?

ADDITIONAL READING

In addition to the sources noted in this section, see Francesco Capotorti, *Study on the Rights of Persons Belonging to Ethnic, Religious and Linguistic Minorities* (1979); Hurst Hannum, *Autonomy, Sovereignty, and Self-Determination: The Accommodation of Conflicting Rights* (1990); Donald Horowitz, *Ethnic Groups in Conflict* (1985); Alan Philips and A. Rosas (eds.), *The UN Minority Rights Declaration* (1993); Patrick Thornberry, *International Law and the Rights of Minorities* (1991). See also Additional Reading at p. 1289, *supra*.

16

Globalization, Development, and Human Rights

Chapter 16 embraces a multitude of subjects within the rubric of 'globalization and development'. The issues have been succinctly defined by UN Secretary-General Kofi Annan: 'the combination of underdevelopment, globalization and rapid change poses particular challenges to the international human rights regime. . . . [T]he pursuit of development, the engagement with globalization, and the management of change must all yield to human rights imperatives rather than the reverse'.[1]

These subjects take us potentially far afield from the traditional focus of human rights, into areas such as trade, development assistance, monetary and financial policy, foreign debt, transnational corporations, and the environment. They require at least a passing acquaintance with the role of institutions such as the International Bank for Reconstruction and Development (IBRD, World Bank) and the International Monetary Fund (IMF). Economic analysis must supplement legal and policy analysis. Finally, these subjects reach well beyond the traditional state-centric framework that is the main concern of most human rights debate, and require a close look at the human rights responsibilities of other actors. Thus corporations and their multinational activities figure importantly in current discussions about minimum labour and environmental standards.

The centrality of these issues to so much of what is happening at both the national and international levels today demands at least a general understanding of their relevance to the human rights agenda. This chapter provides a brief intro-duction to a few of those issues. We look first at the range of challenges to human rights that arise in the context of globalization, and then examine the right to development and its possible implications in terms of aid and debt relief for poor countries. The materials then consider the human rights implications of the increasingly important roles played by the World Bank and the IMF. This chapter concludes with a discussion of multinational enterprises that produce goods in developing countries and of minimum labour standards.

---

[1] UN Doc. A/54/1 (1999), para. 275.

A. THE CHALLENGES OF GLOBALIZATION

Globalization has become one of those protean terms that leads many lives among the commentators on world events who expound it. Consider the analysis of a group of scholars of this phenomenon.[2]

> ... [G]lobalization reflects a widespread perception that the world is rapidly being moulded into a shared social space by economic and technological forces and that developments in one region of the world can have profound consequences for the life chances of individuals or communities on the other side of the globe. For many, globalization is also associated with a sense of political fatalism and chronic insecurity in that the sheer scale of contemporary social and economic change appears to outstrip the capacity of national governments or citizens to control, contest or resist that change. The limits to national politics, in other worlds, are forcefully suggested by globalization.

The authors divide the globalization debate among three types of commentators. *Hyperglobalists* see globalization as defining 'a new era in which people everywhere are increasingly subject to the disciplines of the global marketplace'. The consequence is a 'denationalization' of economies and the related development of 'transnational networks' of production, finance and so on. The 'impersonal forces of the global market' are more powerful than the states (governments) that were in theory supposed to exercise the decisive power in world events. Global and regional institutions further challenge earlier notions of state sovereignty.

Sceptics deny the 'historically unparalleled' character of the economic investment, trade and general aura associated with globalization. They stress the continuing power and significance of national governments to regulate international flows. To the contrary, the *transformationalist thesis* asserts the deep, radical character of the modern trend that blurs longstanding distinctions between the 'international and domestic, external and internal affairs'.

However one describes or assesses this phenomenon, certain characteristic of its context are beyond dispute. Technology has created the essential conditions for a universal trend of this type: the speed of communication of information, of capital flows, of the export of cultural products to countries around the world.

It is not difficult to point to the relationship between these phenomema and the growth and diffusion of the human rights movement, a movement whose very charter bore the term of a *Universal* Declaration. Human rights NGOs have been an important ingredient of the growth of an international civil society, and at the same time have assumed roles and functions that chip away at traditional notions of the sovereignty and hegemony of the state. Intergovernmental organizations foster the growth of a new international consciousness about rights. The norms themselves tower above many states' behaviour and, for most states, find their origin not in national experiences but in international agreements and pressures.

---

[2] David Held, A. McGrew, D. Goldblatt and J. Perraton, *Global Transformations* (1999), at 1.

SHAHID YUSUF, THE CHANGING
DEVELOPMENT LANDSCAPE

36/4 Finance and Development 15 (December 1999)

Since the birth of the modern nation-state, countries have gone back and forth between seeking closer integration with the rest of the world (globalization) and retreating into isolationism and protectionism, while local groups have sought greater autonomy (localization). However, despite the long history of globalization and localization, their impact has been weak and fleeting, until now. The dramatic acceleration of globalization and localization and the enduring changes they have brought about distinguish the closing decades of the twentieth century from earlier periods. . . .

Why globalization?

. . . The word is now common currency and denotes both positive developments, such as the integration of markets for goods and factors of production, and negative developments, such as damage to the environment and the increasing exposure of countries to external shocks that can precipitate banking and currency crises. The growth of international trade and of factor movements was as swift in the first 10 years of the twentieth century as in the century's last decade, but the current phase of globalization is of a different order, in particular because of the increasing share of tradables now exported, advances in technology, changes in the composition of capital flows, and the larger role of international agencies, nongovernmental organizations (NGOs), and transnational corporations. The completion of the Uruguay Round of trade talks in 1994 was a milestone: trade barriers were lowered; the ambit of trade liberalization was expanded to include services, intellectual property rights, agricultural commodities, and textiles; and the new rules of the game that grew out of the talks were anchored in the World Trade Organization (WTO).

In the 1980s, many countries—industrial as well as developing—began dismantling controls on capital movements and adopting policies that encouraged foreign direct investment. Declining transport costs and impressive advances in communications technologies and information processing boosted the integration of goods and capital markets. The adoption of common rules to regulate banking and financial reporting decreased information asymmetry and lent further momentum to globalization, as did the creation of the World Wide Web and international coalescence around product standards such as ISO 9000.

As countries began to welcome foreign direct investment and transacting business over long distances grew easier, companies were motivated to reorganize their activities; [their response] . . . has also reinforced the openness resulting from trade liberalization and the removal of barriers to capital mobility.

Even with these changes, globalization might not have taken off were it not for a seismic shift in attitudes. Countries worldwide have moved to market-based economies and democratic forms of government, the decisive events being the tearing down of the Berlin Wall in 1989 and the spread of democracy during the early

1990s. This broadening of political participation is feeding centrifugal pressures within nations.

The 1990s could be called the decade of globalization. The General Agreement on Tariffs and Trade (GATT) had 102 members in 1990; its successor, the WTO, had 134 members in 1999. Trade in goods and services has grown twice as fast as GDP during the 1990s, with the share of developing countries in total international trade climbing from 23 percent to 29 percent. All forms of capital are circulating more widely and in far larger amounts than ever before. For instance, developing countries received $155 billion (net) of foreign direct investment in 1998, 16 times the amount they received in 1990. . . .

Localization and its causes

. . .

Localization is the demand for autonomy and political voice expressed by regions and communities. It has many causes. Dissatisfaction with the ability of the state to deliver on promises of development is one. The strength of local and ethnic identity—reinforced by education, better communications, and the rising concentration of people in urban areas—is another. A third cause, in a world where globalization is leveling cultural differences, is the desire to deepen a sense of belonging to a place. And a fourth is the sharpening competition between subnational units in an open environment, combined with the reluctance of richer communities to share resources with their less well off neighbors.

The pull of local identity is strikingly manifested by the doubling of the number of nation-states—from 96 in 1960 to 192 in 1998—a development that derived additional impetus from the geopolitical changes that followed the end of the Cold War. Furthermore, the demand for political voice is striking firm roots. . . . In 1980, only 12 of the world's 48 largest countries had national elections. Today, 34 hold both national and local elections.

The political and functional decentralization of both large and small states is another manifestation. Half the countries that decentralized politically also devolved major functional responsibilities—for example, primary and secondary education in Poland, and primary health care and local road maintenance in the Philippines. Often, this devolution has raised the subnational share of public expenditures: for example, from 1987 to 1996, it increased from 11 percent to 30 percent in Mexico and from 21 percent to 50 percent in South Africa.

. . .

One phenomenon driving localization and contributing to the emerging sense of local identity is urbanization. As we enter the twenty-first century, half of the world's population is living in urban areas. As recently as 1975, this share was just over a third; by 2025 it will rise to almost two-thirds. . . .

Globalization and localization enhance the prospects for rapid and sustainable growth in developing countries. The increased availability and more efficient allocation of resources, freer circulation of knowledge, more open and competitive milieus, and improved governance could all contribute to faster growth. But there are also risks. Globalization entails greater exposure to capital volatility—as the financial crisis that erupted in 1997 demonstrated. Decentralizing measures introduced to satisfy local demands may lead to macroeconomic instability if fiscal imprudence by subnational entities is not vigorously disciplined. Moreover, although the concentration of industry and skills in growing urban areas could raise living standards in these areas, the promise of these 'agglomeration economies' could prove elusive in the absence of national policies designed to curb the spread of poverty, violence, and squalor.

...

Globalization and localization demand a multifaceted response. . . . At many levels, institutions will be decisive in making sustainable development a reality.

...

HAROLD HONGJU KOH, INTRODUCTION
US Department of State, 1999 Country Reports on Human Rights Practices
February 25, 2000, www.state.gov/www/global/human_rights/
1999_hrp_report/overview.html

I. The Third Globalization: Transnational Human Rights Networks

Today, all the talk is of globalization. But far too often, both its advocates and its critics have portrayed globalization as an exclusively economic and technological phenomenon. In fact, in the new millennium, there are at least three universal 'languages': money, the Internet, and democracy and human rights. An overlooked 'third globalization'—the rise of transnational human rights networks of both public and private actors—has helped develop what may over time become an international civil society capable of working with governments, international institutions, and multinational corporations to promote both democracy and the standards embodied in the Universal Declaration of Human Rights.

...

... [T]oday, new kinds of networks—linked by air transport, telecommunications, the global media, and the Internet—are helping create transnational communities of shared institutions, shared ideas, and—most importantly—shared values. We are rapidly moving toward a global network of government officials, activists, thinkers, and practitioners who share a common commitment to democracy, the universality of human rights, and respect for the rule of law.

Not surprisingly, the emergence of global telecommunications and commercial networks—the two other new 'global languages'—have served as important driving forces behind this trend. Just as the Berlin Wall once stood as a physical barrier to movement and the free spread of democracy, governments that abuse human rights also seek to build walls that will stop the free flow of information. But the global information revolution has perforated such walls: E-mail, the Internet, cell phones, and other technologies have helped activists from around the globe to connect with one another in ways that were impossible only 10 years ago. The Internet has created a world in which traditional hierarchical, bidirectional models of authority have been replaced by nonhierarchical, multidirectional systems that naturally feed the growth of transnational networks. Similarly, the global commercial revolution has multiplied contact points between open and closed societies. As corporations, banks, international financial institutions, and private investors engage with transitional societies, they increasingly serve as transmission belts for human rights norms and advocates for human rights improvements.

. . .

In addition in areas ranging from environmental protection to human rights, corporations have begun to meet regularly not only with unions but with broader transnational human rights networks to identify how they can work together to solve problems. Corporate social responsibility increasingly has been accepted as a core tenet of global corporate citizenship, generating gatherings from Davos to San Francisco to London, as well as new networks of concern, including the new Global Sullivan Principles, the Fair Labor Association, the Worker Rights Consortium, the SA 8000 initiative, the 'No Sweat' Initiative, and the Apparel Industry Partnership.

The U.S. Government has sought to encourage this trend by interacting and building alliances with multinational corporations that share a commitment to establish a public-private network devoted to human rights advancement. In partnership with American companies, we have developed a set of voluntary Model Business Principles; we also have worked with the business and labour communities as well as the International Labor Organization to promote 1998's Declaration on Core Labor Standards. We are working closely with the garment and footwear industries, trade unions, and community activists to combat the still-too-pervasive reality of sweatshop labour at home and abroad. Most recently, we have been exploring new ways to work together with community activists, human rights NGO's, and corporations working in the extractive industries to promote human rights, support democratic institutions, and strengthen the rule of law, particularly in the three democracy-priority countries of Colombia, Indonesia, and Nigeria.

. .

. . . As international commerce and telecommunications continue to bind the world's peoples together, the United States will remain committed to using the universal language of human rights to build public-private networks to promote democracy and human rights worldwide. . . .

MARY ROBINSON, CONSTRUCTING AN INTERNATIONAL FINANCIAL, TRADE AND DEVELOPMENT ARCHITECTURE: THE HUMAN RIGHTS DIMENSION
Zurich, 1 July 1999, www.unhchr.org

. . .

The design of the post-War international financial system was based on the idea . . . that, in return for economic liberalization on the international level, national governments would provide for the social welfare needs of their citizens. For a long time the separation of the rules for international economic transactions, whether financial or in the area of trade, from the welfare of the individual was carefully maintained. But in recent years concern has been growing at the negative human impact of some economic policies and of structural adjustment programmes in particular. These concerns have been reinforced by the recent financial crisis and have led many to urge that the human impact of policies and actions be considered as an integral part of policy formulation and implementation.

Promoting economic development has, of course, been high on the international agenda. However, as Joseph Stiglitz of the World Bank stated some time ago in a thoughtful speech:

> the experience of the past fifty years has demonstrated that development is possible, but not inevitable. While a few countries have succeeded in rapid economic growth, narrowing the gap between themselves and the more advanced countries, and bringing millions of their citizens out of poverty, many more countries have actually seen that gap grow and poverty increase. . . .

. . .

What can be done to remedy the situation?

It is not beyond the capacity of the international community to devise strategies to help to secure economic, social and cultural rights for all and to honour the often repeated pledges to support the right to development. I would like to suggest five ways in which progress can be made . . . .

(i) Development

A new strategy of development should be adopted which would seek to achieve, not just GDP growth, but society-wide change. The strategy should foster participation and ownership and should embrace the public and private sectors, the community, families and the individual. This approach would place the human person at the centre of the development paradigm. The basis for this approach would be an emphasis on the human rights objectives of development.

(ii) Role of international financial, economic and trade institutions

Human rights must permeate macro-economic policies, embracing fiscal policies, monetary policies, exchange rate policies, and trade policies. To take the example of children . . . , one economist has noted that 'Trade and exchange rate policies may have a larger impact on children's development than the relative size of the budget allocated to health and education. An incompetent Central Bank can be more harmful to children than an incompetent Ministry of Education'.

The international economic institutions should lead the way. They must take greater account of the human dimension of their activities and the huge impact which economic policies can have on local economies, especially in our increasingly globalized world. . . .

(iii) Debt

More and more attention is focussed these days on the crushing burden of debt faced by the poorest countries, a huge obstacle to their meeting economic challenges and, hence, strengthening the human rights of their citizens. . . .

[In June 1999] the G-8 nations agreed to what is being called 'the Cologne Initiative', a package of measures designed to reduce the debt burden of the 33 poorest countries of the world. These countries collectively owe $127 billion to industrialised countries and institutions such as the IMF and the World Bank. Sceptics of debt relief have argued that previous measures did not filter through to ordinary citizens as the savings made were often diverted to wasteful or corrupt purposes. The Cologne Initiative would require debtor nations to show that they are using the benefits primarily for expenditure on education and health.

Properly structured debt relief initiatives could bring tremendous benefits to countries gripped by poverty but committed to economic and political reform. In virtually all of the countries I visit, I encounter a willingness to embrace modern economic practices but I am constantly told of the strangling effect which debt repayments have on governments trying to put their economies on a sound footing. In Mozambique, to quote just one of the most critical examples, 30% of all revenue goes on debt servicing. And this is one of the poorest countries in the world. If debt payments were relieved resources could be freed to restore the health and education systems which are in a dire state.

(iv) The private sector

Undoubtedly, the most powerful player in international economic relations is the private sector. In fact, a great deal of international activity, be it via the World Trade Organization or the International Monetary Fund, is aimed at providing a stable environment for international economic exchanges. On an international level, corporations are indeed important. The largest 100 companies have combined annual revenues that exceed the GDP of half of the world's nations.

Big corporations have the power to bring great benefits to poor communities—but they can cause great damage too: through degradation of the environment, exploitation of economically weak communities, the use of child labour. In recent years there has been an increasing awareness on the part of business that it must face up to its responsibilities in the human rights field. Corporations and business associations contact my office asking for information and guidance. Human rights in business is taking root, through internal ethical statements, corporate codes of conduct, sectoral agreements on issues such as child labour in the clothing industry, or wider codes such as Social Accountability 8000, the International Code of Ethics for Canadian Business and the new Sullivan principles.

. . .

QUESTIONS

1. In broad terms, how would you identify the potential challenges for the international human rights regimes of the trend toward globalization? Of the trend towards localization?

2. What is the nature of the transnational public-private network identified by

Assistant Secretary of State Koh? Are corporations, banks and private investors appropriately seen as 'transmission belts for human rights norms'?

3. The strategies outlined by Mary Robinson, the UNHCHR, are commonly described as 'mainstreaming' human rights. Is this necessarily a good thing or are there some areas which should be kept separate from human rights? If so, what might they be?

NOTE

Most materials in this Section E examine the effects of globalization or different theories and methods of development on human rights norms. What of the reverse inquiry: the effect of those norms on the patterns of globalization and development? Arguments are advanced that current economic trends are not merely consistent with human rights, but indeed are both supported by human rights thinking and point toward those rights' quicker realization. Consider the following comments on such arguments.

HENRY STEINER, DO HUMAN RIGHTS REQUIRE A PARTICULAR FORM OF DEMOCRACY?
in Eugene Cotran and Adel Omar Sherif (eds.), Democracy, the Rule of Law and Islam (1999), at 202

. . .

In this period of rapid and culturally unsettling transformation, forceful argument has asserted (or denied) causal relationships between, for example, the penetration by multinational enterprises of states throughout the world within a regime of free trade and investment, and the gradual inculcation in those states of values associated with human rights generally. For example, the rule of law, so vital to the growth of liberalism and democratic government, is invoked to urge greater predictability in the application of laws bearing on foreign investment and on business generally, a predictability that would serve as a magnet for further investment. In turn, it is argued, heightened business investment and activity under such a legal regime will ultimately strengthen the rule of law with respect to civil and political rights as well. Foreign investment and the development of the local economy in the broad western model thus will contribute importantly toward, if not make inevitable, the realization of democratic and human rights culture.

In such ways, human rights principles have become part of a many-sided argument for globalization and the beliefs informing it: deregulation and free markets under an international regime of free trade, privatization, minimal government, and, perhaps inferentially, the related cultural characteristics [of individualism and materialism] noted above. The causal flows are argued to be reciprocal, as global business activity both inspires and responds to the growth of democratic rule and its associated rule of law. . . .

States or advocates seeking to preserve or develop modes of national life alternative to the West may then perceive their choice to lie between accepting the human rights framework together with the associated economic structures and cultural characteristics of the West, or rejecting important parts of that framework in the effort to protect or develop a different culture. Such an attitude would be deeply mistaken . . . .

Although interest groups or theorists may stress for strategic or policy reasons the complementary and mutually reinforcing nature of different discourses and systems—such as links between globalization, privatization, or deregulated markets on the one hand, and democracy and human rights on the other—these are not linkages proposed, let alone imposed, by human rights instruments. To state the obvious, the ICCPR does not require states to pursue policies of free trade or deregulation of markets as necessary routes towards democracy. Governments' decisions about such vital matters will draw on interrelated factors that touch human rights concerns only in part—for example, the relative political and economic power of states on different sides of these arguments; the economic appeal of and evidence supporting different theories of development and trade and their casual links to the protection of human rights; technological changes in manufacturing, transportation and communication that bind economies and culture to each other more closely than ever.

Over the half century of the human rights movement, arguments about linkages and causation have changed with circumstances, and will continue to. However dominant or persuasive they may appear at a given time, such ideas and advocacy are open to challenge and rethinking from both empirical and normative perspectives. They should not be conflated with a human rights movement with a more restricted agenda whose deep faith lies not in any particular national or international economic system but in the capacity of human beings for critical thought and change.

B. THE RIGHT TO DEVELOPMENT, INTERNATIONAL AID, AND DEBT

Perhaps there was an earlier period that achieved a great consensus over the components and character of 'development'. If so, that period has fled. Today the term is as contested as so many other key concepts. Over the decades, organizations like the World Bank and the IMF have modified to one or another degree their earlier understanding of the concept. Moreover, experiments like the *Human Development Reports* of the UN Development Program have launched innovative ideas and methods for rethinking the ingredients of and thereby changing the statistical measures of development. Amartya Sen (whose related writings appear at pp. 165, 269 and 274 *supra*) is among the thinkers who have contributed importantly to this ferment in thought about development.

AMARTYA SEN, DEVELOPMENT AS FREEDOM
(1999), at 35

Chapter 2: The Ends and the Means of Development

Let me start off with a distinction between two general attitudes to the process of development that can be found both in professional economic analysis and in public discussions and debates. One view sees development as a 'fierce' process, with much 'blood, sweat and tears'—a world in which wisdom demands toughness. In particular, it demands calculated neglect of various concerns that are seen as 'soft-headed'. . . . [T]he temptations to be resisted can include having social safety nets that protect the very poor, providing social services for the population at large, departing from rugged institutional guidelines in response to identified hardship, and favoring—'much too early'—political and civil rights and the 'luxury' of democracy. These things, it is argued in this austere attitudinal mode, could be supported later on, when the development process has borne enough fruit: what is needed here and now is 'toughness and discipline'. The different theories [diverge] in pointing to distinct areas of softness that are particularly to be avoided, varying from financial softness to political relaxation, from plentiful social expenditures to complaisant poverty relief.

This hard-knocks attitude contrasts with an alternative outlook that sees development as essentially a 'friendly' process. Depending on the particular version of this attitude, the congeniality of the process is seen as exemplified by such things as mutually beneficial exchanges (of which Adam Smith spoke eloquently), or by the working of social safety nets, or of political liberties, or of social development—or some combination or other of these supportive activities.

The approach of this book is much more compatible with the latter approach than with the former. It is mainly an attempt to see development as a process of expanding the real freedoms that people enjoy. In this approach, expansion of freedom is viewed as both (1) the *primary end* and (2) the *principal means* of development. They can be called respectively the 'constitutive role' and the 'instrumental role' of freedom in development. The constitutive role of freedom relates to the importance of substantive freedom in enriching human life. The substantive freedoms include elementary capabilities like being able to avoid such deprivations as starvation, undernourishment, escapable morbidity and premature mortality, as well as the freedoms that are associated with being literate and numerate, enjoying political participation and uncensored speech and so on. In this constitutive perspective, development involves expansion of these and other basic freedoms. Development, in this view, is the process of expanding human freedoms, and the assessment of development has to be informed by this consideration.

Let me refer here to an example. . . . Within the narrower views of development (in terms of say, [Gross Domestic Product] growth or industrialization) it is often asked whether the freedom of political participation and dissent is or is not 'conducive to development'. In the light of the foundational view of development as freedom, this question would seem to be defectively formulated, since it misses the crucial understanding that political participation and dissent are *constitutive* parts of development itself. . . . Development seen as enhancement of freedom cannot but address [deprivations of freedom]. The relevance of the deprivation of basic political freedoms or civil rights, for an adequate understanding of development, does not have to be established through their indirect contribution to *other* features of development (such as growth of GDP or the promotion of industrialization). These freedoms are part and parcel of enriching the process of development.

This fundamental development point is distinct from the 'instrumental' argument that these freedoms and rights may *also* be very effective in contributing to economic progress. . . . [T]he significance of the instrumental role of political freedom as *means* to development does not in any way reduce the evaluative importance of freedom as an *end* of development.

. . . The instrumental role of freedom concerns the way different kinds of rights, opportunities, and entitlements contribute to the expansion of human freedom in general, and thus to promoting development. . . . The effectiveness of freedom as an instrument lies in the fact that different kinds of freedom interrelate with one another, and freedom of one type may greatly help in advancing freedom of other types. The two roles are thus linked by empirical connections, as relating freedom of one kind to freedom of other kinds.

. . .

. . . I shall consider the following types of instrumental freedoms: (1) *political freedoms*, (2) *economic facilities*, (3) *social opportunities*, (4) *transparency guarantees*, and (5) *protective security*. These instrumental freedoms tend to contribute to the general capability of a person to live more freely, but they also serve to complement one another. While development analysis must, on the one hand, be concerned with the objectives and aims that make these instrumental freedoms consequentially important, it must also take note of the empirical linkages that tie the distinct types of freedom *together*, strengthening their joint importance. Indeed, these connections are central to a fuller understanding of the instrumental role of freedom. The claim that freedom is not only the primary object of development but also its principal means relates particularly to these linkages.

Let me comment a little on each of these instrumental freedoms. [Discussion of political freedoms omitted.]

Economic facilities refer to the opportunities that individuals respectively enjoy to utilize economic resources for the purpose of consumption, or production, or exchange. The economic entitlements that a person has will depend on the resources owned or available for use as well as on conditions of exchange, such as relative prices and the working of the markets. Insofar as the process of economic development increases the income and wealth of a country, they are reflected in corresponding enhancement of economic entitlements. It should be obvious that in the relation between national income and wealth, on the one hand, and the economic entitlements of individuals (or families), on the other, distributional considerations are important, in addition to aggregative ones. How the additional incomes generated are distributed will clearly make a difference.

. . .

Social opportunities refer to the arrangements that society makes for education, health care and so on, which influence the individual's substantive freedom to live better. These facilities are important not only for the conduct of private lives (such as living a healthy life and avoiding preventable morbidity and premature mortality), but also for more effective participation in economic and political activities. For example illiteracy can be a major barrier to participation in economic activities that require production according to specification or demand strict quality control (as globalized trade increasingly does). Similarly, political participation may be hindered by the inability to read newspapers or to communicate in writing with others involved in political activities.

. . .

Finally, no matter how well an economic system operates, some people can be typically on the verge of vulnerability and can actually succumb to great deprivation as a result of material changes that adversely affect their lives. *Protective security* is needed to provide a social safety net for preventing the affected population from being reduced to abject misery, and in some cases even starvation and death. The domain of protective security includes fixed institutional arrangements such as unemployment benefits and statutory income supplements to the indigent as well as ad hoc arrangements to generate income for destitutes.

These instrumental freedoms directly enhance the capabilities of people, but they also supplement one another, and can furthermore reinforce one another. These interlinkages are particularly important to seize in considering development policies.

. . .

Similarly the creation of social opportunities, through such services as public education, health care, and the development of a free and energetic press, can contribute both to economic development and to significant reductions in mortality rates. Reduction of mortality rates, in turn, can help to reduce birth rates, reinforcing the influence of basic education—especially female literary and schooling—on fertility behavior.

. . .

This approach goes against—and to a great extent undermines—the belief that has been so dominant in many policy circles that 'human development' (as the process of expanding education, health care and other conditions of human life is often called) is really a kind of luxury that only richer countries can afford. Perhaps the most important impact of the type of success that the East Asian economies, beginning with Japan, have had is the total undermining of that implicit prejudice. These economies went comparatively early for massive expansion of education, and later also of health care, and this they did, in many cases, *before* they broke the restraints of general poverty. And they have reaped as they have sown. . . .

. . .

COMMENT ON INTERNATIONAL SOLIDARITY AND THE RIGHT TO DEVELOPMENT

Article 56 of the UN Charter commits all member states to take 'joint and separate action in co-operation' with the UN for the achievement of the purposes identified in Article 55, which includes human rights, 'higher standards of living . . . and conditions of economic and social progress and development' and 'solutions of international economic, social, health and related problems'. Similarly, Article 28 of the UDHR provides that 'Everyone is entitled to a social and international order in which the rights and freedoms set forth in this Declaration can be fully realized'. These provisions, although expressed at a level of great generality, have often been invoked by those who posit the existence of a broad international 'duty to cooperate' or a 'right to solidarity'. In a world of deep-rooted and growing inequalities among nations, the question inevitably arises whether the international community bears some responsibility for assisting states whose resources are inadequate to ensure the human rights of their own citizens, or for providing direct assistance to those individuals in dire need.

Since 1977 much of this debate has been pursued within the field of human rights under the rubric of the 'right to development'. The debate touches upon a number of themes raised in earlier chapters: the basis for recognition of new rights, the priority to be accorded to the different sets of rights, the links between human rights and democratic governance, and the relationship between individual and collective rights (including peoples' rights).

The list of internationally recognized human rights is by no means immutable. Just as the British sociologist T. H. Marshall characterized the 18th century as the century of civil rights, the 19th as that of political rights and the 20th as that of social rights,[1] so too have some commentators over the past three decades put forward claims for the recognition of the new rights, in particular a category known as the 'third generation of solidarity rights'. By analogy with the slogan of the French Revolution these rights have been said to correspond to the theme of *fraternité*, while first generation civil and political rights correspond with *liberté* and second generation economic and social rights with *egalité*. Karel Vasak's list of solidarity rights includes 'the right to development, the right to peace, the right to environment, the right to the ownership of the common heritage of mankind, and the right to communication'.[3]

Far more significant has been the impact of the right to development. First recognized by the UN Commission on Human Rights in 1977, it was enshrined by the General Assembly in the 1986 Declaration on the Right to Development (reproduced in the Documents Annex). It has never ceased to be controversial among governments as well as among academic and other commentators. Efforts to secure its recognition raised the question of the process by which new human rights should be recognized. Some commentators emphasized the need for the catalogue of rights to keep pace with new developments and to be responsive to

---

[3] K. Vasak, 'For the Third Generation of Human Rights: The Rights of Solidarity', International Institute of Human Rights, July 1979, at 3.

new challenges. Others argued that the third-generation approach was a flawed way of seeking to meet such needs.

> Not only is proliferation of rights considered to be dangerous, but also the use of the term 'generation' implies, the detractors say, that the rights belonging to earlier generations are outdated. It is also frequently said that the rights of the new generation are too vague to be justiciable and are no more than slogans. . . .[4]

In the readings below Abi-Saab and Bedjaoui present the case for the existence in international law of a right to development, while Donnelly argues that the right is not only without foundation but is dangerous as well.

GEORGES ABI-SAAB, THE LEGAL FORMULATION OF A RIGHT TO DEVELOPMENT

in Hague Academy of International Law, The Right to Development at the International Level (1980), at 163

[Abi-Saab begins by noting that, for the right to development to be considered a legal right, it must be possible to identify the active and passive subjects of the right and its content. But those elements depend on the legal basis of the right, which in turn depends on whether the right is an individual or collective one.]

It is possible to think of different legal bases of the right to development as a collective right. The first possibility . . . is to consider the right to development as the aggregate of the social, economic and cultural rights not of each individual, but of all the individuals constituting a collectivity. In other words, it is the sum total of a double aggregation of the rights and of the individuals. This version . . . has the merit of shedding light on the link between the rights of the individual and the right of the collectivity; a link which is crucial. . . .

Another way . . . is to approach it directly from a collective perspective . . . by considering it either as the economic dimension of the right of self-determination, or alternatively as a parallel right to self-determination, partaking of the same nature and belonging to the same category of collective rights.

. . .

As far as the beneficiaries or active subjects are concerned, the first answer that comes to mind is that they are those societies possessing certain characteristics which lead the international community to consider them wanting in terms of development and to classify them as 'developing' or 'less developed' countries (LDC). . . .

. . .

. . . Up to now, we have used societies, communities, countries and States as interchangeable, which they are not. In fact, here as with self-determination, the common denominator of these different ways of describing the beneficiary

---

[4] S. Marks, 'Emerging Human Rights: A New Generation for the 1980s?', 33 Rutgers L. Rev. 435, 451 (1981).

collectivity is the 'people' they designate, which constitutes the socially relevant entity or group in this context. . . . Suffice it to say here that the distinction between 'people' and 'State', though in theory it is as important in relation to the right to development as to the right of self-determination, in practice it is not. . . .
. . .

. . . [T]he passive subject of the right to development can only be the international community as such. But as the international community does not have at its disposal the means (organs, resources) of directly fulfilling its obligations under the right to development, it can only discharge them through a category of its members, that of the 'developed' States. . . .
. . .

. . . [S]atisfaction of the collective right is a necessary condition, a condition-precedent or a prerequisite for the materialization of the individual rights. Thus without self-determination it is impossible to imagine a total realization of the civil and political rights of the individuals constituting the collectivity in question. Such rights can be granted and exercised at lower levels, such as villages and municipalities, but they cannot reach their full scope and logical conclusion if the community is subject to colonial or alien rule.
. . .

The same with the right to development, which is a necessary precondition for the satisfaction of the social and economic rights of the individuals. And here, even more than in the case of self-determination, the causal link between the two levels is particularly strong; for without a tolerable degree of development, the society will not be materially in a position to grant and guarantee these rights to its members, i.e., of providing the positive services and securing the minimum economic standards which are required by these rights.
. . .

MOHAMMED BEDJAOUI, THE RIGHT TO DEVELOPMENT
in M. Bedjaoui (ed.), International Law: Achievements and Prospects (1991), at 1182

. . .

14. The right to development is a fundamental right, the precondition of liberty, progress, justice and creativity. It is the alpha and omega of human rights, the first and last human right, the beginning and the end, the means and the goal of human rights, in short it is the *core right* from which all the others stem. . . .
. . .

15. . . . In reality the international dimension of the right to development is nothing other than *the right to an equitable share in the economic and social well-being of the world.* It reflects an essential demand of our time since four fifths of the world's population no longer accept that the remaining fifth should continue to build its wealth on their poverty.
. . .

IV. Basis of the Right to Development

19. The most essential human rights have, in a sense, a meta-juridical founda-tion. For example, the right to life is independent both of international law and of the municipal laws of States. It pre-exists law. In this sense it is a 'primary' or 'first' law, that is to say a law commanding all the others. . . . Thus the right to develop-ment imposes itself with the force of a self-evident principle and its natural foundation is as a corollary of the right to life. . . .

. . .

22. The 'right to development' flows from this right to self-determination and has the *same nature*. There is little sense in recognizing self-determination as a superior and inviolable principle if one does not recognize *at the same time* a 'right to development' for the peoples that have achieved self-determination. This right to development can only be an 'inherent' and 'built-in' right forming an inseparable part of the right to self-determination.

23. . . . [This makes the right to development] much more a right of the State or of the people, than a right of the individual, and it seems to me that it is better that way.

. . .

26. The present writer considers that international solidarity means taking into account the interdependence of nations. One may identify three stages in this search for the foundation of the right to development based on international solidarity:

    (i) interdependence, the result of the global nature of the world economy;
    (ii) the universal duty of every State to develop the world economy, which makes development an international problem *par excellence*;
    (iii) preservation of the human species as the basis of the right to development.

. . .

V. Content of the Right to Development

34. . . . [This right] has several aspects, the most important and comprehensive of which is the right of each people freely to choose its economic and social system without outside interference or constraint of any kind, and to determine, with equal freedom, its own model of development. . . .

. . .

48. . . . [T]he State seeking its own development is entitled to demand that all the other States, the international community and international economic agents collectively *do not take away from it what belongs to it, or do not deprive it of what is or 'must be' its due in international trade*. In the name of this right to development, the State being considered may claim a *'fair price'* for its raw materials and for whatever it offers in its trade with the more developed countries.

. . .

49. This second meaning of the right to development which is due from the international community seems much more complex. It implies that the State is

entitled if not to the satisfaction of its needs at least to receive a fair share of what belongs to all, and therefore to that State also.

. . .

50. . . . [T]he satisfaction of the needs of a people should be perceived as a right and not as an act of charity. It is a right which should be made effective by *norms and institutions.* The relation between the donor and the recipient States is seen in terms of responsibility and reciprocal rights over goods that are considered as belonging to all. There is no place in such an analysis for charity, the 'act of mercy', considered as being a factor of inequality from which the donor expects tokens of submissiveness or political flexibility on the part of the receiving State. The concept of charity thus gives place to that of justice. *The need,* taken as a criterion of equity, gives greater precision to the concept of '*equitable distribution*' which would otherwise be too vague.

. . .

VI. Degree of Normativity of the Right to Development

53. Learned opinion is divided in its view of the legal validity of the right to development. Many writers consider that while it is undoubtedly an inalienable and imperative right, this is only in the moral, rather than in the legal, sphere. The present writer has, on the contrary, maintained that the right to development is, by its nature, so incontrovertible that it *should* be regarded as belonging to *jus cogens.*

. . .

55. It is clear, however, that a right which is not opposable by the possessor of the right against the person from whom the right is due is not a right in the full legal sense. This constitutes *the challenge which the right to development throws down to contemporary international law* and the whole of the challenge which the underdevelopment of four fifths of the globe places, in political terms, before the rulers of the world. . . .

. . .

JACK DONNELLY, IN SEARCH OF THE UNICORN: THE JURISPRUDENCE AND POLITICS OF THE RIGHT TO DEVELOPMENT
15 Calif. Western Int. L. J. 473 (1985), at 482

III. Legal Sources of the Right to Development

. . .

. . . If the right to development means the right of peoples freely to pursue their development, then it can be plausibly argued to be implied by the Covenants' right to self-determination. However, such a right to development is without interest; it is already firmly established as the right to self-determination.

A substantially broader right to development, however, cannot be extracted from this right to self-determination. The right to self-determination recognized in the Covenants does not imply a right to live in a developing society; it is explicitly only a right to *pursue* development. Neither does it imply an *individual* right to development; self-determination, again explicitly, is a right of peoples only. In no sense does it imply a right to be developed. Thus the claim that the right to development is simply the realization of the right to self-determination is not based on the Covenants' understanding of self-determination.

It might also be argued that because development is necessary for self-determination, development is itself a human right. Such an argument, however, is fallacious. Since we will come across this form of argument again, let us look briefly at this 'instrumental fallacy'. Suppose that A holds mineral rights in certain oil-bearing properties. Suppose further that in order to enjoy these rights fully, she requires $500,000 to begin pumping the oil. Clearly A does not have a right to $500,000 just because she needs it to enjoy her rights . . . . The same reasoning applies to the link between development and the right to self-determination. Even assuming that development is necessary for, rather than a consequence of, full enjoyment of the right to self-determination, it simply does not follow that peoples have a right to development.

Allowing such an argument to prevail would result in a proliferation of bizarre or misguided rights. . . .

. . .

The second promising implicit source of a right to development is Article 28 of the [UDHR] . . .

. . .

[O]ne might question whether 'development' falls under the notion of a social and international order referred to in Article 28. 'Development' suggests a process or result; the process of development or the condition of being developed. 'Order', by contrast, implies a set of principles, rules, practices or institutions; neither a process nor a result but a structure. Article 28, therefore, is most plausibly interpreted as prohibiting *structures* that deny opportunities or resources for the realization of civil, political, economic, social or cultural human rights. . . .

. . .

Suppose, though, that Article 28 *were* to be taken to imply a human right to development. What would that right look like? It would be an *individual* right, and only an individual right; a right of persons, not peoples, and certainly not States. It would be a right to the enjoyment of traditional human rights, not a substantively new right. It would be as much a civil and political as an economic and social right—Article 28 refers to *all* human rights—and would be held equally against one's national government and the international community . . .

. . .

[V. Subjects of the Right to Development]

. . .

If human rights derive from the inherent dignity of the human person, collective human rights are logically possible only if we see social membership as an inherent part of human personality, and if we argue that as part of a nation or people, persons hold human rights substantively different from, and in no way reducible to, individual human rights. This last proposition is extremely controversial. . . .

The very concept of human rights, as it has heretofore been understood, rests on a view of the individual person as separate from, and endowed with inalienable rights held primarily in relation to, society, and especially the state. Furthermore, within the area defined by these rights, the individual is superior to society in the sense that ordinarily, in cases of conflict between individual human rights and social goals or interests, individual rights must prevail. The idea of collective *human* rights represents a major, and at best confusing, conceptual deviation.

I do not want to challenge the idea of collective rights *per se* or even the notion of peoples' rights; groups, including nations, can and do hold a variety of rights. But these are not *human* rights as that term is ordinarily understood. . . .

. . .

A further problem with collective human rights is determining who is to exercise the right; the right-holder is not a physical person, and thus an institutional 'person' must exercise it. In the case of a right held by a people, or by society as a whole, the most plausible 'person' to exercise the right is, unfortunately, the state. Again this represents a radical reconceptualization of human rights—and an especially dangerous one.

. . .

NOTE

Ever since the UN Commission on Human Rights asserted or proclaimed the existence of a right to development in 1977 (CHR Res. 4 (XXXIII)), the issue has been a contentious one. Although the international community has underlined the importance of the right on many occasions, including a statement endorsed by the 1993 Vienna World Conference on Human Rights to the effect that it is 'a universal and inalienable right and an integral part of fundamental human rights', extensive efforts to clarify its content and, more importantly, its implications, have yielded little agreement on concrete issues. Subsequent to the adoption of the Declaration on the Right to Development (reproduced in the Documents Annex) in 1986, the UN Commission has established various mechanisms designed to shed light on these issues. They include four different 'working groups', two composed of 'experts' and two of governmental representatives, as well as an independent expert (Arjun Sengupta) appointed in 1998.[5] While a many reports have been produced, they have yet to lead to any consensus about the practical consequences of the recognition of the right.

QUESTIONS

1. Compare the different conceptions of the right to development put forward by Abi-Saab, Bedjaoui, and Donnelly with the text of the 1986 General Assembly Declaration. Key concerns voiced by some of the governmental and other opponents of the

[5] The website of the OHCHR (www.unhchr.ch/) contains a comprehensive set of documents relating to these endeavours.

right to development include objections to collective human rights and especially to any idea that a human right can be vested in a state, resistance to the idea that resource transfers from the North to the South are obligatory, and fears that a right to development gives priority to development over human rights. To what extent does the Declaration provide a foundation for each of these concerns?

2. In 1986, at the same time as it adopted the Declaration, the General Assembly (Res. 41/120) also adopted guidelines that states were to 'bear in mind' in developing new human rights instruments. New rights should (a) be consistent with the existing body of international human rights law; (b) be of fundamental character and derive from the inherent dignity and worth of the human person; (c) be sufficiently precise to give rise to identifiable and practicable rights and obligations; (d) provide, where appropriate, realistic and effective implementation machinery, including reporting systems; and (e) attract broad international support. Does the right to development meet these criteria?

NOTE

The Declaration on the Right to Development (Article 4) says only that 'States have the duty to take steps, individually and collectively, to formulate international development policies with a view to facilitating the full realization of the right' and that 'effective international co-operation is essential in providing [developing] countries with appropriate means and facilities to foster their comprehensive development'. Nevertheless, a claim for some form of global distributive justice runs through much of the governmental discourse from developing countries and some of the literature on the right to development.

The UN's 'independent expert on the right to development' told the UN Commission on Human Rights in 1999 that '[e]very State which recognized the right to development was obliged to take positive action to assist the citizens of other States in realizing those rights'.[6] Other commentators have gone further in suggesting that the right to development requires the provision of aid to developing countries and the elimination of oppressive debt burdens which hinder efforts to ensure respect for economic and social rights. Such suggestions arise not only in relation to the right to development but also in interpretations of Articles 55 and 56 of the UN Charter, Article 28 of the UDHR, and provisions of the ICESCR.

It is important to bear in mind the distinction between the desirability of such measures and the proposition that they are actually mandated by international norms that are now in effect. In the reading that follows Alston and Quinn consider whether the provisions of the ICESCR, especially those calling for 'international assistance and co-operation', might ground an obligation on the part of wealthier countries to provide financial and other types of assistance to poorer countries.

---

[6] UN Doc. E/CN.4/1999/SR. 9, para. 29.

PHILIP ALSTON AND GERARD QUINN, THE NATURE AND SCOPE OF STATES PARTIES' OBLIGATIONS UNDER THE ICESCR
9 Hum. Rts Q. 156 (1987), at 186

. . .

The Covenant contains three provisions that could be interpreted as giving rise to an obligation on the part of the richer states parties to provide assistance to poorer states parties in situations in which the latter are prevented by a lack of resources from fulfilling their obligations under the Covenant to their citizens. The first is the phrase ['individually and through international assistance and co-operation, especially economic and technical'], which appears in Article 2(1). The second is the provision in Article 11(1) according to which states parties agree to 'take appropriate steps to ensure the realization of this right [to an adequate standard of living], recognizing to this effect the essential importance of international co-operation based on free consent'. Similarly, in Article 11(2) states parties agree to take, 'individually and through international co-operation', relevant measures concerning the right to be free from hunger.

Almost inevitably, dramatically diverging interpretations of the significance of these provisions have been put forward. On the one hand they have been said to give rise to quite specific international obligations on the part of industrialized countries and to provide the foundations for the existence of a right to development. On the other hand, the Carter administration, in seeking the advice and consent of the U.S. Senate to U.S. ratification of the Covenant, proposed a reservation to the effect that: 'It is also understood that paragraph 1 of article 2, as well as article 11 . . . import no legally binding obligation to provide aid to foreign countries'.

. . .

The principle of international cooperation is recognized in Articles 55 and 56 of the United Nations Charter. . . .

. . .

During the preparatory work [for the Covenant] it was conceded by virtually all delegations that the developing states would require some forms of international assistance if they were to be able to promote effectively the realization of economic and social rights. . . .

. . . [T]he U.S. representative considered it 'quite essential for the article . . . to indicate the necessity of international co-operation in the matter'. The consensus, however, did not extend much, if at all, beyond that general proposition.

Those arguing in favor of imposing a strong obligation on the developed countries invoked a wide range of justifications. Perhaps the least controversial was the argument based on interdependence. . . .

On occasion, however, this argument was closely linked to the view that international cooperation was owed to the formerly colonized states in reparation for 'the systematic plundering of their wealth under colonialism'. As another representative put it, 'nations that were or had been colonized did not go begging, but called for the restoration of their rights and property'. . . . It was also argued that the absence of a provision relating to international cooperation would render the undertakings of developing countries 'purely academic' because they would be unable to afford to implement them.

The only formal suggestion of the existence of a binding obligation came from the Chilean representative who observed 'that international assistance to under-developed countries had in a sense become mandatory as a result of commitments assumed by States in the United Nations'.

The arguments against that proposition took a variety of forms and came from a significant range of states. France argued simply that 'multilateral assistance could not be mandatory' and an almost identical argument was made by the Soviet Union. In the view of the representative of Greece 'developing countries like her own had no right to demand financial assistance through such an instrument; they could ask for it, but not claim it'.

Other representatives opposed the reference to international cooperation on the grounds that it would enable states seeking to evade their obligations to invoke the inadequacy of international development assistance as an excuse. . . .

. . .

Thus, on the basis of the preparatory work it is difficult, if not impossible, to sustain the argument that the commitment to international cooperation contained in the Covenant can accurately be characterized as a legally binding obligation upon any particular state to provide any particular form of assistance. It would, however, be unjustified to go further and suggest that the relevant commitment is meaningless. In the context of a given right it may, according to the circumstances, be possible to identify obligations to cooperate internationally that would appear to be mandatory on the basis of the undertaking contained in Article 2(1) of the Covenant.

VIEWS ABOUT REQUIRING FOREIGN AID AND FORGIVING FOREIGN DEBT

Keith Griffin and A. R. Kahn, Globalization and the Developing World

(1992), at 90

The most important issue linking human development and international capital revolves around the role of foreign aid. Foreign aid includes the highly concessional loans and outright grants to developing countries from the OECD and other rich countries, channelled both bilaterally and through multilateral development agencies such as the World Bank and the Regional Development Banks. It is often taken for granted that foreign assistance actually assists developing countries. Often, alas, this is not the case. The Committee for Development Planning reflects an emerging consensus when it states that:

> far too much aid serves no developmental purpose but is used instead to promote the exports of the donor country, to encourage the use of (imported)

capital-intensive methods of production or to strengthen the police and armed forces of the recipient country.

But while agreeing that much aid in the past has been wasted, there is evidence that when donor and recipient act responsibly, foreign aid can indeed be of benefit.

The first thing that needs to be done is to depoliticize aid by bringing it under the control of a supranational authority operating under clearly defined and agreed principles. These principles should include both the mobilization and allocation of aid funds. It may be too much to expect that the leading donor countries would agree to channel all foreign assistance through a supranational authority, but it should be possible to reach agreement to channel most foreign aid through such an authority while leaving individual countries free to supplement multilateral assistance with bilateral programmes if they wish to do so. This would not be a radical departure from present practice although it would change the balance decisively in favour of multilateral assistance.

Agreement among donors might be facilitated if it were understood that all multilateral aid would be allocated to countries representing the poorest 60 per cent of the world's population. This implies that only countries with a per capita income of about 700 US dollars or less would be eligible for assistance. Having determined which countries are eligible, the next step is to agree on how the available funds would be distributed among the recipients. We suggest that the criteria for determining the amount of aid to be allocated to eligible countries reflect (a) the severity of poverty as measured by the shortfall of real per capita income from the agreed threshold of 700 US dollars; (b) the degree of commitment to human development as demonstrated by recent success and current programmes; and (c) the size of the population.

The desired total amount of foreign aid available for distribution might be set as an agreed proportion of the combined GNP of all potential recipients. The burden of financing this total should be distributed among the donor countries progressively so that a richer country contributes a higher proportion of its per capita income than a less rich country. This would make the total volume of aid predictable and the distribution of its burden among the contributors equitable.

. . .

Jeffrey Sachs, Release the Poorest Countries from Debt Bondage

International Herald Tribune, June 12–13, 1999, at 8

About 700 million people—the very poorest—are held in debt bondage by the rich countries. The so-called Highly Indebted Poor Countries are a group of 42 financially bankrupt and largely destitute economies. They owe more than $100 million in unpayable debt to the World Bank, the International Monetary Fund development banks and governments, often reflecting the failures of past loans.

Many of those loans were made to tyrranical regimes to suit Cold War aims.

Many simply reflect misguided ideas of the past. The moral and practical case for freeing those countries from their debt bondage is overwhelming.

Jubilee 2000, an organization supported by people as diverse as Pope John Paul II, Jesse Jackson and Bono, the rock star, has called for outright elimination of the debt burden of many of the world's poorest countries. This idea is often scoffed at as unrealistic, but it is the realists who fail to understand the economic opportunities facing the world today.

The financial bankruptcy of the poorest countries has been evident for at least 15 years, but the IMF, the World Bank and the rich countries have delayed real solutions to the chronic problem. . . .
. . .

In 1996 . . . the IMF and World Bank announced a relief program with great fanfare, but without including any true dialogue with the affected countries. Three years later, these plans have failed. Just two countries (Bolivia and Uganda) were given about $200 million, while 40 others continue to wait in line.

In this same period, the stock market wealth of the rich countries has grown by more than $5 trillion, more than 50 times the debt owed by the 42 poor countries.

So it is a cruel joke for the world's wealthy governments to protest that they cannot afford to cancel the debts. . . .
. . .

The commercial banks in total have claims of about $19 billion [most of which is already written off in their balance sheets]. . . .

The United States, for its part, is not so foolish as to count its $6 billion of claims on the poor nations at face value. These loans are already carried on the books at about 10 percent of their face value, or around $600 million. The situation is analogous for other creditor governments.

Rough guidelines might hold that 80 percent or so of the debts would be canceled outright. The remaining 20 percent would be repaid in local currency, for uses in new social programs aimed at overcoming the multiple crises of health, nutrition, water and sanitation that threaten the very survival of these societies.
. . .

C. Denny and L. Elliott, Spark that Lit Global Revolt against Poverty

Guardian Weekly, January 6, 2000, at 7

Five years ago aid agencies and development groups found it difficult to get politicians interested in third world debt. The international institutions argued that writing off debts would only encourage other countries to default, and that any money saved would be wasted on bureaucracy or the military.
. . .

Jubilee 2000 changed the terms of the debate. Drawing on Old Testament ideas, it proposed once-and-for-all loan write-off to coincide with new millennium. The proposal caught the public imagination and turned the discussion on debt relief from a purely technical discussion into a moral argument about justice between rich and poor.

This culminated in the Group of Seven leading industrial countries in Cologne in June [1999] promising to reduce the debt stock of the most severely affected states by $100bn. To qualify, countries have to prove that the money saved on servicing these debts will be spent on anti-poverty measures . . .
. . .

How to Make Aid Work

The Economist, June 26, 1999, at 23

. . .

Over the past 50 years rich nations have given $1 trillion in aid to poor ones. This stupendous sum has failed spectacularly to improve the lot of its intended beneficiaries. Aid should have boosted recipient countries' growth rates and thereby helped millions to escape from poverty. Yet countless studies have failed to find a link between aid and faster economic growth. Poor countries that receive lots of aid do no better, on average, than those that receive very little.

Why should this be? In part, because economic growth has not always been donors' first priority. A sizeable chunk of Saudi Arabian aid, for example, aims to tackle spiritual rather than material needs by sending free Korans to infidels. During the cold war, the Soviet Union propped up odious communist despots while America bankrolled an equally unsavoury bunch of anti-communists. . . . Even today, strategic considerations often outweigh charitable or developmental ones. . . .

Even where development has been the goal of aid, foul-ups have been frequent. Big donors like to finance big, conspicuous projects such as dams, and sometimes fail to notice the multitudes whose homes are flooded. Gifts from small donors are often strangely inappropriate: starving Somalis have received heartburn pills; Mozambican peasants have been sent high-heeled shoes. . . .

Aid faces further hurdles in recipient countries. War scuppers the best-laid plans. A shipment of vaccines was destroyed in Congo when rebels cut the power supply to the capital, shutting down the refrigerators where the medicines were stored. In Afghanistan, Taliban zealots have closed aid-financed hospitals for employing female doctors. Less spectacularly but more pervasively, corruption, incompetence and foolish economic policies can often be relied on to squander any amount of donor cash. . . .

. . .

. . . A recent study by the World Bank[7] sorted 56 aid-receiving countries by the quality of their economic management. Those with good policies (low inflation, a budget surplus and openness to trade) and good institutions (little corruption, strong rule of law, effective bureaucracy) benefited from the aid they got. Those with poor policies and institutions did not. Badly run countries showed negligible or negative growth, and no amount of aid altered this. Well run countries that

---

[7] *Assessing Aid: What Works, What Doesn't, and Why* (1998) and www.worldbank.org/research/aid.

received little aid grew steadily, with GDP per head increasing by 2.2% a year. Well run countries with a lot of aid grew faster, at 3.7% per head a year.

Several things explain these differences. In countries with poor management, aid is sometimes stolen. Its effectiveness is often limited anyway by the fact that it tends to displace, rather than complement, private investment. In countries with good management, aid 'crowds in' private investment: if an economy is growing fast, the returns on road-building or setting up a new airline are likely to be high. A poorly managed, stagnant economy offers private investors fewer opportunities.

It seems clear that aid should be directed towards countries with good management and lots of poor citizens. Yet many donors continue to behave as if it were not. Bilateral aid has tended to favour allies and ex-colonies. . . .

Can aid persuade countries with bad policies and institutions to adopt good ones? It is not easy. For years the IMF and World Bank have made their loans conditional on policy reform, but the record is mixed, to put it kindly. Governments often agree to cut subsidies or tackle corruption, but later backtrack. . . . Even when recipients blatantly flout aid conditions, donors often hand over the money anyway, for fear of sparking an economic collapse or even bloodshed.

Good policies cannot be imposed on unwilling pupils. Attaching conditions to aid can strengthen the arm of governments that are trying to push through wise but unpopular measures. Broadly, however, reforms rarely succeed unless a government considers the reform programme essential, and its own. A recent study by David Dollar and Jakob Svensson found that elected governments were much more likely to implement reforms than unelected ones, and new regimes more likely than old ones.

. . .

Rethinking aid

A condition of the G8's new debt-relief plan is that the cash it frees be spent on worthy things like education and health. The World Bank is well aware of the difficulties in ensuring that this actually happens but many donors are not. Aid-givers often finance specific projects, such as irrigation and the building of schools. Since the schools are usually built and the ditches dug, donors are satisfied that their money has served its intended purpose. But has it? Probably not.

Most evidence suggests that aid money is fungible—that is, that it goes into the pot of public funds and is spent on whatever the recipient wants to spend it on. If donors earmark money for education, it may cause the recipient government to spend more on education, or it may make available for something else the money that it would otherwise have spent on education.

If the government is benign, the alternative may be agriculture or tax cuts. If the government is crooked, donors' funds may be spent on shopping trips to London for the president's wife or fighter planes to strafe unpopular minorities. The important factor is not the donor's instructions but the recipient's priorities. . . .

This does not mean that donors should never support specific projects. Sometimes the real value of a donor-financed dam or telephone network lies in the technology that is transferred, and the advice given on how to operate and maintain the infrastructure. But the fact of fungibility suggests that aid-giving could be greatly simplified if most took the form of unconditional 'balance-of-payments support'. That is, cash.

Rich countries should be much more ruthless about how they allocate their largesse, whether earmarked or not. Emergency relief is one thing. But mainstream aid should be directed only to countries with sound economic management. . . . . . .

QUESTIONS

1. 'The analysis by Alston and Quinn is stuck in the assumptions of the 1950s when most of the ICESCR was drafted. Since then the UN has recognized the right to development. Moreover, the deepening of our understanding of human rights means that it is no longer tenable for people in rich countries to insist that their commitment to human rights brings with it no responsibility for assisting those who live in conditions of absolute poverty that defy any conception of human dignity. Writing off the debt of developing countries is not just a moral but also a legal obligation'. Comment.

2. Thomas Pogge has argued, primarily on the basis of Article 28 of the UDHR, that the global institutional order 'must afford the persons on whom it is imposed secure access to the objects of their human rights' and that there is 'a negative duty not to cooperate in the imposition of this global order if feasible reforms of it would significantly improve the realization of human rights'.[8] What are the reasonable limits of such an obligation? Do national boundaries make a major difference in terms of such obligations? Is it sufficient for the international community to establish institutions devoted to the promotion of different aspects of development? Does it matter if some of these institutions, such as the WTO, explicitly exclude human rights from their fields of activity?

3. Consider the following comments of Mohammed Bedjaoui:[9]

> Why, for example, should not the twentieth century also be equal to the spirituality of the seventh century when the Koran announced to all mankind that 'all wealth, all things, belong to God' and thus to all members of the human community and that consequently the 'Zakat', the act of charity, should be seen rather as a compulsory institutionalized act, a manifestation of human solidarity, making it every man's duty to give away one tenth of his wealth each year?
>
> Is the twentieth century incapable of matching the principles of solidarity stated by the lawyer Emeric de Vattel in 1758 when he affirmed that each nation must contribute, by every means in its power, to the happiness and perfection of the others?

Many proposals have been made for international taxes which would generate funds for development. They include taxes on short-term capital movements (the 'Tobin tax'),

---

[8] Pogge, 'The International Significance of Human Rights', in 4 J. of Ethics 45 (2000).
[9] Bedjaoui, p. 1321 *supra*, at 1196.

on international trade, weapons trade, tourism, carbon emissions, fuel, fishing in international waters, international flights, and even internet usage. Most Western states, and especially the United States, have reacted negatively to all such proposals. What are the human rights-based arguments for and against such an initiative, and what forms of human rights conditionality might reasonably be attached?

C. THE WORLD BANK

The World Bank (formally the International Bank for Reconstruction and Development) is an intergovernmental organization, established in 1944, that currently has 181 member countries. Its importance derives from three factors: (i) it lends $30 billion annually, making it the world's largest source of development assistance; (ii) its imprimatur is, in effect, a prerequisite for loans and investment from many other sources, both public and private; and (iii) it is the single most prolific and influential source of research and policy on development issues. Much of the Bank's work in 2000 is focused on the Comprehensive Development Framework (CDF) which calls for a development plan 'owned' by the country concerned and supported by strong partnerships among governments, donors, civil society, the private sector and other development actors. Among the key issues identified by the Bank in this context are 'structural issues' such as 'good governance and clean government, an effective legal and judicial system, a well-organized and supervised financial system, and social safety net and social programs'.

Although technically classified as a UN Specialized Agency, it keeps itself very much at arm's length from the UN, and strongly rebuffed attempts in the 1960s by the General Assembly to influence its policies towards South Africa. Until the early 1990s human rights issues were entirely absent from the Bank's agenda. Although it has become involved in a growing range of such issues in recent years, it continues to lack a coherent human rights policy. Many of its staff remain convinced that, for the most part, such matters are extraneous to the Bank's mandate and that the addition of a human rights agenda would politicize the institution and undermine its ability to work with governments.

This section considers some of the human rights-type activities that the Bank has recently engaged in. It raises the question of how far the Bank should go in developing a full-fledged human rights agenda of its own, and what such an agenda might look like. Consider at the outset the following excerpts from the Bank's Articles of Agreement (as amended effective February 16, 1989, www.worldbank.org):

Article 1
The purposes of the Bank are:
>   (i)   To assist in the reconstruction and development of territories of members by facilitating the investment of capital for productive purposes, . . .

(ii)   To promote private foreign investment . . .

(iii) To promote the long-range balanced growth of international trade
and the maintenance of equilibrium in balances of payments by
encouraging international investment for the development of the productive resources of members, thereby assisting in raising productivity,
the standard of living and conditions of labor in their territories.

. . .

Article IV, Section 10
The Bank and its officers shall not interfere in the political affairs of any member;
nor shall they be influenced in their decisions by the political character of the
member or members concerned. Only economic considerations shall be relevant
to their decisions, and these considerations shall be weighed impartially in order
to achieve the purposes stated in Article I.

LETTER FROM HUMAN RIGHTS WATCH TO THE WORLD BANK PRESIDENT

December 14, 1999, http://www.hrw.org/press/1999/dec/chech1215.htm

Dear Mr. Wolfensohn:

We are writing to you with the utmost urgency to ask you to withhold payment of
the forthcoming $100 million disbursement under the Bank's structural adjust-
ment loan to the Russian Federation, and to use your relationship with representatives of the Russian government to press for an end to the abuses being committed
in Chechnya. . . .

We understand of course that the Bank is constrained by its Articles of Agreement, as well as its loan agreement with the Russian Federation. As is elaborated
below, however, we cannot accept that these restrictions could be read to require
the Bank to finance a government engaged in activities that so clearly violate
international law and undermine the Bank's fundamental development goals as is
currently the case in Russia.

. . . [I]n Chechnya, . . . tens of thousands of civilians are cowering in the base-
ments of Grozny. They are facing the Russian forces' ultimatum that they leave the
city or face imminent 'destruction' together with Chechen rebels, yet they have not
been able to flee due to on-going aerial bombardment and limited means of
transportation. . . .

The Russian government maintains that it is conducting an 'anti-terrorist'
operation in Chechnya . . . No one doubts the right, and indeed responsibility, of
the Russian government to protect its citizens from terrorism. But the actions of
Russian forces in Chechnya have gone far beyond anti-terrorist measures and have
had a severe impact on the civilian population of Chechnya. Russia is today a party
to an internal armed conflict, and must observe its obligations under the Geneva
Conventions and other international humanitarian law that regulates such
conflicts. To date, in Chechnya, Russian forces have flouted these standards.

. . .

If the Bank pays the forthcoming installment on its structural adjustment loan, it will be implicated in this human suffering and held accountable by citizens of the world who are in fact its ultimate shareholders. As a direct payment to the Russian Central Bank for purposes of general budgetary spending, there is a clear danger that World Bank funds will fuel the military engine at work in Chechnya....

Finally, the Bank should take a stand against the Russian government's actions in Chechnya, because they violate international humanitarian law and reflect a broader disrespect for Russia's international commitments. A government should not be considered a reliable investment partner if it undertakes specific commitments and then blatantly abrogates them, as the Russian government has done [in its dealings with the Organization for Security and Co-operation in Europe]. There is a global system of international law that encompasses the Geneva Conventions and other humanitarian norms as well as international financial agreements; the Russian Federation should not be allowed to pick and choose among its commitments.

The Bank's Articles of Agreement and its loan agreement with Russia must be interpreted in the context of this broader international legal framework. Given the Bank's origins and purposes, there must be an implied understanding in any Bank undertaking that it cannot be allowed through its financing to become complicit in the kinds of violations of international law being perpetrated by Russian armed forces in Chechnya, nor for that matter, to underwrite conduct that is so contrary to its fundamental development goals. Put another way, the Bank is required to weigh only 'economic considerations', but it is further required to do so in a manner consistent with its core purpose.

. . .

. . . [T]he IMF, . . . withheld funds for one set of stated reasons when everyone including the Russian people knows well that it is another. The more credible and effective course is to clearly articulate the real conditions for continued financial support, which should in this case be a clear and verifiable commitment on the part of the Russian government to abide by international law in Chechnya, specifically desisting from attacks on heavily populated areas; implementing well-publicized cease-fires along exit routes to allow civilians to flee; and allowing unfettered access and necessary security for international observers and that of humanitarian organizations seeking to provide relief in Chechnya.

. . .

Kenneth Roth, Executive Director

NOTE

The Bank has become more explicit over the years—surely during the current presidency of James Wolfensohn—in defining its lending policy's relationship to human rights and to closely allied issues such as the alleviation of poverty. That relationship is one of greater engagement, particularly in the light of an evolving conception of the nature and ingredients of development. Consider this excerpt from the introduction to a recent publication of the World Bank.[10]

> The World Bank believes that creating the conditions for the attainment of human rights is a central and irreducible goal of development. . . . And while the Bank has always taken measures to ensure that human rights are fully respected in connection with the projects it supports, it has been less forthcoming about articulating its role in promoting human rights within the countries in which it operates. . . .
>
> . . .
>
> The Bank contributes directly to the fulfillment of many rights articulated in the Universal Declaration. Through its support of primary education, health care and nutrition, sanitation, housing, and the environment, the Bank has helped hundreds of millions of people attain crucial economic and social rights. In other areas, the Bank's contributions are necessarily less direct, but perhaps equally significant. By helping to fight corruption, improve transparency and accountability in governance, strengthen judicial systems, and modernize financial sectors, the Bank contributes to building environments in which people are better able to pursue a broader range of human rights.
>
> . . .
>
> Some believe that [Article IV, section 10 of the Articles of Agreement] prevents the Bank from adequately confronting the issue of human rights. And to be sure, some aspects of human rights do fall outside its mandate. But the Bank's economic and social approach to development advances a comprehensive, interconnected vision of human rights that is too often overlooked.
>
> There is also practical, operational value in the way the Articles are drafted. Because lending decisions are based on the quality of the project, and the effectiveness of the programs in reducing poverty, the Bank has been able to escape the costly experience of committing scarce funds based on short-term political or ideological considerations, which have little to do with relieving the burden of poverty.
>
> None of this means that the Bank views other factors—factors that go to the heart of civil and political rights—as any less important to development. It does mean that, constituted as it is, and with the expertise and resources it possesses, the Bank makes its greatest contribution to development—and simply is able to help more people—by continuing to focus on the important work of economic and social development.

IBRAHIM F. I. SHIHATA, THE WORLD BANK AND HUMAN RIGHTS

in International Commission of Jurists, Report of a Regional Seminar on Economic, Social and Cultural Rights, Abidjan 1998 (1999) at 145.

[Dr Shihata was Senior Vice-President and General Counsel of the World Bank.]

---

[10] 'Development and Human Rights: The Role of the World Bank' (1998), <www.worldbank.org/html/extdr/rights/hrintro.htm>.

In spite of the Articles' clear provisions, both with respect to the mandates of the institutions and the prohibition of political considerations, some academics, politicians and NGO activists suggest that the Bank must recognize the relevance and importance of political rights and democracy to economic development and should use its powers to serve these objectives. The academics base their argument mainly on three grounds. The first is that human rights are indivisible and interdependent. The second is that the Articles of Agreement should not be read literally but should be subject to the overriding values and policies that they are meant to serve, taking into account the evolution of such values and policies over time. In other words, questions of the Articles' interpretation should be addressed as issues of conflict of interests and values where the higher interests and values should be given preference, even if this would contradict the language of the text. The third argument assumes that human rights is of a higher order than the Bank's Articles which should only be read in a manner consistent with that law.

As to the first argument, I agree that human rights are indeed interdependent and mutually reinforcing. This does not mean, however, that each international organization must concern itself with every and all human rights. Each of these organizations is a juridical body, the legal capacity of which is confined by its respective mandate as defined in its charter. It does not belittle any international organization if its charter specifies its specialized functions in a manner that excludes concern for certain aspects of human rights. But it demeans the organization to ignore its charter and act outside its legal powers. This is simply it matter of specialization of international organizations.

As to the second argument, I also agree that the Bank's Articles of Agreement should not always be read literally. This may suggest that they should be interpreted in a purposive, teleological manner. It cannot reasonably suggest that they should be interpreted in a way that totally negates the ordinary meaning of the text in the light of its object. Nor can it require the Bank to do the opposite of the clear injunctions of its charter by taking political considerations into account for the sake of what is perceived as the higher value of the interpreter. To do so would give the interpreter the authority to apply the Articles in any way he sees fit. It renders the text meaningless for practical purposes.

The third argument is really irrelevant, as the Articles of Agreement in no way contradict human rights law.

Some writers, mainly non-lawyers, have tried to belittle the distinction made in the Articles between economic and political considerations, pointing to the inevitable overlapping between the two. Such overlapping exists; it cannot mean, however, that we must or can correctly disregard the Articles' explicit distinction. It can ... allow for taking economic considerations into account even when they originate from, or are otherwise associated with, political factors.

. . .

In my official opinions in the Bank, I have taken the view that the Bank is not authorized in principle to interfere in the political relationship between a member country and its citizens. However, an extensive violation of individual political rights which takes pervasive proportions could impose itself as an issue in the Bank's decisions. This would be the case if the violation had significant direct economic effects or if it led to the breach of international obligations relevant to the Bank, such as those created by binding decisions of the UN Security Council. This position respects the Articles' injunctions that 'only economic considerations' shall be taken into account by the Bank and its officers in their decisions. It realizes, however, that political events can have economic effects, and authorizes the taking of these effects into account when they are clearly established. It also recognizes the supremacy of the UN Charter over other international agreements. But it does not accord the Bank, as an international financial institution, the role of a political or ethical reformer of its members.

NOTE

Consider the allied issue of corruption, so closely related to the strategies relevant to bringing about development. A recent publication of the World Bank states:[11]

> Given the mounting evidence of the costs of corruption and the need for more coordinated approaches at both country and international levels, the Bank requires a broad framework to address the issue. This chapter outlines the emerging strategy for the Bank, which has four channels:
>
> > Preventing fraud and corruption within Bank-financed projects. Helping countries that request Bank support in their efforts to reduce corruption. Taking corruption more explicitly into account in country assistance strategies, country lending considerations, the policy dialogue, analytical work, and the choice and design of projects. Adding voice and support to international efforts to reduce corruption.
>
> . . .
>
> *The Bank's legal mandate*
> Although corruption is a politically sensitive issue in many countries, the Articles of Agreement authorize the Bank to address corruption, within certain limits. In a recent paper on the subject, the General Counsel [Dr Shihata] pointed out that
>
> > the World Bank can hardly insulate itself from major issues of international development policy. Corruption has become such an issue. . . . From a legal viewpoint, what matters is that the Bank's involvement must always be consistent with its Articles of Agreement. The Bank can, in my view, take many actions to help the fight against corruption. It can conduct research on the causes and effects of this worldwide phenomenon. It can provide assistance, by mutual agreement, to enable its borrowing countries to curb corruption. It may take up the level of corruption as a subject of discussion in the dialogue with its borrowing members. And, if the level of corruption is high so as to have an adverse impact on the effectiveness of Bank assistance, according to factual and objective analysis, and the government is not taking serious measures to combat it, the Bank can take this as a factor in its lending strategy towards the country. The only legal barrier in this respect is that in doing so the Bank and its staff must be concerned

---

[11] 'Helping Countries Combat Corruption: The Role of the World Bank' (1997), <www.worldbank.org/html/extdr/corruptn/cor03.htm>.

only with the economic causes and effects and should refrain from
intervening in the country's political affairs....

VIEWS OF THE PRESIDENT OF THE WORLD BANK

Letter to President of Indonesia

8 September 1999

[For the background on the East Timor case see pp. 672–93, *supra*].

Dear Mr. President,

I am writing to seek your personal intervention to restore peace in East Timor, and to ensure that those who would use violence to thwart the result of the referendum do not succeed. The World Bank, as you know, has closely monitored events in East Timor in the months preceding the vote, so we would be ready with appropriate assistance whatever the outcome. In this, we were particularly heartened by the assurances of your government at Consultative Group meeting in Paris that the international community should '*rest assured that . . . we are determined to implement our part of the agreement, and give our full support to the operations of the United Nations in East Timor*'. The CGI donors based their commitments on these assurances. However, reports from Dili and elsewhere in East Timor in the past few days have described military and police personnel standing by as civilians have been wounded and killed by armed militias.

As you know, the Bank and Indonesia have a long and positive relationship, stretching back many years. We have been through many ordeals together, and I am sure we will go through many more. For the international financial community to be able to continue its full support, it is critical that you act swiftly to restore order and that your government carry through on its public commitment to honor the referendum outcome. The World Bank stands ready to do all we can to assist in the long and difficult task of building an independent East Timor, consistent with the decision of the August 30 referendum.

Sincerely yours,

James D. Wolfensohn

James Wolfensohn, Poor Countries Must Have a Free Press

Int'l Herald Tribune, November 11, 1999, p. 9

A free press is not a luxury. A free press is at the absolute core of equitable development, because if you cannot enfranchise poor people, if they do not have a right to expression, if there is no searchlight on corruption and inequitable practices, you cannot build the public consensus needed to bring about change.

. . .

When I came to the bank nearly five years ago, I was told we did not talk about corruption. Corruption was political. It was the 'C-word', and if you could not use the C-word you surely could not talk about press freedom. What could be more intrusive on politicians than a free press? What is it that could enfranchise people more than a free press?

But it soon became very clear to me that corruption and the issue of press freedom, while they may have political impact, are essentially economic and social issues, both key to development.

So we redefined corruption, not as a political issue, but as an economic and social issue. Corruption is the largest single inhibitor of equitable economic development, and in redefining the issue in this way our shareholder countries reacted very favorably.

Indeed, six months later at a meeting of our development committee, ministers all made speeches about corruption and asserted that it was at the core of the problems that affect development.

So, too, is press freedom. Studies at the bank show that the more press freedom a country has, the more it can control corruption. Studies show, too, that there is a strong positive correlation between voice and accountability and measures such as per capita income, infant mortality and adult literacy.

And yet we know from Freedom House that just 1.2 billion people live in countries with access to a free press, that 2.4 billion live without a free press and 2.4 billion have access to a partially free press.

Because we understand better now the links between development and issues of voice, accountability and transparency, the World Bank is running courses for journalists in all regions of the developing world and doing so with government approval.

QUESTIONS

1. How can you reconcile the Bank's policies on East Timor and on press freedom with the Articles of Agreement and the advice provided by the Bank's Legal Counsel?

2. What implications for IBRD loans would you see from the Bank's adopting a position along the lines advocated by Human Rights Watch to the effect that the Bank should never permit itself 'through its financing to become complicit in [serious] violations of international law'? If you were a member of Human Rights Watch, how would you bear out its letter through proposed guidelines about when not to provide financing, or perhaps when to extend financing but only on stated human rights conditions?

3. Are the view of Amartya Sen, p. 1316, *supra*, relevant to the Bank's currently developing policies about human rights? In what directions would those views point for the proposed guidelines referred to in question (2)?

4. Consider the following news stories, all taken from issues of *Development News* produced by the World Bank (www.worldbank.org/news):

14 September 1999: The World Bank country director for Bangladesh told a donors' meeting in Dhaka that 'some recent government actions ... have caused concern about governance and human rights in Bangladesh'.

14 September 1999: The World Bank froze its $1 billion a year programme in Indonesia in a move that will increase pressure on it to end the atrocities in East Timor.

2 February 2000: World Bank Vice-President Severino is quoted as saying: 'if we came to a situation where these governance, democracy and human rights goals were not present in the [Indonesian] government, I don't see how there could be any financial, political or technical support from the international community'.

3 February 2000: In a major policy change, the Bank will take Moscow's war in Chechnya into consideration before releasing loans to Russia. Wolfensohn was quoted as saying 'important issues will need to be addressed if the Bank's full potential for support to Russia is to be realized'.

3 February 2000: The Bank and the IMF might ease sanctions imposed against lending to India after its nuclear tests in May 1998.

3 February 2000: The United States will continue to oppose any World Bank loans to Iran. Iran is on the State Department's list of 'state sponsors of terrorism', and US law requires it to vote against any multilateral loans to such countries.

What reply would you give if, as an assistant to the Bank President, you were asked to provide a clear statement of, and a coherent rationale for, the existing policy towards human rights?

5. In a 1999 analysis[12] the Bank indicated that:

> The protection of human rights depends on the existence of a strong, access-ible, and independent judiciary. The World Bank has long recognized that accessible and efficient courts are essential to the attainment of sustainable and broad-based economic growth. In any society striving to achieve eco-nomic growth, the government must guarantee that contracts are honored and property rights are respected, and that domestic and foreign investors trust it to ensure that their investments enjoy legal protection.
>
> A country's legal system must ... be the ultimate guarantor of equality before the law for rich and poor alike, for the strong and the weak, for the State and its citizens. If the legal system does not function as this guarantor, then corruption, theft, and discrimination will undermine both economic integrity and social stability.

Can a policy of strengthening the legal system and the independence of the judiciary be effectively pursued without also tackling broader human rights issues such as freedom of speech and information, access to justice, and the probity of the criminal justice system?

---

[12] 'Development, Human Rights, and Judicial Reform', World Bank, Press Backgrounder, December 1999, <www.worldbank.org/html/extdr/pb/pbhr.htm>.

D. THE INTERNATIONAL MONETARY FUND

The International Monetary Fund (IMF) was established in 1944 to oversee the international monetary system. Among the purposes listed in its Articles of Agreement are:

> (i) to promote international monetary cooperation through a permanent institution which provides the machinery for consultation and collaboration on international monetary problems; and (ii) to facilitate the expansion and balanced growth of international trade, and to contribute thereby to the promotion and maintenance of high levels of employment and real income and to the development of the productive resources of all members as primary objectives of economic policy. (Article 1).

The Fund's permanent decision-making organ is its 24-member Executive Board. Voting is weighted in accordance with the size of each country's economy and its contribution to the Fund's capital. As of March 2000, the following weights applied: United States—17.35%; Japan—6.23%; Germany—6.08%; France—5.02%; UK—5.02%; the Belgian Executive Director (representing 10 countries)—5.21%; the Dutch Executive Director (representing 13 countries)—4.92%; the Mexican Executive Director (representing 9 countries)—4.32%; the Italian Executive Director (representing 6 countries)—4.23%; etc.

The Fund exercises surveillance over the exchange rate policies of its members through an analysis and evaluation of each country's economic and financial policies. When the Fund lends to a country, it attaches specific policy requirements as conditions for the loan. This 'conditionality' is the source of most of the controversy surrounding the Fund and the basis upon which the Fund is able to influence the domestic policies and programmes of, in particular, a wide range of developing countries. In 1983 one commentator summarized the criticisms made of the IMF in these terms:

> [It is said that] the IMF adopts a doctrinaire monetarist approach, that it is insensitive to the individual situations of borrowing countries, that it imposes onerous conditions, that it is ideologically biased in favor of free markets and against socialism, and that it overrides national sovereignty and perpetuates dependency. Until recent years, the IMF did not respond to such criticisms. Its aloofness seems to have aggravated the critics . . .[13]

In 2000 the same might well be said. The charge remains that the historical models of the structural adjustment programmes required by the Fund as conditions to a loan instituted neo-liberal programmes that generally had the effect of requiring governments to cut back on social welfare programmes and related economic and social rights, to engage in deregulation and privatization, and to stress budget balancing as a vital ingredient of adjustment.

---

[13] J. Williamson (ed.), *IMF Conditionality* (1983), at vii.

In an effort to counter such allegations, the IMF notes that it 'is neither a development bank, nor a world central bank, nor an agency that can or wishes to coerce its members to do very much of anything. It is rather a cooperative institution that 182 countries have voluntarily joined because they see the advantage of consulting with one another . . .'. Seeking to counter the claim that it 'imposes' austerity, the same source says that 'contrary to widespread perception, the IMF has no effective authority over the domestic economic policies of its members. It is in no position, for example, to force a member to spend more on schools or hospitals and less on buying military aircraft . . . It can, and often does, urge members to make the best use of scarce resources . . .'.[14]

But while the formalities of the system might be consistent with this analysis, the reality is that countries in financial difficulty have few, if any, options but to cooperate with the Fund, which means accepting its prescriptions. Oxfam has noted that 'its programmes shape the policy environment in which poverty-reduction strategies developed by national governments and donors are implemented'.[15] The following materials look at the evolving notion of conditionality and consider whether or not the Fund should develop a human rights policy *per se.*

HAROLD JAMES, FROM GRANDMOTHERLINESS TO GOVERNANCE: THE EVOLUTION OF IMF CONDITIONALITY
Finance and Development, December 1998, at 44

. . .

. . . [G]uidelines on conditionality . . . were approved by the IMF Executive Board in 1979. . . . Section 9 of the guidelines stated that they would be 'normally confined to (i) macroeconomic variables, and (ii) those necessary to implement specific provisions of the Articles . . .'. Performance criteria would relate to other variables 'only in exceptional cases when they are essential for the effectiveness of the member's program because of their macroeconomic impact'. In practice, however, the concept of a macroeconomic impact is both quite vague and quite inclusive.

The elaboration of additional ('exceptional') details intended to ensure that the macroeconomic criteria would be observed inevitably drew the IMF into domestic political debates. The shape of IMF programs emerged in discussions between IMF officials and national civil servants and politicians . . .

. . .

Changing role of IMF

In the 1990s, [pre-existing views] of the IMF and its role changed dramatically. In large part, this was a consequence of reflections on the collapse of communism and on the links between political and economic reform. . . .

. . .

---

[14] D. Driscoll, 'What is the International Monetary Fund?', September 1998, www.imf.org/external/pubs.

[15] Oxfam International, *The IMF: Wrong Diagnosis, Wrong Medicine* (1999), at 3.

The collapse of the centrally planned economies or (in the case of China) their movement toward the market was the last stage in creating a new consensus about economic policy, frequently but misleadingly referred to as the 'Washington consensus'. The consequence has been an increasing homogeneity of political outlook, as well as of the economic order. Indeed, one key insight is that the two are linked: that economic efficiency depends on a functioning civil society, on the rule of law, and on respect for private property.

Governance issues

... In August 1997, a new set of guidelines [on governance] promulgated by the IMF's Executive Board instructed the staff that, in policy advice, the IMF 'has assisted its member countries in creating systems that limit the scope for ad hoc decision making, for rent seeking, for undesirable preferential treatment of individuals or organizations'. The IMF suggested that 'it is legitimate to seek information about the political situation in member countries as an essential element in judging the prospects for policy implementation'. At the same time, these guidelines also preserved the nonpolitical vision of Bretton Woods, requiring the IMF's judgments not to be influenced 'by the nature of the political regime of a country'. In particular, recognizing an obvious danger, they specify that 'the IMF should not act on behalf of a member country in influencing another country's political orientation or behavior'.

The IMF's interest in governance was already reflected in a number of very high profile decisions in 1996–97. Conditionality has come to the fore in each of four completely new areas. First, military spending had never been a topic of explicit discussion by the IMF in the era of the cold war. Since 1993, however, it has been discussed in the IMF's World Economic Outlook reports as a major problem of misallocation of resources. In a number of cases, notably those of Pakistan and Romania, it became a central element in IMF discussions. Second, corruption is explicitly addressed: in Africa, but also in Indonesia. Third, so also is democracy addressed, although there is no reference to democracy in the IMF's Articles of Agreement ... Fourth, especially in response to the Asian crisis, ... the concept of 'trust', or of 'strong informal networks' ... was now relabeled and condemned as 'crony capitalism'. This criticism was linked to the attack on corruption, and 'a stable and transparent regulatory environment for private sector activity' was laid out as the solution.

There had been some consideration of human rights issues in the past: in Poland, whose membership application was held up in the 1980s after the imposition of martial law and the internment of political dissenters; or, more discreetly and subtly, in South Africa in the 1980s, where apartheid was attacked as an inefficient labor practice. But the scale of the discussion of political issues in the mid- and late 1990s is novel. The gradual extension of the IMF into these areas is an immediate result of the new consensus about economic practice and of a new world political order that it has helped to produce. But it reflects something more profound—a realization increasingly shared throughout the world that the world economy, and world institutions, can be a better guarantee of rights and of prosperity than some governments, which may be corrupt, rent-seeking, and militaristic. Economic reform and the removal of corrupt governments are pre-conditions both for the effective operation of markets and for greater social justice. Indeed, these two results, far from being contradictory as some critics imagine, are complementary.

Fresh challenges

The new approach will produce greater global prosperity and stability . . . But questions arise concerning the degree to which the IMF can be 'evenhanded' in its treatment of all its members. Addressing the issues of military expenditure, corruption, and undemocratic practices is easier for international institutions in the cases of small countries, or even politically isolated countries. But it is likely to be hard and controversial in large states with substantial military and economic potential—for instance, China or Russia. . . . In other cases, conditionality will be interpreted as a blatant attempt to impose Western values in the hope of restraining or even crippling potential competitors (a criticism frequently voiced, for example, by Mahathir Mohamad, the Prime Minister of Malaysia).

Second, there is the question of the IMF's institutional capacity for implementation. Some recent programs and statements also go into such issues of economic organization as the dismantling of cartels, the improvement of accounting practices, and banking supervision. On the one hand, it is easy to see the macro-economic effects of the organizational or structural flaws criticized by the IMF. On the other hand, correcting them takes the IMF into completely new areas in which it has no previous experience. . . .

Third, and most fundamentally, this process of adding new expectations could create a dangerous momentum of its own. Part of the recent discussion in the U.S. Congress on an IMF quota increase involved the issue of whether to integrate environmental and labor standards into IMF programs. Many of the IMF's member countries rightly feel that economic reform programs must be responsive to social and humanitarian concerns. But the amplitude of such an agenda may produce an expectations trap. The more the IMF is seen to extend its mandate, the more it will be expected to undertake, and, inevitably, the greater the challenge it will face in trying to live up to the demands. The IMF will need to resist institutional overstretch: to ensure that its mandate is limited, clearly defined, and subject to realistic assessment of results.

LARRY ROHTER, BRAZIL COLLIDES WITH I.M.F. OVER A PLAN TO AID THE POOR
New York Times, February 21, 2000, at p. A21

A new Brazilian government plan to spend more than $22 billion on social programs in the next decade has led to a squabble with the International Monetary Fund, which argues that the money should be used to reduce Brazil's indebtedness rather than to fight poverty.

The unusually public dispute has added to the unpopularity here of the I.M.F., which in the past has been accused of provoking recession in Brazil and trampling on the country's sovereignty. It has also given President Fernando Henrique Cardoso badly needed political help . . .

Brazil and the I.M.F. reached agreement in November 1998 on an emergency three-year $41.5 billion rescue package. . . . The accord calls for the Brazilian government to cut spending and raise taxes, and sets targets and timetables for actions like reducing public sector debt and selling state-owned companies.

But nationwide municipal elections are scheduled for October, with the presidential and legislative races to follow in 2002, and the government coalition is eager to offer voters something more than continued austerity. In addition, Mr. Cardoso promised in his 1998 campaign that if elected to a second term, he would take steps to lessen the country's chronically skewed income distribution and other social inequalities.

Though living conditions for the poor improved in the 1990s, economists calculate that at least half the work force in this nation of 165 million still earns the minimum wage of $77 a month or, in the case of millions working off the books, even less. According to government statistics, the poorest 10 percent of the population accounts for only 1 percent of national income, while the richest 10 percent receives nearly half.

As presented to Congress, the government's plan calls for at least $2.25 billion a year over the next 10 years to be funneled into a Fund to Combat and Eradicate Poverty for additional spending on things like education, health and infrastructure. . . .

. . . [I]n an interview last week with the Dow Jones news service, the I.M.F. representative in Brasilia, Lorenzo Perez, said the government plan 'established a precedent that could become dangerous'. 'Brazil already spends a significant amount of money on social programs', he said. 'This money has to be used more effectively'.

The Brazilian reaction was sharp and immediate. . . . [The Minister of Finance] said 'the allocation of budgetary resources has never been a theme of discussion with the I.M.F. and is not within its area of competence'.

A day later, Mr. Perez reversed course, saying that after further study of the plan, 'I don't think its implementation would involve macroeconomic risks'.

QUESTIONS

1. The Fund's 1997 Governance Guidelines acknowledge that 'it is difficult to separate economic aspects of governance from political aspects'. A recent report notes that IMF loan conditions are politicized because they go 'far beyond monetary matters to cover trade liberalisation, privatization, and financial reform', priorities said to 'reflect the strategic interests of major shareholders, notably the USA and France'.[16] How could the Fund seek to take account of civil and political rights-related issues without becoming even more 'politicized' and going far beyond its mandate?

[16] *Ibid.*

2. After an army coup in Pakistan in October 1999 the IMF Managing Director said that Pakistan could lose its IMF aid if democracy were not restored. He noted that 'democracy is in retreat, and when democracy retreats, countries are in danger'. On the same day he stated, in relation to the situation in Chechnya, that if the Russian 'budget is over-shooting because of an uncontrolled increase of military spending, we shall interrupt our support'.[17] Do these statements give cause for concern in view of the fact that the Fund has no specific policy on democracy or human rights, or is this a positive development which simply recognizes the inseparable link between development and respect for human rights?

3. An Oxfam International report claims that in Brazil 'the IMF "rescue" has been accompanied by a 25 per cent decline in spending on early childhood education programmes'.[18] Should such issues be seen in terms of possible violations of economic and social rights, and if so what policy prescriptions might still be consistent with the Fund's aim to restore 'fiscal integrity'?

4. At a press briefing on 12 January 2000, the IMF Managing Director responded to a question by saying: 'You are suggesting that the IMF could have a kind of double standard, being lenient on Russia and being tough on other countries, particularly on Africa. I will tell you that there is not such a thing as a double standard'. Does the fact that, by virtue of the weighted voting arrangements, the industrialized countries are the predominant forces within the IMF, and that the Fund will rarely be in a position to push effectively specific policies for industrialized countries, give pause for thought about the desirability of giving it a potentially powerful human rights mandate?

ADDITIONAL READING

On the right to development and globalization see: A. Orford, 'Globalization and the Right to Development', in P. Alston (ed.), *Peoples' Rights* (forthcoming); A. Clapham, 'Globalization and the Rule of Law', 61 Int'l Comm. Jurists, The Review 17 (1999); Y. Ghai, 'Rights, Social Justice, and Globalization in East Asia', in J. Bauer and D. Bell (eds.), *The East Asian Challenge for Human Rights* (1999), 241; T. Pogge, 'Human Flourishing and Universal Justice', in E. F. Paul et al. (eds.), *Human Flourishing* (1999), 333; D. Weissbrodt and M. Hoffman, 'The Global Economy and Human Rights: A Selective Bibliography', 6 Minn. J. Global Trade 189 (1997); K. M'Baye, 'Introduction', in M. Bedjaoui (ed.), *International Law: Achievements and Prospects* (1991), 1043.

On the World Bank and IMF see: *IMF Survey* (weekly) and *Finance & Development* (monthly); J. Gathii, 'Good Governance as a Counter Insurgeny Agenda to Oppositional Transformative Social Projects in International Law', 5 Buffalo Hum. Rts L. Rev. 107 (1999); L. Pritchett and D. Kaufmann, 'Civil Liberties, Democracy, and the Performance of Government Projects', Finance & Development 26 (March 1998); A. Orford, 'Locating the International: Military and Monetary Interventions after the Cold War', 38 Harv. Int'l L. J. 443 (1997); D. Bradlow, 'The World Bank, the IMF, and Human Rights', 6 Transnat'l L. & Contemp. Probs. 47 (1996).

---

[17] *Development News*, October 13, 1999, www.worldbank.org/news.
[18] See *supra* n. 15.

E. MULTINATIONAL CORPORATIONS

Globalization has contributed to, and in part been driven by, the increasingly central role of multinational corporations (MNCs) in both the domestic and international economies. For human rights proponents this development raises the question of how to ensure that corporate activities are consistent with human rights standards and of how to ensure an element of accountability. In principle, the answer is straightforward. The human rights obligations assumed by each government require it (or should require it) to use all appropriate means to ensure that actors operating within its territory or otherwise subject to its jurisdiction comply with national legislation designed to give effect to human rights.

Several problems arise, however: (1) governments are often loathe to take the measures necessary to ensure compliance by MNCs, especially in relation to labour matters; (2) such measures are costly and perceived to be beyond the resource capabilities of governments in developing countries; (3) in the context of increasing global mobility of capital, competition among potential host countries discourages initiatives that may push up labour costs and make one country less attractive than others with lower regulatory standards (the so-called 'race to the bottom'); (4) the multinational complexity of manufacturing and related arrangements in an era of globalization makes it increasingly difficult to identify who is responsible for what activities and where; and (5) especially in the labour area, difficult issues arise about the different levels of minimum acceptable standards from one country to another.

The following materials look at the approaches adopted by the United Nations and by several leading NGOs, consider some evaluations that have been made, and reflect on what might be the best approach to adopt. Consider at the outset the following observations about the role of MNCs.[19]

> Today, the globalization of production is organized in large measure by MNCs. Their pre-eminence in world output, trade, investment and technology transfer is unprecedented. Even when MNCs have a clear national base, their interest is in global profitability above all. MNCs have grown from national firms to global concerns using international investment to exploit their competitive advantages. Increasingly, however, they are using joint ventures and strategic alliances to develop and exploit those advantages or to share the costs of technological innovation. But the growing globalization of production is not limited to MNC activity, for over the last decades there has been a significant growth in producer-driven and buyer-driven global production and distribution networks . . .
>
> MNCs, however, are the linchpins of the contemporary world economy. Around 53,000 MNCs account for at least 20 per cent (some estimate 30 per cent) of world output and on some estimates up to 70 per cent of world trade. Despite regional concentrations of production, transnational business networks span the three core regions of the world economy, linking the fortunes of disparate communities and nations in complex webs of interconnectedness. Contrary

[19] David Held *et al.*, *supra* n. 2, at 282.

to the sceptics, MNCs are not simply 'national firms with international operations', nor are they, as the hyperglobalizers argue, 'footloose corporations' which wander the globe in search of maximum profits. Rather MNCs play a much more central role in the operation of the world economy than in the past and they figure prominently in organizing extensive and intensive transnational networks of coordinated production and distribution that are historically unique. MNCs and global production networks are critical to the organization, location and distribution of productive power in the contemporary world economy.

. . .

HUMAN RIGHTS WATCH, NO GUARANTEES: SEX DISCRIMINATION IN MEXICO'S MAQUILADORA SECTOR
(August 1996)

Maquiladoras, or export-processing factories, along the US–Mexico border account for over US $29 billion in export earnings for Mexico and employ over 500,000 workers. At least half of the Mexicans employed in this sector, mainly in assembly plants, are women, and the income they earn supports them and their families at wages higher than they could earn in any other employment sector in northern Mexico.

These women workers routinely suffer a form of discrimination unique to women: the maquiladoras require them to undergo pregnancy testing as a condition of employment and deny them work if they are pregnant; if a woman becomes pregnant soon after gaining employment at a maquiladora, in some instances she may be mistreated or forced to resign because of her pregnancy. Maquiladora operators target women for discriminatory treatment, in violation of international human rights and labor rights norms. And despite its international and domestic legal responsibility to ensure protection for these workers, the Mexican government has done little to acknowledge or remedy violations of women's rights to nondiscrimination and to privacy. . . . In fact, government employees responsible for overseeing compliance with and enforcement of Mexico's federal labor law—which explicitly prohibits sex discrimination—inconsistently condemn such discriminatory practices; view themselves as incapable of enforcing the law; and, in one instance, defended the pregnancy-based discrimination as reasonable or legitimate.

. . .

It is difficult for workers—poor, under-educated, and female in a society with 6.3 percent official unemployment . . .—with so few job alternatives to contest maquiladora policies. Most of the women Human Rights Watch interviewed had not finished primary school and had very little work experience outside the manufacturing sector. As a consequence, these women emphasized that their only other opportunity for work is in domestic service, which pays poorly, allows them very little control over their schedules and working conditions, and provides no health insurance or social security. Women repeatedly expressed unwillingness to challenge discriminatory practices in the maquiladoras, given the lack of other comparable employment opportunities.

For the Mexican government, there are economic disincentives to regulating closely the conduct of these companies, given the number of people the maquiladora industry employs and the amount of foreign currency earnings it produces. . . .

. . .

AMNESTY INTERNATIONAL, HUMAN RIGHTS PRINCIPLES FOR COMPANIES
January 1998, AI Index: ACT 70/01/98

Multinational companies have a responsibility to contribute to the promotion and protection of human rights. In an increasingly globalized world economy, their decisions and actions impact directly on governmental policies and on the enjoyment of human rights. The Universal Declaration of Human Rights calls on 'every individual and every organ of society' to play its part in securing universal observance of human rights. Companies and financial institutions are organs of society, and as their operations come under scrutiny around the world, this is increasingly demanded by consumers, shareholders and the communities with whom they interact.

All companies have a direct responsibility to respect human rights in their own operations. Their employees and other people with whom they work are entitled to rights such as freedom from discrimination, the right to life and security, freedom from slavery, freedom of association, including the right to form trade unions, and fair working conditions. Particular care needs to be taken by companies to ensure that their security arrangements do not lead to human rights abuses. Those companies making arms or other military or security equipment also need to help ensure that their products are not used to violate human rights.

Amnesty International believes that the business community also has a wider responsibility—moral and legal—to use its influence to promote respect for human rights. A multinational company's reputation will be increasingly affected by its response—in word and deed—to the violation of human rights and the defence of such rights. Violations of human rights may contribute to civil instability and to uncertainty in the investment climate, but even where this is not the case, companies should not be silent witnesses. Multinational companies have a responsibility to use their influence to try to stop violations of human rights by governments or armed political groups in the countries in which they operate. Large companies regularly try to influence governments' tax and trade policies, their labour laws and environmental rules. The silence of powerful business interests in the face of injustice is not neutral.

Companies may argue that they should not take action in these areas because to do so would be to interfere in domestic politics or offend the values of other cultures. However, the international community has decided, through a variety of covenants and agreements, that the promotion and protection of inherent human rights transcends national and cultural boundaries. Amnesty International has therefore developed an introductory set of human rights principles, based on international standards, to assist companies in developing their role in situations of human rights violations or the potential for such violations. These are outlined below.

Responsibility for Own Operations

Personnel practices and policies

Standards relating to labour rights have been developed by a variety of international organizations, notably the International Labour Organization (ILO). . . .

On complex and sensitive personnel issues such as child labour, companies would find it useful to consult relevant specialists and non-governmental organizations familiar with the implementation of particular ILO Conventions. . . .

The performance of a company's contractors, suppliers and partners (whether government, governmental agencies or otherwise) is perceived to reflect on the performance of the company. The general public does not draw a line between them. It is therefore in companies' own interests to promote similar standards through all third parties who act with them or on their behalf.

Security arrangements

Violence and instability in many countries today have led companies to defend their personnel and property by armed guards and/or by arrangements with state security forces. These arrangements have sometimes directly contributed to human rights violations, such as assaults involving excessive force used against peaceful demonstrators. The reputation of a company itself can also be at stake in such situations.

A company should therefore ensure that its own personnel and any security forces engaged by them should be properly trained in and committed to respect of international guidelines and standards for the use of force, in particular the United Nations (UN) Code of Conduct for Law Enforcement Officials and the UN Basic Principles on the Use of Force and Firearms by Law Enforcement Officials. These standards set strict limitations on when force and firearms can be used, and require a reporting and review process if it becomes necessary in any instance to use minimum force.

. . .

Companies should also, when recruiting security staff, screen backgrounds for any previous involvement in human rights violations and decline to hire any person determined to have been responsible for serious human rights violations.

. . .

Responsibility for Promoting and Upholding Human Rights Standards

Companies should cooperate in creating an environment where human rights are understood and respected. Companies may operate in countries where there is a high level of human rights violations or where legislation, governmental practice or other constraints make it imperative to address specific abuses and devise innovative ways of promoting respect for human rights. For example, if an employee of the company or one of its sub-contractors is arbitrarily arrested, strong protests should be made to the highest levels of government, and the company should actively pursue the employee's release.

. . .

Multinational companies can improve their ability to promote human rights by:

- developing an explicit company policy on human rights
- providing effective training for their managers and their staff in international human rights standards, preferably with input and assistance from appropriate non-governmental organizations
- consulting non-governmental organizations, including Amnesty International, on the level and nature of human rights abuses in different countries
- establishing a clear framework for assessing the potential impact on human rights of all the company's and its sub-contractors' operations.

Implementation and Monitoring

The primary responsibility for monitoring company policies and practices lies with the company itself. However, all systems for monitoring compliance with voluntary corporate codes of behaviour should be credible and their reports should be independently verifiable. . . . [T]here should also be periodic independent verification of these procedures and the reports they generate. In this there is also a role for other stakeholders, such as independent employee associations and trade unions, non-governmental organizations or members of the local community in which the company operates, in order to give greater transparency and credibility to the operation.

. . .

NGO INVOLVEMENT AND INDUSTRY INITIATIVES

Lawyers Committee for Human Rights

Business and Human Rights (2000), www.lchr.org/sweatshop/business.htm

With the rapid growth of the global economy in the last twenty years, the linkages between human rights, trade, the labor movement, and the activities of multinational corporations have taken on new importance. These linkages are evident around the world and have been particularly visible in the United States with the rise of the anti-sweatshop movement and with increased demands being placed on corporations to incorporate greater respect for internationally recognized labor rights in their global business practices.

While the process of globalization and the drive to open markets has spurred growth and development in parts of the world, it has also exacerbated existing problems. As is evident from the public protests at the meeting of the World Trade Organization in Seattle in November 1999, opposition to globalization is rising. This is based at least in part on concerns that an expanding global economy is not adequately addressing human rights, labor rights, and environmental needs.

In the last decade, many multinational companies, especially those in labor-intensive, low-wage industries, such as apparel and toys, have shifted most of their operations from the United States and other developed countries to poorer, developing countries in Asia and Latin America and elsewhere. In these countries, low wages are the result, at least in part, of weak labor laws and enforcement, and restrictions on trade union activity. Such conditions lead in turn to violations of internationally recognized labor rights . . .

. . .

The Lawyers Committee believes that advocating for the global enforcement of internationally recognized labor rights must go hand in hand with the drive to open markets and enhance global competitiveness. . . .

. . .

Apparel Industry Partnership

(1999), www.lchr.org/sweatshop, summary.htm

The Apparel Industry Partnership (AIP) was initiated by the White House in August 1996 to take steps to protect workers worldwide and to give the public the information it needs to make informed purchasing decisions.

The Partnership is comprised of apparel and footwear companies, a prominent U.S. university, human rights groups, labor, religious organizations and consumer advocates.

In April 1997, the AIP released an historic agreement establishing:

- A *Workplace Code of Conduct* addressing problems in 9 key areas (child labor, forced labor, discrimination, harassment, freedom of association, wages, health and safety, hours of work and overtime compensation).
- *Principles of Monitoring* with two components:
  - *Internal Monitoring Principles* that include establishing workplace standards; communicating these standards within the workplace; creating programs to train company monitors; conducting periodic visits and audits to ensure compliance; providing factory workers with confidential reporting mechanisms; developing relationships with local labor, human rights or religious institutions; and establishing a means of remediation.
    - *Independent External Monitoring Principles* that include establishing clear evaluation guidelines and criteria; verifying implementation of internal monitoring principles; providing independent access to and conducting independent audits of employee records; conducting periodic visits and audits (announced and unannounced); developing

relationships with local labor, human rights or religious institutions
(where external monitors are not themselves such organizations); conducting confidential employee interviews; implementing remediation;
and completing evaluation reports.

In November 1998, a working group of the AIP reached an agreement that will
include the following:

Creation of a new non-profit entity, the Fair Labor Association, to oversee
monitoring of compliance with the code and evaluation of company compliance. The Association board will have equal numbers of company and NGO/
labor members with a mutually acceptable chair.

The Association will accredit independent monitors who will inspect a significant number of factories manufacturing products for each Participating
Company that is part of the Association's monitoring process.

The UN Global Compact

(1999), www.unglobalcompact.org

At the World Economic Forum, Davos, on 31 January 1999, UN Secretary-General
Kofi A. Annan challenged world business leaders to 'embrace and enact' the Global
Compact, both in their individual corporate practices and by supporting
appropriate public policies.

Human Rights
   Principle 1: support and respect the protection of international human rights
within their sphere of influence;
   Principle 2: make sure their own corporations are not complicit in human
rights abuses.

Labour Standards
   Principle 3: freedom of association and the effective recognition of the right to
collective bargaining;
   Principle 4: the elimination of all forms of forced and compulsory labour;
   Principle 5: the effective abolition of child labour;
   Principle 6: the elimination of discrimination in respect of employment and
occupation.

Environment
. . .

CHRISTOPHER AVERY, BUSINESS AND HUMAN RIGHTS IN A TIME OF CHANGE

(1999), www.business-humanrights.org

[The background to this analysis is provided in the Global Snapshot at p. 4, *supra.*]

. . .

  5. A case in point: Nike

. . .

  In 1996 accusations were made that Nike's Asian factories were sweatshops where workers were underpaid and mistreated. . . .

. . .

  Nike's response over time was, like other companies that have faced human rights allegations, reactive and slow. . . . Elaine Bernard, Executive Director of the Harvard Trade Union Program, has noted five common stages in a company's response to criticism of their social and labour record in developing countries.

  (i) Denial: The company denies any knowledge of human rights violations or denies that the violations are occurring. 'Most of their denials . . . include statements to the effect that "we meet all the local standards, and are good employers".'
  (ii) Blame others: As the violations are corroborated, the company blames others for the shortcomings, perhaps their suppliers/contractors, or the local government for its failures of enforcement, or the workers themselves for their failure to complain.
  (iii) Damage control: the company engages in damage control by taking the offensive and denouncing its critics who are labelled 'as "zealots" or "troublemakers" or "publicity hounds" . . . the claim is made that the critics have "a political" or "labor agenda".' Sometimes the company threatens to bring a defamation lawsuit.
  (iv) Reassert control over damaged corporate image: The company attempts to recapture the high ground by establishing and publicizing a code of conduct, often with assistance from a public relations firm.
  (v) Give the appearance of compliance: The company may seek to give the appearance of compliance and enforcement of the code of conduct by hiring auditing firms or high-profile monitors. Sometimes the company seeks to 'divide and conquer' its critics by splitting the human rights community between those who support this sort of monitoring and those who insist in more systematic, independent monitoring and enforcement.

[An analysis of Nike's response then follows. The final stage is described below.]

. . . Step towards implementing change; more remains to be done

Nike reportedly has now introduced improvements in its Asian factories. Overtime has been reduced, new ventilation systems have been installed, lead-based paints and solvent-based adhesives have been eliminated. The number of workers at Tae Kwang Vina factory reporting nose and throat complaints reportedly fell to 18% of the labour force in 1998 from 86% in 1997. There is a new system for workers to submit complaints and suggestions into a box for which only union representatives have a key.

Human rights advocates recognize the progress that Nike has made in health and safety issues, but there is continuing concern about wage levels, and about how the factories will be monitored.

Nike has asked the International Youth Foundation (IYF), an NGO based in the U.S., to undertake work at Nike Asian factories to assess worker and community needs and devise projects for workers relating to education, health, nutrition, and vocational skills training. . . . The IYF is to carry out this work through a new IYF division called The Global Alliance for Workers and Communities, a partnership of business, public and non-profit organizations . . .

. . .

Nike has signed on to the Apparel Industry Partnership's Fair Labor Association agreement . . .

Human rights advocates will be closely scrutinizing the various procedures for monitoring Nike's factories, to see how they work in practice. They are watching to see which local NGOs will be involved in the monitoring process, how they will be involved, and whether the fact-finding process is carried out with sufficient independence, expertise and thoroughness.

HUMAN RIGHTS WATCH WORLD REPORT 2000
(2000), www.hrw.org

. . .

. . . The two key [corporate] sectors under fire [during 1999] were the apparel and footwear industry, for labor rights violations, and the energy industry, for complicity in human rights violations committed through partnerships with repressive governments.

Companies that had previously made human rights commitments continued to develop policies and programs to address the potentially negative impact of their operations on human rights. However, even though some companies, such as the Gap and Royal Dutch/Shell (Shell) pledged to implement socially responsible policies, they faced new controversies. A disturbing new trend emerged as well: companies that were mired in controversy seemed to reject human rights considerations out of hand, even though a growing body of evidence clearly indicated a need to change their practices in order to avoid the risk of public criticism, the potential impact on the companies' bottom-line, and potential legal liabilities.

The Apparel and Footwear Industry

. . .

. . . Two key developments increased the pressure on the industry to address labor rights: a series of class-action lawsuits against U.S. companies and their subcontractors manufacturing in the U.S. island territory of Saipan and the emergence of university students as a powerful force against workplace exploitation.

The Saipan Lawsuit

On January 13 [1999], a federal class-action lawsuit in the U.S., a lawsuit in the U.S. territory of Saipan, and a third lawsuit in California state court were simultaneously filed against thirty-two apparel and footwear manufacturers and their subcontractors by Global Exchange and Sweatshop Watch, two California-based labor rights nongovernmental organizations (NGOs), on behalf of approximately 40,000 garment workers employed by manufacturers in Saipan. The suit alleged that workers faced repeated harassment, physical abuse, and poor working conditions . . . Although the lawsuit filed in Saipan was dismissed, four of the defendants . . . reached a settlement . . . and agreed to pay U.S. $1.25 million in order to implement an independent monitoring program . . .

. . .

Student Activism at U.S. Universities

University students emerged as a powerful new voice in the campaign against worker exploitation. Throughout the year, students staged demonstrations at Harvard University, the University of Wisconsin, Duke University, the University of North Carolina, throughout the University of California system, and other universities around the U.S. demanding that their schools only agree to license their university apparel with companies who have credible monitoring programs to ensure respect for labor rights and also urging their universities to support the FLA [Fair Labour Association]. In response to student activism throughout the U.S., more than eighty universities had joined the FLA by the end of 1999.

NEIL KEARNEY, CORPORATE CODES OF CONDUCT: THE PRIVATIZED APPLICATION OF LABOUR STANDARDS

in S. Picciotto and R. Mayne (eds.), Regulating International Business: Beyond Liberalization (2000), at 208

. . .

Corporate codes of conduct, in effect, have privatized the implementation of national labour legislation and the application of international labour standards. Their proliferation is a reflection of the failure of governments to implement effective labour legislation and of intergovernmental institutions, such as the International Labour Organization, to enforce internationally agreed basic minimum labour standards around the world. They also reflect the obsession of many governments in recent years, particularly in the industrialized world, with deregulation. Rather than legislate to eliminate exploitation at home and abroad, many administrations, including that of the United States, preferred to encourage multinational companies to adopt voluntary undertakings on responsibility for the labour standards of their suppliers and business partners.

Corporate codes of conduct are, however, no substitute for national legislation enacted and effectively implemented by governments or for international labour standards enforced around the world; neither can they be a substitute for the right of workers to organize and to bargain collectively with their employers; nor are they shortcuts to more equitable wages and better working conditions. Indeed, unless properly handled, codes of conduct may work to the disadvantage of those they were intended to help. For example, one sports shoe producer in Indonesia recently claimed that as it had accepted a merchandiser's code of conduct there was no need to continue the collective agreement negotiated with the local trade union. Elsewhere, so-called monitoring systems involving NGOs have been put in place which effectively negate the role of the democratically elected union structures in the plants concerned.

In spite of these drawbacks, corporate codes of conduct, if they continue to grow in number and impact, may be the catalyst that will force governments to examine new mechanisms for the enforcement of workers' rights, regardless of the location of employment. Unfortunately, to date the great majority of corporate codes have been little more than public relations exercises—fig leaves for exploitation—the latest in a long title of efforts by firms to escape responsibility for the production conditions from which they profit. . . .

Corporate codes of conduct are, in effect, written statements of principles a corporation will follow regarding working conditions. Despite pressure from unions and NGOs that codes of conduct contain, at a minimum, the core ILO standards, most codes, introduced unilaterally by companies are often less than what is demanded by national law and international labour standards, but typically will include references to the non-use of forced labour and child labour and to the implementation of reasonable health and safety standards. Some include a reference to the payment of minimum wage levels, but, to date, very few have included a commitment to recognizing the right of workers to organize and to bargain collectively. Until recently no company code made a commitment to the payment of a living wage.

COMMENT ON APPROACHES TO REGULATION AND SELF-REGULATION

Issues of activities of MNCs in relation to working conditions have vast economic and political stakes: the volume of trade with respect to both exports and imports, the effects on domestic industry, the effects on consumer groups, the effects on the political branches of government. It is then natural, indeed inevitable, that many interests and groups are brought into the debate and into the political fray about what, if anything, to do. Business firms, labor unions, consumer groups, churches, NGOs and the media have all been involved, whether in advocacy to the general public or in lobbying the Congress. That involvement affects all three of the approaches to regulation of business activity that are noted in this Comment.

Consider first treaties. Several require their parties to enact and enforce legislation on rights affecting relations between labour and management. Article 11 of

CEDAW, for example, requires states to end employment discrimination by ensuring that women benefit from rights on an equal basis with men. The ICCPR provides in Article 22 for freedom of association, including trade unions. Conventions of the International Labor Organization regulate aspects of employment and work conditions. But the strong treaty texts notwithstanding, they have often not been effective in protecting workers' rights. Intergovernmental human rights institutions have not given these issues priority or even concentrated on the problem of slow realization of those rights.

Legislation in some developed countries would seem to promise more dramatic effects. For example, section 301 of the United States Trade Act of 1974 permits trade sanctions against states that fail to observe worker rights. Other legislation also speaks to these issues. Nonetheless, US policy about sanctions for violation of worker rights has been selective, and often politically motivated.

The earlier materials in this Section E have introduced a third approach: self-regulation by business, meaning reliance on market mechanisms involving consumer choice, and agreements among firms as in the apparel industry. The market mechanisms vary. Sometimes consumer activism has led to boycotts of imports. Sometimes strategies move toward 'social labelling' of products that informs consumers whether, for example, child labour was used in their manufacture.

QUESTIONS

1. In what ways, through what types of regulation, might corporations be legally bound to respect human rights standards?

2. The UNDP *Human Development Report 1999* (at 100) concluded that 'multinational corporations are too important and too dominant a part of the global economy for voluntary codes to be enough'. Another observer, however, concluded that: 'The impulse is to call for some global governing body to fix the problem. But there is none and there will be none. The only answer is for activists to learn . . . how to compel companies to behave better by mobilizing consumers and the Internet'.[20] How satisfactory is it, from a human rights point of view, for enforcement to be left in the hands of consumers? Is it correct that there is, and can be, no role for any of the UN monitoring techniques that prior materials have examined?

3. How do you respond to the argument that poor countries must be left to set their own standards in these areas, and that poor economic conditions in developing countries cannot be overcome either by international campaigns or stepped up domestic labour inspections?

4. Suppose that shoes are produced in country X by a MNC with a branch in X and its home office in the United States. NGO reports indicate that labor conditions in X are very poor. The argument made by US trade unions is that poor labor conditions in X allow the MNC to produce the goods cheaply and thus to export to the United States

---

[20] Thomas Friedman, 'The New Human Rights', *New York Times*, July 30, 1999, p. 15

and undercut prices of domestic producers. It argues that X should comply with international minimum labour standards, and that, if it does not, trade sanctions should be imposed on imports into the United States. (a) What are the different ways in which you might understand the reasons for this position of trade unions? (b) What arguments might you expect other concerned groups or interests in the United States to advance? (c) What position on this issue might the government of X take?

ADDITIONAL READING

On corporations and labour standards see: P. Utting, *Business Responsibility for Sustainable Development* (2000); Harvard Law School Human Rights Program and Lawyers Committee for Human Rights, *Business and Human Rights* (1999); R. Mayne, 'Regulating TNCs: The Role of Voluntary and Governmental Approaches', in S. Picciotto and R. Mayne (eds.), *Regulating International Business: Beyond Liberalization* (2000), 235; C. Thomas and A. Taylor (eds.), *Global Trade and Global Social Issues* (2000); C. McCrudden, 'International Economic Law and the Pursuit of Human Rights', J of Int'l Econ. L. 3 (1999); L. Dubin, 'The Direct Application of Human Rights Standards to, and by, Transnational Corporations', 61 Int'l Comm. Jurists, The Review 35 (1999); R. Bhala, 'Clarifying the Trade-Labor Link', 37 Colum. J. Transnat'l L. 11 (1998); S. Cleveland, 'Global Labor Rights and the Alien Tort Claims Act' 76 Tex. L. Rev. 1533 (1998); R. Kozul-Wright and B. Rowthorn (eds.), *Transnational Corporations and the Global Economy* (1998); S. Charnowitz, 'The Moral Exception in Trade Policy', 38 Va. J. Int'l L. 689 (1998); C. Forcese, *Commerce with Conscience? Human Rights and Business Codes of Conduct* (1996); P. Spiro, 'Globalization, International Law, and the Academy', 32 N.Y.U. J. Int'l L. & Pol. 567 (2000).

Annex on
DOCUMENTS

This annex sets forth documents that are essential to an understanding of materials in different parts of the coursebook. Since they have been edited to delete provisions that are unnecessary for an understanding of those materials, you should not rely on any of them as full and official versions. The Annex on Citations that follows provides both the official citation to each document and a reference to a more readily available source in which the complete document can be found.

In the Table of Contents below, there appear within parentheses after the official title of a document the acronym or abbreviated name(s) by which the text or the readings sometimes refer to the document.

CONTENTS

CHARTER OF THE UNITED NATIONS

We The Peoples of The United Nations Determined

to save succeeding generations from the scourge of war, which twice in our life-time has brought untold sorrow to mankind, and

to reaffirm faith in fundamental human rights, in the dignity and worth of the human person, in the equal rights of men and women and of nations large and small, and

to establish conditions under which justice and respect for the obligations aris-ing from treaties and other sources of international law can be maintained, and

to promote social progress and better standards of life in larger freedom,

And for These Ends

to practice tolerance and live together in peace with one another as good neighbours, and

to unite our strength to maintain international peace and security, and

to ensure, by the acceptance of principles and the institution of methods, that armed force shall not be used, save in the common interest, and

to employ international machinery for the promotion of the economic and social advancement of all peoples,

Have Resolved to Combine Our Efforts to Accomplish These Aims

. . .

CHAPTER I. PURPOSES AND PRINCIPLES

Article 1

The Purposes of the United Nations are:

1. To maintain international peace and security, and to that end: to take effect-ive collective measures for the prevention and removal of threats to the peace, and for the suppression of acts of aggression or other breaches of the peace, and to bring about by peaceful means, and in conformity with the principles of justice and international law, adjustment or settlement of international disputes or situations which might lead to a breach of the peace;

2. To develop friendly relations among nations based on respect for the principle of equal rights and self-determination of peoples, and to take other appropriate measures to strengthen universal peace;

3. To achieve international co-operation in solving international problems of an economic, social, cultural, or humanitarian character, and in promoting and encouraging respect for human rights and for fundamental freedoms for all without distinction as to race, sex, language, or religion; and

4. To be a centre for harmonizing the actions of nations in the attainment of these common ends.

Article 2

The Organization and its Members, in pursuit of the Purposes stated in Article 1, shall act in accordance with the following Principles.

1. The Organization is based on the principle of the sovereign equality of all its Members.

2. All Members, in order to ensure to all of them the rights and benefits resulting from membership, shall fulfil in good faith the obligations assumed by them in accordance with the present Charter.

3. All Members shall settle their international disputes by peaceful means in such a manner that international peace and security, and justice, are not endangered.

4. All Members shall refrain in their international relations from the threat or use of force against the territorial integrity or political independence of any state, or in any other manner inconsistent with the Purposes of the United Nations.

5. All Members shall give the United Nations every assistance in any action it takes in accordance with the present Charter, and shall refrain from giving assistance to any state against which the United Nations is taking preventive or enforcement action.

6. The Organization shall ensure that states which are not Members of the United Nations act in accordance with these Principles as far as may be necessary for the maintenance of international peace and security.

7. Nothing contained in the present Charter shall authorize the United Nations to intervene in matters which are essentially within the domestic jurisdiction of any state or shall require the Members to submit such matters to settlement under the present Charter; but this principle shall not prejudice the application of enforcement measures under Chapter VII.

CHAPTER II. MEMBERSHIP

. . .

Article 4

1. Membership in the United Nations is open to all other peace-loving states which accept the obligations contained in the present Charter and, in the judgment of the Organization, are able and willing to carry out these obligations.

. . .

Article 6

A Member of the United Nations which has persistently violated the Principles contained in the present Charter may be expelled from the Organization by the General Assembly upon the recommendation of the Security Council.

CHAPTER III. ORGANS

Article 7

1. There are established as the principal organs of the United Nations: a

General Assembly, a Security Council, an Economic and Social Council, a Trusteeship Council, an International Court of Justice, and a Secretariat.

2. Such subsidiary organs as may be found necessary may be established in accordance with the present Charter.

Article 8

The United Nations shall place no restrictions on the eligibility of men and women to participate in any capacity and under conditions of equality in its principal and subsidiary organs.

CHAPTER IV. THE GENERAL ASSEMBLY

Article 9

1. The General Assembly shall consist of all the Members of the United Nations.

. . .

Article 10

The General Assembly may discuss any questions or any matters within the scope of the present Charter or relating to the powers and functions of any organs provided for in the present Charter, and, except as provided in Article 12, may make recommendations to the Members of the United Nations or to the Security Council or to both on any such questions or matters.

. . .

Article 13

1. *The General Assembly shall initiate studies and make recommendations for the purpose of:*

(*a*) Promoting international co-operation in the political field and encouraging the progressive development of international law and its codification;

(*b*) Promoting international co-operation in the economic, social, cultural, educational, and health fields, and assisting in the realization of human rights and fundamental freedoms for all without distinction as to race, sex, language, or religion.

. . .

Article 18

1. Each member of the General Assembly shall have one vote.

2. Decisions of the General Assembly on important questions shall be made by a two-thirds majority of the members present and voting. These questions shall include: recommendations with respect to the maintenance of international peace and security . . .

3. Decisions on other questions, including the determination of additional categories of questions to be decided by a two-thirds majority, shall be made by a majority of the members present and voting.

. . .

CHAPTER V. THE SECURITY COUNCIL

Article 23

1. The Security Council shall consist of fifteen Members of the United Nations. The Republic of China, France, the Union of Soviet Socialist Republics, the United Kingdom of Great Britain and Northern Ireland, and the United States of America shall be permanent members of the Security Council. The General Assembly shall elect ten other Members of the United Nations to be non-permanent members of the Security Council, due regard being specially paid, in the first instance to the contribution of Members of the United Nations to the maintenance of international peace and security and to the other purposes of the Organization, and also to equitable geographical distribution.

2. The non-permanent members of the Security Council shall be elected for a term of two years ... A retiring member shall not be eligible for immediate re-election.

. . .

Article 24

1. In order to ensure prompt and effective action by the United Nations, its Members confer on the Security Council primary responsibility for the maintenance of international peace and security, and agree that in carrying out its duties under this responsibility the Security Council acts on their behalf.

2. In discharging these duties the Security Council shall act in accordance with the Purposes and Principles of the United Nations. The specific powers granted to the Security Council for the discharge of these duties are laid down in Chapters VI, VII, VIII, and XII.

. . .

Article 25

The members of the United Nations agree to accept and carry out the decisions of the Security Council in accordance with the present Charter.

. . .

Article 27

1. Each member of the Security Council shall have one vote.

2. Decisions of the Security Council on procedural matters shall be made by an affirmative vote of nine members.

3. Decisions of the Security Council on all other matters shall be made by an affirmative vote of nine members including the concurring votes of the permanent members; provided that, in decisions under Chapter VI, and under paragraph 3 of Article 52, a party to a dispute shall abstain from voting.

. . .

Article 29

The Security Council may establish such subsidiary organs as it deems necessary for the performance of its functions.

. . .

CHAPTER VI. PACIFIC SETTLEMENT OF DISPUTES

Article 33

1. The parties to any dispute, the continuance of which is likely to endanger the maintenance of international peace and security, shall, first of all, seek a solution by negotiation, enquiry, mediation, conciliation, arbitration, judicial settlement, resort to regional agencies or arrangements, or other peaceful means of their own choice.

2. The Security Council shall, when it deems necessary, call upon the parties to settle their dispute by such means.

Article 34

The Security Council may investigate any dispute, or any situation which might lead to international friction or give rise to a dispute, in order to determine whether the continuance of the dispute or situation is likely to endanger the maintenance of international peace and security.

. . .

Article 36

1. The Security Council may, at any stage of a dispute of the nature referred to in Article 33 or of a situation of like nature, recommend appropriate procedures or methods of adjustment.

2. The Security Council shall take into consideration any procedures for the settlement of the dispute which have already been adopted by the parties.

3. In making recommendations under this Article the Security Council should also take into consideration that legal disputes should as a general rule be referred by the parties to the International Court of Justice in accordance with the provisions of the Statute of the Court.

. . .

CHAPTER VII. ACTION WITH RESPECT TO THREATS TO THE PEACE, BREACHES OF THE PEACE, AND ACTS OF AGGRESSION

Article 39

The Security Council shall determine the existence of any threat to the peace, breach of the peace, or act of aggression and shall make recommendations, or decide what measures shall be taken in accordance with Article 41 and 42, to maintain or restore international peace and security.

. . .

Article 41

The Security Council may decide what measures not involving the use of armed force are to be employed to give effect to its decisions, and it may call upon the Members of the United Nations to apply such measures. These may include complete or partial interruption of economic relations and of rail, sea, air, postal, telegraphic, radio, and other means of communication, and the severance of diplomatic relations.

Article 42

Should the Security Council consider that measures provided for in Article 41 would be inadequate or have proved to be inadequate, it may take such action by air, sea, or land forces as may be necessary to maintain or restore international peace and security. Such action may include demonstrations, blockade, and other operations by air, sea, or land forces of Members of the United Nations.

Article 43

1. All Members of the United Nations, in order to contribute to the maintenance of international peace and security, undertake to make available to the Security Council, on its call and in accordance with a special agreement or agreements, armed forces, assistance, and facilities, including rights of passage, necessary for the purpose of maintaining international peace and security.

2. Such agreement or agreements shall govern the numbers and types of forces, their degree of readiness and general location, and the nature of the facilities and assistance to be provided.

3. The agreement or agreements shall be negotiated as soon as possible on the initiative of the Security Council. They shall be concluded between the Security Council and Members or between the Security Council and groups of members and shall be subject to ratification by the signatory states in accordance with their respective constitutional processes.

Article 44

When the Security Council has decided to use force it shall, before calling upon a Member not represented on it to provide armed forces in fulfilment of the obligations assumed under Article 43, invite that Member, if the Member so desires, to participate in the decisions of the Security Council concerning the employment of contingents of that Member's armed forces.

Article 45

In order to enable the United Nations to take urgent military measures, Members shall hold immediately available national air-force contingents for combined international enforcement action . . .

. . .

Article 48

1. The action required to carry out the decisions of the Security Council for the maintenance of international peace and security shall be taken by all the Members of the United Nations or by some of them, as the Security Council may determine.

2. Such decisions shall be carried out by the Members of the United Nations directly and through their action in the appropriate international agencies of which they are members.

. . .

Article 51

Nothing in the present Charter shall impair the inherent right of individual or collective self-defence if an armed attack occurs against a Member of the United Nations, until the Security Council has taken measures necessary to maintain international peace and security. Measures taken by Members in the exercise of this right of self-defence shall be immediately reported to the Security Council and shall not in any way affect the authority and responsibility of the Security Council under the present Charter to take at any time such action as it deems necessary in order to maintain or restore international peace and security.

CHAPTER VIII. REGIONAL ARRANGEMENTS

Article 52

1. Nothing in the present Charter precludes the existence of regional arrangements or agencies for dealing with such matters relating to the maintenance of international peace and security as are appropriate for regional action, provided that such arrangements or agencies and their activities are consistent with the Purposes and Principles of the United Nations.

. . .

3. The Security Council shall encourage the development of pacific settlement of local disputes through such regional arrangements or by such regional agencies either on the initiative of the states concerned or by reference from the Security Council.

Article 53

1. The Security Council shall, where appropriate, utilize such regional arrangements or agencies for enforcement action under its authority. But no enforcement action shall be taken under regional arrangements or by regional agencies without the authorization of the Security Council [subject to an exception for measures against 'any enemy state' (as defined), a state related to Second World War hostilities].

Article 54

The Security Council shall at all times be kept fully informed of activities undertaken or in contemplation under regional arrangements or by regional agencies for the maintenance of international peace and security.

CHAPTER IX. INTERNATIONAL ECONOMIC AND SOCIAL CO-OPERATION

Article 55

With a view to the creation of conditions of stability and well-being which are necessary for peaceful and friendly relations among nations based on respect for the principle of equal rights and self-determination of peoples, the United Nations shall promote:

(*a*) higher standards of living, full employment, and conditions of economic and social progress and development.

(*b*) solutions of international economic, social, health, and related problems; and international cultural and educational co-operation; and

(*c*) universal respect for, and observance of, human rights and fundamental freedoms for all without distinction as to race, sex, language, or religion.

Article 56

All Members pledge themselves to take joint and separate action in co-operation with the Organization for the achievement of the purposes set forth in Article 55.

. . .

CHAPTER X. THE ECONOMIC AND SOCIAL COUNCIL

Article 61

1. The Economic and Social Council shall consist of fifty-four Members of the United Nations elected by the General Assembly.

. . .

Article 62

1. The Economic and Social Council may make or initiate studies and reports with respect to international economic, social, cultural, educational, health, and related matters and may make recommendations with respect to any such matters to the General Assembly, to the Members of the United Nations, and to the specialized agencies concerned.

2. It may make recommendations for the purpose of promoting respect for, and observance of, human rights and fundamental freedoms for all.

3. It may prepare draft conventions for submission to the General Assembly, with respect to matters falling within its competence.

4. It may call, in accordance with the rules prescribed by the United Nations, international conferences on matters falling within its competence.

. . .

Article 68

The Economic and Social Council shall set up commissions in economic and social fields and for the promotion of human rights, and such other commissions as may be required for the performance of its functions.

. . .

CHAPTER XI: DECLARATION REGARDING NON-SELF-GOVERNING TERRITORIES

Article 73

Members of the United Nations which have or assume responsibilities for the administration of territories whose peoples have not yet attained a full measure of self-government recognize the principle that the interests of the inhabitants of these territories are paramount, and accept as a sacred trust the obligation to promote to the utmost, within the system of international peace and security established by the present Charter, the well-being of the inhabitants of these territories, and to this end:

    (A) to ensure, with due respect for the culture of the peoples concerned, their political, economic, social and educational advancement, their just treatment, and their protections against abuses;

    (B) to develop self-government, to take due account of the political aspirations of the peoples, and to assist them in the progressive development of their free political institutions, according to the particular circumstances of each territory and its peoples and their varying stages of advancement;

    (C) to further international peace and security;

    (D) to promote constructive measures of development . . .

. . .

CHAPTER XII. INTERNATIONAL TRUSTEESHIP SYSTEM

Article 75

The United Nations shall establish under its authority an internal trusteeship system for the administration and supervision of such territories as may be placed thereunder by subsequent individual agreements. These territories are hereinafter referred to as trust territories.

Article 76

The basic objectives of the trusteeship system, in accordance with the Purposes of the United Nations laid down in Article 1 of the present Charter, shall be:

    (A) to further international peace and security;

    (B) to promote the political, economic, social and educational advancement of the inhabitants of the trust territories, and their progressive development towards self-government or independence as may be appropriate to the particular circumstances of each territory and its peoples and the freely expressed wishes of the peoples concerned, and as may be provided by the terms of each trusteeship agreement;

    (C) to encourage respect for human rights and for fundamental freedoms for all without distinction as to race, sex, language, or religion; and to encourage recognition of the interdependence of the peoples of the world; and

    (D) to ensure equal treatment in social, economic, and commercial matters for all Members of the United Nations and their nationals, and also equal treatment for the latter in the administration of justice.

. . .

CHAPTER XIV. THE INTERNATIONAL COURT OF JUSTICE

Article 92

The International Court of Justice shall be the principal judicial organ of the United Nations. It shall function in accordance with the annexed Statute, which is based upon the Statute of the Permanent Court of International Justice and forms an integral part of the present Charter.

. . .

Article 94

1. Each Member of the United Nations undertakes to comply with the decision of the International Court of Justice in any case to which it is a party.

2. If any party to a case fails to perform the obligations incumbent upon it under a judgment rendered by the Court the other party may have recourse to the Security Council, which may, if it deems necessary, make recommendations or decide upon measures to be taken to give effect to the judgment.

. . .

Article 96

1. The General Assembly or the Security Council may request the International Court of Justice to give an advisory opinion on any legal question.

CHAPTER XV. THE SECRETARIAT

Article 97

The Secretariat shall comprise a Secretary-General and such staff as the Organization may require. The Secretary-General shall be appointed by the General Assembly upon the recommendation of the Security Council. He shall be the chief administrative officer of the Organization.

. . .

Article 99

The Secretary-General may bring to the attention of the Security Council any matter which in his opinion may threaten the maintenance of international peace and security.

Article 100

1. In the performance of their duties the Secretary-General and the staff shall not seek or receive instructions from any government or from any other authority external to the Organization. They shall refrain from any action which might reflect on their position as international officials responsible only to the Organization.

2. Each Member of the United Nations undertakes to respect the exclusively international character of the responsibilities of the Secretary-General and the staff and not to seek to influence them in the discharge of their responsibilities.

. . .

CHAPTER XVI. MISCELLANEOUS PROVISIONS

Article 103

In the event of a conflict between the obligations of the Members of the United

Nations under the present Charter and their obligations under any other international agreement, their obligations under the present Charter shall prevail. . . .

CHAPTER XVIII. AMENDMENTS

Article 108

Amendments to the present Charter shall come into force for all Members of the United Nations when they have been adopted by a vote of two thirds of the members of the General Assembly and ratified in accordance with their respective constitutional processes by two thirds of the Members of the United Nations, including all the permanent members of the Security Council.

UNIVERSAL DECLARATION OF HUMAN RIGHTS

PREAMBLE

Whereas recognition of the inherent dignity and of the equal and inalienable rights of all members of the human family is the foundation of freedom, justice and peace in the world,

Whereas disregard and contempt for human rights have resulted in barbarous acts which have outraged the conscience of mankind, and the advent of a world in which human beings shall enjoy freedom of speech and belief and freedom from fear and want has been proclaimed as the highest aspiration of the common people,

Whereas it is essential, if man is not to be compelled to have recourse, as a last resort, to rebellion against tyranny and oppression, that human rights should be protected by the rule of law,

Whereas it is essential to promote the development of friendly relations between nations,

Whereas the peoples of the United Nations have in the Charter reaffirmed their faith in fundamental human rights, in the dignity and worth of the human person and in the equal rights of men and women and have determined to promote social progress and better standards of life in larger freedom,

Whereas Member States have pledged themselves to achieve, in co-operation with the United Nations, the promotion of universal respect for and observance of human rights and fundamental freedoms,

Whereas a common understanding of these rights and freedoms is of the greatest importance for the full realization of this pledge,

Now, therefore,

The General Assembly,

Proclaims this Universal Declaration of Human Rights as a common standard of achievement for all peoples and all nations, to the end that every individual and every organ of society, keeping this Declaration constantly in mind, shall strive by teaching and education to promote respect for these rights and freedoms and by progressive measures, national and international, to secure their universal and effective recognition and observance, both among the peoples of Member States themselves and among the peoples of territories under their jurisdiction.

Article 1

All human beings are born free and equal in dignity and rights. They are endowed with reason and conscience and should act towards one another in a spirit of brotherhood.

Article 2

Everyone is entitled to all the rights and freedoms set forth in this Declaration, without distinction of any kind, such as race, colour, sex, language, religion, political or other opinion, national or social origin, property, birth or other status.

Furthermore, no distinction shall be made on the basis of the political, jurisdictional or international status of the country or territory to which a person
belongs, whether it be independent, trust, non-self-governing or under any other
limitation of sovereignty.

Article 3

Everyone has the right to life, liberty and security of person.

Article 4

No one shall be held in slavery or servitude; slavery and the slave trade shall be
prohibited in all their forms.

Article 5

No one shall be subjected to torture or to cruel, inhuman or degrading treatment
or punishment.

Article 6

Everyone has the right to recognition everywhere as a person before the law.

Article 7

All are equal before the law and are entitled without any discrimination to equal
protection of the law. All are entitled to equal protection against any discrimination in violation of this Declaration and against any incitement to such
discrimination.

Article 8

Everyone has the right to an effective remedy by the competent national tribunals
for acts violating the fundamental rights granted him by the constitution or by
law.

Article 9

No one shall be subjected to arbitrary arrest, detention or exile.

Article 10

Everyone is entitled in full equality to a fair and public hearing by an independent
and impartial tribunal, in the determination of his rights and obligations and of
any criminal charge against him.

Article 11

1. Everyone charged with a penal offence has the right to be presumed innocent
until proved guilty according to law in a public trial at which he has had all the
guarantees necessary for his defence.
2. No one shall be held guilty of any penal offence on account of any act or
omission which did not constitute a penal offence, under national or international

law, at the time when it was committed. Nor shall a heavier penalty be imposed than the one that was applicable at the time the penal offence was committed.

Article 12

No one shall be subjected to arbitrary interference with his privacy, family, home or correspondence, nor to attacks upon his honour and reputation. Everyone has the right to the protection of the law against such interference or attacks.

Article 13

1. Everyone has the right to freedom of movement and residence within the borders of each State.

2. Everyone has the right to leave any country, including his own, and to return to his country.

Article 14

1. Everyone has the right to seek and to enjoy in other countries asylum from persecution.

2. This right may not be invoked in the case of prosecutions genuinely arising from non-political crimes or from acts contrary to the purposes and principles of the United Nations.

Article 15

1. Everyone has the right to a nationality.

2. No one shall be arbitrarily deprived of his nationality nor denied the right to change his nationality.

Article 16

1. Men and women of full age, without any limitation due to race, nationality or religion, have the right to marry and to found a family. They are entitled to equal rights as to marriage, during marriage and at its dissolution.

2. Marriage shall be entered into only with the free and full consent of the intending spouses.

3. The family is the natural and fundamental group unit of society and is entitled to protection by society and the State.

Article 17

1. Everyone has the right to own property alone as well as in association with others.

2. No one shall be arbitrarily deprived of his property.

Article 18

Everyone has the right to freedom of thought, conscience and religion; this right includes freedom to change his religion or belief, and freedom, either alone or in community with others and in public or private, to manifest his religion or belief in teaching, practice, worship and observance.

Article 19

Everyone has the right to freedom of opinion and expression; this right includes freedom to hold opinions without interference and to seek, receive and impart information and ideas through any media and regardless of frontiers.

Article 20

1. Everyone has the right to freedom of peaceful assembly and association.
2. No one may be compelled to belong to an association.

Article 21

1. Everyone has the right to take part in the government of his country, directly or through freely chosen representatives.
2. Everyone has the right to equal access to public service in his country.
3. The will of the people shall be the basis of the authority of government; this will shall be expressed in periodic and genuine elections which shall be by universal and equal suffrage and shall be held by secret vote or by equivalent free voting procedures.

Article 22

Everyone, as a member of society, has the right to social security and is entitled to realization, through national effort and international co-operation and in accordance with the organization and resources of each State, of the economic, social and cultural rights indispensable for his dignity and the free development of his personality.

Article 23

1. Everyone has the right to work, to free choice of employment, to just and favourable conditions of work and to protection against unemployment.
2. Everyone, without any discrimination, has the right to equal pay for equal work.
3. Everyone who works has the right to just and favourable remuneration ensuring for himself and his family an existence worthy of human dignity, and supplemented, if necessary, by other means of social protection.
4. Everyone has the right to form and to join trade unions for the protection of his interests.

Article 24

Everyone has the right to rest and leisure, including reasonable limitation of working hours and periodic holidays with pay.

Article 25

1. Everyone has the right to a standard of living adequate for the health and well-being of himself and of his family, including food, clothing, housing and medical care and necessary social services, and the right to security in the event of

unemployment, sickness, disability, widowhood, old age or other lack of livelihood in circumstances beyond his control.

2. Motherhood and childhood are entitled to special care and assistance. All children, whether born in or out of wedlock, shall enjoy the same social protection.

Article 26

1. Everyone has the right to education. Education shall be free, at least in the elementary and fundamental stages. Elementary education shall be compulsory. Technical and professional education shall be made generally available and higher education shall be equally accessible to all on the basis of merit.

2. Education shall be directed to the full development of the human personality and to the strengthening of respect for human rights and fundamental freedoms. It shall promote understanding, tolerance and friendship among all nations, racial or religious groups, and shall further the activities of the United Nations for the maintenance of peace.

3. Parents have a prior right to choose the kind of education that shall be given to their children.

Article 27

1. Everyone has the right freely to participate in the cultural life of the community, to enjoy the arts and to share in scientific advancement and its benefits.

2. Everyone has the right to the protection of the moral and material interests resulting from any scientific, literary or artistic production of which he is the author.

Article 28

Everyone is entitled to a social and international order in which the rights and freedoms set forth in this Declaration can be fully realized.

Article 29

1. Everyone has duties to the community in which alone the free and full development of his personality is possible.

2. In the exercise of his rights and freedoms, everyone shall be subject only to such limitations as are determined by law solely for the purpose of securing due recognition and respect for the rights and freedoms of others and of meeting the just requirements of morality, public order and the general welfare in a democratic society.

3. These rights are freedoms may in no case be exercised contrary to the purposes and principles of the United Nations.

Article 30

Nothing in this Declaration may be interpreted as implying for any State, group or person any right to engage in any activity or to perform any act aimed at the destruction of any of the rights and freedoms set forth herein.

INTERNATIONAL COVENANT ON CIVIL AND POLITICAL RIGHTS

PREAMBLE

The States Parties to the present Covenant,

Considering that, in accordance with the principles proclaimed in the Charter of the United Nations, recognition of the inherent dignity and of the equal and inalienable rights of all members of the human family is the foundation of freedom, justice and peace in the world.

Recognizing that these rights derive from the inherent dignity of the human person,

Recognizing that, in accordance with the Universal Declaration of Human rights, the ideal of free human beings enjoying civil and political freedom and freedom from fear and want can only be achieved if conditions are created whereby everyone may enjoy his civil and political rights, as well as his economic, social and cultural rights,

Considering the obligation of States under the Charter of the United Nations to promote universal respect for, and observance of, human rights and freedoms,

Realizing that the individual, having duties to other individuals and to the community to which he belongs, is under a responsibility to strive for the promotion and observance of the rights recognized in the present Covenant,

Agree upon the following articles:

PART I

Article 1

1. All peoples have the right of self-determination. By virtue of that right they freely determine their political status and freely pursue their economic, social and cultural development.

2. All peoples may, for their own ends, freely dispose of their natural wealth and resources without prejudice to any obligations arising out of international economic co-operation, based upon the principle of mutual benefit, and international law. In no case may a people be deprived of its own means of subsistence.

3. The States Parties to the present Covenant, including those having responsibility for the administration of Non-Self-Governing Territories, shall promote the realization of the right of self-determination, and shall respect that right, in conformity with the provisions of the Charter of the United Nations.

PART II

Article 2

1. Each State Party to the present Covenant undertakes to respect and to ensure to all individuals within its territory and subject to its jurisdiction the rights recognized in the present Covenant, without distinction of any kind, such as race, colour, sex, language, religion, political or other opinion, national or social origin, property, birth or other status.

2. Where not already provided for by existing legislative or other measures, each State Party to the present Covenant undertakes to take the necessary steps, in accordance with its constitutional processes and with the provisions of the present Covenant, to adopt such legislative or other measures as may be necessary to give effect to the rights recognized in the present Covenant.

3. Each State Party to the present Covenant undertakes:

(*a*)   To ensure that any person whose rights or freedoms as herein recognized are violated shall have an effective remedy, notwithstanding that the violation has been committed by persons acting in an official capacity;

(*b*)   To ensure that any person claiming such a remedy shall have his right thereto determined by competent judicial, administrative or legislative authorities, or by any other competent authority provided for by the legal system of the State, and to develop the possibilities of judicial remedy;

(*c*)   To ensure that the competent authorities shall enforce such remedies when granted.

Article 3

The State Parties to the present Covenant undertake to ensure the equal right of men and women to the enjoyment of all civil and political rights set forth in the present Covenant.

Article 4

1. In time of public emergency which threatens the life of the nation and the existence of which is officially proclaimed, the States Parties to the present Covenant may take measures derogating from their obligations under the present Covenant to the extent strictly required by the exigencies of the situation, provided that such measures are not inconsistent with their other obligations under international law and do not involve discrimination solely on the ground of race, colour, sex, language, religion or social origin.

2. No derogation from articles 6, 7, 8 (paragraphs 1 and 2), 11, 15, 16 and 18 may be made under this provision.

3. Any State Party to the present Covenant availing itself of the right of derogation shall immediately inform the other States Parties to the present Covenant, through the intermediary of the Secretary-General of the United Nations, of the provisions from which it has derogated and of the reasons by which it was actuated. A further communication shall be made, through the same intermediary, on the date on which it terminates such derogation.

Article 5

1. Nothing in the present Covenant may be interpreted as implying for any State, group or person any right to engage in any activity or perform any act aimed at the destruction of any of the rights and freedoms recognized herein or at their limitation to a greater extent than is provided for in the present Covenant.

2. There shall be no restriction upon or derogation from any of the fundamental human rights recognized or existing in any State Party to the present

Covenant pursuant to law, conventions, regulations or custom on the pretext that the present Covenant does not recognize such rights or that it recognizes them to a lesser extent.

PART III

Article 6

1. Every human being has the inherent right to life. This right shall be protected by law. No one shall be arbitrarily deprived of his life.

2. In countries which have not abolished the death penalty, sentence of death may be imposed only for the most serious crimes in accordance with the law in force at the time of the commission of the crime and not contrary to the provisions of the present Covenant and to the Convention on the Prevention and Punishment of the Crime of Genocide. This penalty can only be carried out pursuant to a final judgement rendered by a competent court.

3. When deprivation of life constitutes the crime of genocide, it is understood that nothing in this article shall authorize any State Party to the present Covenant to derogate in any way from any obligation assumed under the provisions of the Convention on the Prevention and Punishment of the Crime of Genocide.

4. Anyone sentenced to death shall have the right to seek pardon or commutation of the sentence. Amnesty, pardon or commutation of the sentence of death may be granted in all cases.

5. Sentence of death shall not be imposed for crimes committed by persons below eighteen years of age and shall not be carried out on pregnant women.

6. Nothing in this article shall be invoked to delay or to prevent the abolition of capital punishement by any State Party to the present Covenant.

Article 7

No one shall be subjected to torture or to cruel, inhuman or degrading treatment or punishment. In particular, no one shall be subjected without his free consent to medical or scientific experimentation.

Article 8

1. No one shall be held in slavery; slavery and the slave-trade in all their forms shall be prohibited.

2. No one shall be held in servitude.

. . .

Article 9

1. Everyone has the right to liberty and security of person. No one shall be subjected to arbitrary arrest or detention. No one shall be deprived of his liberty except on such grounds and in accordance with such procedure as are established by law.

2. Anyone who is arrested shall be informed, at the time of arrest, of the reasons for his arrest and shall be promptly informed of any charges against him.

3. Anyone arrested or detained on a criminal charge shall be brought promptly before a judge or other officer authorized by law to exercise judicial power and shall be entitled to trial within a reasonable time or to release. It shall not be the general rule that persons awaiting trial shall be detained in custody, but release may be subject to guarantees to appear for trial, at any other stage of the judicial proceedings, and, should occasion arise, for execution of the judgment.

4. Anyone who is deprived of his liberty by arrest or detention shall be entitled to take proceedings before a court, in order that the court may decide without delay on the lawfulness of his detention and order his release if the detention is not lawful.

5. Anyone who has been victim of unlawful arrest or detention shall have an enforceable right to compensation.

Article 10

1. All persons deprived of their liberty shall be treated with humanity and with respect for the inherent dignity of the human person.

2. (*a*) Accused persons shall, save in exceptional circumstances, be segregated from convicted persons and shall be subject to separate treatment appropriate to their status as unconvicted persons;

(*b*) Accused juvenile persons shall be separated from adults and brought as speedily as possible for adjudication.

3. The penitentiary system shall comprise treatment of prisoners the essential aim of which shall be their reformation and social rehabilitation. Juvenile offenders shall be segregated from adults and be accorded treatment appropriate to their age and legal status.

Article 11

No one shall be imprisoned merely on the ground of inability to fulfil a contractual obligation.

Article 12

1. Everyone lawfully within the territory of a State shall, within that territory, have the right to liberty of movement and freedom to choose his residence.

2. Everyone shall be free to leave any country, including his own.

3. The above-mentioned rights shall not be subject to any restrictions except those which are provided by law, are necessary to protect national security, public order (*ordre public*), public health or morals or the rights and freedoms of others, and are consistent with the other rights recognized in the present Covenant.

4. No one shall be arbitrarily deprived of the right to enter his own country.

Article 13

An alien lawfully in the territory of a State Party to the present Covenant may be expelled therefrom only in pursuance of a decision reached in accordance with law and shall, except where compelling reasons of national security otherwise require, be allowed to submit the reasons against his expulsion and to have his case reviewed by, and be represented for the purpose before, the competent authority or a person or persons especially designated by the competent authority.

Article 14

1. All persons shall be equal before the courts and tribunals. In the determination of any criminal charge against him, or of his rights and obligations in a suit at law, everyone shall be entitled to a fair and public hearing by a competent, independent and impartial tribunal established by law. The press and the public may be excluded from all or part of a trial for reasons of morals, public order (*ordre public*) or national security in a democratic society, or when the interest of the private lives of the Parties so requires, or to the extent strictly necessary in the opinion of the court in special circumstances where publicity would prejudice the interests of justice; but any judgment rendered in a criminal case or in a suit at law shall be made public except where the interest of juvenile persons otherwise requires or the proceedings concern matrimonial disputes or the guardianship of children.

2. Everyone charged with a criminal offence shall have the right to be presumed innocent until proved guilty according to law.

3. In the determination of any criminal charge against him, everyone shall be entitled to the following minimum guarantees, in full equality:

(a) To be informed promptly and in detail in a language which he understands of the nature and cause of the charge against him;

(b) To have adequate time and facilities for the preparation of his defence and to communicate with counsel of his own choosing;

(c) To be tried without undue delay;

(d) To be tried in his presence, and to defend himself in person or through legal assistance of his own choosing; to be informed, if he does not have legal assistance, of this right; and to have legal assistance assigned to him, in any case where the interests of justice so require, and without payment by him in any such case if he does not have sufficient means to pay for it;

(e) To examine, or have examined, the witnesses against him and to obtain the attendance and examination of witnesses on his behalf under the same conditions as witnesses against him;

(f) To have the free assistance of an interpreter if he cannot understand or speak the language used in court;

(g) Not to be compelled to testify against himself or to confess guilt.

4. In the case of juvenile persons, the procedure shall be such as will take account of their age and the desirability of promoting their rehabilitation.

5. Everyone convicted of a crime shall have the right to his conviction and sentence being reviewed by a higher tribunal according to law.

6. When a person has by a final decision been convicted of a criminal offence and when subsequently his conviction has been reversed or he has been pardoned on the ground that a new or newly discovered fact shows conclusively that there has been a miscarriage of justice, the person who has suffered punishment as a result of such conviction shall be compensated according to law, unless it is

proved that the non-disclosure of the unknown fact in time is wholly or partly attributable to him.

7. No one shall be liable to be tried or punished again for an offence for which he has already been finally convicted or acquitted in accordance with the law and penal procedure of each country.

Article 15

1. No one shall be held guilty of any criminal offence on account of any act of omission which did not constitute a criminal offence, under national or international law, at the time when it was committed. Nor shall a heavier penalty be imposed than the one that was applicable at the time when the criminal offence was committed. If, subsequent to the commission of the offence, provision is made by law for the imposition of the lighter penalty, the offender shall benefit thereby.

2. Nothing in this article shall prejudice the trial and punishment of any person for any act or omission which, at the time when it was committed, was criminal according to the general principles of law recognized by the community of nations.

Article 16

Everyone shall have the right to recognition everywhere as a person before the law.

Article 17

1. No one shall be subjected to arbitrary or unlawful interference with his privacy, family, home or correspondence, nor to unlawful attacks on his honour and reputation.

2. Everyone has the right to the protection of the law against such interference or attacks.

Article 18

1. Everyone shall have the right to freedom of thought, conscience and religion. This right shall include freedom to have or to adopt a religion or belief of his choice, and freedom, either individually or in community with others and in public or private, to manifest his religion or belief in worship, observance, practice and teaching.

2. No one shall be subject to coercion which would impair his freedom to have or to adopt a religion or belief of his choice.

3. Freedom to manifest one's religion or beliefs may be subject only to such limitations as are prescribed by law and are necessary to protect public safety, order, health, or morals or the fundamental rights and freedoms of others.

4. The States Parties to the present Covenant undertake to have respect for the liberty of parents and, when applicable, legal guardians to ensure the religious and moral education of their children in conformity with their own convictions.

Article 19

1. Everyone shall have the right to hold opinions without interference.

2. Everyone shall have the right to freedom of expression; this right shall

include freedom to seek, receive and impart information and ideas of all kinds, regardless of frontiers, either orally, in writing or in print, in the form of art, or through any other media of his choice.

3. The exercise of the rights provided for in paragraph 2 of this article carries with it special duties and responsibilities. It may therefore be subject to certain restrictions, but these shall only be such as are provided by law and are necessary:

- (*a*) For respect of the rights or reputations of others;
- (*b*) For the protection of national security or of public order (*ordre public*), or of public health or morals.

Article 20

1. Any propaganda for war shall be prohibited by law.

2. Any advocacy of national, racial or religious hatred that constitutes incitement to discrimination, hostility or violence shall be prohibited by law.

Article 21

The right of peaceful assembly shall be recognized. No restrictions may be placed on the exercise of this right other than those imposed in conformity with the law and which are necessary in a democratic society in the interests of national security or public safety, public order (*ordre public*), the protection of public health or morals or the protection of the rights and freedoms of others.

Article 22

1. Everyone shall have the right to freedom of association with others, including the right to form and join trade unions for the protection of his interests.

2. No restrictions may be placed on the exercise of this right other than those which are prescribed by law and which are necessary in a democratic society in the interests of national security or public safety, public order (*ordre public*), the protection of public health or morals or the protection of the rights and freedoms of others. This article shall not prevent the imposition of lawful restrictions on members of the armed forces and of the police in their exercise of this right.

. . .

Article 23

1. The family is the natural and fundamental group unit of society and is entitled to protection by society and the State.

2. The right of men and women of marriageable age to marry and to found a family shall be recognized.

3. No marriage shall be entered into without the free and full consent of the intending spouses.

4. States Parties to the present Covenant shall take appropriate steps to ensure equality of rights and responsibilities of spouses as to marriage, during marriage and at its dissolution. In the case of dissolution, provision shall be made for the necessary protection of any children.

Article 24

1. Every child shall have, without any discrimination as to race, colour, sex, language, religion, national or social origin, property or birth, the right to such measures of protection as are required by his status as a minor, on the part of his family, society and the State.

2. Every child shall be registered immediately after birth and shall have a name.

3. Every child has the right to acquire a nationality.

Article 25

Every citizen shall have the right and the opportunity, without any of the distinctions mentioned in article 2 and without unreasonable restrictions:

(*a*) To take part in the conduct of public affairs, directly or through freely chosen representatives;

(*b*) To vote and to be elected at genuine periodic elections which shall be by universal and equal suffrage and shall be held by secret ballot, guaranteeing the free expression of the will of the electors;

(*c*) To have access, on general terms of equality, to public service in his country.

Article 26

All persons are equal before the law and are entitled without any discrimination to the equal protection of the law. In this respect, the law shall prohibit any discrimination and guarantee to all persons equal and effective protection against discrimination on any ground such as race, colour, sex, langauge, religion, political or other opinion, national or social origin, property, birth or other status.

Article 27

In those States in which ethnic, religious or linguistic minorities exist, persons belonging to such minorities shall not be denied the right, in community with the other members of their group, to enjoy their own culture, to profess and practice their own religion, or to use their own language.

PART IV

Article 28

1. There shall be established a Human Rights Committee (hereafter referred to in the present Covenant as the Committee). It shall consist of eighteen members and shall carry out the functions hereinafter provided.

2. The Committee shall be composed of nationals of the States Parties to the present Covenant who shall be persons of high moral character and recognized competence in the field of human rights, consideration being given to the usefulness of the participation of some persons having legal experience.

3. The members of the Committee shall be elected and shall serve in their personal capacity.

. . .

Article 31

1. The Committee may not include more than one national of the same State.

2. In the election of the Committee, consideration shall be given to equitable geographical distribution of membership and to the representation of the different forms of civilization and of the principal legal systems.

. . .

Article 38

Every member of the Committee shall, before taking up his duties, make a solemn declaration in open committee that he will perform his functions impartially and conscientiously.

. . .

Article 39

1. The Committee shall elect its officers for a term of two years. They may be re-elected.

. . .

(2)(b) Decisions of the Committee shall be made by a majority vote of the members present.

Article 40

1. The States Parties to the present Covenant undertake to submit reports on the measures they have adopted which give effect to the rights recognized herein and on the progress made in the enjoyment of those rights:

(*a*) Within one year of the entry into force of the present Covenant for the States Parties concerned;
(*b*) Thereafter whenever the Committee so requests.

2. All reports shall be submitted to the Secretary-General of the United Nations, who shall transmit them to the Committee for consideration. Reports shall indicate the factors and difficulties, if any, affecting the implementation of the present Covenant.

3. The Secretary-General of the United Nations may, after consultation with the Committee, transmit to the specialized agencies concerned copies of such parts of the reports as may fall within their field of competence.

4. The Committee shall study the reports submitted by the States Parties to the present Covenant. It shall transmit its reports, and such general comments as it may consider appropriate, to the States Parties. The Committee may also transmit to the Economic and Social Council these comments along with the copies of the reports it has received from States Parties to the present Covenant.

5. The States Parties to the present Covenant may submit to the Committee observations on any comments that may be made in accordance with paragraph 4 of this article.

Article 41

1. A State Party to the present Covenant may at any time declare under this article that it recognizes the competence of the Committee to receive and consider communications to the effect that a State Party claims that another State Party is not fulfilling its obligations under the present Covenant. Communications under this article may be received and considered only if submitted by a State Party which has made a declaration recognizing in regard to itself the competence of the Committee. No communication shall be received by the Committee if it concerns a State Party which has not made such a declaration. Communications received under this article shall be dealt with in accordance with the following procedure:

[Article 41 spells out a procedure involving efforts toward resolution, referral of the matter to the Committee, and a report by the Committee to the States Parties concerned that is confined 'to a brief statement of the facts; the written submissions and record of the oral submissions made by the States Parties concerned shall be attached to the report.' Article 42 provides that if the matter is not resolved to the satisfaction of the States Parties concerned the Committee may, with the consent of those parties, appoint an *ad hoc* Conciliation Commission. If no amicable solution is reached, the Commission submits a report to the Chairman of the Committee. The report includes the Commission's finding on all relevant questions of fact, and its views on possibilities of an amicable solution.]

. . .

Article 44

The provisions for the implementation of the present Covenant shall apply without prejudice to the procedures prescribed in the field of human rights by or under the constituent instruments and the conventions of the United Nations and of the specialized agencies and shall not prevent the States Parties to the present Covenant from having recourse to other procedures for settling a dispute in accordance with general or special international agreements in force between them.

Article 45

The Committee shall submit to the General Assembly of the United Nations, through the Economic and Social Council, an annual report on its activities.

PART V

Article 46

Nothing in the present Covenant shall be interpreted as impairing the provisions of the Charter of the United Nations and of the constitutions of the specialized agencies which define the respective responsibilities of the various organs of the United Nations and of the specialized agencies in regard to the matters dealt with in the present Covenant.

Article 47

Nothing in the present Covenant shall be interpreted as impairing the inherent right of all peoples to enjoy and utilize fully and freely their natural wealth and resources.

PART VI

...

Article 50

The provisions of the present Covenant shall extend to all parts of federal States without any limitations or exceptions.

Article 51

1. Any State Party to the present Covenant may propose an amendment and file it with the Secretary-General of the United Nations. The Secretary-General of the United Nations shall thereupon communicate any proposed amendments to the States Parties to the present Covenant with a request that they notify him whether they favour a conference of States Parties for the purpose of considering and voting upon the proposals. In the event that at least one third of the States Parties favours such a conference, the Secretary-General shall convene the conference under the auspices of the United Nations. Any amendment adopted by a majority of the States Parties present and voting at the conference shall be submitted to the General Assembly of the United Nations for approval.

2. Amendments shall come into force when they have been approved by the General Assembly of the United Nations and accepted by a two-thirds majority of the States Parties to the present Covenant in accordance with their respective constitutional processes.

3. When amendments come into force, they shall be binding on those States Parties which have accepted them, other States Parties still being bound by the provisions of the present Covenant and any earlier amendment which they have accepted.

...

PROTOCOLS TO THE INTERNATIONAL COVENANT ON CIVIL AND POLITICAL RIGHTS

(FIRST) OPTIONAL PROTOCOL

The States Parties to the present Protocol,

Considering that in order further to achieve the purpose of the International Covenant on Civil and Political Rights (hereinafter referred to as the Covenant) and the implementation of its provisions it would be appropriate to enable the Human Rights Committee set up in part IV of the Covenant (hereinafter referred to as the Committee) to receive and consider, as provided in the present Protocol, communications from individuals claiming to be victims of violations of any of the rights set forth in the Covenant,

Have agreed as follows:

Article 1

A State Party to the Covenant that becomes a Party to the present Protocol recognizes the competence of the Committee to receive and consider communications from individuals subject to its jurisdiction who claim to be victims of a violation by that State Party of any of the rights set forth in the Covenant. No communication shall be received by the Committee if it concerns a State Party to the Covenant which is not a Party to the present Protocol.

Article 2

Subject to the provisions of article 1, individuals who claim that any of their rights enumerated in the Covenant have been violated and who have exhausted all available domestic remedies may submit a written communication to the Committee for consideration.

Article 3

The Committee shall consider inadmissible any communication under the present Protocol which is anonymous, or which it considers to be an abuse of the right of submission of such communications or to be incompatible with the provisions of the Covenant.

Article 4

1. Subject to the provisions of article 3, the Committee shall bring any communications submitted to it under the present Protocol to the attention of the State Party to the present Protocol alleged to be violating any provision of the Covenant.

2. Within six months, the receiving State shall submit to the Committee written explanations or statements clarifying the matter and the remedy, if any, that may have been taken by that State.

Article 5

1. The Committee shall consider communications received under the present

Protocol in the light of all written information made available to it by the individual and by the State Party concerned.

2. The Committee shall not consider any communication from an individual unless it has ascertained that:

(*a*) The same matter is not being examined under another procedure of international investigation or settlement;

(*b*) The individual has exhausted all available domestic remedies. This shall not be the rule where the application of the remedies is unreasonably prolonged.

3. The Committee shall hold closed meetings when examining communications under the present Protocol.

4. The Committee shall forward its views to the State Party concerned and to the individual.

Article 6

The Committee shall include in its annual report under article 45 of the Covenant a summary of its activities under the present Protocol.

. . .

SECOND OPTIONAL PROTOCOL

The States Parties to the present Protocol,

Believing that abolition of the death penalty contributes to enhancement of human dignity and progressive development of human rights,

Recalling article 3 of the Universal Declaration of Human Rights, adopted on 10 December 1948, and article 6 of the International Covenant on Civil and Political Rights, adopted on 16 December 1966,

Noting that article 6 of the International Covenant on Civil and Political Rights refers to abolition of the death penalty in terms that strongly suggest that abolition is desirable,

Convinced that all measures of abolition of the death penalty should be considered as progress in the enjoyment of the right to life,

Desirous to undertake hereby an international commitment to abolish the death penalty,

Have agreed as follows:

Article 1

1. No one within the jurisdiction of a State Party to the present Protocol shall be executed.

2. Each State Party shall take all necessary measures to abolish the death penalty within its jurisdiction.

Article 2

1. No reservation is admissible to the present Protocol, except for a reservation made at the time of ratification or accession that provides for the application of

the death penalty in time of war pursuant to a conviction for a most serious crime of a military nature committed during wartime.

. . .

Article 3

The States Parties to the present Protocol shall include in the reports they submit to the Human Rights Committee, in accordance with article 40 of the Covenant, information on the measures that they have adopted to give effect to the present Protocol.

. . .

INTERNATIONAL COVENANT ON ECONOMIC, SOCIAL AND CULTURAL RIGHTS

PREAMBLE

The States Parties to the present Covenant,

. . .

Recognizing that these rights derive from the inherent dignity of the human person,

Recognizing that, in accordance with the Universal Declaration of Human Rights, the ideal of free human beings enjoying freedom from fear and want can only be achieved if conditions are created whereby everyone may enjoy his economic, social and cultural rights, as well as his civil and political rights,

. . .

Realizing that the individual, having duties to other individuals and to the community to which he belongs, is under a responsibility to strive for the promotion and observance of the rights recognized in the present Covenant,

Agree upon the following articles:

PART I

Article 1

1. All peoples have the right of self-determination. By virtue of that right they freely determine their political status and freely pursue their economic, social and cultural development.

2. All peoples may, for their own ends, freely dispose of their natural wealth and resources without prejudice to any obligations arising out of international economic co-operation, based upon the principle of mutual benefit, and international law. In no case may a people by deprived of its own means of subsistence.

3. The States Parties to the Present Covenant, including those having responsibility for the administration of Non-Self-Governing and Trust Territories, shall promote the realization of the right of self-determination, and shall respect that right, in conformity with the provisions of the Charter of the United Nations.

PART II

Article 2

1. Each State Party to the present Covenant undertakes to take steps, individually and through international assistance and co-operation, especially economic and technical, to the maximum of its available resources, with a view to achieving progressively the full realization of the rights recognized in the present Covenant by all appropriate means, including particularly the adoption of legislative measures.

2. The States Parties to the present Covenant undertake to guarantee that the rights enunciated in the present Covenant will be exercised without discrimination of any kind as to race, colour, sex, language, religion, political or other opinion, national or social origin, property, birth or other status.

3. Developing countries, with due regard to human rights and their national economy, may determine to what extent they would guarantee the economic rights recognized in the present Covenant to non-nationals.

Article 3

The States Parties to the present Covenant undertake to ensure the equal right of men and women to the enjoyment of all economic, social cultural rights set forth in the present Covenant.

Article 4

The States Parties to the present Covenant recognize that, in the enjoyment of those rights provided by the State in conformity with the present Covenant, the State may subject such rights only to such limitations as are determined by law only in so far as this may be compatible with the nature of these rights and solely for the purpose of promoting the general welfare in a democratic society.

Article 5

1. Nothing in the present Covenant may be interpreted as implying for any State, group or person any right to engage in any activity or to perform any act aimed at the destruction of any of the rights or freedoms recognized herein, or at their limitation to a greater extent than is provided for in the present Covenant.

2. No restriction upon or derogation from any of the fundamental human rights recognized or existing in any country in virtue of law, conventions, regulations or custom shall be admitted on the pretext that the present Covenant does not recognize such rights or that it recognizes them to a lesser extent.

PART III

Article 6

1. The States Parties to the present Covenant recognize the right to work, which includes the right of everyone to the opportunity to gain his living by work which he freely chooses or accepts, and will take appropriate steps to safeguard this right.

2. The steps to be taken by a State Party to the present Covenant to achieve the full realization of this right shall include technical and vocational guidance and training programmes, policies and techniques to achieve steady economic, social and cultural development and full and productive employment under conditions safeguarding fundamental political and economic freedoms to the individual.

Article 7

The States Parties to the present Covenant recognize the right of everyone to the enjoyment of just and favourable conditions of work which ensure, in particular:

　　(*a*)　Remuneration which provides all workers, as a minimum, with:
　　　　(i)　Fair wages and equal remuneration for work of equal value without distinc-

tion of any kind, in particular women being guaranteed conditions of work not inferior to those enjoyed by men, with equal pay for equal work;

(ii) A decent living for themselves and their families in accordance with the provisions of the present Covenant;

(*b*) Safe and healthy working conditions;

(*c*) Equal opportunity for everyone to be promoted in his employment to an appropriate higher level, subject to no considerations other than those of seniority and competence;

(*d*) Rest, leisure and reasonable limitation of working hours and periodic holidays with pay, as well as remuneration for public holidays.

Article 8

1. The States Parties to the present Covenant undertake to ensure:

(*a*) The right of everyone to form trade unions and join the trade union of his choice, subject only to the rules of the organization concerned, for the promotion and protection of his economic and social interests. No restrictions may be placed on the exercise of this right other than those prescribed by law and which are necessary in a democratic society in the interests of national security or public order or for the protection of the rights and freedoms of others;

(*b*) The right of trade unions to establish national federations or confederations and the right of the latter to form or join international trade-union organizations;

(*c*) The right of trade unions to function freely subject to no limitations other than those prescribed by law and which are necessary in a democratic society in the interests of national security or public order or for the protection of the rights and freedom of others;

(*d*) The right to strike, provided that it is exercised in conformity with the laws of the particular country.

2. This article shall not prevent the imposition of lawful restrictions on the exercise of these rights by members of the armed forces or of the police or of the administration of the State.

. . .

Article 9

The States Parties to the present Covenant recognize the right of everyone to social security, including social insurance.

Article 10

The States Parties to the present Covenant recognize that:

1. The widest possible protection and assistance should be accorded to the family, which is the natural and fundamental group unit of society, particularly for its establishment and while it is responsible for the care and education of dependent children. Marriage must be entered into with the free consent of the intending spouses.

2. Special protection should be accorded to mothers during a reasonable period before and after childbirth. During such period working mothers should be accorded paid leave or leave with adequate social security benefits.

3. Special measures of protection and assistance should be taken on behalf of all children and young persons without any discrimination for reasons of parentage or other conditions. Children and young persons should be protected from economic and social exploitation. Their employment in work harmful to their morals or health or dangerous to life or likely to hamper their normal development should be punishable by law. States should also set age limits below which the paid employment of child labour should be prohibited and punishable by law.

Article 11

1. The States Parties to the present Covenant recognize the right of everyone to an adequate standard of living for himself and his family, including adequate food, clothing and housing, and to the continuous improvement of living conditions. The States Parties will take appropriate steps to ensure the realization of this right, recognizing to this effect the essential importance of international co-operation based on free consent.

2. The States Parties to the present Covenant, recognizing the fundamental right of everyone to be free from hunger, shall take, individually and through international co-operation, the measures, including specific programmes, which are needed:

   (*a*) To improve methods of production, conservation and distribution of food by making full use of technical and scientific knowledge, by disseminating knowledge of the principles of nutrition and by developing or reforming agrarian systems in such a way as to achieve the most efficient development and utilization of natural resources;
   (*b*) Taking into account the problems of both food-importing and food-exporting countries, to ensure an equitable distribution of world food supplies in relation to need.

Article 12

1. The States Parties to the present Covenant recognize the right of everyone to the enjoyment of the highest attainable standard of physical and mental health.

2. The steps to be taken by the States Parties to the present Covenant to achieve the full realization of this right shall include those necessary for:

   (*a*) The provision for the reduction of the stillbirth-rate and of infant mortality and for the healthy development of the child;
   (*b*) The improvement of all aspects of environmental and industrial hygiene;
   (*c*) The prevention, treatment and control of epidemic, endemic, occupational and other diseases;
   (*d*) The creation of conditions which would assure to all medical service and medical attention in the event of sickness.

Article 13

1. The States Parties to the present Covenant recognize the right of everyone to education. They agree that education shall be directed to the full development of the human personality and the sense of its dignity, and shall strengthen the respect

for human rights and fundamental freedoms. They further agree that education shall enable all persons to participate effectively in a free society, promote understanding, tolerance and friendship among all nations and all racial, ethnic or religious groups, and further the activities of the United Nations for the maintenance of peace.

2. The States Parties to the present Covenant recognize that, with a view to achieving the full realization of this right:

(*a*) Primary education shall be compulsory and available free to all;

(*b*) Secondary education in its different forms, including technical and vocational secondary education, shall be made generally available and accessible to all by every appropriate means, and in particular by the progressive introduction of free education;

(*c*) Higher education shall be made equally accessible to all, on the basis of capacity, by every appropriate means, and in particular by the progressive introduction of free education;

(*d*) Fundamental education shall be encouraged or intensified as far as possible for those persons who have not received or completed the whole period of their primary education;

(*e*) The development of a system of schools at all levels shall be actively pursued, an adequate fellowship system shall be established, and the material conditions of teaching staff shall be continuously improved.

3. The States Parties to the present Covenant undertake to have respect for the liberty of parents and, when applicable, legal guardians to choose for their children schools, other than those established by the public authorities, which conform to such minimum education standards as may be laid down or approved by the State and to ensure the religious and moral education of their children in conformity with their own convictions.

4. No part of this article shall be construed so as to interfere with the liberty of individuals and bodies to establish and direct educational institutions, subject always to the observance of the principles set forth in paragraph 1 of this article and to the requirement that the education given in such institutions shall conform to such minimum standards as may be laid down by the State.

Article 14

Each State Party to the present Covenant which, at the time of becoming a Party, has not been able to secure in its metropolitan territory or other territories under its jurisdiction compulsory primary education, free of charge, undertakes, within two years, to work out and adopt a detailed plan of action for the progressive implementation, within a reasonable number of years, to be fixed in the plan, of the principle of compulsory education free of charge for all.

Article 15

1. The States Parties to the present Covenant recognize the right of everyone:

(*a*) To take part in cultural life;

   (*b*) To enjoy the benefits of scientific progress and its applications;

   (*c*) To benefit from the protection of the moral and material interests resulting from any scientific, literary or artistic production of which he is the author.

2. The steps to be taken by the States Parties to the present Covenant to achieve the full realization of this right shall include those necessary for the conservation, the development and the diffusion of science and culture.

3. The States Parties to the present Covenant undertake to respect the freedom indispensable for scientific research and creative activity.

4. The States Parties to the present Covenant recognize the benefits to be derived from the encouragement and development of international contacts and co-operation in the scientific and cultural fields.

PART IV

Article 16

1. The States Parties to the present Covenant undertake to submit in conformity with this part of the Covenant reports on the measures which they have adopted and the progress made in achieving the observance of the rights recognized herein.

. . .

Article 22

The Economic and Social Council may bring to the attention of other organs of the United Nations, their subsidiary organs and specialized agencies concerned with furnishing technical assistance any matters arising out of the reports referred to in this part of the present Covenant which may assist such bodies in deciding, each within its field of competence, on the advisability of international measures likely to contribute to the effective progressive implementation of the present Covenant.

Article 23

The States Parties to the present Covenant agree that international action for the achievement of the rights recognized in the present Covenant includes such methods as the conclusion of conventions, the adoption of recommendations, the furnishing of technical assistance and the holding of regional meetings and technical meetings for the purpose of consultation and study organized in conjunction with the Governments concerned.

Article 24

Nothing in the present Covenant shall be interpreted as impairing the provisions of the Charter of the United Nations and of the constitutions of the specialized agencies which define the respective responsibilities of the various organs of the United Nations and of the specialized agencies in regard to the matters dealt with in the present Covenant.

Article 25

Nothing in the present Covenant shall be interpreted as impairing the inherent right of all peoples to enjoy and utilize fully and freely their natural wealth and resources.

PART V

. . .

Article 28

The provisions of the present Covenant shall extend to all parts of federal States without any limitations or exceptions.

. . .

CONVENTION ON THE ELIMINATION OF ALL FORMS OF DISCRIMINATION AGAINST WOMEN

The States Parties to the present Convention,

Noting that the Charter of the United Nations reaffirms faith in fundamental human rights, in the dignity and worth of the human person and in the equal rights of men and women,

Noting that the Universal Declaration of Human Rights affirms the principle of the inadmissibility of discrimination . . .,

Noting that the States Parties to the International Covenants on Human Rights have the obligation to ensure the equal rights of men and women to enjoy all economic, social, cultural, civil and political rights,

. . .

Concerned, however, that despite these various instruments extensive discrimination against women continues to exist,

Recalling that discrimination against women violates the principles of equality of rights and respect for human dignity, is an obstacle to the participation of women, on equal terms with men, in the political, social, economic and cultural life of their countries, hampers the growth of the prosperity of society and the family and makes more difficult the full development of the potentialities of women in the service of their countries and of humanity,

. . .

Convinced that the full and complete development of a country, the welfare of the world and the cause of peace require the maximum participation of women on equal terms with men in all fields,

Bearing in mind the great contribution of women to the welfare of the family and to the development of society, so far not fully recognized, the social significance of maternity and the role of both parents in the family and in the upbringing of children, and aware that the rule of women in procreation should not be a basis for discrimination but that the upbringing of children requires a sharing of responsibility between men and women and society as a whole,

Aware that a change in the traditional role of men as well as the role of women in society and in the family is needed to achieve full equality between men and women,

. . .

Have agreed on the following:

PART I

Article 1

For the purposes of the present Convention, the term 'discrimination against women' shall mean any distinction, exclusion or restriction made on the basis of sex which has the effect or purpose of impairing or nullifying the recognition, enjoyment or exercise by women, irrespective of their marital status, on a basis of equality of men and women, of human rights and fundamental freedoms in the political, economic, social, cultural, civil or any other field.

Article 2

States Parties condemn discrimination against women in all its forms, agree to pursue by all appropriate means and without delay a policy of eliminating discrimination against women and, to this end, undertake:

(*a*) To embody the principle of the equality of men and women in their national constitutions or other appropriate legislation if not yet incorporated therein and to ensure, through law and other appropriate means, the practical realization of this principle;

(*b*) To adopt appropriate legislative and other measures, including sanctions where appropriate, prohibiting all discrimination against women;

(*c*) To establish legal protection of the rights of women on an equal basis with men and to ensure through competent national tribunals and other public institutions the effective protection of women against any act of discrimination;

(*d*) To refrain from engaging in any act or practice of discrimination against women and to ensure that public authorities and institutions shall act in conformity with this obligation;

(*e*) To take all appropriate measures to eliminate discrimination against women by any person, organization or enterprise;

(*f*) To take all appropriate measures, including legislation, to modify or abolish existing laws, regulations, customs and practices which constitute discrimination against women;

(*g*) To repeal all national penal provisions which constitute discrimination against women.

Article 3

States Parties shall take in all fields, in particular in the political, social, economic and cultural fields, all appropriate measures, including legislation, to ensure the full development and advancement of women, for the purpose of guaranteeing them the exercise and enjoyment of human rights and fundamental freedoms on a basis of equality with men.

Article 4

1. Adoption by States Parties of temporary special measures aimed at accelerating *de facto* equality between men and women shall not be considered discrimination as defined in the present Convention, but shall in no way entail as a consequence the maintenance of unequal or separate standards; these measures shall be discontinued when the objectives of equality of opportunity and treatment have been achieved.

2. Adoption by States Parties of special measures, including those measures contained in the present Convention, aimed at protecting maternity shall not be considered discriminatory.

Article 5

States Parties shall take all appropriate measures:

(*a*) To modify the social and cultural patterns of conduct of men and women, with a view to achieving the elimination of prejudices and customary and all other practices which are based on the idea of the inferiority or the superiority of either of the sexes or on stereotyped roles for men and women;

(b) To ensure that family education includes a proper understanding of maternity as a social function and the recognition of the common responsibility of men and women in the upbringing and development of their children, it being understood that the interest of the children is the primordial consideration in all cases.

Article 6

States Parties shall take all appropriate measures, including legislation, to suppress all forms of traffic in women and exploitation of prostitution of women.

PART II

Article 7

States Parties shall take all appropriate measures to eliminate discrimination against women in the political and public life of the country and, in particular, shall ensure to women, on equal terms with men, the right:

(a) To vote in all elections and public referenda and to be eligible for election to all publicly elected bodies;

(b) To participate in the formulation of government policy and the implementation thereof and to hold public office and perform all public functions at all levels of government;

(c) To participate in non-governmental organizations and associations concerned with the public and political life of the country.

Article 8

States Parties shall take all appropriate measures to ensure to women, on equal terms with men and without any discrimination, the opportunity to represent their Governments at the international level and to participate in the work of international organizations.

Article 9

1. States Parties shall grant women equal rights with men to acquire, change or retain their nationality. They shall ensure in particular that neither marriage to an alien nor change of nationality by the husband during marriage shall automatically change the nationality of the wife, render her stateless or force upon her the nationality of the husband.

2. States Parties shall grant women equal rights with men with respect to the nationality of their children.

PART III

Article 10

States Parties shall take all appropriate measures to eliminate discrimination against women in order to ensure to them equal rights with men in the field of education and in particular to ensure, on a basis of equality of men and women:

(*a*) The same conditions for career and vocational guidance, for access to studies and for the achievement of diplomas in educational establishments of all categories in rural as well as in urban areas; this equality shall be ensured in pre-school, general, technical, professional and higher technical education, as well as in all types of vocational training;

(*b*) Access to the same curricula, the same examinations, teaching staff with qualifications of the same standard and school premises and equipment of the same quality;

(*c*) The elimination of any stereotyped concept of the roles of men and women at all levels and in all forms of education by encouraging coeducation and other types of education which will help to achieve this aim and, in particular, by the revision of textbooks and school programmes and the adaptation of teaching methods;

(*d*) The same opportunities to benefit from scholarships and other study grants;

(*e*) The same opportunities for access to programmes of continuing education, including adult and functional literacy programmes, particulary those aimed at reducing, at the earliest possible time, any gap in education existing between men and women;

(*f*) The reduction of female student drop-out rates and the organization of programmes for girls and women who have left school prematurely;

(*g*) The same opportunities to participate actively in sports and physical education;

(*h*) Access to specific educational information to help to ensure the health and well-being of families, including information and advice on family planning.

Article 11

1. States Parties shall take all appropriate measures to eliminate discrimination against women in the field of employment in order to ensure, on a basis of equality of men and women, the same rights, in particular:

(*a*) The right to work as an inalienable right of all human beings;

(*b*) The right to the same employment opportunities, including the application of the same criteria for selection in matters of employment;

(*c*) The right to free choice of profession and employment, the right to promotion, job security and all benefits and conditions of service and the right to receive vocational training and retraining, including apprenticeships, advanced vocational training and recurrent training;

(*d*) The right to equal remuneration, including benefits, and to equal treatment in respect of work of equal value, as well as equality of treatment in the evaluation of the quality of work;

(*e*) The right to social security, particularly in cases of retirement, unemployment, sickness, invalidity and old age and other incapacity to work, as well as the right to paid leave;

(*f*) The right to protection of health and to safety in working conditions, including the safeguarding of the function of reproduction.

2. In order to prevent discrimination against women on the grounds of

marriage or maternity and to ensure their effective right to work, States Parties shall take appropriate measures:

   (*a*) To prohibit, subject to the imposition of sanctions, dismissal on the grounds of pregnancy or of maternity leave and discrimination in dismissals on the basis of marital status;
   (*b*) To introduce maternity leave with pay or with comparable social benefits without loss of former employment, seniority or social allowances;
   (*c*) To encourage the provision of the necessary supporting social services to enable parents to combine family obligations with work responsibilities and participation in public life, in particular through promoting the establishment and development of a network of child-care facilities;
   (*d*) To provide special protection to women during pregnancy in types of work proved to be harmful to them.

   3. Protective legislation relating to matters covered in this article shall be reviewed periodically in the light of scientific and technological knowledge and shall be revised, repealed or extended as necessary.

Article 12

   1. States Parties shall take all appropriate measures to eliminate discrimination against women in the field of health care in order to ensure, on a basis of equality of men and women, access to health care services, including those related to family planning.
   2. Notwithstanding the provisions of paragraph 1 of this article, States Parties shall ensure to women appropriate services in connection with pregnancy, confinement and the post-natal period, granting free services where necessary, as well as adequate nutrition during pregnancy and lactation.

Article 13

States Parties shall take all appropriate measures to eliminate discrimination against women in other areas of economic and social life in order to ensure, on a basis of equality of men and women, the same rights, in particular:

   (*a*) The right to family benefits;
   (*b*) The right to bank loans, mortgages and other forms of financial credit;
   (*c*) The right to participate in recreational activities, sports and all aspects of cultural life.

Article 14

   1. States Parties shall take into account the particular problems faced by rural women and the significant roles which rural women play in the economic survival of their families, including their work in the non-monetized sectors of the economy, and shall take all appropriate measures to ensure the application of the provisions of the present Convention to women in rural areas.
   2. States Parties shall take all appropriate measures to eliminate discrimination

against women in rural areas in order to ensure, on a basis of equality of men and women, that they participate in and benefit from rural development and, in particular, shall ensure to such women the right:

(a) To participate in the elaboration and implementation of development planning at all levels;
(b) To have access to adequate health care facilities, including information, counselling and services in family planning;
(c) To benefit directly from social security programmes;
(d) To obtain all types of training and education, formal and non-formal, including that relating to functional literacy, as well as, *inter alia*, the benefit of all community and extension services, in order to increase their technical proficiency;
(e) To organize self-help groups and co-operatives in order to obtain equal access to economic opportunities through employment or self-employment;
(f) To participate in all community activities;
(g) To have access to agricultural credit and loans, marketing facilities, appropriate technology and equal treatment in land and agrarian reform as well as in land resettlement schemes;
(h) To enjoy adequate living conditions, particularly in relation to housing, sanitation, electricity and water supply, transport and communications.

PART IV

Article 15

1. States Parties shall accord to women equality with men before the law.

2. States Parties shall accord to women, in civil matters, a legal capacity identical to that of men and the same opportunities to exercise that capacity. In particular, they shall give women equal rights to conclude contracts and to administer property and shall treat them equally in all stages of procedure in courts and tribunals.

3. States Parties agree that all contracts and all other private instruments of any kind with a legal effect which is directed at restricting the legal capacity of women shall be deemed null and void.

4. States Parties shall accord to men and women the same rights with regard to the law relating to the movement of persons and the freedom to choose their residence and domicile.

Article 16

1. States Parties shall take all appropriate measures to eliminate discrimination against women in all matters relating to marriage and family relations and in particular shall ensure, on a basis of equality of men and women:

(a) The same right to enter into marriage;
(b) The same right freely to choose a spouse and to enter into marriage only with their free and full consent;
(c) The same rights and responsibilities during marriage and at its dissolution;
(d) The same rights and responsibilities as parents, irrespective of their marital

status, in matters relating to their children; in all cases the interests of the children shall be paramount;

(e) The same rights to decide freely and responsibly on the number and spacing of their children and to have access to the information, education and means to enable them to exercise these rights;

(f) The same rights and responsibilities with regard to guardianship, wardship, trusteeship and adoption of children, or similar institutions where these concepts exist in national legislation; in all cases the interests of the children shall be paramount;

(g) The same personal rights as husband and wife, including the right to choose a family name, a profession and an occupation;

(h) The same rights for both spouses in respect of the ownership, acquisition, management, administration, enjoyment and disposition of property, whether free of charge or for a valuable consideration.

2. The betrothal and the marriage of a child shall have no legal effect, and all necessary action, including legislation, shall be taken to specify a minimum age for marriage and to make the registration of marriages in an official registry compulsory.

PART V

Article 17

1. For the purpose of considering the progress made in the implementation of the present Convention, there shall be established a Committee on the Elimination of Discrimination against Women (hereinafter referred to as the Committee) consisting, at the time of entry into force of the Convention, of eighteen and, after ratification of or accession to the Convention by the thirty-fifth State Party, of twenty-three experts of high moral standing and competence in the field covered by the Convention. The experts shall be elected by States Parties from among their nationals and shall serve in their personal capacity, consideration being given to equitable geographical distribution and to the representation of the different forms of civilization as well as the principal legal systems.

. . .

Article 18

1. States Parties undertake to submit to the Secretary-General of the United Nations, for consideration by the Committee, a report on the legislative, judicial, administrative or other measures which they have adopted to give effect to the provisions of the present Convention and on the progress made in this respect:

(a) Within one year after the entry into force for the State concerned;

(b) Thereafter at least every four years and further whenever the Committee so requests.

2. Reports may indicate factors and difficulties affecting the degree of fulfilment of obligations under the present Convention.

. . .

Article 21

1. The Committee shall, through the Economic and Social Council, report annually to the General Assembly of the United Nations on its activities and may make suggestions and general recommendations based on the examination of reports and information received from the States Parties. Such suggestions and general recommendations shall be included in the report of the Committee together with comments, if any, from States Parties.

. . .

PART VI

Article 23

Nothing in the present Convention shall affect any provisions that are more conducive to the achievement of equality between men and women which may be contained:

  (*a*) In the legislation of a State Party; or
  (*b*) In any other international convention, treaty or agreement in force for that State.

Article 24

States Parties undertake to adopt all necessary measures at the national level aimed at achieving the full realization of the rights recognized in the present Convention.

. . .

Article 28

1. The Secretary-General of the United Nations shall receive and circulate to all States the text of reservations made by States at the time of ratification or accession.

2. A reservation incompatible with the object and purpose of the present Convention shall not be permitted.

. . .

Article 29

1. Any dispute between two or more States Parties concerning the interpretation or application of the present Convention which is not settled by negotiation shall, at the request of one of them, be submitted to arbitration. If within six months from the date of the request for arbitration the parties are unable to agree on the organization of the arbitration, any one of those parties may refer the dispute to the International Court of Justice by request in conformity with the Statute of the Court.

. . .

CONVENTION ON THE RIGHTS OF THE CHILD

The States Parties to the present Convention,

. . .

Bearing in mind that, as indicated in the Declaration of the Rights of the Child, 'the child, by reason of his physical and mental immaturity, needs special safeguards and care, including appropriate legal protection, before as well as after birth',

. . .

Taking due account of the importance of the traditions and cultural values of each people for the protection and harmonious development of the child,

. . .

Have agreed as follows:

PART I

Article 1

For the purposes of the present Convention, a child means every human being below the age of eighteen years unless under the law applicable to the child, majority is attained earlier.

Article 2

1. States Parties shall respect and ensure the rights set forth in the present Convention to each child within their jurisdiction without discrimination of any kind, irrespective of the child's or his or her parent's or legal guardian's race, colour, sex, language, religion, political or other opinion, national, ethnic or social origin, property, disability, birth or other status.

2. States Parties shall take all appropriate measures to ensure that the child is protected against all forms of discrimination or punishment on the basis of the status, activities, expressed opinions, or beliefs of the child's parents, legal guardians, or family members.

Article 3

1. In all actions concerning children, whether undertaken by public or private social welfare institutions, courts of law, administrative authorities or legislative bodies, the best interests of the child shall be a primary consideration.

2. States Parties undertake to ensure the child such protection and care as is necessary for his or her well-being, taking into account the rights and duties of his or her parents, legal guardians, or other individuals legally responsible for him or her, and, to this end, shall take all appropriate legislative and administrative measures.

. . .

Article 4

States Parties shall undertake all appropriate legislative, administrative, and other measures for the implementation of the rights recognized in the present Convention. With regard to economic, social and cultural rights, States Parties shall undertake such measures to the maximum extent of their available resources and, where needed, within the framework of international co-operation.

Article 5

States Parties shall respect the responsibilities, rights and duties of parents or, where applicable, the members of the extended family or community as provided for by local custom, legal guardians or other persons legally responsible for the child, to provide, in a manner consistent with the evolving capacities of the child, appropriate direction and guidance in the exercise by the child of the rights recognized in the present Convention.

Article 6

1. States Parties recognize that every child has the inherent right to life.
2. States Parties shall ensure to the maximum extent possible the survival and development of the child.

Article 7

1. The child shall be registered immediately after birth and shall have the right from birth to a name, the right to acquire a nationality and. as far as possible, the right to know and be cared for by his or her parents.
. . .

Article 9

1. States Parties shall ensure that a child shall not be separated from his or her parents against their will, except when competent authorities subject to judicial review determine, in accordance with applicable law and procedures, that such separation is necessary for the best interests of the child. . . .
. . .

Article 10

1. In accordance with the obligation of States Parties under article 9, paragraph 1, applications by a child or his or her parents to enter or leave a State Party for the purpose of family reunification shall be dealt with by States Parties in a positive, humane and expeditious manner. . . .
2. A child whose parents reside in different States shall have the right to maintain on a regular basis, save in exceptional circumstances, personal relations and direct contacts with both parents. . . .

Article 11

1. States Parties shall take measures to combat the illicit transfer and non-return of children abroad.
2. To this end, States Parties shall promote the conclusion of bilateral or multilateral agreements or accession to existing agreements.

Article 12

1. States Parties shall assure to the child who is capable of forming his or her own views the right to express those views freely in all matters affecting the child, the views of the child being given due weight in accordance with the age and maturity of the child.

2. For this purpose, the child shall in particular be provided the opportunity to be heard in any judicial and administrative proceedings affecting the child, either directly, or through a representative or an appropriate body, in a manner consistent with the procedural rules of national law.

Article 13

1. The child shall have the right to freedom of expression; this right shall include freedom to seek, receive and impart information and ideas of all kinds, regardless of frontiers, either orally, in writing or in print, in the form of art, or through any other media of the child's choice.

2. The exercise of this right may be subject to certain restrictions . . .

Article 14

1. States Parties shall respect the right of the child to freedom of thought, conscience and religion.

2. States Parties shall respect the rights and duties of the parents and, when applicable, legal guardians, to provide direction to the child in the exercise of his or her right in a manner consistent with the evolving capacities of the child.

. . .

Article 15

1. States Parties recognize the rights of the child to freedom of association and to freedom of peaceful assembly.

. . .

Article 16

1. No child shall be subjected to arbitrary or unlawful interference with his or her privacy, family, home or correspondence, nor to unlawful attacks on his or her honour and reputation.

2. The child has the right to the protection of the law against such interference or attacks.

Article 17

States Parties recognize the important function performed by the mass media and shall ensure that the child has access to information and material from a diversity of national and international sources . . .

. . .

Article 18

1. States Parties shall use their best efforts to ensure recognition of the principle

that both parents have common responsibilities for the upbringing and development of the child. Parents or, as the case may be, legal guardians, have the primary responsibility for the upbringing and development of the child. The best interests of the child will be their basic concern.

2. For the purpose of guaranteeing and promoting the rights set forth in the present Convention, States Parties shall render appropriate assistance to parents and legal guardians in the performance of their child-rearing responsibilities and shall ensure the development of institutions, facilities and services for the care of children.

3. States Parties shall take all appropriate measures to ensure that children of working parents have the right to benefit from child-care services and facilities for which they are eligible.

Article 19

1. States Parties shall take all appropriate legislative, administrative, social and educational measures to protect the child from all forms of physical or mental violence, injury or abuse, neglect or negligent treatment, maltreatment or exploitation, including sexual abuse, while in the care of parent(s), legal guardian(s) or any other person who has the care of the child.

. . .

Article 20

1. A child temporarily or permanently deprived of his or her family environment, or in whose own best interests cannot be allowed to remain in that environment, shall be entitled to special protection and assistance provided by the State.

2. States Parties shall in accordance with their national laws ensure alternative care for such a child.

3. Such care could include, inter alia, foster placement, kafalah of Islamic law, adoption or if necessary placement in suitable institutions for the care of children. When considering solutions, due regard shall be paid to the desirability of continuity in a child's upbringing and to the child's ethnic, religious, cultural and linguistic background.

Article 21

States Parties that recognize and/or permit the system of adoption shall ensure that the best interests of the child shall be the paramount consideration . . .

. . .

Article 23

1. States Parties recognize that a mentally or physically disabled child should enjoy a full and decent life, in conditions which ensure dignity, promote self-reliance and facilitate the child's active participation in the community.

. . .

Article 24

1. States Parties recognize the right of the child to the enjoyment of the highest attainable standard of health and to facilities for the treatment of illness and rehabilitation of health. States Parties shall strive to ensure that no child is deprived of his or her right of access to such health care services.

. . .

3. States Parties shall take all effective and appropriate measures with a view to abolishing traditional practices prejudicial to the health of children.

4. States Parties undertake to promote and encourage international co-operation with a view to achieving progressively the full realization of the right recognized in the present article. In this regard, particular account shall be taken of the needs of developing countries.

Article 25

States Parties recognize the right of a child who has been placed by the competent authorities for the purposes of care, protection or treatment of his or her physical or mental health, to a periodic review of the treatment provided to the child and all other circumstances relevant to his or her placement.

. . .

Article 27

1. States Parties recognize the right of every child to a standard of living adequate for the child's physical, mental, spiritual, moral and social development.

2. The parent(s) or others responsible for the child have the primary responsibility to secure, within their abilities and financial capacities, the conditions of living necessary for the child's development.

3. States Parties, in accordance with national conditions and within their means, shall take appropriate measures to assist parents and others responsible for the child to implement this right and shall in case of need provide material assistance and support programmes, particularly with regard to nutrition, clothing and housing.

. . .

Article 28

1. States Parties recognize the right of the child to education, and with a view to achieving this right progressively and on the basis of equal opportunity, they shall, in particular:

    (a) Make primary education compulsory and available free to all;

    (b) Encourage the development of different forms of secondary education, including general and vocational education, make them available and accessible to every child, and take appropriate measures such as the introduction of free education and offering financial assistance in case of need;

    (c) Make higher education accessible to all on the basis of capacity by every appropriate means;

    (d) Make educational and vocational information and guidance available and accessible to all children;

(e) Take measures to encourage regular attendance at schools and the reduction of drop-out rates.

2. States Parties shall take all appropriate measures to ensure that school discipline is administered in a manner consistent with the child's human dignity and in conformity with the present Convention.

3. States Parties shall promote and encourage international cooperation in matters relating to education, in particular with a view to contributing to the elimination of ignorance and illiteracy throughout the world and facilitating access to scientific and technical knowledge and modern teaching methods. In this regard, particular account shall be taken of the needs of developing countries.

Article 29

1. States Parties agree that the education of the child shall be directed to:

(a) The development of the child's personality, talents and mental and physical abilities to their fullest potential;

(b) The development of respect for human rights and fundamental freedoms, and for the principles enshrined in the Charter of the United Nations;

(c) The development of respect for the child's parents, his or her own cultural identity, language and values, for the national values of the country in which the child is living, the country from which he or she may originate, and for civilizations different from his or her own;

(d) The preparation of the child for responsible life in a free society, in the spirit of understanding, peace, tolerance, equality of sexes, and friendship among all peoples, ethnic, national and religious groups and persons of indigenous origin;

(e) The development of respect for the natural environment.

2. No part of the present article or article 28 shall be construed so as to interfere with the liberty of individuals and bodies to establish and direct educational institutions . . .

Article 30

In those States in which ethnic, religious or linguistic minorities or persons of indigenous origin exist, a child belonging to such a minority or who is indigenous shall not be denied the right, in community with other members of his or her group, to enjoy his or her own culture, to profess and practise his or her own religion, or to use his or her own language.

. . .

Article 32

1. States Parties recognize the right of the child to be protected from economic exploitation and from performing any work that is likely to be hazardous or to interfere with the child's education, or to be harmful to the child's health or physical, mental, spiritual, moral or social development.

2. States Parties shall take legislative, administrative, social and educational

measures to ensure the implementation of the present article. To this end, and having regard to the relevant provisions of other international instruments, States Parties shall in particular:

    (a) Provide for a minimum age or minimum ages for admission to employment;

    (b) Provide for appropriate regulation of the hours and conditions of employment;

    (c) Provide for appropriate penalties or other sanctions to ensure the effective enforcement of the present article.

Article 33

States Parties shall take all appropriate measures, including legislative, administrative, social and educational measures, to protect children from the illicit use of narcotic drugs and psychotropic substances as defined in the relevant international treaties, and to prevent the use of children in the illicit production and trafficking of such substances.

Article 34

States Parties undertake to protect the child from all forms of sexual exploitation and sexual abuse. For these purposes, States Parties shall in particular take all appropriate national, bilateral and multilateral measures to prevent:

    (a) The inducement or coercion of a child to engage in any unlawful sexual activity;

    (b) The exploitative use of children in prostitution or other unlawful sexual practices;

    (c) The exploitative use of children in pornographic performances and materials.

Article 35

States Parties shall take all appropriate national, bilateral and multilateral measures to prevent the abduction of, the sale of or traffic in children for any purpose or in any form.

. . .

Article 37

States Parties shall ensure that:

    (a) No child shall be subjected to torture or other cruel, inhuman or degrading treatment or punishment. Neither capital punishment nor life imprisonment without possibility of release shall be imposed for offences committed by persons below eighteen years of age;

    (b) No child shall be deprived of his or her liberty unlawfully or arbitrarily. The arrest, detention or imprisonment of a child shall be in conformity with the law and shall be used only as a measure of last resort and for the shortest appropriate period of time;

    (c) Every child deprived of liberty shall be treated with humanity and respect for the inherent dignity of the human person, and in a manner which takes into account the needs of persons of his or her age. In particular, every child deprived of liberty shall be separated from adults unless it is considered in the child's best interest not to do so and shall have the right to maintain contact with his or her family through correspondence and visits, save in exceptional circumstances;

(d) Every child deprived of his or her liberty shall have the right to prompt access to legal and other appropriate assistance, as well as the right to challenge the legality of the deprivation of his or her liberty before a court or other competent, independent and impartial authority, and to a prompt decision on any such action.

Article 38

1. States Parties undertake to respect and to ensure respect for rules of international humanitarian law applicable to them in armed conflicts which are relevant to the child.

2. States Parties shall take all feasible measures to ensure that persons who have not attained the age of fifteen years do not take a direct part in hostilities.

3. States Parties shall refrain from recruiting any person who has not attained the age of fifteen years into their armed forces. In recruiting among those persons who have attained the age of fifteen years but who have not attained the age of eighteen years, States Parties shall endeavour to give priority to those who are oldest.

4. In accordance with their obligations under international humanitarian law to protect the civilian population in armed conflicts, States Parties shall take all feasible measures to ensure protection and care of children who are affected by an armed conflict.

Article 39

States Parties shall take all appropriate measures to promote physical and psychological recovery and social reintegration of a child victim of: any form of neglect, exploitation, or abuse; torture or any other form of cruel, inhuman or degrading treatment or punishment; or armed conflicts. Such recovery and reintegration shall take place in an environment which fosters the health, self-respect and dignity of the child.

Article 40

1. States Parties recognize the right of every child alleged as, accused of, or recognized as having infringed the penal law to be treated in a manner consistent with the promotion of the child's sense of dignity and worth, which reinforces the child's respect for the human rights and fundamental freedoms of others and which takes into account the child's age and the desirability of promoting the child's reintegration and the child's assuming a constructive role in society.

. . .

3. States Parties shall seek to promote the establishment of laws, procedures, authorities and institutions specifically applicable to children alleged as, accused of, or recognized as having infringed the penal law, and, in particular:

(a) The establishment of a minimum age below which children shall be presumed not to have the capacity to infringe the penal law;

(b) Whenever appropriate and desirable, measures for dealing with such children without resorting to judicial proceedings, providing that human rights and legal safeguards are fully respected.

4. A variety of dispositions, such as care, guidance and supervision orders; counselling; probation; foster care; education and vocational training programmes and other alternatives to institutional care shall be available to ensure that children are dealt with in a manner appropriate to their well-being and proportionate both to their circumstances and the offence.

. . .

PART II

Article 42

States Parties undertake to make the principles and provisions of the Convention widely known, by appropriate and active means, to adults and children alike.

Article 43

1. For the purpose of examining the progress made by States Parties in achieving the realization of the obligations undertaken in the present Convention, there shall be established a Committee on the Rights of the Child, which shall carry out the functions hereinafter provided.

2. The Committee shall consist of ten experts of high moral standing and recognized competence in the field covered by this Convention. The members of the Committee shall be elected by States Parties from among their nationals and shall serve in their personal capacity, consideration being given to equitable geographical distribution, as well as to the principal legal systems.

. . .

Article 44

1. States Parties undertake to submit to the Committee, through the Secretary-General of the United Nations, reports on the measures they have adopted which give effect to the rights recognized herein and on the progress made on the enjoyment of those rights:

(a) Within two years of the entry into force of the Convention for the State Party concerned;
(b) Thereafter every five years.

2. Reports made under the present article shall indicate factors and difficulties, if any, affecting the degree of fulfilment of the obligations under the present Convention. Reports shall also contain sufficient information to provide the Committee with a comprehensive understanding of the implementation of the Convention in the country concerned.

. . .

6. States Parties shall make their reports widely available to the public in their own countries.

Article 45

In order to foster the effective implementation of the Convention and to encourage international co-operation in the field covered by the Convention:

(a) The specialized agencies, the United Nations Children's Fund, and other United Nations organs shall be entitled to be represented at the consideration of the implementation of such provisions of the present Convention as fall within the scope of their mandate. The Committee may invite the specialized agencies, the United Nations Children's Fund and other competent bodies as it may consider appropriate to provide expert advice on the implementation of the Convention in areas falling within the scope of their respective mandates. The Committee may invite the specialized agencies, the United Nations Children's Fund, and other United Nations organs to submit reports on the implementation of the Convention in areas falling within the scope of their activities;

. . .

PART III

. . .

Article 51

. . .

2. A reservation incompatible with the object and purpose of the present Convention shall not be permitted.

. . .

DECLARATION ON THE RIGHT TO DEVELOPMENT

The General Assembly,

. . .

Considering that international peace and security are essential elements for the realization of the right to development,

Reaffirming that there is a close relationship between disarmament and development and that progress in the field of disarmament would considerably promote progress in the field of development and that resources released through disarmament measures should be devoted to the economic and social development and well-being of all peoples and, in particular, those of the developing countries,

. . .

Recognizing that the creation of conditions favourable to the development of peoples and individuals is the primary responsibility of their States,

Aware that efforts at the international level to promote and protect human rights should be accompanied by efforts to establish a new international economic order,

Confirming that the right to development is an inalienable human right and that equality of opportunity for development is a prerogative both of nations and of individuals who make up nations,

Proclaims the following Declaration on the Right to Development:

Article 1

1. The right to development is an inalienable human right by virtue of which every human person and all peoples are entitled to participate in, contribute to, and enjoy economic, social, cultural and political development, in which all human rights and fundamental freedoms can be fully realized.

2. The human right to development also implies the full realization of the right of peoples to self-determination, which includes, subject to the relevant provisions of both International Covenants on Human Rights, the exercise of their inalienable right to full sovereignty over all their natural wealth and resources.

Article 2

1. The human person is the central subject of development and should be the active participant and beneficiary of the right to development.

2. All human beings have a responsibility for development, individually and collectively, taking in to account the need for full respect for their human rights and fundamental freedoms as well as their duties to the community, which alone can ensure the free and complete fulfilment of the human being, and they should therefore promote and protect an appropriate political, social and economic order for development.

3. States have the right and the duty to formulate appropriate national development policies that aim at the constant improvement of the well-being of the

entire population and of all individuals, on the basis of their active, free and meaningful participation in development and in the fair distribution of the benefits resulting therefrom.

Article 3

1. States have the primary responsibility for the creation of national and international conditions favourable to the realization of the right to development.

2. The realization of the right to development requires full respect for the principles of international law concerning friendly relations and cooperation among States in accordance with the Charter of the United Nations.

3. States have the duty to co-operate with each other in ensuring development and eliminating obstacles to development. States should realize their rights and fulfil their duties in such a manner as to promote a new international economic order based on sovereign equality, interdependence, mutual interest and co-operation among all States, as well as to encourage the observance and realization of human rights.

Article 4

1. States have the duty to take steps, individually and collectively, to formulate international development policies with a view to facilitating the full realization of the right to development.

2. Sustained action is required to promote more rapid development of developing countries. As a complement to the efforts of developing countries, effective international co-operation is essential in providing these countries with appropriate means and facilities to foster their comprehensive development.

Article 5

States shall take resolute steps to eliminate the massive and flagrant violations of the human rights of peoples and human beings affected by situations such as those resulting from apartheid, all forms of racism and racial discrimination, colonialism, foreign domination and occupation, aggression, foreign interference and threats against national sovereignty, national unity and territorial integrity, threats of war and refusal to recognize the fundamental right of peoples to self-determination.

Article 6

1. All States should co-operate with a view to promoting, encouraging and strengthening universal respect for and observance of all human rights and fundamental freedoms for all without any distinction as to race, sex, language or religion.

2. All human rights and fundamental freedoms are indivisible and interdependent; equal attention and urgent consideration should be given to the implementation, promotion and protection of civil, political, economic, social and cultural rights.

3. States should take steps to eliminate obstacles to development resulting from

failure to observe civil and political rights, as well as economic social and cultural rights.

Article 7

All States should promote the establishment, maintenance and strengthening of international peace and security and, to that end, should do their utmost to achieve general and complete disarmament under effective international control, as well as to ensure that the resources released by effective disarmament measures are used for comprehensive development, in particular that of the developing countries.

Article 8

1. States should undertake, at the national level, all necessary measures for the realization of the right to development and shall ensure, inter alia, equality of opportunity for all in their access to basic resources, education, health services, food, housing, employment and the fair distribution of income. Effective measures should be undertaken to ensure that women have an active role in the development process. Appropriate economic and social reforms should be carried out with a view to eradicating all social injustices.

2. States should encourage popular participation in all spheres as an important factor in development and in the full realization of all human rights.

Article 9

1. All the aspects of the right to development set forth in the present Declaration are indivisible and interdependent and each of them should be considered in the context of the whole.

2. Nothing in the present Declaration shall be construed as being contrary to the purposes and principles of the United Nations, or as implying that any State, group or person has a right to engage in any activity or to perform any act aimed at the violation of the rights set forth in the Universal Declaration of Human Rights and in the International Covenants on Human Rights.

Article 10

Steps should be taken to ensure the full exercise and progressive enhancement of the right to development, including the formulation, adoption and implementation of policy, legislative and other measures at the national and international levels.

EUROPEAN CONVENTION FOR THE PROTECTION OF HUMAN RIGHTS AND FUNDAMENTAL FREEDOMS

[This text is a consolidation of the Convention pursuant to Protocol No. 11]

The governments signatory hereto, being members of the Council of Europe,

Considering the Universal Declaration of Human Rights proclaimed by the General Assembly of the United Nations on 10th December 1948;

Considering that this Declaration aims at securing the universal and effective recognition and observance of the Rights therein declared;

Considering that the aim of the Council of Europe is the achievement of greater unity between its members and that one of the methods by which that aim is to be pursued is the maintenance and further realization of human rights and fundamental freedoms;

Reaffirming their profound belief in those fundamental freedoms which are the foundation of justice and peace in the world and are best maintained on the one hand by an effective political democracy and on the other by a common understanding and observance of the human rights upon which they depend;

Being resolved, as the governments of European countries which are like-minded and have a common heritage of political traditions, ideals, freedom and the rule of law, to take the first steps for the collective enforcement of certain of the rights stated in the Universal Declaration,

Have agreed as follows:

Article 1

The High Contracting Parties shall secure to everyone within their jurisdiction the rights and freedoms defined in Section I of this Convention.

SECTION I—RIGHTS AND FREEDOMS

Article 2

1. Everyone's right to life shall be protected by law. No one shall be deprived of his life intentionally save in the execution of a sentence of a court following his conviction of a crime for which this penalty is provided by law.

2. Deprivation of life shall not be regarded as inflicted in contravention of this article when it results from the use of force which is no more than absolutely necessary:

    a.   in defence of any person from unlawful violence;
    b.   in order to effect a lawful arrest or to prevent the escape of a person lawfully detained;
    c.   in action lawfully taken for the purpose of quelling a riot or insurrection.

Article 3

No one shall be subjected to torture or to inhuman or degrading treatment or punishment.

Article 4

1. No one shall be held in slavery or servitude.
2. No one shall be required to perform forced or compulsory labour.

. . .

Article 5

1. Everyone has the right to liberty and security of person. No one shall be deprived of his liberty save in the following cases and in accordance with a procedure prescribed by law:

   a.   the lawful detention of a person after conviction by a competent court;
   b.   the lawful arrest or detention of a person for non-compliance with the lawful order of a court or in order to secure the fulfilment of any obligation prescribed by law;
   c.   the lawful arrest or detention of a person effected for the purpose of bringing him before the competent legal authority on reasonable suspicion of having committed an offence or when it is reasonably considered necessary to prevent his committing an offence or fleeing after having done so;

. . .

2. Everyone who is arrested shall be informed promptly, in a language which he understands, of the reasons for his arrest and of any charge against him.

3. Everyone arrested or detained in accordance with the provisions of paragraph 1.c of this article shall be brought promptly before a judge or other officer authorized by law to exercise judicial power and shall be entitled to trial within a reasonable time or to release pending trial. Release may be conditioned by guarantees to appear for trial.

4. Everyone who is deprived of his liberty by arrest or detention shall be entitled to take proceedings by which the lawfulness of his detention shall be decided speedily by a court and his release ordered if the detention is not lawful.

5. Everyone who has been the victim of arrest or detention in contravention of the provisions of this article shall have an enforceable right to compensation.

Article 6

1. In the determination of his civil rights and obligations or of any criminal charge against him, everyone is entitled to a fair and public hearing within a reasonable time by an independent and impartial tribunal established by law. Judgment shall be pronounced publicly but the press and public may be excluded from all or part of the trial in the interests of morals, public order or national security in a democratic society, where the interests of juveniles or the protection of the private life of the parties so require, or to the extent strictly necessary in the opinion of the court in special circumstances where publicity would prejudice the interests of justice.

2. Everyone charged with a criminal offence shall be presumed innocent until proved guilty according to law.

3. Everyone charged with a criminal offence has the following minimum rights:

a. to be informed promptly, in a language which he understands and in detail, of the nature and cause of the accusation against him;
b. to have adequate time and facilities for the preparation of his defence;
c. to defend himself in person or through legal assistance of his own choosing or, if he has not sufficient means to pay for legal assistance, to be given it free when the interests of justice so require;
d. to examine or have examined witnesses against him and to obtain the attendance and examination of witnesses on his behalf under the same conditions as witnesses against him;
e. to have the free assistance of an interpreter if he cannot understand or speak the language used in court.

Article 7

1. No one shall be held guilty of any criminal offence on account of any act or omission which did not constitute a criminal offence under national or international law at the time when it was committed. Nor shall a heavier penalty be imposed than the one that was applicable at the time the criminal offence was committed.

2. This article shall not prejudice the trial and punishment of any person for any act or omission which, at the time when it was committed, was criminal according to the general principles of law recognized by civilized nations.

Article 8

1. Everyone has the right to respect for his private and family life, his home and his correspondence.

2. There shall be no interference by a public authority with the exercise of this right except such as is in accordance with the law and is necessary in a democratic society in the interests of national security, public safety or the economic well-being of the country, for the prevention of disorder or crime, for the protection of health or morals, or for the protection of the rights and freedoms of others.

Article 9

1. Everyone has the right to freedom of thought, conscience and religion; this right includes freedom to change his religion or belief and freedom, either alone or in community with others and in public or private, to manifest his religion or belief, in worship, teaching, practice and observance.

2. Freedom to manifest one's religion or beliefs shall be subject only to such limitations as are prescribed by law and are necessary in a democratic society in the interests of public safety, for the protection of public order, health or morals, or for the protection of the rights and freedoms of others.

Article 10

1. Everyone has the right to freedom of expression. This right shall include freedom to hold opinions and to receive and impart information and ideas without interference by public authority and regardless of frontiers. This article shall

not prevent States from requiring the licensing of broadcasting, television or cinema enterprises.

2. The exercise of these freedoms, since it carries with it duties and responsibilities, may be subject to such formalities, conditions, restrictions or penalties as are prescribed by law and are necessary in a democratic society, in the interests of national security, territorial integrity or public safety, for the prevention of disorder or crime, for the protection of health or morals, for the protection of the reputation or rights of others, for preventing the disclosure of information received in confidence, or for maintaining the authority and impartiality of the judiciary.

Article 11

1. Everyone has the right to freedom of peaceful assembly and to freedom of association with others, including the right to form and to join trade unions for the protection of his interests.

2. No restrictions shall be placed on the exercise of these rights other than such as are prescribed by law and are necessary in a democratic society in the interests of national security or public safety, for the prevention of disorder or crime, for the protection of health or morals or for the protection of the rights and freedoms of others. This article shall not prevent the imposition of lawful restrictions on the exercise of these rights by members of the armed forces, of the police or of the administration of the State.

Article 12

Men and women of marriageable age have the right to marry and to found a family, according to the national laws governing the exercise of this right.

Article 13

Everyone whose rights and freedoms as set forth in this Convention are violated shall have an effective remedy before a national authority notwithstanding that the violation has been committed by persons acting in an official capacity.

Article 14

The enjoyment of the rights and freedoms set forth in this Convention shall be secured without discrimination on any ground such as sex, race, colour, language, religion, political or other opinion, national or social origin, association with a national minority, property, birth or other status.

Article 15

1. In time of war or other public emergency threatening the life of the nation any High Contracting Party may take measures derogating from its obligations under this Convention to the extent strictly required by the exigencies of the situation, provided that such measures are not inconsistent with its other obligations under international law.

2. No derogation from Article 2, except in respect of deaths resulting from lawful acts of war, or from Articles 3, 4 (paragraph 1) and 7 shall be made under this provision.

3. Any High Contracting Party availing itself of this right of derogation shall keep the Secretary General of the Council of Europe fully informed of the measures which it has taken and the reasons therefor. It shall also inform the Secretary General of the Council of Europe when such measures have ceased to operate and the provisions of the Convention are again being fully executed.

Article 16

Nothing in Articles 10, 11 and 14 shall be regarded as preventing the High Contracting Parties from imposing restrictions on the political activity of aliens.

Article 17

Nothing in this Convention may be interpreted as implying for any State, group or person any right to engage in any activity or perform any act aimed at the destruction of any of the rights and freedoms set forth herein or at their limitation to a greater extent than is provided for in the Convention.

Article 18

The restrictions permitted under this Convention to the said rights and freedoms shall not be applied for any purpose other than those for which they have been prescribed.

SECTION II—EUROPEAN COURT OF HUMAN RIGHTS

Article 19

To ensure the observance of the engagements undertaken by the High Contracting Parties in the Convention and the Protocols thereto, there shall be set up a European Court of Human Rights, hereinafter referred to as 'the Court'. It shall function on a permanent basis.

Article 20

The Court shall consist of a number of judges equal to that of the High Contracting Parties.

Article 21

1. The judges shall be of high moral character and must either possess the qualifications required for appointment to high judicial office or be jurisconsults of recognized competence.

2. The judges shall sit on the Court in their individual capacity.

3. During their term of office the judges shall not engage in any activity which is incompatible with their independence, impartiality or with the demands of a full-time office; all questions arising from the application of this paragraph shall be decided by the Court.

Article 22

1. The judges shall be elected by the Parliamentary Assembly with respect to each High Contracting Party by a majority of votes cast from a list of three candidates nominated by the High Contracting Party.

. . .

Article 23

1. The judges shall be elected for a period of six years. They may be re-elected. . . .

. . .

6. The terms of office of judges shall expire when they reach the age of 70.

. . .

Article 24

No judge may be dismissed from his office unless the other judges decide by a majority of two-thirds that he has ceased to fulfil the required conditions.

. . .

Article 27

1. To consider cases brought before it, the Court shall sit in committees of three judges, in Chambers of seven judges and in a Grand Chamber of seventeen judges. The Court's Chambers shall set up committees for a fixed period of time.

2. There shall sit as an ex officio member of the Chamber and the Grand Chamber the judge elected in respect of the State Party concerned or, if there is none or if he is unable to sit, a person of its choice who shall sit in the capacity of judge.

3. The Grand Chamber shall also include the President of the Court, the Vice-Presidents, the Presidents of the Chambers and other judges chosen in accordance with the rules of the Court. When a case is referred to the Grand Chamber under Article 43, no judge from the Chamber which rendered the judgment shall sit in the Grand Chamber, with the exception of the President of the Chamber and the judge who sat in respect of the State Party concerned.

Article 28

A committee may, by a unanimous vote, declare inadmissible or strike out of its list of cases an application submitted under Article 34 where such a decision can be taken without further examination. The decision shall be final.

Article 29

1. If no decision is taken under Article 28, a Chamber shall decide on the admissibility and merits of individual applications submitted under Article 34.

2. A Chamber shall decide on the admissibility and merits of inter-State applications submitted under Article 33.

3. The decision on admissibility shall be taken separately unless the Court, in exceptional cases, decides otherwise.

Article 30

Where a case pending before a Chamber raises a serious question affecting the interpretation of the Convention or the protocols thereto, or where the resolution of a question before the Chamber might have a result inconsistent with a judgment previously delivered by the Court, the Chamber may, at any time before it has rendered its judgment, relinquish jurisdiction in favour of the Grand Chamber, unless one of the parties to the case objects.

Article 31

The Grand Chamber shall

a. determine applications submitted either under Article 33 or Article 34 when a Chamber has relinquished jurisdiction under Article 30 or when the case has been referred to it under Article 43; and

b. consider requests for advisory opinions submitted under Article 47.

Article 32

1. The jurisdiction of the Court shall extend to all matters concerning the interpretation and application of the Convention and the protocols thereto which are referred to it as provided in Articles 33, 34 and 47.

2. In the event of dispute as to whether the Court has jurisdiction, the Court shall decide.

Article 33

Any High Contracting Party may refer to the Court any alleged breach of the provisions of the Convention and the protocols thereto by another High Contracting Party.

Article 34

The Court may receive applications from any person, non-governmental organisation or group of individuals claiming to be the victim of a violation by one of the High Contracting Parties of the rights set forth in the Convention or the protocols thereto. The High Contracting Parties undertake not to hinder in any way the effective exercise of this right.

Article 35

1. The Court may only deal with the matter after all domestic remedies have been exhausted, according to the generally recognised rules of international law, and within a period of six months from the date on which the final decision was taken.

2. The Court shall not deal with any application submitted under Article 34 that

a. is anonymous; or

b. is substantially the same as a matter that has already been examined by the Court or has already been submitted to another procedure of international investigation or settlement and contains no relevant new information.

3. The Court shall declare inadmissible any individual application submitted under Article 34 which it considers incompatible with the provisions of the Convention or the protocols thereto, manifestly ill-founded, or an abuse of the right of application.

. . .

Article 36

1. In all cases before a Chamber or the Grand Chamber, a High Contracting Party one of whose nationals is an applicant shall have the right to submit written comments and to take part in hearings.

2. The President of the Court may, in the interest of the proper administration of justice, invite any High Contracting Party which is not a party to the proceedings or any person concerned who is not the applicant to submit written comments or take part in hearings.

. . .

Article 38

1. If the Court declares the application admissible, it shall

   a.   pursue the examination of the case, together with the representatives of the parties, and if need be, undertake an investigation, for the effective conduct of which the States concerned shall furnish all necessary facilities;

   b.   place itself at the disposal of the parties concerned with a view to securing a friendly settlement of the matter on the basis of respect for human rights as defined in the Convention and the protocols thereto.

2. Proceedings conducted under paragraph 1.b shall be confidential.

Article 39

If a friendly settlement is effected, the Court shall strike the case out of its list by means of a decision which shall be confined to a brief statement of the facts and of the solution reached.

Article 40

1. Hearings shall be in public unless the Court in exceptional circumstances decides otherwise.

2. Documents deposited with the Registrar shall be accessible to the public unless the President of the Court decides otherwise.

Article 41

If the Court finds that there has been a violation of the Convention or the protocols thereto, and if the internal law of the High Contracting Party concerned allows only partial reparation to be made, the Court shall, if necessary, afford just satisfaction to the injured party.

. . .

Article 43

1. Within a period of three months from the date of the judgment of the Chamber, any party to the case may, in exceptional cases, request that the case be referred to the Grand Chamber.

2. A panel of five judges of the Grand Chamber shall accept the request if the case raises a serious question affecting the interpretation or application of the Convention or the protocols thereto, or a serious issue of general importance.

. . .

Article 44

1. The judgment of the Grand Chamber shall be final.
2. The judgment of a Chamber shall become final

    a.   when the parties declare that they will not request that the case be referred to the Grand Chamber; or

    b.   three months after the date of the judgment, if reference of the case to the Grand Chamber has not been requested; or

    c.   when the panel of the Grand Chamber rejects the request to refer under Article 43.

3. The final judgment shall be published.

Article 45

1. Reasons shall be given for judgments as well as for decisions declaring applications admissible or inadmissible.

2. If a judgment does not represent, in whole or in part, the unanimous opinion of the judges, any judge shall be entitled to deliver a separate opinion.

Article 46

1. The High Contracting Parties undertake to abide by the final judgment of the Court in any case to which they are parties.

2. The final judgment of the Court shall be transmitted to the Committee of Ministers, which shall supervise its execution.

Article 47

1. The Court may, at the request of the Committee of Ministers, give advisory opinions on legal questions concerning the interpretation of the Convention and the protocols thereto.

2. Such opinions shall not deal with any question relating to the content or scope of the rights or freedoms defined in Section I of the Convention and the protocols thereto, or with any other question which the Court or the Committee

of Ministers might have to consider in consequence of any such proceedings as could be instituted in accordance with the Convention.

. . .

Article 49

1. Reasons shall be given for advisory opinions of the Court.

2. If the advisory opinion does not represent, in whole or in part, the unanimous opinion of the judges, any judge shall be entitled to deliver a separate opinion.

. . .

SECTION III—MISCELLANEOUS PROVISIONS

Article 52

On receipt of a request from the Secretary General of the Council of Europe any High Contracting Party shall furnish an explanation of the manner in which its internal law ensures the effective implementation of any of the provisions of the Convention.

. . .

Article 57

1. Any State may, when signing this Convention or when depositing its instrument of ratification, make a reservation in respect of any particular provision of the Convention to the extent that any law then in force in its territory is not in conformity with the provision. Reservations of a general character shall not be permitted under this article.

2. Any reservation made under this article shall contain a brief statement of the law concerned.

Article 58

1. A High Contracting Party may denounce the present Convention only after the expiry of five years from the date on which it became a party to it and after six months' notice . . .

. . .

PROTOCOLS TO THE EUROPEAN CONVENTION FOR THE PROTECTION OF HUMAN RIGHTS AND FUNDAMENTAL FREEDOMS

PROTOCOL NO. 1

. . .

Article 1

Every natural or legal person is entitled to the peaceful enjoyment of his possessions. No one shall be deprived of his possessions except in the public interest and subject to the conditions provided for by law and by the general principles of international law.

The preceding provisions shall not, however, in any way impair the right of a State to enforce such laws as it deems necessary to control the use of property in accordance with the general interest or to secure the payment of taxes or other contributions or penalties.

Article 2

No person shall be denied the right to education. In the exercise of any functions which it assumes in relation to education and to teaching, the State shall respect the right of parents to ensure such education and teaching in conformity with their own religious and philosophical convictions.

Article 3

The High Contracting Parties undertake to hold free elections at reasonable intervals by secret ballot, under conditions which will ensure the free expression of the opinion of the people in the choice of the legislature.

. . .

PROTOCOL NO. 4

. . .

Article 2

1. Everyone lawfully within the territory of a State shall, within that territory, have the right to liberty of movement and freedom to choose his residence.

2. Everyone shall be free to leave any country, including his own.

3. No restrictions shall be placed on the exercise of these rights other than such as are in accordance with law and are necessary in a democratic society in the interests of national security or public safety, for the maintenance of *ordre public*, for the prevention of crime, for the protection of health or morals, or for the protection of the rights and freedoms of others.

4. The rights set forth in paragraph 1 may also be subject, in particular areas, to restrictions imposed in accordance with law and justified by the public interest in a democratic society.

Article 3

1. No one shall be expelled, by means either of an individual or of a collective measure, from the territory of the State of which he is a national.

2. No one shall be deprived of the right to enter the territory of the state of which he is a national.

Article 4

Collective expulsion of aliens is prohibited.

. . .

PROTOCOL NO. 6

Article 1

The death penalty shall be abolished. No-one shall be condemned to such penalty or executed.

Article 2

A State may make provision in its law for the death penalty in respect of acts committed in time of war or of imminent threat of war; such penalty shall be applied only in the instances laid down in the law and in accordance with its provisions. The State shall communicate to the Secretary General of the Council of Europe the relevant provisions of that law.

Article 3

No derogation from the provisions of this Protocol shall be made under Article 15 of the Convention.

. . .

PROTOCOL NO. 7

Article 1

1. An alien lawfully resident in the territory of a State shall not be expelled therefrom except in pursuance of a decision reached in accordance with law and shall be allowed:

    (*a*) to submit reasons against his expulsion,
    (*b*) to have his case reviewed, and
    (*c*) to be represented for these purposes before the competent authority or a persons or person designated by that authority.

2. An alien may be expelled before the exercise of his rights under paragraph 1(*a*), (*b*) and (*c*) of this Article, when such expulsion is necessary in the interests of public order or is grounded on reasons of national security.

Article 2

1. Everyone convicted of a criminal offence by a tribunal shall have the right to

have conviction or sentence reviewed by a higher tribunal. The exercise of this right, including the grounds on which it may be exercised, shall be governed by law.

2. This right may be subject to exception in regard to offences of a minor character, as prescribed by law, or in cases in which the person concerned was tried in the first instance by the highest tribunal or was convicted following an appeal against acquittal.

Article 3

When a person has by a final decision been convicted of a criminal offence and when subsequently his conviction has been reversed, or he has been pardoned, on the ground that a new or newly discovered fact shows conclusively that there has been a miscarriage of justice, the person who has suffered punishment as a result of such conviction shall be compensated according to the law or the practice of the State concerned, unless it is proved that the non-disclosure of the unknown fact in time is wholly or partly attributable to him.

Article 4

1. No one shall be liable to be tried or punished again in criminal proceedings under the jurisdiction of the same State for an offence for which he has already been finally acquitted or convicted in accordance with the law and penal procedure of that State.

2. The provisions of the preceding paragraph shall not prevent the reopening of the case in accordance with the law and penal procedure of the State concerned, if there is evidence of new or newly discovered facts, or if there has been a fundamental defect in the previous proceedings, which could affect the outcome of the case.

3. No derogation from this Article shall be made under Article 15 of the Convention.

Articles 5

1. Spouses shall enjoy equality of rights and responsibilities of a private law character between them, and in their relations with their children, as to marriage, during marriage and in the event of its dissolution. This Article shall not prevent States from taking such measures as are necessary in the interests of the children.

. . .

AMERICAN CONVENTION ON HUMAN RIGHTS

PREAMBLE

The American states signatory to the present Convention.

Reaffirming their intention to consolidate in this hemisphere, within the framework of democratic institutions, a system of personal liberty and social justice based on respect for the essential rights of man;

Recognizing that the essential rights of man are not derived from one's being a national of a certain state, but are based upon attributes of the human personality, and that they therefore justify international protection in the form of a convention reinforcing or complementing the protection provided by the domestic law of the American states;

Considering that these principles have been set forth in the Charter of the Organization of American States, in the American Declaration of the Rights and Duties of Man, and in the Universal Declaration of Human Rights, and that they have been reaffirmed and refined in other international instruments, worldwide as well as regional in scope;

. . .

Have agreed upon the following:

PART I. State Obligations and Rights Protected
CHAPTER I. General Obligations

Article 1

1. The States Parties to this Convention undertake to respect the rights and freedoms recognized herein and to ensure to all persons subject to their jurisdiction the free and full exercise of those rights and freedoms, without any discrimination for reasons of race, color, sex, language, religion, political or other opinion, national or social origin, economic status, birth, or any other social condition.

2. For the purposes of this Convention, 'person' means every human being.

Article 2

Where the exercise of any of the rights or freedoms referred to in Article 1 is not already ensured by legislative or other provisions, the States Parties undertake to adopt, in accordance with their constitutional processes and the provisions of this Convention, such legislative or other measures as may be necessary to give effect to those rights or freedoms.

CHAPTER II. Civil and Political Rights

Article 3

Every person has the right to recognition as a person before the law.

Article 4

1. Every person has the right to have his life respected. This right shall be

protected by law and, in general, from the moment of conception. No one shall be arbitrarily deprived of his life.

2. In countries that have not abolished the death penalty, it may be imposed only for the most serious crimes and pursuant to a final judgment rendered by a competent court and in accordance with a law establishing such punishment, enacted prior to the commission of the crime. The application of such punishment shall not be extended to crimes to which it does not presently apply.

3. The death penalty shall not be reestablished in states that have abolished it.

4. In no case shall capital punishment be inflicted for political offenses or related common crimes.

5. Capital punishment shall not be imposed upon persons who, at the time the crime was committed, were under 18 years of age or over 70 years of age; nor shall it be applied to pregnant women.

6. Every person condemned to death shall have the right to apply for amnesty, pardon, or commutation of sentence, which may be granted in all cases. Capital punishment shall not be imposed while such a petition is pending decision by the competent authority.

Article 5

1. Every person has the right to have his physical, mental, and moral integrity respected.

2. No one shall be subjected to torture or to cruel, inhuman, or degrading punishment or treatment. All persons deprived of their liberty shall be treated with respect for the inherent dignity of the human person.

3. Punishment shall not be extended to any person other than the criminal.

4. Accused persons shall, save in exceptional circumstances, be segregated from convicted persons, and shall be subject to separate treatment appropriate to their status as unconvicted persons.

5. Minors while subject to criminal proceedings shall be separated from adults and brought before specialized tribunals, as speedily as possible, so that they may be treated in accordance with their status as minors.

6. Punishments consisting of deprivation of liberty shall have as an essential aim the reform and social readaptation of the prisoners.

Article 6

1. No one shall be subject to slavery or to involuntary servitude, which are prohibited in all their forms, as are the slave trade and traffic in women.

. . .

Article 7

1. Every person has the right to personal liberty and security.

2. No one shall be deprived of his physical liberty except for the reasons and under the conditions established beforehand by the constitution of the State Party concerned or by a law established, pursuant thereto.

3. No one shall be subject to arbitrary arrest or imprisonment.

4. Anyone who is detained shall be informed on the reasons for his detention and shall be promptly notified of the charges or charges against him.

5. Any person detained shall be brought promptly before a judge or other officer authorized by law to exercise judicial power and shall be entitled to trial within a reasonable time or to be released without prejudice to the continuation of the proceedings. His release may be subject to guarantees to assure his appearance for trial.

6. Anyone who is deprived of his liberty shall be entitled to recourse to a competent court, in order that the court may decide without delay on the lawfulness of his arrest or detention and order his release if the arrest or detention is unlawful. In States Parties whose laws provide that anyone who believes himself to be threatened with deprivation of his liberty is entitled to recourse to a competent court in order that it may decide on the lawfulness of such threat, this remedy may not be restricted or abolished. The interested party or another person in his behalf is entitled to seek these remedies.

7. No one shall be detained for debt. This principle shall not limit the orders of a competent judicial authority issued for nonfulfillment of duties of support.

Article 8

1. Every person has the right to a hearing, with due guarantees and within a reasonable time, by a competent, independent, and impartial tribunal, previously established by law, in the substantiation of any accusation of a criminal nature made against him or for the determination of his rights and obligations of a civil, labor, fiscal, or any other nature.

2. Every person accused of a criminal offense has the right to be presumed innocent so long as his guilt has not been proven according to law. During the proceedings, every person is entitled, with full equality, to the following minimum guarantees:

(a) the right of the accused to be assisted without charge by a translator or inter-preter, if he does not understand or does not speak the language of the tribunal or court;
(b) prior notification in detail to the accused of the charges against him;
(c) adequate time and means for the preparation of his defense;
(d) the right of the accused to defend himself personally or to be assisted by legal counsel of his own choosing, and to communicate freely and privately with his counsel;
(e) the inalienable right to be assisted by counsel provided by the state, paid or not as the domestic law provides, if the accused does not defend himself personally or engage his own counsel within the time period established by law;
(f) the right of the defense to examine witnesses present in the court and to obtain the appearance, as witnesses, of experts or other persons who may throw light on the facts;
(g) the right not to be compelled to be a witness against himself or to plead guilty; and
(h) the right to appeal the judgement to a higher court.

3. A confession of guilt by the accused shall be valid only if it is made without coercion of any kind.

4. An accused person acquitted by a nonappealable judgment shall not be subjected to a new trial for the same cause.

5. Criminal proceedings shall be public, except insofar as may be necessary to protect the interests of justice.

Article 9

No one shall be convicted of any act or omission that did not constitute a criminal offense, under the applicable law, at the time it was committed. A heavier penalty shall not be imposed than the one that was applicable at the time the criminal offense was committed. If subsequent to the commission of the offense the law provides for the imposition of a lighter punishment, the guilty person shall benefit therefrom.

Article 10

Every person has the right to be compensated in accordance with the law in the event he has been sentenced by a final judgment through a miscarriage of justice.

Article 11

1. Everyone has the right to have his honor respected and his dignity recognized.

2. No one may be the object of arbitrary or abusive interference with his private life, his family, his home, or his correspondence, or of unlawful attacks on his honor or reputation.

3. Everyone has the right to the protection of the law against such interference or attacks.

Article 12

1. Everyone has the right to freedom of conscience and of religion. This right includes freedom to maintain or to change one's religion or beliefs, and freedom to profess or disseminate one's religion or beliefs, either individually or together with others, in public or in private.

2. No one shall be subject to restrictions that might impair his freedom to maintain or to change his religion or beliefs.

3. Freedom to manifest one's religion and beliefs may be subject only to the limitations prescribed by law that are necessary to protect public safety, order, health, or morals, or the rights or freedoms of others.

4. Parents or guardians, as the case may be, have the right to provide for the religious and moral education of their children or wards that is in accord with their own convictions.

Article 13

1. Everyone has the right to freedom of thought and expression. This right includes freedom to seek, receive, and impart information and ideas of all kinds,

regardless of frontiers, either orally, in writing, in print, in the form of art, or through any other medium of one's choice.

2. The exercise of the right provided for in the foregoing paragraph shall not be subject to prior censorship but shall be subject to subsequent imposition of liability, which shall be expressly established by law to the extent necessary to ensure:

    (a) respect for the rights or reputations of others; or

    (b) the protection of national security, public order, or public health or morals.

3. The right of expression may not be restricted by indirect methods or means, such as the abuse of government or private controls over newsprint, radio broadcasting frequencies, or equipment used in the dissemination of information, or by any other means tending to impede the communication and circulation of ideas and opinions.

4. Notwithstanding the provisions of paragraph 2 above, public entertainments may be subject by law to prior censorship for the sole purpose of regulating access to them for the moral protection of childhood and adolescence.

5. Any propaganda for war and any advocacy of national, racial, or religious hatred that constitute incitements to lawless violence or to any other similar illegal action against any person or group of persons on any ground including those of race, color, religion, language, or national origin shall be considered as offenses punishable by law.

. . .

Article 15

The right of peaceful assembly, without arms is recognized. No restrictions may be placed on the exercise of this right other than those imposed in conformity with the law and necessary in a democratic society in the interest of national security, public safety or public order, or to protect public or morals or the rights or freedoms of others.

Article 16

1. Everyone has the right to associate freely for ideological, religious, political, economic, labor, social, cultural, sports, or other purposes.

2. The exercise of this right shall be subject only to such restrictions established by law as may be necessary in a democratic society, in the interest of national security, public safety or public order, or to protect public health or morals or the rights and freedoms of others.

3. The provisions of this article do not bar the imposition of legal restrictions, including even deprivation of the exercise of the right of association, on members of the armed forces and the police.

Article 17

1. The family is the natural and fundamental group unit of society and is entitled to protection by society and the state.

2. The right of men and women of marriageable age to marry and to raise a family shall be recognized, if they meet the conditions required by domestic laws, insofar as such conditions do not affect the principle of nondiscrimination established in this Convention.

3. No marriage shall be entered into without the free and full consent of the intending spouse.

4. The States Parties shall take appropriate steps to ensure the equality of rights and the adequate balancing of responsibilities of the spouses as to marriage, during marriage, and in the event of its dissolution. In case of dissolution, provision shall be made for the necessary protection of any children solely on the basis of their own best interests.

5. The law shall recognize equal rights for children born out of wedlock and those born in wedlock.

. . .

Article 19

Every minor child has the right to the measures of protection required by his condition as a minor on the part of his family, society, and the state.

Article 20

1. Every person has the right to a nationality.

2. Every person has the right to the nationality of the state in whose territory he was born if he does not have the right to any other nationality.

3. No one shall be arbitrarily deprived of his nationality or of the right to change it.

Article 21

1. Everyone has the right to the use and enjoyment of his property. The law may subordinate such use and enjoyment to the interest of society.

2. No one shall be deprived of his property except upon payment of just compensation, for reasons of public utility or social interest, and in the cases and according to the forms established by law.

3. Usury and any other form of exploitation of man by man shall be prohibited by law.

Article 22

1. Every person lawfully in the territory of a State Party has the right to move about in it, and to reside in it subject to the provisions of the law.

2. Every person has the right to leave any country freely, including his own.

3. The exercise of the foregoing rights may be restricted only pursuant to a law to the extent necessary in a democratic society to prevent crime or to protect national security, public safety, public order, public morals, public health, or the rights or freedoms of others.

4. The exercise of the rights recognized in paragraph 1 may also be restricted by law in designated zones for reasons of public interest.

5. No one can be expelled from the territory of the state of which he is a national or be deprived of the right to enter it.

6. An alien lawfully in the territory of a State Party to this Convention may be expelled from it only pursuant to a decision reached in accordance with law.

7. Every person has the right to seek and be granted asylum in a foreign territory, in accordance with the legislation of the state and international conventions, in the event he is being pursued for political offenses or related common crimes.

8. In no case may an alien be deported or returned to a country, regardless of whether or not it is his country of origin, if in that country his right to life or personal freedom is in danger of being violated because of his race, nationality, religion, social status, or political opinions.

9. The collective expulsion of aliens is prohibited.

Article 23

1. Every citizen shall enjoy the following rights and opportunities:

   (a) to take part in the conduct of public affairs, directly or through freely chosen representatives;
   (b) to vote and to be elected in genuine periodic elections, which shall be by universal and equal suffrage and by secret ballot that guarantees the free expression of the will of the voters; and
   (c) to have access, under general conditions of equality, to the public service of his country.

2. The law may regulate the exercise of the rights and opportunities referred to in the preceding paragraph only on the basis of age, nationality, residence, language, education, civil and mental capacity, or sentencing by a competent court in criminal proceedings.

Article 24

All persons are equal before the law. Consequently, they are entitled, without discrimination, to equal protection of the law.

Article 25

1. Everyone has the right to simple and prompt recourse, or any other effective recourse to a competent court or tribunal for protection against acts that violate his fundamental rights recognized by the constitution or laws of the state concerned or by this Convention, even though such violation may have been committed by persons acting in the course of their official duties.

2. The States Parties undertake:

   (a) to ensure that any person claiming such remedy shall have his rights determined by the competent authority provided for by the legal system of the state;
   (b) to develop the possibilities of judicial remedy; and
   (c) to ensure that the competent authorities shall enforce such remedies when granted.

CHAPTER III . Economic, Social and Cultural Rights

Article 26

The States Parties undertake to adopt measures both internally and through international cooperation, especially those of an economic and technical nature, with a view to achieving progressively, by legislation or other appropriate means, the full realization of the rights implicit in the economic, social, educational, scientific, and cultural standards set forth in the Charter of the Organization of American States as amended by the Protocol of Buenos Aires.

CHAPTER IV. Suspension of Guarantees, Interpretation, and Application

Article 27

1. In time of war, public danger, or other emergency that threatens the independence or security of a State Party, it may take measures derogating from its obligations under the present Convention to the extent and for the period of time strictly required by the exigencies of the situation, provided that such measures are not inconsistent with its other obligations under international law and do not involve discrimination on the ground of race, color, sex, language, religion, or social origin.

2. The foregoing provision does not authorize any suspension of the following articles: Article 3 (Right to Juridical Personality), Article 4 (Right to Life), Article 5 (Right to Humane Treatment), Article 6 (Freedom from Slavery), Article 9 (Freedom from *Ex Post Facto* Laws), Article 12 (Freedom of Conscience and Religion), Article 17 (Rights of the Family), Article 18 (Right to a Name), Article 19 (Rights of the Child), Article 20 (Right to Nationality), and Article 23 (Right to Participate in Government), or of the judicial guarantees essential for the protection of such rights.

3. Any State Party availing itself of the right of suspension shall immediately inform the other States Parties, through the Secretary General of the Organization of American States, of the provisions the application of which it has suspended, the reasons that gave rise to the suspension, and the date set for the termination of such suspension.

Article 28

1. Where a State Party is constituted as a federal state, the national government of such State Party shall implement all the provisions of the Convention over whose subject matter it exercises legislative and judicial jurisdiction.

2. With respect to the provisions over whose subject matter the constituent units of the federal state have jurisdiction, the national government shall immediately take suitable measures, in accordance with its constitution and its laws, to the end that the competent authorities of the constituent units may adopt appropriate provisions for the fulfillment of this Convention.

. . .

CHAPTER V. Personal Responsibilities

Article 32

1. Every person has responsibilities to his family, his community, and mankind.
2. The rights of each person are limited by the rights of others, by the security of all, and by the just demands of the general welfare, in a democratic society.

PART II. Means of Protection
CHAPTER VI. Competent Organs

Article 33

The following organs shall have competence with respect to matters relating to the fulfillment of the commitments made by the States Parties to this Convention:

   (a) the Inter-American Commission on Human Rights, referred to as 'The Commission'; and
   (b) the Inter-American Court of Human Rights, referred to as 'The Court'.

CHAPTER VII. Inter-American Commission on Human Rights
SECTION 1. Organization

Article 34

The Inter-American Commission on Human Rights shall be composed of seven members, who shall be persons of high moral character and recognized competence in the field of human rights.

Article 35

The Commission shall represent all the member countries of the Organization of American States.

Article 36

1. The members of the Commission shall be elected in a personal capacity by the General Assembly of the Organization from a list of candidates proposed by the governments of the member states.

. . .

SECTION 2. Functions

Article 41

The main function of the Commission shall be to promote respect for and defense of human rights. In the exercise of its mandate, it shall have the following functions and powers:

   (a) to develop an awareness of human rights among the peoples of America;
   (b) to make recommendations to the governments of the member states, when it

considers such action advisable, for the adoption of progressive measures in favour of human rights within the framework of their domestic law and constitutional provisions as well as appropriate measures to further the observance of those rights;

(c) to prepare such studies or reports as it considers advisable in the performance of its duties;

(d) to request the governments of the member states to supply it with information on the measures adopted by them in matters of human rights;

(e) to respond, through the General Secretariat of the Organization of American States, to inquiries made by the member states on matters related to human rights and, within the limits of its possibilities, to provide those states with the advisory services they request;

(f) to take action on petitions and other communications pursuant to its authority under the provisions of Articles 44 through 51 of this Convention; and

(g) to submit an annual report to the General Assembly of the Organization of American States.

. . .

SECTION 3. Competence

Article 44

Any person or group of persons, or any nongovernmental entity legally recognized in one or more member states of the Organization, may lodge petitions with the Commission containing denunciations or complaints of violation of this Convention by a State Party.

Article 45

1. Any State Party may, when it deposits its instrument of ratification of or adherence to this Convention, or at any later time, declare that it recognizes the competence of the Commission to receive and examine communications in which a State Party alleges that another State Party has committed a violation of a human right set forth in this Convention.

2. Communications presented by virtue of this article may be admitted and examined only if they are presented by a State Party that has made a declaration recognizing the aforementioned competence of the Commission. The Commission shall not admit any communication against a State Party that has not made such a declaration.

Article 46

1. Admission by the Commission of a petition or communication lodged in accordance with Articles 44 or 45 shall be subject to the following requirements:

a. that the remedies under domestic law have been pursued and exhausted in accordance with generally recognized principles of international law;

b. that the petition or communication is lodged within a period of six months from the date on which the party alleging violation of his rights was notified of the final judgment;

c. that the subject of the petition or communication is not pending in another international proceeding for settlement; and

d. that, in the case of Article 44, the petition contains the name, nationality, profession, domicile, and signature of the person or persons or of the legal representative of the entity lodging the petition.

2. The provisions of paragraphs 1.a and 1.b of this article shall not be applicable when:

a. the domestic legislation of the state concerned does not afford due process of law for the protection of the right or rights that have allegedly been violated;

b. the party alleging violation of his rights has been denied access to the remedies under domestic law or has been prevented from exhausting them; or

c. there has been unwarranted delay in rendering a final judgment under the aforementioned remedies.

. . .

SECTION 4. Procedure

[Article 48 sets forth procedures for the Commission after it receives a petition or communication alleging violation of any protected rights. The Commission is to 'place itself at the disposal of the parties concerned with a view to reaching a friendly settlement of the matter on the basis of respect for the human rights recognized in this Convention'. Article 49 concerns situations where such a settlement has been reached.]

Article 50

1. If a settlement is not reached, the Commission shall, within the time limit established by its Statute, draw up a report setting forth the facts and stating its conclusions . . .

2. The report shall be transmitted to the states concerned, which shall not be at liberty to publish it.

3. In transmitting the report, the Committee may make such proposals and recommendations as it sees fit.

Article 51

1. If, within a period of three months from the date of the transmittal of the report of the Commission to the states concerned, the matter has not either been settled or submitted by the Commission or by the state concerned to the Court and its jurisdiction accepted, the Commission may, by the vote of an absolute majority of its members, set forth its opinion and conclusions concerning the question submitted for its consideration.

2. Where appropriate, the Commission shall make pertinent recommendations and shall prescribe a period within which the state is to take the measures that are incumbent upon it to remedy the situation examined.

3. When the prescribed period has expired, the Commission shall decide by the vote of an absolute majority of its members whether the state has taken adequate measures and whether to publish its report.

CHAPTER VIII. Inter-American Court of Human Rights
SECTION 1. Organization

Article 52

1. The Court shall consist of seven judges, nationals of the member states of the Organization, elected in an individual capacity from among jurists of the highest moral authority and of recognized competence in the field of human rights, who possess the qualifications required for the exercise of the highest judicial functions in conformity with the law of the state of which they are nationals or of the state that proposes them as candidates.

2. No two judges may be nationals of the same state.

. . .

Article 55

1. If a judge is a national of any of the States Parties to a case submitted to the Court, he shall retain his right to hear that case.

2. If one of the judges called upon to hear a case should be a national of one of the States Parties to the case, any other State Party in the case may appoint a person of its choice to serve on the Court as an ad hoc judge.

3. If among the judges called upon to hear a case none is a national of any of the States Parties to the case, each of the latter may appoint an ad hoc judge.

. . .

SECTION 2. Jurisdiction and Functions

Article 61

1. Only the States Parties and the Commission shall have the right to submit a case to the Court.

. . .

Article 62

1. A State Party may, upon depositing its instrument of ratification or adherence to this Convention, or at any subsequent time, declare that it recognizes as binding, *ipso facto*, and not requiring special agreement, the jurisdiction of the Court on all matters relating to the interpretation or application of this Convention.

2. Such declaration may be made unconditionally, on the condition of reciprocity, for a specified period, or for specific cases . . .

3. The jurisdiction of the Court shall comprise all cases concerning the interpretation and application of the provisions of this Convention that are submitted to it, provided that the States Parties to the case recognize or have recognized such jurisdiction, whether by special declaration pursuant to the preceding paragraphs, or by a special agreement.

Article 63

1. If the Court finds that there has been a violation of a right or freedom

protected by this Convention, the Court shall rule that the injured party be ensured the enjoyment of his right or freedom that was violated. It shall also rule, if appropriate, that the consequences of the measure or situation that constituted the breach of such right or freedom be remedied and that fair compensation be paid to the injured party.

2. In cases of extreme gravity and urgency, and when necessary to avoid irreparable damage to persons, the Court shall adopt such provisional measures as it deems pertinent in matters it has under consideration. With respect to a case not yet submitted to the Court, it may act at the request of the Commission.

Article 64

1. The member states of the Organization may consult the Court regarding the interpretation of this Convention or of other treaties concerning the protection of human rights in the American states . . .

2. The Court, at the request of a member state of the Organization, may provide that state with opinions regarding the compatibility of any of its domestic laws with the aforesaid international instruments.

. . .

Article 66

1. Reasons shall be given for the judgment of the Court.

2. If the judgment does not represent in whole or in part the unanimous opinion of the judges, any judge shall be entitled to have his dissenting or separate opinion attached to the judgment.

SECTION 3. Procedure

. . .

Article 67

The judgment of the Court shall be final and not subject to appeal. In case of disagreement as to the meaning or scope of the judgment, the Court shall interpret it at the request of any of the parties, provided the request is made within ninety days from the date of notification of the judgment.

Article 68

1. The States Parties to the Convention undertake to comply with the judgment of the Court in any case to which they are parties.

. . .

AFRICAN CHARTER ON HUMAN AND PEOPLES' RIGHTS

[PREAMBLE]

The African States members of the Organization of African Unity, parties to the present convention, entitled African Charter on Human and Peoples' Rights,

Considering the Charter of the Organization of African Unity, which stipulates that 'freedom, equality, justice and dignity are essential objectives for the achievement of the legitimate aspirations of the African peoples';

Reaffirming the pledge they solemnly made in Article 2 of the said Charter to eradicate all forms of colonialism from Africa, to coordinate and intensify their cooperation and efforts to achieve a better life for the peoples of Africa and to promote international cooperation having due regard to the Charter of the United Nations and the Universal Declaration of Human Rights;

Taking into consideration the virtues of their historical tradition and the values of African civilization which should inspire and characterize their reflection on the concept of human and peoples' rights;

. . .

Considering that the enjoyment of rights and freedoms also implies the performance of duties on the part of everyone;

Convinced that it is henceforth essential to pay a particular attention to the right to development and that civil and political rights cannot be dissociated from economic, social and cultural rights in their conception as well as universality and that the satisfaction of economic, social and cultural rights is a guarantee for the enjoyment of civil and political rights;

Conscious of their duty to achieve the total liberation of Africa, the peoples of which are still struggling for their dignity and genuine independence, and undertaking to eliminate colonialism, neo-colonialism, apartheid, zionism and to dismantle aggressive foreign military bases and all forms of discrimination, particularly those based on race, ethnic group, color, sex, language, religion or political opinions;

. . .

Firmly convinced of their duty to promote and protect human and peoples' rights and freedoms taking into account the importance traditionally attached to these rights and freedoms in Africa;

Have agreed as follows

PART I: RIGHTS AND DUTIES
CHAPTER I. HUMAN AND PEOPLES' RIGHTS

Article 1

The Member States of the Organization of African Unity parties to the present Charter shall recognize the rights, duties and freedoms enshrined in this Charter and shall undertake to adopt legislative or other measures to give effect to them.

Article 2

Every individual shall be entitled to the enjoyment of the rights and freedoms recognized and guaranteed in the present Charter without distinction of any kind such as race, ethnic group, color, sex, language, religion, political or any other opinion, national and social origin, fortune, birth or other status.

Article 3

1. Every individual shall be equal before the law.
2. Every individual shall be entitled to equal protection of the law.

Article 4

Human beings are inviolable. Every human being shall be entitled to respect for his life and the integrity of his person. No one may be arbitrarily deprived of this right.

Article 5

Every individual shall have the right to the respect of the dignity inherent in a human being and to the recognition of his legal status. All forms of exploitation and degradation of man particularly slavery, slave trade, torture, cruel, inhuman or degrading punishment and treatment, shall be prohibited.

Article 6

Every individual shall have the right to liberty and to the security of his person. No one may be deprived of his freedom except for reasons and conditions previously laid down by law. In particular, no one may be arbitrarily arrested or detained.

Article 7

1. Every individual shall have the right to have his cause heard. This comprises:

   (a) the right to an appeal to competent national organs against acts of violating his fundamental rights as recognized and guaranteed by conventions, laws, regulations and customs in force;
   (b) the right to be presumed innocent until proved guilty by a competent court or tribunal;
   (c) the right to defence, including the right to be defended by counsel of his choice;
   (d) the right to be tried within a reasonable time by an impartial court or tribunal.

2. No one may be condemned for an act or omission which did not constitute a legally punishable offence for which no provision was made at the time it was committed. Punishment is personal and can be imposed only on the offender.

Article 8

Freedom of conscience, the profession and free practice of religion shall be guaranteed. No one may, subject to law and order, be submitted to measures restricting the exercise of these freedoms.

Article 9

1. Every individual shall have the right to receive information.
2. Every individual shall have the right to express and disseminate his opinions within the law.

Article 10

1. Every individual shall have the right to free association provided he abides by the law.
2. Subject to the obligation of solidarity provided for in Article 29 no one may be compelled to join an association.

Article 11

Every individual shall have the right to assemble freely with others. The exercise of this right shall be subject only to necessary restrictions provided for by law, in particular those enacted in the interest of national security, the safety, health, ethics and rights and freedoms of others.

Article 12

1. Every individual shall have the right to freedom of movement and residence within the borders of a State provided he abides by the law.
2. Every individual shall have the right to leave any country including his own, and to return to his country. This right may only be subject to restrictions, provided for by law for the protection of national security, law and order, public health or morality.
3. Every individual shall have the right, when persecuted, to seek and obtain asylum in other countries in accordance with laws of those countries and international conventions.
4. A non-national legally admitted in a territory of a State Party to the present Charter may only be expelled from it by virtue of a decision taken in accordance with the law.
5. The mass expulsion of non-nationals shall be prohibited. Mass expulsion shall be that which is aimed at national, racial, ethnic or religious groups.

Article 13

1. Every citizen shall have the right to participate freely in the government of his country, either directly or through freely chosen representatives in accordance with the provisions of the law.
2. Every citizen shall have the right of equal access to the public service of his country.
3. Every individual shall have the right of access to public property and services in strict equality of all persons before the law.

Article 14

The right to property shall be guaranteed. It may only be encroached upon in the interest of public need or in the general interest of the community and in accordance with the provisions of appropriate laws.

Article 15

Every individual shall have the right to work under equitable and satisfactory conditions, and shall receive equal pay for equal work.

Article 16

1. Every individual shall have the right to enjoy the best attainable state of physical and mental health.

2. States Parties to the present Charter shall take the necessary measures to protect the health of their people and to ensure that they receive medical attention when they are sick.

Article 17

1. Every individual shall have the right to education.

2. Every individual may freely take part in the cultural life of his community.

3. The promotion and protection of morals and traditional values recognized by the community shall be the duty of the State.

Article 18

1. The family shall be the natural unit and basis of society. It shall be protected by the State which shall take care of its physical health and moral health.

2. The State shall have the duty to assist the family which is the custodian of morals and traditional values recognized by the community.

3. The State shall ensure the elimination of every discrimination against women and also ensure the protection of the rights of the woman and the child as stipulated in international declarations and conventions.

4; The aged and the disabled shall also have the right to special measures of protection in keeping with their physical or moral needs.

Article 19

All peoples shall be equal; they shall enjoy the same respect and shall have the same rights. Nothing shall justify the domination of a people by another.

Article 20

1. All peoples shall have the right to existence. They shall have the unquestionable and inalienable right to self-determination. They shall freely determine their political status and shall pursue their economic and social development according to the policy they have freely chosen.

2. Colonized or oppressed peoples shall have the right to free themselves from the bonds of domination by resorting to any means recognized by the international community.

3. All peoples shall have the right to the assistance of the States Parties to the

present Charter in their liberation struggle against foreign domination, be it political, economic or cultural.

Article 21

1. All peoples shall freely dispose of their wealth and natural resources. This right shall be exercised in the exclusive interest of the people. In no case shall a people be deprived of it.

2. In case of spoliation the dispossessed people shall have the right to the lawful recovery of its property as well as to an adequate compensation.

3. The free disposal of wealth and natural resources shall be exercised without prejudice to the obligation of promoting international economic cooperation based on mutual respect, equitable exchange and the principles of international law.

4. States Parties to the present Charter shall individually and collectively exercise the right to free disposal of their wealth and natural resources with a view to strengthening African unity and solidarity.

5. States Parties to the present Charter shall undertake to eliminate all forms of foreign economic exploitation particularly that practiced by international monopolies so as to enable their peoples to fully benefit from the advantages derived from their national resources.

Article 22

1. All peoples shall have the right to their economic, social and cultural development with due regard to their freedom and identity and in the equal enjoyment of the common heritage of mankind.

2. States shall have the duty, individually or collectively, to ensure the exercise of the right to development.

Article 23

1. All peoples shall have the right to national and international peace and security. The principles of solidarity and friendly relations implicitly affirmed by the Charter of the United Nations and reaffirmed by that of the Organization of African Unity shall govern relations between States.

2. For the purpose of strengthening peace, solidarity and friendly relations, States Parties to the present Charter shall ensure that:

  (a) any individual enjoying the right of asylum under Article 12 of the present Charter shall not engage in subversive activities against his country of origin or any other State Party to the present Charter;
  (b) their territories shall not be used as bases for subversive or terrorist activities against the people of any other State Party to the present Charter.

Article 24

All peoples shall have the right to a general satisfactory environment favorable to their development.

Article 25

States Parties to the present Charter shall have the duty to promote and ensure through teaching, education and publication, the respect of the rights and freedoms contained in the present Charter and to see to it that these freedoms and rights as well as corresponding obligations and duties are understood.

Article 26

States Parties to the present Charter shall have the duty to guarantee the independence of the Courts and shall allow the establishment and improvement of appropriate national institutions entrusted with the promotion and protection of the rights and freedoms guaranteed by the present Charter.

CHAPTER II. DUTIES

Article 27

1. Every individual shall have duties towards his family and society, the State and other legally recognized communities and the international community.

2. The rights and freedoms of each individual shall be exercised with due regard to the rights of others, collective security, morality and common interest.

Article 28

Every individual shall have the duty to respect and consider his fellow beings without discrimination, and to maintain relations aimed at promoting, safeguarding and reinforcing mutual respect and tolerance.

Article 29

The individual shall also have the duty:

1. To preserve the harmonious development of the family and to work for the cohesion and respect of the family; to respect his parents at all times, to maintain them in case of need;

2. To serve his national community by placing his physical and intellectual abilities at its service;

3. Not to compromise the security of the State whose national or resident he is;

4. To preserve and strengthen social and national solidarity, particularly when the latter is threatened;

5. To preserve and strengthen the national independence and the territorial integrity of his country and to contribute to its defence in accordance with the law;

6. To work to the best of his abilities and competence, and to pay taxes imposed by law in the interest of the society;

7. To preserve and strengthen positive African cultural values in his relations with other members of the society, in the spirit of tolerance, dialogue and consultation and, in general, to contribute to the promotion of the moral well-being of society;

8. To contribute to the best of his abilities, at all times and at all levels, to the promotion and achievement of African unity.

. . .

PART II: MEASURES OF SAFEGUARD
CHAPTER 1. ESTABLISHMENT AND ORGANIZATION OF THE AFRICAN COMMISSION ON
HUMAN AND PEOPLES' RIGHTS

Article 30

An African Commission on Human and Peoples' Rights, hereinafter called 'the Commission', shall be established within the Organization of African Unity to promote human and peoples' rights and ensure their protection in Africa.

Article 31

1. The Commission shall consist of eleven members chosen from amongst African personalities of the highest reputation, known for their high morality, integrity, impartiality and competence in matters of human and peoples' rights, particular consideration being given to persons having legal experience.

2. The members of the Commission shall serve in their personal capacity.

. . .

CHAPTER II. MANDATE OF THE COMMISSION

Article 45

The functions of the Commission shall be:

1. To promote human and peoples' rights and in particular:

   (a) to collect documents, undertake studies and researches on African problems in the field of human and peoples' rights, organize seminars, symposia and conferences, disseminate information, encourage national and local institutions concerned with human and peoples' rights, and should the case arise, give its views or make recommendations to Governments.
   (b) to formulate and lay down, principles and rules aimed at solving legal problems relating to human and peoples' rights and fundamental freedoms upon which African Governments may base their legislations.
   (c) co-operate with other African and international institutions concerned with the promotion and protection of human and peoples' rights.

2. Ensure the protection of human and peoples' rights under conditions laid down by the present Charter.

3. Interpret all the provisions of the present Charter at the request of a State Party, an institution of the OAU or an African Organization recognized by the OAU.

4. Perform any other tasks which may be entrusted to it by the Assembly of Heads of State and Government.

CHAPTER III. PROCEDURE OF THE COMMISSION

Article 46

The Commission may resort to any appropriate method of investigation; it may hear from the Secretary General of the Organization of African Unity or any other person capable of enlightening it.

Communication from States

[Articles 47–54—on communications from states, efforts at amicable solutions, and related reports by the Commission to the Assembly of Heads of State and Government—are omitted.]

Other Communications
Article 55

1. Before each Session, the Secretary of the Commission shall make a list of the communications other than those of States Parties to the present Charter and transmit them to the members of the Commission, who shall indicate which communications should be considered by the Commission.

2. A communication shall be considered by the Commission if a simple majority of its members so decide.

Article 56

Communications relating to human and peoples' rights referred to in Article 55 received by the Commission shall be considered if they:

1. Indicate their authors even if the latter request anonymity,

2. Are compatible with the Charter of the Organization of African Unity or with the present Charter,

3. Are not written in disparaging or insulting language directed against the State concerned and its institutions or to the Organization of African Unity,

4. Are not based exclusively on news disseminated through the mass media,

5. Are sent after exhausting local remedies, if any, unless it is obvious that this procedure is unduly prolonged,

6. Are submitted within a reasonable period from the time local remedies are exhausted or from the date the Commission is seized of the matter, and

7. Do not deal with cases which have been settled by [the] States involved in accordance with the principles of the Charter of the United Nations, or the Charter of the Organization of African Unity or the provisions of the present Charter.

Article 57

Prior to any substantive consideration, all communications shall be brought to the knowledge of the State concerned by the Chairman of the Commission.

Article 58

1. When it appears after deliberations of the Commission that one or more communications apparently relate to special cases which reveal the existence of a series of serious or massive violations of human and peoples' rights, the Commission shall draw the attention of the Assembly of Heads of State and Government to these special cases.

2. The Assembly of Heads of State and Government may then request the

Commission to undertake an in-depth study of these cases and make a factual report, accompanied by its findings and recommendations.

3. A case of emergency duly noticed by the Commission shall be submitted by the latter to the Chairman of the Assembly of Heads of State and Government who may request an in-depth study.

Article 59

1. All measures taken within the provisions of the present Chapter shall remain confidential until such a time as the Assembly of Heads of State and Government shall otherwise decide.

2. However, the report shall be published by the Chairman of the Commission upon the decision of the Assembly of Heads of State and Government.

3. The report on the activities of the Commission shall be published by its Chairman after it has been considered by the Assembly of Heads of State and Government.

CHAPTER IV. APPLICABLE PRINCIPLES

Article 60

The Commission shall draw inspiration from international law on human and peoples' rights, particularly from the provisions of various African instruments on human and peoples' rights, the Charter of the United Nations, the Charter of the Organization of African Unity, the Universal Declaration of Human Rights, other instruments adopted by the United Nations and by African countries in the field of human and peoples' rights as well as from the provisions of various instruments adopted with the Specialized Agencies of the United Nations of which the parties to the present Charter are members.

Article 61

The Commission shall also take into consideration, as subsidiary measures to determine the principles of law, other general or special international conventions, laying down rules expressly recognized by member states of the Organization of African Unity, African practices consistent with international norms on human and peoples' rights, customs generally accepted as law, general principles of law recognized by African states as well as legal precedents and doctrine.

. . .

VIENNA CONVENTION ON THE LAW OF TREATIES

. . .

Article 2

1. For the purpose of the present Convention:

(a) 'Treaty' means an international agreement concluded between States in written form and governed by international law, whether embodied in a single instrument or in two or more related instruments and whatever its particular designation;

(b) 'Ratification', 'acceptance', 'approval' and 'accession' means in each case the international act so named whereby a State establishes on the international plane its consent to be bound by a treaty;

. . .

(d) 'Reservation' means a unilateral statement, however phrased or named, made by a State, when signing, ratifying, accepting, approving or acceding to a treaty, whereby it purports to exclude or to modify the legal effect of certain provisions of the treaty in their application to the State;

. . .

Article 18

A State is obliged to refrain from acts which would defeat the object and purpose of a treaty when:

(a) It has signed the treaty or has exchanged instruments constituting the treaty subject to ratification, acceptance or approval, until it shall have made its intention clear not to become a party to the treaty; or

(b) It has expressed its consent to be bound by the treaty, pending the entry into force of the treaty and provided that such entry into force is not unduly delayed.

Article 19

A State may, when signing, ratifying, accepting, approving or acceding to a treaty, formulate a reservation unless:

(a) The reservation is prohibited by the treaty;

(b) The treaty provides that only specified reservations, which do not include the reservation in question, may be made; or

(c) In cases not falling under sub-paragraphs (a) and (b), the reservation is incompatible with the object and purpose of the treaty.

Article 20

1. A reservation expressly authorized by a treaty does not require any subsequent acceptance by the other contracting States unless the treaty so provides.

2. When it appears from the limited number of the negotiating States and the object and purpose of a treaty that the application of the treaty in its entirety

between all the parties is an essential condition of the consent of each one to be bound by the treaty, a reservation requires acceptance by all the parties;

. . .

4. In cases not falling under the preceding paragraphs and unless the treaty otherwise provides:

> *(a)* Acceptance by another contracting State of a reservation constitutes the reserving State a party to the treaty in relation to that other State if or when the treaty is in force for those States;
>
> *(b)* An objection by another contracting State to a reservation does not preclude the entry into force of the treaty as between the objecting and reserving States unless a contrary intention is definitely expressed by the objecting State;

. . .

Article 21

1. A reservation established with regard to another party in accordance with articles 19, 20 and 23:

> *(a)* Modifies for the reserving State in its relations with that other party the provisions of the treaty to which the reservation relates to the extent of the reservation; and
>
> *(b)* Modifies those provisions to the same extent for that other party in its relations with the reserving State.

2. The reservation does not modify the provisions of the treaty for the other parties to the treaty *inter se.*

3. When a State objecting to a reservation has not opposed the entry into force of the treaty between itself and the reserving State, the provisions to which the reservation relates do not apply as between the two States to the extent of the reservation.

. . .

Article 26
'Pacta Sunt Servanda'

Every treaty in force is binding upon the parties to it and must be performed by them in good faith.

Article 27

A party may not invoke the provisions of its internal law as justification for its failure to perform a treaty . . .

. . .

Article 31

1. A treaty shall be interpreted in good faith in accordance with the ordinary meaning to be given to the terms of the treaty in their context and in the light of its object and purpose.

. . .

3. There shall be taken into account, together with the context:

(*a*) Any subsequent agreement between the parties regarding the interpretation of the treaty or the application of its provisions;

(*b*) Any subsequent practice in the application of the treaty which establishes the agreement of the parties regarding its interpretation;

(*c*) Any relevant rules of international law applicable in the relations between the parties.

4. A special meaning shall be given to a term if it is established that the parties so intended.

Article 32

Recourse may be had to supplementary means of interpretation, including the preparatory work of the treaty and the circumstances of its conclusion, in order to confirm the meaning resulting from the application of article 31, or to determine the meaning when the interpretation according to article 31:

(*a*) Leaves the meaning ambiguous or obscure; or

(*b*) Leads to a result which is manifestly absurd or unreasonable.

. . .

Article 35

An obligation arises for a third State from a provision of a treaty if the parties to the treaty intend the provision to be the means of establishing the obligation and the third State expressly accepts that obligation in writing.

. . .

Article 38

Nothing in articles 34 to 37 precludes a rule set forth in a treaty from becoming binding upon a third State as a customary rule of international law, recognized as such.

. . .

Article 40

Unless the treaty otherwise provides, the amendment of multilateral treaties shall be governed by the following paragraphs.

. . .

4. The amending agreement does not bind any State already a party to the treaty which does not become a party to the amending agreement . . .

. . .

Article 43

The invalidity, termination or denunciation of a treaty, the withdrawal of a party from it, or the suspension of its operation, as a result of the application of the present Convention or of the provisions of the treaty, shall not in any way impair the duty of any State to fulfil any obligation embodied in the treaty to which it would be subject under international law independently of the treaty.

. . .

Article 46

1. A State may not invoke the fact that its consent to be bound by a treaty has been expressed in violation of a provision of its internal law regarding competence to conclude treaties as invalidating its consent unless that violation was manifest and concerned a rule of its internal law of fundamental importance.

2. A violation is manifest if it would be objectively evident to any State conducting itself in the matter in accordance with normal practice and in good faith.

. . .

Article 53

A treaty is void if, at the time of its conclusion, it conflicts with a peremptory norm of general international law. For the purposes of the present Convention, a peremptory norm of general international law is a norm accepted and recognized by the international community of States as a whole as a norm from which no derogation is permitted and which can be modified only by a subsequent norm of general international law having the same character.

. . .

Article 62

1. A fundamental change of circumstances which has occurred with regard to those existing at the time of the conclusion of a treaty, and which was not foreseen by the parties, may not be invoked as a ground for terminating or withdrawing from the treaty unless:

    (a) The existence of those circumstances constituted an essential basis of the consent of the parties to be bound by the treaty; and
    (b) The effect of the change is radically to transform the extent of obligations still to be performed under the treaty.

. . .

Article 64

If a new peremptory norm of general international law emerges, any existing treaty which is in conflict with that norm becomes void and terminates.

. . .

CONSTITUTION OF THE UNITED STATES

We the People of the United States, in Order to form a more perfect Union, establish Justice, insure domestic Tranquility, provide for the common defence, promote the general Welfare, and secure the Blessings of Liberty to ourselves and our Posterity, do ordain and establish this Constitution for the United States of America.

Article I

SECTION 1. All legislative Powers herein granted shall be vested in a Congress of the United States, which shall consist of a Senate and House of Representatives.
. . .

SECTION 7. . . . Every Bill which shall have passed the House of Representatives and the Senate, shall, before it become a Law, be presented to the President of the United States; if he approve he shall sign it, but if not he shall return it, with his Objections to that House in which it shall have originated, who shall enter the Objections at large on their Journal, and proceed to reconsider it. If after such Reconsideration two thirds of that House shall agree to pass the Bill, it shall be sent, together with the Objections, to the other House, by which it shall likewise be reconsidered, and if approved by two thirds of that House, it shall become a Law. . . .
. . .

SECTION 8. The Congress shall have Power To lay and collect Taxes, Duties, Imposts and Excises, to pay the Debts and provide for the common Defence and general Welfare of the United States. . . .

To regulate Commerce with foreign Nations, and among the several States, and with the Indian Tribes;

To define and punish Piracies and Felonies committed on the high Seas, and Offences against the Law of Nations;

To declare War, grant Letters of Marque and Reprisal, and make Rules concerning Captures on Land and Water;
. . .

To make all Laws which shall be necessary and proper for carrying into Execution the foregoing Powers, and all other Powers vested by this Constitution in the Government of the United States, or in any Department or Officer thereof.

SECTION 9. . . .

The privilege of the Writ of Habeas Corpus shall not be suspended, unless when in Cases of Rebellion or Invasion the public Safety may require it.

No Bill of Attainder or ex post facto Law shall be passed.
. . .

No money shall be drawn from the Treasury, but in Consequence of Appropriations made by Law . . . .
. . .

SECTION 10.

No State shall enter into any Treaty, Alliance, or Confederation. . . .

. . .

No State shall, without the Consent of the Congress, ... enter into any Agreement or Compact with another State, or with a foreign Power. . . .

Article II

SECTION 1. The executive Power shall be vested in a President of the United States of America. . . .

. . .

SECTION 2. The President shall be Commander in Chief of the Army and Navy of the United States, and of the Militia of the several States, when called into the actual Service of the United States. . . .

He shall have Power, by and with the Advice and Consent of the Senate, to make Treaties, provided two thirds of the Senators present concur; and he shall nominate, and by and with the Advice and Consent of the Senate, shall appoint Ambassadors, other public Ministers and Consuls, Judges of the supreme Court, and all other Officers of the United States, whose Appointments are not herein otherwise provided for, and which shall be established by Law. . . .

. . .

SECTION 3. . . . [H]e shall receive Ambassadors and other public Ministers; he shall take Care that the Laws be faithfully executed, and shall Commission all the Officers of the United States.

. . .

Article III

SECTION 1. The judicial Power of the United States, shall be vested in one supreme Court, and in such inferior Courts as the Congress may from time to time ordain and establish. . . .

SECTION 2. The judicial Power shall extend to all Cases, in Law and Equity, arising under this Constitution, the Laws of the United States, and Treaties made, or which shall be made, under their Authority;—to all Cases affecting Ambassadors, other public Ministers and Consuls;—to all Cases of admiralty and maritime jurisdiction;—to Controversies to which the United States shall be a Party;—to Controversies between two or more States;—between a State and Citizens of another State;—between Citizens of different States;—between Citizens of the same State claiming Lands under Grants of different States, and between a State, or the Citizens thereof, and foreign States, Citizens or Subjects.

. . .

The trial of all Crimes, except in Cases of Impeachment, shall be by Jury; and such Trial shall be held in the State where the said Crimes shall have been committed; but when not committed within any State, the Trial shall be at such Place or Places as the Congress may by Law have directed.

. . .

Article V

...

The Congress, whenever two thirds of both Houses shall deem it necessary, shall propose Amendments to this Constitution, or, on the Application of the Legislatures of two thirds of the several States, shall call a Convention for proposing Amendments, which, in either Case, shall be valid to all Intents and Purposes, as part of this Constitution, when ratified by the Legislatures of three fourths of the several States, or by Conventions in three fourths thereof, as the one or the other Mode of Ratification may be proposed by the Congress. . . .

Article VI

This Constitution, and the Laws of the United States which shall be made in Pursuance thereof; and all Treaties made, or which shall be made, under the Authority of the United States, shall be the supreme Law of the Land; and the Judges in every State shall be bound thereby, any Thing in the Constitution or Laws of any State to the Contrary notwithstanding.

...

Articles in Addition to, and Amendment of, the Constitution of the United States of America, Proposed by Congress and Ratified by the Several States, Pursuant to the Fifth Article of the Original Constitution

[The first ten amendments constitute the Bill of Rights.]

Amendment I

Congress shall make no law respecting an establishment of religion, or prohibiting the free exercise thereof; or abridging the freedom of speech, or of the press; or the right of the people peaceably to assemble, and to petition the Government for a redress of grievances.

...

Amendment IV

The right of the people to be secured in their persons, houses, papers, and effects, against unreasonable searches and seizures, shall not be violated, and no Warrants shall issue, but upon probable cause, supported by Oath or affirmation, and particularly describing the place to be searched, and the persons or things to be seized.

Amendment V

No person shall be held to answer for a capital, or otherwise infamous crime, unless on a presentment or indictment of a Grand Jury, except in cases arising in the land or naval forces, or in the Militia, when in actual service in time of War or public danger; nor shall any person be subject for the same offence to be twice put in jeopardy of life or limb; nor shall be compelled in any criminal case to be a witness against himself, nor be deprived of life, liberty, or property, without due process of law; nor shall private property be taken for public use, without just compensation.

Amendment VI

In all criminal prosecutions, the accused shall enjoy the right to a speedy and public trial, by an impartial jury of the State and district wherein the crime shall have been committed, which district shall have been previously ascertained by law, and to be informed of the nature and cause of the accusation; to be confronted with the witnesses against him; to have compulsory process for obtaining witnesses in his favor, and to have the Assistance of Counsel for his defence.

Amendment VII

In suits at common law, where the value in controversy shall exceed twenty dollars, the right of trial by jury shall be preserved, and no fact tried by jury, shall be otherwise re-examined in any Court of the United States, than according to the rules of the common law.

Amendment VIII

Excessive bail shall not be required, nor excessive fines imposed, nor cruel and unusual punishments inflicted.

Amendment IX

The enumeration in the Constitution, of certain rights, shall not be construed to deny or disparage others retained by the people.

Amendment X

The powers not delegated to the United States by the Constitution, nor prohibited by it to the States, are reserved to the States respectively, or to the people.

. . .

Amendment XIII

SECTION 1. Neither slavery nor involuntary servitude, except as a punishment for crime whereof the party shall have been duly convicted, shall exist within the United States, or any place subject to their jurisdiction.

. . .

Amendment XIV

SECTION 1. All persons born or naturalized in the United States, and subject to the jurisdiction thereof, are citizens of the United States and of the State wherein they reside. No State shall make or enforce any law which shall abridge the privileges or immunities of citizens of the United States; nor shall any State deprive any person of life, liberty, or property, without due process of law, nor deny to any person within its jurisdiction the equal protection of the laws.

. . .

SECTION 5. The Congress shall have power to enforce, by appropriate legislation, the provisions of this article.

Amendment XV

SECTION 1. The right of citizens of the United States to vote shall not be denied or abridged by the United States or by any State on account of race, color, or previous condition of servitude.

SECTION 2. The Congress shall have power to enforce this article by appropriate legislation.
. . .

Amendment XIX

The right of citizens of the United States to vote shall not be denied or abridged by the United States or by any State on account of sex.
Congress shall have power to enforce this article by appropriate legislation.
. . .

Amendment XXIV

SECTION 1. The right of citizens of the United States to vote in any primary or other election for President or Vice President, for electors for President or Vice President, or for Senator or Representative in Congress, shall not be denied or abridged by the United States or any State by reason of failure to pay poll tax or other tax.
. . .

Amendment XXVI

SECTION 1. The right of citizens of the United States, who are eighteen years of age or older, to vote shall not be denied or abridged by the United States or by any State on account of age.
. . .

Annex on
CITATIONS

Unless otherwise indicated, details of the number of parties to a treaty are current as of 1 March 2000. The principal abbreviations used are as follows: HRLJ for *Human Rights Law Journal*, ILM for *International Legal Materials*, UNTS for *United Nations Treaty Series* and ETS for *European Treaty Series*.

Human Rights Document Collections

Brownlie, I. (ed.), *Basic Documents on Human Rights* (3rd. edn., Oxford: Clarendon Press, 1992).

Hamalengwa, M., C. Flinterman and E. Dankwa, *The International Law of Human Rights in Africa: Basic Documents and Annotated Bibliography* (Dordrecht: Martinus Nijhoff, 1988).

Human Rights: A Compilation of International Instruments, 3 vols. (Geneva: United Nations, 1994–97).

Human Rights in International Law: Basic Texts (Strasbourg: Council of Europe Press, 1992).

International Labour Conventions and Recommendations 1919–1995, 3 vols. (Geneva: International Labour Office, 1996).

Religion and Human Rights: Basic Documents (New York: Columbia University, Center for the Study of Human Rights, 1998).

Roberts, A. and R. Guelff, *Documents on the Laws of War* (3rd edn., Oxford: Oxford University Press, 2000).

Twenty-five Human Rights Documents (2nd edn., New York: Columbia University, Center for the Study of Human Rights, 1994).

United Nations Treaties

Charter of the United Nations, adopted 26 June 1945, entered into force 24 Oct. 1945, as amended by G.A. Res. 1991 (XVIII) 17 Dec. 1963, entered into force 31 Aug. 1965 (557 UNTS 143); 2101 of 20 Dec. 1965, entered into force 12 June 1968 (638 UNTS 308); and 2847 (XXVI) of 20 Dec. 1971, entered into force 24 Sept. 1973 (892 UNTS 119). 188 Member States.

Convention Against Torture and Other Cruel, Inhuman or Degrading Treatment or Punishment, adopted 10 Dec. 1984, entered into force 26 June 1987, G.A. Res. 39/46, 39 UN GAOR, Supp. (No. 51), UN Doc. A/39/51, at 197 (1984), reprinted in 23 ILM 1027 (1984), minor changes reprinted in 24 ILM 535 (1985), 5 HRLJ 350 (1984). 118 states parties.

Convention on the Elimination of All Forms of Discrimination against Women, adopted 18 Dec. 1979, entered into force 3 Sept. 1981, G.A. Res. 34/180, 34 UN GAOR, Supp. (No. 46), UN Doc. A/34/46, at 193 (1979), reprinted in 19 ILM 33 (1980). 165 states parties.

Optional Protocol to the Convention on the Elimination of All Forms of Discrimination against Women, adopted 6 Oct. 1999, GA Res. 54/4 (1999). Not yet in force.

Convention on the Prevention and Punishment of the Crime of Genocide, adopted 9 Dec. 1948, entered into force 12 Jan. 1951, 78 UNTS 277. 130 states parties.

Convention on the Rights of the Child, adopted 20 Nov. 1989, entered into force 2 Sept. 1990, G.A. Res. 44/25, 44 UN GAOR, Supp. (No. 49), UN Doc. A/44/49, at 166 (1989), reprinted in 28 ILM 1448 (1989). 191 states parties.

Convention Relating to the Status of Refugees, signed 28 July 1951, entered into force 22 April 1954, 189 UNTS 150. 135 states parties.

Protocol Relating to the Status of Refugees, opened for signature 31 Jan. 1967, entered into force 4 Oct. 1967, 606 UNTS 267, reprinted in 6 ILM 78 (1967). 134 states parties.

International Convention for the Elimination of All Forms of Racial Discrimination, adopted 21 Dec. 1965, entered into force 4 Jan. 1969, 660 UNTS 195, reprinted in 5 ILM 352 (1966). 155 states parties.

International Convention on the Protection of the Rights of All Migrant Workers and Members of Their Families, adopted 18 Dec. 1990, not in force, G.A. Res. 45/158, reprinted in 30 ILM 1517 (1991). 12 states parties.

International Covenant on Civil and Political Rights, adopted 16 Dec. 1966, entered into force 23 March 1976, G.A. Res. 2200A (XXI), UN Doc. A/6316 (1966), 999 UNTS 171, reprinted in 6 ILM 368 (1967). 144 states parties.

Optional Protocol to the International Covenant on Civil and Political Rights, adopted 16 Dec. 1966, entered into force 23 March 1976, 999 UNTS 171, reprinted in 6 ILM 383 (1967). 95 states parties.

Second Optional Protocol to the International Covenant on Civil and Political Rights, adopted 15 Dec. 1989, entered into force 11 July 1991, G.A. Res. 44/128, reprinted in 29 ILM 1464 (1990). 41 states parties.

International Covenant on Economic, Social and Cultural Rights, adopted 16 Dec. 1966, entered into force 3 Jan. 1976, G.A. Res. 2200A (XXI), UN Doc. A/6316 (1966), 993 UNTS 3, reprinted in 6 ILM 360 (1967). 142 states parties.

Supplementary Convention on the Abolition of Slavery, the Slave Trade, and Institutions and Practices Similar to Slavery, adopted 7 Sept. 1956, entered into force 30 April 1957, E.S.C. Res. 608 (XXI), 226 UNTS 3. 118 states parties.

Other Universal Treaties

Geneva Convention for the Amelioration of the Condition of the Wounded and Sick in Armed Forces in the Field, adopted 12 Aug. 1949, entered into force 21 Oct. 1950, 75 UNTS 31. 188 states parties.

Geneva Convention for the Amelioration of the Condition of Wounded, Sick and Shipwrecked Members of Armed Forces at Sea, adopted 12 Aug. 1949, entered into force 21 Oct. 1950, 75 UNTS 85. 188 states parties.

Geneva Convention Relative to the Treatment of Prisoners of War, adopted 12 Aug. 1949, entered into force 21 Oct. 1950, 75 UNTS 135. 188 states parties.

Geneva Convention Relative to the Protection of Civilian Persons in Time of War, adopted 12 Aug. 1948, entered into force 21 Oct. 1950, 75 UNTS 287. 188 states parties.

Protocol I Additional to the Geneva Conventions of August 12, 1949, and relating to the Protection of Victims of International Armed Conflicts, adopted 8 June 1977, entered into force 7 Dec. 1978, UN Doc. A/32/144 Annex I, 1125 UNTS no. 17512, reprinted in 16 ILM 1391 (1977). 156 states parties.

Protocol II Additional to the Geneva Conventions of August 12, 1949, and relating to the Protection of Victims of Non-International Armed Conflicts, adopted 8 June 1977, entered into force 7 Dec. 1978, UN Doc. A/32/144 Annex II, 1125 UNTS no. 17513, reprinted in 16 ILM 1442 (1977). 149 states parties.

Vienna Convention on the Law of Treaties, adopted 23 May 1969, entered into force 27 Jan. 1980, U.N. Doc. A/CONF. 39/26, reprinted in 8 ILM 679 (1969). 90 states parties.

Other United Nations Instruments

Declaration on the Elimination of All Forms of Intolerance and of Discrimination Based on Religion or Belief, adopted 25 Nov. 1981, G.A. Res. 36/55, 36 UN GAOR, Supp. (No. 51), UN Doc. A/36/51, at 171 (1981).

Declaration on the Elimination of Violence Against Women, adopted 20 December 1993, G.A. Res. 48/104, UN Doc. A/48/29, reprinted in 33 ILM 1049 (1994).

Declaration on the Granting of Independence to Colonial Countries and Peoples, G.A. Res. 1514 (XV), 15 UN GAOR, Supp. (No. 16), UN Doc. A/4684, at 66 (1960).

Declaration on Principles of International Law concerning Friendly Relations and Co-operation among States in accordance with the Charter of the United Nations, G.A. Res. 2625 (XXV), 25 UN GAOR, Supp. (No. 28), UN Doc. A/8028, at 121 (1970), reprinted in 9 ILM 1292 (1970).

Declaration on the Protection of All Persons from Being Subjected to Torture and Other Cruel, Inhuman or Degrading Treatment or Punishment, adopted 9 Dec. 1975, G.A. Res. 3452 (XXX), 30 UN GAOR, Supp. (No. 34), UN Doc. A/10034, at 91 (1976).

Declaration on the Protection of All Persons from Enforced Disappearance, adopted 18 Dec. 1992, G.A. Res. 47/133, 32 ILM 903 (1993).

Declaration on the Right and Responsibility of Individuals, Groups and Organs of Society to Promote and Protect Universally Recognized Human Rights and Fundamental Freedoms, adopted 9 Dec. 1998, G.A. Res. 53/144, Annex.

Declaration on the Right to Development, adopted 4 Dec. 1986, 6.A. Res. 41/28.

Declaration on the Rights of Disabled Persons, adopted 9 Dec. 1975, G.A. Res. 3447 (XXX), 30 UN GAOR Supp. (No. 34), UN Doc. A/10034, at 88 (1975).

Declaration on the Rights of Persons Belonging to National or Ethnic, Religious or Linguistic Minorities, adopted 15 Dec. 1992, G.A. Res. 47/135, reprinted in 32 ILM 911 (1993), 14 HRLJ 54 (1993).

Declaration on the Rights of the Child, adopted 20 Nov. 1959, G.A. Res. 1386 (XIV), 14 UN GAOR, Supp. (No. 16) UN Doc A/4354, at 19 (1959).

Standard Minimum Rules for the Treatment of Prisoners, adopted 31 July 1957, E.S.C. Res. 663C (XXIV), 24 UN ESCOR, Supp. (No. 1) at 11 (1957), extended 13 May 1977, E.S.C. Res. 2076 (LXIII), 62 UN ESCOR, Supp. (No. 1) at 35 (1977).

Universal Declaration of Human Rights, adopted 10 Dec. 1948, G.A. Res. 217A (III), UN Doc. A/810, at 71 (1948).

United Nations World Conference on Human Rights, Vienna Declaration and Programme of Action, adopted 25 June 1993, reprinted in 32 ILM 1661 (1993), 14 HRLJ 352 (1993).

Instruments adopted by United Nations Agencies

Convention Concerning Forced or Compulsory Labour (I.L.O. No. 29), adopted 28 June 1930, entered into force 1 May 1932, 39 UNTS 55. 152 states parties.

Convention Concerning Indigenous and Tribal Peoples in Independent Countries (I.L.O. No. 169), adopted 27 June 1989, entered into force 5 Sept. 1991, reprinted in 28 ILM 1382 (1989). 13 states parties.

Convention Concerning the Abolition of Forced Labour (I.L.O. No. 105), adopted 25 June 1957, entered into force 17 Jan. 1959, 320 UNTS 291. 144 states parties.

Convention Concerning the Protection and Integration of Indigenous and Other Tribal and Semi-Tribal Populations in Independent Countries (I.L.O. No. 107), adopted 26 June 1957, entered into force 2 June 1959, 328 UNTS 247. 27 states parties.

Convention Concerning the Worst Forms of Child Labour (I.L.O. No. 182), adopted 17 June 1999, not yet in force. 10 states parties.

UNESCO Convention against Discrimination in Education, adopted 14 Dec. 1960, entered into force 22 May 1962, 429 UNTS 93. 11 states parties.

Regional Instruments

(a) The Council of Europe

European Convention for the Prevention of Torture and Inhuman or Degrading Treatment or Punishment, signed 26 Nov. 1987, entered into force 1 Feb. 1989, Doc. No. H(87)4 1987, ETS 126, reprinted in 27 ILM 1152 (1988); 9 HRLJ 359 (1988). 40 states parties.

European Convention for the Protection of Human Rights and Fundamental Freedoms, signed 4 Nov. 1950, entered into force 3 Sept. 1953, 213 UNTS 221, ETS 5. 41 states parties.

Protocol No. 1 to the European Convention for the Protection of Human Rights and Fundamental Freedoms, adopted 20 March 1952, entered into force 18 May 1954, ETS 9. 38 states parties.

Protocol No. 4 to the European Convention for the Protection of Human Rights and Fundamental Freedoms, adopted 16 Sept. 1963, entered into force 2 May 1968, ETS 46. 31 states parties.

Protocol No. 6 to the European Convention for the Protection of Human Rights and Fundamental Freedoms, adopted 28 April 1983, entered into force 1 March 1985, ETS 114, reprinted in 22 ILM 539 (1983); 6 HRLJ 77 (1985). 35 states parties.

Protocol No. 7 to the European Convention for the Protection of Human Rights and Fundamental Freedoms, adopted 22 Nov. 1984, entered into force 1 Nov. 1988, ETS 117, reprinted in 24 ILM 435 (1985); 6 HRLJ 80 (1985). 26 states parties.

Protocol No. 9 to the European Convention for the Protection of Human Rights and Fundamental Freedoms, adopted 6 Nov. 1990, not in force, ETS 40 reprinted in 30 ILM 693 (1991). 24 states parties.

Protocol No. 11 to the European Convention for the Protection of Human Rights and Fundamental Freedoms, adopted 11 May 1994, entered into force 1 Nov. 1998, ETS 155, reprinted in 33 ILM 960 (1994), 15 HRLJ 86 (1994). 40 states parties.

European Social Charter, signed 18 Oct. 1961, entered into force 26 Feb. 1965, 529 UNTS 89; ETS 35. Protocol amending Charter, adopted 21 Oct. 1991, not in force, ETS 142, reprinted in 31 ILM 155 (1992). 24 states parties.

Additional Protocol to the European Social Charter, adopted 5 May 1988, entered into force 4 Sept. 1992, ETS 128. 10 states parties.

Protocol Amending the European Social Charter, adopted 21 Oct. 1991, not in force, ETS 142. 16 states parties.

European Social Charter (Revised), adopted 3 May 1996, entered into force 3 July 1999, ETS 163. 5 states parties.

Framework Convention for the Protection of National Minorities, adopted 10 Nov. 1994, opened for signature 1 Feb. 1995, entered into force 1 Feb. 1998, ETS 157, reprinted in 34 ILM 351 (1995). 28 states parties.

Statute of the Council of Europe, adopted 5 May 1949, entered into force 3 Aug. 1949, ETS 1. 41 states parties.

(b) The Organization of American States

American Convention on Human Rights (Pact of San José), signed 22 Nov. 1969, entered into force 18 July 1978, OASTS 36, O.A.S. Off. Rec. OEA/Ser.L/V/11.23, doc.21, rev.6 (1979), reprinted in 9 ILM 673 (1970). 25 states parties.

Additional Protocol to the American Convention on Human Rights in the Area of Economic, Social and Cultural Rights (Protocol of San Salvador), adopted 17 Nov. 1988, entered into force 16 Nov. 1999, OASTS 69, reprinted in 28 ILM 156 (1989), corrections at 28 ILM 573 and 1341 (1989). 11 states parties.

Protocol to the American Convention on Human Rights to Abolish the Death Penalty, adopted 8 June 1990, entered into force 28 Aug. 1991, OASTS 73, reprinted in 29 ILM 1447 (1990). 7 states parties.

American Declaration of the Rights and Duties of Man, signed 2 May 1948, OEA/
Ser.L./V/11.71, at 17 (1988).

Charter of the Organization of American States, signed 1948, entered into force
13 Dec. 1951, amended 1967, 1985, 14 Dec. 1992, 10 June 1993. Integrated text
of the Charter as amended by the Protocols of Buenos Aires and Cartagena de
Indias, the Protocol of Amendment of Washington; and the Protocol of
Amendment of Managua, reprinted in 33 ILM 981 (1994). 35 member states.

Inter-American Convention on the Forced Disappearance of Persons, signed
9 June 1994, entered into force 28 Mar. 1996, reprinted in 33 ILM 1529 (1994).
7 states parties.

Inter-American Convention on the Prevention, Punishment and Eradication of
Violence Against Women, signed 9 June 1994, entered into force 3 March 1995,
reprinted in 33 ILM 1534 (1994). 29 states parties.

Inter-American Convention to Prevent and Punish Torture, signed 9 Dec. 1985,
entered into force 28 Feb. 1987, OASTS 67, GA Doc. OEA/Ser.P, AG/doc.2023/
85 rev. I (1986) pp. 46–54, reprinted in 25 ILM 519 (1986). 15 states parties.

(c) The Organization of African Unity

Charter on Human and Peoples' Rights, adopted 27 June 1981, entered into force
21 Oct. 1986, O.A.U. Doc. CAB/LEG/67/3 Rev. 5, reprinted in 21 ILM 58 (1982),
7 HRLJ 403 (1986). 53 states parties.

Protocol to the African Charter on Human and Peoples' Rights on the Establishment of an African Court on Human and Peoples' Rights, adopted 10 June
1998, O.A.U. Doc. CAB/LEG/66/5. Not yet in force. 3 states parties.

African Charter on the Rights and Welfare of the Child, adopted July 1990, entered
into force 29 Oct. 1999, O.A.U. Doc. CAB/LEG/TSG/Rev. 1. 15 states parties.

Charter of the Organization of African Unity, adopted 25 May 1963, 47 UNTS 39,
reprinted in 2 ILM 766 (1963). 53 states parties.

Convention Governing the Specific Aspects of the Refugee Problems in Africa,
adopted 10 Sept. 1969, entered into force 20 June 1974, 1001 UNTS 45,
reprinted in 8 11-M 1288 (1969). 44 states parties.

(d) The Organization for Security and Co-operation in Europe

Document of the Copenhagen Meeting of the Conference on the Human Dimension of the Conference of Security and Co-operation in Europe, adopted
29 June 1990, reprinted in 29 ILM 1305 (1990); 11 HR LJ 232 (1990).

Document of the Moscow Meeting of the Conference on the Human Dimension
of the Conference on Security and Co-operation in Europe, adopted 3 Oct.
1991, reprinted in 30 ILM 1670 (1991).

Final Act of the Conference on Security and Co-operation in Europe, adopted
1 Aug. 1975, reprinted in 14 ILM 1292 (1975).

Human Rights in the Concluding Document of the Vienna Conference on Security and Co-operation in Europe, adopted 15 Jan. 1989, reprinted in 10 HRLJ 270
(1989).

Index of Topics

Note: This index is intended to be used in conjunction with the extensive table of contents at the front of the book.

Index of Authors